W9-CUB-148

FOR REFERENCE

Do Not Take From This Room

Contemporary
Literary Criticism

Yearbook 1990

Guide to Gale Literary Criticism Series

When you need to review criticism of literary works, these are the Gale series to use:

If the author's death date is:	You should turn to:
After Dec. 31, 1959 (or author is still living)	***CONTEMPORARY LITERARY CRITICISM*** for example: Jorge Luis Borges, Anthony Burgess, William Faulkner, Mary Gordon, Ernest Hemingway, Iris Murdoch
1900 through 1959	***TWENTIETH-CENTURY LITERARY CRITICISM*** for example: Willa Cather, F. Scott Fitzgerald, Henry James, Mark Twain, Virginia Woolf
1800 through 1899	***NINETEENTH-CENTURY LITERATURE CRITICISM*** for example: Fedor Dostoevski, Nathaniel Hawthorne, George Sand, William Wordsworth
1400 through 1799	***LITERATURE CRITICISM FROM 1400 TO 1800*** ***(excluding Shakespeare)*** for example: Anne Bradstreet, Daniel Defoe, Alexander Pope, François Rabelais, Jonathan Swift, Phillis Wheatley ***SHAKESPEAREAN CRITICISM*** Shakespeare's plays and poetry
Antiquity through 1399	***CLASSICAL AND MEDIEVAL LITERATURE CRITICISM*** for example: Dante, Homer, Plato, Sophocles, Vergil, the Beowulf Poet

---

Gale also publishes related criticism series:

CHILDREN'S LITERATURE REVIEW

This series covers authors of all eras who have written for the preschool through high school audience.

SHORT STORY CRITICISM

This series covers the major short fiction writers of all nationalities and periods of literary history.

ISSN 0091-3421

Volume 65

Contemporary Literary Criticism
Yearbook 1990

The Year in Fiction, Poetry, Drama,
and World Literature and the Year's
New Authors, Prizewinners, Obituaries,
and Outstanding Literary Events

Roger Matuz
EDITOR

Cathy Falk
Mary K. Gillis
Sean R. Pollock
David Segal
ASSOCIATE EDITORS

Jennifer Brostrom
Susan M. Peters
Janet M. Witalec
ASSISTANT EDITORS

 **Gale Research Inc.** · *DETROIT* · *LONDON*

Riverside Community College
Library
4800 Magnolia Avenue
Riverside, California 92506

REF
PN
771
C59

STAFF

Roger Matuz, *Editor*

Cathy Falk, Mary K. Gillis, David Kmenta, Marie Lazzari, Sean R. Pollock,
David Segal, Bridget Travers, *Associate Editors*

Jennifer Brostrom, Ian Goodhall, Elizabeth P. Henry, Susan M. Peters, James Poniewozik,
Janet M. Witalec, *Assistant Editors*

Jeanne A. Gough, *Production & Permissions Manager*
Linda M. Pugliese, *Production Supervisor*
Maureen A. Puhl, Jennifer VanSickle, *Editorial Associates*
Donna Craft, Paul Lewon, Lorna Mabunda, Camille P. Robinson, *Editorial Assistants*

Maureen Richards, *Research Supervisor*
Paula Cutcher-Jackson, Judy L. Gale, Mary Beth McElmeel, *Editorial Associates*
Amy Kaechele, Robin Lupa, Tamara C. Nott, *Editorial Assistants*

Sandra C. Davis, *Permissions Supervisor (Text)*
Josephine M. Keene, Denise M. Singleton, Kimberly F. Smilay, *Permissions Associates*
Maria L. Franklin, Michele Lonoconus, Shalice Shah, Nancy K. Sheridan,
Rebecca A. Stanko, *Permissions Assistants*
Shelly Rakoczy, *Student Co-op Assistant*

Patricia A. Seefelt, *Permissions Supervisor (Pictures)*
Margaret A. Chamberlain, *Permissions Associate*
Pamela A. Hayes, Keith Reed, *Permissions Assistants*

Mary Beth Trimper, *Production Manager*
Shanna Philpott-Heilveil, *External Production Associate*

Art Chartow, *Art Director*
C. J. Jonik, *Keyliner*

Since this page cannot legibly accommodate all the copyright notices, the Acknowledgments section constitutes an extension of the copyright notice.

While every effort has been made to ensure the reliability of the information presented in this publication, Gale Research Inc. does not guarantee the accuracy of the data contained herein. Gale accepts no payment for listing; and inclusion in the publication of any organization, agency, institution, publication, service, or individual does not imply endorsement of the editors or publisher.

Errors brought to the attention of the publisher and verified to the satisfaction of the publisher will be corrected in future editions.

The paper used in this publication meets the minimum requirements of American National Standard for Information Sciences—Permanence Paper for Printed Library Materials, ANSI Z39.48-1984. ∞

Copyright © 1991
Gale Research Inc.
835 Penobscot Bldg.
Detroit, MI 48226-4094

Library of Congress Catalog Card Number 76-38938
ISBN 0-8103-4439-4
ISSN 0091-3421

Printed in the United States of America

Published simultaneously in the United Kingdom
by Gale Research International Limited
(An affiliated company of Gale Research Inc.)

Contents

Preface   vii

Acknowledgments   xi

Preface

Scope of the Yearbook

Contemporary Literary Criticism Yearbook is part of the ongoing *Contemporary Literary Criticism (CLC)* series. *CLC* provides a comprehensive survey of modern literature by presenting excerpted criticism on the works of novelists, poets, playwrights, short story writers, scriptwriters, and other creative writers now living or who died after December 31, 1959. A strong emphasis is placed on including criticism of works by established authors who frequently appear on syllabuses of high school and college literature courses.

To complement this broad coverage, the *Yearbook* focuses more specifically on a given year's literary activities and features a larger number of currently noteworthy authors than is possible in standard *CLC* volumes. *CLC Yearbook* provides students, teachers, librarians, researchers, and general readers with information and commentary on the outstanding literary works and events of a given year.

Highlights of *CLC,* Volume 65: *Yearbook 1990* include:

Reviews of popular, prizewinning novels, including A. S. Byatt's *Possession,* E. L. Doctorow's *Billy Bathgate,* and Charles Johnson's *Middle Passage.*

Commentary on the works of 1990 Nobel Laureate Octavio Paz, whose acceptance speech for the Nobel Prize is reprinted in its entirety.

Criticism on the controversial publication *The Book of J,* which contains David Rosenberg's new translations of Pentateuch portions of the *Bible* and commentary by noted critic Harold Bloom, who argues that the original author of these sections was a woman.

Analysis of recent trends in Feminist literary criticism, focusing on essays and reviews published in 1990, and in African-American literary criticism, emphasizing responses to the works of esteemed author Henry Louis Gates, Jr.

Format

CLC, Volume 65: *Yearbook 1990,* which includes excerpted criticism on more than thirty authors and comprehensive coverage of five of the year's significant literary events, is divided into five sections—"The Year in Review," "New Authors," "Prizewinners," "In Memoriam," and "Topics in Literature: 1990."

•**The Year in Review**—This section consists of specially commissioned essays by prominent writers who survey the year's works in their respective fields. Wendy Lesser discusses "The Year in Fiction," J. D. McClatchy "The Year in Poetry," Robert Cohen "The Year in Drama," and William Riggan "The Year in World Literature." For introductions to the essayists, please see Notes on Contributors, page 27.

•**New Authors**—*CLC Yearbook 1990* introduces thirteen writers who published their first book in the United States during 1990. Authors were selected for inclusion if their work was reviewed in several prominent literary periodicals.

•**Prizewinners**—This section commences with a list of literary prizes and honors announced in 1990, citing the award, award criteria, the recipient, and title of the prizewinning work. Following the listing of prizewinners is a presentation of eleven entries on individual award winners, representing a mixture of genres and nationalities as well as established prizes and those more recently introduced.

•**In Memoriam**—This section consists of reminiscences, tributes, retrospective articles, and obituary notices on four authors who died in 1990. In addition, an Obituary section provides information on other recently deceased literary figures.

•**Topics in Literature**—This section focuses on literary issues and events of considerable public interest, including trends in African-American and Feminist literary criticism; the controversial best-seller *The Book of J;* the relationship between literature and political change as exemplified by Václav Havel, the dissident playwright and political activist who was a leader of the democracy movement in Czechoslovakia that culminated with the Velvet Revolution of 1989 and establishment of Havel as President of the first non-communist government in Czechoslovakia since World War II.

Features

With the exception of the four essays in "The Year in Review" section, which are written specifically for this publication, the *Yearbook* consists of excerpted criticism. There are approximately four hundred individual excerpts in *CLC Yearbook 1990*, drawn from literary reviews, general magazines, newspapers, books, and scholarly journals. *Yearbook* entries variously contain the following items:

•An **author heading** in the "New Authors" and "Prizewinners" sections cites the name under which an author publishes and the title of the work covered in the entry; the "In Memoriam" section includes the author's name and birth and death dates. The author's full name, pseudonyms (if any) under which the author has published, nationality, and principal genres in which the author writes are listed on the first line of the author entry.

•The **subject heading** defines the theme of each entry in "The Year in Review" and "Topics in Literature" sections.

•A brief biographical and critical introduction to the author and his or her work precedes excerpted criticism in the "New Authors," "Prizewinners" and "In Memoriam" sections; the subjects, authors, and works in the "Topics in Literature" section are introduced in a similar manner.

•A listing of **principal works** is included for all entries in the "Prizewinners" section.

•**Cross-references** have been included in all sections, except "The Year in Review," to direct readers to other useful sources published by Gale Research: *Short Story Criticism* and *Children's Literature Review*, which provide excerpts of criticism on the works of short story writers and authors of children's books, respectively; *Contemporary Authors*, which includes detailed biographical and bibliographical sketches on more than 95,000 authors; *Something about the Author*, which contains heavily illustrated biographical sketches of writers and illustrators who create books for children and young adults; *Dictionary of Literary Biography*, which provides original evaluations and detailed biographies of authors important to literary history; and *Contemporary Authors Autobiography Series* and *Something about the Author Autobiography Series*, which present autobiographical essays by prominent writers of adult literature and those of interest to young readers, respectively. Previous volumes of *CLC* in which the author has been featured are also listed.

•A **portrait** of the author is included in the "New Authors," "Prizewinners," "In Memoriam," and "Topics in Literature" sections, and **an excerpt from the author's work**, if available, provides readers with a sampling of the writer's style and thematic approach in the "New Authors," "Prizewinners," and "Topics in Literature" sections.

•The **excerpted criticism**, included in all entries except those in the "Year in Review" section, represents essays selected by editors to reflect the spectrum of opinion about a specific work or about the author's writing in general. The excerpts are arranged chronologically, adding a useful perspective to the entry. All titles by the author are printed in boldface type, enabling the reader to easily identify the work being discussed.

•A complete **bibliographical citation**, designed to help the user find the original essay or book, follows each excerpt.

Other Features

•An **Acknowledgments** section lists the copyright holders who have granted permission to reprint material in this volume of *CLC*. It does not, however, list every book or periodical reprinted or consulted during the preparation of the volume.

•A **Cumulative Author Index** lists all the authors who have appeared in the various literary criticism series published by Gale Research, with cross-references to Gale's biographical and autobiographical series. A full listing of the series referenced in the index appears on page 451 of this volume. Readers will welcome this cumulated author index as a useful tool for locating an author within the various series. The index, which lists birth and death dates when available, will be particularly valuable for those authors who are identified with a certain period but whose death date causes them to be placed in another, or for those authors whose careers span two periods. For example, Ernest Hemingway is found in *CLC*, yet a writer often associated with him, F. Scott Fitzgerald, is found in *Twentieth-Century Literary Criticism*.

•Beginning with *CLC*, Vol. 65, each *Yearbook* will contain a **Cumulative Topic Index**, which lists all literary topics treated in *CLC Yearbook* volumes, *Literature Criticism: 1400-1800*, and the Topic volumes of *Twentieth-Century Literary Criticism* and *Nineteenth-Century Literature Criticism*.

•A **Cumulative Nationality Index** alphabetically lists all authors featured in *CLC* by nationality, followed by numbers corresponding to the volumes in which they appear.

•A **Title Index** alphabetically lists all titles reviewed in the current volume of *CLC*. Listings are followed by the author's name and the corresponding page numbers where the titles are discussed. English translations of foreign titles and variations of titles are cross-referenced to the title under which a work was originally published. Titles of novels, novellas, dramas, films, record albums, and poetry, short story, and essay collections are printed in italics, while all individual poems, short stories, essays, and songs are printed in roman type within quotation marks; when published separately (e.g., T.S. Eliot's poem *The Waste Land*), the title will also be printed in italics.

•In response to numerous suggestions from librarians, Gale has also produced a **special paper-bound edition** of the *CLC* title index. This annual cumulation, which alphabetically lists all titles reviewed in the series, is available to all customers and will be published with the first volume of *CLC* issued in each calendar year. Additional copies of the index are available upon request. Librarians and patrons will welcome this separate index: it saves shelf space, is easy to use, and is disposable upon receipt of the following year's cumulation.

A Note to the Reader

When writing papers, students who quote directly from any volume in the Literary Criticism Series may use the following general forms to footnote reprinted criticism. The first example pertains to material drawn from periodicals, the second to material reprinted from books:

[1] Anne Tyler, "Manic Monologue," *The New Republic* 200 (April 17, 1989), 44-6; excerpted and reprinted in *Contemporary Literary Criticism,* Vol. 58, ed. Roger Matuz (Detroit: Gale Research, 1990), p. 325.

[2] Patrick Reilly, *The Literature of Guilt: From 'Gulliver' to Golding* (University of Iowa Press, 1988); excerpted and reprinted in *Contemporary Literary Criticism,* Vol. 58, ed. Roger Matuz (Detroit: Gale Research, 1990), pp. 206-12.

Suggestions Are Welcome

The editors welcome the comments and suggestions of readers to expand the coverage and enhance the usefulness of the series.

Acknowledgments

The editors wish to thank the copyright holders of the excerpted criticism included in this volume, the permissions managers of many book and magazine publishing companies for assisting us in securing reprint rights, and Anthony Bogucki for assistance with copyright research. We are also grateful to the staffs of the Detroit Public Library, the Library of Congress, the University of Detroit Library, Wayne State University Purdy/Kresge Library Complex, and the University of Michigan Libraries for making their resources available to us. Following is a list of the copyright holders who have granted us permission to reprint material in this volume of CLC. Every effort has been made to trace copyright, but if omissions have been made, please let us know.

COPYRIGHTED EXCERPTS IN *CLC*, VOLUME 65, WERE REPRINTED FROM THE FOLLOWING PERIODICALS:

America, v. 160, May 13, 1989. © 1989. All rights reserved. Reprinted with permission of America Press, Inc., 106 West 56th Street, New York, NY 10019.—*The American Book Review,* v. 9, September-October, 1987; v. 10, September-October, 1988. © 1987, 1988, by *The American Book Review.* Both reprinted by permission of the publisher.—*The American Poetry Review,* v. 18, November-December, 1989 for "Thresholds" by Marianne Boruch. Copyright © 1989 by World Poetry, Inc. Reprinted by permission of the author.—*The American Spectator,* v. 24, February, 1991. Copyright © *The American Spectator* 1991. Reprinted by permission of the publisher.— *Américas,* v. 42, 1990. © 1990 *Américas.* Reprinted by permission of the publisher.—*The Antioch Review,* v. 48, Spring, 1990. Copyright © 1990 by the Antioch Review Inc. Reprinted by permission of the Editors.—*Ariel: A Review of International English Literature,* v. 21, January, 1990 for "Henry Louis Gates, Jr. and the Theory of 'Signifyin(g)' " by Brad Bucknell. Copyright © 1990 The Board of Governors, The University of Calgary. Reprinted by permission of the publisher and the author.—*The Atlantic Monthly,* v. 265, March, 1990 for a review of "Paradise" by Phoebe-Lou Adams. Copyright 1990 by The Atlantic Monthly Company, Boston, MA. Reprinted by permission of the author.—*Black American Literature Forum,* v. 24, Spring, 1990 for "Afro-American Criticism and Western Consciousness: The Politics of Knowing" by JoAnne Cornwell-Giles. Copyright © 1990 Indiana State University. Reprinted by permission of the author.—*The Bloomsbury Review,* v. 10, May-June, 1990 for a review of "The Great Letter E" by Leighton Klein; v. 11, January-February, 1991 for a review of "The Book of J" by H. L. Mortimer, Jr. Copyright © by Owaissa Communications Company, Inc. 1990, 1991. Both reprinted by permission of the respective authors.—*Book World,* November, 1990. © 1990, *The Washington Post.* Reprinted by permission of the publisher.—*Book World—Chicago Tribune,* August 13, 1989. © copyrighted 1989, Chicago Tribune Company. All rights reserved. Used with permission.—*Book World—The Washington Post,* August 20, 1989; January 14, 1990; January 28, 1990; February 11, 1990; April 22, 1990; May 29, 1990; June 24, 1990; July 1, 1990; July 15, 1990; September 16, 1990; December 30, 1990. © 1989, 1990, *The Washington Post.* All reprinted by permission of the publisher.—*Booklist,* v. 85, June 15, 1989; v. 86, November 1, 1989; v. 86, February 15, 1990; v. 86, May 1, 1990. Copyright © 1989, 1990 by the American Library Association. All reprinted by permission of the publisher.—*Books in Canada,* v. 18, June-July, 1989 for "The Teeth of Comedy" by Jack MacLeod; v. 19, October, 1990 for "Morley Callaghan 1903-1990: A Tribute" by Joyce Marshall. Both reprinted by permission of the respective authors.—*Callaloo,* v. 11, Summer, 1988. Copyright © 1988 by Charles H. Rowell. All rights reserved. Reprinted by permission of the publisher.—*The Canadian Forum,* v. LXVIV, July-August, 1990 for "The Governor General's Fiction" by Julie Mason. Reprinted by permission of the author.—*Canadian Literature,* n. 126, Autumn, 1990 for "Callaghan" by Bryan N. S. Gooch. Reprinted by permission of the author.—*The Chicago Sun-Times,* July 23, 1990. Reprinted by permission of Associated Press.—*Chicago Tribune—Books,* May 27, 1990 for "Death at Sea, CIA Strife, and Violent Irish Politics" by Frederick Busch. © copyrighted 1990, Chicago Tribune Company. All rights reserved. Reprinted by permission of the author./March 11, 1990; May 27, 1990; July 8, 1990. © copyrighted 1990, Chicago Tribune Company. All rights reserved. All used with permission.—*The Christian Science Monitor,* March 22, 1989 for "Bathgate: Technique Surpasses Tale" by Merle Rubin; April 30, 1990 for "Elegant First Novel Relates a Family Saga" by Merle Rubin; June 15, 1990 for "Stories of Experience" by Thomas D'Evelyn; July 18, 1990 for "Coming of Age with 'Mami' and 'Papi' " by Merle Rubin; October 18, 1990 for "Paz's Poetry Replaces Revolutionary Hope" by Thomas D'Evelyn. © 1989, 1990 by the respective authors. All rights reserved. All reprinted by permission of the respective authors.—*College English,* v. 50, February, 1988 for "Literature, History, and Afro-American Studies" by William E. Cain. Copyright © 1988 by the National Council of Teachers of English. Reprinted by permission of the publisher and the author.—*Commentary,* v. 89, April, 1990 for "Newspeak, Feminist-Style" by Robert Lerner and Stanley Rothman; v. 91, March, 1991 for "Literature by Quota" by Carol Iannone. Copyright © 1990, 1991 by the American Jewish Committee. All rights reserved. Both reprinted by permission of the publisher and the respective authors.—*Commonweal,* v. CXVI, October 20, 1989; v. CXVII, April 6, 1990; v. CXVII, June 1, 1990; v. CXVII, November 9, 1990. Copyright © 1989, 1990 Commonweal Foundation. All reprinted by permission of Commonweal Foundation.—*Critical Inquiry,*—v. 13, Autumn, 1986 for "Talkin' That Talk" by Henry Louis Gates, Jr. Copyright © 1986 by The University of Chicago. Reprinted by permission of the publisher and Brandt & Brandt Literary Agents, Inc.—*Cultural Critique,* n. 6, Spring, 1987. © 1987 *Cultural Critique.* Reprinted by permission of the publisher, Oxford University Press.—*Essays on Canadian Writing,* n. 41, Summer, 1990. © 1990 Essays on Canadian Writing Ltd. Reprinted by permission of the publisher.—*The Georgia Review,* v. XLIV, Spring-Summer, 1990 for "Some Recent Herstories" by Greg Johnson. Copyright, 1990, by the University of Georgia. Reprinted by permission of the publisher and the author.—*The Iowa Review,* v. 18, Spring-Summer, 1988 for a review of "Tomas Tranströmer: Selected Poems, 1954-1986" by Nance Van Winckel. Copyright © 1988 by The University of Iowa. Reprinted by permission of the publisher and the author.—*Ironwood,* 13, v. 7, 1979 for "Recurrent Images in the Poetry of Tomas Tranströmer" by Mary Sears Mattfield. Copyright © 1979 by Ironwood Press. Reprinted by permission of the author.—*The Kenyon Review,* n.s. v. XIII, Winter, 1991 for a review of "God Hunger" by David Baker. Copyright 1991 by Kenyon College. All rights reserved. Reprinted by permission of the author.—*Kirkus Reviews,* v. LVII, November 15, 1989; v. LVII, December 15, 1989. Copyright © 1989 The Kirkus Service, Inc. All rights reserved. Both reprinted by permission of the publisher.—*Library Journal,* v. 115, June 1, 1990. Copyright © 1990 by Reed Publishing, USA, Division of Reed Holdings, Inc./ v. 114, December, 1989 for a review of "The Quincunx" by Cynthia Johnson Whealler. Copyright © 1989 by Reed Publishing, USA, Division of Reed Holdings, Inc. Reprinted from *Library Journal,* published by R. R. Bowker, Co., Division of Reed Publishing, USA, by permission of the publisher and the author.—*The Listener,* v. 123, March 29, 1990; v. 123, May 31, 1990; v. 124, August 16, 1990; v. 124, August 30, 1990; v. 124, September 27, 1990. © British Broadcasting Corp. 1990./ v. 121, March 9, 1989 for "Bearing Witness" by William Scammell; v. 122, September 14, 1989 for "True-ish Crime Stories" by Andrew Clifford; v. 122, December 21-28, 1989 for "God Bless Us, Everyone" by Peter Parker; v. 123, June 7, 1990 for "Walking Wounded" by Rose Tremain. © British Broadcasting Corp. 1989, 1990. All reprinted by permission of the respective authors.—*London Review of Books,* v. 11, January 5, 1989 for "Foreigners" by John Lanchester; v. 11, May 18, 1989 for "Spanish Practices" by Edwin Williamson; v. 11, September 28, 1989 for "Shakespeare the Novelist" by John Sutherland; v. 12, March 8, 1990 for "Prolonging Her Abscence" by Danny Karlin; v. 12, September 13, 1990 for "Dirty Jokes" by Julian Symons. All appear here by permission of the *London Review of Books* and the respective authors.—*Los Angeles Times,* August 29, 1990; October 1, 1990; October 26, 1990. Copyright, 1990, *Los Angeles Times.* All reprinted by permission of the publisher.—*Los Angeles Times Book Review,* March 5, 1989; September 3, 1989; December 10, 1989; January 7, 1990; January 21, 1990; March 11, 1990; March 25, 1990; April 8, 1990; April 15, 1990; April 29, 1990; May 20, 1990; June 24, 1990; July 1, 1990; July 15, 1990; August 5, 1990; October 28, 1990; November 4, 1990. Copyright, 1989, 1990, *Los Angeles Times.* All reprinted by permission of the publisher.—*Maclean's Magazine,* v. 102, March 6, 1989; v. 102, May 29, 1989. © *Maclean's Magazine.* Both reprinted by permission of the publisher.—*The Magazine of Fantasy and Science Fiction,* v. 78, July 1990 for a review of "Destiny Express" by Algis Budrys. © 1990 by Mercury Press Inc. Reprinted by permission of *The Magazine of Fantasy and Science Fiction* and the author.—*Michigan Quarterly Review,* v. XXIX, Winter, 1990 for "The Shape of Women's Lives" by Linda Simon. Copyright © The University of Michigan, 1990. Reprinted by permission of the author.—*Modern Drama,* v. XXXIII, March, 1990. Copyright 1990 *Modern Drama,* University of Toronto. Reprinted by permission of the publisher.—*Modern Fiction Studies,* v. 34, Spring, 1988. Copyright © 1988 by Purdue Research Foundation, West Lafayette, IN 47907. All rights reserved. Reprinted with permission.—*Modern Philology,* v. 88, 1990 for a review of "The Signifying Monkey: A Theory of Afro-American Literary Criticism" by Kenneth Warren. © 1990 by The University of Chicago. Reprinted by permission of the University of Chicago Press and the author.—*The Nation,* New York, v. 248, April 3, 1989; v. 248, May 15, 1989; v. 249, October 2, 1989; v. 249, November 27, 1989; v. 250, January 29, 1990; v. 250, March 19, 1990; v. 251, October 22, 1990. Copyright 1989, 1990 *The Nation* magazine/ The Nation Company, Inc. All reprinted by permission of the publisher.—*The New Criterion,* v. IX, September, 1990 for "Walker Percy, 1916-1990" by Cleanth Brooks; v. IX, February, 1991 for "Victorians' Secrets" by Donna Rifkind. Copyright © 1990, 1991 by The Foundation for Cultural Review. Both reprinted by permission of the respective authors.—*The New England Quarterly,* v. 62, December, 1989 for "Henry Louis Gates, Jr., and African-American Literary Discourse" by Wahneema Lubiano. Copyright 1989 by *The New England Quarterly.* Reprinted by permission of the publisher and the author.—*New Literary History,* v. 18, Winter, 1987. Copyright © 1987 by *New Literary History.* Reprinted by permission of the publisher.—*The New Republic,* v. 202, March 26, 1990 for "The Havels and the Have-Nots" by Robert Brustein. © 1990 The New Republic, Inc. Reprinted by permission of the author./ v. 176, February 26, 1977; v. 191, July 9, 1984; v. 200, January 9 & 16, 1989; v. 200, March 20, 1989; v. 202, January 8 & 15, 1990; v. 202, January 29, 1990; v. 202, June 4, 1990; v. 203, July 23, 1990; v. 204, January 7 & 14, 1991; v. 204, February 4, 1991. © 1977, 1984, 1989, 1990, 1991 The New Republic, Inc. All reprinted by permission of *The New Republic.*—*New Statesman & Society,* v. 2, March 3, 1989; v. 2, September 15, 1989; v. 3, March 16, 1990; v. 3, May 18, 1990; v. 3, June 1, 1990. © 1989, 1990 Statesman & Nation Publishing Company Limited. All reprinted by permission of the publisher.—*New York,* Magazine, v. 22, September 4, 1989; v. 23, October 1, 1990. Copyright © 1991 News America Publishing, Inc. All rights reserved. Both reprinted with permission of *New York* Magazine.—*New York Native,* October 1, 1990 for "Young Enough to Know Better" by Kevin Grubb. Reprinted by permission of the author.—*New York Post,* August 23, 1989. © 1989, *New York Post.* Reprinted by permission of the publisher.—*The New York Review of Books,* v. XXXVIII, January 17, 1991 for "The Long Voyage Home" by Garry Wills. Copyright © 1991 Nyrev, Inc. Reprinted by permission of the author./ v. XXXVI, April 27, 1989; v. XXXVII, January 18, 1990; v. XXXVII, May 31, 1990; v. XXXVII, August 16, 1990; v. XXXVII, November 22, 1990. Copyright © 1989, 1990 Nyrev, Inc. All reprinted with permission from *The New York Review of Books.*—*The New York Times,* August 23, 1989; January 12, 1990; January 15, 1990; February 15, 1990; March 19, 1990; April 3, 1990; April 23, 1990; May 11, 1990; June 27, 1990; July 24, 1990; August 27, 1990; September 20, 1990; September 21, 1990; October 1, 1990; October 12, 1990. Copyright © 1989, 1990 by The New York Times Company. All reprinted by permission of the publisher.—*The New York Times Book Review,* August 14, 1988; February 26, 1989; August 27, 1989; November 5, 1989; January 14, 1990; February 25, 1990; February 26, 1990; March 4, 1990; April 1, 1990; May 6, 1990; June 17, 1990; June 24, 1990; July 1, 1990; July 8, 1990; September 23, 1990; October 21, 1990. Copyright © 1988, 1989, 1990 by The New York Times Company. All reprinted by permission of the publisher,—*The New Yorker,* v. LXVI, January 21, 1991 for "The Female Yahwist" by Edward Hirsch. © 1991 by the author. Reprinted by permission of the publisher./ v. LXVI, July 2, 1990. © 1990 by The New Yorker Magazine, Inc. Reprinted by permission of the publisher.—*News of Atheneum Publishers,* January, 1990.—*Newsday,* September 19, 1990 for "Young Playwrights Work Without a Net" by Jan Stuart. © Newsday, Inc. 1990. Reprinted by permission of the author./ August 23, 1989. © Newsday, Inc. 1989. Reprinted by permission.—*Newsweek,* v. CXV, April 2, 1990; v. CXV, May 28, 1990; v. CXVI, October 1, 1990. Copyright 1990, by Newsweek, Inc. All rights reserved. All reprinted by permission of the publisher.—*The Observer,* November 20, 1988; February 26, 1989; September 10, 1989; March 11, 1990; June 3, 1990. All reprinted by permission of The Observer Limited, London.—*Open Letter,* Seventh Series, Summer, 1990 for "What Is a Nice Feminist Like Me Doing in a Place Like This?" by Janice Williamson. Copyright © 1990 by the author. Reprinted by permission of the author.—*The Paris Review,* v. 31, Winter, 1989 for an interview with Manuel Puig by Kathleen Wheaton. © 1989 The Paris Review, Inc. Reprinted by permission of the Literary Estate of Manuel Puig.—*Partisan Review,* v. LVII, Spring, 1990 for "Feminism and Politics" by Jean Bethke Elshtain. Copyright © 1990 by *Partisan Review.* Reprinted by permission of the author.—*Poetry,* v. CLIV, April, 1989 for a review of "The Collected Poems of Octavio Paz: 1957-1987" by J. D. McClatchy. © 1989 by the Modern Poetry Association. Reprinted by permission of the Editor of *Poetry* and the author.—*Poetry Flash,* n. 212, November, 1990 for "Pardon Him For Writing Well: The Nobel Prize for Octavio Paz" by John Oliver Simon. Reprinted by permission of the author.—*Poetry Review,* v. 78, Spring, 1988 for "From the Tree-line" by Alan Brownjohn. Copyright © The Poetry Society 1988. Reprinted by permission of the author.—*Publishers Weekly,* v. 235, June 16, 1989; v. 236, December 15, 1989; v. 236, December 22, 1989; v. 237, February 9, 1990; v. 237, April 13, 1990. Copyright 1989, 1990 by Reed Publishing USA. All reprinted from *Publishers Weekly,* published by the Bowker Magazine Group of Cahners Publishing Co., a division of Reed Publishing USA.—*Quill and Quire,* v. 55, May, 1989 for "Sex 'n' Drugs 'n' Rock 'n' Droll" by Paul Kennedy; v. 56, October, 1990 for "Morley Callaghan: 1903-1990" by David Staines. Both reprinted by permission of *Quill and Quire* and the respective authors.—*Raleigh News and Observer,* March 11, 1990. Reprinted by permission of the publisher.—*Research in African Literatures,* v. 21, Spring, 1990. Reprinted by permission of Indiana University Press.—*The Review of Contemporary Fiction,* v. 10, Spring, 1990. Copyright, 1990, by John O'Brien. Reprinted by permission of the publisher.—*San Francisco Chronicle,* August 12, 1990. © 1990 *San Francisco Chronicle.* Reprinted by permission of the publisher.—*The San Juan Star Magazine,* February 10, 1991. Reprinted by permission of the publisher.—*Saturday Night,* v. 105, September, 1990 for "Gentle Revolutionary" by George Galt. Copyright © 1990 by *Saturday Night.* Reprinted by permission of the author.—*The Southern Literary Journal.* v. XXIII, Fall, 1990. Copyright 1990 by the Department of English, University of North Carolina at Chapel Hill. Reprinted by permission of the publisher.—*The Southern Review,* Louisiana State University, v. 24, Spring, 1988 for "Written by Ourselves" by Marcellus Blount; v. 26, Spring, 1990 for "Four American Poets" by Sidney Burris; v. 26, Fall, 1990 for "Walker Percy, 1916-1990" by Lewis P. Simpson. Copyright, 1988, 1990, by the author. All reprinted by permission of the respective authors.—*The Spectator,* v. 264, March 3, 1990 for "Eminent Victorians and Others" by Anita Brookner. © 1990 by *The Spectator.* Reprinted by permission of the author./ v. 264, June 9, 1990. © by *The Spectator.* Reprinted by permission of *The Spectator.*—*The Star-Ledger,* September 20, 1990. Reprinted by permission of the publisher.—*Sulfur,* v. X, Fall, 1990. Copyright © *Sulfur* 1990. Reprinted by permission of the publisher.—*Theater,* v. XXI, Summer-Fall, 1990 for "Mac Wellman's Horizontal Avalanches" by Eric Overmyer. Copyright © by *Theater,* formerly *yale/theatre* 1990. Reprinted by permission of the publisher and the author.—*The Threepenny Review,* v. XI, Summer, 1990. © copyright 1990 by *The Threepenny Review.* Reprinted by permission of the publisher.—*Times,* New York, v. 135, January 8, 1990; v. 135, January 29, 1990; v. 135, May 21, 1990. Copyright 1990 The Time Inc. Magazine Company. All rights reserved. All reprinted by permission of the publisher.—*The Times,* London, July 26, 1990; August 28, 1990; October 1, 1990; October 12, 1990. © Times Newspapers Limited 1990. All reproduced from *The Times,* London by permission.—*The Times Literary Supplement,* n. 4489, April 14-20, 1989; n. 4511, September 15, 1989; n. 4535, March 2, 1990; n. 4549, June 8, 1990; n. 4550, June 15-21, 1990; n. 4555, July 20-26, 1990; n. 4561, August 31-September 6, 1990; n. 4573, November 23-29, 1990. © Times Supplements Ltd. (London) 1989, 1990. All reproduced from *The Times Literary Supplement* by permission.—*USA Today,* September 1, 1989. Copyright 1989, *USA Today.* Excerpted with permission of the publisher.—*The Village Voice,* v. XXXV, April 3, 1990 for "Horse Play" by Richard Gehr; v. XXXV, October 2, 1990 for "Same Streets, Other Scenes" by Michael Feingold. Copyright © News Group Publications, Inc., 1990. Both reprinted by permission of *The Village Voice* and the respective authors.—*Virginia Quarterly Re-*

view, v. 66, Spring, 1990. Copyright, 1990, by *The Virginia Quarterly Review,* The University of Virginia. Reprinted by permission of the publisher.—*VLS,* n. 83, March, 1990 for a review of "The Great Letter E" by Jane Mendelsohn. Copyright © 1990 News Group Publications, Inc. Reprinted by permission of *The Village Voice* and the author.—*The Wall Street Journal,* September 1, 1989; January 18, 1990; February 28, 1990; March 9, 1990; August 14, 1990; October 12, 1990. © Dow Jones & Company, Inc. 1989, 1990. All rights reserved. All reprinted by permission of *The Wall Street Journal.—The Washington Post,* May 11, 1990; October 1, 1990. © 1990, Washington Post Co. Both reprinted by permission of the publisher.—*The Washington Times,* February 26, 1990. Reprinted by permission of the publisher.—*West Coast Review of Books,* v. 14, March-April, 1990; v. 15, June-July, 1990. Copyright 1990 by Rapport Publishing Co., Inc. Both reprinted by permission of the publisher.—*The Women's Review of Books,* v. VII, February, 1990 for "Reprint Rights, Reprint Wrongs" by Carol Barash; v. VII, February, 1990 for "The Permanent Revolution" by Sandra Harding; v. VII, February, 1990 for "Lambasting the Liberals" by Victoria Kahn; v. VII, February, 1990 for "At the Crossroads of Culture" by Peggy Pascoe; v. VII, April, 1990 for "Problems for Profit?" by Harriet Goldhor Lerner; v. VII, May, 1990 for "Different Differences" by Amanda Leslie-Spinks. Copyright © 1990. All rights reserved. All reprinted by permission of the respective authors.—*World Literature Today,* v. 64, Autumn, 1990. Copyright 1990 by the University of Oklahoma Press./ v. 64, Autumn, 1990. Copyright 1990 by the University of Oklahoma Press. Reprinted by permission of the publisher.

COPYRIGHTED EXCERPTS IN *CLC,* VOLUME 65, WERE REPRINTED FROM THE FOLLOWING BOOKS:

Byatt, A. S. From *Possession: A Romance.* Random House, 1990. Copyright © 1990 by A. S. Byatt. All rights reserved.—Castedo, Elena. From *Paradise.* Grove Weidenfeld, 1990. Copyright © 1990 by Elena Castedo. All rights reserved.—Chiles, Frances. From *Octavio Paz: The Mythic Dimension.* Peter Lang, 1987. © Peter Lang Publishing, Inc., New York 1987. All rights reserved. Reprinted by permission of the publisher.—DeFerrari, Gabriella. From *A Cloud on Sand.* Alfred A. Knopf, 1990. Copyright ©. 1990 by Gabriella De Ferrari. All rights reserved.—Doctorow, E. L. From *Billy Bathgate.* Random House, 1989. Copyright © 1989 by E. L. Doctorow. All rights reserved.—Edgecombe, Rodney Stenning. From *Vision and Style in Patrick White: A Study of Five Novels.* The University of Alabama Press, 1989. Copyright © 1989 by The University of Alabama Press. All rights reserved. Reprinted by permission of the publisher.—Fein, John M. From *Toward Octavio Paz: A Reading of His Major Poems, 1957-1976.* The University Press of Kentucky, 1986. Copyright © by The University Press of Kentucky. Reprinted by permission of the publisher.—Ferrigno, Robert. From *Horse Latitudes.* William Morrow and Company, Inc., 1990. Copyright © 1990 by Robert Ferrigno. All rights reserved.—Harding, Gunnar. From an interview in *Tomas Tranströmer: Selected Poems.* Translated by Robin Fulton. Ardis, 1981. Copyright © 1981 by Robin Fulton. Reprinted by permission of the translator.—Hijuelos, Oscar. From *The Mambo Kings Play Songs of Love.* Farrar, Straus and Giroux, Inc., 1989. Copyright © 1989 by Oscar Hijuelos. All rights reserved.—Hynes James. From *The Wild Colonial Boy.* Atheneum, 1990. Copyright © 1990 by James Hynes. All rights reserved.—Johnson, Charles. From *Middle Passage.* Atheneum, 1990. Copyright © 1990 by Charles Johnson. All rights reserved.—Jones, Louis B. From *Ordinary Money.* Viking, 1990. Copyright © Louis B. Jones, 1990. All rights reserved.—Kohout, Pavel. From "The Chaste Centaur," translated by Milan Pomichalek and Anna Mozga, in *The Vanek Plays Four Authors, One Character.* Edited by Marketa Goetz-Stankiewicz. Vancouver: UBC Press, 1987. Copyright University of British Columbia Press, 1987. All rights reserved. Reprinted with permission of the publisher.—Lavers, Norman. From *Pop Culture into Art: The Novels of Manuel Puig.* University of Missouri Press, 1988. Copyright © 1988 by The Curators of The University of Missouri. All rights reserved. Reprinted by permission of the publisher.—Leimbach, Marti. From *Dying Young.* Doubleday, 1990. Copyright © 1990 by Marti Leimbach. All rights reserved.—McFarland, Dennis. From *The Music Room.* Houghton Mifflin Company, 1990. Copyright © 1990 by Dennis McFarland. All rights reserved. Reprinted by permission of Houghton Mifflin Company.—Miller, Arthur. From "I Think About You A Great Deal," in *Václav Havel or Living in Truth.* Edited by Jan Vladislav. Faber & Faber Limited, 1987. © Jan Vladislav, 1986. All rights reserved. Reprinted by permission of ICOR, Inc.—Morgan, Seth. From *Homeboy.* Random House, 1990. Copyright © 1990 by Seth Morgan. All rights reserved.—O'Brien, Edna. From *Lantern Slides.* Weidenfeld and Nicolson, 1990. Copyright © Edna O'Brien 1990. All rights reserved.—Palliser, Charles. From *The Quincunx.* Ballantine Books, 1989. Copyright © 1989 by Charles Palliser. All rights reserved.—Paz, Octavio. From *A Draft of Shadows and Other Poems.* Edited by Eliot Weinberger and translated by Eliot Weinberger, Elizabeth Bishop and Mark Strand. New Directions, 1979. Copyright © 1972, 1975, 1976, 1978, 1979 by Octavio Paz and Eliot Weinberger. All rights reserved.—Paz, Octavio. From his speech *In Search of the Present: Nobel Lecture,* delivered on December 8, 1990. Translated by Anthony Stanton. © The Nobel Foundation 1990. Reprinted by permission of the Nobel Foundation.—Quarrington, Paul. From *Whale Music.* Doubleday, 1990. Copyright © 1990 by Paul Quarrington. All rights reserved.—Rodman, Howard. From *Destiny Express.* Atheneum, 1990. Copyright © 1990 by Howard A. Rodman. All rights reserved.—Schor, Sandra. From *The Great Letter E: A Novel.* North Point Press, 1990. Copyright © 1990 by Sandra Schor.—Sterchi, Beat. From *Cow.* Translated by Michael Hofmann. Pantheon Books, 1988. Translation copyright © 1988 by Michael Hofmann. All rights reserved.—Steven, Laurence. From *Dissociation and Wholeness in Patrick White's Fiction.* Waterloo: Wilfrid Laurier University Press, 1989. Copyright © 1989 Wilfrid Laurier University Press. Reprinted by permission of the publisher.—Tranströmer, Tomas. From an excerpt in *Tomas Tranströmer: Selected*

Poems. Translated by Robin Fulton. Ardis, 1981. Copyright © 1981 by Robin Fulton. Reprinted by permission of the translator.—White, Patrick. From "Patrick White," in *In the Making.* Edited by Craig McGregor. Thomas Nelson, 1969. Copyright © Craig McGregor, 1969.

PICTURES AND ILLUSTRATIONS APPEARING IN *CLC,* VOLUME 65, WERE RECEIVED FROM THE FOLLOWING SOURCES:

Jacket of *Middle Passages,* by Charles Johnson. Atheneum, 1990. Jacket illustration by Mark Hess. Jacket design by Wendy Bass. Reproduced with permission of Atheneum Publishers, an imprint of Macmillan Publishing Company: **p. 3;** Jacket of *Above the River,* by James Wright. Farrar, Straus and Giroux, 1990. Jacket photograph: "The Ohio River, Martins Ferry," by Madeline Zulauf. Reproduced by permission of Farrar, Straus and Giroux, Inc.: **p. 9;** Jacket of *The Want Bone,* by Robert Pinsky. Ecco, 1990. Jacket illustration: "The Want Bone," by Michael Mazur, 1989. Reproduced by permission of The Ecco Press: **p. 11;** Jacket of *The Mail From Anywhere,* by Brad Leithauser. Knopf, 1990. Jacket painting by Mark Leithauser. Jacket design by Carol Devine Carson. Reproduced by permission Alfred A. Knopf, Inc.: **p. 12;** *Playbill* ® is a registered trademark of Playbill Incorporated, NYC. Used by permission: **pp. 14, 17, 21;** © Gerry Goodstein: **p. 19;** Jacket of *Omeros,* by Derek Walcott, photographed by McDonald Dixon. Jacket design by Cynthia Krupat. Reproduced by permission of Farrar, Straus, and Giroux, Inc.: **p. 25;** © Cecilia Domeyko: **p. 31;** © 1990 Timothy Greenfield-Sanders: **p. 42;** © Jerry Bauer: **pp. 47, 63, 81, 105, 146, 152, 245, 254, 262, 274;** © Sally Stepanek: **p. 51;** © Brett Hall: **p. 56;** Photograph by Susan Wilson: **p. 67;** Greg Simms Photography, New Orleans, LA: **p. 75;** © Ann Summa: **p. 89;** © Nancy Crampton: **p. 95;** © Rheinstrohm/Gerald Wesolowski: **p. 100;** © Tara Heinemann: **p. 121;** Photograph by Layle Silbert: **p. 134;** Photograph by Mark Gerson: **pp. 160, 166;** © Lütfi Özkök: **p. 174;** Brian Willer/MacLean's: **p. 202;** © Thomas Victor, 1989: **p. 208;** Courtesy of OU News Services: **p. 217;** Gilbert A. Jain/University of Oklahoma: **p. 232;** Photograph by Yolanda G. H. Gerritsen: **p. 239;** Photograph by Jean Bloom, courtesy of Harold Bloom: **p. 289;** Culver Pictures: **p. 305;** Courtesy of Oxford University Press: **p. 361;** AP/Wide World Photos: **p. 406;** Drawing by David Levine; reprinted with permission from The New York Review of Books. Copyright © 1990 NYREV, Inc.: **p. 427;** Photograph by Tess Steinkolk: **p. 445.**

The Year in Review

The Year in Fiction

by Wendy Lesser

It was, in many ways, the year of the family novel. But because the exception proves the rule—and because, after all, there were other subjects and are always other subjects for the novel to pursue—I will start with a work that was not a family novel. I will start, that is, with the novel-as-descendant-of-Daniel Defoe rather than the-novel-as-descendant-of-Samuel Richardson. That these simple-minded divisions in the history of the novel must eventually break down will be part, I hope, of the implied thesis of this essay.

Charles Johnson's *Middle Passage* received a lot of attention this year: it won the National Book Award and was nominated for just about everything else. The fact that both the novel's author and its main character are black accounts for part of the book's appeal, but that needn't embarrass us. Amy Tan could not have accomplished her engaging *Joy Luck Club* without being Chinese-American, and the literary achievements of Bernard Malamud, Saul Bellow, and Philip Roth are intimately tied to their Jewishness. Novels are about what's interesting, and ethnicity, in America, is a central source of interest. Moreover, Charles Johnson's novel has other things to recommend it—in particular, its ambition. *Middle Passage* is squarely in the middle of the nineteenth-century Great American Novel tradition. A sea story of men in conflict with each other and with the elements, a microcosm of the whole American "ship of state" and its complex racial problems, Johnson's novel is part *Huckleberry Finn*, part *Moby Dick*, and a great deal *Benito Cereno*. In fact, Melville is such a strong influence on this work that he almost ruins it, for no remake of those earlier sea stories can help but suffer by comparison. There is wit in this tale, and passion, and cleverness mixed with true feeling, but for me, at least, it failed to strike the deep chords that its explicit analogues have sounded.

America is not, of course, the only country in which race is a central issue, as Nadine Gordimer's *My Son's Story* reminds us. Gordimer's novels are the opposite of something like *Middle Passage,* in that they are in no tradition but their own, and one compares them only to the author's prior work. *My Son's Story* is good Gordimer, with powerfully appealing characters facing persuasively real, uncontrived moral dilemmas. Sonny, the book's hero (to the extent it has one), the father to whom the title's "son" belongs, is a mixed-race political activist in South Africa, married to a beautiful woman (also "coloured") named Aila with whom he has two children, Will and Baby. The connection between his son's first name and that of Shakespeare is made explicit throughout the novel, beginning with the epigraph taken from Sonnet 13: "You had a Fa-

ther, let your son say so." For Sonny is a man who, though he finds the political life necessary, feels his deepest commitments and connections to the realm of literature. Or perhaps it is not quite fair to separate the two, because it is a combination of politics and literature that brings him into relation with Hannah, his white mistress, the woman who knows him most fully. The novel is about Sonny and Hannah's affair, its discovery by his son Will, and the wider social context in which all this takes place, including the eventual political activism of every member of Sonny's family. Gordimer tells the story in two voices—one objectively third-person, the other from Will's viewpoint. But the odd thing is that both these viewpoints are mainly concerned with imagining, or rendering, the interior of Sonny's mind, as if the novel is *really* Sonny's (as the title in fact implies). So that at the end, when Gordimer tells us that both parts of the novel are actually by Will—that this document represents his attempt to think himself into his father's mind—we feel momentarily tricked. And yet even that sense of temporary displacement, of being on unsteady ground, is true to the social and moral universe that Gordimer is trying to convey here.

Another of the year's best novels—and again, warranting comparison only with the author's previous work—is Ian McEwan's *The Innocent.* My own favorite McEwan novel is his previous one, *The Child in Time,* which, in terms of pure tightness of plot and powerful creation of feeling, is possibly the best thing published in English in the 1980s. But many people will no doubt prefer *The Innocent;* indeed, many people seem to have done so, to judge by its strong standing on the British best-seller lists. The intricately plotted tale of a love affair in 1950s Berlin between a British spy and a German woman, *The Innocent* is simultaneously a personal drama involving the two lovers and a political drama about, essentially, the connection between the British spy service and its American counterpart. In fact, McEwan initially thought of calling this novel *The Special Relationship,* and then realized that one aspect of the actual "special relationship"—a phrase describing the collaboration between the CIA and British intelligence—is that only the British know the term. *The Innocent* is in any case a wonderful title for this book, with all its overtones of Hitchcockian and Jamesian guilt and incrimination. The movie of *The Turn of the Screw* was in fact called *The Innocents,* and McEwan—in terms of subtlety of character portrayal, trust in his readers' intelligence, and willingness to combine realistic emotional truth with highly crafted artifice—is the closest thing we now possess to Henry James.

Often compared to Ian McEwan is another British writer, Patrick McGrath, who this year published a chilling little horror tale called *Spider.* Like McEwan, McGrath is interested in the exploration of perverse or disturbing states of mind in combination with some degree of physical violence. Unlike McEwan, he occasionally allows his "literariness" to run away with him, so that at times he seems more aware of his own ability to create haunting or allusive sentences than he does of his characters' pain or even existence. *Spider* is a compelling, creepy, convoluted story told by a mad murderer. Its revelation—the extent to which the madman is lying to himself, and therefore to us—comes upon us gradually and quite effectively. (I am purposely not giving away the twist, because the essence of reading this book is to discover it yourself.) McGrath's intelligence and skill make him a pleasure to read, but *Spider* finally lacks what one would hope for in such a work: the chill of true horror.

Creepy murder and audience deception are the established province of Scott Turow, and his 1990 book, *The Burden of Proof,* builds on the ground he paved in *Presumed Innocent*—literally, in terms of the re-use of characters and setting, as well as figuratively, in terms of its concerns. In this case, murder has been replaced by suicide: the initial and initiating event of *The Burden of Proof* is the death, by her own hand, of Sandy Stern's wife, Clara. (Sandy, you may recall, is the attractively capable criminal lawyer who defended Rusty Sabich in *Presumed Innocent.*) The rest of the novel then takes the form of Sandy's investigation into *why* his wife killed herself, and his simultaneous—and ultimately related—exploration of the financial shenanigans

that are afflicting one of his major clients. As in the previous novel, the wrongdoer turns out to be closer to home than we might have expected: the final point of a Scott Turow novel appears to be that the most dangerous enemies are the most intimate ones. (Since his main characters tend to be heterosexual males, these intimate enemies are inevitably female.) Turow is not a stylist in the sense of McEwan or Gordimer, but he is a solid craftsman of the novel, an author who knows how to fit the pieces pleasingly together, how to pace his tale, and how to construct a sentence that doesn't grate on our ears or irritate our sensibilities. I mean it no less as an indicator of Turow's achievements than of his limitations when I say that his are the kind of novels one enjoys reading while on vacation or recovering from the flu.

Another novel about suicide investigated by an intimate is Dennis McFarland's *The Music Room,* which describes Martin Lambert's attempt to come to terms with the death (by defenestration) of his only brother, Perry. I first read a section of this novel as a story in *The New Yorker,* and that section, which dealt with Martin's memories of his and Perry's boyhood in the grandly neglectful Southern home of their alcoholic parents, was so beautifully written and so moving that I committed the author's name to memory, as a wonderful new writer to watch out for. The book as a whole is somewhat less than its parts, or at least than *that* part: the sections about childhood and youthful memories remain the best, while the contemporary sections, though filled with interesting matter, are less persuasive. Musicians and musical metaphors pervade the story, and those are handled with great skill, for McFarland was himself a professional musician for some years. But like Edgar Allan Poe—whose connection to language was primarily rhythmic and musical, and who felt that the ideal literary work ought to be short enough to be consumed in one sitting—Dennis McFarland may be better suited to the short form, in that it gives more scope to the exact, perfectly tuned striking of notes at which he so excels.

A writer who has mastered the short form and made it supremely her own is Alice Munro, whose *Friend of My Youth* represents her work at its (almost always consistent) best. Munro's short stories are, ironically, like novels: they take us so deep into the lives of their characters and give us so much information about time, place, and lifelong behavior that we feel satisfied and filled by each one, as we do when reading a novel. Hers is not the epiphanic short story of the single illuminating moment, nor the "slice of life" story that gives us one segment to represent or indicate a larger continuity. With Munro, we get a whole loaf packed into the length of a slice. The subjects of *Friend of My Youth* range from a dying mother to adulterous love affairs to divorce to female friendship; (these topics tend to recur—Munro is nothing if not obsessional in her themes). But what marks all of her stories is the concern with the telling voice: the specific acknowledgment of a relationship not only between the narrator and her characters or between the recollecting writer and her own remembered past, but between the author and her readers.

In a Father's Place is another collection of accomplished

short fiction, this one by a newcomer, Christopher Tilghman. Tilghman is more within the mainstream than Munro—his tales, for instance, are both epiphanic *and* slice-of-life, and each one ends with a mild if calculated punch in our collective readerly stomachs—but then he hasn't had nearly as long as she to develop his own style. Being a man, he is more interested in fathers, where Munro is focused on mothers; and being a relatively young man, he spends more time on a father's (or sometimes mother's) relationship with young children than on the older adult's memories of aging or dead parents. But there is evidence, even at this early stage, of the capacity for great empathy in Tilghman's work. He seems to be a writer who is not limited by geography, or class, or occupation, or historical moment; his characters and situations run the gamut. What unites these stories is, I would say, an overriding concern with the spiritual element of existence—not necessarily religion as such, but our collective and individual ways of coping with death, dailiness, impermanence, and continuity.

John Updike's final Rabbit Angstrom book, **Rabbit at Rest,** purports also to be about spirituality and death—or, at any rate, religion and physical decline. As always, Updike is better on the concrete, detailed level than on any other; at that level he may be supreme among his peers. Reading Updike's novels always reminds me of George Orwell's characterization of Salvador Dali: a genius from the wrist down. Heart and even mind get shorter shrift from these masters of minutiae, and that is a big problem in a book that is supposed to be about Final Things. But in many ways I find **Rabbit at Rest** to be the most congenial of the Rabbit books, in that Updike's irritability is frank and unmediated. There's not the furtive pretense of pleasure, the I'm-having-a-better-time-than-the-next-guy self-congratulation, that I felt tinged the earlier books with a high level of bad faith. Rabbit is depressed here, and so is Updike, and therefore the meanspiritedness which has characterized the whole tetralogy makes more sense. Florida, too, provides a welcome new setting (and a host of new satiric targets), a break from the endlessly aging landscape of urbanized Pennsylvania. There is even a kind of affection (though I think that word actually overstates the case) in Updike's retrospective view of Rabbit's life. All the earlier characters make command appearances here, in body or spirit, and some of them even get redeemed. Whether Rabbit himself does, immediately before or after death, is more than Updike is willing to let on.

Meanspiritedness is also at work in Jamaica Kincaid's novel **Lucy,** but here it is raised to the level of art. Jamaica Kincaid is the most terrifying of our new novelists—a kind of Caribbean Nabokov who skewers her human specimens like dead butterflies on the pins of her sharp English sentences. She comes to English, and indeed to writing, as to a weapon with which she can wreak mortal damage, and nobody survives unscathed, not even (or especially not) her autobiographical narrators. The eponymous heroine of this book is a highly intelligent young woman imported from "the islands" to serve as children's nanny to a wealthy, attractive Manhattan family. With unblinkered accuracy and an equal degree of objectivity, she chronicles

the disintegration of the marriage and the husband's flight to the arms of the wife's best friend, meanwhile detailing her own erotic adventures, her escape from her West Indian family, and her progress toward independence. The prevailing metaphor in **Lucy** is one of cold against warmth, not only in terms of climate (New York's winters versus the Caribbean's), but also in terms of emotional tone (Lucy and her author's steely vision, as set against the pampered sweetness of the wealthy young mother). This novel represents truth at the expense of everything else—sentiment, loyalty, amelioration, forgiveness. Although these too are virtues, they come to seem minor when set against the magnitude of Jamaica Kincaid's relentless honesty.

Salman Rushdie weighs in this year with his own argument in favor of truth: **Haroun and the Sea of Stories,** a fairy tale ostensibly composed for the author's young son, whom he has not been able to see since the Ayatollah's death decree drove Rushdie into hiding. Rushdie's version of truth is, characteristically, a version of fiction. Haroun is a boy whose father, Rashid Khalifa, is a professional story-teller with "teller's" block; for various reasons, his sea of stories has dried up. It is Haroun's task (in the old-fashioned, knightly-quest sense of the word) to get into the alternate world where stories come from and unplug his father's pipes. While there, he also saves a few kingdoms and vanquishes the evil dictator who has banned fantasy from his realm and kept his population in miserable thrall. Ravishingly written (as usual with Rushdie), this parable is directly about all the things it seems to be about, and it is ironic that in its wake Rushdie should have repudiated his *Satanic Verses*—should have capitulated, that is, to the demands of a story-hating dictator. But as D. H. Lawrence aptly remarked, "Never trust the artist. Trust the tale."

A whole slew of American novels addressed the parent-child relationship in far less metaphorical terms than Rushdie's. One of the most interesting of these, because the most eccentric, was Nicholson Baker's **Room Temperature.** Though disappointing in comparison to his marvelous debut novel, *The Mezzanine*—disappointing in part because of its stylistic overlaps with the earlier novel—**Room Temperature** is a witty, smartly written, rigorously investigative report of the thoughts that go through a new father's mind as he sits at home feeding his infant daughter. Baker admits to being influenced by Updike, and like Updike he is fascinated by both the physical minutiae of existence and its expression in precisely chiselled language. But unlike Updike, Baker cares deeply for his characters, and grants them (or rather, him—there is always one central Bakerian personality) perceptions and ideas and realizations as intelligent as the author's. What a Baker novel does is to track the digressive, inclusive, allusive motion of an agile human brain—to mimic, in a manner sometimes reminiscent of *Tristram Shandy,* the humorous, appealing, enraptured vacillations of an unfettered mind contemplating no particular problem.

From the eccentric to the conventional, from the enraptured to the flat, is the distance one must travel to get from **Room Temperature** to Sue Miller's **Family Pictures.** Miller is one of those inexplicably overrated novelists who has gotten much further than one could believe on the basis of mere competence. There is nothing overtly wrong with her novels: they are intelligently constructed, realistically rendered, psychologically and sociologically valid portrayals of significant domestic "problems" (child custody in *The Good Mother,* autism and its effects on the family in this one). Perhaps therein lies the flaw. Miller is so busy examining the problem of her choice that the finished book is more likely to appeal to social workers and family therapists than to avid novel-readers. For what we want in a novel, I think, is some sense of the gripping individuality of the characters. In *Family Pictures,* even Miller's stand-in, a photographer named Nina (for "photographer" read "novelist"), is no more and no less compelling than any of her siblings, each of whom represents a different aspect of Fifties-through-Seventies Americana (Vietnam vet, beautiful teenager, family rebel, mental patient, etc.). With the possible exception of the mother, who has some distinctive characteristics, Miller's people are like the snapshots her title compares them to: two-dimensional placeholders in our collective family album that signify, rather than evoke, lived experience.

A vastly *under*rated novelist, in contrast, can be found in Paula Fox, whose book *The God of Nightmares* is the latest addition to her impressive but almost invisible career. Fox is one of those writers who is willing to stray far beyond the world of her known experience (as she did in *A Servant's Tale,* the story of an immigrant housekeeper), but who can also invigorate lives that might seem tediously normal (as she did, to wonderful effect, in her early work, *Desperate Characters*). *The God of Nightmares* is a movingly romantic tale of nostalgia and regret, about a young woman's coming-of-age in New Orleans shortly after the Second World War. The now-remote period, the entrancingly decadent atmosphere of the city, and the violent enthusiasms of youth are all strikingly rendered; but what moved me most about this book was the way it enabled the young woman, in the end grown middle-aged herself, to come to a new vision of people (her dying mother, her husband) whom she had previously pigeon-holed. If this is a novel about recollection (the past as something fixed and determined), it is also about transformation, reconstruction, and the imposition of the unexpected on the previously known. In that sense, *The God of Nightmares* recapitulates and embodies the feeling that we hope for from all good novels: the feeling that the characters' lives are simultaneously fixed and free, the product not only of their authors' determinations but of unfated possibilities as well.

Two novels by talented newcomers chart the coming-of-age process from a much closer vantage point. Melanie Rae Thon's *Meteors in August* and Michael Cunningham's *A Home at the End of the World* are both first novels that demonstrate enormous talent and delicacy. Thon's book is about a girl named Lizzie Macon who grows up in a small Montana town, a backwater complete with born-again fundamentalists, persecuted Indians, worn-out wives, drunkenly brutal husbands, and the usual array of small-town oddballs. What makes *Meteors in August* special, though, is Lizzie's quizzical, self-deprecating, untar-

nished perceptions. Through her eyes we see the flight of her too-attractive older sister, the resulting anger of her father, the mournful decline of her mother, the nastiness of her sometime best friend, and the rude, aggressive sexuality of the boys she knows (including her own loutish cousins). Despite the subject matter, this is not the stuff of made-for-teens Hollywood movies, for the subtlety of Lizzie's tone can only be appreciated by an adult sensibility.

Michael Cunningham's first novel is also extremely well-written, especially in its early sections on Bobby Morrow's and Jonathan Glover's childhoods. The scene in which Bobby's older brother dies of a freak accident is, in particular, a *tour de force.* But when the two boys grow up and move (at different times) to Manhattan, *A Home at the End of the World* loses a little of its evocative power and takes on shadings of a glossy magazine article about gay and straight life in New York. No, that's unfair: the tone of the writing never descends to the reportorial or the merely gossipy. But the subject matter of the book's later sections (a *ménage à trois* among gay Jonathan, straight Bobby, and the woman they both love, which becomes *à quatre* when Bobby fathers her child, and *à cinq* when Jonathan's AIDS-afflicted lover comes to live with them) is a bit much for the musing, delicate style that carries the earlier part of the book so well. I don't think Cunningham could have left the characters in their Midwestern adolescence—unlike *Meteors in August,* this novel asks for more development than that—but it somehow seems a mistake to carry them all the way up to the topical present.

Two oddities, one obscure and one famous, will serve to close my survey of fiction published in 1990. Both are, in a sense, academic novels (that is, they take place primarily in university settings), but beyond that they have nothing in common. Weldon Kees' *Fall Quarter,* the only novel written by this poet who jumped off the Golden Gate Bridge in 1955, has just been published for the first time by Story Line Press. The tale of its earlier near-misses at publication (as told by editor James Reidel in the introduction) is heartbreakingly familiar. Unfortunately, this edition does less than full justice to the work, in that the introduction and the novel itself are typographically run together in a most confusing way. The novel isn't perfect either, though there are some wonderfully amusing passages about drunken assistant professors, terrifyingly awful literary gatherings, and the combination of prudery and prurience that pervades a small college town. Kees is aiming here for something on the order of Nathanael West's darkly comic tone; what he gets more often is Randall Jarrell at his weakest (the Jarrell, I mean, of *Pictures from an Institution*), and even then he's not as funny. But *Fall Quarter* is far better than many things published now (or, I imagine, in 1941, the inauspicious year of its rejection), and it certainly deserved to be salvaged.

If *Fall Quarter* is the epitome of publishing failure, A. S. Byatt's *Possession* is the corresponding model of success. Who would have thought that a "romance" about two Victorian poets (modeled loosely on Robert Browning and Christina Rosetti), along with two modern-day academics investigating the secret love-life of those two Victorians, would have made it to the best-seller lists in both England and America? Like *The Name of the Rose* (another academy-sprung best seller), **Possession** is filled with knowing allusions to the problematic creation of literature, its correspondence (or non-correspondence) to biography, and all the latest deconstructive notions in literary criticism. Like a post-modern building with traditional motifs glued onto its surface, **Possession** also has a heavy share of nineteenth-century pastiche, ranging from diary entries to some unbearably long mock-Tennysonian poems. In contrast to the vast majority of the critics (or, for that matter, the judges of Britain's Booker Prize), I found this literary effort less than charming. It's not that I'm against the basic idea: I loved it when David Lodge executed it more skillfully a couple of years ago in *Nice Work*. But **Possession** takes itself far too seriously, imagines it has important things to tell us about love and life and literature, and meanwhile neglects to create a single literary character who survives beyond the pages of the book. One would do better to read Browning himself. His brief poem "My Last Duchess" has more to say about character, and tone, and artifice, and history, and (yes) *possession,* than does the 550-page novel of that name.

The Year in Poetry

by J. D. McClatchy

In 1948, the Bollingen Prize, funded at that time by the United States government and administered by the Library of Congress, was awarded to Ezra Pound. The controversy surrounding this honor to a traitor led Congress to abandon its recognition of poetic achievement altogether. This year they changed their minds and, in imitation of the governments of England and France, established a national prize to be given biennially to the poet who, in the opinion of the judges, has published the most distinguished book during the two preceding years. In effect, however, the award is for lifetime achievement, and the first winner was James Merrill. The prize is named for Rebekah Johnson Bobbitt (sister of Lyndon Johnson), whose family helps fund the award. Merrill, himself a former winner of the Bollingen Prize, along with a Pulitzer and two National Book Awards, has written eleven volumes of poetry, and is generally now acknowledged as the contemporary master of both the exquisite lyric and the uncanny epic. In their citation, the judges paid tribute to Merrill's extraordinary career, now four decades along:

> "The brilliance of his style, the dazzling range of his interests and techniques, his complex ambitions and casual graces, all serve to reveal those mysteries that crisscross and come to constitute the heart of anyone's life. He has achieved what few poets are permitted: he has found the words to give us a whole new world of flesh and spirit, image and idea."

Of the giving of prizes there is no end. For an art so often considered ignored and impoverished, poetry attracts more than its share of honors and fellowships—given out of guilt or habit in some cases, perhaps, but nonetheless enabling poets to get on with their work. Even more supportive than the federal government—because more intelligent in its sponsorship—is the Academy of American Poets, with its extensive series of awards, publications, and readings. Two of its most significant prizes are the Walt Whitman Award, given to the best first book of poems, and the Lamont Poetry Selection, given to the best second book. For 1990, the Whitman winner was Martha Hollander. Her collection, *The Game of Statues* (Atlantic Monthly Press), is an impressive debut, curious about experience and the perspectives on it that art affords. Hollander writes with emotional confidence and intellectual panache, and wisely raises her fluent descriptions to the level of parable. Whether meditating on the old TV serial "The Twilight Zone," a soccer game in the Munich suburbs, or a Greek *kouros* locked in a museum's storehouse, she weighs each with a sure hand, searching out ironies and values.

Li-Young Lee, born in Indonesia in 1957, was the Lamont winner. *The City in Which I Love You* (BOA Editions), his second book, seems slack despite its deliberately strong material. The persecution of his family, the experience of immigration, bad memories and haunted prospects—these provide Lee's poems with their appeal. His subjects are not always matched with a strong rhetorical control; lines are thin, images vague. Attitude prevails over observation. Too many of the easy clichés of contemporary verse are marshalled to do the hard work of paradoxical thought and true feeling: "I am letting this room / and everything in it / stand for my ideas about love / and its difficulties."

Three first books of 1990 deserve special mention. Daniel Hall was the year's Yale Younger Poet. His *Hermit with Landscape* (Yale) is a quiet book, but in every way an impressive one. He writes with precision about the natural world—whether the Northwest coast or "sunset pitstops" in Utah—and about the underside of our feelings. In one poem, he recounts burning some old love-letters: "Believers in the afterlife perform / this purifying rite. At last / a match is struck: it's done. The past / will shed some light, but never keep us warm." His voice is formally poised but colloquially pitched, and he writes with a shrewd knowledge of the heart's strategies. Wayne Koestenbaum's *Ode to Anna Moffo* (Persea) seems nearly hysterical by comparison. What in less expert hands might have turned whimsical or campy—diva-worship and adolescent fantasies—Koestenbaum makes into a grand opera buffa. If the example of John Ashbery and James Schuyler loom over his shoulder, he has also learned how to inflect (in strict syllabics) the New York School tone into a revved-up voice all his own. Part mad scene, part love duet, his glamorously contrived memories slip like any quick-change *pierrot* from winsome nostalgias into silk-sheathed ironies. It's rare to find a new book that makes a reader grin just before a clutch in the throat about some erotic misadventure. The enchantment lies in Koestenbaum's tenderly wide-eyed take on things:

> I enter the boy
> I used to be, who lies in my bed,
> naked, as if I've purchased him
> from an Arabian sorceress
> who sews the body to its sorrow, invisibly.

Karl Kirchwey's *A Wandering Island* (Princeton) strikes a more earnest note. The book opens with poems set in the past, or in Switzerland and Italy (where the poet has lived), that show Kirchwey prefers long perspectives to short views. History and legend, the Old World and the high style—this poet has set his eye on the world elsewhere, but he travels in order to reach home truths, to discover the intimate in the exotic. The book's second half then wanders forward, closer, in a series of sly poems about holographs, ambulances, nudists. And everywhere in these songs of experience and innocence, Kirchwey beguiles with a rare nobility of gesture, a command of language that is prodigious and richly chromatic.

To move abruptly from young to old, from tyro to master, reminds one that prizes are also in order for publishers—or for those that bring great poets into clearer focus. Farrar, Straus & Giroux, for instance, published two important retrospective collections in 1990. ***Above the River: The Complete Poems*** by James Wright gathers together the work of one of the most talented and influential postwar poets. Though hailed by admirers as a surrealist of the "deep image" school, Wright considered himself a traditionalist, a Horatian clinging to a fastidious neo-classical ideal of clarity and sense. Critics who praised him in the 1960's as a political poet mistook his decorous privacy of vision. His early allegiance to formal verse gave way to an equally literary but more extreme poetic language—open forms and speech rhythms, disjunctive patterns of imagery meant to release buried psychic or emotional energies. His first two books, *The Green Wall* (1957) and *Saint Judas* (1959), addressed their sympathies to social outcasts—murderer, prostitute, lunatic—in an effort to explore and console the experience of isolation. "Loneliness" recurs more often than any other word in Wright's work, but a better term is "aloneness," the harrowing sense of being forever a man apart. *The Branch Will Not Break* (1963) contains some of his best-known poems, with their startling epiphanies. The tenement whorehouses and abandoned mills, the suckholes and freight cars of his native Ohio, have in Wright's spare poems the beauty of old engravings. The second half of Wright's career witnessed a grievous decline in his power; the poems grow blustery and cloying. His last collection, *This Journey,* virtually assembled on his deathbed and published posthumously in 1982, marks a poignant recovery, and is the most Horatian of his books—if by that term we mean what Auden meant: looking on the world with a happy eye but from a sober perspective. As before, his best poems have a grace and intelligence that stand as a rebuke to most of the glib work of his time, and remain among the finest examples of the midcentury American lyric. Probably the best book of the year, ***Above the River*** will remain essential reading for years to come.

Farrar, Straus & Giroux published another important collection by another Wright in 1990—Charles Wright's ***The World of the Ten Thousand Things: Poems 1980-1990.*** This new book makes a pair with *Country Music: Selected Early Poems* (1982), and gathers between its covers three of Wright's most important collections, *The Southern Cross* (1981), *The Other Side of the River* (1984), *Zone Journals* (1988), and a strong group of new poems titled "Xionia." Perhaps the best poet of his generation (he was born in 1935), Wright here is continually searching out luxuriant and experimental ways (through memory-work, narratives, journal notations) to extend and develop his themes. His move to a longer line in hemistiches has the effect of plainsong. He works by what he calls "linkage,"

interconnected and overlapping images. Whether mulling over the quotidian mysteries or ascending to the linguistic sublime, Charles Wright has embarked on spiritual autobiography, and the meanings of his poems shift and shimmer with each re-reading. "I step through the alphabet," he writes in one poem, "The tree limbs shadow across the grass, / a dark language / Of strokes and ideograms / That spells out a different story than we are used to, / A story with no beginning and no end." That story, finally, is one that seeks to translate language into experience, and few poets can do that so well as Charles Wright.

There were other important new books by senior poets—among them James Dickey, John Frederick Nims, Galway Kinnell, Amy Clampitt, and Philip Booth. Mona Van Duyn's ***Near Changes*** (Knopf) has her accustomed technical aplomb and warm human appreciation of the world's curiosities:

> a volunteer
> stalk sprung from sour
> bird-drop this year
> burst in frantic flower.
> The world's perverse,
> but it could be worse.

Set in a zoo or a carwash, adapted from a newspaper item or a friend's postcard, her poems are never merely occasional. Each works steadily and wittily to a moral point. Her poems bristle with ideas, or, rather, with thinking, the

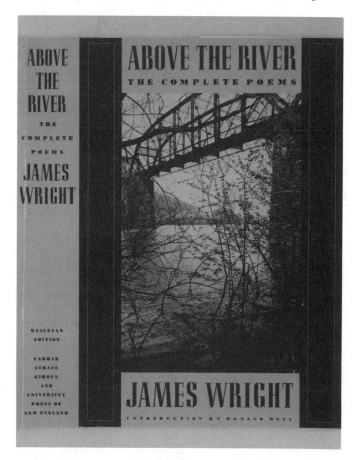

sound of a voice talking sense. She knows, with William James, that ideas are made true by events. And in each poem her sense of things is held up to the incongruities of experience—all of them, from an unruly sex drive to a dirty kitchen counter. Above all, she takes love as her subject—what she calls "married love," the paradigm of all knotty human relationships. Though slighter than some of her books, **Near Changes** includes some of Van Duyn's most charming work. Robert Creeley's **Windows** (New Directions) continues his pointillist project. These quiet poems, over almost before they begin, treat metaphysical matters with a rare composure. Some pieces in this long book are merely ephemeral; others are enriched by the poet's recent stays abroad. "Helsinki Window," for instance, has a northern light: "Old sky freshened with cloud bulk / slides over frame of window the / shadings of softened greys a light . . . " William Jay Smith's **Collected Poems 1939-1989** (Scribners) gathers the work of one of our most versatile and felicitous poets. It's wonderful to be reminded of the tensile delicacy of his early work, wartime poems that capture an era both innocent and menaced. Wryly observed details and neatly turned conceits, in lines that are songlike and surprising, comprise the bulk of his work through the years. Later poems came to favor longer, less epigrammatic lines; they let "the words clean-spun and spiraling orbit that swift-seeing, unseen immensity that will never be contained!" Early and late, these are poems to be grateful for.

Anthony Hecht's first three books, *The Hand Hours* (1967), *Millions of Strange Shadows* (1977), and *The Venetian Vespers* (1979), were reissued in **Collected Earlier Poems** to accompany his new collection, **The Transparent Man** (Knopf), his first new book of poems in eleven years. If Hecht never rushes into print, he also never offers to the public anything that doesn't do supremely well what T. S. Eliot once defined as the poet's job: "to see beneath both beauty and ugliness; to see the boredom, and the horror, and the glory." Hecht's previous books have each contained a long poem of real distinction. *The Hard Hours* (1967) included his powerful meditation on evil in history, "Rites and Ceremonies"; a decade later *Millions of Strange Shadows* gave us "Perepeteia" and "Green: An Epistle," marvels of transformations, like the late romances of Shakespeare; the title poem of *The Ventian Vespers* (1979) dramatized the estrangements of a single life that open out to memories and longings of a nearly unbearable tenderness. Now **The Transparent Man** gives us two long poems, both instant classics: "A Love for Four Voices," based on the movements of a Haydn string quartet and borrowing—to brood on the exegencies of love—the four lovers from *A Midsummer Night's Dream;* and "See Naples and Die," the scarifying diary of a man whose marriage breaks down during a visit to Naples and the nearby site of the traditional entrance to the underworld. In shorter poems as well, throughout the book, Hecht brings an extravagance of conception and high style. Once again, the poems in this new book are marked by the good fortune of their verse and of their understandings, their often vertiginous plunges into doubt, their elegance and slashing gestures, their command of both sensual details and instinctual memory, their narrative invention, the canniness with which they both celebrate and question the

very sense that art can make of things. He writes, as Lucretius did, clear verse about dark things.

The 1990 Pulitzer Prize for Poetry was awarded to Charles Simic's *The World Doesn't End,* a small gathering of prose poems published in 1989. Simic also published a new collection of poems in 1990, **The Book of Gods and Devils** (Harcourt Brace Jovanovich). In this collection, his tenth, all of Simic's characteristic gifts are again on display; a deceptive simplicity is the medium for his unnerving attention to objects and events, for his cognitive traps and dreamy scenarios. He once wrote that his poems exist in a world "where magic is possible, where chance reigns, where metaphors have their supreme logic." As one poem puts it, "Just as I'm about to sink my teeth into the noumenon, / Some old girlfriend comes to distract me. / 'She's not even alive!' I yell at the skies." His metaphysical brio has a genuinely original and deeply satifying wit. The titular gods and devils in this book are those presences that haunt his imagination—and they range from St. Thomas Aquinas and Shelley to Thelonius Monk and St. John of the Cross, who "wore dark glasses / As he passed me on the street. / St. Theresa of Avila, beautiful and grave, / Turned her back on me. / 'Soulmate,' they shouted. 'It's high time.'"

Marvin Bell, a contemporary of Simic's and something of a soulmate too, has built up a body of work over the years that is eclectic, domestic, personable, demotic in its sympathies and accent, busy with the daily round yet with an ear out for the Undersong of Myself. **Iris of Creation** (Copper Canyon) is more muted than his earlier books. "All that was is here, pouring into this moment, / which offers you every chance for tears." This *lacrimae rerum* note sounds throughout the book in its best poems, though there are plenty of merely clever poems as well, little conceptual teasers that solve problems rather than probe mysteries. There are a number of more successful political parables on the subject of American power, our frightening and destructive innocence. But the best poem in this handsome book is the last and longest (twenty 18-line stanzas), "Initial Conditions," a sort of moral instruction manual. Here Bell's voice is expansive, his rhetoric quirky but under sure control, and his themes woven with fine detail. His dampened surrealism and masterful rhythmical instincts move the poem along in unforeseen ways.

Mary Oliver's **House of Light** (Beacon) opens with a question: "Is the soul solid, like iron? / Or is it tender and breakable, like / the wings of a moth in the beak of an owl?" If you can't guess the answer, her ensuing poems—about egrets, terns, snakes, kookaburras, turtles, swans, and their kin—make the point over and over. Oliver writes a plain, exposed, flat poem that asserts its grand generalizations, usually in a concluding cliché. Her attention is focused on her gushy reactions to nature, when her eye should be trained on its manifold wonders and terrors. Her poems are formulaic, and in the end tedious.

Mark Strand was named the nation's new Poet Laureate in 1990, and he also published a new collection, **The Continuous Life** (Knopf), his first in a decade. He has moved on from the warmly expansive poems of nostalgia and landscape that concluded his *Selected Poems* (1980).

Strand's haunting tone, at once vatic and ennervated, has a new luster here. He includes a number of prose poems, droll comentaries on the suburbs of existence. He moves from a rollicking ballad about a grotesque couple to a stunning and plangent poem, "Orpheus Alone," which imagines that first poet's language as "Untouched by pity, in lines, lavish and dark, / Where death is reborn and sent into the world as a gift, / So the future, with no voice of its own, nor hope / Of ever becoming more than it will be, might mourn." Strand never mourns, though he is melancholy—dark, not gloomy, a melancholy over the disparity between what we want ("the blaze of promise everywhere") and what we get. Throughout the book, though, it is rendered with an elegance that sends "Small tremors of love through your brief, / Undeniable selves, into your days, and beyond."

Any new book by Louise Glück is eagerly awaited, and likely to confound. She is among the very best poets of her generation (she was born in 1943), and she began as a blisteringly autobiographical writer, in the manner of Robert Lowell. Her recent books have been more spare and enigmatic; her work has mythic dimensions, and has been concerned to trace the outlines and guage the power of large psychic forces maneuvering our lives—the "thrust and ache" of men and women in their bodies, the "dying orders" of nature, the "ancient repetitions" of family life. Glück's new book, *Ararat* (Ecco), deals almost exclusively with her own family life, with her parents and sister, in poems that may be more immediate, even more vulnerable, than those in her earlier books, but are also less striking. Still, few poets have such an eerie control of their material. Here is "First Memory":

> Long ago, I was wounded. I lived
> to revenge myself
> against my father, not
> for what he was—
> for what I was: from the beginning of time,
> in childhood, I thought
> that pain meant
> I was not loved.
> It meant I loved.

The crisply furious self-knowledge in this poem is somewhat more diluted in others, but throughout are painful poems about envy, enviable poems about pain.

The Want Bone (Ecco) by Robert Pinsky has some of the poet's best work. The book's title signals its themes and recurrent subjects: desire, sexual appetite, romantic love, religious longing, nostalgia, imaginative poverty. At the center of the collection are two fables about Jesus—that is, about the Law and about the Spirit that both giveth life and killeth. Pinsky's use of narrative as a method to devise parables about the emotional life is vivid and convincing. The biblical cadences and tropes that dictate his new, sterner tone of voice in this book are somewhat less appealing. In more personal poems, his virtuosic montage of memories results in a moving eloquence. "Shirt," for instance traces the imagined history of the shirt on the poet's back through Korean sweatshops, the Triangle Factory fire, Scottish mills, planters, pickers, sorters, carders, weavers, loaders, inspectors. By the end of the poem, the plain sportshirt has become a mythological shirt of flame, the burden of history itself.

Winner of the Juniper Prize offered by the University of Massachusetts Press, Edward Kleinschmidt's *First Language* settles comfortably into one of the day's standard styles. It derives in large part from John Ashbery: meditative, associative rambles through surreal details of daily life and the playfulness of idle fantasy. One poem starts this way:

> I trust that the croutons aren't burning. Down-
> Stairs someone's playing *Dies Irae* over and over
>   again on the sax-
> Ophone, and most people who call my answer-
>   ing machine
> Leave nothing but questions.

Kleinschmidt's work is a little shaggy, but quirky and astute.

The notoriety of Brad Leithauser has been cause enough either for a wringing of hands over the success of a genteel triviality or for raising those hands to hail an overdue return to traditional values. His elaborately worked stanzas, their meters and rhymes intricately engineered, lope through *The Mail from Anywhere* (Knopf). If his rhetoric seems stilted at times, and his subject matter deliberately miniaturized, it must still be acknowledged that he writes with an exhilarating bravura. He tends to stick to the surfaces of things, rendering them with loving detail

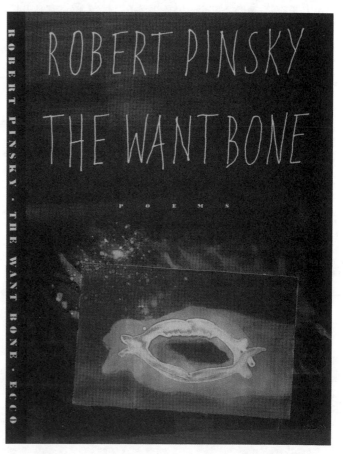

but without much intellectual rigor. On the other hand, faced with so much flatness in book after book of new poetry, one savors this poet's delighted discoveries, his care. He can show off in poems like "A Bowl of Chinese Fireworks" or "Plexal" (about a terrarium filled with pythons), or approach his material in a more relaxed manner, as he does in four Frostian character portraits—including a touching poem about his daughter's conception.

Other books of note to be mentioned briefly are: *Waking* (Chicago) by Tom Sleigh, straightforward poems that complicate important matters; *Cuba Night* (Morrow) by Dave Smith, large-souled accounts of ordinary life by a burly Southern poet in the tradition of James Dickey and Robert Penn Warren; *Powers of Congress* (Godine), Alice Fulton's third collection, boistrous lyrics teeming with metaphors drawn from science and lowlife; *The Dog Star* (Massachusetts) by W. S. Di Piero, chronicles of the provisional patterns in our lives; *Mystery Train* (Pittsburgh) by David Wojahn, thirty-four sonnets and a long envoy that trace the history of rock-and-roll; *The Nowhere Steps* (Sheep Meadow) by Mark Rudman, a long, diverse book of ruminations on history and selfhood; *The 1002nd Night* (Princeton) by Debora Greger, whimsical conceits drawn from the imagination's byways.

It was a quiet year for poetry in Britain. Both John Heath-Stubbs and Peter Scupham issued *Selected Poems,* both from Oxford. Norman MacCaig, regarded as Scotland's leading poet, was represented by *Collected Poems* (Chatto). Ruth Fainlight's *The Knot* (Hutchinson) is idiosyncratic in the intensity with which it pursues personal themes, and mixes them with readings in classical liteature and feminist theory. One of the strongest new talents in Ireland, Eavan Boland, offered *Outside History* (Carcanet); the American edition of the book (from Norton) has been expanded to include selections from her work of the past decade. Love and anxiety, family and history, memories and mysteries—Boland has woven them all into a rich verse fabric. A younger Irish poet, the prodigious Paul Muldoon, whose 1986 *Selected Poems* revealed a dandified sensibility and a nearly Joycean ear for rich linguistic nuance, made a bold advance with *Madoc* (Faber), a long poem in many short episodes, speculating on Coleridge and Southey's 1794 plan to found a "Pantisocratic" community in America, a utopia on the Susquehanna. Muldoon's clever device is to have framed angles on the plan in terms of a history of Western philosophers. The results both puzzle and reward. Dennis Silk, an Englishman long resident in Israel, tries in *Catwalk and Overpass* (Viking), his third book, to challenge entrenched attitudes in his adopted homeland. His wit can be fey and disorienting. A much stronger poet is Peter Sacks, a white South African Jew who emigrated to the United States—and so is several times over an exile. He writes—in *Promised Lands* (Viking), his second collection—about such displacements (his is "a life still folded at the crease of exile") with a voice that approaches the prophetic yet never loses touch with his descriptive (a seasonal sequence) or narrative (poems about travels in South Africa, Israel, and America) purposes.

No book published in either America or England, however, garnered quite the attention that the West Indian poet Derek Walcott's *Omeros* (Farrar, Straus & Giroux) did. It was front page news in *The New York Times Book Review,* and rightly so. Walcott was born in St. Lucia—"a country without a history," he once said—and by forging the indiginous Caribbean culture and the colonial literary heritage into a powerful voice he has created a body of work (both poetry and drama) that encompasses the themes of Caribbean social and racial experience. His poetry has from the start asserted its authority as descriptive impressionism, political analysis, and heroic myth. *Omeros* crowns his career. The book-length poem, in 64 chapters of superbly managed tercets, translates Homer's stories from the *Iliad* and *Odyssey* (the book's title is the Greek form of Homer's name) to a coastal village in the West Indies. Homer himself makes several appearances, as a "white-eyed storyteller" in Africa, as a wandering bargeman, and as Seven Seas, an old blind salt. Hector and Achille are village fisherman, and Helen a local beauty who leaves one man for the other and starts a quarrel. There are many other characters as well, and Walcott portrays them with insight and sympathy. His book displays great richness; the language glitters and flares, the narrative pulses and catches up themes of real moment. In a recent interview, Walcott maintained that

> "when you enter a language, you enter a kind of choice which contains in it the political history of the language, the imperial width of the lan-

guage, the fact that you are either subjugated by the language or you have to dominate it. So language is not a place of retreat, it's not a place of escape, it's not even a place of resolution. It's a place of struggle."

It is the struggle any poet undertakes. Few have won so much as Walcott.

The Year in Drama

by Robert Cohen

One of the advantages of being a student at Yale in the early 1960s was the chance to watch a number of brilliant young American playwrights working up their styles: one who amazed me then was John Guare, who seems now to have perfected a consummate dramaturgy in **Six Degrees of Separation. Degrees** premiered at the Mitzi Newhouse Theatre downstairs at Lincoln Center, and shortly thereafter—following some outstanding reviews—reopened in the larger Beaumont Theatre up top. This is quite a work. Guare has stayed before our eyes all along, of course, with, among others, *Muzeeka, House of Blue Leaves,* and the filmscript of *Atlantic City,* but nothing in his earlier work has provided such a steady jolt of original expressions, seductive engagements, and dramatic body blows as we see here. Staged simply in an elegant midtown apartment—a circular red carpet with two red velvet sofas—Guare's play concerns a young black Harvard man, Paul, who, mugged in Central Park, eases his way into the assistance and good graces of art speculator Flan and his wife Ouisa and then of two other similarly rich white families. But Paul's a liar: he's not from Harvard, nor has he been mugged, nor is he the son of Sidney Poitier, nor is he the casting director for his father's Hollywood film of *Cats.* It's an obvious confidence scheme, but then Paul doesn't steal anything; it seems that it's the confidence itself that he's after. Flan's and Ouisa's children having emotionally deserted them (the college kids of all the families enter the stage cursing and growling), the parent types find themselves attracted by Paul's brilliance, his charm, and most peculiarly by his bereftness: here's someone who *needs* parenting, and who will lie, cheat, and steal in order to get it. It's enchantingly perplexing to them—they who are in need of being perplexed—and they succumb to an appeal which seems even deeper than (though related to) sex.

It is Guare's conceit that we are at most six persons apart: that even the Amazon tribesperson and the Eskimo villager will know someone, who knows someone, who knows someone, who knows someone, who knows *them.* These are the six degrees of separation; when all is said and done, we're not very separate after all. Like virtually all of Guare's dramatized notions, this is unproven and unprovable—it's New York cocktail party chatter—but it holds up: it's a conceit that humbles and provokes, and it seems to evolve organically from his story here. Guare also has much to say about parents and children, which he addresses from both sides of the dividing line, with much attention to *Catcher in the Rye,* assassination, imagination, and the upper-class confidence games played by—let's say—art speculators. It's all just on the edge of comprehensibility, and sounds meaningful even when it's proba-

PLAYBILL

LINCOLN CENTER THEATER AT THE MITZI E. NEWHOUSE

Six Degrees of Separation

bly not. Jerry Zaks' production is funny and spellbinding (this is one of the only plays in recent years that I absolutely hated to see end), and we all emerge from Lincoln Center with a great deal of enchanting confusion. Great Guare.

Back in the days when University English departments taught literature (instead of literary and social theory), students actually read authors like John Steinbeck, and a whole generation of young academics—myself included—came to adulthood with their aesthetic and political consciousness shaped by metaphors as potent, and indelible, as the Joad family in Steinbeck's **Grapes of Wrath.** So it was with an undeniable jolt of illuminated nostalgia that I saw the Joad jalopy chugging its way across the Cort

Theatre stage on Broadway this season, taking its synedochical family from the dust bowl of Oklahoma to the fertile valley of California once again. *Grapes* is theatrical more than dramatic; the story is more ramblingly contextual than suspenseful or compact. Thus the soaring Frank Galati production (Galati wrote and staged the play, first at Chicago's Steppenwolf Theatre, and then on Broadway, where I saw it) proved brilliantly adept at gleaning and fusing Steinbeck's major themes. This production (along with some of its characters) absolutely jumps off the stage; it is the first major non-musical Broadway staging I've seen that bears comparison to the radical theatricality of contemporary German directors and scenographers—it's the sort of production one most usually encounters today in the great avant-garde city theaters of Berlin, Bochum, and Munich. High technology manipulating cardinal (and carnal) elements—fire, water, mud, sex—produce orgasmic thunderstorms, deep-soaking floods, and torrents of nearly-real lightning and rain, which commingle with—and partly inspire—savagely articulate acting (a Steppenwolf trademark), and innately resonant folk cadences: a musical saw, a square dance, and the grimly joyous songs of our American depression. The result is deeply moving and impressive. Kevin Rigdon's (literally and figuratively) brilliant lighting made his appropriately dirty settings, and Steinbeck's troubled characters, almost luminous. The dramatization of novels might be somewhat of a disturbing trend in the modern theater, indicating a move to spectacle rather than well-wrought plays (the dramatist as play-*wright*), but *Grapes* has certainly occasioned the import of bold continental-style staging and passionate Chicago-style acting to a New York audience more accustomed to drawing rooms and well–shaped, rounded tones.

Speaking of which, New York's 1990 season was overwhelmingly a year of English imports, many of which will be described below. Happily for us, however, the best of these plays crossing the Atlantic was by an American, though perhaps an anti-American, Richard Nelson, whose *Some Americans Abroad* was initially commissioned and produced by the Royal Shakespeare Company in 1989. *Americans*'s American premiere (at Lincoln Center in January) showed this subtle, small-scale drama to be quite impressive on its author's native shore. Nelson's subject is rampant Anglophilia—an exaggerated or perverse love of all things English—among "some" Americans; these "some" happen to be a group of U.S. college English professors. Such latter-day Innocents (Nelson's title was lifted from Mark Twain's) are in Albion as the director-chaperones of an annual U.K. theater tour, providing themselves and their student charges with daily overdoses of theatrical Briticulture—at the Barbican, the National, on overnights at Stratford-upon-Avon, and all about the West End. It's twenty-eight plays in four weeks for an increasingly restive (and increasingly randy) student herd, largely female, some of whom are bypassing Shaw and Shakespeare for Harrod's and the cute boys down the hall. The student restiveness, however, comes not so much from theatrical or cultural inundation as from the numbing ineptitude (social, sexual, intellectual) of the American academics who are their putative guides.

Nelson brilliantly limns his four transplanted lit profs,

whose comings and goings and disintegrating relationships (personal and professional) are realized in near-Chekhovian complexity. There's Joe, the department chairman, who is spinelessness epiphanized; passionate on the most abstract of issues ("Jesus Christ, I am a goddamn liberal!"), but unable to subdivide a resturant check, discipline an erring colleague, or tell an untenured Milton lecturer that he's being fired. There's Henry, the sacked Miltonist; he's the only one who doesn't know yet, and whose pathetic efforts at keeping his job are little smiley upchucks of what's being forced down his throat. "Beautifully said, Joe," Henry grimly intones; "I support you, Joe." "You should write an article, Joe; you've got something that's publishable." Gag me. And there's Philip, covertly groping a coed in the back seat of a rented car; and Francie, covertly groping Philip in her hotel room. It's a trenchantly satirized Anglophilia that animates and, for a time, unites them: England—the "Living Education." Team-reading Wordsworth's "Westminster Bridge" on Waterloo Bridge ("wrong bridge," Henry mutters, unheard through his fixed smile), singing "God Save the Queen" (all three verses) under Big Ben as it strikes six in the morning, the profs out-Brit the Brits; they are at the font, fonting.

Critics who saw both London and New York productions of the play say that the satiric edge was sharper in the English version; no doubt it was, but *Some Americans Abroad* exists on many levels, and Nelson's study of the intricacies of American academic politics is accurate, deeply cutting, and wisely funny on a purely domestic level. This play, like *Uncle Vanya,* goes far beyond satire. To Nelson, the intellectual life of the American lit prof—or at least of *some* American lit profs—is aggressively, insistently stupid. It's not just the standard academic bigotry ("His degree, Orson, it's from Case Western Reserve; that's not exactly Harvard,") nor the platitudinous inanity ("The man who wrote *Hamlet* understood that the world was complicated!"), nor the constant praisemaking ("Joe, I want to say that I think you handled this whole problem perfectly"), nor even the ungenerous small-mindedness ("In and out of Hawthorne scholarship in two years! And he writes a book! Junk!") that appalls Nelson. No, it's the profound moral cowardice of (some of) the American professoriat: the cheapness; the abject indecisiveness; the mimicry of style coupled with a near-total retreat from content; in short, the extended distancing of corporeal and ethical life itself. "You always find new things," Joe says, self-admiringly, but Joe is speaking only about literature, and then only formalistically. His "new thing" on *Antony and Cleopatra* is that one scene, "iconographically speaking . . . is a representation not of life, but of another representation." This makes Joe happy: representations of representations—i.e. meta-abstractions—he can deal with. People are another matter. Passion, suffering, and betrayal surround Joe, both in *Antony* and in his tour group, but he's oblivious to them, even when he's in part their cause. Without the passion, without the life connection, even the literature loses its flavor. *Some Americans Abroad* should be abroad for some time.

More Anglophilic Americans are abroad—in England, too—in Caryl Churchill's *Ice Cream,* which was transferred from London's Royal Court Theatre to New York's Public (these theaters enjoy a reciprocal arrangement), but the results are more troublesome. Cultural ambivalence again reigns: "I quite fancy Americans," says Phil, the stumbled-upon British host and lost relative of an oafish American couple, who continues, "I completely loathe the United States of America." OK. Lance and Vera are the quarrelling fortyish American couple hunting up old family in the old world ("America's too damn recent," Lance says); Phil and Jaq are the prey they hunt down—brother and sister Londoners, twentyish, spoiled and spoiling. The transatlantic encounter quickly proves miserable, at least for the statesiders. "They're *both* terrible countries, I guess," hazards Vera in a pathetic attempt to quiet the emerging political row.

But *Ice Cream* isn't, at bottom, political at all: it's sexual (with some attempted, and bungled, cross-coupling of the nationalities) and vicious: there's a murder of an erring landlord, a midnight burial in Epping Forest, and then two more violent deaths back in America (Phil's one—he's hit by a car); plus auto theft, lies, attempted rape, religious fanaticism, and criminal extortion. This is not at all a nice play. Churchill writes with her customary acceleration: scenes (directed in New York by Les Waters) begin with near-mesmerizing tableaux, and then propel themselves forward with dizzying intercuts of dialogue. The situations are immensely provocative, and the combination of acidulous commentary, panicky assassination, and abortive sexual tectonics makes for rapidly spiralling tensions from the first fade-in. But there's nowhere to go, and the story—and characters—simply dissolve before our eyes. Indeed, Churchill seems almost on the verge of starting up a new play when this one closes (Jaq is apparently headed off to South Africa with a new character), and the evening ends not with a bang nor a whimper but a sense of total vacancy. Which, in fact, we mind less than we might, since we've already pretty much lost interest in the proceedings.

Ice Cream (or, as spelled in England, *Icecream;* the title concerning which syllable should be emphasized in spoken American) is finally a frustrating piece of theater from the author of the rousing *Cloud 9* and *Top Girls.* Churchill's talent is enormous and original: she has created a unique (and necessary) system of punctuation in her published playtexts to indicate where speeches interrupt others, continue through others, or follow from speeches prior to the preceding one, and she uses these symbols continually, demonstrating an extraordinary ability to manipulate the syntax of conversational structure into dramatic dialogue. Churchill's capacity to build and sustain dramatic tension, intermixed with sharp social commentary, and wrapped in an acutely contrived dramaturgical form (the rhyme schemes of *Serious Money,* for example; the gender shifts of *Cloud 9*), is perhaps unmatched today. But the main lines of this piece seem ill-formed. On a bill with the shorter and even lesser *Hot Fudge* (sort of a thieves' dialogue, on two levels), *Ice Cream* proves quite a bit less than satisfactory. Another transatlantic transfer was Peter Shaffer's *Lettice and Lovage,* which primarily proved a formula vehicle for Maggie Smith. What makes the venture worthwhile is that the for-

mula is Shaffer's own invention, and that Ms. Smith is very definitely a performing genius, so that the resulting theatrical adventure was unique and, for the most part, quite tasty.

Shaffer's formula—and it must be called that, as he's used it now in at least four plays—is to set a brooding, "civilized" professional next to a brilliant, creative, and nonconforming eccentric. The professional, first trying to nurture or control the eccentric (Act I), soon falls (even collapses) under the eccentric's spell (Acts II and sometimes III). Thus Pizarro and Athualpa (in *Royal Hunt of the Sun*), Dr. Dysart and Alan Strang (*Equus*), Salieri and Mozart (*Amadeus*), and now Lotte Schoen and Lettice Douffet. Lotte is a director at the Preservation Trust in London. Lettice ("it comes from Laetitia—the Latin word for gladness") is, well, the redoubtable Maggie: here, a wayward child of the theater, currently an overexuberant tour guide to what she considers "the dullest house in all England." Faced with pointing out the ogival pattern of the bannister once too often, Lettice has been spicing up her official spiel with exciting—if wholly imaginary—episodes. Tourist audiences are enraptured: "they warm to the thrilling and romantic aspects of our great History," Lettice exults. "Others, however, warm to accuracy," Lotte replies, harshly, when calling Lettice into the Preservation Trust office to summarily dismiss her. End of Act I.

Act II: Lotte now appears at Lettice's basement flat, begging forgiveness. Since firing Lettice, we find, Lotte has been brooding; she's been sitting home in the dark, at "the nondoer's desk," confronting her joyless, merely bureaucratic life. Seeing Lettice's gaily theatricalized apartment throws Lotte into an even deeper despair.

And so a forgiving Lettice leads Lotte out of "the hands of The Mere," and into the rarefied life of the charmingly crazed. Together the two ladies quaff "Quaff"—Lettice's sixteenth-century cordial laced with vodka, mead, sugar and lovage, ("love-ache" Lettice etymologizes)—and set out to reenact the trials and executions of famous men and women: Mary Queen of Scots, Sir Walter Raleigh, King Charles I, etc. Here's anti-bureaucracy, with a vengeance! At the close of the earlier London production (which is the one I saw), Lotte and Lettice are planning to blow up most of modern Britain with medieval petards; in the New York version they are simply planning to lead American tourists (yet more innocents abroad) through London's fifty most disgusting modern buildings, showing how "Beauty has been murdered" by British architects. That's "the single most theatrical idea I ever heard!" cries Lettice. Theater triumphant; professionalism damned.

One suspects that Shaffer's railing against "the Mere" (in *Equus* it was "the Normal," also capitalized and deified, if not Satanified) comes from a personal commitment; there is no question but that it has resonance in the modern theater, where people do come to get in from the cold. Theater audiences have always enjoyed the grotesques—the madwomen of Chaillot and elsewhere—who live out on stage what we daren't in life. The metatheatrical conclusion of *Lettice and Lovage* reinforces this: people going to the theater to be told that life is best lived theatrically.

But the splendor of this play is not in its structure but the actual performance of Maggie Smith; the light plotting and increasing absurdities of Shaffer's text holds together just long enough to permit us the pleasure of watching a hilarious insanity. Let's ignore the hidden contradiction that Ms. Smith's performance is one of an extraordinary professionalism. Inspired silliness might be her, and Shaffer's, best achievement here.

Still yet another American is abroad in the old U.K.—in William Nicholson's **Shadowlands.** She is the Jewish-American poet, Joy Davidman, whose meeting with and marriage to British author C. S. Lewis is the play's celebratory subject. **Shadowlands** is subtitled (in the newspaper ads) as "a Love Story," and the play's thematic proximity to Erich Segal's maudlin work is unfortunately and embarrassingly close: like *Love Story,* this is also the tale of an intellectual, WASPish, aristocratic male who falls in love with, marries, and then loses to hideous cancer a lustier, earthier, pop-ethnic female. The playing out of Joy's disease, wrenchingly enacted by Jane Alexander throughout virtually the entire second act, is saddening in the extreme, but the energy of the play is mainly squandered in dolefulness; it's emotionally exhausting but relentlessly unilluminating. What **Shadowlands** gives us instead is an alarmingly precise view of Oxfordian bigotry and narrow-mindedness, represented by the politely anti-Semitic, anti-American, closet-heterophobic dons at the high table, unwilling even to grieve for their colleague's wife, plus some neo-theological meanderings about why bad things happen to good people and so forth. It also provides the opportunity for some very classy acting by Ms. Alexander, and by Nigel Hawthorne as C. S. Lewis. What we *don't* get from this play, however, is any depth or coloration of this relationship: what in Joy (other than her attention) brings C. S. out of his donnish shell; what in C. S. (other than his reputation) brings Joy across the waters of indifference; what wars of nerves are waged in either of their sexual or aesthetic/scholarly psyches. As a love story, **Shadowlands** is chaste; as a depiction of life before the apocalypse (the "shadowlands" that precede, we gather, a divine enlightenment) it plumbs merely its own murk.

For all the brouhaha in New York last year about David Hare's **The Secret Rapture**—furious public letters back and forth between the author, the producer (Joe Papp), and the *New York Times* drama critic (Frank Rich)—plus considering Hare's reputation as a sharpshooting observer/analyst of postwar European society, one might have assumed that this play was essentially cutting-edge political. It isn't. Despite the presence of a Maggie Thatcher sound-alike (and in this production a look-alike as well), this is a thoughtful and sensitive play about "woman," pretty much on the theme that "a woman responds to the most deplorable things," as expressed by Isobel, Hare's chief protagonist. Isobel not only responds to deplorable things, she tries, haltingly, to do something about them, and for that she's rewarded by calumny and condemnation; finally by five shots in the back. "You can't understand there are actually more important things in life than your wretched sense of honesty," says her sister Marion, the Thatcherite cabinet minister, who only after Isobel's passing recognizes her (and "woman's") value.

This may be sort of a "Good Woman of the West End." Isobel is the good Shen Te, but lacks the rescuing grace of a "bad" Shui Ta. Instead she is done in by her indulgences; she can't separate herself from dependent family members or languishing lovers: "I'm no longer in love with you," she tells her ex-boyfriend, Irwin, "Why don't I just give you the push?" She refuses to protect herself from jealousy, arm herself against rivals, or even acknowledge there could be an evil in the persons she knows, and for these frailties she's roundly hated by all, who are thus associatively exposed by her blanket acquiescences. Well, is this indeed goodness? Hare seems to want us to think so: a final coda mourns Isobel's passing, and effuses with the moral recriminations of her antagonists. Hare has acknowledged that the part was written for his real-life liaison, the American actress Blair Brown. Isobel is certainly, even wanly, winsome. "The big joke is," she moans to Irwin, "by temperament I'm actually an extremely cheerful girl. That's what's so silly." And it is. Still, we share some of the rage and frustration of Isobel's detractors: this is clearly not a woman you would trust to launch the lifeboats if the ship were sinking; she might get tied up leaving milk out for the cat.

The West Coast premiere of **Secret Rapture,** where I saw

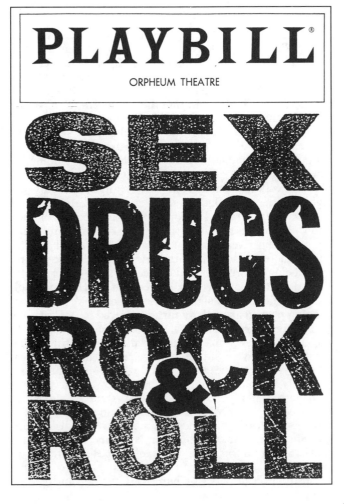

PLAYBILL®

ORPHEUM THEATRE

SEX DRUGS ROCK & ROLL

it (the Broadway production closed shortly after the Frank Rich pan, so I failed to see it there), was entrusted to the doughty South Coast Repertory Company in Costa Mesa, California, with some financial assistance from the British Government to bring over a Brit designer and a couple of English-trained actresses, all of whom harmonized beautifully with the Orange County team. A vigorous and subtle text with riveting performances; it could not have been better in the Big Apple.

And, finally, two more English imports to the Great White Way, both musicals. *Aspects of Love,* is Andrew Lloyd Webber's (failed) attempt to create a multiple cross-generational anti-romance, in other words, a Stephen Sondheim musical. It's in Europe, decadent old Europe, and people who shouldn't fall in love fall foolishly in love: old men with young women, young men with older women, older women with younger women, fathers and daughters, cousins, and just about everybody that moves—one way or another. Ironically, of course. Tragically, too, but only by design.

What makes the evening less than enchanting—less, even, than entertaining—is the numbing score, which reminds me of the sort of musical improvisations ten-year-old children make up when they turn their everyday life into a mock grand opera: "I have to do my hooooome-wooork!—before I go to the baaaaaaath-room!" Very little is spoken in the play: the music begins at the level of a finale refrain, even in the recitatives, and it ascends (or descends) from there, with multiple crescendos, high–octave pitch climbs, and dynamic reversals, all to the most petty words, predictable rhymes, and pedestrian conceits. The final philosophizing of the principals is that one should be "anything but lonely," and it's to this grand theme that Webber brings all his resources. *Aspects* consists of the most banal dialogue propelled and overwhelmed by roiling orchestrations, and the result is simply thundering nonsense.

Aspects began as a 1955 novel by David Garnett, one of the lesser Bloomsbury lights. The story is promising—the notion of "love in the morning and Armagnac after" is seductively appealing, and the multiple love affairs experienced and played at are potentially beguiling. The meta-theatrical aspect of *Aspects* (the leading female is an actress, always making "scenes," and the leading male seeks to "play the lover" with her) adds a tone of self-consciousness to the elegance and philosophizing that prevail, permitting an edge of witty, informed sophistication. But the interrupted coital couplings occur with a frequency known only to farce, and the staging seems grandiose and parodic, particularly when a team of local townfolk arrive, apparently from a nearby production of *Cavalleria Rusticana.* By the end, all possible character shaping and shading is buried under Webber's grossly overblown score, and Maria Bjornson's equally overblown production design.

And then there is *Buddy,* which provided the occasion for the reopening of the Shubert Theatre (after many years of *A Chorus Line*). *Buddy* is a British musical play about the American rock and roll star Buddy Holly, and it's pretty much fun for anyone who likes Holly's music ("Peggy

Sue" "Maybe, Baby"). Indeed, the last third of the show is wholly devoted to a recreation of Holly's last concert, in Clear Lake, Iowa, on February 2, 1959, where Buddy was joined by the Big Bopper ("Chantilly Lace") and Richie Valens (now mostly known for "La Bamba," though at the time his big hits were "Donna" and "Come On, Let's Go.") The next night, all three died in a plane crash: Holly was 22.

There's a great moment in the production, which, unfortunately, comes right at the beginning of the show, where Holly and his "Crickets" are invited to perform at the local Lubbock KDAV radio station. Holly starts out singing a pleasant country tune. Then, just as we're thinking "gee, that's nice," he drops the guitar to his pelvis and breaks into a rip-roaring, foot-stamping rock and roll version of "That'll Be the Day," with the Cricket bassist flopping on his back, viol high in the air. It's terrific, and we get a flood of feeling, a recognition of hidden greatness (or is it just nostalgia for the familiar, momentarily forgotten?). It's just like that moment in *Amadeus* when Mozart picks out Salieri's air on the harpsichord, and then improvises it into "Non Piu Andrai" from *La Nozze de Figaro:* we go from "gee that's nice" to utterly awestruck appreciation in a single segue. Add to that Holly's bright-eyed eagerness (the role brilliantly created and still performed by Paul Hipp), his clean, Southern agreeability, and his boyish charm, and the show starts off with a great thrill.

Amadeus has somewhere to go afterward, however. The play of *Buddy* doesn't give us anything more than a pedestrian retelling of the obvious highpoints of Holly's straightforward life ("I want to do my music my way"), mixed in with what I found to be, by the end, decreasingly wonderful music. It's odd that the producers tell us in the program that "all that happens in the play is based on fact, even those events which seem beyond belief," since nothing that happens in this play is even remotely out of the ordinary: Buddy confounding his critics, Buddy doing his music his way, Buddy marrying despite his and her parents' objections, Buddy's mother wanting him to "eat right" on the road, Buddy's wife having a dream that he'll die in a plane crash. It's formulaic—a "Rocky" of rock and roll—and relentlessly trite in its execution: limp scene endings, contrived confrontations, cheap anachronistic gags. There's also a metatheatrical mishmashing here: from being a Broadway audience at the Shubert we're hauled off to become a black audience at the Harlem Apollo, then a family audience in Cedar Lake; we're continually being pushed around: by turns badgered by MC's ("Are you having a Good Time?"), and shamelessly hounded to applaud, we develop a shifting relationship to the actors. By play's end we don't know if we're applauding the real Buddy Holly or the actor playing him; some of us are probably applauding our own memories of ourselves as teenagers. When you're asked to clap—to play a member of a clapping audience—the drama evaporates: if you're part of the story, you're no longer objective or disinterested, you have a stake in the story's events. But of course you can't *act* on this stake, you can't stop Buddy from getting on the plane. So you are forced back to a now-frustrating objectivity: it's hard to stay entertained.

A scene from Prelude to a Kiss; left to right, Barnard Hughes, Mary Louise Parker and Timothy Hutton. Photo © 1990 Gerry Goodstein.

While I suspect that most of the head-bobbing and hand-clapping Holly-enthusiasts in the audience each night will happily overlook this ontological dissonance, it casts an enervating pall over the last half-hour of this work; the show climaxes joylessly, in mere (if gifted) MC ranting and over-hyped, over-amplified rock and roll decibels. Which makes me grumpy enough to add that the scene design and staging are also well below Broadway professional standards, and a 1950s billboard motif in the multi-scene surround, of questionable merit in the early scenes, looks ridiculous in the Cedar Lake reconstruction.

And so back to the U.S. of A. One can't return home-grown drama any better than with Eric Bogosian's *Sex, Drugs, Rock & Roll,* which is as American as crack cocaine. Bogosian's beguiling fashion is to compile a theater piece out of a dozen-odd character monologues, all created and played by himself, and *Sex, Drugs* is the best by far I've yet seen of this rare genre. The piece begins with a homeless but probably not harmless streetdude leaning against his chainlink fence and glaring at us with a withering, "This is the situation: I need your money!" And from here we move through Bogosian's cast of male Ameri-characters—a career-busting Hollywood exec, a party guy (who hires party girls), a recently unstoned and rehabilitated rock star ("the thing about drugs is you're having such a good time you don't realize what a bad time you're having"), and a still-stoned and un-rehabbed 1960s drop-out, who tells us that we're now living in an "occupied country" run by "fax machines and microwave ovens." Bogosian's deadly cynicism cuts to the core of most contemporary hypocrisies, including (one suspects) his own; there is, quite thankfully, no smug tone of self-righteousness here, nor of false sentimentality. Bogosian simply lays out, in his grimly entertaining fashion, the people (including those resident within us) that we find unavoidable in daily life. We may turn away from them in the street, but in the East Village Orpheum Bogosian allows us to stare at them shamelessly from a safe vantage. *Sex, Drugs* makes for a relatively short evening, and it wrings laughter and insight by turns—and often at the same time—without wringing us out. We will surely look both ways when leaving this theater.

I will quickly segue from Bogosian's to Calvin Trillin's one-man show, *Calvin Trillin's Words, No Music* as it was called at the American Place Theatre. This is not a drama in any shape or form, but it does take place in a theater (the same theater where Bogosian created *Drinking in America* four years ago), and it advertises in the theater pages. I don't exactly know what to make of this. Trillin is an erudite and sparklingly droll humorist, and his spiel was bright and entertaining, but neither more nor less so than in his books or on the pages of *The New Yorker.*

19

There's no character, no acting; it's what we used to call a talk. Do we really need credited scenery and lighting designers for this? A director? A production stage manager? A Who's Who in the Cast? Somebody please get Mr. Trillin a podium and a booking agent.

Two of the plays that occasioned great attention in New York this year I had seen in their earlier, premiere productions. I saw (at Yale) and reviewed (in these pages) August Wilson's remarkable *The Piano Lesson* in 1988, and I see no need to amplify upon my remarks with regard to the current Broadway production. That year I also saw Craig Lucas' *Prelude to a Kiss* at the South Coast Repertory Theatre of Costa Mesa, but did not review it, owing to space limitations. I'm happy I didn't, because Lucas has subsequently revised his script considerably, and I am glad to report upon it now. *Prelude* is one of the most fascinating plays to hit Broadway—and, with an "I love this play" review from Frank Rich, to prove a hit on Broadway—in a long time. It's a fantasy, which makes it a rare breed to begin with, and it's also a romance; this combination is mostly seen on the screen these days (*Ghost, Mr. Destiny, Heaven Can Wait,* etc.). Rita and Peter are Dewars-drinking, yuppie lovers at the play's opening moments, and they turn husband and wife before the end of the first act—whereupon the pretty bride, kissing a mysterious old man at the reception, exchanges souls with him! The rest of the play sorts all this out: the young husband realizing an imposter has infiltrated his wife; the young wife trying, for want of alternatives, to come to terms with new children-in-laws, rotting teeth and a corroded liver. There are elements of intrigue, surprise, and suspense in this well-wrought (and, since the SCR premiere, well re-wrought) play, and there is, above all, an infectious appeal to the principal characters and to the neo-Shakespearean, neo-Churchillian (as in Caryl) trans-aging and trans-genderizing that animates their interplay. Some critics have also seen analogies to AIDS, to homo/hetero sexualities, and to ontological mysteries in the work, all of which quite escape me (I feel no worse for my ignorance), but there's an apparent density to the theme as well as a lightness to the treatment which makes for an enchanting evening of theater. *Prelude to a Kiss* solidifies Lucas' right—staked out with *Blue Window*— to a higher spot on my listing of major American playwrights.

Homo/hetero sexuality is clearly central to David Stevens' *The Sum of Us;* this play has enjoyed a substantial run at the Cherry Lane Theatre off-Broadway, obviously speaking to its audiences with wry effect. A (heterosexual) father and (homosexual) son are the principal integers of the titular sum, and their easygoing mutual affection is both the joy and the curse of their lives. Papa buys homoerotic magazines so as to better understand his son (and maybe learn more about AIDS), but leaving such gay matter around the living room loses him an uptight fiancée by the middle of Act II. Sonny introduces his boyfriends to Understanding Dad, but then sees them go dismayingly limp at his cozifying domesticity. Circular and often redundant, *Sum* is apallingly nice; with all the well-meaning in the world, it trivializes its subjects (and its subject), and leaves you feeling, if anything, that sex oughta be dirty. No relationship, homo, hetero, or platonic-erotic, can sustain

all this well-intentioned third-party supportiveness. Stevens, a Palestinian-born writer of mixed background (English, Australian, African, and now Californian), might want to settle down and sharpen his knives before his next assault on the theatrical Rialto.

Broadway has been on a metatheatrical binge these past few years (Pirandello, thou shouldst be living at this hour!), with at least half the plays on 46th Street and environs taking the theater itself as their principal subject. Thus Rupert Holmes' *Accomplice,* billed as a comedy-thriller, is really a parody-thriller, or a meta-thriller; it's a thriller about people who are themselves rehearsing (or performing) a thriller, and the play keeps jumping levels on you: from "real" action to "staged" action, from rehearsal to improvisation to performance to real (?) life. The play we see begins as a very bad (so bad that it's good) English mystery, set in a cottage on the moors, where characters intone teddibly British sarcasms as, "not trying to make a point, are you dear?" A murder is soon enacted, but it turns out the enactment is merely a rehearsal of a real murder being planned; then the real murder takes place, but that turns out to be part of another rehearsal—for the whole thing up to this point has been a play. By the end of the evening the theater's set has been partly dismantled, the theater program has shown to be full of lies (so has the loudspeaker announcement as the play begins), and the play's (real) author has come up on stage to clarify (or doubly confuse) matters to their final resolution (or irresolution). It's like going to a museum to see a painting, and then realizing that it's not the painting but the frame that you're really supposed to be seeing, and then that it's not the frame but the museum wall that's the actual art work, and then that it's none of those: it's you, having gone to the museum, that's the true subject here. Going the first couple of steps on this route can be enchanting, if frustrating; going much further, however, diminishes the enchantment and increases the frustration (we simply get tired of all the refocusing), and *Accomplice,* for all its brilliant twists and turns, ends up soggy: there's no substance to any of it, and consequently no tension, so the thriller impact never materializes. For all its witty dramaturgy, *Accomplice* doesn't deliver anything, and that—for a thriller—is a fatal flaw; even the laughs die away well before we become *Accomplice*'s accomplice. Still, it's an amusing, audacious, and fitfully entertaining novelty for the Broadway stage, and should be seen often in the dinner and community theater circuits for some time.

Once on This Island is a barefoot Caribbean musical, sort of a story theater opera of *Ondine,* where an aristocratic and engaged man, and a beautiful native girl—there are touches of divinity about her—fall in love, tragically. There's a storm, some hot dancing, good songs that resonate with the French Antilles ("The Sad Tale of the Beauxhommes," "And the Gods Heard Her Prayer"), a single set and no intermission; it is just what you might expect and a little bit more. I found it smooth, pleasant, and entertaining, but exploring little of its potential. We are too close to the lands of neo-colonialism and voodoo to ignore the dramatic issues floating tantalizingly about, just out of this play's attempted reach; I think I would prefer a Haitian version.

Probably the biggest calamity in the American theater during my lifetime was Walter Kerr's *New York Times* pan of *Waiting for Godot* in its 1956 Broadway premiere: a "plastic job for the intellectual fruitbowl," he called it. Kerr's nose has been rubbed in that review more than a thousand times since, but that wasn't the calamity: what really hurts is that theater critics, from then on, have been chary of flailing away at what they perceive as sophomoric inanities, frightened that what they don't understand in the two hours traffic of an evening's entertainment may emerge as the masterwork of the decade, thus subjecting them to the humiliations that Mr. Kerr continues to suffer.

So it is understandable that, even with postmodern neo-absurdity and nonlinear neo-abstracted impressionism pretty much behind us, New York critics struggled to find something interesting in Steve Tesich's **Square One.** But it's hopeless. There's nothing remotely interesting there.

Tesich is a good writer, with an Academy Award (for *Breaking Away*), one well known play (*Division Street*), and others on the way. This one is a two-character pastiche of meeting, courtship and marriage, bearing, however, no relation whatever to the actual sorts of experiences

or problems real humans have encountered in the several thousand years that such events have taken place. Instead we find a series of writerly scenes, linked chronologically but not causally, and styled in what somebody must believe to be a fashionably absurdist, or "stupidist" fashion; which is to say that characters speak only elliptically, smiling blandly while hiding secrets we know we will never uncover, and which we deeply suspect the author has not even begun to think about himself.

That the play seems to be set in the future is a dim way of justifying the inanity and arbitrariness of its conversations and events. The tiresome twosome is comprised of a "third class state artist" (he's striving to become "second class") and a relentlessly enthusiastic older woman, who provides (though at a cost of any cogency or feeling) what energy and amusement the play fitfully delivers. Richard Thomas and Dianne Wiest played the roles in the Promenade Theatre opening, and they're both real pros; they faithfully pretend to enjoy what they're doing, which certainly must be great acting under these circumstances, but they deliver nothing but vapidity. The trouble with a play like this is that it contains absolutely nothing worth watching or hearing: no story, no characters, no eloquence, no ideas, no rhythm, no point. One waits in vain, in a play like this, for a character to do something of even modest interest, like invite you up on stage for a game of chess, or take off his clothes, or stand on his thumb, but it never happens. Anywhere else near Broadway and 76th Street (where **Square One** was performed) you'd have a more theatrical experience looking out the window.

Some plays of note opened in California this year, with serious plans for New York. Athol Fugard's magnificent **My Children! My Africa!** was certainly the play of the year on the West Coast, if not in the nation, and the La Jolla Playhouse production, directed by the author with a superb cast, was captivating, enthralling, and compelling: and while these three adjectives may appear synonymous on the page, each vividly conveys a discrete aspect of **My Children!**'s dramatic and theatrical grandeur.

Simply, even rudimentarily configured for the stage, **My Children!** opens with a school debate: we are students in Classroom Number One, Solile High School, in a small, black township on Cape Karoo, South Africa, in 1984. Immediately we relax, under the benignly cheery and complaisant eye of Anela Myalatya, the widely known and beloved "Mr. M," the town's greying schoolteacher, a self-proclaimed "black Confucius." Debating (on traditional and modern sex roles) are the school's star pupil, Mr. Thami Mbikwana (black), and the debate captain from another school, Miss Isabel Dyson (white). You can probably fill in the rest, but you'll be nonetheless amazed. Yes, the debate moves quickly out of the classroom and onto the street, surging from gender rights to racial wrongs, and from formal and academic to immediate and bloody; and, yes, the teacher's role as mediator, educator, and consolidator degenerates to *sparagmos*—a tearing apart, in a particularly gruesome South African fashion—in the unstoppable onrush of revolutionary fervor, ganging up, and guerrilla assassination. But Fugard, in going for the obvious, makes right for the jugular: in **My Children!** he dramatizes, with crescendoing effect on all fronts, the greatest struggles and dialectics of our time: equality (political, social); justice (racial, sexual); education (canonical, revolutionary); and love (paternal, fraternal/sororal, even romantic). Never have I seen the conflict between personal and social ambitions so beautifully, agonizingly, pointed and propelled on stage.

Fugard gives no answers: every position has dignity and intensity, every argument conveys its own valedictory. "Enthusiasm for your cause is most commendable but without personal discipline it is as useless as having a good donkey and a good cart but no harness," says Mr. M. in the opening scene, and the play wrings every possible variation on that essential theme. The unimpeachable value in this work is friendship, and I have never seen the case for friendship so powerfully and directly pled. The play has no fake drama, nor empty theatrics: there is a single spare (and effective) vulgarism, and no sex, no nudity, no music, no gunshots, and no "production" other than the most tasteful and simple scenery and costume. Basically, it's three exquisite actors (Brock Peters as the teacher, Nancy Travis and Sterling Macer Jr. as the white and black students) and Mr. Peter's school bell, clanged playfully, violently, and at times wildly, and which, in the end, we will ring for him. *My Children! My Africa!* is one of the rarest gifts of the modern theater: an ennobling tragedy.

In the first minutes of *Jake's Women,* the new Neil Simon play that premiered at San Diego's Old Globe Theatre, actress Stockard Channing comes doddering onto the set like a cartoon wife, mouthing idiotic platitudes, and the dismayed audience thinks Simon is off his rocker; this is the cheapest comedy we've seen in decades, harking back not to *Barefoot in the Park* but to Simon's early TV skits for Imogene Coca. But it's just a trick: Channing's not playing Maggie, Jake's wife; she's playing Jake's hallucination of Maggie. Soon afterwards the real Maggie enters, normally enough, and we see that Simon's working in a new level (for him) of stylistic freedom, one that opens his work up to some intriguing possibilities.

Intriguing possibilities, however, are not exactly what Simon's audiences want from him, nor what his critics expect, and *Women* proved so patently unsatisfactory in San Diego that Simon subsequently canceled (or at least "indefinitely postponed") its scheduled New York opening, the first time such a thing has happened in Simon's remarkable history of 25 Broadway shows—mostly hits—in 29 years. A good move, but don't count this play out—not yet.

Jake's women are seven in number: wife Maggie, ex- (and dead) wife Julie, psychotherapist Edith, girlfriend Sheila, sister Karen, and daughter Mollie (at 13 and 21, played by different actresses); the play brings them all onstage, sometimes in their own persons, and sometimes through Jake's distorted imaginings. Thus, Jake can talk to the real Maggie and the imagined Julie at the same time, or to the imagined Maggie and the real Sheila; he can even talk simultaneously to the imaginary Edith (onstage) and the real Edith (on the phone). "Will you let me talk to you?" he hollers to the imaginary Edith, interrupting his phone call to the real Edith. Funny.

But Jake can't rid himself of his imaginings; they have a life of their own, and they crowd out the present. Dead Julie—the idealized first wife—appears with maddening regularity, making Jake's marriage with Maggie a living hell; and when the real Maggie leaves, the imagined Maggie returns to haunt Jake's affair with Sheila. Jake is left impotent; unable to function, to write (he's a novelist), to think straight. Sad.

Unfortunately, Simon has written two plays, not one. As a comic fantasy, *Women* is sort of a double *Blithe Spirit,* with ghosts haunting ghosts as well as people. As a psychological drama, the ghosts are Jake's delusions, hallucinations. Fine on each count, but Simon can't have it both ways. As fantasy, *Women* is good theater: funny, true-to-life (as only fantasy can be), and well-paced. Dead Julie doesn't want to be idealized ("Was I so terrible you didn't want to see me as I really was?") and demands that Jake conjure up their daughter Mollie for her: the recognition scene between Dead Julie and daughter Mollie, reminiscent of the Hermione–Perdita scene in *The Winter's Tale,* is beautifully wrought and emotionally powerful. And as psychological drama, it's an even better play; one senses levels far beneath the autobiographical dramatization (which Simon provided in his *Chapter 2*) of the widower's plight. *Women* gives us levels of mental recess and regression that are infinitely provocative.

Problem is, Simon hasn't brought his two plays together; he's just going for the gag wherever he finds it, eliding fantasy and psychosis, eliminating dramatic tension, and abandoning his characters in the process. Going for the gag is Simon's old game; it's made him the most successful playwright in America, but also kind of a national joke: when an American artistic director wants to announce a serious theater mission he or she simply says "We don't do Neil Simon" and that says it all. A shame, and needless. There's more than joking here, and I, for one, am hoping Simon ultimately brings *Jake's Women* to an integration of its parts, and to a successful re-opening. A year without Neil Simon in New York, after all, has left us all a little uneasy.

The Year in World Literature

by William Riggan

Reverberations from the sociopolitical upheavals of late 1989, particularly in Central Europe and China, began leaving their mark on world literature in 1990. These reverberations resulted in part through the greater artistic freedom now allowed in many areas, in part as a direct response to or description of those events, and in isolated areas such as Albania and Romania in the apparent failure of the revolution to bring about the expected liberalization of the press and the flowering of genuine literature free of ideological restrictions or elaborate statagems for circumventing censorship. Three prime examples were new works by Christa Wolf of East Germany, Václav Havel of Czecho-Slovakia, and Liu Xinwu of China. This was not the only story of the year, however, as world literature also saw the appearance of a wealth of first-rate new works by Asia and African writers both well established and previously little known.

German

Wolf, long a revered beacon of courage and integrity as well as an outstanding prose writer, drew an unexpectedly ferocious firestorm of criticism for her autobiographical novella **Was bleibt** (What Remains), originally written in 1979, which recounts the story of a noted woman writer whose life is suddenly altered when, for reasons unknown, she is placed under twenty-four-hour surveillance by anonymous men in ever-changing automobiles outside her home. Charges of tacit complicity in police-state repression and of opportunism in publishing the work only after the demise of the East German state (GDR) have shaken Wolf badly, though her many admirers—including several writers who suffered imprisonment and/or exile and were treated far worse by the GDR regime—have belatedly begun speaking out more vociferously in her defense. Among her defenders are the bad-boy poet-balladeer Wolf Biermann and the subtle poet and prose writer Günter Kunert. Both writers, now resident in the West for over a decade, also brought out new titles of their own in 1990: Biermann's collected song texts of thirty years, **Alle Lieder 1960-1990** (All the Songs 1960-1990), offers a trove of protest songs, love lyrics, humorous ditties, vicious satires, gentle ballads, and rousing political anthems, together comprising what many have termed the "most German" lieder since Heinrich Heine a century and a half earlier; and Kunert's new verse collection **Fremd daheim** (A Stranger in One's Own Land) presents a series of thoughtful, probing reflections sparked by observations from the author's frequent travels around Germany and abroad.

Max von der Grün's complex modern-day murder mystery cum political thriller **Springflut** (Spring Flood), with its account of an unsettling influx of Polish refugees into a small West German town in the Ruhr industrial district, led an otherwise rather lackluster year in West German letters. Peter Härtling's **Herzwand** (Cardial Wall), which interweaves several autobiographical strands and simultaneously seeks to explain and exemplify the narrative act itself was another notable West German publication in 1990. A stronger showing from Austria included two major new books: **Einander Kind** (Each Other's Child) by Barbara Frischmuth struggled with questions of memory, forgetfulness, despair, and hopeful determination among the inhabitants of a strange, imaginary country that seems at times almost devoid of history or of any understanding of the outside world; and the novelette **Versuch über die Jukebox** (Essay on the Jukebox) by Peter Handke carried the autobiographical narrator to a sleepy Spanish town, where he hoped to write in peace about a fondly recalled super-jukebox from his youth, only to find his intended essay/excursus slowly evolving into a fictional meta-narrative. The gifted Swiss writer Silvio Blatter weighed in with **Das blaue Haus** (The Blue House), a picaresque chronicle covering three generations of the Zinn family's colorful patriarch Johann and his scions.

Slavic Languages

Havel, the dissident playwright turned president of Czecho-Slovakia, became better known as a thinker and artist in 1990 through the international success of **Disturbing the Peace,** (published in Prague as **Dálkový výslech**), a series of interviews, conversations, and commentaries dating from 1986 and touching on such topics as power, reticence, and the absurdist tradition that forms the basis of his political and philosophic outlook. Much less systematic by their very nature than many of his closely reasoned essays, the interviews go a long way toward illuminating Havel as engagingly idiosyncratic, genuinely yet approachably intellectual, thoroughly human, and uncompromisingly moral. His countryman Ivan Klíma provided a well-crafted and provocative look at the 1980s in his homeland with **Love and Garbage,** the multilayered story of the life, loves, and literary efforts of a banned novelist who has taken employment as a sanitation worker. **Too Loud a Solitude** by Bohumil Hrabal (of *Closely Watched Trains* fame) is a typically eccentric romp about a lifelong pulper of printed matter who is also enough of a philosopher and secret rebel to "bless" each bale of pulp he produces with either an art reproduction on the outside packaging or a genuine intact book hidden inside (Kant and Erasmus are his favorites). When technological advances in the "industry" eliminate the possibility of such small subterfuges, he recognizes the end of the world as he chooses to know it and acts accordingly.

Polish literature continued its active resurgence of the 1980s with the publication of several new works both at home and abroad. *Rondo* by Kazimierz Brandys is narrated by the son of a famed Polish general, a connection that proves disastrous for the apolitical, womanizing youth in the postwar years when his supposed rightist connections lead to his imprisonment by the newly ascendant communists. *Bohin Manor* by the prodigiously talented Tadeusz Konwicki recounts the life, loves, and fate of the narrator-novelist's Lithuanian-Polish grandmother in a fashion that mixes nineteenth-century realism à la Tolstoy with twentieth-century introspection and narrative intrusions. *The Beautiful Mrs. Seidenmann* by the former exile and current parliamentarian Andrzej Szczypiorski uses its blonde, blue-eyed Jewish heroine's unsuccessful effort to conceal her true identity in wartime Warsaw as emblematic of a Poland maimed by the systematic destruction of its Jewish citizens.

The prizewinning Belorussian novelist Vasil Bykov was reintroduced to the West through an English edition of his 1986 novel *Sign of Misfortune,* the moving tale of an elderly couple's survival, resistance, and complicity in Nazi-occupied Belorussia during the war years, set against flashbacks to the prewar collectivization's slow destruction of the region's peasantry. The war as seen from exile in Paris provides the backdrop for three novellas by the Russian Nina Berberova—*The Resurrection of Mozart, The Waiter and the Slut,* and *Astashev in Paris*—issued in a single volume titled *Three Novels;* together the three add up to a fine but disheartening portrayal of the Francophile Russian class's pathetic demise within a world they profess to love and admire but which they fail utterly to understand or assimilate. *Goodnight!* by Abram Tertz (the pseudonym of Andrei Sinyavsky) moves backward and forward in time as it weaves an amalgam of fantasy, memories, and history into a fictionalized autobiography that illuminates the author's emergence in the 1960s as a writer and dissident. Particularly impressive are Tertz's accounts of his farcical 1965 interrogation and trial, his imprisonment, his internal exile, and a phantasmagorical scene involving an old clairvoyant who is visited by Stalin on the night of his death. *Arise and Walk* by the seventy-ish novelist and editor Yuri Nagibin marks a strong departure from his usual lyric prose and nature-infused fiction, offering instead a devastating examination of the Bolshevik Revolution's legacy and an outright condemnation of *Homo sovieticus;* all this is conveyed in the spare and seemingly gentle story of a young boy who witnesses his father's arrest and then proceeds to visit him for the next twenty-four years in various camps and prisons across the width and breadth of the Soviet Union.

Asia

Liu Xinwu, a prominent and acerbic chronicler of Chinese society over the last decade who was removed as editor of the influential journal *People's Literature* following the June 1989 suppression of the popular democratic movement, was introduced to English readers with the story collection *Black Walls,* containing works dating from 1980 to 1987. The longest selection, the 1980 novella *The Wish,* is a poignant yet wry depiction of Beijing during the Cultural Revolution, and many of the remaining stories evoke similarly colorful, compassionate snapshots of the capital as it undergoes the pains of momentous transitions. Wang Meng, China's minister of culture from 1986 until his ouster in September 1989, likewise debuted in the West in 1990; his *Bolshevik Salute,* billed as "the first Chinese modernist novel," covers thirty-five years in the life of a dedicated communist trapped between self-knowledge and party dictates. Critics have termed the work a brilliant exploration of the psychology of political identity and alienation, an inside view of the anguish experienced by individuals in modern China trying to remain faithful both to themselves and to the state. Li Cunhao's *Wreath at the Foot of the Mountain* created a sensation in China upon first publication in 1982 for its realistic portrayal of the 1979 China-Vietnam conflict and now has been made available to English readers worldwide as well. The poet Bei Dao's novel *Waves* and Ah Cheng's three-novella collection *King of Children* record the painful years of the Cultural Revolution and track the diverse groups of people—intellectuals, factory workers, drifters, thieves—who represent China's "lost generation" of the 1970s. The stories of Ai Bei's *Red Ivy, Green Earth Mother* present the frankest depiction yet of the lives of women in contemporary China; each focuses on a female narrator—a prison inmate, an abandoned young woman in labor, another young woman confronted by the jealousy of her boyfriend's domineering mother—struggling for social and sexual identity within a repressive society.

Japan's acclaimed novelist Kenzaburō Ōe delved into science fiction in 1990 with *The Healing Tower,* about a twenty-first century resettlement effort on a "new Earth" in a faraway galaxy following the total environmental devastation of our own planet; implicit of course, as in much "green" literature generally, is a strong critique of today's technological-industrial civilization and an advocacy of a more humane, more ethical way of life, if the world is to survive for another generation. Western readers got a first look at Satoko Kizaki and a second glimpse of Saiichi Maruya in the fine short-story collections *The Phoenix Tree* and *Rain in the Wind,* respectively. Kizaki's three novellas, particularly the title piece (winner of the prestigious Akutagawa Prize five years ago) about a handsome older woman who refuses to acknowledge or treat the breast cancer that is slowly killing her, all deal with alienation, focusing on protagonists faced with sudden, prolonged displacement and uncertainty. The title story in *Rain in the Wind* is perhaps best described as a Zen mixture of Eco and Calvino, featuring a modern-day medievalist narrator engaged in an apparently futile search to prove that the drunken monk whose stories so entertained his father in 1940 was the very same *waka* poet who has now posthumously become the rage of literary Tokyo.

India's venerable novelist R. K. Narayan presented readers with another delightful tale from the mythical town of Malgudi in *The World of Nagaraj,* this time focusing on the idle, uninvolved life of the comfortably well-off but resolutely unambitious title character and his desultory efforts at writing the biography of an obscure sage. A slapstick subplot about Nagaraj's adoption of his nephew and the panoply of local characters who are part of his daily routine only add to the novel's charm. The cause of the banned Indonesian novelist Pramoedya Ananta Toer was doubtless helped by the 1990 English-language publication of his slender, poetic 1950 novel *The Fugitive,* a story of treachery, deceit, and survival set amid the Japanese occupation at the end of World War II and the welter of conflicting loyalties—both personal and political—that the complex circumstances generated for such young idealists as the nationalist resistance fighter Hardo and his fellow maquis. Year's end brought a most noteworthy development with the publication of Salman Rushdie's *Haroun and the Sea of Stories,* ostensibly a children's tale (dedicated to the young son the author has not seen since the Ayatollah Khomeini's death edict two years ago) but also a sprightly and inventive allegory relating to the whole *Satanic Verses* controversy and the legal issues surrounding the suppression of literature and the imaginative arts.

Africa

The outstanding and prolific South African writer Nadine Gordimer gave us *My Son's Story* in 1990, fashioning a charged and psychologically complex tale of a black township family caught up in both their own private affairs and the political struggles and changes currently going on in their troubled nation. The work is replete with intricate ironies, not the least of which is the fact that the protagonist's gradual evolution into a human-rights activist directly parallels his betrayal of his wife and son (the narrator) and the dissolution of his tranquil home life. *Age of Iron,* by Gordimer's countryman J. M. Coetzee, takes the form of a long letter from a former classics professor, now dying of cancer, to her daughter in America, charting her own awakening to the death throes of apartheid as well as to her own imminent demise. Among the novel's strongest aspects is the bond of caring solicitude and protectiveness that emerges between the professor and the homeless alcoholic who first only mails her letters but ultimately becomes her confidant, savior, and guardian angel during her final days. The late Bessie Head's *Tales of Tenderness and Power* collected several previously unpublished prose writings along with others not readily available, forming an apt tribute to her versatility and strength as both a storyteller and a commentator.

The noted Nigerian author Amos Tutuola offered *The Village Witch Doctor,* an extraordinary collection of traditional and original stories drawing heavily on Yoruba legend and folklore, and also produced a definitive reworked version of his 1948 novel manuscript *The Wild Hunter in the Bush of Ghosts,* previously published only in a limited scholarly edition eight years ago. Sousa Jamba of Angola produced in *Patriots* an artful and fluent account (in English) of the effects of his country's long civil war on individuals such as himself, an account that is both horrifying in its depiction of suffering and darkly comic in its portrayal of war's moral confusion. Henri Lopes, prime minister of Zaire in that nation's early days, brought out his first novel in nearly a decade, *Le chercheur d'Afriques* (The Seeker of Africas), recounting in alternating sequences the two worlds of its African-European protago-

nist. From North Africa came ambitious and first-rate new French-language works of fiction by Tahar Ben Jelloun of Morocco, *Jour de silence à Tanger* (Day of Silence in Tangiers), and Chantal Chawaf of Algeria, *L'éclaircie* (Clearing Skies).

Caribbean-born Derek Walcott, by any standard one of the finest English-language poets of our time, brought out in August 1990 his long-awaited book-length poem *Omeros,* an epic that borrows from Homer not only its title but also the multiple narrative threads woven by the Greek bard into the *Iliad* and the *Odyssey.* The figure of Homer appears here variously as a blind St. Lucian fisherman, an African griot, and a vagrant bargeman in London. We also find two other fishermen named Hector and Achille, a woman named Helen who is the object of their quarrel, a villager named Philoctete who has an ulcerous leg, and a "phantom narrator" who is a native of the island but now resides in Boston, as does Walcott himself. The scope—nearly nine thousand lines with often complicated meter, rhyme, off-rhyme, and assonance—is daunting, but the poet brings the task off with a skill that is as dazzling as the tale itself is rich. Here is a work that is destined to become one of the touchstones of late-twentieth-century verse.

Near East

The 1988 Nobel laureate Naguib Mahfouz's most highly acclaimed work, the fifteen-hundred-page *Cairo Trilogy,* became available to Western readers in part in 1990 with the publication of the English translation of volume one, *Palace Walk,* which chronicles two years in the life of a

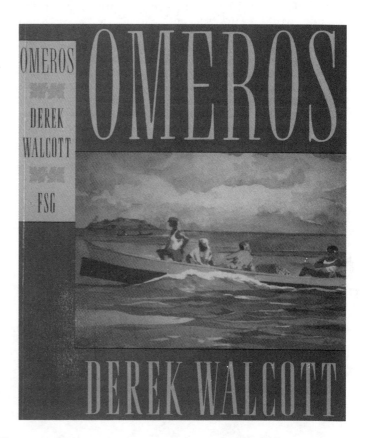

respectable middle-class Cairo family caught up in the so-ciopolitical changes occurring in Egypt in the aftermath of World War I. Mahfouz's pace and style here are stately and, to Western tastes, even a bit anachronistic, much akin to reading Dickens or Tolstoy with a rhetorical over-lay that will recall the *Thousand and One Nights,* but the cumulative effect is surprisingly forceful and pleasurable. Israel's Aharon Appelfeld brought out **The Healer,** a pow-erfully original novel set in prewar Central Europe (like many of his earlier books) and examining the plague of anti-Semitism that haunted both individuals and entire populations during that period, including such "lost Jews" as the ironically named protagonist Felix, who feels himself totally out of place within exclusively Jewish com-munities and genuinely at home only in cosmopolitan Vi-enna. Appelfeld's countryman David Grossman, critically hailed for last year's *See Under: Love,* enjoyed the first En-glish publication of his 1983 novel **The Smile of the Lamb,** a less successful but still compelling work about the ero-sion of values caused by Israel's subjugation of Palestini-ans on the West Bank.

From Iran came first English editions of works by the pop-ular prerevolutionary woman writer Simin Daneshvar and the pseudonymous Manuchehr Irani, considered by his peers as the finest contemporary Persian short story writ-er. Daneshvar's novel **Savushun,** a best seller in Farsi for over twenty years, follows the lives of the members of a prominent family in Shiraz during World War II and their experiences under Allied occupation. Irani's **King of the Benighted** provides a firsthand account of the harsh reali-ties of life under the Islamic Republic, focusing on the hardships endured by a young poet in prison and in the outside world. Turkey's finest living novelist Orhan Pamuk scored a double success in 1990 with the English translation of his third novel, **White Castle,** and the re-lease of his fourth in Turkish, **Kara Kitap** (The Dark Book). **White Castle** is a riveting tale of romantic adven-ture set in seventeenth-century Italy and Turkey with a Borgesian element of reversible identities and magical transformations. **Kara Kitap** is a complex meta-narrative of intertwined tales set in modern-day Istanbul and ulti-mately concerned with the problematic relationship be-tween reality and fiction.

France

An otherwise uninspiring year in French literature was brightened considerably by the dazzling verbal artistry of Hélène Cixous, whose "novel" **Jours de l'an** (Days of the Year) incorporates such disparate elements as anniversa-ries (both imaginary and real) for various dates, medita-tions on death and the irresistibility of night, and fanta-sized voyages across the Styx in the company of the de-ceased authors Clarice Lispector and Thomas Bernhard. In Patrick Modiano's novel **Voyage de noces** (Honey-moon) the narrator tries to come to terms with his long-standing guilt and remorse over his young bride's suicide forty years ago as well as his sudden abandonment by his most recent companion. **Du nerf** (Nerve) by Robert Pinget mixes faulty memory and vestigial longings in a series of understated fragments centering on the creative act of writing, all guided in primly querulous and unreliable fashion by the nevertheless engaging old fool, Monsieur Songe, long familiar to Pinget's readers. Other works of note from France in 1990 included Patrick Grainville's fictionalized autobiography of his childhood and youth, **L'orgie, la neige** (The Orgy, the Snow); Julien Green's journal from the 1980s, **L'expatrié** (The Expatriate); and the complete poems of Edmond Jabès, **Le seuil, le sable** (The Threshold, the Sand), covering the years 1943-88.

Other

The outstanding Dutch-language author Hugo Claus's lengthy but riveting and lively novel **The Sorrow of Bel-gium** details the events and effects of World War II in one corner of one small country as filtered through the eyes and pen of an obnoxious young artist-in-the-making. **Fado Alexandrino** by Portugal's António Lobo Antunes covers some of the same post-Angolan War terrain treated in the author's much-praised earlier novel *South of Nowhere,* but this time more expansively and in a more complex fashion, focusing on the crisscrossed fates of four failed Portuguese combatants in the ten years after the troops returned home from Angola. **Le palais des rêves** (The Palace of Dreams), originally published in 1981 by the Albanian novelist and erstwhile presidential candidate Ismail Kadare, became available in French translation in 1990. This self-proclaimed masterwork is a Kafkaesque fantasy about a state official assigned the task of collecting, sorting, and interpreting all the dreams of all the nation's inhabitants in order to isolate the "master dream" that will predict the country's destiny. The same writer's more recent novel, **Broken April,** tackled the difficult subject of blood feuds and vendettas, unfortunately still a pervasive element in much of present-day Albania. And lastly, the gifted Ro-manian author Paul Goma made his debut in the English-speaking world with the publication of **My Childhood at the Gate of Unrest,** a Proustian exploration of memory and experience centering on a remote Moldavian village that survives the war only to be swallowed up in Stalin's Soviet Union.

A varied and generally excellent year in world literature by any measure.

Notes on Contributors

Wendy Lesser is the editor of *The Threepenny Review*, which she founded in 1980. She is the author of *The Life Below the Ground: A Study of the Subterranean in Literature and History* and *His Other Half: Men Looking at Women Through Art*. Her reviews and essays have appeared in the *New York Times Book Review*, the *Hudson Review*, the *Washington Post*, and elsewhere. She holds a Ph.D in English from the University of California, Berkeley, an M.A. from King's College, Cambridge, and a B.A. from Harvard.

J. D. McClatchy is the author of three collections of poems—*Scenes from Another Life, Stars Principal*, and *The Rest of the Way*—as well as a critical study *White Paper: On Contemporary American Poetry*. He has edited several books, including *Poets On Painters* and a recent anthology, *The Vintage Book of Contemporary American Poetry*. He has taught at Yale, Princeton, UCLA, Columbia, and elsewhere, while serving as poetry editor of *The Yale Review*. His poems and reviews appear regularly in *The New Yorker, The New York Times Book Review, The New Republic*, and other magazines.

Robert Cohen is Professor of Drama at the University of California, Irvine, and the author of the recent *Acting in Shakespeare*. He has written several well known theatre texts and treatises, including *Theatre; Giraudoux: Three Faces of Destiny; Acting Power; Acting One; Acting Professionally; Creative Play Direction;* and *Eight Plays for Theatre*. He contributes essays to various academic and theatre journals and has reviewed "The Year in Drama" for *Contemporary Literary Criticism* since 1986. A professional stage director as well, Cohen is co-artistic director of Theatre 40 in Los Angeles and a regular guest director at the Colorado and Utah Shakespeare Festivals. He holds his Doctorate in Fine Arts from the Yale School of Drama, and has lectured widely on theatrical topics in the U.S. and abroad.

William Riggan is Associate Editor of *World Literature Today* at the University of Oklahoma, with responsibilities for coverage of Third World, Slavic, Anglo-American, and smaller European literatures. He holds a doctorate in comparative literature from Indiana University, is the author of *Picaros, Madmen, Naïfs, and Clowns: The Unreliable First-Person Narrator*, has written extensively on the history and selections of both the Nobel Prize in Literature and the Neustadt International Prize in Literature, and regularly reviews new foreign fiction and poetry for several journals and newspapers.

New Authors

Elena Castedo
Paradise

Castedo was born in Spain in 1937, raised in Chile, and currently resides in the United States.

Paradise is a coming-of-age novel narrated by nine-year-old Solita. After emigrating from Franco's Spain, Solita's family settles in a rundown Chilean boardinghouse. Solita's mother, frustrated with poverty and her two children's bleak prospects, takes them to El Topaz, a wealthy estate that she describes to them as "paradise." Ironically, Solita discovers that the opulent world of El Topaz is more corrupt than the one she has left. The owner of the estate, Tia Merce, has three daughters who mercilessly torment their new companion, and she entertains a series of guests whose decadence and corruption confuse the young girl. Castedo reveals the intrigues of El Topaz through the fragmentary conversations Solita hears but rarely understands, such as the malicious gossip the guests spread about both her father, a union supporter, and her mother, who is plotting to remarry into the local aristocracy. Although some commentators claimed the story was too drawn-out, many commended Castedo's vivid descriptions of the poor immigrant community and the Chilean elite. Most critics hailed *Paradise* as a sensitive depiction of childhood, convincingly presented from Solita's viewpoint. Phoebe-Lou Adams observed: "Ms. Castedo has brought off, with acid wit, the far from easy task of revealing arrogance, folly, injustice, and debauchery through the eyes of an observer who does not know what those qualities are."

Kirkus Reviews

[*Paradise* is a] clever and richly textured first novel by Chilean-reared writer Castedo, now resident in the US, that does not live up to the promise of its premise—namely, that what is thought to be paradise is more corrupt than the fallen world beyond its walls.

Set in Chile just after WW II, the story is told by a child-narrator—Solita—whose family has fled Franco's Spain and then Occupied France, and has come to Chile as refugees. While her parents look for work, they live in a rundown boardinghouse where Solita and her young brother make friends with the other refugees. For Solita, this is a paradise—there are no bombs to fear and the family is all together; but her mother, beautiful and well-born, is not happy. She announces one day that she is taking the children with her to live in a paradise—a luxurious country estate owned by wealthy Chileans. The visit, her mother tells them, is her "big chance." Solita's family is to provide amusement for their hosts, especially their hostess, who depends on Solita's mother for advice and friendship. Solita is to play with the three daughters. This paradise is a self-sufficient enclosed world dedicated to frivolity and inhabited by an eclectic group of guests, wealthy relations, and exotic pets. But paradise is not quite what it should be: the girls torment Solita, her mother ignores her, her father—despised for his union work—seldom visits, and the guests quarrel. Their departure from the estate, though a triumph for Solita's mother, who has dumped Solita's father and ensnared one of her hostess' rich relations, is for Solita the end of that earlier paradise she had enjoyed when her refugee family was all together. Her mother's paradise is too dearly bought.

Casteda's characters are vital and full-bodied, and Solita the child narrator is always correctly childlike, but the story is too drawn out and the metaphor soon exhausted.

Somehow along the way, in more ways than one, paradise gets lost. (pp. 1765-66)

A review of "Paradise," in Kirkus Reviews, *Vol. 57, No. 24, December 15, 1989, pp. 1765-66.*

Publishers Weekly

In [*Paradise*], her first novel, Castedo, who was raised in Chile, recreates the magical world of a group of South American aristocrats just after WW II, but diminishes the charm of her tale by dragging it on too long. The narrator, a lively youngster named Solita, lives in poverty in an unnamed Latin American country where her parents are political refugees from Franco's Spain. While her father dabbles in radical politics, her mother, a renowned beauty, tries to better her family's status by hobnobbing with wealthy eccentrics. One of them, "Tia" Merce, a bisexual fond of Solita's mother, invites the family to her lush country estate, El Topaz. Among Merce's three spoiled daughters, Solita begins an education in the ways of the upper classes. Merce's constant stream of guests, their chatter and their pretensions are vividly conveyed; Solita's naïve, highly accurate descriptions of her elders are often riotously funny. The novel ends with a tragic murder and a resulting loss of innocence for all the children.

A review of "Paradise," in Publishers Weekly, *Vol. 236, No. 25, December 22, 1989, p. 45.*

Barbara Mujica

Paradise is story of survival—spiritual, as well as physical. The story line of Elena Castedo's first novel is deceptively simple: The Prados family, refugees from Franco's Spain, settles in an unidentified Latin American country, where the father continues his activities as a labor agitator. Tired of her husband's endless politicking and the refugee ghetto where they live, Pilar wrangles an invitation for herself and her two children to El Topaz, a huge country estate. It will be Paradise, she tells Solita, almost ten, and four-year-old Neceto. The novel relates their stay at the sprawling *hacienda,* beginning with their arrival and ending with their departure.

As described by Solita, the precocious child-narrator, Paradise is more like hell. A microcosm of Latin American society, El Topaz becomes the training ground where Solita learns what her mother learned years before, first in war-torn Spain and then in Nazi concentration camps: how to survive in an unjust, hierarchical world. Presided over by Doña Mercedes, estranged wife of the estate owner, El Topaz is a gathering place for high-class and not-so-high-class eccentrics. . . . They are catered to by a platoon of servants, and the estate is kept running by a population of peasants, none of whom is of much interest to the inhabitants of the "houses"—the area occupied by Doña Mercedes and her guests. In the distilled atmosphere of El Topaz, a pecking order is strictly observed.

The hostess' daughters, Patricia and the twins Grace and Gloria, make life miserable for Solita, tricking and teasing her incessantly. Only Gloria shows any compassion at all for the little girl, whose name reflects her solitude. Living in a *pensión* in the Spanish ghetto, Solita ran free, only vaguely aware of social stratification and decorum. But her little hostesses are quick to make her understand that she is their inferior. She is poor, without an elegant name or lineage; worst of all, she is a "goth" (the disparaging term for "Spaniard").

The girls manipulate Solita by pretending to know some dark secret about her mother. Pilar was brought to the estate because Mercedes considered her amusing, but according to both the girls and the servants, she has overstayed her welcome. Solita is torn between the desire to spit in the girls' faces and the real psychological need to please her mother, who has instructed her to get along with her hostesses.

Pilar turns on the charm to secure her place among the elite. She has sold out to the system, but she has been through so much that we can hardly blame her. At times her Republican tendencies surface, but Pilar cuts such an attractive figure that Mercedes and her guests consider her liberal views an adorable oddity.

Solita maintains a strong sense of dignity that prevents her from kowtowing to Patricia and the twins, but her loyalty to her mother is so fierce that she puts up with the girls' persecution in order to protect Pilar. For a while Solita longs desperately for her father to come and rescue her, but gradually she realizes that there is no way out. You have to learn to cope: "Long-range plans didn't work; each minute you had to save your skin right then and there, by yourself, and in ways that wouldn't come back to haunt you." When Solita's mother returns from the city with beautiful dolls for the other girls and a cheap one for her, she hides her pain: "I watched the girls take off their dolls' skirts and sweaters. My doll could grow big and invite me to go to Charley's. I accepted. I stayed sensible. I licked wounds."

Through the child's observations of half-understood events, Castedo paints a disturbing picture of a sordid society. The bored clique moves from one amusement to the next. Infidelity, lesbian and homosexual experimentation, and flings with the field hands relieve their tedium—and loneliness.

When Pilar at last plans to leave, Mercedes, who is sexually attracted to her, stages a lavish party to keep her at El Topaz a while longer. The grotesque carnival atmosphere of this last big bash conveys magnificently the hollowness of her guests' existence. Grown men and women dress up in costumes and take part in silly charades. It is bizarre parody of normal affairs at El Topaz, where all the inhabitants are merely role-players.

The behavior of the guests' children mirrors that of their parents. These wealthy youngsters establish their own pecking order. In comparison with the sons and daughters of her mother's millionaire visitors, Patricia and her sisters are nothing. The girls who have tormented Solita for months now struggle desperately to show that they are members of the elite, using Solita as their pawn. They attempt to prove their own superiority by degrading her horribly in front of the others. Solita, who has tried to gain acceptance through her athletic prowess, must come to terms with the fact that in society people are not judged by their talents and contributions, but by their money and power. Surprising developments finally free Solita from the grip of Paradise. She leaves El Topaz with a much clearer notion of how society works, but also with a renewed sense of self.

Elena Castedo has written a brilliant novel in which the narrative voice never falters. Solita is a touching character whose candor filters the harshness of Castedo's view. The child's ingenuous questions point out the absurdity of the rituals and values that govern upper class society, and her commentaries reveal the selfishness and cruelty of adults and children alike. Through Solita, Castedo raises some complex issues about human nature in general, and about Latin society in particular. (pp. 61-2)

Barbara Mujica, "Image and Reality in Latin American Literature," in Américas, *Vol. 42, No. 1, 1990, pp. 60-2.*

Patricia Aufderheide

No one really has a happy childhood. Under the best of circumstances, it's a time of great drama, full of the terror and joy of discovery—nothing so tame as happiness. It takes years of work to strategically forget that wildness, and then we set about raising our own children with the dubious expectation of giving them a "happy childhood."

Elena Castedo has not forgotten. In *Paradise,* she has not only recreated the terrifying heroics and cruelties of youth, but also evoked how they are blandly misunderstood or overlooked by parents and other adults. She has done so in a story whose plot is as idiosyncratic as its themes are universal.

Born in Spain, raised in Chile, now living in the U.S., Castedo is part of the 20th century's international culture of exile. Her central character, a little girl of perhaps 8 or 9, evokes the disruptive conditions of that culture as much as the universal trials of childhood.

Solita (Little Lonely One), a Spanish refugee whose family is living hand-to-mouth in an unnamed Latin American country, narrates the adventures that begin with her mother's announcement that they are moving to "Paradise." Solita, her little brother (who here has the status of an obstreperous puppy), and her mother—who has the flair that Solita so painfully knows she lacks—have been invited to a country estate, where a rich and troubled woman and her three spoiled daughters patronize the refugee family.

Solita's world is aswirl in mysteries, evinced in overheard, half-finished conversations that provide her with clues, which she then diligently interprets (and misinterprets). Why doesn't Solita's daddy come to visit them more often? Where is the daddy of the spoiled little girls? Why does Solita's mom keep urging her to be gracious to the unpleasant man who comes to visit? What's wrong with the mistress of "Paradise," who seems to have everything, but to need something else? Why does the nanny cry at night?

These and other mysteries gradually reveal themselves to be both episodes in a coming-of-age story and also a devastating portrait of a neocolonial society. Solita measures, willy nilly, this rural luxury in which she is, against her own will, a toy for the rich kids, against her earlier experience of poverty and principles in the refugee community. Not that she doesn't value the sudden wealth into which she's been plunged, unfortunately without the accoutrements (her cheap panties have unreliable elastic, for instance, and she's constantly worried they'll fall down). She's as greedy for the candies that every visitor brings as she is conscious of her place in the pecking order for them; she has to compete with the pet animals for the candies her rich hosts drop. Through Solita's struggles to master her environment, Castedo accomplishes, without rhetorical pyrotechnics, a condemnation of a rural elite that, in many places in Latin America, continues a virtually feudal relationship with sharecroppers and tenants.

Solita's rural adventure is also crammed with the typical discoveries of less stress-filled childhoods—the mysteries of sex, the fragility of teachers' authority, the delicate art of boasting in groups. She conducts these adventures virtually alone, although she never forgets she's part of a family conniving to survive. When one of the little girls spits on a piece of food and demands that Solita eat it—proof of her subordination—she almost doesn't, until she remembers that she's part of a game plan she must not betray.

It's a mark of the unobtrusive elegance of this writing that the child who emerges from this tale is not self-pitying, although she is (as children are and should be) self-dramatizing. Solita is a figure who lingers with you, a person of enormous courage and good faith. Particularly poignant is her absolute trust in both her parents' love, as a bedrock in an unstable world.

The narrator's voice is frank and sometimes funny. Castedo is deft at seeming to tell us just as much as Solita would have known, while actually giving us ample information to form our own opinions. So we experience with the little girl the terrible weight of surviving by her wits, and also the depth of an innocent's perception; however, we draw our own conclusions about the responsibility of those around her for her loneliness and abandonment.

Paradise is an ironic title, of course, but it's not just Solita's experience that gives it the twist. The mistress of the estate had hoped to create an idyllic, unworldly atmosphere, a dream world where her children would have a fairy-tale happy childhood. Nothing turns out as she had hoped, and as we learn by the end of the novel, what happens to Solita isn't the worst thing that can happen to someone. (pp. 4, 9)

Patricia Aufderheide, "Down the Garden Path: An Exile's Tale," in Book World—The Washington Post, *February 11, 1990, pp. 4, 9.*

Phoebe-Lou Adams

The narrator of Ms. Castedo's ingenious social satire [*Paradise*] is a girl old enough to observe adult doings and young enough to be regularly bewildered by them. Solita is the daughter of Spanish Republicans who have fled Franco's rule and taken poverty-stricken refuge in a nameless South American country. Solita's mother, invited with her daughter and small son for a long visit at a luxurious country estate, assures the children that it will be paradise. Solita thoroughly detests the place. Ms. Castedo has brought off, with acid wit, the far from easy task of revealing arrogance, folly, injustice, and debauchery through the eyes of an observer who does not know what those qualities are, although she does know a dirty old man when she sees one.

> *Phoebe-Lou Adams, in a review of "Paradise," in* The Atlantic Monthly, *Vol. 265, No. 3, March, 1990, p. 116.*

Merle Rubin

Nine-year-old Solita, the heroine and narrator of Elena Castedo's first novel [*Paradise*], is the daughter of republican refugees who've fled Franco's Spain for the fictional city of Galmeda in an unnamed Latin American country.

While her "Papi" is quick to point out the advantages of life in the New World, Solita's "Mami" has other plans. Tired of her husband's political activities—and of the hand-to-mouth existence they've been leading—she responds with alacrity to a friend's invitation to spend some time at a luxurious country estate called El Topaz. We're going to Paradise, she tells Solita and Solita's four-year-old brother Niceto, who is too young to understand much, but whose babyish charms and big brown eyes (like his mother's) command instant indulgence.

Solita is not so lucky. Removed, albeit temporarily, from her beloved father and from the friendly circle of refugee life in the city, she finds herself alone and without a reliable guide in the treacherous, hothouse anti-Eden of El Topaz, where she is expected to be the deferential companion to the family's three spoiled daughters.

While Solita's mother ingratiates herself with her hostess and the other house guests, Solita is teased and tormented by her new "friends." Patricia, the eldest, is the ringleader. The twins, who are Solita's age, are Grace, who's no better than Patricia, and Gloria, who shows some signs of decency. Idle, mischievous, snobbish, and spiteful, all three are portrayed with appallingly believable accuracy.

El Topaz, seen by Solita's mother as a safe haven from politics and privation, is, as Solita experiences it, more of a fascist country than Franco's Spain and far more physically uncomfortable than the impoverished streets of Galmeda. Forced to go along with the girls' schemes, advised by her mother not to complain about their injustices, Solita feels her basic dignity is at stake. She has no privacy: living in someone else's house, she cannot complain when the girls propose to search her room to see if she has any money.

You can get where you want to go by using other people's roads, Solita's mother explains, but to do so, you have to do things their way. Torn between her natural sense of honor and independence and her feeling that she must protect her mother's position, Solita (whose name is Spanish for little lonely one) must chart her own course amid dangerous waters.

Castedo, whose own family fled Spain for Chile, and who went on to earn advanced degrees in the United States, where she now lives, has done a brilliant job of showing us the world through the eyes of an intelligent child. Solita is an utterly convincing character sharply observant, yet still fresh and innocent; spirited, but not a hoyden. Although she has none of the irritating coyness of a premature sophisticate, this little girl is quick on the uptake.

Seen through her eyes, El Topaz emerges for what it is: a haven for idle, pretentious people, a kind of sexual swap-meet where disgruntled wives, desperate single women, dissolute husbands, and sought-after bachelors play out cynical, childish, and ultimately dangerous games.

In contrasting the young narrator with the material she narrates, Castedo deftly avoids heavy-handed cuteness in favor of understated but powerful irony. This is not the sort of irony that distances narrator from narrative or reader from text: It is an irony based upon the gap between what children are told to do and what adults actually want them to do. Thus, although it contains elements of social satire, *Paradise* also retains the emotional intensity of the youthful experience it describes.

There is a great deal of hilarity, outrage, indignation, and anxiety, but there is subtlety as well: Solita's early sense of superiority about having a caring father is gradually, if not completely, undermined, as the novel goes on to reveal that Solita's idealistic "Papi" may be, in his way, as disappointing a parent as her opportunistic "Mami."

Paradise is a classic coming-of-age novel, in which a girl comes to understand herself, her family, and the complicated social world in which they live. Indeed, it is also an intriguing portrait of certain aspects of Latin American culture and society, from the refugees and immigrants, who are not always welcome in its midst, to the disdained peasantry, whom Solita comes to know, and the cliquish circles of the rich and well-born, who only "know" one another.

> *Merle Rubin, "Coming of Age with 'Mami' and 'Papi'," in* The Christian Science Monitor, *July 18, 1990, p. 15.*

Lyll Becerra de Jenkins

"When my mother told me I was going to Paradise that afternoon, I had no idea what she meant. My father always said Paradise was a hoax invented by priests to seduce nitwits." So reads the opening of *Paradise,* a first novel by Elena Castedo, who was born in Barcelona, Spain, raised in Chile and has, her publisher says, lived on four continents.

Solita, the narrator of *Paradise,* is a bright, not quite 10-

year-old girl. Her family has been invited to a splendid hacienda, El Topaz, to escape the Spanish refugee ghetto in Galmeda, the city in the unnamed Latin American country where they have been living since they exiled themselves from Franco's Spain.

Tia Merce, the owner of El Topaz, introduces her three daughters, Patricia and the twins, Graciela and Gloria, to Solita. She is to be their playmate, but the girls constantly remind Solita that they own everything in view while she owns nothing, and Solita becomes a victim of their cruel pranks.

Among the other long-staying adult guests in El Topaz are a constipated psychiatrist and his wife (with "big upfronts"), a German photographer named Gunther and his companion, Mlle. Vicky, a dancer "with raccoon eyes," as well as a world-famous pianist and a brilliant young poet. There are also a guanaco (a creature like a llama) and a number of dogs with extravagant names.

But nothing in El Topaz seduces Solita. She longs for her father and his stories about her loyalist grandfather, assassinated by Franco's soldiers. "Mami, when is Papi coming to get us?" Solita asks.

El Topaz is "Paradise," the mother says, and Solita and her little brother, Niceto, will "have horses, everything any child would dream of. You're a very lucky girl."

Still, Solita misses the *pensione* in Galmeda with the other refugees, and life with her family reunited as they were before coming to El Topaz.

One of the girls of the hacienda tells Solita that it's boring to play with the same child all the time. " 'Solita, why have you been here so long?' How did I know why? We went from country to country, from place to place, because things happened to us."

Paradise is filled with rich descriptions and vivid scenes. Ms. Castedo's language is exuberant, and she's extraordinary when it comes to rendering the mixture of religious invocations and superstitions that flavors the speech of the *campesinos*.

The reader believes Solita in her innocence as she discovers the New World through El Topaz: we believe that the actions of a powerful man, no matter how outrageous, are to be forgotten or forgiven because "he's very important," that the pain and helplessness of the poor should be dismissed or summarized in witty sentences to dazzle friends. She absorbs the contradictions and absurdities: a rich man, Tío Juan Vicente, saying that "it's not fair for the peasants to be so poor, and he ought to dress like them. So he has Santos, the best designer in Galmeda, put patches on his clothes so he looks like a peasant." The reader accepts Solita's sophistication when she concludes at one point: "We didn't have to worry about bombs in this country, only about the rich."

Solita is puzzled by her mother's behavior in El Topaz, and through the child narrator's eyes the reader sees the woman's motives for remaining there on the estate with her children. Papi's only ambition is to become "*the* labor law expert in the New World." It's up to the mother to

provide economic stability, education and social position for her children.

Paradise is about Solita's coming of age in the New World, losing her father even as she sees her mother immersing herself in the inanities of society at El Topaz, where "you couldn't trust anything. Or anybody. You had to navigate completely on your own." For Solita, true paradise would be to have her family reunited, and to be back in the *pensione* with the Spanish refugees with their dreams and songs and their longing for Spain.

The novel has a strangely static element. The reader needs tension, a current of expectancy. Solita's yearning for her father—a father who doesn't keep his promises to his children—is not enough. The incidents in *Paradise* involving the adults of El Topaz, their banality, rivalries and hedonism as well as the pranks of the rich girls and the dialogues between Solita with her nanny, Fresia, become anecdotal and somewhat repetitive. They achieve transitory echoes, but miss a lasting resonance.

Lyll Becerra de Jenkins, "No Shelter in the Hacienda," in The New York Times Book Review, *April 1, 1990, p. 8.*

An excerpt from *Paradise*

These people were against rebels, and it seemed my mother used to be rebellious, but now was that way only about very few things. You had to decide whether to go along with people who did wrong things or fight them, but it was very difficult, because no matter what you decided, you were going to pay for it. You had to watch how it turned out for other people and see what was best.

José's mother advanced shyly, several children clustered behind her, like one big body with many dusty, blemished legs. My mother talked to her. The woman wiped tears with her dirty apron. The grown-ups became impatient. My mother did these things; she suddenly took matters into her own hands. Once she grabbed a Gypsy girl, bigger than I, saying she was filthy with parasites, and threw her in the pensione's tub. The Gypsy girl screamed that water spirits would kill her and kept trying to climb out of the tub, but she was no match for my mother. The other pensioners were furious, saying they were going to get infected, robbed and cursed. The Gypsy girl left outfitted in my mother's oversized clothes, throwing curses at her, and shiny clean. The pensioners were fed up and complained to my father. He apologized, and told the women that ladies in this pensione had the best fashion taste he had ever seen. He told the men war stories. The pensioners blushed and laughed and patted my father on the shoulder.

Alan Ryan

Elena Castedo was born in Spain, raised in Chile and educated in the United States, where she now lives and writes. She has written a critical study of Chilean theater before this, but it will come as no surprise that her first novel, like so much serious writing in the second half of the 20th century, is about exile and its consequences to the human psyche.

Paradise is set in an unnamed Latin American country that blends features drawn from diverse Central and South American regions: ombu and ilang-ilang trees, mariachi music from Mexico, and *mate,* a drink common in Argentina. Set on an isolated country estate that is redolent of money and filled with an idle, pleasure-seeking aristocracy, it shares some characteristics with other novels using the same device, notably Jose Donoso's *A House in the Country* and Lisa St. Aubin de Teran's *The Tiger.* The setting in each of these novels is central to the book's design, offering ready contrasts between city and country, poverty and wealth, political realities and utopia. And it sets up a painful irony: the colorful and comfortable world of the country can make for the most stinging sort of exile.

Ms. Castedo's principal characters, a mother and her 9-year-old daughter, Solita, are political exiles from the 1930s world of Franco's Spain. Settled now in poverty in a city called Galmeda, they are invited to El Topaz, a country estate, where the mother will entertain the mistress and Solita will be a playmate for her three spoiled daughters. The father of the family, a political activist, is seldom home. The mother, wanting only security and peace, dreads him; daughter Solita, who craves order and normalcy, longs for him. Leaving the city for the country—they are "going to Paradise," says the mother—will change their lives forever.

Ms. Castedo makes Solita (whose Spanish name means "Lonely Little Girl") the narrator of the story, and thus filters through her consciousness not only the physical, cultural, and political exile of the characters but also the universal exile of childhood. This is a difficult technical challenge for a novelist, but Castedo easily conveys a great deal of "adult" information while vividly preserving the limited, and often bewildered, vision of a child.

Survival in an unknown world is the primary challenge of both the exile in the strange land and the child in a world of adults. Elena Castedo links the two themes, illuminating them both, in a novel that is thoughtful, moving and beautifully written.

> *Alan Ryan, "Castedo's Novel of Exile in a Strange Land," in* Raleigh News and Observer, *March 11, 1990.*

Gloria Ortiz

The first chapter [of *Paradise*] sets the tone for a rather simple plot: estrangement and remarriage and its effect on the sensitive first-person narrator. Dissatisfied with their new life in a *pensión* and her Republican husband's involvement in strikes and labor movements, Solita's social-climbing mother leaves with Solita and 4-year-old brother Niceto for El Topaz, which she labels Paradise in an effort to entice them. She invests the entire adventure with multiple dictates to be followed: best behavior, doing as the Romans do, the importance of first impressions, and pleasing others as a means of being liked. Even in this initial stage of the novel, the reader's sympathy goes out to Solita

(who doesn't want to go), to her rebellious cowlick (which won't stay down), and to the surprised, abandoned father who in counterpoint to Solita's Mumsy's description of the colors of the bus that is to take them to El Topaz as garish, pronounces them "superb New World colors."

For the child, the only thing paradisiacal about Paradise are its luxuriant vegetation and the lively menagerie allowed to roam the premises, in particular, the guanaco who has a propensity for spitting dead on target at ludicrous people who say equally ludicrous things.

The human members of the cast are seen by Solita as obstacles to be tolerated or skirted until her vain dream of being reunited with her father and returning to a normal childhood in Galmeda is fulfilled. Ostensibly, Solita goes to El Topaz to play with Tía Merce's children: Patricia, the eldest, and the twins Grace and Gloria. These children hardly veil their sense of superiority (they "own" everything) and subject Solita to cruel pranks, the most ignominious occurring towards the end when Patricia forces the younger child to drink her spit.

Not surprisingly, many of the uncaring adults are referred to most frequently by their nicknames. The big-breasted Mrs. Kaplan, the constipated psychiatrist's wife who carries the fetus of her dead child Lolita everywhere, is called Melons in allusion to her big breasts. The authoritarian head maid is La Mamota. Others, like the Walrus, the straw woman, Marco Polo, the Genius, Werther, and the hipless poet recommended by Pablo (said to be "the number-one poet in the world." Neruda, perhaps?) have their foibles satirized through this means . . . as well they might, since they read like characters who stepped off the screen from Fellini's *Juliet of the Spirits,* or the beggars in Buñuel's *Viridiana* taking over not only the mansion but the airs of the masters.

The eccentric, banal, sometimes amusing goings-on among the adults and the pranks of the children are interspersed by the sporadic, unreliable visits of Julián, Solita's father who, though having improved his position in life as bait to get his wife and children back, cannot sway his materialistic wife. She does as these "Romans" do and ensnares the wealthy Tío Armando who marries her (". . . no need of a divorce, because marriages performed by the Republican militia during the Spanish Civil War aren't recognized either in Spain or abroad") and formally invites the children to see his rare tropical-bird collection. Boarding school in France for Solita is also in the plans.

In the closing pages of the novel, as she leaves El Topaz, Solita swears never to do what Romans did, never to go to Paradise, but rather to "cross the oceans and find love." In token of her new-found awareness, she throws away the ineffective tinfoil ball ironically made of others' discarded candy wrappers, a charm designed to recover her old life. Watching a bus go by she proclaims in words reminiscent of her father's optimism at their first parting: " 'What incredible colors the buses have in the New World.' "

As a richly woven tapestry of eccentricity set against South American exoticism, **Paradise** has its charms even though it is thin on plot. It succeeds best, however, in filtering reality through the eyes of a sensitive child: a reality which is incomplete because only half understood. Castedo unfalteringly gives us that vision, at times alien to the adult perspective because forgotten. Her language coaxes us to go along with Solita, trying to make sense out of seemingly bizarre behavior, half-heard conversations, whispers, to make connections and link loose ends as a child would.

Castedo's first novel, which was a National Book Award nominee, should be read as a sensitive, almost lyrical incursion into human motivation as perceived by a child. There is enough of wisdom and of good writing in it to make us wonder with anticipation what this talented novelist will tackle next.

> *Gloria Ortiz, "'Paradise', a Richly Woven Tapestry of Eccentricity against Latin Exoticism," in* The San Juan Star Magazine, *February 10, 1991, p. 4.*

Timothy O'Leary

There is Mark Twain's Huckleberry Finn, and Harper Lee's Scout in *To Kill A Mockingbird.* To the roll of important or noteworthy youths of American literature add Solita, the protagonist of Elena Castedo's enchanting debut novel **Paradise.**

Solita is a refugee of the Spanish Civil War living in a mythical Latin American country with her parents and younger brother. The mother, weary of ghetto life and her mate's monomaniacal involvement in socialist politics, takes the children to live at El Topaz, a sprawling country estate where Solita experiences luxury, but must cope with the weeds and spines of a dubious paradise. The mother aims to improve the children's lives, and her own, by finding a more worldly and stable mate.

Given Solita's Iberian roots and Latin upbringing, how can she be claimed as one of "ours"?

Miss Castedo, like her principal character, was born in Spain and reared in Latin America, but has spent much time in the United States.

The influences of American culture and literature are evident even in a novel that in several asides mentions the United States merely as a place where used foil may be sold at a handsome profit.

A clue to the novel's "Americanness" comes early. On the first page Miss Castedo describes Solita's stubborn cowlick as "a vexing advertisement of a matching unruly spirit within." "She [Solita's mother] wet it, wrestled with it, pinned it down, although we both knew it would soon dry with the heat of the summer day and spring back up again," Miss Castedo writes.

Solita thus joins a long line of other youthful individualists and nonconformists—Pearl of Nathaniel Hawthorne's *The Scarlet Letter* and Huck come to mind—and the scene is set for the development of a precocious and intelligent child protagonist who rebels instinctively at society's hypocrisy, superficiality, absurdity and immorality.

Life at El Topaz is grand, with its stable of eccentric, permanent guests, the tame exotic and farm animals who meander about, and the colorful peasant servants who instill wonder in Solita's innocent heart with their superstitions and folktales.

But there are snakes in Eden. Solita must survive the pain of her parents' unfolding separation. She must reconcile the glittering beauty of El Topaz with the cruelty of her host's three spoiled daughters, and the social eminence accorded a Supreme Court justice with a fondness for touching little girls. And she must strive to understand why the guests on the estate are white and the servants brown.

The American tradition is evident also in the humor with which Solita's observations are rendered. Long used to her father's tirades against the privileged classes, she notices also that her brother is never reprimanded for wrecking his dolls and toy soldiers. "No doubt about it," she comments, "the rich and 4-year-olds got away with anything."

Like her literary predecessors of the American tradition, Solita makes an effort to get along, but in the end is unable to accept or adapt herself to a society she views as shallow, decadent, confusing and, above all, restrictive. When told by her mother that she must surrender her leading role in a Holy Week play to please the parents of a bratty and less qualified mummer, she balks.

The mother explains, "We all have roles to play, and not always the ones we want. Don't let me hear you're not being cooperative. How many times must I tell you, the best way to get where you want is to please those who own the road." But from Solita's point of view: "Why, why did she want to get to a place where she needed to use these people's roads?"

In the end, after her mother has won the affections and loyalty of her host's aristocratic brother-in-law, Solita resolves,

> When you wanted to go somewhere, you had to take yourself there, but you could choose your own road only if you were grown up. . . . I wasn't going to follow anybody else around, no matter how colossally rich or elevated or anything. And when I grew up, I was never going to go to Paradise, nor do what the Romans did. I was going to do what the Gypsy said: cross the oceans and find love.

Sounds much like Huck's ultimate decision to "light out for the frontier," where he can live by his own rules.

Paradise is not just another American novel with identifiably American symbols, themes and characters. It is a unique hybrid of the best of America and Latin America combined, a delightful and disarming novel in which aspects of each tradition infuse the other with new meaning and dimension. Twain, Lee and Hawthorne are there, but also recognizable are the colorful imagery, the mysticism and the rich, varied characters of Colombia's Gabriel Garcia Marquez, Peru's Mario Vargas Llosa and Chile's Isabel Allende.

Paradise pleases on so many levels, it is difficult to identify them all. A certain stylistic roughness and an extreme devotion to simple declarative sentences are no impediments to an appreciation of its exquisiteness.

Miss Castedo deserves applause for bringing readers of English a fascinating and wonderfully different novel, one that forms a harmonious blend of two rich and fertile literary traditions, Latin America's and our own.

> Timothy O'Leary, "Paradise Found on Author's First Try," in The Washington Times, February 26, 1990, p. E6.

Elena Castedo [in correspondence with *CLC Yearbook*]

[*CLC Yearbook*]: *Comment on the process of writing this work, including the amount of time it took to complete, your writing habits, the process of revision, and significant editorial input.*

[Castedo]: It took me three weeks to complete *Paradise*'s first draft of 300 pages (after waiting for many, many years to have the time to write something other than literary criticism). It needed cleaning and I felt it was a bit too long, so I cleaned and cut and the result was a MS of 400 pages. More cutting and cleaning and I had 500 pages. Another revision and it was nearing 600 pages. It's hard for me to determine time outside of fiction, and I was also concurrently writing some nonfiction pieces, but I think this process took about two years. Then nearly another year to do the real cutting. Then another year plus to re-write it in Spanish.

I write every day for several hours, combining it with other jobs. Since the success of *Paradise,* it has become very difficult to write due to the huge volume of mail, phone calls from several countries for newspaper and radio interviews, regular interviews, including some where the journalist flew in from as far as Spain, requests for readings, lectures, articles, etc. Right now I'm looking forward to finding some uninterrupted time to write.

Working with my editor at Weidenfeld & Nicolson, John Herman, was very rewarding, because in spite of the fact that he suggested cutting the MS to less than 400 pages, (would anyone enjoy cutting her own fingers and toes?) he made excellent suggestions, and never batted an eyelash when I disagreed and wanted to do it some other way. He was also punctilious about accuracy and detail, which is immensely reassuring to a fanatic like me.

Relate the terms of any background research you conducted.

As a maniac for historical accuracy, I researched every detail, such as what kind of wine and from which year would a person from the rural upper class in Chile be drinking during Christmas in 1949, which labor union staged a massive demonstration that year, what kind of weeds grow in a particular geographical area, which commercial products would different people, say servants, use; cosmetics, cleaning, etc.. The Spanish version needed months of sporadic research because each character speaks exactly as someone of his-her own social class, nationality and age group—there are six different groups, each with subgroups—did around 1950.

How is your own experience incorporated into your fiction?

Both Solita, the narrator of *Paradise,* and I were refugee children, and both her parents' and my parents' marriages went sour. Some of the locales are authentic, some are composites. The characters and the situations are invented, and it greatly amuses me that so many readers insist that they "know" who this or that character is; each character apparently has been several people . . .

Whom do you consider your primary literary influences, and why?

Very early my mother told me old Spanish tales, some of them in song form, and I devoured fairy tales as well as the political magazines I found around the house. My parents and their friends would put on impromptu little plays when they got together. It must have fascinated me to see two or three characters live an experience that in some way changed their lives, to see reality re-created in metaphors, and to see how politicians could change the course of events. Later I devoured the typical adolescent literature, such as Swift, Verne and Walter Scott, which must have told me how to enter into different worlds. Then I read classical Spanish literature, which—unlike English and other European literature—since earliest times focused on popular characters, not kings and nobles. For instance, 14th-century *El Lazarillo de Tormes* is an antecessor to Huckleberry Finn; same age, same orphanhood, similar adventures, same biting social commentary; I'm sure both influenced my character Solita. From Cervante's *Don Quixote,* (a book that has dazzled me for almost 40 years, the first modern novel, still the best novel I've ever read) I learned how fiction can observe itself, how it can have different layers (in the area of the reader's understanding this can also be learned from Shakespeare), how fiction and reality mix, and how an entertaining tale with plenty of humor can be far more profound than a humorless one. This I learned before I read Joyce, Kafka, Pirandello, Unamuno and the vanguardists and post-vanguardists. Afterwards I read early 20th-century Latin American literature, with its themes of national identity and the Indian problem; Chilean literature of the forties and fifties, which had an obsession with low-life; the main European literature of the late 19th and early 20th century, American literature of the thirties and forties, etc., all of which I'm sure must have taught me a lot. Theater has always been of special interest to me, and maybe because for many years I was too poor to be able to attend performances, I took plays out of the libraries, which I think has helped me a lot in my use of dialogue.

Describe any works-in-progress.

Aside from an occasional short story and article, I'm writing a novel about several characters who come from different Latin American countries and live in the U.S.

Dolores Moyano Martin

[*Paradise*] is the saga of Solita, a refugee girl, and her family's escape from Spain after the civil war and their exile in a Latin-American country clearly based on Chile. Solita tells us that in the gypsy world of the refugee "long-range plans didn't work; each minute you had to save your skin right then and there," you "went from country to country, from place to place, because things happened." That was why "there were few children left after the war, the exodus, the concentration camp in France, and the exile to faraway countries. I was a survivor, they said."

In this deeply moving and witty exploration of Solita's survival, the author also gives us a brilliant satire of New World pretensions and Old World delusions. With great skill, she brings to life, for lack of a better phrase, the unique "culture of Spanish Republican exile." The personalities and the refugee milieu that she evokes coincide with my own memories of the men, women, and children who arrived in Córdoba, Argentina, in the late 1930s and 1940s. . . .

Solita's narrative of her trajectory from the frugal and breezy world of the refugees into the extravagant hothouse of the Latin-American gentry makes her the best chronicler of one of the most important cultural encounters in Latin America. The influence of Spanish Republican exiles on the region's culture would be profound and long lasting, especially in Mexico and Argentina, where they would affect and change major institutions such as universities and the publishing industry, and challenge the insidious caste system that even to this day prevents most Latin-American countries from becoming meritocracies such as Canada and the United States. . . .

Of the refugees that she leaves behind, Solita tells us that they "lived in rented rooms" or "dilapidated houses," and "they never brought me candy or toys, but sometimes an avocado, a pear or a bunch of dates if they were available in the yard or in a park nearby." But especially they "talked to me," that is to children, "the same way they talked to each other." . . .

Above all, Solita notes, the refugees did not act like *gente decente* or decent folks—the revealing term the so-called well-born of Latin America use to refer to themselves. Refugees, Solita tells us "didn't move slowly, leaning smoothly toward their dinner partners on one side or the other with a soft smile. The refugees were bony, noisy, and plopped themselves anywhere, even on the floor, with their legs and arms sprawled. They argued, got mad, laughed, patted each other, became sour or excited, but never had soft smiles." Vacuous social charm and polite small talk were as alien to the Spanish Republican exiles as was self-pity. They never, ever said or implied that "they were homesick or missed their families." But when they sang, Solita tells us, they left you with a lump in the throat. The untold loss and grief would burst out in their songs, songs that were

> pieces of Spain, hundreds of pieces: a river in the moonlight, hilly villages, old landmarks beloved by a city, the hot chocolate vendor, the coal man, the miller's wife, the iron forger, people doing things, taking mules to the river, dancing, washing handkerchiefs in the fountain, walking back from fields, going on a journey. If you were Spanish, you sang songs.

Until the arrival of the refugees, most foreigners that landed in countries as hard to reach and remote as Argentina and Chile were usually poor immigrants from Europe and the Middle East. But, as Solita shows us, and as I remember, the so-called progressive refugees from Republican and socialist Spain, for reasons and in ways different from the snobbish local gentry, also looked down on immigrants. With her infallible detector for the phoniness of the adult world, Solita tells us that the reason immigrant children's "hair was always perfect; every last one in place" was that—as she had been told—they tended to fuss "with dumb things, something that immigrants tended to do." Implicit in this remark is the refugees' contempt for the aspirations of immigrants, who yearned to become that much dreaded and maligned *bête noire* of both the intellectuals and the gentry of Spain and Latin America: a middle-class creature, the abominable "bourgeois!" Early on, Solita defines the word as having "something to do with being dull, not knowing important things"; later, as an inability to enjoy oneself "intelligently"; and finally, maybe even a tendency to succumb to that gravest of sins, being *cursi,* an affliction which Solita warns is

> the worst thing in the world: gold-trimmed figurines of little shepherds; sugary violin music; lots of big words pronounced slowly (one big word said fast once in a while was good); bouquets in your sofas, drapes, pictures, vases and rugs. After meeting cursi people you laughed at them; they were not to be considered.

Solita's father is one of the most memorable characters of the novel. And Castedo achieves the almost impossible with him by creating not merely a powerful individual, so convincing and alive that he overshadows everyone and everything when he marches onto the page, but also an enduring prototype of a certain species of Spanish and Latin-American intellectuals that has created almost as much havoc in those regions as the self-indulgent elites. Solita's father incarnates a charming and persuasive idealist who is as eloquent as he is generous in the dispensation of lofty opinions and, occasionally, even actions concerning the downtrodden of the earth, but who in dealings with those closest to him is surprisingly uninterested, uneloquent, and ungenerous. A leftist labor organizer, Solita's father forgets more than once to bring his daughter the one item he promised her: a dress of her own. On the other hand, he remembers, upon arriving at El Topaz, to studiously avoid contact with the adults (i.e., "oppressors?") by insisting on dining with the children (i.e. "the oppressed?"), much to the discomfiture of the latter.

At this level, the novel is social commentary in the best tradition of the nineteenth century. Castedo has woven a dense, rich tapestry of interactions that very gradually reveal the subtext, the underlying pattern of power relationships, the connecting threads that control the characters and dictate the preordained design of their lives, a rigid social grid set to highlight and exalt some figures while obscuring and diminishing others. "Everyone in El Topaz," Solita laments, "was trapped below or above somebody, with Tía Merce way up there at the very top," Tía Merce being among those who could have money in her hand anytime she asked, something that in this country, Solita tells us, meant "having total control." And so El Topaz, the *fundo, finca, fazenda, hacienda, estancia,* the great estate—the *Paradise* of the novel's title as Solita's mother refers to it—is a powerful allegory of Latin America, of its escapist and irresponsible elites and their rejection of modernity, of the seductive and wasteful fantasy world they created and retreated into, the immense, irreparable cost of which is becoming apparent in the 1990s.

The "fantasy world" notion is no figure of speech. Like some of the idle gentry I knew as a child, the ones at El Topaz lived not merely in a state of mental fantasy but, off and on, in actual and visible "fantasy worlds" that they could and would set up in a few days. The languid tempo of country life would change overnight, as Solita describes, the entire estate suddenly buzzing with activity, humming with energy, phenomenal energies that were rarely exerted on such a scale for lesser endeavors. In days, country estates would be converted into Egyptian temple cities, gardens metamorphosed into classical Greek settings, living rooms transformed into eighteenth-century French drawing rooms.

The favorite game of Latin-American patricians according to Argentine writer Alejandro Katz "consists in being here but believing—and making others believe—one is there. *There,* of course being Europe."

As a puzzled Solita reports, the dressed-up guests who arrived at these fantasy soirees were invariably "Victor Hugo . . . Socrates . . . Madame Recamier . . . no one was from this country, as if it had no history." In fact, "the way guests talked at El Topaz, only three things had happened in the world: Cleopatra, the Greeks, and some Frenchmen, mostly painters called Impressionists; and only two places existed now, a foggy Paris and a vague Orient."

Thrown to the wolves of El Topaz by her mother, Solita is left alone to survive among that most implacable and cruel breed of uppity-folk: the servants and children of the elite. And so begins the lonely, frightening, heartbreaking, and hilarious pilgrimage of stoic Solita through the Land of Snob. Undaunted by its totems and taboos, armed only with her infallible eye and wonderful humor, our daring young explorer will live to outwit her foes while, fearless anthropologist that she is, reporting back to us (and her mother) on the bizarre beliefs and recondite customs of the tribe at El Topaz.

In appearance, Solita's mother is deceptive, an enchanting woman whose nymph-like beauty, delicacy, and tact hide the unbending will and perseverance of a pioneer. Her zany responses to her daughter's questions are among the many pleasures of this book. " 'Mami,' " Solita informs her one day, " 'the girls say I should be ashamed of my ancestors. Their teachers say Spaniards were cruel and bloodthirsty to the Indians.' " Unfazed, the mother promptly answers, " 'My daughter, tell them those cruel and bloody Spaniards were *their* ancestors. Yours stayed in Spain minding their own business.' " When Solita complains about not wanting to go somewhere, the invariable reply is: " 'What if Columbus had said that? We wouldn't have had a New World to escape to.' " Should Solita refuse to do something because she is afraid: " 'What if El Cid had said that? We would still be wearing veils!' "

There is no doubt in Solita's mind that courage and honor rank equally high on her mother's scale of values. Not so "in country estates" such as El Topaz where, Solita discovers, courage outranks honor by far. There, "the thing to do was to be brave," and "being cowardly was the end." One must be both brave and "aristocratic." But what does *aristocratic* mean in the New World? When Solita reports that having a northern Spanish name in this country meant "you came from Spanish noblemen," her Spanish mother is quick to disabuse here. On the contrary, such names "belonged to poor Spanish land-workers," peasants from the Basque country, Catalonia, Asturias, Galicia, "poor, industrious northern Spaniards who settled here and prospered." And because these northern folk were mostly fair, being "decent" in the New World meant having fair skin, blue eyes and, of course, money. "People in the New World graded each other according to how they looked. In Spain everybody looked the same . . . servants in El Topaz had dark skin, and the guests light skin. Evidently they were different in other ways too. Hair and last names had important meanings" in the New World.

The children soon make it clear to Solita that bragging about ancestors is the thing to do. "I told them my grandfather was Ignacio de Prados. Nobody knew him. 'He was important. He helped the Madrid Philharmonic. He was invited to the palace. The king gave him his portrait signed.' I didn't say that my mother and her sisters always turned the king's portrait upside down because they were Republicans. Having Republican daughters and the king upside down got my grandfather so worked up they had to give him a cold bath in the big tub upstairs." The girls lose no time in alerting Solita that, unlike her, most guests at El Topaz are "aristocrats," or otherwise, "eccentrics." When Solita confesses her ignorance about the latter, the girls inform her that "eccentric" is someone who "does things that everybody says are terrible and everybody loves." And so the complex codes that rule the girls' lives are reported and recorded by Solita: "Elevated people considered you one of them when you agreed their wrongdoings were cute"; "in a country estate everything was done in packs"; "you could be emphatic here about disliking things, never about liking them"; and when greeting people "you didn't lean back with open arms, you leaned slightly forward and shook hands limply." Without any visible money, ancestors, or house, Solita is mercilessly interrogated, criticized, and bullied by the girls until she tells them of the time she threw a rotten squid head, found in a garbage can, at the impeccably braided head of an immigrant girl. The know-it-all girls at El Topaz are, for a change, rendered speechless. " 'Did the squid head have eyes and everything?' " Grace asked respectfully. " 'Yes,' " answers Solita, " 'sad, gummy eyes.' " Silence follows and Solita relishes her victory smiling happily. "From now on, there'd be no insults, no prods, no trampling. Only respect."

When it comes to dealing with that hackneyed topic of Latin-American literature, one much trivialized and easily sentimentalized, the world of the poor (in this case, the servants' world), the author's tone is unerring, her touch deft, and the individuals she brings to life utterly convincing, some so remote they aren't "more noticeable than three shadows," others overwhelmingly omnipresent, none more so than that insatiable busybody, indefatigable bully, incorrigible snob, queen of servants, and scourge of masters: la Mamota.

But it is not among servants or masters, indeed not among humans that Solita would make her best friends in El Topaz. With the eye and ear of a poet, the author conjures a powerful and rich animistic universe of rocks, mountains, plants, flowers, insects, and animals that resonate beyond the story, infusing it with the magic of childhood (e.g., "stray dogs covered with dew"; buzzing bees "sucking the grapes split from sugary old age"; everything "paralyzed by an idle spell of warmth and the locusts' *whirr-whirrs*".) Dogs, cats, goats, horses are as individualistic, mysterious, and complex as the leading human characters, none more so than the ineffable guanaco who liked to be driven around in a convertible and to close "his eyes in the breeze." Not to speak of unseen creatures who lurked in the shadows ready to pounce on the innocent—the dreaded black wolves known as *culpeos*—or other enigmatic beings such as very small children—Solita's brother Niceto who went "around quietly eating rose petals."

Other wonderful characters in this novel include the French governess who blames earthquakes on the savagery of the New World (clearly the citizens of Paris would never put up with them); the enigmatic and wistful Tío Popsy who connects with Solita better than any other adult while eating asparagus from the wrong end; and Padre Romulado, the only adult with a child's sense of justice. Among the best scenes in the novel are the horse-bolting episode and especially an earthquake described with a perfectly balanced mixture of terror and humor.

The real terror in Solita's life, however, is not of earthquakes, or bolting horses, or bullying snobs—all of them temporary passing fears—but of abandonment, the final and lasting terror of all children. And this is what she faces at the end: her own abandonment by the seductive and charming father who wants to save the workers of the New World. In a heartbreaking scene, the mother forces Solita to confront this ghastly truth: that her father is never coming back and that she, the mother, is marrying someone else. Almost as unbearable as her father's abandonment are her mother's and little brother's indifference, their amnesia of their former family life, their obliviousness to a beloved and incommunicable past that is now Solita's alone.

Just as the father abandons his "treasure" (his pet name for Solita), so Solita abandons hers: the sphere of valuable silver foil that she's been carefully constructing from cast-off expensive bon-bon wrappings, the magic ball that was going to buy her way out of charity and the "Paradise" of El Topaz. In the last scene, Solita sheds her last illusion by flinging her priceless ball out of the car that is taking her, her brother, mother, and future stepfather away from El Topaz.

At its deepest level this novel is a poignant and powerful morality play about the discovery of the inevitability, ubiquitousness of sin, suffering, and evil. Ultimately, Solita's exile is our own, the universal exile that lies beyond the loss of innocence, the harmony and wholeness of childhood, our original homeland and native ground, the longing for which is never assuaged, the memory of which will haunt us through an alien world, a purgatory in which all of us are, like Solita, refugees from paradise lost. (pp. 430-37)

Dolores Moyano Martin, "Survivor in the Land of Snob," in Book World *November, 1990, pp. 430-37.*

Gabriella De Ferrari
A Cloud on Sand

Born and raised in Peru, De Ferrari is an art curator and novelist currently residing in New York City.

A Cloud on Sand chronicles the tempestuous relationship between Dora, a narcissistic and often neglectful mother, and her sensitive and reticent daughter, Antonia. Beginning in the tiny fishing town of Artemisia on the Italian Riveria, the narrative traces Antonia's development from a timid young girl manipulated by her mother to a dignified woman and wife of Arturo Rontelli, an Italian businessman living in South America. Filled with feelings of self-doubt as a child, Antonia finds relief in memories of her father, a tycoon who moved to Argentina, and Count Mora, one of Dora's former lovers who remains loyal to Antonia. When her father dies and her mother engages in a number of affairs with wealthy men, Antonia decides to marry the compassionate Arturo and move to Yayaku, a fictitious South American country modeled after Peru. Dora perceives this as thoughtless abandonment and attempts to manipulate Antonia through a series of letters in which she claims despair and hardship. Despite Dora's pleas, Antonia remains in Yayaku, becoming a respected member of her community and a loving mother until unforeseen circumstances force her to visit Italy one last time. While sometimes faulting the plot of *A Cloud on Sand* as melodramatic, critics praised De Ferrari's talent for characterization, shifting points of view, and realistic portrayal of the pressures of family life. Merle Rubin commented: "De Ferrari's novel shows an eye for the idiosyncrasies of characters and the oddities of fate, as well as a subtle understanding of the patterns in people's lives and the surprising turns that cannot be reduced to a pattern."

Publishers Weekly

Set in pre-WWII Italy and wartime South America, this work of psychological realism [*A Cloud on Sand*] tells of the bizarre enchantments touching—and sometimes ruling—human lives. Antonia's mother—the amoral, supremely stylish Dora—lives in an imposing villa built at her request in a seedy section of Artemisia, a small town near Genoa, by a husband who spends most of his time in Argentina. In Artemisia, where Dora grew up poor, she lords it over relatives, neglects Antonia and son Marco, amasses lovers and rare coins, loses servants. One of Dora's conquests, Count Emilio Mora, comes to serve as a surrogate father to the children, installing them in Catholic boarding schools. Both end up in South America—Marco, until he is duped and murdered, running his dead father's Argentinian business, and Antonia as the bride of an Italian living in Yayaku, a Basque-like country north of Chile. Compelled by a tragic sense of fate, De Ferrari's characters are visited by alarming dreams—and in their sleeping and waking hours observe many strange things, from witches to men who melt. The first novelist's impressive control of these uncanny powers in a basically realistic context will suggest comparisons with Marquez, although De Ferrari is in no sense an imitator.

A review of "A Cloud on Sand," in Publishers Weekly, *Vol. 237, No. 6, February 9, 1990, p. 46.*

Joanne Wilkinson

With her quirky, compelling characters and sun-drenched locales, first-novelist De Ferrari has hit the ground running. Through a combination of letters, shifting points of

42

view, and great cinematic chunks of descriptive prose, [*A Cloud on Sand*] lurches forward, giving off a choppy but distinctive sense of time and place. Set partly in Italy during the 1920s and partly in Latin America, the novel revolves around a group of vibrant characters: the imperious Donna Dora, who flaunts her great wealth and many love affairs but remains emotionally hollow; the elegant Count Mora, a wise, kind man who becomes a second father to Donna Dora's neglected children and who can see both her selfishness and her brilliance; the daughter Antonia, who struggles to free herself from her mother's domination; and the world-weary Arturo, who rescues Antonia by marrying her and finds himself rescued in return. De Ferrari suffuses her material with an original artistic vision, so it's not surprising that maverick moviemaker Martin Scorsese has bought film rights to the book. For once, a novel that lives up to the PR hype preceding it.

Joanne Wilkinson, in a review of "A Cloud on Sand," in Booklist, *Vol. 86, No. 12, February 15, 1990, p. 1121.*

Merle Rubin

A hasty plot summary might well leave the impression that this unusual first novel is either a South American version of a North American saga about an immigrant family or an Italian-style "Mommie Dearest." [*A Cloud on Sand*] is, to some extent, a story about the challenge and disorientation of moving from the Old World to the New; and, to an even greater extent, the story of a domineering mother and a daughter who manages to break free from her powerful influence.

But Gabriella De Ferrari has adopted neither the hackneyed plot of the standard family saga nor the searing style of the tell-all confessional in this coolly elegant novel, which is therefore all the more moving for its lack of fireworks.

Donna Dora, the formidable mother of Marco and Antonia, is anything but maternal. She escaped her impoverished background by marrying a rich man, who planned to take her to Buenos Aires, where he made his fortune.

But when the ship was about to dock, the imperious, pregnant Dora insisted she would not have her child on alien soil, and returned to her native village in Italy, where she had a mansion built on the site of her parents' old cottage.

Neither beautiful nor intelligent nor charming, Dora nonetheless possesses a mysterious capacity to attract men: first, when her husband is away on business in South America, where he spends most of his time, and later, after her husband's death. Her attractiveness has something to do with the way she moves, the strikingly original way she dresses, and the sheer forcefulness of her personality. Hardheaded, obdurate, self-willed, she is a kind of monster.

"Remember what it means to be a woman," she advises her daughter, Antonia. "It's the men . . . who have to do the work. We can arrange our lives so that we can get what we want by using these things about women that men

don't understand. Don't forget that. The man builds the house, but the woman dreams it to life."

Most of the time, however, she is not this encouraging toward her daughter, whom she usually berates for being ugly and thick-ankled. Antonia and Marco are neglected children, except for the occasions when their kindly father returns from Buenos Aires and Dora flings herself uncharacteristically, yet wholeheartedly, into the role of perfect wife and mother. The only bright spot of their childhood is the gentle art connoisseur Count Mora, one of their mother's admirers, who is touched by the children's plight and resolves to take care of them.

The children grow up in the 1920s and 1930s, against the disturbing, subtly evoked background of Italy's turn to Fascism. While Dora's brother Roberto is a committed leftist, Dora herself has no qualms about ingratiating herself with whomever is in power, from fascists and Nazi occupiers to American liberators. People suspect her of betraying her brother and his resistance group.

Yet, when the black American sergeant whom she later consorts with gets into trouble for purportedly "fraternizing" with a white woman, Dora boldly—and rather selflessly—comes to his defense by dressing up as a pathetic old crone, for whom the young soldier could only have felt pity.

Antonia is often moved to wonder if her mother is good or evil. Certainly, she is not good. But is she evil, or merely a monster—a sort of horrific, yet impressive freak of nature? And, is Dora really the most intriguing character, the true center of this story, or is it Antonia, whose quiet beauty and untapped resourcefulness win her the love of a good man much like her father, who has also made his fortune in South America? Antonia, unlike her mother, is willing to leave Italy for South America—in this case, for a land even more remote than Argentina, which De Ferrari calls "Yayaku" and locates on the Pacific Coast somewhere between Chile and Peru. Where Dora defied convention and shocked her neighbors with her aggression and ostentation, Antonia's disregard for convention is based on her innate dignity. Where the mother was shrewd, the daughter has learned to be wise.

De Ferrari's novel shows an eye for the idiosyncrasies of characters and the oddities of fate, as well as a subtle understanding of the patterns in people's lives and the surprising turns that cannot be reduced to a pattern.

Merle Rubin, "Elegant First Novel Relates a Family Saga," in The Christian Science Monitor, *April 30, 1990, p. 13.*

Linda Simon

A Cloud on Sand is one of those romantic novels about the struggles between a mother and daughter, set against a background of exotic locales and the distant rumblings of war. The mother is domineering, the daughter reticent; but in the end, the power shifts so that the daughter claims her own life. The story is so familiar that, in the hands of a less talented writer, it would be merely a cliché. But Gabriella De Ferrari, whose first novel this is, has created

An excerpt from *A Cloud on Sand*

Antonia and Donna Dora lived almost totally separate lives. Later, Antonia could remember few times from her girlhood when she felt close to her mother. They were memories she nourished in her heart.

One such memory was of a conversation with her mother when Antonia was fifteen. Dora had returned from a long trip in an unusually happy mood. It was one of the times when there were no servants. Marco was at school and Eliana had gone to stay with a sick relative in Genoa so mother and daughter were alone together for two days.

On the first evening Antonia, not knowing whether to expect her mother, cooked dinner. Dora did come down for dinner. She was dressed in a shiny silk robe with purple flowers on a soft yellow background. She had her hair piled on her head and held in place with a Chinese lacquered comb.

They ate on the little table in the kitchen. "The food smells good," Dora said as they sat down. "You must have a talent for it. Serve me a large portion; I'm very hungry tonight."

"What did you do while I was away?" Dora asked as they began to eat. Antonia was surprised. Dora almost never asked such a question, even when she had been away for weeks.

Antonia described what had gone on in her classes, the history she had been taught, the piece she was learning for the piano. Dora listened quietly, following with her eyes and making no remarks as she usually did.

"Then there was the day I was sent home," Antonia went on.

"Sent home? What for?"

"There was something—wrong with me," Antonia said, gazing into her cup. "I had what—Eliana called it 'the curse.'" She looked up. "Mama, it scares me. Eliana says it will happen over and over."

Dora touched Antonia's cheek. "Don't blush, I will explain it to you," she said gently. "You are young for it, and it is too bad Eliana told you that. It is not the *curse* of woman; it is a price one pays for being a woman."

Dora, in a soft, calming voice, gave her a long, very detailed and accurate description of the entire process and its meaning. It took all of dinner.

"Men try to make us think there is something evil in it," Dora said as Antonia was cleaning up. "They do this because it frightens them; it shows them there are things about women they can never fully understand and control. Remember what it means to be a woman. It's the men, the poor bastards, who have to do the work. We can arrange our lives so that we can get what we want by using these things about women that men don't understand. Don't forget that. The man builds the house, but the woman dreams it to life."

characters of rare charm and set them in a richly detailed context. *A Cloud on Sand* is an impressive debut.

The plot centers on the relationship between Dora di Credi, a grand, flamboyant, unconventional woman, and her daughter, Antonia, at first likely to be subsumed by so ferocious a mother, but who eventually emerges from Dora's domination to become a strong-willed, capable, and beautiful woman. The tension between the two partly is motivated by Dora's need for constant affirmation of her daughter's distinctiveness and her sexuality; she seems to be the wrathful queen who would like Snow White's heart on a platter.

When Antonia is young, Dora usually ignores her quiet, mousy daughter, aiming occasional remarks at her plumpness or bad legs to undermine her confidence and keep Antonia submissive and dependent. When Antonia succeeds in entering a wider world, when she in fact receives attention from admirers, Dora is vengeful. It should come as no surprise that the final rift between them is inspired by a man.

Although there are a few peripheral female characters, the most significant secondary roles in this novel go to men: the elegant Count Mora, an elderly gentleman who for a short time is Dora's lover and for a longer time a surrogate father to her children; Rodolfo, Dora's late husband, revived in flashbacks, who lived in Buenos Aires and made occasional visits to his family; and Arturo, Antonia's husband, an ideal mixture of strength and compassion, authority and sensitivity.

When we meet Dora and her two children—Antonia has a brother, Marco—she is living in a small village on the Italian Riviera, reigning there as Artemisia's most notorious widow, inhabiting a villa far more opulent than any of her neighbors' homes. She is an indifferent mother, often leaving her children in the care of servants while she takes off for Paris, perhaps, or Monte Carlo. Dora does not care what anyone thinks of her—and everyone does think of her: she is impressive and unforgettable, and she nurtures her own legend.

Surely it is difficult to have Dora for a mother, but Antonia, with Count Mora's moral and financial support, manages to make a life for herself. She is training to be a nurse, much to her mother's dismay, when she meets Arturo, a businessman visiting from South America, and decides to marry him. When Arturo presents this proposal to Dora, she tries to seduce him; but Arturo is determined to marry Antonia, and afterwards he quickly carries her away to a small, primitive village in what appears to be Peru.

From this point in the novel, Dora disappears—she writes to Antonia, but her letters are intercepted by Arturo and we do not read them until later. Her absence is missed: she is truly extraordinary, and the other characters simply are not as compelling. Dora, as Count Mora admits, "was like a storm at sea, a typhoon, a force of nature itself. You may not like the typhoon: It may frighten you; it may, of course, even kill you. But you are never more alive than when you are in it." And the novel is never more alive than when Dora is its focus.

Antonia's story, after she leaves Artemisia, is the predictable discomfort of a cultured woman in a peasant society, and we watch Antonia adapt herself as well as she can to life in the New World, gradually earning the respect and love of her neighbors. Arturo, as you may have guessed, eventually dies—he is simply too perfect a man to endure—but we know that Antonia, now with a daughter of her own, will manage very well indeed.

Although the story itself is nothing new, Gabriella De Ferrari writes with clarity and feeling, and there is nothing that escapes her observation. Dora is so palpable a presence because De Ferrari has imbued her every gesture with distinction: when we see her walking down the streets of Genoa we know immediately why Rodolfo was so deeply fascinated. When we see Count Mora's face, "like a round, pink sea with delicate features like tiny islands," we know why Antonia and Marco were so quick to trust him.

At times, De Ferrari complicates the story unnecessarily, for example when she frames Antonia's memories of her life as if she were being interviewed by her niece, Marta. When Marta's husband suggests that Dora, not Antonia, is the real center of the tale, Marta insists that he is "very wrong. . . . Can't you see how she's the center of everything? Her mother may have been flamboyant, but Antonia is the one who triumphed over her. Can't you see that?" But Marta's husband remains unpersuaded and so, I imagine, will most readers.

For all of Antonia's underlying strength and "hidden asymmetry," for all of the "glowing coals" ready to burst into flame, Antonia seems far less complex, far less mysterious than her mother. Dora, says the count, was "the first person I have ever met who had totally invented herself. . . . " Although Dora fails to triumph at the end, although her sense of loss undoes her, although she fails, at last, to understand the meaning of her own life, she stands as the single tragic figure in this novel, and the one who, throughout, commands our attention. (pp. 362-63)

> *Linda Simon, "Soon to Be a Movie," in* Commonweal, *Vol. CXVII, No. 11, June 1, 1990, pp. 362-63.*

Judith Baumel

Gabriella De Ferrari's first novel [*A Cloud on Sand*] is an oddly plotted family saga that takes place in the first half of this century on the Italian Riviera and in South America. Dora, a seamstress with a wild manner and a knack for causing chaos, impulsively marries an aristocrat who has made a fortune in Argentina. They sail to America, but she refuses to set foot on land and returns to Italy. Her husband visits from time to time, staying in the mansion he builds for her on a hill overlooking her family's squalid houses. She has affairs with other men, including a crucial liaison with an intellectual and sensitive count who puts her son and daughter through school and provides them with the stability and companionship their mother can't. Dora's daughter, Antonia, an apparently conventional young woman, seems to live out a variation on her mother's life by marrying the black-sheep son of a Genoese

bourgeois family, who has become wealthy in the fictional country of Yayaku, which seems to resemble Ms. De Ferrari's native Peru. After two weeks of courtship, with Italy on the brink of World War II, Antonia goes to Yayaku. There, by relying on the wildness inside herself and a strength she has inherited from her mother, Antonia comes to terms with the reduced life of a frontier town. Though the novel spends much time with Dora, this is really Antonia's story, and it is a wonderful one. But Ms. De Ferrari doesn't know quite where to concentrate her energies—on the exotic details of Antonia's experiences, on the many characters in her life or on the grand gestures of history. Nor does her prose seem to settle down into a consistent style. Although it provides occasional suggestions of the later Gabriel Garcia Márquez or the early Mario Vargas Llosa, the novel has, for the most part, the feel of a plodding historical melodrama.

> *Judith Baumel, in a review of "A Cloud on Sand," in* The New York Times Book Review, *June 24, 1990, p. 21.*

De Ferrari on writing *A Cloud on Sand*

By the time a cloud is reflected in the sand, the image is barely what first appeared in the sky. By the time this book was finished, the people whose stories I wanted to tell became new and very different people: Dora, Antonia, Marco, Arturo, and many others. Strong and determined individuals who not only led unconventional lives but also confronted the displacement and opportunity that comes to those who move to a different culture. It is also the story of the people whose lives they touched, of the places they lived, and of the changes they inspired. I have known many such brave people in my life, this is a story about them.

Susie Campbell

In the preface to *A Cloud on Sand,* Gabriella De Ferrari writes that she has lived in many of the places she describes. This firsthand knowledge emerges powerfully in the conviction and freshness with which she conveys a sense of place in one or two economic sentences. A first view of Buenos Aires: 'a city of mud. The thick, brown, lazy water of the Rio de la Plata surrounded the ship like a rancid sauce and the city itself barely rose above it on the horizon.' De Ferrari is fascinated not just by the larger scene but 'by minute things'. 'A crack in a yellow wall, a pool of azure and gold, soft rustlings of the pigeons over a plaza', is how her central character Antonia, squinting against the glare of its cultural magnificence, perceives Venice.

The book moves between Europe and South America, Genoa and Pica, as it follows the story of Antonia Di Credi, daughter of the appalling but irresistible Donna Dora. Like her mother before her, Antonia marries an Italian who has made his fortune in South America. She emigrates to Pica just as Mussolini takes Italy into the Second World War. Antonia recalls her first impressions of

Pica and its contrast with the small Italian village where she grew up: 'It sort of spilled out over the desert, as if it were a pool of grey-green water. I remember thinking how different it was from Artemisia, which was packed right up to the hills with no space wasted and the houses right on top of each other'.

Antonia is only one of several characters in the book who are, as De Ferrari puts it, 'displaced' and have to make sense of belonging to two different cultures, while attempting to make new lives for themselves away from the families and communities in which they grew up. De Ferrari writes with sympathetic insight and, again, firsthand experience of the impact this kind of upheaval can have. For Antonia, repressed throughout her childhood by an eccentric and overpowering mother, it is both a liberation and a frightening loss of equilibrium. She has to struggle against this sense of 'unbalance' but, in doing so, discovers the excitement of being uprooted.

However, Donna Dora, Antonia's mother and surely one of this year's most spectacular fictional creations, throws into shadow even this attractive treatment of the theme of displacement. Bestriding the text on her much vaunted 'magnificent legs', Donna Dora dominates the story every time she makes an entrance. She is 'impenetrable', an amoral 'mystery', a 'force of nature itself'. Count Mora, one of her ex-lovers, continually tries to interpret and mediate her bizarre, apparently callous behaviour. But his repeated assurances that, despite all appearances to the contrary, Dora loves her children, remain unsubstantiated and unconvincing to the end of the book. Her letters to Antonia are masterpieces of spite. She writes, 'I hope you will now take my advice and not have any more children, or your body will degenerate . . . not that you had much of a body to begin with. Do nurse the baby. Your breasts are too small, and that way they will be fuller, at least for a while.'

For all this, Dora has a vitality and a power of self-determination that make moral strictures seem petty and irrelevant. The Count sees her as 'the first person I have ever met who had totally invented herself, who had risen out of the sea like some shivering Venus.' Even for Antonia, Dora is finally a positive force. The years of struggling to liberate herself from her mother bring her finally to the realisation: 'Sometimes I think I'm my mother inside out.' The Count agrees: 'you are continuing the tradition and inventing your own self in Pica.'

Sometimes, particularly near the beginning, the narrative itself falters, as if De Ferrari loses confidence in her ability to control all the elements of her story and feels the need to supply missing patches of narrative with rather unconvincing conversations, explanations or letters. 'How did you happen to become a nurse' one chapter begins, a crude excuse for the story of Antonia's attempt to take up a career. This might work very well on a chat-show, but it is unconvincing in a novel. As a writer, De Ferrari is not yet as skilled at constructing narrative as she is at characterising people and places.

However, each time the narrative gets itself going, it gathers pace and conviction. As its focus narrows from the broader sweep of pre-war Italy and South America to Antonia's particular attempts to establish her own independent life, so the story fires into life with no further need for kicks and pushes. Its triumphant revelation of how the different parts of an individual's life, thrown into disarray by displacement, can be reformed—in the parlance of the novel, re-invented—as something new and whole, make any doubts about the novel's success seem ungenerous. (pp. 32-3)

Susie Campbell, "Wives and Daughters," in The Listener, *Vol. 124, No. 3184, September 27, 1990, p. 32-3.*

Robert Ferrigno
The Horse Latitudes

Ferrigno is an American novelist and journalist.

A crime thriller set in southern California, *The Horse Latitudes* follows reformed marijuana dealer Danny DiMedici as he searches for his ex-wife Lauren, who divorced him when he abandoned his criminal occupation. Danny is subsequently implicated in the brutal murder of Lauren's new lover and finds himself pursued on his quest by a bizarre cast of characters, including biochemically enlarged twins and a mad scientist. The intrigue of the novel is interspersed with scenes in which the protagonist takes late night swims in the Pacific Ocean to clear his mind and reflect on his life decisions. Critics praised Ferrigno for skillfully juxtaposing portraits of a fast-paced, materialistic lifestyle with depictions of Danny's personal anguish, often comparing the author to Raymond Chandler and Elmore Leonard. Margaret Carlson commented: "With a magic all his own, [Ferrigno] has written an illuminating novel that never fails to entertain but also, surprisingly, makes us feel."

Tom Nolan

The horse latitudes are a dead-calm area of high atmospheric pressure at the edge of the trade-wind belt. On their way to the New World, ships often got stalled there, it is said; in order to escape those doldrums, captains and crews had to jettison cargo—including horses, whose terrible screams forever echoed in their memories.

In the '60s, this bit of lore inspired a grotesque song by the Los Angeles rock band, the Doors. Now former Long Beach newspaper writer Robert Ferrigno has used it to title his debut novel, ***The Horse Latitudes,*** a lurid thriller set in contemporary Southern California. . . .

This walk-on-the-noir-side seems to have the ingredients of a best seller: hallucinatory sex, homegrown and designer drugs, kinky violence, a cast of California high- and low-life crazies, a few dark chuckles and a sleek prose "look" worthy of a music video.

What's been jettisoned from this fiction vessel are understandable protagonists and a believable plot.

Danny DiMedici is the book's central character: a former anthropologist type who abandoned academia for drug dealing (grass only), then gave up dope and crime when one of his deals turned deadly. As the story begins, Danny is taking nightly swims in the frigid waters near Long

Beach and trying to get over his recent divorce from Lauren Kiel, a beautiful and successful motivational psychologist who left him because he abandoned the outlaw life. ("God hates a coward," his ex-wife explains.)

Police surprise Danny with the news that Lauren is missing, the walls of her beach house spattered with blood. DiMedici sets out to find her—ostensibly to clear himself as a suspect in her disappearance, but also to dispel his existential malaise and possibly effect a reconciliation. Despite mounting evidence that his former mate is a manipulative sociopath, Danny can't help but hope they might yet make it all work. *The Horse Latitudes* is as much romance as crime story, and a weird romance it is: sort of like *Casablanca* crossed with *Fatal Attraction*.

DiMedici's not the only one hunting the missing psychologist. A pair of muscle-bound twins and a spooky ex-Intelligence type also are on the scent, all at the behest of a maniacal pharmaceuticals manufacturer who thinks Lauren has absconded with his youth-serum research. At least *The Horse Latitudes* doesn't lack a clearcut villain. Dr. Arthur Reese, with his office full of big-game trophies and his laboratory full of floating fetuses, must be one of the most flamboyant fictional mad scientists since Fu Manchu.

DiMedici shuns cooperation with the police and goes his own route, getting various friends hurt or killed in the process. At the end, even the cops forgive him, which is no more or less plausible than anything else that's happened in these curious waters.

> Tom Nolan, "The Dark Side of the California Dream," in The Wall Street Journal, *March 9, 1990, p. A-11.*

Gary Dretzka

The Horse Latitudes follows retired marijuana dealer Danny DeMedici as he tries to find his ex-wife, Lauren Kiel. The sexy, amoral blond vanished after her scientist lover was found slain in gory, ritualistic fashion in her southern California beachfront home. Danny is a suspect in the disappearance and murder; and he, in turn, is pursued by two dogged Newport Beach police officers— former debutante Jane Holt and a likable old-timer, Karl Steiner.

So far, so standard. It doesn't take long, however, for the sun-soaked craziness to begin.

Also hunting for Danny and Lauren are a pair of physiologically enhanced twins ("They were massive, but at 5 feet 7 inches, the symmetry was off. Instead of looking developed they looked inflated. And the pressure had been kept on too long."); their uncle, a mad scientist; his henchman, a stork-like professional killer; and a Cuban exile dope fiend.

Danny is suffering midlife doldrums, as well—thus, the title—for which he takes therapeutic late-night swims beyond the marker buoys in the bay.

The chases, kidnapings, beatings, blackmail and extortion attempts that result after this crazy California salad is tossed are imaginatively rendered and make for a quick, chilling, often humorous read.

The book's biographical note makes it clear that Ferrigno is no stranger to the world of crime, having grown up in a neighborhood where illegal activities took precedence over Little League. His reporter's eye obviously was keenly developed as a youth and has served him well here. . . .

About the beautiful, rich and whacked out Lauren Kiel, he writes:

> "She was probably everything an ivory-tower type like Tohlson [the murder victim] had ever dreamed about: a cultured intellectual with French underwear."

The non-police characters in *The Horse Latitudes* are desperate folks, pushing the limits of excessive behavior to reach the goal of unlimited wealth in early, smog-encased retirement.

Holt is a by-the-book officer who wants to become the first woman police chief of a major department, while Steiner more closely resembles a pre-pension Columbo. DeMedici could be Philip Marlowe's illegitimate son.

At 294 pages, the novel feels a bit short. This is because Ferrigno's characters are so imaginatively drawn and immediately believable that any one of the minor parts could be given a few dozen pages more to develop—especially the twins, who would fit nicely in a novel by Harry Crews. The key question of why the stolen scientific research was so valuable also could have been fleshed out a bit.

But Ferrigno's pacing and dialogue are good, and the violence is as nasty as it can be. And the affluent Orange County setting provides some unique wrinkles to the by-now familiar Southern California crime picture.

> Gary Dretzka, "Hardboiled Updated," in Chicago Tribune—Books, *March 11, 1990, pp. 6-7.*

Christopher Lehmann-Haupt

"This would *not* be happening if we were in Kansas," says Danny DiMedici at midpoint in *The Horse Latitudes* as he watches a mostly naked model he hardly knows seductively waxing her legs. "I don't care what they say about 'one nation indivisible.' "

No, it wouldn't happen in Kansas. But it's California where Robert Ferrigno's superior first crime thriller is set. And as another character observes: "Like they say, all the fruits and nuts roll to California."

It's the Southern California coast specifically, in Mr. Ferrigno's imagination a catchall for drug dealers and big-game hunters, for body builders and health food addicts, for bikinied narcissists and seekers after kinky sex, for burned-out Vietnam vets and Cuban ex-convicts, for a mad pharmaceutical tycoon and an industrial spy who wants his secrets, and, at the center of the bin, for a bespectacled scientist named Tohlson who has been strung up by his wrists from a chandelier, punctured to death and castrated.

Out of these weird elements, Mr. Ferrigno has concocted a striking if lurid poetry of violence. A former syndicated feature writer who lives in Long Beach, Calif., Mr. Ferrigno writes of "a tidal wave of blood," of storm clouds that "boil," of "the life fountaining out of " a machine-gunned man, and of cops whose voices are "the verbal equivalent of a twirled nightstick."

In one of the novel's more violent passages, Danny DiMedici shoots in self-defense a rival drug dealer who happens to be wearing a Hawaiian shirt. "Danny emptied the MAC-10 into Wilson's chest. The hula girls kicked and swayed, wiggled their hips as the shirt turned red. Their grass skirts flew everywhere. They saved the last dance for me, Danny thought. He had always had a way with women."

Happily, Mr. Ferrigno has a wry sense of humor to go with his bloody-mindedness. "Those flowers are spoiling the ground-zero effect you've worked so hard to achieve around here," Danny tells his ex-wife's brother, who lives and trades commodities by computer inside a small cinder-block bunker on the edge of an oil field. . . .

Astonishingly, Mr. Ferrigno has fashioned a form of morality tale out of all this dark and bloody mayhem. Sure, Danny DiMedici was a drug dealer. But he never sold anything heavier than pot, and that shootout with the Hawaiian-shirted man took all the fun out of the game. So he has given it up when the novel begins. Quit dealing entirely.

And before he started, Danny was an archeologist. "He had a gift for nonsyllabic languages. Picture languages, Egyptian, Sanskrit, Babylonian, Mayan glyphs in particular." That was how he and Lauren Kiel had met, "when Danny was leading a university group to Copán.

"It was his favorite Mayan site, a ceremonial city in the middle of nowhere. . . . Their last day together . . . they stayed up till dawn smoking hash on top of one of the pyramids. . . . He had never hated a sunrise so much."

So the reader can identify with Danny and his pain over the loss of Lauren, who divorced him after the shootout

---

An excerpt from *The Horse Latitudes*

Danny slouched in the light of the open refrigerator, calmly drinking Evian from the bottle. Steiner headed straight for the black leather armchair and settled himself in with a hiss of the cushions. Holt stayed in the doorway, hands on hips, her hard green eyes surveying the room with distaste.

She was the best dressed cop Danny had ever seen, and wore a tailored gray suit too clingy for Sunday mass and too conservative for a good table at Trumps. Her thick red hair was bound by an ornate antique gold clip. She looked like old money, the kind that got a Yale law degree but felt it was her civic duty to spend a few years with a good PD on the way to a federal judgeship.

She finally stepped in, but kept to the edges of the room, as though wanting to avoid walking on the Oriental carpet. It was a cramped studio apartment with the dining area turned into a bedroom nook. Against one wall was a battered wooden desk piled with books and papers. Overlooking the desk was a map of the dark side of the moon and a velvet painting of the young Elvis. Shirts hung off the doorknobs; towels were piled in the corner. No TV. No plants. No pets.

Danny sat down in the rattan lawn chair next to Steiner, both of them looking into a fake terra-cotta fireplace with a photo of a roaring campfire taped inside.

"This here's real leather, isn't it?"—Steiner beamed, patting the armchair—"The real McCoy." The pockets of his suit bagged from years of shoving sandwiches and arrest reports into them. His tie had a yellow "I Love Grandpa" pattern on a black background. "Got a La-Z-Boy myself, just Naugahyde, though. Always wanted one of these leather jobs . . . " He leaned forward and sniffed the arm of the chair. "Yep. You can always tell."

---

because the spirit had gone out of him. And the reader feels for Danny when he sets out in search of Lauren, after the police report her murdered and name Danny the leading suspect. . . .

In a note at the beginning of the novel, Mr. Ferrigno explains his title *The Horse Latitudes* was an area in the Atlantic Ocean where the trade winds died, becalming sailing ships on their journey to the New World. . . . The most severe and profound doldrums could be escaped only by abandoning their most precious cargo—horses.

"Once the frightened animals were pushed over the side," Mr. Ferrigno concludes, "the sails began to fill. The horses swam after the ships for miles before they drowned. Their screams haunted the superstitious sailors for the rest of the voyage."

One suspects that those sailors weren't so much superstitious about what they had to do as simply sorry for the suffering of innocent beasts.

Some readers will feel similar qualms about *The Horse Latitudes,* but the majority will enjoy the violent, darkly comic and strangely haunting voyage that Mr. Ferrigno has taken them on.

> Christopher Lehmann-Haupt, "Sex, Drugs, Gore and Guns in Southern California," in The New York Times, *March 19, 1990, p. C20.*

Richard Gehr

In many respects, *The Horse Latitudes* reads like nothing more, or less, than one of the most stylish screen treatments ever written. When we meet Danny DiMedici, whose confident profile belongs "on a Roman coin," he's in a becalmed funk. His beautiful and amoral bitch-goddess wife, corporate motivation specialist Lauren Kiel, ditched him two years earlier when he lost his edge—he abandoned a flourishing high-grade pot dealership after a traumatic shakedown. Danny's road to redemption begins with a visit from two police detectives, Steiner and Holt, an old workhorse and his dishy female partner. ("She was the best dressed cop Danny had ever seen. . . . She looked like old money.") Their visit concerns his missing ex and the bloody mess—remnants of a ritualistic murder—left in her "Moorish Modern" beachfront home.

Lauren's absence, the killing, and Danny's ensuing quest all suggest the California comic-noir tradition of Raymond Chandler and the two Rosses, Thomas and MacDonald. But Ferrigno's cartoonier cast smacks more sharply of Elmore Leonard's demented Southern characters. Danny's cocaine-dealing buddy Cubanito, for example, has an immigrant's faith in American prosperity: " 'You worry about your cash flow, the pussy take care of itself. . . . Money's better, Danny,' he said gently. 'Men like us, it's too late for love.' " . . .

As Danny cruises from set piece to set piece in his '68 Mustang—disabling a Samoan bodyguard here, giving Lauren's lesbian lover a bikini wax there—Ferrigno journalistically inventories a cornucopia of conspicuous consumables, occasionally threatening to initiate a new literary subgenre: the lifestyle thriller. Parking lots overflow with fashionably expensive cars whose brand names are dutifully ticked off. Meanwhile, friendlier emotions are subsumed by manifestations of cash. Lauren's memory of a perfect married moment features a bacchanal of orchids and hundred-dollar bills, while Danny's flashback to their honeymoon boasts yet another pile of Franklins. In his Belmont Shore world, even coffee-shop waitresses drive vanity-plated Porsches.

The best moments of *The Horse Latitudes* occur in Danny's smart-alecky brain, especially during his buddy-picture carousings with Cubanito. ("He could hear Detective Holt's ever-so-solicitous inquiry: 'Do you have problems with your temper, Mr. DiMedici?' 'I have problems with everything, lady.'") Ferrigno's gift of wiseass gab sees Danny through some real dumbass West Coast situations, and that's the novel's greatest appeal. Because, in spite of his stylish attire and lovelorn cynicism, he's just another lost sailor on the make. Or perhaps he more closely resembles the jettisoned horse Jim Morrison described in his own "Horse Latitudes," the one drowning "In mute nostril agony / Carefully refined and sealed over."

Richard Gehr, "Horse Play," in The Village Voice, *Vol. XXXV, No. 14, April 3, 1990, p. 76.*

Aram Saroyan

[From the beginning of *Horse Latitudes*], there's no mistaking the mood indigo of Danny DiMedici, a retired dope dealer who pines for his ex-wife, Lauren Keil: "There were nights when Danny missed Lauren so bad that he wanted to take a fat man and throw him through a plate-glass window."

Lauren, brainy as well as beautiful, is still out in the fast lane leading cutting-edge seminars for executives and scientists while Danny idles in a rented apartment in Newport Beach with a phony fireplace. Having had to kill a man, he's lost his appetite for dealing. But don't be fooled, he still has the moves. . . .

Ferrigno is a skillful writer, good with dialogue, who occasionally skimps in setting a scene so the reader experiences a sort of prose jump-out. But the real problem with *The Horse Latitudes* is that Danny isn't revealed deeply enough to provide a narrative center of gravity. This is rather a designer *noir* novel where the bodies and the clothes, the cars and the food, the sex and the dope, the fine furniture and all the fancy talk stand in for the pleasures of a story that actively plumbs its depths.

Sometimes the trouble seems to be that Ferrigno's journal-

istic instincts undercut those of the novelist in him. For example, as he tracks the thoughts of Det. Steiner's female partner, Jane Holt, we learn that "Newport Beach was affluent, educated and white, a quiet, button-down community with three Ferrari dealerships and no public transportation. The supermarkets stocked Black Forest truffles and Dom Perignon, and commodities fraud was more common than murder . . . "—which is straight reportage in the guise of a character's thought process.

Or consider that late in the book Danny visits a local cafe, and we learn more about the life of its proprietor, Grace, than we know about virtually any other character—and she doesn't appear again. We never find out where Danny comes from, who his parents are or where he was educated. The book is all high-resolution front-story, and any back-story remains opaque. The scenes unfold like animate panels in a hip comic-strip. There's no depth of field.

For this reason, perhaps, *The Horse Latitudes* doesn't have much narrative momentum. Much of the action takes place off-stage. With all the elements in place for a high-tech thriller, the book dissolves into an oddly desultory Southern California travelogue cum character study with the moments of intimacy few and far between. Danny regrets his murder, yearns for Lauren and moves from scene to scene, from person to person, with a querulous aplomb that seems to lie on top of a couple of burning questions that never get asked.

Late in the book, Danny and Lauren briefly discuss the loss of one's moral compass while on drugs. Lauren tells him: "Because of the drugs, I was exploring a different moral and logical universe. . . . " Danny has his own memory of "a shimmy of right and wrong, good and bad. In that room, on that morning, it . . . made sense."

It seems a shame Ferrigno didn't pull out all his stops and try to fully render the moral valences implicit in such a moment. His skill indicates that he might have brought it off, and it's exactly what this book needs: a highly charged novelistic epiphany involving moment-to-moment psychology and perception; *who* as opposed to all the insistent *what.*

Then too, the experience of temporary alchemy with irreversible consequences might just be the real *noir* behind this book's high black gloss.

Aram Saroyan, "Newport Beach Noir," in Los Angeles Times Book Review, *April 8, 1990, pp. 2, 8.*

James Hynes
The Wild Colonial Boy

Hynes is an American novelist, born in 1956(?).

A political thriller, *The Wild Colonial Boy* is set in contemporary Northern Ireland and concerns the terrorist activities of the Irish Republican Army (IRA). Brian Donovan, a charming, feckless American, is recruited by his family to deliver ten thousand dollars to his cousin Maire, an IRA sympathizer, on behalf of his dying grandfather, an exiled veteran of the movement. Brian completes his mission, but is soon coerced by Jimmy Coogan, Maire's husband and a radical terrorist, to smuggle plastic explosives into Great Britain. Coogan hopes that by using the explosives to create a terrorist incident at London's National Gallery, he and his comrades will undermine support for Joe Brody, the morally ambiguous leader of the IRA who seeks to negotiate with the British. In the week that follows, Brian slowly awakens to the complexities of the IRA and their struggles as he travels from Belfast to Dublin and finally to London, where he must take responsibility for his part in the violent outcome of Coogan's plans. Although some critics characterized *The Wild Colonial Boy* as conventional, most lauded the novel as a tense, well-plotted thriller that incisively portrays the psychological and political motivations underlying Northern Ireland's troubled legacy. Jack Holland observed: "What emerges most prominently from [the novel's] pages is the IRA—an organization that has so completely obsessed itself with Irish independence that it has absorbed the cause for which it is supposedly fighting, making any compromise tantamount to betrayal. . . . This is a peculiar form of ideological narcissism, and *The Wild Colonial Boy* is a powerful testimony to its alarming potential."

George V. Higgins

What we have here [in *The Wild Colonial Boy*], if he keeps his nerve and tells us some more stories, is the debut of a master storyteller in the person of James Hynes. This, ladies and gentlemen, is the real stuff. Never mind if the double sawbuck in your wallet ought to go for gas or groceries on your way home tonight, and forget about the wait-list at the library—it's going to be long. Go out today and get this book, and plan on doing nothing else but reading it tonight. I don't know James Hynes from a load of goats, who he is or where he hails from, but I know stories when I see them, and this is the finest kind.

Brian Donovan's a feckless lad, native of Detroit, whose poor judgment led him to be born into a family of micks

whose doomed mission on this earth was to demonstrate, time and again, that the great Gaels of Ireland are the men that God made mad. Except that he doesn't mean to get into the wars that have been smoldering since Easter 1916, and before that back to Cromwell, and wouldn't have but for the fact that his more feckless cousin broke his damned-fool leg and therefore cannot serve as courier of $10,000 ready cash, to the Provisional IRA.

All their wars are happy, but the songs that they sing now are American, no longer merely sad but irrelevant to the cause they think that they advance. We have Joe Brody, the Sinn Feiner who cannot take his elected seat in Parliament, because to do so would be to commit political suicide with his co-religionists in Belfast. Quite willing, one might add, to trade his IRA brethren to the British Special Branch to preserve his dominance. We have Jimmy Coogan, gone quite nuts in his determination to prevent Brody from doing that, and therefore more than willing to commission his wife, Maire, to meet the courier with the cash.

But the surprises, not a one of them ringing a false note, each of them in retrospect quite predictable given the characters involved, start to arrive. Maire is tougher than Jimmy. The 10 pounds of plastique Brian finds himself transporting to London proves more burdensome in all respects than the money he took to Northern Ireland to buy ammo to kill British soldiers. Brian is a lippy kid, which gets him in trouble a lot, and Clare Delaney [Brian's love interest] . . . has a saucy attitude as well. You can find out for yourself about the treacherous monk and the reporter named McGuire, sculling himself out of Boston with no talent and no luck. Oh, and then there's the National Gallery in London—you can read about that yourself, too.

While you are doing that, you will be reading dialogue that rings as true as a pure silver coin dropped on its edge. John O'Hara was right when he insisted that there is no such thing as a first-rate writer who cannot write dialogue, and given O'Hara's unavoidable absence (by reason of death), I do not hesitate to say in his place that Hynes writes first-rate dialogue. So, again presuming to speak for the shade of O'Hara, I say that Hynes is a first-rate writer.

Far be it from me to spoil any of it for you. There's a certain magic to be had in the thrall of a good writer, and James Hynes lays irrefutable claim to that title with this lovely, mean story. He does not cheat. The line holds true. No character betrays his nature. No cheap gods intervene. Hynes plays it honest. He knows the people and he knows the places. He knows the mores and the morals; he worked hard on this. I might make some changes in structure and progression, but then, so might you. Still, neither of us wrote this book, nor should we have. James Hynes knows what he is doing.

The ending in my estimation is exactly what it should have been. Welcome to the lodge, Brother Hynes. We can't have too many good writers, nor too many good stories. Are there more of you at home?

George V. Higgins, "A Pawn in the Patriot Game," in Book World—The Washington Post, *April 22, 1990, p. 5.*

Jack Holland

Political problems always seem simpler, the solutions more obvious, the farther away one lives from them. This truth is very quickly brought home to Brian Donovan, the youthful Irish-American hero of James Hynes's first novel, *The Wild Colonial Boy,* when he arrives in Ireland, backpack in place, but with a money belt bulging with $10,000 for the Irish Republican Army. The money has been sent from his dying grandfather in America, himself an I.R.A. veteran eager to help the cause one last time, to Brian's activist cousin Maire in Belfast. Unfortunately for Brian, Maire and her husband, Jimmy Coogan, a well-known Belfast I.R.A. man, are involved in an internal dispute with the movement's leadership, which Coogan thinks is becoming more interested in ballots than bullets. The sirens of normal politics are singing their old song of compromise, and Coogan has a murderous plan to stop it.

Brian is a genial and rather droll young man whose poli-

tics have no more clarity than that bestowed by an innate sense of decency and a commitment to a united Ireland. But he is bullied and shamed into doing Jimmy Coogan one more favor: transport a packet of Semtex plastic explosives across the border from Northern Ireland into the Irish Republic, where it supposedly will be picked up by one of Coogan's faction. The situation, however, grows increasingly complicated and deadly. Brian is inexorably drawn deeper into the I.R.A. dispute, which like all before it quickly degenerates into a bloody feud.

In the meantime, Brian has become involved with Clare Delaney, a bona fide American tourist backpacking around the country. Their "boy meets girl on vacation" romance is conducted against some of Ireland's most charming scenic spots, but with the prospect of a paramilitary outrage looming in the background.

On the face of it, this is a rather improbable tale. But Mr. Hynes, who was born in Michigan and who has written television criticism for *Mother Jones* and other magazines, has made it into a compelling narrative. He has a sharp eye for detail: his descriptions of Belfast and Dublin are outstanding; the relationship between Clare and Brian is drawn sensitively, with an unobtrusive touch of youthful eroticism; and Brian's character is captured with a light stroke, his genial irony offsetting the narrow and obsessive ambitions of Maire and her husband. If anything the Irish characters are somewhat too narrow—as if the author can't quite believe that anybody can be politically committed without having a one-track mind.

Although there are twists in the story that are too far-fetched (Brian and Clare's ruse to elude a dangerously nosy reporter, for instance), the novel is usually convincing and at times powerfully so. The scenes where Maire is arrested, searched and interrogated realize vividly the possibilities for fear, humiliation and psychological cruelty that exist within a society like Northern Ireland.

The politics of it all hardly matter. There is some attempt by Brian and Clare to put the Irish situation into focus, but for Brian it is only an extension of his flirting as he tries to impress Clare. That is, *The Wild Colonial Boy* is not mainly about the Irish struggle or even about an Irish-American's awakening to its complexities. What emerges most prominently from its pages is the I.R.A.—an organization that has so completely obsessed itself with Irish independence that it has absorbed the cause for which it is supposedly fighting, making any compromise tantamount to betrayal. Die-hard activists like Coogan are no longer able to judge whether their violent deeds have any realistic hope of achieving their goal. This is a peculiar form of ideological narcissism, and *The Wild Colonial Boy* is a powerful testimony to its alarming potential.

Jack Holland, "In the Land of Short Fuses," in The New York Times Book Review, *May 6, 1990, p. 13.*

Frederick Busch

In *The Wild Colonial Boy* James Hynes writes of young Americans of Irish descent who are drawn across the sea and into the Irish tragedy. Brian is on an errand for Irish-American elders, and Clare is on a rucksack trip to see the state of the Old Country. Before long, the money Brian has been carrying to the Provos has been exchanged for plastic explosives and more trouble than he can handle. Maire, Brian's Irish cousin, and Jimmy Coogan, whom she loves, and who is violent and driven, make the broth richer and more dangerous. Glib politicians, pragmatic fighters, and immature pawns like Brian and Clare, are mixed and shaken, and the result is a suspenseful novel written with commitment and clarity. Most of the men are part boy; Clare is a considerable woman; Maire, who is in love with Ireland and darkness, is most memorable.

Frederick Busch, "Death at Sea, CIA Strife, and Violent Irish Politics," in Chicago Tribune—Books, *May 27, 1990, p. 4.*

An excerpt from *The Wild Colonial Boy*

Then he was on. One of the Dublin lads took his coat. The door pulled open and one of his regular bodyguards, a burly Belfast lad, beckoned him in, and Brody stepped through the door into the light. The roar of conversation fell away from the back of the hall to the front as he walked up the central aisle into a deafening silence. In spite of all the delegates on the floor and the observers in the gallery, the room was chilly, smelling of varnished oak and musty drapery. A rustle came from the balcony as people edged forward against the rail, their faces white against the ornate cornices. The delegates seated on the floor turned to watch him pass, their seats creaking in a rolling wave that followed him toward the dais. Brody ignored their eyes, though, gazing steadily ahead at the black lectern, at the words Ard Fheis in old Gaelic lettering enclosed by gold piping. Behind the lectern a huge, dark green banner hung without stirring from the balcony, with more old Gaelic lettering proclaiming SINN FEIN: ONE PEOPLE ONE NATION.

He stepped up onto the dais with just a nod to those at the tables on either side, and he edged along behind their chairs, his back stiff and numb. Some he could depend upon; others, like Peter, he was not certain of; Coogan had not left him time to marshal his support. At the lectern he lifted the speech to the polished wood and smoothed it flat, frowning at the thicket of microphones before him, red and gold and black. Collins and de Valera had stood here and looked out on this room, at faces like these, pale and indistinct and expectant; but others had refused to enter this place, preferring to spill their own blood and the blood of others in the pursuit of an ingrown and autistic idealism, vicious and blind with frustration, unable or unwilling to participate in the difficult and unspectacular bricklaying of a modern nation. Brody stood before the delegates like a man at the very edge of the precipice, ignoring the long, fatal drop at his feet, and he paused a moment longer to pour himself a glass of water from the carafe at his elbow. Then he curled his hands around the edges of the lectern and, clinging for dear life, lifted his face to the light and began to speak.

The New Yorker

Mr. Hynes is a first novelist with a real story, intelligently

imagined, to tell, and he does so in a strong, plain style that owes nothing to the literary fashions of the moment. The title [of *The Wild Colonial Boy*] refers at once to an old Irish song and to a young Irish-American, named Brian Donovan, whose dying grandfather, a bloodstained veteran of Irish rebellion, entrusts him with a ten-thousand-dollar contribution to the Provo cause in Northern Ireland, to be delivered by hand to a Belfast cousin. Brian's mission is successful—so successful that he lets himself be mesmerized into undertaking a further mission for the cause. Mr. Hynes, though a Middle Western American, seems to have a vigorous understanding of life and death in the Six Counties, of the mind of an Irish politician, and, in the person of Brian's cousin's husband, of the nature of a terrorist.

A review of "The Wild Colonial Boy," in The New Yorker, *Vol. LXVI, No. 20, July 2, 1990, pp. 73-4.*

Tom Nolan

Jimmy Coogan, renegade battalion commander of the Irish Republican Army, is the first person we meet in James Hynes' exciting and very well written first novel, [*The Wild Colonial Boy*], a tightly-wound chronicle of the continuing troubles in contemporary Ireland.

Coogan, a 15-year veteran of guerrilla warfare, is a Provo leader without any men, following a shoot-out three months ago between his unit and a "suspiciously lucky" British patrol. Furious with the IRA chief of staff he thinks is about to sell out the movement by taking a seat in Parliament, Coogan is planning an unauthorized terrorist strike, "something spectacular" in England to spoil the chances of any politician's compromise.

Driving alone past the flinty farms and open moorland north of Belfast, with ten pounds of Czech plastic explosives stuffed in an Adidas carryall, Jimmy Coogan is an outraged banner headline waiting to happen.

But Coogan needs help. Sought by the Provos and shunned by the locals, his only ally is Maire Donovan, the Sinn Fein city councilor for West Belfast to whom he is secretly married. An outspoken public figure, Maire is in no position to participate in her husband's scheme to get the explosives into the sympathetic hands of the London Brigade. The wanted Coogan dare not try to carry the *plastique* into England himself. Where is the unknown innocent Coogan can use as an accomplice?

Enter Brian Donovan, Maire's American cousin. Amiable, at loose ends, coasting on charm and good intentions, young Donovan has been deputized at the last moment to bring his dying grandfather's $10,000 from Detroit to Ulster and the Provos pension fund. To Jimmy Coogan, Brian sounds the perfect choice to tote explosives past border guards.

Maire is not so sure. "Americans are like children," she tells Coogan. "They come here like tourists to see a bit of aggro, get their thrill, and go home. It's like . . . Disneyland to them, Ulsterworld." When she encounters her cousin, he is even more unsuitable than she'd feared, seeming "less a foreigner than someone from another planet entirely."

Still, she arranges for Brian and Coogan to meet. Coogan sugarcoats his request with reassuring falsehoods. The apolitical American, following momentum and impulse, is drawn in.

There are no real heroes in this taut thriller. Nearly everyone's actions are compromised by obsession, ambition or willful ignorance. Coogan is not averse to causing a bloody IRA schism to turn things the way he wants. Joe Brody, the seeming moderate Coogan is opposed to, shops his enemies to "trigger-happy" British troops.

Maire Donovan is caught between her husband's plotting and her own better judgment, and the incriminating Polaroid she takes of her cousin to insure his loyalty eventually causes all kinds of grief, Brian's fumbling efforts to do the right thing are spoiled by his failure to confront hard realities; his less-than-complete honesty with Clare, a sweet and even more innocent American abroad, leads them both to the edge of disaster.

Brian at least means well. Much more distasteful are the ethical twists and turns made by Tim McGuire, the obese free-lance journalist Coogan bullies into assisting him. "Here he had the story of a lifetime," McGuire reflects after Coogan lets him in on his discontent, "and he couldn't print it. . . . He *believed* in the Republican movement . . . and if he printed what Jimmy Coogan had just told him, he'd be siding with those who wanted to bring it down . . . " Besides, McGuire asks himself, what if Coogan fails and Brody wins? "Then I'd be out in the cold forever, he thought, reviled as Jimmy Coogan's publicist, the end of my career in the North . . . " Better all the way around to betray Coogan, McGuire decides.

If Hynes offers no unequivocal good guys, what he does deliver is a terrific read, filled with believable and memorable characters who are as dimensional and full of surprises as the folks you meet in real life. They charm, they startle, and often they make you laugh.

The tension that builds throughout the book is leavened by wry humor, with Maire seeming to have the best lines. (She also gets perhaps the most powerful scene in the novel, an unexpected and flesh-chilling Gaelic wail of grief.)

With this impressive debut, novelist Hynes stakes a fair claim to part of that morally complex modern political terrain mapped out by the likes of Graham Greene, Joseph Conrad and Robert Stone. His characters meet fates that seem appropriate and even inevitable, while the larger issues remain realistically unresolved.

A brief exchange occuring halfway through the book seems emblematic of a struggle that seems to know no end.

"Are we winning, Joe?" an old Belfast Brigade vet asks Joe Brody.

"No," Brody answers, "but we're not losing either."

"Oh, aye," the old man concludes, "that'll have to do for now."

Tom Nolan, "No Heroes in Ulsterworld," in Los Angeles Times Book Review, *August 5, 1990, p. 12.*

Donna Rifkind

Brian Donovan is a young University of Michigan dropout with no clear direction in his life. But his days of drifting end abruptly when his family asks him to deliver $10,000 in "gun money" to his fighting cousins in northern Ireland.

According to family lore, Brian's grandfather, Patrick Donovan, had killed a policeman in his youth and been forced to leave Ireland forever. He went on to strike it rich in America, settling in Detroit, but has never failed to send regular donations to support the Republican cause back home. Now in failing health, and sensing that this may be his last contribution, Patrick insists that it be delivered personally by a Donovan family member. Young Brian gets the assignment.

So begins James Hynes's first novel, *The Wild Colonial Boy,* a political thriller with a conventionally twisting plot that, because of its setting, raises a few moral questions for the reader—if only occasionally for Brian, an innocent and sometimes a fool. Brian, who likes to call himself a socialist and harbors some sentimental sympathies for his grandfather's birthplace, is essentially naive about the frustrations and dangers of everyday life in war-torn Belfast.

It doesn't take one of his Irish cousins, a beautiful, passionate city councilor for West Belfast named Maire, much time to realize that Brian would make the perfect courier for some stolen Czech-made plastique. Maire's husband, the leader of an extremist branch of the IRA named Jimmy Coogan, plans to use the explosives to protest what he sees as a sellout to the British.

Only slowly does Brian begin to understand some of the complexities of a situation mired in history and local infighting. Traditionally, elected Republican officials from Northern Ireland who are entitled to take a seat in the Irish Dail, or Parliament, have abstained in protest. But now there are rumors that a current IRA leader, Joe Brody, plans to break tradition by taking his seat in the Dail and, in a step toward reconciliation, is making overtures to the British left.

Jimmy Coogan sees Brody's political maneuverings as a betrayal of traditional IRA militancy and he responds in the traditional manner of the IRA militant, choosing a civilian bomb target to express his disapproval: London's National Gallery, to him a symbol of the detested, elitist Thatcherite government. (Never mind that the Thatcher government can hardly be accused of coddling its cultural institutions.) Coogan isn't about to transport the explosives himself—his face is too well-known to both the British and Brody's men. The arrival of Brian, the quintessential American tourist, is a godsend for Coogan.

Soon, Brian is packing the plastique into his rucksack, recognizing his own foolhardiness, yet unable to resist Jimmy's dare. Complications arise almost immediately, most troublesomely in the form of a pretty American tourist, Clare Delaney, to whom Brian is instantly attracted. As they travel together, Clare is never quite sure why Brian gasps every time a policeman comes into view, but she likes him just the same.

In the meantime, Maire is arrested and interrogated by the British, who find her [with] . . . Brian's money belt. Not long thereafter, Jimmy is gunned down by Brody's men as he is heading back into Northern Ireland, just a hundred feet from the border. Left behind are his operatives, who are waiting to detonate Brian's bomb in the National Gallery.

"The whole Irish past seems like yesterday," the critic Hugh Kenner has written. And although the Ireland of James Hynes's novel boasts as many fast-food restaurants as pubs, with billboards of Sylvester Stallone looming over the Dublin landscape, its political climate seems eerily frozen in time. Mr. Hynes observes the same gaunt, haunted young men in Belfast as must have paced the streets during the time of the civil war in 1922. Jimmy Coogan compares Brody's sellout to that of past Irish heroes who have "lost sight of the goal": Michael Collins in 1921 and Eamon de Valera 10 years later. Then as now, lives continue as factional violence threatens everyday existence in a devastated country.

The Wild Colonial Boy (the title comes from an Irish song) suffers from uneven characterization. Mr. Hynes's emphasis is fixed on Maire, Jimmy and Brian, while Joe Brody, a potentially fascinating and pivotal character, remains shadowy. Neither is it easy to believe that even someone as feckless as Brian would really be dumb enough to carry 10 pounds of plastique all the way to London.

On the whole, however, Mr. Hynes has produced a competent, well-plotted thriller. He is judicious in his use of melodrama, a favorite device in thrillers; when he employs it (in one scene, Maire, having been told of Jimmy's death while in prison, angrily sings an ancient Celtic song to the British authorities), he generally manages to exercise restraint. The author is sensitive in his handling of the sickening violence that spreads through this sad terrain. And while he understands the forces that drive a man like Coogan to terrorism, he also dwells on the horrifying results of fanaticism—in this case the death of 11 innocent people. What sets *The Wild Colonial Boy* apart from other books of its kind is Mr. Hynes's clear compassion for every one who suffers in the Irish predicament, a compassion that lends weight and depth to an otherwise rather standard adventure novel.

Donna Rifkind, "The Troubles Never End," in The Wall Street Journal, *August 14, 1990, p. A14.*

Louis B. Jones
Ordinary Money

Jones is an American novelist.

A chronicle of two old high school friends struggling to support their families in a working-class neighborhood in Marin County, California, *Ordinary Money* satirizes the American pursuit of money and pleasure. Randy Potts and Wayne Paschke unintentionally enter into a scheme involving one million perfectly counterfeited twenty-dollar bills after Randy responds to a mysterious advertisement and goes to work for the elusive Bim Auctor. Bim soon entrusts Randy with ten crates of money and instructs him to deposit the cash in various safe-deposit boxes while spending the excess as he wishes. After Bim disappears, Randy involves Wayne by convincing him to store one of the suspicious crates in his garage. The resilient and enterprising Randy sets up a number of bank accounts and buys an expensive house and car before realizing that his money has not brought him satisfaction; Wayne, more cautious and ruminative, vacillates between his sense of morality and his desire for wealth before deciding to ignore the crate and continue working for "ordinary money." Wayne's struggle with temptation is the emotional crisis at the center of *Ordinary Money,* providing Jones with a moral battleground by which he exposes the complexities of greed, desire, and self-gratification. Critics generally responded positively to Jones's social satire and musings. Calling *Ordinary Money* "a first novel of charm and intelligence," Jonathan Yardley commented: "Though it bears a certain superficial resemblance to the 'K-Mart realism' now popular in the writing schools, *Ordinary Money* goes well beyond the limits of that tiny genre; the experiences and emotions of his characters are real rather than contrived, and Jones regards them with sympathy rather than condescension."

Richard Eder

In *Ordinary Money,* Louis B. Jones writes old-fashioned verities in arrestingly original fashion. To spell out just what these verities are would be self-defeating, since it would make *Ordinary Money* sound like a sermon, which it is not. It satirizes the futility with which money and pleasure are pursued in our culture, but it delivers the message through the delicately far-fetched things that befall two ordinary American families when 20 million dollars are mysteriously dumped upon one of them.

Wayne and Randy, who were high school buddies and are still friends, live in the brackish lower reaches of the

American Dream, and in an unfashionable part of Marin County. Wayne is a house painter; a long-suffering, dependable man undependably employed. Randy is itchy and mercurial and holds a variety of nondescript jobs. Both would like to be rich and don't expect to be.

Through an ad, Randy goes to work for Bim Auctor, small and finely built, who, as his name suggests, could have come from outer space but is actually a mad genius. One day, Auctor tells Randy to take charge of 10 crates containing 1 million 20-dollar bills and deposit them in safe-deposit boxes under his own name. Auctor, who cannot be contacted, will send him further instructions. Meanwhile, Randy is to spend what he needs as if the money were his own.

Auctor is never heard from again. Randy goes on a restless and unsatisfactory spending binge. The money seems imaginary; so do his new big house and red Ferrari. Eventually, a group of federal agents catches up with him and questions him, but then seem curiously hesitant about making an arrest.

This part of the plot—its major strand one might say, and an ingenious one—develops around the question of whether the money is real or counterfeit. Rigorous tests show no flaws. This does not mean it is real, though. Auctor seems to have developed a method of producing perfect forgeries. This is so alarming, so potentially destabilizing to the national and international economies, that it may be better for the government to pretend it is real and let Randy keep it.

There is a wicked dose of social satire in all this, along with some intriguing questions: How real is money anyway? How real is the pursuit of it; how real is what it buys? When Randy's daughter, Cindy—we will come to her in a moment—receives an expensive motor scooter, it makes her sick to the stomach. Love is what she needs. The comic spectacle of federal agents, lawyers, mysterious academics and high-level officials arguing over what to do—while Randy goes on shopping joylessly—is more than comedy.

If a message, somewhere between funny spoof and sharp parable, is the organizing principle of **Ordinary Money,** the book is considerably more than that. Randy, though useful and funny, is fairly thin. But Jones, somewhat in the style of Stanley Elkin, knows how to make some remarkably rounded and touching characters flourish among his messages.

Money, success, liberation, self-gratification are the desiccating fevers in Jones' America. Randy dries up; so does his awful divorced wife, Mary, a monster of fashionable selfishness with a fount of clichés about inner space, liberation and self-fulfillment.

Cindy, their daughter, is their sad and appealing victim. Nobody has time for her; she keeps a collection of suicide notes and ransom notes stuffed inside her Kermit doll; she takes them out sometimes and reads them. And when Randy briefly abducts her for a trip to England, she checks to see if her mother has carried out her threat to put out a Missing Child notice. When she discovers that she hasn't bothered, she is heart-broken; and our hearts develop their own stress lines.

And we still have not reached Wayne, the book's bitter, puzzled and beautifully drawn hero. He aches; he desperately wants money; he struggles against the knowledge that he will never make very much. Kim, his daughter, was born with a harelip and a missing nipple; the plastic surgery that has restored her wholeness has left him with colossal medical bills.

He is tempted to take some of Randy's money. He keeps opening up the crate of bills Randy has left in his garage. Laid off as a house painter, he is suckered into working for a telemarketing operation that swindles those who work for it in hopes of making a fortune. Jones is fiendishly clever at describing the swindle and the supersalesman who cons Wayne into putting his wife's savings—all they own—into it.

Wayne is a battleground. He is prey to the dream of success and the other fashionable lusts of the age. He dabbles at seduction with a bar pick-up; suddenly, they find themselves in her apartment having—to their mutual relief—nothing more than a little wine and a friendly chat. And finally Wayne pulls back, goes to work for himself as a house painter and accepts his wife's pregnancy, which up to then had seemed like one more persecution. Ordinary money is worth far more than outer-space millions.

Wayne draws much of his strength from Laura, his wife. She is spunky, sexy and utterly independent of the illusions around her. She is also written with a shade too much of familiar wonderfulness. Kim, on the other hand, is a burning original. She flowers out of her handicap. "How could anyone understand how it feels to be the girl of whom there are no baby pictures?" she asks in pain. By the end, she has healed herself into an earnest and charming love affair with the school nerd.

It doesn't all work. The end is too sweet. There is an insipid and diluting side-plot about a conceptual artist and his eccentric English father. It takes a little effort to figure out just what the government people are up to in their concern over the 20 million dollars. Their elliptical dialogue is comically appropriate, but it also clouds things.

Still, to be smart, funny, uplifting, tender and merciless, all at once, is a remarkable achievement for one novel—particularly, for a first one. (pp. 3, 13)

> *Richard Eder, "The Root of All Evil," in* Los Angeles Times Book Review, *January 7, 1990, pp. 3, 13.*

Jonathan Yardley

Wayne Paschke and Randy Potts are good old boys, California-style: amiable, laid-back, fun-loving, slightly but not terminally irresponsible. Wayne is an unemployed house-painter with a patient, loving wife and an impatient teenaged daughter; Randy is a carpenter, divorced from his wife but burdened nonetheless by his own impatient teenaged daughter. Neither man is getting very far in life, neither is getting there very fast and neither seems inclined to do anything about it.

Then into their lives comes a mysterious man who calls himself Bim Auctor but who could just as well go by the name of God. Quite from out of nowhere he enters Randy's life, charging him with the possession of a million $20 bills: "All I know is, this guy in a big white car met me in the parking lot behind a McDonald's and gave me specific verbal instructions to take care of his money. That's the complete story. I was his employee. He made a point of never telling me anything. He designed the whole thing that way." Use the money as you need to, he tells Randy; "set up a number of accounts in safe deposits," put the stuff in "a great number of storage sites" and—above all—"trust *me.*"

True to character, Randy goes with the flow. He sets up various bank accounts, he buys an expensive car and a big old house, he nudges his standard of living upward a few notches—and he leaves a wooden crate containing $2 million in $20s in Wayne and Laura's garage, just for safe-keeping. He's careful, though:

> He didn't want to spend too much money at one time; he didn't want to attract the notice of the Internal Revenue Service. From now on, he would be more cautious. He had heard that big-time criminals hide large flows of cash by owning laundromats or liquor stores. Maybe he should buy laundromats, on timid little down payments, and then hire a sleazy lawyer to help him do his taxes. He almost wished blasphemously that the money had never entered his life: he would almost rather be here at this big troublesome house as a hired carpenter than as the owner. But he had decided to cooperate with fate, to observe himself with detachment going through the motions of this new force. His idea was, as long as he remains a basically nice guy, everything will turn out all right. Wasn't that right? He hadn't manufactured it. He had simply been given a great deal of "money." It hadn't been his idea to begin with.

That's the way Lewis B. Jones has ordered his little universe in **Ordinary Money,** a first novel of unusual charm and intelligence. It's not exactly an ambitious book—its range is narrow and its themes are perhaps less provocative than Jones believes them to be—but it's admirable all the same. Though it bears a certain superficial resemblance to the "K-Mart realism" now popular in the writing schools, **Ordinary Money** goes well beyond the limits of that tiny genre; the experiences and emotions of his characters are real rather than contrived, and Jones regards them with sympathy rather than condescension.

At one level **Ordinary Money** is fantasy, but its center is deeply rooted in reality. Bim Auctor and his weird beneficence may be creatures from another planet, but the two families affected by them are real and immediately recognizable: basically nice guys, as Randy would put it, but caught in a squeeze between hopes and actualities that is all too familiar to the millions of Americans who got left on the platform when the '80s Express roared out of the station. Even in the Age of Greed, most people don't get rich, don't get more than a distant vicarious apprehension of the platinum life, don't have the luxury of a reprieve from the daily struggle to keep from being crushed by the burden of their ordinary obligations; **Ordinary Money** is a novel about those kind of people, and thus one to which innumerable readers should respond with empathy and appreciation.

Bim Auctor's millions, and the musings they provoke about the meaning and function of money, ultimately are little more than sideshows in this surprisingly populous and busy novel. There's a lot going on here, and Jones controls it with a sure hand: Wayne's gradual discovery that it's about time to get responsible and his bumbling attempt to do so by signing on as a telephone salesman for a marketing scam; the various intrigues undertaken by the two 15-year-old daughters, best friends and allies in the campaign to rid Kim Paschke of her maidenhead; Kim's shy romance with Eric DeBono, a singularly unlikely but hugely appealing Romeo; Randy's relationships with his former wife, a child psychologist who has drifted into the

heaviest weather of echt-Californian psychobabble, and with his daughter, Cindy (the other half of the dynamic teenaged duo); the old friendship of Wayne and Randy, who years ago had made a pact "to drop out of high school together and thus elevate themselves morally into permanent sarcasm."

Ordinary Money will remind certain readers—there can't be many of them—of Tom Lorenz's first novel, *Guys Like Us,* published a decade ago. Both books are about the peculiar rituals of friendship among American men and about the ways that women and children both intrude upon and enrich those friendships; both books also are funny, irreverent, imaginative and, by contrast with so much contemporary fiction, refreshingly unpretentious. It's to be hoped that **Ordinary Money** will get a better break than *Guys Like Us,* which like all too many meritorious first books by unknown writers was permitted to sink without a trace, almost upon the instant of publication; Louis B. Jones deserves better than that, just as Tom Lorenz did.

> *Jonathan Yardley, "Pennies from Heaven," in* Book World—The Washington Post, *January 14, 1990, p. 3.*

An excerpt from *Ordinary Money*

Wayne leaned back in his chair. How had he, in the legendary time of infancy and childhood, suffered the original loss of confidence? It had seemed so logical, his imaginary picture of financial crash. But enslavement to mere logic is exactly what true success transcends. Every failure is perfectly logical. Things always looked bad when he started letting himself think of Marketrend as stupid. The very word *stupid,* freighted with slow pain, came down to him from high school, the years when the word was most often in his mouth, the years when he and Randy Potts went around town barefoot, hated by waitresses and shopkeepers—when, amidst assassinations and undeclared wars, things stopped meaning anything, or when things first started to mean their opposite; when he and Randy learned their incessant sarcastic "talking in quotes," in the specious baritone of ad announcers. It provided a refuge, a personal charmed protection against the school system that was designed to weed him out, against "wars" and "presidents." Even at the dramatic moment of walking out of Miss Roup's economics class, when Randy leaned over and whispered, "Hey, 'Let's Drop Out,' " even then the words had been enclosed in quotes. When they walked out the school's front door, Randy said, "Now We Enter the Ranks of America's Disaffected and Disillusioned."

"Here's to Success!" Wayne had jeered later, lifting a beer above the horizon: he and Randy lay side-by-side on the golden hillside above town on that May afternoon of the Nixon administration. It was Randy, always ahead, who had taught him how to surround everything with treacherous irony. Even at his wedding, Randy was elbowing him and murmuring of "Becoming a Solid Citizen" and "Being a Loving Husband and Responsible Father," alluding to the irrecoverable days before girls when they were a pair of untrappable outlaws. For once in his life, if only to save himself, Wayne had to do something whole-hearted.

Marianne Gingher

Early on in Louis B. Jones's wacky first novel, a lackluster California teen-ager, Kim Paschke, is complaining to her voluptuous adolescent pal and mentor, Cindy Potts. "God, you have the nicest dad," says Kim. "My dad is such a blop."

Wayne (The Blop) Paschke, the unlikely hero of ***Ordinary Money,*** is a dreamy, gullible, unemployed house painter whose midlife spoils are mere dregs of the American dream: a rented house in Marin County, a dented truck and merciless hospital debts for the cosmetic surgery and prosthetics required by his daughter, who was born with one ear and one nipple. Wayne's only defense against misery is his marriage to Laura, a sweet and steady pack animal of a wife who works at a Denny's restaurant and is pregnant with their (unplanned) second child.

It's not exactly "Father Knows Best" at Wayne's place, but there's a persistent familial grace in this household that feels downright nostalgic. In contrast, the modern world at large is filled with the refugees of domestic ruin: est-saturated divorcees, mouthy high school kids for whom the death look is in, bachelor millionaires with their "asexual sheen." Cindy Potts, whose parents have split, stuffs her Kermit the Frog doll with practice suicide notes.

But life for the Paschkes takes a dramatic turn when the seedily glamorous Randy Potts—Wayne's buddy from high school and Cindy's dad—cruises up in a glitzy new truck with a mysterious crate that turns out to be stuffed with perfectly minted counterfeit bills. Or *are* they counterfeit? "You always had to expect the unexpected from Randy Potts, who once picked up a girl at Rumplestiltskins during Happy Hour by throwing croutons and cheddar cheese dice across the room at her bare shoulders; who still wore the same size jeans as in high school; who had divorced Mary neatly and with good humor in a series of hectic anecdotal comedies."

"[Jones has] assembled a cast of lively, delightfully flawed people, folks 'too obviously simple-hearted to do anything against the law.' Then he sat back to watch them reveal the loopholes in their consciences. I'll bet he laughed a lot too."

Marianne Gingher

Randy cons Wayne into storing the suspicious crate in his garage. Meanwhile, Wayne's daughter, who is afflicted with "the Paschke generosity in being habitually surpassed," defers to Cindy in a sexpot make-over scheme that's designed to help Kim lose her virginity. The plan backfires, but through their mischievous association the girls discover the money crate. Soon all of Terra Linda High School is talking, and Randy becomes a sleazy version of Robin Hood, admired by wayward teen-agers.

But is the money really counterfeit? The F.B.I., to whom Wayne mails a sample, claims the bill is genuine.

Randy has come into the money by way of his employment as general lackey to the enigmatic Bim Auctor, a balmy-voiced Ken doll of a mastermind. Bim arranges meetings with Randy in the parking lots of fast-food restaurants, where he instructs Randy in the art of dispersing $20 million in iffy money. But after entrusting Randy with the loot, Bim mysteriously vanishes. For good. And, after a few twists and turns of the plot, the F.B.I., the Secret Service, the Treasury Department and even the State Department eventually swoop down on Randy.

Ordinary Money is an uproariously satirical book, the product of an opulent imagination. Mr. Jones's writing is lush and flamboyant: someone's eye color, for example, is described as "lunatic lashless violet"; someone's mouth is "a huge orange grin like a baseball mitt"; someone walks with "the wounded gait of pregnancy." Although the author's lavish use of imagery sometimes borders on the spendthrift, I say spend it.

It would have been timely for Mr. Jones to play moral accountant in ***Ordinary Money*** and write a sobering book about the imbroglios of contemporary greed. But he's essentially an old-fashioned writer, a man who trusts his characters to call all the shots. And so he has merely assembled a cast of lively, delightfully flawed people, folks "too obviously simple-hearted to do anything against the law." Then he sat back to watch them reveal the loopholes in their consciences. I'll bet he laughed a lot, too.

> *Marianne Gingher, "The $20 Million Secret," in* The New York Times Book Review, *January 14, 1990, p. 7.*

Christopher Lehmann-Haupt

At the beginning of Louis B. Jones's ***Ordinary Money***—a wonderful first novel that might be described as a funny, intelligent version of the film *It's a Mad, Mad, Mad, Mad World*—Wayne Paschke receives in the mail from Randy Potts a $20 bill that Randy wants Wayne to send to the Secret Service for a test of the bill's authenticity.

Randy and Wayne are two lower-middle-class California guys who, "in a single summer, dropped out of high school together and served as best man at each other's weddings in the Silverado Room at the Holiday Inn, their smirks keeping the marriages safely facetious." That happened back during the Nixon Administration, when, "amidst assassinations and undeclared wars, things stopped meaning anything, or when things first started to mean their opposite."

As it turns out, the $20 is one of a million similar bills that a mysterious character named Bim Aucter has hired Randy to do whatever he wants with. Since Bim Aucter has been good enough to keep the source of the money secret from Randy to protect him, Randy decides to do the same thing for Wayne. While the single bill is being tested by the Secret Service, he asks Wayne to store in his garage a wooden crate stuffed with 100,000 more of the bills (or $2 million). He tells Wayne it's just "a bunch of stuff left over from the divorce, like probably pots and pans."

But when the single bill comes back pronounced absolutely genuine, Randy tells Wayne what's really in the crate, and the fun and agony commence. Randy starts spending the money and he not only begins to find his life turning false, but also discovers that the authorities are closing in. Meanwhile, Wayne refuses to touch the crate in his garage though he's repeatedly tempted to do so because of his dwindling income and mounting debt. As a reward for his abstinence, he finds his life moving in the opposite direction of Randy's.

Now the moral that this summary suggests would seem to be straight-forward enough: that money can't buy happiness or even make you very comfortable in your misery. But things are never so simple in the world of **Ordinary Money.** First, they are complicated by Mr. Jones's prose, which has a comically offbeat way of poking fun at reality. "Promise me you won't take yourself too seriously today," Wayne's wife, Laura, says to him on the morning he receives the $20 bill, and though Wayne doesn't take such advice to heart, the novel's omniscient narrator certainly seems to.

Then there is the plot of **Ordinary Money,** which further complicates matters amusingly. As the Secret Service keeps insisting, Randy's money appears to be genuine. This means that Bim Aucter, who disappears early in the story, has somehow achieved what every government must dread: the creation of a perfect counterfeit currency. And, because Randy genuinely doesn't know the money's source, he can't be convicted of trafficking in the "false" currency.

Meanwhile, though Wayne refuses to spend what could be passed off as real money, he allows himself to be roped into a scheme of selling coins for investment over the telephone. In the novel's cleverly satirical treatment, this has all the appearance of a pyramid scam. But if you stop to reflect, it is actually an attempt to traffic in real currency that fails because no one believes in the value of the coins.

And while Wayne's wife is happily content to be a waitress in a Denny's restaurant, serving meals like "Tater Tots and Salisbury steak," Randy's ex-wife, Mary, is so busy pursuing the self-realization that broke up their marriage that she is now driving her unhappy daughter Cindy, further into misery.

In short, the counterfeit is real and the real is counterfeit in **Ordinary Money,** and every sad or funny detail reflects this ambiguity. When Randy buys a mansion in a rich neighborhood, his next-door neighbor turns out to be an artist who got his start as a Velvet Underground groupie buying cans of Campbell's tomato soup so Andy Warhol could sign the labels and sell them as art.

The more Randy tries to buy the love of his daughter with his newfound wealth, the more bereft Cindy becomes. She is even deserted by her best friend and high-school class-

mate, Kim Paschke, who is of course Wayne and Laura Paschke's daughter. Kim was born without an ear, a nipple, and part of her lip, which have had to be counterfeited by plastic surgery at a cost that has placed Wayne and Laura under a mountain of debt. The doctor who rebuilt Kim may possibly have been Bim Aucter, the creator of the perfect $20 bills.

Out of misguided pity for Kim, Cindy has tried to trick her into a physical liaison by writing phone letters to the class nerd, Eric DeBono. But confronted by counterfeit sex, Kim and Eric resort to friendship. And with companionship, the counterfeit melts away—changed

> by the many late hours they'd spent in his family's rec room, slipping through each other's shifting embraces, sliding toward that precipice of pleasure where her self-consciousness of her body fell away and a dark muscular angel arose within her, an angel that could carry them both.

So just as Cindy is crushed by the really false, Kim emerges from false reality. Is there any way out of the novel's endlessly spiraling funnel of ambiguity? One is tempted to quote the conclusion of a paper Cindy Potts writes comparing and contrasting Greek and Roman civilization: "Another comparison/contrast of the Greeks and Romans is, the Greeks were very sane. For example, Plato and other world-famous philosophers pondered the greatest questions of all time. Plato believed that everything was ideal. This is still true today."

But those characters in **Ordinary Money** who pursue the ideal can be very crazy as well as "very sane." So the only way out of the novel's moral puzzles is to read it straight through to the end. Happily, that's an unfailingly entertaining experience. Mr. Jones . . . not only writes originally, he thinks originally as well. One can't help looking forward to whatever he does next.

Christopher Lehmann-Haupt, *"Lives Made No Better by Counterfeit Cash,"* in The New York Times, *January 15, 1990, p. C18.*

Jane Mayer

Louis B. Jones's first novel, **Ordinary Money,** is a kind of comic love letter about ordinary Americans living out their sunny days in their sherbet-colored, suburban tract houses, with their oil-stained driveways, their Salisbury steak and Tater Tot dinners, their sphinxlike teen-age offspring, and their own fading high-school dreams.

But into these skillfully drawn ordinary lives falls a most extraordinary fortune: $20 million to be exact. Randy Potts, a high-school-educated good-time boy, answers a help-wanted ad for a "general secretary/handyman, w/some financial savvy." After several "oddly diagonal interviews" with a mysterious character named Bim Aucter, he finds himself guardian of a huge number of $20 bills, neatly stashed in an abandoned warehouse.

Is the booty real? Counterfeit? Stolen? He can't find out because his bizarre benefactor has vanished without explanation. At first Randy tries to get answers; imploring his longtime friend, an unemployed house painter named

Wayne Paschke, to send a greenback to the feds for testing. It comes back certified legal tender. They try it again, and get an annoyed letter requesting that they stop bothering the government. What to do? *Start spending.*

The money begins to course through the suburban cul-de-sac, turning up first in Paschke's mailbox, then on Randy's teenage daughter Cindy's refrigerator door, saving her from shoplifting some new earrings. Quite a bit more gets spent by Randy on more predictable boy toys, like a bright red Porsche.

The pacing is quick and suspenseful. From the first pages it becomes clear that these warmly drawn suburbanites, so bent on their ant-like satisfactions, are, despite their good fortune, ever more in peril. And soon, Randy, Wayne and Wayne's pregnant waitress wife, Laura, all are snared in what turns out to be a counterfeit scheme so big and so perfect, it threatens to disrupt the global monetary system.

A striking feature of **Ordinary Money** is the contrast between its meticulously realistic characters and settings and this wildly improbable plot. The plot is far more complicated than the characters, and is actually baffling to them as they struggle to figure out what kind of a mess they are in. It seems like a parodistic turn on the squeezed American middle class, struggling fitfully to get a grasp on economic forces that almost defy explanation.

This point becomes explicit when Randy Potts, by this time in peril of being prosecuted, is treated to a dizzying lecture by a Stanford University genius whom he can't even understand, on why the perfect fake bills in his wallet may plunge the world into a global recession.

The question of what is real or counterfeit becomes an amusing vehicle in itself for exploring truth and fraud in the American dream. It also throws open the question of luck, which has dumped this putative good fortune on these people just as inexplicably as it did on John Paul Getty. Once asked by a magazine to write a short article explaining the origin of his success, he wrote only, "Some people find oil, Others don't."

Faced with opportunity, these characters try to do the American thing: Randy social climbs (and collects art), Wayne takes just a big enough wad of cash to betray his pregnant wife and pick up a very available girl in a cocktail lounge—only to find himself too nervous, too moral and too sickened by the color of her carpet. "The carpet was as orange as Tang, so astonishingly orange that he set foot on it warily."

In fact, the divergent paths of Randy and Wayne, one canny enough to get ahead, the other so ploddingly honest he lives up to his daughter's description of him as, "such a blop," make for a nice exploration into who succeeds, why, and at what cost.

Mr. Jones has a fine ear for loopy dialogue and precise, almost camp description. Pubescent Cindy, left alone by a divorced and constantly dating mother, examines the "soft flannel cushion of her lower lip," only to conclude that, "such beauty was not meant for this world: that would be the feeling of the mourners at her funeral service." She keeps a stash of melodramatic suicide notes, written during study halls, in the zipper back of her Kermit-the-frog doll, flattening her favorites out against her thigh, day-dreaming as only an adolescent girl can of how great she'd look lying in state.

Cindy's mom, Randy's ex-wife, is a parody of California psycho-babble, chiding her lonely daughter to,

> Remember the quality of your experience . . . You're a big girl now and you can't keep making me responsible for the quality of your experience.

All of this might be too programmatic were it not for the skill of Mr. Jones's writing—sharp, fresh and humorous—all the more impressive because it resists the usual new novelist's temptations to show off, and instead tells a truly rich story about "ordinary" America.

> *Jane Mayer, "A Handyman, a House Painter and $20 Mil," in* The Wall Street Journal, *February 28, 1990, p. A12.*

Joanne Kirschner

Who could be more of a skeptic, and an amazingly funny one at that, about money, wealth and the American Dream than a budding new novelist? In this offbeat work of comedic fiction, Louis B. Jones proves himself to be just that.

Jones creates a lovable, lifelike cast of characters that won't soon be forgotten by anyone who gets involved with their hysterically funny set of circumstances. Some very ordinary Californians, namely blue-collar Randy Potts, his equally blue-collar buddy Wayne Paschke, Wayne's pregnant wife, Laura, and Randy and Wayne's respective 15-year-old daughters, Cindy and Kim, become rather innocently involved in a counterfeiting scheme gone awry.

It all starts when Randy becomes the caretaker of $20 million, which he must deposit in various banks under phony names, ultimately involving his friend Wayne, an unemployed housepainter who's involved in a get-rich-quick pyramid scam.

These guys are about as far from criminals as one can get—in fact, they're just like anybody else who dreams of "money" and "luck,"—grabbing at whatever they can, hoping it will work for them yet resigned to the fact that they may simply lose out in the end. Jones has made these people as convincing as your next-door neighbor, or, if you happen not to live in a blue-collar suburb, then perhaps your hapless cousin Ralph or your old high school chum who dropped out of college and never quite "made it."

The teenagers in this book are so authentic they may remind you of kids you know. When soul-searching Randy thoughtfully asks his daughter "what she really wants," she glares at him and replies, smart-mouthed, "Braces, Dad."

You will love these people, feel for them in their plights, and regret leaving them at the end of the story. In the meanwhile, though, what will become of them? Will

Randy go to prison? Will Wayne lose all his money in the pyramid scam, spend his wife's savings (tip money earned from her waitressing job at Denny's) and break into the evil crate containing $2 milliion which lurks under his workbench in the garage? Will Wayne and Laura's daughter, Kim, figure out how to land the boy of her dreams? And what has become of the mysterious Bim Auctor, who supposedly printed the troublesome money only to disappear from sight? To find out, read this all-too-human tale of a couple of hapless losers who find out finally, that they aren't the losers they'd deemed themselves to be.

> *Joanne Kirschner, in a review of "Ordinary Money," in* West Coast Review of Books, *Vol. 15, No. 3, March-April, 1990, p. 23.*

Marti Leimbach
Dying Young

Leimbach is an American novelist, born in 1963.

Hilary Atkinson, the narrator of *Dying Young,* is a twenty-seven-year-old veterinary assistant who leaves her job and her mother's home to care for Victor Geddes, a leukemia victim. Against the wishes of his aristocratic father, Victor has chosen to abandon chemotherapy, thus hastening his death. After Victor and Hilary move to the Massachusetts coastal town of Hull, Hilary begins a romance with him, although aware of his impending death. She subsequently has an affair with Victor's friend Gordon, but comes to reassess her relationships with both men as Victor's health wanes. While some critics considered Hilary's passive narrative voice too distant to gain sympathy from readers, most praised Leimbach's vivid descriptions of her characters and their conflicts. Michelle Heinemann noted: "It is Hilary's clear and wry perspective which gives *Dying Young* its sharp focus. She is intimate with us about the most banal aspects of these people's lives, yet the weighted emotion of the story is delivered lightly; a balancing act, which Leimbach usually pulls off."

———————

Paul Gray

Victor Geddes, 33, [a character in Marti Leimbach's *Dying Young,*] suffers from leukemia. Abandoning his chemotherapy, he places an ad in the Boston *Globe* for a companion and caretaker; Hilary Atkinson, 27, applies for the job. Soon these two fall in love and move to the anonymity of a rented room on the Massachusetts coast. There, as winter sets in, they meet Gordon, 30, who becomes Victor's friend and, on the sly, Hilary's lover. The situation is messy, but at least members of the ménage can foresee one outcome for certain: Victor will die soon.

This premise promises a grim and lugubrious read. . . .

There has always been a healthy market for doomed romance. Furthermore, this novel plays upon a current preoccupation—explicitly stated in its title—without raising the troubling specter of AIDS. Finally, Leimbach, 26, proves herself to be both a deft writer and a shrewd judge of just how much sentimentality her traffic will bear.

The author's smartest move is letting Hilary tell the tale. This young woman seems peculiarly passive and affectless, not the sort to dwell on or even recognize pathos or tragedy. All perceptions—grocery displays, radio chatter, the sight of Victor vomiting in a bathroom—pass through her consciousness with equal weightlessness. Hilary con-

stantly learns things that anyone her age should probably already know. She removes some pictures from the room she and Victor have rented: "When I took them from the wall I noticed that the spaces the frames had occupied were a darker shade than the rest of the wall." When she feels the need to conduct a reality check, Hilary looks in the mirror: "I have clear skin and nice, square shoulders. My hair shines like it did when I was seven and I have a smart-looking face."

She also has the chance to live out a fantasy: two men devoted to her, one of them virile and the other literally dying in her arms. Whether Leimbach intends Hilary to be as dim-witted as she seems is immaterial. The trick finally works. Near the end, something dawns on Hilary that is not a truism. As Victor's imminent death begins to seem real to her, she realizes that he "has made it seem that the future of a relationship is not as important as I once imagined." It would be nice to hear Victor on whether dying is a price he willingly pays to teach Hilary about life. But she has the last and only words.

Paul Gray, "Fantasy Life," in Time, *New York, Vol. 135, No. 2, January 8, 1990, p. 74.*

Jill McCorkle

When a novel's title alerts you to the fact that someone is dying—and, more specifically, that it's someone *young*—you discard the possibility of a happy ending and seek other satisfactions. When you discover that the character is dying of leukemia, though this is an all-too-real and serious scenario, you fear that the story will slip into an all-too-familiar fictional pattern.

In her first novel, ***Dying Young,*** Marti Leimbach manages to bring us to a satisfying ending, creating along the way a Massachusetts landscape that intensifies the cold desolation of the narrator and her two lovers. Ms. Leimbach also manages to avoid any obvious manipulation of the reader's emotions. What she emerges with, however, is a novel that sets us too much at a distance, a novel whose characters are difficult to appreciate or understand.

In order to escape living with her mother in a small apartment and working as a veterinary assistant, the novel's narrator, 27-year-old Hilary, responds to an ad placed by a man named Victor in the *Boston Globe.* Soon thereafter she has moved from the city to the coastal town of Hull, where she takes a job caring for Victor, a leukemia patient who at age 33 has opted to die in seclusion rather than continue treatment in a hospital. As a result of this choice, Victor is now estranged from his wealthy father and their old Bostonian world.

Within a short time, Hilary and Victor become lovers, although it is unclear just why she feels such a strong attachment to him. He is affected and obnoxious, ridiculing her and quizzing her about books she has not read. "Read something decent for a change," he sneers. "Kant, Schopenhauer, Wittgenstein, Nietzsche! Lacan, Jung, Freud for godsakes!"

Victor's temper tantrums are almost constant, leaving Hilary to fluctuate between love and hate. She offers vague examples of Victor's virtues—his "rich man's voice and stance," his explanations of "what exists as fact in a rich man's obliging world"—as a rationale for her commitment. She even tells us that "in normal circumstances, someone like Victor would never be with someone like me." Perhaps this revelation explains her attraction to Gordon, also her lover, whom she describes as "a marvel of normality." And yet Gordon is not free of baggage either. He is in Hull because his artist wife has left him; at the end of their marriage, he discovered that he was not the natural father of the little girl he thought was his daughter.

Dying Young is a novel about desperate people in desperately needy situations. But while the immediacy of its present-tense narrative keeps it a safe distance from what could quickly become a melodramatic situation, that very technique also sacrifices the opportunity to develop its narrator into a complex and believable personality. We

know that Hilary shoplifts, and Ms. Leimbach does allow us a glimpse into the origins of the problem, telling how Hilary began her thievery at the age of 4 and later, in the midst of her parents' divorce, began stealing objects from one home and planting them in the other, a child's attempt at forcing a reconciliation. There is a genuineness in this excursion back into memory that we don't feel in the present, when Hilary speaks to Victor or tells a story to Gordon; it is this neglected voice that could carry the novel, but for the most part it is withheld.

The character who temporarily breathes some life into Ms. Leimbach's book is Estelle, an elderly eccentric who reads tea leaves and tarot cards, tints her hair in shades of pink or green and speaks openly about death. Yet for all her wise words, Estelle proves to be shallow and uncaring. In the end, what real sympathy we feel for Victor is not the result of any heroism on his part, but rather a product of the weaknesses of the other characters.

In its surface descriptions of people and places, ***Dying Young*** is quite accomplished. And, even with the weight of the plot, its ending is not easy or predictable. But there is a disconcerting hollowness about this novel, all the same. Despite Ms. Leimbach's best efforts, she fails to give us the emotional understanding we need in order to bear witness to these characters' most intimate and vulnerable moments.

Jill McCorkle, "Desperately Seeking Someone," in The New York Times Book Review, *January 14, 1990, p. 22.*

Bruce Bawer

The dust-jacket illustration for Marti Leimbach's first novel, ***Dying Young,*** reminds one of the cover of a teenage romance. It shows three young people, all of them pretty in the same vapid, square-jawed, Barbie-and-Ken way. Two are male—one blond, one dark-haired and bespectacled—and the third is our heroine (also blond), whose tormented expression, as she gazes up at these hunks, indicates that she just can't choose between them.

This drawing neatly sums up Ms. Leimbach's familiar love-triangle plot. Hilary Atkinson is a lower-middle-class Bostonian whose lack of self-esteem has led her into an affair with Victor Geddes, a patronizing Back Bay aristocrat who is dying of leukemia. Victor is everything the 27-year-old Hilary wishes she were: rich, erudite, articulate, self-possessed. Enter Gordon, a bright, affectionate local boy whom she begins seeing on the sly. The questions before us, of course, are as follows: Will Victor find out about this liaison? Will Hilary ditch Victor and move in with Gordon? If so, what will become of Victor?

Many a serious reader will not care one way or another. For, despite its extensive pre-publication hype (as the reviewer's kit brags, Ms. Leimbach received a total of $500,000 in advances and subsidiary rights), ***Dying Young*** reads like a typical drugstore-paperback love story: The characters lie lightly on the page; the symbolism, mostly death-related (a sinking ship, a decayed seal on the beach, a parachute jumper on TV whose chute doesn't open), is astonishingly obvious and contrived; and the mundane, chatty narrative (written in the first person and present tense) consists almost entirely of simple declarative sentences.

Bruce Bawer, "Notable Debut Novels," in The Wall Street Journal, *January 18, 1990, p. A16.*

An excerpt from *Dying Young*

Victor knows. I stole someone else's shirt from the launderette and, just my luck, the woman's name was sewn into the collar. I'll have a new gadget—a windup replica of the Flintstones' Dino or a design-your-own stamp set that he knows I didn't want and he'll ask if I stole it. He'll notice the chocolate bar I'm eating and say, "A 'gift'?" and I'll nod.

This habit of stealing has embarrassed my parents for years—ever since my mother found an unexplained package of gum in my coat pocket when I was four years old. My father was bewildered by my later thievery—particularly my habit of stealing for others, which caused him some ethical dilemmas as he pondered the appropriate punishment for his grade school daughter who had stolen a gold lighter for her dad's birthday. Later, after the divorce, I stole from the two separate homes of my estranged parents, planting things from one apartment in the other. I put my father's favorite beer mug on my mother's cabinet shelf. I dropped my mother's address book into the mail basket on my father's desk top. I left his tie clip on her bookshelf, her nail polish in his medicine cabinet, his after-shave in the drawer of her nightstand. I wanted them to get back together but, instead, my father remarried. He even moved into a house, a real house, not an apartment. When I was in junior high school I stole a nightgown from my mother and hung it in the closet at my father's new house. His wife saw it and he called me, his anger exploding into the phone. Then I stopped visiting my father.

Julie Morrice

I faintly remember an episode of *Batman* where the eponymous super-hero is imperiled by a giant birthday cake, on top of which he is standing and into which he is slowly sinking. Similarly, Marti Leimbach's first novel is a struggle between a tough little idea and an overwhelming, sugary narrative, but in this case it is the birthday cake that survives to fight another day.

Had it not already been done in *Love Story*, **Dying Young** would have made a great movie. One can almost see the titles flashing up on the quirky first scene, and the credits (and tears) rolling over the final catharsis. The plot is pure soap opera. Girl answers advert for companion for young man with leukaemia. They fall in love and remove to chilly solitude of holiday resort in winter, where he declines and she becomes involved with big, healthy divorcee. All ends lachrymosely, affirming possibility of eternal love, courage in the face of death, etc.

To the author's credit this half-baked story line is quite nicely crisped up. Leimbach is a dab hand with dialogue, her snappy descriptions have a decent bite to them, and

her prose rises to the occasion of the more lyrical moments. **Dying Young** is pleasant, intermittently moving and periodically stimulating.

It might have been more. In little asides and pretty, unspoken metaphors, Leimbach hints at the very different book she could have written. The theme of this non-existent novel is a young woman's struggle to stop seeing herself in relation only to the men she loves.

The female narrator of **Dying Young** is painted as an old-fashioned object of desire. 'Can I tell you something?' one of her admirers asks. 'Can I tell you that if I weren't dying I would make a life out of learning how to love you.' Instead of slamming the car door on his fingers, she puts up with this sort of remark, and lets slip a word here and there which reveals her sense of inferiority. Her life's ambition has been to train as a vet. 'But I don't know anything about animal medicine,' she says, 'I only know how to take directions from someone who does.' Self-expression for this intelligent but inarticulate woman is simply a matter of notching up relationships with impressive, articulate men. Her painful dilemma over which of her lovers to choose is a false one—somebody that insecure needs all the men she can get to shore up her precarious ego.

In the ending of her novel, and at rare moments throughout it, Leimbach appears to understand her heroine, and gives voice to her confusion, but for the most part the author succumbs to her own sweet story.

Julie Morrice, "Sugar and Spice and Nothing Nice," in The Listener, *Vol. 123, No. 3167, May 31, 1990, p. 23.*

Jo-Ann Goodwin

American writers seldom seem to suffer from failure of nerve. Other qualities may be lacking, but not the big idea and the bravado to carry it through.

So at the tender age of 25 Marti Leimbach sets out in her first novel to explore mortality, sexuality and the nature of love. According to the publicity blurb, which compares **Dying Young** not only to *Love Story,* but to *Terms of Endearment* and Mann's *Death in Venice* as well, she has succeeded in a remarkable way, and indeed the film rights already rest with 20th Century Fox.

The novel tells the story of three people. Victor and Gordon are friends. Hilary is Victor's long-time girlfriend and sleeps with Gordon. The difference being that Victor has leukemia and is dying.

Set in Hull, a summer resort on the north Atlantic coast, now godless and deserted in early winter, the three protagonists struggle to make sense of the situation in which they are caught. Victor is obsessed with his right to die as he chooses, and bent on avoiding the pain, lassitude and indignity of yet another hospital "cure". Hilary is increasingly drawn to the uncomplicated normality of Gordon, his shiny, floppy hair, clear eyes and physical competence.

Occasionally the grand themes of fidelity, sexuality and death threaten to overthrow the balance of the writing, the character of Hilary becoming, at times, little more than a cipher for the investigation of large philosophical or symbolic schemes. Yet *Dying Young* constitutes an impressive debut, most especially in the depiction of Victor, whose complex, often selfish, but entirely understandable attitude to his illness is convincing and ultimately moving. (pp. 38-9)

Jo-Ann Goodwin, "The Big Idea," in New Statesman & Society, *Vol. 3, No. 103, June 1, 1990, pp. 38-9.*

Michelle Heinemann

Marti Leimbach writes smoothly about a prickly subject—death: dying young, to be precise. Her literary début, which has been acclaimed in the United States, is a simply told tragic love story. The narrator of *Dying Young* is Hilary, who, at twenty-seven, "is always going towards something, but never quite arriving". She has Victor, her "confident and tempestuous" boyfriend, who chucks a life of chemotherapy to face his death head-on. Hilary and Victor have bland Gordon—Hilary's not-so-clandestine lover and Victor's late-in-life friend. The three of them have clairvoyant Estelle, in her outlandish pink sunglasses and lime-green hair. And eventually they all have Victor's father, Mr Geddes, who respects modern medicine more than he respects his son. Hilary says they "are a reckless bunch". The whole cast is entangled in Victor's tragedy, played out mainly in coastal Hull, Massachusetts, and sometimes in Boston, a forty-minute ferry ride away.

It is Hilary's clear and wry perspective which gives *Dying Young* its sharp focus. She is intimate with us about the most banal aspects of these people's lives, yet the weighted emotion of the story is delivered lightly: a balancing act, which Leimbach usually pulls off. Victor has an opinion on everything; Hilary looks to others to shape her ideas. Victor is cynical, inquisitive, and not especially nice; Gordon naively trusting, a paragon of American goodness. Estelle is outrageous and powerful; Mr Geddes barely manages to be conservative and weak. Everyone is understood in comparison with someone else. The final effect is that Hilary trusts herself in exact proportion to Victor dying and we don't mind too much. The strength of *Dying Young* is its clarity; but it leaves the reader hungry for something a bit more substantial.

Michelle Heinemann, "Arriving in Proportion," in The Times Literary Supplement, *No. 4555, July 20-26, 1990, p. 782.*

Dennis McFarland
The Music Room

McFarland is an American novelist, born in 1950.

The Music Room is an unsentimental portrait of a family overwhelmed by alcoholism. Critics praised the work's finely-crafted structure through which McFarland evokes the mystery and pathos of his characters. A musician himself, McFarland delineates musically-gifted parents whose destructive relationship and incessant drinking has led to the deterioration of their family, wealth, and talent. Their sons, Martin and Perry, develop successful musical careers, but are haunted by their troubled past. At the novel's opening, Martin, the protagonist, is mourning his broken marriage when he learns of his younger brother's suicide. Martin's struggle to understand his brother's death leads him to New York, where he has a brief, grief-stricken affair with his brother's girlfriend and is surprised to learn that Perry worked with abused children. As Martin laments Perry's suicide, his long-buried childhood memories surface. These visions are rendered with vivid imagery and sensuous detail, and the narrative continually shifts from past to present and from dreams to reality.

Reviewers have interpreted Martin's quest for knowledge as an exploration of his identity and his painful past, as he is ultimately drawn to his childhood home in Norfolk, Virginia, where he confronts his alcoholic mother. Although some reviewers considered the novel's ending overly optimistic, others maintained that McFarland's exquisite imagery effectively conveyed Martin's insight into the consuming power of his family's illness, his acceptance of Perry's death, and his realization of his own addiction. Josephine Humphreys asserted: "What is most magical about *The Music Room* is its fabric: thick, rich, mysterious, *true*. . . . Instead of narrowing to a solution, it opens onto territory unforeseen, and revelations larger than those that might have been expected." Humphreys added: "[The novel] builds to a comprehensive vision, remarkable from its beginning to its surprising, satisfying end."

Merle Rubin

The phrase *dysfunctional family* rolls trippingly off the tongue nowadays, summoning up a wealth of damage, anger and confusion, yet seeming somehow to compress all the pain into a neatly manageable category.

Dysfunction can range from extreme cases of child abuse of the sort that horrify hardened police officers, to the kinds of emotional neglect that are so commonplace as to

seem almost endemic: parents who refuse to be—or who are unable to be—parents; bad marriages in which children become the victims; families in which attention and affection are short-circuited by dependence on drugs or alcohol—each unhappy family, as Tolstoy put it, unhappy in its own special way. Yet, certain patterns do emerge, which, *pace* Tolstoy, give the stories—and case histories—of dysfunctional families something of a familiar ring to the postmodern, therapy-trained ear.

Dennis McFarland's first novel [*The Music Room*] (part of which first appeared, in slightly different form, in the *New Yorker*) deals with a classically dysfunctional family, yet manages to state the obvious without sounding clichéd. The mother, a former Las Vegas showgirl, spends her afternoons in a drunken haze, aided and abetted by a pair of boozing buddies. The father, scion of a wealthy, alcoholic Virginia family, withdraws into his music room, where he spends his days quietly imbibing oblivion and brooding over his failure to attempt—let alone achieve—

his dream of a musical career. Martin and Perry, the two sons, born four years apart, share similar experiences growing up in this milieu, but certain differences of temperament give each a subtly and significantly different perspective on those experiences.

The novel opens in 1976, when Martin Lambert, nearly 30, head of a small San Francisco record company, is summoned East by a phone call from the New York City police notifying him of his younger brother's suicide. Trying to cope with the shock of Perry's death, searching for reasons that might explain it, Martin is plunged into a dazed, dreamlike state, in which lost memories resurface and the past slowly acquires shape, color and weight.

Martin is further agitated by meeting up with a sympathetic and attractive woman named Jane Owlcaster, Perry's lover before the break-up in their relationship that occurred shortly before his death. Jane, like everyone else in Perry's life, is initially stunned by Martin's physical resemblance to his brother. She and Martin sense the dangers of falling in love with each other, yet they also sense the possibility of consolation and renewal in such a relationship sometime in the indefinite future.

Pondering Perry's death, Martin can find no single immediate cause that triggered his leap from a hotel window. Yet underlying causes seem scattered like combustible materials throughout Perry's childhood—and his own; alcoholic parents locked in a cool, yet deadly stand-off of disappointment and recrimination; a wife whose contempt for her husband turns his life into a kind of slow suicide. The desperation of the situation is disguised by the seeming ordinariness of their squabbling:

> Father finds Mother in the library playing solitaire . . . cursing the cards under her breath, cigarette hanging from her lips, its ash about to drop. 'You're *drunk*,' he says to her from the doorway, disgusted. 'You're *drunk*,' Mother says to Father in the music room as he lies on the couch staring at the ceiling. . . . In the entryway, gripping her braceleted wrists—is she about to hit him?—he says to her (a harsh whisper, for there are guests in the library), 'You're *drunk*.' Long before I knew what the word meant, I identified it as the meanest thing they said to each other. And when I finally knew that it was what you got from drinking whisky, it seemed a very strange thing to accuse each other of, since they were always drinking whisky.

As Martin struggles to extricate himself from his family's ill-fated tendencies, he comes to see that his parents' marriage was even worse than he knew. Only Perry, who was less of an onlooker, more of an emotionally involved participant, had a clear view of it all, and this clarity of vision may well have contributed to his suicide. But Martin, unlike Perry, recognizes the part played by alcohol in exacerbating the family's problems.

Baldly summarized, the story sounds like an Alcoholics Anonymous parable. As handled by McFarland, it is something more. He is too sensitive a writer to hit us over the head with the obvious: Even when they seem to exemplify casebook histories, his characters retain a measure of mystery that lends dimension.

It would be fair to say that this is a reasonably "faultless" first novel, carefully observed, self-scrutinizing without excessive self-consciousness, and written so seamlessly that you don't really notice the writing. Is it also fair to criticize a novel for being somehow too perfect? McFarland's professional polish seems less a personal trait than a characteristic acquired from repeated and prolonged immersion in professional writing programs. The well-tempered but undistinctive style of his writing is suitable enough, but one suspects it would suit almost any other young novelist just as well.

For all its virtues, *The Music Room* remains a novel that inspires appreciation and respect rather than astonishment and delight. *Pace* the hyperbolic publicity material, it is hardly (and I quote the encomium by storyteller Frank Conroy) "the kind of book you press into people's hands telling them if they don't read it you'll never speak to them again."

Insofar as one's friends may have qualities that make them irreplaceable, and this novel, though valuable, does not, I, for one, would think twice before presenting them with the alternative.

> *Merle Rubin, "Stinking Drunk, and in Front of the Kids," in* Los Angeles Times Book Review, *April 8, 1990, p. 8.*

Christopher Lehmann-Haupt

At the opening of Dennis McFarland's beautifully written first novel, *The Music Room,* Martin Lambert, the 29-year-old owner of a record company, is cleaning out his San Francisco apartment. He is in the nursery, which in a happier time he had decorated with "a hundred self-adhesive stars and moons that glowed in the dark (better than any real starlit sky the night I brought my pregnant wife into the room and switched off the light to show her my handmade heaven)."

His wife, Madeline, has gone to live with her mother after her second miscarriage, and he has decided to give up the apartment, where he has pointlessly remained, "a rambling monk with only random visitation rights to my past."

> As I vacuumed away the cobwebs, I discovered that the little stars and moons had become dry over the months, and when I passed the vacuum across the surface of the wall, they let go easily. This was just the sort of thing I needed, the sort of thing I'd been needing for weeks. And as I stood there sucking the stars and moons from the nursery walls, and crying like a baby myself, the phone rang in the kitchen: a detective with the New York City police department's homicide unit, informing me that early that morning my brother, Perry, had fallen to his death from the twenty-third floor of a midtown hotel, apparently a suicide.

Now, as Marty Lambert makes plans to head back East

and learn why his brother chose to end his life, the reader's heart sinks a little. After all, people as complex as Mr. McFarland's characters seem to be tend not to reveal the motives behind acts as mysterious as suicide. One doubts that Marty will succeed in his mission.

But before this problem can do any serious harm to *The Music Room,* the novel's many virtues begin to assert themselves. As Marty flies East, he starts recalling his family's haunted past in a series of tragicomic flashbacks. He is descended from a long line of Italian musicians named Lamberti whose talent has had trouble expressing itself ever since Marty's grandfather, a concert pianist who settled in Virginia and married a tobacco and coal heiress, died with his wife when he crashed his Piper Cub into a mountainside in Colorado.

Marty's father, Rudy, had nursed his minor gift for the piano, married a Las Vegas showgirl, and then dissipated both himself and his fortune. In a typically evocative childhood memory, Marty recalls himself and Perry lying belly down one summer evening on the gentle slope of the front lawn to their home in Norfolk, Va., watching through the windows of the library. . . .

> Mother, whirling, collapses onto a sofa. Father jerks her erect, they both fall against a desk, sending a lamp crashing to the floor, and their immense shadows break across the library ceiling. It's a spectacular thing, and vaguely frightening, and when I turn to Perry, I see no mixture of emotions on his face. He likes it very much.

Meanwhile, in the novel's present, Marty arrives in New York City and goes about the sad business of winding up Perry's affairs. This involves him with Perry's ex-girlfriend, a conductor's assistant named Jane Owlcaster, who faints at her first sight of Marty because of his striking resemblance to Perry, and then proceeds to fall in love with him in what she realizes is a vain pursuit of Perry's ghost.

Past and present interweave as the novel builds to its moving climax. True, nothing dramatically original happens. Marty discovers how destructively his madcap mother has treated his father. He grows increasingly aware of his own unconscious rivalry with Perry. He finds himself sliding into alcoholism. He learns that Perry changed his will shortly before his death. And he sets out to look at the new beneficiary, a special home for abused children in Brooklyn.

But the details of Mr. McFarland's prose are brilliantly vivid, whether they invoke the Lamberts' almost romantically intemperate past, or Perry's doomed search for redemption, or Marty's sometimes comically tortured dreams. "Once, I had a very elaborate Shakespearean dream full of suicide, fratricide, patricide and conspiracy in which all the characters had the brand names of Scotch: MacGregor, Sir Dewar, King Henry IV, Glenlivet and his doppelganger Glenfiddich."

And in the final pages, the family's wasted musical talent is at last put to some redemptive purpose. It's impossible to sum up the details here. But a passage describing the

laying to rest of Perry's ghost conveys a sense of the ending's poetry.

> Then there was an abrupt silence during which something passed through me, something subtle but definite, like the moment when a school of fish turns in precise unison and there's a flash of brilliance from the mosaic of their scales, like a sustained orchestral chord's changing colors: I felt him so dramatically on the stairs that I had to sit for a moment. Immediately I believed that nothing had prepared me for this, and yet somehow I knew to say goodbye. I said it aloud, then closed my eyes and whispered it.

Through an alchemical process worked by the novel's language, Marty has accepted Perry's death and has taken up the burden that was his life.

> *Christopher Lehmann-Haupt, "Peering into a Family's Haunted Past," in* The New York Times, *April 23, 1990, p. C14.*

Josephine Humphreys

It is a rare pleasure when we can yield immediately to a novel—when its invitation is so persuasive as to banish hesitation, eliciting an instant *yes.* The invitation must intrigue, convince, promise—like this one in Dennis McFarland's first novel, *The Music Room:* "In the bicentennial year of our country's independence from Great Britain, a time when I imagined the American masses celebrative and awash with a sense of history and continuity, my wife of only four years decided it would be best for both of us if she moved in with her mother for a while."

The Music Room is a novel of almost organic integrity, and that first sentence sounds its themes: history and continuity, independence and separation. The narrator, 29-year-old Martin Lambert, is a man detached from his own history, his own family. Interestingly, that condition seems to entail detachment from the larger community as well—from those celebrative American masses, a phrase that gains import in the novel's resolution.

Martin's is a family from which one might well wish to detach: alcoholic, wealthy, incapacitated by disappointment. His father, a failed pianist, drank himself to death 10 years before the action of the novel opens; his mother, an ex-showgirl in her 60's, lounges in silk and feathers at the family mansion near Norfolk, Va., under the care of an aging houseboy, getting "house-drunk" with a couple of horrid hangers-on. Some years back, she accidentally burned down the wing of the house containing the music room. Martin and his younger brother, Perry, grew up isolated by wealth and talent, aware from earliest consciousness of the abysmal doom of their own parents, and necessarily bound to each other by love and rivalry. Perry apparently managed to escape to New York and to serious composing. But the paradox of bad families is that the worse they are, the more unlikely is the possibility of escape, except by self-destruction.

When Martin's wife, childless after two miscarriages, leaves him for another man, he cleans out his California apartment. . . . "And as I stood there sucking the stars and moons from the nursery walls, and crying like a baby myself, the phone rang in the kitchen: a detective with the New York City police department's homicide unit, informing me that early that morning my brother, Perry, had fallen to his death from the twenty-third floor of a midtown hotel, apparently a suicide."

Perry has left Martin's name as the "person to notify" in case of emergency, and Martin flies to New York to make funeral arrangements. He is gradually drawn into a search, initially for the immediate reasons behind Perry's death but eventually for deeper secrets. At first he wants only "to unclutter the thing. I wanted it to be tidy, without echo."

But nothing in this novel is tidy or without echo. Martin's memories come fast and unbidden. Flashbacks are hard to handle even for the most experienced of novelists; they run the risk of flashing, and of distracting attention from the story's flow. But here they are muted and dreamlike, told in the present tense. If the technique seems too clever (present action rendered in past tense, past in present), it nevertheless works—often stunningly, as in Martin's early memory of lying with Perry on the lawn at night, the boys 9 and 5 years old, watching the lighted windows of their house. . . .

Mr. McFarland runs many risks, taking on some of the most difficult (and important) tasks a novelist can choose: the search into childhood for secrets of identity, the depiction of alcoholism and shocking parental failure, the interior landscape of a troubled mind, the mystery of self-knowledge. Yet even as the novel probes these various recesses, it retains a generous, hopeful and often comic underpinning, which does not falter. In the darkest moments there may be hope; in the worst of families there may be great love and the opportunity for redemption.

Strangely, Martin experiences not only flashbacks but flash-forwards. Bits of the future appear in premonitions and dreams; once, he is able to see the future as it might have been. Always these glimpses seem perfectly credible, evidence not of clairvoyance but of the subconscious at work, struggling for understanding. At the same time, events move forward at a fast pace. In New York, Martin falls in love with Perry's lover, Jane; he inherits Perry's dog, tracks down Perry's psychiatrist, and eventually discovers what, in the final days of his life, Perry had been doing. He begins to think Perry might be trying to contact him from beyond the grave. Returning twice to Norfolk, he uncovers ancient memories and new truths about himself, as well as his mother. And it is an accomplishment of a skilled novelist to be able to show that Helen Lambert, in spite of her maternal incompetence and what can only be called family crimes, has an inner strength all her own, and actually turns out to be somewhat endearing.

What is most magical about *The Music Room* is its fabric: thick, rich, mysterious, *true*. Constructed like a detective story (an unexplained death, a detective, clues to a buried past) and pressing forward with the detective story's speed, it is nevertheless an opposite of that genre. Instead of narrowing to a solution, it opens onto territory unforeseen, and revelations larger than those that might have

been expected. The story of Perry's death is not like the tabloid stories his mother has clipped from papers, "nutshell suicide stories," as Martin calls them, "immediately comprehensible—anybody could see the reason in them at a glance—the grisly harbored secret, the terrible twist of fate. That was the sort of answer I had wanted, and the sort I was not to have."

In fact, it is a premise of *The Music Room* that answers are complex and lives are surprising, even the parts that are over and the parts that are yet to come. Past and present and future are beautifully layered, impinging upon one another and shifting unexpectedly, so that the resulting perspective is finally as comprehensive as possible. In one startling realistic scene after another, with evocative description and a fluid, natural language, *The Music Room* itself builds to a comprehensive vision, remarkable from its beginning to its surprising, satisfying end.

Josephine Humphreys, "Secrets Deeper than a Brother's Death," in The New York Times Book Review, *May 6, 1990, p. 11.*

Dennis McFarland   [Interview with Max Berley]

It was music—which plays a large part in Dennis McFarland's first novel [*The Music Room*]—that led him, indirectly, to consider a career as a writer. "I didn't become a writer the way a lot of other people do, because I grew up in a home where there were a lot of books or because I read a lot. I only took one English class in college," he admitted in a telephone interview from his home in Watertown, Mass.

"I became a writer when I realized, after studying piano and musical composition, that I had a debilitating case of stage fright and could never perform in public. I knew that I needed to do something that took place in a room by myself."

The 40-year-old author describes the "hysterical reception" of *The Music Room*—which has been greeted with a six-figure movie option and rave early reviews—as exceeding his "wildest dreams and indeed well beyond the expectation of any author publishing a first novel."

"When they see a well-received book by an unknown," Mr. McFarland said, "a lot of aspiring writers think that you succeed as a writer overnight. You don't. It took me 10 years of hard work to learn to be able to write this way. Writing involves a lot of privations, anguish and hard work."

Mr. McFarland, who teaches writing at Emerson College, said that he believes his novel responded to a "hunger and desire" on the part of readers for literature "more complicated and richer in detail" than the minimalist style that has dominated American writing in the past decade.

Moreover, in his view the appeal of *The Music Room* stems from its emphasis on family relations. "It's basically the story of a family that had big troubles and addictions. The effects of these troubles have been long-lasting and devastating. This description would fit an enormous percentage of American families, and people find resonance in these problems."

Dennis McFarland, "We Owe This Book to Stage Fright," in an interview with Max Berley in The New York Times Book Review, May 6, 1990, p. 11.

An excerpt from *The Music Room*.

Marion is seated on one of the couches, facing the piano, holding Perry in her lap—clearly against Perry's will, which is considerable now that he is nearly two. In addition to quite a bit of English, Perry has acquired a repertoire of grunts and squeals that sound as if they come straight from a medieval torture chamber. He rehearses a number of these as he writhes and fidgets and strains in Marion's lap.

Father, with a whisky just to the right of the music stand, is giving a piano recital, annihilating a Beethoven sonata, making slush of passage work and banging out chord clusters (instead of the written chords) in the melodramatic manner of a very large-scale loser. When Perry sees me, he wrestles free of Marion and runs toward me, shrieking; as Marion lunges for him, he stumbles, his chin connecting audibly with the hardwood floor. Father's piano stops abruptly, and somehow he manages to upset the tumbler of whisky, which crashes to the floor and explodes in a starburst of glass splinters. Father curses, Marion calls out a warning about the broken glass, Perry screams at a pitch that could open graves—a pitch reserved for serious pain—and from somewhere upstairs Mother's voice cries, "What was that? For God's sake, what's happened?" Though it is not yet three in the afternoon, she has already begun the extensive ritual that will culminate in whatever plans she and Father have for dinner that evening, and when she appears in the doorway of the music room, she is wearing a lavender dressing gown and an abundance of fragrance. Marion has got Perry into an upright position, and then there is this moment—the sound of Father's piano still ringing in our ears, the room reeking of perfume and whisky—this moment in which everyone in our family converges on Perry, and we partake in a small struggle for actual possession of him: a confusion of hands, a repetition of the word "come," I hear my own voice saying, "Let him go!" and Perry is in my arms—I am running with him out of the room, out the front door, and down the lawn toward the line of dark cypress trees that signals the beginning of our neighbor's horse farm and the end of our yard, the end of our parents' property.

David Gates

Since about the only glaring period detail in ***The Music Room*** is a police detective's wide paisley tie, why does Dennis McFarland bother to set his book back "in the bicentennial year of our country's independence"? (These are the first words in this first novel.) The bad reason: easy irony. The narrator's wife has left him (independence, get it?) at "a time when I imagined the American masses . . . awash with a sense of history and continuity." The subtler reason: to suggest the narrator, a good—not great—cellist named Martin Lambert, must have remained sturdy enough to survive the events in the book for over a decade.

We soon have reason to worry—on page two, Martin learns his brother has committed suicide—but McFarland's beginning amounts to a happy ending.

Those first two pages are enough to show that McFarland is a brilliant writer with an occasionally heavy hand. Martin gets the call about his brother Perry as he's vacuuming "self-adhesive stars and moons" off the walls of what was to have been a nursery before his wife miscarried. Images of the moon keep coming back: a pair of doorbells are "lit ivory like little moons." And children and parents are the central obsession. While trying to find out why Perry killed himself, Martin learns that their mother tried to abort Perry, that Perry's girlfriend is pregnant and that Perry had been working with abused children. And he comes to recognize that he himself has inherited his parents' alcoholism.

Martin's cosmos disintegrates in the big bang of the first two pages, but McFarland is a Divine Watchmaker of a novelist. He balances character against character: competent cellist Martin and gifted composer Perry, Martin's cheating wife and Perry's faithful girlfriend, a kindly effeminate houseboy and a selfish, drunken gay houseguest. He prefigures Perry's plunge from a hotel window with his earlier dive from a cliff into dangerously shallow water. (Perry had also made a leap of faith; he'd taken to attending a socially activist Roman Catholic church.) Near the beginning of the novel, Martin waves at a white-clad nurse in a distant window; she turns away. Near the end, he sees another nurse in another window who waves "a friendly hello."

Some of these symmetries—the nurses (who don't figure in the plot) and the one-chance-in-365 coincidence that Martin and Perry share a birthday—are just gewgaws. And here in the real world, we could all use a Creator as attentive as Martin's, who throws in his path an abused-child cellist needing tips on left-hand technique. But McFarland more than compensates for first-novelistic excesses with dialogue you can hear—especially in the drunk scenes—and detail you can see. A desk in a precinct house is "one of those sad gray metal obstructions with a rubber-coated top scored by countless fingernail gashes." Best of all, you care whether Martin stays sober, whether Perry's child gets a good upbringing. There's no Dickensian last chapter telling what happened to everybody, but—since this *is* a modern novel—if things had gotten worse we would have heard.

David Gates, "The Writer as Divine Watchmaker," in Newsweek, Vol. CXV, No. 22, May 28, 1990, p. 74.

Robert Towers

[McFarland's ***The Music Room***] is commended by many worthy writers, among them both the late patriarch and the current doyenne of Southern literature, Walker Percy and Eudora Welty. One reader is reminded of listening to Mozart; another read it in a condition that he said could only be described as rapt; still another said she was made to catch her breath by some of the writer's sentences and even by a mere word. The reviews have been equally praising.

Narrated in the first person by a young man named Martin Lambert, *The Music Room* begins with a string of misfortunes. . . . The telephone rings with the news that his younger brother Perry has fallen from the twenty-third-floor window of a Manhattan hotel, apparently a suicide. Martin himself is clearly in a very shaky condition. As he hurries to New York and sets about trying to understand what could have led his twenty-five-year-old brother to kill himself, his dreams begin, in their frequency and intensity, to verge on madness, while much of his recorded action consists of draining a glass of Scotch and pouring himself another. His inquiries involve him not only with Perry's girlfriend, Jane Owlcaster, and other friends in New York, but with a fragmented search for his own past.

Memory rushes in, with scenes (painful or lyrical or both) from the family's house in Norfolk or at the cottage in Newport where his alcoholic parents led their futile, self-indulgent lives. The father, Rudy, is a failed musician who has inherited millions from his mother, a Norfolk coal and tobacco heiress; his wife, Helen, is a former chorus girl whom he met at a craps table in Las Vegas. The father secludes himself in the music room playing Schubert sonatas and drinking, while the mother plays cards and gets "house-drunk" with two repellent hangers-on. The two boys, alternately neglected and indulged, cling together. Marty is fiercely protective of Perry, who at sixteen is a "dead ringer" for James Dean; furthermore, the brothers look so much alike that people often mistake one for the other. By the end, Martin, increasingly sodden with drink and recalling the hatreds and resentments of a lifetime, abruptly reforms and goes to work for a refuge for abused children that Perry had supported before his still-unexplained suicide.

In recounting these events, Dennis McFarland displays considerable virtuosity. Again and again he sets up an episode and then leaps away from it, laterally or into the past. When, for instance, Martin gets the initial telephone call about Perry's death, he does not react with anguish or incredulity but instead:

> Stupidly, I asked the man to hold the line for a moment. I returned to the nursery, then moved to the French windows that overlooked the garden. On the south fence, a hummingbird darted in and out of a passionflower vine, and in a distant window . . . I could see a young nurse in a white uniform and cap; I waved to her, but quite sensibly she didn't wave back, and moved away out of sight. When I returned to the kitchen, I saw that the receiver of the cardinal-red telephone lay on the bare floor. I picked it up and spoke into it. I relied on extreme politeness to get through the rest of the conversation.

This is unexpected and effective (though I'm inclined to question that wave to the nurse). The constant shuttling back and forth—between present and past, between dream and waking reality—is handled with ingenuity. Apart from a shift in tense that seems too schematic—past episodes and dreams are always rendered in the present, present action in the past—the narrative moves forward

smoothly. McFarland evokes the past with strongly registered sensuous detail, as in this account of a teen-age beach party:

> As someone throws more driftwood onto a huge bonfire on the beach, twisted screens of sparks fly up, are caught by the wind, and die. Someone plays white, city-kid blues on a guitar. Couples stroll away and are swallowed up by the blackness outside the circle of fire. Couples return arm in arm. Small groups, mostly of boys, leave—somebody's got dope—and return. Many of the girls and boys are darkly tanned. The sharp smells of the fire and of the sea air dominate, but underneath, there are the sweeter, more tribal odors of coconut oil, cocoa butter, baby oil and iodine.

Yet, despite the cleverness of *The Music Room* and the felicity of some of its passages, I felt throughout a nagging sense of inauthenticity. To a Virginian such as the reviewer, the Norfolk setting, for one thing, is all wrong—topographically, architecturally, botanically, and socially, with its horse farms, stone walls, and a columned house set on a hill. In his effort to achieve a romantically southern effect, McFarland seems to confuse the sprawling suburbs of a city notable for its strip developments, tidal inlets, and a major naval base with the horse country of northern Virginia on the one hand and a Louisiana plantation on the other. A Norfolk debutante in 1923 (Marty's grandmother) would be most unlikely to have had a fortune of $15 million from whatever source, and rich Virginians would not have spent their summers in a twelve-room stone cottage in Newport, however prosperous they were. The Newport settings seem nearly as phony as the Virginian; only the New York scenes ring true.

More important, the inauthenticity extends to the characterizations and to the novel's sentimental ending. The melancholy musician father and the former-chorus-girl mother seem too obviously an incongruous and unlikely pairing. Almost everything they say or do is connected with drinking, which gets monotonous, and their situation is never more than pathetic. While Perry dominates the narrator's thoughts, appearing in vivid flashes as a boy with a gift for the unexpected, his personality never fully coheres, and one is left with a sense of false starts. Martin himself fails to make clear why his immersion in the past should have had such a therapeutic and morally redemptive result as the novel's ending proclaims; the hints in the book that Martin has homoerotic and murderous feelings toward his brother are left dangling. The confrontations that the subject seems to call for are ducked and we are left with a novel in which sleight-of-hand effects take the place of substance. (pp. 45-6)

> Robert Towers, "Inconclusive Evidence," in The New York Review of Books, *Vol. XXXVII, No. 13*, August 16, 1990, pp. 45-6.

Anthony Quinn

A chronicle of disintegration recounted by a young man almost bowed in pain, *The Music Room* manages also to be a spooked testimony of survival. It takes the suicide of his brother Perry to make Martin Lambert retrace his steps through their past, turning out hidden pockets of memory so as to recover the source of his family's wretchedness. The source turns out to be *the* sauce, an addiction which Martin seems to have inherited: Scotch has become the anaesthetic to his sense of failure, recently compounded by the break-up of his marriage. Dennis McFarland conducts us through this emotional wreckage with a sensitivity and assurance that would be noteworthy in any writer—that this is his first novel seems extraordinary.

When a detective from the New York City police department calls to tell Martin that his brother has thrown himself from the 23rd floor of a midtown hotel, the news marks the starting-point of a complicated education in feeling. . . . He begins to discover things about Perry, notably that he had a girlfriend; on meeting her at the police station she faints as though having seen a ghost. In a way, of course, she has: Martin bears a disquieting resemblance to his dead younger brother and, at odd moments in the novel, is actually mistaken for him. Spookier still is the fulminant passion between brother and lover, as if both are trying to make a final connection with the man they loved.

It comes as a further shock to Martin when he learns of Perry's recent conversion to Catholicism, and his involvement in a church support programme, teaching music to local children. In the meantime his thoughts are transported back to childhood days and the cosseted privilege of his parents' home in Virginia. His mother and father hardly seem an ideal match: he is withdrawn, pensive, gentle; she is brittle, insecure and given to vulgar display, a legacy of her years as a Las Vegas showgirl. All they have in common, it appears, is a penchant for travel and a ruinous attachment to drink. Their peregrinations in Europe and decline into alcoholism add up to the kind of neglect that only the very rich can provide for their children. Martin and his brother draw closer as parental attention recedes into a haze of afternoon Scotches round the card-table. He recalls one period, however, when their father tried to pull himself back from oblivion. He took to practising the piano in the music room and gave a handful of public recitals—then Martin's mother intervened and the music suddenly stopped. Martin finds out why, though first he must replay his father's slide into spiritual inertia and financial ruin, which only an early death could relieve: 'Ironically, sadly, it was the impact of his death, not of his life, that endured. His death had fallen on us like a moon falling into the sea whose tides it used to govern—displacing us, setting us loose, sending us thousands of miles apart. And, more or less, we stayed that way'.

These recollections unfold in a series of ghostly tableaux and, couched in the present tense, they are lent an unsettling vividness. McFarland seems to be bringing back the dead in much the same way that old photographs can. Scenes are evoked with a cool, almost draughtsmanlike precision and then replayed at intervals like 'elusive chords from a complicated fugue', as the blurb puts it with unwonted eloquence. *The Music Room* often has the brooding air of a chamber piece written for spectres, though its gloom does not overpower. McFarland's thoughtful characterisation and settings ensure that his

book will not be easily forgotten. Much of the writing is terse and witty, and everyday images are marvellously transformed in a few brief strokes. A downpour on Fifth Avenue, becomes 'A few ruined umbrellas—black fluttering omens of defeat—lay in the gutters, torn, inverted, metal ribs exposed'. Some may object to the story's upbeat ending—its optimism does seem a little pat—but when one contemplates the desolate places it has been, 'up' is perhaps the only direction it could have taken.

Anthony Quinn, "Drinking Song," in The Listener, *Vol. 124, No. 3180, August 30, 1990, p. 23.*

Stephen Amidon

Dennis McFarland's first novel [*The Music Room*] is a mystery story without a solution, a search for answers where the clues bring confusion instead of illumination. The question is simple—why did Perry Lambert, a gifted young music student, jump to his death from the twenty-third floor of a Manhattan hotel without leaving a note? . . .

Martin Lambert is an unlikely gumshoe. At thirty, he seems lacking in clues about his own life, let alone his brother's. Recently divorced, failed as a musician and disillusioned with his work as a record company executive, the only thing Martin seems devoted to is his incipient drinking problem. Yet he is the only one willing to take up the case, which leads him to New York, where he encounters Perry's pregnant ex-girlfriend. Martin breaks the first rule of detective work by falling recklessly in love with her, but she fails to provide either solace or answers. Their short affair, haunted by Perry's ghost, soon dissolves. Martin also discovers that his previously irreligious brother had become a Roman Catholic and left his considerable trust fund to the school for abused children where he gave music lessons. A visit to Perry's psychiatrist is yet another dead end, providing only vague evidence of a "philosophical crisis". A drunken and despairing Martin finally travels to his family home in Virginia, where his alcoholic mother sheds more darkness on the subject.

It is here that Martin's real investigation begins. For the secret to Perry's despair lies not in the plodding accumulation of disparate clues about his last days, but rather in the sifting of the more distant past. He realizes that the causes of Perry's spiritual crisis are to be found in their ruined family and its tangle of love, jealousy and frustration. Their father was a failed concert pianist who drank himself to death before he reached fifty, leaving his sons a legacy of alcoholic doom. Their mother also abandoned them for booze at an early age, regrets her failures as a parent as well as her refusal to let her husband pursue his genius, and harbours a rather laboured "dark secret" which has forever poisoned her relationship with Perry. As Martin relieves his childhood, spent, often literally, as his brother's keeper, he realizes that the evidence for Perry's suicide is as murkily inconclusive as the rest of the torments which wrack the Lambert family. It is a knowledge that allows him finally to drop the case and come to terms with his brother's ghost.

The Music Room is a deeply felt novel that only occasionally sags into bathos. In Martin, McFarland has created a strong narrator, the use of the past tense for current action and the present for flashbacks brings home the idea that it is in the past that Martin's answers really lie. Not surprisingly, the surviving members of the Lambert family—Martin and his mother—are the most effectively drawn, complex and angry sufferers who are left holding the bag after the book's shallower creations, Perry and his father have checked out.

It is only at the end that McFarland fails to sustain narrative power, slouching into sentimentality by having Martin take up his brother's work among abused children. But this only partially detracts from a strong novel which has the courage to avoid answers in order to keep the vital questions very much alive.

> *Stephen Amidon, "Clueless," in* The Times Literary Supplement, *No. 4561, August 31-September 6, 1990, p. 916.*

Seth Morgan
Homeboy

Morgan, an American novelist, was born in 1949 and died in 1990.

Through a frenetically paced narrative, *Homeboy* portrays the picaresque adventures of Joe Speaker, a drug dealer and strip-joint barker in the red-light Tenderloin district of San Francisco. Joe is immersed in the local underworld of drugs, gang violence, prostitution, and pornography, before he is sent to the regional penitentiary after an attempted robbery goes awry. The remainder of the novel chronicles Joe's involvement in brutal conflicts among the prisoners of the institution until his eventual release. Critics perceived strong autobiographical elements in the novel derived from Morgan's personal experience as a drug addict and convict. Although *Homeboy* is occasionally faulted for incongruous language and gratuitous graphic detail, numerous commentators applauded Morgan's use of street vernacular and especially praised his verbal energy and playful neologisms. Deborah Mason asserted: "The great success of *Homeboy* is in the way Mr. Morgan mocks the limits of language to create an unnerving and utterly persuasive rendition of hell, one that affirms him as an important new novelist."

Deborah Mason

If ever the id were to stake out a homeland of its own, it would be the teeming San Francisco nether world of junkies, pimps, drag queens and hookers Seth Morgan conjures up in *Homeboy,* his savagely comic and often brilliant first novel. . . . A former convict with personal knowledge of the San Francisco street drug culture, Mr. Morgan writes with the picaresque authority of a Joycean Hell's Angel.

The novel's early pages depict the citizens of "the Strip" as larger-than-life projections of the fevered images and bizarre impulses that infiltrate our sleep—fun-house mirror versions of what we most desire and fear. Rosemary Hooten is a runaway Valley girl who celebrates her liberation with her rescuer, a biker named Sugarfoot. "Three days later, when she came to, [the] lollisucker of the shopping mall . . . was transmogrified into Rings 'n' Things, shedevil bike bimbo and certified Satan's Slut. Dozens of cheap golden hoops dangled from her ears, nostrils, nipples," and her body was coated with fresh tattoos from neck to ankles—"emblazoned on her schoolgirl tummy . . . a sort of freeway centaur, half mad biker, half flamethrowing shovelhead Harley-Davidson."

Rigoletto La Barba, "a bloatchested dwarf" who is a combination pusher, strip-joint barker and porn-film star, is the owner of Crystal Blue Persuasion, a battery-powered 1962 Impala lowrider tailored to cruise the Strip "just inches above the pavement," and outfitted for seduction with a miniature crystal chandelier and, "next to the ivory Virgin atop the minklined dash, a keyboard on which he could play 'Besame Mucho' [and] 'Don't Cry for Me, Argentina.'"

The Strip's residents mock the straight world even as they service its secret kinks and obsessions to pay for their own—usually a serious dope habit.

Joe Speaker, the eponymous "homeboy" of the title, uses his sinecure as barker for the Blue Note Lounge to hustle the dentists who wear white vinyl loafers and matching belts (known on the Strip as "the Full Cleveland") and to push the plastic bags of heroin he has stashed in his cheek—always reserving one for his own use. He gives away more bags than he sells, usually to down-and-out hookers or burned-out con men.

The venal overlord of the Strip is Baby Jewels Moses, superpimp and snuff-film king, who turns into Joe's bête noir when Joe inadvertently comes into possession of the rare gem Baby Jewels wants—to cover up some messy business of his own.

A literary descendant of William Burroughs and Henry Miller, Mr. Morgan describes in relentless, graphic detail the grisly rituals of drug ingestion at "the Troll's subterranean shooting gallery" and the highly imaginative forms of sexual gratification required by the johns. At other times, he shifts into hallucinogenic prose that ranges from Rings 'n' Things' manic "Valleyshriek" to a rich Joycean patois of double-entendres (a murdered hooker is named Gloria Monday) and sly wordplay (the drag queen Bermuda Schwartze "stood hipshot fixing Joe with a slantendicular dogeye").

The cute names and conspicuous raunchiness could be adolescent. But not on Mr. Morgan's pages: it is in describing the Strip's most lurid abominations that he comes into his own. His style is literary Grand Guignol at its most flamboyant and most refined. He clearly means to shock, then takes the provocation further by casually tossing in a bombshell of outrageous humor—maybe just to be certain that the catharsis has taken before he moves to the next terror.

The juicy irony of *Homeboy* is that despite the fact that its *mise en scène* is the urban sprawl of drugs, AIDS and gang warfare, at its heart it is an old-fashioned novel. Joe may be a dissipated street punk, but he has an impeccable literary lineage: Mr. Morgan has imbued him with the innocence and good-heartedness of Dickens's Pip and Fielding's Tom Jones. *Homeboy* is even a *Bildungsroman* of sorts, the classic coming-of-age novel in which the hero, often an uninteresting young man like Joe, accrues character, nuance and compassion from his adventures in the world (and his liaison with an honest whore like Kitty Litter). Mr. Morgan regularly advances Joe's cause by hairbreadth escapes and near-farcical coincidences of overheard conversations and chance meetings that are the stuff of 18th- and 19th-century fiction.

Like those of his literary prototypes, Joe's adventures are also strongly informed by issues of patrimony. Joe has no idea who his father is but is aided by several mysterious benefactors along the way, most notably—when he is sent to jail—a convict who evokes Pip's protector, Magwitch.

Prison is a self-circumscribed universe few outsiders can even imagine, let alone understand, and most prison authors seem to write not for the elucidation of the reader but for themselves—to reaffirm their survival each day, to make sense of and transcend the brutality around them.

[Mr. Morgan] has created a narrative that is both riveting and fully accessible. With a reportorial eye and a dramatic sense of the absurd, he details the byzantine bartering of information, drugs and kickbacks that it takes simply to survive. He shows the teeming prison yard where San Francisco drag queens and Los Angeles barrio punks, generals of the Aryan Brotherhood and Chinese crime lords converge daily to work out, to reforge loyalties, to take in the gay weddings and, finally, to riot. He creates the extraterrestrial goon squad of Teamster guards swathed in black polyester chain mail to protect them from AIDS-infected blood when they beat the prisoners.

Then, in the midst of this purgatory, Mr. Morgan will suddenly inject a scene so tender, so affecting that the reader is startled. He writes with particular poignancy of Joe watching as two friends—one blind, the other a paraplegic sick with AIDS and chained to his wheelchair—are paraded across the prison yard after they have tried to liberate the rest of "the plaguers." Joe's agony attests to the emotional education he has received in prison, and foreshadows the crucial role he will be called on to play as the book ends.

But with his growing compassion, Joe is never quite so compelling a character as he is a symbol: the freaks and drag queens who surround him—even the villains—are tough competition. There is a stylized, artificial ring to the intimate conversations and inner thoughts that would otherwise round Mr. Morgan's portrait of Joe and help him to emerge as a full-blooded person. It is his observations, not the depth of his persona, that allow Joe to convey the sweep and the fearlessness of the novel's vision.

The great success of *Homeboy* is in the way Mr. Morgan mocks the limits of language to create an unnerving and utterly persuasive rendition of hell, one that affirms him as an important new novelist. (pp. 13-14)

> *Deborah Mason, "Hell's Angels in Purgatory,"* in The New York Times Book Review, *May 6, 1990, pp. 13-14.*

Robert Campbell

[In *Homeboy*] Seth Morgan makes the ugly streets of San Francisco's Tenderloin, the peep shows, naked shows, skin shows; the gonnifs, whores, drifters, dopers, pimps, snuffers, cops and square johns; the prisoners, snitches and guards of Coldwater Penitentiary into mythical characters and places, much larger than life, highly colored, speaking a vivid language in a Hogarthian hell viewed from a very special angle, slightly skewed, sometimes caricatured, the characters all too human.

The jacket biography mentions that Morgan is a survivor of the street drug culture and has served some time. The book is dedicated to Frederick Morgan, his father, and the poem on the quotation page is by Frederick Morgan. If he is the author of such works as *A Book of Change, Death Mother & Other Poems* and *The Tarot of Cornelius Agrippa*—and I feel certain that he is—then Seth Morgan has clearly been given a gift of words at birth.

I'm assuming that the habit he's kicked has been replaced by a better one; here is a writer stoned on words.

Get these characters:

Gloria Monday, a whore murdered for stealing.

Baby Jewels Moses, a monstrous pimp and snuff-film impresario.

Quick Cicero, his henchman.

Rings 'n' Things Hooten, who took a biker's "solemn word that chasing a fistful of Seconals with a quart of Thunderbird was the righteous way to celebrate her liberation," when she ran away from home.

Joe Speaker, barker for the Blue Note Lounge, who robbed one store, killed one man and crossed one power broker too many and ended up in the slam.

Kitty Litter, the trick stripper and love of Joe's life, who waits for his return.

Fay DuWeye, a junkie whore.

Oblivia DeHavilland, a drag queen.

A detective lieutenant of the SFPD named Tarzon, who is haunted by his failure to keep his daughter clean and safe.

LaBelle Cakes, Rooski, Rigo La Barbra, Judge Trepanian, Kool Tool Raul, Whisper Moran, Belly Buster, Mocha Monsoon and Rowdy McGee—you know these are nothing like those gentler folk with quirky monikers created by Ring Lardner or Damon Runyon. These streets are really and truly mean, these folks truly fighting for their lives. All of them are in search of, connected to, held in thrall by a diamond as big as a baby's fist known at the Blue Jager Moon. . . .

Sometimes he goes a word—a phrase—too far. "It was a fire-gutted Victorian on Treat Street, pooled with black water, where wind through the gashed roof dirged and the homeless and hunted found hospice." "He wagged his neckless glabrous head, shivering jowls talced like sugared aspic . . . " "Rings was dancing with herself by the jukebox flaming in the corner when she lamped this prime side of USDA beef at the counter slumped on his forearms . . . "

Sometimes he falls off the edge into language as obscene, scatalogical and pornographic as any I've read, just this side of that line that people argue about and which we all make up our minds about for ourselves. It's language meant to assault your senses and shock your sensibilities, and it's not always necessary to get his message across. But that's okay. When somebody's hitting the piano with a hammer, playing new tunes, you can't start picking individual offending notes and riffs out of the debris. You read it or you don't.

If you read [the novel], you'll have a wild ride and you might even go around with your head chattering with Morgan's outrageous rhythms, the tragic-comic telling of a well-constructed tale, a few fascinating hours spent with people I doubt many of us would want to meet outside of fiction.

If you don't read it, you could be missing something, the first offering of a new talent who writes well and wide and deep and who will, I predict, write with greater and greater control to greater and greater effect for a wider and wider audience.

Robert Campbell, "Stoned on Words," in Book World—The Washington Post, *May 20, 1990, p. 10.*

John Skow

[In *Homeboy*] the boy is Joe Speaker, small-time heroin peddler and barker for the Blue Note Lounge, a scumbucket strip joint in San Francisco's Tenderloin. The home is prison, out of which he is not likely to stay long. This is partly because his dim sidekick Rooski foolishly shot a Chinese druggist when the two of them were fumbling what was supposed to be a peaceful, harmless burglary. The main reason is that Joe belongs in jail, feels comfortable there. Not secure, understand, because dope selling in the lockup is even tougher than it is on the streets. Everyone there is a villain, and every villain has at least a shank, a homemade knife. Black and Aryan gangs feud murderously. Studs and lovers brutalize each other. And Joe, of course, misses Kitty Litter, his stripper girlfriend. But he is an outcast, and jail is where, when you go there, they have to take you in.

Seth Morgan began writing this first novel during a prison term for armed robbery. The cuff marks show, and not just in detail that seems accurate. The novel is funny and fast moving, but its air stinks slightly of decay. As it should. A couple of Nelson Algren's low-life adventures come to mind, such as *A Walk on the Wild Side* and *The Man with the Golden Arm*. Algren was a better writer and a more lyrical artist, but Morgan is better acquainted with dead souls.

There is more than a slight whiff of jailhouse self-pity: Joe loves Kitty, goes to the lockup, survives the schemes of bad villains with the help of good villains, and gets out to find true-blue Kitty and the child he has never seen waiting for him. The best of the book is Morgan's wildly reinvented con lingo. His ear fails him occasionally, when he uses lace-curtain language—"caparisoned," "implacable mien"—that some editor should have yanked from the manuscript with tongs. But at other times he's cooking:

> Saturday night movies in the Gym were the social climax of the week. Everyone put on the Big Dog. The hucklebuckin hambones Afropicked and jerrycurled their cornrows . . . the vatos and street bravos wrapped their cleanest bandannas around Dippity-Doed razorcuts . . . the whiteboys splashed on fifi water . . . the Q Wing punks and B CAT queens greased on party paint and shimmied into tightass state blues.
>
> (pp. 80, 83)

John Skow, "Jailhouse Blues," in Time, *New York, Vol. 135, No. 21, May 21, 1990, pp. 80, 83.*

Aram Saroyan

Hail the conquering literary hero! Seth Morgan's *Homeboy* is a big, densely plotted, lyrically and idiomatically written first novel about sex, drugs and rock 'n' roll, with murder thrown in left, right and center.

An excerpt from *Homeboy*

The Strip itself was awakening; dressing itself in lights, cloaking the stink of backbar rot and curbside garbage with a fresh admixture of popcorn, beer, stray bottled scents. Spitting banks of neon began their nightcrawling, hissing and humming the names: The Casbah, Blue Note, Gaslight Follies, Pepper Patch; Kyoto's Oriental Massage, Fleur de Lis Nude Encounter Clinic, the Tender Trap, Lucky Louie's Sexporium, the One-Stop-Smut-Shop. Everywhere red, yellow, blue, and green bulbs flashed promises as old as they were empty.

The purveyors of these promises were arriving with the rise of a gibbous moon. Dropped from cars and cabs, on foot; strippers lugging gym bags, hookers out for early luck, sleevegartered bartenders masked with professional boredom, barkers wearing loud clothes and practiced leers.

One of these last, a pale joker in his late twenties with slickedback hair, squashed nose, and a nervous smirk, was already at his station in the laserblue neon haze fogging the entrance of the Blue Note Lounge. On the back of his black velveteen jacket was embroidered a dragon amid constellated Chinese characters. A toothpick traversed his mouth in sync with the restless eye gunning the street, identifying in less time than it took to name the hookers, hustlers, thieves, and thugs; pennyweight ponces and flyweight flimflammers; diddyboppers, deadbeats, and dopefiends. Cops he could feel with every sentient fiber; highrollers scent as a shark does blood. . . .

"Murder one," is how Joe Speaker pitched his merchandise to the evening's first customer, a bloatchested dwarf in top hat and tails who barked at the Pepper Patch; adding "Knock yer dick inna dirt," as if Rigoletto's had far to go. A special munchkin was Rigoletto, twice a freak by virtue of a monstrous member which qualified him to moonlight for Climax Produxions, the porno movie mill owned by Baby Jewels Moses.

"Whip me a deuce, homeboy," piped the dwarf.

This familiarity bunched Joe's nostrils. A homeboy was someone you trusted more than money, and Joe trusted Rigoletto less than himself. Not that he hesitated spitting twice in his fist and shaking the dwarf's nubby hand, palming in exchange for his folded twenties the balloons Rigoletto stashed in his mouth by covering it to cough. They stood side by side surveying the populating Strip like livestock bidders sizing up cattle chuting into auction pens.

"Dentist convention in town," the dwarf noted. "Fat City tonight."

"Every night's the same to me," said Joe. By which he meant that Maurice, the Blue Note's manager, no matter how often or eloquently he promised a bonus percentage of gross receipts over a certain figure, always kicked the same lousy fifty dead presidents across the bar at closing. Not that Joe cared. He would have stood each night in the Blue Note's door for free, talking more shit than a Chinese radio—because in between felonies he supported his own oilburning habit slinging the same dope he shot. Barking at the Blue Note was a license to stand in one public spot for eight straight hours without attracting police attention, a pusher's wetdream.

And there was a further bonus. Kitty Litter, his squeeze, stripped at the Blue Note, and Joe pimped her to its customers to make up the nut when he shot more dope than he could sell. For this heroin absolved him of guilt, becoming its own morality. Its fleet sweet spell reprieved Joe of the conscience he couldn't otherwise abide.

Morgan's working-class hero is Joe Speaker, a heroin-addicted pimp and strip-joint barker in San Francisco wanted by the police after a robbery in which his unschooled older partner panicked and killed a man. Joe's main squeeze, Miss Kitty Litter, who performs at the bar he pitches for, is in love with him because, as she explains to him:

> I met a fella who wanted to love but couldn't. He believed in love, he'd just never known it. And watching him I realized I was watching myself, and I seen that wanting to love, struggling for it, is more real than just loving. It's deeper, stronger, more honest. The other's too easy and cheap. For cheap, easy people. The sort who fall in love like falling off a horse. Our kind has to suffer.

As the police close in, Joe sets up his partner, Rooski, who is killed, and his guilt over this act is at the center of the redemptive process that begins with his imprisonment.

Morgan writes in the third person, jump-cutting from place to place, protagonist to protagonist, male to female, with impressive energy and ease. Joe's opposite number is a Lt. Tarzon, a man with a past and an ever-present Hav-a-Tampa Jewel cigar, and by convolutions of the remarkable plot, a second robbery involves the two in a murder that goes to the center of power in San Francisco on both sides of the law, and threatens Joe's life behind bars. Indeed, people die with amazing narrative dispatch in this novel: Getting dropped into a boiling vat, being sodomized, with the collapse of a prison balcony, being decapitated in a pornographic snuff movie.

Morgan writes up a storm, sometimes too literally: "Then thunder cracked the sky like a hammer striking a gourd, spreading electric branches overhead; and the rain fell in fat drops, plucking silver nipples from the flagstones without." One chapter, aptly titled "Hotshot," begins with this howler: "Day broke like a wine cooler smashed suddenly on the curb of the sky, splashing the derelict building with lemon and peach, drenching its concrete crevices cherry, inking the lacework shadows of exterior catwalks and ladderways in grape."

Say what? And when people talk in *Homeboy,* frequently they seem to be setting each other up for zingers, as when Joe tells his friend Earl, the intimate prison photographer who has confessed to him his dream of an armadillo farm: "F Stop, I don't know what's eatin' your brain worse, Alzheimer's or Weisenheimer's."

But these gaucheries are more than balanced by moments when Morgan, who did time himself for armed robbery, writes with clear authority of life behind bars: "I was just thinking," Joe tells Earl, "that the aim of prisons is to correct criminals, make adults out of overgrown children. The first object you'd think would be to force them to stop having fantasy lives. But that's all prison is, fantasy finishing school. I never learned how to direct my dreaming until I got here."

Seth Morgan, 41, grew up on Manhattan's upper East Side and attended Hotchkiss prep school. In 1970, he was a heroin addict and Janis Joplin's dealer and lover. Later a pimp and alcoholic, he eventually went to prison. The upper East Side, it is gradually becoming clear, isn't the optimal environment in which to grow up. This reviewer, who also grew up in that stretch of concrete and apartment buildings a few miles square, personally knew half a dozen suicides who shared the environs. The desolation and poverty of this novel's milieu, while ostensibly at the other end of the social and economic spectrum, seems emotionally and metaphorically parallel.

Over the long haul, there is something sturdy and likable about the hard-writing Morgan and *Homeboy,* a big beast of a novel with a beating and evolving human heart at its center. Morgan's women are awfully simple souls, whores with hearts "as big as Texas" who seem to come out of another era of human relations, and one can quibble with a generally simplistic tendency in most of the other characters portrayed as well. But a novel can fail or succeed on a larger and deeper principle than these details indicate.

Homeboy is full of the reality of human suffering and of a central intelligence taking it in and, by effort and fortitude and simple love of life, moving on. Morgan has come through several hells to make a unique literary debut. Hail again.

> *Aram Saroyan, "Where Day Breaks Like a Wine Cooler," in* Los Angeles Times Book Review, *July 15, 1990, p. 2.*

Nick Hornby

Homeboy is the story of Joe Speaker, a strip-joint barker arrested for armed robbery and sent to State Prison in California. It is a long book—it runs to nearly 400 pages—and quite relentlessly unpleasant in its depiction first of the bleak nexus of prostitution, addiction and violent crime, and then of the mind-bogglingly hellish world of Coldwater Prison. Think of the most disgusting perversion you have ever heard of. Now double it. Nope, you're not even close.

What saves the book from being unreadable is Morgan's ambition. The first few chapters, in which we are introduced to some 30 characters (all with names to die for: Rings n' Things, Baby Jewels, F Stop Fitzgerald) in several different locations, are particularly impressive in this regard; and though he cannot keep all the plates spinning all the way through the book, and has to overstuff the denouement, one cannot but respect him for aiming considerably higher than might have been expected.

There is equal pleasure to be found in the author's command of an extraordinary and bewildering demotic: yegg, jones, halfgainer, ditz, ducat (as in 'How can they ducat me?') gumbas, popstand, psych jacket, kasj . . . maybe I won't bother with the spellcheck after all. . . . There are passages where this reviewer was convinced that he had been inadvertently asked to read the Albanian translation; although Morgan does his best to help us along with some of the more recondite expressions (and in the process lumbers himself with some of the most ponderous dialogue . . . , in which characters explain to each other

technical terms they should have known for years), inevitably many of the lines are left to stand in their own glorious mystery.

There is a quite beautiful exchange between two ironpumping black cons, Moonpie Monroe and Dr Raggedy Mouth, whose chants of mutual encouragement drip with the kind of lewd poetry that would have had Robert Johnson scrabbling for his notebook: 'Pie yous a covershaker / unna sweet slatbreaker / one sweet babymaker / yous a binder Pie / a shonuff grinder / unna weak spot finder . . . cradleshaker / whoretaker / lovefaker'. In the world of Coldwater Prison, this is about as close as they get to the Song of Solomon.

In the end Morgan's affection for his characters provides the book with a series of improbably happy endings, whereby junkies kick habits and settle down with babies, and whores sail off on the arms of policemen, ready to take up office work. (Really!) But there is a unique voice to be heard here . . . , even if *Homeboy* proves to be the only song it can sing. . . .

> *Nick Hornby, "Jailhouse Jock," in* The Listener, *Vol. 124, No. 3178, August 16, 1990, p. 32.*

Julian Symons

[*Homeboy*], though in substance horrific, is in manner distinctly jokey. Seth Morgan, his publisher tells us eagerly, is 'a survivor of the San Francisco street drug culture and a former convict', and ditto his central character, dope addict Joe Speaker. To describe the activities of Joe and his acquaintances Morgan has fashioned a style like that of an addict on a permanent high. The account of how Bermuda Schwartze, headliner at the clip joint where Joe is a barker, got her 'fortyfour triple-D bionic bumpers' is typical:

> Bermuda's barometric bazooms were a standing joke on the Strip to all but her. She'd gotten her boobjob back in the days before implants. A Van Nuys surgeon had simply injected a couple of gallons of silicone into her chest with a syringe the size of a cake decorator. And all he asked in payment was to be strung up by an engine hoist in his garage and sodomised with a caulking gun. 'But you get what you pay for,' Bermuda philosophised: the first cold snap the miracle mammaries lumped up like two sacks of golf balls.
>
> Only when both the thermometer rose and the barometer dropped would the silicone decongeal and jiggle as it ought.

Funny? I thought so, but one can't take too much of it, and too much of everything is what Seth Morgan is out to give us. There are reminders of Runyon, occasional echoes of Chester Himes's [detectives] Coffin Ed and Grave Digger in the dialogue's street-smart cynicism, but the resemblances are superficial. Morgan's book has the form of a thriller which begins when the Fat Man, Baby Jewels Moses, tortures the prostitute Gloria Monday to reveal the whereabouts of a necklace (' "Necklace" the Pimp Bimp coyly simped'), and has her strangled by his sidekick when she hands it over. If one accepts that the animal level of behaviour is right for these people in this place, Morgan's eagerness to describe violence in detail still seems gratuitous (when Gloria dies 'one rolledup eye bulged big as a pingpong ball' and 'the other was sprung from its socket, hanging by optic fibers'), but *Homeboy* is just one among a wave of similarly violent American thrillers, of which the cult novel *The Silence of the Lambs* is the most viciously unpleasant. (pp. 16-17)

Julian Symons, "Dirty Jokes," in London Review of Books, *Vol. 12, No. 17, September 13, 1990, pp. 16-17.*

Charles Palliser
The Quincunx

Born in 1948?, Palliser is an American novelist.

The Victorian setting, sinister characters, intricate plot, and strong moral tone of *The Quincunx* prompted many critics to compare the novel to the works of Charles Dickens. Its protagonist, a boy named John Huffam, struggles to uncover the conspiracies of five families linked by their claims to a vast estate. When John and his mother refuse to surrender the codicil that proves they are rightful heirs, they are threatened by covetous relatives and flee from their rural village to the slums of London, where they descend into poverty and squalor. As he gradually solves the mysteries surrounding his relatives, John is repeatedly betrayed; he is victimized by theft, sent to an isolated prison farm, and apprenticed to a gang of thieves. The product of twelve years of research, *The Quincunx* was praised for its graphic, unsentimental portrayal of early nineteenth-century London and its vivid depiction of the stormy English landscape. Critics were also impressed by Palliser's ability to maintain suspense throughout the novel's length of nearly eight hundred pages. Christopher Lehmann-Haupt stated: "The detail and the language of *The Quincunx* are overwhelming in their richness. And one is swept along by those enduring emotions that defy modern art and a random universe: hunger for revenge, longing for justice and the fantasy secretly entertained by most people that the bad will be punished and the good rewarded."

Quincunx," in Booklist, *Vol. 86, No. 5, November 1, 1989, pp. 498-99.*

Denise Perry Donavin

[In Charles Palliser's *The Quincunx,* a] quincunx of roses makes up the family crests for the Huffams, Mompessons, Palphramonds, Maliphants, and Clothiers, clans linked by a bewildering chain of inheritance and murder. The quincunx is also is a symbol that comes to mean calamity for John Huffam and his mother, Mary, who seek sanctuary from family pressure and greedy relatives. Mother and son move from a comfortable home and three servants in the English countryside to London, where the theft of nearly all of their possessions and the perfidy of their relations drive them into a squalid domicile and life-style. Regency England at its worst is on display here, while readers observe John's search for answers and allies. Many will be enchanted by this lengthy tale of power, deceit, and passion; others will fail to wade through even one family history to uncover the calamitous links among them all. (p. 499)

Denise Perry Donavin, in a review of "The

Kirkus Reviews

Palliser's first novel [*The Quincunx*] is an extraordinary achievement: a triple-decker (800-page) Victorian pastiche, obviously modeled on *Bleak House,* unfolding the staggeringly complex tale of young John Huffam's attempts to ward off ruin and death until he can solve multiple family mysteries.

Everybody wants the codicil to long-dead Jeoffrey Huffam's will. But since John's mother Mary refuses to sell it to the lordly Mompessons (who want to destroy it before it impeaches their claim to Jeoffrey's estate) or surrender it to her mysterious enemy (who will inherit the estate if he can place the codicil in Chancery and arrange to outlive John and Mary), everybody sets out to get it by fair means or foul, ruining them through gullible Mary's weakness for speculation and driving the two from their modest country home to London—where they find poverty, illness, and death, all described with a wealth of period detail. Every revelation of a new branch of John's grasping family—the Clothiers, the Palphramonds, the Malaphants—brings new threats to John, betrayed at every turn by false friends who steal his property, apprentice him to a gang of thieves, send him to an isolated prison farm to die, and commit him to a madhouse. Coincidences turn out to be the product of intricate conspiracies, relatives ceaselessly using John to get at each other as he narrowly escapes a kidnap attempt; gets nailed into his father's coffin; toils for pennies in the London sewers; and keeps taking refuge with precisely the wrong people. Meanwhile, the Chancery tug-of-war becomes more and more tangled—until promised revelations of who killed and defrauded whom and what John's connection is to the Regency social fabric that's been rotting around him all along bring his grandly interminable tale to an end.

Exhaustively researched and exhaustingly plotted. If you've been longing for a new Wilkie Collins, this will keep you stylishly bamboozled for a week. (Illustrated with maps and genealogies—and you'll need them all.)

> A review of "The Quincunx," in Kirkus Reviews, Vol. LVII, No. 22, November 15, 1989, p. 1627.

Cynthia Johnson Whealler

[In *The Quincunx*], Palliser combines an eye for social detail and vivid descriptions of the dark side of 19th-century London with a gift for intricate plotting and sinister character development reminiscent of 19th-century novels. He weaves a complicated tale of a codicil containing a crucial entail, the possible existence of a second will, and a multiplicity of characters—all mysteriously related—seeking to establish their claims to a vast and ancient estate. Related by a young boy who often appears too worldly for his sheltered upbringing and wise beyond his years, the story occasionally bogs down in innuendo and detail which become tedious rather than suspenseful. Nevertheless, overall, this is a gripping novel. Highly recommended. (pp. 173-74)

> Cynthia Johnson Whealler, in a review of "The Quincunx," in Library Journal, Vol. 114, No. 20, December, 1989, pp. 173-74.

Publishers Weekly

The epic length of this first novel [*The Quincunx*]—nearly 800 densely typeset pages—should not put off readers, for its immediacy is equal to its heft. Palliser, an English professor in Scotland, where this strange yet magnetic work was first published, has modeled his extravagantly plotted narrative on 19th-century forms—Dickens's *Bleak House* is its most obvious antecedent—but its graceful writing and unerring sense of timing revivifies a kind of novel once avidly read and surely now to be again in demand.

The protagonist, a young man naïve enough to be blind to all clues about his own hidden history (and to the fact that his very existence is troubling to all manner of evildoers) narrates a story of uncommon beauty which not only brings readers face-to-face with dozens of piquantly drawn characters at all levels of 19th-century English society but re-creates with precision the tempestuous weather and gnarly landscape that has been a motif of the English novel since *Wuthering Heights*. The suspension of disbelief happens easily, as the reader is led through twisted family trees and plot lines. The quincunx of the title is a heraldic figure of five parts that appears at crucial points within the text (the number five recurs throughout the novel, which itself is divided into five parts, one for each of the family galaxies whose orbits the narrator is pulled into). Quintuple the length of the ordinary novel, this extraordinary tour de force also has five times the ordinary allotment of adventure, action and aplomb.

> A review of "The Quincunx," in Publishers Weekly, Vol. 236, No. 24, December 15, 1989, p. 56.

Peter Parker

[Palliser's *The Quincunx* presents] almost 800 closely-printed pages, some 120 characters (listed alphabetically at the back), street maps, family trees, heraldic devices, and a plot that twists and turns with the speed, skill and unexpectedness of an international wing-quarter. There is not a single slack passage or dull page in the entire book.

Set in the early 19th century, the novel is subtitled *The Inheritance of John Huffam,* and follows the young narrator's adventures as he gradually uncovers a complicated and lethal network of conspiracies concerning ancient wills and codicils. Each of the books which make up the novel is named after one of five interconnected families, all of whom have an interest in a valuable estate, and at the end of each book there is a revised family tree, with a few more branches filled in (readers are urged not to peek in advance). John's age is never given, but when the novel opens he is still in the charge of a nursemaid, and lives with his mother in a village. A succession of mishaps force the family to give up their home and travel to London, where their fortunes decline still further as they percolate through society right down to its pitiful and brilliantly realised dregs.

Palliser has great fun in supplying and withholding material, so that vital parts of the story come piecemeal or in garbled form: a confused, misspelled journal kept by John's mother, from which essential pages have been torn, or the recollections of a crazed old man who muddles generations. Indeed, although *The Quincunx* is ostensibly a reverent pastiche of a 19th-century novel—employing archaic spelling, inventive illiteracy ('crowner's inkwich' for 'coroner's inquest'), and a great deal of thieves' slang—the author subverts the very genre he is celebrating. Dickens is the most obvious model ('John Huffam' being Charles Dickens' middle names), and parts of the book are more-or-less straightforward borrowings from *Nicholas Nickleby* (the appalling Yorkshire 'school,' which is Dotheboys Hall without the laughs, *Oliver Twist* (the criminal underworld) and *Bleak House* (a long-running Chancery case). Palliser creates vivid characters, but he disdains Dickensian comic caricature; the book's humour lies rather in the way the author raises expectations (luring the reader as skilfully as his characters gull the unfortunate Huffams) only to confound them.

For instance, the splendidly colourful gang of criminals with whom John becomes involved owe something to Fagin and Sikes, but the boy's rescue by a well-to-do family takes the Brownlow strand of that novel and turns it on its head. Although Palliser filters most of the novel through John's consciousness without authorial interference, there are moments when the reader is clearly expected to find the boy priggish, pompous and humourless. When, as a street-trader of dolls, he is warned off someone else's patch, he assures the reader: 'Indignant at this threat to the native liberties of an Englishman, I continued to sell.'

In spite of this, John remains a sympathetic character, a true innocent abroad. Unlike most of the characters, he is not motivated by rapacity, but by a desire to see justice done: 'Only justice gave the world back a pattern, for without it there was nothing but incoherence and confusion.' Quite what constitutes justice is one of the searching questions this intelligent entertainment explores.

The novel took 12 years to research and write, and not least among its many pleasures is Palliser's remarkably (but unobtrusively) detailed recreation of early 19th-century life: the social hierarchy below stairs in an aristocratic household, Law and Equity (the novel's guiding principles), sewers and lunatic asylums, crime and punishment, death and burial, and the hand-to-mouth existence of a vast proportion of the population. Strong wrists may be required to read *The Quincunx,* but not strong stomachs, for although Palliser depicts a society that is brutal and squalid, he avoids the cardinal Dickensian fault of sentimentality. The novel's resolution is both exciting and entirely satisfying without being (in the traditional sense) a happy ending.

The Quincunx may be an historical novel, but the world Palliser presents so graphically, where greed is paramount and losers go to the wall, is horribly familiar; while a society whose finances rely upon dubious shareholdings, bill-dealing and vast loans against 'expectations' is uncomfortably close to the current economic climate of junk bonds, 'financial futures' and limitless credit at extortionate rates.

Dickens believed that his Christmas books in particular might shock people into a more compassionate outlook on life. Perhaps a copy of this extraordinary novel should be sent as a Christmas offering to Number 10 Downing Street?

> *Peter Parker, "God Bless Us, Every One," in* The Listener, *Vol. 122, No. 3145, December 21-28, 1989, p. 67.*

An excerpt from *The Quincunx*

Now I was hungry and the fact that I had no money forced me to think about my future. I thought of the vastness of London with its teeming millions close-packed in streets and squares, or tiny courts and alleys. In all that huge crowd—each member of it preoccupied with his selfish concerns—I knew nobody to whom I could apply for aid, nobody who cared whether I lived or died, nobody at all—except perhaps Miss Quilliam, and she could do little enough for me. My head spun at the thought of the huge, meaningless, uncaring city around me and at the realization that I had no idea what to do next. Justice! That was the idea to hold onto. Only justice gave the world back a pattern and therefore a meaning, for without it there was nothing but incoherence and confusion. I would go to Miss Quilliam and perhaps she would help me to secure justice against the Mompessons, for they had done her harm; and with this thought I set out for Coleman-street.

As I was hurrying through Soho I noticed on a high narrow house in a dark street a brass door-plate bearing the legend "James Lampard: School of Anatomy". I remembered that name on Isbister's lips and now I understood what the point of his dreadful trade must be. I could not shake the thought of it off, and as I walked along I saw all those I encountered as pigs, brutal animals, self-interested, creatures of mere appetite. I did not wish to belong to such a race. Everywhere I saw jowls heavy with self-satisfaction, starched linen framing faces of utter bestiality, bare arms displaying jewelled bracelets. Perfumed beasts, animals strutting in stolen finery—that was all my fellow beings seemed to me.

Don G. Campbell

[For] a research job that really blows the mind, dip into Charles Palliser's slice of early-1800 England, *The Quincunx.* A quincunx, incidentally, is a geometric pattern of five designs—one in each corner and one in the center, as on the No. 5 die in a set of dice—which runs throughout this first novel by English scholar and lecturer Palliser. While this is the story of young John Huffam and his efforts to unravel the mystery of his birth, the circumstances of murder involving his grandfather and the hanky-panky of his own disinheritance, the real protagonist in *The Quincunx* is London and the English countryside as they were at the birth of the 19th century.

In mood, color, atmosphere and characters, this is Charles Dickens reincarnated—the grinding poverty of the homeless in London's slums, the acrid pall of smoke from open fires, the stench of a city without sanitation. It's a complex plot of dirty deals, land scandals and murder, and little John, time and again, is in danger of his life as he skirts the fringes of London's underworld and toils 20 hours a day as the lowest-of-the-lowest in the household staff of a wealthy family—all the while in search of the elusive truth of his past. And what wonderful names—Digweed, Bellringer, Limpenney, Umphraville, Thackaberry, Vamplew. It is an immersing experience. You're there . . . you feel the biting cold of the London winter with only a thin shirt on your back . . . the terror of being caught in the tides of London's underground sewers. The 12 years that Palliser spent researching the period pay off handsomely in a remarkable book.

> Don G. Campbell, in a review of "The Quincunx," in Los Angeles Times Book Review, January 21, 1990, p. 12.

Charles Palliser [in correspondence with *CLC Yearbook*]

[*CLC Yearbook*]: *Comment on the process of writing the work, including the amount of time it took to complete, your writing habits, the process of revision, and significant editorial input.*

[Palliser]: I was writing **The Quincunx** for about twelve years—though for much of that time I was doing other things as well. (In fact, I began making notes for it even earlier than that: at least as early as 1974. In a sense it goes back to an idea I had when I was eighteen.) Only for the last five or six of those years was it my sole project.

At one point I worked for three years (off and on) on the storyline alone and ended up with a synopsis that ran to 80,000 words. I also compiled an account of the action of the novel in chronological order so that there would be no inconsistencies in the chronology. At a certain stage the novel was about 750,000 words long but I cut a lot of material out.

I wrote **The Quincunx** in long-hand and had it typed, until about 1983 or 1984 when I switched to using a word-processor. I found this a miraculous improvement to the drudgery of writing and re-writing. This is probably because I am an endless, obsessive reviser and rewrote every sentence in **The Quincunx** many times.

There was virtually no editorial input. My editor for the first publication saw the book for the first time when it was complete and wrote only two pages of notes. When the book went into paperback for the first time, another editor contributed a couple more pages of notes.

The answer to the question of why I wrote the book is not easy. One reason is that, as writers often say, it wouldn't let go until I had written it. That is to say, I felt that all those people and events had happened and needed me to make them accessible to other people. And once I'd started I wanted to find out more about the characters I had discovered. Though it sounds rather winsome, I didn't really think of it as inventing but rather as a process of finding out about people and things that were real.

Another reason I wrote the book is that I wanted to recapture the intensity of my first reading of Dickens (and other Victorian novelists) as a child. There was also my admiration for the ingenuity of Wilkie Collins and my interest in the intricate plotting of the best detective novels.

In a sense, too, it was the crystallisation of ideas I'd had most of my life. I've long been interested in the idea of "family oral history"—the accumulation of information and stories that is handed down and the way children are made full members of a family by being initiated into the mythology. And it is a mythology rather than a history,

for the family's "oral history" is always characterised by suppressions and distortions.

And so this connects with the issue in the novel of the extent to which my hero, John's, destiny is determined for him before he is born because of the way he is born into an existing situation over which he has no control. In the course of the novel he searches for freedom which he imagines to involve full knowledge of the past. But in the process of seeking this knowledge, it might be said that he in fact—paradoxically—enslaves himself by taking over a collection of responsibilities and commitments. This has, I hoped to suggest, both positive and negative implications for him.

There was also my interest in that period which has no simple name because it falls between other, better-defined, periods and so gets one or other awkward label: Late Regency, Late Georgian, or pre-Victorian. What interests me is that it was a time when so many of the reforms that made Victorian England seem to be the beginning of the modern era were only just being introduced. So there was still a medieval system of local government and administration of justice, virtually no central state government authority, and an economic system untrammeled by laws protecting workers or consumers. In the social history of the period there are rich pickings for a novelist: the madhouses, the horrific poverty, the widespread prostitution, the huge class differences, the brutality of the penal system, etc. But what makes it particularly interesting is the emergence at that time of a strikingly modern consciousness. So you have the striking contrast between a near-medieval barbarism in many respects and a newly-awakened modern conscience associated with Romanticism and the Religious Revival—Methodism and Evangelicalism. This means that you have all these terrible things along with people who have almost our own horror at them.

Relate the terms of any background research you conducted.

I do my research in two stages: First I make a broad sweep in the earliest stages in order to avoid making fundamental errors when I'm structuring the plot. Then once I start to work on the novel, I find out what I am going to need to know in more detail and then go back later to search for specific bits of information.

As well as looking for specific things, I'm also on the alert for bits of "local colour". I try to incorporate bits of actual historical reality—expressions and vocabulary of the period, names (none of which I invented in **The Quincunx**), and places. In the case of that novel, I needed to feel that it all could have happened even though it didn't actually occur. So I followed my characters around London on actual maps of the period.

Because I find the past so fascinating, I find it difficult to balance the need to remain open to new discoveries against the danger of being side-tracked. For example, while writing my first novel I came across an actual *Diary of a Resurrectionist* which had been written by a real grave-robber in about 1812. This cost me about a year's extra work because I could not resist the temptation to make use of it.

For that novel, I must have read all or parts of several thousands works. Apart from fiction of the period, I read academic history, contemporary letters and diaries, autobiographies, newspapers, etc. I also studied paintings and engravings as a way of picking up information and getting insight into the "mind-set" of the period.

How is your experience incorporated into your fiction?

I use my own experience only very indirectly, if at all. This is because one of the main impulses that drives me to write is the desire to find out what it's like to be someone wholly different from myself, or to see how someone rather like me would behave in circumstances totally different from any that I've ever encountered.

Was there a particular event or person that inspired you to compose this work?

Far too many things over a very long period lay behind the impulse to write *The Quincunx* for me to be able even to begin to list them. In the case of *The Sensationist* [Palliser's second novel, published in the United States in summer, 1991], however, the very clear starting-point was a very vivid dream I had of being in a tall building at a party and looking out at a vast city. In the novel, although there are several dreams recounted, this becomes an actual incident.

What do you hope to accomplish through your writing?

One of the strongest motives that drives me to write is curiosity. I write in order to find things out. In the most obvious sense, writing lets me research things I don't know about already. (I sometimes think it's no more than an excuse to read the books and visit the places and meet the people I am already interested in.) But in another sense, writing enables me—or, rather, requires me—to find out things that I already know. It's a way of forcing myself to think hard about difficult issues, to try to go beyond the evasions and half-truths that I'm satisfied with in my own life but which are ruthlessly exposed within a novel.

As you write, do you have a particular audience in mind or an ideal reader?

My ideal reader is usually myself, so I try to imagine what it would be like to be me but not to have written what I'm writing.

Whom do you consider your primary literary influences, and why?

I admire dozens of writers—living and dead. Some of the ones I admire most have probably not influenced me very much—unfortunately! (I'm afraid I can't plausibly claim Shakespeare, Dostoyevsky, or Joyce as precursors.) The ones I've consciously tried to learn from are the great craftsmen: Flaubert, James, Conrad, Faulkner, Waugh. Obviously while I was writing *The Quincunx* I immersed myself in Austen, Dickens, the Brontës, Wilkie Collins, and Hardy—all of whom I revere. Less obvious writers whom I admire enormously are: Constant, Balzac, Gogol, Zola, Kafka, Golding, Grass, Vargas Llosa, Malamud, Bellow, and Updike.

Describe any works-in-progress.

I am at the moment working on a number of different projects. One of my main preoccupations is with a group of linked novellas whose setting and form are very different from each other. One is set in Hollywood in 1928 and concerns the arrival of the "talkies" and the impact this had on some of those working in the movie industry. Another is set in a railway train in the Highlands of Scotland in about 1915 when circumstances bring together a disparate group of people with some strange and hidden connections between them. Another takes place in contemporary Glasgow and deals with an academic who becomes implicated in a series of gruesome and bizarre murders. Yet another deals with the relationship between a contemporary (popular and successful) novelist and an impoverished writer of talent and integrity. The link between the novellas is that they are all parodies of or exercises in the detective-genre. But I'm not sure yet how many or which of these will be used.

Frederick Busch

Charles Palliser owes everything to Dickens except his novel's title, [*The Quincunx*], which refers to secret codes made of sets of five. Indeed, Palliser's protagonist, John Huffam, is born on Feb. 7—the date of Charles Dickens's birth.

This is the long, long story of a boy contending with the secret forces marshalled against his innocent, loving mother (modeled, surely, on David Copperfield's mother) and against him. Mrs. Huffam dies in the grim London of the Regency (1811-1820). Through John's adventures, we see the fruits of Palliser's long and thorough researches into pre-Victorian England, high and low.

Palliser researched not only the period but Dickens, who, born during the Regency, set his early books in that time. The novel opens (as does each of its five sections) with meetings among the evil forces who contest for a codicil, in Mrs. Huffam's possession, to a will. They discuss how they will steal the codicil or force Mrs. Huffam to sell it to them. It will prove that John Huffam is the heir to a great estate contested in Chancery Court, where it has been fought over for years. The forces, referred to as Arrogance, Society, etc., are declaimed upon by a narrative voice that rants, "we condemn it at the bar of the Court of Conscience that is seated within the breast of each of us!"

Of course, this is Palliser's version of the voice Dickens employs in *Bleak House*—*his* novel about Chancery Court, wills, codicils, conscience, etc. . . . Dickens's anger galvanized his prose, and he was a genius. On Palliser's pages, the voice is at best a nag.

If Dickens did it, Palliser tries it too. For example, the vivifying of the inanimate, a device we associate with Dickens's children when they're frightened, and his murderers in flight—coffins that chase people, say, or a house (in *Little Dorrit*) that "had had it in its mind to slide down sideways." Palliser's version is about an inn that "seemed to lean into the road as if peering sideways for possible customers"; later, cottages must touch "as if each were trying to support itself by leaning against the other."

Palliser uses what he has learned from Dickens's fiction about Regency England, not what he invents or perceives. He makes Dickens-noises well enough, I suppose; but he has no vision, nothing of his own to say that urgently makes new language, images, or events. This is bright recitation, not invention. The orphaned boy who is chased in his terrors through the countryside (*Copperfield*) and the London underworld (*Oliver Twist*) because of greed (all of Dickens), and whose future is governed by a secret (*Great Expectations*) expressed in a legal document (*Bleak House, Dorrit, Oliver Twist*), whose heart is broken by a girl and then woman growing colder, more distant (*Expectations*), with excursions into fallen womanhood (*Copperfield, Dorrit, Dombey and Son*)—this story could be original only if the author had original thoughts that went beyond his research.

He hasn't. But that research is excellent, and you can learn how the London poor worked in the reeking sewers; what downstairs life was like; how the rural poor suffered; the labyrinthine workings of speculation "bubbles"; the desperation of the homeless.

At the end, John confronts his beloved Henrietta near the ruined gardens of the ancestral house. It is Palliser's revisitation of the Pip-Estella scene at Satis House in *Great Expectations*. Pip has become a grown-up; Estella has discovered how to feel. But in *The Quincunx,* John is the same, only older. Henrietta is deranged (and Palliser's fascination with instability and paranoia runs deep). But the characters aren't changed: they were never well-enough established to be changed. That the story stops at page 781 is a mercy, but not a necessity of construction or characterization.

Do salute Charles Palliser for his hard work. Then return to Dickens for the darkness of our lives, and for great prose.

> Frederick Busch, "What the Dickens!" in Book World—The Washington Post, *January 28, 1990, p. 7.*

Paul Gray

[Palliser's *The Quincunx*] is a novel, written during the waning years of the 20th century, that passes itself off as a product of 19th-century British fiction. No fooling. Charles Palliser does not resuscitate this old form—which stretched from Jane Austen to Thomas Hardy—in order to play modernistically with its conventions, as John Fowles did in *The French Lieutenant's Woman.* Never does Palliser's Victorian mask slip to reveal the ex post facto knowledge and anxieties of the present era. Pastiche is not a means to an end but the whole point of this enterprise.

It takes a brave or foolhardy author to court competition with the 19th-century masters, to write an ersatz novel when dozens and dozens of the real things are on the library shelves. That Palliser succeeds in capturing this distant world of Victorian fiction—with its careful plotting and moral punctiliousness—is impressive enough for

openers. That he makes *The Quincunx* a gripping read throughout most of its length is practically miraculous.

Set in England during the 1820s and '30s, the novel is chiefly narrated by a character who first appears as a young boy named John Mellamphy. He lives with his mother in a small village; he has no knowledge of his father, nor does he realize that Mellamphy is not his real surname. Gradually, he comes to understand that his mother possesses something that a number of other people desperately want. It is the codicil to an old, disputed will concerning the immense Huffam estate. The present holder of that property, Sir Perceval Mompesson, wants to obtain the codicil so he can destroy it. But another, mysterious enemy can lay claim to the estate if he can 1) get his hands on the codicil and then 2) engineer the deaths of John and his mother.

These details by no means exhaust the plot; they simply set in motion John's long, arduous journey toward self-discovery. The idea that, somewhere, a powerful person has designs on his life soon changes into an ominous reality for the boy. Strangers try to abduct him. His mother's small inheritance is wiped out through bad investments, all recommended by an attorney who is supposed to protect her anonymity and interests. The two of them are forced to flee from their village and hide in the capaciousness of the capital: "Long before I saw London I smelt it in the bitter smoke of sea-coal that began to prickle my nostrils and the back of my throat, and then I saw the dark cloud on the horizon that grew and grew and that was made up of the smoke of hundreds of thousands of chimneys."

The Dickensian overtones are impossible to ignore. John's situation seems a direct conflation of *Great Expectations* and *Bleak House:* he has the hope that his fortunes may improve and the knowledge that, if he survives, he may spend the rest of his days in fruitless litigation. But his adventures call to mind a host of other Victorian novels as well. He is sent briefly to a Yorkshire school and enters the harsh world of *Nicholas Nickleby;* he overhears a former governess tell her life story, and the events and diction take on the coloration of *Jane Eyre.*

Fortunately, such echoes do not make *The Quincunx* a mausoleum of older books. Palliser brings his scenes, no matter how familiar, vividly to life. John's hunted movements through London expose him to the full expanse of the sprawling city and to all tiers of its society. He appears before the Chancery judge in Westminster Hall and marvels wryly at the pomp: "The Master was wearing a costume in which it was so impossible to believe that he had knowingly attired himself, that it seemed that it was only by a polite conspiracy among his observers that no-one drew his attention to it." At one of his nadirs, the boy searches for coins among the appalling muck of Thames-side sewers.

For all its vibrancy, *The Quincunx* occasionally seems to be too much of a good thing. In order to wring maximum suspense out of each encounter, Palliser allows his narrator some shameless stalling. "Not so fast," one character remarks, when asked a leading question, and the reader is inclined to mutter, "Faster." John's mother is particularly maddening in her refusals to answer her son's questions. A typical response: "No, I won't tell you that. Not yet. One day you'll know everything." Postulate a more forthcoming parent, and the novel would be 200 pages shorter.

Still, patient readers will find their investment of time worthwhile. The book's leisurely pace contributes to the overall effect of uncanny impersonation. Victorian novels were not brisk because people had plenty of time to spend with them. Now it is difficult to go home after work, put some wood in the fireplace, light candles or gas lamps, and settle in for a long, peaceful evening. *The Quincunx* suggests how much fun that could be.

Paul Gray, "A Mask That Never Slips," in Time, *New York, Vol. 135, No. 5, January 29, 1990, p. 74.*

Christopher Lehmann-Haupt

[Palliser's *The Quincunx*] is a novel to get lost in for a year of Sundays. Lost in the best sense of the word, for the story is at times so compulsively absorbing that reality disappears and you find yourself irritated at the people who want you to stop reading and eat dinner. But you get lost in a negative sense too, for the plot gets so complex that trying to keep it all straight makes you feel as if your head were about to explode.

The novel has more than 500,000 words. It has 8 maps of London; 5 coats of arms; 5 genealogical tables, 4 of which repeat the preceding one in progressively greater and more intriguing detail, and an alphabetical list of more than 150 names, which serves as a useful reminder of the book's characters and places whenever you get lost, but never reveals more about them than what the plot has already told.

The story of *The Quincunx* is almost impossible to describe. Simply, it is about a boy named John with great expectations if a chancery suit involving a great estate can be settled in his favor. Impossibly, his chances depend on a piece of parchment in his mother's possession, the codicil to a will that a thousand mysterious enemies seem to be after.

In John's Dickensian first-person narrative, these unscrupulous enemies cheat his naïve mother of her small living and force her to flee with him from a sheltered cottage in the north to the bowels of London. There they are betrayed wherever they turn, and they sink down, down through the lower depths of society; down through cheap lodgings with people who trick John into working with a grave-robbing gang; down through the pits of the London underworld; down, down, until John ends up slogging through the city sewer system, searching through the muck for discarded coins.

Periodically, the author's persona breaks in to address the reader and reveal the evil machinations of various greedy conspirators:

Let us imagine that we are standing, on a wintry

afternoon some years ago, in the west-end of Town. . . . Standing beside us on the pavement is an individual in a shabby great-coat who has the brim of his hat pulled down over his eyes. He is looking up at one of the houses. We, likewise, raise our heads, averting our eyes from the sight of Poverty and gazing instead towards the haunts of Wealth, Arrogance, and Power.

The detail and the language of *The Quincunx* are overwhelming in their richness. And one is swept along by those enduring emotions that defy modern art and a random universe: hunger for revenge, longing for justice and the fantasy secretly entertained by most people that the bad will be punished and the good rewarded.

And on *The Quincunx* goes, with another villain twirling his mustache, with another would-be friend stepping forth to reveal in another endless monologue yet another piece of the ultimate design, which turns out to be not just a single quincunx, but a "quincunx raised to the power of two, a quincunx of quincunxes," which in turn represents the five families whose complex histories end up providing John with the key to his birthright.

How does the author keep it all straight? It must have taken a computer program to track the details. How can he have been sure what the reader would be thinking? Is one supposed always to know so much more than John does? Oh, no. Not another betrayal. Oh, no. How can John be so stupid and trusting?

After a while, it does get a little tiresome. True, John is seasoned by his experiences. As he grows toward his majority, he keeps reaching new stages of understanding. But so many of the characters are so two-dimensional. So many incidents are so melodramatic. "Then this changes everything," a lawyer exclaims on page 750. But everything has been changed so many times that you almost have to laugh at this announcement.

Yet having come so far, you have to keep going, if only to solve the puzzle finally, if only to finish the game of Adventure. And maybe the plot is meant to grow increasingly artificial. Maybe Mr. Palliser is showing off how completely he's hooked the reader, as if he were an animal trainer making a tiger leap with the lifting of an eyebrow.

Is *The Quincunx* worth the huge investment of time? Looking back on it, one sees an antique artifact, a huge pastiche of a Victorian novel combining every 19th-century English writer from Thackeray to Trollope to Hardy. (Near the end, Mr. Palliser even pays homage to *The Return of the Native* by referring to his narrative as "a concatenation of events.")

But you don't recall any particular feeling or mood that the book evokes. You picture 19th-century London, yes, but it's a costumed, museumed London, a London stuffed and mounted for exhibition. You recall John's struggle, but it seems endless and shapeless. What you mainly remember about the book is the sensation of compulsively reading. This may be the whole and successful point of *The Quincunx.* Simply to make you keep reading.

Christopher Lehmann-Haupt, "Farrago of Greed and Deceit in 19th-Century London," in

The New York Times, *February 15, 1990, p.* C25.

Howard A. Rodman
Destiny Express

Rodman is an American novelist, journalist, and scriptwriter.

A fictional account of filmmaker Fritz Lang's last year in Germany, *Destiny Express* relates Lang's anguish over the failure of his marriage to scriptwriter Thea von Harbou and the events preceding his flight to Paris following Adolf Hitler's rise to power. Best known for his films *Metropolis* and *M*, Lang fled Berlin in 1933, following the completion of *The Testament of Dr. Mabuse,* a film banned by Nazi censors. In *Destiny Express,* Rodman embellishes limited biographical information to meticulously describe Lang's daily activities and interactions with other important figures of the period. For example, the narrative describes his purported meeting with Nazi propagandist Joseph Goebbels, as well as his estranged relationship with von Harbou, who collaborated on many of Lang's early works but remained in Berlin to write film scripts under Nazi rule. Many critics praised Rodman for accurately depicting the atmosphere of Lang's films, which often portray bleak urban scenes distinguished by dark shadows and sharply defined geometrical buildings. While some commentators questioned the accuracy of Rodman's historical research, others considered *Destiny Express* a worthy rendition of a pivotal time both in world history and in Lang's life. A critic for *West Coast Review of Books* observed: "[*Destiny Express*] offers imaginative insight into the personal characters of Lang and [von Harbou], allowing the reader to share their detachment and concern over their future in Germany."

Howard A. Rodman

[The following interview was originally published as a press release.]

Why did you choose to write your first novel about [Fritz Lang]?

[Rodman]: I have always been fascinated by Fritz Lang. He would have been one hundred years old this year, and was one of Germany's—and the world's—greatest filmmakers. One of the true pioneers of cinema, his career as a director started just after WWI with *Doctor Mabuse, M,* and *Metropolis*—still considered among the all-time best. He fled Germany in 1933, and eventually settled in Hollywood where, with films like *The Big Heat,* he continued his precise, troubling "film noirs."

What first attracted you to [Lang and von Harbou's] story?

One day, avoiding work, I wandered into a movie theater. It was showing the complete version of the Lang/von Harbou *Doctor Mabuse*. I wandered out, six hours later, with my mind on fire, having seen—as happens all too rarely—a piece of film which changed my life, which commanded me to look at everything with new eyes. I knew, almost at once, that I would have to find a way to render my love for that play of light and shadow—and for all the films which *Mabuse* made possible.

What happened next?

I came upon the famous, wonderful story of Lang's departure from Germany—and sensed that it would make a terrific armature for a piece of fiction. But quite soon after beginning my research I became obsessed with something far more difficult: the relationship between Lang and von Harbou. In short, the two—the most intimate of lovers and collaborators—worked as one for more than a decade, until the Nazis came to power. He left, fleeing the new regime; she stayed and made films for it. How could two people be at once so close and so far apart? And what does that tell us about the films—indisputably masterpieces—that they made together? Films, it must be said, possessed of far more power and genius than either one was ever able to create separately.

What else were you trying to do?

Thea von Harbou was one of cinema's great women—far more talented and complex than the due she's been given by postwar historians. I wanted to rescue her from the neglect imposed upon her by those who could not see beyond her decision—tragic, terrifying—to live and work in Nazi Germany.

How much of the novel is true?

It's a sandwich. Which is to say, all the small details are scrupulously true—the weather, for instance, in Berlin on February 28, 1933. And the grand events—about Brecht, Goebbels, Lang, von Harbou—are also true. But in between—a thick layer of wild, lying fictionification. I wanted to write a book informed by the world of the extraordinary films the two made, without slavishly copying the plots or the characters, of any of them. I wanted, more importantly, to create, in the black of print on the white of paper, a world of light and shadow that would be as haunting and obsessive as my hero and heroine deserve—a world where everything seemed possible, where film could change everything—except, of course, history.

> *Howard A. Rodman, in an interview published as a press release in* News of Atheneum Publishers, *January, 1990.*

Deborah Mason

The last days—of a century, of a civilization, of a love affair—unfold according to the laws of their own mysterious logic, their own persuasive propaganda. Living under the shadow of an ending changes everything: everyday reality suddenly turns thick with clues and symbols, as in ***Destiny Express,*** the first novel by the scriptwriter and journalist Howard Rodman, which tracks the last Berlin days of the film director Fritz Lang.

The novel is set in 1933, when Lang made *The Testament of Dr. Mabuse,* a film that was ultimately banned by Hitler. For Lang, the period was a disorienting twilight in which he was forced to face an ending he had suspected might come, but found agonizing to play out in real life—the end of his film career in Germany, the end of his marriage.

Until then, the director, a cool, imperious Viennese whose monocle, people joked, was removable only by surgery, had reigned as the emperor of German film. Collaborating with his wife, the screenwriter Thea von Harbou, Lang created elegiac monuments such as *Metropolis, Destiny, M* and *Dr. Mabuse the Gambler.* In such films, Lang used his characters' private apocalypses to construct dark parables of the manic, lyrical decadence and the growing depersonalization of pre-Hitler Germany.

With *The Testament of Dr. Mabuse,* Lang's symbolism turned pointedly political. This time, he made his perennial archcriminal Mabuse embody a more pernicious evil, the evil that infiltrates a nation's soul, determined, in Lang's words, "to destroy everything a people holds dear." The new Mabuse, inhabiting the body of a decent man, a Dr. Baum, dictates his orders by phone or from behind a curtain—an anonymous, soulless *Übermensch* who demands absolute obedience from his growing army, well disguised in their bland good-citizen masks.

Within days of the first screenings of *Testament,* everything Lang himself held most dear began to quietly, almost imperceptibly slip away. It is this unraveling of Lang's life that Mr. Rodman embroiders with fiction, and he does this in an extraordinary way: his novel portrays Lang as Lang himself portrayed the central characters in his own dark, feverish movies—as an innocent man whose actions have somehow thrown him into the way of fate. To summon up the miasma of growing dread both in Lang's life and in Germany, Mr. Rodman calls up Lang's arsenal of symbols—ominous grids of slanted light, lush Bauhaus geometry and the surreally menacing streets of Berlin, where what could be a movie arc lamp following an actor turns out to be a police spotlight tracking a man running from the Nazis.

This is a curious book, one that turns on the imperatives and conceits of film making: the image that is the most cinematic, cuts the most dashing figure, always prevails. An enterprise like this is premised, unabashedly, on a derivative creativity; its style and mood are built in, determined to a large degree by film technique and movie nostalgia. This is not literature for purists. The surprise is, given its flamboyant, mirror-within-a-mirror theatricality, that **Destiny Express** turns out to be, on the whole, a crisp and engaging novel.

Mr. Rodman tells the story alternately through the eyes of Lang and his wife, Thea, but Lang's version of the events is infinitely more compelling in its precise, convincing detailing of how it feels to have the ground you walk on give way beneath your feet. The director's first confused intimations that the people around him are no longer quite what they seem unfold as if in a dream: at a screening of *Testament,* Lang imagines his projectionist has slipped someone into his booth to see the film; at his dentist's office, he suddenly has an inkling that the two men in the waiting room have been shadowing him all day. At first, Lang blames his own forgetfulness, the fact that he has misplaced a face, or been careless about a commitment, as in his marriage.

The sleek facade of Lang and von Harbou's marriage is depicted in the novel with the artfulness of one of their exquisitely structured screenplays. The couple is given to looking at themselves in mirrors and smoking unusually large numbers of cigarettes. When Thea, with her elongated body and angled, blue-black hair, enters their apartment, she is "all silhouette, a long trapezoid of spilled hallway light at her feet." Fritz and Thea's brainy, brittle dialogue is dizzyingly self-referential: they reprise images and lines from their old films and ransack their daily lives for scenes and special effects. Even their passion is fueled by the narcissistic eroticism of the creative act—and the unshakable conviction that making films is one of the most important tasks in the world.

It is in the scenes in which Thea eludes Fritz's cautious but quietly desperate gestures to keep her from slipping out of his reach that Mr. Rodman, too, allows both characters to break free of their own fraught symbology—sometimes so insistent that it feels like a game of Trivial Pursuit for film students—and turn human. Thea's affair with a young American expatriate is serious, her allegiance to the Fatherland clearly more zealous than his, and her ambition to direct boundless. Mr. Rodman's description of Lang's alarming yearning for his wife and the deep black pool of loss that lies beneath is sparely, deeply poignant. " 'Have I told you,' he found himself asking, and was immediately sorry, even as he said it, that he'd let the words out, 'how much I love you?' Thea said, 'Yes.' She was bent over the table again. Her hair covered the side of her face, and he could not see her lips as they formed the reply. He could only hope he'd not ruined all."

As happened in real life, Lang in the novel is offered the opportunity to manipulate a new set of symbols and collaborate on a new breed of film—not with Thea, but with [Joseph] Goebbels—as the architect of the new National Socialist film program. Mr. Rodman has Lang, repelled by the job offer, demur by reminding Goebbels that his mother is Jewish; Goebbels replies that the Reich welcomes "converts." Lang stalls, even as he secretly plots the end of his own story: escape from Germany.

When the real Lang moved to Hollywood in 1935, he swore off the use of symbolism in his films; in America, he said, a person's character, rather than outside forces, determines his fate. But for Lang's riveting escape to Paris in 1933, Mr. Rodman reprises the symbol that has so infatuated psychoanalysts and film makers (including Lang, who relented and used it in *Human Desire,* 1954)—a train. In a book heavy with self-important symbols, this one has lean, inarguable force: the train enables Lang to outwit his destiny; later, it will rob thousands of Jews of theirs. (pp. 13-14)

Deborah Mason, "Fate Calls for Fritz Lang," in The New York Times Book Review, *March 4, 1990, pp. 13-14.*

Ernest Callenbach

In her exquisite small novel, *Light,* Eva Figes told her story through the eyes of the French Impressionist painter who was its central figure. Howard Rodman has tried something similar [in ***Destiny Express***]: telling the story of the great film director Fritz Lang's "escape" from Germany, as the Nazis came to power in 1933, through the eyes of Lang and his scriptwriter wife, Thea von Harbou.

It's an intriguing idea, since Lang's visual world was strongly defined—a jagged, powerfully geometrical place of great good and great evil, often expressing grim forebodings that Hitler's rule was soon to render murderously concrete.

Unfortunately, it's a very difficult world to convey in words, compared to the soft, sensuous flow of the Figes

book, and Rodman brings it off only fitfully, never really making Lang's world look like a Lang film. But this is not the only reason why the book is not very satisfying; puzzlingly, for more than half its pages, Rodman keeps the dramatic materials of the legend off-stage, and even a reader who knows the basic legend is likely to find this frustrating.

Lang assiduously propagated the story (embroidering it more as the years passed, his biographer Lotte Eisner wrote) that the very day Joseph Goebbels, Hitler's newly installed and demonic minster of propaganda, asked him to head the Nazi film industry, the half-Jewish Lang got on the train and escaped to Paris—not even waiting a day to get his money out of the bank, the banks having closed when he left Goebbels' office. Instead of presiding over the Nazi "Potemkins" and "Ninotchkas" that Goebbels offered him, Lang's later career took him to Hollywood, while Von Harbou remained in Berlin, working under the Nazis.

Rodman holds this back, the heart of his tale, until late in the book, preceding it with an oblique and tedious account of the deteriorated relationship between Lang and his collaborator-wife, who is having an affair with a mysterious American. Tiny clues to the surrounding political developments in Berlin pop up here and there, but unless you already care about Lang and know something about the unhappy history of the times, you probably won't care too much about his emotional frame of mind concerning Von Harbou.

Rodman does a decent job of conveying how Lang might have seen his domestic world (he's good at Lang's perceptions of light and shadows, for instance), but he doesn't make it matter much to us. Lang and Von Harbou, in their own stories, were hardly so reticent; they slapped the premises of their films right in the viewer's face, and if Rodman had tried to follow their aesthetic in the framing of his story as well as in details of its narration, he might have written a much more compelling book.

There also is a little problem about Rodman's use of Lang's legend: The legend recently has been proven false. As Swedish historian Gosta Werner has found (an article about all this will appear in the spring issue of *Film Quarterly,*) Lang's passport has turned up in the German archives. It shows that Lang in fact went in and out of Germany several times after his probable interview with Goebbels (which is not mentioned in the evil doctor's usually meticulous diary); that he didn't really leave Berlin for good until many months later; that he did take a sizeable sum of money with him on at least one occasion.

Nor was Lang so immediately allergic to the Nazis as he later implied: He was one of the four major founders of the NTBO, set up to provide guidance to the film makers of the new Reich a few days before he probably saw Goebbels.

All this notwithstanding, Lang was one of the great film makers of all time, and all Lang fans will find a certain fascination in Rodman's effort to dramatize the legend—a part of Lang's creative life even if not of his real life.

Ernest Callenbach, "The Great Escape that Never Was," in Los Angeles Times Book Review, *March 11, 1990, p. 5.*

Peter Matthews

In 1932, the German director Fritz Lang staged the conflagration of a chemical factory for his highly implausible thriller, *The Testament of Doctor Mabuse.* The Nazis banned the film and, as though under secret orders from Lang's megalomaniacal arch criminal, burned the Reichstag. The movies have often proved most uncannily accurate at their most grotesque and fanciful. Cowardly and self-serving, they look away from the scenes of historical disaster, but by a seemingly inexorable law are compelled to figure them obliquely, at second hand, in cryptic imagery and ponderous melodrama.

Ever since Nathanael West's *The Day of the Locust* and Isherwood's *Prater Violet,* novels about movies have been fascinated by their duplicity, their innocent barbarism—as if the movies were a suitably corrupt art form to announce the end of the world, but the moviemakers themselves would be the last to know it. Howard A. Rodman's novel about Fritz Lang [*Destiny Express*] appears at first sight to belong to this lineage. For most of its short length, Lang and his wife and collaborator, Thea von Harbou, haunt the streets of Berlin like somnambulists, oblivious to the portents all around them. Or like neutral recording apparatuses, they see—cinematically—but do not know, their heightened, haphazard perceptions seeming to immobilise their faculties of judgment.

Lang and von Harbou were not, of course, as stupid as that. Nor is the novel actually concerned with them—or the other legendary personages, like Brecht and Helene Weigel, who wander through—but instead with what is now modishly termed their simulacra. Glibly agnostic about our access to history, it fills in the void with archetypes, leitmotifs, even camera angles lifted from Lang's films. Nor for the first time in recent fiction, the past is recollected as an outsize film set. And Lang himself, like Peter Lorre as the child murderer in *M,* is blindly led through a crisscross of his own expressionist lighting to a studio-processed assignation with fate.

Lang's romantic, doom-laden cinema, where, as Siegfried Kracauer has said, "the law triumphs and the lawless glitters", was certainly ambiguous enough to appeal to a regime that had collapsed such distinctions. The ornamental patterns of mass suffering in *Metropolis* impressed Dr Goebbels who, with a certain justice, invited Lang to head film production for the Third Reich. In Rodman's version of their famous interview, the aestheticisation of politics is enacted quite literally: the young and glamorous Minister for Propaganda keeps his best profile continuously before Lang, like a rising star.

Since communists and fascists are equally well-rehearsed automatons in this novel, Lang's eventual flight on the night train to Paris seems a perfunctory, almost meaningless action. Rodman's rather trifling pastiche is pathetically ill-equipped to convey anything of the tragedy of a generation of German artists and intellectuals in exile, most of them, like Lang, finishing up inevitably in Hollywood. The book is impeccably researched—not in itself much of a recommendation—but pays at best a shallow tribute to Lang's memory in the year of his centenary.

Peter Matthews, "Simulacra," in New Statesman & Society, *Vol. 3, No. 101, May 18, 1990, p. 39.*

Triva Ponder-Cohen

Destiny Express is mostly a love story or rather, the end of a love story, as these main characters, while sharing a marriage, are no longer in love. Filled with passion and talent, Lang is tormented by the affair his wife is having although he tries desperately not to admit it to himself. Making the black hole in his life seem deeper are his various friends in the film industry who leave the country, fearing their safety as German Jews. This book offers imaginative insight into the personal characters of Lang and Harbou, allowing the reader to share their detachment and concern over their future in Germany.

Rodman is successful in portraying realistic concerns coupled with realistic action. Although this novel is only slightly more than 200 pages, it offers readers a glimpse into the lives of various fictional and non-fictional German celebrities such as Joseph Goebbels, Otto Merz and Rudolf Klein-Rogge during a very dark time period in Germany's history.

Triva Ponder-Cohen, in a review of "Destiny Express," in West Coast Review of Books, *Vol. 15, No. 4, June-July, 1990, p. 34.*

Algis Budrys

[It] seems to me that [*Destiny Express*] captures something that no other book has done quite as well if at all: the glorifying effect of Nazism on the insufficiently talented.

This has not been sufficiently understood. But one of the many effects of Nazism was to provide opportunities for career advancement that could have come in no other way. First of all, the first-raters, in this case in the film industry, tended to get out while there was still time, barely. Rodman's book is replete with the names of people who next turn up in Hollywood, in the front ranks for years thereafter. Second of all, the Nazis were uncomfortable with first-rank talent; they saw it as undisciplined and inclined to go its own way, when what was wanted was a vigorous film industry cranking out goods intended to make the German people feel good about specific things. So they simply declared the second-raters first rate, and gave them all the privileges of the first rank.

I would like to see a book about a second-rate film maker gradually realizing that he is second-rate. Because that must have happened; despite all the limousines and the parties that were almost (but not quite) what they should have been, the simple fact remains that there must have been times when a man's reach and a man's grasp both fell short; when what appeared on the film was, simply, cli-

---

An excerpt from *Destiny Express*

The ether was sweet, overwhelmingly so, like gardenias, or the aniline cement in the UFA screening room; but after a while Lang found it less difficult to take the ether all the way down, hold it there. He saw twin wheels of wire mesh—much the same material of which the mask was made—spinning against each other, the left clockwise, the right counterclock, and the small silhouette of a man at their juncture, growing smaller.

He had been filming Thea's scenarios for ten years, and had forgotten what writing might be like, without her. Sometimes when they had worked together they had not been on the best of terms; but things were different now, and he could not visualize the two of them at their desk.

The wheels were spinning more slowly. Lang could see ripples, and moirés, in the pointed oval where the disks intersected. Then he discerned once more the silhouette of a man walking, it seemed, down a railroad track, becoming smaller but not, somehow, more distant. He could see the tracks now. The crossties sank below him, one by one. Sprocket holes appeared, at the ties' outer edges. For a while he was unsure whether he were looking at a railroad track or a strip of film. The rectangles sank, one by one. The silhouetted man became still more tiny. Then the spinning disks reasserted themselves, obliterating all between them. There was a horrible grinding sound as the disks grated against one another.

---

ched despite its maker's best efforts, and a certain pale wraith began stalking the gilded corridors. But that's another book.

In Rodman's book, set in Fritz Lang's last few days in Germany, Lang appears as a two-sided fellow. On the one hand, he pines for von Harbou to a point of obsession, a case which is made worse by the fact that, thanks to repairs on the home where she now usually stays, she is living with him in the Berlin apartment which was originally just a *pied a terre* for him. Living with him, but seeing Sam pretty constantly, a fact which is signalled by a red rose in a vase in the foyer, to tell Lang not to wait up for her.

In this involvement, Lang tends to remind one of the stricken professor of *The Blue Angel;* it takes him forever to realize that *The Testament of Dr. Mabuse* is never going to be released as it was made, the two men in the Mercedes are secret police, etc.; he simply does not pay attention until ludicrously late in the game.

On the other hand, he wakes up quick enough when Joseph Goebbels offers him the chance to supervise all films being made in Germany in the future. This is the artist being addressed, and even before Goebbels stops speaking, he is planning exactly how he will catch the train to Paris and thence Hollywood.

Thea has to stay. Under the new regime, she has been offered a chance to direct. True, the first film is a piece of *kitsch,* but the one after that, or the one after that, will be a real film, she is sure.

Rodman tells all this—and much more—with a quiet deft-

ness that is all the more impressive when you realize that he has no actual idea, for instance, of how a Lufthansa plane ride would have gone in those days—he has it exactly right, by my mother's account; the experience would be almost impossible to duplicate with any of today's equipment.

I think it's a hell of a book. Thank God I never wrote one like it. (pp. 32-4)

Algis Budrys, in a review of "Destiny Express," in The Magazine of Fantasy and Science Fiction, *Vol. 78, No. 6, July, 1990, pp. 32-4.*

Andrew Hislop

When he was a young Bohemian artist, Fritz Lang was an unwitting partner in fraud. He was commissioned in Belgium to paint new pictures over "old" paintings which were then used to trick the New York customs into certifying incorrectly that the covered-up art was genuine.

Destiny Express, Howard Rodman's novel about Lang's last days in Berlin in 1933 before fleeing Nazi Germany to France, is a compelling account of an extraordinary period of history and a peculiar personal relationship—between Lang and his second wife, the German nationalistic writer Thea von Harbou, who collaborated with him on his most famous German films. But Rodman's fictional covering only adds to our confusion about the genuineness of the story behind it.

Destiny Express has some linguistic oddities, due in part to the problems of writing about Lang's German period in English: Lang's "I so attest", when asked by his dentist whether his toothache was an emergency, seems out of time and place with his "What kind of shit is this?" to his head of production. But for the most part, the novel is neatly turned, poignant, even moving. Lang is shown not as the dictatorial master of the film set but as a more vulnerable figure, suffering not only from toothache but from a now unrequited love for Thea, who sleeps with an American, Sam Harrison, and who shows more sympathy than Lang for the Nazis. In his personal and political alienation, Lang begins to write again without Thea—the nostalgic, humorous tribute to his Viennese origins, *The Legend of the Last Viennese Faker* (a scenario which was never filmed). Thea too is portrayed with some understanding. When Lang flees Berlin (and Thea) immediately after his celebrated meeting with Goebbels in which he was asked to head the Nazi film industry, she is shown rushing to the station with his forgotten scenario, an ending worthy, as is the rest of the novel's plot and construction, of a film.

But as much as the novel fascinates, it also irritates, since only the most knowledgeable of Lang scholars can enjoy Rodman's playful *cinéaste* composition without yearning to know the truth—not an objective truth of Lang's life, which must elude even the most discerning biographer, but the truth of its construction from historical sources.

Though ***Destiny Express*** does not fill a gap in the history of the novel, which has long cross-fertilized narrative tricks and tropes with film, it does highlight the lack in cinema history of a proper biographer of Lang (who discouraged biographical speculation).

Great historical novels transcend their subject-matter but ***Destiny Express*** teases us with its material only to be subsumed by it. Its very construction demands deconstruction. Lang's meeting with Goebbels is well known, but did he really, as in the novel, bump into "Bert Brecht" at the station when the playwright was fleeing the country? Is Harrison a real character? Thea may indeed have had a map of Germany's lost provinces stitched into her coat lining but did she always leave a rose in a vase when she was not coming home at night? And what evidence is there that this would send Lang searching to see if her diaphragm was missing? Has Rodman found a secret diary of Lang? If so, such a work, however self-deceiving, could not but trump Rodman's liberty with concealed truth.

Andrew Hislop, "Meetings at the Station," in
The Times Literary Supplement, *No. 4550,*
June 15-21, 1990, p. 653.

Sandra Schor
The Great Letter E

Schor (1932?-1990) was an American novelist.

The protagonist of *The Great Letter E* is Barry Glassman, a Jewish optometrist living in Bayside, New York, who rigorously studies the works of the seventeenth-century philosopher Baruch Spinoza. Like Glassman, Spinoza earned his living grinding and polishing lenses as he attempted to explain events as indisputable acts of God, whom he equated with nature. Spinoza also contended that God has no moral designs for the world, but that one can learn to accept the seeming randomness of life when one is aware of one's place in and unity with all of nature. Although Glassman struggles to adopt Spinoza's viewpoint, he must reassess his beliefs in the face of personal tragedies: his business is failing, the congregation of his synagogue opposes his views, and his wife Marilyn leaves him for his best friend and rival optometrist, forcing him to move to Brooklyn. There Glassman falls in love with his cousin, Enid Moscow, a physicist, who in turn falls in love with another man. When Glassman faces his thirteen-year-old son who has run away from home, he realizes that, unlike Spinoza, he must be satisfied with the few parts of life that he can understand.

Critics hailed *The Great Letter E* as a unique blend of humor and insight. Several passages in the novel consist of Glassman's philosophical musings and daydreams about Spinoza's life. Although some commentators claimed that these passages disrupted the book's generally straightforward narrative style, others judged them an effective tool for revealing the protagonist's thoughts. Joan S. Boudreaux observed: "Schor weaves Spinoza's ethics through this poetic account of a modern man's isolation, . . . unraveling as much universal truth as did Penelope. Her command of the English language along with her wisdom about human nature combine to make this an unforgettable novel, one worth reading again and again."

Stephen Stark

Baruch (Barry) Glassman, the occasionally infuriating narrator of Sandra Schor's first novel [*The Great Letter E*], is a New York optometrist with the worst kind of impaired vision, that which is self-imposed. Obsessed with the work of Baruch Spinoza, Barry allows everything he does to become so obscured by the hazy lenses of philosophy that he can't see his life disintegrating around him. His business is failing, his wife is having an affair with a

rival optometrist, and the congregation of his synagogue is ready to heave him into the street for his depredations on its religious philosophy. But it's not until his wife forces him out of his home in Queens and into a chilly apartment in Brooklyn that Barry begins to come out of himself. He begins an uneasy friendship with Bernard Messenger, the blind son of his landlady, and has an affair with his cousin, the physicist Enid Moscow. Then 40 of his colleagues are killed in a plane crash on their way to an optometry convention. His rabbi decks him. His 13-year-old son disappears in a religious and perhaps hormonal frenzy with the gentile girl from across the street. It is here, when the novel begins to draw back from its tight focus on Barry and broadens its tender, lunatic field of vision, that its power overwhelms the many narrative tricks that could undercut it. Certain situations—the painful funerals of Barry's friends and the peculiar irony that their deaths reinvigorate his business—are denied their full impact by the distance Ms. Schor puts between narrator and reader. Philosophical musings impede too much of the action and muddy otherwise superb characterizations. Yet despite its shortcomings, *The Great Letter E* gradually blossoms, and in the end it has become so affecting that one wishes for more of Barry Glassman's humane clarity of vision.

Stephen Stark, in a review of "The Great Letter E," in The New York Times Book Review, *February 26, 1990, p. 24.*

Jane Mendelsohn

Halfway through Sandra Schor's first novel [*The Great Letter E*], Barry Glassman, an amateur philosopher, attempts to lift himself out of an abysmal depression by huddling under the covers with a pile of Mounds bars and listening to old tapes of his favorite college professor lecturing on Spinoza. "No one can blame God," the professor paraphrases, "because he has given him or her an infirm nature or an impotent mind. For it would be just as absurd for a circle to complain that God has not given it the properties of a sphere." This insight elicits from Glassman a belated wish that he had received a higher grade on the final exam of a course taken some 20 years before. Spinoza's call to be a stoic Jew escapes him; the very idea becomes, through the lens of Glassman's comic misery, an oxymoron. Yet *The Great Letter E* attempts to make sense out of this calling; it is a novel about living the ethical life with a sense of humor. With its strange, sad comedy and lighthearted, almost giddy tempo, it charmingly depicts Glassman's gradual acceptance of his decidedly circular self.

Glassman is a man with "a gene for God." Like his hero, Baruch Spinoza, he is an optometrist by trade, yet in his heart he is a philosopher. Rather than lend his life clarity, however, philosophy obscures his vision like a fingerprint on the front of his glasses. He tucks brief messages about atheism into his son's bar mitzvah invitations, infuriating his rabbi and alienating his son. Although he admits that according to his own best reading of Spinoza's *Ethics,* his estranged wife, Marilyn, is virtuous, he finds himself unable to love her. He feels that to relinquish his philosophy in order to win her back "would be like waging nuclear war to save a front tooth." But when he loses her to another optometrist, his business to competitors, and his son to a Talmud-reading girlfriend, he exiles himself to Brooklyn in despair. It's at this point that he huddles under the covers with the Mounds bars. In an effort to shake off his loneliness by completing his life's work, he struggles over a theoretical essay concerning the effects of metropolitan pollution on rainbows. For consolation, he continues to read Spinoza, whose euclidean system of logical propositions and corollaries calms him. When his sister asks him if he's suicidal, he tells her "No. I still get my reading done. Unhappiness is a moral state. I'm looking into it."

In this self-deprecating, self-absorbed hero, Schor blends a familiar mix of lovable comedian and unbearable egotist, a combination that can seem unsympathetic, or clichéd. Although Glassman never descends to either depth, the relentlessly comic nature of his predicament does confuse the seriousness with which we are supposed to view his mid-life crisis. Schor doesn't possess the resources of a

[Philip] Roth to sustain one long complaint. While not intended to read as a smoothly flowing stream of consciousness, but more as a journal jotted down in the present tense, the novel nevertheless suffers from abrupt alternations between Glassman's internal meanderings and the external world of divorce, religious ceremony, bankruptcy, and even plane crashes which so dramatically shapes the story.

At times, even the transitions among aspects of Glassman's imagination reflect this structural weakness. His visions of Spinoza, obsessive reveries concerning life in 17th-century Amsterdam, come across as too poetic in contrast to the parodied philosophizing that sets the tone for much of the book. They draw unnecessary attention to themselves; it's as if passages from Plato were inserted in bubbles in a comic book. And yet despite the awkwardness of their integration, the daydreams do produce lovely writing. In one instance, Glassman imagines the cold attic in the van der Spyck home, where Spinoza rented a room; when the "servants hung wet nightgowns there to dry, ice crystals stiffened them into corpses with pleading arms." In another daydream, Glassman envisions an incident in which Spinoza's peers unleashed their hatred for him and his brilliant, heretical scholarship:

> One winter night, outside a theater, two of his classmates stepped out of the shadows, one seizing him while the other plunged a knife into his shoulder. He might have been dying, and no one to come to his rescue. He felt lonely and luckless. But rather than flee to the synagogue to ask God's forgiveness and help, he pressed his cape to the wound, feeling in its depths the oozing of his fate. God does not control my fate, he thought, God *is* my fate, and I will love my fate because it is all I have.
>
> It is thought that the thickness of the cape in fact saved his life.

Writing like this saves the book from relying too heavily on the funny and the philosophical. When Schor works simply with words she creates remarkable scenes and interesting people. Transported to a different environment, Glassman in Brooklyn takes on bright new colors as he falls in love with his cousin Enid, a sexy, insecure physicist. She, however, falls in love with Glassman's downstairs neighbor, Bernard, a handsome, blind genius who studies Pascal. This unlikely trio turns out to be surprisingly engaging. They move in a timeless, junior high school world of field trips, neighborhood intrigue, and stolen kisses in Prospect Park. Glassman's unsatisfied passion for philosophy repeats itself in his similarly sweet but adolescent obsession with Enid. At one point, dazed by her facility with the mathematical computations involved in his essay on optics, he compares himself to one of those literary girls he knew as a teenager who read Amy Lowell and worshipped the "mathletes." He doesn't understand, of course, until it's too late, that, like any pubescent boy, what he loves about Enid is that she asks nothing from him.

The crisis that jolts Glassman into this belated revelation comes when his 13-year-old son, Michael, runs away.

After years of searching for philosophical answers and months of waiting for Enid, Glassman recognizes in his son's disappearance the final impossibility of complete gratification. Having lost almost everything, he can now see through the imprisonment of living life as a logical construct. This clarity of vision is the culmination of an optical imagery sustained, almost too well, but in the end successfully, throughout the book. What begins as a novel of ideas transforms itself into a book about a father and son, about the optical illusions and distortions their relation creates. Through its many mutations, the story's theme remains the same, that of accepting a human, and therefore not necessarily consistent picture of the world, of love, and of family. The sense that life is an unfulfilled wish with no one to blame, that we are circles and not spheres, emanates from the novel's last pages so well that the work succeeds despite its flaws. This final call for mature renunciation, not a particularly delicious pill to swallow, is sweetened by the book's cheerful tone and lovely language. Even Spinoza would have to smile.

> Jane Mendelsohn, in a review of "The Great Letter E," in VLS, No. 83, March, 1990, p. 9.

Janet Hadda

Poor Barry Glassman. It's bad enough that he has to contend with a struggling optometry business in a rough Manhattan neighborhood, a wife who is having an affair with his childhood friend and business rival, a pint-size son, and a sister who discards husbands the way others get rid of clothes. In addition to these hardships, the protagonist of *The Great Letter E* must carry within himself the spirit—and, to some extent, the fate—of Baruch Spinoza, the phenomenally brilliant 17th-Century Jewish philosopher.

Barry's condition corresponds to Spinoza's in certain surface ways: He shares his Hebrew name; he grinds lenses in order to make a living while remaining devoted to metaphysical concerns; his ideas are despised and maligned by some, treated with respect and acknowledgment by others.

Unlike Spinoza, however, who remained single, Barry looks to philosophical enlightenment as a guide to help him work out the mess of his marriage. He leaves his physically attractive but vestigially phobic wife, thereby suffering the loss of daily contact with his son, of whom he is immensely fond.

His mean little Brooklyn apartment is woefully far from properly brewed coffee and the Bayside garden he had cherished. He longs to rechannel his procreativity into a new sexual relationship, but his romantic forays are neither forceful nor successful.

The problem with Sandra Schor's often amusing and touching first novel is that Glassman is no Spinoza. He is neither phenomenal nor brilliant, and the author's attempt to infuse her character with the depth and conflict of the man who was excommunicated by the Amsterdam Jewish community for the provocative radicalism of his views hangs on the pages.

Barry grapples with his belief that everything comes from God; God is the universe and is therefore beyond good and evil. Yet how can he accept this thought when he feels so betrayed by his old buddy Donahue, now raking in the money with a chain of eye-wear stores and sleeping with his wife? On the surface, reading Spinoza helps buttress his conviction that he should not be consumed by loss and loneliness. "A free man thinks of nothing less than of death," he quotes to himself. It makes sense to him that, "since substance must exist, death subtracts nothing from the universe" and, therefore, that "some powerful law of compensation exists."

Yet he cannot help but feel for his dead father, lying alone in his grave, abandoned by Barry's mother, who—in a final burst of free thinking—has had herself cremated. And what is he to make of the fact that, on an ill-fated plane that he nearly took himself, 41 optometrists, including a number of his friends, are killed—thereby expanding his business without his having to lift a finger?

The answer, the author seems to be telling us, lies in the fact that mere humans cannot know the ways of the world except in a fragmentary way. Thus, the cause of the plane crash is never discovered, and this lapse in understanding is metaphysically fitting. The theme of humankind's limited vision is brought to the fore through the characters of Bernard Messenger, Barry's blind but perspicacious Brooklyn neighbor, and Enid Moscow, his myopic, elusive and sexually irresistible cousin.

Bernard cannot see the way Barry does with his perfect eyesight, yet he is able to feel his way through life, getting what he needs; and Enid—the heart and soul of the book—bumbles her way along.

Bernard and Enid accept the unravelled mysteries of their lives: why it was Bernard's fate to be stricken blind through a bout with meningitis at age 8; why it was that Enid's brother disappeared one day in 1968 while taking a Civil Service exam, never to be heard from again. From them, Barry learns that there is existence beyond puzzling the unfathomable, and the transformation is salutary. By the book's end, he has discovered that the greatest E of all is not on the eye chart, nor is it Spinoza's *Ethics,* nor even Espinosa (Spinoza) himself. Rather, it stands for Enid and the power of love and friendship.

In the end, as many loose ends as the novel itself leaves—proving that the form of a work can illustrate its thematics—and despite some conspicuous symbolism, there is a cheer about the book that lingers.

On Yom Kippur, the Jewish Day of Atonement, he hears a proverb: "If you see a blind man, kick him, lest you be kinder than God." Suddenly, a bit of religious truth dawns on him: The proverb is wrong. Everyone—Bernard, he himself, his wife, even Enid—is blind in a different and separate way, and the reasons for this are unknown.

Thus, compassion is always in order. After all, why risk being meaner than God?

> Janet Hadda, "Spinoza on the Half-Shell," in Los Angeles Times Book Review, *March 25, 1990, p. 9.*

An excerpt from *The Great Letter E*

Bernard Baruch made me proud to be his namesake, sharing the Hebrew name Baruch, used for Torah readings, burials, Hebrew school, and the naming of a child. Baruch College makes me proud, since I am its graduate. But Baruch Spinoza is my teacher and master: from him I learn that our knowledge is partial, we are partially free, partially in ignorance. From him I learn to exist without bitterness and pride. I am what I am, or, in Jehovah's words, I am that I am. I will not complain that I am an optometrist and not an ophthalmologist; that the pathology of that tremulous organism is too specialized for me; that I have one five-foot soprano son and not three six-foot baritones; and have been cuckolded by a lifelong friend. Quests and accommodations are my destiny, as is my unfailing study of the Infinite. But I am no Spinoza! My B+ intellect fails me at crucial moments, most recently as I work my tail off on refraction formulas. Just yesterday morning what a rainbow that was! Walling myself into work and away from the disappointments of marriage, I stepped out into the driveway for a breath of early air, and there it was! I immediately thought of Marilyn and the wonders of another chance. Between the blue and the violet, a deep, sheer, diaphanous streak, a blazing indigo—and then it vanished. Which compound in our polluted city produced that soft and spiritual blue baffled me. God, what a color! But even Spinoza surrendered to the vastness of Nature and recognized that he owed his defects to the fragmentary vision of man, even he had limits to what he knew, had to live in a finite house, sleep in a bed, work in a rectangle of a room covered with glass dust, at a wooden lens-grinding machine, until his lungs failed. Amsterdam in the seventeenth century. A malodorous place at the brink of new thought. The new philosophies, after Descartes, were in the smelly air, in the cold chrome light that swept across the Waterlooplein on an October night. Ten years ago I dragged Marilyn to Holland (she wanted Spain and the Alhambra!) and we toured the sacred places where Spinoza lived, studied, died. Oh, if only life were so simple as to begin at birth!

The Antioch Review

[*The Great Letter E*] is a wonderful novel—a *first* novel at that. Barry Glassman is a West-Side optometrist with a "gene for God," the God of Spinoza (also a dealer in lenses), the God we know through *reason*. Disputing his way with his some-time wife, his about-to-be-Bar-Mitzvahed son, his mistress, Rabbi, neighbors, and business competitors, Glassman roils the clutter of his untidy life. Phrases from Spinoza's writings dominate our hero's reflections. Both Glassman's difficulties and Spinoza's are seen to come from their common devotion to reason as the way to know God. Like Spinoza, Glassman has a theory of the rainbow, a theory that he, and some of his supporters, hope to see published. (Some of the plot hinges on the fate of this manuscript.) Spinoza is such a central character in the novel that it is both his life and Glassman's that are offered for our reflections. A warm, funny, intellectually nourishing book.

A review of "The Great Letter E," in The Antioch Review, *Vol. 48, No. 2, Spring, 1990, p. 262.*

Joan S. Boudreaux

As adept as D. H. Lawrence at portraying female characters, Sandra Schor [in *The Great Letter E*] reveals Barry Glassman's male mind in the turmoil of a marriage gone wrong. The Bayside, New York, setting in autumn lends credence to the paradox in Glassman's life. The first conflict in the novel that keeps readers engaged is the one centered on Barry's and Marilyn's son Michael, who is preparing for his bar mitzvah. The couple, already estranged emotionally (but not sexually), plan to separate soon after their frail, thirteen-year-old's ceremony; however, a great source of contention is created when Barry chooses to add Spinoza's philosophy to his part of the traditional presentation. Not only is Marilyn up in arms about the phrase "Blessed art thou God or Nature, in whose extended greatness we all dwell . . . " which Barry has added to the traditional father's part of the presentation, but also the rabbi and Marilyn's orthodox relatives "use guilt to goad" Barry into giving his speech at the bar mitzvah in the traditionally accepted way.

Family, church, and community opposition reinforce Barry's philosophy: "The philosophic life is a self-centered life that deludes itself into thinking it's not." Schor parallels Barry with Baruch Spinoza, revealing his aloofness when he moves out of his wife's bedroom and into the damp basement until after Michael's bar mitzvah, and later when he moves into an attic apartment because the attic room suits his "need for aloofness."

Barry's Spinozaic philosophy comforts him throughout his estrangement from wife, church, and community. Imitative of his idol, Barry grinds lenses and writes philosophy while the community scorns his heresy, his wife seeks refuge in another optometrist's arms, and the church literally blackens his eye (via Rabbi Mordecai Mayberg).

We sense Marilyn's motivation for adultery in the seven philosophic questions Barry lists early in the novel just after he learns his wife is sleeping with her boss and Barry's archrival, Bob Donahue, another lens grinder, who, unlike the protagonist, has gotten rich selling glasses, two pairs at a time, while the former, obsessed with Spinoza, has eked out an income giving "twelve months of evenings" to the *Spinoza Review,* and persuading poor patrons at his Eighth Avenue optical shop not to buy expensive glasses.

Schor weaves Spinoza's ethics through this poetic account of a modern man's isolation, and weaves, unraveling as much universal truth as did Penelope. Her command of the English language along with her wisdom about human nature combine to make this an unforgettable novel, one worth reading again and again. (pp. 308-09)

Joan S. Boudreaux, in a review of "The Great Letter E," in The Review of Contemporary Fiction, *Vol. 10, No. 1, Spring, 1990, pp. 308-09.*

Leighton Klein

"God is unimaginable! Perfect and complete as a carrot." A free thinker trapped by his own faith in reason, Barry Glassman can't understand why his rabbi bridles at such statements. When Barry's wife Marilyn takes up with his best friend, he asks himself if anything is worth losing her for. His answer takes the form of a two-page list that starts calmly with a discussion of the ethics of the situation, then leaps off into a comic vision of himself as a cripple at Lourdes, segues to reminiscences about personal ads never sent ("Redheaded violinist. Afternoons. Manhattan."), and finally ends where it started, asking a rhetorical question for which he does not have an answer.

In *The Great Letter E*, her first novel, Sandra Schor has created one of the more vivid characters in recent fiction. Optician, iconoclast, dedicated student of the seventeenth-century Dutch philosopher Spinoza, Barry Glassman is reckless for knowledge, mad with reason, and racked by lust and doubt. His contradictory impulses and elliptical beliefs are unerringly detailed in this funhouse ride through one man's psyche. The book begins with Barry already separated from his wife, the two of them attempting to keep up appearances until their son Michael's bar mitzvah. Simultaneously serene, confused, and demented, Barry tries to intellectually understand a world that is tying his guts up in knots. His faith in knowledge is his talisman; everything else is so much stuff, disorder jammed in a single room through which he, unseeing, tries to thread his way.

Glassman's infatuation with Spinoza and his world is a lens that distorts and transforms everyone around him. Exiled to the basement of his own home, he sees himself, Walter Mitty-like, in the court of Emanuel the First of Portugal, healing his marriage and the King's daughter with an ancient recipe for oil of mustard and with hot bricks. Bernard Messenger, the blind son of his Brooklyn landlord, becomes for a moment an acolyte of the false messiah Sabbetai Zevi, "self-possessed and handsome, but blinded by ecstacy, floating, as blind people often seem to do, from village to village in the Europe of the seventeenth century."

The other characters are just as dynamic, each one jostling and pushing, trying to elbow their way to the front of the action. Schor sketches them elegantly and swiftly, making each one breathe in the space of a single sentence: Enid Moscow, the "rumply sexy gritty take-charge take-a-chance Brooklyn intellectual," Barry's assistant Feliz, "the gossip and master meddler in two languages," and his long-dead mother, "Her excitement came through in the emphatic way she lectured us and in the distracted way she threw dinner together." Above all of these, Glass-man's own voice soars on crooked wings; a wild, giddy creation:

> They need me; I believe it, as I believe in Substance and in light bending and in eye banks. Even Marilyn deserves better, though she was always impetuous. A July night; the bus stopped on the Grand Concourse and Fordham Road; she foretold our marriage, heavy dark hair swinging, an arm thrown around the belt of my pants, fingers hooked in my belt loops as we boarded; we tossed our quarters together into the hopper, symbolizing the joint casting of our lots, she, looking out for bats all the way up the Concourse as a small piece in the newspapers had warned of an invasion of bats from Sullivan County. I was a blind risk, but she took it, bit the bullet, as they say now, said I was not like the other guys, knew instantly she could trust me with her life—*so what if you are a universalist; in my heart I believe, come fire, earthquake, or wild dogs, that you will rush in and save me first.* (Within two years I had cured Marilyn of an irrational fear of German shepherds by instilling in her a belief in the oneness of all the beings in the universe.) Fortunately, I was never put to the test.

These idiosyncratic characters trip their way through a book packed with quirky events that somehow seem perfectly reasonable. Business at Glassman's shabby office improves after a plane filled with rival opticians crashes on the way to a convention ("Making money off of one's dead buddies is like picking your teeth after eating your pet dog," he says), his son runs away with a fireman's daughter, and the Manhattan Board of Education is poisoned by chicken livers. Far from being mere comic devices, each crisis pushes Barry toward a more complete understanding of himself.

There are several small flaws in *The Great Letter E:* one of the longer interior monologues is unconvincing, and a few of the female characters are thinly rendered. Overall, however, this is an accomplished and thoroughly delightful novel, one that does not stoop to a neat ending. Barry emerges blinking and disoriented from his failed marriage, having gained just a glimpse of the potential for human happiness in this life. "Digging is better than thinking about digging," Bernard Messenger tells him, and for once Barry Glassman listens.

Leighton Klein, in a review of "The Great Letter E," in The Bloomsbury Review, *Vol. 10, No. 3, May-June, 1990, p. 21.*

Beat Sterchi

Cow

Sterchi is a Swiss novelist, born in 1949.

Cow addresses themes of xenophobia, corruption, and human alienation. The novel's protagonist, Ambrosio, is a Spanish expatriate who finds employment on a traditional Swiss dairy farm owned by Farmer Knuchel. Although Knuchel admires Ambrosio's work, the local community's distrust of foreigners leads to Ambrosio's dismissal and subsequent employment in a slaughterhouse that exploits cheap, foreign labor. Sterchi, trained as a butcher, vividly describes the daily horrors of the abattoir. Seven years after his dismissal, Ambrosio recognizes Farmer Knuchel's prized cow, now diseased, emaciated, and being prepared for slaughter, and experiences an epiphanic moment in which he identifies with the cow's passivity toward her fate. Some reviewers claimed that *Cow*'s narrative, alternating between scenes at Knuchel's dairy farm and the slaughterhouse rather than following Ambrosio's story chronologically, became tedious. Other critics, however, praised the novel's depiction of human and animal degradation. Valentine Cunningham observed: "Sterchi's protest against our civilisation's reliance on dirty work and wasted people equals Charles Kingsley's anger over the 'Human Soot' that was the by-product of Victorian industrialism."

Valentine Cunningham

Flounders, tin-drummers, midnight's children, glass cathedrals in Australia: our most exciting novelists have returned to Dickensian technique, taking the startling angle of vision, the weird emblem, the queer standpoint that's designed to get under your guard. In this line of country, Swiss novelist Beat Sterchi almost beats the band. His subject [in **Blösch,** published as **Cow** in the United States,] is foodstuffs—milk, meat, especially cow's meat.

Blösch is an unlikely heroine. She's a Swiss cow, a great red-coloured provider of calves and milk and dung, proud leader of a prospering dairy herd in a tight-knit Swiss village. Sterchi is a kind of a prose Ted Hughes: the archaic and archetypal joys of the udder were never more joyfully or lengthily celebrated. But these sweets of utopian udderness turn out to be backed by darker othernesses. For the plump, pure, even puritan villagers depend on *Gastarbeiter*—like the man Ambrosio, enticed away from his family and poverty in southern Spain to come and milk cows for the well-off Swiss.

Local xenophobia, though, never lets its dark little brother settle. Ambrosio is hounded by the mayoral guardians of hygiene—he has no health certificate. Eventually his employer has to farm him out for ghastly employment in the local abattoir. And here the truer story of bovine existence unfolds.

The abattoir is a deep circle of hell, a dump for ill-paid Spaniards and Italians and awkward-squad Swiss. Here the guestworkers have a truly awful career alongside the gigantic natives—the big boys too strong and stupid for well-paid brain work. This tribe of butchers get their living by wading through waste—blood, guts, tripes, excrement. They kill to live and often it's their own fingers that get cut off, their bellies that fatally spout blood.

The abattoir is presented as a war zone, a Red Front but without hope of revolution's changes. The workers mimic the organisation of the Home Guard the Swiss are so pleased with. Such disconcerting parodies mount up accusingly. The novel's citizenry push pleasant foodstuffs, especially cow-products, into their mouths; they eat well. The *Doppelgänger* in the bloody underground of that food's production do not eat well. They shove a deadly international Babel of cigarettes constantly into their mouths: Rossli Stumpen, Parisienne, Mary Long. These fags are the only women in their regulated lives.

Constantly intercut through the novel, an official discourse of hygiene and tidy-mindedness publicises the State's failure to keep darkness and horror at bay. What's more, mutedly, but mutinously, the train-loads of animals being led to the slaughter insist on reminding you of the fate of the Holocaust Jewry. His countrymen, Sterchi implies, have a way of shutting their eyes to slaughterhouses.

Sterchi's astonishing fiction never relents—even to the point of arranging an analogy between Ambrosio and the beast Blösch. The parallelism defies the corniness it risks. Sterchi's protest against our civilisation's reliance on dirty work and wasted people equals Charles Kingsley's anger over the 'Human Soot' that was the by-product of Victorian industrialism. And *Blösch's* larger affinities are as forceful and clear: they lie with Hardy's Jude, modernism's stuck pig, and Kafka's K, scapegoat of scapegoats. *Blösch* is a memorable and great fiction: hurt, and about hurting, with the power for (one hopes) positive hurt.

> *Valentine Cunningham, "Udder-Worldliness," in* The Observer, *November 20, 1988, p. 44.*

John Lanchester

Beat Sterchi's stir-causing first novel [*Blösch,* published in 1990 as *Cow* in the United States,] was published in German in 1983: it describes the experiences of Ambrosio, a Spanish *gastarbeiter* in Switzerland. Ambrosio works on Farmer Knuchel's dairy farm in Innerwald, where the small, wiry southerner is baffled by the prosperity, stoicism and size of everything around him—dogs as big as cows, cows as big as elephants. His viewpoint gives the Innerwald chapters of the novel a gentle, lyrical flavour, while also allowing Sterchi to stress the exhausting difficulty of the manual work Ambrosio performs, and the nastiness of the local peasantry. Some of the best passages in the book evoke the smugness, small-mindedness and xenophobia of Sterchi's compatriots: he seems to be about as fond of his fellow Swiss as Thomas Bernhard is of his fellow Austrians.

These chapters alternate with what is happening seven years later. Driven out of Innerwald by the locals, Ambrosio now works in an abattoir—one of the places where stiff Swiss restrictions on the employment of foreign labour are found to be more flexible. The slaughterhouse chapters describe the events of a single day, and set out to evoke the brutality and monotony of the work through a fractured, modernistic style which spares the reader nothing of the horror of 'the cow-demolition process'. One of the strongest scenes in the novel has Ambrosio staggering out of the slaughterhouse, blood all over his abattoir clothing, and confronting an appalled group of engineers waiting for the beginning of their working day: 'What kind of process was it that spat out blood-rinsed foreigners as a by-product,

and allowed them to wander out through the gates?' The novel imposes the engineers' discomfort on its readers.

The eponymous *Blösch* is the novel's other central character, if 'character' is the right word: she's a cow, the star cow on Farmer Knuchel's Alpine homestead. (The name 'Blösch' is traditionally given to any cow with a hide of 'sheer and unbrindled red'.) Cow-herds have strictly-defined internal hierarchies, apparently, and Blösch is the lead cow on Farmer Knuchel's herd, the first cow through the gate and the first into the trough; she thrives on Knuchel's low-tech, old-fashioned approach to his animals. To Ambrosio, the enormous Simmenthal cattle embody 'morbid forbearance and dignified passivity', with at the same time 'a civilised readiness to compromise on serious matters'; 'the warmth they radiated, their incessant inner activity, their endless ruminating, digesting, multiplying, lactating, producing-even-while-they-slept, all that impressed Ambrosio in spite of himself.' But the animals are doomed. 'Every cow in Knuchel's shed had a vertebra that one day would be split. All of them would one day climb unwept and unsung the shit-smeared ramp of a cattle-truck and disappear in the direction of the slaughterhouse.'

Seven years later, Ambrosio recognises a pitifully shrivelled Blösch among the cattle that have arrived at the abattoir to be slaughtered. The recognition precipitates a crisis for Ambrosio, a crisis which eventually leads to him walking out of the slaughterhouse, and which makes the politics of the novel—a blend of Marxism and animal rights—explicit for the first and only time. 'What had been taken from the cow had been taken from himself. . . . He had laughed at Knuchel's cows for their passivity and meekness, but the display of unconditional obedience, of obsequiousness and motiveless mooing that he had witnessed on the ramp, he had also witnessed in himself, to his own disgust. In Blösch on that Tuesday morning, Ambrosio had recognised himself.'

Any novel needs to earn the reader's confidence before it can get away with making its own moral as clear as that. *Blösch* does so by the strictness with which it has hitherto avoided explicit statement of that moral. The processes of dehumanisation and alienation in the workplace are shown rather than told. But the very thoroughness with which we are shown this loss of humanity goes some way to leaching the interest and the imaginative freedom of movement out of the characters who work in the slaughterhouse: an effect compounded by the way Sterchi forsakes a gradual movement towards horror for repeated immersions in it. When the slaughterhouse workers make their final gestures of the novel—two of them walking out, the others drinking in turn a ladle of blood from a cow's freshly cut throat—it's hard for the reader to feel that the redemptory actions amount to much. But perhaps it's appropriate that *Blösch* offers no consolation or uplift, while the scenes and conditions it depicts are still with us. (p. 22)

> *John Lanchester, "Foreigners," in* London Review of Books, *Vol. 11, No. 1 January 5, 1989, pp. 22-3.*

Publishers Weekly

The premise of [the] ambitious, sometimes monotonous but ultimately disturbing novel [*Cow*] is that mechanization, genetic tinkering with animal stock, and an eye for profit has dehumanized the Swiss dairy industry and the slaughterhouses it services. Its implication is wider, however, provoking reassessment of the mechanistic quality of modern life. Sterchi segues between the Alps dairy farm where the Knuchel family still does things in the "old way"—eschewing milking machines, growth hormones and the like—and a nearby slaughterhouse which is being modernized. Ambrosio, a Spanish guest worker hired as a milker by the Knuchels, is fired under pressure from the Knuchels' intensely xenophobic neighbors. He becomes a butcher in the slaughterhouse. The brutal, repetitive activities that take place there make for highly uncomfortable reading. Sterchi's focus on the plight of a guest worker in a foreign land is sometimes lost amid muckraking, but this first novel is still a powerful piece of fiction.

> *A review of "Cow," in* Publishers Weekly, *Vol. 23, No. 15, April 13, 1990, p. 54.*

John Brosnahan

Here's a novel that comes with a publisher's warning that makes it out to be a bovine equivalent of *The Satanic Verses.* Certainly, *Cow* is not for the squeamish, but if the reader can stomach one of the more vivid episodes of "All Creatures Great and Small," there should be no problem with Sterchi's very realistic story of a milk cow's life, from pasture to slaughterhouse. The human element in this tale is a Spanish immigrant who comes to the Swiss Tirol as a guest worker and who, despite many linguistic and cultural obstacles, finds himself at home with the animals, if not with the local populace. Sterchi's novel also raises some hard food-chain issues: where does our daily sustenance ultimately come from, how safely and humanely is it produced, and will the reader gag on the next Big Mac that is ordered up? Certainly the relationship between human and animals has never been portrayed with such intimacy and power as in the pages of this novel, nor have the implications of this animal-human dependency been illustrated on such an elemental level.

> *John Brosnahan, in a review of "Cow," in* Booklist, *Vol. 86, No. 17, May 1, 1990, p. 1686.*

Paul E. Hutchison

The pastures of Hans Knuchel's Swiss farm blossom with happily grazing cows. At the herd's lead walks Blösch, the biggest cow Ambrosio has seen since leaving Spain to become a guest worker in "the prosperous land." While he had expected large cows, he had not expected the hostility of the Swiss toward foreigners, their harsh looks and harsher treatment. Yet he endures first the old-fashioned ways of the Knuchel farm and then the creeping modernization he finds at his later job in the slaughterhouse. Sterchi's first novel [*Cow*] is an imaginatively structured narrative on the topic of bovines, one that will excite few readers. This is not *The Jungle,* and Sterchi seems painfully aware that he falls short by comparison: references to Sinclair's masterpiece abound. Topic aside, however, the three-part focus glued together with the character of Blösch shows real skill.

> *Paul E. Hutchison, in a review of "Cow," in* Library Journal, *Vol. 115, No. 10, June 1, 1990, p. 186.*

Merle Rubin

Beat Sterchi trained in his father's trade as a butcher but left his native Switzerland to study and work abroad and become a writer. His first novel, *Cow* (published in Switzerland in 1983 as *Blösch*), is an impressive, unsettling, monumental, yet in some ways disappointing chronicle of the life and death of a magnificent domestic animal from the rich green Eden of the dairy farm to the blood-smeared hell of the slaughterhouse.

Blösch, we are told, is the name given to calves born with a pure red hide, and Blösch is the name and color of the lead cow at Farmer Knuchel's pristine dairy farm high in the scenic Innerwald. We first see Knuchel and his cows through the eyes of Ambrosio, a *Gastarbeiter* (guest worker) newly arrived from Spain. . . . (p. 2)

Although Ambrosio finds the big Swiss cows rather bovine compared to the fiery bulls of his native Spain, he adjusts well to life at the Knuchel farm. Knuchel is an exemplary farmer who runs his place the old-fashioned way: The cows are fed on home-grown hay in winter and in summer graze in pastures fertilized by homemade manure. The newfangled tricks of artificial insemination and milking machines are anathema to Knuchel, who has his cows properly mated with live bulls and insists that the cows be milked by hand.

Although he steadfastly resists such outlandish new ideas, Knuchel is delighted by his new foreign worker's capacity for honest labor and his sensitive knack for dealing with cows. Unfortunately, other Innerwalders, though quick to adopt industrialized farming methods, are downright xenophobic about the dark-skinned foreign workers in their midst. A succession of minor incidents serves to propel Ambrosio out of the farm and into a job at the city slaughterhouse, where, seven years later, he is astonished to encounter the once-splendid Blösch, now a sickly bag of bones about to fall victim to the butcher's knife:

> The emaciated body that had been dragged out of the cattle-truck . . . that had mooed so pathetically into the morning mist, that body was also Ambrosio's body. Blösch's wounds were his own wounds, the lost lustre of her hide was his loss . . . what had been taken from the cow had been taken from himself. . . . Yes, he had laughed at Knuchel's cows for their passivity and meekness, but the display of unconditional obedience, of obsequiousness and motiveless mooing that he had witnessed on the ramp, he had also witnessed them in himself, to his own disgust.

Between Ambrosio's introduction to the farm and his epiphanic encounter with Blösch in the slaughterhouse, there are more than 300 pages of narration and description that fully flesh out the slime and muck of the cattle industry, down to the last detail. As portrayed in these pages, it is a relatively well-regulated industry, with the usual corruptions that creep in, with more than the usual soul-destroying elements found in the modern industrial workplace. Although there are many horrific scenes of slaughter, evisceration, dismemberment, of industrial corruption and so forth, this novel is not an exposé of industrial corruption (like Upton Sinclair's *The Jungle*), but rather, a confrontation with the more essential corruption—human and animal—that seems to be inseparable from eating, working, living and dying.

An excerpt from *Cow*

And then it was Ambrosio's turn to show what he could do.

Having first rather awkwardly pushed his sleeves back as far as the shoulder several times, and then dipped into the can of milking fat, he cleared his throat and spat, as he did in Spain, to help the flow. He had buckled on the one-legged milking stool as tight as it would go, and then stepped out onto the floor behind the cows. The towering structures of the cows' hindquarters had risen up in front of him, like mountains that he had to move. He had to make a breach there, to get them to part, to reach the full udder of Flora, had to grab hold of the flailing tails, hold onto them and tie down their bushy ends, but the blind lunks of hide and bone didn't want to move, not an inch, and however he cow-shouted at them, however he pounded on their flanks left and right, the back legs of the animals remained knock-kneed and obdurate, their hooves were rooted in the ground, and at the front, in the thick skulls at the end of their long necks, they weren't overly concerned about this stranger who even on tiptoe couldn't see over the top of them.

Flora, who the day before had been persuaded to reach ambitious new heights in her performance, was today making common cause with her neighbour May. They were rubbing against one another with such fervour that even Knuchel was unable to get access to Flora's udder for Ambrosio. 'What a carry-on!' he exclaimed angrily. 'A right pair you are. Anyone would think they were complete novices. Now come on! Take May first this time!'

And then Ambrosio was milking.

Cow is a novel of monumental ambition in that it is clearly intended to be the definitive work on its subject as well as a statement of universal resonance. It is poignant, grisly, powerful, grimly comic, and sometimes lyrical. Richly detailed, it straddles the gulf between realism and allegory: Its grittiest naturalistic particulars seem rife with symbolic significance.

But in addition to being exhaustive, it tends to be exhausting, sometimes to the point of tedium. Some of the tedium is deliberate and appropriate: meant to replicate the mind-numbing labor of farmhands, pig-stickers, meat-cutters, tripe-handlers and intestine-washers. But there's also a te-

dium in the way that Sterchi has elected to structure his novel.

Instead of simply narrating the story chronologically, Sterchi alternates between the earlier days of Ambrosio's farm experience and the later days spent at the slaughterhouse. Thus, by the second chapter, Ambrosio is already at the slaughterhouse, already astonished to meet up with Blösch. Subsequent chapters unfold a little more of how each came to this pass, but in a sense, it's a foregone conclusion for the reader. Structurally, the lack of a conventionally suspenseful story line would not be an insurmountable problem, if only one felt that the novelist's chosen structure were building up toward a revelation as dramatic and profound as the energy of his descriptions seems to promise.

Sterchi is nothing if not thorough. In addition to Ambrosio, we learn the histories of other workers in the meat trade: the gigantic Gilgen; the harried veal-dealer Schindler; the triper Rötlisberger, labeled a "Red" agitator on account of his protest against working conditions; Buri, who lost a leg in an accident in the meat plants of Chicago, but who still boasts of his experience of the big time in America; and many more. The passivity with which these strong, vigorous men find themselves shepherded into their forms of livelihood has obvious parallels with the courageous, helpless passivity of the animals they slaughter.

The novel culminates in a moment of recognition, in which the men rise up from their usual deadening routine to enact a ritual that restores grim meaning to the endless slaughter:

> The cow stood and bled, and it was as though she knew the long history of her kind, as though she knew that she was one of those mothers cheated of their rich white milk, who had offered their teats for thousands of years, and for thousands of years been devoured in recompense. . . . It was as though this cow knew about her ancestors, understood that she herself could only be a pale reflection of the mighty aurochs, who with his curved, arm-length horns had established a dominion that stretched from the bright woods and rich parkland of central Europe as far as the distant heart of China. . . . It was as though this little cow understood the scorn and contempt that had been leveled at her subjugated species since that time, but as though she could still hear . . . a vague rushing, a softened roar that filled her head . . . that could be none other than her ancestors' hoofbeats as they thundered across the steppes . . . and it was as though this rushing and roaring showed itself unmistakably in the eyes of the little cow.

Neither a celebration nor a condemnation of the world it so unflinchingly depicts, *Cow* is a massive and forceful attempt to make us see the obvious and the elemental. This is no small virtue. But in a novel of this size and scope, a novel with such large ambitions, one cannot help wishing there had been something more. (pp. 2, 11)

Merle Rubin, "Kith and Kine," in Los Angeles Times Book Review, *July 1, 1990, pp. 2, 11.*

John Crowley

We humans are sentimental about mothers and children, about what we call Nature, about the past and rural life. But about nothing are we more sentimental than about our relations with the domestic animals from which we get our living. *Cow*—a first novel of considerable ambition—comes from Switzerland, the land of Heidi, the land bucolic at its cutest; but the book aims to describe not simply the pretty part of the food chain, but the whole length, and fully.

Two stories are told by turns in the novel, though in fact one story precedes the other in time. One story takes place on a Swiss dairy farm, the other in a nearby abattoir. We understand early on how the one is connected to the other, just as we understand it in our daily lives—though rarely will we have considered the connection in such detail.

Farmer Knuchel loves his cows. He heals their sores, ponders their diet, follows their quarrels over rank. He milks them by hand, holding modern milking machines in contempt; he won't have them artifically inseminated either. Above all he loves Blösch, an all-red Simmental, lead cow of his herd, champion milk producer whose only fault is an unbreakable habit of producing bull calves.

The work is hard, and Knuchel has hired a Spanish *Gastarbeiter* (migrant worker) to help out. Ambrosio's responses to the huge cows, the big Swiss farm people, the vast dung heap neatly constructed, have a delicate Chaplinesque comedy; the highly colored descriptions of the Knuchel herd, of dairy work, have a cartoonlike distinctness that is quite unlike the pastorals of Thomas Hardy or Hamlin Garland. Appealing as these pages are, they convey well the utter symbiosis of man and his customized slave species, a symbiosis that is made to seem the more ineluctable with every vivid detail of milking and calving.

The final turn of that circle of symbiosis is the slaughterhouse; it is Ambrosio's destination too, as we are aware from the novel's first page, and it is to be Blösch's. The village officials, suspicious from the first of the dark-skinned Spaniard who speaks no German, have excluded Ambro-

sio from the collective creamery, fussed over his papers, badmouthed him to his employer and finally got him fired. Offered no other options, he moves from extracting milk from live cows to extracting meat from dead ones.

The slaughterhouse scenes, which form the greater part of the book, are as rich in detail as the farm scenes, and are at first just as appalling as they were no doubt meant to be; but as the slaughtering, bleeding, beheading, disemboweling and mincing go on and on a tedium sets in, and we begin to read more critically. One of Ambrosio's fellows, an apprentice butcher and a former student too sensitive for his trade and drowned in existential horror, becomes the ruling consciousness in these episodes, and we remember that this is a first novel and suspect it is of the Awful Summer Job variety. The young author adopts a stream-of-consciousness, sentence-fragments style, hoping no doubt to convey immediacy, but in fact loses it by inserting a literary device between his readers and his matter.

Ambrosio is nearly lost sight of; the carefully constructed Swiss village evaporates as we are given brief biographies of all the staff of the slaughterhouse in turn. We cannot even properly attend to the death and sacrifice of the cow Blösch, because the facts of her story (what did she sicken of? what did Farmer Knuchel feel when he led her to the slaughterhouse? why is her meat declared poisoned by the inspector?) are left untold or so buried in the flow as to have no effect. . . .

Beat Sterchi, himself the son of a Swiss butcher, has written a compelling, if grueling, first novel. He has bitten off more than he could chew (if the figure may be allowed), as a great writer ought to, but has not then found the literary means to chew it, as a great writer will. It may seem frivolous to concentrate on matters of style when the book asks us to attend to the matter of butchery and the deaths on which we live, but it is the author's own inexperience that has put the literary questions between us and his story and obscured our view. When the subject is the extremes of existence, blood and guts, what is wanted is not less art, but more.

John Crowley, "Beef Interlude," in The New York Times Book Review, *July 8, 1990, p. 9.*

Christopher Tilghman
In a Father's Place

Born in 1948(?), Tilghman is an American short story writer.

In a Father's Place contains short stories notable for their surprising revelations about ordinary people as well as society as a whole. Centering upon familial relationships, Tilghman addresses such topics as tradition, class differences, death, and religion in a vital, evocative manner. Setting is an integral part of Tilghman's narratives; Michiko Kakutani noted that "the land itself emerges as a kind of character in many of these stories." In "On the Rivershore," for example, Tilghman vividly portrays the bay locale of a small town in Maryland. In this tale, enduring opposition between farmers and watermen is temporarily overcome when members of both sides agree to cover up the murder of a town troublemaker. Many characters in Tilghman's stories espouse traditional family values and often find themselves in search of a lost past, or a more stable present. In "Hole in the Day," Lonnie suddenly leaves her husband while pregnant with their fifth child. Her husband follows her across South Dakota and Montana in a desperate search that is eventually fulfilled through the inspirational presence of their youngest child. While critics note that at times Tilghman's stories rely upon contrivances of plot and a self-conscious perspective that weaken the effect of the author's impressionistic style, most commentators concur that his compact, dramatic tales are successful character portrayals based on substantive themes. Kakutani maintained: "*In a Father's Place* is a moving and pictorially vivid collection—a collection that signals the appearance of a gifted new writer, blessed with an instinctual feel for the emotional transactions that make up family life."

mansions, their pecans and honey locusts like sails, seem to be making their way, somewhere, on the shimmer of the bay."

For good or ill, nature shapes these people's lives and invests them with a believable grandeur. As a result, they possess an almost Dickensian sense of drama and possibility. In ["**In a Father's Place**"], for example, an aging father, in the face of a brewing storm, finally asserts himself and boots his son's churlish girlfriend out of his house. Then he wonders, out of habit, how he will explain himself. "But the wind that had already brought change brushed him clean of all that and left him naked, a man. He could not help the rising tide of joy that was coming to him. He was astonished by what had happened to him. By his life." (pp. 59-60)

Malcolm Jones, in a review of "In a Father's Place," in Newsweek, *Vol. CXV, No. 14, April 2, 1990, pp. 59-60.*

Malcolm Jones

Christopher Tilghman is in most respects a spare and careful craftsman whose prose is always tucked in and buttoned down. Likewise, his characters are resolutely unexotic, mostly middle-class people, with jobs and families and usually some money in the bank. They struggle to find what society expects of them and what they expect of themselves as fathers, mothers, sons and daughters. Otherwise the seven stories in [*In a Father's Place*] are very audacious. Tilghman sets his tales in places of sweeping greatness: the high plains, the open sea, the vast Eastern Shore of Maryland, where "the rolled farmland and mirrored water meet so seamlessly that on hazy days the big

Michiko Kakutani

In the title story of this radiant new collection [*In a Father's Place*], an aging patriarch learns that his son, Nick, is writing a book, and he asks his son's girlfriend what the book is about. "Well, I guess what it's really about is you," she replies. "Not really you, but a father, and this place"—this place, meaning Nick's boyhood home, the family manse, the community his family has lived in now for generations.

The same might well be said of all the stories in this debut volume by Christopher Tilghman. Each one measures the emotional distance a man or woman has traveled since leaving home, each one traces the vestigial hold that childhood memories and a familial past continue to exert on an individual life.

In many of the tales, a man or woman returns—after the space of many years—to a family home. In **"Loose Reins,"** a man by the name of Hal goes back to Montana, to visit his widowed mother who has just announced her marriage to a ranch hand named Roy. As Hal revisits his favorite boyhood haunts, he realizes that all he sees is overlaid with another map that exists only in his imagination, a map of memories and emotions he thought he'd lost when he moved back east.

He sees the kitchen table where his taciturn father used to preside silently over dinner, staring out the window looking for rain. He sees his mother at work in the garden, and remembers how she moved to this desolate land from the East so many years ago. And he sees the ranch hands' bunkhouse and remembers how Roy used to sleep there, how he nearly froze to death there one winter during a violent blizzard. The image of Roy in the bunkhouse is juxtaposed, now, with the image of Roy giving his mother "a light, dancing kiss on the top of the head" as they sit on the veranda sipping coffee in the warm mid-morning sun. . . .

[The] compression of a character's life into a couple of brief pages distinguishes all the stories in this volume. Though many revolve around a single dramatic anecdote—a man's attempt to find his wife, who's run away from home; a father's attempt to talk with his son during a strained family reunion; a sailor's attempt to make a choice between his marriage and his love of the open sea—they unfold to reveal an entire life, a complete emotional history. In this sense, the central anecdote simply serves as a touchstone by which Mr. Tilghman's hero may re-evaluate his relationship with the past, with his family and their world.

Indeed, Mr. Tilghman demonstrates a remarkable gift in these stories for delineating the complexities and complications of familial love: the ways in which one embraces or rebels against family tradition, the ways in which one is tied to other family members by loss, crisis and a shared sense of place, as well as by straightforward affection. Many of his people come to see their lives as defined not only in terms of their immediate families, but also in terms of generations within the arc of history.

In **"Loose Reins,"** Hal's mother, who gave up a debutante's life for the hardships of Montana, says she understands "what the pioneer wives felt as they waited in the wagons, dreaming of the green hills of Ohio, while husbands made homes out of sod and buffalo skin." And Grant, the hero of **"Hole in the Day,"** who is driving west across Montana in pursuit of his wife, thinks of his great-grandfather, who traced a similar route westward to the Pacific, and all the others who once left their homes in search of an elusive frontier.

In fact the land itself emerges as a kind of character in many of these stories. The wilds of Montana, the clay banks of Maryland's Eastern Shore, the sun-dappled landscapes of Chesapeake Bay—such places are giving way, in Mr. Tilghman's stories, to homogenized suburbs with "miracle miles and plastic strips." But they remain implanted in his heroes's imaginations, as powerful, if receding, memories that help define who they are.

It is Mr. Tilghman's sure sense of his characters' histories that lends these stories their form and their emotional chiaroscuro. When he abandons this impressionistic method in favor of more self-conscious, structural conceits, the results tend to be weaker. **"Mary in the Mountains,"** which relies upon excerpts from a woman's letters to her estranged husband, gives the reader an oddly disembodied account of a middle-aged woman's fractured life. And **"A Gracious Rain"** stands as an awkward ghost story about a young father who dies from a sudden heart attack, and then returns to watch over his family.

Such tales, however, are exceptions. *In a Father's Place* is a moving and pictorially vivid collection—a collection that signals the appearance of a gifted new writer, blessed with an instinctual feel for the emotional transactions that make up family life.

> Michiko Kakutani, "Going Home Again, and Finding You Can't," in The New York Times, April 3, 1990, p. C17.

Richard Eder

The cartoon fox chases the cartoon rabbit around a clump of trees. And since panic is quicker than desire, after a few circuits, the rabbit is chasing the fox.

Literature starts with an emotion in pursuit of a writer. The course is tricky and keeps doubling back on itself. The solitary workroom, the dry holes, the exercise that depletes instead of fortifying, the struggle to jam the ghost into running shoes—no wonder it so often ends with the writer padding along after the emotion.

Christopher Tilghman's first collection of short stories runs the race both ways. Almost all display moments that are triumphs: a phrase that switches on the light, a sudden impulse of thought or feeling that calls a tide on the point of turning. In many of them, though, we get the sense that the author has seized an occasion to write very well. In two, it is as if the occasion had seized the author and given voice through him.

The people in Tilghman's stories—set mostly in rural areas or in small or middle-sized towns—are value-seekers. They look in themselves, their past, their communities for signs of life and meaning. Somewhat unfashionably, they care a lot and prize their own caring.

In the beautifully drawn **"On the Rivershore,"** Tilghman poises everything upon a series of frontiers. It is set in Maryland's Chesapeake Bay Country, where the farmland lies so low and flat that it seems to merge with the water. "On hazy days," he writes, "the big mansions, their pecans and honey locusts like sails, seem to be making their way, somewhere, on the shimmer of the Bay."

The frontier may be hazy, but it is there. The farmers and the watermen form two separate and mutually wary communities. When a farmer kills a fisherman who has been abusing his daughter, a war is on the point of erupting. Two cooler heads prevail, one on each side; an abuse has been committed and paid for, they conclude.

But there are other frontiers, and Tilghman delicately superimposes one upon the other. There is youth and age; the killing and the subsequent confrontation are witnessed by the farmer's 12-year-old son. In the showdown that ends peaceably, he will hear—and later, as an adult, understand—the restraint imposed by a different frontier, between past and present.

A way of life is passing on the land and the water. The farms are slipping from the hands of their proprietors; the watermen's prosperity will slip away as well, and with it, their clan pride. We hear the times changing in the troubled words of accommodation spoken by Ray, the farm overseer, and Morris, the older of the two crabbers.

A different growth into understanding is told in the lovely **"Hole in the Day."** A South Dakota farm wife, desperate at being pregnant with her fifth child, slams her legs together one night as her husband is making love, jumps out of bed, packs some clothes and drives off.

> She ran from that single weathered dot on the plains because the babies that kept coming out of her were not going to stop, a new one was just beginning and she could already feel the suckling at her breast. Soon she will cross into Montana, or Minnesota, or Nebraska; she's just driving and it doesn't really matter to her where, because she is never coming back.

In these few opening lines, Tilghman captures her drowning despair, the flash of her revolt, and also its fragility.

Grant, the husband, sits rigidly for hours in the chair from which he'd watched her pack. "He feels as if the roof of his house had been lifted," Tilghman writes. Come morning, the four children wake up; Leila, age 8, numbly takes charge. Unable to move, Grant hears the sounds of the children coping: "In the kitchen the baby wails as he is passed around."

After the explosion and the subsequent silence of the crater, movement returns. Grant packs his pickup truck, drops Leila with a neighbor and two of her brothers with his mother. Nobody will accept the 2-year-old, so he takes him along. He doesn't know where Lonnie, his wife, has gone, but he will find her.

The search—farmer and baby driving from town to town—is grand folly. But it is also a grand act of faith. Tilghman's story of the trip is the story of a man, out of a suddenly purified love, casting himself upon fortune. The baby—"a buddy, willing and cheerful to go along, always surprised by events"—is his talisman. Without him, he reflects after he has found Lonnie and they have made peace, his instinct would have failed; he would not have sensed where to go.

It is touching and comic, this mad search and peaceable reunion. Something has been learned. And Tilghman has accomplished what only a true storyteller can do: make the impossible inevitable.

In other stories, the characters and their discoveries are less convincingly joined. **"A Gracious Rain"** is a contrived, *Our Town*-like sketch of a factory worker who dies and returns in spirit to sit on his front porch and to reflect that death is just as inconclusive in a small town as life is. **"Mary in the Mountains"** describes the lethal coldness in the heart of a gentle woman. Tilghman has fashioned a target out of her, and shot it.

The same feeling of a target, of a story as an occasion for literature, comes in the title piece. Like **"Riverroad,"** it is set in Maryland and tells of an era passing. The setting—a shore mansion filled with things from a more gracious time—and Dan, its protagonist—an old lawyer who has vegetated since his wife died—are well drawn, if familiar. Dan's son, a writer, has come home for a brief visit.

With Nick, the son, comes Patty, his girlfriend. She is an intolerably sharp-tongued, arrogant and greedy young woman who "tore up"—in Nick's admiring if cowed words—the English Department at Columbia. She prowls the house with price tags in her eyes, flaunts a book by Jacques Derrida, the fashionable literary deconstructionist, and prods Nick to work faster on his novel.

It will, she assures a dismayed Dan, "deconstruct" the family. At night, Dan overhears her giving Nick directions to her orgasm. An explosion comes, with a total lack of surprise. Patty is not simply a mean effigy; she is a regular Guy Fawkes stuffed to the sneer with gunpowder.

"Norfolk" tells of the estrangement between a '60s couple when he goes off to sea in the Navy and finds he likes it, and his wife stays at home to be arty. It arranges its characters woodenly, though there is some lovely writing in it.

"Loose Reins" recounts a son's distress when his mother, widow of a rancher, marries a broken-down cowhand. It too is stiffly arranged around its point, although it boasts one shining scene. The cowhand picks up a crystal bowl that the son has brought as a wedding present, and his words challenge the young man's simplistic contempt. "I've never seen nothing so pretty that I can hold in my hands," he says. "It's like mountain water."

Tilghman's ladders, rising like Yeats', out of the human heart, are fine ladders, and when they sit firmly, they give a glorious view. Too often, though, they slip on the strewed rags and bones of which he does not yet seem ready to take account.

Richard Eder, "The Flash and Fragility of Revolt," in Los Angeles Times Book Review, April 29, 1990, pp. 3, 7.

John Casey

[*In a Father's Place*] is a wonderful surprise. Each [story] starts with assurance, opens into a cluster of lives, a precise evocation of place and a gathering current of action, reaction and reflection. Each story becomes increasingly charged with feeling and yet increasingly clarified; quick reflective realizations guide the narrative. A good helmsman, Christopher Tilghman doesn't oversteer. I read eagerly, with an eye to what comes next, but two or three times in every story I was surprised by a smooth turn, a reorientation that left me startled with pleasure. . . .

It is as hard to summarize what happens in these stories as it is to categorize what they are about. The first, **"On the Rivershore,"** has as its precipitating event the shooting of a waterman by a farm worker. The story is told from the point of view of the farm worker's son, who sees the killing. It is, of course, about the son's horror and loyalty, but the story also involves the vertical landlord-tenant hierarchy of the [town] as well as the horizontal ill will between watermen and farmers. They work out a resolution that avoids the law in favor of an act that is truer to their community and their sense of the reach of their lives.

"Loose Reins" is set in Montana (though one of the *things* in the story is a wedding present transported from Shreve, Crump & Low in Boston). The plot has some of the abrupt complexity of comedy. A widowed mother of two sons, grown and gone away, announces that she has married an old ranch hand, once a pathetic drunk, whom she has salvaged. The older son flies out from the East with his wife to do the right thing and to see what's up. But comedy is squelched early on, when he and his mother are driving to town:

> "There is perhaps one more thing you should know. There's no sex between us."
>
> "Good God," said Hal.
>
> "Not that you have a right to know or care, but it seems something worth clearing up."
>
> "Not that I *want* to know or care." He looked out at the fence posts flashing by like newsreel frames. "But what is it, then? Can you imagine what it's going to be like during the winter?"
>
> "Of course we talk, most of the time about——"
>
> Hal interrupted. "You tell him all about the 1937 Cotillion and he tells you about squeezing Sterno in Missoula."
>
> "Is that a joke, dear?"

The obvious way for the story to go is mother-son conflict or reconciliation. But Mr. Tilghman summons other story lines: the family history of the ranch and the transformation of the mother from a nice young lady from back East into someone who knows what she's doing in Montana, Hal's old troubles with his petrified father and quicksilver

brother and, most important, Hal's relationship, before and now, with the man who has married his mother. All these past hauntings and present circumstances come at a good pace, opening up Hal's character in a way that would be enough by itself to justify the story. But the story isn't just Hal's; it's about what all of these people have worked out with one another, the way the place works them loose from the predestinations of family and class.

"Norfolk, 1969" is about much younger people, a new Navy ensign and his bride. There are several pulls of place—the dismaying heat and sprawl of Norfolk, a ship at sea, an antiwar demonstration in Washington. The point of view is the ensign's, conveying his initial dislike of the Navy, his aching for his wife, his eventual love of being at sea, his attempts to fit into the life his wife has arranged for herself while he's away for so long. But his point of view includes a valiant effort to understand his wife. Both of them are decent in love and sorrow, and vulnerable to each other. There is anguish in their relationship, but no self-pity. The yes/no of their love is recorded in part from a calmer time afterward, as is the conflict of the two subcultures they have grown into. Their differences aren't argued out in ideology (they're both against the Vietnam War) any more than they are in sexual conflict (they're both faithful). What they find to comfort themselves with, in each other's absence, becomes stronger than their young marriage. Each of their new allegiances is understandable to the other but, in the end, is not reachable.

These plots sound plausible and intelligent, but Mr. Tilghman's stories are much more than that. I remember Peter Taylor blithely telling a class to write 15-page short stories that "do the work of novels." I know he didn't mean stuffing a story with larger and longer action. I'm pretty sure he meant suggesting the slow forces of life through details that are not only immediately vivid but that also imply a character's accumulated life, presenting family and society in tuned resonances, like the unplucked but sympathetically sounding strings of certain Renaissance instruments.

In this, his first book, Mr. Tilghman has written stories, usually between 20 and 30 pages long, that do the work of novels with that sort of detail, with what Turgenev called "the life-giving drop." I can't pick a favorite, and there's not one of the seven that doesn't belong with the others. There's a metaphysical wrinkle in **"A Gracious Rain,"** but it leads to a vision that is more than worth the jolt. The title story, **'In a Father's Place,"** has the only onstage villain of the whole book, and I worried about whether Mr. Tilghman endorsed the father's view of this villain, who is his son's lover. She and the father have a winging fight, and the second time I read the story I began to root for her, at least a little bit. She says that she disapproves of the manorial life the family leads on their Maryland estate:

> "I think you're all in a fantasy."
>
> Dan made a show of looking around at the walls, the cane-and-wicker furniture. . . . He shrugged. "People from the outside seem to make a lot more of this than we do."

Of course, after a remark like that she retaliates, and they're at it hammer and tongs. The father explodes: "Oh, cut the crap about his work. You want his soul, you little Nazi, you want any soul you can get your hands on." Then he cuts off her attempt to talk back and asks her to leave the house. *If* the author's view of her is that of the father, the story ends up a little pat, though it's still riveting in its progress.

"Hole in the Day" and **"Mary in the Mountains"** are, like all the others but the title story, elegantly balanced. **"Hole in the Day"** in particular has the virtue of telling a genuinely sweet story in contrastingly dry and gritty detail. It and the other six stories, all variations on the theme of the powers of the family, form a wonderfully satisfying cycle. *In a Father's Place* is a beautiful book, making emotions as vivid and rich in perspective as a loved landscape.

> *John Casey, " 'Is That a Joke, Dear?' " in* The New York Times Book Review, *May 6, 1990, p. 12.*

Joan Motyka

Christopher Tilghman started writing fiction in 1971 when he left the Navy, but it wasn't until 1986 that his first story was published. Between those years, he worked as a carpenter and in a sawmill, he renovated buildings and apartments in exchange for rent and he wrote copy for corporate reports. Some years, he wrote no fiction at all.

"If there were anything resembling a career path for fiction writers, there would be enormous gaps in the résumé, like mine," he said in a recent telephone interview from the partly renovated Shaker meetinghouse in Harvard, Mass., where he lives with his wife and two young sons. But, he added, the tales that make up his first collection of stories, *In a Father's Place,* could not have been written "if I hadn't spent all those years doing what I did. I couldn't have written it at 25. I didn't *know* it at 25."

The stories, set in places as diverse as a Montana ranch and an antiques-stuffed mansion on the Eastern Shore of Maryland, provide a road map of where the 43-year-old Mr. Tilghman has lived and traveled. But they also tell of families and the intersecting lives of the people in those families.

Mr. Tilghman's fascination with place and family, cornerstones of the Southern literary tradition, was strongly instilled in him during childhood summers on a Maryland farm that has been in his family since the 17th century. "I sit down to write a story," he said, "and the word 'father' appears in the first paragraph." The family, in Mr. Tilghman's view, "is the one inescapable fact of life, the measure of what we accomplish personally and professionally."

Mr. Tilghman said his own family has been a strong support since he began writing. But in those long unpublished years, what really kept him going was the pleasure of weaving tales. "It's fun to do, to make stories," he explained. "It's been full-time work or a primary hobby, depending on what stage I've been in. But it has never ceased to be fun."

> *Joan Motyka, "Road Maps of His Life," in* The New York Times Book Review, *May 6, 1990, p. 12.*

Ann Hulbert

In the last of the stories in [*In a Father's Place*], an aloof and spiritual woman describes how she takes her elderly neighbor on walks in the New Hampshire woods and tells her stories from her life: "When I repeat myself, she starts jabbing a deformed knuckle into my side to urge me to get on to the parts she loves, about trains, and about people who fear for their souls." Christopher Tilghman's stories are also about journeys and travails, but he is far from aloof. His first collection unfolds at a serene pace, the calm born not of detachment but of devoted interest in small details, which open onto larger spaces. There's no rushing him to the parts about (in his case) boats and about people whose souls are unsteady but sturdy, afloat in a world that inspires them with doubt.

Inspires rather than daunts them: "Hope had kept him going, but it was the doubt that gave him joy," Stanley Harris, recently dead, reflects in **"Gracious Rain"** as he looks back over a life that has seemed to him inexplicably blessed in its accumulation of mostly happy accidents. The revelation of this unusual story, which nonchalantly steps into the afterlife as though barely a doorsill stood in the way, is that for Stanley, dead too soon of an unhappy accident, "The quest was not over. He had been spared once again, spared the end of doubt, preserved from eternal rest. Life, in other words, went on."

What is distinctive about the transcendent impulse that surfaces in so many of Tilghman's stories is that it doesn't take the characters away from the world so much as return them to it. Rather than shattering everyday life, the epiphanies that happen here put errant pieces of ordinary days into a new shape—rarely a well-rounded or fixed shape, but that is usually the point. At his best, Tilghman doesn't stage easy leaps out of confusion, but merely turns a corner to find a moment of greater clarity about the confusion—a moment that, it seems clear, isn't likely to last.

As the title of this collection of seven stories suggests, life for the characters goes on mostly within the confines of the family. Like many American fiction writers lately, Tilghman is a master of mundane realism—doesn't miss the wet Pampers, the hot kitchens, the rumpled beds. But at the same time that he's watching the eddies of need and desire inside the house, he also has his eye on history, and on nature. And it's while he's doing that, as Stanley's experience shows most explicitly, that Tilghman looks across yet another threshold, reaching for a timeless perspective on the passage of time, on the "passionate daily traffic in perishables," as Leslie Farber once described the essential drama of family life.

Landscape matters in these stories, and Tilghman plants his characters all over the country—in Montana; in Norfolk, Virginia in the summer, charmless and hot; on roads leading out of the plains and into the mountains; and, the place he's most at home, on Maryland's Eastern Shore, on "land just barely afloat on fragile banks of clay and sand," the Chesapeake Bay always encroaching and the Bay Bridge rising in the background, a reminder of a mainland that seems far away. Big cities, it's worth noting, don't appear, except in the background, and it is hard to imagine Tilghman keeping his calm pace amid urban bustle. Not that his scenes are placid. Nature is usually a physical and psychological challenge in the foreground of his characters' lives, tiring them out, making them feel trapped. But if their roots in the places they have settled are sometimes constricting, ultimately their groundedness is a liberation to their spirits.

History haunts them in a very different way. Tilghman unfolds their far-flung lives against a common background: the advent of the post-Vietnam era, with its mood of doubt about the direction of public life, and about the traditional bonds of private life. That's not to suggest that this collection is facilely contemporary, another contribution to the genre of certifiably up-to-date dramas of disillusionment and unhappiness. On the contrary, there is a refreshingly anachronistic air about these stories. Tilghman's imagination is unobtrusively historical, not superficially sociological. He's as interested, if not more, in the old ways of life that were overturned not so long ago as in the contemporary changes that have replaced them. And the doubt that has accompanied the changes is anything but enervating.

These are stories with real plots. Tilghman catches his characters at moments of transition, when their lives have suddenly taken a turn, and he leaves them with a new perspective not just on themselves, but on the world—an unusual push beyond psychological drama to social observation and then to moral reflection. As its title promises, **"Norfolk, 1969"** is the one story in which Tilghman writes directly about the tumultuous era that occupies a quiet but important place in the background of the collection, and it shows just how out of the conventional currents his vision runs. Charlie and Julie Martin, young and newly married, arrive in Norfolk, where Charlie is about to begin his three-year stint with the Navy. It's clear from the start that a saga of troubled love is in store, but it's only slowly and subtly that the political contours of that trouble emerge—and just as subtly they are complicated by a deeper, unideological perspective.

Charlie sails away from his wife full of ambivalence, both about leaving Julie and about having ended up in the Navy: the unspoken, important fact about Charlie is that he didn't evade the draft. But while he's at sea this diffident draftee is suddenly overcome with loyalty to his ship:

> The farther the *Jupiter* plowed toward the center of the ocean, the more an elemental soul asserted itself, swells of time, growing over a million square miles. . . . None of the anguishes of the age, none of the compromises that had been forced on him, none of the political confusions in his head, mattered anymore.

Back on shore, Julie has meanwhile discovered what counterculture there is in Norfolk and now occupies a central place in a circle of anti-war activists, among whom Charlie

feels awkward on his return, though he tries to join in. One night when the group gathers over marijuana, talking about quiet communion with nature, Charlie is roused from his usual silence to describe his ecstasy at sea—only to be met with stony silence. At that moment he suddenly sees how far away from their certainty he feels, though he joins Julie in the march on Washington, still grasping for a sense of political and social solidarity, for "a place in his time." A story that risks slipping into the *Coming Home* genre follows a more complicated course and finally embraces muddle rather than melodrama. When Charlie looks back years later, trudging in a now widened "middle of the road," what he remembers is how truly at sea he was—out on those infinite "swells of time."

The water is again an arbiter in a very different story, **"On the Rivershore,"** in which Tilghman conjures up a world that existed back on the other side of the war. Like almost all of his stories, it opens with an evocation of place: it's a beach on the Eastern Shore, and the description is metaphorically as well as physically telling: "The sand is fine enough, but it is sharp with oyster shells and rough with stones the color of oxblood and ginger. There's always a tangled line of seaweed running the length of the last high tide." This is a story about one bloody day in the 1950s when the line dividing the local watermen—oystermen, clam diggers, and seine haulers—and the farmers back on shore was suddenly tangled, a prelude to much more drastic dislocations to come.

Here, too, the larger scene quietly builds around a smaller domestic drama. Twelve-year-old Cecil Mayberry has just seen his father, a tenant farmer, shoot Tommie Todman, a troublemaking waterman, in the head. There's a slow-motion feel to the prose in which Tilghman traces the consequences of an act that, as the stunned boy half-realizes but can't quite believe, threatens to wreak havoc on the shoreline world that is his life. But the water swallows up the trouble, and for a time at least the local peace is kept. Out on the Bay, where Cecil, his father, and his father's boss go to dump the body, a battle with avenging watermen is averted when, in a sudden moment of understanding, the men realize it isn't worth disrupting the delicate balance of Bay life for the likes of no good Tommie.

They all watch as the body sinks to the depths; the law and local codes of honor have been superseded by a community's instinct for self-preservation. But there's no romanticizing here: that instinct is all too soon overwhelmed. Thirty years later when Cecil, now a father himself and long since gone from the land, comes back for his father's funeral, the old ways have disappeared amid much larger feuds. His boyhood friend, the son of one of the watermen on the Bay that day, has come back from Vietnam "changed forever, and the catch is down and the oystermen go to war with the clam diggers and the seine haulers give up for good." (pp.40-1)

There's plenty of land in these stories, not just water and wind. And there is also fire, since Tilghman, though he knows the tug of transcendence, doesn't leave more lowly human passions out of the picture. In **"Hole in the Day,"** Lonnie, the young mother of four, has fled her husband, her babies, and the oppressive plains where she keeps on having more babies. But as she reaches the mountains she's been heading for, she's pulled back by merciless domestic demands, which suddenly loom up around the thought of her chipped baby spoon, decorated with ducks whose beaks have long since faded:

> She has held that spoon for four babies, scooped in the first mouthfuls of pears and custard, given those four babies their first tastes of life on that spoon. Even now she can feel through the handle the cleaning tug of the baby's lips when he or she is hungry, and the resistance of the tongue that moves her hand aside when he's not. She's given her children everything on that spoon, and now she wants to hold it and look at those beakless ducks.

Almost without our noticing, the homely image has been transformed: the ducks on the spoon have become Lonnie's babies. In the ample vision of Tilghman's stories, small metamorphoses always matter. (p. 41)

> *Ann Hulbert, "Leaps of Faith," in* The New Republic, *Vol. 202, No. 23, June 4, 1990, pp. 40-1.*

Thomas D'Evelyn

Christopher Tilghman has been writing these stories since he got out of the Navy in 1971. He's also worked as a carpenter and corporate newsletter writer; he's gotten married and had children. These stories reek experience.

Tilghman is now over 40. *In a Father's Place* is his first book. It sounds, however, like a last book—seven stories sifting spiritual from ephemeral things. There's also Tilghman's rhetoric. No plastic-spastic postmodern prose for him: He plays the whole piano. Tilghman listens to his sentences, his paragraphs, until he hears the inner shape, then shows it. The sound completes the meaning.

Another thing: These stories are about families. That is, they are about fathers, mothers, and children. They are about memories and places, about homes. . . .

Tilghman makes no apologies for the emotional scope of his stories. On the contrary, he takes risks; one thinks of great Southern writers—Faulkner, O'Connor, Percy—who also plunged into the beyond. But his stories, like theirs, grow from soil rich in perception. Tilghman has tracked the senses for years, noticing how they carry information, how they interpenetrate. Synesthesia is not too big a word for some of his effects—"the electric blue snap of the welder sparking deep in the shadows."

Tilghman is wonderful with children. **"Hole in the Day"** is about a baby accompanying his father to find Lonnie, wife and mother. This baby loves to see the big trucks file down the passes in Montana. "Turk," he sings: "Turk."

In **"A Gracious Rain,"** we see the children of Stan and Beth run through the gamut of emotions at the wake of their father, who has died suddenly at work one day. The story seems nearly perfect. Stan was a quiet, thoughtful man in life, and he's the same in death. Tilghman manages

the transition from this character's life to his afterlife without skipping a beat.

These stories about fathers feature strong women. In **"Norfolk, 1969,"** notable for its evocation of life on a huge Navy vessel, a young married couple go their own ways. No adultery. She's on shore and gets involved in antiwar activism; he's on the high seas. Experience proves stronger than love.

The title story, **"In a Father's Place,"** recreates the Civil War. A Chesapeake Bay mansion is invaded by grown children and a girlfriend, Patty Keith. She is the terror of the Columbia University English department, an arrogant radical with an eye for antiques. The father is sure she's a witch. As soon as he gets a chance, he throws her out. Seductive in her own way, Patty Keith is not the last word on the untameable woman.

The final story recapitulates the book: past and present alternate, father exerts authority, the promise of family life divides as well as unites. **"Mary in the Mountains"** moves from place to place, from New Hampshire to Boston to Paris to Wellesley, Mass. Mary is writing a letter to her ex-husband. She writes with the vehemence of Sylvia Plath and the aching wisdom of Emily Dickinson. The narrative shifts between letter writing and memories (the memories are in italics), with recollections as lucid as a dream.

Tilghman's eloquent stories are works of intelligence, craft, and time. They deal with topics that are so charged today as to be labeled "political": patriarchy, abortion, family tradition, class tension, religious belief, and the divine. But they deal with these topics wisely, through art making them transparent for meanings beyond them.

Taken together these stories bear witness to the ancient truth that man's happiness lies beyond self. These stories grow on one. We need companions such as these.

> *Thomas D'Evelyn, "Stories of Experience," in* The Christian Science Monitor, *June 15, 1990, p. 13.*

Robert Towers

Christopher Tilghman is a writer who does not duck issues or short change his reader. Each of the seven short stories in his impressive first collection, *In a Father's Place,* works like a novel in miniature. Each is grounded not only in a richly detailed setting but in a family history and in the psychologically complex relations among parents and children, husbands and wives. The first story, **"On the Rivershore,"** opens with a landscape:

> Between the clay banks of the Eastern Shore of Maryland and the brackish waters of the Chesapeake Bay there is a beach a thousand miles long. The sand is fine enough, but it is sharp with oyster shells and rough with stones the color of oxblood and ginger. There's always a tangled line of seaweed running the length of the last high tide. Except for this narrow divider, the rolled farmland and mirrored water meet so seamlessly that on hazy days the big mansions,

their pecans and honey locusts like sails, seem to be making their way, somewhere, on the shimmer of the Bay.

Then the story closes in on the main character:

> On one spot of this beach along the Chester River, there is a boy sitting on the polished curve of a washed-up loblolly pine. His eyes are dry now, but the dirt on his cheeks is streaked and there is salt on his lips. He is holding a crab net and an empty bushel basket, and his broad-brimmed straw hat floats in the water at his feet.

The boy is Cecil Mayberry, aged twelve, the son of a farm hand who works for the owner of the local manor; he has just witnessed his beloved father shoot and kill a "crazy son-of-a-bitch," a local waterman named Tommie Todman, who has been forcing himself upon Cecil's elder sister. The boy knows he has to tell someone—because "even if the buzzards eat Tommie clean up and no one cares or misses him ever, he knows his daddy, and sooner or later, after milking is done today probably, he's going to walk into Officer Stapleton's office and turn himself in." He decides to tell his father's employer, Mr. McHugh, who lives at the Big House, and he thus sets in motion the burial of Tommie's corpse in the bay and a confrontation between the local farmers and their hereditary enemies, the watermen. In only twenty-two pages a small society, with its occupations, its class structure, and its codes (e.g., no waterman learns how to swim), has been revealed.

Tilghman seems perfectly at ease in a variety of milieus. In **"Loose Reins,"** the leading character, Hal, is the son of a well-to-do Yale graduate who had moved to Montana in the late Thirties with his Philadelphia debutante wife and became the owner of a prosperous thousand-acre ranch. Now, decades later, his widow, Jean, has suddenly married a battered, formerly drunken ranch hand called Roy, whom she had befriended over the years, and Hal and his wife are traveling west from Boston to see them. Not only is the Montana landscape evoked carefully and knowledgeably but so are the language and attitudes of the old ranch hand who now preposterously has become Hal's stepfather. In the story's climactic scene, Roy, whom Hal has always regarded as little better than a half-wit, is sent to retrieve Hal from a local bar, where he has gone to drown with bourbon his dismay over his mother's new situation. There Roy startles Hal by revealing an unexpectedly acute insight into the family's life.

> "I never really knew your dad. No one did. But this was sure: nothing came natural to the man. Nothing at all." It sure wasn't ranching, Roy went on, though he'd become one of the best ranchers in Montana. And it sure wasn't raising a family.

> "I'll give it to you straight," said Roy. "I hated the man. And there's one thing I'll never forgive his memory for. It was the way he looked at his family and saw right through them, right out the other side, as if there was nothing to take pride in."

> "Good God," said Hal. "You knew that?"

> "Just because I was drunk didn't mean I was deaf. I used to watch you and Markie [Hal's younger brother] fighting over who would sit next to him in the pickup. I coulda told you to forget it. It made me sad, seeing you kids try to please him."

In **"Hole in the Day,"** a young mechanic, Grant, and his wife, Lonnie, live in an isolated spot on the endless grassy plains of South Dakota. He has grown up there and likes it, but Lonnie, who has already had four children and discovers she is pregnant again, can stand her life no longer. One night she stops her husband in the middle of their lovemaking and drives off. We follow Grant as he tries to deal with his children; he leaves the older ones with his dour mother and sister in Nebraska, and sets off—accompanied by the baby whom no one will take—in successful pursuit of his wife. Tilghman dramatizes the situation of the desperate young couple without condescension and the children are remarkably real.

In only one story does Tilghman's touch seem less than sure, and that is in the title story, **"In a Father's Place."** Like **"On the Rivershore"** and **"A Gracious Rain,"** it is set on the eastern shore of Maryland. A middle-aged lawyer, Dan, the owner of a fine old house that has been in his family since the seventeenth century, is visited by his daughter, Rachel, his son, Nick, and Nick's girlfriend, Patty. Patty is presented as a shrewish young deconstructionist who, according to the admiring but dominated Nick, "tore the English Department at Columbia *apart*." She is pushing Nick to complete a novel which, according to him, is "not really *about* anything, not a plot, anyway." "I know she's not for everyone," Nick continues, attempting to explain Patty to his father, "but I've never known anyone who takes less shit in her life." Tilghman seems ill at ease in presenting the intellectual credentials of this fierce young woman and the deepening conflict between her and Dan. The portrait of the father who is both burdened and sustained by his family's past and must now face the dispersal of his children and the end of an increasingly untenable way of life is, however, movingly done.

One begins the stories in Tilghman's collection with no idea where each will lead. But after finishing several of them, the reader is confident that something eventful and even surprising lies ahead. *In a Father's Place* leaves me impatient to see what he will write next.

Robert Towers, in a review of "In a Father's Place," in The New York Review of Books, *Vol. XXXVII, No. 13, August 16, 1990, p. 46.*

Prizewinners

Literary Prizes and Honors

Announced in 1990

•Academy of American Poets Awards•

Fellowship of the Academy of American Poets

Awarded annually to recognize distinguished achievement by an American poet.

William Meredith

* * *

The Lamont Poetry Selection

Established in 1952 to reward and encourage promising writers by supporting the publication of an American poet's second book.

Li-Young Lee
The City in Which I Love You

* * *

Peter I. B. Lavan Younger Poets Award

Established in 1983 to annually recognize three accomplished American poets under the age of forty.

George Bradley
Jorie Graham
Mary Jo Salter

* * *

Walt Whitman Award

Secures the publication of the first book of a living American poet.

Elaine Terranova
The Cult of the Right Hand

•American Academy and Institute of Arts and Letters Awards•

Academy-Institute Awards

Given annually to encourage creative achievement in art, music, and literature.

M. H. Abrams, Rick DeMarinis,
Debora Greger, Rachel Hadas,
Shelby Hearon, Maxine Hong Kingston,
David Lehman, Edmund S. Morgan
(Awards in Literature)

* * *

Witter Bynner Foundation Prize for Poetry

Established in 1979 and awarded annually to recognize an outstanding younger poet.

Jacqueline Osherow

* * *

Sue Kaufman Prize for First Fiction

Awarded annually to the best first fiction published during the preceding year.

Alan Gurganus
Oldest Living Confederate Widow Tells All

* * *

Richard and Hilda Rosenthal Foundation Award

Awards given annually for accomplishment in art and literature. The literature award recognizes a work of fiction published in the preceding year which, while not a "commercial success," is considered a literary achievement.

Daniel Stern
Twice-Told Tales

* * *

Morton Dauwen Zabel Award

Presented in alternating years to poets, fiction writers, and critics, to encourage progressive, original, and experimental tendencies in American literature.

Paul Auster

•James Tait Black Memorial Book Prize•

Sponsored by the University of Edinburgh and awarded annually for the best work of fiction and the best biography published during the previous year.

James Kelman
A Disaffection
(fiction)
(see *CLC*, Vol. 58)

•Rebekah Johnson Bobbit National Prize for Poetry•

Established in 1990 by the Library of Congress to recognize a collection judged to be the best book of poetry by a U.S. citizen published during the preceeding two years.

James Merrill
The Inner Room

•Booker Prize for Fiction•

Britain's major literary prize is awarded annually in recognition of a full-length novel.

A. S. Byatt
Possession
(see entry below)

•Governor General's Literary Awards•

To honor writing that achieves literary excellence without sacrificing popular appeal, awards are given annually in the categories of prose fiction, prose nonfiction, poetry, and drama. Officially known as the Canadian Authors Association (CAA) Literary Awards.

Paul Quarrington
Whale Music
(fiction)
(see entry below)

Heather Spears
The Word for Sand
(poetry)

Judith Thompson
The Other Side of the Dark
(drama)

Pierre Desruissaux
Monème
(fiction)

Louis Hamelin
La Rage
(poetry)

Michel Garneau
Mademoiselle Rouge
(drama)

•Drue Heinz Literature Prize•

Established in 1980 to recognize and encourage the writing of short fiction, this annual award is given by the University of Pittsburgh Press.

Rick Hillis
Limbo River
(see *CLC*, Vol. 66)

•Hugo Awards•

Established in 1953 to recognize notable science fiction works in several categories.

Dan Simmons
Hyperion
(novel)

Lois McMaster Bujold
The Mountains
(novella)

Suzy McKee Charnas
"Boobs"
(short story)

•Ruth Lilly Poetry Prize•

Awarded annually to an outstanding American poet.

Hayden Carruth

•Lenore Marshall/*Nation* Poetry Prize•

Established in 1974 to honor the author of the year's outstanding collection of poems published in the United States.

Michael Ryan
God Hunger
(see entry below)

•Los Angeles Times Book Awards•

Awards are given to authors in various categories to honor outstanding technique and vision.

Edna O'Brien
Lantern Slides
(fiction)
(see entry below)

John Caddy
The Color of Mesabi Bones
(poetry)

•National Book Awards•

Established in 1950 to honor and promote American books of literary distinction in the categories of fiction and nonfiction.

Charles Johnson
Middle Passage
(fiction)
(see entry below)

Saul Bellow
(Distinguished Contribution to American Letters)

•National Book Critics Circle Awards•

Founded in 1974, this American award recognizes superior literary quality in several categories.

E. L. Doctorow
Billy Bathgate
(fiction)
(see entry below)

Rodney Jones
Transparent Gestures
(poetry)

•Nebula Awards•

Established in 1965 to honor significant works in several categories of science fiction published in the United States.

Elizabeth Ann Scarborough
The Healer's War
(novel)

Geoffrey A. Landis
"Ripples in the Dirac Sea"
(short story)

•Neustadt International Prize for Literature•

Awarded every two years for outstanding achievement in literature.

Tomas Tranströemer
(see entry below)

•New York Drama Critics Circle Award•

Awards are presented annually in several categories to encourage excellence in playwriting.

August Wilson
The Piano Player
(best play)
(see *CLC,* Vol. 63)

Peter Nichols
Privates on Parade
(best foreign play)
(see entry below)

•Nobel Prize in Literature•

Awarded annually to recognize the most distinguished body of literary work of an idealistic nature.

Octavio Paz
(see entry below)

•Obie Award•

Awards in various categories are given annually to recognize excellence in off-Broadway and off-off-Broadway theater productions.

Craig Lucas
Prelude to a Kiss
(see *CLC,* Vol. 64)

Suzan-Lori Parks
Imperceptible Mutabilities in the Third Kingdom

Mac Wellman
Bad Penny, Crowbar, and *Terminal Hip*
(see entry below)

(best new American plays—tie)

•PEN American Center Awards•

Ernest Hemingway Foundation Award

Awarded annually to encourage the publication of first fiction by young American authors.

Mark Richard
The Ice at the Bottom of the World

* * *

Faulkner Award for Fiction

Annually recognizes the most distinguished book-length work of fiction by an American writer published during the calendar year.

E. L. Doctorow
Billy Bathgate
(see entry below)

•Edgar Allan Poe Awards•

Mystery Writers of America awards these prizes annually in recognition of outstanding contributions in mystery, crime, and suspense writing.

Helen McCloy
(grand master)
Larry Gelbart
City of Angels
(best mystery play)
(see *CLC*, Vol. 61)

•Pulitzer Prizes•

Awarded in recognition of outstanding accomplishments by American authors in various categories within the fields of journalism, literature, music, and drama. Literary awards usually recognize excellence in works that concern American life.

Oscar Hijuelos
The Mambo Kings Play Songs of Love
(fiction)
(see entry below)

Charles Simic
The World Doesn't End
(poetry)

August Wilson
The Piano Lesson
(drama)
(see *CLC*, Vol. 63)

•Rea Award•

Presented annually to recognize outstanding achievement in the short story genre.

Joyce Carol Oates

•Tony Awards•

Officially titled the American Theatre Wing's Antoinette Perry Awards, this prize is presented in recognition of outstanding achievement in the Broadway theater.

The Grapes of Wrath
adapted by Frank Galati
(best play)

•United States Poet Laureate•

Created in 1986 by an act of Congress to honor the career achievement of an American poet.

Mark Strand

A. S. Byatt
Possession: A Romance

Award: Booker Prize for Fiction

An English novelist, critic, and editor, Antonia Susan Byatt was born in 1936.

Possession: A Romance focuses on two contemporary literary scholars, Roland Michell and Maud Bailey, who unwittingly stumble upon evidence that links two Victorian poets in a passionate love affair. Roland is a languid postdoctoral student researching the famous Victorian poet Randolph Henry Ash, and Maud, a lecturer at the University of Lincoln, is an expert on Christabel LaMotte, an obscure poet and writer of fairy tales who has been recently rediscovered by lesbian feminist scholars. While working at the London Library, Roland chances upon written correspondence between the highly respected and married Ash and a woman Roland suspects is LaMotte. Excited by the possibility that he has discovered a secret romance, Roland steals the letters and searches out Maud, who possesses a number of LaMotte's unpublished papers. Together they pursue the secret of the poets' hidden passion and eventually engage in a love affair of their own. By juxtaposing the two relationships, Byatt scrutinizes the nature of love and romance from both modern and Victorian perspectives while utilizing a number of voices and genres to illuminate the differences and similarities between the two relationships. Byatt's creation of the poetry of both Ash and LaMotte also allows her to experiment with Victorian syntax and provide a multilayered text in which to explore the intricacies of desire and self-gratification, as well as the repercussions of biographical inquiry. *Possession: A Romance,* replete with academic satire and shifting literary styles, has received widespread critical and popular acclaim. Jay Parini commented: "*Possession* is a tour de force that opens every narrative device of English fiction to inspection without, for a moment, ceasing to delight."

(See also *CLC,* Vol. 19; *Contemporary Authors,* Vols. 13-16, rev. ed.; *Contemporary Authors New Revision Series,* Vol. 13; and *Dictionary of Literary Biography,* Vol. 14.)

PRINCIPAL WORKS

NOVELS

The Shadow of a Sun   1964
The Game   1967
The Virgin in the Garden   1978
Still Life   1980
Possession: A Romance   1990

OTHER

Degrees of Freedom: The Novels of Iris Murdoch   (criticism)   1965
Wordsworth and Coleridge in Their Time   (criticism)   1970
Iris Murdoch   (criticism)   1976

Richard Jenkyns

Roland Michell is a dullish young man with a doctorate and a bleak part-time job as a research assistant working on an edition of the famous Victorian poet R. H. Ash. Maud Bailey is a lecturer at a plate-glass university and an expert on Christabel LaMotte, an obscure Victorian poet and writer of fairytales, lately rediscovered by feminists. Little is known of LaMotte's life except that she shared a house in Richmond with one Blanche Glover, who killed herself in 1860; thereafter she lived as a virtual recluse in the Lincolnshire home of her sister Sophie's family. A chance find of Roland's reveals a connection between the two Victorians and brings him into contact with Maud. A complex plot, worked out with much skill, involves the two of them, and a clutch of rival professors, in a quest for the full story of Ash and La Motte's brief love-affair.

We hear that Ash is known for his "ventriloquism" and "unwieldy range"; and in *Possession* A. S. Byatt sets out to match him. There are forty pages of correspondence between Ash and LaMotte, long extracts from their poetry and from the journals of Miss Glover, Mrs Ash and Christabel's Breton cousin Sabine, and more besides. It must enthusiastically be said that Byatt's ventriloquism is a *tour de force.* . . . Occasionally a phrase does not quite have the true Victorian ring. But pedantry must quickly give way to admiration for a brilliant achievement of sheer technique.

The impersonation of Christabel is a triumph. She owes something to Christina Rossetti, more, perhaps, to Emily Dickinson, who provides a model for Christabel's eccentric punctuation as well as for the blend of spareness and intensity in her lyrics. We are able to walk round Christabel and see her from different angles: we understand both why earlier critics saw her as a poet of sweet resignation or domestic mysticism, and why a newer school sees her as a proto-feminist, probably lesbian, although we realize that neither view is very close to the truth. We feel her both as a child of her time and as an individual: in her letters we meet a keen intelligence wrestling with some awkwardness and angularity, in her verse a passionate reticence, a quirky lyricism, nervous but refined. But Byatt is wise enough not to tell us everything; Christabel keeps some of her secret, including the nature of her feelings for Blanche Glover, and that is as it should be. Beatrice Nest, the editor of Mrs Ash's journal, is muddly and pathetic, but she is on the side of the angels because she recognizes in it the "mystery of privacy", in contrast to the smart omniscience of more successful academics. Byatt is at her most sensitive in the half-disinterment of buried lives. Blanche Glover's suicide letter is very eloquent, defiant and defeated, mixing an honourable earnestness with spasms of genteel bitterness; and its poignancy is much increased by our sense that there lies behind it a story of passion, aspiration and failure, unspoken and irrecoverable. Blanche was a painter, who tried to dedicate her life to her art; but her paintings have all been lost.

Ash bears some general resemblance to Browning, though one detects elements of Arnold, Morris, perhaps Carlyle too. This impersonation is also remarkable, though less wholly successful. Byatt never quite removes the suspicion that he is a wordy bore. His letters do give the sense of a forceful, widely curious mind—no easy task—but Byatt has a slight tendency to suppose that pompous polysyllables will give the Victorian tone: Ash's letters speak of "vegetable aliment" and "woolly integuments"—indeed even Christabel's verse includes "pensile foliage", surely the kind of eighteenth-century diction that the nineteenth century despised. Whereas Christabel emerges as a distinctive imagination within her age, Ash is perhaps too

perfectly of his time to come fully alive; his interests exemplify the entire "Victorian frame of mind", faith and doubt, geology, amateur biology, Darwinism, spiritualism, comparative mythology. Few people represent their period so neatly. The ventriloquism is impressive, none the less, and the struggle between conscience and passion in his and Christabel's letters finely realized.

Possession is sure to get plenty of praise, as it deserves; it has earned the right to be judged by high standards, and so it is worth probing its weaker side. In its twentieth-century parts the characterization can be cardboard, and we sometimes have the feeling that we have been here before; one suspects not imitation but the lapse into a conventional cast of mind. Roland remains shadowy, and Maud never comes alive. She is an upper-middle-class lecturer in English, whose hair is her most glorious feature (though she tries to conceal the fact), with a former lover who spouts post-structural jargon and an admirer who is her social and intellectual inferior—in all these respects like Robyn Penrose in David Lodge's *Nice Work*. She lets down her golden hair and we are encouraged to think of Rapunzel, as in Dennis Potter's *Pennies from Heaven*. The supporting cast includes a baronet who waves a shotgun at intruders and says things like "stone-age chappie" and "Never had any use for poetry myself ", and the usual gallery of academic types. There are Beatrice Nest, fat, scatty and obsessional, like Rose Lorimer in Angus Wilson's *Anglo-Saxon Attitudes;* Professor Blackadder, sarcastic and disillusioned like most dons in fiction (Linton Hancox, for instance, in Margaret Drabble's *The Ice Age*); and Fergus Wolff, a seducer whose conversation lurches from deconstruction to Mills and Boon ("We two are the most intelligent people here, you know. You are the most beautiful thing I have ever dreamed about, I want you, I need you, can't you feel it, it's irresistible").

There are also two Americans. Leonora Stern is a loud lesbian feminist who talks dirty and is allegedly never dull; the half-hearted scene in which she half-heartedly attempts to seduce Maud is close to a similarly perfunctory episode in Alison Lurie's *The Truth about Lorin Jones*. Mortimer Cropper wants to know every single thing possible about Ash, like Zapp in *Changing Places,* before Lodge spoiled his most exuberant invention by taking him seriously. Cropper is an acquisitive collector of Ash's relics for his university, and our first sight of him is beautifully comic, skulking in a suburban bathroom in the small hours, furtively photographing a letter by Ash belonging to the lady of the house. But the extracts from Cropper's life of Ash are perhaps Byatt's least successful pastiche; she does not quite catch the anglophile mandarin accent, and she conflates it with another, more middlebrow American tone ("my lovely parental home . . . not far from where Robert Dale Owen University is so beautifully situated"). And Cropper proves to be a mother's boy, sexually messed up. Compare Waugh's Mr Joyboy. Aren't Americans funny?

It is bad luck on Byatt that her book should follow Lurie's *Lorin Jones* (1988), also built around a scholar's pursuit of the truth about a dead artist. Lurie gives us a sequence of kaleidoscopically shifting pictures of Jones, differing yet recognizably of the same woman and each with its partial truth; the subtlety and agility of this performance are outside Byatt's range. Each new discovery about Ash or Christabel more or less "corrects" the earlier view in a way that seems comparatively a little ponderous. Still, the book presents itself as a Quest, and it is apt that a quest should move towards a determinate goal; nor is it unfitting that a novel with a Victorian theme should proceed with a certain weightiness. Its texture is made dense with allusion, cross-reference and symbolism in a fashion not easily summarized. Byatt is aware of the risks here: when Sabine hears a fairy story turned into a neat allegory, she thinks of a net drawing up a shoal of dull dead fish. We are perhaps not to take the symbols too solemnly; they are a high civilized entertainment, glancing and suggestive, where the fancy may play. At moments the symbolism seems to drive the story into a mechanical pattern: why should the beautiful Maud retreat, implausibly, into a chilly celibacy if not so that Childe Roland may possess the Bailey as Ash possessed the Motte? But on the whole the symbolic game enriches the fabric and coheres with a book that explores the relation between life and the literary imagination.

Possession is full of comparisons to other books: its characters liken the events in which they are caught up to *As You Like It, Jane Eyre.* . . . But *Possession* does gain much of its *élan* from the way in which it bursts out of the confines of the campus novel to revel in the delights of a boldly romantic narrative, with a gloriously melodramatic climax—grave robbery and sexual consummation in a night of howling storm. Indeed, it is subtitled *A Romance,* and begins with an epigraph from Hawthorne which distinguishes the "latitude" of romance from the "minute fidelity" of the novel. Yet ironically it is the book's more spectacular and improbable events that bring it closest to the novel's great tradition: to *Great Expectations* . . . where unlikely but not impossible happenings drive forward the narrative of a basically naturalistic fiction. There is a defensive note in this talk of romance, as though Byatt is thinking of critics rather than readers, and this seems a pity. Boldness is best: it is a mistake to have Roland reflecting that his situation has become implausibly romantic, because one can only agree. Worse still are one or two passages of would-be post-modern self-reflexiveness, which merely take us back to the university novel at its most arch and banal. "It is possible for the writer to remake. . . . Novels have their obligatory tour-de-force . . . "—enough of these drabblings. Here Byatt misunderstands the virtue of her own book, which lies in its solidity. It is grounded in specific times and places; even that climactic melodrama is precisely datable—to October 1987, the night of the hurricane. Byatt is good at evoking places: the Lincolnshire Wolds, the North Yorkshire Moors, the Breton coast. And she suggests that those who genuinely love literature may apprehend the real world more keenly: seeing the Wolds, Roland suddenly realizes the exactness of a description in Tennyson; walking down a passage in a neo-gothic country house, the word "drugget" comes into his mind from a poem by Ash. Conversely, poetry should be rooted in the actual world. Feminists have supposed the landscape in LaMotte's *Melusina* to be symbolic and anatomical. So it may be, but it is also, we

find, the Yorkshire background of her brief adventure in passion.

Sense of place is bound up with sense of the past. Ash holds that the life of the past persists in us and we must try to possess such fragments of it as we can. But how? Cropper's greed to possess the past destroys its life by entombing it in an air-conditioned museum. Leonora is more sympathetic, but in her indignation at the decay of the mouldering churchyard where Christabel is buried she seems to understand less than Maud, who with generations of English gentry in her blood feels that the return to nature and oblivion is fitting. Christabel's house in Richmond has been so slickly Victorianized by its present occupants that it has lost its Victorian character—another kind of greed for the past destroying the very thing that it seeks to possess. Roland remarks that it would have looked older when it was younger. But conversely Maud, driving past a wood, thinks of the trees when they were saplings and reflects on the young vitality of the past, upon which her own scholarly prying feeds like a ghostly thing.

Byatt is celebrating the vigour not just of the past but of this past; for *Possession* is another of those books that restore the Victorians to honour, with an especial admiration for their emotional lives. Both Maud and the author in her own voice contemplate the modern world's knowing chatter about sex and its consequent fear of talking boldly about love. Attempting to have sex with his dispiriting girlfriend, Roland finds that he has to think of a Victorian woman in petticoats and black bodice to maintain his erection; we may contrast this drab coupling with the intensity of passion released by Ash and Christabel in a kiss. When Roland finally "possesses" Maud's body, their lovemaking is triumphant, but that, we may infer, is partly because their relations hitherto have been marked by an almost Victorian restraint and decorum. Quite how far Byatt wishes to praise the last century may be a moot question. The comparatively conventional depiction of the present-day characters accidentally points up the romance and vividness of the Victorian part of the story; and elegantly self-conscious though the book is, one wonders if there is not a repressed Byatt, more robustly reactionary than she knows, longing to burst out and declare that traditional country life is best, and the modern world is scruffy and smutty, and what a girl needs is a strong, handsome man to look after her.

All the same, she is sharp enough to tease our expectations. Blackadder is interviewed on television by an Indian woman about his efforts to keep Ash's letters from going abroad. Surely, we think, the liberal novel will exercise some positive discrimination on behalf of the immigrant. But no, she is ignorant, arrogant and superficial, and he does pretty well, because he really cares. This is indeed a kindly book: most of the major characters are allowed some sort of secular redemption—all perhaps except Wolff and Cropper, the two most avaricious for possession. Roland, who began his quest by purloining a document, confesses and hands it back, a "dispossession, or perhaps the word was exorcism"; Maud, who has clung to her self-possession, becomes willing to give herself. If this seems tidy and moral, like the end of a Victorian novel—well, is that not appropriate?

And in fact Byatt has a last surprise in store. The omniscient author takes over, and we learn something that her twentieth-century characters will never discover. It would be an unkindness to Byatt's readers to give away the twist; those familiar with Edith Wharton's *The Age of Innocence* will recognize a device that in a way seems sure of its effect, yet to risk sentimentality. Byatt brings it off, in part because she is not afraid; the scene, in a flowery summer meadow, is unashamedly idyllic, and its simplicity touching in contrast to all the elaboration that has gone before. One other clue: the scene includes a small girl who in a special sense is a link between the nineteenth and twentieth-century parts of the novel; she is given a message to carry, but goes off for a game with her brothers and forgets it. And so the book ends . . . with a child playing, innocent of the portentous meaning of what it hears. This is poignant in itself, but it also fits the novel as a whole. "There are things which happen and leave no discernible trace," Byatt begins her epilogue, "are not spoken or written of, though it would be very wrong to say that subsequent events go on indifferently, all the same, as though such things had never been." The tone and sentiment recall George Eliot, surely by intention; we may learn from her that a multitude of small, forgotten acts and experiences makes the texture of the world in which we are embedded. Children are a generation's link with its future, and yet the charm of a child lies in the unselfconsciousness which makes it lose so much that posterity would wish to have had preserved. But the way to possession is through dispossession; we can apprehend the past rightly only by letting it work in its own natural way, absorbing so much that is precious into the mysteries of privacy and oblivion. Byatt has contrived a masterly ending to a fine work; intelligent, ingenious and humane, *Possession* bids fair to be looked back upon as one of the most memorable novels of the 1990s. (pp. 213-14)

> *Richard Jenkyns, "Disinterring Buried Lives,"
> in* The Times Literary Supplement, *No. 4535,
> March 2, 1990, pp. 213-14.*

Anita Brookner

Antonia Byatt's publishers compare *Possession* with [John Fowles's] *The French Lieutenant's Woman* on the not unreasonable grounds that both are Victorian dramas secured to the present day, and are therefore both exploratory and disabused. The comparison is inevitable but *Possession* is the superior of the two novels, which means that it is very good indeed. Subtitled *A Romance,* for reasons which become clear only at the very end, it deals, essentially, with a group of 20th-century scholars engaged on various aspects of the work of Randolph Henry Ash, a mid-19th-century poet, much of whose life remains obscure. Letters are involved, and diaries, and the reader should be warned that the works of Randolph Henry Ash are quoted at very great length. The startling intrusion of blank verse into a late-20th-century novel is compounded by long extracts from the work of Ash's great love, Christabel LaMotte, all done in impeccable 19th-century paro-

dy and in very much smaller type. The actual narrative which contains all these diversions, and which explores the detective work of the scholars working on the original texts, is comparatively slight but is strong enough both in form and content to articulate what might at first seem a thoroughly disconcerting and discontinuous collection of testimonies. The novel is capacious, ambitious, occasionally overwrought: it is marvellous.

Randolph Henry Ash, speculative and verbose Victorian poet . . . is the author of *Ragnarök, Gods, Men and Heroes, The Garden of Proserpina,* and *Ask to Embla.* He is a cross between Browning and Mr Casaubon: his verses put one in mind of the Bishop ordering his tomb in St Praxed's Church. Roland Michell, research assistant to Professor Blackadder at Prince Albert College in the University of London, discovers an unpublished letter from Randolph Henry to an unknown woman. The letter reveals intense admiration and intense sexual attraction. It proves not too difficult to identify the recipient as Christabel LaMotte, author of *Last Things, Tales Told in November, The Fairy Melusina,* and many short lyrics. Christabel is an altogether grittier Victorian subject, and here the comparison with *The French Lieutenant's Woman* is valid, for Christabel is passionate, secretive, virtuous, pure and slightly mad. Her work, also quoted at length, derives more from *The Eve of St Agnes,* while her shorter lyrics reveal her to be a forerunner of Emily Dickinson.

The main sources for the life and works of Christabel LaMotte are in the hands of Dr Maud Bailey at the University of Lincoln. Christabel has aroused feminist interest: Dr Bailey is herself the author of a study of liminality in Christabel's work, while Professor Leonora Stern of Tallahassee profers an exuberant Lacanian interpretation of *The Fairy Melusina.* A lot of this sort of thing goes on these days. Simultaneously, the works of Randolph Henry Ash are in the hands of his biographer, Mortimer Cropper, of the Stant Collection, Robert Dale Owen University, New Mexico, and Professor James Blackadder, who, in the impoverished tradition of his university, is allowed a room in the basement of the British Library. There is also a Dr Beatrice Nest, of whom no one takes much notice, and who has been working for 25 years on the journal of Randolph Henry's wife Ellen—also quoted at length, as is the entirely unconnected but crucial journal of Sabine de Kercoz, Christabel's cousin. Making guest appearances are extracts from Cropper's luxuriant biography of Ash, interjections from the diary of Blanche Glover, LaMotte's one-time companion, and of course the full flowery correspondence between Ash and LaMotte, which is put together by the joint efforts of Maud Bailey and Roland Michell.

The scholarship involved begins by being weary and self-interested but quickens into a chase for the possession of the correspondence, each half of which is known separately. When the letters are put back together the story they contain proves combustible. Randolph Henry and Christabel of course had a love affair, as do Roland and Maud, but this bald summary cannot convey how remarkable these love affairs turn out to be. The ominous Victorian taboos which encircle Randolph Henry and Christabel are like an enchantment: the imagery is of Merlin and Vivien and of various plants and sea creatures, tentacular. Roland and Maud have their own inhibitions: in each case sex with the wrong person has made them indifferent. The terrible passion of Randolph Henry and Christabel (or rather *her* terrible passion) involves deceit—lifelong—and death. Randolph Henry, after a stolen month, returns to his wife, whose complacent journal also conceals a secret.

Possession, or the act of possession, indicates not only love and its requirements, but the desire of scholars to gain exclusive control of the evidence. The metaphors are astonishingly thoroughly worked out: this is a novel *de longue durée.* The subtitle is also ambiguous. This is not a romantic novel, or not primarily a romantic novel: it is a Romance, in the original sense of the word, i.e. something fictive. The concept is applied to the conclusion, which I found flurried and almost impertinently unconvincing. Here the canny author reminds the dazed reader that a Romance is what it says it is, and need not necessarily be bound by the familiar laws of logic.

Possession is inordinate, but not indiscriminate; it is unfashionable; it is generous, teeming with more ideas than a year's worth of ordinary novels. An occasional unpruned sentence cannot diminish the high style of the whole. A brilliant start to the publishing season, and one which it will be very difficult to overtake.

> Anita Brookner, "Eminent Victorians and Others," in The Spectator, Vol. 264, No. 8434, March 3, 1990, p. 35.

Danny Karlin

Possession is a big book, a spectacular novel of ideas and intrigue, spectacular both in its shortcomings and its successes; it has vaulting literary ambitions and is unafraid to crash. Moreover it moves decisively away from the familial and social territory which Byatt has been cultivating in her most recent novels, *The Virgin in the Garden* and *Still Life.* The oddly-linked hands of George Eliot and Proust lay a little heavily at times on these densely artful fictions. *Possession,* no less dense and artful in its own terms, has the feel of a writer who has broken bounds. (p. 17)

The book's genre is hard to pin down—teasingly so, I imagine. Its literary ancestry is richly diverse. The depiction of the small world of literary criticism, in which romance and fairy-tale motifs are intertwined with contemporary academic and sexual politics, clearly owes a good deal to David Lodge; the theme of the lost literary legacy invokes *The Aspern Papers;* James might be cited . . . in relation to the book's punning deployment of 'possession' as a term of material, erotic and demonic significance, an association that also reminds you of Dickens; indeed, the Dickens of *Bleak House* (family romance, Gothic quest, detective thriller) displaces the moral arbiter George Eliot as chief Victorian precursor. Then, of course, there are the literary origins of the two Victorian poets, Ash and LaMotte. Ash descends (swervingly) from Robert Browning; LaMotte is compounded from (but again, not reducible to) Elizabeth Barrett Browning, Christina Rossetti and Emily

Dickinson. . . . But the name LaMotte leads to an original for both poets: Friedrich, Baron de la Motte Fouqué, the German poet and novelist whose fairy-tale 'Undine', about the water-sprite who kills her faithless lover with a kiss, was one of the most famous and influential texts of European Romanticism. La Motte gives his name and interest in water-spirits to Christabel, whose major work is an epic poem on the subject of the French water-spirit Mélusine, and his other literary interests (in Norse mythology—his dramatic trilogy *Der Held des Nordens* was based on the Icelandic *Edda*) to Randolph Henry Ash, who writes a dramatic monologue called *Ask to Embla* and a 12-book 'Christianising of the Norse myth' called *Ragnarok.*

The playful erudition with which these invented or quasi-historical figures are conjured up is, of course, a Browningesque trait, and so is the plurality of voices and styles in which the story is told, and which represents in another way its refusal of conventional classifications. There is straightforward omniscient-author narrative; *style indirecte libre;* poetry and fiction by both Ash and LaMotte, and not in token amounts, either; academic criticism and biography; letters and diaries from characters present and (crucially) past. Ash's poems are a fair pastiche of Browning, although they make you realise how difficult it is to catch his manner (as opposed to his mannerisms, which are prominent but misleading). Some of LaMotte's are, by contrast, very good, particularly the Dickinson-like lyrics, complete with stray capitals and eccentric dashes. But the Ash-LaMotte writings also expose a serious weakness in Byatt's design, which is nothing to do with whether their period feel is completely convincing.

How could it be, after all? Byatt's forgeries of Victorian poems and letters don't purport to be the Turin Shroud, and need not be carbon-dated in some literary-historical laboratory. They are required to pass muster in a 'romance', and generally do so, with occasional lapses and occasional moments of inspired rightness. (I am less irritated by a few false notes or anachronisms in this area than I am by Professor Blackadder still compiling his edition with slips of paper and index cards.) What matters is the use which is made of this material, and here Byatt is too knowing and too coercive. It is fatally convenient to invent your Victorian poets rather than take them as you find them; the temptation is to *make* them write or do whatever suits your purpose. In **'Precipice-Encurled'**, a story from Byatt's 1987 collection **Sugar,** the historical Robert Browning made an appearance memorable for its convincing use of a multiplicity of details gleaned from his life and writings: they were all *there,* the art was in the gathering and sorting. With Ash and LaMotte, just because they both are and are not their historical originals, the detail can be supplied where it is wanting. LaMotte is required to be too many kinds of writer, for example: some of her poems don't go well with each other, don't seem the product of a single mind (as those of her models emphatically do). The Norse and Celtic myths, and other artistic topics in which she and Ash are interested, dovetail together too neatly, a feature of Byatt's compulsion to make everything resonate with everything else. As a result, the novel's patterns of association, its networks of coincidence and connection, too often seem forced. Roland and Maud decide to take a day off from their tracking of Ash and LaMotte to visit a beauty-spot *not,* as far as they know, connected with their quarry. 'There's a nice place on the map called the Boggle Hole,' Roland says. 'It's a nice word—I wondered—perhaps we could take a day off from *them,* get out of their story . . .' But there's no getting away from *them,* of course: later on it turns out that Ash and LaMotte have been there too. The 'significance' of this episode is overshadowed by its denial of human contingency, a failing for which Byatt rightly criticises literary scholarship but which she does not recognise closer to home, in her own sweeping exercise of the novelist's providential powers. (pp. 17-18)

Danny Karlin, "Prolonging Her Absence," in London Review of Books, *Vol. 12, No. 5, March 8, 1990, pp. 17-18.*

Christina Koning

Antonia Byatt's new novel [*Possession: A Romance*] is an erudite work, displaying a scholarly familiarity with the work of Browning, Tennyson, Ruskin and Christina Rossetti, as well as a detailed knowledge of nineteenth-century preoccupations, from evolution theory to spiritualism. On a more contemporary note, *Possession* is a debate on the nature of literary scholarship. . . .

The novel opens with the discovery of a letter from a Victorian poet, Randolph Henry Ash, to an unknown lady, by Roland Michell, an impoverished research assistant. Researching Ash's work for a definitive edition of his poems, and intrigued as much by the letter's tone as its contents, Roland decides to pursue the matter further. He consults another expert on Victorian poetry, Dr Maud Bailey, whose explorations into an obscure nineteenth-century woman poet, Christabel LaMotte, lead into the next stage of the conundrum.

Ash is presented, initially, as the quintessential Victorian Man of Letters, feted during his lifetime and celebrated since his death, his work extensively researched, his memorabilia collected. LaMotte, on the other hand, has been as overlooked by posterity as she was by her contemporaries, her poetry of interest only to feminist critics anxious to reconstruct her as a lesbian feminist bluestocking. Byatt has a great deal of fun at the expense of assorted Freudians, feminists and deconstructionists, and points up the danger of imposing doctrinaire readings on multilevelled and elusive texts in her handling of the book's central relationship.

The clandestine affair between Ash and LaMotte is presented in the form of contemporary documents. Not only do we get to read their letters, but also extracts from journals, stories and—in one of the novel's most daring touches—whole poems, ranging from dramatic monologues over 400 lines long to short lyrics, written by the protagonists as part of their courtship. The sureness with which these passages of verse and prose pastiche are handled is considerable. That they are postmodernist texts—pastiche rather than fake—is never in doubt, however; they are too knowing, too self-referential, to be anything else.

Possession, then, is not entirely what it seems. While appearing to write a faithful imitation of a romance, even down to the final scenes in which the villain is unmasked, the will read and the fatherless child acknowledged, the author in fact subverts the form. The reader is simultaneously beguiled by traditional narrative expectations and made aware of the author's deconstruction of them through the verse pastiche, which provides a kind of commentary upon the action. Ironically, as Maud and Roland become preoccupied with the biographical details of their subjects' lives to the exclusion of the texts through which they survive, it becomes apparent to the reader that the texts are all there is. Ash and LaMotte exist no more than their twentieth-century counterparts. They are all part of what one of Byatt's characters calls a 'postmodernist mirror-game', a game the reader will enjoy as much for its stylistic elegance as for its playfulness with ideas.

Christina Koning, "Ladies of Letters Look in the Mirror," in The Observer, *March 11, 1990, p. 68.*

An excerpt from *Possession: A Romance*

Roland had learned to see himself, theoretically, as a crossing-place for a number of systems, all loosely connected. He had been trained to see his idea of his "self" as an illusion, to be replaced by a discontinuous machinery and electrical message-network of various desires, ideological beliefs and responses, language-forms and hormones and pheromones. Mostly he liked this. He had no desire for any strenuous Romantic self-assertion. Nor did he desire to know *who* Maud essentially was. But he wondered, much of the time, what their mute pleasure in each other might lead to, anything or nothing, would it just go, as it had just come, or would it change, could it change?

He thought of the Princess on her glass hill, of Maud's faintly contemptuous look at their first meeting. In the real world—that was, for one should not privilege one world above another, in the social world to which they must both return from these white nights and sunny days—there was little real connection between them. Maud was a beautiful woman such as he had no claim to possess. She had a secure job and an international reputation. Moreover, in some dark and outdated English social system of class, which he did not believe in, but felt obscurely working and gripping him, Maud was County, and he was urban lower-middle-class, in some places more, in some places less acceptable than Maud, but in almost all incompatible.

All *that* was the plot of a Romance. He was in a Romance, a vulgar and a high Romance simultaneously; a Romance was one of the systems that controlled him, as the expectations of Romance control almost everyone in the Western world, for better or worse, at some point or another.

He supposed the Romance must give way to social realism, even if the aesthetic temper of the time was against it.

Elaine Feinstein

This is a poet's novel in several senses, being at once about a brief affair between two 19th-century poets, the fierce passion for poetry, and itself charged throughout with a breathtaking use of language. Byatt can describe the many greys of gardens in the moonlight (she identifies silver pewter and lead) and the dusty heaps of brooches and paperknives in a northern shop window with the same exuberance. That the novel nevertheless has all the page-turning compulsion of a mystery story is a triumph in itself.

The hero, suitably named Roland, is a post-doctoral research student. Working in the London Library on the Victorian poet Ash, he comes upon an interchange of letters between Ash and an unknown woman which excites his normally tepid spirits. He steals the letters. A series of clues lead him to believe the recipient of Ash's affections might be Christabel Lamotte, a Victorian poet of much interest these days to feminist critics, and his quest for information about Lamotte leads him to the beautiful scholar Dr Maud Bailey. . . .

Both Victorian poets are invented very successfully, but it is the characterisation of Christabel Lamotte that is central. Lamotte's passion for the making of poems gives her the ability to live a withdrawn life which rewards her with a freedom women in the 20th century hardly recognise. She and her companion would inevitably these days have been mistaken for Lesbian. Indeed, we never do discover the full nature of her relationship with poor Blanche Glover, who is driven to suicide when Lamotte departs with Ash.

But it is Byatt's creation of Lamotte's poetry which is quite remarkable, in a way that the word pastiche does not convey. Certainly, Lamotte is given themes that recall Christina Rosetti and some of the syntax of Emily Dickinson, but the lovely poem about spinster aunts who "sorted—cleaned—and ordered/What lay in feckless heap" is decidedly more than that. It is almost as if Byatt had taken on the persona of a felt 19th-century counterpart in order to write poems of her own.

The other 19th-century figure, Ash, has all the concerns of his time: religious doubt, Darwin, world mythologies and so forth. Byatt makes him an enchanting letter writer, and gives his poems an admirably vigorous Browningesque quality. It is not Ash and Lamotte's love affair, but the intellectual intimacy in the letters between them which arouses our envy.

There are many other contemporary academic figures in the book, some of whom might inhabit a David Lodge novel: Mortimer Cropper, with his American chequebook and horridly precise notion of everyone's financial expectations; Professor James Blackadder, his frustrated English counterpart, who turns out kindlier than seemed likely; Dr Nest, steered into working on Ash's wife Ellen because she is a woman herself; and a bouncy bisexual American, Leonora Stern, who is inclined to read the landscapes in her texts as if they were human orifices.

It is on Maud Bailey, however, that the wish for freedom Lamotte so beautifully articulates in her reading of the Mermaid fairy story is focussed. Maud finds herself much drawn to Roland, who at that stage of the novel looks to-

tally unemployed. It is not an easy situation for a dedicated scholar, as Maud observes: "If he went out of the room it would be grey and empty. If he did not go out of it, how could she concentrate?"

This ambitious novel goes part way to questioning the centrality of sexuality in our time, and makes some claim for the passionate intensities of work and retreat which the Victorians found so much more acceptable than we do. Nevertheless, there is an ending altogether suitable to a novel subtitled *A Romance,* and an exquisite floral postscript. I doubt if we shall see a bolder novel this year.

> *Elaine Feinstein, "Eloquent Victorians," in* New Statesman & Society, *Vol. 3, No. 92, March 16, 1990, p. 38.*

Jay Parini

As anyone who has read her previous novels, including **Shadow of a Sun,** or her stories or her critical studies knows, the British writer A. S. Byatt is a gifted observer, able to discern the exact but minor details that bring whole worlds into being. **Possession** begins in 1986 in the Reading Room of the London Library, where Roland Michell—a postdoctoral research assistant at London University and the novel's hero of sorts—is rummaging through an old book that once belonged to the man he worships: Randolph Henry Ash, a famous Victorian poet and obvious stand-in for Robert Browning.

"The book," Ms. Byatt writes, "was thick and black and covered with dust. Its boards were bowed and creaking; it had been maltreated in its own time. Its spine was missing, or, rather, protruded from amongst the leaves like a bulky marker. It was bandaged about and about with dirty white tape, tied in a neat bow." (p. 9)

[This] begins an unlikely but dazzling quest for what literary critics and historians once, with unfounded confidence, referred to as the Truth.

Along the path, Michell, an old-fashioned scholar, falls in love with Maud Bailey, a feminist academic, but he cannot trust anything so out of date as a "self" that falls in love. Ms. Byatt writes: "Roland had learned to see himself, theoretically, as a crossing-place for a number of systems, all loosely connected. He had been trained to see his idea of his 'self' as an illusion, to be replaced by a discontinuous machinery and electrical message-network of various desires, ideological beliefs and responses, language-forms and hormones and pheromones."

The consequences of this highly improbable self-view are devastating, as it turns out. Michell has been living in a damp basement flat in London with a feckless woman by the name of Val, and what they call their "relationship" is distinctly uninspired. They eat and sleep together in a low-keyed, almost mournful way that neither especially likes.

The pace of everything in Michell's life picks up, however, when he (almost inadvertently) begins a mad, intensely private search for the truth concerning the mysterious letters, which he has secretly tucked into his wallet. An ingenious literary detective, he soon discovers that the letters were sent to another poet, Christabel LaMotte—whose life is based on Christina Rossetti. (pp. 9, 11)

Dr. Maud Bailey, the leading LaMotte scholar, lives "on the outskirts of Lincoln" and spends her time writing articles about "liminality" in the poems of LaMotte, who (it so happens) is her distant ancestor. In what becomes the most charming part of the story, Mitchell and Bailey steal away to a magnificent country house, not far from Lincoln, where LaMotte lived most of her life in seclusion. The house, and its current master, Sir George Bailey, who seems to have walked right out of the pages of P. G. Wodehouse into a novel by David Lodge, are summoned with consummate wit and parodic skill.

As **Possession** progresses, it seems less and less like the usual satire about academia and more like something by Jorge Luis Borges. The most dazzling aspect of **Possession** is Ms. Byatt's canny invention of letters, poems and diaries from the 19th century. She quotes whole vast poems by Ash and LaMotte, several of which struck me, anyway, as highly plausible versions of Browning and Rossetti and are beautiful poems on their own. The painful and quintessentially Victorian love story of Ash and LaMotte is retold in their "own" words, offering an ironic counterpoint to the contemporary story of Mitchell and Bailey, who both eventually do fall into something like "love."

Then, as the narrative moves from Quest to Chase (as Mitchell himself puts it), the novel intensifies. It so happens that Michell and Bailey are not the only scholars with a vested interest in the Ash-LaMotte story. There is Professor Leonora Stern, a heavyset lesbian from the United States who is possessed by LaMotte's romantic attachment to a woman called Blanche Glover. And there is Professor James Blackadder—a Dickensian figure who has been editing Ash's Complete Works in "what was known as Blackadder's Ash Factory" since 1951 and is Michell's dour mentor. Blackadder's archopponent is Mortimer Cropper, an American scholar entrepreneur, devilishly caricatured by Ms. Byatt as a cross between Leon Edel and Liberace. Cropper's greatest desire is to possess everything that once belonged to Ash, including a metal box buried in the poet's grave that—Cropper suspects—contains a Big Secret.

All the interested parties converge in an archetypal Sussex churchyard on an archetypal dark and stormy night. And the Big Secret is, finally, divulged. It's a supremely Dickensian one, as it were, that plays wittily with the convention of coincidence. I won't be so churlish as to give away the end, but a plenitude of surprises awaits the reader of this gorgeously written novel. A. S. Byatt is a writer in mid-career whose time has certainly come, because **Possession** is a tour de force that opens every narrative device of English fiction to inspection without, for a moment, ceasing to delight. (p. 11)

Jay Parini, "Unearthing the Secret Lover," in The New York Times Book Review, October 21, 1990, pp. 9, 11.

Carolyn See

Now is the time to lament the perhaps insignificant fact that there is no feminine word for "masterpiece." Because A. S. Byatt, student and biographer of Iris Murdoch, explicator of Wordsworth and Coleridge, has crafted in this just-announced Booker Prize winner [**Possession: A Romance**] a masterpiece of wordplay and adventure, a sampler of styles, a quilt of scholarly methods and a novel that compares with both Stendahl and Joyce: Characters *race* to their destinies, but stop, on the way, to rejoice in language in all its ramifications. The history of English literature is encompassed; the state of scholarship is brutally examined (and found wanting), but the world itself is praised, and the humans who quest—as in any real romance—after knowledge swim in adventure and drown ultimately, in happy endings. (p. 2)

Remember, when the author calls this narrative a "romance," she doesn't mean a bodice-ripper. Byatt is taking all that material that originally came from Brittany, the place in our literature where the natural and the supernatural embrace, at a magic threshold, as it were, where humans may meet—or turn into—angels or devils or goblins. It may not be absolutely necessary to remember that the medieval "Roland" was Charlemagne's sidekick and a hero of France; that "Maud" was made immortal by Alfred, Lord Tennyson; that with a boss named Blackadder, you *could* be in some trouble.

Maud is as chilly as she is beautiful. But when she hears that *her* Christabel may have had something to do with Roland's Ash, she too becomes possessed. She is related distantly to Christabel's family, and she and Roland set out, in rain and gloomy weather, to a decaying castle where . . . they find the correspondence! Letters that could change the history of a nice chunk of English literature. For if the boring Randolph Henry Ash is the "possession," by now, of the stolid middle-of-the-road white male academy, Christabel LaMotte, with her frail, morbid poems and her mordant tales for children, has become the property of militant feminists, who are busily building a myth around her and her friend—perhaps lover—Blanche Glover, who lived together in a mild perversion of Coventry Patmore's idealized domesticity. These two "Angels in the House" made jams and jellies—and probably made love.

So in the real world, as [Roland's dispirited girlfriend] Val (only she really is going to turn out to be Valiant) reminds us, people are poor and people are dying, and a few scribbled lines mean "nothing" in the scheme of things. But in the *really* real world of the imagination, and the pure search for knowledge, the correspondence of Randolph Henry Ash and Christabel LaMotte, who did love, means everything. It means the whole world. And everyone in this small academic world wants part of it.

[An academic rival of Roland, the vulpine] Fergus Wolff wants to further his career with these letters. As a byproduct, he'd like to "deconstruct" Maud, for the mean hell of it. Blackadder, his life lived in the British Museum basement (in total subservience to the memory of Ash), is frantic when he hears of the letters, and of Roland and Maud's blatant thievery.

And over from America come two particularly peculiar American specimens. Mortimer Cropper, who believes that to possess the object is to possess poetic magic, has bought manuscripts and letters and the poet's watch, as if that mechanism could give him a heart. Prof. Leonora Stearn pens ferocious and absolutely unreadable feminist criticism, but in person she's even more scary—absolutely determined to sleep with every man and woman she comes up against.

Will Roland and Maud come into possession of the letters, and of their own rightful lives? Will they ever get to fall in love? (Unlike their 19th-Century predecessors, they must distrust love, especially romantic love, as a faulty ideological construct.) We're given hundreds of pages to find out. Many of these pages are taken up with Ash's long poems, and LaMotte's short ones. Or LaMotte's fables, which really aren't for children. . . . You learn to love these poets who love so tragically.

And you read with fascinated horror the self-serving blather of Mortimer Cropper and are bored stiff with Leonora's turgid feminist rant. And then, just because she's showing off, Byatt throws in the 19th-Century journal of a precocious adolescent in Brittany. You're encouraged to think about "thresholds": If artists strive and pine and yearn to live on, through their work, into the future, it's the scholars, with equal tenderness and yearning, who lean and look, further and further back into the past, willing, finally, to lose themselves in the search for those lost artists. They meet on the threshold where knowledge is.

Byatt believes that all these people should get their happy endings. About 80 pages from the finish, she begins pitching them out: Something for Val. Something for a self-effacing guardian of Ash's wife's journal. Something for Blackadder. Maud finds out who she is. Roland, noble knight, finds the real object of his quest. (And who said there could only be one?)

You sail on the wind in this book. You give yourself up to it. And it rewards you a thousand times. (pp. 2, 13)

> *Carolyn See, "At a Magic Threshold," in* Los Angeles Times Book Review, *October 28, 1990, pp. 2, 13.*

Ann Hulbert

In our era of theory-saturated literary studies, it takes a tenured professor to set a clever novel in the groves of academe. Who else knows the orthodoxies cold, and has the liberty and leisure to have readable fun with them? The key is to be suitably self-conscious about anything so simple as a "story" or a "character," and then proceed to create just that. Handle it right, and you can offer old-fashioned mystery, comedy, and romance tricked out in newfangled, self-reflexive style. You can, as A. S. Byatt does in her tour de force of university fiction, write a book that is packaged like a fat, glossy romance—and win the Booker Prize, too.

The escape from criticism into creative writing, as Byatt tells it, occasions a kind of conversion in one's attitude toward the word. One of her protagonists, Roland Michell, a dogged postdoctoral researcher at Prince Albert College, London, describes his heady sense of enlightenment when, toward the end of *Possession,* he suddenly thinks he might be a poet:

> He had been taught that language was essentially inadequate, that it could never speak what was there, that it only spoke itself. . . . What had happened to him was that the way in which it *could* be said had become more interesting than the idea that it could not.

Just how subversive a revelation that can be, challenging the reigning theories of linguistic indeterminacy, Byatt only slowly reveals. Her immediate aim is to make the most of multiple meanings and voices: her novel is the occasion for an exhilarating, virtuosic, and at times exhausting exploration of the many ways language has of speaking. A scholarly authority on George Eliot, the Romantics, and Iris Murdoch, Byatt puts her expertise to energetic use. In *Possession* she becomes a nineteenth-century ventriloquist, and she ingeniously juxtaposes the previous century with the hothouse world of the contemporary academy. The donnish novels of Murdoch (to say nothing of David Lodge, John Fowles, Umberto Eco, and others) have clearly inspired her.

True to the requirements of up-to-date university fiction, *Possession* is full of the fashionable rhetoric of literary theory. Byatt proves herself, as she says of Roland, "trained in the post-structuralist deconstruction of the subject." But it soon becomes clear that her facility with the professional jargon is accompanied by a mounting frustration with it. The two characters in the historical foreground of the novel, Roland and his equally sober literary companion, Maud Bailey of Lincoln University, "know all . . . about how there isn't a unitary ego—how we're made up of conflicting, interacting systems of things. . . . We know we are driven by desire. . . . " They often lapse into semiotic chatter, and the talk about textuality and sexuality is almost always an occasion for a satiric dig, not least at their emotionally straitened lives. It is also a prelude to serious doubt for Roland and Maud about the literary orthodoxy they officially endorse.

For as Byatt sends them off on one extraordinary quest—to uncover the secret romance between the famous (married) Victorian poet Randolph Henry Ash and the lesser known (and until now purportedly lesbian, or asexual) poet Christabel LaMotte—she also burdens them with another mission: to confront the glacial anti-romanticism at the heart of their studies and their lives so far. What better way to scrutinize the postmodern, post-Freudian, "knowing" attitude than to compare it with the doubting, inhibited Victorian spirit? Especially since the juxtaposition offers an unexpected twist: lives in the age of sexual ultra-sophistication turn out to be frigid, and passion thrives in the age of repression.

In playing out this contrast, Byatt takes a conventional novelistic approach: she interweaves the paths and preoccupations of her two couples. But within that old-fashioned structure, she mixes up styles, genres, voices in good postmodern manner. The tale of her contemporary pair is a detective story, and the mystery at its heart is the tale of her Victorian pair, which is a romance. The thriller is launched when Roland, browsing among his hero Ash's papers in the library, discovers drafts of an urgent personal letter to an unidentified woman. Roland immediately recognizes the note as a possible clue to an unknown side of the fiercely intellectual poet renowned for his calm, exemplary life. In a moment of uncharacteristic impulsiveness, Roland slips the letters into his own Oxford Selected Ash and leaves the library, and the sleuthing begins.

In pursuit of Ash's mysterious correspondent, whom he quickly identifies as Christabel LaMotte, Roland is led to Maud Bailey, who is a distant relative of the poetess, an expert on her, and the guardian of some of her unpublished papers. They turn out to have more than a professional subject in common: they are both full of diffidence about personal entanglements. From here on, Roland and Maud's story, as they pursue the Victorian secret, traces the erosion (slowly) of their literary certainties and (even more slowly) of their emotional uncertainties.

The quest for the poets' hidden passion is a formal challenge to the scholars' habits. Roland, a dedicated textual editor of Ash, and Maud, a psychoanalytic critic of LaMotte, are at once queasy and excited about the personal probing they are suddenly drawn into. Byatt captures their ambivalence, and their initially combative relation, in a characteristic bit of well-tuned dialogue, initiated by Roland:

> "I've never been much interested in places—or things—with associations—"
>
> "Nor I. I'm a textual scholar. I rather deplore the modern feminist attitude toward private lives."
>
> "If you're going to be stringently analytical," Roland said, "don't you have to?"
>
> "You can be psychoanalytical without being *personal*" Maud said. Roland did not challenge her.

Inevitably, their pursuit becomes very personal, as they unearth letters that chart the at first hesitant, then increasingly intense conversation between Ash and LaMotte—and that break off at precisely the moment when the young scholars (in spite of their purist approach) are dying to know what happened next. Was the relationship ever consummated, or did Christabel in the end retreat into the quiet house she shared with her spinsterish companion? Roland and Maud set out to trace Randolph Ash's natural history expedition to North Yorkshire in June 1859, hoping to discover, by reading various clues in a new light, whether Christabel accompanied him.

Just because Roland and Maud depart from their strictly textual methods doesn't mean that Byatt endorses old-fashioned biographical hounding, or the newer feminist variation on it. She may be skeptical of high-flown theory, but she's also dubious about more reductive approaches. As she follows Roland and Maud in their tramp through Yorkshire on the trail of the poets, she interweaves her

most merciless satire of two of the cruder varieties of literary analysis. Her targets are Americans, Professor Mortimer Cropper, keeper of the most complete collection of Ash relics at Robert Dale Owen University in New Mexico, editor of Ash's correspondence, and author of *The Great Ventriloquist,* a pompous biography of Ash; and Professor Leonora Stern, from Tallahassee, author of *Motif and Matrix in the Poems of LaMotte,* a study in which discussions of creativity inevitably return to discussions of female sexuality.

Roland and Maud dip into those tomes on their trip, and so do we, thanks to Byatt's skillful parody of several pages of each. Writing of LaMotte's long poem *The Fairy Mélusine,* for example, Leonora Stern discourses on feminine landscapes as erotic terrain and emphasizes the relation between watery scenes and orgasmic pleasures:

> The male fountain spurts and springs. Mélusine's fountain has a *female* wetness, trickling out from its pool rather than rising confidently, thus mirroring those female secretions which are not inscribed in our daily use of language (*langue,* tongue)—the sputum, mucus, milk, and bodily fluids of women who are silent for dryness.

By now prepared to be impatient with their colleagues, Roland and Maud see that they completely miss the point. Stern digresses about LaMotte and autoeroticism, and Cropper speculates about the fear of sterility and decline lurking behind Ash's new interest in nature's procreative powers, but the younger scholars are onto the truth, which is precisely the opposite: the Yorkshire journey was the occasion of an all-consuming affair between Ash and LaMotte, and their poems can't look the same once that secret has been glimpsed.

Byatt's aim is to show that Maud and Roland are guided to their discovery by a much more imaginative sense of what words can mean than either of the Americans begins to grasp. The key to the young scholars' sympathetic comprehension of the poets is the opposite of sophistication. "Something primitive," they acknowledge, seizes them in their reading: "narrative curiosity." And something else, equally primitive, overtakes them at the same time: stirrings of their own desire—this from a pair who agree that their ideal is "a clean empty bed in a clean empty room, where nothing is asked or to be asked. . . . Maybe we're symptomatic of whole flocks of exhausted scholars and theorists." Though still studiously avoiding any admission of their growing interest in each other, they pore over the works of their heroes with new energy and vision.

Here Byatt agilely plays off the divergences and convergences between the circumstances of her two couples. Roland and Maud are inspired by the act of sympathy required to bridge what they see as a huge gap separating them from Ash and LaMotte. "It makes an interesting effort of imagination," Roland puts it in his understated way, "to think how they saw the world"—and saw each other. Byatt invites her readers to join in that effort, plunging us into the same freighted material the professors peruse. She puts all her linguistic, parodic skills on display, almost as if she had set herself the challenge of imitating and interweaving as many Victorian genres as possible: short poems, long poems, personal letters, public letters, stories, journal entries (Ash's and his wife's, as well as those of LaMotte's companion and her niece), and more.

The effect of the sometimes dizzying collage is at first just as Roland says: there's a sense of real distance separating us from them. But before long that comfortably detached vantage is unsettled. Juxtaposing her contemporary style—abrupt swerves between documents and time frames—and the poets' old-fashioned style, Byatt unfolds a curiously anachronistic story. The great drama of their lives, as Christabel steps forth from her well-guarded seclusion and Randolph ventures onto uncharted emotional terrain, begins as a Victorian tale told in musty letters but becomes a surprising modern story of liberation followed by abandonment. In the chapter that culminates the poets' affair, Byatt springs free of her documentation and claims imaginative license to follow them on their fateful Yorkshire trip. As she begins, using only "the man" and "the woman," it's momentarily unclear whether the excitedly apprehensive couple on the train are Randolph and Christabel or Maud and Roland.

Several further, suspenseful turns in the detective story reveal that the poets' lives have a ragged modern ending, their paths leading off in different directions and their messages to each other lost in transmission. The young professors, meanwhile, are on their way to an old-fashioned happy ending, two chilly souls warming each other at last. Having quoted Hawthorne in her epigraph ("When a writer calls his work a Romance . . . he wishes to claim a certain latitude, both as to its fashion and material . . . "), Byatt calls on the conventions of Romance to wind up the many threads of her mystery in a pleasantly implausible way.

But Byatt the literature professor can't resist a last word. Though the lives she has spun out have been fascinating, it's the books that finally count, she instructs near the end: language and imaginative reading shouldn't be eclipsed by biographical sleuthing. As she explains in a Victorian authorial intrusion, it's not easy to prevent words from fading into the background amid the drama of tumultuous lives: "It is possible for a writer to make, or remake at least, for a reader, the primary pleasures of eating, or drinking, or looking on, or sex. . . . [Novels] do not habitually elaborate on the equally intense pleasure of reading." That's because it's a tricky, self-reflexive matter, calling attention to the experience of reading in the course of that experience; it requires rousing "the brain" and "the viscera" so that the pleasure of encountering words on a page isn't merely "papery and dry."

That is the challenge Byatt has immodestly set for herself in her elaborate patchwork of "original" texts. There's a triumphant, sometimes slightly irritating, exhibitionism at the core of that aim, for the many words we're meant to thrill to are, of course, all finally Byatt's own. At the close of the novel, just in case her readers haven't already fully enjoyed such pleasure and watched her characters enjoy it, she gives Roland a classic moment of readerly ecstasy. He goes back to a poem of Ash's with his new knowledge of the poet's passionate life:

> Roland read, or reread, *The Golden Apples,* as though the words were living creatures or stones of fire. . . . He heard Ash's voice, certainly his voice, his own unmistakable voice, and he heard the language moving around, weaving its own patterns, beyond the reach of any single human, writer or reader. . . . He saw too that Christabel was the Muse and Proserpine and that she was not, and this seemed to be so interesting and *apt,* once he had understood, that he laughed aloud.

Byatt assiduously tends to all the "primary pleasures" of description in her novel, entering into her characters' lives and above all their loves. She sees to it that Roland gets his girl in the end, though as he's said earlier, that's "vulgar romance," certainly compared with the Victorians' high passion. But the real feat of her novel is in making it plausible—and important—that those poets wrote poems from their heads and hearts, and that Roland and Maud can now read them more fully than they ever have before. It's the kind of lesson more literature professors could stand to teach. (pp. 47-9)

Ann Hulbert, "The Great Ventriloquist," in The New Republic, *Vol. 204, Nos. 1 & 2, January 7 & 14, 1991, pp. 47-9.*

Donna Rifkind

One of the curiosities of 1990 in the publishing world was the popularity of a novel by the British writer A. S. Byatt entitled *Possession.* In October it was announced that Miss Byatt's novel (her fourth) had won the Booker Prize, England's most prestigious literary award. At the same time came news that Miss Byatt had also picked up the Irish Times-Aer Lingus International Fiction Prize. Together, the two awards netted the author just a bit under ninety thousand dollars and a good deal of priceless publicity. In this country, the book remained for weeks on the *New York Times* best-seller list, was universally praised by critics, and occupied a prominent position on just about every roundup of the most distinguished books of the year.

Possession marks a departure from Miss Byatt's previous novels—*The Virgin in the Garden* (1978), say, or its sequel, *Still Life* (1985)—which are big, messy, plot-heavy books, full of somber theoretical reflections on life and art, religion and society. These books owe a clear debt to the fiction of Iris Murdoch (one of Miss Byatt's nonfiction works is a study of the older novelist entitled *Degrees of Freedom*) and are, like Miss Murdoch's novels, absorbing while read but forgettable once they are finished. That a good deal of *Still Life* takes place at Cambridge is not surprising: the university is clearly a world Miss Byatt knows well, having taught English and American literature at University College, London.

While *Possession* can be called a university novel as well, it has a distinctly new focus, concentrating less on traditional plotting and more on literary game-playing. Subtitled *A Romance,* the novel takes its epigraph from the preface to *The House of the Seven Gables.* In writing a romance, Hawthorne noted, the goal is "to connect a bygone time with the very present that is flitting away from us."

The writer of a romance, he continues, "wishes to claim a certain latitude, both as to its fashion and material, which he would not have felt himself entitled to assume had he professed to be writing a Novel."

Miss Byatt's novel assumes latitude galore, especially in the way it attempts to connect a "bygone time" and the "very present." Half the book tells the story of a secret love affair between two well-known British Victorian poets of Miss Byatt's imagination: Randolph Henry Ash, who bears some resemblance to Robert Browning, and Christabel LaMotte, a demure figure somewhat reminiscent of Emily Dickinson, whose poetry is, in the late 1980s, enjoying a widespread popularity among modern scholars. The other half of the plot concerns a cadre of contemporary academics, each of whom is intent on uncovering the details of the love affair for his or her own professional glory.

One of the curiosities of 1990 in the publishing world was the popularity of a novel by the British writer A. S. Byatt entitled *Possession.*

"Latitude" of some sort also shows itself in Miss Byatt's re-creation of the art of her fictional Victorian poets. Not content merely to have her modern scholars rave about its quality (though they do plenty of this), she invents pages and pages of poetry, prose, diaries, and letters by Ash and LaMotte in order to give readers a look at the primary material that has all of her academics gaga over their subjects' private life.

Many reviewers of *Possession* have lavishly praised these inventions. The poetry struck Jay Parini in *The New York Times Book Review* [see excerpt above] as "highly plausible versions of Browning and Rossetti and . . . beautiful poems on their own." But it must be said that, whatever Miss Byatt's familiarity with the genre, she is deplorably inept at creating imitations of important Victorian poetry. Here, for example, is a brief quotation from Ash's 1840 pseudo-epic *Ragnarök,* a twelve-book poem (mercifully, in this case we are only given four pages) "which some saw as a Christianizing of the Norse myth":

> And these three Ases were the sons of Bor
> Who slew the Giant Ymir in his rage
> And made of him the elements of earth,
> Body and sweat and bones and curly hair,
> Made soil and sea and hills and waving trees,
> And his grey brains wandered the heavens as
>   clouds.

Christabel LaMotte's poetry, while no better, generally has at least the virtue of brevity. Here is a representative bit of banality that serves as the introduction to Chapter 8:

> All day snow fell
> Snow fell all night

> My silent lintel
> Silted white
> Inside a Creature—
> Feathered—Bright—
> With snowy Feature
> Eyes of Light
> Propounds—Delight.

If Miss Byatt's intention had been to offer these "poems" as parodies of nineteenth-century literature at its worst, they might perhaps have had some narrative punch. But she presents them unsmilingly, without so much as a hint of irony, as if they were comparable to "Porphyria's Lover" or "Fra Lippo Lippi."

The parody in *Possession* is reserved for easier targets: the contemporary scholars who are squabbling over the literary remains of Ash and LaMotte. The academic treated most kindly—if not unsatirically—by Miss Byatt is her hero, Roland Michell, a twenty-nine-year-old with a doctorate from Prince Albert College in London and a bleak future. (When a teaching job comes up in his department, there are six hundred applications.) Trained in "the post-structuralist deconstruction" of the poetry of Randolph Henry Ash, Roland now finds himself with no hope of employment, and spends his time doing donkey work for his former professor, an expert on Ash named James Blackadder.

Roland is keenly aware that he has missed the chance to reap the benefits of trendy literary scholarship in its heyday: gone is the time when an opportunistic academic could rise to superstardom. Yet against all odds, Roland manages to make a major academic discovery one morning in the Reading Room of the London Library. Leafing through an overlooked copy of Vico from the Ash archives, he discovers two love letters written by Ash and deduces, after some research, that the object of Ash's illicit devotion must be Christabel LaMotte. For years it had been taken for granted among scholars that Ash was entirely faithful to his devoted wife Ellen, while Christabel thrived in what the feminists had been enthusiastically assuming was a happy lesbian relationship. So Roland's discovery, which he at first keeps entirely to himself, is decidedly momentous.

But Roland cannot continue for long on his own: he is familiar enough with Ash's life, but needs more information about LaMotte's. Rather reluctantly, he forms an alliance with Maud Bailey, a LaMotte expert who is herself an indirect descendant of the poetess. Together the two scholars sift through their combined archives in search of clues; step by step, in an atmosphere of mounting scholarly excitement, they uncover evidence for what turns out to have been a steamy sexual liaison which may or may not have resulted in the birth of an illegitimate child.

Before too long, however, other academics begin suspecting that something is up and scramble to join the chase. This pack of bloodhounds includes Mortimer P. Cropper, Ash's American biographer and curator of a huge archive of the poet's artifacts. Cropper drives a long black Mercedes and is known to be both unscrupulous and unbearably pompous; he is certainly meant to be regarded as a figure of fun, as is dour Professor Blackadder (Roland's mentor) and his office-mate Beatrice Nest, who has been dispiritedly trying to produce a volume of Ellen Ash's diary and letters for twenty-five years.

Miss Byatt lavishes most of her satirical attention on Professor Leonora Stern, a radical feminist at Tallahassee University who shares with Maud Bailey the distinction of being the world's foremost expert on Christabel La-Motte. Leonora is "a majestically large woman, in all directions," who claims both Creole and Indian ancestry. After chucking her first husband, "a happily meticulous New Critic [who] had totally failed to survive Leonora and the cut-throat ideological battles of structuralism, post-structuralism, Marxism, deconstruction and feminism," she bore a son to a hippie named Saul Drucker, then left him for an Indian woman professor of anthropology. "After the professor," notes Miss Byatt, "there had been Marge, Brigitta, Pocahontas and Martina."

However ridiculous this oh-so-contemporary personal history may appear to be, the most pointed lampooning in *Possession* is in its characterization of the novel's hero and heroine, Roland and Maud. Throughout the book we are teased into hoping that, in the process of uncovering the facts of a bygone love affair, Roland and Maud will have their own fling. But this repeatedly fails to happen, on purpose: Miss Byatt's intention here is to point out the irony in the fact that Ash and LaMotte, a pair of properly repressed Victorians, managed to be a lot sexier than today's sexually well-informed scholars. Although Roland and Maud are attracted to each other, they are utterly incapable of "any strenuous Romantic self-assertion":

> They were children of a time and culture that mistrusted love, "in love," romantic love, romance *in toto,* and which nevertheless in revenge proliferated sexual language, linguistic sexuality, analysis, dissection, deconstruction, exposure. They were theoretically knowing: they knew about phallocracy and penisneid, punctuation, puncturing and penetration, about polymorphous and polysemous perversity, orality,

good and bad breasts, clitoral tumescence, vesicle persecution, the fluids, the solids, the metaphors for these, the systems of desire and damage, infantile greed and oppression and transgression, the iconography of the cervix and the imagery of expanding and contracting Body, desired, attacked, consumed, feared.

The most effective aspect of *Possession* is not its satire of contemporary academic warfare, its literary self-consciousness, or the complexity of its detective-story plot, which ends melodramatically with all the scholars perched over Ash's grave in a storm, ready to exhume its surprising contents. Nor, finally, is it Miss Byatt's prodigious (and largely failed) attempts to imitate Victorian literary artifacts. The most effective thing—the only truly memorable thing, in fact—about this novel is its eloquent declaration of a single simple point: that Roland and Maud, highly trained specialists in the very latest theories about sexuality and the ego, do not know the first thing about finding sexual fulfillment for themselves.

And yet the convincing articulation of this very postmodern dilemma is not a satisfactory explanation for the widespread success of *Possession.* Roland's and Maud's is, after all, a most specialized kind of arrested love affair, one which requires a thorough knowledge of semiotics in order for all its ironies to be properly understood. The best that can be said of this novel is that it is a kind of intellectual cult book: instead of possessing the more popular appeal of a novel by David Lodge or Kingsley Amis, both of whom have written brilliantly about the foibles of academics, Miss Byatt's book has a far more segregated readership. It is hard to imagine, once the wheels of the publicity machine have ground to a halt, that *Possession* will be regarded as anything other than an outdated literary curio, and a rather overwrought one at that. (pp. 77-80)

Donna Rifkind, "Victorians' Secrets," in The New Criterion, *Vol. IX, No. 6, February, 1991, pp. 77-80.*

E. L. Doctorow
Billy Bathgate

Prizes: National Book Critics Circle Award; PEN/Faulkner Award.

Born in 1931, Doctorow is an American novelist, short story writer, editor, essayist, and dramatist.

Billy Bathgate explores the decline of gangsterism in post-Prohibition New York through the eyes of its fifteen-year-old narrator and title character. Billy comes of age under the tutelage of the criminal Dutch Schultz—a character based on the historical figure—who is desperate to hold on to his dwindling empire. As he witnesses brutal murders, has an affair with Dutch's lover that endangers his life, and leaves New York City for the first time, Billy develops a personal moral code and ultimately inherits Dutch's fortune. Comparing the author to Twain and Dickens, Garry Wills stated that Doctorow "sees adult possibilities in 'the boy's book'—the tale of an orphan, not yet socialized into ordinary adult life, who acquires an outlaw mentor. . . . Billy, outside accepted moral systems, must create his own code of responsibility, as Huck [Finn] does."

Critics marveled at Doctorow's vivid descriptions of New York City in the 1930s and of the horrific murders committed by Dutch and his gang. Some considered Billy's immense vocabulary unbelievable for a fifteen-year-old high school dropout. Billy explains this inconsistency at the end of the novel, however, telling the reader that he has since completed an Ivy League education and is narrating the story of his boyhood fifty years later. Reflecting on the image of the American gangster, Doctorow has provided what some critics believe to be a "fairy tale about capitalism." Dutch's accountant, Abbadabba Berman, soliloquizes about the new universal language of numbers which "don't lie" and opens the doors for Billy to gain a fortune. As many critics have observed, Doctorow in *Billy Bathgate* has rewritten several "fairy tales" into one novel, merging the excitement and violence of the 1930s, the American Dream of striking it rich, and a boy's coming-of-age story.

(See also *CLC,* Vols. 6, 11, 15, 18, 37, 44; *Contemporary Authors,* Vols. 45-48; *Contemporary Authors New Revision Series,* Vol. 2; *Dictionary of Literary Biography,* Vols. 2, 28; *Dictionary of Literary Biography Yearbook: 1980;* and *Concise Dictionary of American Literary Biography: 1968-1988.*)

PRINCIPAL WORKS

NOVELS

Welcome to Hard Times   1960

Big as Life   1966
The Book of Daniel   1971
Ragtime   1975
Loon Lake   1980
World's Fair   1985
Billy Bathgate   1989

SHORT FICTION

Lives of the Poets: Six Stories and a Novella   1984

PLAYS

Drinks before Dinner   1979

Merle Rubin

[In *Billy Bathgate*], E. L. Doctorow appears to have based his story on the shaky assumption that his teen-aged hero's fixation on the Dutch Schultz gang is as universally resonant as Faust's thirst for hidden knowledge, Cathy's passion for Heathcliff, or Huck Finn's need to get away from civilization. Doctorow builds his novel, undoubtedly a tour de force of sorts, out of two opposing lines of tension: The first is the perception that crime is glamorous and that criminals are daring, self-reliant warrior-heroes. The second is the revelation that crime can be brutal, disgusting, and nauseating.

So we have crime as a celebration of vitality versus crime as a humiliation of life itself. The contrast is neatly balanced, but the contrasted ideas are never developed beyond the stage of truism.

The eponymous young narrator, who names himself "Bathgate" after a market in his native Bronx, manages to attach himself as a kind of errand boy, mascot, and apprentice to the notorious Dutch Schultz gang in the 1930s. He witnesses some horrifying murders that do not accord with his idea of criminal heroics, but the horror he feels is mitigated by the money he makes and by the excitement he gets from being so close to a source of raw power.

Billy first catches Schultz's attention because of his skills as a street juggler. Juggling comes to serve as a metaphor for the way Billy will juggle his conflicting attraction and revulsion, anxiety, and admiration. It is also a metaphor for the orderly "spin" of the organized crime machinery: the flow of money (bribes, payoffs, extortion, numbers, and other rackets) and the ebb and flow of the criminal acts that elude the mathematics of profit and loss (suspicion, betrayal, revenge, and rage, the commodities in which Schultz himself deals).

Billy enters the world of this peculiar solar system just as it is starting to break down, as the juggler's spinning plates begin to wobble, careening off course in shattering, unpredictable trajectories. Unnecessary murders are messing up the criminal arithmetic of "orderly" retribution (Billy is as much attracted by the quasi-military "order" of gang life as by its lawlessness). The killer/leader is increasingly off-balance, in constant danger of overstepping a line his fellow outlaws, who have no qualms about overstepping the ordinary bounds of law, would nonetheless consider beyond the pale.

Technically, *Billy Bathgate* is an accomplished piece of fiction. Intellectually and thematically, it is less interesting than Doctorow's earlier work, including his almost forgotten . . . novel, *The Book of Daniel,* a fictional extrapolation of the story of the children of the executed "atom spies" Ethel and Julius Rosenberg. Like much of Doctorow's previous work, *Billy Bathgate* takes its imaginative nourishment from the image-rich storehouse of American history. Whether Doctorow feeds off history or enriches it remains a moot point.

The structure of this book, however, is an object lesson in novelistic technique. The scene shifts brilliantly from the backrooms, alleys, and nightclubs of Manhattan to the quiet neighborhoods of City Island, to the bucolic upstate town of Onondaga, where Dutch and his gang ingratiate themselves with the locals who will sit on the jury at his upcoming trial.

These changes of setting are quite as dramatic as the development of the plot: in some sense, they *are* the plot, more so than Dutch's unpredictable but monotonous mood swings that set the killing action. There is less and less that Billy can learn from Dutch, but his apprenticeship does give him the opportunity to see more of the world than he did from his narrow Bronx tenement.

The other remarkable feature of this book is Billy's narrative style. The long, run-on sentences that sound excited and reflective at once are clearly the voice of a young man eager to set down all he's getting to see, while trying to make some sense of his experience. The trouble is, Billy never quite succeeds at the latter endeavor.

Billy's voice is central to the story and apparently, to judge from a cursory survey of the book's reception so far, it has sufficient appeal to elicit a chorus of uncritical praise from book reviewers. They are too dazzled by the polished technique, however, to notice that this gangster story has little more depth than a B-movie.

> Merle Rubin, *"Bathgate: Technique Surpasses Tale,"* in The Christian Science Monitor, *March 22, 1989, p. 13.*

Anne Tyler

Billy Bathgate [E. L. Doctorow's] eighth novel, takes us . . . to the Bronx of the 30's. It is Mr. Doctorow's shapeliest piece of work: a richly detailed report of a 15-year-old boy's journey from childhood to adulthood, with plenty of cliff-hanging adventure along the way.

The title character is a rough, tough high school dropout living by his wits in the Bronx. His father has long ago disappeared, his mother is an impoverished laundry worker given to periods of "distraction" (some might say insanity) and Billy himself possesses only one distinguishing feature: he knows how to juggle.

One day, while performing an unusually difficult juggling feat, he attracts the attention of the notorious gangster Dutch Schultz. Dutch is considered a local hero; so when he calls Billy a "capable boy," it means something. But Billy's capability, as he himself realizes long after he has carved out a niche for himself in Dutch's gang, is not only for juggling; it is for worship, for wholeheartedly admiring "that rudeness of power of which [Dutch] was a greater student than anybody, oh and that menace of him where it might all be over for anyone in his sight from one instant to the next . . . the danger he was really a maniac."

So what we have here is something considerably darker than Huck and Jim floating down a river together. The fact is that Dutch Schultz is a scary man. His position in Billy's life is much like that of a powerful but capricious parent. (pp. 1, 46)

Prohibition has already been repealed (although the gang maintains its old neighborhood beer drops, as if for the sheer romance of it all), and the legal hounds are closing in on several matters of tax evasion; but most important, Dutch seems to be undergoing some personal deterioration as well. He murders more frequently and more senselessly, losing control of his temper and flailing out at whoever is handy. As Billy puts it, "He needed more death, he was using up his deaths so quickly now he needed them faster and faster." Merely to stay alive around such a man takes some doing.

Billy's narrative reveals first, of course, that he does stay alive (since it's written in the first person) and second, that he's astonishingly articulate. This causes the reader some anxiety. When a nearly uneducated street urchin uses words like "undulant," "coprolitic," "animacy" and "imprimatur," you can't help noticing the author himself lurking behind the backdrop. True, we're told at the end of the book that Billy eventually received some further education, but the tone is very much here-and-now—a boy's tone, vital and brisk. It sounds like anything but an old man's long, fond backward look.

There's a trade-off, though. What the novel loses in authenticity, it gains in eloquence. Kindly agree to grant Billy his gift of language and you'll be rewarded with passages of writing so intense, so breathtakingly vivid, that you'll trust the story in spite of yourself, and that face behind the backdrop will miraculously fade.

For instance, in the opening scene, which sets the stage for everything to follow, Billy describes the killing of a man named Bo Weinberg. It's the kind of crime most commonly referred to as a "gangland murder"—a body will wash up later sporting cement overshoes, as the comedians like to put it—but seen through Billy's clear eyes it seems almost artistic, a piece of skilled craftsmanship. It reveals details we never before stopped to wonder about: the neat rolling of the victim's trousers, the baring of his long white feet, the gingerly manner in which, "like some princess at a ball," he takes a henchman's arm and steps into a laundry tub full of wet cement. The cement itself, Billy tells us, makes "a slow-witted diagram of the sea outside, the slab of it shifting to and fro as the boat rose and fell on the waves." Then the victim's hands are tied with clothesline "still showing the loops it came in from the hardware store, and with . . . perfect knots between the wrists like a section of vertebrae." His expression, as he watches these proceedings, is one of "distracted admiration," and you might say the same for the reader's expression as well.

Billy's style of vision is fresh and unprejudiced and almost comically bemused. He tells us that the victim "was staring at his feet, perhaps because feet are intimate body parts rarely seen with black tie, and following his gaze, I felt I had to commiserate with what I was sure he was thinking, that for all our civilization we go around on these things that are slit at the front end into five unequal lengths each partially covered with shell." A spell of lightheadedness at sea brings the realization that "water is a beast of another planet," while the boat's rails and bolts strike him as "good news, that something like a boat could be so much of a construction, all according to the rules of the sea, and that there was a means of making your tenuous way across this world that clearly reflected a long history of thought."

Given this beginning, then—which is as elegantly woven as a poem—we take heart. This is going to be an easy ride. And it is; *Billy Bathgate* is the kind of book you find yourself finishing at three in the morning after promising at midnight that you'll stop after one more page. One scene glides into the next, and yet each is so complete in itself, so fully and precisely observed, that it seems to be encapsulated in a tiny glass paperweight.

For example, early in his career Billy is sent to a certain street corner to report on something that will happen there—what, he has no idea. First, therefore, he observes the general action: the coconut-drink stand, the water wagon, the delivery truck delivering racks of bread, the dance studio spilling forth "Bye Bye Blackbird." Then he zeroes in on two window washers on a scaffold high above him, and he knows somehow that this is what he was meant to watch: the rope on one side snapping and a window washer plummeting to the ground, while everything below appears to freeze.

"I don't know if I shouted," he tells us, "or who else saw it happen or heard it, but while he was still several stories up, some seconds above his death, the whole street knew. The traffic was stopped as if every vehicle had been pulled up taut on the same string. There was a collective screech, a total apprehension of disaster on the part of every pedestrian for blocks around, as if we had all been aware all along of what was going on above our heads in the sky, so that the moment the composition was disturbed everyone knew instantly."

It's a moment that illustrates not only Mr. Doctorow's ability to encompass an event, to view it in uncanny entirety, but also his deep feeling for city life. Over and over, Billy unrolls before us the most complex and oddly beautiful New York street scenes, full of grime and energy and color. Other sites strike him as poor imitations. A trip to New Jersey chills his heart; the streets are the wrong width and the passers-by seem lost. A sojourn with the gang in a little country village is pleasant but unsettling; the nights are too dark, the sky is too empty, and one of the mobsters asks where a person would go to take a walk. Even more unsettling—to the reader as well as to Billy—is Billy's reaction when he returns to the city. All at once he can see the squalor and smell the cinders, and we worry, for a moment, that he's lost the sense of his own place. But then he readjusts, and the book's final paragraph—a hauntingly lovely hymn of praise to the East Bronx of Dutch Schultz's day—will make you feel downright homesick.

This is not to say that *Billy Bathgate* is a novel only of period and geography. It boasts a plot that's almost perfectly constructed—a long, graceful arc of a plot, marred only by one strange lapse (a highly unlikely surprise arrival in the next to the last paragraph, just when we thought we were home free). And it abounds in character as well. Dutch Schultz, with his buzzing voice and clumsy style of dressing, walks right off the page. His financial advisor, the dapper mathematical genius Abbadabba Berman, is someone whose appearances we learn to look forward to, and Dutch's high-society girlfriend is irresistible— dazzlingly insouciant, proceeding through real peril at a casual saunter.

Even the various gangsters are multidimensional. Bit by bit, they begin to seem . . . well, ordinary, which in this case is a compliment. We wouldn't go so far as to relax around them, but on the other hand we do start to realize how unexpectedly funny and homely they can be. . . .

But the star, of course, is Billy Bathgate himself. He is kindhearted, sharp-witted, original, likable and always completely believable. He's Huck Finn and Tom Sawyer with more poetry, Holden Caulfield with more zest and spirit—a wonderful new addition to the ranks of American boy heroes. (p. 46)

> *Anne Tyler, "An American Boy in Gangland,"* in The New York Times Book Review, *February 26, 1989, pp. 1, 46.*

Richard Eder

A king is known by the tone of his retinue. E. L. Doctorow elevates the story of the gangster, Dutch Schultz, into a cycle of rise, fall and renewal by using the lofty voice of a prodigious 15-year-old apprentice-boy.

Like virtually all of Doctorow's work, ***Billy Bathgate*** uses some of the features of a period piece to do something quite different. Here, the period is the 1930s, when Schultz flourished in his own ferocious fashion until state prosecutors—notably, the late Thomas E. Dewey—began pressing him hard, and a rival gang rubbed him out.

Doctorow's novel makes full and loving use of the manners, the artifacts, the savors and the rhythms of the '30s. He is marvelously skillful at getting into the thoughts and the lingo of the time.

But that is not all. There is also a contemporary sensibility at work at some mid-point between the author and his narrator. The Billy Bathgate of the title, the 1930s apprentice, recalls his story today in the 1980s.

It is, as ***Ragtime, Loon Lake, World's Fair*** were, a dialogue between two eras. And Doctorow's ultimate purpose, aside from entertaining and enthralling—which perhaps he has never done so well as here—is only apparently to re-create the past through this dialogue. In fact, it is to give an edge, an unsettling undertone to the present.

Billy is an apocryphal figure amid a lot of real, or only partly embroidered New York history. The Schultz that Billy remembers—his idol, his mentor and, in the way symbolic fathers are, his victim—is both real and transfigured. It is the difference between a 6th-Century Welsh chieftain and the myth-enshrouded King Arthur of Thomas Malory.

The Arthurian comparison goes further. Billy is a Bronx slum-kid who catches Shultz's eye. He is a protégé but in a distant, mysterious fashion. Like some Arthurian Round-Tabler, he is sent on a quest, marked by lethal puzzles and ordeals. In this case, the object is not the Grail, but a seat at the gangster-king's right hand.

Billy becomes an errand boy at numbers-racket headquarters. As an initiation, he is taken to watch the arranged death—by apparent mishap—of a troublesome window washer in a union that Shultz controls.

Billy is tutored in detail by Schultz's accountant, Abba-

dabba Berman, a cripple and a mathematical genius. Schultz himself is alternately remote and close, benevolent and threatening. Billy never knows when he is in favor and when he may be liquidated.

It is the truest apprenticeship. Schultz's own life of perpetual combat and deadly gambles is mirrored in Billy's uncertainty about his position, and even his life.

He becomes a busboy-cum-informer in a Schultz-controlled bar. He witnesses Schultz's personal liquidation of a lieutenant suspected of treachery. He is a kind of chaperon and companion to the gangster's high-society mistress, and briefly—though he is only 15—her lover.

Still 15, and still wearing short pants, he is assigned to shadow Dewey. Schultz, unhinged by the net closing about his operations, wants to kill the prosecutor. And Billy is there, in a New Jersey restaurant, when the Mafia chieftain, Lucky Luciano—fearful that such a scheme will ruin them all—has his men kill Schultz and his lieutenants.

Billy's voice is by turns flowery, baroque, mystical and down-to-earth. It is mannered talk, yet supple enough to accommodate both the questing 15-year-old, as recalled by his older self; and Doctorow's own vision.

After Schultz is gunned down in the New Jersey bar, Billy slips away, unnoticed. He has the combination to his master's safe, and clues to where the rest of his fortune is stashed. Later, he tells us, he will use the money to build up his own empire.

He does not tell us who he has become, nor whether he is still connected to the gangs. It does not matter, he implies. Gangs and "legitimate" enterprises come and go; the money is unchanging and immortal.

So much for the dark thread that runs . . . through a gaudy and elegant book. It is a binding thread, a governing one.

And there, perhaps, is the underlying weakness of ***Billy*** despite its beguilement. As in his other recent books, Doctorow governs his work as a craftsman governs his material. The pulse and pattern his characters move to seem implanted; he has given them a life-like mechanism, not life itself.

At his best, that is, his novels are prodigious toys. When they end—even his placement in a past time makes their endings seem like an off-switch—the thread is in his hand. The toy goes back to him. We open our eyes just where we have closed them.

> *Richard Eder, "Siege Perilous in the Court of Dutch Schultz," in* Los Angeles Times Book Review, *March 5, 1989, p. 3.*

John Bemrose

E. L. Doctorow, the celebrated chronicler of America . . . , opens his new novel, ***Billy Bathgate,*** with a murder scene as chilling as any in recent fiction. Dutch Schultz, the Depression-era gangster who is one of the book's main characters, has decided to eliminate a disloyal gang member called Bo Weinberg. Schultz takes Weinberg on a night boat ride out of New York City harbor into the open Atlantic, where he orders him at gunpoint to stand in a basin of wet cement. Then, while the cement is hardening, he takes Weinberg's girlfriend, Drew Preston, into a nearby cabin—apparently to rape her. The two-pronged torture is highly effective. Weinberg, who can face his own death at the bottom of the Atlantic with some equanimity, is completely unmanned by the attack on Drew. By the end of the chapter, he can only moan for his mother and beg Schultz's henchmen to shoot him—an act of mercy that they steadfastly refuse to perform.

Doctorow describes that event—and several others like it—with a kind of surgical exactness, an exquisite attention to detail that reveals how much his imagination is galvanized by the nearness of violent death. Like another American writer before him, Ernest Hemingway, Doctorow frequently depends on the charge inherent in depictions of physical danger to keep his images bright and his long, lyrical sentences taut and clean. The book's narrator, Billy Bathgate, describes Bo Weinberg's death with a vividness that permeates the whole novel. Billy misses nothing, right to the last moment when all that can be seen of Bo above the surface of the Atlantic is "the shot white cuffs and the pale hands reaching for heaven."

Yet *Billy Bathgate* is a celebration of life as well, particularly the life of youth, with its boundless resilience and illusions of immortality. Now in his 60s, Billy re-creates his past as a fatherless 15-year-old in the Bronx of the 1930s. While his mother works in a local laundry, Billy—like his peers—goes to school only sporadically, steals a little and worships the mystique of Schultz, whose territory includes Billy's neighborhood. Then, one day, Schultz drops by to visit a warehouse he owns and sees Billy juggling two balls, a navel orange, an egg and a black stone. As wily as he is dexterous, Billy pretends to be so impressed at seeing the famous gangster that he drops everything. Pleased and impressed himself, Schultz compliments Billy and gives him a crisp $10 bill. From that moment on, Billy becomes obsessed with joining Schultz's gang. He hangs around their hideout until they adopt him as a sort of errand boy. Eventually, he wins their full confidence, finding in the mobsters a substitute for the father who deserted him and his mother years ago.

Billy's new family is a strange one, a motley collection of professionals as dedicated to their craft as any doctor or lawyer. They are perhaps a bit too colorful to be wholly convincing, drawn as much from Hollywood as from their real-life models. But it is hard not to like a character such as Abbadabba Berman, Schultz's master accountant and numbers-racket man, who slips Billy money and teaches him how to shoot a gun. Even Billy's number 1 foster-father, Schultz himself, has a kind of crude geniality. But he is also given to violent, unpredictable rages. As Schultz's empire shows cracks, and he turns increasingly on his own colleagues, Billy realizes that closeness to the gangster is a dubious advantage.

Still, he manages to stay out of harm's way—until the arrival of Drew Preston in Schultz's entourage. The beautiful young woman has taken up with her lover's murderer

without any apparent qualms of conscience. Billy, because he is only a boy, is considered a trusty escort for Drew when Schultz is occupied elsewhere. But Billy falls in love with her—and indeed *makes* love to her in a scene of powerful eroticism set in, of all places, a swamp—and so turns himself into his benefactor's betrayer.

The oedipal triangle between Billy, Drew and Schultz has enormous narrative promise. But instead of exploiting it to the full, Doctorow backs off the conflict before it takes form. Billy learns that the fickle Schultz wants to kill Drew because she was a witness to Bo's murder. So he cunningly arranges to have her whisked away by her rich homosexual husband, who does not seem to mind her sleeping around. Schultz is none the wiser, and Billy goes back to playing his faithful follower—right up to the climactic moment when Schultz and his gang are gunned down by rival mobsters.

Doctorow's refusal to fully explore Billy's conflicting loyalties underlines the novel's astute avoidance of any deep feeling. It is a romantically compelling fable of surfaces: of the sheen of gunmetal, of the neighborhoods of New York City, of the look and feel of expensive cars and clothes. Nothing characterizes that quality better than Billy himself. He witnesses his first murder—and all the subsequent ones—with an odd lack of emotion. He does not feel so much as observe and calculate. At times, he seems less a boy than a stylized literary device whereby Doctorow can present his darkly exciting poetry of violence.

Billy's character may create a problem for readers who bear in mind, even as they enjoy the teenager's adventures, that society is being plagued by an upsurge of violent crime connected mainly to the drug trade. Such readers might well ask how Doctorow can so deliberately romanticize a life outside the law, and how he can pretend that a 15-year-old could thrive in his association with murderers.

The answer to those objections is that *Billy Bathgate* is intended as pure myth, a sort of Robin Hood for grown-ups. Other novels may be more psychologically subtle or emotionally resonant. But few of those celebrate, as well as *Billy Bathgate* does, the raw, sometimes amoral energy of life, so often feared by the timid and the primly virtuous. That is what Doctorow suggests in Billy's closing words of triumph. Billy reveals that he has had a happy, prosperous life—funded partly by Schultz's ill-gotten fortune, which he steals—and he gives thanks to God for "my life of crime and the terror of my existence." Something in human nature identifies with the outlaw and his rebellion against what is false and overbearing. *Billy Bathgate,* with its driving rhythms and hair-trigger images, is as bracing as a shot of Dutch Schultz's bootleg scotch. (pp. 58-9)

John Bemrose, "Growing Up in Gangland," in Maclean's Magazine, Vol. 102, No. 10, March 6, 1989, pp. 58-9.

Alfred Kazin

The Bronx-born gangster Arthur Flegenheimer, professionally "Dutch Schultz," not one of your nice Jewish boys, was killed on October 23, 1935, mown down in a New Jersey chophouse with his immediate entourage. This consisted of his accountant, a mathematical wizard known as "Abbadabba" Berman, and his bodyguard, "Lulu" Rosencrantz. [In his novel *Billy Bathgate*] Doctorow has added, invented, a taciturn, horribly perfect man-of-all-work, "Irving," who never killed anyone, but did many a preliminary job that enabled Dutch and company to kill and kill.

The "Dutchman" was big in policy (the numbers racket), beer (which he compelled saloons to buy even after Prohibition), and unions (the window washers and waiters). He had committed quite a few murders himself with spectacular brutality, and had ordered many more. Though there were rival gangs, like Lucky Luciano's Mafia mob, that loved him not, Schultz might have lived beyond his 33rd year had he not, with his usual crazy rashness, plotted to have Thomas E. Dewey himself murdered. As Manhattan district attorney, Dewey was cutting the wide swath through New York gangsterdom that was to make him governor of New York and twice a candidate for president of the United States.

In his deliciously irreverent and quite wonderful novel about the life and death of Schultz, E. L. Doctorow has him murdered by Lucky Luciano's gunmen. In the novel, Luciano stands witness to Schultz when the latter has himself very cunningly converted to the Roman Catholic faith in order to impress the small upstate town where he is to stand trial for income tax evasion. Luciano is, in the novel, understandably alarmed by the thought of having Dewey murdered.

Dutch did not die all at once. Strange to relate, he lingered long enough for an amazing monologue to be taken down. This became famous in its own right and has often been featured as a literary curiosity; it is so unlike what you would expect of gangster Schultz at his end. William Burroughs wrote a play, *The Last Words of Dutch Schultz.* Young professors of English, understandably looking for novelty, have found in Dutch's ravings a stream of consciousness "worthy of Joyce." "Please, mother! You pick me up now. Please, you know me." "I want to pay, let them leave me alone." Doctorow has kept some of the "last words," has invented others in the style of "A boy has never wept, nor dashed a thousand kim."

Doctorow has cleverly adapted and recast Schultz's last words to the services of his plot and somehow finds the thread of the ingeniously versatile style of his novel in these words. *Billy Bathgate* relates in *his* own words the adventures inside the Schultz gang of a 15-year-old boy who takes his last name from the once flourishing market street Bathgate Avenue in the Bronx. His Jewish father has skipped, his Irish mother is demented. He finds a kind of father in "Abbadabba" Berman, who reduces all existence to numbers, thus allowing Billy to dream that numbers can be changed to words. And Billy is understandably spellbound by the sheer hulking presence of Dutch Schultz himself, who in bulk exercises the kind of power over others that Billy comes to think of as another element of existence. (pp. 40-1)

Like Huck [Finn, Billy] is encased in a violence not his own. Like Huck, he is so sentient, self-dependent, and in a sense self-"educated" that he brings a special style of his own to the book. This is quite lyrical at times and amusingly overdrawn in a style that rises at times to Joyce and descends to the darling vernacular of Damon Runyon. Billy is his own man in every sense, and so (this is one of Doctorow's jokes) he alone finds the clues in Dutch's last words that enable him to discover the millions that Dutch stashed away. With these Billy grows up to become an Ivy League graduate, U.S. Army officer in World War II, and a corporate entrepreneur.

The plot is a fairy tale of sorts, and there is a joke in the plot. With Doctorow's usual irony about the moneyed goings-on in the upper levels of American society, he has Billy conclude that the gangster world is not untypical of, at least, corporate America. But more immediately the joke is in Billy's narrative style. This is perfectly straight and chillingly vivid in giving us Dutch's looming presence and murderous rages, but becomes "inspired," gives itself a lift, which is the sheer joy of reporting a Bronx kid's ascent in life, when Billy is in communion with his own feelings. . . . (p. 41)

As Huck is all country, Billy is all city. Each urban detail, right down to the hexagonal tiles on the park side of Fifth Avenue and the view from the El passing along Third, is wonderfully real to a boy whose gangster life gives him the whole city to take advantage of, and for all the risks, to be safe in. "The city has always given me assurances whenever I have asked for them."

Indeed it does. To the point where Billy, rounding out the fairy tale he has lived up from Bathgate Avenue, recovers Schultz's money. But—the Doctorow note—the money when recovered is clearly associated with junk and garbage. Though Dutch's gang is all gone, "Nothing was over, it was all still going on, the money was deathless, the money was eternal and the love of it infinite."

There are those who will bridle at the destined conclusion of the fable and the all too assured tone in which the grown and successful Billy identifies the slipperiness he has survived with the corporate America in which he now rules. Is it just Billy speaking here and not Doctorow? Bridle at the conclusion or not, it is all less serious in the end than what has come before. And if the conclusion is shocking, it is no less shocking because it is so amusing. (p. 42)

Alfred Kazin, "Huck in the Bronx," in The New Republic, *Vol. 200, No. 12, March 20, 1989, pp. 40-2.*

John Leonard

Though *Billy Bathgate* meditates on many matters— mobsters and orphans, the East Bronx and the Great Depression, the politics of sex and the psychology of class, "how a ritual death tampers with the universe" and "the amphibian journey" from desire to identity—think of it, like Horatio Alger's *Ragged Dick* or F. Scott Fitzgerald's

The Great Gatsby, as a fairy tale about capitalism. And color it wonderful.

Of course, this capitalism is in its first stages of primitive accumulation, by extortion, murder and the numbers racket. The gangster Dutch Schultz dies of his failure to evolve into the higher, monopolistic forms. Dutch lacks the corporate vision of a Lucky Luciano. Still, like the church, the army, trade unions and professional sports, organized crime has always been a launching pad for the upwardly mobile. And dirty money is the medium through which young Billy in 1935 levitates out of boyhood and the Bronx into "a large, empty resounding adulthood booming with terror" and "even greater circles of gangsterdom than I had dreamed, latitudes and longitudes of gangsterdom." This is the modern world, where everybody lives alienated ever after.

Billy is a 15-year-old high school dropout and amateur juggler. His immigrant Jewish father abandoned him in infancy. His immigrant Irish mother, who works in a laundry, is the neighborhood crazy. . . . Like any Horatio Alger hero, he wants glamour, status, a destiny, "the mythological change of my station." . . .

But fairy tales in the West tend also to be Oedipal. Billy wants a father, too, and in gangsterdom he has his choice. There's bossman Dutch, born Arthur Flegenheimer, all passion, energy, menace and "rudeness of power," a sort of bad-seed Henderson the Rain King. And there's Abbadabba Berman, the gang's accountant, a natural pedagogue, wise in his numbers, a dandy even if a humpback in his "summer yellow double-breasted suit and a panama hat."

Dutch is capitalism's past: social Darwinism. He moves in a "realm of high audacity," "contriving a life from its property of danger, putting it together in the constant contemplation of death," in "an independent kingdom of his own law, not society's." The law, he says, "is the vigorish I pay, the law is my overhead." Each hit's "a planned business murder as concise and to the point as a Western Union telegram. The victim after all had been in the business. He was the competition." And this laissez faire attitude toward the morality of economic relations translates into an equally laissez faire attitude toward the economy of moral conduct: "I like the idea of women, I like that you can pick them up like shells on the beach, they are all over the place, little pink ones and ones with whorls you can hear the ocean." Even his sudden conversion to Catholicism has this greed about it: "I give you my word I couldn't be more sincere, Father. I brought it up, didn't I? I live a difficult life. I make important decisions all the time. I need strength. I see men I know take their strength from their faith and I have to think I need that strength too. I fear for my life like all men. I wonder what it's all for. I try to be generous, I try to be good. But I like the idea of that extra edge."

On the other hand, Abbadabba Berman is capitalism's future: the managerial revolution. Having seen this future, he knows it belongs to Luciano. It's like railroads: "You look at the railroads, they used to be a hundred railroad companies cutting each other's throats. Now how many

are there? One to each section of the country. And on top of that they got a trade association to smooth their way in Washington. Everything nice and quiet, everything streamlined." (p. 454)

Why do you suppose gangsters show up so often in the novels of serious male writers like Doctorow, William Kennedy and Saul Bellow? Maybe because, to the immigrant trying to Americanize himself, one myth is as good as another—baseball, Hollywood, Tin Pan Alley, Murder Inc. Or maybe it's otherwise hard to think about our American romance with money—the unmentionable in Henry James, the ponderous obsession of Dreiser, the peculiar poetry of Fitzgerald. Lionel Trilling said somewhere that money is "the great solvent of the solid social fabric of the old society," the jumping beans of a new culture and a new status system. And surely its absence is an oppression. Yet, for the most part ours is a literature of loners and losers. We can't talk about serious money from the point of view of deerslayers, whaling captains, river pirates or the Lone Ranger—not even a private eye, not even Huck Finn. And so, sorting among pop icons, we arrive at the urban outlaw. We drop, as if by bathysphere, into the primordial greed and consult the original crab. We inquire into metastasis.

Doctorow has as much fun as Kennedy, and more than Bellow, among these low-lifes. He seems especially to enjoy their mannered violence, their arabesques. To be sure, he writes beautifully about everything from food and water to sex and horses, from corrupt unions to the country poor, from "the contours of the ocean bed" to "the contours of the white Miss Drew." As Billy levitates by money, Doctorow levitates by language, through circles of light and suspensions of childhood, the deepest chords and finest blood threads, on his way from the cityscapes "where we come out sliming . . . where we . . . make our tracks and do our dances and leave our coprolitic spires" to "the black mountains of high winds and no rain," where moral awareness waits in ambush.

But to the executions of a West Side numbers boss (in a barbershop, after the hot towel has been applied, "wrapping it the way they do like a custard swirl, so that only the tip of the nose is visible") and "Bye Bye" Weinberg (dainty "as some princess at a ball" on the tugboat, placing one foot at a time in the tub of wet cement, which "made a slow-witted diagram of the sea outside, the slab of it shifting to and fro as the boat rose and fell on the waves"), he brings such fierce relish, such lovely precision, that we either blush or gasp. The absurd is dignified.

And yet Doctorow obviously doesn't *like* these gangsters as much as Kennedy and Bellow seem to. It's as if, for all their "supernatural warrior spirit," they'd somehow let him down. Unlike the bootleg dreamer Gatsby, they don't know what to do with the money once they've got it: "It was all for survival, there was no relaxed indolence of [their] right to it." And so Doctorow takes the poetry of their money, their imaginative capital, and gives it to the white Miss Drew. For Doctorow, as much as for the smitten Billy, Drew Preston, half a tourist in the underworld and half Persephone, is what the magic of money is really all about. Which is why Billy must rescue her from a

Dutch who "needed more death, he was using up his deaths so quickly now he needed them faster and faster"—like Third World markets. (pp. 455-56)

This tiresomely insouciant Miss Drew, American aristocrat, golden girl, Daisy chain, "covered her tracks . . . trailed no history . . . would never tell her life because she needed no one's admiration or sympathy or wonder, and because all judgments, including love, came of a language of complacency she had never wasted her time to master." So what if "she took her clothes off to gunmen, to water, to the sun"? "Life disrobed her." And so on. This is why we kill our fathers. It's also an awful lot for any 22-year-old to have to carry around in any novel's scheme of things. No wonder she disappears. It's a vanishing act, like Alan Ladd's in *Shane*. The white Miss Drew seems to me to be not so much a woman, not even a Persephone, as a credit card, by means of which Billy is enabled to multiply his opportunities for social and erotic disappointment. In her, sex and money and Freud and Marx are more mixed-up than Leslie Fiedler, than Herbert Marcuse. And hard as it is to believe in *her,* the baby in a basket is impossible.

Never mind. Doctorow's whole point is to call into question the authenticity of Billy's identity-making, his juggling act. So much for the "metaphysical afflictions" that inspire "art, invention, great fortunes, and the murderous rages of the disordered spirit." The Dutchman dies, going out with a tantrum, a delirium. And so, too, does Abba-dabba die, though *his* last words are the combination of a lock. . . .

For Doctorow, language is the agency of moral awareness. Moral awareness is the content of any serious discourse. This works for a writer of his quality, and for Toni Morrison, and almost nobody else. Is it sufficient for Billy? His decoding of the Dutchman's "cryptic passion" will make Billy rich. (Happy is some other category.) But to do what? An adult Billy isn't saying. "Who I am in my majority and what I do, and whether I am in the criminal trades or not, and where and how I live must remain my secret because I have a certain renown." Among the several endings to this subversive fairy tale—a mother rescued from her "distractions," a lovely hymn to the Bronx that was, a surprise package from Persephone—we are encouraged to choose for ourselves the one we need. I found a bitter chocolate sadness in Billy's floating, his tumble in freefall, his vertigo among the memory candles. . . .

It seems to me that Billy—like Bo Weinberg in concrete on the tugboat, like the window washers falling from the midtown skyscraper because they didn't pay their dues, like his own lost father in the long history of the big chance, like the Max and Dora Diamond orphans—is singing "Bye Bye Blackbird." Once upon a time he'd had a huge heart, our Billy, Billy Budd, Huck Finn, call him Ishmael; but they broke it forever. (p. 456)

John Leonard, "Bye Bye Billy," in The Nation, *New York, Vol. 248, No. 13, April 3, 1989, pp. 454-56.*

Donald E. Pease

[The] setting to which Doctorow obsessively returns is that of New York City at around the time of his birth (1931). In **World's Fair,** Doctorow brings everyday life in the Bronx of the 1930's back into recollection with a historian's clear eye for detail and texture. In **Billy Bathgate,** Doctorow returns to the Bronx of the 1930's to restore another dimension to that life.

Billy Bathgate is a child of the Depression. He lives in the East Bronx with his mother; his father had abandoned them years earlier leaving Billy to make it on his own and Billy's mother in a state of permanent mental distraction. Billy learns control over the powerful forces threatening his life in two unrelated activities: reading about gangland heroes and juggling on Bathgate Avenue. Billy's story begins on a day in 1935 when these unrelated activities come into magical relationship with one another. On this day, Billy's juggling act brings him the attention of Dutch Schultz, the notorious gangster from the news stories, who like Billy began in the East Bronx. Dutch Schultz catches Billy's juggling act, calls him a "capable boy," then returns to his world. In Billy's mind, these words of recognition were not casual but magically removed him from the East Bronx, where he was the helpless plaything of forces that seemed to juggle with his fate and placed him in hands that had learned to control these forces.

Gangsters like Dutch Schultz took advantage of the defensive Puritanism the Depression induced in everybody else. Firm believers in the spirit of capitalism even in the era of the Depression, gangsters constructed an underworld that released Americans from the economic virtues they produced out of their everyday fears. Here a different ordering of the relationship between needs and their satisfaction prevailed, transforming the need for thrift into the wish to get rich quick at the numbers and the enforced temperance of prohibition into the casual drunkenness of the speakeasies. Gangsters based their power on everybody else's fears about the economy; they regulated their power with a code of rough justice. A victim of economic fear, Billy looks to Dutch Schultz's outlaw gang for an alternative code with which to take possession of his life. But Billy joins up with the Dutch Schultz gang at the time when it is in trouble with the F.B.I. for income tax evasion and with competing gangs for Schultz's repeated violations of the code.

Billy looks to Dutch Schultz as a surrogate father, a magical personification of the control missing from his life, but he finds in Dutch's behavior only a manifestation of his own impotent rage. In his brief time with the Schultz gang, Billy moves through a series of adventures—involving robbery, extortion, prostitution, racketeering and murder—with all the breathtaking speed of someone dropped from a great height. The only forces powerful enough to break his fall through these events are supplied by Billy's language. Like his talent for juggling, Billy's gift for fluency takes hold of events otherwise falling out of the time of his life, brings them into momentary equilibrium, then recirculates them through the medium of the time kept by other events in the 1930's. Instead of quite belonging to the Schultz gang, Billy articulates for it the only order capable of preserving it from oblivion. Without Billy's language to redefine them, the other members of the gang—Abbadabba Berman, Lulu Rosencrantz Irving and (on occasion) Miss Lola—threaten to decompose into aspects of Dutch Schultz's rage.

An excerpt from *Billy Bathgate*

It was juggling that had got me where I was. All the time we hung around the warehouse on Park Avenue, and I don't mean the Park Avenue of wealth and legend, but the Bronx's Park Avenue, a weird characterless street of garages and one-story machine shops and stonecutter yards and the occasional frame house covered in asphalt siding that was supposed to look like brick, a boulevard of uneven Belgian block with a wide trench dividing the uptown and downtown sides, at the bottom of which the trains of the New York Central tore past thirty feet below street level, making a screeching racket we were so used to, and sometimes a wind that shook the bent and bowed ironspear fence along the edge, that we stopped our conversation and continued it from mid-sentence when the noise lifted—all the time that we hung out there for a glimpse of the beer trucks, the other guys pitched pennies against the wall, or played skelly on the sidewalk with bottle caps, or smoked the cigarettes they bought three for a cent at the candy store on Washington Avenue, or generally wasted their time speculating what they would do if Mr. Schultz ever noticed them, how they would prove themselves as gang members, how they would catch on and toss the crisp one-hundred-dollar bills on the kitchen tables of their mothers who had yelled at them and the fathers who had beat their ass—all this time I practiced my juggling. I juggled anything, Spaldeens, stones, oranges, empty green Coca-Cola bottles, I juggled rolls we stole hot from the bins in the Pechter Bakery wagons, and since I juggled so constantly nobody bothered me about it, except once in a while just because it was something nobody else could do, to try to interrupt my rhythm by giving me a shove, or to grab one of the oranges out of the air and run with it, because it was what I was known to do, along the lines of having a nervous tic, something that marked me but after all wasn't my fault. And when I wasn't juggling I was doing sleight of hand, trying to make coins disappear and reappear in their dirty ears, or doing card tricks of trick shuffles and folded aces, so their name for me was Mandrake, after the Hearst *New York American* comics magician, a mustached fellow in a tuxedo and top hat who was of no interest to me any more than magic was, magic was not the point, it was never the point, dexterity was to me the point, the same exercise as walking like a tightrope walker on the spear fence points while the trains made their windy rush under me, or doing backflips or handstands or cartwheels or whatever else arose to my mind of nimble compulsion. I was double-jointed, I could run like the wind, I had keen vision and could hear silence and could smell the truant officer before he even came around the corner, and what they should have called me was Phantom, after that other Hearst *New York American* comics hero, who wore a one-piece helmet mask and purple skintight rubberized body garment and had only a wolf for a companion, but they were dumb kids for the most part and didn't even think of calling me Phantom even after I had disappeared into the Realm, the only one of all of them who had dreamed about it.

As the gang's means of preserving itself in memory, Billy's language opposes Schultz's anger. Whereas Schultz's rage appropriates everything to his need to destroy, Billy's words bear permanent witness to whatever is threatened with impermanence. Billy discovers this gift when he witnesses Schultz's gangland execution of his former lieutenant, Bo Weinberg: "Kid, I want you to look on Bo Weinberg for your own sake and understand the terrible usage of such a man, look him in the eye, look him in the eye if you can so you will never forget this as long as you live."

Doctorow begins the novel with Billy's account of Bo Weinberg's execution and structures the remainder of the narrative around Billy's reflection on its implications. The part of Billy that is loyal to Dutch Schultz gives himself over utterly to the transitory intensities of his adventures; the part of Billy that is loyal to Bo Weinberg preserves those adventures as if they, like Bo (and Dutch Schultz), are otherwise threatened with oblivion. In composing *Billy Bathgate* out of a boy's divided loyalties, E. L. Doctorow has restored to the memory of American culture the era of the Great Depression it has tried to forget. In recovering the cultural legacy of the Depression era, Doctorow has produced a book that promises to remain as permanent an addition to its culture as *The Adventures of Huckleberry Finn,* its cultural predecessor. (pp. 458-59)

> *Donald E. Pease, in a review of "Billy Bathgate," in* America, *Vol. 160, No. 18, May 13, 1989, pp. 458-59.*

Salman Rushdie

The idea of the Star, of the human individual who radiates celestial light, is a quintessentially American one, because America is in love with light. Just listen to its national anthem: 'star-spangled banner', 'dawn's early light', 'twilight's last gleaming', 'rocket's red glare'—was there ever such an ode to illumination?

But if America sees itself as the Light Incarnate it knows its Darkness, too, and loves its dark stars, loves them all the more because it fears them: Al Capone, Don Corleone, Legs Diamond and the demon-god of *Billy Bathgate,* the barbarian Arthur Flegenheimer who stole a dead man's name and became Dutch Schultz.

A secular nation hungry for gods, America made of men like the Dutchman dark deities in whom it desperately wanted to believe, as 15-year-old Billy, Doctorow's narrator, wants to believe in Schultz. But what America loves most, needs most, more than light or darkness, more than gods or demons, is the myth of itself. Mythical America, its writers tell us constantly, is the real America, and myth demands, among other things, that heroes fall as well as rise. *Billy Bathgate* is the story of the Dutchman's long, last dive.

It's also the story of Billy's rise. Billy the punk, the 'capable boy' who catches the great hood's eye by juggling objects of different weight on the sidewalk outside one of the racketeer's beer drops. Billy with the crazy mother who nailed her departed husband's suit to the floor of her room, spreadeagled as if it were a man. Billy whose best friend is a scavenger named Arnold Garbage and who, at 15, takes 14-year-old Rebecca up to the roof of the orphanage and screws her twice for a dollar. Billy who dreams of greatness and pursues it the way he tells the story, in a great rush of language and scheming and love of danger and fear of death and determination to survive; and whose one chance of greatness lies with the Schultz gang and depends on the boss's murderous whim. Knowing he could die at any moment, for seeing too much or learning too little, Billy seizes his chance with all the hunger of the street. 'I think these days for the real training you got to go right to the top,' he dares to say right in to the Dutchman's face, and gets away with it. . . .

What he learns: how to shoot a gun, and (from Schultz's financial genius Abbadabba Berman) the secrets of numbers, including the numbers racket, and what you feel when your god arranges to have your nose broken, and how some people feed on death, and what it means to a racketeer when the bent politicians refuse to take his money any more, and how dying gangsters, gasping out their last words, will give up their greatest secrets if you know how to listen right. He learns how to fall in love and, above all, how to live to tell his tale.

Love comes to Billy in the form of Drew Preston, society beauty and tramp. . . . Drew makes herself available to Billy as well, and although she is beautiful as all hell and the Dutchman is crazy about her and she almost splits the gang and Billy winds up saving her life at the Saratoga racetrack by an ingenious scheme involving bouquets of flowers and boxes of candy and also her husband Harvey, the fact is that she's the least convincingly drawn character in an otherwise flawless book; she reads like she's waiting for Michelle Pfeiffer to play her in the movie. The book does read at times too much like the movie it will obviously be pretty soon but, what the heck, the story is so terrific you really don't care to complain.

American novelists have always been readier than their European counterparts to demonstrate that the art of literature can adopt the form of popular entertainment without losing an iota of seriousness, and *Billy Bathgate* is Doctorow's most brilliant proof of this to date. In fact, were it not as robustly vulgar as it is, it would fail as art, because Billy himself is after all the incarnation of the street, he has named himself after Bathgate Avenue in the Bronx, 'this bazaar of life, Bathgate', and so it is right that he and his book should be as pell-mell and clattering as that raucous thoroughfare.

Doctorow's gift for evoking the actuality of street-life is unrivalled, and he vividly evokes Bathgate, the market where the barrow-boys sell grapefruit and Georgia peaches and 'the aristocracy of the business' have real stores selling 'your chicks still in their feathers', and lox and whitefish and pickles and everything else as well; and just as vivid as Bathgate Avenue is the boy who takes its name and is like it dedicated to money, to the pursuit of money in America, and to the gangsters who are paradigms of that single-minded and ruthless pursuit, who are its most exalted and malign embodiments, who are to Bathgate Avenue as the monarch is to the punk.

The gangsters in Doctorow's novel . . . draw their self-belief, their sense of solidity and permanence, from the metropolis itself, which suggests that only those who can believe in the permanence of the city are able to survive its transformations, its tricky changes of light and lethal shadowplays, because it's that belief that keeps you one step ahead, with money in your pocket and the world at your feet, until you come up against somebody who believes even harder than you.

Salman Rushdie, "Billy the Streetwise Kid,"
in The Observer, *September 10, 1989, p. 51.*

Andrew Clifford

Doctorow's trademark of using historical fact to brew up brilliantly imaginative fiction has helped him stake a claim to be the present-day Great American Novelist.

For Doctorow uses his true-ish stories to examine America and her institutions, often by scrutinising certain key individuals. *Billy Bathgate* is an account of the institution of crime—which for Doctorow bears a complex kinship to capitalism at its worst.

He is interested not in the abstractions of corruption, but in the simple, emotional things of the criminal existence— what it feels like to be a gangster, what moral and psychological universe one inhabits, its day-to-day mechanics and, perhaps most importantly, how one survives a life of violence. Thus, underneath the soft prose of Billy's voice, we are given glimpses of the murderous danger of the criminal life, and how the people who live it, particularly its leaders, keep their heads above water.

Unfortunately, moments that take us beyond the novel's precisely located world are disappointingly rare. Doctorow does not do enough spadework in *Billy Bathgate* to lift us out of our somewhat nostalgic, Warner Bros image of the criminal Thirties.

Dutch Shultz (the gangster who spots Billy juggling, and who is based upon a real-life gang-leader) is a fascinating thug who never quite emerges out of cameo—perhaps because Billy admires him too much. He has sidekicks with colourful names—Abbadabba Berman, and Mr Dixie Davis the lawyer; he falls temporarily in love with a femme fatale; and his speech, reminiscent of *Guys and Dolls,* is pitched somewhere between ignorance and knuckly wit. Consequently, his very real cruelty and violence rub shoulders with an amusingly psychopathic gentility, blurring the more grim and pointed analysis Doctorow is sometimes trying to construct.

But it is the cracks in the character of Billy Bathgate himself which cause most damage to the novel. He is an overtly naive narrator, and Doctorow expects us to note that he is somewhat overwilling to poeticise his experiences. Because of the opportunities it affords for irony at Billy's expense, this device should enable Doctorow to offer a more accurate, between-the-lines account of the cruelty of the criminal fraternity, while at the same time casting the same humane eye over the gangsters as his innocent boy hero. But instead, Billy seems simply rather careless when, for example, he describes the most gruesome deaths in charming and adjectival prose. As we follow his adventures—from office boy, through his affair with Shultz's moll, to the novel's tender but gory climax—it is impossible not to wonder why Billy doesn't turn his back on the whole nasty bunch. It is all too rare that Doctorow manages to disentangle himself from Billy's selfish, prettified version of events. This is more than a mere technical failure. One feels not only Billy but the author behind him is curiously bland or amoral, unable to set appropriate margins to the narrative, unsure what position to take up towards his material.

The lack of a moral centre wouldn't matter if Doctorow was trying to write a *Prizzi's Honour* or even a *Godfather.* But Doctorow is a serious, committed writer, unusually exact and political, and his artistic ambitions are mountain-high. Although beautifully written, with his usual painstaking establishment of each scene and many excellent set pieces, the novel fails to climb the usual heights.

It would certainly be a pity if new readers turned to this book for their first taste of Doctorow. His other works prove what *Billy Bathgate* offers only circumstantial evidence for—that Doctorow can be a moving, profound and breathtakingly versatile artist. A far more capable juggler, than Billy himself.

> Andrew Clifford, "True-ish Crime Stories," in The Listener, *Vol. 122, No. 3131, September 14, 1989, p. 29.*

Boyd Tonkin

What chivalry did for the medieval epic, organised crime does for the American imagination. To writers and filmmakers it grants an endless fund of knights and monsters, passions and betrayals, round tables and holy grails. E. L. Doctorow has already made his fortune as a mythographer of the 20th century, his chronicles too full of dragons and miracles for a sober historian to trust. *Billy Bathgate* is his Arthurian novel, hitched to the perennial American tale of a boy's growing-up into the "realm of high audacity" inhabited by men who start as demigods and end as beasts.

The street-smart, fatherless kid who calls himself Billy catches the eye of gang-leader Dutch Schultz—who did exist—in the raucous Bronx of 1935. As he recalls a brief career as the bootleg beer baron's factotum, Billy speaks a strange but addictive hybrid language. One part of it reeks of the sidewalk and the speakeasy; the other soars into a novelist's dream of vivid adolescence where the garbage-men empty trash-cans with "the tympanic carelessness of their profession". No one ever spoke like Billy. But this bardic high style whisks the reader breathless through his story, from the slow-motion drowning of a gang-member in New York harbour at the outset to the predictable but still stomach-churning shoot-out of its finale.

For Billy, crime becomes a means of grace. Intimacy with Dutch Schultz and an affair with his discarded moll, Miss Lola Miss Drew, stretches the spirit and sharpens the senses. Living in "the constant contemplation of death"

transforms each dreary episode of low-grade vice into an epiphany. . . .

As he drily admits, Billy's account "differs from what you will read if you look up the old newspaper files". Some will blame Doctorow for it, and denounce the craze for "faction". Billy, however, has a long ancestry on his side. The novel was debauched in its cot with legend and rumour. From the days of Fielding's *Life of Jonathan Wild the Great* it battened on to first-division rogues whose exploits mocked and mirrored the deeds of monarchs or heroes. Doctorow's Dutch Schultz belongs in their company. He will also rank high in American fiction's legion of false fathers, those giants of childhood who shrink to midgets in the eye of memory.

> Boyd Tonkin, "A Round Table Story," in New Statesman & Society, *Vol. 2, No. 67, September 15, 1989, p. 37.*

Michael Wood

Gangsters in novels and movies are such nice guys: hard-working, courageous, loyal to the family, or at least to the Family. It's true they rub a few folks out now and again, but only in the line of business and when their patience has been sorely tried. It's curious that we should so enjoy this myth of kindly, violent people, and that it should last so long. It says something about the place we should like to find for violence but can't; says even more about our slightly truant feelings towards the law. The myth is sentimental and evasive, of course, and so unlikely that we wouldn't even entertain it if we didn't have, as William Empson says in another context, "obscure reasons" for wanting what the myth offers. But then these reasons are just what makes the myth interesting. The narrator of *Billy Bathgate* distinguishes between mere "government justice" and "the real justice of a sanctified universe" which is then paradoxically connected to crime: real justice, we dream, is where the right crimes are permitted.

E. L. Doctorow specializes in reviewing American myths and rubbing their noses in history—although only a little history, and not too hard. In *Billy Bathgate,* a picaresque, stylized, smooth-running novel, he expertly evokes the Depression and the colourful legends that dark time threw up. Billy is our narrator, a survivor of the period's gang wars, a man who picked up the stashed treasure no one else could find, and who now sounds rather like Moll Flanders having come into her good luck. "Who I am in my majority and what I do, and whether I am in the criminal trades or not, and where and how I live must remain my secret because I have a certain renown." Does this make him a politician or a racketeer, and why do our minds turn so readily to those alternatives?

Billy is telling us about a year of his young life, which includes the decline and death of Dutch Schultz, the Jewish mobster who had himself baptized into the Catholic Church in order to foster an underworld alliance, and was then killed by his distrustful new Italian partner. There are those who claim that Schultz was killed by the police, but this novel accepts the rival gang theory. Schultz is danger and glamour to the fifteen-year-old Billy, waiting on the mean streets of the Bronx for a chance to show his talents, his appetite for risk and rising in the world. Schultz takes Billy under his erratic wing, allows him to see or know about a murder or two—cement on the feet before the dip in the river, the throat slit in the barber's shop—and lets him join his small band of intimates: the dim and angry Lulu Rosenkrantz, the meticulous Irving, the silent Mickey, and Abbadabba Berman, wizard with numbers and keeper of Dutch Schultz's mind. There is also Drew Pearson, the haughty and randy young socialite who hangs out with gangsters for kicks, and whose life Billy narrowly saves. If this sounds more like *Bugsy Malone* than *Scarface,* that is probably almost right. We are not in the world of crime but in the world we dream for crime, which can be light or lethal depending on the mood of our "obscure wishes".

Or light *and* lethal. What is real in the novel is the strength and reach of the gangsters, the allure of their refusal of ordinariness, and the horror of their revenges; more subtly, the attraction of their strength, and even of the horror. On the very first page Billy tells us that he was capable of worshipping the "rudeness of power", and that Dutch Schultz's unpredictability was part of the "thrill" he provoked: "he really was a maniac". And yet Billy remains curiously innocent through all this; guilty only of curiosity and a taste for adventure, and of being a little too close to the grown-up practice of murder. He is not innocent in his own mind, and one of the best things in the book is the sense of Billy's fast-fleeing childhood, his nostalgia for the time when he knew less. But he is innocent for us, just a kid after all, and I worry about what such innocence means, all the questions it eludes.

Doctorow manages to catch both the charm and the horror of the Schultz myth, and this can't have been easy. On the contrary, the writing is plainly full of craft and care. Billy seems to have swallowed not the dictionary but several portions of *Ulysses* and most of Faulkner, along with, conceivably, a dash of García Márquez. "So I rode as a secret rider there at the cold railing through several minutes of my irresolution, and the strings of lights on the bridges behind me made me sentimental for my past"; "and then there was peace between us, and we lay as we were with such great trust as to require no words or kisses, but only the gentlest slowest and most coordinate drift into sleep". Even the gangsters tend to talk like this, or rather to keep lurching from this sort of language to slangier, more modern speech, and then lurching back. Exile from the city, one of them says, "has been a tough son of a bitch for every one of us and it will be all for naught if love conquers all". There is spoof on spoof here, a fine travesty of fine writing. But the effect finally is lyrical rather than critical, the lilt and the music of the prose turn it into something like the stylistic equivalent of Billy's innocence. There is blood everywhere, but it touches no one, fades in the soft focus, leaves no serious trace: an American romance. Doctorow, I take it, wants us to feel the rage and killing in the plot all the more forcefully because of the lilt of the narrative. But then this is something of a gamble. We may well be able to resist the romance, or at least, as we fall for it, still see the heartless reality it implies. But what if the gamble doesn't come off, if we just

fall? Well, we get an elegant, light-hearted tale of modern butchery, a stylish new relative for *The Godfather,* an offer we could hardly refuse.

Michael Wood, "*Light and Lethal American Romance,*" *in* The Times Literary Supplement, *No. 4511, September 15, 1989, p. 997.*

John Sutherland

Although it plays with the motif, **Billy Bathgate** does not fit the *de casibus* convention of the gangster genre. Dutch Schultz is the found father of myth, whose patriarchal power the son must eventually steal. Patriarch he certainly is, but as a criminal Dutch is also the last of his line. His brand of pure reflexive violence—bred in the anarchy of Prohibition—is anachronistic in 1935. He is being hounded by two 'organisations': by the IRS and by the Italians under Lucky Luciano. Dutch's accountant—Abbadabba Berman—is a wizard with numbers and foresees a future in which crime is just another American industrial conglomerate. . . . The massacre of Dutch (and his loyal accountant with him) in the appropriately named Palace Chophouse is just part of that streamlining. Dutch Schultz is a wart on the ass of progress. . . .

Billy Bathgate is half-fairy-tale, half Puzo-style shoot-em-up thriller. Doctorow taps expertly into the inexhaustible curiosity which America has for its gangster heroes. . . . The novel is wonderfully easy to read and in its last pages gripping. But what makes **Billy Bathgate** consistently entertaining and yet strangely worrying is its idiom. Doctorow fashions a specifically new prose instrument for each of his novels. **Ragtime** had a syncopated 'plink' to its short sentences. **Billy Bathgate** starts with a sentence which is 144 words long. Immensely extended syntax is the novel's stylistic signature and the looping intricately-linked clauses witness to Billy's skill as a verbal juggler. But there is also a mystery embedded in the diction of Billy's confessions, something that seems implanted to tease the ear of the reader. In an uncharacteristically brief coda, Billy informs us that, enriched with Schultz's millions, he 'made the leap' to Townsend Harris High School in Manhattan for exceptional students, then the 'even higher leap' to an Ivy League college 'which I would be wise not to name'. He went on to serve his country as an officer in World War Two. 'Who I am in my majority,' he concludes, 'and what I do, and whether I am in the criminal trades or not, and where and how I live, must remain my secret because I have a certain renown.' It doesn't ring true. Would someone who had gone through the speech regimentation of Harvard and officer's training use Runyonisms like 'the criminal trades', 'in my majority' and 'I have a certain renown'? This is the eloquence of Nick the Greek and Liverlips Louie. Billy's constant overreaching for the ten-dollar word and turn of phrase belies the grand CV which he presents to us. Baloney. Billy Bathgate is another Billy Liar. (p. 26)

John Sutherland, "*Shakespeare the Novelist,*" *in* London Review of Books, *Vol. 11, No. 18, September 28, 1989, pp. 26-7.*

Oscar Hijuelos
The Mambo Kings Play Songs of Love

Award: Pulitzer Prize for Fiction.

Born in 1951, Hijuelos is an American novelist and short story writer.

The Mambo Kings Play Songs of Love follows the lives of two Cuban immigrants on their quest for, and ultimate disillusionment with, the American dream of success. The novel received widespread praise for its poignant representation of the immigrant's simultaneous disassociation with the past and expectation for the future. Written as Cesar Castillo's reflections on his past as he drinks himself to death in a New York City hotel, *The Mambo Kings Play Songs of Love* recounts Cesar's and his brother Nestor's arrival in New York in 1949, their striving for stardom and one moment of fame as guest musicians on the *I Love Lucy* television show, and their subsequent decline into anonymity. Cesar yearns for the exciting night life and sexual escapades associated with the heyday of Cuban mambo music; Nestor retreats into his memories of the woman he left behind in Havana, and ultimately dies an early and tragic death. The sixty-two-year-old Cesar ends his life isolated in the United States, estranged from his family in Fidel Castro's Cuba.

Critics extolled Hijelos's representation of the musical and social atmosphere of the 1950s, when a wave of Latin American immigrants generated a fascination with the rumba and the mambo in the United States. Descriptions of tedious daily life and menial occupations are offset by the characters' evenings, which are filled with music and dance. While some commentators considered Hijuelos's style overly detailed and excessive, most lauded his prose for its lyrical tone that accurately captured the melancholy and passion of the characters. Joseph Coates observed: "[*The Mambo Kings Play Songs of Love*] leaves one with [a] chill, a sense of some voracity at the heart of the American dream that chews up talented people and spits out what's left, that magnifies personal faults, along with rewards, and turns them into self-destruction, into the litany of missed chances and bad choices that Cesar recites in his final agony."

(See also *Contemporary Authors,* Vol. 123.)

PRINCIPAL WORKS

NOVELS

Our House in the Last World   1983
The Mambo Kings Play Songs of Love   1989

Joseph Coates

"Many years later, as he faced the firing squad, Colonel Aureliano Buendia was to remember that distant afternoon when his father took him to discover ice."

This famous sentence not only unfurled the long, luminous scroll of Gabriel García Márquez's *One Hundred Years of Solitude,* published in Argentina in 1967, but it also began something that is still echoing and that can be heard in the opening sentence of Oscar Hijuelos' new novel [*The Mambo Kings Play Songs of Love*]:

> Nearly twenty-five years after he and his brother had appeared on the *I Love Lucy Show,* Cesar Castillo suffered in the terrible heat of a summer's night and poured himself another drink.

This something—literary influence or sensibility—by now extends beyond the works in Spanish that coalesced around *Solitude.* It amounts to a playful new way of looking at the hemisphere's experiences of uprootedness, migration and attempts at community, and it can be found in several works in English.

Such books often evoke Genesis and Exodus in their descriptions of failed efforts to realize a lost or imagined Eden—which in García Márquez's version is "a truly happy village where no one was over thirty years of age and no one had died." And several, including Hijuelos' novel, differ from earlier treatments of the immigrant experience by dealing as fully with the old worlds the migrants left as with the new ones they find or establish.

The Mambo Kings Play Songs of Love achieves the long backward look characteristic of such novels by dealing with pre-Castro Cubans who came to New York City immediately after World War II and whose experiences provide a generation's worth of historical perspective for the waves of Third World immigration that have washed ashore since then.

Most important, it connects the American dream its pilgrims pursue with the Popcult world created by the postwar rise of television. . . . Cesar Castillo, the elder Mambo King, unreels an epic in his head as he looks back at his life. It is 1980, and Cesar—already long gone in cirrhosis—has holed up with a case of whiskey in the Hotel Splendour, scene of his most memorable erotic triumphs, to drink himself into one last new world while listening to the scratchy 78s that represent his life's accomplishment in this one. . . . Cesar has a visual aid to focus his memories, the flickering black-and-white reruns of the 1955 "I Love Lucy" episode on which he and his melancholy brother, Nestor, appeared as guest musicians after the show's stars, Desi Arnaz and Lucille Ball, caught their act in a nightclub. This apparently trivial 24 minutes of entertainment, reprised throughout the book, becomes the mythical hinge of a considerable epic. And it is Hijuelos' achievement to make clear both the silliness and seriousness of this consummately American apotheosis: the Guest Appearance on National TV.

For one thing, the Castillos are serious musicians who work long days at menial jobs for the privilege of practicing their art most of each night in dance halls that pay them nothing, or next to it. . . . For another, Nestor wrote the hit song that attracts Arnaz, "Beautiful Maria of My Soul," out of a tragic love affair that blights the rest of his short life.

Having been validated by television, the Mambo Kings reenact the national myth, the crossing of the continent, on a coast-to-coast tour that embodies some of the unobtrusive ironies to be found in the novels of Wright Morris, who often sends his modern-day characters on the same trek. "The brothers loved the immensity of the United States," and "Cesar, delighted all his life with cowboy movies, saw his first bowlegged, drawling cowpokes leaning up against a bar [in Denver] . . . a rinky-dink piano jiving through 'The Streets of Laredo.' " The heartland's treatment of their black musicians also lets the band feel "an Arctic coldness of spirit that made New York seem like Miami Beach."

The novel leaves one with the same chill, a sense of some voracity at the heart of the American dream that chews up talented people and spits out what's left, that magnifies personal faults, along with rewards, and turns them into

self-destruction, into the litany of missed chances and bad choices that Cesar recites in his final agony.

Maybe Hijuelos is saying that America itself is a kind of inferno. Early in the novel, Delores Fuentes, the young girl who eventually marries Nestor, has a moment of sexual confusion involving her father, and "[i]n that moment, which she would always remember, she felt her soul blacken as if she had committed a terrible sin and condemned herself to the darkest room in hell. She expected to turn around and find the devil himself standing beside her, a smile on his sooty face, saying 'Welcome to America.' "

Joseph Coates, "When Cuban Musicians Dream the American Dream," in Book World—Chicago Tribune, *August 13, 1989, pp. 6-7.*

Bob Shacochis

[In *The Mambo Kings Play Songs of Love,* the] brothers Castillo—born, like [Desi] Arnaz, in Oriente Province—have played the dance halls and plazas throughout the island countryside and worked in Havana as "strolling troubadors and in a cheap social band," but have fallen, like so many others, under the spell of the stories they've heard about Cubans who left for the States: Cesar Romero, Xavier Cugat, their own triumphant village export, crooning his trademark, *Babalu!* "Visas in hand and sponsored by their cousin Pablo" in Harlem, Nestor and Cesar Castillo arrive in New York in the winter of 1949 "as part of the wave of musicians who had been pouring out of Havana since the 1920s, when tango and rumba crazes swept the United States and Europe . . . It was stay in Cuba and starve to death or head north to find a place in a rumba band." . . .

Hijuelos's American dream is as strong and rich and sweet as a Cuban coffee, exhilarating and exuberant and passion-rocked, but it also unfolds in paradox, flawed by the very characters pursuing it (we'll get to that in a minute). The Castillo brothers are destined to be "Stars for a Night. Stars of buying drinks, stars of friendly introductions, stars of female conquest." In no time at all, their orchestra is being booked all over Manhattan and in the hippest ballrooms in the Bronx and Brooklyn, and before the Mambo Kings disband after the tragic death of Nestor, they have "packed clubs, dance halls and theaters around the East Coast," toured cross country in a flamingo-pink bus, cut 15 records—"black brittle 78s"—and participated in "an item of eternity"—a guest appearance on the *I Love Lucy* show, where they play Ricky Ricardo's singing cousins and, at the Tropicana, perform their biggest hit, Nestor's agonizingly romantic bolero, "Beautiful Maria of My Soul."

It's not unfair to assume that Hijuelos, born in New York City in 1951 and fluent in northern urbanisms, has no personal history of exile. He has, however, inherited a communal one and out of this has created a story, both structurally and thematically, of remembrance. The frame is significant, for perhaps no one has a more self-destructive memory than the exile, blinded by nostalgia, incapacitated by homesickness, motivated by regrets. When Hijuelos has finished his fastidious reporting of the *cu-bop* music scene of the '50s—cataloguing all the band jobs, songs, sexual conquests, clothes, drinks, dances and food—the consequence of this act of remembering serves as the novel's slippery narrative premise. The exile's memory can be, in fact, a siren voice or non-stop argument in favor of suicide (a tradition in Cuban history, never more practiced than in the past decade). There appears to be no political agenda here, but Cesar Castillo is most certainly an exile—dislocated by his ambition from his homeland, emotionally estranged from the purer world of music once his younger brother is killed.

So it is that we are first introduced to Cesar Castillo on the last day of his life, aged 62 but looking 75, deliberately drinking himself to death in the Hotel Splendour in upper Manhattan, listening over and over to the album that provides the title of the book, dissipated and "desolately bored," a straight razor within reach in case the booze somehow fails him. "It seemed that all he had were memories," Hijuelos writes, "that where his pleasures resided now was in the past." Playing the extravagant, idealized, maudlin songs of love recorded by the two brothers 25 years ago, Cesar Castillo discovers the ultimate irony— that he who has sung about love has lied about its true nature.

It's not easy to build an emotional involvement with the Castillo brothers and the melancholy and lust that infect them. It takes a reader as long as it takes Cesar Castillo to get below the surface of his life—which is to say, the entire book. Early on it begins to look as if Hijuelos is using the melodramatic boleros of his characters to explore something endemic in their culture. Here is Hijuelos writing about Nestor's absurd pining for a lost love: "He didn't know what was going on. Cubans then (and Cubans now) didn't know about their psychological problems. Cubans who felt bad went to their friends, ate and drank and went out dancing. Most of the time they wouldn't think about their problems. A psychological problem was part of someone's character."

It's this self-destructive pining that is machismo's dark shadow. It undoes Nestor; indeed, he welcomes his destruction. And it's the same pining—for lost years, faces, places, women's flesh—that buries Cesar Castillo and his version of the American dream, and the same pining that makes Eugenio, Nestor's only son, a haunted young man.

On second thought, maybe I'm wrong to think Oscar Hijuelos is writing without a socio-political subtext in mind. With each turning of the page, his *cu-bop* music scene gathers credibility as a grand metaphor for the splitting of a national family that took place in 1959. Because only a Cuban-American writer of the new generation could write a book that is so critical of the disease of memory afflicting his people. (p. 2)

        Bob Shacochis, "The Music of Exile and Regret," in Book World—The Washington Post, *August 20, 1989, pp. 1-2.*

Margo Jefferson

The Mambo Kings Play Songs of Love follows a family and a culture from one world to the next in the form of several generations of Latin music. The habanera, the rumba, the *son*—all made their way from Cuba to America, to be translated, truncated and elaborated for Yankee and Latin-immigrant ears and feet. Where the music went the musicians followed, and so in 1949 Cesar and Nestor Castillo (just two of many) came to New York City, on the heels and the beat of the rumba's intricate, exuberant successor, the mambo. (p. 1)

And for a time, destiny works as it should. Cesar and Nestor establish their own orchestra, the Mambo Kings, and put out records—brittle plastic 78's that sell for 69 cents apiece and feature a Miss Mambo pinup girl on each cover. They record songs like "My Cuban Mambo," "The Subway Mambo," "Twilight in Havana," "Conga Cats and Conga Dolls," "Mambo Inferno!" and "The Sadness of Love." They play to cheering audiences on the East Coast and tour the country in flamingo pink and black suits, generally thrilling the natives but occasionally, just occasionally finding excrement rubbed on the windows of their flamingo pink bus.

In 1955 they have their moment in the bright sun of pop America. Desi Arnaz spots them performing in a New York club one night and invites them to appear on "I Love Lucy," playing his cousins. It's a lovely moment as described by Nestor's son, Eugenio, who never tires of watching the reruns. There is a gentle rap on Lucy's stage set door. She calls out, "I'm commmmmming," in her dotty housewife way, and there, standing in her doorway, are two men "in white silk suits and butterfly-looking lace bow ties, black instrument cases by their side and black-brimmed white hats in their hands." The scene shifts to Ricky Ricardo's show at the Tropicana Club. The brothers enter; Cesar strums his guitar; Nestor lifts his trumpet, and with Desiderio harmonizing they perform their languorous and mournful bolero, "Beautiful Maria of My Soul." When the song ends, Desi whips up his hand and shouts, *"Ole!"* The brothers bow, acknowledging the applause, then they exit from the set and from the lives of Mr. and Mrs. America.

But they have just entered ours. In this near-mystic moment, Eugenio sees his dead father and his aging, dying uncle resurrected—young, fresh and flush with what they do and love best. That the world sees them too thrills him, but one of the best things about this novel is the fact that it doesn't center on the Castillos' longing to cross over into the American dream; it leads us across into their dreams instead.

Mr. Hijuelos notes and orchestrates the lives of the Castillos, their friends and their families with multiple emotional rhythms. Garrulous, florid Cesar, filled with both kindness and cock-of-the-walk macho; Nestor, growing more and more withdrawn each year, trying to fortify himself with daily readings of a Dale Carnegie-like book called *Forward America!;* Delores, Nestor's wife, serious, dreamily ambitious, yearning to go to college; women and men who work as maids, clerks, janitors or butchers by day and fill the ballrooms at night, their manners a gorgeously inflected blend of formality and abandon.

The novel alternates crisp narrative with opulent musings—the language of everyday and the language of longing. When Mr. Hijuelos falters, as from time to time he does, it's through an excess of self-consciousness: he strives too hard for all-encompassing description or grows distant and dutiful in an effort to get period details just right. Still and all, you finish feeling as Cesar's first music teacher in Cuba told him audiences should feel when a song ends—ready to throw up your arms and cry, *"Qué bueno es!"* Mr. Hijuelos is writing music of the heart, not the heart of flesh and blood that stops beating, "but this other heart filled with light and music . . . a world of pure affection, before torment, before loss, before awareness." (p. 30)

> *Margo Jefferson, "Dancing into the Dream,"* in The New York Times Book Review, *August 27, 1989, pp. 1, 30.*

Grace Edwards-Yearwood

[It] was a pleasure to read **The Mambo Kings Play Songs of Love.** Against [a] background of Latin and jazz, Oscar Hijuelos, a writer of considerable talent, introduces Nestor and Cesar Castillo, two brothers newly arrived from Batista's Cuba to make their way in New York's music world.

At that time, the Cuban nightclubs and casinos—controlled by American gangsters, where white musicians entered through one door and mulatto and black musicians entered through another and the pay was wretched for all—offered no future.

Told in a series of flashbacks through the eyes of Cesar, the older brother, this story bares two dramatic struggles: of Nestor, who loved too much, and Cesar, who never learned how.

The story opens with Cesar, now a physical and emotional wreck at age 64, holed up in a small room in the seedy Hotel Splendour on 125th Street in Harlem, the scene of many of his past rendezvous. He has brought with him a battered cane suitcase containing some old recordings, faded photos, and letters—mementos from his glory days as the Mambo King. He has also brought a huge quantity of whiskey with which he plans to drink himself to quick and merciful death rather than continue to suffer the ravages of end-stage congestive heart failure.

The first quarter of the novel is crammed with more than enough information to satisfy any musicologist interested in the 1950s scene. (pp. 1, 10)

Cesar and Nestor arrive in New York at a time "When every Cuban knew each other" and, after sitting in with other bands, decide to form their own group, the Mambo Kings. They play the halls and clubs and sing songs of love. The high point comes when they are discovered by Desi Arnaz who invites them to Hollywood to appear on the "I Love Lucy" show.

An excerpt from *The Mambo Kings Play Songs of Love*

For me, my father's gentle rapping on Ricky Ricardo's door has always been a call from the beyond, as in Dracula films, or films of the walking dead, in which spirits ooze out from behind tombstones and through the cracked windows and rotted floors of gloomy antique halls: Lucille Ball, the lovely redheaded actress and comedienne who played Ricky's wife, was housecleaning when she heard the rapping of my father's knuckles against that door.

"I'm commmmmming," in her singsong voice.

Standing in her entrance, two men in white silk suits and butterfly-looking lace bow ties, black instrument cases by their side and black-brimmed white hats in their hands—my father, Nestor Castillo, thin and broad-shouldered, and Uncle Cesar, thickset and immense.

My uncle: "Mrs. Ricardo? My name is Alfonso and this is my brother Manny . . . "

And her face lights up and she says, "Oh, yes, the fellows from Cuba. Ricky told me all about you."

Then, just like that, they're sitting on the couch when Ricky Ricardo walks in and says something like "Manny, Alfonso! Gee, it's really swell that you fellas could make it up here from Havana for the show."

That's when my father smiled. The first time I saw a rerun of this, I could remember other things about him—his lifting me up, his smell of cologne, his patting my head, his handing me a dime, his touching my face, his whistling, his taking me and my little sister, Leticia, for a walk in the park, and so many other moments happening in my thoughts simultaneously that it was like watching something momentous, say the Resurrection, as if Christ had stepped out of his sepulcher, flooding the world with light—what we were taught in the local church with the big red doors—because my father was now newly alive and could take off his hat and sit down on the couch in Ricky's living room, resting his black instrument case on his lap. He could play the trumpet, move his head, blink his eyes, nod, walk across the room, and say "Thank you" when offered a cup of coffee. For me, the room was suddenly bursting with a silvery radiance. And now I knew that we could see it again.

Here, the description of the technical aspects of television production gets in the way, slowing the forward action, but this is a minor complaint because the characters are so skillfully rendered. The story really comes to life when Nestor meets Delores, a young Puerto Rican girl who works as a maid for a Park Avenue man "so rich he is unhappy."

Through this relationship, we are taken via yet another flashback to Cuba, to an earlier love affair Nestor has had with Maria, "the beautiful Maria of my soul." The affair, obsessive, passionate and explicitly detailed, ends before the brothers emigrate but this love remains the source of Nestor's melancholia.

By turns, Cesar reflects on his own tumultuous relationships. His short, unhappy marriage ended in disaster but his macho posture continued to play havoc with every woman he meets. While Nestor's pain is all-consuming, the Mambo King, as Cesar comes to be called, keeps right on going.

The band achieves a small measure of fame—if not fortune—in the local dance halls. Hijuelos captures in poignant detail the life of the musicians: men who work menial, sometimes back-breaking jobs during the day and play to crowded dance halls at night. The life is sad, precarious, boisterous, exciting, and sometimes dangerous.

Night time is the glory time as they sweat through hot rumbas and mambos and soulful ballads, and at 3 a.m. crowd into family kitchens to feast on huge platters of pork chops, paella, yellow rice, fried plantains and more rum.

The story weaves back and forth in time contrasting the present. Cesar, a swollen wreck who has taken to wearing a girdle and whose urine is now streaked with blood, to the young virile man of 30 years ago who was attractive to legions of women.

He studies the photos and listens to the recordings of the Mambo Kings. And drinks. Each glass of whiskey produces more, and sadder, memories. He is plagued by the circumstances of Nestor's tragic death, the breakup of the band, the difficulty of trying to live up to a reputation he no longer deserves.

He reminisces about his trip to Cuba and his failure to establish a relationship with his estranged daughter. Castro's revolution has changed everything and everyone; his wife has now married a high-ranking official in the regime and his daughter is a member of the state-sponsored ballet. Ideologically and emotionally, these women and everything they represent are now beyond his reach. He returns to New York to witness more change: the intrusion of a different type of music, hard drugs, more crime, the deterioration of a sense of community.

And saddest of all is the change in his latest relationship with a much younger woman named Lydia, who tolerates him because he is generous and good to her two children.

The affair is initially invigorating, then gradually degenerates into scenes of rage, fear and jealousy as he struggles to come to terms with the fact that, despite his enormous sexual capacity, time has passed and he—the Mambo King—has grown old.

Hijuelos has painted an erotic and desolate landscape where people surge to life and diminish with terrifying exactitude. And where macho men like Cesar—handsome, proud, and mired in the disillusionment of change—find no way out. (p. 10)

> Grace Edwards-Yearwood, "Dancing to the Cuban Beat," in Los Angeles Times Book Review, September 3, 1989, pp. 1, 10.

Nick Hornby

The Mambo Kings Play Songs Of Love is the story of two brothers, Nestor and Cesar Castillo, who arrive in New York in 1949 from Havana and set out to make their mark in the Big City. Nestor is sensitive and introverted, Cesar flash and brash (Hijuelos is not of the Jamesian school of character delineation); they find jobs and women, form the eponymous band and mambo their way through the jazz clubs of NYC. They make a little money and blow it. They run into Desi Arnaz, Cuba's most visibly successful émigré, and get invited to make a guest appearance on the *I Love Lucy* show, the touchingly pathetic highlight of their lives. All this is recalled by Cesar as he lies, prematurely old, dissipated, lonely and on the point of death, in a seedy hotel room, listening to the young couple next door making love.

This is especially galling to the Mambo King, because the novel is in effect about three characters: Nestor, Cesar and Cesar's penis, the latter being not only larger than life, but apparently larger even than its owner. Its exploits are detailed with alarmingly loving care and though there are hints that Hijuelos has an ironic perspective on all this machismo, they come none too frequently. Here, of course, we have the old Dennis Potter Paradox: can a male writer get away with torrid sex scenes by placing them in inverted commas, or is he just a dirty old man anyway? It is distinctly possible that those male readers who watch *thirtysomething* and buy from the Body Shop will end up feeling that they have ploughed their way through a common-or-garden smutty book, acceptably ethnic though it may be.

The novel suffers from the absence of a strong female character with whom we can sympathise. One of the many strengths of *Our House In The Last World,* Hijuelos's first novel, is that women are depicted from the neck up, and the consequences of the feckless behaviour of the men can thus be presented with a more convincing sense of ambivalence. It covered territory broadly similar to its successor: like Nestor and Cesar, Alejo and his wife Mercedes leave Cuba for New York, but their story is more downbeat, certainly more internal, and perhaps as a consequence the author's prose is much tauter and more lyrical (and for lovers of Magic Realism, Mercedes turns into an orchid 30 pages from the end, so stick with it). One of the problems with *The Mambo Kings* is that the relentless carousing of the book's first half seems to sap the writing of much of its strength.

Its other major disadvantage is that it is wildly underedited, at just over 400 pages one is left with the feeling that there is a great short story in here struggling to get undressed. Hijuelos seems to be trying to capture at great length the rhythms and resonances of the music in the writing: memories and songs percolate into each other, resulting in the kind of trade-offs and changes of mood that improvisational music provides. That's the theory, anyway, but in practice the effect is more Black Sabbath than Charlie Parker, and phrases and incidents are repeated over and over without any discernible modulation.

Photographs feature strongly in both these novels: characters look and remember and mourn and yearn, and this kind of aimless nostalgia is characteristic not only of Cesar and Nestor Castillo but also of Hijuelos. In the end one is left with the inescapable impression that he has gathered a collection of two-dimensional static images, shuffled them around and flicked through them in a desperate attempt to give the impression of life and movement. Even the potent and evocative music can't help to pull it off; after all, it's extraordinary how cheap potent music can be.

Nick Hornby, "Cuban Heels," in The Listener, *Vol. 123, No. 3158, March 29, 1990, p. 33.*

Charles Johnson
Middle Passage

Award: National Book Award: Fiction

An American novelist, essayist, short story writer, and scriptwriter, Charles Richard Johnson was born in 1948.

Set in 1830, *Middle Passage* chronicles the misadventures of twenty-two-year-old Rutherford Calhoun, a well-educated, mischievous freed slave from southern Illinois. Released in New Orleans by his former master—a clergyman who provided him with a broad education—Rutherford revels in the city's sordid underworld. Intending to escape his numerous creditors and an impending marriage to a priggish schoolteacher that would free him of his debts, Rutherford boards the first available boat, which, to his horror, is a slave clipper bound for Africa. On the dangerous round-trip voyage, recounted in the form of a ship's log, Rutherford becomes divided in his allegiance to his white American crewmates and his sympathy for the suffering Allmuseri tribesmen. Rutherford ultimately sides with the captives when they mutiny and, through his traumatic experience with his oppressed shipmates, gains new knowledge about slavery, race relations, and himself.

Although Johnson received mixed criticism for anachronistically interspersing modern idioms, nineteenth-century maritime jargon, and naturalistic prose, many commentators lauded his adroit blending of such genres as the picaresque tale, historical romance, sea yarn, slave narrative, and the philosophical novel. Arend Flick observed: "[*Middle Passage* is] informed by a remarkably generous thesis: that racism in general, and the institution of slavery in particular, might best be seen as having arisen not from political or sociological or economic causes, not (God help us) from pigment envy, but from a deep fissure that characterizes Western thought in general, our tendency to split the world into competing categories."

(See also *CLC*, Vols. 7, 51; *Contemporary Authors,* Vol. 116; *Dictionary of Literary Biography,* Vol. 33; and *Black Writers.*)

PRINCIPAL WORKS

NOVELS

Faith and the Good Thing   1974
Oxherding Tale   1982
Middle Passage   1990

OTHER

The Sorcerer's Apprentice (short fiction)   1986
Being and Race: Black Writing Since 1970 (essays)   1988

Arend Flick

In his highly readable though densely philosophical fiction, Johnson gives us characters forced to chart a middle passage between competing ways of ordering reality: sensual or ascetic, Marxist or Freudian, Christian or pagan. They quest for a unity of being beyond all polarities, for what the heroine of his first novel [*Faith and the Good Thing*] calls "the one thing all . . . things have in common. And happily for them and for us, they usually find it."

Johnson describes *Middle Passage* as an effort at "serious entertainment," a blurring, in other words, of another ancient pair of opposites, philosophy and art. He shares with his mentor, the late novelist and critic John Gardner, the Tolstoyan conviction that all true art is moral, not the promulgating of doctrine (which inevitably distorts morality) but the exploration and testing of values.

The formula fits *Middle Passage.* Though never preachy, it's informed by a remarkably generous thesis: that racism generally, and the institution of slavery in particular, might best be seen as having arisen not from political or sociological or economic causes, not (God help us) from pigment envy, but from a deep fissure that characterizes Western thought in general, our tendency to split the world into competing categories: matter and spirit, subject and object, good and evil, black and white. One of the novel's epigraphs, from the *Upanishads,* grows increasingly rich in implication as we read *Middle Passage:* "Who sees variety and not the Unity wanders on from death to death."

Rutherford Calhoun, a newly freed 22-year-old slave from southern Illinois, drifts into New Orleans in 1829 and experiences a shock of recognition. For Rutherford, who narrates the story, the city is a place of sensory overload, an assault of smells, "if not a town devoted to an almost religious pursuit of Sin, then at least to steamy sexuality." The city suits his desire for adventure, experience, excess; it seems to be himself. His opposites are the Creoles downstream, who "sniffed down their long Continental noses at poor, purebred Negroes" like him. So he falls in among the thieves and gamblers upriver and becomes one of them.

Rutherford further defines himself in opposition to Woman. Isadora Bailey, whom he encounters one morning at the waterfront, is pretty "in a prim, dry, flat-breasted way," and everything Rutherford isn't: "frugal, quiet, devoutly Christian." She is completely, in other words, out of place in New Orleans. Rutherford regards this daughter of a large Boston family free since the Revolutionary War as "positively ill with eastern culture." Naturally, she wants to reform him. Naturally, he resists reformation—to the point of stowing away on a slave clipper bound for Africa to escape marriage to her. (She has arranged the marriage with his creditor by paying off Rutherford's debts.)

By turns mimicking historical romance, slave narrative, picaresque tale, parable, and (finally) sea yarn, indebted (among many other writers) to Swift, Coleridge, Melville, and Conrad, *Middle Passage* invites but frustrates categorization. And that's exactly its point. The storytelling sounds historically credible at first (Johnson's research and command of language are impressive), but the counternaturalistic signals begin early, and they're intended. Idioms have sometimes a distinctly modern flavor: "down to earth" to describe Isadora's father, "hung over" to describe Rutherford. All the characters in *Middle Passage,* in fact, sound as if they're double majors in classics and philosophy. "It seemed so Sisyphean," says Rutherford of a lovelorn fellow sailor, "this endless seeking of a single woman's love . . . in all others, because they would change, grow old, and he'd again be on a quixotic, Parmenidean quest for beauty beyond the reach of Becoming." His narrative comes to resemble an act of ventriloquism, a dreamlike projection of 20th-Century writer into the voice of roguish ex-slave, the writer winking behind the mask at time, blurring past and present. There's no clear

line between Rutherford's world and our world, his journey and our journey. All polarities collapse by design here.

The opposition between Ebeneezer Falcon and Peter Cringle, captain and first mate of the metaphorically named "Republic," furthers Rutherford's process of self-definition on the passage to Africa. Cringle is Isadora in drag: a gentleman whose "whole air spoke of New England gentility."

Falcon, by contrast, is a carnival sideshow: a pederast, solipsist, and dwarf. He too seems to have taken a first in philosophy. Dualism is a permanent biological condition, he tells Rutherford:

> Subject and object, perceiver and perceived, self and other—these ancient twins are built into the mind like the stempiece of a merchantman. We cannot *think* without them, sir. And what, pray, kin such a thing mean? Only this, Mr. Calhoun, they are signs of a transcendantal Fault, a deep crack in consciousness itself. . . . Slavery, if you think this through, forcing yourself not to flinch, is the social correlate of a deeper, ontic wound.

No wonder Cringle plans to set him adrift.

Between Cringle and Falcon, Rutherford can't choose, though both try to force him to. He can't find his loyalties, though he seems to take up and put down each of their perspectives at times. His unwillingness to choose makes sense, since Johnson blurs all ethical categories, showing the ministerial Cringle unable to "see himself, his own blighted history, in the slaves," the satanic Falcon ("known for his daring exploits and subjugation of the colored races") capable of generosity in the end. Not until "The Republic" takes on its cargo in Africa—40 Allmuseri tribesmen and their mysterious totem—does Rutherford finally begin to declare an allegiance.

Johnson creates the Allmuseri for pretty obvious thematic reasons. An ancient tribe of magicians, they are less a biological clan than one held together by shared values. For Rutherford, who feels "the presence of countless others in them," they are the "Ur-tribe of humanity itself." Without fingerprints, incapable of abstract thought, unable to distinguish the white crewmen as individuals, the Allmuseri envision Hell as the failure to experience "the unity of Being everywhere." And their god—which Falcon has plundered for the most Western of reasons, fame and fortune—is King Kong, Tolkien's ring and Spielberg's ark all rolled into one. Even Falcon recognizes it's beyond dualism: "The Allmuseri god," he tells Rutherford, "is everything, so that the very knowing situation we mortals rely on—a separation between knower and known—never rises in its experience."

The Allmuseri become Rutherford's vehicle for self-knowledge, providing him with a passage beyond categories, beyond opposites, beyond desire and fear, and toward what we would want for him, and for ourselves. *Middle Passage,* suffused with the quasi-Buddhist sensibility that seems increasingly common in Western writing today, ends quietly, surprisingly.

What always saves the novel from the intellectual scheme

that would otherwise kill it is the sheer beauty of its language. Here is Rutherford's vision of his father's death 20 years earlier:

> I beheld his benighted history and misspent manhood turn toward the night he plotted his escape to the Promised Land. It was New Year's Eve, *anno* 1811. For good luck he took with him a little of the fresh greens and peas Chandler's slaves cooked at year's end (greens for "greenbacks" and peas for "change"), then took himself to the stable, saddled one of the horses and, since he had never ventured more than ten miles from home, wherefore lost his way, was quickly captured by padderolls and quietly put to death, the bullet entering through his left eye, exiting through his right ear, leaving him eternally eight and twenty, an Eternal Object, pure essence rotting in a fetid stretch of Missouri swamp.

Philosophy and art are not simply joined here. They are one. (pp. 1, 7)

> Arend Flick, *"Stowaway on a Slave Ship to Africa,"* in Los Angeles Times Book Review, June 24, 1990, pp. 1, 7.

Thomas Keneally

There are problems with Charles Johnson's [*Middle Passage*] that might seem to call forth from a reviewer the old cheap-shot treatment. But the genre switches of *Middle Passage,* from period bodice-ripper to metaphysical drama, are—like every other aspect of this fairly short book—heroic in proportion. There's an endearing and determined recklessness at work here, for Mr. Johnson, who is a professor of English at the University of Washington and the former director of its creative writing program, manages to break with heretic abandon many of the cherished axioms of the writing academies.

Mr. Johnson violates not only the genre-switch rule but Chekhov's "rifle" dictum (that if there's a rifle on the wall, it has to go off before the curtain descends). The assumption that anachronisms are permitted in Elizabethan literature but should be researched out of modern fiction also goes by the board. . . .

All this roughshod riding is achieved with such panache, however, that I wound up wanting to cheer him, even though the scribe in me might disapprove. In fact, I found Mr. Johnson forcing me back to the ultimate question, the one high-toned reviewers are supposed to avoid at any cost: how does the book read? And the answer is: you'll certainly want to go on reading *Middle Passage.*

In the summer of 1830, Rutherford Calhoun, freed slave from Illinois and flamboyantly learned scoundrel, escapes marriage to a cat-loving schoolmarm in New Orleans and hides aboard a slaver called the Republic. Calhoun's former master has given him a humanist education, and his narration of an extraordinary voyage is spiked with 19th-century maritime argot as well as such terms as "velleities," *"haecceitas"* and *"quidditas."*

The Republic is bound for the Gulf of Guinea to take on

African slaves. Rutherford's peculiar position, as a former slave and an American patriot aboard a ship devoted to the enslavement of a fresh set of Africans, provides the lens through which bondage is considered. But Mr. Johnson further enriches this perspective. In the coastal trading post at Bangalang, the tormented dwarf Captain Falcon takes aboard not only a cargo of Allmuseri tribesmen, thought by slavers everywhere to be premium-grade slaves, but also their god. Barely glimpsed and packaged in a crate, the divinity is lowered into the hold. From that point, the Republic seems to the reader to be both massively laden and held together by threads. Mr. Johnson has us by the throat.

Rutherford Calhoun, the manumitted slave, knows how the god unbalances the ship. The Allmuseri are dangerous enough on their own, since they practice an elegant, dancelike form of unarmed combat. And although *they* can be chained and guarded, their many-faced god, packed into an insecure crate, churns in the darkest recesses of the hold like a nuclear reactor on the edge of meltdown.

Middle Passage is a novel in the honorable tradition of *Billy Budd* and *Moby-Dick.* We are often told by the berserk scholar-captain, Falcon, that a ship is "a society, if you get my drift. A commonwealth, Mr. Calhoun." The Republic is therefore also a republic—one with a literal underclass, the Allmuseri, who suck their innate cleverness deeply into themselves in their prison in the bilges. Young Rutherford is torn between loyalty to his white American comrades on deck and his empathy for the pulses of sorrow that emanate from the hold. And this loose federation is likely at any second to be eaten whole, to be reduced to atoms. For the divine force that the mad president of this "commonwealth" has chosen to take aboard is not only vaster than the ship but than the whole damned ocean.

With such a setup, Mr. Johnson's book just about transcends its faults, one of which is a frequent straining for meaning, an unnecessary portentousness. Surely some of the conversations Captain Falcon has with his unwilling confidant, Rutherford, in a cabin booby-trapped in case of mutiny are the fanciest possible ways of expressing the sentiment, "I know slaving's wrong, but it gives me a kick." . . .

But then maybe Mr. Johnson is reminding us that a little metaphysics is the beginning of evil. (p. 8)

The most important device of all, the cosmic rifle that only partly fires, is the Allmuseri deity. When Rutherford Calhoun encounters it, it takes on a form from his past. We are not told that this confrontation with Rutherford slakes the god of his thirst for souls. In fact, it is Rutherford himself who is pretty much extinguished by the meeting. We understand from the aura of threat that Mr. Johnson has managed to build up that the god transcends the elements and is eternal. By contrast, we know from the time we see the slaves being loaded onto the Republic that the ship will ultimately vanish from the tale. And yet, once the Republic does go, the Allmuseri deity is also no longer in the book.

In the end, there is a rescue involving a handsome clipper ship, where the tables are glibly turned upon a Creole gangster and slavemonger named Zeringue, whom we first met in the book's opening chapter. But with Zeringue, after being so long in Melville territory, we are back in a neatly whimsical arm of the sea. The cosmic has been supplanted by a variety of nautical sitcom. The question of whether the Allmuseri's enormously powerful god might not come ravening over the gunwales one night is not addressed. The question of how Rutherford can live with himself, having sailed on a slaver and even devoured human meat, seems resolved in the end by an artificial jollity.

Nevertheless, **Middle Passage** is still an engrossing book and—to say it again—one that leaves a reader unsure whether its almost willful failures are not sometimes its very point. This is fiction that hooks into the mind. Above all, it speaks of the legacies and griefs the peculiar institution has brought to the life of the American Republic. (p. 9)

> *Thomas Keneally, "Misadventures in the Slave Trade," in* The New York Times Book Review, *July 1, 1990, pp. 8-9.*

Joseph Coates

Long after we'd stopped believing in the Great American Novel along comes a brief, spellbinding adventure story that may be just that, without being grandiose about it—and from a source where, inexcusably, we seldom look for it: the black experience of America.

Even hearing its author, Charles Johnson, tell how "I've devoted myself to developing a genuinely philosophical black American fiction, which I don't think existed before the work of Jean Toomer, Richard Wright and Ralph Ellison" doesn't quite prepare the reader for what Johnson has accomplished in **Middle Passage** which, he says, "is intended to be serious entertainment, one that takes black fiction in America into hitherto unexplored regions of our cultural life."

Middle Passage does that, and a lot more. And it's no accident that this tale presents itself as a simple sea-story in its simplest form, ". . . the logbook you [the reader] presently *hold* in your hands," which describes the few months' experience of an Illinois black freedman named Rutherford Calhoun who unwittingly becomes a stowaway aboard the slave clipper Republic.

The first sentence of the first of the log's nine entries (June 14, 1830) should bring the briny scent of another sea story to American noses: "Of all the things that drive men to sea, the most common disaster, I've come to learn, is women." Like Ishmael, Calhoun sees "the watery part of the world" as "the analogue for life," but unlike him he puts polymorphous human sexuality and racism at the center of his story rather than veiling those subjects, as Melville did in *Moby-Dick.*

Middle Passage is both a deliberately brief counter-epic to that oceanic book and a reading of it that shows, among other things, that Ahab's quest for his pale killer whale represents American society's self-destructive obsession with its own dangerous whiteness.

Like Ellison's *Invisible Man,* Johnson's book is less about black experience per se (though it's certainly about that, too) than it is about white blindness to black experience.

Along the way it echoes and partly recapitulates much of the experience of the white Western culture Calhoun so painfully encounters, resonating off everything from Israel's bondage under the Pharaohs (the newly freed Calhoun arrives in New Orleans from southern Illinois—Little Egypt) to the pre-Socratic philosophy of Parmenides to Odysseus' return to Penelope.

Calhoun's Penelope is the prim schoolteacher Isadora Bailey whose "civilizing" intent he went to sea to escape, like Huck Finn fleeing down the big river from Miss Watson. (p. 6)

At the center of the book is Captain Ebenezer Falcon, born in the early hours of the new American nation, "a Faustian man of powerful loves, passions, hatreds: a creature of preposterous, volatile contradictions"—a man of such truly demonic impressiveness that he makes Ahab look like a Rotarian on a Saturday-night fling.

Falcon, a dwarf, is emblematic of the white man's fear that he is the black man's physical inferior; and he assumes that all American blacks he meets are mentally vacant. And in his dealings with Falcon, Calhoun, extensively educated by the guilt-ridden clergyman who inherited him as a slave, shows us how blacks in subordinate positions are forced into feigning the stupidity whites presume they possess.

Falcon's ship is as emblematic as its captain. The Republic "was physically unstable, perpetually flying apart and reforming during the voyage, falling to pieces beneath us," so that "Falcon's crew spent most of their time literally rebuilding the *Republic* as we crawled along the waves. In a word, she was, from stem to stern, a process."

As for the crew, the "Republic was, above all, a ship of *men*. . . . [E]veryone felt the pressure, the masculine imperative to prove himself equal to a vague standard of manliness in order to be judged 'regular,'" which led to "a tendency to turn themselves into caricatures of the concept of maleness." . . .

Johnson has given us the first real conceptual advance in imagining a true American hero since Saul Bellow's Augie March, who likewise was skeptical of and hostile to other people's definitions of his being.

With Rutherford Calhoun, Johnson transforms Ellison's black victim of white society—who transcends his fate only by an act of will—into a laughing, sensual rogue, fully equipped intellectually, who exults in his difference from white Americans and from the blacks who stereotype themselves in the white image. Calhoun sees the members of both groups as the real slaves—either of bourgeois uptightness or of the rigid code of disreputable maleness that imprisons even those who "light out for the territory" by isolating them from the women who, for Calhoun, make life worth living.

In a marvelous act of the imagination, Johnson has created for us the first really free native American who is not a Native American and who does not have to renounce his citizenship to claim his freedom. (p. 7)

> *Joseph Coates, "Uncharted Waters," in* Chicago Tribune—Books, *July 8, 1990, pp. 6-7.*

An excerpt from *Middle Passage*

New Orleans, you should know, was a city tailored to my taste for the excessive, exotic fringes of life, a world port of such extravagance in 1829 when I arrived from southern Illinois—a newly freed bondman, my papers in an old portmanteau, a gift from my master in Makanda—that I dropped my bags and a shock of recognition shot up my spine to my throat, rolling off my tongue in a whispered, *"Here, Rutherford is home."* So it seemed those first few months to the country boy with cotton in his hair, a great whore of a city in her glory, a kind of glandular Golden Age. She was if not a town devoted to an almost religious pursuit of Sin, then at least to a steamy sexuality. To the newcomer she was an assault of smells: molasses commingled with mangoes in the sensually damp air, the stench of slop in a muddy street, and, from the labyrinthine warehouses on the docks, the odor of Brazilian coffee and Mexican oils. And also this: the most exquisitely beautiful women in the world, thoroughbreds of pleasure created two centuries before by the French for their enjoyment. Mulattos colored like magnolia petals, quadroons with breasts big as melons—women who smelled like roses all year round. Home? Brother, for a randy Illinois boy of two and twenty accustomed to cornfields, cow plops, and handjobs in his master's hayloft, New Orleans wasn't home. It was Heaven. But even paradise must have its back side too, and it is here (alas) that the newcomer comes to rest. Upstream there were waterfront saloons and dives, a black underworld of thieves, gamblers, and ne'er-do-wells who, unlike the Creoles downstream (they sniffed down their long, Continental noses at poor, purebred Negroes like myself), didn't give a tinker's damn about my family tree and welcomed me as the world downstream would not.

In plain English, I was a petty thief.

Melvin Dixon

Middle Passage reflects the same fascination with history and narrative as Johnson's previous novels, *Faith and the Good Thing* and *Oxherding Tale. Oxherding Tale* plays upon the slave narrative and demands the manumission of readers and writers alike from the constraints of the first-person viewpoint. That novel begins with a single joke: Master and slave in a drunken revel decide to swap wives. Andrew Hawkins, born from this confusion, is raised a slave until he escapes bondage. *Middle Passage* ventures into this same period of history and play but fares less well. Here, the single joke (former slave stowaway on a slaveship) does not support the novel's plot. The novel remains unsure of its tone and direction, falling short of seriousness or high comedy. It lacks the brilliant, sustained, outrageous humor of Ishmael Reed's *Flight to*

Canada or the compelling seriousness of Sherley Ann William's *Dessa Rose.* And for all of Johnson's inclusion of references to Kant and Thomist theology (Calhoun was raised in such an intellectual household, you see), he never broadens our understanding of the elusive past and its presence in contemporary letters the way, say, Toni Morrison's *Beloved* demands a total re-reading of history.

Many African-American novelists in recent years have wrestled with the past and the power of historical imagination. They have loosened the stranglehold of popular stereotypes and, at the same time, have poked good-natured fun at history's uncanny ability to repeat itself. Johnson's *Middle Passage* is part of a larger quest to save us from our self-induced cultural amnesia by recovering a lost history and examining its impact on us today. Yet Johnson relies on so many received texts and situations that he loses his own. Scenes that recall Melville's *Moby-Dick* abound, and Johnson even borrows characters such as Babo, Atufal and Delano from Melville's classic tale "Benito Cereno." The situation of reverse navigation (towards Africa by day, America by night) draws from period accounts of Cinque's rebellion aboard the Amistad.

These elements of 19th-century American fiction and history are all present in *Middle Passage* but without the necessary critique and playfulness usually present in satire or parody. Johnson's language ranges from the anachronistic cliche ("What's a nice girl like her doing in a city like this?") to near eloquence: "Standing aft, looking back at the glittering lights ashore, I had an odd sensation, difficult to explain, that I'd boarded not a ship but a kind of fantastic, floating Black Maria, a wooden sepulcher whose timbers moaned with the memory of too many runs of black gold between the New World and Old." Yet Johnson hasn't brought us closer to Rutherford Calhoun because the protagonist himself takes nothing seriously enough to sustain the reader's empathy with his unwieldy predicament or to share his absurd delight in confronting such an unruly past.

> *Melvin Dixon, "Mutiny on the Republic," in* Book World—The Washington Post, *July 15, 1990, p. 6.*

Michael E. Ross

[In *Middle Passage*]—a rousing adventure yarn that resonates with and echoes the spirit of earlier sea stories—Johnson has fashioned a tale of travel and tragedy, yearning and history, and done so from a different, rarely explored viewpoint. (p. 1)

Middle Passage is a story of slavery, often brilliant in its structure and riveting in the way it's told. The novel amounts to a ship's log, written by a stowaway from life, a man as much adrift at sea as he was in America.

Rutherford Calhoun—a black 22-year-old thief, roue and ne'er-do-well transplanted from Illinois to the licentious New Orleans of 1830—is faced with a daunting proposition: In order to repay a multitude of debts, he must either marry a female acquaintance he's not inclined to wed or suffer the dire, physical consequences administered by one of the city's underworld bosses. Calhoun, in a fit of desperation, finds a way out by stowing away aboard the Republic, a ship he believes is bound for Africa on a supply expedition.

Aboard ship he encounters a gallery of misfits and malcontents that would have gladdened Melville's pen: Josiah Squibb, the rummy, affable cook; Cringle, the first mate and quartermaster with a heart of quiet sorrow; and Ebenezer Falcon, the cruel, calculating, eccentric master of the Republic.

Calhoun, forced into service without pay by the captain, also discovers the true reason for the ship's voyage—to pick up slaves to bring back to America.

Therein lies one of the book's more intriguing constructs, plumbing the relationship between Calhoun—the sole black member of the crew—and the slaves he now has a complicity, however reluctant, in imprisoning.

Some of the most charged, powerful language in the book concerns the agony of the slaves in the hold below decks. "There's not a civilized law that holds water . . . once you've put to sea," Falcon remarks, and the pestilential conditions Johnson depicts give weight to Falcon's observation.

Calhoun has parallels with other vagabonds in the world of literature. Johnson said he sees him as "a bit like Huck Finn and, to a certain extent, Odysseus."

The book rings with the language and terminology of the naval world of the 19th century. But rather than writing his sea tale entirely in the style of that period, Johnson has invested much of the story with the rhythms of modern English. It makes for a highly readable and accessible novel, one whose idioms and style teasingly ricochet between past and present.

Johnson sees *Middle Passage* as an effort to put a different spin on the established idea of novels about sailors at sea. "We don't really have any sailors in African American literature," he said. "There's lots of books about slavery and Africa, but very little about the ships as they crawled their way back to the New World." (pp. 1, 11)

Much of the Johnson canon has at its root the links between race, sex and class. His books also address philosophical ideas—the ways in which knowledge is gained—as much as the concrete aspects of reality. His 1982 novel, *Oxherding Tale,* is written, he said, "in the form of a slave narrative, a meditation on the meaning of freedom." Likewise, he said, his novel *Faith and the Good Thing* (1974) is "a philosophical novel about a quest for the good."

Middle Passage contains similar metaphysical scrutiny: Calhoun thinks of the life he's lived—a life that in some ways he thinks he's wasted—and he and other characters ruminate on the nature of life, love, work, good and evil. (p. 11)

> *Michael E. Ross, " 'Passage' Author Detects New Currents in Modern Black Fiction," in* San Francisco Chronicle, *August 12, 1990, pp. 1, 12.*

Garry Wills

Rutherford Calhoun [the protagonist of *Middle Passage*] is a naive wiseacre, a freed slave brought up on a remote Illinois farm, where an abolitionist stuffed his head with learning to arm him against a hostile white world, then set him loose on the streets of New Orleans where, at age twenty-two, he whores and steals, gambles and runs up debts, and tries to control danger with a distancing ridicule. As Charles Johnson presents him, he sounds like a stand-up comic wandered back into the 1820s:

> You have seen, perhaps, sketches of Piltdown man? Cover him with coal dust, add deerskin leggings and a cut-away coat tight as wet leather, and you shall have Santos's younger, undernourished *sister.*

Santos is the monstrous slave bred up as a bare-knuckled fighter and freed into the service of "Papa" Zeringue, the Creole who presides over that world of interracial crime Calhoun has slipped into. Calhoun finds here a new form of slavery when his debts are bought up by a pious black schoolmarm who takes in crippled pets. Papa decrees a marriage with this reform-minded lady; but Calhoun sees himself sinking, like his brother, into a "gentleman of color". . . . Fleeing to a New Orleans bar, Calhoun falls in with seamen. . . . So to sea he goes, on a voyage that is part Robert Louis Stevenson and part Sebastian Brant, the fifteenth-century author of *Ship of Fools.* His ship, the *Republic,* is a process, always on the verge of sinking, remade with desperate patchings and repairs throughout the journey. The crew, too, seems assembled of replaceable parts, of eye patches, hand hooks, peg legs. . . .

The mad capitalist captain, who has stashed his cabin with spoils of the cultures he preys on, is shrewd and naive, more Melville's Captain Delano than his Ahab. . . .

Johnson's method is to build neat little structures of period detail, then shatter them with a defiant anachronism. The captain explains why he cannot give Calhoun a paying share on the boat. Calhoun might make a passable mate, but he is not one "to *advance* the position, or make a lasting breakthrough of any kind." . . .

Without realizing it, Calhoun has shipped onto an illegal slave ship, still bringing captives through the Middle Passage in 1830. On the shores of Africa, the comedy turns bitter:

> How could I feel whole after seeing it? How could I tell my children of it without placing a curse on them forever? How could I even dare to *have* children in a world so senseless?

The most powerful two pages of the novel occur when Calhoun must throw a dead slave, a young man about his own age, overboard. The boy's decomposing flesh seems to seep into Calhoun's body as he handles it, effecting a weird transubstantiation.

Yet Calhoun continues to feel as distant from the captive "Allmuseri" as from their white captors. Even when an eight-year-old Allmuseri girl, Baleka, adopts him as her father, he has no trusted place with the Africans. They are as strange as their god, whom the captain has crated up (like a supernatural King Kong) and put in the hold—his climactic seizure of a foreign culture's soul. This is a god who feeds on the people who go near the crate, absorbing them into him and infusing himself into them.

When the inevitable mutiny comes, Calhoun is caught between the first mate and the captain, like Jim Hawkins torn between Long John and Doctor Livesey. But at the crisis—when he finally understands his own brother's nobility because he has come to care for someone (the Allmuseri girl)—he betrays both white factions to the Africans, who swarm up out of the hold bearing names taken from *Benito Cereno.* . . . In the aftermath of the revolt, Calhoun and some Allmuseri allies have trouble with an African demagogue, who wants to draw up new maps uncontaminated by the white man. Sorting out his own attitudes toward Africa, Calhoun finally goes down into the hold, sent there by the girl Baleka, to face the mystery of his own origins in the native god.

As the voyage doubles back to its beginning, Calhoun sees previously hidden aspects of his New Orleans—the schoolmarm has revealed her odd charm, so that the Creole boss Zeringue is about to marry her, a suitor to Penelope. She has been delaying him by knitting booties for her stray pets and unraveling them by night. In a loving send-up of *The Odyssey,* Calhoun thwarts Zeringue with an Allmuseri martial arts trick (like Odysseus' bow feat) and a revelation from the ship's log (the secret of Odysseus' bed).

Johnson's previous novels were not entirely saved from the pretentiousness of his own graduate training in philosophy by the wit that keeps his fictional *Republic* poising over the abyss. Here he has used an even older skill—Johnson's first trade was as a cartoonist. The novel's language is inventive in zany ways, full of learned and slangy inventions (glim, chaosmos, pungled, flimmer, mubblefuddled, turngiddy).

It is ironic that Johnson's book won the National Book Award in a panel that was accused, by a judge on it, of choosing ideology over merit. Johnson's merit is as obvious as his opposition to ideological formulas. In the novel as in his critical writing, Johnson resists the idea of expressing "black experience" as opposed to a black's experience of his or her inevitably multicultural world. In the *Republic* every person is changed—for good and ill—by the presence of all the other persons on the ship. The process remakes the passengers as the boat is itself remade, by the task of sailing on. Everyone aboard goes to school to the others' terrors. Even when he has cast his lot with the African rebels, Calhoun does not, like them, yearn back toward a home in Africa:

> The States were hardly the sort of place a Negro would pine for, but pine for them I did. . . . If this weird, upside-down caricature of a country called America, if this land of refugees and former indentured servants, religious heretics and half-breeds, whoresons and fugitives—this cauldron of mongrels from all points on the compass—was all I could rightly call *home,* then aye: I was of it. There, as I lay weakened from bleeding, was where I wanted to be. Do I sound like a patriot? Brother, I put it to you: What Negro, in his heart (if he's not a hypocrite), is not?

Garry Wills, "The Long Voyage Home," in The New York Review of Books, *Vol. XXXVIII, Nos. 1 & 2, January 17, 1991, p. 3.*

Carol Iannone

[Charles Johnson] holds the profoundly heterodox belief that black artists should be allowed to write as individuals rather than as "spokesmen for the race." "I find it very difficult to swallow the idea that one individual, black or white, can speak for the experience of 30 million people," he asserts in an interview with the Washington *Post.* "Would anyone ask John Updike to be a spokesman for white America?" Like Ralph Ellison, the first black novelist to win the [National Book Award] (1953), Johnson especially resents the demand that a black writer limit himself to ideological or "protest" novels. He concludes passionately, "All my life, that's what I've fought for, the absolute freedom for the black artist that we extend to the white artist."

The statement is admirable, even courageous, and it is only a pity that *Middle Passage* does not live up to it. Although in some ways a lively and enjoyable book, the novel falls short at least partly *because* it is a deliberate attempt to counter the plight-and-protest school of novelwriting. In place of the numbed, semi-literate, often brutal and inarticulate characters who people such novels, *Middle Passage* is narrated by Rutherford Calhoun, a newly freed slave who is also highly educated and intensely verbal. Upon his arrival in New Orleans, Calhoun falls in with thieves and gamblers and eventually stows away aboard a ship in order to escape from a forced marriage. Once aboard he discovers that the ship, allegorically named the *Republic,* is sailing to Africa to fetch a shipment of slaves, members of the mystical, magical Allmuseri tribe.

Far from being a marginal outsider, Calhoun freely identifies himself with the motley, restless, roaming, exploratory American spirit that the *Republic* embodies; indeed, *Middle Passage* as a whole gleefully embraces the expansive Western tradition, and teems with echoes of Homer, Coleridge, Melville, and Conrad. At the same time, Calhoun must confront the challenge presented by the Allmuseri in their symbolic role as the "Ur-tribe of humanity itself," a people in touch with "the unity of Being everywhere" and thus a countertype to the spirit of Western philosophical dualism.

To describe *Middle Passage* is to begin to suggest some of its shortcomings. As one otherwise admiring reviewer remarked, the characters "sound as if they're all double majors in classics and philosophy." What is more, these characters often seem less important than the ideas or social types they all too obviously express or stand for. It does not take long to surmise, for example, that the reason the captain of the *Republic* is a dwarf is to suggest the stunted humanity implicit in the pure rationalism he represents, the reason he is a homosexual is to suggest its sterility, the reason a pederast to suggest etc., etc. Of course

Johnson is hardly the first to deploy physical traits as marks of psychological or spiritual reality, but the reader of *Middle Passage* more often finds himself piecing together an intellectual puzzle than fathoming the depths of human feeling and behavior.

There are other problems, too. Johnson has fashioned a jocular tone for Rutherford Calhoun that is meant to convey his Whitmanesque nature, but the tone works against the tragic revelation that is attempted at the end of the plot. And the book's self-consciously anachronistic quality, which derives from Johnson's deliberate molding of a 19th-century tale to our current social and cultural dilemmas, sometimes produces inadvertently comic effects. Here is the *Republic*'s captain denouncing, of all things, affirmative action:

> I believe in *excellence*—an unfashionable thing these days, I know, what with headmasters giving illiterate Negroes degrees because they feel too guilty to fail them, then employers giving that same boy a place in the firm since he's got the degree in hand and saying no will bring a gang of Abolitionists down on their necks. . . . Eighty percent of the crews on other ships, damn near anywhere in America, are *incompetent,* and all because everyone's ready to lower standards of excellence to make up for slavery, or discrimination, and the problem . . . the *problem,* Mr. Calhoun, is, I say, that most of these minorities aren't ready for the titles of quartermaster or first mate precisely because discrimination denied them the training that makes for true excellence.

In short, although much in this novel is engaging, and though Johnson's larger ambitions are noble, it is hard to take his prize-winning book seriously as literature. (pp. 51-2)

Carol Iannone, "Literature by Quota," in Commentary, *Vol. 91, No. 3, March, 1991, pp. 50-3.*

Peter Nichols
Privates on Parade

Award: New York Drama Critics Circle Award for best foreign play

Born in 1927, Peter Richard Nichols is an English playwright, scriptwriter, and autobiographer.

Nichols is a respected playwright whose typical concerns are the mores, anxieties, and institutions of the English middle class. In *Privates on Parade,* as in his earlier works, Nichols exploits both the serious and comic aspects of his themes, using black humor to lighten otherwise troubling issues. Described by the author as "a play with music," *Privates on Parade* is loosely based on Nichols's experience as a member of an entertainment unit stationed in Southeast Asia after World War II. Private Steven Flowers, the naive young protagonist generally believed to be based on the author, learns about love from a native woman performing with the troupe. The discovery of her pregnancy leads to one of the comic crises in this multifaceted play, as Flowers insists on marrying her and is subjected to a barrage of snobbish lectures by the incompetent, uptight Major Flack.

Privates on Parade is interspersed with amateurish magic shows and song-and-dance routines with satirical lyrics—also written by Nichols—performed by men in women's clothing. While some critics questioned the efficacy of interrupting dramatic action that raises such issues as colonialism, racial and sexual prejudices, and the horrors of war, with skits based on traditional music-hall routines, others commended *Privates on Parade* as a thoroughly enjoyable farce. John Simon remarked: "Nichols achieves—comically, gravely, brilliantly—the total interpenetration of routine army life with its absurdities, army shows with their sentimental escapism and transvestite humor, and the reality of war with its maiming and dying."

For overviews of Nichols's life and work, see *CLC,* Vols. 5, 36; *Contemporary Authors,* Vol. 104; and *Dictionary of Literary Biography,* Vol. 13.

PRINCIPAL WORKS

PLAYS

A Day in the Death of Joe Egg   1967
The National Health; or, Nurse Norton's Affair   1969
Forget-Me-Not Lane   1971
Chez Nous   1974
The Freeway   1974
Privates on Parade   1977
Passion Play   1981
Poppy   1982

Clive Barnes

[*Privates on Parade*] offers problems on a number of levels, especially, I think, for American audiences. It certainly requires some kind of translation, not, of course, of language, but of style.

And even when that leap of translation has been achieved, Nichols' own dramaturgical purpose still remains distinctly cloudy, a cloudiness which some say was largely cleared up in the movie version, which I still have to catch up with.

Anyone who has served with the armed forces of either the United States or the United Kingdom (do other nations have such traditions—the Germans or the Japanese?) will know about that institution the troop show—whether it was provided by the U.S.O. or, in its British versions, E.N.S.A. or C.S.E.

There were differences—the U.S.O. aspired to the slick subtlety of the Bob Hope Show (and, not infrequently, with Bob Hope himself), while the British style was altogether less slick, less subtle, and owed almost everything to the now virtually lost traditions of the English music hall.

Privates on Parade, with its cheery, essentially unmemorably yet cleverly pastiched music by Denis King, is, in large part, an odd tribute to that kind of show, here set immediately after World War II in the Southeast Asia of 1948.

Nichols is a British playwright who sometimes uses the theater as a means of investigating and reviewing his own life, a psychiatrist-couch potato approach that provides some of his plays—*A Day in the Death of Joe Egg,* for telling example—with a highly personal sense of pain.

Privates is based on Nichols' own experiences as a Royal Air Force draftee with a forces touring troupe north of Singapore, during what Britain called the Malayan Emergency, and which turned out to be a primitive precursor of the French and American Vietnamese wars.

Like Nichols' later musical vaudeville *Poppy,* the show is part revue, part play, and the narrative line (a perfectly straightforward tale about a young man growing up rather suddenly) is satirically counterpointed by a larger imperial theme of Britain and loss of Empire, or Mad Dogs, Englishmen and what went wrong with the combination.

Steven Flowers is a young man who finds himself losing his virginity through love in a hot climate, and behaving despicably in the process.

The trouble with the show is that its strength comes in skits and spurts, while the more serious themes, both private and public, personal and political are sounded without really being stated.

Steven's engagement with a seductive Anglo-Indian charmer is never fully realized dramatically, any more than is his relationship with the idiotic, jingoistic, Bible-thumping Major who is in charge of this Fred Karno-like Army, or his liberalizing introduction to a homosexual lifestyle totally remote from his upbringing.

As for the political implications of Britain's fast-fading colonialism, these are suggested merely by the random violence of unexplained terrorists.

Meanwhile, at the drop of an idea, everything stops for either a song, or a revue imitation by Terri Dennis, who is the civilian star of the troop's troupe.

There remains something indestructibly engaging about the musical—even though I found I liked it less here than I did originally with the RSC in London. It has, I think, dated in the years between.

For most New York audiences, *Privates on Parade* will not have the same resonance it would still command in London, yet as a shock trip to a strange culture it can still amuse, ingratiate and, hopefully, even move.

> Clive Barnes, "High-Ranking 'Privates'," in
> New York Post, *August 23, 1989.*

Mel Gussow

With his gymnastic wit and droll body, Jim Dale places his signature on whatever character he chooses to play, as he demonstrates anew in the New York premiere of Peter Nichols's *Privates on Parade.* In the comedy, which opened last night at the Roundabout Theater Company, he is Acting Capt. Terri Dennis, a vaudevillian who specializes in female impersonation. It is an exceedingly flamboyant role that benefits from Mr. Dale's bold brand of clowning. . . .

Terri is the queenpin of the Middlesex Regiment, a special service unit of military misfits on hyperactive duty in Malaysia several years after the end of World War II.

The comedy in *Privates on Parade* is an amalgam of old jokes and music hall routines, but none of this matters much when Mr. Dale is center stage.

Despite its occasional suggestions of seriousness, the play is outranked by other works by the author, beginning with *A Day in the Death of Joe Egg* and *Forget-Me-Not Lane* (which has still not been presented in New York). As a satiric commentary on colonialism, *Privates on Parade* is shadowed by Caryl Churchill's *Cloud 9.*

In its favor, it has an easygoing spontaneity. The characters are unabashed about their own amateurism as performers. Repeatedly, the dialogue stops for a song, with enough parody numbers to make the play a musical revue. The score (music by Denis King and lyrics by Mr. Nichols), is a nostalgic pastiche of a period when Hollywood ruled Britannia.

Terri and his conscripted countrymen are doomed to perform their vaudeville shows in theaters filled with non-English-speaking natives. At one point, the troupe—at the behest of its misguided major—puts on a show in a hostile section of the Malaysian interior. When guerrillas cut the power circuit, one actor does his magic act in the dark. More than anything, this reverse sight gag is representative of the lack of communication between the actors and their audience, between the English army and Malaysians.

In the late 1940's, the playwright was himself a member of such a special service unit. His alter ego in the play is a young recruit quick to mimic his elders while undergoing his own rite of passage.

> Mel Gussow, "Comically Carrying Culture to
> the Colonies," in The New York Times, *August 23, 1989, p. C13.*

Linda Winer

Those tangerine lips, those ruffled panties, that fabulously limp wrist. When Peter Nichols entertains the British troupes, he isn't exactly thinking Bob Hope.

Nichols' *Privates on Parade,* which took 12 years to have its New York premiere, finally opened last night at the Roundabout Theater with the wicked and delightful Jim Dale as Acting Captain Terri Dennis—a song-and-dance soldier in mascara and fishnet hosiery.

The "play with music," which Nichols based loosely on

his own experiences in a Southeast Asian entertainment unit after World War II, is a stylishly tacky and touching—though not especially hilarious or brilliantly cutting—satire of war, prejudice and the nature of power in the declining British empire.

Jim Dale's Dennis, of course, is no more a soldier than Brooke Shields is. Being gay and an entertainer in homophobic 1948, he has found an odd stardom as the Marlene Dietrich and Carmen Miranda of remote forces protecting Britain from nobody-quite-knew-what in the "Malaysian Emergency"—a kind of Vietnam guerrilla action that lasted until 1960.

Nichols, best known here as the author of *Joe Egg, The National Health* and *Georgy Girl,* comments on senseless wars and dubious military ethics and intolerance and the human pawns of colonial egos. But he also is celebrating the British music-hall traditions—the variety shows, magic, revues and the transvestite "panto Dames"—he saw as a child.

Not all British humor travels as jauntily as Monty Python, of course. That fact, along with the similarities to our own Vietnam experience, and our reluctance to make light of it, may explain New York producers' reluctance to stage *Privates* when it was fresh and new.

In Larry Carpenter's capable—if not sparkling—production, the play feels about 30 minutes too long and a bit leisurely for its antics. On the other hand, the unrelenting double entendres, male nudity (backsides in the shower scene) and naughty irreverence (Dennis calls Jesus "Jessica Christ") actually seem a bit outspoken—a frightening thought—in our newly conservative climate.

Dennis is the most outrageous character in Nichols' "Jingle, Jangle, Jungle Jamboree," but he is hardly the only one around. The plot, such as it is, hinges on the coming-of-age of Private Flowers, a new soldier who loses his virginity to Sylvia, the half-breed East-Indian battered slave of the evil Sergeant-Major—and the only woman in the troup.

The other soldiers are either gay or, like Corporal Len, married but like "to be taken care of." And then there are the Asians, Lee and Cheng, who wait on the foreigners, listen ominously, and wait for them to stop meddling and return—amid news-reel hurrahs—to proper queen and country.

Although not described as a musical, *Privates* includes shamelessly sophomoric production numbers against the painted jungle foliage. Denis King's music suggests English standards, which may have greater meaning to the English, and Nichols' lyrics are loaded with sly and not-so-sly ironies about the Empire and home. There also are dance numbers with beefy men twirling parasols and negotiating chorus lines with rifles between their legs. A little one-joke humor goes a long way here, but Nichols has more than one idea to justify the journey.

Linda Winer, "A Gay Old Time, 12 Years Later," in Newsday, *August 23, 1989.*

David Patrick Stearns

Any playwright who combines equal parts of *South Pacific, Apocalypse Now* and *Torch Song Trilogy* would have to be either wildly creative or completely mad. Peter Nichols shows signs of both, having accomplished such a synthesis before *Apocalypse* or *Torch Song* existed.

The play is *Privates on Parade,* a British hit 12 years ago, now making its New York debut. It must have been ahead of its time back then. Now, this story about a musical comedy troupe entertaining British troops occupying Malaysia in 1948 is a bit dated.

But only a bit, especially when produced so irresistibly by the Roundabout Theater Company and performed so winningly by Jim Dale. As a flamboyant homosexual ringleader of the comedy troupe, Dale impersonates Marlene Dietrich, delivers double entendres with bravura and infuses his monologues with affecting honesty. Throughout, he seems intoxicated by the moment. And so are we.

Director Larry Carpenter keeps the heavy-handed antiwar sentiments precise and articulate, showing us its relevance in this age of Olliegate. Even if one of the officers weren't selling arms to the enemy, the cavalier attitude toward basic human values would still be resonant.

Nothing short of a rewrite, though, can help the play's style—absurdist political satire bordering on surrealism, presented so coyly it can drive you crazy. It does have enough effective scenes to justify this major production, with its onstage rainstorms and thoughtful sets and costumes.

Most important, though, is that the play's heart is in the right places—it exudes compassion for gays, Asians, even stuffy officers.

David Patrick Stearns, " 'Parade' Marches Along Amusingly," in USA Today, *September 1, 1989.*

Laurie Winer

[In *Privates on Parade,*] Terri Dennis is a British civilian-entertainer—serving in her majesty's army in Malaya in 1948. He is the star of a band of fortunate soldiers (the rest of them draftees) whose job it is not to fight the guerrilla war against the Malayan People's Anti-British Army but to entertain the men who are doing the fighting. Dennis's troupe is known as SADUSEA—the Song and Dance Unit of Southeast Asia. Their corny skits and pastiche musical numbers are meant to enliven the fighting soldiers' spirits and give them respite from the gloom of wartime. But because the numbers were written by an enormously gifted playwright (Mr. Nichols supplied the lyrics to the songs, which were composed by Denis King), the musical interludes in *Privates* also reveal invaluable information about the characters who perform them and about the mores of the society those characters have been drafted to maintain.

An unrepentant homosexual struggling to maintain his dignity in an eerily conservative culture, Terri uses the shabby, fragile glamour of army show business as an escape from reality. His audience might snigger when he dresses up as Carmen Miranda or Marlene Dietrich for the show, but Terri puts his whole heart and soul into the charade. When he meets the newest member of the troupe, a likable young private named Steve Flowers, Terri recalls his own young romantic ideals and the necessarily cruel emotional deflowering of his early dreams.

In a monologue halfway through the first act, Mr. Dale shows us the ache that fuels Terri's constantly convivial chatter. He remembers a time when "nothing sordid or unforgivable could happen," when "nobody could use you or chuck you off like an old pair of drawers when they'd finished with you." For a moment Terri's hands stop their busy fussing and his tongue stops playing erotically over his teeth, and his face—upon which rouge and powder have been defiantly yet tastefully applied—lets slip its cheery mask. At that moment, Terri Dennis—the man who loves finery—is naked in his long-suppressed pain. And for Mr. Dale, it's an acting coup; he piercingly reveals a complex, complete human being.

Terri Dennis may be the play's most empathetic character, but he is not its protagonist. That role goes to Private Flowers, the kid who learns to be a man in the army. Unfortunately, the kind-hearted Terri is only briefly his mentor; Flowers is soon taken under wing by a much more "suitable" role model, Maj. Giles Flack. Maj. Flack is that wonderful specimen that British playwrights so love to draw (remember Clive, Caryl Churchill's colonialist in Africa in *Cloud Nine?*)—the ostensibly paternal British representative in one of the they-ought-to-be-grateful colonies.

Unlike Ms. Churchill's more brutal comic portrait, Flack is a more fully drawn man with sincerely beneficent impulses. He wants to assist the young private out of a "spot of bother"—Flowers has fallen in love with and impregnated Sylvia Morgan, a 28-year-old Eurasian woman who sings and dances with the troupe.

Flack, an unquestioning patriot and philistine who blathers on about God and King and who once saw half a film and walked out, sees the boy's impending marriage to a Eurasian woman as an irreversible social disaster. Like Terri he is touched by the boy, and he sees him as his natural successor, not only in the army, but in the world at large (he has no sons). He infiltrates Flowers's mind with his opinions and suggests that Sylvia wants to marry him only for the free trip to Britain. He tells Flowers that Eurasian women may be handsome early on but that they "tend to put on weight rather soon."

If in its colonies Britain is waging a war for the souls of the natives, *Privates on Parade* delineates how a country also wages war for the souls of its young men—through the intensity of wartime bonding it persuades them to relinquish whatever idiosyncratic personal instincts that arise in them. It teaches them to conform. In the character of Flack, Mr. Nichols also makes clear how, for the bored older generation, the one that has suppressed every natural impulse, waging war is a way of relieving boredom and of getting away from the "not very brilliant company . . . [of] only my wife and the Labradors," as Flack says.

Laurie Winer, "Jim's Dandy in Army Tale," in The Wall Street Journal, *September 1, 1989.*

John Simon

What a marvelous play—musical—show Peter Nichols's *Privates on Parade* is, and how nearly impossible to get across to a standard American audience. It is so full of English history, theatrical history, and social commentary, of army slang and other Britishisms, that it would tax even the most sophisticated New York theatergoers, let alone the good folks who subscribe to the Roundabout. No wonder a number of them walked out during the second act (if not sooner), yet what a fine thing they were missing! My heart goes out to everyone: to the Roundabout, which cannot really be blamed for the incurable acoustics of its theater; to the cast, doing its damnedest with those difficult accents; to the absent playwright, who has written such a smashing play only to lose much of it in transit; to the befuddled viewers, even though some audibly enjoy themselves; and to myself, trying to sell this show to you while having to admit how hard it is to follow.

I wonder how many people in the audience understand the double entendre in the title (which is not the one, by the way, Nichols would have chosen) *Privates on Parade,* i.e., "genitals on display"? In any case, this is the story of a bunch of men and one woman civilian in an entertainment unit of the British army in Singapore, 1948. That was the beginning of the Malayan Emergency, a run-through for the Vietnam war, during which British and colonial forces tried to hold the Malayan peninsula and Singapore against some 5,000 Chinese Communists, who managed to harass them until the Communist state of Malaysia came about.

Here, then, are Major Giles Flack, an eccentric army regular; Acting Captain Terri Dennis, an unemployed pantomime actor and self-styled raving queen; Sergeant Major Reg Drummond, ex-bobby, bully, secret trader of arms and supplies to the Communists, pimp of young Malayan boys to army personnel, and lover of the aforementioned civilian, Sylvia Morgan; Sylvia herself, an Anglo-Indian dancer, also a part-time prostitute, and more British than the king; Private Steven Flowers (the author's stand-in), a twenty-year-old virgin and nice small-town boy; who wants to become a teacher, has been transferred here from an Intelligence unit, and is suspected by Reg of spying on his activities, even though Steven, a former clerk, wouldn't begin to know how.

The group further includes Leading Aircraftman Eric Young-Love, bespectacled, homely, and yearning for his fiancée in Blighty; Corporal Len Bonny, accordionist turned quartermaster, an army regular with a wife back home; his lover (Len likes to be taken care of), Lance Corporal Charles Bishop, a confirmed homosexual but, unlike Terri, a guilt-ridden one; and Flight-Sergeant Kevin Cartwright, an ordinary sort of bloke who has had a number of women but never a white one. Two native servants, Lee and Cheng, perform a variety of roles, including some that are scary. Red, brown, yellow, white, and true-blue in skin and/or ideology, they are a motley crew, and Nichols, who served with such a unit, fashioned them in part out of observed reality.

Privates is about the everyday interaction of these characters, which includes Steven's initiation by Sylvia into love and sex; about what happens to all of them in what is, after all, a war; and about the musical numbers they put on for mighty strange audiences, not least a regiment of Gurkhas who don't understand beans. Nichols achieves—comically, gravely, brilliantly—the total interpenetration of routine army life with its absurdities, army shows with their sentimental escapism and transvestite humor, and the reality of war with its maiming and dying. Metaphors become real: the *warfare* of love, the *theater* of war, the brave *show* put on in life as on the stage. It's more than Pirandellian: Illusion and reality don't merely get mixed up, they lose all meaning in a world where craziness enfolds craziness, chaos without end.

It's amazing how little it takes Nichols to create a character: a couple of sentences, a gesture or footling action, an attitude, and, presto magico, there's a person—and one to care about.

> *John Simon, "Near Misses," in* New York
> Magazine, *Vol. 22, No. 35, September 4, 1989,
> pp. 62, 64.*

Thomas M. Disch

[*Privates on Parade*] is a more than usually lifelike play, in that it is consistently interesting, often quite funny, full of memorable characters, but doesn't in the end seem to add up. This may be simply because, like Nichols's *Joe Egg,* it is based on the events of his own life, in this case the time, in 1947, when he served in the British Army in Malaya in a theatrical touring troupe. Into this inherently absurdist situation Nichols introduces a male ingénue, Private Steven Flowers, who must choose between buggery (of the five other men in the troupe, three are bent) and "Les Girls" (the title of Flowers's first musical number and the choice he makes). Sylvia Morgan, the girl he favors, is the mistress of the brutal Sergeant-Major Drummond, whose offstage villainies include running a ring of boy prostitutes, selling guns to the Communist enemy, beating Sylvia and knocking her up. On stage he harasses gays. Drummond is so bad that no one even has to argue with him: Chinese Communist infiltrators kill him off at the end of Act One, and good riddance!

By the end of Act Two the entire troupe has had a run-in with the Commies as a result of a silly decision by Major Flack to tour the show through enemy strongholds in the interior; in the aftermath the butchest of the three gays is dead, one of the two other straights besides Flowers has lost his manhood and the other an eye, and Flowers himself has gone back on his promise to marry Sylvia and so provide her with a visa to England. To rectify this the star of the show and of the show within it, the exceedingly fruity Captain Terri Dennis, saves the day by marrying Sylvia himself. What this says either about the nature of British imperialism in the Far East or about homosexuality is beyond my comprehension—and, I suspect, beyond Peter Nichols's.

I might not have bothered trying to take a sum from all the addends of the plot if the musical component of the show had been less perfunctory. *Privates on Parade* won Nichols and composer Denis King a prize for Best Musical in 1978; it has been made into a successful movie. But none of the songs rise above the original piffle they travesty, and so there is no way that Jim Dale, [the actor who portrays Terri Dennis,] in his various transvestite turns (as Marlene Dietrich, Carmen Miranda and Vera Lynn), can take off into the wild blue yonder of Show Biz Significance as did (the obvious comparison) Joel Grey as the M. C. in *Cabaret.* The material just isn't there, and so the drag acts have no other dramatic necessity than to signal to the audience that this is a play about homosexuals.

Except that it isn't. For [Terri Dennis], sexuality is a matter of fond reminiscence; in the play at hand, it is his destiny to become the genderless escort of the leading lady. Of the three sexually active men in the play, two are murdered and the third, Flowers, forswears sex. As sex is represented in this play, one can scarcely blame him.

Director Larry Carpenter has done a superb job of disguising these blemishes, and the sets by Loren Sherman provide some genuine moments of Gosh! Wow! . . . Two rainstorms, *and* a shower scene (with the promised privates coyly on parade), and singing and dancing and Jim Dale in drag. If it doesn't add up, it does zip along. Anyone hungry for a musical will find it worth the price of admission.

> *Thomas M. Disch, in a review of "Privates on
> Parade," in* The Nation, *New York, Vol. 249,
> No. 10, October 2, 1989, pp. 362-64.*

Gerald Weales

While *Sweeney Todd* is making a welcome return to Broadway, *Privates on Parade,* another product of the late 1970s, is in New York for the first time—if you do not count the 1982 movie version of the 1977 "play with songs." The Peter Nichols-Denis King show has had a spirited production at the Roundabout. Jim Dale seems to be having a marvelous time with his role as a flamboyantly high camp actor-director. It lets him move from the stage within the stage, on which he plays Marlene Dietrich, Noel Coward, and Carmen Miranda, sometimes chewing up the songs for the sake of broad imitation, to backstage where he can flounce his way through minefields of double-entendres and rest occasionally for a sentimental moment. Simon Jones, who had a small part in the original Aldwych production, plays Major Flack (the role John Cleese played in the film) as a perfect model of a sincerely priggish Christian warrior. The musical numbers, most of which had thematic or character point in the original, have made it to the stage with the fun intact, but the play has undergone some odd changes.

It is set in Singapore and the Malayan jungle in 1948, at the beginning of the guerrilla action which was called the Malayan Emergency ("softly, softly officialese" for war, says Major Flack), and it concerns an army song-and-dance unit caught in an ambush. The play—and even more the film—was as tough as *Sweeney Todd* in its view of a world in which the consequences of colonialism and the British class system make pawns and victims of ordinary men. This version, which seems to be an amalgam of the play and the movie with important hunks of plot and color cut away, is more amiable, except for a scene in which one soldier mourns his dead friend and lover while the major speaks platitudes on the other side of the stage.

Aside from the system, the chief villain of the original piece is Reg, the sergeant-major who stages a fake death for himself and then organizes the attack on his comrades-in-arms. Reg is still a villain at the Roundabout—a woman-beater, a gunrunner, a black marketeer—but his death is real, an event that renders both his early scenes and the attack confusing.

There are a great many small cuts, mostly of very English references in the mouth of Sylvia, the Welsh-Indian woman who has never seen England. Their absence does no great harm to the script; however, the play loses some of its resonance because the England Sylvia has invented out of her dead father's memories and the *London Illustrated News* is no more imaginary to the ordinary soldiers than the Berkshire world Major Flack lives in when he is home. No one is going to worry about the cuts and changes in **Privates on Parade** (except for the occasional niggling scholar of modern drama like me). There is still enough direct and oblique social criticism to feed the playgoers who like a little substance with their fun. For the rest, there is the fun itself.

Gerald Weales, in a review of "Privates on Parade," in Commonweal, *Vol. CXVI, No. 18, October 20, 1989, p. 567.*

Edna O'Brien
Lantern Slides

Award: Los Angeles Times Book Award

Born in 1932, O'Brien is an Irish novelist, short story writer, dramatist, scriptwriter, autobiographer, and editor.

Praised for their sensitivity and universality, the short stories in *Lantern Slides* focus on O'Brien's familiar theme of victimized women who grieve for lost love or struggle to overcome their pasts. Her story "Storm" is frequently cited for its poignant depiction of the quiet suffering experienced by a middle-aged woman recently abandoned by her lover. While vacationing with her son and his girlfriend, the woman grows resentful of the young couple's exclusivity, but only further alienates herself when she vents her anger. Critics consistently praised O'Brien's deep exploration of such human experiences as isolation and loneliness, occasionally likening her characters to those in James Joyce's short story collection *Dubliners*. The title work, "Lantern Slides," for example, has been favorably compared to Joyce's story "The Dead" for its compassionate portrayal of lonely people drawn together by desperate hopes at a birthday party. Human tragedy caused by entrenchment in the past is also a prominent motif of several stories, including "The Widow," in which a woman's decision to remarry sparks the scathing criticism of her peers.

During her prolific literary career, O'Brien has been widely regarded as an artist dedicated to evoking emotions, rather than one who experiments with fictional form. Nevertheless, numerous critics have contended that the distinct style of *Lantern Slides* is influenced by the Irish Gothic tradition of fable, as well as O'Brien's own childhood in rural Ireland. Thomas Cahill asserted: "[O'Brien] is a storyteller, an Irish storyteller, one of an ancient tradition of storytellers, people who tell the truth. In old Ireland, the words of a truthful poet were both sought and feared: They could kill. Her best work has the sound of something prehistoric—palpable, thrilling, incantatory—about it. It should be read aloud, like poetry. It is, indeed, not prose, at least not in any modern manner."

(See also *CLC*, Vols. 3, 5, 8, 13, 36; *Contemporary Authors*, Vols. 1-4, rev. ed.; *Contemporary Authors New Revision Series*, Vol. 6; and *Dictionary of Literary Biography*, Vol. 14.)

PRINCIPAL WORKS

NOVELS

The Country Girls   1960
The Lonely Girl   1962
Girls in Their Married Bliss   1964
August is a Wicked Month   1965
Casualties of Peace   1966
A Pagan Place   1970

Zee & Co.   1971
Night   1972
I Hardly Knew You   1977
The High Road   1989

SHORT FICTION COLLECTIONS

The Love Object   1968
A Scandalous Woman and Other Stories   1974
Mrs. Reinhardt & Other Short Stories   1978; also published in the United States as *A Rose in the Heart*, 1979
Returning   1982
A Fanatic Heart: Selected Stories   1985
Lantern Slides   1990

PLAYS

A Pagan Place   1973
Virginia   1981

OTHER

Mother Ireland   (autobiography)   1976
Seven Novels and Other Short Stories   1978

Jack Fuller

If Molly Bloom had James Joyce's gift for story and didn't ramble on so, she might have written fiction like Edna O'Brien's.

O'Brien's stories are earthy, wry, direct. They owe a debt to the Irish master, and they pay it. The title piece of this most recent collection [*Lantern Slides*]—set at a dinner party—is so honest about its antecedents in *Dubliners* that its main male character takes the name of Mr. Conroy, straight from "The Dead."

But O'Brien does not see Irish women, as Joyce saw Gerty McDowell on the beach, from a yearning distance. Her characters sometimes speak directly to the reader, sometimes not, but either way their voices are intimate and presented without sentimentality or the wishfulness of lust.

O'Brien's women most commonly are people who have lost the love of their life, or the illusion of it. The Blazes Boylans of the world are no better today than when Joyce wrote. And the women have the same weary romanticism, believing that somehow, someday an Irishman might live up to his lies.

Many of the stories in this volume are a sort of Irish gothic. O'Brien is very hard on the national peculiarities and she has a taste for raw-edged tales about cruel towns and the indifferent city. One could read the first piece in the collection, " 'Oft in a Stilly Night,' " as a kind of commentary on Dylan Thomas' *Under Milkwood*. Unlike Thomas' Welsh, the Irish characters in this "small somnolent village" are not forgiven through the miracle of sweet lyricism. O'Brien makes the drunks mean, the God-wracked ladies insane, the dalliance assaultive or at least crude. And in the end she asks, "Now I ask you what you would do? . . . You would probably drive on, is that it? Perhaps sequestered your own village is much the same. Perhaps everywhere is."

This is no author's vain boast of universality. O'Brien's stories have a reach way beyond the eccentricities of the land in which they are set. Hers are tales of people leaving love, of returning years later to find what is left. At their rawest, they are as cruel as a carving knife: the incestuous sister in **"Brother"** coolly planning to do away with his wan, newfound mate. And then O'Brien will surprise you with a moment so sweet and round that it seems it might redeem all humankind.

"Epitaph," for example, is a soliloquy of a woman whose love was spurned and then rekindled. In the end, she is the one who turns aside. But not in anger or despair.

> If was understood that we might meet in that other country. Might. . . . Meanwhile, I had that picture of you in my mind, my secret Odysseus returned from his wandering, reunited with his wife, his retinue, his dog. We said goodbye, three or four times; we clung. To think that it happened as cleanly as that.

The effects O'Brien achieves are so elegant that it is possible to overlook her subtlety.

Sometimes it is to be found in the perfect choice of word. A man and woman wander on the beach where they each once had tarried in love. The man has hopes, the woman memories. She describes the sand as being as white as salt-petre.

Sometimes it is the perfect detail: a woman visiting her emotionally distant father in a nursing home sits in the overheated bedroom as he shuffles off into the bathroom and fails to close the door. She finds herself "listening, while trying not to listen."

Sometimes the effects come from the shape of the piece as a whole. In **"Storm"** a mother on holiday has sharp words with her son and his girlfriend, they go off for a sail, a storm blows up and when they do not come home, she becomes frightened that she has lost them. The natural conditions mirror the tempest of her own relationship with them and her feelings of remorse. It is just that simple. And yet the grace is in the ending. The couple comes home, having eluded danger, and everyone acts as if nothing happened." 'Tomorrow,' they say, as if there were no storm, no rift, as if the sea outside were a cradle lulling the world to a sweet, perpetual, guileless sleep."

Guilelessness is not the same as innocence, which is one of O'Brien's favorite themes. Nor is innocence like virginity, which can be lost but once. It is rather something that is eroded steadily by time.

In the story **"Another Time"** a famous woman pays a visit alone to a town of her youth and meets there a woman who, as a girl, walked away with her flame. The man, she learns, had spoken of her often in later years. "You were a feather in his cap, especially after you appeared on television," she is told. Another story, **"Dramas,"** as a whole is both an innocent farce and a tale of the end of innocence.

Ultimately, what makes these pieces so wonderful is that, like the masterpieces of the Irish literary tradition, they come straight from the soil of genuine experience. Convention-bound as Irish society is, its literature gets behind this to the sources of human behavior that convention attempts to reform or hide. Nor are literary conventions sacred either. You don't find very much easy affection or easy despair in O'Brien's pieces. Their elegance is in the way they render the complexity of human interchange and emotion.

It is peculiar that it was James Joyce who, more than anyone else, launched writers of fiction into a relentless and ultimately dead-ended pursuit of formal invention. Perhaps his own inventions were lighted with genius simply because, as an Irishman, he was still rooted in the rich, loamy earth of human concern (all too human, as he said), from which the value and deepest pleasures of literature grow.

O'Brien's work springs from the same fields. She is not particularly interested in chasing the chimera of structural novelty. Rather she has a more modest but more insatiable interest in finding ways to say things that are true. And time and again, in small ways and large, she succeeds. (pp. 1, 3)

Jack Fuller, "Wryly Irish," in Chicago Tribune—Books, *May 27, 1990, pp. 1, 3.*

Valentine Cunningham

[**Lantern Slides**], Edna O'Brien's latest collection of stories—affectionate and affecting about ordinary Irish lives lived in a fug of incense and familial nosiness, marinaded in cabbage, bacon and gossip—is as approachable as an old mitten. In **Lantern Slides** locked-up selves, missed chances, unspeakable lusts, plaintive recollections, are all lodged behind serene lace curtains.

A great array of pitiable women throngs the stage—widowed, abandoned, batty, priest-ridden. These tales are where you find out what bachelor farmers are thinking of out in the byre, what Maisie knew about incest, how it feels to collect a pregnant sister from her convent school and what the neuroses of brash *nouveaux riches,* brought about by Modern Irish Marriage, currently consist of. Edna O'Brien's stories are expert on the quirkiness breeding in the dry ground of memory and desire. None of these fictions disappoints.

Valentine Cunningham, "Down and Out in Dublin," in The Observer, *June 3, 1990, p. 62.*

Rose Tremain

In Edna O'Brien's early novels, gullible young girls left rural poverty for the lure of the wicked city, fell in love with the wrong men and were abandoned by them. Now, in her recent stories [in **Lantern Slides**], these same people have reached middle age. They've known passionate love, some have had marriages and children, but mainly they're on their own again, filled with vague longings and old dreams. Life is in the past. The present is ugly and solitary.

In **"Epitaph"**, the female narrator addresses the married man she's loved all her life, he seemingly content with his double existence, she withering away in 'atrocious solitudes'. She recalls their meetings, some passionate, some awkward. She breaks the narrative to tell him the story of her aunt Bridget, driven out of her own house by a selfish son and daughter-in-law. The message is: we women suffer so, you would not believe it. Very often we are 'sodden with wine and grief' and no wonder, when so little care is taken. In **"Long Distance"**, a similar lifetime's betrayal is recounted. The narrator has a final meeting with her married lover, in which he dangles before her starved soul the offer of a trip to Thailand. 'Every bit of her wanted to say yes. Her eyes said it and the eyes at the tip of her fingertips said it and the flesh at the back of her throat ached at the thought. . . . ' But she won't let herself go, in the knowledge that the returning will be too painful to endure and the story ends with a rather peculiar observation on the nature of love: 'first it fruits, then it flowers, then it seems to wither, then it goes deep, deep down into its burrow, where no one sees it, where it is lost from sight and ultimately people die with that secret buried inside their souls.'

Grown-up children provide no comfort for O'Brien's abandoned women. In **"Storm"**, Eileen, 'recently jilted', has gone to Italy with her son Mark and Mark's girlfriend, Penny, but their sexy self-absorption and their thoughtless untidiness make Eileen resentful and, returning from dinner one evening, she comes out with a tirade against them. Mark is appalled. Now 'it is his turn to explode. His rage is savage and she realises that a boy who has been mild and gentle all his life is cursing her vehemently.' The following day, Mark and Penny go off sailing and Eileen is left alone to 'dream of her lover on a swing with his wife'. A storm gets up and she imagines her son and his girl drowned. But they are not drowned. Even though for them 'the holiday must seem a fiasco' they return chattering about a new restaurant they've found, where they promise to take Eileen. The mutual hurt is bandaged. The wounds will not be further probed. Nothing, of course, has been made more bearable for jilted Eileen; merely she has understood that her son cannot cope with the burden of her pain.

O'Brien is adept at delineating the heroic patience middle-aged women bring to their suffering, but the sobbing and sighing pall after a while. Most successful are the stories in which women—though victims yet again—decide to climb back into the ring and go a few rounds with the enemy. In the beguiling and original **"Brother"**, ugly Maisie lives in bog-ignorant incestuous splendour with a brother whose chief erotic delight is to hear her say, 'I've eaten to my satisfaction and if I ate any more I'd go flippety-floppety.' Maisie's monopoly of his 'rise in the wet evenings' is threatened when he announces he is going to marry plump Tilly from the next farm. With delicious venom, Maisie plans a strategy. She will fawn upon and flatter the new bride for a while. Then, she'll 'lure her to the waterfall to look for eggs' and give her a shove into the abyss. Maisie is determined that nobody will ever replace her and she sums up the situation with exquisite terseness: 'I'm all he has. I'm all he'll ever have. Roll on, nuptials. Daughter of death is she.'

In **"What a Sky"**, a dutiful daughter pays a visit to her elderly father in a nursing home. She's gone planning to cheer up his monotonous routine by taking him out to lunch in a hotel, but at the last moment 'something awful gets between her and the nice gesture'. She is aware that all her life she has tried to please her father and found no real love in return. Her refusal to honour him now is an act of self-preservation and yet she knows, too, that 'she has missed something, something incalculable'—the need to forgive those who have done you wrong before they die. This tale has a perfect coherence, every changing emotion beautifully captured. In its simplicity and truth it succeeds far better than the title story, **"Lantern Slides"**, which eavesdrops on a motley of desperate souls gathered in a crumbling Irish mansion for a surprise party. O'Brien's Irish eccentrics, unlike Molly Keane's, are never funny, only miserable and mad and thus in essence very little different from the demented, man-starved heroines at the heart of all her fiction.

Rose Tremain, "Walking Wounded," in The Listener, *Vol. 123, No. 3168, June 7, 1990, p. 27.*

An excerpt from "Storm"

The sun gave to the bare fields the lustre of ripened hay. That is why people go, for the sun and the scenery—ranges of mountains, their peaks sparkling, an almost cloudless sky, the sea a variety of shades of blue, ceaselessly flickering like a tray of jewels. Yet Eileen wants to go home; to be more precise, she wishes that she had never come. Her son Mark, and his girlfriend, Penny, have become strangers to her and, though they talk and go to the beach and go to dinner, there is between them a tautness. She sees her age and her separateness much more painfully here than when at home, and she is lost without the props of work and friends. She sees faults in Penny that she had not noticed before. She is irked that a girl of twenty can be so self-assured, irked at the languid painstaking way that Penny applies her suntan oil, making sure that it covers each inch of her body, then rolling onto her stomach imploring Mark to cover her back completely. At other times Penny is moody, her face buried in a large paperback book with a picture of a girl in a gauze bonnet on the cover. There are other things, too: when they go out to dinner Penny fiddles with the cutlery or the salt-and-pepper shakers, she is ridiculously squeamish about the food, and offers Mark tastes of things as if he were still a baby.

On the third night, Eileen cannot sleep. On impulse she gets out of bed, dons a cardigan and goes out on the terrace to plan a strategy. A mist has descended, a mist so thick and so opaque that she cannot see the pillars and has to move like a sleepwalker to make her way to the balustrade. Somewhere in this sphere of milky white the gulls are screaming, and their screams have a whiff of the supernatural because of her not being able to see their shapes. A few hours earlier, the heavens were a deep, a hushed blue, studded with stars; the place was enchanting, the night balmy and soft. In fact, Penny and Mark sat on the canvas chairs looking at the constellations while waiting and hoping for a falling star so that they could make a wish together. Eileen had sat a little apart from them, lamenting that she had never been that young or that carefree. Now, out on the terrace again, staring into the thicket of mist and unnerved by the screaming gulls, she makes herself a firm promise to go home. She invents a reason, that she has to do jury duty; then, like a sleepwalker, she gropes her way back to bed.

Louise Doughty

Most of the characters in Edna O'Brien's new collection of stories, *Lantern Slides,* have secrets of one sort or another. In **"Another Time"**, a woman re-visits a seaside resort and encounters her past—an envied childhood friend now overweight and pitiable. **"The Widow"** is Bridget, a book-keeper who has lost the perfect husband: in fact the husband was a suicide and just before a potentially happy re-marriage Bridget wraps her car round a tree. In this story, as in others, O'Brien displays human idiosyncrasies with a fine mix of black humour and precision. We are on familiar O'Brien territory; isolated people yearning for past dreams, a landscape of poignant human histories. The reader turns voyeur, peeping over hedges and under bed-covers for a brief glimpse of the truth.

This is particularly true of the stories set in rural Ireland. **" 'Oft in the Stilly Night' "** is a tale of gentle country folk full of gentle, in-bred, country eccentricities: "You would never dream that so many restless souls reside here, dreaming of a different destiny." Ita, who arranges the flowers in the local church, is obsessed with Father Bonaventure, an evangelical missionary who comes to the village to preach. She goes berserk one night and hence becomes part of the local folklore, the lunatic old lady forking manure on the farm. This story, like some of the others, is somewhat spoiled by an address to the reader at the end: "perhaps pity is a luxury and deliverance a thing of the past". O'Brien has a tendency to indulge in these little epigrams, as if she doesn't quite trust us to get the point. She avoids it in those stories which have a first-person narrator, such as **"Brother"**, where the slightly portentous authorial voice is replaced by a hilariously lunatic spinster plotting to murder her new sister-in-law. Sex lurks in the woodshed. The incestuous village siblings may be archetypes but O'Brien handles them with consummate skill.

The rural tales are in sharp contrast to stories such as **"Epitaph"**, a raw account of the death of a relationship between a woman and a well-known public figure. On the subject of loneliness, O'Brien is excellent. The same precision with which she portrays landscape is applied to human emotions; there isn't a single character in these stories who is unconvincing. O'Brien continues to display acute powers of observation in a prose that is always neat and often immaculate.

> *Louise Doughty, "Restless Dreaming Souls,"* in The Times Literary Supplement, *No. 4549, June 8, 1990, p. 616.*

Gabriele Annan

[*Lantern Slides*] is Edna O'Brien's first collection of stories for eight years, and all of them are sad. Each one centres on a lone female figure, sometimes a little girl, more often a middle-aged woman; the middle-aged woman will have been left by her husband or jilted by her lover. The weather is terrible: dank, if not pouring with rain, often stormy. 'The wind keened like a banshee'. It would. Most of the stories are set in the west of Ireland (though even in a Mediterranean holiday village a threatening tempest blows up) and they are not free from cliché and other kinds of carelessness: 'The crows were incorrigible', for instance; had anyone tried to correct them? . . . It makes no difference whether the stories are told in the first person or the third, by a child or an adult: the voice is always the same—sad and somehow resigned and urgent at once. There is even a second-person story addressed to a distant lover and recalling his final departure. Second-person narratives are risky. They can sound over-insistent and make one want to go away.

Still, Edna O'Brien's imperfections are part of her powerful appeal, her verve and spontaneity. She is either incredibly cunning and puts them in on purpose, or else she is natural; someone with a tremendous gift for writing who is not interested in writing at all, but only in telling. Of course this makes her very unmodern and puts her at the opposite end of the spectrum from writers like, say, Martin Amis or Philip Roth, whose novels, implicitly or explicitly, are all about what can be done with fiction. Nor is she interested, like Margaret Drabble (and Martin Amis again, for that matter), in what is happening to the world: she is a romantic novelist, but a disappointed one. Bitterness is her theme.

Her defenceless heroines are tormented either by their lovers or by their families. There is an opening here for feminist sentiments and propaganda, but it's not taken. Sometimes there's spite, with dreams of vengeance and 'cold rodent glances', but more often it's just sadness and yearning. Over every story there hovers the image of an ideal woman who might—just might—triumph over the fate of being a woman: 'her radiance, this woman in a black dress, composed and at the same time reeking of wildness.' The black dress is significant; the woman is a vamp, though a vamp with profound passion, and if she isn't the heroine (as in the story from which the quotation comes), then she's what the plain spinsters or oppressed little girls dream of being.

The Ireland where they dream is lowering, and not just because of the weather. The title story is set at a birthday party, 'a smart gathering in a select part of the outskirts of Dublin', in a plush house where 'the big flower arrangements were all identical—pink and red carnations, as if these were the only flowers to be found.' Show-off car dealers and sexy doctors make jokes about jacuzzis and embarrassing speeches about the birthday girl—a middle-aged woman whose husband left her years earlier. The ghastly vulgar milieu comes so brilliantly to life that all one wants is to go home.

But home would be another place to escape from, a small town in western Ireland where happiness comes only in brief flashes and upsets the neighbours. A widow becomes engaged to a decent man who had broken off an earlier, impossible engagement. 'Her happiness was too much for people to take; they called her a hussy, they predicted another breach of promise, they waited for the downfall. Some of the older women went to the parish priest about it.' They needn't have bothered: the widow dies in a car crash before the wedding. In another story a little girl looks forward to a day's outing in a hired car to the convent where her sister is a pupil. Various contretemps spoil the day, and when they finally arrive it is too late for the expected delicious tea. The sister turns out to be ill and needs to be taken home. She seems to have put on weight, and that very night, in the room she shares with her little sister, she begins to howl with pain as the birthpangs come on.

Everyone is always peering, interfering. Every husband is a lush, every wife a shrew. Children expect their parents to be always quarrelling, and their expectations are fulfilled. Hidden behind net curtains of sleazy gentility there is violence, illegitimacy, incest, but none of these are as bad as the cruel demeaning snobbery and poisonous envy under every roof. At her most Zolaesque, O'Brien is as impressive as she is depressive. (pp. 40-1)

Gabriele Annan, "Bitterness is Her Theme," in

The Spectator, *Vol. 264, No. 8448, June 9, 1990, pp. 40-1.*

Leigh Allison Wilson

Edna O'Brien's sixth collection of short stories [*Lantern Slides*] marks the 30th anniversary since the publication of her first book, *The Country Girls,* and displays a style notable for the quality of its grace. Such a style, as Chekhov would have it, consists of "making the most movement with the least effort." . . . O'Brien's territory ranges from the rural to the urban, from the farm country of Ireland to the coast of Italy to the apartments of London. And in all of these territories she shows a deftness of vision that locates not only character but also its connectedness to time and place.

Love, that difficult "rubric against death," is a theme in all these stories. "Devour" and "dementia" are words that crop up throughout the pages: Characters are devoured by passion or the memory of passion; they devour smells and sights as though their senses might leave them; they are demented with grief, with isolation, with unfulfilled desire.

Even children are not immune to the mysteries of hope and desire, loss and madness. In **"A Demon"** young Meg goes on a trip with her parents to bring home a "repining" sister from a convent. There is a special guest, the doctor's wife, whose social attentions Meg's mother has been courting for years, a rather gross woman whose very presence lends a pathetic quality to the mother's anxious overtures. For Meg this trip is a grand adventure that steadily declines into its own sorts of anxiousness: a lost coat, lost directions and, finally, an utterly lost sister, whose "demon"—and the family's social standing—will be witnessed and exorcised by the doctor. As Meg, near hysteria, thinks, "in a few hours' time their lives would be destroyed."

The mothers of children also find the borders of hope and loss a frightening negotiation. **"Storm"** finds Eileen, her son, Mark, and his moody lover, Penny, on vacation together, a vacation that has become an accumulation of small irritants, like grains of sand in a well-made bed. In their youth and their tentative, selfish passion, Mark and Penny have isolated Eileen, who has herself been recently jilted by a lover. A furious row occurs after a seemingly innocuous dinner; Eileen, appalled even as she does it, vents her rage in a series of petty grievances; Mark turns savagely against her, making clear his allegiance to Penny in these matters of the heart. The story swells on, ominous as the sea, until an uneasy truce is made, though not without cost: "They have each looked into the vortex and drawn back, frightened of the warring primitive forces that lurk there . . . 'Tomorrow' . . . " they say, "as if there were no storm, no rift, as if the sea outside were a cradle lulling the world to a sweet, perpetual, guileless sleep."

" 'Oft in the Stilly Night' " recounts some eerie stories about a "somnolent" village through the voice of an unnamed narrator who adopts the pose of a gossip in love with her people (and what narrator is not a loving gossip in the end, although this one is more forthright about it).

Desire and thwarted desire skirt the edges of madness, a layering of difficult lives and monstrous detail that O'Brien manages brilliantly to universalize: "Now I ask you, what would you do? Would you comfort Ita, would you tell her that her sins were of her own imagining . . . or would you drive on helter-skelter, the radio at full blast? Perhaps your own village is much the same, perhaps everywhere is." This loving, graceful voice, and its ability to punch the stuffing of narrow lives into the fabric of Everyman or Everywoman, is at the heart of O'Brien's latest collection.

But the best piece is the title one, **"Lantern Slides."** In its particulars and its nuance the story is reminiscent of Joyce's "The Dead" (the kind of comparison O'Brien is no doubt sick of hearing over the years, though the story invites it and, frankly, deserves it, in all the best ways). The select of Dublin are present at a surprise birthday party in the home of one of their own. There is Miss Lawless, whose memory of her youthful lover, Abelard, is rekindled by a visit home, and whose hopes in love are also rekindled by the presence at the dinner of a man who could, just perhaps, take that Abelard's place. There is Mr. Conroy, the escort and confidant of Miss Lawless, who entertains hopes of more than her confidences. There are others, too, all hoping and striving for romance or willing to settle for a bastardization of it; it is a dining room full of hope, however tenuous, and full of secret despair, however rationalized. It is, in fact, a glimpse of all Ireland (or else, of all of us), and as O'Brien has written, "At least it does not leave one pusillanimous." **"Lantern Slides"** ends with the living and not the dead, with a sudden surge of outrageous hope and not the other, darker thing: "It was as if life were just beginning—tender, spectacular, all-embracing life—and she, like everyone, were jumping up to catch it. Catch it."

Edna O'Brien moves from the flower of innocence to the taint of self-consciousness and back again as easily as if she were a force of nature. Perhaps she is, for the grace of her characters moves one to reach out, open the senses, extend the fingers, and catch this book in one's arms.

Leigh Allison Wilson, "By Love Obsessed," in Book World—The Washington Post, *June 24, 1990, p. 9.*

David Leavitt

[O'Brien's stories] divide almost without exception into two types: those that describe the lives of worldly, urban women with a penchant for vacationing in exotic climes and (usually) an obsessive attachment to a charismatic, powerful and married man; and those in which Ms. O'Brien—to borrow the title of an earlier collection—finds herself "returning" to the Ireland of her childhood. In these latter stories, we see once again the country girl, living in a blighted village with her house-proud mother and drunken father; but we also see, somewhere in the distance, the city woman, sitting at her writing table, puzzling out the mystery of how she got from there to here, and in the process delineating, with ever-increasing exactitude, the tragic world into which she was born.

Lantern Slides, her superb new collection, continues the quest for origin and explanation that has preoccupied Ms. O'Brien these past decades. Though she covers little new ground here, she also digs deeper into the old ground than ever before, unearthing a rich archeology. Tragedy is the central theme of the stories, but not the blind tragedy of car wrecks and earthquakes. Rather, what concerns Ms. O'Brien is those tragedies that come about as a result of ordinary passion, stupidity or stubbornness. The epigraph to the book—"Each human life must work through all the joys and sorrows, gains and losses, which make up the history of the world"—is from Thomas Mann, but it could just as well be from Shakespeare or Joyce, two omnipresent ghosts here, and it is echoed throughout the stories. "Ours was a small tragedy in comparison with the big ones," one narrator observes to her married lover, "the world gone off the rails, righteous chants of madmen, rapine, pillage; ordinary mortals, feeling as insignificant as gnats." But, as Ms. O'Brien shows us, ordinary mortals can love and suffer keenly.

In a story called **"Dramas,"** an ebullient, probably homosexual shopkeeper, arriving in a steely Irish village with the intention of starting a theatrical company, is quickly dissuaded from his original intention of producing Shakespeare or Chekhov: "The locals were suspicious, they did not want plays about dead birds and illegitimate children, or unhappy couples tearing at each other, because they had these scenarios aplenty." As the tension between the villagers' puritanism and the shopkeeper's flamboyance moves toward its inevitably awful climax, yet another episode of sordidness and humiliation is recorded in the O'Brien annals. High drama, we see, is not merely the province of the playwrights.

In **"Epitaph,"** a woman addresses the unreliable married lover with whom she has been obsessed for years, and who has been for years driving her to the brink of self-destruction. "You see, everyone is holding on," she tells him. "Just. If their skins were peeled off, or their chest bones opened, they would literally burst apart." Such ruthlessly surgical peeling and cracking might also describe Ms. O'Brien's method as a writer; the follies that can result from passion are subjected, in story after story, to an analysis so unsparing it verges on a kind of mutilation. Like the mother vacationing with her son and his girlfriend in **"Storm,"** Ms. O'Brien is constantly looking "into the abyss . . . frightened of the primitive forces that lurk there"; unlike the narrator, however, she never succumbs to the impulse to draw back.

In this literary universe, passions govern and casually destroy lives; cruelty and pain are as familiar as furniture. In **" 'Oft in the Stilly Night,' "** a married woman whose shoes have been stolen by a "tinker woman" loses "her heart for retribution" upon seeing the unfortunate thief in a courtroom and asks the judge "in tearful tones to overlook [the crime] and to exercise clemency." But the judge will have none of it, will not even heed the woman's request that the tinker be allowed to keep the shoes, and the woman leaves the courtroom carrying them "limply, as if she would drop them the moment she got outside."

People often go mad in these stories. In one, an old sacristan is driven into a life of delusion for love of a priest, while in another a brother's repeated molestation of his sister compels her to plot the murder of his arriving bride. Elsewhere, tragedy results merely from a stubborn refusal to admit the truth, as in **"A Demon,"** in which a family making a visit first to a son in a monastery and then to a daughter who is ill in a convent endures with increasing anxiety and terror a journey fraught with mishaps—a late start, many wrong turns. Only in the end are the family members obliged to confront the true source of their anguish—not the journey but the daughter's mysterious "illness," which remains unnamed until its truly catastrophic implications can no longer be ignored.

The title story is the collection's masterpiece. A long, lilting paean to Joyce's own masterpiece, "The Dead," it travels the emotional terrain of a huge surprise party in contemporary Dublin, a celebration held to honor the birthday of a woman named Betty, whose husband has recently left her. The narrative voice—alternately wistful and funny—moves effortlessly among the points of view of the different guests, returning periodically, as if to center itself, to a young woman named Miss Lawless. (Most of Edna O'Brien's heroines could be named Miss Lawless.)

The stories that link the party guests usually begin with love and end with some kind of disaster or humiliation: a discovered tryst, a miscarriage, an abandonment. The owner of a flower shop that is about to go bankrupt searches frantically for a rich man to save her; a mentally ill girl whose "particular quirk was to keep walking, always walking, as if looking for something," wanders through on her way to somewhere else; a woman who has avenged herself on her philandering husband, and thereby earned the contempt of most of their friends, prays "with all her heart and soul for a seizure to finish her off, but she just grew thinner and thinner, and tighter and tighter, like a bottle brush."

Then "miniature trees with tiny lights as thin as buds" drop from the ceiling, "so that the room took on the wonder of a forest." A cake appears; a dog barks, suggesting the last-minute arrival of Betty's estranged husband, and the members of the crowd turn toward the door, "each rendered innocent by this moment of supreme suspense." As the story concludes, Miss Lawless, like the others, is caught up in the spell, the fantasy of the knight in shining armor arriving to save them all. "It was as if life were just beginning—tender, spectacular, all-embracing life—and she, like everyone, were jumping up to catch it. Catch it."

That repetition is vintage O'Brien—a stuttered last grasp at a fleeting sensation, and at the same moment an imploring plea to the reader, bringing to mind E. M. Forster's exhortation to "only connnect." In the hands of a lesser writer, such a finale might seem melodramatic; but here, and elsewhere, Ms. O'Brien writes with a degree of assurance and commitment that can render even the most melodramatic gesture utterly credible.

With a few exceptions—**"Epitaph,"** most notably—I tend to find Ms. O'Brien's stories about cosmopolitan, contemporary women less satisfying than her Irish stories. Some-

thing is missing in them—a kind of gumption, a humorous vigor. Perhaps this is because the narrators of the city stories tend to speak into looking glasses and to live in the stasis of passionate attachments to married men that they cannot or will not break. The narrators of the Irish stories, by contrast, are engaged in investigations of the past—a past rich with fable and incident.

In a story called **"Another Time,"** a successful television announcer named Nelly decides to spend a holiday at an Irish hotel near her hometown, a hotel that, in her youth, she thought the height of glamour. There her past returns to her, "the rooms and landings of childhood, basins and slop buckets that oozed sadness." Nelly's homecoming prompts a rush of catharsis, "as if doors or windows were swinging open all around her and . . . she was letting go of some awful affliction."

For Edna O'Brien as well as for Nelly, the past—particularly the Irish past—provides a way into knowledge. Her stories unearth the primeval feelings buried just below the surface of nostalgia, using memories to illuminate both what is ridiculous and what is heroic about passion. Like Nelly, by going backward, Ms. O'Brien goes forward, "a river that winds its way back into its first beloved enclave before finally putting out to sea."

David Leavitt, "Small Tragedies and Ordinary Passions," in The New York Times Book Review, *June 24, 1990, p. 9.*

Thomas Cahill

A writer's life is filled with lies, most of them not of her own making.

"Poor Mrs. O'Brien," says the countrywomen of rural Clare in speaking of Edna O'Brien's late mother. "Sure, she tried to hold her head up, but . . . (shrug) well, y'know, with a daughter like That Wan. Ah, the poor t'ing, didn't she travel all the way to London to visit That Wan and when she got there didn't she find there wasn't a stick of proper furniture to be found in the entire flat—just pillows on the floor?" Of course, the content of That Wan's novels and stories lie beyond all possibility of comment. They are, literally, unspeakable. Far easier to pronounce authoritative condemnations on her decor.

In Dublin, whither Edna fled her rural life, they recall her mad, shop-girl involvement with a prominent Anglo-Irish statesman, who, they aver, "taught her to be above herself, to have notions." They recall her marriage to a mild, reticent man ("You wouldn't know he was in the room"), who taught her to write ("She hadn't a clue"). Note the nice balance in this analysis: He was of no account, yet he was wholly responsible for her later fame and fortune. From these years came *The Country Girls Trilogy,* first novels that tore across the literary sky like comets whose tails we have yet to see the last of.

In London, whither she fled her provincial Dublin life, they speak of her with admiration and a kind of tender pity as for one "beautiful and . . . (shrug) well, doomed, rather"—a hopeless Celt who finds tragedy everywhere, especially in all those places where the English find reason only to titter and be smug. A romantic among the impervious Nigels and Beryls. And yet, the spell O'Brien casts does have its uses. "I always take along an Edna O'Brien to read on trains," confided one Beryl, "because then I'll always be picked up by the right sort." Quite.

On her occasional sallies into New York, O'Brien leaves a sea of dazed admirers in her wake, all dazzled and bewitched by her unearthly beauty, her diabolical talent. Her reputation, both here and in London, almost threatens to overwhelm her work—to elevate her to that High Empyrean where, with a few other living figures like Graham Greene, she may exist beyond criticism or reproach.

But all these lies and half-truths cannot really disguise the permanent, universal value of her work. The fictional Irish village she returns to again and again is her village and your village. In " **'Oft in the Stilly Night,'** " the opening story of *Lantern Slides,* she tells us of a woman sacristan who goes mad:

> Now I ask you, what would you do? Would you comfort [her], would you tell her that her sins were of her own imagining? . . . Would you loiter with the drunkards and laugh with the women gorging the white bread; would you perhaps visit the grave to say an *Aye* where Angela . . . and the errant husband lie close together, morsels for the maggots, or would you drive on helter-skelter, the radio at full-blast? Perhaps your own village is much the same, perhaps everywhere is, perhaps pity is a luxury and deliverance a thing of the past."

In **"A Little Holiday"** in the same collection she gives us a 9-year-old Everychild whose first holiday adventure proves an immense disappointment. She had thought to escape the crabbedness of her own household by visiting a seaside aunt and uncle, whose domestic establishment proves to be even more bleak than her parents'. Hysterical and forlorn, she is returned home in disgrace.

> Part of me wanted to volunteer to go back with them, while another part admitted that that would be absurd. Either way, I knew that I had lost some part of my parents' love and God only

knows how long it would take to win it back—days, weeks maybe, of slaving and washing up and shining at school. But even then it could come up at any time, this failure of mine, an added incentive for an outburst, another blind grope in which my mother and father were trying to tell each other how unhappy they were.

She is a storyteller, an Irish storyteller, one of an ancient tradition of storytellers, people who tell the truth. In old Ireland, the words of a truthful poet were both sought and feared: They could kill. Her best work has the sound of something prehistoric—palpable, thrilling, incantatory—about it. It should be read aloud, like poetry. It is, indeed, not prose, at least not in any modern manner.

Her plots are devastating, not a happy one among them, though they are intensely full of sensuous joys. Her scenes are both archetypal and resolutely naturalistic—the claustrophobic, incestuous farmhouses of Ireland, the soiled beds of England, the desperate pleasures of a Mediterranean holiday.

She writes with the sureness and conviction of a priestess or prophet, one of a long procession of prophetic Irishwomen—from Briget and Ita in late antiquity, through Dark Eileen O'Connell (whose Sophoclean "Lament for Art O'Leary" is one of the world's great poems), to Lady Gregory and Mary Lavin and Maeve Brennan—surely the boldest tradition of women writers in all literature.

Edna O'Brien writes about love and death, the only two things that can ever matter to a great writer. She tells the truth.

And no one should expect to be thanked for telling the truth.

Thomas Cahill, "On Edna O'Brien's 'Lantern Slides'," in Los Angeles Times Book Review, *November 4, 1990, p. 11.*

Octavio Paz

Nobel Prize in Literature

A Mexican poet, essayist, critic, nonfiction writer, dramatist, editor, journalist, and translator, Paz was born in 1914.

Paz has earned international acclaim for poetry and essays in which he seeks to reconcile divisive and opposing forces in life. Paz's writings accommodate such antithetical elements as culture and nature, the meditative and the sensuous, and the linear and the circular nature of time, stressing that language and love can provide means for attaining unity and wholeness. His works reflect his knowledge of the history, myths, and landscape of Mexico as well as his interest in surrealism, existentialism, romanticism, Eastern thought, and diverse political ideologies. In his verse, Paz experiments with form and strives for clarity and directness as well as vitality and vivacity. He stated: "Wouldn't it be better to turn life into poetry rather than to make poetry from life? And cannot poetry have as its primary objective, rather than the creation of poems, the creation of poetic moments?" Paz's essays are praised for their lyrical prose, witty epigrams, and insightful explorations of art, literature, culture, language, and political philosophies. The first Mexican to receive the Nobel Prize in Literature, Paz was commended by the Swedish Academy "for impassioned writing with wide horizons, characterized by sensuous intelligence and humanistic integrity."

Paz began his literary career in his late teens by founding *Barrandal,* an avant-garde literary journal, and publishing his first volume of poems, *Luna silvestre.* From 1937 through the 1940s, Paz's extensive travels in Spain, France, and the United States exerted a profound influence on his political and literary views. In Spain, he became involved in antifascist activities, and in France he was exposed to the aesthetic and political tenets of existentialism and surrealism. While traveling in the United States, Paz became acquainted with the formal experiments of such modernist poets as William Carlos Williams and Wallace Stevens. He solidified his international reputation as a major literary figure during the 1950s with the publication of some of his most celebrated works, including *La laberinto de la soledad* (*The Labyrinth of Solitude*), a sociocultural analysis of Mexico, and *Piedra de sol* (*Sun Stone*), a long poem generally considered his finest achievement in verse. Paz became ambassador to India in 1962 and served in this position until 1968, when he resigned in protest following the massacre of student demonstrators in Mexico City by government forces. *Posdata* (*The Other Mexico: Critique of the Pyramid*) examines the political upheaval of that time and details the reasons for his resignation. Since relinquishing his ambassadorship,

Paz has taught at several American universities and continued his extensive travels.

In his early poetry, Paz experimented with such diverse forms as the sonnet and free verse, reflecting his desire to renew and clarify the Spanish language. He often employed the surrealist technique of developing a series of related or unrelated images to emphasize sudden moments of perception, a particular state of mind, or a fusion of such opposites as dream and reality, life and death. Topics of Paz's formative verse include political and social issues, the brutality of war, and love and sexuality. *¿Aguila o sol?* (*Eagle or Sun?*), one of his most important early volumes, is a sequence of visionary prose poems concerning the past, present, and future of Mexico. Paz's next major collection, *Sun Stone,* poetically records the psychological processes of an individual attempting to make sense of existence. Mirroring the Aztec calendar, *Sun Stone* is comprised of 584 eleven-syllable lines that form a circular sentence, blending myth, cosmology, social commentary, and personal and historical allusions.

The variety of forms and topics in Paz's later verse reflects his many interests. *Blanco,* widely considered his most complex work, consists of three columns of verse in a chapbook format that unfolds to become a single page; each column develops four main themes relating to language, nature, and the ways in which an individual makes sense and order of life. In *Ladera este, 1962-1968,* Paz employs simple diction within complicated syntactical structures in poems that investigate Eastern philosophy, religion, and art. In the long poem *Pasado en claro* (*A Draft of Shadows*), Paz examines selfhood and memory by focusing on poignant moments in his life in the manner of William Wordsworth's autobiographical poem *The Prelude. The Collected Poems of Octavio Paz, 1957-1987* presents Paz's poems from this time period, many appearing for the first time in English translation, including *Arbol adentro* (*A Tree Within*), his most recent collection, which was issued concurrently in a separate volume.

Paz's numerous essays on culture, art, politics, and language are collected in several volumes. *The Labyrinth of Solitude,* in which Paz explores Mexican history, mythology, and social behavior, is his most famous prose work. According to Paz, modern Mexico and its people suffer a collective identity crisis resulting from their mixed Indian and Spanish heritage, marginal association with Western cultural traditions, the influence of the United States, and a recurring cycle of war and isolation. While critics debated Paz's contention that this description also symbolizes the modern human condition, *The Labyrinth of Solitude* received widespread praise. Several of Paz's other nonfiction works concern linguistics, literary theory, or literary history, including *Corrente alterna* (*Alternating Current*), *El mono gramático* (first published in France as *Le singe grammairien; The Monkey Grammarian*), and *Los hijos del limo: Del romanticismo a la vanguardia* (*Children of the Mire: Modern Poetry from Romanticism to the Avant-Garde.*

(See also *CLC,* Vols. 3, 4, 6, 10, 19, 51, and *Contemporary Authors,* Vols. 73-76.)

PRINCIPAL WORKS

POETRY

Luna silvestre   1933
Raiz del hombre   1937
Entre la piedra y la flor   1941
¿Aguila o sol?   1951
   [*Eagle or Sun?*   1970]
Piedra de sol   1957
   [*Sun Stone*   1963]
Salamandra, 1958-1961   1962
Selected Poems   1963
Blanco   1967
La centana: Poemas, 1935-1968   1969
Ladera este, 1962-1968   1969
Early Poems, 1935-1955   1973
Pasado en claro   1975

[*A Draft of Shadows*   1979]
Selected Poems   1984
Arbol adentro   1987
   [*The Tree Within*   1987]
The Collected Poems of Octavio Paz, 1957-1987   1988

ESSAY COLLECTIONS

El laberinto de la soledad   1950
   [*The Labyrinth of Solitude*   1962]
El arco y la lira: El poema, la revelación poetica, poesia, e historia   1956
   [*The Bow and the Lyre: The Poem, the Poetic Revelation, Poetry, and History*   1973]
Corrente alterna   1967
   [*Alternating Current*   1973]
Conjunciones y disjunciones   1969
   [*Conjunctions and Disjunctions*   1973]
Posdata   1970
   [*The Other Mexico: Critique of the Pyramid*   1972]
El mono gramático   1974
   [*The Monkey Grammarian*   1981]
Los hijos del limo: Del romanticismo a la vanguardia   1974
   [*Children of the Mire: Modern Poetry from Romanticism to the Avant-Garde*   1974]
Tiempo nublado   1984
   [*One Earth, Four or Five Worlds: Reflections on Contemporary History*   1985]
On Poets and Others   1986
Convergences   1987

OVERVIEWS

John M. Fein

[Every] great writer we study is to some degree unattainable, no matter how clear or moving his literary creation may be. This incompleteness, which is perhaps more the reader's than the author's, is particularly applicable in the case of Octavio Paz, whose poetic goal is the expression of what he feels to be basically incommunicable. The reader, therefore, can only approach the author's work and accept with mystery, frustration, or pleasure the realization that his comprehension will be imperfect.

The undisputed intellectual leadership of Paz, not only in Mexico but throughout Spanish America, rests on a dichotomy of achievements. In the field of the essay, he is the author of twenty-five books on subjects whose diversity—esthetics, politics, Surrealist art, the Mexican character, cultural anthropology, and Eastern philosophy, to cite only a few—is dazzling. In twenty-one books of poetry spanning more than fifty years, his creativity has increased in vigor as he has explored the numerous possibilities opened to Hispanic poets from many different sources. His success in diversified fields is heightened by the ways in which his essays and his poetry are complementary: the core of his creativity is a concern for language in general and for the poetic process in particular.

Like most intellectuals, Paz is more the result of his rigorous inquiry and self-discipline than of an educational system. The family into which he was born in Mexico City in 1914 represented, in its combination of indigenous and Spanish heritage and of Catholicism and nonbelief, and in its impoverishment after the Revolution, the history of his country. As a child he led a rather solitary life in a crumbling mansion and attended a French religious school, having been tutored in that language by an aunt. He had access to his grandfather's library, which introduced him to Latin, Greek, and Spanish classics, nineteenth-century French authors, and writers in Spanish who were popular around the turn of the century.

At fourteen he showed the dedication to poetry and the autodidacticism that were to shape his life. Although his family persuaded him to attend the schools of Arts and Letters and Law at the university, he did not receive a degree. His enthusiasm for poetry turned to the Spanish generation of 1927; only later did he discover their predecessors of the post-modernist period. At nineteen, when he published his first book of poems, *Luna silvestre,* Paz was an active member of literary groups, a contributor to literary reviews, and the founder of two. He was in the center of a productive and eclectic activity that introduced the most innovative French, English, and Spanish writers to Mexico.

A key event in Paz's life was the invitation, at the suggestion of Pablo Neruda, to attend a congress of anti-fascist writers in Spain in 1937. At the height of the Civil War, he met not only the leading Spanish writers (Cernuda, Alberti, Altolaguirre, Antonio Machado), but also Spanish Americans (Neruda, Huidobro, Vallejo). An even more important result of the experience in Spain was the feeling of solidarity, which Paz was to call, in another context, "communion."

He continued to express that feeling in his work on behalf of Spanish Republicans, particularly those in exile in Mexico, and in his collaboration in *El popular,* a politically oriented newspaper sponsored by Mexican workers. In 1940 he broke with *El popular* and with Neruda as a result of the Russian-German pact. His literary prestige grew through his contributions to three literary journals (*Taller,* 1938; *Tierra nueva,* 1940; and *El hijo pródigo,* 1943) and his role in the introduction of Surrealism to Mexico.

With the support of a Guggenheim grant in 1944, Paz visited the United States, where he began the brilliant essay on Mexican character, *El laberinto de la soledad* (*The Labyrinth of Solitude*), that was to attract international attention when it was published in 1950. The first edition of his collected poetry, *Libertad bajo palabra,* appeared in 1949. His appointment to the diplomatic service took him to Paris, where he strengthened his knowledge of, and connection with, French writers, particularly Breton and the Surrealists. (pp. 1-3)

Paz's numerous books of essays offer ample evidence of his productivity as a thinker. Just as the meaning of history underlies his analyses of society, so does the significance of language connect his numerous essays on Hispanic and French poetry and art. Ranging from *El arco y la lira* (1956)—a brilliant interpretation of poetry as language, process, and social phenomenon—to his broad history of the evolution of modern poetry, *Los hijos del limo: Del romanticismo a la vanguardia* (1974) (*Children of the Mire: Modern Poetry from Romanticism to the Avant-Garde*), he views the distillation of language not as an adornment of mankind but as a key to its comprehension. His seminal study of the French artist, *Marcel Duchamp o el castillo de la pureza* (1968) (*Marcel Duchamp, or the Castle of Purity*), provides insights into contemporary hermetic expression, including his own work. The massive *Sor Juana Inés de la Cruz, o, Las trampas de la fe* (1982) is equally revolutionary in its scholarship on the remarkable philosopher, scientist, and authoress, and in its intellectual history of the Colonial period.

Paz's poetry and prose represent two aspects of a concern for the predicament of modern man, whom he is not unique in viewing as fragmented and mutilated. In fact, all of his work is unified by a utopian wish for the fulfillment of man's wholeness in individual creativity and in the building of society, offering an ennobling vision of man to an uneasy world. This vision underlies his attempts to reconcile opposites, especially those of passion and reason, linear and circular time, society and the individual, and word and meaning. (pp. 3-4)

There are two major characteristics of Paz's work that are particularly challenging to his critics. The first is his relationship to the Surrealists, among whom French poets figure more significantly than their Hispanic counterparts. It is obvious that Paz, who is trilingual in Spanish, English, and French, feels a great affinity with French culture and history of ideas. His veneration of André Breton, for example, clearly delineated in Jason Wilson's excellent book, suggests that his affiliation with Surrealism is part of the origin of his hermeticism. The difficulties for the critic are obvious: how can one define the theme of a poem that is so intensely personal that its ultimate definition rests within the text itself? How can one assume a common response from readers when the poem in fact invites multiple responses, each of which is justifiable and may conflict with, if not exclude, the alternate readings?

Another significant critical problem is posed by Paz's concept of poetry, which has developed over the period of many years and can be seen most clearly in his essays. These, as has often been observed, are the basis for comparing him to the late Alfonso Reyes, not only in their breadth and brilliance, but particularly in their contribution to critical theory and to an understanding of the role of poetry in society. Paz's first effort in this field, **"Poesía de comunión y poesía de soledad,"** is as meaningful today as when it first appeared in *El hijo pródigo* in 1943. Some of the ideas outlined there were the nucleus for the best developed and most readable volume on poetic theory that Latin America has produced, *El arco y la lira* (1956). The observation of Paz's evolution as a critic is in itself an educational process. Paz himself is the first to note rectifications and clarifications (see Rodríguez Monegal's article on the differences between the editions of *El arco y la lira*), but the concepts underlying his theories remain basically unchanged. Central to his critical thought are the desire to make poetry more meaningful to man and the conviction that poetry must go beyond the text to (and through) the individual's response. The essence of the poem, he believes, is unwritten, and therefore silent. It is analogous to the pauses in musical composition that express as much meaning as the sounds. If the poem ends in silence, the critic is reluctant to intrude with his own interpretation of meaning.

The constants of Paz's concept of poetry can be stated in a series of paradoxes. The poet writes only for himself but must communicate to an audience. The poem is a mystery whose creation can never be accurately described, yet man cannot receive it without thinking about the process that created it. Language is a defective but indispensable instrument for conveying what is incommunicable. Poetry is an ecstasy that both denies and transforms reality; although it cannot be grasped, it is essential to man's concept of himself and to the functioning of society.

Perhaps the most troublesome of Paz's paradoxes is his rejection of analysis as an aid to understanding contemporary poetry. Even his notes to *Ladera este,* limited to geographical and historical explanations, are regarded by Paz with reluctance and suspicion:

> Since in some passages there appear words and allusions to people, ideas, and things that might puzzle the reader who is not familiar with that part of the world, several friends advised me to include at the end of this volume a few notes to clear up those difficulties—and others not less superfluous. I accede to them with the fear (hope?) that these notes, far from dissipating the enigmas, will increase them.

It is significant that the notes are omitted in the collected poetry of *Poemas.* A more important distrust of critical interpretation appears in Paz's essay **"Hablar y decir,"** in which he supports Maistre's observation that thought and word are synonymous and Breton's similar belief that poetry is the perfect equivalence between sound and meaning, rendering any further statement superfluous. It is, Paz maintains, meaningless to ask what a poem means: "Poems cannot be explained or interpreted; in them the sign stops signifying: it is." The clearest summary of Paz's anticritical stance is the conclusion of his introduction to *Poesía en movimiento:* "The meaning of poetry, if it has any, is neither in the judgments of the critic nor in the opinions of the poet. The meaning is changing and momentary: it comes from the encounter between the poem and the reader."

The diminishment, if not the elimination, of criticism's role in understanding poetry results in increased responsibilities for the reader. In the same way that contemporary drama experiments with the location of the stage and with the distinction between actors and audience to abolish the latter's passivity, so does Paz seek to enable the reader not only to respond to the poem, but to assist in its creation. His objective is to reduce the differences between poet and reader, so that the two can work together in a common purpose. He is aware, of course, of the paradoxical nature of his mission: just as to reach ultimate expression he must abolish words, so must the reader and poet communicate by transcending the poem. As early as 1938, Paz referred to "the reader of poetry who is more and more a true reconstructor of it." In recent years he has developed this concept to its logical conclusion, transforming the reader into a poet by confronting him with demanding literature: "According to this view of reader participation, the interpretive act becomes synonymous with the creative process itself."

In her very perceptive essay, Ruth Needleman traces the origin of Paz's concept of the reader to the fundamental change in his view of language that took place between the two editions of *El arco y la lira* in 1956 and 1967. In the first he denied the possibility of separating language from its human context. In the second he notes the loss of that context and the substitution of a multiplicity of meanings: "Coherence, as a result, has ceded its place to fragmentation, so that the meaning, no longer immanent, resides in the very search for meaning." The poem, consequently, becomes variable according to the experience and the capacity of the reader: "The meanings are inherent in the poem, and the reader realizes them by rendering them conscious." Whether the average person can measure up to this responsibility is a serious question that Needleman answers indirectly.

Paz's poetry is consistent with his theories in the multiple possibilities it presents for interpretation. The reader who is not acquainted with those theories may feel that the poems are inconclusive, or even unconcluded, presented as sketches or notes. If he persists, however, he will understand that the poet invites him to feel his own version of the poem. Brotherston's statement in *Latin American Poetry* that Paz is "a poet of movement, defined by successive moments" succinctly classifies not the end of the reader's response but the beginning. Paz's description of Duchamp's work as the bridge between the polarities of the absence of meaning and the necessity of meaning is helpful in comprehending his own intentions. Perhaps more clearly than any other critic, Gabriel Zaid has urged us to have new objectives:

> When one examines it carefully, the work of Octavio Paz does not yield ultimate meanings. It is not a work derived from ultimate demands, but originating at the source of the ultimate demands. The final meaning of Paz's work is not a meaning but a living act: to move itself and to move us to the place of the final meanings.

In addition to the constants noted by critics (the desire for transcendence, the symbolism of the paradox, the quest for origins, and the polarities of solitude and communion), there is one less documented constant: Paz's attempts to shape through his poetry a more sensitive, independent, and enlightened reader. This is an additional goal for a poet who assigns a high priority to forging a new—or at least clearer—medium of communication. One feels that in Paz the order of urgency is, if not reversed, simultaneous. He would not be satisfied to write a different kind of poetry unless he had the hope that it would create a reader with a different set of expectations. (pp. 5-10)

John M. Fein, in his Toward Octavio Paz: A Reading of His Major Poems, 1957-1976, *The University Press of Kentucky, 1986, 189 p.*

Frances Chiles

> The charm of myths does not lie in their religious nature—these beliefs are not ours—but from the fact that in them poetic storytelling transfigures the world and reality.

Octavio Paz, *Children of the Mire*

Myth occupies a central place in the art of Octavio Paz, both in his theory of the meaning and function of poetry in the modern world and in the use of mythological themes and symbolism as a medium of poetic expression. Along with some of the greatest poets and thinkers in the modern Western literary tradition, Paz believes that the old myths gave a cohesion and meaning, lacking in our modern world, to the existence of ancient man. He proposes, therefore, that poetry, functioning as myth, affords to modern man a greater understanding of the human condition, as well as a means of transcending it in the here-and-now without outwardly altering his actual historical situation. Like myth, poetry is a unique verbal expression of a reality which, paradoxically, includes yet transcends man's historical experience. As in the actualization of the myth in ritual, so in the creation and re-creation of the poem man momentarily experiences the fullness of being: the simultaneous unification of himself with his fellow man, with woman, his complementary opposite, and with the natural world.

A thorough study of Paz's complete works to date reveals that his conception of myth and its parallels to poetry is derived from eclectic sources, including the vast knowledge of anthropologists, philosophers, psychologists, historians of religion, literary critics, and other writers who have sought to establish a theory of the "true meaning" of myth. While their definitions and theories reflect their diverse interests and disciplines, there is a consensus that far from being merely an account of the fantasy world of primitive man, myth is a repository of universal humanist values and a cultural history of mankind, fulfilling a function that is simultaenously transcendental and pragmatical. It reconciles man with a sacred timeless reality beyond the limits of "profane" time and space in which, Mircea Eliade maintains, "No true orientation is now possible, for the fixed point no longer enjoys a unique ontological status: it appears and disappears in accordance with the needs of the day."

Through myth, too, the world becomes more intelligible to man in that it explains and justifies the universal order of things and man's place, in particular, within that order. According to Joseph Campbell, whose "unitary mythological science" is based on a correlation of world mythology with the vast data of natural history, religion, archaelogy, art, and psychology, there are four essential functions of myth in the history of mankind, from the primitive beginnings to modern times. The first of these is numinous in that it reconciles the "waking consciousness of the *mysterium tremendum et fascinans* of this universe as it

is," the second is to render a cosmology or "an interpretive total image of the same;" the third function serves to establish, support and enforce a moral order: "the shaping of the individual to the requirements of his geographically and historically conditioned social group;" and the fourth function, the most vital of all, is to "foster the centering and unfolding of the individual in integrity, in accord with d) himself (the microcosm), c) his culture (the mesocosm), b) the universe (the macrocosm), and a) that awesome ultimate mystery which is both beyond and within himself and all things."

Paz shares the views held by some scholars of myth and by many of his literary predecessors and contemporaries as well that modern poetry has grown out of myth and has perpetuated it, and that it is the modern poet's task as myth-user and myth-maker to transform the ancient myths into the new myths of poetry. His program for poetry as the new myth of mankind is inseparable from his view that the modern human condition is a constant and all-encompassing feeling of alienation and isolation, consubstantial with existence itself:

> When we are born we break the ties that joined us to the blind life we lived in the maternal womb, where there is no gap between desire and satisfaction. We sense a strange or hostile atmosphere. Later this primitive sense of loss becomes a feeling of solitude, and still later it becomes awareness: we are condemned to live alone, but also to transcend our solitude, to re-establish the bonds that united us with life in a paradisiac past.

For man's acute consciousness of his alienated state is always accompanied by an equally intense awareness of "la otredad constitutiva," the constitutive otherness of his being—that is to say, the awareness of being himself and at the same time being someone or something "other" than the conscious self; of being existent in profane time and space, but always longing to make the Kierkegaardian "spiritual leap" beyond the phenomenal world to "la otra orilla," the other shore of reality.

Traditionally, access to the other shore or the return to a previous Edenic existence has been through religion; but during the past century the progressive erosion of religious belief, Paz remarks, "has made a desert of the soul of Western man;" moreover, it has left the modern world bereft of the spiritual and psychological catharsis of ritual or "fiesta:" "In ritual, man communes with all ages, time is dissolved in a magic present—a present that is repeated because it is inscribed in the sacred calendar."

The religious dimension having been forfeited, in consequence the world has become secularized and fragmented. It is Paz's opinion that modern technology has destroyed the ancient cosmological order and has made it virtually impossible for us to return to the myths and rites that imitated and sustained that order. At the same time, it has failed to provide us with a new world image in which, as in antiquity, "man would contemplate the world and the trans-world as a totality." Technology has placed barriers between us and our natural surroundings and has made us subordinate to, if not victim of, the mechanical objects of our own creation.

Throughout the history of mankind, as Paz shows in *El laberinto de la soledad* (*The Labyrinth of Solitude*), it has been necessary to revitalize and reconstitute a society facing decline by creating a new religion, a new utopia, or a new myth. Although our universe has become "desacralized" and we exist in alienation, there are other modes of universal communion which can fill the spiritual void left by the failure of organized religion and unfulfilled prophecies of various political systems of a secular golden age. Paz argues that even in the midst of quotidian life we may recover our primordial "otherness," at least momentarily, in existential encounter, love—particularly erotic love—, and certain other spiritual experiences which he calls for lack of a more precise phrase, "poetic experiences." And while all of these experiences are individual and personal, they may be relived collectively through the medium of the poem:

> Each time the reader truly relives the poem, he reaches a state that we can call poetic. The experience can take this form or that, but it is always a going beyond oneself, a breaking of the temporal walls, to be another. Like poetic creation, the experience of the poem is produced in history, is history, and, at the same time, denies history.

The common ground of ancient myth and poetry which is evident in their spiritual function also extends to their common modes of expression and the similar manner in which they are created. Frederick Clarke Prescott, one of the earlier myth critics, has said that myth is the mass from which modern poetry has slowly evolved; and the mythmaker's mind is "the prototype of the poet's mind which is still essentially mythopoeic." Like the so-called "primitive" myth-maker, the poet tends to envision the universe as "the great society of life," a phrase that Paz borrowed from Ernst Cassirer, which the latter describes further as a "fundamental and indelible *solidarity of life* that bridges over the multiplicity and variety of its single forms." For Paz as for Cassirer, both the poet and the mythmaker create poems and myths by giving concrete names to things and by universal analogy: by observing the similarities between different forms of life and by establishing metaphorical correspondences between subject and object, man and nature. Both utilize the common language which, in the act of poetizing or mythmaking, is transformed into another timeless mode of expression that eclipses all linguistical, historical, and cultural barriers.

In his study on the structural components of myth, Claude Levi-Strauss shows that it is precisely the universal and timeless nature of myth that identifies a myth as such. A myth is created by a particular society at a specific time and place, but, he maintains, "Whatever our ignorance of the language and the culture where it originated, a myth is still felt as a myth anywhere in the world." The gross constituent units of the language of myth, known as "my-themes," phrases or combinations of words whose arrangement within the context of the narrative establishes "bundles of relations," produce the myth's unique double structure that is simultaneously historical and ahistorical, diachronic and synchronic. The combination of these two

dimensions of language produces a third timeless dimension which, though it remains linguistic, is different from the other two in that it functions at a level "where meaning succeeds practically at "taking off " from the linguistic ground on which it keeps on rolling." In telling, listening to or ritually re-enacting the myth, the third timeless dimension is actualized and the participants "enter into a kind of immortality."

Using Levi-Strauss's theory on the structural composition of myth as an analogue, Paz further establishes the similarities between myth and poetry and, in the process, refutes the noted anthropologist's notion that, because of its timeless dimension and untranslatable language, myth is more analogous to music than to poetry. Paz maintains that music, like all of the arts, can be considered a language in the sense that it is a form of communication; but it is not verbal. "In order to transcend something it is necessary to pass through that something and go beyond it: music does not transcend the articulated language because it doesn't pass through it." On the other hand, the poem, like the myth, is a singular verbal form capable of expressing the inexpressible and is inexplicable except in itself:

> Touched by poetry, language is more completely language and, simultaneously, it ceases to be language: it is a poem. An object made up of words, the poem opens into a region that is inaccessible to words.

The constituent unit of the poem, the equivalent of the mytheme, is the poetic phrase composed of rhythms and images; and the combination and interrelationship of these structural components give the poem the same unique coherence and meaning characteristic of the myth.

Rhythm in poetry distinguishes it from all other literary forms and also reinforces its connection with myth. It is clear that to Paz poetic rhythm is not limited to prosody, but includes something else close to magic:

> Rhythm engenders in us a state of mind that will only be calmed when "something" happens. It puts us in an attitude of waiting. We feel that the rhythm is a moving toward something, even though we may not know what that something is.

Rhythm is something that is already being expressed wordlessly and at the same time a conjuration or summoning of the words to verbalize it.

Poetic rhythm also reflects a particular image of the world; it is an imitation of the cyclical movements of the planets and the seasons; and the poet, creating by analogy, attempts to bring his own rhythms into harmony with those of the universe. In a sense, then, rhythm is to the poem what ritual is to the myth: it is invocation and convocation; a repetition of the original, archetypal time:

> Poems and myths coincide in transmuting time into a special temporal category, a past that is always a future and always capable of being present, of *presenting* itself.

The image, the other constituent of the poetic phrase, is in essence articulated rhythm, the utterance of something that is otherwise unutterable. In Paz, the poetic image—whether classified as metaphor, symbol, simile, allegory, or any other figure of speech—responds to a dialectic uniquely its own. Unlike the signs and abstractions of discursive language, the poetic image is dynamic rather than static or fixed; it expresses a plurality of meanings and affirms simultaneously the concrete, individual identity of things: "The poet names things: these are feathers, those are stones. And suddenly he affirms: stones are feathers, this is that." The image is an instantaneous reconciliation of opposites, the bridge between the name and the object and between the poet and all that surrounds him. By virtue of the word, "The universe ceases to be a vast storehouse of heterogeneous things" and becomes instead "an immense family" in constant communication and transformation.

As evidenced in *Los hijos del limo* (*Children of the Mire*), Paz's admirable essay on the modern poetic tradition, the genesis of his mythopoeic conception of poetry and of its function in contemporary society goes back to Romantic literature. His first long poems published in the 1930's and his seminal essay on poetics, **"Poesía de soledad y poesía de comunión"** (**"Poetry of Solitude and Poetry of Communion"**), published in 1942, reveal that his affinity for the Romantic writers emerged very early in his career. More recently, the poet himself has confirmed that much of what he has written has been a deliberate attempt to insert himself into the mainstream of the Western literary tradition which began with certain German and English Romantic poets.

As M. H. Abrams has shown in *Natural Supernaturalism,* the Romantics represented themselves as poet-prophets and seers and assimilated what was valid in their Classical and Judeo-Christian cultural inheritance into new secular modes of thought and personal mythological systems. While each writer had his own distinctive voice and preoccupations, Abrams observes, collectively they concerned themselves with solving the problems of their time:

> When, therefore, they assumed the visionary persona, they spoke as members of what Wordsworth called the "One great society . . . / The noble Living and the noble Dead," whose mission was to assure the continuance of civilization by reinterpreting to their drastically altered condition enduring humane values, making whatever changes were required in the theological systems by which these values had earlier been sanctioned.

The Symbolist and Surrealist movements, which inherited and perpetuated the world view and many of the literary tendencies initiated by the Romantic authors, also contributed to Paz's poetic formation, as did the rich and extensive Hispanic literary tradition. And in Mexico Paz and his generation of writers were the immediate beneficiaries of the legacy of "Los Contemporáneos" (The Contemporaries), a group of eminent Mexican authors, including Alfonso Reyes, José Gorostiza, Xavier Villaurrutia, and Carlos Pellicer, among others, that published a literary journal of the same name between 1928-1931. It was primarily through the translation and publication of the works of the Romantics and of contemporary authors

such as T. S. Eliot, D. H. Lawrence, St. John Perse, and Andre Breton in *Contemporáneos* that Paz was exposed at an early age to some of the greatest works of the modern literary tradition, which have had an enduring influence on his poetry and thought. Paz considers not only his own works but also those of all Latin American poets both a prolongation and a transgression against this tradition which, he remarked to an interviewer some years ago, "despised" the Latin American writer until recently; and it is for this reason that the latter affirms "with the same desperation and exasperation—his Latin American origins and his part in world tradition." (pp. 11-18)

Paz has long been recognized as one of a number of outstanding contemporary writers who have dominated Hispanic letters and who, at the same time, have made a significant impact on contemporary literature internationally. This is attested by the numerous literary awards that Paz has received, and by the fact that his works have been widely translated—not only into English and the modern European languages, but also into languages as diverse as Japanese and Serbo-Croatian. (p. 20)

Frances Chiles, in her Octavio Paz: The Mythic Dimension, *Peter Lang, 1987, 224 p.*

An excerpt from "Waking"

        I looked through the window:
not a soul under the streetlamp;
snow already dirty, dark houses,
telephone poles, cars asleep, and the brave
cluster of oaks, tall skeletons.

The night, white and black; the drawn
figures of the constellations, illegible;
the wind and its blades. I looked
without understanding—looked with my eyes
in the empty street, the presence.
The presence without body.
Being in its fullness, is quiet.

I looked inside. The room was my room
and I wasn't in it. Even without us,
being lacks nothing. Outside,
still hesitant, clarities:
dawn among the confusion of rooftops.
Already the constellations were being erased.

—translated by Mark Strand

Eliot Weinberger

The figure in the landscape

As an adolescent, Octavio Paz discovers French modernism in *Anabasis*. A 1945 memorial essay on Tablada, emphasizing both the haiku and Mexican motifs, hopes to rescue the poet from oblivion—though the poems will remain out of print for nearly thirty years. In 1952, his first visit to Japan; the poem **"Is there no way out?"** [¿**No hay salida?**] is written there. In 1955 the Mexican haiku of *Loose Stones* [Piedras sueltas] and the first Western translation of Bashō's poetry and prose travel journal, *Sendas de Oku* [in Cid Corman's translation, *Back Roads to Far Towns*] written with Eikichi Hayashiya. Erotic haiku in *Salamander (Salamandra).* Throughout the 1960s and 1970s, translations of Chinese and Japanese poets. *East Slope (Ladera este),* arguably his best book of poetry, takes its title from the Sung dynasty poet Su Shih, who wrote under the name Su Tung-p'o (East Slope). The pages on Taoism and Chinese eroticism in *Conjunctions and Disjunctions (Conjunciones y disyunciones)*. That same year, Paz collaborates with Charles Tomlinson, Eduardo Sanguineti and Jacques Roubaud on the quadrilingual *Renga.* In 1970, a major essay, "The Tradition of the Haiku" in the second edition of the Bashō book (reprinted in English in *Convergences*). In the 1970s and 1980s, short essays on Tu Fu, Wang Wei, Han Yu and other Chinese poets. In 1976, the Japanese translation of *The Labyrinth of Solitude,* the first of many Paz books to be translated into that language. In 1979, *Hijos del aire / Airborn,* a variation on renga written with Tomlinson. In 1984, a visit to Japan and pilgrimage to Bashō's hut. In 1989, Duo Duo, the young Chinese poet most avidly read by the students demonstrating in Tiananmen Square, remarks that his favorite poet is Octavio Paz.

> *The god that emerges from an orchid of clay*
> Born smiling
> From ceramic petals:
> A human flower.

Like the invention of *mole* in a convent in Puebla: the adaptation of Eastern techniques, employing indigenous Mexican materials, in an essentially Western context. The poem, from *Loose Stones,* is of course written in Spanish, and not Nahuatl or Japanese; its form is a loose haiku; its subject the tiny Jaina god—a god, by the way, identical to the *apsaras* emerging from lotuses in the exactly contemporaneous T'ang art. A tropicalization of the haiku not invented by Paz—in the 1930s the Guatemalan Flavio Herrera was writing haiku like: "Happy / to be Indian, it smiles: / an ear of corn."—but perfected by him.

What Paz, as so many others, found in the haiku was verbal concision, a precision based on close observation of the world, particularly the natural world, and the sense that a poem remains permanently at the verge of completion, never arriving, as Western art once attempted, at a finished totality. The reader always supplies the rest of a haiku, and it changes with each reading. The haiku is a tiny graph of relations within the natural world—a world that includes its human observers—but these relations, according to Buddhism, are as illusory as the interacting beings. For both poet and reader it is a sudden act of the discovery and affirmation of a comradeship in illusion.

1955 as a turning-point in a work that keeps turning: In 1952, his one poem written in Japan, **"Is there no way out?"** begins, in Denise Levertov's translation, "Dozing I hear an incessant river running between dimly discerned, looming forms, drowsy and frowning." The language, as in the other poems of this period, is lush, vague, rhetorical, Surrealist, unchained, interior. (Japan, of course, is notable for its absence of any major river.) After 1955 and his actual working with haiku—*Loose Stones* and the Bashō

translation—Paz is able to bring the period to a close by joining the luxuriant rhetoric to a precise imagery that is far more concrete than anything previous in his or any one else's Surrealism: the incantatory **Sun Stone** (*Piedra de sol,* 1957):

> a crystal willow, a poplar of water,
> a tall fountain the wind arches over . . .

And from there, the almost inevitable move is toward an adaptation of Pound's "ideogrammic method": the stepped lines, the free-floating images forming configurations of meaning, the simultaneity of **Days and Occasions** (*Días hábiles,* 1961):

> Night in the bones
>   skeleton night
> the headlights touch your secret plazas
> the sanctuary of the body
>   the ark of the spirit
> the lips of the wound
> the wooded cleft of the oracles

Four poets in four languages meet for five days to write a series of collective poems. *Renga* (1969), the experiment, is an ideogram composed of many of Paz's essential elements: The belief, from Lautréamont, that in the future poetry will be composed by the multitude, not the individual. The disappearance of the author, as it comes out of the Surrealist practices of automatic writing and the painters' "exquisite corpse," and, more recently at the time, French structuralism. Buddhism's sublimation of the ego as the first step toward the recognition of *sunyata,* emptiness. Hindu and Buddhist emphasis on relation rather than substance. The pluralism and multilingualism of the 20th century. Translation as the creation of a third language somewhere between the "source" and the "target"; and equally, as the creation of a third poet. A collaborative, quadrilingual poem as the expression of an era, rather than an author. The Western adaptation of a traditional Eastern form, applying some of its methods, but few of its rules.

And yet *Renga,* the book, remains a disappointment: the poems lack even the vivacity of the linked haiku collaboratively written by the Beats ten years before. Perhaps the problem is that *Renga* is not renga.

Renga is a chain: a three line haiku by one poet, then two additional lines by the next to form a five-line tanka, then three more lines, added to the two above to form another tanka. Two discrete tanka out of eight lines: the end of one is the beginning of another. And so on forever, or until other more elaborate rules—refined over the centuries—declare the chain is over.

Renga is an endless series of permutations, changing over time. But *Renga* is a group of 28 sonnets in four groups of seven; each author contributing a quatrain or tercet, and the entirety of one of the final sonnets. Unlike renga, the form is closed: the effect is that of four painters, each painting a quarter of 24 canvases (but, unlike the "exquisite corpse," aware of what the others are doing). Canvases that are painted simultaneously, four at a time: the process is visible, but the product is dominant.

Nor do the authors vanish: each is made visible by his language, though there is some leakage from one language to the other, and each is the sole author of one of the sonnets. (Sanguineti's sonnet, however, is silence.) And, stuck in a basement in a Paris hotel, instead of outside where renga is usually composed, the poems are filled with the interior bric-a-brac of four erudites observing, not the moon or the plum blossoms, but each other, writing.

A modern renga would be more like a multi-authored *Cantos:* its end could not be predicted from its beginning; it would often proceed by association; it would be a babble of unidentified voices (its authors, if multilingual, writing in each other's languages); its pace would be that of time-lapse cinematography, a single cell swiftly multiplying into hundreds of organisms; it would be abandoned rather than finished; it would be an emblem of restless change.

Since the mid 1950s Paz has continued to practice haiku and to learn, from Chinese poetry, to record the instantaneous moment in the natural world. Yet he has never indulged in Orientalism. One of his most "Chinese" poems, **"Concord"** (dedicated to Carlos Fuentes):

> Water above
> Grove below
> Wind on the roads
>
> Quiet well
> Bucket's black   Spring water
>
> Water coming down to the trees
> Sky rising to the lips

takes its first two lines from the *I Ching* (the 28th hexagram, Ta Kuo: "The lake rises above the trees: The image of 'Preponderance of the Great.' Thus the superior man, when he stands alone, is unconcerned, and if he has to renounce the world, he is undaunted.") The poem's middle lines are an observed Indian landscape; its last line one of the most beautiful Surrealist images. And somewhere behind it all, as nearly always in Paz, a tiny piece of Mexico is transformed; in this case, a 1912 poem by Alfonso Reyes, "Cluster of Sky":

> Rage above:
> Calm below.
> Weather vanes rattle,
> the blinds weep.
>
> The celestial cattle slowly rise
> from the diaphanous courted sheep.

Idle speculations:

Had Paz not discovered the disappearance of the author in automatic writing and renga, would he not have found it in the Nahuatl tradition, which does not distinguish between poet and poem, where a poet can declare: "God has sent me as a messenger. / I am transformed into a poem."? And had Pound not invented the "ideogrammic method," would not Paz have evolved a similar theory, based on the Maya glyph?

The glyphs, after all, like Chinese characters, are conglomerates of component parts: simple pictographs (a jaguar for "jaguar"), phonetic signs (each representing a single syllable), logographs (non-representational representa-

tions of a word), and semantic determinatives (specifiers of particular meaning).

For those who cannot read them—and this was articulated most notably by Charles Olson in the Yucatan in the 1950s—the glyphs have a concreteness, a weight, that does not exist in alphabetic writing: the word is an object. And more: it appears, to the outsider, that each glyph, each word, has the *same* weight. The glyph-covered stela becomes the ideal, irreducible, poem.

For those who can read them—as has become increasingly possible—the glyphs become even more like poetry, for each word could be represented in pictographic, geometric or syllabic form (which corresponds to Pound's *phanopeia, logopeia,* and *melopeia*). There are seemingly unlimited ways to represent any given word, and the continual invention of glyphs was a dazzling display of association, homophony, and punning. Laid out in a grid, these metamorphosing word-clusters could be read in a variety of ways, both horizontally and vertically. The Maya "text," as far as we now know, was a net of continually changing correspondences, and reading an intricate game for skilled players.

There is a line from Palenque to *Blanco* that does not pass through Mallarmé.

The figure is the landscape

As an adolescent, Octavio Paz discovers Anglo-American modernism in *The Waste Land*. First visit to India in 1952; the poem **"Mutra"** is written there. From 1962 to 1968, Ambassador to India. Meets and marries Marie-José Tramini. The poems of *East Slope,* including *Blanco.* The essays on Buddhist logic, Hinduism, caste, published in *Alternating Current* (*Corriente alterna,* 1967). In 1969, his major meditation on East and West, *Conjunctions and Disjunctions.* In 1970, Paz organizes the first exhibition of Tantric art in the West, at the Galerie Le Point Cardinal in Paris; the catalog contains the important essay, **"Blank Thought"** ("El pensamiento en blanco"). The same year he writes his "unraveling novel" of a pilgrimage to Galta in Rajasthan, *The Monkey Grammarian* (*El mono gramático*). In the 1970s and 1980s, although there are no major poems or essays dealing specifically with India, references, particularly to Buddhism and Tantrism, are made throughout. In 1985 Paz revisits India.

The god Vishnu appears at the cave of an ascetic, Narada, who has been practicing austerities for decades. Narada asks the god to teach him about the power of *maya,* illusion. The god beckons Narada to follow him. They find themselves in the middle of a burning desert. Vishnu tells Narada he is thirsty, and asks him to fetch some water from a village he will find on the other side of the hill. Narada runs to the village and knocks at the first door, which is opened by a beautiful young woman. He stares at her and forgets why he has come. He enters the house; her parents treat him with respect; and the following year they are married. He lives in the joys of marriage and the hardships of village life. Twelve years go by: they have three children; his father-in-law has died and Narada has inherited the farm. That year, a particularly fierce monsoon brings floods; the cattle are drowned, their house collapses. Carrying his children, they struggle through the water. The smallest child slips away. He puts the two children down to search for her; it is too late. As he returns he sees the other two children swept off; his wife, swimming after them, is pulled under. A branch strikes Narada on the head; he is knocked unconscious and carried along. When he awakes he finds himself on a rock, sobbing. Suddenly he hears a voice: "My child! Where's that water you were bringing me? I've been waiting nearly half an hour." Narada opens his eyes and finds himself alone with Vishnu on the burning desert plain.

Is this not the "plot" of the first two sections of *East Slope?* The book opens with the lines "Stillness / in the middle of the night"—the poet is alone on a balcony overlooking Old Delhi—and then it immediately fills, overflows, with Indian stuff: monuments, landscapes, a jungle of specific flora and fauna, painters, musicians, gardens, gods, palaces, tombs, philosophy, temples, history, bits of Indian English, a large cast of strange and funny characters—the only characters in Paz's poetry—and, central to it all, the lover / wife. In the end, in **"A Tale of Two Gardens" ("Cuento de dos jardines"),** it all vanishes: "The garden sinks. / Now it is a name with no substance. / / The signs are erased: / I watch clarity." The poet is not in the desert, but in the middle of the equally empty ocean on a boat leaving India. (Although—this being poetry and not philosophy—his wife, rather than Vishnu, is with him.)

Maya is made manifest by time. The Indian cosmos is a map of ever-widening concentric cycles of enormous time: millions of human years with their perpetual reincarnations are merely one day and night in the millions of years in the life of Brahma, who is himself but one incarnation in an endless succession of Brahmas. The function of yoga and other meditation practices is to break out of these cycles of illusory births and rebirths, off the map (out of the calendar) and into the undifferentiated bliss of *nirvana* (which the Buddhists would later say was equally illusory).

Myth is a similar rupture of time. Its time is intemporal time, and though its narration unfolds in measured minutes and hours it abolishes time with its narration. Narrator and auditor are projected into a sacred space from which they view historical time and all its products: a world to which they must return, but to which they return educated.

The poem too, though heard in a time that has its own precise measurements (prosody), erases time by projecting us into a world where everything looks the same but is more vivid, where we speak the language but it doesn't sound like the language we speak, where ideas and emotions become concrete particulars, and the concrete is a manifestation of the divine.

The first two sections ("East Slope" and "Toward the Beginning") of *East Slope* are "travel poetry": a poetry of verifiable landscapes, things and people which are foreign to the author. But they are among the few instances in the last two hundred years of a travel poetry worth reading. (Poets, since the birth of Romanticism, have tended to

write their travels in prose and letters.) One reason is its precision of observation, its glittering language, intellectual cadenzas, emotional and erotic rhapsodies. But more: on nearly every page are synonyms of silence and stillness. The poems are simultaneously located in India and in a not-India, a somewhere else.

As Aztec shamans would travel out of the earth to a place where all time was visible in a state of total immobility. There they could observe the life-force of the *tonalli* at any given moment before it occurred in human life. The shaman's task was to alter the tonalli, to effectively rewrite the future.

As the first two sections of *East Slope* observe the world from a world where the wind comes simultaneously from everywhere, where "the present is perpetual" and bodies "weigh no more than the dawn."

Paz, above all, is a religious poet whose religion is poetry. This does not mean that the poet is a "little God," as Huidobro dreamed, with extraordinary powers. Rather it is the poem that opens a hair-line crack in time through which the poet, in astonishment, slips through.

The final third of *East Slope*—the long poem **"Blanco"**—is both the most "Indian" poem in the book, and the one with the fewest images of India. (In fact, only three words in the poem pertain specifically to India: the *neem* tree and the musical instruments *sitar* and *tabla*. Only three more refer to phenomena that exist in India and other places, but are not universal: *crow, jasmine, vulture.*)

The form of the poem, originally published on a single vertical folded sheet in black and red type—"black and red ink" in Nahuatl means "wisdom"—is usually described as a hybrid descended from Mallarmé's *Un Coup de Dés . . .* and Indo-Tibetan mandalas. Neither is accurate. Mallarmé's poem, though it plays with varying typefaces and blank space, still uses a traditional (though oversize) page as its playing-field: it exists to end up in a book. It is more likely that the Western grandparent of *Blanco* is the original 1913 edition, designed by Sonia Delaunay, of Cendrar's "Prose of the Transsiberian." It too is a floor-to-ceiling vertical sheet with different typefaces in black and red, but unlike **"Blanco"** the words are not surrounded by emptiness: every inch is covered with Delaunay's hallucinogenic color, itself a kind of Indian festival.

On the Eastern side, the poem is not really a mandala, although it has been described by Paz as such: mandalas are complex configurations of circles within squares, filled with iconic images of the gods. **"Blanco"** of course has no gods, other than poetry, and its representational imagery tends to be abstract. The poem, rather, is more like the yogic and tantric vertical scrolls depicting the ascent of the *kundalini* (the "serpent power" of latent energy). Such scrolls represent the human body, though an outline of the body itself is rarely shown. From bottom to top are images of the seven *chakras,* the energy centers that run from the base of the spine to the top of the head, and through which the kundalini ascends during yogic meditation or tantric practice. Each of the chakras has a host of attributes: elements, colors, senses, planets, emotions, philosophical concepts, and so on.

"Blanco," which must necessarily be read down the page (it not being written in Maya) can be seen, loosely, as an upside-down diagram of the chakras. Its first two vertical sections (before it splits into left and right) correspond to the first chakra at the base of the spine, Muladhara, which means "the foundation" (the first two lines of the poem are: "el comienzo / el cimiento" or "the beginning / the foundation") and which is associated with the *bija,* the syllable-seed (the next two lines are: "la simiente / latente" or "the seed / latent") from which all sound, all language, and everything in the cosmos is born. Other attributes of the Muladhara chakra are the earth ("escalera de escapulario"—an earth-body pun meaning both "mine shaft / scapulary ladder") and the color yellow (which appears in "Blanco" as the "yellow chalice of consonants and vowels").

From there the kundalini rises as the poem descends through the other chakras—though not strictly: most of the attributes of the chakras are present in "Blanco," though not quite in the same order. It never reaches the final, seventh chakra, the illumination of the void: to do so, in a poem, would be less presumptuous than impossible: at that point poetry ceases to be written. But it does, following this schema, reach the sixth, called Ajna ("power"). That is the point between the eyebrows (the last word of the poem is *mirada,* "gaze"), where all the elements return in purified form (as they do in the poem), and whose "color" is transparency ("transparency is all that remains"). Its reigning god is Ardhanarishvara, who is the half-male, half-female incarnation of Shiva, the union of all opposites ("No and yes" and the many other pairs which unite in this section of the poem). And it is associated with *nada,* cosmic sound, which becomes a complex Spanish-Sanskrit pun in "Blanco": "son palabras / aire son nada" (with "son" meaning both "sound" and "they are"; "nada" both "nothing" and "cosmic sound"): "sound (they are) words / air sound (they are) nothing (cosmic sound)." The seed-syllables, though made of air, form words, form the cosmic sound, form the universe. The three are inextricable, and equally illusory: Sanskrit *nada* is Spanish *nada.* (There is a form of meditation, rather like "Blanco," called *nada-yoga,* which consists of focusing on a succession of sounds as they emerge from and retreat into silence.)

Further, in this map of the Hindu body and of "Blanco," there are three "nerves" or "veins" which convey sacred breath and the body's subtle energies. The left, *lalana,* is feminine and associated with the moon, wisdom, emptiness, nature, the Ganges river, vowels. The right, *rasana,* is masculine and associated with the sun, intellect, compassion, method, the Yamuna (the other great river in India), consonants. In the center is *avadhuti,* the union of the two veins and all their attributes. Again, a schema followed loosely in the poem through its left, right and center columns.

The map of the body is a map of the earth is a map of the cosmos (or time) is a map of language. Most of Paz's work is, and has always been, concerned with the tangle of correspondences among these four elements, their identicalness, their transformations into one another. He is surely

poetry's primary "inventor of India for our time" (as Eliot called Pound the inventor of China); but he is equally an invention of India: "Indian" readings are possible for poems he wrote long before he went there.

Much has been written about the connections between "Blanco" and the ritual copulation practiced in Tantrism: an escape from the world (and a return to the original unity of the world) through the union of all opposites as incarnated in the actual bodies of the male and female adepts. (The best texts on this are still Paz's pages in *Conjunctions and Disjunctions* and the essay "Blank Thought.")

Robert Duncan, in the era of "action painting" in the 1950s, used to emphasize that the poem "is not the record of the event, but the event itself." "Blanco," though far too structured to be an "event" of writing in the processual sense developed by the Black Mountain poets, demands reader participation in the creation of the text by offering a list of variant readings that is, moreover, deliberately left incomplete. Writer and reader are yet another pair of opposites who unite in the poem. But "Blanco" goes even further: with its male center column and female split columns, it is, uniquely in erotic poetry, a poem that makes love to itself. (As, in India, the syllable-seeds engender language without human assistance.) The author has closed the door behind him on his way out; the reader may or may not be peering through the keyhole.

Tantric texts are written in *sandha,* which Mircea Eliade translates as "intentional" language. Each word carries a long string of associative possibilities, like those attributed to the three yogic "veins" above: the spiritual words have materialist and erotic meanings, and vice-versa. (The "right-hand" group of Tantrists believes that all of the material words should be taken only as metaphors for the spiritual; the "left-hand" group believes that all of the spiritual words are merely code names for aspects of the rituals, which, like copulation on a cremation ground, are scandalous to outsiders.)

There is a pair of sandha-words in the *Hevajra Tantra* (a line of which Paz rewrites as an epigraph to "Blanco") that is particularly intriguing: *preksana* (the act of seeing) is *agati* (the act of arrival or achievement). In India the primary act of daily worship among Hindus is *darshana* (seeing): it is both a "viewing" of the gods as they are manifest in the temple and wayside images, and something more: in darshana the eyes literally touch the gods; sight goes out to physically receive the god's blessing.

"Blanco" ends at the chakra between the eyes. Its last line reiterates an earlier couplet ("The unreality of the seen / brings reality to seeing") in the context of a ritualized copulation: "Your body / spilled on my body / seen / dissolved / brings reality to seeing." The poem, then, never erases the world, never enters the "plentiful void" of nirvana (as the last canto of *Altazor* does: a void filled with syllable-seeds) or the "empty void" of sunyata. In the unreality of the world the poem ends by affirming the reality of a seeing which is touching which is writing.

Tantric art is notable for its representation of the cosmos in a simple or complex geometric drawing: the *yantra.*

Paz's India (India's Paz) is a yantra composed of a triangle (seeing-touching-writing) within a square (body-world-cosmos-language) within a circle (which in India stands for a vision or a system—or is it a poet's political button?—or an O for Octavio?).

In the meditation, the yogin imagines a lotus blossoming on his navel. On the petals of the lotus are the letters of the mantra ARHAN. Smoke appears, rising from the letter R. Suddenly a spark, a burst of flame, and the lotus is consumed by fire. The wind picks up and scatters the ashes, covering him from head to toe. Then a gentle rain falls, and slowly washes them away. Bathed, refreshed, the yogin sees his body shining like the moon. (pp. 26-36)

Eliot Weinberger, "Paz in Asia," in Sulfur, *Vol. X, No. 2, Fall, 1990, pp. 17-37.*

AWARD ANNOUNCEMENTS

Sheila Rule

Octavio Paz, a writer of vivid surrealistic verse and penetrating social essays, won the Nobel Prize in Literature today, becoming the first Mexican writer to win literature's highest award.

The Swedish Academy of Letters said in its formal announcement that Mr. Paz had won the award "for impassioned writing with wide horizons, characterized by sensuous intelligence and humanistic integrity."

The academy said Mr. Paz's poetry consisted "to a very great extent of writing both with and about words" and that in his "surrealistically inspired thought, the words are endowed in this way with new, changeable and richer meanings." The academy quoted a 1976 poem in which Mr. Paz was seen as articulating his literary stance:

> Between what I see and what I say
> Between what I say and what I keep silent
> Between what I keep silent and what I dream
> Between what I dream and what I forget:
> Poetry

The 76-year-old Mr. Paz, an influential political commentator often attacked by Marxists and nationalists, is probably best known for his many essays. In one major work, **The Labyrinth of Solitude,** published in 1950, he offered an analysis of modern Mexico and the Mexican personality in which he described his fellow countrymen as instinctive nihilists who hide behind masks of solitude and ceremoniousness.

Mr. Paz published his first collection of poetry while a teen-ager. Still active as a writer and critic, he has founded and edited several magazines and has been publishing a literary monthly called *Vuelta,* which means return, since 1976. He also served as Mexico's Ambassador to France, Switzerland, Japan and India before resigning from the diplomatic service in 1968 after the Mexico City police fired at young demonstrators protesting Government repression of student activists and spending on the Mexico Olympics.

Describing himself as a "disillusioned leftist," Mr. Paz has since the late 1970's led a personal crusade against what he perceives as a threat of Soviet and Cuban intervention in Latin America. He has also devoted himself to writing and lecturing, in particular at Harvard, where he received an honorary doctorate in 1980.

Mr. Paz, whose distinctive verse has broad appeal and has been well received by critics internationally, has long been mentioned by Swedish publishers and cultural editors as a front-runner for the award. Prof. Sture Allen, who is the secretary of the Swedish Academy and who announced the selection of Mr. Paz, said that the poet had been a finalist for several years. . . .

The academy, an assembly of Swedish authors and academics, selects Nobel winners by consensus. This year's decision by the academy, some of whose past choices have been criticized as obscure, was greeted with enthusiasm by publishers and literary critics who gathered to hear the announcement in a room of the academy in the Stock Exchange building in the Old Town.

Mr. Allen said that the selection of Mr. Paz fit the academy's pattern of trying to encompass varying styles, languages and cultures with the award but that the will of Alfred Nobel, who established the prize, stipulated that the award should be "given to the best writers, irrespective of whether they are Scandinavian, Mexican, Nigerian or Australian." . . .

Mr. Paz was born in 1914 in Mexico City. His mother was Spanish, from Andalusia, and his father, a lawyer and politician, was Indian and Spanish. The poet, the academy said, "embodies this union of cultures—it is in his blood."

Mr. Paz's grandfather was a public official with liberal ideals and a novelist who was one of the first to write sympathetically about Mexico's Indian population. Mr. Paz's love of literature flowered in his grandfather's extensive library and it was the poet's father who planted the seeds of the commitment to social reform found in Mr. Paz's writing.

Mr. Paz was greatly influenced by the Spanish Civil War, which he witnessed in Madrid. After returning to Mexico in 1938, he became a founder of the journal *Taller (Workshop)* and exerted strong influence on contemporary literature as one of its contributors. In 1943, he traveled to the United States as a recipient of a Guggenheim award. In 1981, he was awarded the Cervantes Prize, the most important award in the Spanish-speaking world. The following year he received the prestigious Neustadt Prize.

One of the high points of Mr. Paz's poetry is the long poem **Sunstone,** published in 1957. It was inspired by an Aztec calendar stone, which is based on the conjunctions of Venus and the sun. The 584 days of the cycle, carved into the stone, are matched by the 584 lines of the poem. The academy said this "suggestive work, with its many layers of meaning, seems to incorporate, interpret and reconstrue major existential questions, death, time, love and reality."

Sheila Rule, "Octavio Paz, Mexican Poet,

Wins Nobel Prize," in The New York Times, *October 12, 1990, p. C33.*

Philip Howard

This year's Nobel Prize for Literature has been given to Octavio Paz, the Mexican poet, intellectual, polemicist and disillusioned diplomat. In its adjudication the Swedish Academy of Letters said Paz, aged 76, had been awarded the four million Swedish krona (£363,000) prize "for impassioned writing with wide horizons, characterised by sensuous intelligence and humanistic integrity". . . .

Paz published his first collection of poetry when he was aged 17. His meeting with André Breton, one of the founders of surrealism, was a potent influence. He is a founding father of the trendy modern Latin American export of magical realism. In particular, he takes a surrealist view of love and poetry as ways of subverting the day-to-day world.

It is an unconventional point of view for a professional statesman. He has described himself as a disillusioned left-winger. After seeing the Spanish civil war, he wrote of his disenchantment with the Mexican Revolution and the failure of socialism, and couched in stunning imagery his ideas about the relationship between the individual and society.

The theme of self and other, the problem of fragmentation and rootlessness, the quest for timeless experience, all converge in one of his finest poems, *Piedra del Sol* (1957), published in English as *Sun Stone* in 1963.

Paz, who is in New York to give a lecture at the Metropolitan Museum of Art, said yesterday: "This is something very important for me and for Mexican and Spanish-American literature. I was always interested in international culture, and I think writers must be a bridge from one culture to another."

He lives in an apartment on Paseo de Reforma, one of the main streets of Mexico City, and still edits and publishes his literary monthly, *Vuelta.* He annoyed his fellow countrymen in *The Labyrinth of Solitude,* which analysed them as being instinctive nihilists, who hide behind masks of solitude and ceremoniousness. He annoys *bien pensant* Latin American intellectuals by his crusade against the threat of Soviet and Cuban intervention in Latin America.

He is an intellectual so various that he seems to be not one, but all eggheads epitomised, discussing anthropology and art, as well as literature and politics. In *The Monkey Grammarian,* published in English in 1981, he plunged into the midden of deconstruction, putting language itself into question, and treating grammar as "a critique of the universe". I found it jolly hard going.

The academy's awards are always controversial. That is the point of awards. But it has seemed odd that Paz has not got the Nobel before, as Gabriel García Márquez observed when he won it, back in 1982.

No doubt Paz is an awkward chap; but he is the grand old man of Latin American literature. Or as the academy put it, in its stately honorific Nobelspeak, it is "honouring a

writer with a wide international perspective". They can say that again.

Philip Howard, "Nobel Prize for Literature Goes to Octavio Paz," in The Times, *London, October 12, 1990, p. 12.*

Amy Gamerman

As he took his place at the lectern in a conference room of the Drake Hotel in midtown Manhattan, the Mexican poet and essayist Octavio Paz still seemed surprised to be this year's winner of the Nobel Prize for Literature.

"Two years ago, I knew I was being considered, and I was in some way waiting, but this time I didn't have the slightest idea," said the soft-voiced, blue-eyed 76-year-old writer. Mr. Paz was in New York for the opening of the Metropolitan Museum's Mexican art show, for which he wrote the catalog introduction, when the news came from Stockholm.

Apparently, the 18 life-appointed members of the awards committee had just been biding their time. Citing his "impassioned writing, characterized by sensuous intelligence and humanistic integrity," the Swedish Academy chose Mr. Paz from an impressive list of contenders that included, according to one quasi-official list, Milan Kundera, Nadine Gordimer, Gunther Grass and Carlos Fuentes.

This year's winner has a dual life as poet and social critic. The author of 13 collections of verse (the first was published while he was still in his teens) and 30 volumes of essays, Mr. Paz also publishes the political journal *Vuelta* (*Return*). He is a well-known political commentator toward the conservative end of the spectrum in Mexico. He also is the first Mexican to receive the Nobel Prize in any category.

But if Mr. Paz is Mexican in heritage, his perspective is unabashedly international. Of mixed Spanish and Indian ancestry, he has made himself at home in the cultures of Europe and East Asia. His poems are as likely to refer to ancient Greek mythology and Buddhism as they are to Aztec legend.

Mr. Paz spent many years in France, where he hobnobbed with the likes of Albert Camus. His poetry has its roots in the European surrealist movement, and he has written several essays about Marcel Duchamp, the influential dada painter.

But if Mr. Paz has served as a Latin American conduit for European ideas, he has continued to explore his heritage as a Mexican and a Latin American in such works as *The Labyrinth of Solitude* (1950), an eloquent examination of his country's turbulent colonial history and its struggle to modernize.

Mr. Paz also has devoted himself to the scholarly analysis of Mexico's greatest poet, Sor Juana Ines de la Cruz, in a 1982 biography that showed how a country girl became the leading author in the Spanish language in the 17th century (*Sor Juana: Or the Traps of Faith*).

Mr. Paz's multicultural yet always Mexican approach

fairly flaunts itself in *Sunstone* (*Piedra de Sol*), a poem he wrote in 1957. Few works could be more rooted in Mexican soil than these 584 lines that stand for the 584 days of the Aztec stone calendar representing the conjunctions of Venus and the sun. But *Sunstone* reflects a native American light over an international cast of heroes and villains, Agamemnon and Brutus, Robespierre and Trotsky, felled by an assassin's ice ax in Mexico. All these culture heroes merge in the cosmopolitan poet of *Sunstone*:

> Mary, Persephone, Heloise, show me
> your face that I may see at last
> my true face, that of another,
> my face forever the face of us all,
> face of the tree and the baker of bread,
> face of the driver and the cloud and the sailor,
> face of the sun and the stream,
> face of Peter and Paul, face
> of this crowd of hermits, wake me up
> I've already been born.

The man behind those masks was born in Mexico City in 1914. He studied law but never took a degree, lighting out for the Spanish Civil War instead. On his return to Mexico in 1938, he helped found the literary journal *Taller* (*Workshop*). . . .

Mr. Paz's politics and poetry fit together naturally and inextricably, just as they did, he observes, for Dante, Milton and T. S. Eliot. He told reporters yesterday: "I see myself as a poet, but I belong to a special tradition of Western literature . . . Dante had very clear political ideas, and he is a model."

For Mr. Paz, the act of writing itself is a social and moral act. "Language is a common property . . . a writer is only the guard of language," he said. "To be a guard of language means you must think, talk with precision."

He refuses to categorize himself as belonging to the political right or the political left, but insists on his role as a detached social observer and critic. In 1979 he told an interviewer, "As a young man, I adopted a maxim of Andre Gide's as my own: 'The writer must learn to swim against the tide.'" Apparently, that maxim continues to guide him.

"Our society needs criticism," Mr. Paz said, his voice barely carrying in the crowded conference room. "Especially now . . . especially when we see trends toward nationalism, fundamentalism and fanaticism in the world."

Mr. Paz fell easily into the role of sage and public spokesman. He has been doing the same thing in Mexico for decades. At home, his face is perhaps even better known than his prose.

"He's on TV a lot," said Pablo Marentes, the acting Mexican consul general in New York. "He can be very controversial, but he's admired. He's outspoken, very outspoken."

Mr. Marentes isn't complaining. "This is our first Nobel Prize," he said. "It sort of feels like it's won by everybody."

Amy Gamerman, "Mexico's Nobel Winner,

Octavio Paz," in The Wall Street Journal, *October 12, 1990, p. A10.*

An excerpt from "January First"

> The year's doors open
> like those of language,
> toward the unknown.
> Last night you told me:
>   tomorrow
> we shall have to think up signs,
> sketch a landscape, fabricate a plan
> on the double page
> of day and paper.
> Tomorrow, we shall have to invent,
> once more,
> the reality of this world.
>
> I opened my eyes late.
> For a second of a second
> I felt what the Aztec felt,
> on the crest of the promontory,
> lying in wait
> for time's uncertain return
> through cracks in the horizon.
>
> But no, the year had returned.
> It filled all the room
> and my look almost touched it.
> Time, with no help from us,
> had placed
> in exactly the same order as yesterday
> houses in the empty street,
> snow on the houses,
> silence on the snow. . . .
>
> You were beside me
> and I saw you, like the snow,
> asleep among appearances.
> Time, with no help from us,
> invents houses, streets, trees
> and sleeping women.
>
> When you open your eyes
> we'll walk, once more,
> among the hours and their inventions.
> We'll walk among appearances
> and bear witness to time and its conjugations.
> Perhaps we'll open the day's doors.
> And then we shall enter the unknown.
>
> *—translated by Elizabeth Bishop*

Thomas D'Evelyn

Born in 1914, Paz has been long acquainted with political violence. Both his grandfather and father were part of the Mexican revolution. During the Spanish Civil War, Paz went to Madrid in support of the republicans.

In Madrid, his own revolutionary poetics took root in the soil of European surrealism. Paz's belief in a reality beyond conventional appearances has born fruit for over half a century. In essay and poem, Paz has measured the world against the ideal poem.

His first prose proved to be his most popular work. *The Labyrinth of Solitude* (1950) explained Spanish Americans to themselves. Having seen the Mexican revolution turn sour, Paz wrote: "History has the cruel reality of a nightmare, and the grandeur of man consists in making beautiful and lasting works out of the real substance of nightmare."

Twenty years later he would attack the condescending idea of "underdeveloped country" because it uses economic development to measure the success of a nation rather than the broader human culture. By that time he had turned against the revolutionary promise of the Marxists. And he had seen the cause of revolution spread to the "developed" countries.

Poetry filled the vacuum left by the diminishment of revolutionary hope. In his mature poetry, Paz witnesses a time beyond time. As a self-described member of the "repentant avant-garde," Paz has re-envisioned poetry so it can bear the weight of hope once born by revolutionary ideology and violence. His vision owes much to his last foreign-service post. From 1962 to 1968 he served as an ambassador to India (where he met his wife). Paz says he learned there how to integrate the silence of the page into the poetry. Praised by the Nobel committee for his sensuous intellect, Paz is in fact far more conceptual than most popular poets. Some critics use the word mystic to describe his point of view.

In a word, Paz's poetry is strange; it would be a disservice to pretend otherwise. As he says of Dante, "Among the many ways we may read the great books of the past, there is one which I prefer: to look in them not for what we are, but for the thing which denies what we are. I return to Dante, precisely because he is the least up-to-date of the great poets of our tradition."

Now he celebrates a postmodern poetry of the present. In *Children of the Mire,* he says that the new poetry is "Pure time: heartbeat of the presence in the moment of its appearance/disappearance."

Thus Paz's chastened view of modern politics has yielded a counterbalancing view of poetry. But he saved something else from the old surrealism. Paz is a great love poet. Perhaps that is why he likes both Dante and e. e. cummings!

Paz's way with love and art is illustrated by a little lyric called **"With Eyes Closed"**. The old Pygmalion tale of the sculptor falling in love with his statue comes alive for Paz as he deploys his most powerful word. Not I, as with so many modern poets, but you: you the reader, you the lover, you the other, you the work. The difference with Paz is that both "I" and "you" have our eyes closed and so know each other. For Paz, this intimacy, equally poetic and erotic, is a great consolation.

> *Thomas D'Evelyn, "Paz's Poetry Replaces Revolutionary Hope," in* The Christian Science Monitor, *October 18, 1990, p. 13.*

John Oliver Simon

The 1990 Nobel Prize for Literature, which the Swedish Academy awarded last month to Octavio Paz, is a grand validation of Latin American writing, and a crowning glory for Mexican poetry. Paz becomes the sixth Nobel lit-laureate from Latin America, joining Miguel Angel Asturias, Juan Ramón Jiménez, Gabriela Mistral, Pablo Neruda and Gabriel García Márquez, and he is the first Mexican writer to receive the honor. . . .

Octavio Paz began publishing his poetry in 1931, when he was seventeen years old. The years 1937-38 found him in Spain, attending a conference of anti-Fascist writers and working for the Loyalists; he left the Communist Party after the Nazi-Soviet pact. This experience of conversion and apostasy indelibly marked his thinking. Wherever the Party comes up in his writing, it is superimposed on the hierarchical Church, as in **"Nocturno de San Ildefonso"**:

> Good, we wanted good:
> > to set the world right.
> We didn't lack integrity:
> > we lacked humility.
> What we wanted was not innocently wanted.
> Precepts and concepts,
> > the arrogance of theologians,
> to beat with a cross,
> > to institute with blood,
> to build the house with bricks of crime,
> to declare obligatory communion.
> > > Some
> became secretaries to the secretary
> to the General Secretary of the Inferno.

A Guggenheim Fellowship brought Paz to the United States in 1944, and his reflections on Mexico from that perspective because *El laberinto de la soledad (The Labyrinth of Solitude),* often considered the most profound self-portrait of the Mexican character, and notorious for its analysis of the verb *chingar.* Going to France in 1945, Paz allied himself with Andre Breton and the Surrealists, and brought their program into the Spanish language, while adding a Latin American element to the great movement.

Juvenal Acosta, a Mexican poet now living in the [San Francisco] Bay Area, calls Octavio Paz the premier intellectual in Latin America. "I mean intellectual in the European sense, in the French style," Acosta says. "The guy is completely mistaken politically, but as a poet he is very brilliant. Octavio Paz sensed the lack of a definition of Mexican culture. *The Labyrinth of Solitude* permitted what is Mexican to enter into universal play. Paz became the Mexican Pound, the Mexican Breton and Eliot, rolled into one. The Europeans don't have that problem of self-definition; they can jump right away into theory, into meta-literature."

Francisco X. Alarcón has his Latin American Studies students at UC Santa Cruz read, and criticize, *The Labyrinth of Solitude.* Alarcón finds its logic "surprisingly simplistic, classist and misogynist." In the first chapter, "On the Pachuco and Other Extremes," Paz dismisses the authenticity of the Mexican living in the United States. (p. 1)

A certain Eurocentric disdain, signalled here, surfaced in

a 1977 article in the London *Times,* in which Paz stated that Latin America had never had original intellectual movements, and the Spanish language has never had a true critical thinker. Questioned on this point by an interviewer from *La Gaceta,* the millenial Guatemalan man of letters Luis Cardoza y Aragón (b. 1904) replied, "what you have read me by Octavio is absolutely a self-portrait. His thinking is always exaggerated, and in this exaggeration of Paz I find his bravery, his strength and also his weakness."

Paz's collected poems up to 1949 appeared as **Libertad bajo palabra** (the wordplay Frenchified in translation as **Freedom Under Parole**—*palabra,* the *word,* is key). The significance of this title is sketched by editor Fernando García Ramírez:

> Freedom to say, to sing, expressive freedom, moral, erotic freedom—more than a single influence stimulating Mexican poets . . . we salute in Paz the generous and passionate writer, the poet in love with woman, with the city and with history; poet of love and of the moment, whose poems do not exclude indignation and adventure. The word is at liberty, and freedom is under the word.
>
> (p. 4)

His work brought the cultures of Asia into the Spanish language, above all in the essay **El mono gramático** (**The Grammatical Monkey,** 1974), a meditation on Hanuman and the temple-monkeys of Galta, and in the poems of **Ladero Este** (East Slope). "Octavio Paz opened Mexico towards the Orient," comments Alberto Blanco, winner of the 1989 Carlos Pellicer Prize for his book, *Cromos.* "His influence forms a mandala. He opened a path towards Japan and India and China. He opened us to the United States, to Europe through the Surrealists, and to Latin America. And he opened Mexico to ourselves, from the center to the inside."

Octavio Paz's central poem is surely **"Piedra de Sol"** (**"Sunstone"**). Muriel Rukeyser wrote,

> This is a poem of opposites seen in a swift cycle, cypher of star, woman, season, the tree over water, graces and ferocities. All the shifts of experience, the acrobatics of inward turning, the bite and venom of the moment, are seen in a long period of 584 days [the cycle of Venus]—the 584 lines of the poem—as they are marked on the Aztec Calendar Stone.

I first read **"Piedra de Sol"** in a night of insomnia in an old hotel in the center of Mexico City, the center of the universe, and it did not conduce to sleep.

Rereading **"Piedra de Sol,"** the shape-shifting woman's face dissolves into a whirlwind of rooms and streets, lovers remaking the world, Madrid in 1937, war and the deaths of famous men, Lincoln, Robespierre, Madero, a seamless interlace of pronouns, a mystical communion that returns us in impeccable vertigo to the opening arrival. " 'Piedra de Sol' is a masterpiece," enthuses Francisco X. Alarcón. "I really celebrate that poem. It may be the best poem ever written by a Mexican."

The heart of Paz's keystone poem is the passage where the walls of oppressive culture, be they bourgeois or Marxist, tumble to give us a vision of our simple, transcendent humanity. And inevitably, cantankerously, at the core of this key transition Paz takes off the gloves for a personal swipe at his greatest rival among Mexican poets of their generation, the militant leftist Efrain Huerta, universally nicknamed *el cocodrilo:*

> everything's transfigured and is sacred,
> the center of the world is every room,
> it is the first night, the first day,
> the world is born when two people kiss,
> a drop of light with transparent entrails,
> the room half-opens like a fruit
> or explodes like a taciturn star
> and the laws gnawed away by rats,
> the iron bars of banks and prisons,
> the bars of paper and barbed-wire,
> the seals and stamps and spurs,
> the mellifluous scorpion in cap and gown,
> the top-hatted tiger, president
> of the Vegetarian Club and the Red Cross,
> the pedagogical burro, the crocodile
> turned savior, father of nations,
> the Chief, the shark, the architect
> of the future, the uniformed pig,
> the favorite son of the Church
> who washes his black dentures
> with holy water and takes classes in
> democracy and English, the invisible
> walls, the rotten masks
> that divide man from men
> man from himself
>   they tumble down
> for an immense instant and we glimpse
> our lost unity, the vulnerability
> of being human, the glory of being human
> and sharing bread, the sun, and death,
> the forgotten wonder of being alive

The parallel between the totalitarian Church and the ecclesiastical Party is clear. Robert Hass notes that Czeslaw Milosz makes the same identification: two Nobel poets, both disillusioned ex-Communists, reacting against authoritarian Catholic educations. (pp. 4-5)

In 1986, Paz published a massive biography of the seventeenth century Mexican poet Sor Juana Inéz de la Cruz, **Sor Juana, o las trampas de la fe** (**Sor Juana, or the Traps of Faith**). Sor Juana, arguably the greatest world poet of her era, was stifled by the Inquisition, censored as a poet and a woman, and forced to recant, to give up her library and abandon her writing. Paz projects Sor Juana as a model for the contemporary writer of conscience in the Gulag.

Writing in the magazine *Textual* in February of this year, . . . Paz puts on his Grand Inquisitor's hat and speaks *ex cathedra:* "Historical changes—whether of taste, ideas or social convictions—condemn to Purgatory poets who have been celebrated when alive. For example, Neruda, Aragon and Eluard are paying today for their political sins. I say *sins* [emphasis his] because Stalinism, more than an error, was a wrong (*ùna falta*)."

And what of the political sins, or errors, or wrongs, of Octavio Paz? *Vuelta,* the well-funded magazine he edits, has served as the platform for a shrill series of attacks on Nicaragua, providing the most prominent podium in Latin America for the intellectual destabilization of the Sandinistas. Paz's own most controversial discourse, **"El diálogo y el ruido" ("Dialogue and Noise")** was delivered in Frankfurt, Germany, in 1984, when he declared that Nicaragua was irreversibly headed down the road to a Cuban-style military-bureaucratic dictatorship, and pointed to Duarte's El Salvador as a model for Latin American democracy. For this unpopular opinion, Paz was burned in effigy in front of the American embassy on the Reforma in Mexico City. We are dealing here, Robert Hass suggests, with "the consequences in the world of a politics so pure as to be practically untenable."

At a presentation last July of Paz's most recent book of essays, *Pequeña crónica de grandes días* (*Small Chronicle of Great Days*), historian Hector Aguilar Camin delivered a balanced judgment: on the one hand, Paz has consistently pointed out "the theoretical rigidity of the authoritarian paradigm of the Latin American left," where others kept convenient silence. On the other, "his almost evangelical emphasis . . . has led him to underestimate other aspects . . . I think of the almost total absence, in his perspective . . . of the poverty, the inequality, the social injustice, whose moral urgency is the genuine source of the utopian, egalitarian and revolutionary movements Paz has combatted with such fervor." Alberto Blanco discerns a larger message of reconciliation beyond the bitter polemics. "It is not coincidence that Octavio Paz and Mikhail Gorbachev should receive the Nobel Prize at the same time," Blanco points out, noting that Paz's criticisms of Communism "prefigure the changes in the socialist countries."

In 1984, the Instituto de Bellas Artes put on a grand Homenaje to Octavio Paz in Mexico City on the occasion of his 70th birthday. . . . The event was a more or less naked campaign rally for the Nobel, which has now been justified. What I found strange, though, was how speaker after speaker trooped to the microphone not only to elucidate the excellence of Paz, but to negate the very possibility of a political poetry. "Poetry is over here; politics is over there," said Argentine minimalist Roberto Juarroz. "There is nothing more dangerous for the poet than politics." What should the poem be about? Juarroz approvingly quoted Paz to the effect that the poem is "an object made of language" and Wallace Stevens saying that the theme of the poem is poetry itself.

This rhetoric is disingenuous: Paz's major poems, such as **"Piedra de Sol," "Nocturno de San Ildefonso"** and **"El Cántaro Roto,"** are political down to their socks. What Paz is hoping to forestall, rather, is poetry that disagrees with his own politics. The young editors of a 1990 anthology, *La Sirena en El Espejo* (*The Mermaid in the Mirror*), repeat the lesson dutifully: "many of the propositions presented by Octavio Paz remain valid . . . the new poets no longer understand poetry as a sublime act, and possibly few believe that poetry can change society . . . the new poets have rejected the possibility of utilizing poetry as a political, ideological, didactic or moral instrument . . . "

Lewis Hyde put his finger exactly on the problem of this exclusionary thinking, talking about Jesse Helms and obscenity in last month's *Poetry Flash* ("Bringing Back the Dirt," an interview by Dorianne Laux and Ron Salisbury); if you say an artist cannot touch obscenity (if you say a poet cannot touch politics), "it's almost like saying to a scientist, we want you to continue to explore biological questions, but you're not allowed to consider any ideas of evolution." Paz himself could not have written under these stipulations. Once the poetic gaze is averted from any large sector of experience, quotidian data and sensory reality tend to disappear, and what's left, in a lot of young Mexican poets, is a vitiated submarine narcissism: the Mermaid in the Mirror. In a 1988 issue of the magazine *Plural,* Mónica Mansour was the only one of seven women poets who neither began nor ended a poem with the image of "shadows."

Arbol Adentro (*The Tree Within*), published simultaneously in Spanish and in graceful English translation by Eliot Weinberger in 1987, is at least Paz's twenty-fifth book of poetry, and it is no longer major work. The long prophetic line of **"Proem"** and **"I Speak of the City"** is static. The occasional poems, such as **"Between what I see and what I say,"** cited by the Nobel committee, are both slight and ponderous, didactic without illuminating.

> Poetry
> speaks and listens;
> it is real.
> And as soon as I say
> *it is real.*
> it vanishes.
> Is it then more real?

But at this stage we are speaking of an institution more than an individual poet. Octavio Paz has concentrated more literary-political power at his fingertips than anyone outside of recent Writer's Union bureaucracies in Communist countries can easily imagine. Paz and his closest disciples have edited the most important anthologies for the last thirty years. The Mexican government has initiated an exemplary program of handsome grants to poets; it goes without saying that Paz chooses the grantees. At the same time, *Vuelta* publishes the approved young poets, many of them magnificent to be sure. "Granted that Paz wrote some great poems," Mónica Mansour told me. "But he did not become the *cacique* (boss) of Mexican poetry because he wrote **'Piedra de Sol,'** but because of his skill in manipulating power and human relations."

How are people reacting to the Nobel Prize in Mexico? Alberto Blanco finds a general consensus of "enjoyment and celebration," amid a healing of old wounds. Blanco was at an international poetry festival in Guadalajara when the award was announced. Such well-known leftist poets as Argentina's Juan Gelman came up to him with "joy and recognition" at the honor for Paz. "People's reaction depends on what side they're on," disagrees Mónica Mansour. "A lot of people are suddenly on Paz's side. Some people say this is good; he's been soliciting the prize for ten years; now he'll calm down. Others say he'll be more arrogant and powerful than ever."

In one of Octavio Paz's greatest poems, **"El Cantaro**

Roto" ("The Broken Pitcher"), he laments the passing of all that is sacred and beautiful:

> The corn-god, the flower-god, the water-god, the
>   blood-god, the Virgin,
> have they all died, gone away, broken jars by the
>   blind fountain?
> Only the toad lives,
> only the green toad glistens and shines in the
>   Mexican night,
> is only the fat cacique of Cempoala immortal?

The fat cacique of Cempoala was the quisling who welcomed Cortez to the Mexican shore, who first converted to the alien creed; here he is identified as well with the Mexican Presidency. It is ironic that the poet, monstrously inflated beyond his own poetry, becomes this self-portrait. It is fashionable to say, love the poetry, hate the politics, or love the poetry, discard the essays. But the writer and the work are one: it is a machinery fixated on hateful Church and Party, and doubtless armored out of ancient wounds of childhood, that propels the furious energy of poetic vision from the very core of Octavio Paz across sixty years of literary achievement.

Paz, himself, meditating on the value of those Stalinist poets whose politics he despises, finds solace in quoting Auden's "On the Memory of W. B. Yeats." The lines will serve as well for a judgment on Octavio Paz:

> Time that with this strange excuse
> Pardoned Kipling and his views,
> And will pardon Paul Claudel.
> Pardons him for writing well.

(pp. 5-6)

John Oliver Simon, "Pardon Him For Writing Well: The Nobel Prize for Octavio Paz," in Poetry Flash, *No. 212, November, 1990, pp. 1, 4-6.*

Octavio Paz: Nobel Lecture

I begin with two words that all men have uttered since the dawn of humanity: thank you. The word gratitude has equivalents in every language and in each tongue the range of meanings is abundant. In the Romance languages this breadth spans the spiritual and the physical, from the divine grace conceded to men to save them from error and death, to the bodily grace of the dancing girl or the feline leaping through the undergrowth. Grace means pardon, forgiveness, favour, benefice, inspiration; it is a form of address, a pleasing style of speaking or painting, a gesture expressing politeness, and, in short, an act that reveals spiritual goodness. Grace is gratuitous; it is a gift. The person who receives it, the favoured one, is grateful for it; if he is not base, he expresses gratitude. That is what I am doing at this very moment with these weightless words. I hope my emotion compensates their weightlessness. If each of my words were a drop of water, you would see through them and glimpse what I feel: gratitude, acknowledgement. And also an indefinable mixture of fear, respect and surprise at finding myself here before you, in this place which is the home of both Swedish learning and world literature.

Languages are vast realities that transcend those political and historical entities we call nations. The European languages we speak in the Americas illustrate this. The special position of our literatures when compared to those of England, Spain, Portugal and France depends precisely on this fundamental fact: they are literatures written in transplanted tongues. Languages are born and grow from the native soil, nourished by a common history. The European languages were rooted out from their native soil and their own tradition, and then planted in an unknown and unnamed world: they took root in the new lands and, as they grew within the societies of America, they were transformed. They are the same plant yet also a different plant. Our literatures did not passively accept the changing fortunes of the transplanted languages: they participated in the process and even accelerated it. They very soon ceased to be mere transatlantic reflections: at times they have been the negation of the literatures of Europe; more often, they have been a reply.

In spite of these oscillations the link has never been broken. My classics are those of my language and I consider myself to be a descendant of Lope and Quevedo, as any Spanish writer would . . . yet I am not a Spaniard. I think that most writers of Spanish America, as well as those from the United States, Brazil and Canada, would say the same as regards the English, Portuguese and French traditions. To understand more clearly the special position of writers in the Americas, we should think of the dialogue maintained by Japanese, Chinese or Arabic writers with the different literatures of Europe. It is a dialogue that cuts across multiple languages and civilizations. Our dialogue, on the other hand, takes place within the same language. We are Europeans yet we are not Europeans. What are we then? It is difficult to define what we are, but our works speak for us.

In the field of literature, the great novelty of the present century has been the appearance of the American literatures. The first to appear was that of the English-speaking part and then, in the second half of the 20th century, that of Latin America in its two great branches: Spanish America and Brazil. Although they are very different, these three literatures have one common feature: the conflict, which is more ideological than literary, between the cosmopolitan and nativist tendencies, between Europeanism and Americanism. What is the legacy of this dispute? The polemics have disappeared; what remain are the works. Apart from this general resemblance, the differences between the three literatures are multiple and profound. One of them belongs more to history than to literature: the development of Anglo-American literature coincides with the rise of the United States as a world power whereas the rise of our literature coincides with the political and social misfortunes and upheavals of our nations. This proves once more the limitations of social and historical determinism: the decline of empires and social disturbances sometimes coincide with moments of artistic and literary splendour. Li-Po and Tu Fu witnessed the fall of the Tang dynasty; Velázquez painted for Felipe IV; Seneca and Lucan were contemporaries and also victims of Nero. Other differences are of a literary nature and apply more to particular works than to the character of each literature. But can we say that literatures have a *character*? Do they possess a set of shared features that distinguish them from other literatures? I doubt it. A literature is not defined by some fanciful, intangible character; it is a society of unique works united by relations of opposition and affinity.

The first basic difference between Latin-American and Anglo-American literature lies in the diversity of their origins. Both begin as projections of Europe. The projection of an island in the case of North America; that of a peninsula in our case. Two regions that are geographically, historically and culturally eccentric. The origins of North America are in England and the Reformation; ours are in Spain, Portugal and the Counter-Reformation. For the case of Spanish America I should briefly mention what distinguishes Spain from other European countries, giving it a particularly original historical identity. Spain is no less eccentric than England but its eccentricity is of a different kind. The eccentricity of the English is insular and is characterized by isolation: an eccentricity that excludes. Hispanic eccentricity is peninsular and consists of the coexistence of different civilizations and different pasts: an inclusive eccentricity. In what would later be Catholic Spain, the Visigoths professed the heresy of Arianism, and we could also speak about the centuries of domination by Arabic civilization, the influence of Jewish thought, the Reconquest, and other characteristic features.

Hispanic eccentricity is reproduced and multiplied in America, especially in those countries such as Mexico and Peru, where ancient and splendid civilizations had existed. In Mexico the Spaniards encountered history as well as geography. That history is still alive: it is a present rather than a past. The temples and gods of pre-Columbian Mexico are a pile of ruins, but the spirit that breathed life into that world has not disappeared; it speaks to us in the hermetic language of myth, legend, forms of social coexistence, popular art, customs. Being a Mexican writer means listening to the voice of that present, that presence. Listening to it, speaking with it, deciphering it: expressing it . . . After this brief digression we may be able to perceive the peculiar relation that simultaneously binds us to and separates us from the European tradition.

This consciousness of being separate is a constant feature of our spiritual history. Separation is sometimes experienced as a wound that marks an internal division, an anguished awareness that invites self-examination; at other times it appears as a challenge, a spur that incites us to action, to go forth and encounter others and the outside world. It is true that the feeling of separation is universal and not peculiar to Spanish Americans. It is born at the very moment of our birth: as we are wrenched from the Whole we fall into an alien land. This experience becomes a wound that never heals. It is the unfathomable depth of every man; all our ventures and exploits, all our acts and dreams, are bridges designed to overcome the separation and reunite us with the world and our fellow-beings. Each man's life and the collective history of mankind can thus be seen as attempts to reconstruct the original situation. An unfinished and endless cure for our divided condition. But it is not my intention to provide yet another description of this feeling. I am simply stressing the fact that for us this existential condition expresses itself in historical terms. It thus becomes an awareness of our history. How and when does this feeling appear and how is it transformed into consciousness? The reply to this double-edged question can be given in the form of a theory or a personal testimony. I prefer the latter: there are many theories and none is entirely convincing.

The feeling of separation is bound up with the oldest and vaguest of my memories: the first cry, the first scare. Like every child I built emotional bridges in the imagination to link me to the world and to other people. I lived in a town on the outskirts of Mexico City, in an old dilapidated house that had a jungle-like garden and a great room full of books. First games and first lessons. The garden soon became the centre of my world; the library, an enchanted cave. I used to read and play with my cousins and schoolmates. There was a fig tree, temple of vegetation, four pine trees, three ash trees, a nightshade, a pomegranate tree, wild grass and prickly plants that produced purple grazes. Adobe walls. Time was elastic; space was a spinning wheel. All time, past or future, real or imaginary, was pure presence. Space transformed itself ceaselessly. The beyond was here, all was here: a valley, a mountain, a distant country, the neighbours' patio. Books with pictures, especially history books, eagerly leafed through, supplied images of deserts and jungles, palaces and hovels, warriors and princesses, beggars and kings. We were shipwrecked with Sinbad and with Robinson, we fought with D'Artagnan, we took Valencia with the Cid. How I would have liked to stay forever on the Isle of Calypso! In summer the green branches of the fig tree would sway like the sails of a caravel or a pirate ship. High up on the mast, swept by the wind, I could make out islands and continents, lands that vanished as soon as they became tangible. The world was limitless yet it was always within reach; time was a pliable substance that weaved an unbroken present.

When was the spell broken? Gradually rather than suddenly. It is hard to accept being betrayed by a friend, deceived by the woman we love, or that the idea of freedom is the mask of a tyrant. What we call "finding out" is a slow and tricky process because we ourselves are the accomplices of our errors and deceptions. Nevertheless, I can remember fairly clearly an incident that was the first sign, although it was quickly forgotten. I must have been about six when one of my cousins who was a little older showed me a North American magazine with a photograph of soldiers marching along a huge avenue, probably in New York. "They've returned from the war" she said. This handful of words disturbed me, as if they foreshadowed the end of the world or the Second Coming of Christ. I vaguely knew that somewhere far away a war had ended a few years earlier and that the soldiers were marching to celebrate their victory. For me, that war had taken place in another time, not here and now. The photo refuted me. I felt literally dislodged from the present.

From that moment time began to fracture more and more. And there was a plurality of spaces. The experience repeated itself more and more frequently. Any piece of news, a harmless phrase, the headline in a newspaper: everything proved the outside world's existence and my own unreality. I felt that the world was splitting and that I did not inhabit the present. My present was disintegrating: real time was somewhere else. My time, the time of the garden, the fig tree, the games with friends, the drowsiness among the plants at three in the afternoon under the sun, a fig torn open (black and red like a live coal but one that is sweet and fresh): this was a fictitious time. In spite of what my senses told me, the time from over there, belonging to the others, was the real one, the time of the real present. I accepted the inevitable: I became an adult. That was how my expulsion from the present began.

It may seem paradoxical to say that we have been expelled from the present, but it is a feeling we have all had at some moment. Some of us experienced it first as a condemnation, later transformed into consciousness and action. The search for the present is neither the pursuit of an earthly paradise nor that of a timeless eternity: it is the search for a real reality. For us, as Spanish Americans, the real present was not in our own countries: it was the time lived by others, by the English, the French and the Germans. It was the time of New York, Paris, London. We had to go and look for it and bring it back home. These years were also the years of my discovery of literature. I began writing poems. I did not know what made me write them: I was moved by an inner need that is difficult to define. Only now have I understood that there was a secret relationship between what I have called my expulsion from the present and the writing of poetry. Poetry is in love with the instant and seeks to relive it in the poem, thus separating it from sequential time and turning it into a fixed present. But at that time I wrote without wondering why I was doing it. I was searching for the gateway to the present: I wanted to belong to my time and to my century. A little later this obsession became a fixed idea: I wanted to be a modern poet. My search for modernity had begun.

What is modernity? First of all it is an ambiguous term: there are as many types of modernity as there are societies. Each has its own. The word's meaning is uncertain and arbitrary, like the name of the period that precedes it, the Middle Ages. If we are modern when compared to medieval times, are we perhaps the Middle Ages of a future modernity? Is a name that changes with time a real name? Modernity is a word in search of its meaning. Is it an idea, a mirage or a moment of history? Are we the children of modernity or its creators? Nobody knows for sure. It doesn't matter much: we follow it, we pursue it. For me at that time modernity was fused with the present or rather produced it: the present was its last supreme flower. My case is neither unique nor exceptional: from the Symbolist period, all modern poets have chased after that magnetic and elusive figure that fascinates them. Baudelaire was the first. He was also the first to touch her and discover that she is nothing but time that crumbles in one's hands. I am not going to relate my adventures in pursuit of modernity: they are not very different from those of other 20th century poets. Modernity has been a universal passion. Since 1850 she has been our goddess and our demoness. In recent years there has been an attempt to exorcise her and

there has been much talk of "postmodernism". But what is postmodernism if not an even more modern modernity?

For us, as Latin Americans, the search for poetic modernity runs historically parallel to the repeated attempts to modernize our countries. This tendency begins at the end of the 18th century and includes Spain herself. The United States was born into modernity and by 1830 was already, as de Tocqueville observed, the womb of the future; we were born at a moment when Spain and Portugal were moving away from modernity. This is why there was frequent talk of "Europeanizing" our countries: the modern was outside and had to be imported. In Mexican history this process begins just before the War of Independence. Later it became a great ideological and political debate that passionately divided Mexican society during the 19th century. One event was to call into question not the legitimacy of the reform movement but the way in which it had been implemented: the Mexican Revolution. Unlike its 20th century counterparts, the Mexican Revolution was not really the expression of a vaguely utopian ideology but rather the explosion of a reality that had been historically and psychologically repressed. It was not the work of a group of ideologists intent on introducing principles derived from a political theory; it was a popular uprising that unmasked what was hidden. For this very reason it was more of a revelation than a revolution. Mexico was searching for the present outside only to find it within, buried but alive. The search for modernity led us to discover our antiquity, the hidden face of the nation. I am not sure whether this unexpected historical lesson has been learned by all—that between tradition and modernity there is a bridge. When they are mutually isolated, tradition stagnates and modernity vaporizes. When they are joined, modernity breathes life into tradition, while the latter responds with depth and gravity.

The search for poetic modernity was a Quest, in the allegorical and chivalric sense that this word had in the twelfth century. I did not find any Grail, although I did cross several wastelands, visiting castles of mirrors and camping among ghostly tribes. Still, I discovered the modern tradition. For modernity is not a poetic school but a lineage, a family dispersed over several continents, which for two centuries has survived many changes and misfortunes: indifference, isolation, and tribunals in the name of religious, political, academic, and sexual orthodoxy. Because it is a tradition and not a doctrine, it has been able to survive and to change at the same time. This is also why it is so diverse: each poetic adventure is distinct, each poet has sown a different plant in the miraculous forest of speaking trees. Yet if the works are diverse and each route is distinct, what is it that unites all these poets? Not an aesthetic, but a search. My own search was not fanciful, even though the idea of modernity is a mirage, a bundle of reflections. One day I discovered that I was returning to the starting point instead of advancing, that the search for modernity was a descent to the origins. Modernity led me to the source of my beginning, to my antiquity. Separation became reconciliation. Thus I discovered that the poet is a pulse in the rhythmic flow of generations.

The idea of modernity is a byproduct of our conception

of history as a unique and linear process of succession. The origins of this conception are in the Judeo-Christian tradition, but it breaks with Christian doctrine. In Christianity, the cyclical time of pagan cultures is supplanted by unrepeatable history, which has a beginning and will have an end. Sequential time was the profane time of history, an arena for the actions of fallen men, yet still governed by a sacred time that had neither a beginning nor an end. And after Judgment Day, there will be no future either in heaven or in hell. In the realm of eternity there is no succession, because everything *is*. Being triumphs over becoming. The new time, our concept of time, is linear like that of Christianity, but it is open to infinity, it makes no reference to Eternity. Ours is the time of profane history, an irreversible and perpetually unfinished time that marches toward the future and not toward its end. History's sun is the future. Progress is the name of this movement toward the future.

Christians see the world, or what used to be called the *seculum* or worldly life, as a place of trial: in this world, souls can be lost or saved. In the new conception, by contrast, the historical subject is not the individual soul but the human race, sometimes viewed as a whole and sometimes through a chosen group that represents it: the developed nations of the West, the proletariat, the white race, or some other entity. The pagan and Christian philosophical tradition had exalted Being as changeless perfection overflowing with plenitude, but we adore change; it is the motor of progress and the model for our societies. Change articulates itself in two ways, as evolution and revolution. The trot and the leap. Modernity is the spearhead of historical movement, the incarnation of evolution or revolution, the two faces of progress. And progress takes place by means of the dual action of science and technology, applied to the realm of nature and to the use of her immense resources.

Modern man has defined himself as a historical being. Other societies chose to define themselves in terms of values and ideas different from change: the Greeks venerated the *polis* and the circle, yet they were unaware of progress. Like all the Stoics, Seneca was much exercised by the eternal return; St. Augustine believed that the end of the world was imminent; St. Thomas constructed a scale of being, linking the smallest creature to the Creator; and so on. One after the other, these ideas and beliefs were abandoned. It seems to me that the same decline is beginning to affect our idea of Progress—and, as a result, our vision of time, of history, of ourselves. We are witnessing the twilight of the future.

The decline of the idea of modernity, and the popularity of a notion as dubious as "postmodernism," are phenomena that affect not only literature and the arts. We are experiencing the crisis of the essential ideas and beliefs that have guided mankind for over two centuries. I have dealt with this matter at length elsewhere. Here I can only offer a brief summary.

In the first place, the concept of a process open to infinity and synonymous with endless progress has been called into question. I need hardly mention what everybody knows: natural resources are finite and will run out one day. In addition, we have inflicted what may be irreparable damage on the natural environment and our own species is endangered. Finally, science and technology, the instruments of progress, have shown with alarming clarity that they can easily become destructive forces. The existence of nuclear weapons is a refutation of the idea that progress is inherent in history. This refutation, I add, can only be called devastating.

In the second place, we have the fate of the historical subject, mankind, in the 20th century. Seldom have nations or individuals suffered so much: two world wars, tyrannies spread over five continents, the atomic bomb and the proliferation of one of the cruellest and most lethal institutions known by man: the concentration camp. Modern technology has provided countless benefits, but it is impossible to close our eyes when confronted by slaughter, torture, humiliation, degradation, and other wrongs inflicted on millions of innocent people in our century.

In the third place, the belief in the necessity of progress has been shaken. For our grandparents and our parents, the ruins of history (corpses, desolate battlefields, devastated cities) did not invalidate the underlying goodness of the historical process. The scaffolds and tyrannies, the conflicts and savage civil wars were the price to be paid for progress, the blood money to be offered to the god of history. A god? Yes, reason itself deified and prodigal in cruel acts of cunning, according to Hegel. The alleged rationality of history has vanished. In the very domain of order, regularity and coherence (in pure sciences like physics) the old notions of accident and catastrophe have reappeared. This disturbing resurrection reminds me of the terrors that marked the advent of the millennium, and the anguish of the Aztecs at the end of each cosmic cycle.

The last element in this hasty enumeration is the collapse of all the philosophical and historical hypotheses that claimed to reveal the laws governing the course of history. The believers, confident that they held the keys to history, erected powerful states over pyramids of corpses. These arrogant constructions, destined in theory to liberate men, were very quickly transformed into gigantic prisons. Today we have seen them fall, overthrown not by their ideological enemies but by the impatience and the desire for freedom of the new generations. Is this the end of all Utopias? It is rather the end of the idea of history as a phenomenon the outcome of which can be known in advance. Historical determinism has been a costly and bloodstained fantasy. History is unpredictable because its agent, mankind, is the personification of indeterminism.

This short review shows that we are very probably at the end of a historical period and at the beginning of another. The end of the Modern Age or just a mutation? It is difficult to tell. In any case, the collapse of Utopian schemes has left a great void, not in the countries where this ideology has been proved to have failed but in those where many embraced it with enthusiasm and hope. For the first time in history mankind lives in a sort of spiritual wilderness and not, as before, in the shadow of those religious and political systems that consoled us at the same time as they oppressed us. Although all societies are historical, each one has lived under the guidance and inspiration of a set of metahistorical beliefs and ideas. Ours is the first age that is ready to live without a metahistorical doctrine; whether they be religious or philosophical, moral or aesthetic, our absolutes are not collective but private. It is a dangerous experience. It is also impossible to know whether the tensions and conflicts unleashed in this privatization of ideas, practices and beliefs that belonged traditionally to the public domain will not end up by destroying the social fabric. Men could then become possessed once more by ancient religious fury or by fanatical nationalism. It would be terrible if the fall of the abstract idol of ideology were to foreshadow the resurrection of the buried passions of tribes, sects and churches. The signs, unfortunately, are disturbing.

The decline of the ideologies I have called metahistorical, by which I mean those that assign to history a goal and a direction, implies the tacit abandonment of global solutions. With good sense, we tend more and more towards limited remedies to solve concrete problems. It is prudent to abstain from legislating about the future. Yet the present requires much more than attention to its immediate needs: it demands a more rigorous global reflection. For a long time I have firmly believed that the twilight of the future heralds the advent of the now. To think about the now implies first of all to recover the critical vision. For example, the triumph of the market economy (a triumph due to the adversary's default) cannot be simply a cause for joy. As a mechanism the market is efficient, but like all mechanisms it lacks both conscience and compassion. We must find a way of integrating it into society so that it expresses the social contract and becomes an instrument of justice and fairness. The advanced democratic societies have reached an enviable level of prosperity; at the same time they are islands of abundance in the ocean of universal misery. The topic of the market is intricately related to the deterioration of the environment. Pollution affects not only the air, the rivers and the forests but also our souls. A society possessed by the frantic need to produce more in order to consume more tends to reduce ideas, feelings, art, love, friendship and people themselves to consumer products. Everything becomes a thing to be bought, used and then thrown on the rubbish dump. No other society has produced so much waste as ours has. Material and moral waste.

Reflecting on the now does not imply relinquishing the future or forgetting the past: the present is the meeting place for the three directions of time. Neither can it be confused with facile hedonism. The tree of pleasure does not grow in the past or in the future but at this very moment. Yet death is also a fruit of the present. It cannot be rejected, for it is part of life. Living well implies dying well. We have to learn how to look death in the face. The present is alternatively luminous and sombre, like a sphere that unites the two halves of action and contemplation. Thus, just as we have had philosophies of the past and of the future, of eternity and of the void, tomorrow we shall have a philosophy of the present. The poetic experience could be one of its foundations. What do we know about the present? Nothing or almost nothing. Yet the poets do know one thing: the present is the source of presences.

In this pilgrimage in search of modernity I lost my way at many points only to find myself again. I returned to the source and discovered that modernity is not outside but within us. It is today and the most ancient antiquity; it is tomorrow and the beginning of the world; it is a thousand years old and yet newborn. It speaks in Nahuatl, draws Chinese ideograms from the 9th century, and appears on the television screen. This intact present, recently unearthed, shakes off the dust of centuries, smiles and suddenly starts to fly, disappearing through the window. A simultaneous plurality of time and presence: modernity breaks with the immediate past only to recover an age-old past and transform a tiny fertility figure from the neolithic into our contemporary. We pursue modernity in her incessant metamorphoses yet we never manage to trap her. She always escapes: each encounter ends in flight. We embrace her and she disappears immediately: it was just a little air. It is the instant, that bird that is everywhere and nowhere. We want to trap it alive but it flaps its wings and vanishes in the form of a handful of syllables. We are left empty-handed. Then the doors of perception open slightly and the *other time* appears, the real one we were searching for without knowing it: the present, the presence.

> *Octavio Paz, "In Search of the Present: Nobel Lecture," delivered on December 8, 1990. Translated by Anthony Stanton. Permission granted by the Nobel Foundation.*

REVIEWS OF *THE COLLECTED POEMS OF OCTAVIO PAZ, 1957-1987*

Joel Lewis

Any comprehensive survey of American poetry of the last thirty years will have to take into account the influence that modern Spanish verse has had on the look and shape of the contemporary poem. Just as French Symbolist verse influenced High Modernism, and French Surrealism had a decisive effect on post-World War Two poets as different as James Wright and Frank O'Hara, the poets of Spain and the Americas have long become part of the daily poetic climate. . . .

In the same year (1961) that Grove Press issued the selected poems of [Pablo] Neruda and New Directions issued a selection of [Federico Garcia] Lorca, the Mexican poet Octavio Paz's 1950 prose meditation on his homeland, **The Labyrinth of Solitude,** was published in its English translation. The following year brought Muriel Rukeyser's translation of **Sun Stone,** the first volume of Paz's poetry in English translation. Although Paz had been publishing his poetry since 1933, it was these two books that established his North American reputation. In the following years, Paz published a dizzying stream of books that reflected his wide interests: books on art, politics, culture, history, anthropology, and contemporary Mexican society established him as one of the most important intellectuals in the western hemisphere. And, of course, Paz continued to write poetry all during this period; and blessed with sensitive poet/translators such as

Elizabeth Bishop, Paul Blackburn, Muriel Rukeyser, and Denise Levertov, Paz's work has been widely available for English readers.

The Collected Poems of Octavio Paz, 1957-1987, edited and mostly translated by Eliot Weinberger, is a massive overview of the mature work of a poet who is, sadly, better known in this country for prose writings and, when his poetry does come under consideration, is often categorized as yet another Spanish surrealist. Although surrealism has had a great influence in his writing and philosophy, Paz is the last of the Modernists—not the Modernism of Pound and Eliot, sidetracked by elitist political aspirations, but the visionary poetry of Kenneth Rexroth and André Breton that imposed no hierarchy on the differing world cultures and saw art as a means toward daily liberation in mass society.

Paz was well prepared to begin the poetry of his maturity in 1957, the year from which this collection proceeds. Born in Mexico City in 1914 to the religious daughter of Spanish immigrants and an often-absent father, a journalist/lawyer who defended Zapata and helped introduce agrarian reform in postrevolutionary Mexico, Paz was educated by Marist brothers and came of age at the beginning of the world economic crisis that followed the 1929 Wall Street crash. He published his first poem at age seventeen and, two years later, his first book, *Luna Silvestre.* He spent a year in Republican Spain as a noncombatant, becoming involved in left-wing political activity and meeting many of the writers who went to the Iberian peninsula in support of the Loyalists, including Neruda and Machado.

Paz returned to Mexico and wrote for the left-wing newspaper *El Popular.* He founded the literary review *Taller* and continued espousing revolutionary politics in his prose and poetry. But, like many Marxist intellectuals around the world, Paz became disillusioned with Soviet Marxism in the wake of the Hitler-Stalin pact. In 1941, he broke with his friend Neruda (then Chilean consul general in Mexico City and now believed to have been one of the Stalinist agents culpable in the assassination of Leon Trotsky) over the latter's subservience to dogmatic political partisanship—these two giants of Spanish letters not to meet again until 1967. By 1943, finding himself isolated by his break with Marxism, he took advantage of a Guggenheim fellowship to leave Mexico for a two-year sojourn in the United States. He then went to Paris in 1945, becoming a cultural attaché to the Mexican embassy the next year. It was this decade abroad that set the stage for Paz's mature poetry. He was introduced to André Breton by the surrealist poet Benjamin Peret, whom Paz had befriended in Spain, at a Parisian cafe. Paz's ensuing friendship with the founder of surrealism would have a profound effect on his writing. Paz, however, was attracted not to the prosody of surrealist verse, "automatic writing," and other techniques to liberate the unconscious, but to the moral implications of surrealism, primarily Breton's insistence upon the freedom of the artist along with the society he/she existed in. Years later, in the poem **"Clear Night,"** he recalled the significance of that encounter:

> We scattered in the night

> my friends went off
> I carried their words like a burning treasure
> . . . We have lost all the battles
> each day we win one
>
>   Poetry

Paz stayed in Paris until 1951, then traveled to Japan and India—whose cultures were also to influence his writing. When he returned to Mexico in 1952, after a decade's absence, he had evolved into a poet with an internationalist perspective who just happened to write in Spanish, bringing with him the accumulation of his travels and of his wide readings. **"Sunstone,"** which opens the *Collected Poems,* is one of the great contemporary long poems. He has described this poem's central theme as "the recovery of the amorous instant as a recovery of true freedom" and he frames this theme within a structure that is modeled after the Mayan calendar—the 584 hendecasyllables of the poem relate to a Mayan cycle that signifies the ending and beginning of another epoch. The poem is intended to be read in a rush (it is constructed without any stops or breathing space), and Weinberger's new translation captures the energy of this surging text:

> there is nothing inside me but a large wound,
> a hollow place where no one goes,
> a windowless present, a thought that returns
> and repeats itself, reflects itself,
> and loses itself in its own transparency,
> a mind transfixed by an eye that watches
> it watching itself till it drowns itself
> in clarity:

Also in 1957, Paz began a serious practice as translator with his version of Basho's writings. In the ensuing years he was to do book-length translations of William Carlos Williams and Apollinaire, as well as many individual poems from the French, English, Chinese, and Japanese. In 1962 he was appointed Mexican ambassador to India. The long poem **"Blanco"** (1966) is a product of Paz's scholarly interest in Indian culture. Combining Mallarme's notion of poetry as process and the radical eroticism of the Tantra, **"Blanco"** offers the reader a number of ways of making meaning from the poem:

> The spirit
> is an invention of the body
> The body
> is an invention of the world
> The world
> is an invention of the spirit
> No   Yes
>   the unreality of the seen
> transparency is all that remains

Paz resigned his ambassadorial post in 1968 as a protest against his government's massacre of student demonstrators during the Mexico City Olympics. Since then, he has devoted his time to writing and to teaching, mostly at American universities. In his great study of the poetic process, *The Bow and The Lyre* (1956), he notes that "the poetry of our time cannot escape from loneliness and rebellion, except by a change of society and man himself. The action of the contemporary poet can only be exerted on individuals and groups. In this limitation, perhaps, lies his present effectiveness and his future fecundity." In his elegy

A Draft of Shadows (1974), he reaffirms the power of the poem even over the poet's personal history:

> My memory: a puddle.
> A muddy mirror: where was I?
> My eyes, without anger or pity,
> look me in the eye
> from the troubled waters
> of the puddle my words evoke.
> I don't see with my eyes: words
> are my eyes. We live among names;

Although Paz's work has been readily available in English for many years, half of the 200 poems appearing in the **Collected Poems** are appearing in an English language edition for the first time. Equally significant is the translation of Paz's **A Tree Within,** which collects the poetry of the years 1976-1987. Appearing simultaneously with the Spanish edition, it gives us a rare opportunity to be informed of the poet's most current work.

The depth and variety of Paz's mature writing make the **Collected Poems** a volume that demands serious engagement by the reader, one that will give up its "secrets" only when the reader gives up the same level of energy that it took to create these poems.

> Joel Lewis, "Ink and Transfers," in The American Book Review, *Vol. 10, No. 4, September-October, 1988, p. 11.*

J. D. McClatchy

In the prologue to his magisterial study of Sor Juana [*Sor Juana, or the Traps of Faith*], as part of a meditation on "the system of implicit authorizations and prohibitions" in modern culture, Octavio Paz speculates that the democratic and progressivist societies dominant in the West since the late eighteenth century are constitutionally hostile to certain literary genres. Bourgeois rationalism and poetry, for instance, are oil and water. The methods and attitudes, the very nature of poetry has grown hostile to the dogmas of the day and the cult of the future, to the moral pieties of modern society. Poetry is a violation. Baudelaire and the Symbolists, the pioneers of Modernism, the Surrealists—these were enemies within the walls, and remain the champions of all those forces opposed to the relentless progress of twentieth-century life.

There is more than a little truth in Paz's view of history, and more than a little self-justification. Certainly those champions have been his masters, and his career has been devoted to the idea that as "an operation capable of changing the world, poetic activity is revolutionary by nature; a spiritual exercise, it is a means of interior liberation." Though it reveals the world and its *correspondances,* it denies history. It is simultaneously the voice of the people, the language of the elect, and the word of the solitary. Like those of his Modernist masters, Paz's poems have preferred the fragmentary and ecstatic, the discoveries of chance and dream, the infernal landscape of the city, nostalgic glimpses of paradisal literature from the past, the unredeemable self *in extremis.* Such views derive largely from European models, and have put Paz in one camp (along with Borges, he has been a sort of major general)

of a continuing battle that rages (or used to) in Latin America as in its northern neighbor. He himself tells the story of meeting, decades ago, Gabriela Mistral. She had just won the Nobel Prize, and asked the young, unknown Paz to show her his poems. He sent a slim volume. A few days later, she greeted him at a party with that slightly too formal politeness one understands to be a reproof: "I like your poems," she said, "though they are not at all what I feel. You could well be a European poet; for my taste, you are not *telluric* enough." What she meant by the peculiar term is that Paz was airborne rather than deeply rooted, a cosmopolite rather than a native. Any Latin American writer, he would counter, is actually both, working between the traditions of European civilization and the realities of American culture. The convergence appears even, or first, in the language itself. The Spanish of Spain is pure, solid, substantialist; the Spanish of Latin America is a hybrid, "sometimes a mask, sometimes a passion—never a habit."

Masks and passions would likewise describe the surface, the *sound,* of [**The Collected Poems of Octavio Paz, 1957-1987**]. The book picks up where **Early Poems: 1935-1955,** published fifteen years ago by New Directions, leaves off, and with these two volumes the reader will have most of Paz's poems, attractively presented and fluently translated. The past three decades have taken Paz far afield, most notably during his years as the Mexican Ambassador to India, and resulted in some of his strongest work. But I'll confess I have always preferred Paz's essays to his poems. Only in prose does the full range of his extraordinary mind stand revealed, its breadth of reference and brilliance of analogy. The poems, oddly, seem more one-dimensional. They are nearly always lyrics; there is no narrative, little portraiture or evocation of specific places, not much variety of tone. He is a poet of phrases, what he calls "a succession of signs," as if sustained argument would somehow handicap a poem's spontaneity. Surrealist gestures, "the apple of fire on the tree of syntax," electrify by moments, but are often merely scintillant sparks. Other rhetorical gestures are more grandiose, but hollow:

> The things were buried deep in themselves
> and my eyes of flesh saw them
> weary of being, realities
> stripped of their names. My two eyes
> were souls grieving for the world. . . .

There are worse examples of this same sort of vatic mannerisms throughout the new collection, though it is fair to say it sounds flatter in English than in Spanish.

What here seems a fault is elsewhere a virtue of Paz's restless search for the world behind the world. "Poetry is not truth," he says in **"San Ildefonso Nocturne,"** "it is the resurrection of presences." The best poems here are rites. What we get is an invocation of powers, a litany of images, the ascent to vision, and the ritualistic struggle of opposing psychic and mythic forces. If Paz sometimes seems impatient to get beyond language, at other times he celebrates the textuality of the self. Here is an exuberant Whitmanian flourish:

> entering yourself you're not leaving the world,
>   there are

rivers and volcanoes inside your body, planets
   and ants,
empires, turbines, libraries, gardens sail through
   your blood,
there are animals, plants, beings from other
   worlds, galaxies
wheel through your neurons,
entering yourself you enter this world and the
   other worlds,. . . .

                    (pp. 29-31)

[*Collected Poems*] falls into three parts. At the heart of the earlier work here is the long poem that first brought Paz to the attention of an international audience, **"Sunstone"** (1957). Reading it is rather like listening to Messiaen's *Turangalila:* you're overwhelmed, but don't want to repeat it very often. Memory's "swimming flame"—at once sensuous and metaphysical—flickers in corners of his life, and on the faces of women he has loved. And it's right that this poem be placed first in a volume that is obsessed with women: with real women, like his wife and mother; with the idea of woman, fertile and mysterious, Mother India or the *anima mundi* or "the feminine void"; and finally with woman as the type of the muse, the lyric, the imagination, *la palabra,* the word itself, "stainless / promiscuous / speechless / nameless."

With **Ladera Este** (**East Slope,** 1968) we move with Paz to India, and to material congenial to his mystical temperament but also exotic enough to be transcribed into poems much denser, richer than before. Like India itself, these poems are a collage of details both elemental and quotidian. The waking dream of Orientalism calls forth from Paz some of his most sharply observed and powerful lines. Let this brief excerpt from **"A Tale of Two Gardens"** stand for his intentions:

             It rained,
the earth dressed and became naked,
snakes left their holes,
the moon was made of water,
              the sun was water,
the sky took out its braids
and its braids were unraveled rivers,
the rivers swallowed villages,
death and life were jumbled,
dough of mud and sun,
season of lust and plague,
season of lightning on a sandalwood tree,
mutilated genital stars
               rotting,
reviving in your womb,
               mother India,
girl India,
drenched in semen, sap, poisons, juices.

Paz does not always take the panoramic view. His close-ups, with their posed images and eerie stillnesses, can be very affecting. (pp. 31-2)

In 1968 Paz resigned his post in New Delhi to protest the massacre by government troops of student demonstrators in Mexico City. After a stay in England and the United States, where he taught at Harvard and Texas, he returned to Mexico in 1971, and the title of his next book, **Vuelta** (**Return,** 1975), indicates his spiritual turn back towards Mexican themes. The title poem itself is a stinging jeremi-

ad that scans from the hilltop of indignation the city which has swallowed up his native village. . . . (p. 33)

Paz's most recent work, **Arbol Adentro** (**A Tree Within,** 1988) is the last section of this book, but as a courtesy to readers who have all the earlier books it has also been published simultaneously and separately by New Directions. Though it contains a remarkable poem, **"Preparatory Exercise,"** which speculates about his own death, this generous group is hardly valedictory; it includes some of Paz's most vigorous work. There is a suite of poems addressed to painters—among them, Balthus, Miró, Duchamp, Rauschenberg, Matta, and Alechinsky—that set out to recreate the surfaces and moods of their paintings. In other poems too, the economy of the visionary and the descriptive, the prophetic and the panegyric, is wonderfully balanced. I finished this book convinced that Paz stands out like a ziggurat in the literary landscape of Mexico. And though to North American tastes much of his poetry will seem like a rather inflated throwback, Paz remains, at seventy-five, one of the truly imposing figures in the cultural life of the New World. (pp. 33-4)

> *J. D. McClatchy, in a review of "The Collected Poems of Octavio Paz: 1957-1987," in* Poetry, *Vol. CLIV, No. 1, April, 1989, pp. 29-34.*

Arthur Terry

Octavio Paz is unquestionably one of the finest poets writing in any language, a fact which [his **Collected Poems**] should make abundantly clear to English readers. Though earlier selections have done much to convey the quality of his poetry, only a thorough reading of his work of the past three decades can bring out the often subtle relations between individual poems and an overall structure of great ambition and integrity. At the same time, as readers of his prose can confirm, the integrity of Paz's vision is not purely a poetical matter: his continuing reflections on a multiplicity of themes, from art and anthropology to the contingencies of world politics and the society of his native Mexico, bear witness to an intelligence which both feeds off, and feeds into, his activity as a poet.

Something of the nature of this relationship emerges from one of Paz's best-known statements: "Poetry is the *other* voice. Not the voice of history or of anti-history, but the voice which, in history, is always saying something different." What this means in practice is that any poem involves a "breaking of silence" or, as he puts it in his note to **Blanco** (1966), "the passage of the word from silence before speech to silence after it". This already suggests Paz's affinities with both Mallarmé and the Surrealists: where Breton, for instance, rejects the notion of an "external theme" in poetry, Paz sees the poem not as a means of representing the world but as a way of reproducing it through the behaviour of language itself. Thus each of his major poems, from **"Piedra de sol"** (1957) to **"Carta de creencia"** (1987), forms a kind of "itinerary" in which the composition of the poem is made to reflect the actual experience of reading a poem. This is not to say that external reality is excluded from the poem, but rather that such references as there are—to outside events or to moments in the poet's own experience—tend to lead back into the verbal structure of the text. As for the nature of the "itinerary", this more often than not takes the form of a movement towards a particular moment which remains fixed in the poem, where it acts as a mirror for the poet's own consciousness.

What prevents this from being merely narcissistic is Paz's sense of "the Other": in poem after poem, the individual consciousness is made to confront that which is not itself in an attempt to reach the unity which, in Paz's view of things, lies beyond this essential duality. In the course of the process. Otherness assumes a number of forms—language, the human body, the world itself—each of which is interchangeable with the others. Hence the eroticism which is central to Paz's poetry is never an isolated force: its subversiveness owes something to Surrealism, but sexual love is both a way of escaping from the constrictions of the self and a metaphor for a kind of fusion which language itself can only hint at. The line which occurs near the beginning of **"Piedra de sol"**—"the world is now visible through your body"—is both the starting-point of the poem and the axis around which the whole complex sequence of images revolves. Similarly, **"Blanco"**—Paz's most "experimental" poem, in which a single poem breaks up into a constellation of shorter sequences, each self-sufficient yet complementary to the others—may be read simultaneously as a love poem and as a meditation on knowledge and on the nature of poetic language.

Paz's achievement as a poet rests ultimately on his power to create a kind of poetry which both exemplifies, and at the same time questions, the ability of language to come to terms with the world it claims to know. The kind of transaction this implies, he would argue, can never be more than provisional; as he says in **"El mono gramático"**, probably his finest prose text, "fixity can only be momentary", and the final poem in his most recent volume ends, simply and movingly, with a sense of new beginnings:

> Perhaps to love is to learn
> to walk through this world.
> To learn to be silent
> like the oak and the linden of the fable.
> To learn to see.
> Your glance scatters seeds.
> It planted a tree.
>   I talk
> because you shake its leaves.

The collection from which this comes, *Árbol adentro* (*A Tree Within*), forms the last section of Eliot Weinberger's massive and beautifully produced bilingual edition, which contains virtually all of Paz's poetry from his first major poem, **"Piedra de sol"** (**"Sunstone"**), to the present. . . .

[*Collected Poems*] deserves to be widely read, and one must applaud the efforts of both editor and publisher in making available a body of work which engages so lucidly and on so many levels with the possibilities and limitations of modern poetry.

Arthur Terry, "Back to the Other," in The Times Literary Supplement, *No. 4489, April 14-20, 1989, p. 402.*

Edwin Williamson

Octavio Paz occupies a unique position in the Spanish-speaking world. He is the foremost living poet of the language as well as being one of the most authoritative interpreters of the Hispanic situation, a *pensador* in the tradition of Unamuno, Ortega y Gasset, Rodo and Mariategui. Poetry, however, has always been the vital source of his ideas. His work as cultural historian, political essayist and editor of *Vuelta,* the most influential journal in Latin America today, is rooted in his belief that the poetic conscience must be brought to bear on the central issues of contemporary history. The **Collected Poems** brings together for the first time Paz's mature work in a splendidly produced bilingual edition. Over half of the poems have not been rendered into English before and it is very gratifying to find here the most recent collection, the superb *A Tree Within,* which came out in 1987. . . .

The collection begins appropriately with **Sunstone,** an extended reverie which incorporates the sum of his poetic experience until 1957. The title refers to an Aztec calendar stone whose cycle of 584 days is reflected in the number of lines of the poem. This correlation evinces Paz's perennial concern to escape contingency by looking for a mythic dimension to personal experience. The Surrealist influence—his friendship with André Breton in the late Forties left an indelible mark on his poetry—is evident in the visionary intensity of the language. But despite its oneiric strangeness, the poem describes a purposeful quest for a fullness of being which time routinely denies the poet except for intermittent epiphanies granted him in the love of woman, the universal 'other'. The poem undulates through successive states of consciousness, interweaving memories of war and atrocity with personal recollections of people, places and events. Impelled by its own inner momentum, its flow is punctuated by sudden spasms of joy until it eventually finds its way back to the beginning:

> a course of a river that turns, moves on,
> doubles back, and comes full circle,
> forever arriving:

These lines repeat the opening sequence of metaphors and, ending with a colon, trace an image of history as eternal recurrence, though 'forever arriving', lacking the final spurting rhythm of *y llega siempre,* fails to capture the narrowness of this victory over the contingent and the terminal.

Salvation for history through love and poetry was to remain the romantic heart of Paz's enterprise. From 1959, when he returned to live in Paris, the search for pure being was extended under the influence of Mallarmé, from whom he derived a metaphysics of the poetic word as a primal reality buried under layers of dead language. The desire to cleanse the word from the slime of functional usage led to experiments with phonic resonance—intensive punning and internal rhyme—and typographical layout: spaced-out lines, stanzas suspended in mid-page, counterpointed islets of text, with the odd word exiled to a margin. Such experiments can be seen at their most radical in **Topoemas** (1968), a cross between Apollinaire's *calligrammes* and oriental ideograms.

Though the linear text remained the norm, Paz would continue to break up or displace lines to allow white spaces to show through, creating a pleasing effect of airiness which corresponded graphically to his belief in the transcendent potential of poetic language. Indeed, at their best, Paz's disjointed texts read with the freshness of a breeze: words appear to have been swept up by a wave of air and relieved of their burden of reference, to circulate in some undetermined space between the material world and whatever might lie beyond it. When they fail to come off, such poems are like arrested mobiles, with inert images hanging off a predictable set of ideas.

The mystical strain was more fully developed after 1962, when Paz became Mexican Ambassador in India for six years. His reactions to a new landscape and a new human reality are recorded in *East Slope* (1962-1968), a miscellany ranging from snapshots of nature or ironic sketches of social types to long meditations prompted by monuments and places where, surprisingly, as in **'Happiness in Herat'**, the quietism of Hindu mysticism is rejected for a more dynamic vision of a natural world transfigured into the 'perfection of the finite'. In the East, Paz recognises the Europeanness of his heritage as a Mexican: he refuses to discount material reality in the quest for plentitude of being.

Perhaps for this reason, he was drawn to the sacred eroticism of Tantric rites. The major works of his Indian interlude are indeed love poems. It was in India that he met his second wife and there that he most fully deployed his extraordinary powers of evoking sexual union in language that fuses exhilarated sensuality with religious awe. Eroticism and Mallarméan experimentation are combined in **Blanco** (1966), the most ambitious poem of this period. Conceived as a sort of verbal kaleidoscope, it consists of 14 texts that can be read separately or in a variety of interlocking permutations. The aim is to generate a changing interplay of images and rhythms that will figure forth the oppositions and polarities that divide consciousness, and whose reconciliation is achieved only in the ecstatic moment of erotic fulfillment:

> No and Yes
> together
> two syllables in love

Blanco now seems to be too beholden to the vapid spirituality of the Sixties to convince in its entirety. But the headiness of the Indian years did not distract Paz from the grim realities of history. In 1968 he resigned his post as ambassador in protest at the massacre by government troops of several hundred student demonstrators at Tlatelolco before the Olympic Games were due to open in Mexico City.

Back in Mexico, he began his intellectual journey to discover a new political ethic for Latin America. *Return* (1969-1975) contains poems of terrible desolation:

> the blind in combat beneath the noon sun
> thirst panting anger
> beating each other with rocks
> the blind are beating each other
> the men are crushing
> the stones are crushing
> within there is a water we drink

> bitter water
> water whetting thirst
> where is the other water?

In this harsh wasteland the poet must find the resources to avoid becoming a 'gardener of epitaphs'. The two masterpieces of these years are **'San Ildefonso Nocturne'** and *A Draft of Shadows* (1974). Both reflect upon his own childhood—a new preoccupation—and on the ghastly proliferation of Mexico City, which had devoured the village where he was born and raised. Paz is forced back into an inner world:

> I close my eyes,
> I hear in my skull
> the footsteps of my blood,
>
> I hear
> time pass through my temples.
> I am still alive.

Sheltering in that last redoubt, yet perturbed by the strange allure of death, he finally submits to the 'errant clarity' of the Moon, and contemplating his sleeping wife ('she too is a moon'), brings his poem to an end by placing his trust in the woman's 'quiet flowing'. Attenuated now from what it was in **Sunstone,** his faith in woman as the saving 'other' still serves to overcome despair and the obliteration of the cherished landmarks of childhood.

A Draft of Shadows, one of his most moving compositions, begins by alluding once more to those 'footsteps in the mind' which tread

> the path of echoes
> that memory invents and erases.

A long complex poem about the substance of personal identity, it has none of the attitudinising which sometimes mars the earlier works. There are intimations of a divine presence, a 'bodiless god' who refuses to be named in 'the language of the body'. This realisation cuts the poet down to size: his poem is nothing but

> air that sculpts itself and dissolves,
> a fleeting allegory of true names.

Yet if this is all that can be expected of poetry, it is also the sum of what can be salvaged from the ruin of time, for the self is simply 'the shadow my words cast'. Released now from his anxiety to be a hierophantic visionary, Paz accepts the humbler calling of a mere boxer of shadow-words. His reward is the discovery of a new voice.

In **'A Tree Within'**, the brief but charming title-poem of his latest collection (1976-1987), the poet tells how he felt a tree growing inside him, lighting up his whole body. Paz's new voice is gentler, more accepting of the world as it is, yet suffused with the roguish humour of a man entering old age who has come across a garden, not of epitaphs, but of images and sensations that repeat the 'great exclamation with which the world begins each day'. He now writes in a well-modulated, unforced, surrealist manner, with graceful clarity and no perceptible loss of the power to strike beautiful images, as in the surprisingly coltish **'The Dryad War'**, with its sparkling stream of fancies, or in the unerring metaphors of **'A Fable of Joan Miro'**. The advent of death is contemplated with a serenity that commands respect. In **'A Small Variation'** his last moment is imagined as one of those instants of communion which have formed the axes of his life as a poet, an instant which

> opens under my feet
> and closes over me and is pure time.

> (p. 20)

Edwin Williamson, "Spanish Practices," in London Review of Books, *Vol. 11, No. 10, May 18, 1989, pp. 20-2.*

Paul Quarrington
Whale Music

Award: Governor General's Literary Award: Fiction

Born in 1954(?), Quarrington is a Canadian novelist, scriptwriter, and playwright.

Whale Music is a comic novel concerning the reclusive former lead singer of a rock group called The Howls. Desmond Howell, the novel's protagonist, is an overweight alcoholic and drug addict hiding from his therapist and the outside world in a well-secured mansion overlooking the ocean in California. Desmond's on-going project is a symphony of whale music he is composing in honor of his brother, whose spectacular suicide car crash into the ocean attracted nearby whales. During the course of *Whale Music,* Desmond forms a relationship with Claire, an escaped mental patient who appears on his doorstep one day; her abrupt departure after an argument is the catalyst that forces Desmond out into the world again to search for her. While some critics were uncomfortable with the similarities between the protagonist and Brian Wilson, the former leader of The Beach Boys band, who suffered a mental breakdown following the suicide of Dennis Wilson, his brother and fellow band member, others praised Quarrington's witty yet penetrating treatment of such matters as the rock and roll lifestyle, drug addiction, and death. Jack MacLeod wrote: "There is comic capering [in *Whale Music*] and the rush of epiphany, but there is also a taut control evident here, an artistic restraint and even a suggestion of wisdom, qualities reflecting not just the craft of the entertainer but the confident art of the mature writer."

Whale Music, Quarrington's sixth novel, relies more heavily on the author's personal experiences than his previous works; Quarrington toured for six years with a Canadian rock group before he became a writer. Quarrington is best known for his lighthearted approach to baseball in *Home Game,* and hockey, in *King Leary,* which won the Stephen Leacock Memorial Medal for Humour. Since *Whale Music,* Quarrington has published *Logan in Overtime,* a novel about the longest overtime hockey game in history, and his play, *The Invention of Poetry,* was produced in Toronto.

PRINCIPAL WORKS

NOVELS

Home Game 1983
The Life of Hope 1985
King Leary 1987
Hometown Heroes 1988

Whale Music 1989
Logan in Overtime 1990

Paul Kennedy

[In] *Whale Music,* Quarrington has produced a major work of fiction that confronts the age-old themes of love and death and power and corruption and—more than anything else—art.

This isn't to say that Quarrington has lost his sense of humour. The protagonist of *Whale Music* is a parody of a hideously fat, ageing rock musician. Des Howell now lives in Hollywood. His house might have been designed by Hunter S. Thompson. Platinum records are alternately used as frisbees and as trays for snorting coke. Henry Mancini lives across the street behind a tiny moat with a huge neon sign proclaiming it to be "MOON RIVER." Des has become a hopeless drug and alcohol abuser and a recluse. When Dr. Tockette comes to the front door, with his medical degree from the Betty Ford Center and his personal mandate to unravel the patient's peculiar sex life, Des screams through the keyhole, announcing his own death.

He's obviously crazy. But in the not-too-distant past, Des was the musical genius behind one of the biggest rock bands of the 1960s, the Fabulous Howl Brothers. He composed the tunes that got everyone in his generation laid (except himself). With his brother Dan he recorded a string of hits that reached the top of the charts and put the Howl Brothers on the cover of *Time*. In their heyday, Des and Dan Howell rivalled the Beatles in popularity.

John, Paul, George, and Ringo make cameo appearances in *Whale Music.* So do Bill Haley, Elvis Presley, Jimi Hendrix, and Jerry Lee Lewis. The rest of the characters are Rabelaisian figments of Quarrington's vivid imagination. They bear about as much resemblance to real '60s heroes as Des Howell of the Howl Brothers does to Brian Wilson of the Beach Boys. One of my favourites is an erstwhile spiritual leader named Babboo Nass Fazoo. As the plot advances Babboo disappears from view, but he resurfaces near the end of the book—now simply named Bob—slobberingly drinking mescal in a sleazy California bar. Then there's Freaky Freddy Head, who acts as the recording engineer on all of the Howl Brothers' records. Fred discovers drugs and sex simultaneously in San Francisco during the Summer of Love. Not long after, Fred is thrown in jail for propositioning a pre-pubescent teenager.

The character Freaky Fred is actually a foil for the underlying artistic or creative theme of *Whale Music.* He performs a miraculous studio mix on the electronic masterpiece that Des has been composing during his few lucid moments in the course of the narrative. Des's creation is called Whale Music. It's a celebration of whales and whale-like bodies, a dirge, and a paean to love and to life itself. The fact that it's never adequately described is probably the book's major disappointment. But it's far from a fatal flaw. And it's an indication of Quarrington's success that by the final page of *Whale Music,* most readers will sincerely want to know, and try to imagine, just how wonderful Whale Music sounds.

> *Paul Kennedy, "Sex 'n' Drugs 'n' Rock 'n' Droll," in* Quill and Quire, *Vol. 55, No. 5, May, 1989, p. 20.*

John Gault

Paul Quarrington seems poised to become a major Canadian novelist.

If he finds that notion humorous, it is at least partly because he finds humor in most of life's situations—as befits a man who has published four funny novels since 1983 and who earned the 1987 Stephen Leacock Memorial Medal for Humour. His latest book, *Whale Music*—a send-up of sex, drugs and rock 'n' roll—may have "commercial success" written all over it, but that is not really something

that occupies the author's thoughts. He says that he wants to "get a lot of things out there," and that is precisely what he is doing. This fall, his first play, *The Invention of Poetry,* will open at Toronto's Canadian Stage Company theatre. He has completed three original screenplays—all of them commissioned and now in the hands of film producers—and one is at the casting stage. His newly completed novel, *Logan in Overtime,* is scheduled for publication next year, while the early chapters of another novel, *An Encyclopedia of All Things Animate,* are stored in his Apple computer.

His two musician brothers, Tony and Joel, suggest that Quarrington might not have produced all that work if he had made it big in the rock scene. He toiled for six long years as a bass guitarist with Joe Hall and the Continental Drift, playing short engagements in Toronto clubs and often touring the country. The author says that his brothers are wrong and points out that he wrote most of his 1983 baseball novel, *Home Game,* during the band's last tour. His rock 'n' roll years, however, prepared him for *Whale Music,* which features a composer-lyricist hero called Des Howell. Des—a character patterned slightly on the author himself but more strongly on Brian Wilson of The Beach Boys—does battle with all the mundane and cosmic forces that plague a superstar's existence.

Like his previous works, *Whale Music* is very much a novel of character. "I know plot is not what grabs people about my books," Quarrington said. His first-person narrator, Des, is a drunkard, drug-user and doughnut addict who manages to outmanoeuvre all manner of evil and exploitation, from his mother on through to his record producer. From the opening sentence, Quarrington weaves a bond of friendship with the lovable madman. Des and his brother Danny once formed the nucleus of the Howl Brothers, a fictional 1960s American supergroup that rivalled The Beatles in popularity. Then Danny (whose demise echoes the drowning of Beach Boys drummer Dennis Wilson) drove his silver Porsche full blast through a guardrail and out into the Pacific. The car exploded, and whales gathered to watch the conflagration. Now, the stricken Des, a recluse in his beachfront home, writes music only for whales. Deftly and seductively throughout the novel's 213 pages, Quarrington has the reader straining to hear the chords, anticipating the concert, cheering for Des to complete his lonely suite.

Quarrington wrote *Whale Music,* he says, because after writing novels on baseball (well received by critics, *Home Game* brought Quarrington his first real recognition) and hockey (*King Leary* won the Leacock award), friends and acquaintances urged him to write about something he knew from firsthand experience. And somewhere in the not-too-distant future, he says, there will likely be a Quarrington novel on a subject with which he has just become acquainted: fatherhood. . . . Quarrington is now planning a novel in which the president of the United States fathers his first child while in office. As a result, the leader gets a whole new sense of what is important in life, and dedicates himself and his country to saving the world's children.

Despite the earnest sound of that plot, it is unlikely that

the novelist with a gift for comic outrageousness is going to get serious. When a Quarrington hero saves the world, he will have a loony gleam in his eye.

John Gault, "Loony Tunes: Paul Quarrington Sends Up Rock 'n' Roll," in Maclean's Magazine, Vol. 102, No. 22, May 29, 1989, p. 61.

Jack MacLeod

The adjective "comic" is frequently applied to a writer in a disparaging way or as a synonym for "minor," (although exceptions are made for Shakespeare, Cervantes, or Dickens), but *Whale Music* is a comic novel of the most serious sort. It's a book about music, fame, drugs, whales, sex, accidents, and money. That it evokes chuckles is a grand bonus.

In 1986 Quarrington was named one of the 10 best Canadian writers under the age of 45. Now, at age 35, he has published his fifth novel and sixth book. For a man who spent seven years as a rock musician, with Joe Hall and the Continental Drift, that's not a bad record, even without the 1987 Leacock Award for *King Leary.* It is not known whether there are any earnest Ph.D. theses being written on him yet, but that too will happen.

In [*Whale Music*] Des and Danny Howell—The Howl Brothers—were rock sensations in the '60s, contemporaries of the Beatles. Fame and wealth and drugs blew their minds. Des, who is reminiscent of the fat boy in *A Confederacy of Dunces,* may be based on Brian Wilson, the chubby and reclusive lead singer of The Beach Boys. Des ambles around his oceanside house, hallucinating, eating jelly doughnuts, and composing a rock symphony for whales on a monster Yamaha 666 keyboard. Intruders and the sharp teeth of life keep snapping at him and force him into grim and funny grapplings with what the world calls real. To Des it is not always clear whether he is defending his privacy, fighting for his art, guarding his gold, or riding shotgun on a garbage truck. Somehow a whole plausible/incredible world is created—which is what superior writing is all about.

Apart from warmth and laughter, the book is full of effective one-liners and aphorisms. When a demented singer proclaims an Era of Free Love, the response is: "Sounds okay. It's been costing me a fortune." Failure to do what his lover demands makes Des "suffer in a little hell that makes Hades look like Disneyland." With the whales, Des communicates. The book, like Des, has good vibes.

Unlike some of his earlier work, where his talent seemed untamed and his exuberance unbounded, *Whale Music* demonstrates that Quarrington can write a lean, spare prose. There is comic capering and the rush of epiphany, but there is also a taut control evident here, an artistic restraint and even a suggestion of wisdom, qualities reflecting not just the craft of the entertainer but the confident art of the mature writer.

Moving from the humorous big boffolas to the wry and sly is a long leap, and Quarrington has made it. The book is a joyous affirmation of a major—yes, serious—talent. (pp. 25-6)

Jack MacLeod, "The Teeth of Comedy," in Books in Canada, Vol. 18, No. 5, June-July, 1989, pp. 25-6.

An excerpt from *Whale Music*.

Let's review the pristine American upbringing, let's look at this childhood painted by Normie Rockwell. Here we see the Howells at dinner: the father, the mother, Danny, and Desmond. What are they eating? No one knows. It was cooked by the mother, and she has the best insight, but she identifies all of her dishes with a kind of crippled continental French that the boys have long since given up trying to decipher. The father doesn't care what it is. The father eats with fork and spoon. Apparently he never mastered the knife, the knife is beyond him, the whole concept of knife goes over the father's flat, brush-cut head.

Daniel picks at the meal. Desmond devours with gusto.

"This is good," Danny offers. "It tastes like in a restaurant."

Mother looks up dreamily. She names the dish. We are baffled.

"It is good," I say. "I'm having seconds."

"Hey, Dezzy-do," says the father. "You're turning into a real porker."

"He's big-boned," says my mother quietly.

" 'Sides," offers Dan, turning toward the father, "he's not as fat as you."

"Put a lock on it."

"Henry," says my mother, and that single word snaps the father's head up. "What's happening with Jimmy Cohn?"

Cohn being one of many weasel-like men that my father had music-related business with.

"That guy," snarls the father. "He wouldn't know a smash-hit number-one socko boff if it came up and kissed his ass."

"Please. *Les enfants.*"

Margot Mifflin

The story of the Beach Boy Brian Wilson is a tangled yarn of excess, knotted with the kind of pathetic drama only actors and rock stars seem capable of living. Brian Wilson has been riddled with mental problems, is 96 percent deaf in one ear, has snorted an entire gram of cocaine in one breath, used to keep his piano in a sandbox and, in the early 1970's, stayed in bed for the better part of four years. . . . [His life story] would strain credulity even if it were printed as fiction.

Paul Quarrington's *Whale Music* is, redundantly enough, a fictionalization of Brian Wilson's life. A comic writer who won Canada's Stephen Leacock Award for his previous novel, *King Leary,* Mr. Quarrington has a ribald, animated prose style all his own. Unlike many novelists who write about rock, this one has done his pop culture homework: he played bass in a Canadian rock band for six years, and his writing betrays not only his knowledge of music but his love of it. He likens the sound of Jerry Lee Lewis's fingers on the keyboard to "sailors on shore leave."

Whale Music concentrates on the period of Brian Wilson's recovery after his brother's death, when, with the help of a psychiatrist, he emerged from a haze of isolated unreality and took his first steps toward human contact. To lure Desmond (read Wilson), the superannuated popster, back into the world of light, Mr. Quarrington concocts Claire, a quirky 20-year-old with pretty toes, newly escaped from a mental institution, who shows up without explanation at Desmond's house. The author manages to sustain the tragic hilarity of Desmond's warped mental state through most of the novel's ambling plot. But he hits a snag when he has Desmond wrestle his girlfriend Claire out of a strip joint and lands him at a police station, where Desmond signs a new contract and delivers Claire permanently from institutional life. This final inexplicable drama is clumsily designed to expedite an infuriatingly happy ending in which Desmond's romantic and artistic dreams are realized, courtesy Claire.

Mr. Quarrington is an exceptionally inventive writer whose ability to create rounded and colorful characters almost compensates for his novel's lack of originality. He draws arbitrarily from Brian Wilson's life, basing about two-thirds of his story on fact, embroidering and complicating other real-life incidents for no apparent reason and overlooking the one aspect of Brian Wilson's history ripe for literary plunder—the irony of his band's apple-pie image, given its sordid private affairs. (In 1968, the group included Charlie Manson's "Cease to Exist" on the "B" side of one of their 45's, thereby landing a mass murderer-to-be on the charts.)

Entertainingly written but ill conceived, *Whale Music* will be best appreciated by Beach Boys non-initiates, who won't be hampered by Mr. Quarrington's peculiar manipulations of fact. But be forewarned: if curiosity sends you running to consult a biography, as it did me, you'll find that truth, where the Beach Boys are concerned, is not only stranger than fiction, it's better.

> *Margot Mifflin, "Bad Vibrations," in* The New York Times Book Review, *February 25, 1990, p. 12.*

Tom Schnabel

Give me a well-researched and well-written biography and I can't put it down. But while I'm no expert on the Beach Boys, not even much of a fan, I had plenty of problems with Paul Quarrington's fifth novel, *Whale Music.*

The Canadian novelist's book is a *roman à clef* about Brian Wilson's life after his brother's death, with plenty of flashbacks about family life and the rise to fame of one of the most popular groups of all time.

The Beach Boys took California sunshine and surf and splashed its happy message all over the world: a mythic American youth of surfing, girls, your first set of wheels. . . .

The Beach Boys' paean to California youth culture sours abruptly when you look at the harrowing lives of Brian and Dennis Wilson. Perhaps no greater disparity exists than that between the utter wholesomeness of their all-American music and their messed-up lives.

Dennis Wilson jumped off a moored yacht in 1983, hit his head on the Marina del Rey bottom, and died. Brian Wilson is still with us, although his creative output has ground to a halt. His psychiatrist, Dr. Eugene Landy, co-wrote the lyrics on the solo album that came out about two years ago. Brian Wilson seemed the shell of his former self.

And it is at this point that *Whale Music* picks up the saga of the superannuated star. In Quarrington's fictionalized account, we find Desmond Howell perched on a cliff overlooking the Pacific in a million-dollar home protected by about every security device except a moat and live crocodiles.

Howell fiddles with his state-of-the-art Yamaha 666 on his latest project, the whale music. The majestic sea creatures seem a sort of idealized metaphor: They don't fall victim to the complex emotions that wrack our lives, and certainly not to the emotional paralysis and inertia that taint Howell's daily life. In music and in life, the cetacean state of grace is something Howell aspires to, and a little booze and drugs probably will smooth his path in getting there.

Howl tells us his story in the first person: his early talent for music, his idolization of his brother Dannie, the ambitious and conniving father (Wilson's own father was an opportunist who in the late '60s sold the publishing rights to all of Brian's songs for quick big bucks).

The book is about the rise and fall of the famous Howl Brothers whose first big hit, "Torque, Torque," launched them into superstardom (substitute The Beach Boys' 1962 hit, "Surfin' "). Desmond Howell, who has spent the last few years horizontal in his hermetically sealed seaside manse, is pulled out of his semi-permanent torpor by Claire, a mental-hospital escapee from Toronto and a former groupie of a metal band whose members are into Satan worship and other lovely things.

One day Claire shows up at Desmond's place. (We find out later that she was really looking for the now-departed Dannie.) Twenty-year-old Claire passes her days wandering around the house and pool, clothing optional. Desmond Howl, for his part, takes refuge in bed, but also rummages around for any drugs or alcohol that might have been stashed out of sight of his therapist and well-meaning friends.

Sometimes he gets lucky, and thus inspired, enters the music room, wherein sits the Beast, the Yamaha 666, the contraptual equivalent to having the Berlin Philharmonic in your living room. Better than the redoubtable orchestra, the Beast can imitate sounds of nature so well that it would make Paul Winter green with envy. Like whale music, for instance.

Claire lures Howell out of years of lethargy, and the two manage to become intimate a few times. By the time Claire has become quite at home, and Desmond has rediscovered a long-dormant sexuality and starts to be able to reach out again to another person, the two quarrel over uninvited guests she's let into the house, and she splits.

Howell then is forced to come out of his shell, leave his seaside fortress and go searching through the seedier side of Los Angeles to find her. This he does, in a downtown strip joint from which he successfully delivers her. He takes her back home, lands a new recording and publishing contract, and the two presumably live happily ever after. Or so the artificial and utterly implausible ending would seem to imply. (Desmond Howell is very clear-witted and a clever conversationalist for a guy who can barely tie his shoelaces, and will probably have a hit on his hands with his whale music album.)

Whale Music is stylishly and inventively written, often charming and certainly entertaining. But the subject matter, in my opinion, is ill-conceived. Why write about a burned-out rock star who never made it into any 12-step program? And why so thinly veiled this fictionalized account? I would have felt more comfortable with either straight biography or a new set of characters not so transparently linked to real people, dead or alive.

Don't misunderstand me. *Whale Music* is dazzling prose. At the beginning of the book—which the author calls "a novel, sort of"—Desmond Howell reflects on his and his brother's lives:

> We were all of us born too late, that's a sad fact.
>
> This age is a strange new neighborhood, cheaply constructed and stuck out in the middle of nowhere. None of us belongs. Daniel should have been a medieval warlord. Dan-Dan should have wandered throughout the barren earthworks, a butt of malmsey in his paw, tweaking the bosoms of handmaids. . . .

At times like this, the narrative resembles an existential portrait out of Heidegger.

The fact that I'm not enamored of the Beach Boys and don't give a hoot if I ever hear a Beach Boys song again no doubt colored my lack of appreciation for *Whale Music.* I'm probably in the minority.

If you've followed popular music and the lives of the people making it, *Whale Music* is a witty, off-beat little tale that you might just love.

Tom Schnabel, "Beach Boy in An Ebb Tide," in Los Angeles Times Book Review, *April 15, 1990, p. 8.*

Julie Mason

In 1970, Robert Fulford wrote, "My generation of Canadians grew up believing that, if we were very good or very smart, or both, we would someday graduate from Canada." Like Fulford's generation, we had to teach ourselves to hear, value and create our own uniquely Canadian story, and to measure our success by a Canadian yard-stick. Yet, in the last few years, we have abandoned our Canadian jobs, Canadian expertise and Canadian institutions in exchange for an elusive continental economic revival. Now, in spite of three decades of literary nationalism, [the 1990] Governor General's list seems to show that we are also willing to reward those writers who abandon our unique Canadian voice in exchange for the bland tones of a continental literature.

Paul Quarrington's winning *Whale Music,* Anne Copeland's delicate *The Golden Thread* and Helen Weinzweig's disquieting *View From the Roof* are all interesting and deserving works. Each in its own way is appealing, vibrant and daring. Yet, even taken together, they seem lacking as the best of Canadian writing.

The problem begins with setting. *Whale Music* is set on the California coast, *The Golden Thread* in the eastern United States, and Helen Weinzweig's stories take place in the United States, Europe, Mexico and sometimes Canada. But nowhere do you find in these works the shock of recognition, the sense of knowing the place, of having met the people, as you do in W.P. Kinsella's Iowa cornfield or Timothy Findlay's war-ravaged Europe.

Just as the landscape is unfamiliar, so too is the voice. Like the flat unaccented cadences of American news announcers, these stories carry no identifying Canadian sensibility. They could be written by authors from anywhere.

There's no doubt that Paul Quarrington's *Whale Music* is immensely likeable. It's impossible to resist the perverse charm of 300-pound, drug-addled rock musician Des Howell and his eccentric cast of hangers-on. Following the death of his younger brother, Des has cocooned himself among his synthesizers and mixing boards, existing on jelly doughnuts, drugs and royalty cheques from his now-defunct group, the Howl Brothers.

His self-imposed exile is constantly disturbed—by greedy record executives, a possessive psychiatrist, rock musician friends in various stages of collapse, his manipulative family, and by the memory of his past with his brother Danny. Into his slide toward self-destruction comes burned-out groupie Claire, "a gamine from the Planet Toronto". In a deft blend of memory and drug-hazed reality, Des and Claire weave their way through his music to forgiveness and back into the world.

In sharp contrast to the brash and chaotic world of Des Howell is the order and nuance of Claire Delaney's life in *The Golden Thread.* Like Des Howell, Claire is removed from the world by her own choice. As a young student at a Catholic girl's high school, she longs to become a nun. (pp. 28-9)

These works by Weinzweig, Copeland and Quarrington show good writers at the top of their form. *Whale Music* is an engaging book, funny and poignant and rich with eccentrics. Copeland's writing in *The Golden Thread* is as delicate and lyrical, and in the end, as strong and resilient as Claire Delaney herself.

Given their quality, it seems almost churlish to object to the selection of these books for the Governor General's awards. Yet reading them is like getting together with

American friends: they are intelligent, provocative and likeable, yet in some small but vitally important way, we do not really talk to each other.

The Governor General's Literary Awards are the place to recognize the very best of Canadian fiction. They should reward excellence and skill, certainly, but they should also look further to reward those good writers that tell us something about ourselves, who enrich our sense of what it is to be Canadian, and who expand and reclaim our mythologies. (p. 29)

Julie Mason, "The Governor General's Fiction," in The Canadian Forum, *Vol. LXVIV, No. 791, July-August, 1990, pp. 28-9.*

Michael Ryan
God Hunger

Award: The Lenore Marshall/*Nation* Poetry Prize

Ryan is an American poet born in 1946.

In *God Hunger,* Ryan addresses themes of love, death, the ego, and emotional distance. Unlike the poet's first two volumes, *Threats Instead of Trees* and *In Winter,* which contained oblique, often surreal language, *God Hunger* employs a narrative voice that reflects an underlying desire for meaning in commonplace events. In the long poem "A Burglary," for example, a straightforward account of a robbery becomes an expression of the poet's feelings of alienation and solitude. Some of the pieces in *God Hunger* are rhymed, metrical quatrains and villanelles while others are written in free verse in conversational tones. Some critics suggested that Ryan's style occasionally becomes verbose and imprecise; however, most commentators lauded Ryan for effectively melding objective accounts of situations and events with very personal reflections. Marianne Boruch stated: "[The poet Seamus Heaney remarked] that 'poetry is more a threshold than a path,' and the force of Ryan's [*God Hunger*] stems in part from this power—those moments, either sprung forward or longed for, which turn one inward, yet out to the world, in swift simultaneous motion."

(See also *Contemporary Authors,* Vols. 49-52 and *Dictionary of Literary Biography Yearbook: 1982.*)

PRINCIPAL WORKS

POETRY

Threats Instead of Trees   1974
In Winter   1981
God Hunger   1989

Jim Elledge

Nominated for a National Book Award for his first collection and winner of a National Poetry Series award for his second, Ryan investigates, in [*God Hunger*], the mysteries embedded in the everyday. So much love appears on page after page—not only the romantic, erotic variety, but also and more importantly the spiritual union of the poet with the world—that one is left humbled by witnessing such visionary power. The volume's opening poem, **"Not the End of the World,"** prepares us for the poet's affair. Yet there is never a hint of sentimentality. Instead, Ryan

walks a tightrope between subjectivity and objectivity, offering the reader neither too much of one nor not enough of the other. A distinctive collection.

> *Jim Elledge, in a review of "God Hunger," in* Booklist, *Vol. 85, No. 20, June 15, 1989, p. 1774.*

Publishers Weekly

Ryan's disarming voice in [*God Hunger*], his third poetry collection (after *In Winter* and *Threats Instead of Trees*), is a quietly intimate one: "I think of myself as dust of bones / mornings when I awake / to find the fine white ash / lining the bottom of my box stove." Revelations like these occur at odd, unexpected moments—as the poet tends a bird that flies down the chimney into his wood stove, or contemplates a newspaper clipping about a prison marriage, or watches Bertolucci's film *1900,* or recalls an incident from his oppressive childhood. There are occasional pieces (**"Meeting Cheever," "A Burglary"**), a villa-nelle, free-form verses and metrical quatrains tinged with the wistful irony of W. D. Snodgrass. With almost reportorial detachment, Ryan meditates on a friend's suicide, the Holocaust, severely injured children in a hospice. Nearly all of the poems are marked by the control of a meticulous craftsman seeking transcendent meanings in ordinary events.

A review of "God Hunger," in Publishers Weekly, *Vol. 235, No. 24, June 16, 1989, p. 64.*

Carol Muske

"Brilliant John Cheever is a handful of ash. / I would be finished with what I was," Michael Ryan proclaims in *God Hunger*—and he then sets out in 38 masterly poems to exorcise the "fiction of the self." Admirers of Mr. Ryan's previous books, ***Threats Instead of Trees*** and ***In Winter,*** will recognize his unassailable technical proficiency (streamlined villanelles, tight rhyming octaves) and a witty, self-deprecating conversational style. But they may not be prepared for the sea change that marks this poet's entrance into major work.

It is not by chance that he calls on great prose masters ([Henry] James, [Anton] Chekhov, [Leo] Tolstoy, Cheever) to witness his disavowals of the "fictions" of existence, for these are poems obsessed with narrative and the impossibility of sequential narrative, what he terms the lie of telling. The "truth" here is implicit in the technique, which explodes the narrative process.

Mr. Ryan dismisses what he calls James's "late concerti of almost inaudible ephemerae on the emotional scale," but the denial is self-reflexive and dissembling. He, like James, works at creating (then denying) the self through ephemerae: dreams, memories, random images surfacing with the dark connective intent of the subconscious. He employs another Jamesian technique to startling advantage, the "double alternating center" (as described by James in the preface to *The Wings of the Dove*), which James used to unite two (often opposed) characters, bringing them side by side in a shared obsession, an emotional convergence.

In **"My Dream by Henry James,"** the narrator dreams a line presumably written by James and identifies with a youth approached on a beach-front hotel terrace, perhaps sexually, by the old writer ("the young man doesn't know how to feel"). Mr. Ryan gracefully moves him through the poem's central double image (a cloud above a pond that mirrors it) and out the "other side" into an ostensibly unrelated but magnificently revelatory memory of the narrator's early childhood; he is at the side of the pond with his mother, who is teaching him how to feel:

> when with both hands she turned my face
> toward the cloud captured in the water
> and everything I felt in the world was love for
> her.

This charged duality gives the poem two simultaneous worlds, two emotional vocabularies, even two painterly lights (from impressionistic oceanside pastels to neo-Expressionist clear cloud and water) and two distinct bodies joined by a single "heart." James's vision becomes maternal in this exchange.

This approach serves Mr. Ryan brilliantly in poem after poem, most notably in **"Tourists on Paros"** (joy and grief, a new marriage and a funeral are wed to the astonishing image of the "shaggy orange beard" of an Orthodox priest, like a "wild, high-pitched laugh"), **"First Exercise," "Smoke," "The Crown of Frogs," "A Splinter"** and **"Winter Drought"** (here the haunted image of the drowned body of a young man, a suicide, surfaces, and the poet pleads with the past, "Tell me what you want"). Such direct address to the past acquires a mad, fragmented fastidiousness in **"A Burglary"** and ambivalent power in **"Switchblade,"** where two "hidden" encased objects (a violin and a switchblade knife) link the potential acts of artistic creation and aggression forever in the poem's double center, the frightening Manichaean sides of the narrator's father. If the effort of freeing the self from the narrator's character gets at times too prodigious, Mr. Ryan knows how to "put on the wind like a gown of light linen / and go be a king in a field of weeds."

Michael Ryan's new narrative symmetries and self-consciousness have broadened the expression of his poetic gift immeasurably. Life's "almost inaudible ephemerae on the emotional scale" have no better contemporary poet-apologist.

Carol Muske, " 'Go Be a King in a Field of Weeds',"in The New York Times Book Review, *November 5, 1989, p. 32.*

Thomas M. Disch

Ryan strikes me as the very model of the workshop poet, in the pejorative sense. He comes with many laurels: His first book was nominated for a National Book Award; his second was selected for the National Poetry Series. [*God Hunger*] is published by Viking, and its poems have appeared in such venues as *Poetry, The New Yorker, The Nation* and *American Poetry Review,* where Ryan is a regular contributor. Despite all this, so large has the kingdom of poetry grown that I'd not heard of Ryan before reading *God Hunger,* and I can take an oath that my poor opinion of his poems is based strictly on their internal evidence. Yet, since Ryan writes about almost nothing except himself and his various foul moods, from self-pity to reproachfulness, it is hard to speak of his poems as though they had an existence independent of his personality as he has chosen to dramatize it. In disliking his poems I feel I am disliking a person, and this bespeaks a kind of mimetic achievement: Were Ryan a worse poet, one might have less cause to dislike the self he depicts.

Ryan is often concerned to show himself in his uniform as a poet, as when, in his account of **"Meeting Cheever"** (Iowa City, 1973), he sees himself as a "wounded-by-the-world angry young poet / who became me as strangely as years become today." In another poem reproaching a doppelgänger who committed suicide, we see the same face in the mirror: "a pushy kid who loved poetry, / one more young man alone in his distress." Ryan the Wounded Poet truly comes into his own in the book's longest poem, **"A Burglary,"** which begins with a moment of immortal false modesty: "It was only of my studio at Yaddo / a twenty-by-twenty cabin in the woods / whose walls are nearly all windows, and all they got was a typewriter and stereo." Ryan admits this is "a loss / which even to me did not sound great / within the world's constant howl of misery," but he is wretched anyhow, and can substantiate his woe with a quotation from Hannah Arendt's *Thinking:*

> with my underscoring and stars in the
>   margin—
> "Solitude is being with oneself.
>   Loneliness
> is being with no one."—I felt again
> a desolation I had almost forgotten.
> At Yaddo I could hear it whisper
> like the voice of another person
> mocking all I said outwardly calm or
>   kind,
> and for months, teaching classes or at
>   dinner with friends,
> my mind might blank as if slammed
> by a wave, and I'd struggle to pretend
> I wasn't somersaulting underwater
>   unable to breathe.

Ryan escapes his desolation by attending a party to which he'd been invited by two dentists' wives he'd met at a local disco. At the party,

> The guests were all dentists, their
>   wives, and hygienists;
> all had long been curious about Yaddo
> which stands like a Vatican in their
>   midst.
> In twos and threes, all twenty of them
>   talked to me
> ("You're a poet? What do you *do*?"),
> and someone's unemployed kid
>   brother
> who could have passed for Arthur
>   Bremer
> recited his own personal poems to me
> endlessly. I tilted my ear toward him
>   and listened.
> I thought this something I could do.
> Maybe for this reason, if for no other,
> everyone came to seem to feel pleasure
> in my being there. I began enjoying
>   myself, too,
> until we heard, from the den this time,
> the host dentist screaming at his wife:
> "What the hell are you doing inviting
>   to our *home*
> some strange guy you met in a bar?
> To humiliate me? Or are you crazy?"

Ryan considers sticking around but, recalling a knife fight he'd witnessed in a Mexican movie theater, thinks better of it and goes back to the disco, where he guzzles "shot after shot of bourbon" and then drives back drunk to Yaddo, where, switching to six-packs, he drinks till dawn. At the end of the poem he learns that the dentist whose party he'd visited is divorcing his wife. The tone throughout the poem, throughout the book, is self-aggrandizing, lachrymose and condescending toward all who are den-

tists and not poets (but who, even so, must see Yaddo as "a Vatican").

And these qualities, I would submit, are precisely the ones that have won Michael Ryan the approval of his peers. For if self-portraiture and self-mythologizing are his only competence, then it must be that the self Ryan exhibits is one that registers as not only viable but worthy of emulation. And it is not an unfamiliar myth: the hard drinking, the hints of having been a brawler, the womanizing and litanies of reproach to the women who won't put out but just lie there: "your luminous eyes wide open, three miles deep in yourself / rooted in poison." This is Hemingway country, denuded though it may be of those narrative virtues that make Hemingway worth reading, but even this territory is considered genuinely admirable by some readers, because they either live there or suppose they'd like to. In pop music there is Bon Jovi and Guns n' Roses; in the movies there's Chuck Norris and Sean Penn; in poetry there is Michael Ryan, and doubtless many more. (pp. 634-35)

Thomas M. Disch, "The Rhyme Scheme," in The Nation, *New York, Vol. 249, No. 18, November 27, 1989, pp. 632, 634-36.*

Marianne Boruch

[In] Michael Ryan's **God Hunger,** [the] eye is fixed on *story* to carry it, a surface willfully external and accessible, kept remote and mysterious only by an inner terror which coils meaning tight, ready to spring. In a sense, however, these are what [Seamus] Heaney would call "usual poems" that "keep faith with the way we talk at the table." Yet unlike such poems, they often go dangerous, take the flintier turn, hardly the usual poem's "hymn-singing effect," and rarely "its action as a dissolver of differences."

"The Crown of Frogs" begins idly enough, its opening lines generalizing us into Bertolucci's *1900*, though things edge up quickly enough as the focus narrows to scenes like this: the poor half-brother bitterly against his privileged sibling, sewing living frogs into a crown, until its seems "his brain / turned inside out, squirming, bleeding / . . . the wire . . . / down into these pale underbellies of despair. . . ." But this is mere overture for the larger witness, the fiction of the theater left behind for the fact of life, and its far more fearful inventions. Here, further into the past, is the entirely believable patio, two sets of parents "with Windex-blue drinks," the host's son drawing the speaker back to his yard's "secret place" where he performs torture upon toads, hanging each in a little wire noose until "choked and swayed to rest and hung / plumb and quiet for that endless minute." Such a moment, of course, is one of abrupt consciousness for the speaker— *this boy is not me*—but in hindsight, Ryan allows that to deepen into compassion. "The toad instead of himself," he tells us, "it now seems obvious." But back there—*then*—it is relief, pure rescue, when his mother holds out her hand to him as he steps back onto the patio which "felt like an ice floe in a sea of oil." And from here, the high aerial view of the last lines hits us, the bland stunned wake of a terrible knowledge. "We all just sat there, /" Ryan says, ". . .

—two silent little boys, / one crazy, and four adults: soft pale people / in black elastic knee socks and plaid Bermuda shorts."

It's [W. H.] Auden's dictum here, come to rest from Heaney's own quoting, that "in so far as poetry can be said to have an ulterior purpose, it is by telling the truth, to disenchant and disintoxicate. . . ." If Ryan skillfully puts the gas to whatever Pollyanna vision we might have cherished, he manages at the same time a greater understanding of that end. In **"Switchblade,"** where the speaker recalls years of watching his father at the dining room table in a ritual cleaning of three violins as alike in their cases as "three infant sisters whose hearts had stopped for no reason," it is the boy's patience that rewards him, and puts the surreal scene in context. In equal ritual, the father will produce the gleaming switchblade and the fierce stories that go with it after the violins—the music—are put away. The knife, this "sleek prehistoric fish," flashes open "with the terrible click." But even this dark and dramatic enchantment with the great world will alter, be derailed, that click sounding at last, which is to say *now,* "like just a *tsk* of disappointment, it has become so sweet and quiet." In ["The Government of the Tongue," Heaney] remarks that "poetry is more a threshold than a path" and the force of Ryan's new work stems in part from this power—those moments, either sprung or longed for, which turn one inward, yet out to the world, in swift simultaneous motion. (pp. 21-2)

> *Marianne Boruch, "Thresholds," in* The American Poetry Review, *Vol. 18, No. 6, November-December, 1989, p. 21.*

Sidney Burris

Michael Ryan, although a poet obsessed with the tessellated psychology of need, has never indulged the consoling historical investigations that characterized the genealogical writing of, say, Robert Lowell, nor has he concocted the extensive cultural autobiography that has engaged, for example, Seamus Heaney. Ryan has been doing quieter, odder things with recognized distinction: his first volume, **Threats Instead of Trees,** won the Yale Series of Younger Poets Award and his second book, **In Winter,** was chosen by Louise Glück as one of the five volumes in the National Poetry Series for 1981. His new collection, **God Hunger,** so thoroughly eclipses his previous work, certainly in its newfound ambition and, to my mind, in its glaring accomplishment, that Ryan seems once again the new poet on the block. I search in vain through his earlier work for a sensibility that would yield this etched stanza, the first one of **"Through a Crack":**

> That bird's odd chirp behind the fence
> I thought the rasp of garden shears
> I used as a boy to edge the lawn
> late Saturday afternoon for years.

But Ryan is not guilty of New Formalism; here is ["**God Hunger**"], two quatrains romping with Ryan's familiar surrealistic invention, yet newly measured by his implicit recognition of the stanza's boxy efficiency:

> When the immutable accidents of birth—
> parentage, hometown, all the rest—
> no longer anchor this fiction of the self
> and its incessant *I me mine,*
>
> then words won't be like nerves in a stump
> crackling with messages that end up nowhere,
> and I'll put on the wind like a gown of light linen
> and go be a king in a field of weeds.

In the long narrative poem of this volume, **"A Burglary,"** Ryan had headlined himself as "The Lapsed Catholic [who] Still Sees Through Lens of Religion," and throughout this new collection Ryan continually confronts the disjunctions of an imagination where "the pressure of reality," to use Wallace Stevens's phrase, is often depicted as a kind of secularization and where the poet is seen as a "king in a field of weeds." An innately American image, it neatly avoids the democratic embarrassment of privilege, yet claims, in its colloquial way, the consolations of the majestic perspective.

Much of Ryan's new verse, while strenuously sounding the lyrical register, encompasses a broad-based social critique that is new to his writing. The social matrix of a poem often proves to be the aspect of the poem most impervious to discussion; the lyric voice in English and American poetry stolidly resists attribution, insisting on the veiled and mystified provenance that many theorists nowadays see as the deceiving metaphor of artistic production in a capitalistic society. Although clearly viewing himself as separate from the carnivalesque rabble he encounters in **"County Fair,"** Ryan's eye continually lights on the subtle continuities—they are too delicate, too finely etched to bear the weighty word "traditions"—that bind generation to generation. He and a companion have attended a local fair where they have witnessed the alluringly amateurish performance of a "bunch of pre-teens from a local dance school"; they have seen the Mary Kay Cosmetics booth offering a "fabulous-free-complete makeover"; and they are heading home as he recalls the mothers who taught their daughters, their "pre-teens," the songs for the dance:

> The mothers who had helped them practice
> for months in front of every mirror in the house
> were easy to pick out. They were marching, too,
> almost imperceptibly, mouthing a song
> one of them might remember
> without knowing where it came from
> out on her evening walk or watering the lawn
> when her daughter has grown daughters
> already starting families of their own.
> "You forgot your free makeover," I said driving home,
> and, smiling, you reached over and pinned my hand to the horn.

Mothers and daughters marching in time, daughters growing up to become mothers, the unconscious song that binds them, and all of these representations of American life rendered within the refining context of a carnival—this is a brilliant evocation of the diverse, social continuities lying just behind the dominant myth of diversity that has so often organized our perception of American culture, and Ryan's verse is extraordinary in its continual attempt to ferret out these continuities and transform them into poetry. **"A Burglary,"** the long poem of the volume remarkable for its own sustained evocation of the social incongruities that inform, often humorously, the artistic and "bourgeois" communities in America, comprises a masterful narration of the poet's stay at Yaddo in New York State, and I can only sketch the work's incisive and thoroughly original accomplishment. Taking as its definitive emotion the feelings of invasion and defilement that inevitably follow a burglary, the poem chronicles the poet's movements through the artistic community at the retreat and through the professional community in the town where Yaddo "stands like a Vatican." Partly picaresque in its intention, **"A Burglary,"** after many readings, evolves into a vastly metaphysical travelogue documenting a day in the life of a late twentieth-century poet, and all of the clanging abstractions reserved for the postmodern performance come under a quick and severe scrutiny here. Alienation, humiliation, deprivation, and rejuvenation—these are terms that Ryan has authoritatively rede-

---

"This Is Why" (from *God Hunger*)

He will never be given to wonder much
if he was the mouth for some cruel force
that said it. But if he were
(this will comfort her) less than one moment
out of millions had he meant it.

So many years and so many turns
they had swerved around the subject.
And he will swear for many more
the kitchen and everything in it vanished—

the oak table, their guests, the refrigerator door
he had been surely propped against—
all changed to rusted ironwork and ash
except in the center in her linen caftan:
she was not touched.

He remembers the silence before he spoke
and her nodding a little,
as if in the meat of this gray waste
here was the signal

for him to speak what they had long agreed,
what somewhere they had prepared together.
And this one moment in the desert of ash
stretches into forever.

They had been having a dinner party.
She had been lonely.
A friend asked her almost joking
if she had ever felt really crazy,

and when she started to unwind her answer
in long, lovely sentences like scarves within her
he saw that this was the way
they could no longer talk together.

And that is when he said it,
in front of the guests,
because he couldn't bear to hear her.
And this is why the guests have left
and she screams as he comes near her.

---

fined for us in his extravagant poem, and we use them now, having once come under his spell, with a wink and a nod. (pp. 460-62)

Sidney Burris, "Four American Poets," in The Southern Review, *Louisiana State University,* Vol. 26, No. 2, Spring, 1990, pp. 456-65.

The Virginia Quarterly Review

[*God Hunger* is a] splendid volume, packed with warmth and wit, pathos and surprise. Most of these poems tell stories of ordinary life—beautiful, memorable, well-crafted vignettes that take us from the wood stove to the county fair, from meditations on the Virginia landscape to a superb elegy for the poet's father (the finest poem in the volume). They are exquisitely paced, maintaining a relaxed tone but building unnoticeably to a pitch of emotional intensity. Ryan dares to write in an undefensive style, to speak in a voice that is open, unpretentious, strong. Eminently readable, sure to gain wide esteem.

A review of "God Hunger," in The Virginia Quarterly Review, *Vol. 66, No. 2, Spring, 1990, p. 64.*

Tony Hoagland

What distinguishes Michael Ryan from the herd of other meditative poets is that his abstract drive has its deep source in anger, and this lends his thinking both pressure and a certain hostile incisiveness. Ryan has an unusual willingness and ability to confront the ugly sides of life with a matching poetic brutality. His special subject area is that of the great Unquenchables, the anger or desire at the self's core which vandalizes the ability to be. His revenge is in the shapely power of his poems. In *God Hunger,* Ryan enlarges his field of action, from that of his personal estrangement to a sympathy with and sensitivity to the woe that is in everything.

Ryan's thematic obsessions—death, sex, fidelity, the separateness of consciousness—are generally persistent in his new work, but in *God Hunger* these preoccupations are more settled and better understood in the poet's mind. Such familiarity hasn't cost the work its poetic edge; rather, his more assured self-knowledge has made for less abstract thrashing around, and more calm, clear delineation, as in the visionary conclusion of **"Winter Drought,"** in which the poet confronts the ghost of a teenage suicide. . . .

The notable technical advance of *God Hunger* over Ryan's earlier work lies in his increased ability to let observation and description do more of the meditative work in his poems. This is evident in a poem like **"TV Room at the Children's Hospice."** Though the terrible, sensational topic seems made for exploitation, whether by poetry or an episode of *Geraldo,* Ryan manages to avoid sentimentality by keeping the poet almost entirely out of the poem, letting charged descriptions and imagery make his statement for him:

Red-and-green-leather-helmeted

maniacally grinning motorcyclists
crash at all angles
on Lev Smith's pajama top

and when his chocolate ice cream
dumps like a mud slide down its front
he smiles, not maniacally, still nauseous
from chemotherapy and bald already.

In this poem, with its ample opportunity for melodrama and self-promotion, the speaker appears only once, and then only, and essentially, to understate and disown the power of his presence. The narrator speaks to one of the catastrophic children's mothers, while they sit before a television:

I say it's amazing how life can change
from one second to the next
and with no apparent disdain
for this dismal platitude

she nods yes, and yes again
to the gameshow's svelte assistant
petting a dinette set, and yes
to Lev Smith's grandma

who has appeared beside her
with microwaved popcorn
blooming like a huge
cauliflower from its tin.

"TV Room" illustrates the grim, corkscrewing force of Ryan at his poetic best, and *God Hunger* is a fine book in part because of the care with which it manages the poet's self. Ryan is a first-rate craftsman who consistently focuses on the gravest subject matter; as he continues to mature, as age makes self-centeredness less necessary and less interesting, his attention moves more regularly outward. This latest book shows Ryan's ability to document the lives of others with clarity and insight, as well as the relentlessness which is his trademark.

> *Tony Hoagland, "Mythologies of Self," in* The Threepenny Review, *Vol. XI, No. 2, Summer, 1990, pp. 21-2.*

William H. Pritchard

Michael Ryan's three books of poetry have followed one another at a fairly deliberate pace. His first one, *Threats Instead of Trees* (1974), was a Yale Younger Poets selection; *In Winter* (1981) was chosen as a volume in the National Poetry Series; now our panel of judges has awarded *God Hunger* (1989) the Lenore Marshall/*Nation* Poetry Prize. Unlike too many poets who tumble into print at the first twitch of feeling, Ryan takes time to listen to himself, and such listening contributes immeasurably to the subtlety of his address to the reader. In the opening of the first poem in *God Hunger,* "Not the End of the World," a note is struck that will be heard more than once in this book:

What flew down the chimney
into the cold wood stove
in my study? Wings
alive inside cast iron
gave the cold stove a soul
wilder than fire, in trouble.
I knocked the window-screen out

with a hand-heel's thunk,
and dropped the shade over
the top half of the window,
and shut the study door,
and wadded the keyhole,
hoping whatever it was
would fly for the light,
the full, clean stream of light
like the sliding board from heaven
our guardian angels slid to earth on
in *The Little Catholic Messenger.* . . .

Something like "the sound of sense" (Robert Frost's phrase) can be experienced in these rhythms, while the poem's protagonist comes across as humanly sound, a person of thoughtful good sense in his procedures to assist the "dull brown bird no bigger than my fist" which soon hops "modestly" out of the stove. Although, as in almost all of Ryan's poems, the style of address is rather soberly couched, that address is not without wit—as in the momentary glance at "the sliding board from heaven" remembered from what I take to have been a magazine for good Catholic children.

There is very little, however, in Ryan's two earlier books that prepares one for the flexibility and variety of speech found in the new poems—although there were hints of those qualities in the last two sections of *In Winter.* By contrast with the somewhat toneless voice that permeates so much of Ryan's previous work, the prevailing tone in *God Hunger* is very much a *speaking* one, and at times it becomes downright virtuosic in the attempt to create its breathing space. Consider the final, attractively tortuous sentence of "Pedestrian Pastoral":

But I do walk
happily in this mild Virginia winter

unable to feel absolutely sure
I won't be here forever
almost like this, a pure observer,
for once oblivious

to the spurs of ego and desire
that—whatever death is
or is not—could be paradise
to finally do without.

This "pastoral" impulse, found in a number of the poems, is another way of naming what the book's title has in view. Robert Pinsky calls it, in a comment on the dust jacket, "the unfillable craving people feel for some generosity of meaning beyond the circumstances of the self." That craving, in "Not the End of the World," may be toward restoring a wounded bird to some of its lost freedom of flight; or, in "Pedestrian Pastoral," a momentary experience of a freedom and purity beyond finite human constraints. Or, in "Crossroads Inn," it is the impulse to reach back into history for confirmation of something altogether larger than and rightfully humbling of the single individual. In "Crossroads Inn" a man contemplating the hills of Virginia (Ryan has lived in Virginia) has something turn in his mind as he looks at the road below him and thinks that

two hundred years ago,
needing rest and company,

a drover walking livestock

to a nearby river port
stopped here overnight
and in the evening sat on this rock
thinking *What will be here*
two hundred years from now
and the surging hills answered
Nothing that you know.

This sudden surge of feeling in the poem is beautifully engendered by those answering hills with their eternal lack of consolation.

It would be a mistake, though, to see Ryan as mainly a locked-in sensibility, brooding upon himself and the infinite. Much of the vagueness and surreal atmosphere that characterize his earlier poems have been replaced, in the new volume, by a sharper, more dramatic sense of situation and—along with it—a more poised tone. Accordingly, the sense that our life is on the whole a pretty grim business (a sense there from the start in Ryan's verse) is less portentously stated than it is thoroughly articulated within a particular poem's texture. The shocks and brutal changes composing the ills flesh is heir to are rendered powerfully in poems placed near each other early in this book, like **"Winter Drought"** (about a suicide) or **"Meeting Cheever"** (with the striking line, "Brilliant John Cheever is a handful of ash") or the painfully graphic **"TV Room at the Children's Hospice."** What's most interesting about these poems is that Ryan finds himself calling upon the uses of rhyme and stanza unit even as his chosen subjects become more harsh and intractable. In **"Boy 'Carrying-In' Bottles in Glass Works"** both rhyme and stanza are employed to create a figure at least partially adequate to the great piercing detail from Lewis W. Hine's photograph of the child laborer looking out at us with eyes that have seen it all:

What makes his face heartbreaking
is that he wouldn't have it so—
just one of many boys working
amid splinters of glass that throw
such light they seem its only source
in this dusky photograph.
A random instant of the past.
And the brutal factory, of course,

is only one memory of brutality
on the world's infinite list.

So it begins, and continues with rhymes that enhance rather than impede fluidity by never insisting on themselves, as if they were discovered by an artistry that need not pause to admire its particular effects. In the past, Ryan's prevailing vice was solemnity, or rather a tendency to confuse the merely solemn with the truly serious. *God Hunger,* by caring more about the minute particulars Blake said all experience consists in, also manages to care more tellingly about the larger, frequently sad, truths that must be drawn from life.

But the life from which these truths are drawn, for all its sadness, has vitality and a tough staying power that impels the poet to make a story out of it. These poems have beginnings, middles and ends; they are the product of a strong narrative impulse that shows the storyteller caught up in

the intransigent otherness of his subjects, like the girl turning herself into a sex object in **"Portrait of a Lady":**

Was it only the new old chemical
    stirrings
that made her shoplift purple
    corduroys
and squeeze into them out of her
    mother's hearing
to discover what noises could come
    from boys?

"Like sleepwalking on stilts," she
    laughed years later
about the cheap spiked heels
    wobbling under her feet.
The lip-smacks and wolf-whistles she
    remembered
as fainter than the slamming of her
    own heartbeat

when she appeared to herself in the
    overlit mirror
that Saturday afternoon in the
    shopping mall john.
All the stoned girls quit primping
    and stared.
And time stopped. Then one stuck out
    her tongue.

This is the beginning of a tale about an adventurer who soon declines into a mere wife and mother, and the tale is told without condescension or the pitying superiority of "understanding." In the book's longest (and strangest) poem, **"A Burglary,"** Ryan's narrative interest seizes upon a typewriter and stereo stolen out of his Yaddo studio in order to explore, in vividly idiomatic language, some ramifying events and troubling questions.

In his comments about *God Hunger,* Robert Pinsky quoted William Carlos Williams's famous words about how "it is difficult / to get the news from poems" but how very much we stand in need of that news. In Michael Ryan's poetry the news issues from a human being with a history who lives in a country we can recognize as contemporary America, filled with furniture from our own lives and speech heard over our individual airwaves. The book reminds us on every page that poems can be about lives, and about them in ways most urgent and delicate; such is the challenge set for itself, and impressively met, by *God Hunger.* (pp. 460-62)

William H. Pritchard, "The Lenore Marshall/'Nation' Poetry Prize—1990," in The Nation, *New York, Vol. 251, No. 13, October 22, 1990, pp. 460-62.*

Anthony Thwaite

Philip Larkin once wrote that "what I want readers to carry away from the poem in their minds is not the poem, but the experience; I want them to live something through the poem, without necessarily being conscious of the poem as a poem." This may seem surprising, coming as it did from a writer who was so conspicuously a maker of objects that were constructed, finished, in the best sense *refined,* in a way that never confuses the reader into thinking the objects aren't poems. Yet it is sympathetic, too: Larkin recognized that there is such a thing as subject-matter, which can seldom be evaded by a mere show of technique. There will always be some readers (perhaps mainly other poets) whose concerns are primarily technical. But most readers look for an "experience," and lose interest when it doesn't seem to be there.

Not that it is enough for the poet to be "confessional," or even plain "sincere." The magazines (and books) are full of poems that are one or the other, and sometimes both; and most of them are bad or boring, and sometimes both. To first come across a poet who has written at least half a dozen poems that say something unfamiliar in a way that catches one's interest, that make one carry away the experience (in Larkin's terms), is refreshing and exciting.

I have found this in Michael Ryan's *God Hunger.* The title at first put me off, drawing on a poem that, though it begins well, is not one of Ryan's best. He takes a number of risks in a lot of his poems—risks of a sort that don't always pay dividends: risks of nakedness, of banality, of casualness, pushing an anecdote too far or an emotion too hard. For example, there is the final stanza of **"Her Report":**

> Nothing I can tell you now
> will say how much I missed you then.
> I thought you were dying, yet all I
>   cared about
> was that I would never see you again.

But at his best Ryan fuses the story, the manner and the emotion in such a way that the experience is memorably re-created: in **"Boy 'Carrying-in' Bottles in Glass Works"** (which looks at a 1911 photograph from West Virginia, reproduced on the cover), in the haunting anecdote **"Meeting Cheever,"** in **"Portrait of a Lady,"** in the significantly-titled **"Larkinesque,"** and (taking a risk with a form that has been perilously in and out of fashion) in **"Milk the Mouse."** . . .

[**"Milk the Mouse"**] is, quite plainly, a "personal" poem, a reminiscence; but it is not plainly done, it uses the peculiarly formal and complicated and dangerous resources of the villanelle to achieve that reminiscence. The result is a brilliant harmonious union, in which the impulse and the form come inevitably together. Ryan can almost equally well follow through less strict measures to get his effects, as in **"Crossroads Inn,"** seven casual quatrains that concentratedly fix a real moment now and a presumed moment 200 years ago in a single timeless nexus; in **"Switchback,"** which draws on the same sort of background as **"Milk the Mouse"** but which does so in a controlled free verse; and in **"One,"** which gropes through a half-remembered image ("from nowhere particular—/ books or movies or newspaper / stories") of a little girl in a death-camp having her head shaved, itemising the details in short-breathed lines, without pleading but with terrible effect.

Ryan is so good at his best that some of the time I was helplessly, and uselessly, pushing the prerogative of the editor—suggesting a cut here, a re-phrasing there, a reversal somewhere else. **"A Burglary,"** for an example, is an enticing anecdote that outstays its welcome and becomes

a long shaggy-dog story. Sometimes Ryan is prattlingly verbose, and he can too slackly push forward reminiscences and emotions, as in **"Two Rides on a Bike"** and **"County Fair."** And he can be too complicated and overloaded, as in **"The Crown of Frogs,"** which yokes together a sadistic sequence from a Bertolucci movie and a sadistic story from Ryan's own childhood. But my impotent editorialising should indicate how very impressive I think Michael Ryan is. Most new poems one reads are beyond such fussing: They are irredeemably what they are, too raw or too cooked, and one passes by on the other side.

> *Anthony Thwaite, "Poems and Experiences," in* Book World—The Washington Post, *December 30, 1990, p. 8.*

David Baker

Michael Ryan, in his new collection *God Hunger* as in his earlier two books, is . . . fascinated by psychic violence, by the inner damages we do to each other and to ourselves unintentionally, often in our attempts to love. This formula, in fact, provides Ryan with his favorite subjects—the inability of love to compensate for the harm it does, and the inherent grief and shame of the lover whose knowledge, even foreknowledge, of these facts nonetheless rarely prevents harm. Ryan is one of our most moving and wise singers of love's difficulties, solitudes, and inevitabilities. Ryan knows that pain can make us sing our finest songs, and few poets can sing so beautifully sadly as he can.

In one of his most dire love poems, **"Sea Worms,"** Ryan's speaker desperately tries "to make a joke" of

> Five-foot red-headed sea worms
> that peek out of tubes they live in
> [and that] don't look exactly in the photo
> like rampant uncircumcision. . . .

Here, as often in his poems, he's got a nearly perfect pitch in balancing the grotesque and/or humorous with the serious and sad. The deeply submerged sea worms in their "sulfurous plumes of water / from vents in the bottom crust" are finally less sexual than isolated, mirroring the speaker's and his lover's inherent state. He hopes that "when you plunge / into your black, internal pit / something lovely and strange / will emerge from it," and then admits that his futile, boyish joke was intended only to try to balance against the bleak knowledge that, as Chekhov reminds him, " 'the soul of another lies in darkness.' " Apologetic, he catalogs the reasons for his joke. Even the ordering of his explanation demonstrates how his attempt to charm quickly disintegrates into self-aware futility:

> because I wanted you to laugh,
> because I couldn't touch you,
> because my love was useless. . . .

It's as if he tries, through lightheartedness, to prevent his lover from floating away, to postpone the inevitable separateness which is a condition of their love, but finally must admit that the condition of apartness is a constant. The poem's final lines describe the painful proximity of the lovers, a distance—short as it may be—that can never be fully eliminated:

. . . I feel your cells call to mine
across the abyss of inches between us
when we lie in darkness together,
your luminous eyes wide open,
three miles deep in yourself
rooted in poison.

The "abyss of inches" may as well be a distance equivalent to the depth of the ocean, as the speaker verifies the essential "poison" of isolation and solitude inherent in any lover.

As in his other most successful poems, here Ryan has composed lines that arrive by subtle means at terror and failure. It's one of his powerful devices—to speak in a casual, calm voice about devastating subjects. Ryan's poems typically work because he is so deliberate, so painstakingly careful, to join this casual yet knowing voice to a tight formal structure. In **"Sea Worms,"** for instance, the nearly hidden half-rhymes in the second and fourth lines of each quatrain lend a kind of restraint to the voice, a hushed, implosive control; some of the quatrains find their dramatic end in a shortened, two-stressed line that follows three previous, longer, often three-stress lines. The result is a severe, blunt, bitten-off effect. Throughout *God Hunger,* in fact, Ryan shows himself to be a superior formalist—that is, subtle, effective, various—for whom formality is less a quality to flaunt than a necessary means of articulation and control.

Ryan's particular strength lies, I believe, in his short, tight, dramatic lyrics. When he tries to extend his poems, as in a few cases here, the power of his poetry tends to dissipate. **"A Burglary"** is an example of Ryan's difficulty with the longer narrative. At ten pages, this poem is really rather tedious. About a stay at the writers' colony at Yaddo and the resultant robbery of "a discontinued Smith-Corona, a decent stereo, maybe a stapler, / and a goose-neck desk lamp that belonged to Yaddo," the poem is too often mundane, merely personal. Many things conspire here against Ryan—flat detail, loose and prosey language, and in fact a whole lot of talk about a relatively insignificant event; lots of people have much more trouble than a writer socked away at a writer's colony who gets his typewriter stolen, so his sense of shock and vulnerability rings pretty thinly. To infuse this long poem with dramatic importance, Ryan tries several times to raise the circumstance's philosophical import and its literary "meaning." . . . The whole thing becomes overblown and sentimental, and Ryan doesn't seem to locate a sufficiently compelling *poetic* impulse or center to drive the fairly chatty, loose narrative. There are a couple of other poems in *God Hunger*—**"The Crown of Frogs"** and **"The Ditch,"** for instance—which also strike me as occasionally flat and

self-indulgent, poems for which even Ryan's rather winning charm can't quite atone.

But of course these are relatively rare, untypical of this poet whose best work is severe and taut and whose gift is to be able to turn the apparently personal into the public and important. The predominant characteristic of Ryan's poems is their precision and subtle drama—their willingness to acknowledge love's terror and, still, to love. The presiding impulse of his best poems is not complaint but confession; the threat in his finest work is not loss but annihilation: "I think of myself as dust of bones / mornings when I awake," he writes in **"Fire."** And even the opening lines of the brilliant love poem, **"Tourists on Paros,"** function to allow for absence despite the lovers' happiness:

> If I die or something happens to us
> and a stray breeze the length of the house
> takes you alone back to that June on Paros . . .
> I hope the memory gives you nothing but plea-
>   sure.

While this poem purports to recall the two lovers' relaxed time on the island of Paros "when we wrote every morning in a whitewashed room / then lay naked in the sun all afternoon," the speaker inevitably transforms the scene into an elegiac one: "But if you also suddenly feel the loss / snap open beneath like a well covered with grass, / remember our stumbling in T-shirts and shorts / onto that funeral party." Over and again in *God Hunger,* Ryan insists on this doubleness, that love and loss are concurrent, unreasonable, always inevitable partners. Therefore, the figure on which he elects to end **"Tourists on Paros"** is neither the lovers, nor the funeral party's young widow, "nor the grief that filled the air and seemed boundless":

> but the brawny, red-haired Orthodox priest
> whose shaggy orange beard over his black-
>   smocked chest
> was like an explosion from a dark doorway
> of a wild, high-pitched laugh.

It's a masterful, vibrant, and frightening touch to conclude with the figure of the priest—so full of life, both faithful and on fire—who marries and buries us. The simile of his final, unreasonable laughter bears our ultimate fear and fascination. Like the best of Michael Ryan's poetry, it's so unavoidable, so passionate, and so thoroughly alone. (pp. 200-02)

David Baker, in a review of "God Hunger," in The Kenyon Review, *n.s. Vol. XIII, No. 1, Winter, 1991, pp. 192-202.*

Tomas Tranströmer

Neustadt International Prize for Literature

(Full name Tomas Gösta Tranströmer) A Swedish poet and translator, Tranströmer was born in 1931.

The most internationally respected poet now writing in Swedish, Tranströmer is praised for his use of nature imagery, through which he explores both contemporary and traditional themes. His poems are often constructed around one concrete image which serves as a link between the conscious and unconscious, providing a context in which to investigate the mysteries of time, identity, and reality in a manner often compared to that of the French Surrealists. Tranströmer's poetry, first published in Sweden in 1954, became available in English translation in 1970 with the publication of his fifth volume, *Mörkerseende* (*Night Vision*). This volume, while comprised of only eleven poems, evidences Tranströmer's mastery of metaphor and imagery and established his reputation among English-language readers as an important contemporary poet. In addition to winning the Neustadt Prize for career achievement, Tranströmer was awarded the prestigious Petrarca Prize in 1981 and the Bonniers Poetry Prize in 1983. Sven Birkerts summarizes the distinctive characteristics of Tranströmer's verse: "In Tranströmer's poems the image is dominant, prevailing over the line, and the individual poem progresses by way of stacked perceptual units. This is where Tranströmer reveals his mastery: he is an engineer of uncanny effects."

Tranströmer's first collection of poetry, *17 dikter,* gained widespread popularity in Sweden, prompting many young Swedish poets to imitate his elegiac tone and use of formal metrical structures. A celebration of Swedish landscapes that features recurring images from Rummarö, an island in the Swedish Archipelago, *17 dikter* does not attempt to didactically define life but rather presents contrasting images of a universe replete with both malevolence and tenderness. Tranströmer's second collection, *Hemligheter på vägen,* draws upon the poet's experiences in the Balkans, Turkey, and Italy and includes verse inspired by artists Vincent van Gogh and Francisco Goya. While many reviewers praised this volume's striking imagery, Tranströmer's exploration of traditional themes of travel was faulted by some as unimaginative.

Tranströmer's first two volumes are considered more positive in outlook and more formal in structure than his subsequent works. In Tranströmer's third volume, *Den halvfärdiga himlen,* the poet begins to move toward a dark optimism through which he concedes the widespread existence of human suffering while extolling the virtues of love and nature. In addition to these themes, Tranströmer continues his travel impressions and includes a number of

new, lyrical poems—among them "C Major," "Nocturne," and "Allegro"—in which music becomes a prevalent subject. In *Klanger och spår,* Tranströmer experiments with looser poetic structures, placing less emphasis on form while continuing to address topics derived from his worldwide travels.

Tranströmer's next volume, *Night Vision,* is considered more autobiographical in nature than his earlier works. This collection addresses such topics as death, the loss of identity, and the destruction of nature. *Windows and Stones: Selected Poems,* featuring verse from Tranströmer's first four volumes, introduced English-speaking audiences to his earlier works. *Östersjöar* (*Baltics*) is commonly considered one of Tranströmer's most accomplished and complex works. Divided into six loosely connected sections, this volume examines the nature of family legacies, social history, and time through Tranströmer's memories of childhood summers spent with his grandparents in the Swedish islands. In *Baltics,* Tranströmer uses contrasting images of the sea to examine humankind's relationship with nature and to symbolize regeneration of the collective human consciousness. Sven Birkerts commented: "*Baltics* plaits history and locale, personal and communal memory, and generates an affecting texture of tenuously interconnected lives."

Sanningsbarriären (*Truth Barriers*) contains four sections of poems written primarily in loose, informal free verse and prose in which Tranströmer considers such topics as art, hallucinations, and dreams. In this volume Tranströmer attempts to overcome a pessimistic worldview by affirming the possible existence of supernatural forces. Tranströmer's *Selected Poems* of 1981 includes all of *Truth Barriers* and *Baltics* in English translation, while his *Selected Poems, 1954-1986* features both new and previously published works. Tranströmer won the Grand Prize of the Nordic Council for his most recent collection, *För levende och döda* (*For Living and Dead*).

Tranströmer's poetry has been translated into thirty languages with large selections in Dutch, French, Polish, Spanish, and English. This has caused some commentators to suggest that much of Tranströmer's international popularity lacks viability since readers are responding to modified versions of his poetry. Yet those qualities which continue to garner attention are considered to survive in translation: Tranströmer's striking imagery, his explications of the complexity of nature, and his merging of the inner and outer life. Critics suggest that the continuing appeal of Tranströmer's verse is due in part to his concentration on catalytic metaphors rather than on individual lines or words. Tranströmer stated: "My poems are meeting places. Their intent is to make a sudden connection between aspects of reality that conventional languages and outlooks ordinarily keep apart."

(See also *CLC*, Vol. 52, and *Contemporary Authors*, Vol. 117.)

PRINCIPAL WORKS

POETRY

17 dikter   1954
Hemligheter på vägen   1958
Den halvfärdiga himlen   1962
Klanger och spår   1966
Three Poems   1966
Twenty Poems   1970
Mörkerseende   1970
   [*Night Vision,*   1971]
Windows and Stones: Selected Poems   1972
Citoyens   1974
Östersjöar   1974
   [*Baltics,*   1975]
Sanningsbarriären   1978
   [*Truth Barriers,*   1980]
Selected Poems   1981
Det vilda torget   1983
   [*The Wild Marketplace,*   1985]
Collected Poems   1987
Tomas Tranströmer: Selected Poems, 1954-1986   1987

†*För levende och döda*   1989

*These works were published as *Kvartett* in 1967.

†Selections from this volume appear in English translation in Robin Fulton's *Four Swedish Poets: Tranströmer, Ström, Sjögren, Espmark,* 1990.

Tomas Tranströmer and Gunnar Harding

[*The following interview was originally published in the Swedish magazine* Lyrikvännen *in 1973.*]

[Tranströmer]: I started writing as a child. But it wasn't "literature." It was "science." Zoology and things like that. I was precocious then and was interested in science, most of all zoology and most of all insects, which occupied me a great deal and I wanted to produce books on the subject. . . . I have a feeling that the usual boys' books passed me by without making any special impression compared with the reality I thought I met in, say, travel books. The first literary classic to make a strong impression on me was *The Pickwick Papers.* I must have been about 13 then, but that was still a long way from poetry. That didn't come before—I think I was 16 before I could take poetry. Till then I'd associated poetry with unpleasant occasions, e.g. end of term ceremonies at school, standing up and reading out patriotic verses. Poems were solemn and painful things. Then I went to senior high school, in the Latin line at Södra Latin in Stockholm, and found myself surrounded by people who from a literary point of view were quite advanced, which I wasn't at all. I did have artistic interests, mostly music and to a certain extent painting, but literature least of all. And it was very much through the influence of classmates that I got round to reading poems. . . . Naturally I thought the poets of the forties were silly and incomprehensible before I'd even read them. And it's pleasant to think that the first properly modern book I read was Peter Weiss's collection *From Island to Island.* I borrowed it from the library when it had just been published. Of course at first I thought it was stupid, but at the same time I was affected by it in a way no poetry had affected me before. We have strange ideas about the length of time certain things lasted. What I'm talking about gives the impression of having lasted a long time but in fact it all happened within a few weeks or months that I progressed from a poetic illiterate to an enthusiastic and well-informed reader of modernist verse. . . . I'd become friends with someone in the class below me in school (Bo Grandien, who of course became a considerable author) and he was following the same interests. Together we cultivated our more or less surrealist passions and then gradually developed a predilection for Swedish classics—Stiernhielm, Wallin, Tegner and so on. In a way I came into poetry through the back door, via difficult modern poetry and gradually coming to grips with traditional poetry. Usually it's the other way around. And what I think is important here is that I began writing poetry at about the same time as I started reading it. And of course I wrote very modernistically and imitated the poets of the forties. (pp. 153-54)

[Harding]: *What makes you start on a poem?*

Mainly a very special kind of ignition when a strong outer pressure suddenly meets a strong inner pressure. And then a spark jumps between the two poles, and so a poem's under way.

Is it more difficult in your usual surroundings? Most of your poems are written from places where you don't actually live.

Yes, there's a very simple explanation: in my usual surroundings I find it very difficult to get peace to work. Besides, I travel a lot in my job [as a psychologist] and so when I'm on a journey I'm alone, I can't be reached by telephones, I can't be reached by the usual duties which stream in on me. Then I have a feeling of concentration so that it's easier for me to write. . . . But my normal surroundings are never like that, though I do value very much being part of a family. Still, I'm helpless in the face of all the distractions at home, the piano, and so on.

Let's talk about music. It's meant a lot to you. . . .

Yes, more than literature.

Does it still?

Yes, in the sense that I have an innocent relationship to music, it's not something I'm involved in professionally, it's just something I help myself to. . . .

Did you ever think of going in for music?

In my mid-teens I wanted to be a composer pure and simple. I remember a fugue my piano teacher thought was neat. But I still get certain musical impulses and at times they come in connection with a poem, so that it's like a shadow of the poem emerging tonally. This doesn't get written down but it does exist in a way in my consciousness.

How can you explain that?

I guess it's the banished composer knocking on the coffin-lid.

But you seldom compose your poems musically—it's normally the visual factor that is pronounced rather than any kind of word music.

Word music in the sense that you labor over vowels and consonants has never had any special attraction for me. On the other hand when I was younger I had the ambition to try and carry over musical forms into poetry—though that was a very common ambition at the time, in the late forties. . . .

Has pictorial art meant much to you?

I've written seven or eight pieces based on impressions from pictorial art, but mostly from so-called primitive art or medieval art, more anonymous creations. Pictures as such appear only once I think—

The van Gogh picture in "After an Attack"?

Yes, there.

It's a picture in a hospital ward. . . .

It was part of the milieu in that room where I worked as a very inexperienced psychologist. I was testing an epileptic who'd had a lot of severe fits and had hurt himself. I describe him there, and in the background there was a van Gogh reproduction, the sort you see in places like that.

In reviews they sometimes talk of you as a mystic and sometimes as a religious poet. What do you think of that?

Very pretentious words, mystic and so on. Naturally I feel reserved about their use, but you could at least say that I respond to reality in such a way that I look on existence as a great mystery and that at times, at certain moments, this mystery carries a strong charge, so that it does have a religious character, and it is often in such a context that I write. So these poems are all the time pointing towards a greater context, one that is incomprehensible to our normal everyday reason. Although it begins in something very concrete.

Have you anything to say about your working method?

No, I've no typical working method. There are poems which have come into being very quickly and almost as if dictated from the subconscious. And there are poems which have been sifted out through long and difficult processes. And there are poems which never became more than magnificent fragments. But then it's hard to know what we really mean by writing for there's a kind of inner writing that goes on all the time and it doesn't need to finish up on paper. . . .

You're now for the first time writing a proper long poem, **Baltics.** *You've been at it for about two years. Does it take up a lot of your time?*

Not in the sense that I sit writing at it every day but clearly it's there in my mind.

Is it ready in your mind as a completed whole or is it something that grows step by step?

What makes it in a certain way pleasant to write is that I don't know how it will end and I've no idea which way it'll go. Besides, I'm more talkative and relaxed in this poem and this is a good change for an old so-called "spare" poet.

You've said that in your earlier writing you felt a certain joy which has diminished with the years. . . .

If you have a strong need to express yourself artistically then clearly it feels good to achieve something, but earlier I had the feeling of having achieved something marked by beauty, while that is a feeling I very seldom have now. And anyway that's no longer my ambition in the way it sometimes used to be. In general it's important to make something beautiful but my ambition now is to be as truthful as possible. And that doesn't necessarily make you happy. A sense of liberation perhaps. And what I write about now is often more marked by tensions, difficulties, anxiety sometimes.

How does your writing relate to your other work as a psychologist?

It's difficult to know. I believe there is a very close connection, though it can't be seen. Everything one writes is an expression of a gathered experience. And the problems one meets in the world at large are present to a very great extent in what I write, though it doesn't always show directly. But it's close to hand, all the time. That's what makes me feel under such a pressure when I write. What I put down on paper must be able to exist together with that, the total and rather dark picture of the world. And that's true even when I'm writing about something which doesn't seem to touch that total picture.

Do you have any sense of poetry changing things?

Yes, I think poetry can open a breach in the wall of conventional thinking and seeing people have, we all have it most of the time. . . .

*In **Seeing in the Dark** there's a poem called **"Night Duty"** which touches on some of the things we've been talking about. There are clear reminiscences of your daily work in the first stanza:*

> Tonight I am down among the ballast.
> I am one of the silent weights
> which prevent the vessel overturning.
> Obscure faces in the darkness like stones.
> They can only hiss: "don't touch me."

In this verse, yes. It's my most pessimistic poem, if you like. I'd been working at an institution for young offenders for six years and of course I've lived with social problems since then. Besides, the verse is a kind of image of myself, of my situation. This poem was written in the winter of 1968. It is a picture of a person who remains silent and doesn't want to take part in the colossal turmoil of public opinion that's going on. This is a very simplified expression but there is a touch of passive resistance in this verse. Yet it is also an attempt to work out a statement in the middle of this silence. It's an image of a sailing vessel where someone is sitting like a stone, a piece of ballast that prevents the ship capsizing. I imagine there's a huge crowd of people running around on deck trumpeting in different directions or trying to steer the ship on different courses. Well, all this isn't conscious enough to have been written like this, but it's a kind of rationalization after the event. . . . And at the same time it's an identification with these people at the bottom of society, who from the point of view of society at large have no useful function.

This poem talks both about your function as a poet and about your work as a psychologist?

And also about the situation of those people who are rejected. It's a sort of double exposure. It's a strange verse. It's very compressed, and difficult to defend rationally, I must admit. A configuration of complex history. Then in the second stanza it's a little easier to explain things in the usual way.

> Other voices throng, the listener
> glides like a lean shadow over the radio's
> luminous band of stations.
> The language marches in step with the execu-
>   tioners.
> Therefore we must get a new language.

There one is no longer silent but is trying to find a new language because conventional language is marching in step with the executioners. It's a disgust with—a refusal to speak these propagandist languages when it's a question of something important.

If we go on to the third stanza:

> The wolf is here, friend for every hour
> touching the windows with his tongue.
> The valley is full of crawling axe-handles.
> The night-flier's din overruns the sky
> sluggishly, like a wheelchair with iron rims.

Well, I understand many have found this difficult to grasp, and from the start I did too. It's one of those things that are more or less dictated from underneath. I know it should be like this and that it is meaningful but what in fact is the meaning? Looking back on it, we can say: "The wolf is here, friend for every hour," that must be a variation on the phrase "hour of the wolf," i.e. the hour immediately after midnight when ghosts and fear dominate. Here, it's the hour of the wolf right round the clock, for twenty-four hours. "The valley is full of crawling axe-handles." I don't know what associations you get there. I knew absolutely that the line should be like this but it wasn't till afterwards that I properly understood why. In part, of course, it's an image, a little sickening and frightening, where you see these axe-handles crawling round like eels. . . . Yet as an instrument of execution there's no blade on it, it's not an axe, so to say. It's only a half complete instrument of violence. And of course in Swedish "axe-handle" is a very loaded expression. In the background, for someone who has read history, there's Gustav Vasa's saying: "Everyone wants to see the axe at work, but no one wants to hold the shaft." And also that silly old story about "Good day, Axe-shaft!"—the phrase suggesting a situation where someone gives absurdly irrelevant answers, like a deaf person not admitting he hasn't heard the question properly. An image of a grotesque lack of contact. But also there's something else here like a ghost, which I wasn't aware of when I wrote it. I don't know if you remember Lester Maddox, who featured in the papers a few years ago. He was a restaurant owner in Georgia who handed out axe-shafts to his white customers to keep the Negroes away. That was when the restaurants were integrated and he became very popular because of this and in due course was elected governor. But an American public—I've read this poem in the States—immediately associates this image with him so this too is one of the associations of primitive violence in the phrase "axe-handle." So it's a very compound story. We have "Good day, Axe-shaft," we have this violent character in Georgia, we have "No one dares hold the shaft," and we have the purely concrete image of crawling axe-shafts and what is only half present in it, the incomplete. All of these work together in the stanza and give it a special character and one is not perhaps directly conscious of any of the separate associations. But they are there, subconsciously.

And that's then followed by the lines about the night-plane which is transformed into a wheelchair.

There's this image of someone who's very mobile, the night-flier, someone traveling at great speed, in great freedom. At the same time I introduce a wheelchair as an image of someone who's imprisoned. The association comes through the sound. This seems very speculative when we talk about it but the poem was quite spontaneously written. It's afterwards, like this, we can sit thinking it out. . . .

> They are digging up the town. But it is silent
>   now.
> Under the elms in the churchyard:
> an empty excavator. The scoop against the
>   earth—
> the gesture of a man who has fallen asleep at a
>   table
> with his fist in front of him.—Bell-ringing.

The fourth stanza, I don't have much to comment on here. It's an image of a churchyard in Vasteras, near the cathedral, and they are digging it up and restoring it. I saw all this, the elms in the churchyard, an empty digging machine, and then an image of someone who has fallen asleep at a table in a pub and then the bells ring. It's exactly what happened, then and there, as I stood looking.

It's different bits of different realities you've experienced, that you fit together.

It's a sequence of short poems really, not one continuous poem but four short movements. But with a common atmosphere. It opens out a little at the end with this bell-ringing—even if it doesn't directly express any liberation it is at any rate a new element coming in, which can mean that we're getting free from all this. It can also be a death-knell but I don't really see it that way. A departure, anyway. This poem is a kind of zero-point and I wouldn't say it was in any sense typical, that it gives any picture of a total attitude to life. It's a question of an attitude to life at certain moments.

*In **Paths** there's a poem called "The Outpost." Would you like to say something about it?*

. . . It began almost as a joke. It began very modestly. There was no intention it should become such a serious business, it was more something I passed the time with. The situation is this: I'm on a military exercise and get posted out to a heap of stones, a situation one experiences as quite absurd. And to cheer myself up a little I wrote the opening lines. I didn't mean any poem to come out of it. These first verses were written very easily just because I didn't have any feeling of "now this is serious, you must achieve something." But then gradually the poem came to deal with how I find myself in an absurd situation in life generally, as I often do. Life puts us in certain absurd situations and it's impossible to escape. And that's where the poem becomes very serious, in the fifth verse, which ends:

> I am the place
> where creation is working itself out.

And that's a kind of religious idea which recurs here and there in my poems of late, that I see a kind of meaning in being present, in using reality, in experiencing it, in making something of it. And I have an inkling that I'm doing this as some sort of task or commission. It recurs further on in the book at the beginning of **"December Evening 1972"**—

> Here I come, the invisible man, perhaps em-
>   ployed
> by a Great Memory to live right now . . .

It's a purely personal experience really, that I fulfill some function here, in the service of something else. This sounds pretentious and because of that the tone in such circumstances often becomes a little frivolous. Well, so you've enticed me into making a commentary and pointing my finger and telling readers how they should understand my text and so on, something which I really don't want to do.

There seem to be two sorts of reading which need not conflict with each other—the readers have their own subjective experience although they can see the author himself has another. How much freedom do you give the reader to use the poem himself and read into it what he wants?

A great deal. (pp. 155-62)

> *Tomas Tranströmer and Gunnar Harding, in an interview in* Tomas Tranströmer: Selected Poems, *translated by Robin Fulton, Ardis, 1981, pp. 153-62.*

Mary Sears Mattfield

Since his first published volume in 1954, Transtömer has been recognized as a powerful voice in Swedish poetry, and with the publication in 1971 of May Swenson's admirable translations of his selected poems (**Windows and Stones**), an overview of his development has been available to American readers. The poet's work—an extension of many contemporary lines of approach to poetry—is presented here in reverse order of composition, and hence should really be read in reverse order as well by a reader interested in his development. Transtömer's vision as illustrated in this volume has undergone no abrupt or radical change, but a gradual evolution. In a valuable introduction, Leif Sjöberg sums up the more than twenty years of growth from tighter form and more native Swedish themes, through wider and more international landscapes with less dependence upon form, to a more autobiographical and darker poetry concentrated upon the idea of the present. In addition, the reader will observe that the overall tendency is a development away from formal rhetorical and sequential "logic" toward greater fluidity and compression of images, a more stripped and stronger poetry which is more open to the irrational and therefore of tremendous significance to an international audience.

A professional psychologist as well as a poet, Transtömer has moved through the five volumes of his collected poems on a genuine journey of discovery. He has assimilated private, national, and universal experience into poetic awareness, and has opened that awareness to his readers. Free of the excesses of the "confessional" poet, he speaks as directly to the reader and offers a vigorous and exciting direction in the development of modern poetry.

Many elements of Tomas Transtömer's poetic practice richly repay a close examination. The question of rhythms, for example, is a vital though not a readily translatable matter. Another aspect, relevant to the changing poetic temper and need of our times, which translates more readily is Tranströmer's use of the image. Much of the strength of his work derives from his ability to fuse inner with outer space, to gain spiritual force through what Rilke called *"die Befreiung der dichterischen Figur."* In her preface to **Windows and Stones,** May Swenson has called this tension between inward and outward images the "double exposure"—a useful description of the exciting moment when the hard, clear, literal picture sharply plunges into the unconscious and illuminates truth. A number of recurrent images perform this function and serve as intermediaries between two states of being. Among these are the "windows" and "stones" in the title of Swenson's translation; water images; images from music; images of travel. A closer examination of some of these will serve to suggest at least in part the brilliance of the poet's craftsmanship. It is a process which inevitably invites comparison to techniques of painting, even to psychiatry, but perhaps the best description of Tranströmer's method is his own direct statement in **"Preludes,"** a poem from the 1966-1970 volume **Dark Adaptation (Mörkersende):**

> Two truths approach each other. One comes
>   from within,
> one comes from without—and where they meet
>   you have
> the chance
> to catch a look at yourself.

Recurrent images which give both poet and reader that chance to catch a glimpse of the self are many. It is a temptation, among others, to pursue the flight of birds, from the chirpers of **"Epilogue"** to the blackbacked gull of **"Morning and Evening"** (in which both bird and stone images come together) and the osprey of **"Prelude"**—all from *17 Poems,* 1948-1953, (the earliest volume)— through the falcon of **"A Man from Benin,"** the eagle of **"Siesta,"** and the vulture of the title poem from *The Half-Made Heaven,* 1958-1962, to the swallows and eagles of **"Winter's Formulae,"** from *Eagles & Traces,* 1963-66. It would be interesting to relate them to the total work, and also to the "glass-clear" subject of the early poem called **"Stones,"** to the "starved" stones from **"Five Stanzas to Thoreau,"** to the stones which "begin to emanate light" in **"Upright"** from *Dark Adaptation*—all of which may be rather less "opaque" than the translator assumes in reading *Stone* as "the opaque, impenetrable, absolute," and *Window* as its "opposite symbol of clarity, openness, together with the risk of vulnerability," as opposing forces in these poems. The reader may question also the comment in the otherwise excellent introductory statement that the "startling juxtapositions reminiscent of dream flight" are noticeably less frequent in the later books. Though these books are indeed more personal, more autobiographical, it is precisely for that reason that many of the later poems do in fact bring together unexpected images with the real potency of dream, in particular images from nature (especially trees) and images of motion (especially of flight).

The most complete statement from the earliest volume is the poem called **"Epilogue,"** a title which suggests the place of the poem in the poet's achievement to that point. It is a long and rather ambitious youthful work upon which any reader should have predicated serious expectations for the poet's future. The images which are to remain continuing preoccupations are all present here: the ship, the sea, the bird, the stone, the omnipresent trees. The poet is already in command of his materials, though not yet of his methods. The images are solidly located in the literal, and already reflect the intense perceptions and insights of which Tranströmer disposes in all his work. The poem begins directly:

> December. Sweden is a hauled-up,
> unrigged ship. Stark in twilight stand
> her masts. And twilight lasts longer
> than day. The way here is stony:
> not until noon comes daylight,
> when winter's colosseum is revealed,
> lit by unreal clouds. . . .

(pp. 123-25)

The concrete natural imagery of **"Epilogue,"** however exact and haunting, remains for the most part external. Though true to his vision, the poet has not here fully employed his resources to extend the range of his sensibility, and there is more direct statement, more sequential rhetoric, than we find in subsequent work. However brilliant the individual line and the glittering pictures of the changing landscape, the persona here is detached, reflective, cold. The "I" who appears so fleetingly at the close of the third verse paragraph is external to the poem. The facts of the outer world crowd in, take over, and **"Epilogue"** remains (like so much American poetry of the same period) an impersonal construct independent of the poet. Had Tranströmer continued to follow this line, however skillfully, it is doubtful that he would be today a poet of international stature.

Another poem from this first volume, **"Prelude,"** demonstrates the same perception and power to transmit the exact which we find in **"Epilogue,"** while linking the archetypal tree image more closely to the poet's later practice. Although **"Prelude"** is written in the third person, it seems a more inward and personal poem. Like **"Secrets on the Way," "Awakening to Song Over the Rooftops," "The Name," "Nocturne,"** and others, **"Prelude"** shows us the poet typically exploring one of the states between sleep and waking which are most open to the dream-state and hence to the creative impulse. "Awakening," the poem begins, "is a parachute jump from the dream." And the skydiver sinks toward "huge tree-root systems / like branchings of subterranean chandeliers" through trees which stand "with lifted arms, as if listening / to the beat of invisible pistons," into the "dazzling crater" of summer, "trembling under the sun's turbine." (p. 126)

"Prelude" is a more interesting poem than **"Epilogue,"** in part at least because it anticipates a technique found in many of the best of the more recent poems. Through the skydiver, piston, and turbine references forced together with the "tropical flood" of greenery by means of the "double exposure" of May Swenson's felicitous phrase, the poem gains tension from the powerful fusion of human, natural, and mechanical forces. The treeroots of **"Prelude,"** like the "immortal / or half-immortal root-system" in the much later poem from *Dark Adaptation,* **"A Few Minutes,"** function as do so many of Tranströmer's underground and underwater images to penetrate the unconscious and suggest the underground truths so often opened up by the poet through this fusion.

In addition to the "huge tree-root systems" of **"Prelude,"** images of trees in the first volume range from the gray tree of **"Connection"** through which "Infinity has trickled" to the mythic giant oak of **"Autumn in the Skerries"** and the greenwood into which the "crafty and hopeful" poet of **"Five Stanzas to Thoreau"** vanishes. None of these, however, goes much beyond the range of the poet's contact with the objective world, however intensely experienced. In the poem **"Tree and Sky,"** from the third volume, *The Half-Made Heaven,* the hurrying tree walking in the rain significantly "has an errand in the universe," but it is still separate, objectified, distinct from the poet. This is in marked contrast to the highly successful later poem from *Dark Adaptation* called **"Breathing Room: July"**:

> Lying on his back under tall trees
> he is also up there. He rills into thousands of
>   twigs and branches,
> is swayed back and forth,
> as if in a catapult seat outflung in slow motion.

In many of the later poems, these references to trees are less literal and more a means to transcendence and communion with inner truths. Not all are so luminous, so joyous, as in **"Breathing Room: July"**; the escape from corporal limits may bring a much darker vision. In **"The Name,"** also from *Dark Adaptation,* it is "under the trees / by the side of the road" that the driver falls asleep and on waking experiences "fifteen seconds in / the dark hell of amnesia" in which his identity, his sense of the self, is wiped out and then restored. The deepening vision may move toward a heightened awareness of mutability and mortality: in the interesting recent poem from *New Poems* (1970-71) called **"Sketch in October,"** the tugboat is "freckled with rust," while the trees that "wave wild colors: signals to the other shore" and the "horsetail mushrooms . . . from the grassy turf " cause the poet to conclude that "We are the earth's." But whether joyous or dark, it is a maturing vision, in closer touch with the truest roots of poetry.

In addition to the tree imagery illustrated by **"Prelude,"** the arresting parachute figure in that poem is also related to the many other recurrent references to means of transportation. The reader will note dozens of ships, trains and train whistles, automobiles, busses, trucks—"all the rolling wheels that contradict death!" as the speaker exclaims at the conclusion of **"The Four Temperaments"** in *Secrets on the Way,* (1954-1958). In **"Nocturne,"** an effective poem from the 1958-1962 collection *The Half-Made Heaven,* it is the speaker's driving at night through a sleeping village and a forest where the silent trees, theatrically illuminated, appear to follow him home, that proves to be the force which opens him in the dream-state to the possibilities of significant communication from within and beyond himself. **"Tracks,"** from *Secrets on the Way,* and **"Journey,"** from *The Half-Made Heaven,* use the image of train travel to accomplish a similar illumination. The poem **"Traffic"** from *Dark Adaptation* which probes deeply into problems of communication and ultimate

meaning in a mechanistic and industrialized modern society begins its terrifying downward journey with a highly successful instance of the use of this type of transportation image:

> The long-distance truck with its trailer pushes
>   through fog,
> the huge silhouette of a dragonfly's larva
> slowly stirring the silt on the lake's bottom.
>
> Our headlamps meet in the dripping gloom.
> We can't make out each other's faces.
> Floods of light plunge through pine needles.

Images of air travel are particularly potent in Tomas Tranströmer's work. Helicopters and jet aircraft buzz and drone through a number of interesting poems, among them the small but nearly perfect **"Awakening to Song Over the Rooftops"** from *Secrets on the Way;* **"Summer Plain"**; **"Under Pressure"**; and the very important poem **"In the Clear"** (all from *Echoes & Traces*); as well as **"Night Work"** and **"The Open Window"** from *Dark Adaptation.* In **"The Open Window,"** the literal buzzing of the speaker's electric razor moves by dream-association into the sound of the helicopter-vision of life greedily perceived as if for the last time; dream-flight forces him into seeing acutely the "dialects of green" of the natural world as well as the "red of the timbered housewalls" of human existence.

In a final and most impressive poem, **"Guard Duty,"** from *New Poems,* 1970-1971, the image of flight dispenses with the need for mechanical means to transcend space and time. The speaker in this poem tells us that he is "ordered out into a pile of stones" to some essential confrontation. This sense of compulsion carries through the poem: in the fourth quatrain he is "whistled back from the distance"; the final image makes him a passive agent of transmission. The situation of the poem is firmly rooted in the literal; the speaker, rising before dawn, is impelled to leave the tent where his companions lie sleeping warmly and still in human communication. He goes out into the darkness where, still in the literal setting, he finds a "pile of stones" where he orients himself in the dark and cold. The stones suggest the remote and historic past. He intimates that they are like a prehistoric burial cairn, and he sees himself ironically as a warrior or hero out of the past—from the "iron age" of Hesiod or of our own degenerate time— propped up for burial. *Cold* reinforces this implication. Meanwhile the speaker, awake, is aware of the sleep of his fellows "fanned out like spokes in a wheel." He has left this warm circle of security and humanity, and the vividly hissing serpent of the fire, for the cold and solitude of the night. The poet must break out of the circle in order to achieve the necessary loneliness and silence. Though it is cold, it is almost dawn, and it is spring, a hopeful season. At this point the speaker is open to possibilities. That there are in this poem no explicit images of travel is hardly crucial. To have arrived at this spatial point, this cold outpost where the frail tent and the fire are abandoned for the quiet of the "cold stones," obviously *implies* previous literal motion in the physical body.

In the third verse paragraph, of course, the speaker does "begin to fly," as he soars in the dream-flight of imagination into the recent or personal past. Using the "shaman's" power to control and interpret, he reaches a level at which he responds wholly to a very lovely sexual image in which the power of organic nature ("the moss was warm") functions to help him gain understanding. But this is not enough. The past will not permanently sustain the poet. While he can "brush near those warm moments," he "cannot stay there for long," and he is again under compulsion "whistled back from the distance," dragged out of the past, forced to confront the "Here and now" of the present. This is a poem in which the truth of the self must be confronted. While it is easy to recognize the importance of the here and now, what is more significant is how the poet maneuvers himself from one end of the poem to the other: not *that* he accepts his responsibility as a poet, but *how* he does.

The stones recur in the fourth stanza, both as concrete image and as link between the orders of the opening line of the poem and the very important abstract statement of the fifth stanza. Here we have the explicit assertion of the poet's acceptance of his responsibility:

> Mission: to be where I am.
> Also, in my silly and solemn role,
> I am the place
> where creation works on itself.

Mission echoes the title, the conception of the poet as a man under orders, a lonely sentinel. The self-deprecation and humility of *silly* pick up the wryly ironic view of himself as "noble corpse" in the second line of the poem: Tranströmer has gained a lively sense of the irrational aspect of poetry while deepening his commitment to it. To assent to being "the place / where creation works on itself" is to have gained as well a mature understanding of the process of the poet's craft.

In the sixth stanza of **"Guard Duty,"** truths from outside the self—the dawn, the trees—are the agency of inner enlightenment. Even though "sparse" and "frostbitten," tree trunks have color and "forest / flowers send a search party / for anyone who's lost in the dark" (a magically effective surreal image which fuses inner with outer space and liberates real poetic energy). The natural world is as vividly present in this poem as it was in Tranströmer's most youthful work, but here the poet is fully present too, without detachment or the reservation of an impersonal objectivity. The seventh quatrain reiterates the poet's duty: "to be where I am. And wait." In this acceptance of his "mission," however, he has no pretensions to complete understanding; he remains "anxious, stubborn, confused."

In the final stanza, the speaker's quasi-mystical experience has opened him totally to the "murmuring crowd" of "future events" which "already exist" and which "want to enter," though he still asks "Why?" The startling concluding figure works admirably. As a modern-day Gate of Horn, the commonplace subway turnstile through which the spiritual truths travelling from "outside the barricade" of consciousness "come / one by one" strikingly conveys the workmanlike unpretentiousness with which Tomas Tranströmer submits himself wholly to poetry.

Merely to point out the obvious, that images of transportation and of trees recur with astonishing frequency in that poetry would be a fruitless exercise. What makes these recurrences truly significant involves what Jung called the "participation mystique" that occasions true artistic efficacy. The reader responds so directly to these potent images that, without risking the intentional fallacy, we can safely make some useful inferences about the meaning of an image to the poet on the basis of the reader's response to it, and by observing its apparent *function* in a number of successive instances.

The mechanical images—all those motors felt through their throbbing and forward motion—are more than mere emblems of literal (or even psychological) journeys of discovery, though they certainly are that as well, and have in a sense helped to transport the poet from the youthful guardedness and objectivity of **"Epilogue"** toward the splendid openness of **"Guard Duty."** In most individual instances, the images of travel and flight function as the catalyst or liberating agency in the poem which impels the poet toward his perception of the natural world. The natural images—mosses, mountains, especially trees—have their being deep in inner realities, truths of nature, the unconscious self. When these "two truths approach each other" as Tomas Tranströmer himself put it, when they are not merely pictures from the objective world but an extension of the poet's own substance, then the human response to this juxtaposition of mechanical and natural imagery makes the fusion functional, the poetry powerful. (pp. 126-31)

Mary Sears Mattfield, "Recurrent Images in the Poetry of Tomas Tranströmer," in Ironwood, *13, Vol. 7, No. 1, 1979, pp. 122-31.*

An excerpt from "The Outpost"

> Mission: to be where I am.
> Even in that ridiculous, deadly serious
> role—I am the place
> where creation is working itself out.
>
> Daybreak, the sparse tree-trunks
> are colored now, the frost-bitten
> forest flowers form a silent search party
> for someone who has vanished in the dark.
>
> But to be where I am. And to wait.
> I am anxious, stubborn, confused.
> Coming events, they're there already!
> I know it. They're outside:
>
> a murmuring crowd outside the gate.
> They can pass only one by one.
> They want in. Why? They're coming
> one by one—I am the turnstile.

Gary Lenhart

Tomas Tranströmer's poems occupy "the slot between waking and sleep." He is a poet of strong, controlled feelings who with quiet surrealist effects describes an oneiric landscape, but one that is ordinary and definite—at once tangible and mysterious. Despite the recurring Baltic fog, the objects in his dreams have sharp edges and a particular insistence.

He writes, "Poems are active meditations, they want to wake us up, not put us to sleep." So the movement in his poems [in *Tomas Transtrӧmer: Selected Poems, 1954-1986*] is from grogginess to consciousness. They don't disorient our senses, but wake us to transcendent lights that may have been obscured by the brouhaha of getting and spending. In a slight but significant poem, **"Espresso,"** he eulogizes the dark brew that like "black drops of profundity" gives us "a healthy push" to open our eyes. Typically, this profound waking leaves us not in some fantastic landscape, but alert at a sidewalk cafe.

I'm not given to identify darkness and profundity, but they recur often and usually together in Transtrӧmer's work. Again and again he returns to darkness and "the deep" to carry more into the light of day. To anyone who is familiar with the poetry of one of his principal translators, Robert Bly, the vocabulary of contraries (darkness and light, the eagle and the mole, the earth and the sky) is familiar. Like Bly, Transtrӧmer is a poet of few ideas, but his ardent faith in those ideas suffuses his every thought and perception. He is enough the craftsman that feelings and faith come across. His Romantic vocabulary is refreshed by the exotic landscape he inhabits—the bracing Baltic climate with its dramatic range of light. What he writes of the Baltic jellyfish could also be said about his poems:

> if you take them out of the water all of their
>   shape disappears,
> as when an indescribable truth is lifted up out of
>   the silence
> and formulated into a lifeless mass, yes, they're
>   untranslatable,
> they have to stay in their element.

(This volume was prepared for an audience ignorant of Swedish, as is this reviewer; I'm speaking now of the context of landscape and ideology.) Like George Crabbe or John Clare, Transtrӧmer is best served by an extended immersion in his work. He isn't an anthology poet, despite the relative concision of most of his poems. His early poems have a distinctly nineteenth-century sensibility. They are meditations that acknowledge Thoreau and Gogol as inspiration and announce the author's decision to flee into the greenwood, the world of forest and sea. They are loaded with images of Nordic landscape: snow, sleds, fog, sailors, storms, ships, clouds. The concerns are expansive and metaphysical, the form cramped. The poems are economic and spare, as sober and stern as the cold-water vision they proclaim. The past weighs heavy, not as history but as dead souls animating the landscape. It is a Kierkegaardian vision of the individual confronted with all of creation, made anxious and guilty and getting damn little help from his freiends.

Transtrӧmer's mystic vision exists in tension between the insistent phenomena of the material world and a conception of the poem as a place where spiritual polarities resolve. For him the truth is imminent. He is suspicious of the power of words to do more than circle the real, and in approximating the real, distort it. He writes that "the wild does not have words." And he is more interested in the "wild," taking it for the genuine, than in human efforts to impose a social significance upon the world, efforts he obviously believes are doomed to failure and mischief. His concerns are only implicitly social. His is a road of dream, of solitude and not common history. Where history intrudes, it is the story of individual ghosts reminding us of their travails, their courage, their endurance, their artifacts. For Transtrӧmer there is something more important ("deeper") than all this folderol, and it is glimpsed in silence and solitude. He obviously believes that words lack the actuality of trees. Because the world exists with its own truths, independent of their utility for us, he has the courage (and maybe the fate) to be unpopular. Other voices contribute little to his confrontation with the existing.

Though Transtrӧmer speaks much of freedom, it is a psychological freedom, an internal freedom that resents material necessity as much as political oppression. Human history is but a fleet, unimportant episode against the abiding backdrop of earth, rocks, seas, sky, darkness. All questions are returned to the stern bedrock where they are measured against, if not eternity, the distances of the universe. . . . For Transtrӧmer, writing is a moral act, one that he frequently compares to composing music. His homages to composers (Grieg, Schubert, Balakirev, Haydn) are among his finest poems. (Unfortunately, whatever music inheres in the poetry is minimized in translation.) In **"Allegro,"** he ends a "black day" by playing Haydn.

> The music is a house of glass standing on a slope:
> rocks are flying, rocks are rolling.
>
> The rocks roll straight through the house
> but every pane of glass is still whole.

This is an idealist philosophy, unlike Haydn's music, which recalls a specific place and time. But as in a successful piece of music, the clarity and integrity of the poet's emotive expression cut through the mist like a foghorn, and travel across oceans, translators, and selected editions to move quietly, but irresistibly. . . .

[In *Tomas Transtrӧmer: Selected Poems, 1954-1986*], the poems are arranged chronologically, and as one moves through the work, the press of suburban blight becomes more urgent and disheartening. The anxiety becomes particular as the things the poet stands by come to be undervalued by the community that derives its character from them. The "eternal verities" that give some perspective on temporary ills seem to wobble and disappear. The world is awash in junk and we are rudderless.

In the later poems, the poetic line lengthens until, in **"Baltics,"** Transtrӧmer discovers a long Whitmanic line that strikes me as more contemporary, more flexible, more personal, and (I would guess) less difficult to translate without great costs. Figures are more dominant in the landscape, but they are not familiar. Though without personality, they are not without character, totems of geography as much as civilization.

Though it's a regional color that first comes to mind when I think of Tranströmer, it should be mentioned that he is an avid tourist. There are many small pleasures in the diary-like notations he has made of trips to such exotic venues as the Nile Delta, the Sahara, Shanghai, Turkey, and Oklahoma. His spiritual obsessions travel with him and modify the landscape (in Shanghai, he observes, "Behind each one walking here hovers a cross that wants to catch up to us, pass us, join us. / Something that wants to sneak up on us from behind and cover our eyes and whisper, Guess who?"). But the demands of the landscape also counter his subjectivity. Tranströmer is by no means an exteriorist. The force of his descriptions owes more to evocation than to sharp outline. Though he sometimes sounds like Jeremiah, his attractive reticence and sheer politeness make him never overbearing.

Finally, I must admit that I find few sparks here, few flashes of the surprising speech or lightning move of mind with which poems most often engage us. But the light is clear and steady, a light of constant attention, in which private, brooding vision becomes eloquent public occasion, as it might have for the medieval artisans who so fascinate Transtömer, the craftsmen who left their sign on artifacts like baptismals and prows, whose impress can still be glimpsed when the light strikes their handiwork at the right angle.

> *Gary Lenhart, "Hard Edge Fog," in* The American Book Review, *Vol. 9, No. 4, September-October, 1987, p. 10.*

Alan Brownjohn

Tranströmer's poetry has been available in this country [since 1970], in small (and very good) samples of translations by Robert Bly, Robin Fulton and John F. Deane. But Fulton's new *Collected Poems* translation provides the entire sequence of the Swedish poet's work from the beginning, an enthralling series of very short individual books between the covers of this one paperback; and even brings us commendably up-to-date with some recent pieces published only in magazines. It deserves to be welcomed avidly as an opportunity to attune to a major voice in European poetry.

Tranströmer had the stamp of a major poet from the start. The *17 Poems* of 1954 (a small puzzle: I count only fifteen here) and the following book, *Secrets on the Way* (1958), occasionally toy with an uneasy, semi-surrealist shuffling of topographical properties:

> A man like an uprooted tree with croaking fo-
> liage
> and lightning at attention saw the beast-smelling
> sun rise up among pattering wings
>   **("The Four Temperaments")**

But already the silent, haunted openness of the Swedish landscape, its lakeshores and mists, is delivered in images of arresting visual precision. This apparently timeless and unchanging panorama is constantly and mysteriously on the move ('Old villages are on / their way, retreating further into woods / on the seasons' wheels with magpie-creaking') and moving *through* the poet: he will later ac-

knowledge his sense of himself as someone through whom natural forces and 'gathered experience' are mediated:

> Mission: to be where I am.
> Even in that ridiculous, deadly serious
> role—I am the place
> where creation is working itself out
>   **("The Outpost")**

Where he is, in the newly-married poems of *The Half-finished Heaven* (1962), is not only a home landscape where happiness orders the elements ('The sunshine stuck to all the fur caps like pollen on bees') but foreign places which produce some startling poems of travel (**"The Palace"**, **"Syros"**, **"In the Nile Delta"**). These leave darker traces, and for the next decade, in three impressively varied volumes (*Seeing in the Dark* is the title of the 1970 book) he seems principally to be concerned with understanding that darkness: near to death in a car accident, watching the spread of urban desolation on building sites and in traffic lines, attending like a ghost the bulldozing of the city churchyard:

> The wolf is here, friend for every hour
> touching the windows with his tongue.

Then he expands into the wholly different, broad vision of *Baltics* (1974), a long poem about ancestry, history, travel, time and the incursion of the outer world on this region: this challenges comparison, in theme and magnificence, with some of Whitman, with Eliot's *Dry Salvages*, with Lowell's Quaker graveyard. What follows, in the two most recent books, *The Truth-Barrier* (1978) and *The Wild Market-Square* (1983) is even bolder and clearer, poems that are ready to draw directly and vividly on dream and fantasy material, more alarming, and with an elaborate grandeur of theme and manner. This is a *Collected* to read, re-read and absorb. . . . (p. 22)

> *Alan Brownjohn, "From the Tree-line," in* Poetry Review, *Vol. 78, No. 1, Spring, 1988, pp. 22-3.*

Nance Van Winckel

Only when the poet sees his imagination become the light in the minds of others, says Stevens, is he fulfilled. The imagination illuminates the murky spaces through which the poem struggles to isolate "what will suffice." And what makes Transtömer's poems so remarkable is the great beauty of his particular illuminating imagination. Furthermore, it seems only reasonable that Transtömer should be interested in how these illuminating perceptions take place. Such processes are often the subjects of his poems. [In *Tomas Transtömer: Selected Poems, 1954-1986*], Transtömer shows us the spirit in motion as it tries to untangle itself from the world, and as it tries to reconnect.

"Track"

> 2 A.M.: moonlight. The train has stopped
> out in a field. Far off sparks of light from a town,
> flickering coldly on the horizon.
>
> As when a man goes so deep into his dream

he will never remember that he was there
when he returns again to his room.

Or when a person goes so deep into a sickness
that his days all become some flickering sparks,
   a swarm,
feeble and cold on the horizon.

The train is entirely motionless.
2 o'clock: strong moonlight, few stars.

I've quoted all of this poem since it shows so well how Tranströmer's peculiar light-effects of the imagination work. I'm struck first by the way this poem pushes farther and farther into the complete quiet and motionless depth of consciousness, which for Tranströmer is often lonely, filled with eerie foreboding. But it's also a curious and provocative place, sweetly cunning. Such a place, one we feel Tranströmer knows so intimately, taunts us with its elusiveness, as if to remind us that no matter how deeply we enter the spirit, we barely glimpse the "flickering lights at the edge of town." (pp. 178-79)

Those lights. Tranströmer makes me think of them in another way too: as the inner reflection of a busy, chaotic external world, a world that also beckons and beguiles us, and similarly taunts us with its elusiveness. Yet the understanding that matters most to Tranströmer is that which moves us toward a balance between inwardness and the societal world. For Tranströmer, the self, try as it may, cannot remain disconnected from what's around it. It too lives on, indeed thrives on, *context.* So we must look in and out, and at the same time.

Working for many years in Sweden as a psychologist, Tranströmer treated delinquent boys and the occupationally handicapped. But we see Tranströmer the physician only insofar as we are struck by his keenly observant eye and by the way he enters the mind with such courage and strength, and with such relish and intrigue. These powers propel the poems, energizing their every odd movement. In **"A Man from Benin"** the photographic image of a man pulls another man, an observer, closer and closer, until the observer establishes a connection to the one observed. It's a subtle, quiet movement toward that union, and it's the movement, not merely union itself, that drives the poem so forcefully. The poem shoots forward with such strength that when the last line suddenly stops it, everything seems to reverberate as if from impact: *"I am come to meet him / who raises his lantern / to see himself in me."* (Tranströmer's italics.)

Yet perhaps the greatest beauty of [*Selected Poems, 1954-1986*] is how well the translations allow Tranströmer to sing as he undoubtedly does in his native Swedish. . . . Earlier collections in English, like those of May Swenson, Robin Fulton, and Robert Bly, have been uneven and leave readers uncertain of Tranströmer's lyric voice. For Tranströmer is above all a lyric poet, one of the best of our time. And what a tribute to this volume that at last Tranströmer's lovely lyrical voice can make itself so consistently felt to English readers. (pp. 179-80)

In **"Morning Birds,"** to mention just one of many examples, the singing's own beautiful force in the poem convinces us of the powerful truth of the ending:

Fantastic to feel how my poem grows
while I myself shrink.
It is growing, it takes my place.
It pushes me out of its way.
It throws me out of the nest.

And how appropriate that the poem has been filled with so *many* birds, so many voices competing for one's attention, until finally amid all this squawking, the one song of the poem/bird is gathered and lifts over the others to be heard.

It is no coincidence that song, especially in the form of music, often appears in Tranströmer's poems, for the similarities between music and his own poetry are many: that lovely melodic voice and the resonant, often odd reverberations of image laid upon image, like sound upon sound. Indeed, sound can be something visual for Tranströmer. Synesthesia. Consider, for instance: "The sound [playing Haydn] is spiritual, green, and full of silence." (p. 180)

As with music, the imaginative reverberations given off by Tranströmer's layering of images make for a wild, jazz-like music. A poem entitled simply **"Loneliness"** is a good example. In its two sections, the poem presents two very different views of loneliness. In section I, a man facing his own demise in the swift moment before it's about to arrive watches it come toward him. He has swerved into the lane of oncoming traffic. The headlights keep approaching, as toward "a boy in a playground surrounded by enemies." This is the frightening and often isolating loneliness the imagination can reveal to us, the one that Plath and Lowell and many others were so mesmerized by and drawn to. Nearing it, the spirit squeezes so tightly into itself it threatens to disappear. Then we read section II, where we see a beautiful and demure side of solitude and loneliness. A man walks out "on the frozen Ostergotland fields" and makes something like a plea *for* isolation:

To be always visible—to live
in a swarm of eyes—
a special expression must develop.
Face coated with clay.

We must live both within the world and within our deepest selves at the same time. We cannot turn our backs on either. I can't think of a poem that takes on this modern dilemma in any better, tougher, or truer way.

Another way Tranströmer syncopates movement in these poems is through his unique combination of sparse language and dramatic, riveting imagery. It was to this combination that the deep image poets, Bly and Wright, were so drawn. Bly, for instance, was one of Tranströmer's first translators. Yet none of Tranströmer's American counterparts strike quite the same intriguing weights and rhythms between language and image. It is his very studied, sure-footed movement toward inwardness that so compels me. "In the slot between waking and sleep / a large letter tries to get in without quite succeeding." With what perfect clarity this image speaks, evoking a whole state of consciousness with one deftly perceptive stroke.

Tranströmer's images often strike me this way, as if they had simply been around in just that form all along waiting for someone to pass by and "see" them. In the prose poem,

"The Blue House," when someone who lived in the house died, it was repainted. "The dead person does the painting, without a brush, from within." Through a steady reexamination of its past, Tranströmer makes the house, as a kind of reliquary of memory, stand firm.

Titles. Like Stevens here too, Tranströmer is a master. But Tranströmer's titles may seem deceptively simple. Take the poem **"Track"** quoted in the beginning. Moving into the poem, we sense the hook to the title quite literally: a man's life paused on its track to take stock of itself. But

---

Laureate's Words of Acceptance

I want to draw attention to a fairly large group of men and women who share this prize with me, without getting one single cent: those who have translated my poems into different languages. No one mentioned, no one forgotten. Some are my personal friends; others are personally unknown to me. Some have a thorough knowledge of Swedish language and tradition, others a rudimentary one (there are remarkable examples of how far you can get with the help of intuition and a dictionary). What these people have in common is that they are experts in their own languages, and that they have translated my poems because they wanted to. This activity has brought them neither money nor fame. The motivation has been interest for the text, curiosity, commitment. It ought to be called *love*—which is the only realistic basis for poetry translation.

Let me sketch two ways of looking at a poem. You can perceive a poem as an expression of the life of the language itself, something organically grown out of the very language in which it is written—in my case, Swedish. A poem written by the Swedish language through me. Impossible to carry over into another language.

Another, and contrary, view is this: the poem as it is presented is a manifestation of another, invisible poem, written in a language behind the common languages. Thus, even the original version is a translation. A transfer into English or Malayalam is merely the invisible poem's new attempt to come into being. The important thing is what happens between the text and the reader. Does a really committed reader ask if the written version he reads is the original or a translation?

I never asked that question when I, in my teenage years, learned to read poetry—and to write it (both things happened at the same time). As a two-year-old child in a polyglot environment experiences the different tongues as one single language, I perceived, during the first enthusiastic poetry years, all poetry as Swedish. Eliot, Trakl, Eluard—they were all Swedish writers, as they appeared in priceless, imperfect, translations.

Theoretically we can, to some extent justly, look at poetry translation as an absurdity. But in practice we must believe in poetry translation, if we want to believe in World Literature. That's what we do here in Oklahoma. And I thank my translators.

—A transcription of Tranströmer's acceptance speech after being awarded the Neustadt International Prize for Literature on June 12, 1990 at the University of Oklahoma.

---

as the poem moves and allows us to look elsewhere, we cannot forget that track. It is always there, always running through that very dark and lonely field.

A title I like even more is **"After the Attack."** Here are the first two stanzas:

> The sick boy.
> Locked in a vision
> with tongue stiff as a horn.
>
> He sits with his back towards the painting of a
>   wheatfield.
> The bandage around his jaw reminds one of an
>   embalming.
> His spectacles are thick as a diver's. Nothing has
>   any answer
> and is sudden as a telephone ringing in the night.

So what attack, we wonder. We read on. We read about a painting the sick boy sees nearby, and we begin to realize we're slowly entering his sensations, no longer those of the voice who'd been observing the boy in the earlier stanzas. The title stays in our minds. What attack? Then, as the details of the painting begin to take control of the poem, we realize it's the painting itself that has attacked the boy, and as quickly as that hits home, the poem scores *its* little blow. It's made its attack as well. And I come back again and again to that bandage around the boy's jaw—the other attack—and think how he'll never see the world in quite the same way again. His perceptions of everything have been altered. Now everything has the power to lurch forward and connect to him—like an attack. (pp. 181-82)

Nance Van Winckel, in a review of "Tomas Tranströmer: Selected Poems, 1954-1986," in The Iowa Review, *Vol. 18, No. 2, Spring-Summer, 1988, pp. 178-83.*

Robert Bly

Tomas Tranströmer seems to me the best poet to appear in Sweden for some years. He comes from a long line of ship pilots who worked in and around the Stockholm Archipelago. He is at home on islands. His face is thin and angular, and the swift, spare countenance reminds one of Hans Christian Andersen's or the young Kierkegaard's. He has a strange genius for the image—images come up almost effortlessly. The images flow upward like water rising in some lonely place, in the swamps, or deep fir woods.

Tranströmer's poems, so vivid in English, show the ability of certain poetry to travel to another culture and actually arrive there. As Tranströmer said in a letter to the Hungarian poets, published in the magazine *Új Írás* in 1977:

> Poetry has an advantage from the start. . . .
> Poetry requires no heavy, vulnerable apparatus
> that has to be lugged around; it isn't dependent
> on temperamental performers, dictatorial directors, bright producers with irresistible ideas.

He also remarked, "Poems are active meditations; they want to wake us up, not put us to sleep." At many places I go in this country, I meet people for whom Tranströmer is an awakener. They receive the fragrance of the depth from him; they see the light suddenly released by one of his brief quatrains. His work has become a strong influence now on many younger American poets. (p. 570)

The early fifties were a rather formal time, both here and in Sweden, and Tranströmer began by writing highly formal poems, all elements measured. His first book, *17 dikter (17 Poems)*, published in 1954, contains several poems written in classical meters adapted from the Latin. That collection includes many baroque elements in its language. Tranströmer's language has gradually evolved into a more spoken Swedish, and he has written both prose poetry and free verse; but, as he remarked during a recent interview published in *Poetry East:*

> Often there is a skeleton somewhere in the poem with a regular number of beats and so on in each line. You don't have to know that, but for me it's important.

Tranströmer's second book, *Hemligheter på vägen (Secrets on the Road)*, contained fourteen poems and appeared four years later. In 1962, after another gap of four years, he published *Den halvfärdiga himlen (Half-Finished Heaven)*, with twenty-one poems—fifty-two poems in all in about ten years. In 1966 came *Klanger och spår (Resonance and Foot-Tracks)* and in 1970 *Mörkerseende* (Eng. *Night Vision*). Three years later he published *Stigar* (**Paths**) and in 1974 a long poem, *Östersjöar* (Eng. *Baltics*), describing the island where his family on his father's side have lived for generations.

Tranströmer's early poetry could be described as baroque romantic, with elements visible from both the eighteenth and the nineteenth century. Like the romantics, Tranströmer loves to travel, and a chance encounter may evolve into a poem; but Göran Printz-Påhlson notes a crucial difference between Tranströmer's work and that of the romantics: "The traveler is brought to a halt, and the experience is imprinted with ferocious energy, but not interpreted." Tranströmer works slowly and steadily on poems and often writes only seven or eight a year. That may be one reason why his poems have so much weight. (pp. 570-71)

Tranströmer's three most recent books have been *Sanningsbarriären* (Eng. *Truth Barriers*) in 1978, *Det vilda torget* (Eng. *The Wild Marketplace*) in 1983, and last year a fine new collection, including some of his strongest poems, *För levande och döda* (Eng. *For Living and Dead*).

Tranströmer values his poems not so much as artifacts but rather as meeting places. Images from widely separated worlds meet in his verse. In the letter to the Hungarian poets he said, "My poems are meeting places. . . . What looks at first like a confrontation turns out to be connection." The poem **"Street Crossing"** describes an encounter between the ancient Swedish earth and a Stockholm street.

> The street's massive life swirls around me;
> it remembers nothing and desires nothing.
> Far under the traffic, deep in earth,
> the unborn forest awaits, still, for a thousand
>   years.

He remains "suspended" so as to hear things.

> one evening in June: the transistor told me the
>   latest
> on the Extra Session: Kosygin, Eban.
> One or two thoughts bored their way in
>   despairingly . . . I saw heard it from a sus-
>   pension bridge
> together with a few boys. Their bicycles
> buried in the bushes—only the horns
> stood up.

                                   (**"Going with the Current"**)

He likes this "suspension," where objects float in a point of view that cannot be identified as "Marxist" or "conservative," right or left. During the sixties many critics in Sweden demanded that each poet commit himself or herself to a Marxist view, or at least concede that documentaries are the only socially useful form of art. Tranströmer has received several attacks for resisting that doctrine. Art still needs the unconscious, he believes; that has not changed. He also believes that a poem needs a place for the private, the quirky, the religious, the unexplainable, the human detail that the collective cannot classify. **"Out in the Open,"** for example, is neither a nature poem, nor a political poem, nor a religious poem. One of its purposes evidently is to draw from all these sections of psychic experience without choosing among them. . . .

One of the most beautiful qualities in Tranströmer's poems is the space we feel in them. I think one reason for this is that the four or five main images which appear in each of his poems come from widely separated sources in the psyche. His poems are a sort of railway station where trains that have come enormous distances stand briefly in the same building. One train may have some Russian snow still lying on the undercarriage, and another may have Mediterranean flowers still fresh in the compartments and Ruhr soot on the roofs.

The poems are mysterious because of the distance the images have come to get there. Mallarmé believed there should be mystery in poetry, and he urged poets to get it by removing the links that tie the poem to its occasion in the real world. In Tranströmer's poems the link to the worldly occasion is stubbornly kept, yet the poems have a mystery and surprise that never fade, even on many readings.

Tranströmer has said that when he first began to write, in the early fifties, it still seemed possible to compose a nature poem into which nothing technological entered. Now, he says, he feels that many objects created by technology have become almost parts of nature, and he makes sure in his poetry that technology and its products appear. Some sights brought about by technology help him see more vividly a countryside scene: "All at once I notice the hills on the other side of the lake: / their pine has been clear-cut. They resemble the shaved / skull-sections of a patient about to have a brain operation." Perhaps nature can help you see a semi: "The semi-trailer crawls through the fog. / It is the lengthened shadow of a dragonfly larva / crawling over the murky lakebottom." Man-made objects are not necessarily without life. (p. 571)

Recent poems bring forward a fresh emphasis: the poems circle in an intense way around the experience of borders, boundaries of nations, the passage from one world to the next, the weighty instant as we wake up and step from the world of dream to this world, the corridors through which the dead invade our world, the intermediate place between life and art, the contrast between Schubert's music and Schubert, "a plump young man from Vienna" who sometimes "slept with his glasses on."

The title of a recent collection, *Sanningsbarriären,* translated as both *Truth Barriers* and *The Truth Barrier,* suggests a customs gate. Tranströmer remarked that truth exists only at the border between worlds. On this side of the border there is doctrine, and on the other side infinity, so that we experience truth only at the moment of crossing. But, alas, there are guards who do not want us to cross.

In **"Start of a Late Autumn Novel"** Tranströmer, inside an uninhabited island house, finds himself neither asleep nor awake: "A few books I've just read sail by like schooners on the way to the Bermuda Triangle, where they will disappear without a trace." This description is rueful and funny. He's right: sometimes we finish a book and can't remember a word. As the poem continues, he lies half asleep and hears a thumping sound outside. He listens to it—it is something being held down by earth. It beats like a heart under a stethoscope; it seems to vanish and return. Or perhaps there is some being inside the wall who is knocking, "someone who belongs to the other world, but got left here anyway, he thumps, wants to go back. Too late. Wasn't on time down here, wasn't on time up there, didn't make it on board in time." So apparently a successful passage to the other world and back has to do with timing: the Celtic fairy tales also emphasize that. The poem ends with his amazement the next morning when he sees an oak branch, a torn-up tree root, and a boulder. When, in solitude, we see certain objects, they seem to be "left behind when the ship sailed"; Tranströmer says they are monsters from the other world "whom I love."

A poem called **"December Evening '72"** begins: "Here I come the invisible man, perhaps in the employ / of some huge Memory that wants to live at this moment. And I drive by / the white church that's locked up. A saint made of wood is inside, / smiling helplessly, as if someone had taken his glasses." The first two lines suggest that Transtömer as an artist believes himself to be a servant of the Memory. He writes a poem when some huge Memory wants to cross over into this world; and this view of art seems more European than American. Often in America the artist believes his or her job is to tell the truth about one's own life: confessional poetry certainly implies that. Following that concept of art, many workshop poets comb their personal memory and write poems about their childhood, filling the poems with a clutter of detail. This clutter sometimes ensures that the piece will remain "a piece of writing" and will not become "a work of art."

Transtömer has the odd sense that the Great Memory can only come in when the artist is alert to it. While on guard duty in a defense unit a few years ago, he wrote:

> Task: to be where I am.
> Even when I'm in this solemn and absurd
> role: I am still the place
> where creation does some work on itself.

> Dawn comes, the sparse tree trunks
> take on color now, the frostbitten
> forest flowers form a silent search party
> after something that has disappeared in the
>   dark.

> But to be where I am . . . and to wait:
> I am full of anxiety, obstinate, confused.
> Things not yet happened are already here!
> I feel that. They're just out there:

> a murmuring mass outside the barrier.
> They can only slip in one by one.
> They want to slip in. Why? They do
> one by one. I am the turnstile.

>   **("Sentry Duty")**

He experiences the Great Memory as "somebody who keeps pulling on my arm each time I try to write." Again we feel ourselves at a boundary, being influenced by something on the other side. In **"From the Winter of 1947"** the dead press through into our world, as the stains in wallpaper: "They want to have their portraits painted." And in **"Street Crossing,"** for one second as he crosses a busy Stockholm street, the poet has the sensation that the street and the earth below it have eyes and can see him.

Transtömer begins his Schubert poem by describing New York from an overlook, "where with one glance you take in the houses where eight million human beings live." He mentions subway cars, coffee cups, desks, elevator doors. Still, "I know also—statistics to the side—that at this moment in some room down there Schubert is being played, and for that person the notes are more real than all the rest." And what are notes? When sounds are absorbed and shaped by and inside, say, a string quartet, they contain vibrations that resonate somewhere inside us and awaken "feelings" that we seem not to have felt in daily life. There is evidently a layer of consciousness that runs alongside our life, above or below, but is not it. Perhaps it is older. Certain works of art make it their aim to rise up and pierce this layer, or layers. Or they open to allow in "memories" from this layer. Some artists—Transtömer, Pasternak, and Akhmatova come especially to mind—keep the poem spare and clear so it can pierce the layers, or leave room for the Memory.

The art of Schubert puts Transtömer at a boundary between worlds, and at such a boundary he sees astonishing truths.

> The five instruments play. I go home through
>   warm woods
> where the earth is springy under my feet
> curl up like someone still unborn, sleep, roll on
>   so weightlessly
> into the future, suddenly understand that plants
>   are thinking.

Art helps us, he says, as a banister helps the climber on a dark stairwell. The banister finds its own way in the dark. In certain pieces of music happiness and suffering weigh exactly the same. The depths are above us and below us at the same instant. The melody line is a stubborn "humming sound that this instant is with us / upward into / the depths."

Swedish magazines often fill themselves with abstract hallucinatory poetry, typewriter poetry, alphabet poetry—poems that are really the nightmares of overfed linguists, of logical positivists with a high fever. Tranströmer, simply by publishing his books, leads a movement of poetry in the opposite direction, toward a poetry of silence and depths. (pp. 572-73)

> *Robert Bly, "Tomas Tranströmer and 'The Memory',"* in World Literature Today, *Vol. 64, No. 4, Autumn, 1990, pp. 570-73.*

Lasse Söderberg

To what extent can Tomas Tranströmer's poetry be said to reflect something specifically Swedish? The question was put to me in Oklahoma, very likely out of pure politeness toward me as a fellow countryman of the 1990 Neustadt laureate, but, judging by the urgency of the question, also in the hope of a characterization beyond the handbooks, based on such insights as only a well-informed compatriot might be expected to possess. I must admit that in that very moment I was left speechless. What, if anything, I wondered to myself, could be termed specifically Swedish? Our legendary uncommunicativeness and reserve, our well-known love of nature, our notorious proclivity to suicide? Our assiduous but contradictory work for world peace? Our blue-eyedness, not purely as a distinctive physical feature but also in the secondary sense that the expression possesses in Swedish: gullibility? Could this, or anything else we saw in ourselves, be applied to Tranströmer's poems and thus shed light on them?

For my own part I have always paid less attention to the national and more to the international in Tranströmer's poetry: the connection to the admittedly meandering yet effective modernistic tradition with its insistence on clarity of image. He appears to me to be considerably closer to a number of foreign poets than to the most influential among our own. Of course this does not exclude the possibility of a local connection, in terms either of literature or of a more general social sense. But, I immediately ask myself, is there any particular reason to emphasize this? I am reminded that, as early as the beginning of the last century, one of our greatest authors, Carl Jonas Love Almqvist (1793-1866), ascertained that "Swedishness consists in being Swedish, more than in crying out that one is Swedish." The distinction is less superfluous than it may appear: it distinguishes the genuine from the ostentatious. It also relieves the concept of its more unpleasant associations—we know only too well where loudmouthed patriotism can lead. Still, it is not certain that I would have had the same misgivings if the object of my study had come from somewhere else; then I would probably have dwelled with pleasure on the national characteristics. One of the peculiarities of the Swedes, though, is that they are ashamed of their peculiarities.

What part then does the literary inheritance play for Tomas Tranströmer? One is a bit startled by the expression "national grandiloquence," used by the most brilliant observer of the Swedish poetry scene, Göran

Printz-Påhlson, in his essay "Tranströmer and Tradition," published in the special 1979 issue of *Ironwood* on Tranströmer [see Further Reading]. That forces one to recall patriotic outpourings of a sort which hardly are found in poetry any more. What Printz-Påhlson refers to, however, is the kind of stylistic qualities in the young Tranströmer—his wording concerns *17 dikter* (*17 Poems;* 1954)—that are reminiscent of our belated baroque poetry with its richly rendered emblematics. (p. 573)

[If] one goes back to Carl Jonas Love Almqvist and continues reading in his exceptional pamphlet "Om den svenska fattigdomens betydelse" (The Importance of Swedish Poverty), from which I have already quoted, it is hard to deny that certain trains of thought become uncommonly striking, in connection not only with Tranströmer but also with a line of Swedish poets among which he can be counted: those sharp-sighted ones who unite objectivity with imaginative ability. The concept of *poverty* in Almqvist does not refer primarily to an economic situation, as one might suspect, considering the fact that Sweden was among the European countries in the greatest distress in his time. "The Swede is poor," states Almqvist, "and if he comprehends this, he has won the kernel of his nationality and is invincible. *To be poor is to be restricted to one's own resources.*"

The polite inquiry in Oklahoma appeared to me to be a challenge, in this case to a rereading of Tranströmer's ten volumes of poetry, those more than two hundred pages (in the latest pocket edition) which he has produced in thirty-five years: 128 poems, just over three-and-a-half poems per year, but they are poems which to a great extent are crystallized from experience and attain their effect above all through their high degree of *concentration*. I italicize the word because I also find it in Almqvist: "With the Swede, poverty actually means concentration: staking one's strength on a single card of the personality, or tapping an inner individual wellspring with an inexhaustible vein."

More than thirty years ago I wrote a poem that paid homage to Tranströmer. It is referred to quite often, and I therefore in turn permit myself now to quote two lines: "Du står i det hemligas flackande sken / och i hjärtat flödar vårt fattiga språk" (in Stephen Klass's translation, "You stand in the flickering conundrum-light / and in your heart our poor tongue is in flood").

Our impoverished language? Even Almqvist points out that, "strangely enough," the Swedish language is poor in terms of vocabulary and word forms, "just as the land is in terms of people, and the way of life [is poor] in variegated external events." Others would certainly agree. The question, though, is whether there is not a romantic misconception in this. In comparison with English the Swedish language of course does not possess a large vocabulary, but its *expressiveness* need be no less for all that. The spareness of the language is compensated for by a certain syntactic flexibility. The words we have fortify one another. If our language is poor, it nevertheless "flows," in our best (Swedish) poets and not least in Tomas Tranströmer. His language is compressed but not complicated. The images are dense but not impenetrable. "Reduce!" runs his call, placed in the mouth of the composer Edvard Grieg, but

Tomas Tranströmer accepting the 1990 Neustadt International Prize for Literature.

still to a great extent his own. He skillfully avails himself of the capacity for expressiveness that Swedish provides. This goes for compounds such as *barvinterdagar* or *paltbrödsmörk,* expressions so permeated with Nordic experience as to be almost untranslatable. When Robin Fulton translates them as "bare winter days" and "the distant pine," it is correct per se, even if the adjective in the first case by necessity has been disconnected from the subject and refers to the latter rather than the former part of the expression and the adjective in the second case loses its topographical association. . . .

Neither syntactic liberties nor references to specifically Nordic phenomena or landscapes constitute insurmountable barriers for translators. This is a truth which is not restricted to Tranströmer or to any other language area. In fact, one can maintain that the *original*—and to the original belongs the adjacent—stimulates that kind of retransmission. Tranströmer is among the most often translated Swedish poets and may also be one of the few, not to say the only one, who has exerted a notable influence beyond the borders of Sweden and Scandinavia. This is true especially of the English-speaking world, where such like-minded poets as Robert Bly and Robin Fulton have eagerly set about translating Tranströmer's poems and have also allowed themselves to be permeated by them. . . . (p. 574)

Two words, both capitalized, appeared in the poem that concluded Tranströmer's debut collection [*17 Poems*]. They were terms that many of us others at that time in our radicalism would not even have dreamed of using, except possibly with an irreverent purpose. . . . To him the two words came naturally, since they were associated with experiences which were fundamental for him. The first was the word *Sweden.* The second was *God.* As rendered by May Swenson and Leif Sjöberg, the poem begins: "December. Sweden is a hauled-up, / unrigged ship. Her masts stand stark / in the twilight. And the twilight lasts longer / than day." As in an old copper engraving, Tranströmer here evokes the supreme desolation that characterizes our country in wintertime. The stillness at the beginning of the poem is façade, however. Soon we have moved, not geographically but in time; the region is filled with the most disturbing events, until "the year kicks off its boots / and the sun shinnies higher, trees take leaf, / are filled with wind and sail out freely," and all of a sudden summer has arrived. Even if the crowding of images in these eighty-five verse lines almost gets out of hand—the young poet does not yet manage to keep them together— one notices that his language, with its "vestiges of national grandiloquence," is certainly imaginative yet always deeply rooted in his perception. He knows what he is talking about.

In the middle of all this objectivity another kind of experience breaks in: "And finally: / God's spirit, like the Nile, flooding / and sinking in a rhythm calculated / in texts from many epochs" (tr. Robin Fulton). I don't know if the religiosity that Tranströmer sometimes expresses, with great moderation, can be defined in relation to his nationality. If so, it can be seen as the result of the progressive secularization in a country with a state church and represents that which has been salvaged from the petrification of organized religion. He does not preach, is never elevated (except perhaps in the lines just quoted). To Tranströmer religion is a private matter, very little in need of theological commentary. "We're in the church of keeping-silence, in the piety according to no letter," he says in the remarkable poem **"Guldstekel"** (**"Golden Wasp"**), which ends his most recent collection, *För levande och döda* (1989; Eng. *For Living and Dead,*) for which he received the Grand Prize of the Nordic Council.

The divine shows itself only by glimpses, "in the texts from varied epochs" or in certain privileged and most often unguarded moments, in nature or in dream. This is what happens, for instance, in a poem from the 1962 collection *Den halvfärdiga himlen* (*The Half-Finished Heaven*), in which the divine once again is connected to the great Nile River of Africa, although this time it refers to a real visit **"In the Nile Delta,"** as the poem is called, a journey on which the poet, after a heartrending encounter with dirt and desolation, falls asleep "curled up into a 'no' ": "A dream came. He was on a sea voyage. / In the gray water there rose up a disturbance / and a voice said: 'There is one who is good. / There is one who can see without hating' " (tr. Eric Sellin). There is someone speaking for God here without mentioning his name. God himself does not speak, does not intervene. He is not a higher power but rather one mystery among others, or a mystery which in itself includes other mysteries, inaccessible to speculation. "The executioners gather stones, God writes in the sand," we read in *Det vilde torget* (1983; Eng. *The Wild Marketplace*). "But," he says in **"Epilogue"** . . . , "He is also unchangeable" and, as a consequence of unchangeability, "seldom noted here."

It looks like a conscious clue that both the problematic words in **"Epilogue"** recur already in the opening poem of *Hemligheter på vägen* (*Secrets on the Way;* 1958), "in many ways the key poem for Tranströmer's development at that time, being both his most 'traditional' and also his boldest attempt at Surrealist imagery," as Printz-Påhlson says in the abovementioned essay. Here too God is hidden, unseen, but this very fact lends itself to inspiring a kind of paradoxical hope, as if an intercession could not come about: "Let them feel without alarm / the camouflaged wings / and God's energy / coiled up in the dark" (tr. Robin Fulton). The title of this poem—"chillingly descriptive," says Printz-Påhlson—is **"Svenska hus enslgt belägna"** (**"Solitary Swedish Houses"**). It makes me think of Tacitus, who in his *Germania* relates of the tendency of the Nordic peoples to construct villages with detached houses, "whether this is done for protection against fire or from lack of knowledge in construction work." We are few and far between in this sparsely populated land, even when we crowd together in cities. To what avail? The country

distances stretch out inside us. The city, says Tranströmer in the poem following next—one of the many dealing with waking up—is a *fäbod,* a châlet. The simile would not have occurred to him, if we did not historically find ourselves so close to preindustrial, rural Sweden. This goes not only for Tranströmer but for many other poets as well: at heart we are small farmers, coastal fishermen, or, like Tranströmer, pilots.

To be sure, Tranströmer was born and brought up in a city, Stockholm, and for years he has resided in another, Västerås; but he has his roots in the skerries from which his maternal ancestors came. This archipelago, exploited in literature by many authors since Strindberg—relentlessly exploited one might sometimes think—has been present with him ever since the sapphic verses of *17 dikter,* later brought together under the rubric **"Höstlig skärgård"** (**"Autumn in the Skerries"**). To that region, to the sea and the cliffs, "the wonderful labyrinth of islands and waters" and the inherited house with its wood "impregnated with four times joy and three times sorrow," he returns year after year, both physically and in his poems. The high point, of course, is the long poem called *Östersjöar* (1974; Eng. *Baltics*), which touches not only upon the place but also, as remaining components of the place, upon those who once lived and worked there.

Tacitus makes a curious observation concerning the burial habits of the Teutons: "It is the women's task to mourn, the men's to remember." For Tranströmer memory is a strongly inspiring factor, not least the personal but deeply buried memory which preserves and supplements the finest, most abortive external impulses: a communication route inward. Memory creates kinship. "No telling / bones of the dead from bones of the living," we read in *Stigar (Paths;* 1973). And in his latest collection he writes, "They have something to say, the dead," conscious that he himself "will hurry through the streets as one of them." In the same collection he sees himself as a "mummy resting in the blue casket of the forests," counterpart and at the same time descendant of the slain Bocksten Man, who for six hundred years lay preserved in a peat bog and whose discovery Tranströmer lingered over in an early poem. "It is easy to love fragments which have been on their way for a long time," he says. It is as if the poem were groping its way through the ages while the poet moves in the opposite direction, encircled in his inescapable present: "Here I come, the invisible man, perhaps employed / by a Great Memory to live right now." The term *employed* suggests a relationship of dependence, as if the poet has been entrusted the task of decoding and passing on the messages from the past. The present would be intolerable if it did not also include a past. Every moment includes all moments. "The seconds," he says in *Klanger och spår (Bells and Tracks;* 1966), "grew as big as hospital buildings." Tranströmer's masterful skill consists in his ability to open up, to make himself accessible in the throng of reality—"I am a water-spout for impressions"—and at the same time to know exactly where and when the image he calls to life expresses something. It does when, as Tranströmer says, "what looks like a confrontation turns out to be a connection." That is when he makes the scales fall from our inner eyes. Is he invisible? At any rate, one who makes visible.

Swedishness implies, of course—concerning other nations—different, sometimes contradictory qualities. If Tomas Tranströmer is Swedish in his poetry, he is so in the same way that Harry Martinson or Werner Aspenström is, but not like the national poet Gustaf Fröding (1860-1911) or the programmatic Gunnar Ekelöf (1907-68). He is no confessional poet. He is suspicious of his own ego—already in *17 dikter* he wishes to "leave behind his self-disguise"—and does not exude melancholy or agitated words. He does not keep his eyes fixed on a distant, more bearable (to the sensitive) place or on an impossible horizon of thought. He is not torn apart. In a way entirely different from Fröding and Ekelöf, he is equipped with what I would like to call creative equanimity. He is the Observer who asserts from a generally confident basic view, "Mission: to be where I am"—i.e., as is revealed two lines farther down in the poem **"The Outpost,"** "the place / where creation is working itself out." Once again the wonder. That place is a meeting place, "a turnstile," as he says. There is something stable, something tangible in this. The turnstile spins securely. Through it one exits. Through it one enters.

The Swede has, says Almqvist, "but little of the culture which Europe recognizes as culture and designates as such. But he has very much the manner of seeing quickly and straight through things, which customarily is called sound Swedish sense." There is much of this to be found in Tomas Tranströmer, and, in addition, an innocence, which I have always envied him. Almqvist has a wonderful expression for this: "Actually, it is a young state of mind: it is 10 o'clock in the morning in the head and in the heart." (pp. 575-76)

> *Lasse Söderberg, "The Swedishness of Tomas Tranströmer," translated by Leif Sjöberg, in* World Literature Today, *Vol. 64, No. 4, Autumn, 1990, pp. 573-76.*

Eric Sellin

[Upon first opening the books *17 dikter* and *Hemligheter på vägen* in 1959], I was struck by the generous margins or what we might call "paginal aeration." Upon reading the texts themselves, I admired Tranströmer's talent for juxtaposing remote yet seemingly relevant elements in an imagery which combined rupture and symbiosis and whose dynamics reinforced the sense of aeration.

Tranströmer's imagery, grounded as it is in the real world and personal experience, nevertheless goes far beyond mere analogy. His images are, as it were, moths on the windowpane that are like "tiny pale telegrams from the world," to use one of the poet's own images. As Åke Lundqvist has said of Tranströmer's poetry, it seems to "exist in an invisible link with *something other* than what we call reality."

Indeed, Tranströmer's great and well-deserved reputation as one of the world's major poets seems to be based largely on his consummate use of imagery. Critic after critic has commented on his powerful and unusual images, which somehow link the objects and experiences of daily life to overarching cosmic intuitions. In fact, Tranströmer's images are sometimes so disjointed in their flexion between the empyrean and the mundane that we wonder how the imagery manages to work—but it does. His imagery seems so dominant and so patent that one feels it would be easy to become a major poet merely by emulating Tranströmer's curious blend of referents; but if one tries to imitate Tranströmer's style, the result will, more than likely, be totally wooden. The master seems to be he who can make the great look easy, whether in sports or in art. Typical of the many comments on the importance of Tranströmer's imagery are those of Robert Bly ("He really has an amazing gift for the image—he knows just how much room the image needs to expand and resonate, and he keeps everything quiet and spacious around it. The poem is like a violin body"), Robin Fulton ("One thing that makes Tranströmer's poetry so widely accessible [in spite of the loss in translation of its original Swedish music] must be the startling clarity of its imagery and its surprising changes of perspective"), and *votre serviteur* ("One can adequately translate the poetry of Tranströmer . . . with minimal aesthetic heat loss, if he has the rudiments of the language and a basic sympathy with modern poetics").

Tranströmer's characteristic imagery is especially noticeable because many of his poems end on what I would call a "cosmic image," by which I mean an image that opens up extensive vistas of possibilities at the close of the poem rather than wrapping up the material in a logical closure as is the case with many poems. . . .

A corollary of the stress on imagery in Tranströmer's work is the number of translators who have rendered his poems into other languages, especially English. As Robin Fulton has pointed out: "Every poem in every collection has been translated into English, and the majority of his poems exist in two or more English versions."

Having said the above, I would like now to turn to other, less frequently considered aspects of Tranströmer's poetry, especially his musicality. The same analysts who have emphasized his imagery have tended to minimize his musicality and his metrical talents. I myself have been guilty of this, having suggested, as in the quotation above, that his attraction for translators may be due to the fact that there is "minimal heat loss" in the translations as a result of Tomas's reliance on imagery at the expense of musicality and metrics. However, the poet's images are to some degree floated, so to speak, on his other less recognized yet manifest gifts of metrical mastery and musical appropriateness. . . . (p. 598)

The so-called concentration of "heat" in the imagery does not mean that there are not other factors; however, the salience of the imagery tends to tone down other poetic elements by comparison. Expressed metaphorically, we may liken the emphasis on imagery in Tranströmer's poetics to the hot spots on an infrared heat-analysis picture. The red masses in the poems are the images (including the mute portions of the image, when the poet makes unsaid transitions or leaves voids in which the image can reverberate), the magnets which draw our attention and interest; but there are as well the other orange, blue, and black areas, which contribute to the overall thrust of text, notably metrics and musicality.

Many of Tomas's poems are essentially in free verse; however, as a young poet he was influenced by Greek and Latin poetry and wrote poems in Swedish metrics (stress-based, as in English), but using classical forms. Whereas the unique imagery that has remained his trademark was evident in the very first poems of *17 dikter,* his versification has evolved from a more even-length line and adoption of classical forms to a freer rhythm. . . .

The most complex yet most faithful reflection of classical modes is perhaps **"Strof och motstrof,"** in two stanzas of nine lines, the second of which thematically repeats the varied line length of the first. In *17 dikter* other poems written in the traditional Swedish metrical system (e.g., the tetrameter or pentameter) and/or using classical verse patterns include **"Epilog," "Upprörd meditation," "Sång,"** and **"Elegi."**

Tranströmer moved slowly toward freer verse, including more and more frequent use of the prose poem, as well as toward longer poems, especially with and after *Ostersjöar* (1974); yet the metrical mastery evident in the early works surely remains a constant, albeit a more attenuated, more subtly crafted one.

In poetics, musicality hinges on the poet's use of such factors as alliteration, assonance, rhyme, and the selection of vowels and consonants whose sounds somehow evoke in the reader or listener feelings in concord with the imagery and the content of the poem. A poet with the gift of musicality has the knack for making the sounds and alliteration support rather than cancel out the imagery. . . .

Tranströmer's poetry is not unmusical—to the contrary!—but in it the music is simply less evident than the masterful imagery. It would be astonishing, in fact, were Tranströmer's verse not musical, for he is a great lover of music. He plays the piano for pleasure, and many of his poems bear witness to this passion, containing reference to musicians (Haydn) or composers (Balakirev) and making use of musical terms for titles: **"C-dur," "Lamento," "Allegro," "Nocturne."** (p. 599)

Musicality exists, for better or for worse, in all words. It is merely a matter of how sensitively the sounds and their repetition are handled and how the sounds that prevail are successful in creating, on the one hand, sound associations which emphasize the visual, tactile, gustatory, auditory, and olfactory imagery and, on the other, tremolos and other such interactions above and around the imagery.

In a very revealing extract from an interview with Gunnar Harding [see excerpt dated June, 1973], Tranströmer acknowledges the fact that he is more concerned with pictures than with musical wordplay; but he stresses the profound influence music has had on his life and maintains that his interest in music is somehow transferred to the poetic process.

> [Harding]: *Let's talk about music. It's meant a lot to you. . . .*
> [Tranströmer]: Yes, more than literature.

Does it still?
Yes, in the sense that I have an innocent relationship to music, it's not something I'm involved in professionally, it's just something I helped myself to. . . .
Did you ever think of going in for music?
In my mid-teens I wanted to be a composer. I remember a fugue my piano teacher thought was neat. But I still get certain musical impulses and at times they come in connection with a poem, so that it's like a shadow of the poem emerging tonally. This doesn't get written down but it does exist in a way in my consciousness. . . .
But you seldom compose your poems musically—it's normally the visual factor that is pronounced rather than any kind of word music.
Word music in the sense that you labor over vowels and consonants has never had any special attraction for me. On the other hand when I was younger I had the ambition to try and carry over musical forms into poetry—though that was a very common ambition at the time, in the late forties. . . .

Another reason for Tranströmer's worldwide reputation as an imagist is the fact that many translations simply do not convey the subtle music of the originals. Robert Hass regrets, in the preface to his Ecco Press edition of Tranströmer's *Selected Poems, 1954-1986* (1987), that he felt he could not include "the rich blank verse '**Sång**' from *17 dikter,* which needed to be in fairly regular blank verse in English and has so far resisted the metamorphosis." Indeed, much of the beauty of the long poem **"Sång"** resides in its sustained, dignified tone, blending sea sounds and cosmic images. . . . The poem is full of examples of successful alliteration: "med sång i fjärden som ett fågelsträck"; "en flodvåg mörk med måsar ridande"; "men fläckad av förbjudna kusters rökar."

I have been rereading a number of the translations of Tomas's work. When the translation does sing, it is often in places where the original does not and vice versa. Obviously one cannot achieve every nuance in transferring the lyric energy from one language to another. To do so one would have to change the language and the imagery. To do so would be to substitute Tomas's trump card with a low card. The density of Swedish syntax in some instances defies exact equivalence, as in the close of **"Skepparhistoria"** ("Där den ende överlevande får sitta / vid norrskenets ugn och lyssna / till de ihjälfrusnas musik"), whose terse, powerful lines have been translated by Robert Bly as "There the sole survivor sits by the furnace / of the Northern Lights, and listens to the music / coming from the men frozen to death," a discourse which sounds natural but loses the density of the original music. Robin Fulton's version of the text, though a bit tighter, does not capture the essence of the original, seeming instead stilted and unnatural: "Where the sole survivor may sit / at the borealis stove and listen / to the music of those frozen to death."

Occasionally the translator brings a *different* music to a poetic phrase. For example, Bly's idiom in the last line of **"Kväll—Morgon"** has a more noticeable alliterative music than does Tomas's original. Tomas's line reads, "Halvkvävda sommargudar famlar i sjörök"; Bly's rendition, beautifully manipulating consonance and assonance, reads: "Half-suffocated summer gods grope in the sea-smoke." There is great musicality here, in both the original and the translation, but they move in two entirely different modes.

Tomas Tranströmer established himself as one of Sweden's most promising poets with his first book. With his next two books, *Hemligheter på vägen* and *Den halvfärdiga himlen* (1962), he became, for many enthusiasts, Sweden's foremost contemporary poet, a ranking that he has continued to consolidate with subsequent volumes and which has recently been commemorated by several major prizes, including the 1990 Neustadt International Prize for Literature. Such eminence could not be achieved by a poet whose lyre has but one string. Tranströmer's unique verse is grounded in innovative imagery, but the imagery is sustained as well by a mastery of metrics and a deep respect for the role musicality plays in poetry. (pp. 599-600)

Eric Sellin, "Musical Tranströmer," in World Literature Today, *Vol. 64, No. 4, Autumn, 1990, pp. 598-600.*

Jaan Kaplinski

[Tranströmer] is a disciple of Swedish poets of both recent and earlier times, but also, what is equally important, of the French surrealists. He learned their language as a young student, but he never accepted their philosophy. Perhaps he was too much a rationalist or simply a Northerner with a strong sense of nature, firmly rooted in his native rocks, spruce forests, and small islands.

Perhaps the most important difference between Tranströmer and many other modernist poets is his emphasis on the human dimension, on suffering, loneliness, and the threat from hostile forces both outside and inside us. He seems always keenly aware of our insecurity and anxiety. In a sense, his poetry is a dialogue between someone asking the questions basic to any serious religious and philosophical discussion. These are questions about human suffering and insecurity, questions that he, in some other form, had to put to thousands of people, working throughout his life as a professional psychologist helping young delinquents and immigrants. From the esthetic point of view such questions seem trivial and naïve; they repeat, with minimal variations, what Buddha, Ecclesiastes, or Shakespeare asked long ago: "To be or not to be?"; "What to do about all this pain and suffering?"

There is always a discrepancy between the religious and the esthetic ways of expression. Religious texts do not avoid repetition and truisms; literary texts shun them. For that reason what is called religious poetry is most often dull and even kitschy. This is definitely not the case with Tranströmer. His poetry distances itself from conventional religiosity. Nowhere does he address a "Thou" over there. Any personal God is absent from his poetry; the "I-Thou" relationship is reserved for human beings. Still, the feeling of awe and wonder, the other basic element of a religious attitude toward the world, is certainly present. One of the recurrent themes in his poetry is the presence of something strange, great, and mysterious. We meet it already in his first youthful collection, *17 Poems:* "And culture is a whaling- / station where the stranger walks / among white gables, playing children, and / still with each breath he takes he feels / the murdered giant's presence" (**"Elegy"**). About thirty years later he writes: "I lie on the bed with my arms outstretched. / I am an anchor that has dug itself down and holds steady / the huge shadow floating up there, / the great unknown which I am a part of and which is certainly more important than me" (**"Carillon"**).

These poetic insights have their counterparts in philosophy, religion, and science. Most definitely, what we know is tiny compared with what we do not know but is constantly with us, influencing us. This is a simple truth that people around the year 1900 tended to forget. The scientific parallel to Tranströmer's metaphor of "the great unknown" he holds steady can well be the so-called Mach principle, which states that every single inertial movement, let us say the spinning of a whirligig, is dependent on the total mass of matter in the universe. A child on a merry-go-round feels with its body the weight of the whole cosmos, although it does not know much about it. The great unknown is one of the major forces that create us and influence us. We are part of them. The unknown penetrates us too, works in us and through us: "I am the place / where creation is working itself out" (**"The Outpost"**).

Besides the Mach principle, modern science knows many theories of interdependence between microcosm and macrocosm—i.e., the physics of elementary particles and cosmology—between subjective and objective, as seen in quantum mechanics or the theory of probabilities. To be more philosophical or poetic, we can say that as tiny is dependent on huge, huge is dependent on tiny.

The Swedish historian of religions Martin P. Nilsson speaks about religion as man's search for meaning. In this sense Tomas Tranströmer is certainly a religious poet and Mach, Einstein, Schrödinger, and other scientists are religious too. The theories of cosmic interdependence help us find a meaning to our existence in this strange world. The cosmic process needs us; we are "places where creation is working itself out."

Man is not only a part of the cosmos, however, but also a part of mankind. Tranströmer speaks about "the battlefield within us / where we Bones of the Dead / fight to become living" (**"An Artist in the North"**). Man has his place and meaning in human society too; most often it is called his duty. It has two facets. You have to study and to understand yourself; and you must open yourself to others, to understand and to help them. It is what the psychologist Tomas Tranströmer has done for thirty years, and in many of his poems he has reflected about duty: "Tonight I am down among the ballast. / I am one of the silent weights / which prevent the ship overturning!" (**"Night Duty"**).

Born into a family with a long tradition of seamen, Tranströmer often uses the image of seafaring as a metaphor of our human condition. Seafaring is dangerous, but we must do it—*navigare necesse est*—to be truly ourselves and to fulfill our duty before other people. Drowned seamen's souls returning home are something we find in both his earliest and latest poems (**"Sailor's Yarn"** in *17 Poems,* **"The Forgotten Captain"** in *For Living and Dead*). In his perhaps most famous poem, **"Baltics,"** man's relationship with the sea is a simile for his relationship with his destiny, with a life full of constant danger. We are all seafarers who must face storms, drifting mines, and fog. If life were not such a common thing, it would be heroic. For Transtömer, as for his ancestors, Swedish seamen and peasants, it is simply work, and work must be done. The work is a "great unknown of which we are part and which is certainly more important than us." Work binds us together; work is something we have inherited from our forefathers to continue.

Work is also what unites us with our dead, our common heritage. Tranströmer is very conscious of everything we have inherited: our houses, books, life histories, works of art, even cemeteries; and the meaning of life is certainly more in work than in fame. Fulfilling your duty is certainly more important than struggling to have your name written in the annals of history, in a codex. We should accept anonymity and oblivion, as have those countless generations before us: "Total oblivion. It's a kind of exam / taken in silence: to step over the border without anyone noticing" (**"Codex"**).

We see that Tranströmer, a disciple of French surrealists, a globetrotter who has written travel poems about Oklahoma, Molokai, the Nile delta, Iceland, Central Africa, and Greece, is at the same time a true inheritor of the world view of the Nordic peasants and seamen. He is a traditionalist, valuing modern individualism less than group solidarity, hard work, and veneration of the dead ancestors.

Is such a traditionalist attitude really a solution to the problems of the modern world? In a way it is, if we see the difference between the essential and nonessential. A positive attitude toward human community, toward work, and toward the dead is not something that belongs exclusively to the village society of the past. It can well exist in the modern global village too. Don't some of our evils come from the fact that our culture has inherited a system of values that originates mostly in the aristocratic and clerical traditions in the past and shuns the hardworking peasant tradition? Is not our culture too individualistic, competitive, pleasure-oriented, and esthetic? Is not its use of language too rigid, too theological? What we lack is openness and real work, practice. If we had both, our life and psychology would be more balanced and we would feel what we might call a Presence, as Tranströmer did.

Our intellectual tradition has, from the Greeks on, had a theoretical bias; practice or work was considered mostly a necessary evil, something that should be left to slaves, wives, or machines. The idea that doing hard work with a proper, open state of mind could be something absolutely essential for our humanness, for achieving real happiness and peace of mind, is alien to the Platonic tradition and certainly unpopular in a consumption-oriented society.

There are two ethical attitudes in the history of Western civilization: orientation to pleasure and orientation to work. The orientation to work has been more prevalent in the North, where the aristocratic and clerical traditions were not so strong and the older peasant one better preserved; and certainly people had to work harder in the more extreme ecological conditions in the North. (pp. 602-04)

Perhaps it is not an exaggeration to say that in the Scandinavian socialist movement two traditions—the Marxist one and the old local one—overlap. What they have in common is their understanding of the humanizing and the liberating quality of work. Such attitudes are represented also in the Indian conception of karma-yoga and in Far Eastern Zen Buddhism, where work was an essential part of monastic practice, an idea that would sound familiar to many monks and nuns in Europe too.

My first impression of Tranströmer was that he possesses the ability to reconcile and unite in his poetry many things that are considered opposites in our thinking. He is both a modernist and a traditionalist, as I have attempted to prove. He is certainly a citizen of the world, but at the same time firmly rooted in his Swedish soil. He is a religious person who has distanced himself from every formalized religion. He is keenly aware of the troubles of the modern world, but he has refused to become engaged in any political party or movement. In his poetry he has succeeded in merging abstract truths with concrete details of his everyday environment. He has blended together surrealism and autobiographical realism. His poetry is very musical, yet he has written practically no rhymed verse. To put it briefly, his work is very interesting and important to every one of us. (p. 604)

> *Jaan Kaplinski, "Tomas Transtömer and the Mach Principle," in* World Literature Today, *Vol. 64, No. 4, Autumn, 1990, pp. 601-04.*

FURTHER READING

Bly, Robert, and Tranströmer, Tomas. "Two Poets Translating." *Translation* IV (Spring-Summer 1977): 47-58.
> Documented conversation between Tranströmer and one of his principal translators. Bly and Tranströmer discuss the process of translation and the problems involved in presenting a fair and powerful translation of the original text.

Friebert, Stuart. "All Over Again." *Field,* No. 38 (Spring 1988): 54-75.
> Favorable overview of Transtömer's works and career.

Fulton, Robin. "The Poetry of Tomas Transtömer." *Scandinavica* 12 (1973): 107-23.
> Issue devoted to Scandinavian poets in which Fulton provides a detailed scholarly analysis of Transtömer's poetic development from *17 dikter* to *Mörkerseende.*

Ironwood 7, No. 13 (1979): 13-24.

Special issue devoted to Tranströmer's career, including translated poems as well as analyses by Robert Hass, Mark Rudman, and Goran Printz-Pahlson.

Sellin, Eric. "Tomas Tranströmer and the Cosmic Image." *Scandinavian Studies* 43, No. 1 (1971): 241-50.
Asserts that Tranströmer's international success is largely due to the ease of translating his primarily imagistic poetry.

Steene, Birgitta. "Vision and Reality in the Poetry of Tomas Tranströmer." *Scandinavian Studies* 37, No. 3 (August 1965): 236-44.
While considering imagery an integral element in Tranströmer's poetry, Steene concludes that other qualities are equally important, including "dynamic movement, paradoxical . . . use of language, and rhythmic verse."

World Literature Today 64, No. 4 (Autumn 1990): 591-95.
Special issue devoted partly to Tranströmer following his acceptance of the Neustadt Prize for Literature. Includes essays by Risa Lesser, Staffan Bergsten, and Lars Gustafsson.

Mac Wellman

Bad Penny, Crowbar, Terminal Hip

Award: Obie

Wellman is an American playwright, born in 1945.

A prolific and innovative dramatist, Wellman has been a leading figure in off-Broadway theater since the mid-1970s. He considers himself a "language-poet" playwright, employing words more for their sound than for their meaning. His unconventional use of puns, oxymorons, slang, repetition, and neologisms, has prompted comparisons to James Joyce, Lewis Carroll, and Gertrude Stein. The *Village Voice* awarded the 1990 Obie to Wellman for three of his most outstanding plays. *Terminal Hip* displays Wellman's extravagant wordplay, using lengthy monologues to satirize American politics, culture, advertising, and speech. *Bad Penny,* a site-specific work that instructs actors to shout their lines across a lake in New York's Central Park, was described by Eric Overmyer as "an exhilarating theater poem, a comic sonata of urban life, alienation, and pastoral respite interrupted by insanity and death." *Crowbar,* another site-specific piece, is set in the Victory Theatre on 42nd Street in New York. The play traces the varied history of this venue from its opening in 1900 to the present. By relating fragmented stories of celebrities associated with the Victory Theatre as well as those of people who died from murder, suicide, and accidents near the establishment's opening date, Wellman relies upon the show-business tradition of haunted theaters and suggests a correlation between the problems occurring outside and inside the building. Eric Overmyer summarized Wellman's work: "The plays of Mac Wellman are like a horizontal avalanche. A sliding flood of images, language, ideas, which moves the viewer out of his or her accustomed habitation as relentlessly and inexorably as a wall of mud."

Mel Gussow

Terminal Hip, Mac Wellman's "Spiritual History of America Through the Medium of Bad Language," is a post-Joycean Jabberwocky. Expect no exegesis. Just sit back and enjoy the torrent of language, as Mr. Wellman zigzags through time, space and participle.

This riff is a crazy quilt of slang and circumlocutions, double negatives and oxymorons gathered under a baldachin, or ornamental canopy of the mind. Listening to it, one repeatedly reaches for a mixed metaphor as steering wheel.

Terminal Hip is a word processor gone awry, garbling "grammatical shibboleth" on a scrambled screen.

Occasionally, the playwright strikes a note of clarity, trashing beachfront condos, assailing United States foreign policy in Central America (Presidents who "jubilate with successive Somozas") and parsing the component parts of the panda. For fun, there is a replay of Abbott and Costello's "who's on first" routine. If all this sounds illogical, that's for a reason. Think too hard about meaning, or listen for "chtonic murmurs," or primitive sounds, and one might be overcome by vertigo.

Amazingly, the actor Stephen Mellor tones and tames the monologue so that it seems to have an organic flow. Mr. Wellman and Mr. Mellor, who have often worked together, are quite a team, especially as evidenced in this play and in last summer's *"Bad Penny." "Bad Penny"* made a certain sense, as Mr. Mellor's character summed up a mad tourist's underview of New York. In contrast, *"Terminal Hip"* whirligigs its way without a thought about destination while taking theatergoers for a wild word-busting ride.

With all its convolutions and neologisms, the text must be impossible to memorize, but then who, except for Mr. Wellman, could tell if Mr. Mellor missed a word—or made up a word? The dream-of-consciousness principle is the thing. . . .

If the play is "a maniacal hubbub," it is a literate, amusing hubbub. It may be true, as the author says, that "any airhead can play an air guitar," but only Mr. Wellman could have written this play and only Mr. Mellor could have imbued it with such histrionic variety.

> Mel Gussow, "Language as a Toy, In One-Man Comedy," in The New York Times, January 12, 1990, p. C3.

Thomas M. Disch

Crowbar [is] a performance piece staged by En Garde Arts at the Victory Theater on 42nd Street. En Garde Arts is the "site-specific" theater company founded in 1985 by Anne Hamburger, who has a talent for turning unlikely nooks and crannies of the world at large—Central Park, the Chelsea Hotel, the Brooklyn waterfront—into de facto theaters. Her latest and largest inspiration has been to take over a real theater on the brink of annihilation and to commission from playwright Mac Wellman and composer David Van Tieghem a kind of *son et lumière* pageant celebrating the building's history, from its opening night premier of *Sag Harbor* in 1900 (in which the actors eat real clam pies and gingerbread right on stage) down through the decades as it becomes a burlesque house, a movie theater and, until just yesterday, a porn palace.

Wellman and Van Tieghem have risen to the occasion with a theatrical event of genuine inspiration. Not a drama, perhaps, since there is next to no story line; rather, they have provided a simulated haunting with musical accompaniment, a spookhouse for sophisticates. As the audience sits onstage and in a bank of seats at the front of the orchestra, a cast of eight actors, backed up by a chorus of twenty, are deployed all about the theater, on the stage, in the wings, in the boxes, aisles and balconies—even aloft in the dome. They represent a cross section of real-life New Yorkers who suffered mischance or killed themselves at the time the theater opened (their deaths were culled from contemporary newspapers). Included is one ghost, who had been killed by the crowbar of the title as it fell from the dome during the building's construction.

The style of this haunting varies from the high-polish realism of the apparition of David Belasco (many of whose works premiered here) to the deliciously ditzy monologues of an aggrieved, mad Polish housewife . . . , with a midrange of specters whose identities keep slipping away from them to beautiful effect. . . .

To suggest the overall effect of *Crowbar* I would have to hark back to the glory days of Judson Church, when Al Carmines was producing his best work there, especially the work he based on texts by Gertrude Stein. Wellman's text often uses repetition as Stein might have, and Richard

Caliban's direction steers a similar exhilarating course between the cozily quotidian and the gracefully weird. As an evocation of ghostliness I can't recall seeing anything in live theater to equal it, and as an evocation of the ill-fated Victory Theater it is genuinely poignant. One experiences a particular *frisson* in watching a play that is designed for this unique space and can never be transferred, meaningfully, elsewhere. (p. 396)

> Thomas M. Disch, in a review of "Crowbar," in The Nation, *New York, Vol. 250, No. 11, March 19, 1990, p. 396.*

Robert Brustein

Mac Wellman's *Crowbar* is a blunter work than [Richard Nelson's] *Some Americans Abroad* and its social ideas are cruder, but it deserves some marks for ambition, if not for originality. *Crowbar* is not only being performed at the Victory Theatre—a newly renovated house on 42nd Street. It is, in effect, a history of that theater, first called the Republic when owned by Oscar Hammerstein, then named for David Belasco after he refurbished it for his spectacular productions (starting with *Sag Harbor* in 1900), then renamed the Republic when it featured movies, burlesque, and porno films, and finally called the Victory, having reverted to its former legitimate glory. Besides being a history of the theater, *Crowbar* serves as something of a theater tour, minutely examining, with floodlights and flashlights, every corner of the ancient stage and auditorium, and especially the gorgeous, cupid-decorated overhead dome. The audience is seated both on stage and to the side, with most of the action in the orchestra and balconies, affording a clear view of the actors—and of a critic for the dailies snoozing in his chair.

Billed as a "pataphysical compilation"—a reference to Alfred Jarry's School of Pataphysics—culled from newspaper stories around the turn of the century (the date of *Sag Harbor*'s opening), *Crowbar* is intended as a ghost story, its dust-covered spirits being the various suicides, homicides, infanticides, and lunatics of the time. A mostly female chorus stomps through the house like a spectral chain gang, a limber figure with saxophone provides the exposition, a Polish woman wails about the changes in management over the past ninety years and the plight of her poor benighted country (which "doesn't exist most of the time"). Her bewildered husband tells us that "America is an empty theater and all the theaters are haunted," and finally David Belasco materializes to extol his ingenious technical improvements and to regret "the infamy of consuming time."

Although well executed, the production spinoffs of *Marat/Sade* and *Phantom of the Opera* tire one rather quickly, and so does the inflated style of the playwright's dialogue. (One is tempted to ask, along with one of his characters, for "a little reduction of the garrulity.") Because they are content to substitute rhetorical tirades for dramatic speech, Wellman's historical ghosts never manage to escape their tabloid origins. And the wider theme seems to have a tabloid imprint, too. I'm not certain how much more I know about my country after being told it's an empty, haunted theater. I'm not even sure how much more I know about the theater after hearing it described as "a kind of big place—with red walls—like the inside of a human heart—but not as empty." But then I have never been numbered among those who grow weak-kneed and wet-eyed about endangered Broadway houses. I did not join the chorus of outrage when the Morosco and the Belasco were being threatened. And while I am delighted whenever such legitimate theaters as the Victory in Times Square and the Majestic in Brooklyn are rescued from urban decay and porno nude shows, I confess to being much more interested in what goes on inside these buildings than in the ghosts and ornaments of their past.

What's going on inside the Victory at the moment is a riot of environmental techniques, performed with all the enthusiasm, and some of the limitations, of an advanced drama-school exercise. This En Garde Arts production seems imitatively avant-garde. Wellman possesses, at times, a certain daffy Joycean eloquence that augurs well for future better-formed plays. . . . But in view of all that's happening in the world these days—during a time when at least one playwright has things on his mind urgent enough to dominate the affairs of an entire country—*Crowbar* seems peculiarly theater-enclosed. For all its technical ambitiousness, it's another melancholy sign of how little American art seems to matter in the universe at large. (pp. 28-9)

> Robert Brustein, "The Havels and the Have-Nots," in The New Republic, Vol. 202, No. 3923, March 26, 1990, pp. 28-9.

Gerald Weales

Mac Wellman's *Crowbar* is the first production I have seen of En Garde Arts, which was founded in 1985 to produce site-specific pieces, often performed outside where passers-by can become part of the audience. I did see the script of Wellman's *Bad Penny,* one of the three *Plays in the Park* that En Garde Arts offered in Central Park last year. Although it has its fascinations on the page, the presumably accidental confluence of five strangers needs the Bow Bridge setting for which it was written. The Victory Theatre on 42nd Street was the setting and the subject of *Crowbar.*

The Victory was a derelict theater with a grand history when En Garde Arts moved in on it. It opened as the Republic in 1900 when Oscar Hammerstein presented *Sag Harbor,* James A. Herne's last play. David Belasco took over the theater in 1902, fancily renovated it, and renamed it after himself. When he moved on to 44th Street to the new Belasco Theatre, the Republic reclaimed its name and ran, first as a legitimate, then as a burlesque house until the early 1940s when, now the Victory, it became a movie theater. It declined to porn flicks and finally to abandonment. This history, told in slides and direct explanations, is part of what *Crowbar* is about, but this is not a simple celebration of a theater. The audience is grouped on the stage and at the front of the auditorium (stage right), while in the rest of the theater—the boxes, the aisles, the balco-

nies—figures appear to assert that old show-business platitude—that all theaters are haunted.

Although the ghosts of Belasco and Hammerstein are on hand, for the most part these are not conventional theatrical ghosts—the great performers of the past. Wellman, who combed turn-of-the-century newspapers for deaths, has peopled—or rather ghosted—his piece with the victims of violence—murders, suicides, accidents that took place on or near the opening date of the Republic in 1900. The main performers play multiple roles or, more often, single figures whose identities keep shifting, changing from one victim to another. This mélange of half-told stories, carefully orchestrated confusions, presumably is allied to the changing nature of the theater, always itself under various guises. There is also an implied connection between disasters inside and outside the theater, between theatrical role-playing and unanchored identities. Mr. Rioso is a saxophone-playing guide, somewhat menacing in manner, who tries to introduce a blustering, solid-citizen character—under various names, having suffered various deaths—into the mysteries of theater. His assurance is shattered at the end, when the ghost of William Gorman . . . slams a crowbar down on stage, unmasking Rioso as a laborer who was killed during the Belasco renovations when a falling crowbar—dropped by Gorman—smashed his skull. This dramatic final moment grows out of nothing in the play—no line of narrative, at least—and gets whatever force it has from the theatrical gesture itself. It does explain the title for playgoers who like to know what titles mean. (pp. 223-24)

The chief charm of the piece is the setting, the theater itself, a demirep of a building, plainly down-at-heels but with touches of past elegance still in place. Beyond the site, the best things are the long monologues provided by Wellman, a virtuoso mixer of wit, eloquence, and incoherence. Belasco has a lovingly detailed description of his theater, based on a real interview with Djuna Barnes. Since she did not become a journalist until 1913, he is probably talking about the 44th Street Belasco; not that that matters since the theater he is creating is visible only in his words. A woman sitting in a box—a dead actress apparently—has a slippery speech about time, death, sex, what have you which . . . was oddly funny, strangely sensible. Best of all, was Nora Dunfee's first-nighter (the action ostensibly takes place during an intermission of the opening play), who begins by talking about *Sag Harbor,* speculating on what will happen when the play recommences; she indicates what she does not want to see in the rest of Herne's play, then in any play, then in theater for the ninety years since Herne's first-act curtain came down. It is a gem of a speech.

Crowbar was popular—probably to the surprise of everyone involved—and it was extended for two weeks beyond its original limited run. Even so, it will be gone by the time you read this. That is the trouble with site-specific productions, pieces for occasion. They cannot be reviewed or, if they are, they become something else in the process. Now that the crowbar has fallen, don't look for its ghost. (p. 224)

> Gerald Weales, "Prying Open the Past," in

Commonweal, *Vol. CXVII, No. 7, April 6, 1990, pp. 223-24.*

Eric Overmyer

Mac Wellman's plays are political in every line. Because at bedrock they are about language, and because of their formal strategies, they are simultaneous, multifaceted critiques of American politics, culture, jargon (and the modern degradation of language in the political, economic, and cultural realms), and American theater itself (Wellman is reflexive, in the post-modern tradition). Wellman's plays are not: blunt, didactic, polemical, single-minded, propagandistic, crude, simple-minded, topical, ideological. Which is what most people mean by Political Drama. State your Topic, State your Point of View, Construct Some Straw Villains, Demolish Them, Preach to the Converted, Go Home Smug.

Wellman's plays are not direct, They are oblique. Ironic. They have multiple, even contradictory meanings. They are dense texts. Their narratives are rebukes to more ordinary ways of thinking about and writing for the theater. (I always feel slightly chastised after a Wellman play—why haven't I been more adventurous? Why haven't I ventured further out on the theatrical ledge?) In a word, poetic. They resonate. For these reasons, they are not recognized by cruder critics as political.

The plays of Mac Wellman are like a horizontal avalanche. A sliding flood of images, language, ideas, which moves the viewer out of his or her accustomed habitation as relentlessly and inexorably as a wall of mud. Wellman's subject is often simply language itself, its "thingness," its palpable existence, its matter, its uses and perversions. Therefore, by extension, his subject is also, inevitably, American culture and politics. To my mind, the three seminal works of the Wellman oeuvre (to date) are *Harm's Way, Bad Penny,* and *The Bad Infinity.*

Harm's Way is a Western (or a Midwestern). The Western is largely unexplored territory in the theater, though the subject's importance to American culture seems stunningly self-evident. . . . *Harm's Way* is a meditation upon violence, the language of violence, the American culture of violence, the conquest of the frontier, American foreign policy, American myth, and American history. It is dark, ugly, brooding, and twisted. Its hero, Santouche, is a gunfighter, a glorified psychopath, and a serial killer. The play ends with Santouche shooting "his" woman, a whore named Isle of Mercy, in the back, saying "People get what they deserve," and a chorus of children taunting the gunslinger: "You gonna kill everyone, Mister? You gonna kill everyone, Mister? You gonna kill everyone, Mister? You gonna kill everyone, Mister?" *Harm's Way* is a dark reflection upon the American Way in the World. (p. 55)

I take a Bad Infinity to mean a system, a flawed system which replicates itself forever. Like most human systems. More correctly, the term is from Hegel, and means any series of logical operations which never reaches a final result or reaches another level, a dialectic which never synthesizes and transcends itself. In *The Bad Infinity* Wellman explores a number of such systems: geopolitics, fashion, economics, international banking, crime, criticism, media, language, and the theater itself, or rather, the conventions of the conventional theater. A Bad Infinity if ever there was one. (pp. 55-6)

I think *Bad Penny* is Wellman's masterpiece, a text in which his language and his concerns both theatrical and worldly converge beautifully. A "site-specific" piece designed for a particular spot in Central Park, *Bad Penny* is an exhilarating theater poem, a comic sonata of urban life, alienation, and pastoral respite interrupted by insanity and death. . . .

Much of Wellman's recent work, like *Terminal Hip* and *Cellophane,* is pure language, long monologues which harangue the culture and reinvent an American speech which has been scarred and twisted by advertising and mendacity. I find Wellman's work occasionally frustrating as if he is pursuing an ideology of obfuscation, a strategy of deliberate inaccessibility in order to escape the received ideas of the theater. But when I connect with his work, I understand it as I understand poetry, on a deep, cellular level. Much in life is unexplained, unexplainable, mysterious. So are Wellman's plays. (p. 56)

Eric Overmyer, "Mac Wellman's Horizontal Avalanches," in Theater, *Vol. XXI, No. 3, Summer-Fall, 1990, pp. 54-6.*

In Memoriam

Morley Callaghan

September 22, 1903—August 25, 1990

(Full name Morley Edward Callaghan) Canadian novelist, short story writer, journalist, playwright, and autobiographer.

Described by Edmund Wilson as "perhaps the most unjustly neglected novelist in the English-speaking world," Callaghan was the author of many acclaimed novels and short stories but is perhaps best known in the United States for his memoir *That Summer in Paris: Memories of Tangled Friendships with Hemingway, Fitzgerald, and Some Others.* Callaghan's allegorical fiction, in which he infused seemingly ordinary human relationships with complex moral, psychological, and religious significance, includes such novels as *The Loved and the Lost,* for which he received the 1952 Governor General's Literary Award, and *The Many Coloured Coat.* Callaghan is regarded as a major figure in twentieth-century Canadian literature.

For an overview of Callaghan's life and work see *CLC,* Vols. 3, 14, 41; *Contemporary Authors,* Vols. 9-12, rev. ed.; and *Dictionary of Literary Biography,* Vol. 68.

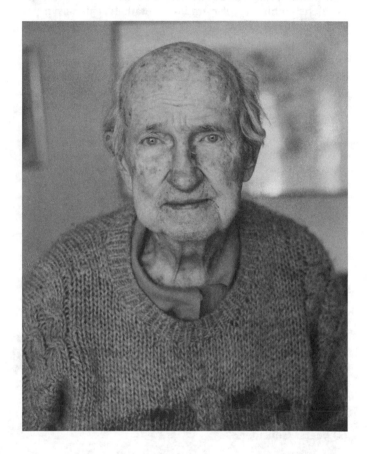

REVIEWS OF CALLAGHAN'S RECENT WORKS

Gary Boire

[The appearance of Callaghan's novel] *A Wild Old Man on the Road* has already prompted blurbists to whirl dervish-like into rhapsody, claiming it as a triumph of both age and talent. The league of Callaghan detractors will take a decidedly less enthusiastic line, seeing it more as a victory of perseverance over discretion. As is so often the case with Callaghan, the truth lies between polarized extremes—somewhere inside the dialectic between reader and elusive text. I doubt that the book will "take its place alongside his finest works"; but it will stand as one of Callaghan's most intriguing experimentations with language, moralist ideology, and self-conscious self-revisionism.

In one sense *A Wild Old Man* uncomfortably recalls many of Callaghan's more problematic aspects. It has a lumpy, vaguely boring plot, more than occasional examples of cretinous dialogue, the characteristic pared-down style, and one of the most fatuous heroes in Canadian literature. Mark Didion, a macho cub reporter, is of a piece with many of Callaghan's earlier impulsive nincompoops (James McAlpine, Sam Raymond, Harry Lane, *et al.*);

that is, he's a rebellious young man with an inarticulated cause—but he's also a transparent medium for Callaghan's reader in dire search of exactitude. Following his father's death in Toronto and the discovery of his long-secreted diary, Mark retraces his elder's Parisian experiences of the twenties. Within multiple echoes of both *That Summer in Paris* (1963) and *A Fine and Private Place* (1975), he meets the enigmatic Jeremy Monk, an old revolutionary writer who "was a revered cult figure concerned only with truthful reporting." As Monk seems progressively to get religion and betray the grand old cause, Mark becomes obsessed with Monk's mysterious young wife, Cretia Sampari. By engaging with both, he travels the long road of experience and comes to grips with birth, sex, death, truth, betrayal, loyalty, art, literature, and all the other conventional Callaghan ambiguities.

Amidst such clichés, overdone Svengali figures, and sexist attitudes, there is much that Callaghan detractors might rightly question. Most prominent are the characteristic "advertisements for myself": the book is punctuated with acerbic swipes at avant-garde writing, ironic nonreminiscences of Joyce and Hemingway, vitalist pleas to see life "for the first and the only time," an almost naïve wonderment at the mysteries of the individual, and a ubiquitous self-justifying defence of "a good straightforward style." Ever since the publication of **"Looking at Native Prose"** in *Saturday Night* (1928), Callaghan has consistently pontificated on the virtues of his own crisp reportorial manner that minimizes baroque extravagance while exploiting the inherent ambiguity of mundane detail. In this unsympathetic vein, *A Wild Old Man* reads as a shrill self-defence. . . . (pp. 16-17)

But this kind of sniping is not only mean-spirited, it's inaccurate. For all its obvious shortcomings, almost in spite of these grotesque excesses, the book somehow *works*. Over 20 years ago Milton Wilson touched on this paradox when he ingenuously remarked,

> I . . . have a liking for the peculiar distinctions of Callaghan's fiction. But I despair of justifying it to any skeptic. . . . What for one critic is the degree of distortion proper to parable, for the other is implausible and incompetent plotting; what for one is an austere rejection of witty epigrams and ingenious metaphors, for the other is an inability to handle words with grace, invention, and precision—a lack of proper respect for language.

Despite the most glaring defects of style and thought, *A Wild Old Man on the Road* sustains this ambivalent response: while monosyllables may dominate, it nonetheless has the implicatory allure of the fairy tale, an almost elemental mystique that pervades language usage, plot, and characterization. This is vintage Callaghan, warts and all. And what makes this particular vintage outstanding is that it is critically retrospective. This is a watershed type of novel wherein many of Callaghan's past reflex habits are foregrounded, a retrospective that both sustains and interrogates much of the thought and writing of the past 60 years. Consider.

One of Callaghan's most overlooked features is his almost compulsive tendency to recycle, to take an early story or vignette (usually either a personal experience or an irritatingly mundane predicament), and then to recast it, over and over again, into a series of subsequent forms. The revisions, in turn, develop both the literary and philosophical significance of the original situation. Even a superficial glance over part of the canon turns up an extraordinary number of these "re-visions," moments of rewriting that tease out a verbal ambiguity or moral pleonasm. What makes *A Wild Old Man* so interesting is that throughout the novel Callaghan plays this revisionistic/autobiographical hand with ironic perfection.

Obviously the book is a puckish rewriting of *That Summer in Paris*—Mark, Cretia, and Jeremy all relive versions of experiences recorded by Callaghan in 1963. More piquant, however, is that as Mark retraces, and in some senses tries to rewrite, his dead father's Parisian diary (an act that highlights Callaghan's lifelong interest in fathers and sons), he also reenacts his author's own writerly practice.

Callaghan plays resurrectionist throughout the text, minutely recasting, revising, and ironically complicating many of his past key ideas and techniques. The result is a peculiar kind of double-focusing or pastiche, with the reader of *A Wild Old Man* eerily aware of spectral presences in adjoining rooms. What initially appears to be a straight-forward plea for original and transparent style is often an echo (a self-plagiarism), and as such transforms into an ambiguous meditation on both the relativity of truth and the impossibility of dealing with it in an original way. Likewise . . . , and, most enigmatically, the entire final section replays the latter half of *A Passion in Rome,* one of Callaghan's most problematic texts.

As the mystery surrounding Jeremy Monk builds to a crescendo, the Pope sickens and dies: Mark and Cretia then relive the agony and ecstasy of Sam Raymond and Carla Caneli. As in the earlier text, Callaghan here plays with the polarities of sacred and profane, suggesting that polarities themselves are perhaps delusions, and that all extremes meld ultimately into one ongoing lemniscate. Intriguingly, this novel of resurrection ends not with *A Passion in Rome*'s exultation and wonderment, but with a suicide. A mysterious throwaway note stuffed in the pocket of an old man is directed to Callaghan's reader, *"As I said once . . . about what I am doing now, don't worry. It's just like opening a door into another room."* Typically, Callaghan's last sentence offers little hope of definitive closure to the conservative reader; on the contrary, it stands as a mischievous tantalization—an invitation to be puzzled.

In a recent interview with Bette Laderoute, Callaghan confided that *A Wild Old Man on the Road* is about betrayal, more specifically the betrayal of one's personal muse. The book does have weaknesses, that is undeniable. But in its ironic self-reference, experimental verbal play, and difficult moral representation, Callaghan remains steadfast; in no way does he commit the crime of his own personal Monk. (pp. 17-19)

> *Gary Boire, "Rewriting Callaghan," in* Essays on Canadian Writing, *No. 41, Summer, 1990, pp. 16-19.*

Bryan N. S. Gooch

The appearance of *The Man with the Coat* (originally published in *Maclean's,* 16 April 1955) and *A Wild Old Man on the Road* is a reminder of the continuing strength of their author's hand and points to many of the reasons why Morley Callaghan has occupied such a notable position in our cultural milieu for over five decades. An unerring sense of human nature (realistic and compassionate), a capacity to capture character and to suggest nuances of speech and movement, a superb control of pace and disclosure—the very characteristics which marked the early novels and became especially memorable in *Such Is My Beloved* (1934) and *They Shall Inherit the Earth* (1935), for instance—are present in the latest book, just as they are in *The Man with the Coat* from the mid-1950's.

Indeed, *The Man with the Coat* is utterly compelling, a short, tense novel, set in Montreal, which has as its central figure one Harry Lane who suffers rejection for his actions at the fraud trial of his sometime friend Scotty Bowman (who commits suicide in jail) and who obstinately continues to wear a suit with ruined (ostensibly faulty) lining made by ex-fighter, tailor, and Bowman-supporter Mike Kon. The questions of responsibility and consequent guilt, the problems of misunderstanding and lack of communication permeate the story, which ends in Lane's sudden death in a scuffle with Kon, the latter's subsequent clearance on a manslaughter charge, and his pathetic attempts, in conversation, to square accounts, as it were, with Lane's memory. The cast of characters is relatively small, but vivid and varied and always relevant in some way—the focus is intensely urban but the light falls on Callaghan's involved circle; the lack of diffusion, of digression to any detailed consideration of a wider scene, adds to the impression of concentrated power.

The Man . . . served as a basis for an expanded and slightly different story, *The Many Coloured Coat* (1960). Here Lane survives and refuses, in the end, to appear at Kon's trial for assault. As in *The Man . . .* , the Bowman incident and death precipitate matters, and the coat with its embarrassing lining serves as the central irritant in the continuing conflict. But *The Many Coloured Coat,* with all its strengths, is neither a better nor an inferior book. And it is not what *The Man . . .* should have been in the first instance. Both novels stand firmly on their own ground, neither one suffering by comparison with the other. That this should be so is a reflection of the Callaghan craft, that sense of the justness of the narrative and control of material.

The qualities which mark *The Man . . .* and its later transfiguration are also to be found in *A Wild Old Man on the Road.* To say that this is vintage Callaghan is to do it justice and not to deride it as literary wine which is past its prime or, indeed, which is less interesting because our palates have become dulled by over-indulgence. It concerns what is essentially a spiritual quest for the aging writer and early-day idealist Jeremy Monk and the attempt of young Mark Didion, hero-worshipper and luster after Monk's wife, Cretia, to come to terms with his own character and with what for him are inexplicable changes in the philosophy of his idol, Monk. Like *The Man . . .* , this is an urban narrative, but it reaches beyond our shores to find settings in Paris and in Rome. It is a cosmopolitan piece—in the best sense—and its shifts in venue never cause disintegration of structure but, rather, serve, in this case, to enhance the interest and tension of the narrative. As in earlier novels, the dialogue is central to character development, and handling of voice is absolutely sure: temperament and age are impeccably and consistently reflected. Further, like *The Man . . .* , *A Wild Old Man on the Road* has a splendidly visual quality, a deftness of character and scene-painting that is as remarkable for its economy as for its resultant realism.

In their own ways both books are about truth—about assumptions, evasions, about appearances and realities, about charity and the folly of ill will. They speak of human nature, of our society and parts of its sometimes seemingly tangled fabric. And if they speak of truth, they speak of

human nature truthfully. What more could we want from fiction in its best moments? (pp. 148-49)

Bryan N. S. Gooch, "Callaghan," in Canadian Literature, *No. 126, Autumn, 1990, pp. 148-49.*

OBITUARIES AND TRIBUTES

Wolfgang Saxon

Morley Callaghan, a Canadian writer who lived in Paris in the 1920's and mixed with Ernest Hemingway and F. Scott Fitzgerald, died Saturday, his son Barry said today. He was 87 years old and lived in Toronto. The cause of death was not disclosed.

Through his long writing career, Morley Callaghan's hard-boiled style won him critical praise in his native Canada and throughout the English-speaking world. Less famous than some of his fellow expatriates, he survived them and continued writing well into his 80's. The critic Edmund Wilson considered Mr. Callaghan a far more important writer than the public generally thought. . . .

Mr. Callaghan's spare style and detailed realism has been compared to Hemingway's and Erskine Caldwell's. Though he often wrote in the same genre as Hemingway, Caldwell and William Faulkner, critics nevertheless noted his own unmistakable voice in Mr. Callaghan's novels and short stories.

But the single incident in his life best remembered by most readers involved Hemingway and Fitzgerald in a casual bout of fisticuffs in which the young Mr. Callaghan floored Hemingway, a totem of American macho.

There were several versions of the episode, differing more as time passed. Mr. Callaghan's was contained in his most successful work, *That Summer in Paris* (1963), a highly acclaimed memoir of the months in 1929 when his friendship with the two Americans, as well as the close relationship between the latter two, ended in bitterness.

Mr. Callaghan was a college student working part time for *The Toronto Star* in 1920 when Hemingway was its star reporter. The writer was impressed with the younger man's literary ambitions, and they struck up a friendship.

Meeting in Paris in 1929, Hemingway proposed that they box at the American Club. At 6 feet and 200 pounds, Hemingway was four inches taller than Mr. Callaghan, who was out of shape but figured that, being 14 years younger, he might come out ahead.

At some of those matches Joan Miró, the Catalan painter, served as volunteer timekeeper. But at the most famous meet, Fitzgerald took that ringside position. According to Mr. Callaghan's memoir, the boxers agreed on one-minute rounds with two-minute rests in between. Hemingway, he recalled, bore in fast, using up his wind; Fitzgerald, engrossed with the Canadian's counterpunches, forgot to call time; and when Hemingway lunged, Mr. Callaghan struck him squarely on the jaw, bloodying him and downing him hard on his back.

"Oh, my God," Fitzgerald supposedly cried in anguish, "I let the round go four minutes." But Hemingway, according to Mr. Callaghan, thought the lapse had been deliberate, causing the incident to take on mythic proportions in the Hemingway legend and prompting tensions and estrangement among the three men.

Edmund Wilson, in a 1960 essay called Mr. Callaghan "perhaps the most unjustly neglected novelist in the English-speaking world." At the same time, Wilson conceded that his subject "belonged to the literary scene of the 20's" and that even people who remembered him probably thought "he was dead."

But Mr. Callaghan continued writing. His early work had been encouraged by praise from the likes of Hemingway, Ring Lardner and Wolcott Gibbs, and it was published by Ezra Pound, Ford Madox Ford and Harold Ross.

Born in Toronto, Mr. Callaghan trained as a lawyer but never practiced. He moved to Paris after the publication of his first novel, writing full-time. Before returning to Toronto, he also lived in New York and on a farm in Pennsylvania.

Mr. Callaghan once observed that success may have come to him too early, with three novels published by Charles Scriber's Sons, before he turned 30. In Wilson's view, the underestimation of Mr. Callaghan's true stature

> may have been a general incapacity—apparently shared by his compatriots—for believing that a writer whose work may be mentioned without absurdity in association with Chekhov's and Turgenev's can possibly be functioning in Toronto.

In 1970, the Canada Council, a quasi-Governmental body, partly made up for the neglect by honoring Mr. Callaghan with a Molson Award carrying $15,000.

His best-known titles also include *They Shall Inherit the Earth* (1935), *The Loved and the Lost* (1955), *The Many Colored Coat* (1960), *A Passion in Rome* (1961) and *A Fine and Private Place* (1975).

> *Wolfgang Saxon, in an obituary in* The New York Times, *August 27, 1990, p. D12.*

The Times, London

Morley Callaghan belonged securely in the company of such outstanding Roman Catholic novelists of this century as Georges Bernanos, François Mauriac, Graham Greene, Julien Green and Evelyn Waugh. But he never attained the critical status which his readers believed he deserved—except in his own country and in the minds of discerning critics, who invariably recognised that he was of the calibre of these writers. The late Edmund Wilson indeed once described Callaghan as "the most unjustly neglected novelist in the English-speaking world."

Of his 18 volumes of fiction (five collections of stories and 13 novels), almost all were published in the United States as well as Canada—but only five in this country. Here he was most famous for his Paris memoirs of the late 1920s: *That Summer in Paris: Memories of Tangled Friendships with Hemingway, Fitzgerald and Some Others* (1963). Many of the grateful British readers of this invaluable record remained unaware that he was a major novelist.

His genius first fully revealed itself in the novel *Such Is My Beloved* (1934), about the relationship between a Catholic priest and two young prostitutes. This book, which came under fire from conservative Catholics, was both highly religious and socially indignant. The priest, in his efforts to give of his best, is bitterly criticized; the message, that Christian charity is more important than the letter of the church law, was obvious. *The Loved and the Lost* (1951), published here only 10 years later, was certainly a novel of social protest, although the main interest lies in the brilliant and subtle portrayal of the strange female protagonist. The book is set in Montreal, of whose cafe society it gives an incomparably vivid impression.

Of his 13 novels it is, however, *The Many Coloured Coat* (1960) that is regarded as his finest (it appeared here in 1966). This, which combines a powerful naturalism with a rare and intuitive sense of Christian compassion and what it truly means, is the story (as the title implies) of a gifted and beloved man who drifts into good fortune, but has many bitter trials on the way. The novel has been acclaimed for the picture it gives of urban life which it depicts as being both squalid and full of beautiful moments (as of true communication between people). His fine and craftsmanlike short stories were collected in *Stories* (1959, in this country in two volumes, 1963-4). This was followed by a further collection, *No Man's Meat, and The Enchanted Pimp,* published in Canada only in 1978.

Morley Edward Callaghan was of Irish descent on both sides. He was educated at St Michael's College in the University of Toronto, graduating in 1925. He then trained as a lawyer at the Osgoode Hall Law School, Toronto, obtaining his LLB in 1928. He was admitted to the Ontario Bar in the same year.

Callaghan had already served on a newspaper, the Toronto *Daily Star,* between university and law school, and had met Ernest Hemingway, who encouraged him. In 1928 he decided to become a full-time writer, and went to live in Paris for a year, where he met most of the American writers then living there, and of whom he left such a vivid and discerning record in *That Summer in Paris.* But during the 1930s he did sporadically practise law, though he devoted most of his time to writing. During the second world war he worked with the Canadian navy on assignment for Canada's national film board.

Callaghan was always a devout Roman Catholic, but never one uncritical (if, usually, only by implication) of certain of the more rigid aspects of the administration of his church. Callaghan's earlier stories and novels did not really show his potential. He was very much the disciple of his friend Hemingway, as well as of Erskine Caldwell and even of William Faulkner. He wrote in clipped sentences, with a deliberately cold objectivity, although critics already noted a "lyrical . . . sympathy". He also wrote two plays, both produced in Toronto—his home for virtually the whole of his life—a book for children, and the commentary for a book, *Winter,* of evocative photographs by John de Visser (1974).

Although Callaghan has not had the recognition he deserves outside Canada and in some quarters of the United States, it can only be a matter of time for his *oeuvre* to be recognised as belonging to the very best Roman Catholic tradition of our century. Among several studies of his work, the most perceptive essay appeared in Edmund Wilson's *O Canada.*

Callaghan was in his younger days a "short, stocky man, with black, curly hair, a small moustache, and bright blue eyes". He was an outstanding athlete at college, and an effective public speaker. He was universally liked and admired for his modesty and for his sympathetic nature. He received several Canadian honours, including the Governor-General's Award (1952). In 1967, however, he publicly refused the Medal of Service in a Canadian honours list which had been instituted for that year's centenary celebrations, on the grounds that such awards set up a pecking order among writers.

An obituary in The Times, *London, August 28, 1990.*

Myrna Oliver

Morley Callaghan, a highly respected Canadian writer who was a contemporary of Ernest Hemingway and F. Scott Fitzgerald, has died in Toronto. He was 87.

Callaghan's son Barry, also a writer, said his father died on Saturday after hospitalization and surgery for an undisclosed illness.

The elder Callaghan's novels included **The Loved and the Lost, They Shall Inherit the Earth, The Many Colored Coat,** and *A Fine and Private Place.*

His more than 100 short stories were published in major magazines including the *New Yorker,* the *Saturday Evening Post, Harper's Bazaar* and *Esquire.* . . .

"Although four inches shorter than the 6-foot-tall, 200-pound Hemingway, Callaghan knocked him down. Fitzgerald was the timekeeper, and the furious Hemingway blamed him for deliberately letting the round go on too long."

—*Myrna Oliver*

Callaghan, who published three novels before he was 30, shared Hemingway's and Fitzgerald's editor at Scribner's in New York, Maxwell Perkins.

Born in Toronto, Callaghan first became friendly with Hemingway in 1920 when Callaghan was still a student and working part time on the *Toronto Star,* where Hemingway was a seasoned reporter. When Callaghan moved to Paris in 1928, he again encountered Hemingway, who continued to encourage him in his literary efforts.

Callaghan was invited to box with Hemingway at the American Club in Paris, an event he later believed clouded his entire career.

Although four inches shorter than the 6-foot-tall, 200-pound Hemingway, Callaghan knocked him down. Fitzgerald was the timekeeper, and the furious Hemingway blamed him for deliberately letting the round go on too long. . . .

The much-discussed incident led to tensions and estrangement of all three writers and caused Callaghan to lament in his later years: "I'm probably better known for boxing with Hemingway than for anything I've written."

Although Callaghan was well received by literary critics, including Edmund Wilson, who likened his work to that of Chekhov and Turgenev, the Canadian writer felt he suffered by repeated comparisons with Hemingway and Fitzgerald.

Myrna Oliver, in an obituary in Los Angeles Times, *August 29, 1990.*

Joyce Marshall

Morley Callaghan, who died on August 25 at the age of 87, was so much a person, so firmly, even stubbornly his own self, that I find that I can only write personally about him. We had a curious friendship, going back for more than 40 years—longer if I twist the word to mean friendship on my side even though not yet on his.

I first saw him during the fall of 1938. He was walking in the twilight on Yonge Street near Bloor, round the corner from where I was living. I'd been told that he often came down from his house in Rosedale and walked about the streets, "thinking out his books," and here he was—a rather short, broad man with a great head of very dark hair. . . . I saw him frequently after that, at the same hour and in the same neighbourhood, but though I'd studied **Such Is My Beloved** and read his other novels and his stories, it didn't occur to me that I might speak to him. I was even in the same room with him once—a meeting held to hear a talk by Ed Cecil-Smith, who'd commanded the Mackenzie-Papineau Battalion that had fought on the Loyalist side in the Spanish Civil War. Callaghan slipped in, sat to one side near the door and, as soon as the talk ended, he slipped out again. This is what a writer should do, I thought. He comes to increase his experience, not to engage in social chitchat—or to be introduced to people like me. For I thought of him as a forbidding figure, inhabiting a world that wasn't yet mine and that I had no right to try to enter.

Finally, in 1946, we met. My first book had just been published and I was introduced to him as "one of our most promising younger writers." Morley's smile was bemused, surprised, a shade mischievous—he had many rather complicated sorts of smiles. "But that's what they always say about me," he said. And as far as I was concerned, I was in, Morley Callaghan had accepted and welcomed me. I'd always been a writer in my own mind. Now I was one in fact.

After that I always felt that Morley and I knew each other. He must have felt something of the sort himself for it was his way to come up to me at literary gatherings—we never met socially in the ordinary sense—and without formal greeting begin to talk, about his work or mine, whatever happened to be in his mind. Once he informed me without preamble that I should get married. (I think what he had in mind for me was a wife, something every writer needs. He had a splendid one himself in Loretto.) To me he was always the same, though as the years went by his strong dark hair whitened and became skimpy, the flesh of his face fell away and we saw that there'd been a gnome hiding underneath. In his last years he was a small, even a tiny man but still full of energy. And he still had his variety of complicated smiles.

Before I leave the purely personal, I want to acknowledge a debt I owe him. Sometime during the 1950s I showed an early version of a story of mine called "The Old Woman" to a magazine whose name I no longer remember. Morley had some editorial connection with the magazine and sent a message to me that if I'd call him he'd talk to me about it. I called and, very simply and plainly, he told me what the story was really about and how I could rearrange the material to give it pacing, clarity, and point. "Now get at it," he concluded. I did and, though the magazine had perished before I was finished, I soon got the story published and it has become through the years my most frequently reprinted story. I never thanked Morley Callaghan for this. Why? Perhaps I simply assumed that he knew. I thank him now.

I thank him also for his books, though it isn't as easy to find words for what they mean and have meant to me. Morley Callaghan was his own writer just as he was his own person. It's interesting to note that he never started a school and, though all Canadian fiction-writers are aware of the debt they owe him, none to my knowledge has ever cited him as a major influence. He was for many years neglected in this country, though not, I maintain, by other writers. Honours that should have come to him earlier came late—but they did come: a first Governor General's Award for *The Loved and the Lost* in 1952, the Molson Prize, the Royal Bank Award, and other honours and prizes. And in 1982 he was named Companion of the Order of Canada.

For me, when I first read *Such Is My Beloved,* Morley Callaghan was a miracle. I'd been searching for some written words that spoke of my own place and people, and found nothing to satisfy me in the works of Frederick Philip Grove and Mazo De la Roche. And now here was someone who was Canadian, who wrote (though never in very explicit detail) about this country, and who wrote well. Furthermore, he'd made it. I admired his books, I rather liked the style, its determined plainness, its avoidance of elaborate figures or metaphors, of "fine writing" of any

sort. But weren't the books themselves a little too simplified, the characters as well as the events? A child of my time, I admired two sorts of writing: the stream of consciousness (Woolf, Joyce, Faulkner) and the realist political (Dos Passos, Caldwell). And here were novels I couldn't help liking that fell into neither of these categories. Did I just like them, I wondered, because Callaghan was one of ours and I thought I should?

I was less troubled by the stories—**"Last Spring They Came Over," "Now that April's Here," A Predicament,"** and the others. Stories after all are supposed to be stripped, to omit, to hone in, and the Callaghan stories do this so magnificently, so often making something strong and beautiful out of what might be in less skilful hands a minor, even trivial incident—a decision to buy a certain hat or bring a young man home.

I see now what I wasn't subtle enough to see when I was younger, that I was wrong to think that the novels required more than they contained—more facts, a more complex rendering of character and motive. Everything is there that needs to be there. "Strip the style," he himself wrote in *That Summer in Paris,* "and make the style, the language, all the psychological ramifications, the ambiance of the relationships, all the one thing, so the reader couldn't make separations. Cézanne's apples. The appleness of apples. Yet just apples." This he did and, when his method worked, the result is cool, simplified certainly, but finally and essentially more real than the real. George Woodcock has called the three novels of the 1930s, *Such Is My Beloved, They Shall Inherit the Earth,* and *More Joy in Heaven*—which, like most of us, he considers Callaghan's finest work—"novels of consequence." I would call them fables—fables of innocence betrayed by social and moral forces it can never more than partly understand.

I believe that these novels, like the stories, still repay rereading. Though they're rooted in the mean poverty of the Depression, they have a strong moral force and do not date. I also admire *The Loved and the Lost,* a story of faith and lack of faith, and *A Passion in Rome,* which could be called a variant of the Pygmalion legend.

There were later novels, the last, *A Wild Old Man on the Road,* only two years ago, and the occasion for a tribute to the author at that year's Harbourfront International Authors Festival and a most amusing reading by "the old rascal" (as he's been called) himself. But these are not vintage Callaghan. Though he'd always been the least intrusive of writers, he seemed now to be writing more for himself than for us—with bitterness in his picture of the neglected writer in *A Fine and Private Place* and nostalgically in what is clearly a search for the lost Paris of his youth in *A Wild Old Man on the Road.*

He was at work on a novella, we're told, when the final illness struck. I'm sorry he won't be able to finish it, sorry above all that he won't be present among us, old and frail but still writing indomitably as he had done for almost 70 years—and from time to time smiling one of his smiles. (pp. 11-12)

Joyce Marshall, "Morley Callaghan, 1903-

1990: A Tribute," in Books in Canada, Vol. XIX, No. 7, October, 1990, pp. 11-12.

David Staines

That Summer in Paris, Morley Callaghan's "memories," according to its subtitle, "of tangled friendships with Hemingway, Fitzgerald, and some others," suggests many features of its author and his writing.

Here are Callaghan the narrator, standing back to allow his characters centre-stage; Callaghan the reporter, recording with careful accuracy; Callaghan the writer, bringing to life a place and an era; and Callaghan the Canadian, observing with detachment an American expatriate colony.

Here, too, is Callaghan's literary creed. "The trouble with writing was that poets and story-writers used language to evade, to skip away from the object, because they could never bear to face the thing freshly for what it was in itself." Writing should be "the right relationship between the words and the thing or the person being described: the words should be as transparent as glass, and every time a writer used a brilliant phrase to prove himself witty or clever he merely took the mind of the reader away from the object and devoted it to himself."

Readers of *That Summer in Paris* remember a boxing match where Callaghan knocked down Hemingway, while Fitzgerald, as time-keeper, looked on. When will we realize that Callaghan was, more importantly, a better writer than Hemingway?

> "Callaghan holds a special place in the literary landscape of his own land. The father of modern Canadian fiction, he brought the fledgling Canadian novel from its rural sentimentality into the urban world of the 20th century. By his example and his care, he was a model for generations of writers."
>
> —David Staines

Callaghan's logic is not burdened by American, stereotyped gender roles. And being Canadian, Callaghan never became, as did Hemingway, "such a big public personality," to use Callaghan's description; that personality interfered with writing.

So often compared incorrectly with Hemingway, Callaghan deserves proper appreciation as a disciple of international literature. Wyndham Lewis wisely saw Callaghan as closer to Tolstoy than to Hemingway, and Edmund Wilson associated him with Chekhov and Turgenev.

The first full-time writer in Canada, Callaghan was born in Toronto. . . . He graduated from the University of Toronto and Osgoode Law School. In 1928, the year he was called to the bar, he published his first novel, *Strange Fugitive.*

Fiction remained his vocation; he never practised law. The Toronto *Globe* failed to review *Strange Fugitive,* but a letter to the editor complained about the novel's offensive reality. "If the book portrays a true picture of the average citizen of the city, then God help the city, and God help the present and future generations of Torontonians."

In *Saturday Night,* editor B. K. Sandwell denied *Strange Fugitive* the status of Canadian novel because the setting was not the traditional rural landscape of Canadian fiction: "Toronto and Montreal are just aggregations of population at places where passengers and freight are taken out of one conveyance and put into another."

"Go on in your own way," Sinclair Lewis advised Callaghan in 1929. And so he did, maintaining his residence in Toronto, perfecting his craft, and writing 20 novels and more than a 100 shorter works of fiction (not to mention essays, plays, and reviews). Naturally and unobtrusively, for nearly seven decades he pursued his vocation, recording the dramas in ordinary lives and their moral consequences. His characters struggle to act with dignity in a world of often hostile social forces and institutions. Hope rests in the individual, in his or her capacity for compassion, goodness, and choice.

Callaghan holds a special place in the literary landscape of his own land. The father of modern Canadian fiction, he brought the fledgling Canadian novel from its rural sentimentality into the urban world of the 20th century. By his example and his care, he was a model for generations of writers.

When Malcolm Ross convinced a reluctant Jack McClelland in the mid-'50s to begin a new paperback series, to be called New Canadian Library, Callaghan's fourth book, *Such Is My Beloved,* was chosen to be the first book. When McClelland told Callaghan of the enterprise, adding that he believed the series would be far from profitable, Callaghan—to show his support—offered to take one-half the standard royalty. After a few years, with the series' survival, the royalty was adjusted and Callaghan received the standard payment.

Thirty-five years later, Callaghan agreed to pen an afterword to Raymond Knister's *White Narcissus* for the newly redesigned series. "You won't have another one like this," he taunted. His afterword, a memory in the style of *That Summer in Paris,* captures Toronto in the 1920s. A few factual details, however, jarred with my own knowledge of Knister. Callaghan maintained that these were his memories, which he believed were accurate. Reluctant to challenge him, I did research the facts, only to discover that some accounts of Knister's life were incomplete or inaccurate and Callaghan's memory was infallible.

That summer Callaghan had intended to dictate his memoirs to his son Barry.

On August 25 Callaghan passed away in Toronto. At the time of his death he had completed the first draft of his 21st novel and revised its opening chapter.

"Does the dolphin or the rose flourish with an eye on eternity? Death for me was a painful, gloomy, inevitable experience," he wrote in *That Summer in Paris.*

> Our job . . . was to be concerned with the living and it seemed to me it would be most agreeable to God if we tried to realize all our possibilities here on earth, and hope we would always be so interested, so willing to lose ourselves in the fullness of living, and so hopeful that we would never ask why we were here on this earth.

> David Staines, "Morley Callaghan: 1903-1990," in Quill and Quire, Vol. 56, No. 10, October, 1990, p. 8.

Rick Marin

Famous for knocking down Ernest Hemingway in a boxing match in Paris, Morley Callaghan was one of the hottest young literary properties of the 1920s and became one of the handful of writers that Canada has produced with a claim to the adjective "great." Yet, when he died in August of last year at the age of 87, his obituary did not make the front page of the *Globe and Mail,* Canada's newspaper of record. To be slighted even in death was the story of Morley Callaghan's life.

Called by Edmund Wilson "the most unjustly neglected writer of the English-speaking world," Callaghan published his first novel, *Strange Fugitive,* at twenty-five and his last, *A Wild Old Man on the Road,* sixty years later. Though still widely available in Canada, none of his two dozen titles is in print in the United States today. Bookstores well-stocked with inferior Canadian imports (Margaret Atwood, Robertson Davies) have never heard of him. The only place to find Callaghan here is a library, or second-hand shop, which is where I recently came across a worn paperback of *That Summer in Paris,* his 1963 memoir of Hemingway, Fitzgerald, et al. Somehow I'd managed to spend the first two decades of my life in Toronto, in a house not minutes from Callaghan's own, without having read (or at least retained) anything he had written. I saw him walk past our front door many times and once at a reading of his penultimate novel, *A Time for Judas.* He was a small, frail old man with a surprisingly forceful voice. It was impossible to believe he had ever knocked down anyone, let alone Ernest Hemingway.

Callaghan met Hemingway at the *Toronto Star,* where they worked together in the mid-1920s, one a cub reporter, the other a swaggering foreign correspondent. Hemingway thought Callaghan's stories "big-time stuff " and encouraged his awed acolyte to keep at it. (One such story, published in *American Caravan,* got him an invitation to New York from Maxwell Perkins at Scribner's.) In 1929 he made the pilgrimage to Paris with his wife Loretto, and soon found himself steeped in the liquid life and poisonous gossip of The Quarter's expatriate colonists: James Joyce, Ford Madox Ford, Sylvia Beach, Robert McAlmon, Michael Arlen. Caught between Hemingway and Fitzgerald's prickly feuding, he exacerbated it during the boxing contest that, despite his efforts to play it down, would be-

come the most celebrated event in Morley Callaghan's long life.

The two sparred regularly at the American Club. The time Callaghan knocked Hemingway to the mat, Fitzgerald was keeping time and became so engrossed by the bout that he let the round go longer than three minutes. Hemingway was furious:

> "Christ!" Ernest yelled. He got up. He was silent for a few seconds. Scott, staring at his watch, was mute and wondering. I wished I were miles away. "All right, Scott," Ernest said savagely. "If you want to see me getting the shit knocked out of me, just say so. Only don't say you made a mistake," and he stomped off to the shower room to wipe the blood from his mouth.

In later years Hemingway would dismiss the affair as a drunken lark, though Callaghan maintains that they were all quite sober.

What's most remarkable about Callaghan's memoir *is* its sobriety. Dispassion would be the wrong word; he shows remarkable compassion for these vain, brilliant egotists around him. Hemingway, he observes, "kept death in his work as a Medieval scholar might have kept a skull on his desk." The most junior of the group, this clear-headed, self-assured Canadian seems even then to have had the oldest soul. After nine months he packed it up and took it home.

In his native Toronto, Callaghan would write many good novels and a few great ones. Their themes: faith, justice, innocence, and experience. A young priest devotes himself to the material and spiritual salvation of two indigent prostitutes, sacrificing his collar and sanity to his obsession (*Such Is My Beloved,* 1934). An ex-con trying to go straight is hounded by his underworld past (*More Joy in Heaven,* 1937). For brightening a banker's drab life and blamelessly ending it, a well-liked public relations man becomes a pariah, falsely accused and feverishly bent on vindication (*The Many Colored Coat,* 1960). Outcasts, social misfits, martyrs—these are the painfully isolated protagonists of Callaghan's spare prose. His Biblical titles and mad priests invite comparisons to Graham Greene, but Greene's prescriptive moral tone is absent. Callaghan never subscribes to political messianism, even in his novels of the 1930s. He is profoundly concerned with moral behavior but loath to judge. His Catholicism, influenced by his friend Jacques Maritain, inclines toward charity and tolerance. His sinners are usually forgiven.

"The truth about any man is pretty hard to tell," a character says in *The Many Colored Coat,* "because someone else always has another angle on him." The book's two bitter enemies, divided over the death of a mutual friend and the eponymous garment, become prisoners of their "angles" on each other. They meet on a Montreal street:

> It was an awkward moment. They both wanted to speak, reach a peaceful settlement. But they were so far apart now that neither one trusted the first words he would have to use, or any words needed to tell what was in his heart; they shared for the moment that helpless angry feeling. There was no way of communicating, nor

showing any recognition of what they felt almost furtively as a desperate need. There was nothing left to say.

Modernist by way of daily newspapering, Callaghan shared Hemingway's affinity for direct speech and his distrust of literary ornament. He admired the "appleness" of Cezanne's apples. . . . Metaphors and descriptive indulgences are rare in Callaghan's writing. Everything serves the panoptic narrative, whose rise and fall he plots with expert calibration. Declared another admirer, Sinclair Lewis: "Here is magnificently the seeing eye."

Callaghan's intense curiosity about the motives of human action and his quietly sympathetic voice exert an inexorable pull. You hardly notice the sly, subtle tug of his prose, his gift for snapshot description with telling cadences, as when he describes a young priest's vacillation between human and divine love:

> He saw that Midge was getting sleepy. Once he yawned himself. They both lay back and began to doze. Then Father Dowling sat up abruptly, saw Midge's eyes closed, saw how long her lashes were, and how her lips were parted and her breast was softly swelling, and he went out without disturbing her.

I was loyal to my search for the sacramental in the daily lives of people," Callaghan told an interviewer in 1983. "To find the extraordinary in the ordinary—this used to be the great and only aim of art." A modernist in style and theme, he seems never to have been a "contemporary" writer. His fictional lives are decorated with a minimum of period detail, and the moral dilemmas his characters face up to have as much relevance to secular as religious readers. His sincerity, sensible balance of reason and emotion, strong but self-effacing voice, shrewd sense of irony—all these seem identifiably Canadian traits, though Callaghan was never a cultural nationalist. His novella **The Varsity Story** (1948), routinely dismissed as a nostalgic valedictory to the University of Toronto, is in fact a cleverly disguised inquiry into his country's elusive national identity.

Edmund Wilson tried to revive Callaghan's reputation in a series of articles for the *New Yorker* in the 1960s. The first was a review, extremely favorable, of **That Summer in Paris,** praising its author's "gift of moral objectivity" and kindred ability to rise above the expatriate fray. Allowing that Callaghan's prose lacked the lyricism and emotion of Fitzgerald or Hemingway, he deemed his art "more subtle" and his intelligence "more mature." Callag-

han, Wilson wrote, "is so much interested in moral character as exhibited in other people's behavior that, unlike his two exhibitionistic friends, he never shows himself at all." The conventional Canadian wisdom on Callaghan was always that he was a master of the short story but wanting as a novelist. "Very interesting failures," one assessment patronizingly deemed his long fiction. Wilson, in a letter, reported getting in trouble for making the opposite claim: that the novels were more interesting than the stories for their larger themes and the depth of their characters. This audacious heresy was viewed as Yankee imperialism. But he was right.

Although his countrymen conferred prizes and accolades upon Callaghan throughout his career, although his stories were published in American magazines and anthologies, he always felt underestimated beyond his own borders and underappreciated within them. His reputation fell victim to what Wilson identified as

> the general incapacity—apparently shared by his compatriots—for believing that a writer whose work may be mentioned without absurdity in association with Chekhov's and Turgenev's can possibly be functioning in Toronto.

For a decade (1938-48), which he called "the dark period of my life," he stopped publishing fiction altogether, and became a full-time radio commentator for the CBC. In *A Fine and Private Place* (1975), an American critic bearing a strong resemblance to Wilson champions a neglected Toronto novelist who bears a strong resemblance to Callaghan. Even though the book is deeply autobiographical—the novelist even lives on the same street as Callaghan—its central character is not the novelist but the young scholar studying him. It's also, as the title makes clear, not in the least self-pitying. Callaghan *chose* to live and work in Toronto. He regarded his relative obscurity with ironic resignation, not bitterness. The title page of one of his plays reads "Published from The House of Exile/20 Dale Avenue, Toronto"—his home address.

Callaghan once remarked that while studying law—he was called to the bar the year before he left for Paris—he read "case books on human nature." In his fiction he learned to write them. (pp. 36-7)

Rick Marin, "Morley Callaghan, 1903-1990," in The American Spectator, *Vol. 24, No. 2, February, 1991, pp. 36-7.*

Walker Percy

May 28, 1916 — May 10, 1990

American novelist and essayist.

Best known for his first novel, *The Moviegoer,* for which he won the National Book Award, Percy explored such conditions of modern life as alienation, malaise, and conformity. Drawing upon the religious and philosophical ideas of Søren Kierkegaard and Gabriel Marcel and imbued with his knowledge of semiotics, science, Southern history, and popular culture, Percy's works promoted Christian and existential values as a means for counteracting contemporary psychological and social ills.

For an overview of Percy's life and work, see *CLC,* Vols. 2, 3, 6, 8, 14, 18, 47; *Contemporary Authors,* Vols. 1-4, rev. ed., 131; *Contemporary Authors New Revision Series,* Vols. 1, 23; *Dictionary of Literary Biography,* Vol. 2 and *Dictionary of Literary Biography Yearbook: 1980.*

Cleanth Brooks

Walker Percy was an excellent literary artist and a remarkable man. In his fiction he was keen and witty, and in his social criticism and satire he was brilliantly perceptive. As a man he was genial, gracious, a wonderful conversationalist, and apparently cheerfully comfortable in a world in which he was quite at home. Yet the great theme of his fiction was man's alienation from the familiar world of here and now in which we pass our daily lives.

He insisted, in essays and interviews, that he was not writing the "Southern Novel" and that he had not the slightest intention of imitating William Faulkner. Yet he greatly admired Faulkner—and we may add, for he himself added them, Eudora Welty, John Crowe Ransom, Allen Tate, R. P. Warren, Flannery O'Connor, and other Southern writers of our century. As for being Southern himself, I can't think of anyone who knew the South better or who could more precisely set forth the people, black and white, rich and poor, in their appearance, their customs, their thinking, and their speech. Percy could faultlessly address any Southern speaker in his own proper dialect.

Percy was indeed deeply Southern, and he moved about in his chosen Southern world easily and with enjoyment. Why, then, was his basic theme man's alienation from the dominant society? Why, for example, should Will Barrett, the principal character in Percy's *The Last Gentleman,* experience his peculiar loneliness? After several years in Manhattan, Barrett comes home to his native South. But the South he came home to "was different from the South

he had left. It was happy, victorious, Christian, rich, patriotic and Republican."

Percy is very emphatic in stressing this new happiness of the South. As the returning Will Barrett saw it, "The happiness of the South was very formidable. It defied you to call it anything else." It certainly defied Barrett to call it anything else. But in spite of his determination to join the home folks and be happy "and at home, too," Barrett does not succeed. He remained an alienated man.

Though he came of planter stock, and was reared by a foster father, William Alexander Percy, who was a man of letters, Percy chose to major in chemistry and to go on to the Columbia University Medical School. He received his M. D. in due course and was serving as an intern at Bellevue in New York City when he contracted tuberculosis while doing an autopsy. So his planned career as a physician came, in fact, to an end before it had really begun: it was only then that he seriously engaged himself in a career as a writer.

Percy's knowledge of science was to be of great importance to him as he set out to write about the new South still full of its old customs and ideas but eager to embrace the new technological society which had made the rest of America rich. A firm grasp of the proper domain of scientific work, its methods of verification, and its limitations as an oracle dispensing truth, was useful to a writer who had been a serious reader of thinkers like Kierkegaard, Sartre, and Camus and had become a convert to Catholicism. In an age of general confusion such as ours is, the man who has a definite position and knows how to defend it, speaks with authority. This is especially true when such a man is also an accomplished artist and has a natural command of the language.

Percy's first novel, *The Moviegoer* (1961), attracted serious attention at once. Yet being a Southerner as well as being a Catholic has its liabilities. He was thoroughly aware of this fact. He entitled a lecture published in 1982 "How to Be an American Novelist in Spite of Being Southern and Catholic." He specifies there the difficulties. But the situation was not hopeless and indeed there were actual positive advantages. One great advantage, Percy tells us, is

> that the Southerner can see the American scene from both the inside and the outside—inside because living as he does in the resurgent Sunbelt, he is more American than ever; from the outside because he's still Southern whether he likes it or not, which is to say he can still see the American proposition from a tragic historical perspective. He knows in his bones that things can come to grief and probably will. And whether he is a believer or not, he is also more likely to know that Man is tragically flawed and is born to trouble as the sparks fly upward.

This is a very acute observation and applies to many other Southern writers, but the form of the statement is pure Walker Percy. He has here got down clearly the character of his vision of America. The way in which he describes it is characteristic of his own personality.

Problems of all sorts do exist for the Southern writer and the Catholic writer, problems that cannot be simply brushed aside. For example, the Sunbelt, Percy remarks, is now "informed . . . by a species of triumphant Christendom." In this Sunbelt Christendom, there has been a "devaluation of the Christian vocabulary. . . . The old words, God, grace, sin, redemption . . . now tend to be rather exhausted, worn slick as poker chips and signifying as little, or else are heard as the almost random noise of radio and TV preachers." Percy goes on to point out that the grim roadside signs of the "Christendom of the Old South, such as 'Prepare to Meet Eternity,' served the novelist's purposes better than Oral Roberts' cheerful announcements that Something Good is Going to Happen to You."

How does Percy treat his alienated characters in his novels? Do they emerge from their alienation triumphantly? Do they enter the Catholic Church? Only one of Percy's main characters, Dr. Tom More, who appears in two of his novels, is a Roman Catholic, and More frankly calls himself a "bad Catholic." Binx Bolling, Will Barrett (who like More appears in two of the novels), and Lancelot Andrewes Lamar are not believers at all. "Seekers" would be a more accurate term for them. Something significant, even transformative, does happen to all of these alienated men. But what happens occurs so quietly that its full significance is sometimes missed by even a sensitive reader. I recently received a letter in which a reader reported to me that the ending of one of Percy's novels had left her quite puzzled. Why did this able novelist seem to play down so much the ultimate recoveries and resolutions of problems—that is, if these recoveries and resolutions did, in fact, occur?

The simplest answer is that Walker Percy was a novelist and that as a novelist he had special problems in presenting his truths. He remarks in one of his lectures that "The South has been called a Jesus haunted country. A believer would not want to escape His haunting presence. There are two things Southern writers have always been stuck with, blacks and Jesus." But Percy goes on to observe that if the writer is a believer, he is also in trouble. "He finds himself in bed with the wrong bedfellows."

One can easily imagine who some of these wrong bedfellows would be. But furthermore, the believing artist must refuse to be a mere spokesman. He must render his ideas dramatically rather than argue a case or bring forth a brief. The literary artist must not tell his reader how he should react and what he ought to feel. He must allow the reader to draw his own conclusions from the circumstances the novel has set forth. The literary artist may be a devout believer himself; but as an artist he is not writing an essay or preaching a sermon. He must be content to be an artist and not a mere spokesman for a church or any other institution.

In *The Moviegoer,* perhaps Percy's most beautifully crafted work, young Binx Bolling is a thoroughly disenchanted young man. He is well-born and well-educated. His family like him and have the power to promote his interests. He has a good job, a comfortable life, a bright future. Even the secretaries in his office are pretty and attractive. But Binx is not happy. His life lacks conviction and does not seem to be quite healthy or even real. In fact, Binx finds that the local movie house provides him with something closer to reality than he can find in Gentilly, the New Orleans suburb in which he has chosen to carry out his career of a half life.

The novel succeeds in the difficult task of making the reader aware of Binx's disorder, and it shows the steps—some serious, some comic—through which he proceeds as he comes to discover what matters most. But Binx's quest does not conclude with his becoming converted to Catholicism. As the novel ends, Binx is married to Kate, a girl who also has serious problems and needs not only love but responsible care. On the last page of the novel, Binx is asking Kate to do him a little favor, to go downtown and pick up some legal papers for him. It's a small task but Kate is genuinely unsure of herself. He reassures her with precise directions. His final words to her include not only reassurance but a pledge that he will be thinking of her all through her little task. It even includes a tenderly spoken command. His rather commonplace words imply something deeper, of course, something like "I'm trying to face up to reality now and so must you. I will try to help you to do so. We are in this thing together."

We have much the same sort of ending in Percy's last novel, *The Thanatos Syndrome.* Though full of action, some of it exciting and quite violent, this novel also ends with a very minor event, one whose significance has probably eluded—or at least temporarily misled—a good many readers. Tom More, the hero of the novel, is now at home: his wife has been restored to him. Financially he is not in good shape. Worst of all, as a physician he has lost most of his patients. But he has succeeded in one or two of his larger endeavors and now toward the very end of the novel one of his old patients returns rather suddenly. She tells him that everything is fine, but that she is terrified of something she feels is about to happen; she dreads something, but doesn't know what it is. The dream she used to have has been recurring. It has to do with the smell of winter apples in her grandmother's farmhouse in Vermont and the dream also includes the feeling that a stranger is coming. She believes that the stranger is a part of herself trying to tell her something and Dr. More encourages her by saying "Well?" Something important is afoot. But then the book ends here.

What is it that commits Percy to such artistic reserve and understatement? Is it perhaps part of his dread of being dismissed as no novelist but a spokesman for an institution? (Percy has been charged with this by some reviewers.) Or perhaps his forbearance and lightness of touch are simply parts of his personality? Whatever the cause, writing about the new Sunbelt South did not daunt Percy in the least. He rather relished the challenge. Listen to him on the subject of a Middlewesterner come to Louisiana: a man who has made two billion dollars in oil leases, who lives in an antebellum mansion in New Orleans, who has never read a novel in his life, and who is "so absorbed in dealmaking that he is a stranger to his friends and family." "Maybe he can't use me," Percy writes. "But I can sure use him." There is a jovial confidence in a statement like this—something perfectly characteristic of this remarkable man. Would that Percy had lived to deal with this character from the Middlewest or others like him.

Of course, there were other sides of Walker Percy's warmth. I had the opportunity to experience one of them two or three years ago. When Percy heard that my wife was dying of cancer he generously offered to come up from Louisiana to New Haven and drive us around New England for a week to visit and dine at some of the old inns. It was a thoroughly handsome offer. I told him immediately that I could not accept so generous an invitation, and that, in any case, it was impossible. My wife was now on oxygen. Only a properly equipped ambulance could allow her to leave the house or her hospital bed.

I was emboldened, however, to ask him for a favor. I knew that *The Thanatos Syndrome,* though it had not yet appeared, was going through the press. I told him that my wife and I had so much enjoyed hearing him read an excerpt from it the year before that I wondered whether he had an extra proof that he could send for her to read in

her hospital bed. A typed copy with corrections appeared within a few days. It proved to be my wife's last reading matter.

In losing Walker Percy, we have lost a remarkable figure in American literature and a generous man. Some of us have lost a very kind and dear friend. (pp. 82-5)

Cleanth Brooks, "Walker Percy, 1916-1990," in The New Criterion, *Vol. IX, No. 1, September, 1990, pp. 82-5.*

Eric Pace

Walker Percy, a Southern author who wrote about modern man's search for faith and love in a chaotic world in *The Moviegoer* and other novels, died yesterday at his home across Lake Pontchartrain from New Orleans.

A complex, ruminative man, Mr. Percy lived and wrote for years in Covington, a small town in southeastern Louisiana. As a young man, he went north and earned a medical degree from Columbia University but he did not make medicine or psychiatry his career. He became a Roman Catholic in 1946 and wrote essays on questions of philosophy and faith before becoming a writer of fiction.

When *The Moviegoer* was published, it was acclaimed by literary arbiters, Lewis Gannett, Herbert Gold and Jean Stafford, the judges who chose it for the National Book Award, issued a statement praising it in these words:

The Moviegoer, an intimation rather than a statement of mortality and the inevitability of that condition, is a truthful novel with shocks of recognition and spasms of nostalgia for every— or nearly every—American. Mr. Percy, with compassion and without sentimentality or the mannerisms of the clinic, examines the delusions and hallucinations and the daydreams and the dreams that afflict those who abstain from the customary ways of making do.

In the years that followed, various aspects of his writing won praise. The critic and teacher Cleanth Brooks, Gray Professor Emeritus of Rhetoric at Yale University, wrote in 1989 in the journal Humanities that "Walker Percy knows as much about how the people of the Deep South act and speak as anyone that I can think of."

"He knows what is limited, narrowminded and even grievously wrong in the social fabric of the Old South," he added.

In *The Times Book Review* in 1983, the novelist Francine du Plessix Gray called Mr. Percy "our greatest Catholic novelist since Flannery O'Connor." And Robert Giroux, his editor for years at Farrar, Straus & Giroux, once called him a loner with "a very original cast of mind," who was to a great extent "unlike any other Southern writer."

Mr. Percy's distinctive way of thinking reflected his early shifts of interest. In 1966 he wrote: "What began to interest me was not the physiological and pathological processes within man's body but the problem of man himself, the nature and destiny of man; specifically and more immediately, the predicament of man in a modern technological society."

He once said he turned to writing fiction after "reading the French—writers like Sartre."

"The American novelist tends to distinguish between reflections on our universal predicament and what can be told in fiction," he said, "whereas the French see nothing wrong with writing novels that address what they consider the deepest philosophical issues."

As a novelist, Mr. Percy wrote from within the tradition of such European existentialists as Sartre and Kierkegaard, who focused on the question of the individual's relationship to God or the universe.

Yet Mr. Percy cast his net more broadly. Ms. Kakutani wrote in *The New York Times* that in his novels as well as in his essays, "behavioralist theory is contrasted with the author's own existential outlook, scientific positivism with a more old-fashioned brand of Christian humanism."

Among some critics, it was Mr. Percy's talents as a storyteller rather than as a philosopher that won him praise. Jonathan Yardley wrote in *The New York Times Book Review* in 1979 that what was extraordinary about Mr. Percy was "not that he can claim to be a Christian existentialist philosopher-theologian of the first rank, but that he can bring all this heavy artillery to the typewriter and make good fiction out of it."

The psychiatrist and author Robert Coles wrote in his admiring 1978 book, *Walker Percy: An American Search,* that Mr. Percy believed "in the obligation men and women have to assume responsibility for their lives." "That is to say, he believes that we are 'not pigs, nor angels,' " he wrote. "We are, he says, pilgrims—wayfarers on a journey."

And so the narrator of *The Moviegoer,* the film fan Binx Bolling, says: "The search is what anyone would undertake if he were not sunk in the everydayness of his own life. To become aware of the possibility of the search is to be onto something. Not to be onto something is to be in despair."

Thomas Nagel, a professor of philosophy at New York University, wrote in *The New York Review of Books* that *The Moviegoer* offered a pure and precise "description of that malady of extreme detachment from perception and action which allows the victim to make contact with reality only when he is first dislodged, with greater or less violence, from his accustomed perch."

Mr. Percy was good at other sorts of description and analysis, too. Joyce Carol Oates wrote in *The New Republic* that he had been "wonderfully alive to the sounds and textures and odors of life." She said his novels were "artistically and humanly rich, and beautifully crafted."

And the author and critic V. S. Pritchett wrote in *The New York Review of Books* that Mr. Percy was praiseworthy for "moving about, catching the smell of locality, and for a laughing enjoyment between his bouts with desperation and loss."

Mr. Percy also built satire and symbolism into his fiction. The writer and editor Alfred Kazin once called him "the satiric Dostoyevsky of the bayou." And Professor Brooks, in the *Humanities* article, wrote, "Percy's language is the kind of instrument that any good satirist must have at hand."

Both the fictional superstructure and the messages in his novels were sometimes attacked by reviewers. Christopher Lehmann-Haupt wrote in *The New York Times* that in *Lancelot* the "narrative voice is uneven and unconvincing." Writing in *The Times Book Review,* Richard Locke said the book included ranting, sermonizing and much blather.

Yet both aspects of *The Second Coming* were praised in a front-page review in *The Times Book Review* by John Romano, an instructor of English at Columbia University. He declared it to be "among recent novels, masterly and superior" and, as a book of ideas, "splendid and engrossing." It, too, was nominated for an American Book Award.

Mr. Percy also set out his views and beliefs in two nonfiction books [*The Message in the Bottle* and *Lost in the Cosmos*].

Eric Pace, in an obituary in The New York Times, *May 11, 1990, p. D17.*

Bart Barnes

Walker Percy, 73, the critically acclaimed novelist, essayist and philosopher who wrote of angst, despair, neurosis and malaise in the subdivisions, country clubs and cities of the contemporary American South, died of cancer [May 10] at his home in Covington, La.

Mr. Percy was best known as the author of the novels *The Moviegoer, The Thanatos Syndrome, Love in the Ruins, The Last Gentleman, Lancelot* and *The Second Coming.* He was never an evangelist, but his books reflected a belief in the value of faith and spirituality, good works and family, and his characters seemed to be searching for something to help them overcome their despair.

He also was a brilliant satirist and a gifted storyteller, and because most of his stories had Southern settings, he was often considered a "Southern novelist" in the tradition of William Faulkner, Flannery O'Connor, Robert Penn Warren and Eudora Welty.

But Mr. Percy never accepted that label. "I lived a hundred miles from William Faulkner, but he meant less to me than Albert Camus," he told *The New York Times Book Review.*

"One does not immediately sense the South in Percy's work," observed *Washington Post* book critic Jonathan Yardley, "because he is telling us that the South is not the South any more, that it has been absorbed into the crassness and possibly the hopelessness of America. Percy's South has been violated not by Sherman's marauders but by . . . the masters of commerce and technology."

Robert Coles, a psychiatrist and Harvard professor whose

1978 study, *Walker Percy: An American Search,* is one of the foremost works about the author, said Mr. Percy had "a sharp eye for all the pompous, self-important and self-centered baloney that is eating away at American secular culture—its moral drift, its egoism, rootlessness and greed. He's on to both the liberals and the conservatives. He hits the blind spots in both camps."

Trained as a physician, Mr. Percy did not publish his first novel, *The Moviegoer,* until 1961, when he was 44 years old. Although the publisher, Alfred A. Knopf, did little to promote the novel, it was discovered and won a National Book Award.

Critics would see in it many of the themes that came to dominate much of Mr. Percy's subsequent writing. It was a first-person narrative about the uneventful and unchallenging times of Binx Bolling, a well-bred Southern gentleman whose life in New Orleans is characterized by meaninglessness and inauthenticity.

[Percy] graduated from the University of North Carolina where he studied chemistry, then enrolled in medical school at the Columbia College of Physicians and Surgeons, where he received a medical degree in 1941. That same year, he began a residency at Bellevue Hospital in New York.

Working as a pathologist in New York, he performed many autopsies on indigent alcoholics, many of whom had died of tuberculosis, and within a year he caught the disease. He spent much of the next three years in a sanitorium, and for much of that time he was flat on his back reading. He studied French and Russian literature, philosophy and psychology.

In 1944, Mr. Percy had recovered sufficiently to return to work, and he taught pathology at Columbia until he suffered a relapse and decided to quit medicine altogether.

It was his illness that led to his career in literature. "If the first great intellectual discovery of my life was the beauty of the scientific method, surely the second was the discovery of the singular predicament of man in the very world which has been transformed by this science," he told *Bookweek.* "An extraordinary paradox became clear: that the more science progressed and even as it benefited man, the less is said about what it is like to be a man living in the world."

Living on an inheritance, Mr. Percy married Mary Bernice Townsend in 1946. Raised as a Presbyterian, he converted to Catholicism in 1947. As he rejected the notion of being considered a Southern writer, he also rejected the idea of being considered a Catholic writer, although he acknowledged the conversion had an impact on his work.

"It entails a certain view of the way people are. In a technical sense, it entails anthropology, a theory of man, that man is a fallen creature."

Moving to Covington from New Orleans, Mr. Percy wrote two unpublished novels before beginning work on *The Moviegoer,* which today is an internationally acclaimed classic.

It was followed in 1966 by *The Last Gentleman,* which

shared the protagonist, Will Barrett, with *The Second Coming,* in 1980. In the first book, Barrett is afflicted with amnesia; in the second, he suffers from acute memory attacks that bring back a painful past.

Two other novels, *Love in the Ruins,* and *The Thanatos Syndrome,* also shared a common protagonist, Dr. Tom More, based loosely on the Tudor-era martyr, Sir Thomas More, and dealing with moral bankruptcy and political polarization in an America where scientists use technology to twist human souls.

> *Bart Barnes, in an obituary in* The Washington Post, *May 11, 1990.*

Josh Getlin

New York—On a chilly afternoon, as Manhattan's rush hour filled the streets and sidewalks, friends and admirers of the late Walker Percy gathered in a hushed midtown church Wednesday to remember his living legacy as a writer.

Percy, whose powerful novels about the South are studies in human faith and despair, was called a titan of American letters by such luminaries as Eudora Welty, Shelby Foote, Wilfrid Sheed, Mary Lee Settle and Stanley Kauffmann.

"He was, quite simply, the best we've got," said Welty, speaking in a frail voice to a crowd of more than 400 at St. Ignatius' Church.

"He'd always say, it's the job of the novelist not to notice how things are, but [to show] that people don't notice how awful things are. . . . He said there's something worse than being deprived of life. It's being deprived of life and not knowing it."

Percy, the author of novels including *The Moviegoer, Love in the Ruins* and *The Thanatos Syndrome,* died of cancer on May 10 in Covington, La. Although he suffered a painful death, those who knew him best spoke of the lanky, good-humored author in the present tense, as if he was somehow listening to them in a pew at the back of the church.

"I heard of his passing by reading an obituary, and I suddenly felt a cold draft, as if somehow I had left the window open," said writer Wilfrid Sheed. "But just looking at his wonderful books reminds me of how easily he can be brought back to life . . . and that's why this day is a celebration."

Percy came to the writing craft late in life, publishing his first novel, *The Moviegoer,* in 1961, when he was 45. Earlier, he had received a medical degree from Columbia University, but contracted tuberculosis after performing autopsies on derelicts and spent two years in a sanitarium.

There, undergoing an epiphany like the character of Hans Castorp in Thomas Mann's *The Magic Mountain,* Percy decided to drop medicine. Instead, he would explore himself and the world around him by becoming a writer.

In his six novels, Percy was one of the first American authors to depict the New South—a land of suburban malls, fast-food and spiritual pain cut loose from its historical moorings. A devout Roman Catholic, he portrayed the drabness and normalcy of modern life in a search for higher meaning, blending themes of existential doubt and religious faith.

Percy won the National Book Award for his first novel in 1962 and gained widespread recognition for his works thereafter. An accomplished essayist as well, Doc Percy, as he came to be known, was once described by critic Alfred Kazin as "the satiric Dostoevski of the bayou."

"I didn't know him, but I was his pupil," said author Mary Settle. "He taught me really for the first time that everything can be magic . . . a trunk in an attic, the ninth green on a golf course. An old greenhouse could become a castle."

Kauffmann, now a critic who edited *The Moviegoer* when it was published by Alfred A. Knopf, recalled a humorous side to the then-fledgling author. Although the first draft was brilliant in parts, he said, it needed to be rewritten. Percy obliged, retooling the book twice in 14 months.

When it was published, the novel was "favorably reviewed, but irritatingly, briefly reviewed," Kauffmann said. He tried to cheer up Percy, telling him his career would take off, but didn't think he was too convincing.

A year later, when the novel won the coveted National Book Award, Kauffmann said it was "lifted from oblivion to the top ranks of American literature, where it belongs. And Walker called me after he heard the news. For one minute, we laughed and laughed. Laughing with Walker Percy, it was a privilege, let me tell you."

Author and historian Shelby Foote recalled that Percy once told the producers of the "Today" show that he couldn't appear on their program, because he had no socks that would cover his calves.

But Foote grew somber as he recalled his last letter from Percy, when the author was fighting a losing battling against cancer. His friend of 60 years wrote him that "hospitals are no place for anyone, let alone a sick man." The author noted that "death is no big thing," because he still had his faith, but it was "an expense to others . . . and an indignity."

"There was never anything sentimental between us. We didn't want it to end that way," Foote said, his voice breaking.

Toward the end of the ceremony, Patrick Samway SJ, recalled Percy's May 12 funeral, noting that most of the attendees didn't know each other.

"But all had come because of this one man who had charmed them in so many ways, by word and deed. And so we say to Walker: *Requiescat in pace.*" (pp. E1, E4)

Josh Getlin, in an obituary in Los Angeles Times, *October 26, 1990, pp. E1, E4.*

Lewis P. Simpson

Walker Percy was graduated from the College of Physi-

cians and Surgeons of Columbia University in 1941. The following year, while doing autopsies as an intern at New York City's Bellevue Hospital, he contracted tuberculosis. Even as the fair courts of life opened before him, it would seem, the promising young physician had been dealt a crippling blow. Yet Walker Percy never considered this ironic stroke of fate to be anything but great good luck. He regarded his two-year confinement in the Trudeau Sanatorium in Saranac Lake, New York, to be sure, as the seminal moment in his life: the time when a thirty-year-old student of medical science from Greenville, Mississippi, had shattered the mold of the southern patriciate into which he had been born, with its moral requirement that he become a lawyer, doctor, or planter. Otherwise Percy might well have honorably pulled his stint in the World War II American army and, directed by the same sense of honor and responsibility, thereafter become a conventional practitioner of medicine, instead of a free-lance philosopher and novelist.

Of course if he had been able to benefit from advances in the treatment of TB that were soon to come, and thus had had a rapid recovery from his illness, the story of the young Dr. Percy would no doubt have been different. But as it was, he had the great advantage of "taking the cure" at "an old-fashioned sanatorium" that he once described somewhat hyperbolically as being like the one in Thomas Mann's *The Magic Mountain.* Yet, although it hardly offered an exotic community of patients and doctors, emblems of a dying European culture, like that Hans Castorp encountered at the Swiss sanatorium in the years immediately preceding World War I, Trudeau Sanatorium did afford Percy the opportunity, in the context of life in a community of displaced fellow sufferers, to pursue a personal quest into the mystery of existence.

His quest had a strong motive in the circumstances of Percy's rearing. His father a suicide when he was eleven, his mother the victim of an accident a year or so later, Walker Percy had known disorder, sorrow, and displacement early in life. The trauma of the experience was markedly alleviated by the fact that the orphaned Percy children (Walker and his two brothers) had been adopted by a bachelor cousin whom they loved and revered, William Alexander Percy ("Uncle Will")—author of *Lanterns on the Levee,* gentleman-poet, and disciple of Marcus Aurelius—whose home was the center of the "high culture" of the Mississippi Delta. The comparatively early death of W. A. Percy in 1941 meant to Walker Percy the loss of a second father and a second home. The onset of tuberculosis and his admittance to the sanatorium at Saranac Lake was a final displacement.

Afforded the leisure at Saranac Lake to read what he would, Percy became absorbed in the writings of Søren Kierkegaard, Charles Sanders Peirce, Gabriel Marcel, Ludwig Wittgenstein, Jean-Paul Sartre, and other students of the nature of man in the modern age. The result was that, not unlike Hans Castorp, he became aware of the representational—the symbolic—quality of his own singular existence in the historical culture of which he was an inextricable part. Indeed, his physical illness enabled the ex-Bellevue pathologist to unmask the symptoms in himself of a more insidious disease than TB, these belonging to that affliction of the spirit—pervasive in a post-Christian society dominated by the rational, scientific approach to knowledge—Søren Kierkegaard refers to as "the sickness unto death," a disease characteristically expressed in the individual human consciousness by a despair that does not know itself. Pursuing the subtle and devious etiology of the modern malaise, Percy—who actually was allowed by the mild nature of his own case of TB (a lesion on one lung) to serve as a physician at Trudeau even as he was a patient—diagnosed the cause of the sickness unto death as being not the reaction to the highly touted Nietzschean death of God, but the anxious reaction to the widespread sense of the loss, or displacement, of God. Bringing this sense into a tension with his scientific training—especially with respect to the "classical behaviorism" he had been taught as a pre-med at Chapel Hill and the "idea of the mechanism of disease" he had heard expounded at Columbia—Percy began to suspect that "Science can say everything about a man except what he is in himself." Questioning more and more the validity of the psychoanalytical quest for the self—which he had personally pursued for three years after Uncle Will's death by visiting a Freudian psychiatrist five days a week—the young doctor-patient at Trudeau found himself profoundly attracted to the Christian concept of the pilgrimage of the soul. But it was 1952 before Percy formally identified himself as a Christian pilgrim, this when he and his wife "Bunt" (Mary Bernice Townsend of Mississippi, whom he had married in 1946) both became converts to Roman Catholicism. By this time they had ended a period of residence in the New Orleans French Quarter and moved across Lake Pontchartrain to establish a home on the bayou called Bogue Falaya ("river of mists" or "river of ghosts") in Covington, Louisiana. As might be expected of a Catholic convert heavily influenced by a crucial Protestant thinker like Kierkegaard, Percy came into a close but rather tense association with the Church. A member of the confraternity of Benedictine monks of St. Joseph's Abbey near Covington, he was recognized by the Church in various ways as time went on, his honors including not only such conventional distinctions as the Campion Medal of the Catholic Book Club but an ultimate distinction, election to the Vatican's Pontifical Council of Culture.

Although he had by 1952 long since given up any thought of practicing medicine, Percy (who was blessed with an inherited income) did not formally signify his adoption of the literary vocation until two years after his conversion, when in a series of appearances in various journals of limited circulation (*Thought, Commonweal, America, Philosophy and Phenomenological Research, Partisan Review,* and others), he began a career as a prophetic essayist. Devoted to the exploration of the critical alienation of the self in post-Christian Western culture, Percy's brilliant periodical essays—among them, **"Symbol as Hermeneutic in Existentialism," "The Man on the Train: Three Existential Modes,"** and **"The Message in the Bottle"**—are now known to a wider audience than the original one. His literary career remained obscure, until—having discovered that the major treatment of his subject is in "the modern novel," which is wholly about "alienation . . . about man as dislocated, disoriented, uprooted, homeless"—Percy

turned from the essay to the novel, with its endless satirical and ironic possibilities, as his primary means of expression. After a false start or two, he wrote what in balance may well be his classic work, *The Moviegoer.*

By then it was 1961, and Percy had reached the mid-forties, hardly the optimum age for a beginning novelist. But there were two things in his favor. The historical moment was right. In the age of the flower children there was a response to Binx Bolling, Will Barrett, and Thomas More that would not have been possible before the sad, ironic decade of the 1960s, which occurred one hundred years after that other sad, ironic decade in American history, the 1860s, when the citizens of the new Republic had slaughtered each other in a catastrophic civil struggle—a struggle that had been essentially provoked by the same issue basic to the strife of the 1960s: that is to say, the fundamental modern issue, the nature of man. A second thing the overaged novelist had going for him was the historical fact that he belonged to the autumnal generation of the twentieth-century "Southern Renaissance." He himself would have rejected such an interpretation; in fact, he did explicitly reject it, insisting that he was distinctly different from writers of the preceding generation like Faulkner and the Agrarians in that he used the southern scene only as "a backdrop." But in protesting the interpretation of his work as that of a "southern" author, Percy himself in effect denied his own protest. In the act of storytelling and, most notably, in the creation of his characters, he implicitly identified his sense of the land and the people of his nativity with his sense of his vocation as a modern novelist. His difference from Faulkner or Allen Tate, we realize, is one of generational perception. As with Faulkner, the context of Percy's stories is the history of the South, past and present, as an integral representation of the modern world; like Faulkner his deep, underlying motive is a sense of the novelist's responsibility for dramatizing and interpreting the modern crisis of self in its relation to human nature and human history. Peculiarly at the heart of the remarkable efflorescence of literature in the twentieth-century South, this crisis has one of its most memorable novelistic formulations in the story of the displaced young southerner in *The Last Gentleman,* Williston Bibb Barrett. Like all southerners, Will has "trouble ruling out the possible," tending not to act unless he is acted upon, as when war makes the possible actual. In this respect Will bears a resemblance to all those young southerners who in one way or another are summed up in the memory-obsessed, suicidal Quentin Compson. But, as Percy's novel goes, it was different with Will. It was "more than being a Southerner"; it was worse maybe, Will's incapacity for decision making being rendered total by his recurrent fugue states. In one such state he "wandered around northern Virginia for three weeks, where he sat sunk in thought on old battlegrounds, hardly aware of his own name." Does Will's state of mind and emotion actually reflect more than being southern, or does it simply reflect a more refined and subtle dimension of being a patrician southerner (to refer to the words of Romana Guardini in the epigraph to *The Last Gentlemen*) at "the end of the modern world"? Percy's story about Will Barrett is not only about Will but about himself.

With Walker Percy's death on May 10, 1990, the last generation of southern writers to write with a knowledge of the high culture of the patrician South in their bones has all but disappeared. After the celebration of the Mass of the Resurrection at the Church of St. Joseph's Abbey on May 12, standing at the gravesite in the cemetery reserved for the Benedictines and the members of their confraternity, I found myself remembering Percy's feeling—as different as the two were in important respects—for a relationship between himself and another physician writer, Anton Chekhov, and about how Walker had told me once about the experience of giving one of his infrequent lectures to the audience at a Chekhov festival held at Cornell University. I suppose I remembered this because, following the word of his death, I had—for no particular reason, save perhaps that I might imagine hearing his voice again—started reading randomly in Lewis Lawson's and Victor Kramer's comprehensive collection of interviews with Walker. I had been struck with an odd comment or so in a 1977 interview in which he had recalled the title of his Cornell lecture, **"The Novelist, Diagnostician of the Contemporary Malaise."** Chekhov, Walker said, "was a doctor, like me, who also didn't particularly like medicine." Dr. Walker Percy failed to say that Dr. Anton Chekhov was also like him in that he was a tubercular—who, possessing the sharp, exquisite sensibility of a cultural patrician and the gifts of the literary artist, lived at the end of a world; and both lived and wrote of its death and—the indistinct possibility, at once tantalizing and terrifying—of its transmutation into another world. In the depths of a warm, muggy south Louisiana spring day, amid the lush greenery of the cemetery at St. Joseph's, I seemed to know why Percy said that Chekhov "has influenced me a lot." But I am no more able to put this into words than I was then. (pp. 924-28)

Lewis P. Simpson, "Walker Percy, 1916-1990," in The Southern Review, *Louisiana State University, Vol. 26, No. 4, October, 1990, pp. 924-28.*

Manuel Puig

December 28, 1932—July 22, 1990

Argentine novelist, screenwriter, and nonfiction writer.

A leading contributor to the international prominence and popularity of contemporary Latin American literature, Puig is best known as the author of the novel *El beso de la mujer araña* (*Kiss of the Spider Woman*). In this and other acclaimed works such as *La traición de Rita Hayworth* (*Betrayed by Rita Hayworth*) and *Cae la noche tropical,* Puig employed an innovative narrative style that synthesizes the conversations and interior monologues of his characters with fragments from newspapers, soap operas, Hollywood movies, and popular songs to investigate how individuals escape painful truths through fantasy.

For an overview of Puig's life and work, see *CLC,* Vols. 3, 5, 10, 28; *Contemporary Authors,* Vols. 45-48; *Contemporary Authors New Revision Series,* Vol. 2.

Norman Lavers

It is more than usually helpful, in the case of a writer like Manuel Puig, to know something of his background and how he came to be a writer. Biographical details neatly explain his techniques, his themes, and, particularly, his materials. It is especially in his materials that we see one of the most unique characteristics of this entirely unique novelist: his use of debased or subliterary forms of language and art—the tango and bolero, the soap opera, the detective story, serial fiction, the *fotonovela,* and, above all else, the Hollywood movie.

"El fenómeno Puig," the great reception Puig's novels have received in Latin America and the critical attention that is accorded them—almost as much is written about Puig each year as is written about García Márquez—has been a fact of Latin American literary life since his first book was published in 1968. In the United States at least since the mid-1970s Puig has been a favorite of avant-garde writers and readers, and all of his novels are available in English translation. But it was not until the success of the award-winning movie made from his novel **Kiss of the Spider Woman** that he received the wide attention in this country that his unique but quite accessible novels deserve.

Puig, like the characters in his first two novels, was born (in 1932) in a flat, dusty, landscapeless town in the Argentine pampas. The setting was not only physically ugly but also morally oppressive, with its ethic of unremitting machismo. Those too sensitive to flourish in such an envi-

ronment escaped to the town's movie theater to merge and identify with and to shape their dreams from the images of 1930s and 1940s Hollywood films. Ultimately for these sensitive ones (Puig among them) the movies became reality, and the harsh life of the town outside the theater became a B movie they had been placed in through an error in casting.

Puig himself was thirty years old before he escaped the enchantment sufficiently to turn back and write about it in his extraordinary novels, which are compassionate at the same time that they miss absolutely nothing. In the bleak pampas the institutionalized oppression—boys over girls, men over women, a dictator over the state—was laid bare, but when his novels left the pampas and moved into the centers of civilization they found the same oppression there, but everywhere concealed and at the same time reinforced by the anodyne popular culture of tangos, soap operas, and Hollywood films. It is not a surprise that **Kiss of the Spider Woman** should be so popular as a film. It may be his best novel as well, at least insofar as it has captured all his themes within the most perfect imaginable metaphor: two men literally imprisoned by their culture, in this case in the penitentiary in Buenos Aires, who, with a constant threat of torture and destruction hanging over them, must face each day the annihilating monotony of their incarceration. It is Puig's version of *Waiting for Godot*. To pass the time, one tells lovingly remembered plots of Hollywood films to the other, and this becomes their necessary reality—even though in subtle ways the films are the purest expression of what has imprisoned them.

Perhaps biography explains Puig's sources too neatly. What we know about his origins comes chiefly through his remarks in numerous interviews. I do not mean to suggest he is mythologizing his past, but in his insistence on casting himself as a naif who fell into his extraordinary novel-writing techniques by chance and force of circumstances there may a degree of simplification. When he speaks of himself as timid and feckless it must be kept in mind that he is a sophisticated world citizen, fluent in five languages (he has written novels in three), that he studied film directing with De Sica and screenwriting with Zavattini, and that in all his writing and his discussions of his writing he shows himself to be an extremely self-conscious artist and technician. Still, as Henry James said, if you give an artist an inch, he will take an ell, so it is quite possible simple causes fashioned richly proliferating and almost instantaneous results in his waiting sensibility.

The first detail to know about him is that his background is not literary. He insists on that. Now that he is a figure in Latin American literature, there is some effort being made to show how he fits into it—but if he does fit, it is in the sense of Eliot's "Tradition and the Individual Talent," where the individual writer alters the whole of the preceding tradition in order to make his place in it. The truth is that Manuel Puig is not like any other Latin American writer. He knows the other writers now, has met them in conferences, and no doubt has read some of their books. But this was not the case when he was starting. He did not then esteem literature highly—he still does not read much fiction. He did not read literature written in Spanish, and most certainly he did not read literature from his native Argentina. He gives his reasons:

> I was born in a town in the pampas where life was very hard, very difficult—almost like the *Far West*. The prestige of strength. No one questioned machismo. Authority had the most prestige possible. . . . These were the coordinates. Weakness, sensibility, had no prestige. A world I rejected [interview with Saul Sosnowski, *Hispamérica* 1 (May 1973)].

Rejecting this world meant, for him, rejecting its literature. . . . (pp. 1-3)

That does not mean his background was not artistic, only that another form held dominance. "For me literature was a secondary thing . . . like listening to music, like looking at a painting. . . . All my expectations, all my attention, was on movies" (Sosnowski).

It is worth examining the psychology of his relationship to movies, because it influences the shape of his writing, and because it penetrates the psychology of his characters.

> In this town there was *one* means of escaping reality: movies. One single theater that gave a different picture every day. I went with mama at least four times a week. Little by little I changed the terms: that which was reality changed into a class Z movie in which I had been stuck by mistake. Reality . . . was what happened in the movies, not what happened in town, which was a western from Republic. (Sosnowski)

Since movies meant everything to him it seemed natural, when it came time for him to choose a career, to try to enter the movie-making industry. The way to enter the world of the movies, he felt, was through language. This meant, preeminently, English, since that was the language of the Hollywood films he most esteemed. He learned French also, and latterly Italian, since in the period we are talking about, right at the end of the Second World War, the Italian neorealist film was gaining prestige. Puig had nothing but contempt for the undeveloped Argentine film industry. So he studied these languages, and won a scholarship in 1956 to study at Cinecittà in Rome.

He was immediately disenchanted. Instead of finding a beautiful world of technicolor and romantic love, a place of saints like Norma Shearer, a place where sensibility always triumphed, he found the same power-jockeying, the same prestige for authority and for nothing else. Even directing was simply another kind of exploitation, of forcing one's will on another. As an escape from this, in his free time he began coming at movies from the direction of screenwriting. Significantly, he wrote not in his rejected Spanish but in the English of Hollywood.

> I knew English pretty well, but not well enough to write in. . . . For me English was the language of film. This first screenplay was a "sophisticated comedy" of the thirties written in 1958, a time of total derision for the thirties. I wrote it with great enthusiasm. While I was writing it I felt good. When I finished it, I didn't. It was an abortion. Horrible. . . . What I had wanted was to prolong my times as an infantile spectator. To rewrite some movie that had really impressed me, but it cost me three screenplays to find that out. Naturally I didn't sell them. . . . I realized that what I enjoyed in making films was copying. Creating didn't interest me at all. What I wanted was to re-make things from another epoch, things already seen. To recreate the moment in childhood in which I had felt safe in the dark hall. (Sosnowski)

The situation was serious. When he was a child in a small town in the pampas, everything was regulated by power, by machismo, and no esteem was given to sensibility, which was the only thing the boy had. When he went to secondary school and to the university in the big city, in Buenos Aires, he expected everything to be different. But he found it was just the same thing again, the same power and authority, the same exploitation of the weak. His escape had always been the movies, but when he finally arrived in Italy and got inside the fabled precincts themselves, he found it was once more the same thing.

> I was in Rome, thirty years old, without career, without money, and discovering that the vocation of my whole life—cinema—had been an error, a neurosis and nothing more. (Sosnowski)

Friends of his, who were far enough outside his problem to have some perspective on it, saw why his screenplays were failing. They counseled him to write in his native language and to write about things he knew, something particular that he had experienced.

> I tried to write a screenplay about the loves of cousins in my town. It was autobiographical material that was deep inside me and that I couldn't see with the necessary distance. To make the characters clearer to me I decided to make, before the dialogue, before shaping the plot, etc., a small description of each one to make them clear to me. These descriptions weren't to show to anybody . . . They were, for the first time, in Spanish. How to do it? I didn't know how to describe characters. I didn't find the vocabulary. But I remembered the voice of an aunt. Her voice came to me very clearly, things this woman had said while washing clothes, while cooking, twenty years before. I began to record that voice. The description that was going to be two pages ended up being thirty. It was material that flowed by itself. I quickly realized that the voice I heard was material that I could handle. In spite of the fact that I was returning to a reality I had rejected, I was interested in going on with it. It ended up as a kind of interior monologue. (Sosnowski)

I think we must believe Puig when he tells us he had rejected the experience of his childhood so utterly that he had even rejected his own language. And thus we must see it as a psychological as well as an artistic breakthrough when in his desperation he was able to return to both the experience and the language in which it was cast. Having freed himself from the blockage, he could free himself also from the device he had used to escape the misery of his childhood. (pp. 3-6)

The movies had been an escape, "a neurosis and nothing more," but when he fell suddenly into novel writing, there is no sign that it was simply a new escape to replace the original, failed escape. There is no more blindness, no more unrealistic expectation. Immediately he is making artistic decisions, immediately he is making realistic assessments of his strengths and his weaknesses.

> I didn't know how to do anything but write interior monologues because pure Spanish made me tremble. The only thing I wanted to do was register voices. But I wasn't just a recorder. Afterward I manipulated the material, I cut it . . . I did any experiments I liked with it, but the material was always the spoken language. . . . But in the interior monologues . . . there came a certain moment when I began to repeat myself. I needed some other techniques. Third person was not possible, because my Spanish was lost, I had no confidence in it [he had been out of Argentina for eight years]. I didn't even have any reading material in Spanish. . . . I needed something that was neither interior monologue nor third

> person. Then it came to me . . . : casual writing, that is to say, people writing, people who could commit errors writing. I figured if I knew the psychology of the character, I could make him write. I had these characters write letters, intimate diaries, scholarly compositions, and in this way completed the novel escaping third person. (Sosnowski)

Puig was not simply, however, avoiding the difficulty of third person. He quickly perceived the utility of what he was doing.

> I was not only afraid to use third person, but I also didn't feel it was an instrument adequate for the work I wanted to do. I was especially interested in characters I knew in my childhood who handed over to me their secrets, their intimacy. I had lots of facts about them but one can never know the totality of a person. One can try to reconstruct it in some way, but I was not too sure about being able to reconstruct them, although it occurred to me that listening to them speak or having them write a letter, they alone were going to reveal themselves to me. (Sosnowski)

Puig was in fact reinventing the novel. There is an uncanny similarity between his words and those of the first inventor of the modern novel, Samuel Richardson. Richardson also was a sensitive, precociously intelligent, perhaps effeminate young boy to whom people confessed their intimate secrets. . . . When he began to write *Pamela*—and Richardson too was a very self-conscious artist knowing exactly what he was doing—he developed his famous epistolary style, remembering that a person's own writing could reveal the truth of his soul more subtly and more completely than pages of authorial description in the third person.

So it is a pleasant irony. What seems so new, so modern in Puig, what makes the first and strongest impression on the reader, Puig's extreme objectivity, his refusal to appear as narrator, is in fact the oldest and first trick of the novel genre, forgotten by succeeding generations of writers, and reinvented by Puig in almost the same way that it first was. I don't mean for a moment to say that Puig is not original. Precisely what the truly original artist does is to reinvent his form, recast it with the stamp of his freshness and uniqueness.

Although virtually all of Richardson's fictions are cast in the form of exchanges of letters, Richardson, as did Puig, recognized the need for polyphony. In the letters one finds monologue, third-person narrative, in moments of stress something close to stream-of-consciousness, and very often scenes of almost pure dialogue (Richardson was strongly influenced by Restoration and eighteenth-century drama, just as Puig was influenced by Hollywood movies). But Puig has shown much more interest in the effects of putting different kinds of writing and different narrative styles side by side. At least here he concedes that he had a literary influence.

> I have never read *Ulysses* all the way through. In truth, all I did was peruse it. I haven't even read all of Molly Bloom's monologue. But what I saw in the book was the immense freedom,

which was very stimulating, very liberating to me. I learned that there was no need to tell the story with just one technical device. [Interview with Ronald Christ, *Partisan Review* 44 (1977)].

Puig's own telling of how he became a novelist can lead to a suggestion that everything happened by default, that he had no aesthetic control over material that, in fact, simply wrote itself. But such a conclusion annoys him, as it annoyed Richardson. Richardson was at some pains to describe the artistic use he made of his materials, the indirect way he revealed the psychology of his characters, the suspense he created by having his characters writing "to the moment," when they themselves did not know the outcome. Puig too insists on his aesthetic control.

> To live in terms of beauty, that's what I wanted. What helped me in literature was that I could put both things together—reality and beauty. If not in life, at least in literature. For myself at least, my books are always investigations, researches, certain ways of looking at problems that are mine, and not only mine, I hope. That research, however, has to be done with an esthetic rigor. The reality must be recreated and sustained at the same time and analyzed at the same time by a wish to create beauty. Beauty, in this case, is form.

> *Many readers seem to have missed the point of the form.*

> That happened with my first two novels. With the third I got a little more respect. People would say, oh, those books are just taped records of reality; you went out into the streets and recorded the voices of the people, that's all. That made me furious. Even if the characters' voices were the only material—and they were not—I was "editing" them just as other writers edit cultured, written language. This was a matter that I had made clear to myself from the first day that I started to write literature: the fact that I was dealing with reality wasn't enough; reality had to be told in terms of beauty, otherwise there was no satisfaction for me. (Christ)

His original priority had been beauty and escape from the sordidness of reality. Later he still wanted the beauty, but he wanted to create it out of reality, out of the sordidness, out of those things he had rejected. There was at least in part a kind of therapeutic reason.

> I always start with an obsession, a subject that haunts me, that I need to develop. Such subjects are problems of my own that I can't deal with consciously—personal problems. And I feel relieved if I develop the subject as a story. Once I have that subject, I look for the best shape to give it. (Christ)

The neurotic solution, which failed him, had been to escape from reality through the beauty of Hollywood movies. The healthy solution, which now sustains him, is to come to terms with reality by converting it into beauty. Here indeed we are close to the center of Puig's art, and close to unraveling the theme that runs through each of his works. All of Puig's characters, just as Puig was himself, are faced with the sterility, the cruel oppression, of

their lives. This life is the given; there is no escape from it (there is nowhere else to go), there is only the illusion of escape. Therefore, if their lives are not to be rendered meager and meaningless, the characters must redeem themselves, and they can only do so by rearranging the sordid and banal terms of their reality, converting them somehow into meaning and beauty. Puig has shown one way, converting the vulgarity of language, the sentimental banality and deceit of subliterature and other forms of popular culture, into his fine novels. At thirty he measured his life a failure, because he still had not learned to do this, so it is no wonder that thirty is often a critical age in the lives of his characters, and it is not surprising he feels compassion for those who fail. When they do succeed, however, it is not because they have spurned the materials they had to work with, but because they have somehow transcended them.

Often it is because they have become, as Puig became, *bricoleurs.* A number of commentators have made the connection between Puig's techniques and the idea of bricolage advanced by Claude Lévi-Strauss. Lévi-Strauss was distinguishing between primitive science and modern science. Whereas a modern scientist creates new tools and materials to engineer a solution to problems, a primitive scientist makes use of what is preexistent in his world to improvise solutions. Lévi-Strauss took the term *bricoleur* for that early scientist, because in modern French the term refers to a sort of odd-jobs man who can make or fix anything from whatever materials are at hand. The key point is that in solving problems he never uses new materials specifically acquired for the job, but limits himself to these things at hand. The materials at hand are the cast-off ready-mades of society, but through recombining them he transcends and redeems their cast-off quality. There is not much profit in trying to compare Puig to a primitive scientist, but the term *bricoleur,* once it is mentioned, is so exactly descriptive of Puig's methods that I want to retain it. Gladys, the artist in **The Buenos Aires Affair,** has a life that parallels Puig's in many ways. She too at thirty is at a stall, having failed in life, having taken all the wrong turns.

> That night I felt lonelier than ever. Imprisoned by despair I returned to the cottage and, almost crazed, I had an inspiration. I couldn't sleep. At five the dawn found me on the beach, for the first time picking up the debris that the surf had left on the sand. Flotsam, I only dared to love flotsam, anything else was too much to dare hope for. I returned home and began to talk . . . with a discarded slipper, with a bathing cap in shreds, with a torn piece of newspaper, and I started to touch them and to listen to their voices. That was my work of art, to bring together scorned objects to share with them a moment of life, or life itself.

Lévi-Strauss says, "Further, the 'bricoleur' also, and indeed principally, derives his poetry from the fact that he does not confine himself to accomplishment and execution: he 'speaks' not only *with* things, as we have already seen, but also through the medium of things: giving an account of his personality and life by the choices he makes between limited possibilities." Jorgelina Corbatta, in an interview with Puig [in *Revista Iberoamericana* 49 (April/Sept. 1983)], quotes the passage from *The Buenos Aires Affair* I have just given, concerning Gladys on the beach making her collages, and connects it to Lévi-Strauss's *bricolage.* Corbatta asks Puig, "What relationship exists between all this and your concept of art?" Puig replies, "I share totally Gladys's concept of art."

Who were the people whose voices Puig remembered, and what was the language they spoke and wrote in, and why were they so completely trapped by the shoddiest parts of their culture?

> It is necessary to remember that in Argentina, the great mass of the population was formed at the beginning of the century and was formed by immigrants (peasants who speak Galician, Catalan, Basque, Italian, Polish). These immigrants wanted to enter the middle class, to be small merchants, employees, and they couldn't pass any cultural heritage to their children, they couldn't even pass on a language. These children had to learn Spanish in the streets: everything in the house was "dubious," nothing in the house served because it was already superceded; so the models of language handy were those of the songs, those of the cheap press, those of the serials that circulated at that time, and were always a language "highly charged," an unreal language, high-sounding, too florid. The language of the tango, for instance. Why is the language of the tango always so truculent? Because it was directed at very simple people, who you have to impress with effects, and which, in some ways, is a language difficult to repeat because it is not real. The Argentine, then, the Argentine of the first generation and his children, sees that there is a language of the home that includes dialectal forms, and that is spontaneous, and another, a language of the street, that one uses when the time comes to express yourself: a declaration of love, writing a letter, discussing something at a bar. (Corbatta)

> As I have worked much with the language of my characters, I have had, of necessity to work with the songs of the period, with the radio of the period, big influences on the language of these characters. . . . This first generation had a little to invent a language; they had to seize whatever models were at hand. The models closest were the radio, the songs, the tango; in the forties the boleros from Mexico and Cuba; the subtitles of American films and very much the women's magazines, the fashion magazines. (Sosnowski)

Puig is in no way parodying or being satirical of these characters. If their language is inadequate, it is not through a fault in the characters, but because this is the language the culture has given them to live their lives in, to express their deepest feelings in, to have their thoughts and dreams in. (pp. 6-13)

> I hate the word "parody"; I think it is misleading. I'm often embarrassed when someone says to me: "You mock the way poor people speak." That isn't my intention, and I'm sorry if it comes out that way. The point is that the ordinary speech of these people is already a parody. All I do is record their imitation. This is why I think the word "parody" may lead people to the wrong conclusion. [*Translation* 2 (1974)]

Perhaps it is for this reason that Puig, in many statements, has denied satiric or parodic intent of any kind. But the truth is that his attitude toward his materials is shifting and complex. In Juan Carlos's obituary notice in *Heartbreak Tango,* or in the opening passages of *The Buenos Aires Affair* or *Pubis Angelical,* Puig is clearly having fun parodying subliterary language. When he casts his novels in the form of serials or detective thrillers he claims that he means to be redeeming these useful forms for literature, but in fact he has altered the forms so greatly for his purposes that the real audience for those forms would put down his novels in puzzlement after the first few pages.

The form of popular culture with the most far-reaching effects on Puig himself, of course, is the Hollywood movie. . . . [Movies are important] as materials in his novels, as influences on the lives of his characters, providing them not only a language but also a mode of living, a mark to aspire for, a pattern for values, a metaphor, however unreliable, for life. But in less overt ways movies provide formal patterns for Puig's writing and structuring. His professional training, after all, is in the movies.

> I don't have obvious literary models, because, I think, there are no great literary influences in my life. This space is filled by the influence of the movies. I believe that if someone took the trouble he might find influences of Lubitsch in certain of my structures, of Von Sternberg in this love of certain atmospheres. A lot of Hitchcock. . . . (Corbatta)

> I believe there are affinities with Von Sternberg, with *Dishonored* by Von Sternberg. It is a picture that, when I see it—ay! how close he is to what I am doing! (Corbatta)

When Puig was asked if he kept his reader in mind when he was writing, he said:

> I always have the readers before me. I write for a reader with my limitations. A reader with certain difficulties concentrating on reading, which, in my case, proceeds from my formation as a watcher of movies. Therefore I try not to ask for special strengths of attention on the part of the reader.

> *JC:* But don't you think these switches, these parallel stories or the same story told on different levels, causes . . . ?

> *MP:* It causes reflection, that is another kind of mental operation. For me what is hardest is to follow a story that has no determined thread. . . . I don't mean I am thinking of a stupid reader but of a reader with a certain need for speed. I believe that the movies are this, before all, that they have provoked in us a need for speed. (Corbatta)

> I wouldn't say I was mad about the movies of today. The movies of today are not much interested in "story telling" . . . and this is the part that's interesting, the art of narration. This is

what the movies of today don't do, and the movies of the thirties did do. (Sosnowski)

Indeed, though he came at it in his own way, his attitude and his practice are not dissimilar to many modern innovative writers—Borges, Hawkes, Kosinski, to name a few—who exploit the techniques and materials of subliterary genres—detective fiction, pornography, spy thrillers, and so on. These writers both parody and profit by the sensational materials and strong plotting of such forms, just as the reader in part keeps an amused ironic detachment and in part enjoys the sex and violence on the lowest level. What is special about Puig is that the popular culture gives him not only forms and materials to utilize but also his themes. One theme, developing more and more clearly as Puig continues writing and thinking, is first how this secondhand culture strangles and destroys his characters and finally how that culture is manipulated by a self-serving state to hold its citizens in thrall. The popular culture is a sinister net, and it is frightening how few of his characters slip through it, even momentarily, and horrifying how the culture seeks to take revenge on them when they do.

Yet some few can wrest, even out of the destructive materials themselves, a few moments of salvation. It will be my theme in this book to see how Puig as novelist, and his characters as creators of their own lives, take the degraded, secondhand, ready-made materials of their world (*bricoleurs* by necessity) and try to create with them moments of beauty. The stakes are mortal, the success rate is low. But—so miraculous is the human spirit—it is higher than a first reading of the novels might suggest. (pp. 13-15)

> Norman Lavers, *"Art Out of Scorned Objects,"* in his *Pop Culture into Art: The Novels of Manuel Puig, University of Missouri Press, 1988, pp. 1-15.*

Manuel Puig   (Interview with Kathleen Wheaton)

[Wheaton]: *What is the difference between movie and book material?*

[Puig]: In my experience, an epic story translates very well into film. Realistic novels—the kind made up of small details and constructed using a certain analytical approach—don't make good films. Films are synthesis. Everyday grayness, everyday realism is especially tough to translate to the screen. I remember discussing this once with a filmmaker, who said, "Yes, but look at the realistic films the Italians made, such as De Sica's *Umberto D."* I disagreed. There's nothing of everyday grayness in *Umberto D*—it's about suicide, about deciding whether to kill yourself or not. It's an epic film *disguised* as an everyday realistic one. What I like to do in my novels is to show the complexity of everyday life; the subtexture of social tensions and the pressures behind each little act of ours. That's very difficult to put into film. I feel much more comfortable with films dealing with allegorical, larger-than-life characters and stylized situations.

Is that why you liked American films of the 1940s?

Sure. They were dreams, totally stylized—the perfect stuff

of films because dreams allow you the possibility of a synthetic approach.

Have you ever found that the dialogue of those 1940s films helped with fictional dialogue?

I learned certain rules of story-telling from the films of that time. Mainly how to distribute the intrigue. But what interests me more about those films is examining the effect they had on people.

On the people you grew up with?

Well, yes—on my characters. My characters have all been affected by those cinematic dreams. In those days, movies were very important to people. They were their Mount Olympus. The stars were deities.

Obviously you were intrigued by movies as a child. What about books?

One of the very first books I read was André Gide's *Pastoral Symphony.* In 1947 he won the Nobel Prize. At the same time a film had been made of the novel, so he had come into the territory of my immediate interest, which was, of course, film. I read the novel and was immensely impressed. Soon after, I remember being impressed by Faulkner's *The Wild Palms.* Such contrasting authors—Gide all measure and economy, and Faulkner sprawling all over the place.

Did you read The Wild Palms in English?

No, I read Borges's Spanish translation, which is a beautiful work. I read Faulkner's other books in English. I never went back to *The Wild Palms,* but for me it's always an example of intuitive writing.

So a writer's imagination is either calculated or intuitive?

It goes from one extreme to the other. In between you have all these shadings. I have trouble reading fiction these days. So I've lost that immense realm of pleasure. Thank God I still enjoy movies and plays.

You mean you don't read any fiction now?

Writing has spoiled the pleasure of reading for me, because I can't read innocently. If you are an innocent reader, you accept the fantasy of others; you accept their style. These days another writer's problems of style immediately recall my own stylistic problems. If I read fiction, I'm working; I'm not relaxing. My only sector of interest now is biographies. Those I read with great relish, because the facts are real and there is no pretense of style.

Even your later novels are concerned with 1940s films. Do you ever go to contemporary movies?

Rarely. I simply got tired of walking out in the middle. It's a pity, because I know I may be missing some good things, but the price of viewing hours and hours of trash is too high. Of course, I receive films from all over the world—very strange films from Barcelona, Rome, Los Angeles, London. I barely have time to see *them.* (pp. 131-33)

Do you find it easy to adapt yourself to different cultures?

I learn languages easily, except German. My experience in Rome, New York, and Mexico was that you have to either integrate yourself or leave. For me there's always this desire to belong and become part of the country. Here in Brazil I had a very bad experience with the literary establishment and at the same time a very positive one on the human side.

What was the bad experience?

I published a book with a Brazilian setting called ***Blood of Requited Love;*** the literary establishment here decided to ignore it, as if it hadn't even been published.

Wasn't the Josemar character in the novel a carpenter who worked on your house?

There are very few words in the book that are not his. I simply edited our conversations. Mainly my job was to bring all the material out of him, put him in a mood to talk and express himself.

Did he ever read the book?

He barely reads. It was odd because he received a huge amount of money. He made more money on that book than I did. I thought it was going to be a big success—here, especially—so we made a fifty-fifty arrangement. But then he preferred to get a fixed amount and with that he bought himself a new house. It was ironic, because his tale was about the loss of a house; by telling it he got a new and better house. I felt very good about all this. Not only had I written a new novel, but I had helped someone. I expected gratitude, at least to inspire a warm feeling. But it wasn't the case.

He felt burdened by your help?

He tried to blackmail me. After the book was published, he said he'd had threats against his life and had had to give people money. I reminded him of the contract, which said that he was responsible for any references made to living persons. I had changed the names of the people and places, there was no publicity about his identity. That was enough to dissuade him. What he'd said was all lies. If it had been true, he would have come to me in despair. Thank God I had a very good contract. I was really appalled. The fact of telling me the story, of unburdening himself, was already positive for him. What's more, I paid him per hour while he was talking.

The reverse of psychoanalysis.

Yes. And on top of it all he got a house, which was so symbolic of all he had lost. The book is really about the loss of a father, so similar to my own ***Betrayed by Rita Hayworth.*** I felt terribly identified with him. I always write about people who somehow reflect my problems. In general they are similar to me, though I make many changes. In this case, the guy was Brazilian, not Argentine. He was thirty, not fifty. He was extremely strong and handsome; I am not. He has fantastic health, which I don't have. He was illiterate; I was supposed to be a writer. He doesn't question machismo, while machismo for me is the basic question of my existence. What we shared was this father problem—a ghost of a father. By the end there was such a brotherhood between us. It came to nothing as far as human relations go, but I'm very glad it happened because

the novel has a certain interest; and I'm glad because I helped him.

Was the process of writing that novel different from that of your other books?

Very much so. I'd never worked with a tape recorder. With ***Eternal Curse on the Reader of These Pages*** there was also a real character present, but the writing process was different. I created a character myself—the old man Ramirez—so I could establish a dialogue with him. I didn't have much trouble feeling and imagining myself as Ramirez, because in 1978 and 1979, when I was working on the book, I was going through a very dark period.

So you wrote the novel from the dialogue that was going on between the two of you as one between Ramirez and this other person.

We practically wrote it together. He was beside me the whole time; it was a sort of psychodrama typed as it happened.

Using this extraordinary method, how do you control your material?

If you know a character—as much as it's possible to know another—and you put that person into a certain circumstance, you should be able to predict the reaction, especially the verbal reaction.

Doesn't the book take all sorts of unexpected turns?

It should be the opposite. It should be a situation where, well, I know all about them and I can probably guess what their reactions would be in a given situation. So it's just a matter of watching. But of course, they are delicate relationships. You cannot impose anything on characters. They help you, they give you all, but you have to respect them.

So you get to know your characters and then turn them loose.

You should be able to put a character in a situation that never happened in real life and predict what that character would have done or said.

What if a person you're interviewing says or does something different from what you had in mind?

Both in ***Blood of Requited Love*** and ***Eternal Curse on the Reader of These Pages*** I didn't have anything that the characters hadn't said. Of course, I did my own weaving. The yarn is presented by the characters and I work with that.

What most writers like about fiction is the idea of making up characters and having them do whatever they want.

Oh, no, no, no, no. I try to respect my characters. If you know them well, you won't make them do any nonsense.

If you're reproducing real conversation verbatim, what is the difference between this kind of fiction and . . . well, documenting?

My characters' ways of thinking and talking have their musical and pictorial qualities. I take these qualities and I do my own embroidery. In aesthetic terms, a writer can use any method he wants. What counts, and what makes it fiction, is how it's done. The writer who uses the third person in his fiction is using an orthodox, established method or code. I am interested in the individual kinds of speech, however flawed and limited, of real people. That may limit me, but the use the writer makes of whatever method is limited only by his talent.

What kind of characters do you pick as these "collaborators"?

I can only tell a story about a character who reflects my most burning problems. I believe in characters as vehicles of exposition. Their voices are full of hidden clues, and I like to listen to them. That's why I work so much with dialogue. What they *don't* say sometimes expresses more than what they *do* say. Mine is not the classic third-person voice.

Obviously you have to edit them.

In my novels I try to reproduce everyday language. Of course, there's a certain concern about length. You can't have people expounding on themselves forever in novels the way they do in real life.

Is it easier to write in the first person?

Yes. When I deal with first-person dialogue and I know the character well, it's just a matter of lending an ear.

You prefer not to have the novelist in the novel?

I'm not interested in listening to my voice that much. I have no ego.

But the voice of Manuel Puig is always there.

My view of things comes out in the long run, let's hope. I remember at the beginning of my career a very nasty established writer said, "Oh, I know how Manuel Puig's characters talk but how does *he* talk? He doesn't have a persona." I thought the world of movies and acting provided the pure height of vanity, but I was mistaken.

There's a lot of jealousy among writers.

They're supposed to be people with more insight and distance, but it's not always the case.

In some of your novels, particularly **The Buenos Aires Affair,** *it seems as though people live in an artistic world because they can't live in the day-to-day world. Do you ever yearn for a life that has nothing to do with art?*

It's not a solution. With that book I meant to suggest there are other sources of energy and strength. But a life totally devoid of the imagination would be very boring.

Do you think fiction can show people how to live?

Direct experience is best, but then you'd need a thousand lifetimes. Books have that wonderful quality of showing you other lives. They can be a great nourishment.

What are the easiest and hardest parts of writing for you?

The beginning is exciting because I get an idea. Then I start looking for the shape to use to present it. The content always comes from the form, in my case. I think it should be like that, but I know other writers work differently.

Then comes the critical moment, when I look for the voices of the narrators. Sometimes it's easy; sometimes not. If I find the narrator quickly, that's great, but it doesn't always happen that way. I have to find a voice that convinces me, and that's very difficult. Only when I believe in the narrator does it fall into place. Actually, the hardest part of writing for me is the typing and tidying things up. I don't dare try a word processor. I find it useful to type the different drafts—going from the rough draft to the second. As you're typing a clean copy you make decisions. I have been writing novels for almost thirty years, and I'm used to a certain technique of polishing. I've been told, "Try that machine, that processor, you'll love it." But not yet. Maybe next time. I like to keep track of the first draft. I like to see the scratching in ink. I do a lot of scratching.

Are your revisions very radical?

It depends. **Kiss of the Spider Woman** had almost no corrections. I wrote that novel with the greatest ease. **The Buenos Aires Affair** and **Pubis Angelical** were the toughest, because there were many changes in narrators. The last one, **Cae la noche tropical,** came out quite easily.

How much of the book do you have in mind before you start?

Most of it. But with this last novel, something very peculiar happened. I was shaping it, working on a real character—Ferreira in the book—but then he just disappeared. I couldn't get all the information I needed from him. So somehow another interesting person—actually someone I was considering for another story—came into the picture. I thought perhaps I could shift him into this novel. Absolutely accidental. But then *he* disappeared. It was very, very strange. Both were people in the neighborhood whom I could talk to and both of them disappeared. But that gave the final shape to the novel. The fact that they would disappear was essential. It was their nature. At a certain point they couldn't take the responsibility and they would leave. So it was reality, absolutely dictating the course of the novel. Nothing like that had ever happened to me before. But it wasn't a problem; it turned out to be an advantage.

Do you think that people are determined by their circumstances?

This is the awful thing: we are all *so* determined by our culture. Mainly because we learn to play roles. For me it starts with the very unnatural and hideous sexual roles. I think that sex is totally banal, devoid of any moral meaning or weight. It's just fun and games, innocence itself. But at a certain point somebody decided that sex has a moral weight. A patriarch invented the concept of sexual sin to distinguish between the saintly woman at home and the prostitute on the street.

And men have a very different morality applied to them?

Men are subject to no morality! A man full of sexual energy is a stallion, a model of health. A woman with strong sexual needs, up to a certain time ago, was considered a victim of her glands. She was not trusted, because it was thought that if she had sex so easily there must be something wrong with her, physically and mentally. The minute sex becomes of moral importance, horrible problems are created needlessly. The principle of sex is pleasure, that's all. I consider sex to be an act of the vegetative life, vegetative in the sense of eating and sleeping. Sex is as important as eating or sleeping but as devoid of moral meaning.

At the end of **Pubis Angelical,** *when Ana realizes she's sexless, like an angel, she begins thinking about the people whom she loves. It seems like you're saying that once people get over sex they can begin to love each other.*

Yes, once that problem is settled—or you don't imagine it as a problem. Once you've eliminated sex as a means of superiority or inferiority, sex is of no meaning. (pp. 134-43)

In **The Kiss of the Spider Woman,** *there is a little utopia created under dire circumstances in the prison cell. Did you feel that Molina and Valentin transcended their traditional roles?*

It happens. I'm not just fantasizing; what I know comes from experience.

If you weren't a writer, could you imagine yourself in another occupation?

Something I'd enjoy? I'd like to sing, but I have no voice. Or maybe play an instrument. I'd enjoy anything creative. I wasn't bad at drawing, but I never developed it.

Why did you become a writer? Do you feel it's something you need to do?

For me it was a blessing. At first, I thought films were my thing, but I didn't like the work on the set and collaborating with lots of people. So I decided to write film scripts. I never sold them; they were training, pre-literary practice. Later when I finally started writing novels I found them to be the great solution—because what I'd wanted to do all along was to tell stories. With images, or with words, it didn't matter; I like to recreate reality in order to understand it better. But writing was something I could do on my own. I could do all the revisions I wanted and without the pressures of budgets. I could make a living out of it, and also it was an enjoyable activity. Of course, there are the secondary aspects which are a little bothersome.

Like being interviewed?

Well, more or less. Even worse is the accounting, dealing with the publishers, all that. But what's really a bore and downright unpleasant is the relationship with the critics. They can be very irresponsible people. There are exceptions, but few. I've been rescued in a way by the colleges. There you find a different attitude. But it comes much later; when you've just published a book, what you feel immediately is the contact with the press.

Universities don't pick up books for several years.

No, and their reaction doesn't have much impact. But it's wonderful to know that somebody accepts your work. The reviewers from newspapers and magazines just want to amuse the person who buys the paper. They do it at the expense of the authors. Many, many times it's dishonest

as well, because the critics belong to groups that don't like you—it's a horror. I'm published in twenty-four different languages, so I know critics. In Spanish I have to deal with the attitudes of the Mexicans, of the Argentines, of the Chileans. Each Spanish-speaking country has a special syndrome. I don't find it stimulating at all.

Do you worry much about this?

Well, critics have power, unfortunately. With time the book will outlive anything. But they have the power to retard it a lot. I've had a very bad relationship with the critics. I don't have to say thank you to them.

Do you think that writing is something that can be taught?

No, but you can discuss it. What I did when I taught at City College and at Columbia University was to discuss my own experiences and then suggest exercises. I don't like to go into a classroom and sit and listen to somebody reading.

Did teaching help your writing at all?

It always does, because you're always discussing the questions that plague you. (pp. 144-46)

Do you have a reader in mind when you write?

I could say that each novel has been written for somebody, to convince somebody in particular. It's almost an act of seduction. If not seduction, at least an attempt at explaining something to somebody.

Tell me about your schedule as a writer. Do you write every day?

I adore routine. I cannot work away from it. It has to be the same thing every day. It takes a long time for me to wake up, so in the morning I write letters, revise translations—things that don't demand too much. At noon, I go to the beach and swim for twenty minutes. I come back, eat, and take a nap. Without that nap there is no possibility of creation. From four to eight I really work. Then I have dinner and that's it. I cannot work after eating. I stop and see something on the video machine. I hate to interrupt this for weekends. Then it's very hard to go back to work.

You can't pretend that the weekends are weekdays?

Friends take me out of my routine.

Which of your novels do you like best?

It's difficult to say. There isn't one I dislike more than the others. They all have their problems, but I must admit if I published them it's because I believe that there's something worthwhile in them. That I cannot hide from you. (p. 147)

Manuel Puig and Kathleen Wheaton, in an interview in The Paris Review, *Vol. 31, No. 113, Winter, 1989, pp. 129-47.*

John T. McQuiston

Manuel Puig, the Argentine novelist whose work *The Kiss of the Spider Woman* was made into an award-winning film, died on Sunday in Cuernavaca, Mexico. He was 57 years old. . . .

Mr. Puig was an experimental realist who searched for what he called "a new form of popular literature."

Literary critics found Mr. Puig, like William Faulkner, a master of occluded narrative. He liked to recount the ordinary melodramas of everyday life in novel ways. And he would often let his characters tell their own stories without comment, in a cinematic style.

The Hollywood films of the 1930's and 40's animated and empowered Mr. Puig's entire literary career. In his novels, he repeatedly fused details of ordinary lives with vivid images from films, both actual and imagined.

In an interview in 1985, Mr. Puig recalled how movies had a liberating influence on his life. He observed that "not everybody is born in a big country with access to other forms of culture, education."

"There are many people who live in the sticks and have no means," he said. "They are soaking in machismo, in a hostile environment. What do they do? They have no choice.

"The movies provided them, as they did me, an alternative. They help you to not go crazy. You see another way of life. It doesn't matter that the way of life shown by Hollywood was phony. It helped you hope."

His first novel, *Betrayed by Rita Hayworth,* published in 1971 by E. P. Dutton, was a critical success. It evoked the drama, pathos and humor of moviegoing as a way of life in the Argentine provinces.

The book was somewhat biographical, in that it was essentially a story as told by Toto, a boy born in 1932 in the bleakest flatland pampas of the Argentine.

Mr. Puig was himself born in 1932 in the small town of Vallegas, on the arid pampas far from Buenos Aires.

His mother was a confirmed moviegoer and introduced Manuel to this pastime when he was 3 years old. The first film he remembered was *The Bride of Frankenstein,* which he said he expected to haunt him as long as he lived.

In 1946, he went to Buenos Aires to attend an American boarding school. Four years later, he enrolled at the University of Buenos Aires, where he studied philosophy.

He also studied English, French and Italian, for these were the languages spoken in the films he saw. At the age of 23 he traveled to Rome where he studied at an experimental film school, and worked on the special effects of the David O. Selznick film *A Farewell to Arms.*

Five years later, he returned to Argentina and started to write *Betrayed by Rita Hayworth.* It was panned by Argentine critics and had problems with censorship, but received favorable reviews in France and the United States.

His second novel, *Heartbreak Tango: A Serial,* published by Dutton in 1973, conveys the sense of growing old pathetically and bitterly as the romantic illusions of youth fade.

That same year, Juan Perón returned to power in Argentina and Mr. Puig went into self-imposed exile, with stays in Mexico, Brazil and the United States.

Among his other novels were *The Blood of Requited Love, The Buenos Aires Affair* and *Eternal Curse on the Reader of These Pages.*

The Kiss of the Spider Woman, published by Alfred A. Knopf in 1979, was made into a film in 1985 starring William Hurt, whose performance won him an Academy Award, and Raul Julia. The novel is a running dialogue between two men in an Argentine prison cell, a Marxist student (Mr. Julia) and an apolitical homosexual (the role played by Mr. Hurt) who recounted plots of old romantic movies.

The novel was also made into a musical written by Terrence McNally, with a score by John Kander and Fred Ebb, and directed by Harold Prince, which had a limited run this summer as part of the New Musicals series in Purchase, N.Y.

Mr. Puig had lived in Cuernavaca, 50 miles south of Mexico City, since last October. He is to be buried in a family plot in La Plata, Argentina.

He is survived by his mother, Maria Elena de Puig, a brother, Carlos Puig, and two sons, [Javier] Labrada and Agustin García Gil, all of Cuernavaca.

John T. McQuiston, in an obituary in The New York Times, *July 24, 1990, p. B15.*

The Chicago Sun-Times

Argentine writer Manuel Puig, who gained international fame for his novel *Kiss of the Spider Woman,* died of a heart attack Sunday. He was 57.

Mr. Puig, who was suffering complications from gallbladder surgery, had earned a reputation as a leading member of the younger generation of Latin American writers for his novels written in a cinematic, non-narrative style.

His works often explored the relationships between his characters' impoverished lives and their rich, if unfulfilled, fantasies.

Mr. Puig wrote several books, and some were made into successful movies. Among his novels are *Betrayed by Rita Hayworth, Eternal Curse on the Reader of These Pages* and *Heartbreak Tango.*

Brazilian filmmaker Hector Babenco's 1985 film version of *Kiss of the Spider Woman* starring William Hurt and Raul Julia brought the novelist a larger international audience. Hurt won an Academy Award for that performance.

The novel *Kiss of the Spider Woman* was set in a bleak Argentine prison cell shared by a Marxist guerrilla and a homosexual.

Mr. Puig also wrote numerous plays and movie scripts over the past 30 years.

He was born in the small town of General Villegas, on the arid pampas of Argentina.

As a youth, he spent much of his free time in the local movie theater watching popular American and Argentinian films that influenced his later work.

In 1946, he went to Buenos Aires to attend an American boarding school. Four years later, he enrolled at the University of Buenos Aires, where he studied philosophy.

After leaving the university, Mr. Puig sought to launch a career in the film industry and began to write screenplays.

One such screenplay developed into the autobiographical novel, *Betrayed by Rita Hayworth.*

It was panned by Argentine critics but received more favorable reviews in France and the U.S.

With the return of Juan Peron to power in Argentina in 1973, Mr. Puig felt increasingly alienated from his country. He went into self-imposed exile, eventually settling in Mexico, where he wrote *Kiss of the Spider Woman.*

He moved to New York in 1976, partly because of a heart condition, and later settled in Rio de Janeiro.

When he died, Mr. Puig had just finished revising the English translation by Susan Jill Levine of his most recent book, *A Tropical Nightfall,* his son, Javier Labrada said in an interview in Mexico.

Mr. Puig is survived by his mother, Maria Elena de Puig; a brother Carlos Puig; Labrada and another son, Agustin Garcia Gil, all living in Cuernavaca.

Mr. Puig had lived in Cuernavaca, 50 miles south of Mexico City, since October.

He will be buried in a family plot in La Plata, Argentina, Labrada said.

> *An obituary in* The Chicago Sun-Times, *July 23, 1990.*

The Times, LONDON

Although known by the Anglo-Saxon media exclusively for his part as the author of the original of the 1985 Hector Babenco film—and *Kiss of the Spider Woman* was his most powerful, if possibly not quite his best, work—Manuel Puig had been a best-selling author in Argentina in the 1960s and 1970s and was already known to critics outside Latin America. Puig indeed played an important role expanding the narrative techniques of the modern Latin American novel.

Born in the culturally remote small town of General Villegas situated in the immense province of Buenos Aires, Puig's first novel, an immediate critical success, was *La traición de Rita Hayworth* (1968) which was translated in the United States by S. J. Levine as *Betrayed by Rita Hayworth* (1971). This in certain ways reflects Puig's own adolescence, although it cannot be taken as entirely autobiographical. Toto, a boy, views life exclusively from the framework of Hollywood films. So, too, as he himself said, did Puig. Toto's alienated family, an immigrant one, is viewed by him entirely through an interior monologue amalgamating all the films he has seen. The banal mental

processes of other characters are similarly presented. The Argentinian provincial middle-class, with its day-to-day language based on films, TV and radio soap opera, women's magazines, advertisements and the like is exposed as ersatz. But a sense of the real, *"gaucho"* tradition of the country of the pampas is conveyed, thus highlighting, with sadness as well as irony, the emptiness and rootlessness of an immigrant culture.

Although he gained in power, it is possible that Puig never really surpassed this work, although it would not have been suitable for filming—for obvious enough reasons. The strong emotional tie that Toto feels to this sort of material is the same one as Puig himself felt: he hated, criticised and satirised it, but he was also its victim.

The satirical edge of Puig's later fiction became blunter as he concentrated on areas of sexuality which involved his own personality: self-tormenting sexual fantasy, homosexuality and auto-eroticism. It is true that *The Buenos Aires Affair* (so titled, 1973), a bizarre study of an art critic (Leo) and a sculptor (Gladys), in the form of a detective story, does implicitly question the ideal of loveless sex (and the values of the film world). But there were many readers for whom the whole did not ring altogether true and who saw Puig's book as faintly meretricious in its blend of every fashionable modernist technique (such as interior monologue, lists of objects, footnotes) and, as well, in its real theme of people driven to insanity by their sexual obsessions.

But *Boquitas pintadas,* published in 1969, had been a cult best-seller in Argentina and elsewhere in Latin America. Described by one critic as "an effort at 'popular literature'," this is divided into red and other-coloured "painted" sections. It has been called "minimalist" and "toneless", and not all its readers may have got through it. But parts of it, especially the ironic ones satirising Argentinian vulgarity, as expressed in the words of pop songs and tangos, are undoubtedly pointed and effective.

It was with *El beso de la mujer araña* (*Kiss of the Spider Woman*), first published in 1976, that Puig found international success. This is also his most fully realised imaginative work, and it led to a superb film, which starred William Hurt and Raul Julia. Its plot, concerning sexual fantasy, treachery and final sacrificial loyalty to an ideal, has its roots less in overtly modernist works than in Graham Greene, François Mauriac and other novelists often grouped as "Catholic", and in the spy thriller.

Puig had always wanted to achieve success in the cinema—specifically as a director, despite his satirical view of its function. But this eluded him. He had studied photography in Rome; then, when he went to New York as an employee of Air France, he wrote what he described as many poor film scripts. He enjoyed his notoriety as the originator of *Kiss of the Spider Woman* and this enabled him to enter more fully into his own character as a happily overt homosexual: "I love boys", he told an American friend, "and New York is my Mecca!" Sadly, all the hard work he put into a projected musical version of the *Kiss* was wasted since it never opened on Broadway as had been planned. He is survived by his two sons.

An obituary in The Times, *London, July 26, 1990, p. 2C.*

Américas

A letter from Manuel Puig lies on my desk, unanswered. I meant to write to him, of course. It was just one of those things I didn't quite get around to doing. All I needed was a day or two more, but before I found time, Argentine author Manuel Puig had died in Mexico, at age 58, of complications from an operation.

To me, that letter symbolizes all the business that was left unfinished by Puig's untimely death. One of the most energetic, promising novelists and playwrights of the postboom generation, Puig was in the midst of several projects when he died. One was a production of his play *El misterio del ramo de rosas* (*The Mystery of the Bouquet of Roses*), planned for next April in Spain. Another was a novel, which he had already outlined, that would have taken place in a town in the Pampa during the 40s. Although Puig said that he would not be the protagonist of his new book, he himself was born in the town of General Villegas, in the Province of Buenos Aires, and spent his early years on the Pampa. In the work he was projecting, he intended to explore the repression inflicted by society on the individual and also the constraints the individual places on himself.

Puig's first love was film, and as a young man he studied directing at the Centro Sperimentale di Cinematografia in Rome. According to him, he was too timid and unsure of himself to give orders, and soon turned to writing. His first novel, *La traición de Rita Hayworth* (*Betrayed by Rita Hayworth*), published in 1968, was a largely autobiographical account of growing up in a small town on the Pampa, where the only diversion was the movies. In this book Puig explores the pressures on a young boy who is too sensitive and unathletic to fit into the macho mold imposed by his father and other men. His next novel, *Boquitas pintadas* (*Heartbreak Tango*) (1969), on which a film was based, is a kind of detective story inspired by the newspaper serials that were once popular in Latin America and elsewhere. Like Puig's first novel, *Boquitas pintadas* exposes the boredom, pettiness, and hypocrisy of small-town life and examines the influence of popular culture—movies, magazines, tangos—on the people. Perhaps his best-known novel is *El beso de la mujer araña* (*Kiss of the Spider Woman*) (1977), which also became a movie. It revolves around two prison inmates, one of whom is a homosexual and the other, a political activist. Over a period of time a strong attachment develops between them, and both discover facets of their personalities that had previously been hidden.

Because of Puig's criticism of government repression in *The Buenos Aires Affair* (1973), the author was forced to leave Argentina. He lived in Berlin, Mexico, New York, and Rio. Puig situated novels in nearly all of these cities, and even wrote in foreign languages. *Pubis angelical* (1979) takes place in Mexico; *Maldición eterna a quien lea estas páginas* (*Eternal Curse on the Reader of These Pages*) (1980) takes place in New York and was written in English; *Sangre de amor correspondido* (*Blood of Requited Love*) takes place in Brazil and was written in Portuguese. Adapting to new circumstances was a challenge Puig was always ready to meet.

Manuel Puig made a major contribution to Latin American fiction by breaking down barriers. He dealt with subjects—homosexuality, machismo, pressures on children, female sexuality—that were previously taboo. He exposed the loneliness and alienation of modern men and women. He depicted homosexuals and others who live on the margins of society with humor and tenderness. Although he often said that he had no formal training in literature and did not consider himself to be a stylist, his novels were innovative both technically and structurally.

But Manuel Puig was not only a fine writer. He was also a kind, gentle, compassionate man and a good friend. Who knows what further contributions he might have made. Who knows how much business he left unfinished. (pp. 62-3)

"Goodbye to Manuel Puig: Unfinished Business," in Américas, *Vol. 42, No. 5, 1990, pp. 62-3.*

Patrick White

May 28, 1912—September 30, 1990

(Full name Patrick Victor Martindale White) English-born Australian novelist, playwright, memoirist, short story writer, and poet.

Widely considered Australia's foremost fiction writer, White was awarded the Nobel Prize for Literature in 1973 for, in the words of the Nobel Academy, "an authentic voice that carries across the world." White's novels are stylistically complex explorations of isolation, often featuring inarticulate and abnormal characters. His unflattering portrayal of Australian society together with the intricacy of his narrative style denied him the stature within Australia that he enjoyed elsewhere. White is best known as the author of such novels as *The Eye of the Storm, Voss, The Aunt's Story, The Tree of Man,* and *The Solid Mandala.*

For an overview of White's life and work, see *CLC,* Vols. 3, 4, 5, 7, 9, 18, and *Contemporary Authors,* Vols. 81-84.

OBITUARIES

Tracy Wood

Nobel Prize-winning author Patrick White, whose complex novels made him among the best known writers about his Australian homeland, died Sunday after a lengthy illness. He was 78.

No cause of death was given.

A private, retiring man most of his life, White in recent years began boldly speaking out on Australian political issues, denouncing what he perceived as dishonesty in some areas of government, urging Australia to better itself and raising the alarms against pollution, consumerism, the plight of the aborigines and other topics.

"As a homosexual I have always known what it is to be an outsider," he said earlier this year in championing one political cause. "It has given me added insight into the plight of the immigrant. . . ."

As novelist, poet and playwright, White repeatedly returned to the theme of man's isolation, an alienation he described in his 1982 autobiography, *Flaws in the Glass.*

In 1973 he was awarded the Nobel Prize for literature for introducing "a new continent" to literary art. A history of asthma forced White to send a substitute to accept the award for the novel, *Eye of the Storm,* a portrait of the final days of an elderly woman whose greedy relatives

await her demise. The work also explored Australians' attitudes toward their European cultural roots.

Born on May 28, 1912, in London, Patrick Victor Martindale White spent his childhood in Australia. In his early teens, he was sent to public schools in England where, he said, he felt isolated and, with the acquisition of a British accent, rejected by Australians. White also described in his biography feelings that he had disappointed his parents, who would have been happier if he had been a lawyer or had followed in his father's footsteps. His father was a sheep rancher.

Educated at King's College, Cambridge, White served as an intelligence officer in the Royal Air Force during World War II.

He credited Manoly Lascaris, his companion of more than 40 years, as "this small Greek of immense moral strength, who became the central mandala in my life's hitherto messy design."

White's first novel, *Happy Valley*, published in 1939, was awarded the Australian Literary Society Gold Medal, as was *The Tree of Man*, published in 1955.

Considered one of Australia's leading authors, his works were required reading in many high schools and universities.

Essayist Margaret B. Lewis, in the 1986 reference work, *Contemporary Novelists*, described White as "a writer who makes serious demands of his readers, straining prose to the utmost poetic limits, putting severe pressure on syntax and vocabulary and stretching credence to an unusual degree in his search for the transcendent in the lives of his idiosyncratic characters."

> *Tracy Wood, in an obituary in* Los Angeles Times, *October 1, 1990.*

New York Times

The novelist Patrick White who won the Nobel Prize in Literature in 1973 as an authentic voice of Australia, died today at his home here. He was 78 years old and had been ill for several weeks.

Although Mr. White won international acclaim, his portrait of Australia was harsh and unflattering and little loved by many of his countrymen.

The author received the Nobel Prize from the Swedish Academy for his 1973 novel *The Eye of the Storm* (published in the United States by Penguin, as were most of his other major works). In awarding the prize, the academy said he had wrestled with the English language to take it almost beyond the limits of its expressive power. It added that he had given Australia "an authentic voice that carries across the world."

But Mr. White, whose best-known novels include *Voss, The Aunt's Story* and *The Tree of Man*, said of the Nobel Prize in 1988: "I really was rather horrified. I would have liked to refuse it because of all the publicity it made in this childish country."

A tall and craggy man with deep-set dark eyes, he was a staunch left-winger who attacked the policies of his country governing aborigines and boycotted official celebrations in 1988 of 200 years of white settlement in Australia.

Although for many years he supported the Australian Labor Party, he fell out with Labor Prime Minister Bob Hawke in the 1980's and began voting Communist instead.

Mr. White's unflattering references to Australia did not increase his local popularity: he had also criticized "the march of material ugliness" here and had spoken of "the great Australian emptiness."

But he had his admirers outside Australia. The South African novelist Nadine Gordimer said, "There is no other contemporary writer in English who uses the language with such conventional mastery and demotic flair."

Mr. White's parents were wealthy farmers and he was born during one of their periodic trips to England, in Lon-don on May 28, 1912. He spent most of his boyhood in Australia, to which his great-grandfather had emigrated in 1826.

Mr. White worked on sheep stations before returning to Britain to study languages at Cambridge University and joined the Royal Air Force during World War II, serving as an intelligence officer in the Middle East.

After the war, he returned permanently to Australia. His first success, *Happy Valley*, was published in 1939 and won the Australian Literature Society's gold medal. It was followed by a second novel, *The Living and the Dead*, in 1941.

His third novel, *The Aunt's Story*, was published in 1946. But he remained little known until *The Tree of Man*, which brought him international recognition, appeared in 1955.

His other novels included *Riders in the Chariot* (1962), *The Solid Mandala* (1966), *The Vivisector* (1970), *The Cockatoos* (1974), *A Fringe of Leaves* (1976), *The Twyborn Affair* (1979) and *Memoirs of Many in One* (1986).

In 1976 he resigned as Companion of the Order of Australia, which he had been awarded the previous year.

Mr. White lived the last part of life in Centennial Park, Sydney, with Manoly Lascaris, his male companion for 46 years.

> *An obituary in* The New York Times, *October 1, 1990, p. B11.*

The Times, London

Patrick White was not the only indisputably major novelist to emerge from Australia this century. The great—and still underrated—trilogy, *The Fortunes of Richard Mahony* by Henry Handel Richardson, must come into any reckoning of Australia's contribution to the modern movement. But Patrick White did more than any other writer to put Australian literature on the international map. This has something to do, of course, with his Nobel prize, though that carried with it dangers in the Grand Old Man status it conferred on White. But, Nobel prize or no, he would in any case have warranted a place in the history of the novel for his visionary power and for taking risks, which few other writers dared to take, in order to give full rein to his imagination. Without doubt *The Tree of Man*, *Voss* and *The Solid Mandala* are among the most important novels of the century in any language; and as a whole his tormented *oeuvre* is that of a great and essentially modern writer. . . .

His first novel, *Happy Valley*, was published by Harrap in 1939, and in 1940 by Viking Press in the USA. This was his first success, and won the Australian Literature Society's gold medal. It was a gloomy, caustic and almost Hardy-esque study of Australian farm life. While "wandering", half fascinated and half repelled, in America during 1939 and 1940 White wrote *The Living and the Dead* (1941), which he set in pre-war England and which is his weakest novel.

Critics of his early novels compared him to James Joyce and found him difficult to read: "He carries the stream-of-consciousness method to almost its ultimate extreme", wrote one. But another critic made a more accurate prophesy when he pointed out that White's chief preoccupation was "deviation from the psychological norm".

In the autumn of 1940 Patrick White joined the Royal Air Force. He served as an intelligence officer in Sudan and Egypt until he was demobilised in 1945.

In 1945 White returned to Australia, to a property in Castle Hill, 25 miles from Sydney. He bred Schnauzers and Saanen goats, cultivated olives and citrus fruit, and lived "more or less" off his own produce. He was also writing his first major novel, *The Aunt's Story* (1948). This met with a mixed reception, but most critics recognised White's powers and his ability to evoke the mental processes of inarticulate and "abnormal" people. *The Aunt's Story* is a half-surrealistic, visionary account of the painful flowering of an Australian maiden-aunt, who eventually finds a new life in the American desert. *The Tree of Man* (1955) is an Australian epic, sombre and shot through with fire and drought, and menacing symbolism, centred on one couple's growing up in a growing land. *Voss* (1957), regarded by most as his greatest achievement, is based on the life of the German explorer, Leichardt, who with a group of men penetrated the Australian outback in a desperate and difficult journey.

At this point White became Australia's leading novelist—he has even been said to have established a "stranglehold" on Australian letters rather as Goethe did in Germany. White had now begun his sceptical and painful search for what he called "some meaning and design", and he did not eschew the paranormal, the savagely and scathingly satirical, or the mystical. *Riders in the Chariot* (1961), a novel combining the stories of four eccentrics, also concentrates with peculiar venom on the folk of Sarsparilla (based on a suburb of Sydney). It is satirical attitude and uncompromising loathing of the commonplace did not make it popular with all Australian readers. *The Solid Mandala* (1966), his own favourite, is an updated Cain and Abel story of two brothers. *The Vivisector* (1970) is in some ways a sort of imaginative autobiography of White's internal life: an adopted child becomes a painter, and becomes lost in his own mysticism.

The Eye of the Storm (1973) is apparently more realistic, in dealing with the last years of a rich old lady in Sydney. It incorporates a scene of incest in its bitter account of her power struggle with her son and daughter. In the year of its publication White became the first Australian writer to win the Nobel Prize for Literature. The historical *A Fringe of Leaves* (1976) followed. *The Twyborn Affair* (1979) is his most explicitly autobiographical novel, though its story is different from White's own in terms of outward events. Eddie Twyborn runs away from marriage, becomes the "wife" of a wealthy old male Greek, then transforms himself into a first world war hero and ends as the sexless madame of a posh London brothel. While writing this novel White felt that "everyone was going to hate" it. *A Flaw in the Glass: A Self-Portrait* (1981), an autobiography, explains many of his difficul-

ties, including his coming-to-terms with his homosexuality. He also wrote several collections of stories and a number of plays, none of which was really successful—although almost all were produced. . . .

White was a difficult and sometimes cantankerous man, who had many quarrels, notably with Australia's distinguished artist Sidney Nolan, a feud which dragged on for many years. He also made headlines when he made outspokenly uncomplimentary remarks on television about a visit to Australia by the Prince and Princess of Wales on the occasion of Australia's bicentenary celebrations in 1988. He made few concessions to readers or interviewing journalists, and in his latter years had become more reclusive and eccentric.

In general White paid a high price for what was an essentially religious quest. But he was also very generous, especially in the matter of money for other writers. The strongest single influence on him was Nietzsche, whom he was able to read in the original and thus never misunderstood, as so many others did.

> *An obituary in* The Times, *London, October 1, 1990.*

Richard Pearson

Patrick White, 78, the Australian novelist whose explorations of the human saga through epic narrative descriptions of the lives of pioneers in his country's lonely outback helped win him the 1973 Nobel Prize for literature, died yesterday at his home in Sydney. The cause of death was not reported.

The Swedish Academy, in awarding him the Nobel, said Mr. White "for the first time has given the continent of Australia an authentic voice that carries across the world."

The academy called his novel *Voss* (1957), the story of a tragic 19th-century German explorer of Australia, "an intensive character study against the background of the fascinating Australian wilds."

Perhaps ironically, Mr. White, who wrote of an Australia that was hard, unforgiving and at times downright vicious, was not particularly popular in his own country.

The academy also hailed his more recent works, "which show White's unbroken creative power, an ever deeper restlessness and seeking urge, an onslaught against vital problems that have never ceased to engage him and a wrestling with the language in order to extract all its power and all its nuances, to the verge of the unattainable."

Among his other best-known novels are *The Eye of the Storm, The Aunt's Story* and *The Tree of Man.* He also is the author of plays and poems as well as the 1981 autobiography *Flaws in the Glass.*

Critics have long been divided by Mr. White's work. Some have hailed it as brilliant, comparing it to the work of Charles Dickens, D. H. Lawrence, James Joyce and Gertrude Stein.

Others have found his style overly rich in cadence and imagery with overly complex structure and themes. One critic simply called his work "unreadable."

He wrote of seemingly ordinary people contending with enormous difficulties, often in small communities in the isolated outback. But these same works also were packed with symbols and allegory, as well as references to both eastern and western myths and folk tales. One critic referred to one of his works as containing "choking thickets of imagery."

South African novelist Nadine Gordimer said: "There is no other contemporary writer in English who uses the language with such conventional mastery and demotic flair."

Australian poet and critic A.D. Howe wrote of Mr. White's "pretentious and illiterate verbal sludge." David Tacey, a literature professor, said Mr. White, who was gay, could do virtually anything, write the most ordinary work, "and somehow it is all justified under the wondrous banner of gayness."

Mr. White's writing often took religious or philosophical turns. He wrote of a man's search for meaning in a meaningless world, of individuality and alienation from society, and ultimately, of loneliness. Although most of his novels took place in Australia, they were really set in what one critic called "the country of the mind."

Happy Valley, the fourth novel he wrote but the first to be published, appeared in 1939. This was followed in 1941 by *The Living and the Dead,* which was set among London's Bloomsbury set. His next novel, *The Aunt's Story* (1948), was the tale of a drab Australian spinster who achieves a kind of life through madness.

The first novel he wrote after returning to Australia after World War II was *The Tree of Man* (1955), which recounted the struggle of a pioneer couple in the outback. This novel brought him a degree of international fame.

His 1961 allegorical and religious novel, *Riders in the Chariot,* baffled many critics. These novels were followed by *The Solid Mandala* (1966), another allegorical tale, and *The Eye of the Storm* (1974), the story of a vicious, predatory and egotistical woman on her deathbed. . . .

Patrick Victor Martindale White was born May 28, 1912, in London, where his Australian parents were vacationing.

He spent the early part of his youth on an Australian sheep ranch before being sent to boarding school in England. After graduating in 1935 from Cambridge University's King's College, where he read modern languages, he wrote and traveled.

During World War II, he was an intelligence officer in Britain's Royal Air Force. He served in the Sudan, Egypt and Greece.

He returned to Australia to make his home in 1946, settling on a six-acre duck farm in New South Wales, where he lived off produce he grew, cultivated olive and citrus trees, and raised Saanen goats and schnauzers.

Richard Pearson, in an obituary in The Washington Post, *October 1, 1990.*

OVERVIEWS

Laurence Steven

In [*New Left Review,* No. 18 (1963)] Margaret Walters established the terms for a solid, balanced response to White's work:

> The grandeur of White's aspirations, and his often compelling brilliance, are undoubted. In fact it is because of this "grandeur" that we need so urgently to discriminate in his work between the false rhetoric and the truly exploratory use of language; between the passages which are pretentious and mystifying, and those which reveal new depths of experience. The central question raised by his works is whether he establishes significance in dramatic terms—or whether in the last count his attempt to work through myth and symbol is an evasion of the complexities of actual life, and of artistic creation as well.

My contention is that while White often establishes significance in dramatic terms—and with a compelling force that warrants the term "major"—at the same time he strains away from that significance by attempting to place the centre of novelistic interest and human value solely within the one character who has a direct link to a transcendent realm of wholeness. The result of his wanting to locate wholeness beyond the world we live in, is an overt devaluing of human life. White forces a split between the transcendent realm of significance to which his visionaries gain occasional access, and the banal, quotidian actuality in which we live our alienated lives. This "gap" leads to the dualisms which are everywhere apparent in White: mind/body, spirit/flesh, individual/society, permanence/flux, abstract/concrete, deformity/health, and so on.

The dualisms are only symptoms of a deeper problem. Patrick White is a man dissociated, a man who strives for surety, permanence, and the ideal, while knowing all too well the empirical reality, the contingent, temporal world which undermines schemes of permanence. The dissociation urges him into restless experimenting. He seeks surety by imposing mental constructs on the novels; symbolic patterning overshadows the life that arises through the interaction of characters. The cerebral aspect of White's sensibility comes to dominate emotion and intuition. Intent on surety, White largely misses the fulfilment, though not permanence, human life can offer, and to which his novelistic art can direct him through dramatic realization. He clings to extrinsic systems while knowing they are stopgap measures.

The tension thus generated forces complex human issues into the forefront of his fiction—primarily the issue of how we find and maintain meaning and value in human life. In a large part of his canon, the desire for surety results in an "evasion of the complexities of actual life" through the suggestion of a transcendent realm glimpsed by the elect in epiphany and only reached in madness or death. Overarching symbolic designs make the novelistic experience point one way, while the author's "oracular statements" reinforce the dualistic split between significance and banality. But this evasion through symbolism and assertion accompanies a sincere, if wrongheaded, response to the complexity of the situation. If misanthropy and solipsism attend the sincerity they do not cancel it. White is consistently concerned with discovering meaning and value in a world he feels is devoid of them. Witness the sheer technical skill and imaginative energy he displays in his continued wrestlings with the task he has set himself: to help "people a barely inhabited country with a race possessed of understanding." Witness, too, the genuine life that does get into the novels.

White's spiritual and ethical concerns—being real concerns, and those of a novelist—necessarily involve him in close exploration of characters' lives. The characters he invests with life then threaten to escape his confining grasp—that part of White that wants to impose a symbolic pattern of significance. He responds by thwarting the growth, truncating development before it escapes from his control completely. He may, consequently, as John Colmer says [in "Duality in Patrick White" (*Patrick White: A Critical Symposium*)], often be presenting only a "symbolist form . . . as a solution to a humanist dilemma," but in finding this solution he joins the prestigious company of the high modernists. White warrants major status with us because the sincerity of his concern, his continual wrestling with the issue, finally forces him out of the *cul de sac* his desire for surety had forced him into. He recognizes that the symbolist route is no solution unless the symbolism is firmly rooted in human experience. The terms of this recognition are what White explores so fruitfully in *A Fringe of Leaves.*

Through *Fringe* may be his most unequivocal success, a substantial part of White's corpus manifests the powers of an assuredly major figure. The portions which genuinely "reveal new depths of experience," however, are seldom separate from problematic contexts. Within parts of works, within certain relationships, when the material grips him firmly, we see White's novelistic genius. In Theodora Goodman's childhood, and her later relationship with Huntly Clarkson in *The Aunt's Story,* in Himmelfarb's relationships with his wife Reha and with Mary Hare in *Riders in the Chariot,* in Hurtle Duffield's relationship with Nance Lightfoot in *The Vivisector,* there is much to show us, before authorial impositions stifle creativity, what being fully human means. (pp. 1-3)

While there are critics who judge, who openly oppose the doctrine of alienation in White's fiction, or who are skeptical of White's grand designs, too often their stridency or the looseness of their arguments warrants the dismissal levelled by Alan Lawson: "All of the skeptical writers on White have proceeded [by] blaming the novelist for not measuring up to the critic's hypothesis." The breadth of the swathe Lawson cuts here, however, suggests that to question White's vision at all is tantamount to revealing one's inability to read White. [See "Meaning and Experi-

ence: A Review-Essay on Some Recurrent Problems in Patrick White Criticism," *Texas Studies in Literature and Language* XXI (Summer 1979).] (pp. 4-5)

His work itself challenges us to recognize the hints and promptings of a way beyond the modernist doctrine of alienation. Though the doctrine imposes the concepts of transcendent wholeness, epiphany, human baseness and banality on the novels, and though multiple detail convinces us that White has an absorbed awareness of the empirical world he inhabits, there is also the ability to present dramatic situations which render human experience with a subtlety and delicacy the grand designs cannot approach. Here rather than in some imported hypothesis criticism will find the standard against which to judge the dissociation in White's work. That work challenges the critic to develop an ability to see, within the restrictive compass the author's symbolic designs impose on the novels, the "new shoots," as Lawrence would have it, which indicate new life, new creativity, and which point toward a wholeness which human beings can embrace as their own.

As well as not seeing adequately the genuine life in White's canon, criticism has rarely recognized how White's development over the years shows an increasing awareness and acknowledgment of this life, of the reality that can close the gap in his fiction by pulling together the extremes of idealism and empiricism. John Colmer, for example, implies that *A Fringe of Leaves* comes out of nowhere when he says its appearance "invites us to see the whole of White's fiction in a fresh perspective." Colmer appreciates the moving authenticity of *Fringe;* a closer look at the issues involved would have caused him to recognize that authenticity as a gradually evolving element in White's fiction. White wrestles more and more directly with his own doctrine of alienation—which comes increasingly to look like self-indulgent escapism—until he triumphs with the wholeness of *A Fringe of Leaves.* The elements of this triumph were there all along, but demanded a genuinely engaged and courageous criticism which could evoke their power. The only person who has made the sufficient criticism is White himself. The development from the straitjacket of *Riders in the Chariot* to the wholeness of *A Fringe of Leaves* is ample proof of this. If *The Twyborn Affair* and *Memoirs of Many in One* swing indulgently the other way again, this does not mean that White has lost the knowledge of *Fringe.* It means that he is a human being living in a dissociated century, and that for him, as for the rest of us, wholeness is a state which demands our constant creative engagement—it is never achieved, once and for all. In the face of the diminished corner of life that our cultural doctrine of alienation tells us is *all* of life, we are tempted to self-indulgence, to narcissism, to resignation. Real courage is necessary to even attempt to come out of the corner; the work of our major authors, White included, is a record of such attempts.

I am concerned to show that the dualism we meet in White's work is not the settled state of humanity, that wholeness does not entail a transcendent realm which arbitrarily harmonizes earthly conflict. This does not mean that I see White's work expressing secular humanism, as

Leonie Kramer does [in "Patrick White's Götterdämmerung," *Quadrant* 17 (June 1973)]. To do so would simply be advocating the other side of the dualist position. Rather, I see White's work gradually overcoming the split between significance and banality, transcendent reality and human nullity, as it expresses his understanding of the wholeness that creative relationship can bestow. The spiritual dimension in White is transformed gradually from an arbitrary and unconvincing imposition into a moving reality which gains in authenticity by being the natural outcome of, and on a continuum with, human relationships. (pp. 5-6)

The Aunt's Story (1948) presents Theodora Goodman's solipsistic quest for wholeness through madness as an alternative to the intractable banality of the world she inhabits. This is the solution White had found to Joe Barnett's question in *The Living and the Dead:* "I love Eden, he said, but what can this do for the world, the sick, stinking world that sits in the stomach like a conscience? He was helpless." In both *Happy Valley* (1939) and *The Living and the Dead* (1941) White tries to deal with a social world from the outside and finds that he can't do it. Theodora's option is the result, though White is clearly not wholly convinced by it. *The Tree of Man* (1955) and *Voss* (1957) both extend White's exploration of the possibility of illumination and transcendent wholeness. But both, as articles by Margaret Walters and others suggest, fail to engage the problems entailed by an exploration in this direction. *Riders in the Chariot* (1961) embodies these problems in their most extreme manifestation. *The Solid Mandala* (1966) is a lesser work in the same vein as *Riders,* and though it does begin to question some of the premises of the earlier novel, the real questioning appears in *The Vivisector* (1970). White cannot extend the novelistic condemnation of Hurtle Duffield's vivisectory mode of living to the point that it becomes a sustained criticism of the solipsistic quest for significance; but he is certainly aware of the "new world outside" and only lacks the courage to climb through the break his own creativity has made in the wall. In *The Eye of the Storm* (1973) he stands on the threshold, so to speak. The possibility of illumination exists side by side with the wholeness to be found in relationship. This dual tension would be remarkable if we could say it was wholly a study of Elizabeth Hunter. We can't, however; White is still entangled with his protagonist. In *A Fringe of Leaves* (1976) he achieves the necessary distance and presents a study of human wholeness emerging from dissociation. (pp. 11-12)

> *Laurence Steven, in his* Dissociation and Wholeness in Patrick White's Fiction, *Wilfrid Laurier University Press, 1989, 163 p.*

Rodney Stenning Edgecombe

It is, I think, not too harsh a judgment on Patrick White, great novelist that he is, to suggest that the early works (like the fragments of Waldo) seem to have been prompted more by the urge to be a writer per se than by an impulse to communicate a vision. That vision took form, of course, between *The Aunt's Story* and *The Tree of Man* when, on his back in the mud of Castle Hill, he cursed the Deity he

---

Patrick White on Writing

I always like to write three versions of a book. The first is always agony and chaos; no one could understand it. With the second you get the shape, it's more or less all right. I write both of those in longhand. The third draft I type out with two fingers: it's for refining of meaning, additions and subtractions. I think my novels usually begin with characters; you have them floating about in your head and it may be years before they get together in a situation. Characters interest me more than situations. I don't think any of my books have what you call plots. I used to take notes, once upon a time; and sometimes I begin with a very slight skeleton. But I always think of my novels as being the lives of the characters. They are largely something that rises up out of my unconscious; I draw very little on actual people, though one does put a bow or a frill on from here or there. I find the actual bits, if you do use them, are most unconvincing compared to the fictitious bits. . . .

I am interested in detail. I enjoy decoration. By accumulating this mass of detail you throw light on things in a longer sense: in the long run it all adds up. It creates a texture—how shall I put it—a background, a period, which makes everything you write that [much] more convincing. Of course, all artists are terrible egoists. Unconsciously you are largely writing about yourself. I could never write anything factual; I only have confidence in myself when I am another character. All the characters in my books are myself, but they are a kind of disguise.

---

had theoretically discarded. From this point the fiction develops a fervor that burns away the affectation of the self-advancing early prose, and finds a function for the quirkishness of an idiom that before was simply that—mannered quirkishness. Even so, although the break between *The Aunt's Story* and *The Tree of Man* is a radical one, the stylistic assurance of the later novel, separated from its predecessor by seven years' maturation, is not absolute. White's newfound problem of expressing the inexpressible causes him to founder with such notorious cruces as the equation—too baldly made—of God and spittle in the final pages of *The Tree of Man.* He avoids this sort of crassness in *Voss* by resorting to an altogether looser, allegorical mode. Carolyn Bliss [in *Patrick White's Fiction*] has expounded this allegory with her usual sensitivity and penetration, though even she has finally to admit that some of the equivalences slip, slide, will not stay in place, will not stay still: "If this seems imprecise and unsettled, White probably intended that effect." In *Riders in the Chariot* the author opts for a crisper, cleaner design and a more explicit prose, though Peter Wolfe [in Laden Choirs] has objected that the "book's effects are too rigged and its plot too diagrammatic," and other critics have also found the authorial control overbearingly evident. (p. 150)

Be that as it may, my concern is with texture rather than design, even if the two are obviously closely connected. Once the greater thematic purpose has been clarified, the local purpose of each sentence can be established and its success appraised. Such purpose being imperfectly realized in large segments of *The Aunt's Story,* the style runs amok. This is not the case in the great novels though. As John Weigel [in *Patrick White*] observes, "White's commitment asks the reader to believe in him, to trust that his words always signify." The point is well taken, especially in its stress on words, for if the reader too intently assimilates the novels to the perennial philosophy or to some Jungian scheme of psychic health, the temptation to devalue and sidestep the rich integrity of the style will become irresistible. Peter Beatson's account of the novels [*The Eye in the Mandala: Patrick White: A Vision of Man and God*] is suggestive, but slightly impoverished in this regard. White might be a mystic, but, like all mystics, he is entrapped in the flesh. Words, by the same token, entrap the mystic dimension of the novels, and while these might seem to be pushing toward a beatific state of wordlessness, they have de facto to give an account of the sensuous reality in which the divine is immanent. This they manage in a spectacular and memorable way, and . . . they manage it through style.

At its most perfect (which is to say its most functional), White's is essentially a mimetic mode of expression. Almost every detail of the expression serves a thematic or corporealizing end. His fragmentary syntax is not a tic, not an uncontrollable stylistic spasm. When he uses it, he uses it with meaning. The memorable opening of *Voss* provides one of countless instances:

> "There is a man here, miss, asking for your uncle," said Rose.
>
> And stood breathing.

The angularity and intractability of the second paragraph suggest the gauche presence of the woman, steadfast and awkward; and the breathing fills the space allotted to it as stertorously as it does the room. In fact, the very incompleteness of the sentence suggests the effort of breath, while the opening "and" connects a visual complement to her utterance. Rose's position is uncompromising, and the syntax endorses it. There is something figural about the deployment of the half-sentence. It is not Rose herself, but Rose registered in the appropriate stylistic manner.

Leech and Short provide an illuminating discussion of this phenomenon in *Style in Fiction:*

> Iconicity is inherent in the language in a way that the mention of odd words like *miaow* and *thunder* does not begin to show. The phonetic shape of words is in fact one of the less promising areas in which to explore the phenomenon of language imitating nature. Words are conventional and stereotyped units; but . . . it has been recently suggested by Bolinger that above the word, iconicity takes a 'quantum leap,' the syntactic relations between words characteristically imitating relations between the objects and events which those words signify.

Such iconicity abounds on every page of the great novels. Almost all the "aberrant" features of the prose can be justified in these terms, as can its documentary texture. So when Adrian Mitchell [in "Eventually White's Language: Words and More than Words," *Patrick White: A Critical Symposium*] mischievously suggests that much of White's detail is otiose, he deserves rebuttal:

> White rather wastefully if splendidly heaps up enormous sets of details that ultimately don't signify though by that he may achieve a semblance of continuity; or if you want to hear that said much more bluntly, he conceals a relatively simple sense of character within the complexity of his patterns of symbols and metaphors, the literary allusions and the enigma of his mandalas and so forth, devices that in the end just don't matter.

If an imagination is so fecund as to be prodigal with its discoveries, who would wish it more restrained? Music critics have, in terms similar to Mitchell's, described the opening melody of Tchaikovsky's Concerto in B-flat Minor as "wasteful" because it is not absorbed into the musical argument. Yet who would wish it away? Plenitude deserves gratitude. Even so, the issue of wastefulness scarcely arises because . . . the detail, in all its abundance, *is* significant. And over and above its place in the thematic schemes of the novels, it supplies a ballast of "accidentality" without which they would remain inexpressive theorems of salvation. What Mitchell presents as a case against White, his "simple sense of character within the complexity of his patterns," could be brought against any novelist one might choose to mention. The most rigorously documented naturalism will, at the right critical distance, resolve into a pattern of archetypal motifs, and behind the realism of countless novels there lurks the stylization of romance. This supposed "simplicity" scarcely holds if one devotes attention to what is revealed in its vehicle, the elaborate specificity of the style.

Indeed, a striking feature of White's expression is its concrete rendition of abstract thought, manifest above all in his characteristic use of synesthesia. Carolyn Bliss is quite right to point out that in "White's hands, (it) becomes another instrument for undermining familiar distinctions, such as those among sensory functions, thus establishing a disquieting sense of flux counterpointed with a reassuring sense of comprehensiveness," but this does not exhaust its Whitean possibilities. If, as Coleridge has said, the poetic imagination is esemplastic, then White's synesthesia is a means toward the end of whole-forming, toward the restoration of a "primitive" vision that affirms the continuity of the physical with the intangible world. The synesthesia of *The Aunt's Story* tends, if one might venture a summary judgment, to serve the rather puerile function of administering repeated stylistic shocks. That of *The Solid Mandala,* by contrast, is unassertively taken up into the book's theme: "In the beginning there was the sea of sleep of such blue in which they lay together with iced cakes and the fragments of glass nesting in each other's arms the furry waves of sleep nuzzling at them like animals."

Although the adjective "blue" is partly accommodated by the sea metaphor (whether it be the sea of amniotic fluid or oceanic consciousness), one still experiences a synesthetic fusion once removed. The blueness of the sleep is a measure of its sanctity (as witness Himmelfarb's name and Duffield's final painting), for blue is the color of the infinite, a connection already hinted by the Johannine start to the paragraph. "Iced cakes" image the frosted confections that are the delight of childhood, but could also be regarded as a child's projection of the icebergs never to be seen, but which, in a visionary dream, will crumble into manna-like mandalas. Similarly the "furry waves of sleep," while they might suggest the ermine tufts of foam on each wave, could just as easily evoke the texture of a blanket drawn up to Arthur's chin as a wave flattens up along a beach. The synesthesia in both cases is organic, erasing adult distinctions to posit a primal unity of experience. (pp. 150-53)

An aspect of White's style related to the figurative dimension of his language is its poise upon the threshold of allegory. Quite often an external description will be taken into the mind of the spectator and invested there with a secondary level of meaning. Duffield's final renunciation of Sunningdale is handled in this way:

> The half darkness through which he was climbing seemed to be developing an inescapable form: of a great padded dome, or quilted egg, or womb, such as he had seen in that da Vinci drawing. He continued dragging round the spiral, always without arriving, while outside the meticulous womb, men were fighting, killing, to live to fuck to live.

What begins as an ascent up a (no doubt curving) suburban staircase is allegorized into a surrealistic, inwardly realized journey, with hellish touches of Sisyphus ("always without arriving") and prenatal suffocation. The "round, domed room" mutates into a womb unnaturally soundproofed and cushioned against outside realities, realities documented in harsh Anglo-Saxon diction and an unbreakable chain of infinitives—"to live to fuck to live."

An additional touch of phantasmagoria is supplied by the detail of Hurtle's having "outgrown" the room as though he were a latterday Alice in Wonderland:

> Outside the room he had outgrown, the night was rocking back and forth. A wind sounded like rain in the glittering trees. On the way across the sky mounds of intestinal cloud began to uncoil, to knot again, to swallow one another up. A fistful of leaves flung in his face as he leant out had the stench of men, of some men at least, who have overexerted themselves, of Pa Duffield, who was his actual father, in an old grey flannel vest, counting the empties as he piled them under the pepper tree.

The idea of motion without purpose is exemplified in the night which rocks back and forth, paralleling Hurtle's goalless ascent of the staircase, and the hissing wind and glitter of the trees provide only the *semblance* of fertilizing rain. By the same token, the self-engulfing clouds, "intestinal" in their tubular shape, are likewise intestinal in the way they image Alfreda Courtney's attempt at engulfing Hurtle with her dubious love. The leaves that sting his face by reminding him of his social disclassification also suggest the leaves of Sibyl, flung oracularly on the wind. What is remarkable in all this is the delicacy, belied by my critical pouncing, with which the equivalences between inner and outer states are gestured—sometimes so lightly that what White ultimately presents is more a scaffold of objective correlatives than the equations of allegory.

He can, however, be slightly too ready to connect. The internalization of lightning to image passion has an automatic, unreflective feel in this extract from *Riders in the Chariot.* The outer storm has been only implied, its mental ingestion made to seem too pat: "Soon the boy's memory was lit by the livid jags of the metho love the two had danced together on the squeaky bed."

In *The Twyborn Affair* also there is an over-ready allegorization of detail: "Madame Reboa's ulcer is by no means pretty, but most of us have one, while concealing it." Here the ulcer has too much medical specificity to be taken up into the general human condition, just as the following metaphoric gradations from skirt to dragnet to eyes do not helpfully establish a sexual differentia though they attempt to do so in a portentous way:

> The scents your skirt drags from the borders of a garden: the dragnet skirt is one of the advantages a man can never enjoy.

> On the other hand there is not much that escapes those old dragnet eyes of his. Angelos is a specialist in dredging up the moral wreckage of others, while inclined to remain impervious to his own.

Although this feature could be rationalized as an index to White's sense of continuity between the inner and outer worlds, not enough has gone into establishing the transition, and the reader is put in mind of Laura's adolescent enthusiasms about "rocks of prejudice, and, yes, even hatred" in *Voss.* Such flaws are minor, however, and do not seriously blemish the worked verbal scabbards in which the novels are sheathed.

Given White's persistent finesses in gauging and executing his effects of style, it is extremely important for the reader to give due attention to the word-structure of the novels. In an otherwise sensitive article ["The Novelist and the Reign of Necessity: Patrick White and Simone Weil," *Patrick White: A Critical Symposium*] Veronica Brady has suggested that they be taken as "a kind of Wisdom literature," advice which, taken too far, might involve the sacrifice of style to vision. Yet style without vision can be a sterile thing. It would be an intemperate judgment that *denied* vision to *The Twyborn Affair* and *Memoirs of Many in One;* but there can be no doubting that the vision has been curtailed, even stinted, and the style sometimes resembles a beautifully wrought seashell, no longer holding the organism it was designed to. If *The Tree of Man* marks Patrick White's artistic coming of age and shows him sloughing all meretricious excrescences of style, *The Twyborn Affair* marks a falling off from the great phase of achievement, for the great cohesive vision has been suspended and less weighty concerns examined in its stead. The prose has all the lucidity and poise that one finds in the great fiction (one critic, Peter Wolfe, has even detected a unique simplicity that eludes me), but its function is often only local, and the jeweled egg sometimes seems to be enclosing a vacuum.

For whereas *The Solid Mandala* explores androgyny as the imaginative extension of human identity, *The Twyborn Affair* seems caught up in the altogether more superficial concerns of transvestism—literally superficial, since in this most fetishistic form of sexual unorthodoxy, emphasis falls heavily on costume, on outer surface. While these surfaces are for the most part documented with immense sensitivity, the novel fails to satisfy when it is judged by White's own best standards. One feels, in the febrile brothel sequences toward the end of the work, that one has been returned to the claustrophobic, overheated atmosphere of the *Jardin Exotique*. And with this apparent "regression" goes a sense of bewilderment, of being less than entirely sure about the author's intentions. For all the reverently "meaningful" metonymy of this excerpt, nothing less banal than oral compensation seems be at the bottom of it all:

> . . . ordering Ada, Ida and Vi to fetch the dishes of salted almonds, oily olives, sheathed pistachios which blunt Anglo-Saxon fingers avoided entirely, or on being caught out, heeled under velvet fringes of sofa or divan, or in the case of more reticent or passive clients, waiting for expert nails to split the phallus-shaped pistachio and pop it, if not an oily olive, into a complacently fleshed, or thin and chapped, though equally greedy, male mouth.

The Aunt's Story seems also to be present, though in a faint, palimpsestic way, in White's most recent novel, *Memoirs of Many in One,* which, for all its surface brilliance, also tends to leave the reader unsatisfied. The cause, as with *The Twyborn Affair,* must be sought in content, not style, since the writing is light and sprightly and conspires with the novel's satiric conception in whisking the reader forward. The pace prevents him or her from pausing to seek for depths, and even seems to trench on *reductio ad absurdum* of all the great, grave tenets of the middle period. An example of the way in which the clipped, rapid exposition takes on a deflationary force can be found in a sequence such as this: "There is an old man with matted hair and a hand down his back scratching. Probably a mystic." While some of the mystics in the great novels have been social outcasts, it hardly follows, as Alex here seems to think, that most outcasts must be mystic, and the fault of logic becomes the more satirically blatant for the bald way in which it is presented.

What renders the tone of *Memoirs of Many in One* even more difficult to construe is our uncertainty about the status, whether moral or ontological, of the narrative. Patrick White's stance toward his characters has frequently been ambivalent, but the first person here removes all vestiges of authorial control, a problem complicated further by the author's self-dramatization in the figure of Patrick. The reader is rushed through the experiences of Alex Gray in various avatars as nun, actress, and invalid, sequences which are clearly imaginary and which yet seem to have clothed small grits of reality like baroque pearls. In what amounts to a spirited, satiric survey of many Whitean materials and motifs, Alex becomes a familiar compound ghost, made up from bits of Theodora Goodman, Elizabeth Hunter, and Hurtle Duffield. But the satire, different from the compassionate irony of the great novels, always seems to reduce and parody the materials it processes. If the following passage were placed in the context of the

middle fiction, it would seem a profoundly moving epiphany of wholeness and spiritual calm, reverberant as it is with echoes of *Voss, Riders in the Chariot, The Solid Mandala,* and *The Eye of the Storm:*

> I walk on into the plain beyond, a carpet of dust, almost a mattress. A few ghost trees console the revenant I have become. Small birds skitter across the desert, larger ones rise by the grace of a stately basketwork of wings. I bow my head under the increasing weight of heat, my eyes humbled by the sheets of metallic light opening out, swingeing at me from the distance. If I were at least a shadow, but I am not, I am nothing now that my ghost trees have evaporated in the heat and glare. Not even an insect. Louse fallen from a bird's wing. Grain of mica.

This rapt, radiant moment is part of a fantasy—Alex's tour of the outback. How, then, is one to take its intensity? The spirit, as if inevitably, returns to its source in the primal (Neoplatonic) light, a return celebrated by the presence of sacral birds (the birds at the eye of the storm or in the garden with Sister de Santis). It is marked also by the characteristic humbling of the visionary, whose access to grace is shadowed by the technical "grace" (*gratia*) that lifts the improbably heavy bodies of the pelicans skyward. White registers the stripping of the self in the behavior of the landscape (the ghost trees evaporate) and in the gradual contraction of the sentences, which shed even their articles as they crumble. A shift from animal to mineral is also carefully gauged. But when we put this poised and prayerful writing back into the novel, we find it forerun by a reductive statement that the likes of a Waldo Brown might have uttered: "O God! I don't know why I should invoke the name of one who probably does not exist." This, and the very status of the vision as part of an imaginary experience, calls its restorative function into question, one of the many difficulties posed by a fascinating but ultimately lightweight work.

In advancing the work from *The Tree of Man* to *A Fringe of Leaves* as a canon of great novels and regarding the run-up and the aftermath as comparatively flawed achievements, I have invoked as my yardstick the continuity of vision and style. While the early works are marred by a style whose rampancy lacks the discipline of a focused theme, the most recent apply the perfected prose of the mature pieces to a vision so reconstituted as to seem circumscribed and even self-satirizing. Words, despite White's frequent disclaimers, are an inescapable *donnée* of his art, and he is indubitably their master in his great middle period, especially in the subtlety and resourcefulness of his commentary prose. If the plays seem disappointingly thin, that is because his characters are denied the right he exercises on their behalf in the novels—the right to speak to the reader in a language rich, adaptable, and mimetic. (pp. 154-59)

Rodney Stenning Edgecombe, in his Vision and Style in Patrick White: A Study of Five Novels, *The University of Alabama Press, 1989, 169 p.*

Obituaries

In addition to the authors represented in the In Memoriam section of this *Yearbook,* several other notable writers passed away during 1990:

Reinaldo Arenas
July 16, 1943—December 7, 1990
Cuban novelist, poet, and short story writer

Marked by an imaginative embellishment of history and reality, Arenas's works reflect Cuba's turbulent political environment. Arenas was imprisoned by the Castro regime for publishing his writings abroad and for his homosexuality. He escaped to the United States in 1980, and at the time of his death had five novels under contract and a newly completed autobiography, *Before Night Falls.* Arenas was awarded France's coveted Prix Medici in 1969.

Anatole Broyard
July 16, 1920—October 11, 1990
American critic

Broyard was a daily *New York Times* book critic for nearly fifteen years and served for three years as editor of *The New York Times Book Review.* Broyard primarily reviewed fiction in his critical writings, often emphasizing the author's use of language. Broyard's collections *Aroused by Books* (1974) and *Men, Women and Other Anticlimaxes* (1980) offer a selection of his humorous, intelligent book reviews and essays. He also contributed short stories and articles to such periodicals as *The Partisan Review, The New Republic,* and *Commentary.*

Roald Dahl
September 13, 1916—November 23, 1990
Welsh author of children's books, novelist, and short story writer

Dahl was an original voice in children's literature whose macabre, witty explorations of the dark side of human nature remain extremely popular. A highly acclaimed satirist of adult mores and values, Dahl claimed that the key to his success was to conspire with children against adults. While he was often accused by critics of infusing his tales with excessive violence and cruelty, such works as *James and the Giant Peach* (1961) and *Charlie and the Chocolate Factory* (1964) are regarded as classics.

Sergei Dovlatov
September 3, 1941—August 24, 1990
Russian novelist, journalist, short story writer

Dovlatov was a successful journalist who was censored for his irreverent fictional portraits of his homeland, and consequently emigrated to the United States in 1978. His novels were published and became widely admired in the Soviet Union only after the advent of *glasnost* in the late 1980s. Often compared to Anton Chekhov, Dovlatov employed an unemotional narrative voice that humorously offset his sly critique of Soviet life. Dovlatov's works published in English translation include the novels *The Invisible Book: Epilogue* (1979), *The Compromise* (1983), and *Ours* (1989), and the short story collection *The Zone* (1985).

Lawrence Durrell
February 27, 1912—November 7, 1990
Indian-born English novelist, poet, playwright, and translator

An influential novelist and poet, Durrell wrote in an intense, baroque style, often employing words in their associative rather than denotative capacity. Largely influenced by the works of D. H. Lawrence and Henry Miller, Durrell explored in prose and verse the human psyche and the primacy of sexuality. His most famous work, *The Alexandria Quartet,* consisting of the novels *Justine* (1957), *Balthazar* (1958), *Mountolive* (1959), and *Clea* (1960), utilizes theories of Einstein and Freud in its inventive structure and multiple narrative viewpoints and features an evocative prose style that emphasizes sensuality and the spirit of place.

Friedrich Dürrenmatt
January 5, 1921—December 14, 1990
Swiss playwright, novelist, and critic

Dürrenmatt is among the most celebrated German-language dramatists to emerge after World War II. Writing in an expressionist manner akin to that of Bertolt Brecht, Dürrenmatt focused on the subject of hypocrisy, most notably in *Der Besuch der alten Dame: Eine Tragische Komödie* (1956; *The Visit: A Tragi-Comedy*). Regarded as a major contemporary play, this work centers on the residents of an impoverished town who decide to murder a fellow citizen for profit.

Michael Glenny
September 26, 1927—August 1, 1990
English translator

Recognized as an important translator of Russian literature, Glenny introduced Soviet novelist and playwright Mikhail Bulgakov to the English-speaking world with translations of *The Master and Margarita, The White Guard,* and *A Country Doctor's Notebook.* His other translations include Aleksandr Solzhenitsyn's *August 1914* and Zinovy Zinik's *The Mushroom-Pickers. The London Times* stated: "[Glenny is likely] to be remembered for the skill with which he could enter a novelist's world and appropriate his style and the voice of his characters."

Rosamond Lehmann
February 3, 1901—March 12, 1990
English novelist and translator

Lehmann was an acclaimed romantic novelist whose technical proficiency and exquisite prose style were lauded throughout her long career. She achieved success with her first novel, *Dusty Answer* (1927), which concerned lesbianism and was commended for its acute perception into female psychology. After a twenty-year hiatus from writing fiction, Lehmann published *A Sea-Grape Tree* (1976), renewing interest in her earlier works, many of which were subsequently reprinted by the British feminist press Virago. Along with *Dusty Answer,* Lehmann is best known as the author of such novels as *A Note of Music* (1930), *Invitation to the Waltz* (1932), *The Weather in the Streets* (1936), and *The Ballad and the Source* (1945).

Michel Leiris
April 20, 1901—September 30, 1990
French autobiographer, poet, essayist, and novelist

A distinguished anthropologist and surrealist poet, Leiris was perhaps most respected for autobiographical writings that expanded the boundaries of confessional literature. His acclaimed memoir, *L'age d'homme* (1939; *Manhood: A Journey from Childhood into the Fierce Order of Virility*), differs from most autobiographies in its emphasis on its author's shortcomings rather than his life history. By revealing personal deficiencies, Leiris hoped to purge inhibitions that he believed were ruining his life and to express the ultimate meaning of his existence.

Ivar Lo-Johansson
February 23, 1901—April 11, 1990
Swedish novelist, short story writer, nonfiction writer, and poet

Author of more than sixty works, Lo-Johansson was one of Sweden's most prolific and influential twentieth-century writers. Lo-Johansson's fictional portrayal of the plight of impoverished workers greatly influenced social reforms in his homeland and brought comparisons to John Steinbeck and Erskine Caldwell. His most notable novels include *Godnatt, Jord* (1933), *Statarna* (1936-37), and *Jordporletärerna* (1941).

Thomas McGrath
November 20, 1916—September 19, 1990
American poet, critic, scriptwriter, and novelist

Often compared to Walt Whitman for his expansive and humanistic verse, McGrath was considered the premiere Marxist poet of his generation. Although McGrath encountered discrimination throughout much of his professional life for his political views, he was awarded a senior fellowship from the National Endowment of the Arts. McGrath's poetry is marked by belief in the empowerment of community, rejection of religion and religious institutions, and reverence for humanity and the environment. His long-sequence poem *Letter to an Imaginary Friend,* which extended to four published volumes at the time of his death, is his best known work. McGrath's *Selected Poems: 1938-1988* received the prestigious Lenore Marshall/*Nation* Poetry Prize in 1989.

Alberto Moravia
November 28, 1907—September 26, 1990
Italian novelist, short story writer, poet, and dramatist

The author of nearly two dozen novels, Moravia produced popular and critically acclaimed fiction throughout the six decades of his literary career. His irreverent portrayal of Italy as a society dominated by sexual passion and emotional alienation made him a controversial figure in his predominantly Catholic homeland. Italian President Francesco Cosiga hailed Moravia as a "sharp but very sensitive narrator of 20th-century Italian society, its contradictions, bewilderments and anxious search for values."

Yannis Ritsos
May 14, 1909—November 12, 1990
Greek poet

Ritsos was considered Greece's most popular contemporary poet. His verse was frequently inspired by his dedication to Communist politics, and the Soviet Union awarded him the Lenin Peace Prize in 1977. "O Epitafios," one of Ritsos's best known poems, reflects his characteristic tone of pessimism and anguish in its portrayal of a mother grieving for her murdered son.

W. M. Spackman
May 20, 1905—August 3, 1990
American novelist, essayist, and critic

Characterized by idiosyncratically ornate prose, Spackman's novels of manners concerning the romantic affairs of the upper-class frequently drew comparisons to the works of Henry James and F. Scott Fitzgerald. His best-known novels include *An Armful of Warm Girl* (1978), *A Presence with Secrets* (1981), and *A Difference of Design* (1983).

Irving Wallace
March 19, 1916—June 29, 1990
American novelist, nonfiction writer, and scriptwriter

A prolific and popular author whose works have been translated into more than thirty languages, Wallace created suspenseful, well-researched novels that explore such diverse topics as religion and sexual maladjustment. Wallace is best known for his novels *The Chapman Report* (1960), which traces the impact of a sexual survey on suburban housewives; *The Prize* (1962), a fictional account of the complex process of awarding the Nobel Prize; and *The Word* (1972), which centers on the discovery of a lost portion of the New Testament.

Topics in Literature: 1990

The Book of J

The Book of J consists of new biblical translations by David Rosenberg and commentary by noted critic Harold Bloom. Rosenberg's translation is restricted to parts of the Pentateuch, the first five books of the Hebrew Bible and the Christian Old Testament, supposedly written by the author referred to as "J." Although Jewish tradition identified Moses as the author of the Pentateuch, eighteenth- and nineteenth-century scholars, led by Julius Wellhausen, discerned four distinct authors, the first of whom called God by the name "Yahweh" or "Jahweh" and was therefore referred to as "J." In his controversial commentary in *The Book of J,* Bloom proposes that J was in fact a woman and was a creative writer equal to Shakespeare. He postulates that J lived during the reign of three kings of Israel: David, Solomon, and Rehoboam. While King David, the founder of Israel, ruled gloriously, Rehoboam's decadent regime led to revolt and division of the Hebrews into two kingdoms, Judah and Israel. Bloom's J, who exalted David's reign, was disillusioned by Rehoboam's decline and may have fashioned her Yahweh in the founding king's image.

To support his theory of a female J, Bloom cites the author's unequal treatment of male and female characters. Her male characters, including Yahweh, are impish and childish, while her female characters are strong and have more developed personalities. Another indication of J's feminity, Bloom claims, is found in her description of creation. The relation of Eve's creation is six times as long as that of Adam's, implying that Yahweh improved on his first attempt. While many critics were intrigued by Bloom's analysis of J's preferential treatment of women, some argued that this alone was not sufficient support for the theory of a female J.

Rosenberg's accompanying translation of J's passages remains close to the original Hebrew, attempting to avoid later interpretive influence. Some critics observed that Rosenberg's translation was sometimes inconsistent in its use of tenses, points of view, and modern language, and cited what they considered incorrect transliteration. Others, however, considered the sparse prose appropriate for Bloom's detailed interpretation of J's writing, and acknowledged the personal voice that surfaces when the "J" passages are isolated from the rest of the Pentateuch.

Although the idea that a woman wrote parts of the Bible is not unprecedented, Bloom furthered speculation on J's identity, proposing that she was a creative rather than a religious writer. Comparing her to authors such as Shake-

Harold Bloom

speare and Kafka, Bloom emphasizes J's awareness of her characters' psychological complexities and her artistic talent as a prose poet. J's identity as a writer of religious doctrine and history, he claims, is the fault of centuries of misreadings by translators and interpreters of the Pentateuch. Admitting that he cannot prove the accuracy of his hypotheses on J's identity, Bloom adds: "This J is my fiction, most biblical scholars will insist, but then each of us carries about a Shakespeare or a Tolstoy or a Freud who is our fiction also. As we read any literary work, we necessarily create a fiction or metaphor of its author." John Barton voiced the opinion of many commentators who praised Bloom's astute and convincing work: "[*The Book of J*] may be brilliant, or it may be wildly anachronistic—I suspect it is both—but it is not a book one can ignore."

(For further information on Harold Bloom, see *CLC,* Vol. 24 and *Dictionary of Literary Biography,* Vol. 67)

Barbara Probst Solomon

The Book of J is a collaborative effort between David Rosenberg, who has given a fresh, interpretative translation of the salient portions of the "J" sections of the Pentateuch—the first five books of the Hebrew Bible and the Christian Old Testament—and Harold Bloom, our reigning literary terrorist critic. The parts of Genesis, Exodus and Numbers that scholars have ascribed to the unknown writer they call "J" include the stories of Creation, Eden, Cain and Abel, the Tower of Babel, Abraham and his wife Sarai in Egypt plus the majority of the stories involving the Patriarchs: Isaac and Rebecca, Jacob and Rachel, Joseph, and, most important, the narrative of Moses. Bloom, bent on knocking out of the ring adversaries presumed to have the wrong theories as to the origins of the Old Testament, presents his view that the "J" portions were, in fact, the work of a woman—a worldly sophisticate of royal blood of the house of David living in Jerusalem during the 10th century B.C.

In candidly admitting that his idea that "J" is a woman is an intuition born of his ear for poetry, rather than based on concrete fact, Bloom disarms his readers. After he has us well accustomed to accepting J's womanly gender, well toward the end of the book, Bloom somewhat disingenuously informs us: "I cannot prove anything about 'J,' not even that she existed, or whether she was a woman, or when she lived, or what was her rank or class, or whether her home was Jerusalem." It is the tough-mindedness of the sturdy woman characters and, in contrast, the childlike behavior of Yahweh in the J sections that most convince him of J's gender.

Such claims are not new: Samuel Butler maintained that Homer was a woman; the French critic, Jean Wahl, said he didn't care what great writer turned out to have been a woman, so long as Corneille was left in peace. Subjectively, I delight in the idea that the greatest literary narrative of all time, that from which flowed our three major religions—the Judaic, Christian and Moslem—was born of womankind. But, standing back a little, as a critic, I am more interested in Bloom's feat for its shrewd sleight-of-hand rather than as a true possibility.

Had not Bloom reimagined J as a sort of stunning intellectual princess, what would he have been left with? Myriad scholars have done the hard, nitty-gritty work on the Old Testament—it already has been sorted out into its different parts: in addition to J, other divisions include E, P and D. The 1964 Doubleday Anchor Bible, with commentary by E. A. Speiser (who also supervised the translation), makes clear that J is considered by mainstream scholarship to be the work of one of the world's greatest literary geniuses. Speiser, like Bloom, has observed that the Yahweh created by the writer J is far more a personal participant in the lives of the patriarchs than the Yahweh of other writers. He also perceives J as a writer sophisticatedly aloof from his material, indeed, frequently critical of the messy behavior of the characters. Moreover, since in the Jerusalem of the 10th century B.C. the art of writing was not an equal-opportunity affair, and, as the family-minded Old Testament so meticulously concerns itself with status

relationships, it would seem likely J had to come from the highest social caste.

But Bloom immediately heightens his drama, and separates it from traditional biblical and literary scholarship, by establishing his J as a foil for the Yahweh she has invented. Thus results a creation within a creation within a creation. We have Bloom creating J, who, in turn, creates Yahweh, who, in turn, creates Adam and then Eve.

> [J] begins her account of the natural and the human with Yahweh, all alone, standing in a mist that comes from within the earth that he has made. There, in that mist, for no stated reason or cause, he scoops up a handful of wet earth and shapes it into what we would call an earthling. But this earthling is still a mud pie . . . until Yahweh blows his own breath, 'the wind of life,' into the nostrils he had formed . . . It would be like the lovingly ironic J if her childlike Yahweh breathes from his own nostrils into the child of her art.

Abruptly, albeit cleverly, Bloom shifts J from being a literary genius writing in a received tradition—one which has at its core monotheism in its first representation, "Yahweh"—to being, herself, the individualist inventor of her form of monotheism. "J is the most monistic of all Western authors," writes Bloom, "even as Saint Paul is one of the most dualistic. There is for J no split between body and soul, between nature and mind. So far as I can tell, such monism was J's invention, whereas the creation out of clay was not." He then adds, "I venture the speculation that J's power as a writer made Judaism, Christianity, and Islam possible, if only because the furious liveliness of her Yahweh presented tradition with an unforgettable and uncanny being."

Bloom no longer is interpreting the Old Testament; instead he is revealing to us the wills, desires and caprices of his mighty Princess J. Since nobody is a higher authority on Princess J than Bloom, he is, of course, in absolute charge. If one is willing to suspend judgment on Bloom's method and accept his *donnees* as pleasurably heightened literary drama, his scatterings of earthly delights have considerable allure. In mixing erudition with poetic leaps of the imagination he has a noble precedent in Robert Graves's "historical grammar of poetic myth," *The White Goddess,* which also involves a search for the *ur*-female hidden behind the obvious patriarchal bent of the Judeo-Christian religion.

Bloom particularly entices in his vivid description of Princess J and her strong rendering of Biblical women. He sweeps aside any notion of religious, moral or historical possibility in his J—since she is the greatest of all literary geniuses, why must these profound areas be absent in her work?—in order to highlight his view that Yahweh was merely her own literary creation: She had no need, therefore, to be in awe of him. Bloom almost novelistically places on one side J and her women, on the other, a weak, childlike, male Yahweh, who is no match for their female superiority.

In Bloom's reading, the aged Sarai ridicules Yahweh for suggesting that she beget a child with her husband Abraham—"now that I'm used to groaning, I'm to groan with pleasure? My lord is also shriveled." A gritty Rachel holds on to her father's property by sitting on top of his idols; she tells the embarrassed Laban that due to her period she cannot rise from her seat. Bloom's favorite heroine though is Tamar, who nervily pushes her way into a story that she was not born into. Undaunted by the weakness of Judah's two sons, who, each in his turn, leave her childless, she seduces her father-in-law. Through her psychological insight into his behavior, she manages to take care that her sons, the ancestors of David, are born without stigma. She discreetly gets Judah to acknowledge legally his paternity while making it clear to him she will not make this disgraceful information public. "Most crucially, she knows that she is the future, and she sets aside societal and male-imposed conventions in order to arrive at her truth, which will turn out to be Yahweh's truth, or David."

Bloom's main aim is to nail down his Princess J as the absolute source and equal of Shakespeare, Tolstoy, Kafka, Freud, et al. Since she is his personal hostage, he is also staking his own claim to the methods he means to maintain in judging their work. By stressing J and her women as equal to—indeed, at times, more powerful than—Yahweh and the patriarchs, he has directed our imagination to contemplate in a roomy way the unguilty child born of J's great prose narrative, that child being not religion, but literature. (pp. 5, 14)

> Barbara Probst Solomon, "Moses and Feminism," in Book World—The Washington Post, September 16, 1990, pp. 5, 14.

Christopher Lehmann-Haupt

> Before a plant of the field was in the earth, before a grain of the field sprouted—Yahweh had not spilled rain on the earth, nor was there man to work the land—yet from the day Yahweh made earth and sky, a mist from within would rise to moisten the surface. Yahweh shaped an earthling from clay of this earth, blew into its nostrils the wind of life. Now look: man becomes a creature of flesh.

So reads the opening of David Rosenberg's new translation of *The Book of J,* a neglected version of the Bible that the critic Harold Bloom defines and explains in his brilliant accompanying commentary and interpretation. . . .

From the standpoint of normative Judaism, Christianity and Islam, J is the most blasphemous writer that ever lived.
—Harold Bloom

[As] Mr. Bloom almost but not quite warns us, reading *The Book of J* comes as a shock in this new translation. Where is the magnificent music of the King James Version? Where is "the darkness . . . upon the face of the

deepe"? "Now look" instead of "Behold" comes as a shock, and so do the frequent changes of tense, the sudden shifts in point of view, the seemingly uneven, fragmentary quality of the work.

Yet Mr. Bloom asks that the reader absorb these shocks in this book of surpassing originality and critical penetration. More precisely, he asks one to scrape "through three stages of varnish, plastered on by the rabbis, the Christian prelates and the scholars, stages that converted J into Torah, Torah into Hebrew Bible, and Hebrew Bible into Old Testament." (Elsewhere, he adds that the reader must work back through "twenty-five hundred years of institutionalized misreading, a misreading central to Western culture and society.")

Mr. Bloom proposes that J was a resident at or near the court of Solomon's son and successor, King Rehoboam of Judah; that J was "not a professional scribe but rather an immensely sohpisticated, highly placed member of the Solomonic elite, enligthened and ironic"; that J was an artist of the stature of Homer, Chaucer, Shakespeare and Cervantes, among other titans; and, for reasons that he propounds at length and with considerable subtlety, that J was a woman.

Does he succeed in persuading the reader of all this? Not at once. There is the strangeness of the text by Mr. Rosenberg—a poet and former editor in chief of the Jewish Publication Society—which takes time and repeated reading to get used to. There are the conventional moral attitudes one tends unconsciously to impose: that Adam and Eve's Fall had something to do with original sin, or that the Cities of the Plain were destroyed for the sexual perversity of their inhabitants. There is a persisting tendency to attribute the work's highly elliptical quality to its having been composed from fragments.

Yet it doesn't really matter whether Mr. Bloom is literally correct or not. As he writes: "This J is my fiction, most biblical scholars will insist, but then each of us carries about a Shakespeare or a Tolstoy or a Freud who is our fiction also. As we read any literary work, we necessarily create a fiction or metaphor of its author."

His J is a great character: a tragedian and comedian; like Shakespeare the creator of a genre that embraces and transcends all genres; withal "uncanny, tricky, sublime, ironic, a visionary of incommensurates," by which Mr. Bloom apparently means a dramatist of the impossibly uneven conflict between Yahweh and his creatures of flesh, "and so the direct ancestor of Kafka, and of any writer, Jewish or Gentile, condemned to work in Kafka's mode."

And the book Mr. Bloom reads is a great work of literature. In the space of its ellipses, he sees J's mind at play. In the creation: "It is not just that J has given six times the space to woman's creation as to man's; it is the difference between making a mud pie and building a much more elaborate and fairer structure. . . . Surely J's ironic point is that the second time around, Yahweh has learned better how the job ought to be done."

As for conventional morality: neither sex nor sin is at issue in J's version of the Fall. Being a monist, she could not conceive of the body disobeying the mind by lusting. To eat of the forbidden tree was simply to know the limits of being human. As Kafka put it: "Why do we lament over the fall of man? We were not driven out of Paradise because of it, but because of the Tree of Life, that we might not eat of it."

The failings of Sodom and Gomorrah did not lie in sexual perversity, but rather in the cities' inhospitality, "now as then a betrayal of the nomadic ideal," and this "contempt" weighed on Yahweh's sense of human vitality, the supreme joy of his creation.

In Yahweh, Mr. Bloom sees J's greatest character, God with a demonic streak, Shakespeare's naked Lear unfettered by Goneril's and Regan's inhospitality, Freud's superego punishing the discontented children of Moses. "From the standpoint of normative Judaism, Christianity and Islam," Mr. Bloom writes, "J is the most blasphemous writer that ever lived, far surpassing the beleaguered Salman Rushdie."

But Mr. Bloom holds out a promise. If you can brave the blasphemy, if you will strip off the multiple layers of traditional religion's varnish, "if you will do the work, then as Kierkegaard says, you will give birth to your own father."

As Mr. Bloom concludes his extraordinary probe of history's psyche: "Yahweh and Superego are after all versions of yourself, even if the authorities have taught you to believe otherwise. To say it another way, J's Yahweh and Freud's Superego are grand characters, as Lear is a grand character. Learning to read J ultimately will teach you how much authority has taught you already, and how little authority knows."

> Christopher Lehmann-Haupt, "New Words and Views on Roots of the Bible," in The New York Times, *September 20, 1990, p. C18.*

Frank Kermode

Who is this J, described by Harold Bloom in *The Book of J* as one of the greatest of all writers? Hitherto, J has been a mere patchwork of passages, by an unknown author or authors, in the first five books of the Bible. Biblical scholarship has, by long and minute labor, and with continuing controversy, established that these books are a redaction of at least four separate documents (some say more). One of these, usually regarded as the earliest, was given the label J, because it refers to God by the name Jahweh or Yahweh. Another is known as E because he calls God by the plural word Elohim, a word J uses only for angels. Later came P, a priestly contributor, who wrote Leviticus, and D, who contributed largely to Deuteronomy. Finally there was R, the Redactor who, after the return from the Babylonian Exile, put all the books into something like their present form.

Nobody knows who J, as the author of J has come to be called for short, was, and many believe there were several J's; but Mr. Bloom, while agreeing that all these different authors were involved, is quite sure there was only one J, whom he takes to have been a writer living in Jerusalem about 3,000 years ago, during the decadent reign of Reho-

boam. This person venerated the semidivine David and contributed to the cultural splendors of Solomon's court, along with another great writer, the author of II Samuel, who was probably a close friend.

Mr. Bloom has further decided that J was a woman, first arguing playfully that this assumption is no more and no less a fiction than the assumption that J was a man, and then, more positively, by adducing evidence for her feminine preferences. Thus J's most striking characters are women; her males are often childish. Even her Yahweh behaves like a headstrong, petulant boy, and is treated with a maternal indulgence tempered by irony. This hypothesis is advanced with the learning and ingenuity, the charm and the cheek, that characterize Mr. Bloom at his brilliant best. I can only hope that it will not cause such a stir that the rest of this fascinating book gets inadequate attention.

Mr. Bloom, the author of *The Anxiety of Influence* and many other books, has written quite a lot about J over the past few years, most recently and notably in *Ruin the Sacred Truths* (1989), where he calls J "a vastly eccentric great writer whose difficulty and originality are still obscured to us"—an *uncanny* writer, he likes to say; a sublime writer. In Mr. Bloom's view there is no difference whatever between sublime sacred and sublime secular literature; J is no more a religious writer than Shakespeare, whom she resembles in certain Bloomian respects. That J should be regarded as having to do with religion is the result of centuries of misreading by Jews, Muslims and Christians. Mr. Bloom's project is to strip away all these accretions and reveal for the first time what kind of book this woman wrote. He can even discuss lost passages, deleted or muted by her successors, that he knows by intuition she must have written.

So Mr. Bloom, connoisseur of sublimity, unveils and proceeds to adore Lady J, now seen to be a royal princess, perhaps a daughter of Solomon: a superb aristocrat, a rationalist, a comedian, a feminine ironist, one of Mr. Bloom's "strong" poets. He believes, correctly, that people rarely talk much sense about texts without thinking of them as having authors; hence this historical construct. It is there to enable him to have his remarkable say about J's book, which he does in an introduction (in which, by the way, he mentions me along with other critics who have analyzed the Bible) and a longer commentary.

Inserted between the two is a new translation of the J material by the poet David Rosenberg, the former editor in chief of the Jewish Publication Society. Mr. Rosenberg welcomes Mr. Bloom's thesis about J, even venturing a guess that J was in her 40's at the time of writing. He offers a rendition of her book intended to stay close to her rugged Hebrew, avoiding the accents of the King James Version (which, superb as it is, tends to make J and E and the rest sound the same) while avoiding also the blandness of the modern versions.

This bold and deeply meditated translation attempts to reproduce the puns, off-rhymes and wordplay of the original. In some respects, however, it seems misguided. Dryden said that Spenser, in imitating the ancients, "writ no language," and to write modern English as if it could simulate the terseness and the rhythms of biblical Hebrew is to risk writing no language at all.

Here are a few cavils: "The man named his wife Hava; she would have all who live, smooth the way, mother" (Genesis 3:20) is hardly English. Nor is " 'No', he said now, 'your sides split count on it' " (Genesis 18:15). Sometimes the attempt to avoid modern flatness itself falls flat: "What drama have you brought us?" (Genesis 26:10). And what are we to make of Esau's complaint (Genesis 27:36), "Was he named Jacob, heel-clutcher . . . that he might jaywalk behind me, twice?" What has jaywalking to do with the theft of birthright and blessing?

The Book of J says "The eyes of Leah were exquisite." Perhaps the Hebrew word is obscure; the King James Version says "tender eyed" (Genesis 29:17), the New English Bible, "dull-eyed." I looked it up in the Septaguint, the Greek Jewish Bible, reckoning that the Jews who wrote it, being 2,300 years closer to the original, might have some idea what it meant. They said Leah's eyes were *astheneis,* which means "sickly," "feeble," and the lexicon gives no hint whatever that it could be used to describe an attractive feature.

The tale of Dinah also is made to sound odd. When she went to see some "girlfriends in the country," Shechem seized her: "Lying with her, her guard was broken." Here is a dangling participle, as well as a peculiar maidenhead. Shechem, however, "had fallen in love" with her (the King James Version has "his soul clave unto Dinah" (Genesis 34:3), and the Greek is closer to that). Finally, one can't imagine a great writer giving Moses the line, "My lord, for what have you brought your people into this sad situation?" (Exodus 5:22). All the same, we may think that from time to time we hear, in this translation, the voice of Mr. Bloom's great, unexpected, uncanny author.

Mr. Bloom, connoisseur of sublimity, unveils and proceeds to adore Lady J, now seen to be perhaps a daughter of Solomon.

If one were to be severe, Mr. Bloom's contribution could be said to contain some chatter and repetition, but it is so beguiling that complaints of that kind would be churlish. He will say whatever he needs, however surprising, to discover J's "plain sense." Misunderstood for several millenniums, venerated for the wrong reasons by a long series of traducers, this sophisticated, comic, even on occasion ribald writer is closer to Kafka than to Torah as we now know it. Her "sublime fiction" has nothing to do with piety. Her manner is abrupt, ironic; she never judges, never blames. Her account of the disobedience of Adam and Eve has nothing to do with a Fall, only with an arbitrary and disproportionate punishment. Her version of the creation of Adam gives us a wanton Yahweh breathing life into a mud pie; but Eve's creation is lovingly dwelt on, for she is Adam's natural superior.

J's delight in these folk tales does not diminish her interest in the politics of her own time, and her book, we are told, is, at one remove, a lamentation for the decay of the kingdom, the tarnishing of the blessing handed on by David.

In *The Book of J* bright ideas gleam, vanish and are replaced by more. It pains a reviewer to be able to discuss so few of them. Believers, fundamentalists, may be shocked, but the effect on others will surely be refreshing, with just a little of the jolt that one sometimes gets from looking at a familiar painting newly cleaned. And even those who doubt whether Mr. Bloom has truly identified and fairly described his 3,000-year-old genius will surely not withhold a tribute to this author. Prolific and gifted though he has always been, this is his best book. (pp. 1, 24)

> *Frank Kermode, in a review of "The Book of J," in* The New York Times Book Review, *September 23, 1990, pp. 1, 24.*

Kenneth L. Woodward

After God, Victor Hugo once remarked, Shakespeare invented the most. But then Hugo had never heard of "J," the writer who may have invented God.

In modern Scripture scholarship, J is the label experts use to designate those scattered passages that refer to God as Jaweh or Yahweh. But in a controversial new book [*The Book of J*], Harold Bloom, Yale's iconoclastic literary critic, challenges the long-accepted interpretation of J's writings about the Creator. According to Bloom, Yahweh—the God of Abraham, Isaac and Jacob, the prototype of the Christians' God the Father and of the Muslims' Allah—is the literary invention of a sophisticated Israelite woman who lived 3,000 years ago during the decline of the Solomonic empire. Witty, ironic and not conventionally religious, this unknown author, Bloom says, fashioned the original stories of Adam, Noah, Abram and Moses, and above all the figure of Yahweh. Thus, Bloom argues, Yahweh was actually *the central character in a book of fiction* before he became the object of religious belief and worship. Unfortunately, says Bloom, later rabbis reworked her material and blended it with other texts to produce the Pentateuch, or first five books of the Hebrew Bible.

In his introduction to *The Book of J,* Bloom attempts to scrape away the layers of "varnish, plastered on by the rabbis, the Christian prelates and the [religious] scholars" to reveal something which he regards as superior to the Bible: the scattered remnants of a brilliant work of imaginative literature. Thus emancipated from "the prison" of Holy Writ, J emerges in Bloom's estimation as a "sublime" prose-poet on a par with Shakespeare, a "Jewish Chaucer" whose fictional portrayal of God is "blasphemy" by later Jewish or Christian standards.

At the center of *The Book of J* co-author David Rosenberg, a poet, gathers the passages attributed to J and translates from the Hebrew. Bloom then provides detailed commentary as if he were explicating a major poet. In Bloom's interpretation of Rosenberg's text, women like Tamar and Rebecca turn out to be stronger figures than Abram or

Moses—one sign, he says, that J was a woman. Another sign is the narration of Eve's creation: it is six times longer than the story of Adam's.

J's Yahweh, Bloom demonstrates, is an anthropomorphic figure of superhuman power and passion—not transcendent holiness. He often acts impulsively, more like an "impish" master of the universe than a judgmental deity. "Sin is not one of J's concepts," Bloom avers. Thus, J attaches no guilt to Adam and Eve's disobedience. In J's telling, the primal pair are merely rebellious children who show contempt for Yahweh's rules and are disproportionately punished by their unpredictable Maker. To be sure, Yahweh *does* destroy Sodom. But his revenge is inspired by the contempt the citizens showed for Yahweh, women and strangers, not because they routinely buggered unwary outsiders.

Bloom reads J's stories as high-spirited comedy. Her Yahweh wants his creatures to enjoy his blessing—a blessing which, says Bloom, means sharing the sort of vitality that God himself possesses in profusion. But many of J's heroes are weaklings: Moses is especially timorous, and for a while Yahweh contemplates killing him. Of all her male figures, the lyrical David, with his charm and outsize passions, comes closest to what J thinks God wants his people to be. Yahweh's own greatest attribute, says Bloom, is "an endless exuberance of energy." That—not holiness or progeny—is the blessing he offers his people.

Bloom argues [that] Yahweh was actually *the central character in a book of fiction* before he became the object of religious belief and worship.

Bloom is not a religious believer and there is in his interpretation much of William Blake's identification of energy with godliness and not a little of Freud's psychodynamics. Since J's God is a figure of the imagination, it is no wonder that Bloom's analogies are mostly literary. "I want the varnish off," Bloom writes, because "such a writer is worth more than many creeds, many churches, many scholarly certainties."

Most Biblical scholars agree that the Yahweh depicted in the J material is closer to King Lear than to the God of the Torah. But they disagree about whether that material is the work of one hand or of many. Bloom seems resigned to his theory of a sole, female author being "condemned as a fancy or a fiction"—but one that nevertheless helps readers to think of the J material as human script, not holy scripture.

Hebrew scholar Richard Elliott Friedman, author of a book on Biblical sources, says Bloom and Rosenberg have erroneously credited J with passages from other sources—rather like including *War and Peace* among the complete works of Dostoevsky. The controversy in fact has just begun. Yet to be heard from are scholars who still believe that God had a voice in telling his own story.

Kenneth L. Woodward with Larry Wilson, "The Woman Who Invented God," in Newsweek, *Vol. CXVI, No. 14, October 1, 1990, p. 62.*

Jack Miles

Harold Bloom has a lot of nerve, but then again he may not have nerve enough. *The Book of J,* Bloom's commentary on David Rosenberg's punning, experimental translation of portions of the books of Genesis, Exodus, and Numbers is both less and more than it seems.

It is less than it seems when Bloom writes, at the end of his introduction:

> I am aware that it may be vain labor, up Sinai all the way, as it were, to seek a reversal of twenty-five hundred years of institutionalized misreading. . . . Yet the book of J, though fragmentary, is hardly Mr. David Rosenberg's creation or my own. All I have done is to remove the book of J from its context in the Redactor's Torah and then to read what remains, which is the best and most profound writing in the Hebrew Bible.

Lay readers may be excused if they take away from that paragraph the mistaken impression that what Bloom calls the book of J, though not his creation, is at least his discovery, a discovery reversing "twenty-five hundred years of institutionalized misreading."

The inconvenient truth is that nothing in biblical interpretation is more thoroughly "institutionalized" than the notion that the Bible—and in particular the Pentateuch—is an edited work. The use of the letter *J* as the scholarly tag for the oldest of the four documents that after editing became the Pentateuch is a century old. The letter stands for *Jahve,* the German spelling of the reconstructed Hebrew god-name later respelled in English as *Yahweh.* Not even the separate publication of the Yahwist document is a new idea. In 1968, Peter Ellis published the Jerusalem Bible translation of J, with commentary, as *The Yahwist: The Bible's First Theologian.*

Bloom does not deny any of this. But he is not, as we say these days, quite "up front" about it either. Not until deep in the translator's first appendix do we learn that the authors have relied on Martin Noth, a German scholar whose major work is now two generations old, for their determination of just which portions of the Pentateuch should be regarded as part of J.

Bloom's main claim to originality, however, is not the isolation of J but the discovery or invention of "the author J," to whom he devotes the first sixty pages of this book. "As we read any literary work," he writes, "we necessarily create a fiction or metaphor of its author. That author is perhaps our myth, but the experience of literature partly depends on that myth. For J, we have a choice of myths, and I boisterously prefer mine to that of the biblical scholars. I will put all my cards on the reader's desk here, face up. My J is a *Gevurah* [*sic*] ("great lady") of post-Solomonic court circles, herself of Davidic blood, who began writing her great work in the later years of Solomon, in close rapport and exchanging influences with her good friend the Court Historian, who wrote most of what we now call 2 Samuel."

Boisterously, let me suggest that Bloom's most important card is not on the reader's desk at all. Bloom has lifted the notion that the author of J may have been a woman from Richard Elliott Friedman, who proposed it in *Who Wrote the Bible?* (1987). Bloom cites this work in another connection but does not credit Friedman for the provocative hypothesis that Bloom has placed at the center of his own work.

Nor is this Bloom's only unacknowledged debt. Frank Moore Cross, Hancock professor of Hebrew at Harvard University until his recent retirement, has been for a generation the learned and subtle proponent of a thesis crucial to *The Book of J;* namely that Israel's epic—Adam, Noah, Abraham, Jacob, Joseph, Moses—must be read in the light of the beliefs and prejudices of the Davidic dynasty. Bloom mentions Cross, as he mentions Friedman, in passing, but here too he fails to acknowledge his indebtedness where it counts.

Does this mean that Bloom's work is without originality? Not quite: *The Book of J* is a work of modest, if finally truncated, originality.

But before taking up its originality, I would digress for a moment on the background question of the recent use of historical-critical scholarship by literary critics. The moment seems to me to be one of rich irony.

Critical scholarship of the sort that began with Richard Simon's 1678 *Critical History of the Old Testament* and that came to a climax with Julius Wellhausen's 1883 *Prolegomena to the History of Israel* was essentially just a close reading of the text in the relative absence of theological preconditions. Though Simon called his work a critical history, you cannot really write the history of a thing using only the thing itself as source. Biblical history in the modern sense became possible only when archeology, including the recovery by archeology of lost languages and entire lost literatures, made possible the independent correction, completion, and, not infrequently, the confirmation of the Bible's own version of the events it reports. It was archeology, then, that turned critical scholarship into *historical-*critical scholarship.

Now, as to its tone and style, twentieth-century historical-critical Bible scholarship is very remote from literary appreciation. Though a literary text may remain historical-critical scholarship's ultimate object, it approaches that object through hieroglyphic, cuneiform, dendrochronology, comparative Semitic epigraphy, historical linguistics, and a score of ancillary disciplines of daunting complexity and negligible literary charm. The charge has quite properly been brought against such scholarship that it too often exchanges ends and means, reducing the Bible to data for the reconstruction of the politics and history of the ancient Near East.

Interestingly, however, a similar charge is regularly leveled against the neo-historicist criticism of modern literature that has lately become so influential on American campuses. What I find ironic is that this newest generation of *outré* literary criticism should have so much more in common with the staid older generation of highly technical Bible criticism than it does with the likes of Bloom, Frank Kermode, and Robert Alter. The latter, all professors of modern literature who have recently written on the Bible, are relative conservatives within their own field, radicals only when they set their caps against the "institutionalized misreading" of the Bible by historical-critical scholarship. A true literary radical like Michel Foucault, mucking about in the Bibliothèque Nationale, has more in common with a classic Orientalist like William Foxwell Albright, squinting at a squiggle on a scrap of parchment, than he does with an aesthete like Bloom. Foucault and Albright represent, even now, the threat of a literary leveling. Bloom, by contrast, represents the faintly antique folly of a literary exaltation.

What paleo- as well as neo-historicists object to in their more humanistic or literary colleagues is that the boys tend to get their facts wrong or only half right. In the present instance, Bloom denies, ignorantly and without argument, that oral tradition is possible or that literary creativity may be exercised by a community as well as by an individual. The folk tale, the folk song seem to be, for him, metaphysical impossibilities; no evidence can count in their favor. Bloom never adjusts his Bible interpretation by a hair's breadth in the light of an artifact or the evidence of literary parallels from elsewhere in the ancient Near East, and yet he is capable of reassigning a verse or an incident from another source to J simply because he finds it congenial. While, on the one hand, he takes the key findings of critical scholarship as given, on the other, he remains uncritically devoted to the romantic ideal of the genius writer, or perhaps the neo-romantic ideal of the genius writer read by the genius critic.

But so far, so fair: when historical-critical scholarship has done its best (or worst), it cannot and does not deny that there are genius writers and genius critics. The proof of this pudding, to return to the question of Bloom's originality, must be in the eating. What does this pudding taste like?

Bloom's method is circular and unabashedly subjective but, in my view, legitimate and, on occasion, brilliantly brought off. He infers a personality for his "great lady" from what she has written. Then, allowing the inference to feed his imagination, he reads the text again seeking what he might at first have missed. The text, now more deeply and artistically understood, further specifies the imagined personality of the author. And so on until text and writer (not to speak of critic) stand in a fully achieved reciprocity, creators of each other, as it were.

This method leads Bloom to four principal assertions:

1. J and her character Yahweh are both in love with David. In another Pentateuchal source, man is created in the image and likeness of God. In Bloom's J, Yahweh is

created in the image and likeness of Israel's exuberant founding monarch.

2. J and Yahweh are decidedly cool toward the stammering Moses and oddly detached, even ironic, toward the Mosaic religion. "The Yahwist herself is not *a* Yahwist," Bloom writes.

3. The theomorphic David aside, J and Yahweh respond more to vigorous women than to even the most vigorous men. "There is a grand hardness in J's women," Bloom writes, "in Sarai, Rebecca, Rachel, Tamar, and Zipporah, a hardness that perhaps J found in herself, or in Solomon's mother, Bathsheba. . . . "

Among all these women, it is, please note, Tamar whom J and Yahweh love best. An Adullamite married in turn to two of Judah's sons, both of whom die, Tamar seduces her father-in-law not just to avoid childlessness but also to claim a part in Israel's blessing and destiny. Bloom writes:

> Of all J's heroines, Tamar is the most vivid, and the most revelatory of J's identity. . . . I will go further and observe that Tamar, despite her brief appearance in only a single chapter, Genesis 38, is the most memorable character in the book of J. . . . Jacob wins the new name of Israel; even more gloriously, Tamar wins the immortality of her own name, and a central place in the story that she was not born into and so had to usurp for herself.

4. J and Yahweh are cool not just to Moses but also to the Israelite rank and file. They are aristocrats, in a word; their affections go to the chosen among the chosen: "A life-long monarchist, as I read her, a distruster of priests and people alike, she had more faith in David than in Yahweh."

More than can appear in such an enumeration, these are earned insights. Bloom may go perversely to those verses that most critics find peripheral or even undecipherable and ignore those verses, even in J, that most critics find central. The result, nonetheless, has impressive internal coherence. Bloom's essays, "The Representation of Yahweh" and "The Psychology of Yahweh" present a god with a daylight clarity that can be stunning.

It is in this sense that **The Book of J** is more than it seems. And yet there is, even on Bloom's own aesthetic and free-wheeling terms, a structural weakness in this work and even, as noted, a failure of nerve.

Bloom never thinks to ask about the overall aesthetic effect of the removal of those other materials that were combined with J by the ancient redactor. We may grant that their removal throws J into relief. What else does it do?

The fact is that this removal produces an effect rather like that of an opera cut to just the arias or a film with all the dissolves and fade-outs, all the "continuity," eliminated. Looked at one way, J without the rest of the Pentateuch is clean and masterful narrative; looked at another way, it is just "Bible stories" for children. Bloom writes, intuitively (and defensively): "We need to be like wise children in reading or listening to J, because her mode, and not just

in the primeval history of humankind, is like a more sophisticated kind of children's literature than we now possess." True, but perhaps all too true. There is a question here that needs more than Bloom has given it.

So much for the structural weakness. The failure of nerve is Bloom's failure to see how directly his evidence suggests that his "great lady," his *Gevurah,* is Bathsheba. The wife of a Hittite and almost certainly a Hittite or Canaanite herself, Bathsheba—as a nubile young woman—seduced the much older David even as Tamar, the Adullamite, seduced the older Judah. If Bathsheba is Bloom's J, we need not wonder that her sympathies tend so powerfully toward Tamar, that earlier gentile who forced her way into Israel's destiny.

No wonder, either, that David's queen should be so in love with her king as to take him as her model for the personality of God. Or that this foreign woman should look with such studied coolness on Moses and on the fiercer, more moralistic stand of Yahweh-worship that he represented. As we read in 1 Kings, Bathsheba was deeply involved in the court intrigues that brought her son, Solomon, to the throne. Among the things she did not blush to check up on, during that period, was whether Abishag, David's last concubine, was still a virgin after he had begun to sleep with her (she was). It is entirely possible that this indomitable queen mother survived her son as well as her husband, taking herself—quite as Bloom suggests—as the model for all those "hard" women of the patriarchal narratives, not least for the two—Sarai and Rebecca—who make impolite jokes about the sexual limitations of elderly men.

And finally, once her hapless grandson Rehoboam has betrayed the Davidic legacy, who better than the dowager queen to weave regal indignation into the warp and woof of Israel's foundation myth?

It all fits. Why does Bloom, otherwise so acute, fail to see it? He fails, in my view, because he has in **The Book of J** an agenda which requires the repudiation of the very insight that made his reputation in *The Anxiety of Influence.* In that book, Bloom taught us that a literary successor can escape the humiliation of being merely a successor by a "strong misreading" of his predecessor, strong misreading being the kind of deliberate, calculated error that brings new truth into view.

In **The Book of J,** by sharpest contrast with *The Anxiety of Influence,* Bloom wants history to stop. The earliest stratum of Yahwism is the only one worthy of consideration. No strong misreadings here, if you please. All successors, beginning with Moses himself, are to be seen as weak misreaders, mere corrupters.

But are they so in fact? Bloom, Yahweh's psychoanalyst, cannot fail to see the intrinsic interest in watching God's character change as the rest of the Hebrew Bible comes into being. But then can that process of becoming be called to a halt at the end of the Hebrew Bible? What is there, in principle, to prevent Israel's masterpiece from becoming, as Bloom bitterly puts it, "the Protestant Bible, in which the Hebrew Scriptures dwindle down to that captive prize of the gentiles, the Old Testament?"

The New Testament is, of course, the strongest, most outrageously successful misreading in history. If Bloom had the nerve to honor that misreading in the same spirit in which he honors Tamar for winning "a central place in the story that she was not born into and so had to usurp for herself," then he could also recognize all the greatness that intervenes—the greatness of Moses, not to speak of Jeremiah (whom he professes to despise) and Isaiah and Job. And if he could do all that, then he might have the nerve to face the implication in his own research that part of the Hebrew Bible was a gentile "captive" in its opening moments; that, in sum, Bathsheba invented Yahweh.

I don't know that a serious case can be made that Bathsheba was the Yahwist; but if we are in the realm of the boisterous rather than the serious, fictionalizing her is certainly a better bet than fictionalizing a German abbreviation. Bathsheba is a real woman, full of all the appetites of which fiction is made. Her career begins with lust in the dawn of Davidic glory and ends with ambition in its twilight. The possibilities for an imaginative (and heuristic) elaboration of her role are endless, particularly if we recall that the Solomonic era represented the high tide of Israelite openness to Canaanite and other foreign cultural influences, not just in art and architecture but also in literature and religion. Solomon himself, late in life, became an Astarte worshipper, according to 1 Kings 11. It is not implausible, in principle, that a foreign writer—whether Bathsheba or another—could have had a hand in writing some of the fledgling kingdom's first scriptures and could have introduced a subversive note of hostility to the exclusive covenant that Israel understood itself to have with the god of its fathers, whom it had boldly identified with El, the universal Semitic high god, and then declared the only true god.

Bloom's charge that the gentiles, with their New Testament, make a hostage of the Hebrew Bible is true but deserves to be handled as something more than a side-of-the-mouth slur. The New Testament is indeed a literary and religious raid on the Jewish covenant, but it only continues a struggle that began much earlier. That struggle was full-blown centuries before the rise of Christianity; and Christianity's resolution of it via a new covenant, though dramatically successful, is not the only possible resolution.

Tamar the Adullamite, Rahab the Canaanite, Uriah the Hittite, Naaman the Aramean, Ruth the Moabite—the list of gentiles whose virtue the Old Testament flings in the face of Israel is long and shocking. Among ancient literatures, that of ancient Israel is in this regard utterly without parallel. No other nation has so calculatedly undermined its own national myth.

Now, just here, in this process of subversion and counter-subversion is where we might have expected Bloom to excel. If he is not the leading literary critic of the day, he may be at least the leading diagnostician of literary strategy. When the Hebrew Bible celebrates gentiles, it gives evidence of an ancient quarrel, whether that quarrel be regarded as between contending ideas in the mind of Israel or between contending groups sharing the life and worship of Israel. This quarrel is the perfect subject for a critic with Bloom's gifts.

Regrettably, he ducks it. Determined to trump the New Testament, Bloom dismisses the subject of testaments or covenant altogether. J, he says, responds to "vitalism" and "impish" anarchy, not to covenant and stifling order: "Her Yahweh moves her at the rare moments when he is Davidic." What Bloom loses by this dismissal, this default, is nothing less than the plot of the Hebrew Bible. A high price to pay for tweaking the beard of the Apostle Paul. (pp. 639-42)

Jack Miles, "The Book of B: Bloom, Bathsheba & The Book," in Commonweal, *Vol. CXVII, No. 19, November 9, 1990, pp. 639-42.*

John Barton

I remember my surprise when a student of mine wrote a paper about the book of Job, and referred to the author throughout as "he or she." Perhaps such evenhandedness is now standard in North America, but it certainly isn't in Oxford. But I realized that I had simply assumed the author was male, without examining the reasons. Nonreligious feminist critics become angry at the patriarchal attitudes in much of the Bible, while Jewish and Christian feminists often argue that, within the assumptions of an admittedly patriarchal society, the Bible scores quite highly for its treatment of women. But until now no critic known to me has argued that any substantial part of the Bible had a woman as its author.

Professional scribes in the ancient world were men: so much we know or think we do. But was every book in the Bible written by a professional scribe? Probably not. Were women literate? Some, perhaps. By arguing [in *The Book of J*] that a singularly important section of the Hebrew Bible may have been written by a woman, Harold Bloom enlarges our ideas about ancient Hebrew literature. The balance of probability is against him, but the idea is intriguing and must not be dismissed.

Bloom thinks an important strand in the early part of the Bible, designated by many scholars as "J," was written by a princess of the line of King David, probably in the early years of David's successor but one, Rehoboam (922-915 BCE). She had lived through the golden age of Solomon (961-922 BCE), David's son and heir, and then had seen Solomon's achievements squandered by the ineptitude of the new king. The detailed history of this period can be found in the latter part of the Second Book of Samuel and in 1 Kings 1-12. Most of 2 Samuel was written by her contemporary, the so-called "Court Historian": Bloom thinks they used to compare notes. Be that as it may, the existence of the Court Historian is accepted by most biblical scholars, though they do not always agree about how close he was to the events he chronicled. Bloom here builds on a theory of the German biblical scholar Gerhard von Rad, still widely influential among students of the Hebrew Bible, that the age of Solomon was a period of cultural "enlightenment," worthy to be compared with the European Enlightenment: a somewhat secularized era, in which many old beliefs were questioned. It is from this age that many of the best narratives in the Bible come: works with as much power as the Homeric poems, yet even earlier in date.

But where in the Bible is the work of "J"? "J" belongs to a hypothesis about the composition of the Five Books of Moses (the Pentateuch, or Torah as the Hebrew Bible calls them). Even if one reads the Pentateuch in the sonorous King James version, one soon becomes aware that it is a very strange work to have been written by Moses or indeed by any single author. Versions of the same story appear more than once (compare Genesis 12:14-20 with Genesis 20), and some passages are so convoluted that any attempt to reduce them to a single narrative thread is soon defeated. In the story of the Flood, for example (Genesis 6-8), incidents are repeated needlessly, and the duration of the flood is virtually impossible to calculate even though many explicit figures are provided, because so many of the figures are mutually incompatible.

Detailed studies of such problems led, during the eighteenth and nineteenth centuries, to a widely accepted solution, given its definitive shape by Julius Wellhausen (1844-1918). This hypothesis used textual analysis to argue that there were four separate documents or sources of widely differing dates: "J," the earliest; "E," a fragmentary, alternative, and bowdlerized version of "J"; "D," mainly found in the book of Deuteronomy, and written not long before the Jewish exile to Babylon (587 BCE); and finally "P," the work of priests in the Second Temple period (around 450 BCE). Add to this the "redactor" (or a whole series of redactors) who spliced and edited the four "sources," and you have the Wellhausen hypothesis. Wellhausen himself thought that "J" came from the ninth century, the age of Elijah and Elisha, but some scholars—notably von Rad—have argued for a tenth-century date, and Bloom has based his work on the tenth-century hypothesis.

Identifying "J" sections of the Pentateuch is not hard. They comprise almost all the best stories, beginning with the creation of human beings in Genesis 2, and ending with the death of Moses. Bloom thus draws on a long tradition of biblical criticism, without weighing the detailed objections that the Wellhausen hypothesis has been subjected to, though he is plainly aware of them. But traditional criticism has tended to see "J" as a collector of older stories, and not so creative a writer as Bloom would have us believe. The great charm of Bloom's book is the way he proceeds, by a close reading of the text, to establish "J" as an author in her own right—the earliest but also the best of all Hebrew writers.

Among current literary critics of the Bible Bloom is heretical in commenting on a reconstructed "source" rather than on the finished text as it lies before us. It is something of a dogma now that traditional biblical criticism has been, as the University of California critic Robert Alter puts it, "excavative": it has always been looking "beneath" or "behind" the biblical text for hypothetical earlier, underlying sources or fragments. Alter himself has insisted on the present form of the text to such an extent that he considers even textual emendations of the most obvious kind doctrinally impure, and to be eschewed. Since the various sources were fused in the text we now have, Alter

believes that the text should not be pulled apart. The injunction to "read what is put before you" is the motto of most articles in *The Literary Guide to the Bible,* edited by Alter and by Frank Kermode. This literary dogma joins hands easily with a traditional Jewish or Christian belief that the books of the Bible just as they stand are divinely inspired, and that it is a form of impiety to probe behind them. Thus a highly secular and a highly religious response to scripture produce, strangely enough, the same effect.

Bloom will have none of this. He maintains that the composite nature of the Pentateuchal narratives is obvious to any sensitive "literary" reader. "J" would eventually have been discovered by such readers even if it had not been reconstructed by (largely Christian) biblical scholars. The author of "J" was a literary genius, whereas the other sources are quite pale and bland: the difference, for Bloom, leaps out of the page. Biblical scholars who have recently tried to defend their traditional "excavative" craft against Jewish or Christian fundamentalists, and their more sophisticated recent descendants, have constantly had the ground pulled out from under their feet by an appeal to the style of current "secular" (hence, it is implied, religiously unbiased) literary criticism. For if critics of the stature of Kermode and Alter find no reason to base their work on analyses of different "sources," who are these philistine biblical scholars to cut beautifully constructed texts up into little bits?

Bloom's work comes as a shaft of sunlight into this murky debate, showing us how worthwhile "fragmentation" can be if it gives us access to a writer as inventive and remarkable as "J." The final chapter, "The Greatness of J," argues for placing "her" in the same class as Shakespeare. Like Shakespeare, Bloom's J is a pioneer who is uniquely aware of her characters' psychological complexity, and whose genius is not bound by the genres available in her culture. She welds together all the available genres to make a prose poem, neither epic nor romance nor tragedy nor comedy yet all these at once. She stands at the beginning of the Hebrew narrative tradition, but like Homer she is greater than all who come after her.

The use of the letter "J" in biblical exegesis derives from the German "Jahwe," spelled "Yahweh" in English. The earliest of the Pentateuchal sources is called after "Yahweh" because in it God has been invoked by this name since very soon after the creation of humankind (Genesis 4:26). Later sources, especially "P," maintain that the name was first revealed to Moses (Exodus 3:13-15, compare also 6:2-3), and hold (probably mistakenly) that it had something to do with the verb "to be"—hence the paraphrase of the name as I AM THAT I AM in Exodus 3:14. The foundations of what we now recognize as Judaism were laid in the period when "P" was writing, some time in the fifth century BCE, and within Jewish tradition it came to be thought blasphemous to utter the name. When a reader was confronted with its four consonants (YHVH) in a biblical scroll, he said instead *"Adonai,"* which means "Lord." English Bibles with rare exceptions have followed this custom, but print LORD in capitals to indicate that it stands for the sacred Tetragrammaton (or four sacred consonants) and not for the actual Hebrew word *Adonai*. (A much later custom of writing the consonants of Yahweh with the vowels of *Adonai* produced the strange hybrid form "Jehovah," but this is a word that never existed in antiquity.) When J was writing, none of these taboos yet existed. For the people of the tenth century BCE "Yahweh" was simply the name of Israel's God, freely used both in invocation and in narration.

Now this shift from directness to reverence in the use of the divine name is a representative example of a much wider development. The Yahweh of J, Bloom argues, is not the holy, utterly transcendent, totally good God of later Judaism, Christianity, and Islam. He is a character in J's story, and his main characteristic is not holiness or morality but exuberance (or zeal or zest, as he sometimes puts it). J's Yahweh is an imp, unpredictable and tricky—not unlike Jacob, the patriarch who was to inherit the blessing of his father Isaac but did so mainly by deceit. J does not worship Yahweh; she takes a detached view of him as one of her best characters. In a sense Yahweh is the "hero" of J's narrative, if by "hero" we mean "central character." But in another sense J has no heroes, only heroines.

> None of J's male personages, Yahweh included, ever surmount their childlike and also childish qualities. The only grown-ups in J are women: Sarai, Rebecca, Rachel, Tamar. Isaac is always a baby, Abram and Judah easily fall into childishness, and the two men of acute sensibility—Jacob and Joseph, father and true son—remain wonderfully spoiled and gifted temperaments, childlike in the extreme, until they die.

The formation of the Pentateuch, for Bloom, is one long tale of backpedaling from this daring and exuberant vision of the national god. It is rather as if the skeptical Euripides had been the first great Greek tragedian instead of the last. The normative religious tradition in Judaism became nervous of the god of J, as well it might, and ensconced Yahweh firmly in the holy of holies in the temple, safe from prying and mischievous eyes such as hers. Yahweh became remote, dwelling in unapproachable light. Contact with him could be established only through the approved rituals overseen by the official priesthood. Already in Ezekiel, perhaps an older contemporary of P (mid-sixth century), we find a vision of God which describes what the prophet saw as "the appearance of the likeness of the glory of the LORD" (see Ezekiel 1:28). Later writers would not even venture so far, and Saint John's Gospel reminds Christians that "no one has seen God at any time" (John 1:18).

J's Yahweh walks in the garden of Eden to enjoy the evening breeze, and comes down to have a picnic with Abram; and he shuts the door of Noah's ark with his own kindly hands. But he is not to be trusted, and this is the other and blacker side of J's vision. He attacks Moses himself for no good reason; and he blesses the trickster Jacob instead of his elder and more honest brother, Esau. Yahweh, in J's narrative, is not nice to know: he is a fascinating character, but he is not the God that Jews or Christians worship, he just happens to share the same name. "I am afraid," Bloom writes,

this means that Judaism is just as far away from the Yahwist as Christianity is. The great rabbis, say Hillel and Akiba, are in the service of a God who is very different from J's Yahweh. Like every other religion, Judaism asserts more continuities in its history than actually exist. . . . What is totally unassailable is the vast gulf between the Yahweh of the Book of J and the God of Judaism.

Jewish and Christian commentators on J thus stand both accused of reading back their own spiritual and theological interests into the Hebrew Bible. Even those who have recognized that there is change and progression from J to P—from the Yahwist's Yahweh to the priestly writers' LORD—have usually made the mistake of seeing progression as progress. "Anthropomorphism," correctly used to describe J's homely yet at times sinister (*unheimlich*) Yahweh, has become a derogatory term for a belief in God which has not yet attained to full monotheism, a belief without the subtleties of the Judaeo-Christian exaltation of the supreme Creator.

> The long history of what is called "the problem of anthropomorphism" brought about by J's depictions of Yahweh constitutes one of the curious cultural comedies of Western religious tradition. Embarrassment caused by the impishness of J's Yahweh presumably began with the early revisionists, attaining a first culmination with the work of the Redactor, . . . and became far more overt . . . during the last two centuries before the common era. Greek philosophy demanded a dehumanized deity, and Jewish Hellenists rather desperately sought to oblige, by allegorizing away a Yahweh who walked and who argued, who ate and who rested, who possessed arms and hands, face and legs.

But Bloom also suggests that the nineteenth-century German scholarship that gave us back J was, unfortunately, tainted with this same opposition to anthropomorphism in portraying the deity, which it saw as something crude and unsophisticated.

> The crucial nineteenth-century biblical scholars were the triad Karl Heinrich Graf, Wilhelm Vatke, and Wellhausen. . . . Unfortunately, these grand savants were all Hegelians, and like Hegel, they saw Israelite faith as a primitive preparation for the sublimities of the true religion, high-minded Christianity. . . . The idealist anti-Semitism of this biblical Hegelianism is almost enough to explain the strong resistance of normative Jewish scholars to the Documentary Hypothesis.

All credit to Bloom that he does not do so. But in taking over the common accusation that Wellhausen, like Vatke, was a Hegelian, he deprives himself of the chance to call the most valuable possible witness in favor of his own reading of J. Like Bloom, Wellhausen thought J's picture of Yahweh anthropomorphic and therefore more admirable than the pale priestly religion which eventually overlaid and concealed it. For Wellhausen was decidedly not a Hegelian; he regarded Hegelianism as long-outmoded nonsense (see L. Perlitt's study *Vatke und Wellhausen*, which refuted the charge of Hegelianism definitively as long ago as 1965). So far from endorsing the Hegelian view that Judaism had slowly advanced from the crudities of J, Wellhausen saw even simple philosophical monotheism, let alone "priestly" religion, as a sign that Hebrew faith was becoming ossified and rigid. J was anthropomorphic, according to Wellhausen, because it came from a period of direct spontaneity in religious response, a "natural" religion that had not yet been handed over to the theologians. Certainly, one does not find in Wellhausen that J is a sly and sophisticated author, as one does in Bloom's interpretation; but nor does one find any appreciation for the dry and bookish religion of the priestly writers who came after. Bloom should look at Wellhausen again, and would find a man much more after his own heart than he has realized.

The Book of J has a complicated structure, and divides into five parts—it is pentateuchal, in fact, unsurprisingly. The first part establishes the identity of the J material, and goes on to reconstruct the author, or to "imagine" the author, as Bloom puts it. One can never be sure how far his proposals about the author's sex and identity are meant seriously, and how far they may be a way of playing the reader like a fish with sparkling ideas that are in part pure whimsy. Sometimes Bloom is a sober literary historian; at others he is playing a kind of "reader response" game with us, telling us that it will be more fun to pretend that J was a princess of the Davidic line than a boring man of letters.

The second part consists of a new translation of the J material by David Rosenberg. Then Bloom provides a section-by-section commentary on almost this text. I say "almost," because there are a few incidents which Bloom regards as by J but which Rosenberg does not translate. For example, Bloom draws out the humor in the story of Jacob and the striped and spotted goats (Genesis 30) but unfortunately the story cannot be found in Rosenberg's text—or perhaps this is a meta-joke. There follows an "After Commentary" arranged thematically, on such matters as the representation and the psychology of Yahweh in J, and the way J has been woven into the finished Pentateuch. Lastly Rosenberg provides a commentary on his own interpretative choices in the translation.

This is a translation people will either love or loathe. It reminds me a little of Tony Harrison's version of Aeschylus, with a spare, sinewy strength and no frills of any kind. Since the message of Bloom's work is that we should recapture the original J by stripping away all later accretions and interpretations, this style is a good vehicle for the commentary. It does not sound anything like what we think of as "biblical English." It is deliberately alien and unfamiliar. . . .

For my taste the mixture of high-toned and colloquial language in this translation does not work very well, and I would not use it apart from Bloom's commentary. But what is a modern Bible translator to do? Almost all possible styles have already been tried, and so will not do the job of presenting the reader with the sense of an ancient, alien text. Some of Rosenberg's attempts to render wordplay produce rather excruciating puns: " 'May this son en*joy safe*ty from Yahweh,' said Rachel. So it was: Rachel had Joseph." (*joy/safe* = Joseph). But the alternative

would be a footnote, and then we should be into a commentary by Rosenberg as well as by Bloom.

Some features I found merely irritating: "Now look," which is used many times for "behold" (*hinneh* in Hebrew), conveys too much meaning; it sounds admonitory, even critical, in a way that the Hebrew does not. Modern English, unlike French (*voilà*), has no word of this kind, so more subtle strategies are needed to convey the necessary degree of surprise, delight, or emphasis.

But taken together with Bloom's commentary, the translation is acceptable and useful. Now look: *The Book of J* should be read by students of general literature and of the Bible alike. It may be brilliant, or it may be wildly anachronistic—I suspect it is both—but it is not a book one can ignore. (pp. 3-4)

> *John Barton, "It's a Girl!" in* The New York Review of Books, *Vol. XXXVII, No. 18, November 22, 1990, pp. 3-4.*

H. L. Mortimer, Jr.

The recent controversy surrounding secular interpretations of sacred icons, such as Salman Rushdie's *Satanic Verses* and Martin Scorsese's *The Last Temptation of Christ,* would be enough to frighten away any novice covenant hunter. But Harold Bloom, consummate literary critic and Yale professor, now dares to assert [in *The Book of J*] that the oldest strand in the Pentateuch—what scholars call the Yahwist, or J text (c. 950-900 B.C.E.)—was never intended to be read as holy scripture. Rather, the stories of Adam and Eve and the apple, Cain's slaying of Abel, Noah, Moses and the Israelites, and others, were all composed by an author of supreme literary genius, a predecessor to the likes of William Shakespeare and Franz Kafka. Bloom further proclaims that this enlightened and ironic author J was neither Moses nor a professional scribe, but a woman related by blood or marriage to the royal house of David.

Although Bloom's bold assertions may inspire controversy among devout Jews and Christians alike, he writes that it was never his intent to further the interests of any religious group. Instead, his interpretation of poet David Rosenberg's startling translation of J challenges 3,000 years of Jewish and Christian revision that have obscured "the best and most profound writing in the Hebrew Bible."

> Before a plant of the field was in earth, before a grain of the field sprouted—Yahweh had not spilled rain on the earth, nor was there man to work the land—yet from the day Yahweh made earth and sky, a mist from within would rise to moisten the surface. Yahweh shaped an earthling from clay of this earth, blew into its nostrils the wind of life. Now look: man becomes a creature of flesh.—*The Book of J.*

The history of J's reduction began with the Elohist, or E, whose revision (c. 850 B.C.E.), according to Bloom, mixes a variety of material from sources that are now lost in an attempt to reduce J to a normative text. The Deuteronomists and the Priestly Authors made their slight but damaging revisions between 650 and 500 B.C.E. However, for Bloom, the real villain is the Redactor, R, who may have "performed a work of *avodah*, of service, to Yahweh," by producing the Torah of today. Unfortunately, though, this scribe completely shattered J's imaginative genius.

J's text can be distinguished from that of her successors by her use of what Bloom calls dramatic irony. Her uncanny ability to create incongruities between what develops in the narrative and what the characters comprehend is rivaled only by Shakespeare. This ability is also, as Bloom notes, the main cause of J's misinterpretation. For instance, the story of Adam and Eve, as told by J, does not involve a Fall. J portrays the original couple as disobedient children who simply succumb to their curiosity and temptations. Yahweh, it seems, is just as much to blame for he put the sacred tree of "good and bad" within easy reach.

> Now the woman sees how good the tree looks, to eat from, how lovely to the eyes, lively to the mind. To its fruit she reached; ate, gave to her man, there with her, and he ate. And the eyes of both fall open, grasp knowledge of their naked skin.

To J, the expulsion from the Garden derives from Yahweh's worry that the couple, having opened their eyes to everything, will want to eat from the tree forever.

> "Look," said Yahweh, "the earthling sees like one of us, knowing good and bad. And now he may blindly reach out his hand, grasp the tree of life as well, eat, and live forever." Now Yahweh took him out of the Garden of Eden, to toil—in the soil from which he was taken.

Yahweh throws his creations out, not as punishment for their sexual awakening but because he fears their potential rivalry.

What do we make of Yahweh's jealous and selfish behavior? According to Bloom, J's Yahweh is completely unlike the God of Judaism, Christianity, and Islam. He strolls around the Garden; he sits under the terebinth trees at Mamre to eat veal calf and curds; he even appears to Moses with murderous intent, for no reason. And unlike the ancient "maker-gods" of Egypt and Mesopotamia, who stood in front of a potter's wheel to perform their creation, Yahweh molds Adam from a handful of clay, "rather like a solitary child making a mud pie."

Yahweh, J's word for God, is a literary character of Shakespearean dimension. His "incommensurateness" is a metaphor for man's desire for fame, to be god-like. Modeled after J's idol, King David, he is a sophisticated creation unmatched in J's time. J's Yahweh is also an "antithetical imp," in Bloom's eyes, a mischief-maker whose anthropomorphism has been a thorn in the side of normative Jews for centuries. But this "human-all-too-human" behavior seems, to Bloom, to be a deliberate scandal. Where most scholars view the ancients as solemn and orderly, Bloom believes that Yahweh was no divine bureaucrat. It is his conviction that the original model for the

God of Judaism and Christianity is a child "who behaves sometimes as though he is rebelling against his mother, J."

Throughout the book, Bloom refers to J as a woman, but nowhere does he construct a defense of his hypothesis. In fact, he merely suggests that it is just as much a fiction or fantasy to suppose that *The Book of J* was written by a man. He is not the first to make this proposal: Scholars, such as Gerhard von Rad and Frank Moore Cross, have also assumed one Yahwist author writing under the sponsorship of the enlightened Solomonic royal court.

However, Bloom does point out several reasons why he sticks to this theory of J's femininity. First, J devotes approximately six times more space to the creation of woman than to man. Bloom is struck not by the quantity but by the quality of the creation. Eve was born from flesh, not clay, and she is presumably animate at birth and does not need to be inspirited by the breath of Yahweh. Clearly, "J's ironic point is that the second time around, Yahweh has learned better how the job ought to be done."

Second, Bloom makes the observation that J has no heroes, only heroines. Women such as Sarai, Rachel, and Tamar are much more admirably portrayed than their husbands, brothers, and fathers. J's vision of human reality differs greatly from that of her descendants, the Prophets. She views power as familial rather than royal, communal instead of courtly, like "a wise woman." Her genius, Bloom believes, is to retell her people's story so that the Patriarchs become the connecting links between the origins of humankind and the return of the Jewish people to their own land.

Bloom is not a theologian seeking to uncover new source material. He is not a "believer" or historian. He is foremost a literary critic, and as one his concern is to flesh out, as he says, the "vagaries of the Sublime." He does not seek to read religion out of the Bible. Rather, he is restoring to it the literary value that he feels it once had. Recovering J as a writer of unprecedented sophistication will not shed new light on the Bible, nor will it bring the reader closer to God. Bloom's task does, however, expertly reveal a writer who is "worth more than many creeds, many churches, many scholarly certainties." (pp. 15, 19)

> *H. L. Mortimer, Jr., in a review of "The Book of J," in* The Bloomsbury Review, *Vol. 11, No. 1, January-February, 1991, pp. 15, 19.*

Edward Hirsch

It takes a leap of readerly imagination for us to consider the actual nature of the archaic Hebrew writer, or writers, who inscribed the oldest stories in what scholars have come to think of as an extremely heterogeneous and composite text: the first five books of the Bible. No one really knows who composed or edited those books, which Jews call the Torah (invariably and somewhat narrowly translated as "Law") or the Pentateuch (which derives from a Greek term meaning "the book of the five scrolls") or the Five Books of Moses, but they have shaped our sensibilities so profoundly that we can scarcely understand how much we are their inventions. No one who grew up reading these Biblical stories, so deeply familiar and yet fundamentally strange, or listened to them—as I did—as if history itself were speaking, can ever be entirely free of their influence. The cycle that runs from the creation of Adam to the death of Moses has had an incalculable hold on our imaginations; indeed, what designs these texts have on us, and who in turn designed them, has inspired so much commentary that it could probably be used as landfill for the Dead Sea. Even so, if the literary critic Harold Bloom and the translator David Rosenberg are correct in their audacious new work of reconstruction, *The Book of J,* then we have misunderstood some of the most critical dimensions of these narratives. And we have weakly underimagined the author who composed them.

Who is this J that Harold Bloom has called "a vastly eccentric great writer," a genius equal to Dante and Shakespeare, an ironic precursor of Tolstoy, Mann, and Kafka? Previously, J has been considered a documentary source, or sources; a traditional process of accretion, revision, and interpretation; a patchwork of laconic narrative passages. Through a long and arduous process, beset by continual disagreements and controversies, Biblical scholarship has identified at least five main strands that have come together in the final text of the Pentateuch. J, known as the Yahwist, because of a distinctive use of the name for God (Yahweh, or, in German, Jahweh, misspelled as Jehovah), is the most ancient and radically original of these strands. J's text is embedded in the books now called Genesis, Exodus, and Numbers, and constitutes the largest single narrative block in the Pentateuch. Most of the great early Biblical stories—from the Expulsion to the Exodus—originated with J, perhaps sometime between the mid-tenth and the late ninth century B.C.E. Yet the question of whether or not there ever was an individual J remains open. Hans Schmid, in his book *The Putative Yahwist* (1976), takes the position that the J text developed over a period of four or five hundred years, and that "instead of speaking of the Yahwist as a single collector, author and theologian, one should rather speak of an (inner-) Yahwistic process of editing and interpretation."

There is no consensus on the full dimensions of the J text, because the Yahwist was followed by a long succession of other sources, who edited, revised, and, as Bloom would have it, "censored" the original body of stories. After J came E (known as the Elohist, because he refers to God by the plural Elohim, a name that J uses for angels), D (the Deuteronomist), and then P, the priestly sources who reworked earlier material and spliced their own didactic interpretations onto it, diluting the combined JE and adding extensive passages of Levitical laws. It is most likely the priestly writers and editors, with their theological, cultic, and institutional concerns, who developed the preliminary canon of the Hebrew Bible. R represents the last stage of the process: the Redactor, or redactors, who selected, changed, and fused all the scrolls together sometime after the Babylonian exile. It was R, conventionally placed in the Academy of Ezra around the year 400 B.C.E.—as much as six hundred years after J—who gave the Torah its decisive formulation.

R was one of the supreme synthesizers of the Hebrew Bible. Critics who have made convincing cases for the literary unity of the Pentateuch—such as Robert Alter, in *The Art of Biblical Narrative* (1981), and Northrop Frye, in *The Great Code* (1982)—are, in effect, praising R's work. As David Damrosch suggests in *The Narrative Covenant* (1987), the later redactors tried to create a text, seamless and whole, that concealed its own compositional history. And what R hoped to obscure approximately twenty-four hundred years ago is precisely what Bloom and Rosenberg have struggled to excavate. Their strategy is to lift the J text from its contextual surroundings in R's Torah and then to translate and interpret it. The result is nothing less than a very old and a very new work of literature, a hypothetical "Book of J."

In a playful, speculative, and brilliant disquisition on the "Author J" Bloom situates an individual Yahwist in Jerusalem nearly three thousand years ago. He asserts that J was not a professional scribe or copyist, as has sometimes been suggested, even less a court theologian, but, rather, an erudite member of the Solomonic élite who lived at or near the decadent court of King Rehoboam of Judah, Solomon's son and successor (922-915 B.C.E.), and wrote in friendly competition with the Court Historian, the writer responsible for what is now known as II Samuel. Bloom's most startling surmise is that J was a woman—a *gevurah,* or "great lady," possibly related to the Court Historian by either blood or marriage, possibly even a princess, one of Solomon's daughters. It is this writer of Davidic royal blood whom Bloom exalts to the highest literary throne, where she somewhat ironically presides, along with Shakespeare, over the spiritual consciousness of Western literature.

Bloom is well aware that his version of the historical J is a fiction, but then, as he suggests, all versions of the early Biblical authors—no matter how well grounded in research or attested to by faith—are fictions. Yet his admittedly free speculations are not entirely outside the line of modern Biblical scholarship. Like scholars before him, he dismisses the idea of a Mosaic authorship for the Pentateuch as a religious fabrication. As long ago as the twelfth century, Abraham Ibn Ezra circumspectly pointed out that passages in the Torah were inevitably post-Mosaic, and in the seventeenth century Spinoza identified some of the internal discrepancies, divisions, anachronisms, and duplications in the received text, thus inaugurating the "higher" Biblical criticism. More recently, such scholars as Gerhard von Rad and Frank Moore Cross have contravened the so-called Documentary Hypothesis (definitively formulated in the nineteenth century) by assuming that there was in actuality only one Yahwist working in the Solomonic period. It was von Rad who first perceived the possible subtext in the J work which connected it to the achievements of the United Monarchy, under David, and to the Solomonic Enlightenment. And it was the late E. A. Speiser, editor of the superb edition of Genesis in the Anchor Bible Series, who deduced a relationship between the Yahwist and the Court Historian. In *King and Kin* (1986) Joel Rosenberg fleshes out the political context of these two possibly companion works, Genesis and II Samuel, and in *Who Wrote the Bible?* (1987) Richard Friedman identifies at least six different places where the Yahwist linguistically improvises on the Hebraic root of Rehoboam's name. Mr. Friedman also points out that the J stories are much more sympathetic to women than were later stories by E, and, though he stops short of concluding that J was a woman, he opens up the possibility by suggesting that "we cannot by any means be quick to think of this writer as a man." Bloom relies heavily on this previous scholarship, and takes it one step further to assert that J and the Court Historian not only worked together but did so during two distinct periods of history. They share, in his words, "a nostalgia for David, a dubiety about the Solomonic splendor, and an ironic disdain for Rehoboam." The consequences of such a hypothesis are enormous. For example, in this reading of the J text the story of the expulsion from the Garden of Eden becomes less a parable of the Fall, as it has so often been read in Christian revisionism, than a metaphor or trope for the painful transition from Solomon to Rehoboam, and the subsequent reduction and dispersal of the kingdom. Many have pointed out that J's work, unlike the revisions of the redactors, is profoundly narrative, earthbound, and humanistic.

Bloom departs from Biblical scholarship in his insistence on reading J's work exclusively as a secular text, no more sacred than Tolstoy's novels or Shakespeare's *King Lear*. He disregards oral tradition, declares that distinctions of genre are irrelevant in relation to J's writing, and argues that she was deliberately *not* creating a national epic. His J was neither a religious nor a historical writer but an aristocratic storyteller. Yet his own critical reading is continually shadowed by the theological aura that surrounds J's greatest literary creation, the character of Yahweh. (No one prays to King Lear.) Indeed, Bloom's boisterous and self-proclaimed antithetical aim is nothing less than to undo a couple of thousand years of institutionalized misreading of J—to cut through the layers of varnish that converted J first into the Torah, then into the Hebrew Bible, and then into the Christian Old Testament. He likes to cite William Blake's maxim that religious history consists of "choosing forms of worship from poetic tales."

Most of the attention that *The Book of J* has thus far received has focussed on the polemical contention that J was a woman, a claim that is asserted rather than proved. Part of the argument rests on J's representation of women. For evidence, Bloom suggests that J devoted six times as much space to the creation of woman as to that of man, that she has no heroes but only heroines (Eve, Sarah, Rebecca, Rachel, Tamar, and Zipporah), that human reality is for her domestic and familial rather than royal or priestly, that she undermines and mocks rather than endorses patriarchal authority, and that she exalts women as tougher and more vital than men. This case is intuitively appealing but rationally flawed. From these essentialist arguments one would have to infer, for example, that the creators of *Anna Karenina* and *Madame Bovary* were women.

Bloom has written about J before—most notably in his contribution on Exodus to the book *Congregation* (1987), edited by David Rosenberg, and in the first chapter of his expanded Charles Eliot Norton Lectures at Harvard, *Ruin the Sacred Truths* (1989). The Yahwist also stands as one of his three paradigms for poetic originality in *The*

Breaking of the Vessels (1982). In these works Bloom outlined J's quintessential features as a writer of the "Hebraic sublime," but apparently he still considered the Yahwist a male author. As a literary critic Bloom is well known for his spirited defense of Romanticism and for his agonistic theory of misreading, which is defined in a tetralogy on literary revisionism—*The Anxiety of Influence* (1973), *A Map of Misreading* (1975), *Kabbalah and Criticism* (1975), and *Poetry and Repression* (1976). He tells us it was in response to feminist critiques of that theory as patriarchal that in the past year he began to develop the notion of a female Yahwist. He was led to it by what he has come to think of as the ironic representation of the Biblical patriarchs. In a certain sense, the idea of J as a woman serves as a feminist line of defense for his theory of "strong" poets and their aggressive appropriation of literature. No critic has shown a more Nietzschean will to interpretative power over literary texts. He has also resurrected the historical Yahwist with a vengeance against those literary theorists who have proclaimed the so-called "death" of the author. Perhaps more important, the idea of J as a woman serves as a Bloomian metaphor for the originality he finds in the Yahwistic text. The question of J's sexual identity inevitably points to the issue of J's difference. What is new in J? How does J's Yahweh differ from the God of normative Judaism? Bloom's most engaging idea may be not that J was a woman but that she was essentially a comic writer, a supple and uncanny ironist.

The key to Bloom's conception of J as a Kafkaesque dissembler and a "visionary of incommensurates" hinges on her portrayal of Yahweh. How, he asks, are we to conceive of an all-powerful Yahweh who also haggles with Abram or tries to slay Moses or sits under the trees at Mamre eating veal and curds? Yahweh walks in the garden in the cool of the evening; he shuts Noah's ark himself; he inspects the Tower of Babel. A later proverb such as "The fear of the Lord is the beginning of knowledge" (Proverbs 1:7) seems completely alien to the spirit of J, who shows neither awe nor fear in Yahweh's presence but instead treats him, in Bloom's words, like "an imp who behaves sometimes as though he is rebelling against his Jewish mother, J." And yet he is also God the Father, who makes a sacred covenant with the Jewish people. The Yahweh who is represented as simultaneously human and supreme seems to come from a more archaic tradition of Judaism, now lost to us forever. The heart of the Bloomian argument about the revolutionary originality of J is that the deliberate blasphemy of her work "always was and still is a Yahweh at once human-all-too-human and totally incommensurate with the human." That Blakean Yahweh is exuberant and free of inhibition, willful, possessive, extremely dynamic. At times, he operates like the Freudian superego. He is vastly different from the immeasurable, unnameable God of normative Judaism. The writer who dared to imagine that very sly and formidable Creator, Bloom argues, was not a moral theologian but a secular monist, an ironic visionary. But she was first of all a teller of earthly tales.

David Rosenberg's bold new translation of *The Book of J*—sandwiched between commentaries by Bloom—is especially alert to the abundant wordplay and the elliptical nature of the text. He presents a work that is, in Erich Auerbach's resonant phrase, "fraught with background." His translation allows us to read J apart from the context of the redactors. Rosenberg is not the first to have isolated and reproduced the J text in translation, but his rendition is by far the most literary. He has scrapped the chapter divisions that were retrospectively imposed on the J text, and has adopted a sequence of much shorter chapters, which read like multiple scenes from a longer prose work. This structure remains faithful to the gaps and ruptures in the text even as it allows us to consider what remains of the sequence as a whole.

J's text begins not with God's majestic creation of Heaven and earth, which was written by later priestly sources, but in the Judean season of spring when Yahweh scoops up a handful of moistened red clay, shapes it into a human being, and animates it with his own breath. The very name for man (*adam*) is a permanent reminder that human beings come from the earth (*adamah*).

> Before a plant of the field was in earth, before a grain of the field sprouted—Yahweh had not spilled rain on the earth, nor was there man to work the land—yet from the day Yahweh made earth and sky, a mist from within would rise to moisten the surface. Yahweh shaped an earthling from clay of this earth, blew into its nostrils the wind of life. Now look: man becomes a creature of flesh.

Yahweh plants a garden in Eden, molds the clay into "all the creatures of the field and birds of the air," and brings them to man curious to see what he will name them. This is the beginning of human language, the primal act of poetic creation. But man still lacks an equivalent being, and so Yahweh puts him into a deep sleep and then takes one of his ribs and shapes or builds it into a nameless woman, the first living being forged not from earth but from another living being. This is what Keats called Adam's dream, comparable to the Imagination: "He awoke and found it truth." The Hebrew word for "man," *ish* (used in the sense of an individual being, as opposed to the word *adam*, which is generic and undifferentiated), appears here, connecting him permanently to woman, *isha*. Bloom's commentary on the creation of a second sex is especially amusing: "Surely J's ironic point is that the second time around, Yahweh has learned better how the job ought to be done."

Rosenberg's translation of the next passage suggests that man is both consoled and haunted by a sense of lost unity and wholeness with the woman, whom he later names Eve, or Hava (*hawa*). (pp. 89-92)

What follows is the story that has had such a scandalous history in our culture—the tale of Adam and Eve and the serpent. J's version reads less like a theological parable of temptation, sin, guilt, and punishment—in other words, less like the Christian Fall—than like the story of an aggrieved parent and his offending children. It enacts what Bloom calls their "wounding estrangement" from God, playing out a painful family triangle and romance. (p. 92)

Anyone who has tried to translate even a small portion of the Pentateuch knows how difficult the task can be. One has to contend with classical Hebrew, with thousands and thousands of pages of religious commentary and Biblical scholarship, with a heavily revised and bowdlerized text, with the majestic splendors of the King James Bible, or Authorized Version (1611), which has set the standard for English prose since the seventeenth century. "That old tongue with its clang and its flavor," Edmund Wilson said. "We have been living with it all our lives." There is also the modern competition of the Revised Standard Version (1952); the Jerusalem Bible, which is Catholic (1966); the New English Bible, which is Protestant (1970); and the New American Jewish Version (1982). Of course, in all those translations J is effaced, and incorporated into the larger rhythms of the Hebrew Bible.

Rosenberg's innovative translation struggles to re-create J's distinctive voice, a tone of modulated ironic grandeur. His version is replete with self-conscious puns, verbal pyrotechnics, and elaborate repetitions, words echoing within words. Dazzling as it is, this idiom can seem forced and unnecessarily convoluted, as in Chapter 6 when Yahweh questions Adam:

> "Who told you naked is what you are?" he asked. "Did you touch the tree I desired you not eat?"

Certainly, we think, Yahweh could have learned to speak English more naturally than this. And it's hard to know what to make of Esau's complaint to his father:

> "Was he named Jacob, heel-clutcher . . . that he might jaywalk behind me, twice?"

These anachronisms and verbal contortions create a literary text that is at times unusually difficult to read.

Rosenberg follows J in continually shifting between past and present tenses. He also reproduces what seem in the Hebrew to be purposely ambiguous pronouns, which often make it difficult to distinguish who is speaking. What was translated as "and" and "behold" in older versions, and as "when," "if," "then," etc., in more recent versions, he has rendered as "now" or "now listen" or "now look" or "watch" or "so it was," depending on the context. This creates a sense of genuine directness but also a jumpy, offbeat rhythm, a music that is filled with jolts and jumpstarts—*The Book of J* rendered in the fractured idiom of John Berryman's *Homage to Mistress Bradstreet* or *77 Dream Songs*. Ezra Pound's description of William Carlos Williams' characteristic "volts, jerks, sulks, balks, outblurts and jump-overs" sounds a bit like the language of Rosenberg's J. And, just as in Berryman and Williams, the American version of J can have a surprising offhanded eloquence, as in:

> Now Abimelech proclaimed for all: "One who touches this man and his wife has felt his own death."

Or:

> They moved on from Sukkot, marked out their camp at Eitam, at the border of the desert. Yahweh walks ahead of them each day in a pillar of cloud, marking the way: at night, in a pillar of fire. Day or night, the people can walk. Ahead

The Creation of Eve, by Michaelangelo. *From the Fresco on the Ceiling of the Sistine Chapel.*

of them, it never disappears: a pillar of fire by night, a pillar of cloud by day.

In these passages it is possible to detect the splendors of the writer that Bloom and Rosenberg have constructed for us.

After reading **The Book of J,** one can never consider the oldest strand in the Hebrew Bible in quite the same way as before. J seems as poignantly real and fictive a figure as Homer or Shakespeare or the Court Historian who was supposedly her friend. She is an elusive presence; indeed, we are not convinced that she ever existed, and yet we become collaborators in imagining her. There is a Midrash on Psalms which says that the Torah was written "in black fire upon white fire." I think of the author who inscribed those flames. She is using the Phoenician—Old Hebrew script and writing on papyrus with a reed pen in one of Rehoboam's courtyards. Or maybe she is carving words into a leather scroll with a dull knife. With what political nostalgia does she daydream about the days of King David. With what fierce joy does she imagine Yahweh walking through a grove of trees or moving across the desert at night in a pillar of fire. With what tragic sense of wonder does she write:

And look: they are naked, man and woman, untouched by shame, not knowing it.
(pp. 92-3)

Edward Hirsch, "The Female Yahwist," in The New Yorker, *Vol. LXVI, No. 49, January 21, 1991, pp. 89-93.*

David Stern

Harold Bloom will appreciate better than anyone the fate of being misread. Having devoted the better part of his career as a literary critic to explicating the necessity of misreading as a prerequisite for what he calls "strong" poetry, it seems poetically just that Bloom's own writing—*The Book of J* in particular, his most recent and best book— should be misinterpreted by nearly everybody, misconstrued as a work of literary criticism about the Bible when in fact it is an audacious if flawed attempt at theology.

Bloom, who emerged in the late '50s and early '60s as one of several young critics instrumental in restoring the Romantic poets to the literary canon, has earned for himself surely the most prodigious and provocative reputation of any American critic of his generation. He first won wider fame with the publication of *The Anxiety of Influence* in 1973. Subtitled "A Theory of Poetry," it recast the history of post-Enlightenment English poetry into the image of a Freudian family romance, "the story of how poets as poets have suffered from other poets." In Bloom's account, every emerging poet, or "ephebe," is engaged in an Oedipal struggle for literary life with his precursors, or poetic fathers. Anxious from too much influence, from the feeling of being overwhelmed to the point of creative asphyxiation by the originality of his predecessors, the ephebe's response comes in the form of one or another psychopoetic defense. These defenses amount to the essential tropes of all poetry, indeed to poetry itself. "A poem is the poet's melancholy at his lack of priority," Bloom wrote in one of his more eloquent moments.

One consequence of this anatomy of poetic melancholy was a revised lineage of "anxious" and "belated" poets, extending in English poetry from Milton to the Romantics, and in American poetry from Emerson and Whitman to Stevens and Ashbery. This lineage drastically altered the shape of the modernist canon, demoting most of modernism itself to a kind of blocked Romanticism. But the most influential idea of *The Anxiety of Influence* was its notion of "misreading." An umbrella term for all the poetic and critical strategies that an ephebe employs in defending himself against a predecessor's influence, "misreading" is how a poet gains the creative nerve to write his own poems. Hence, as Bloom wrote in what has since become his most quotable slogan, "the meaning of a poem is always another poem," by which he really meant that every poem is a misreading, a misprision, of an earlier poem's meaning.

Bloom himself has always been an "antithetical" critic, as John Hollander notes in his graceful, admiring introduction to *The Poetics of Influence,* a helpful anthology of Bloom's writings over the years. Bloom has invariably tended to write against something or someone: the New Criticism, Northrop Frye, structuralism, the varieties of poststructuralism. Yet if there is a single presence in all literary history, past or present, with whom Bloom has himself struggled as ephebe with precursor, it is the colossal figure of T. S. Eliot.

Eliot's influential essay of 1920, "Tradition and the Individual Talent," stands behind *The Anxiety of Influence* like a headache behind a bad mood; virtually every claim in the latter can be read as a renunciation of a corresponding assertion in the former. If Western literary history was, for Eliot, "an ideal order of monuments" to be "if ever so slightly, altered" whenever a new work is introduced into "the ideal order," so as to attain "conformity between the old and the new," for Bloom it is more like a series of palace revolts and familial coups staged by ambitious but insecure young princes against their imperious fathers. For Eliot, the creative act was a "continual surrender of self," the "extinction of personality." For Bloom, it is a continual assertion of self, a relentless attempt at impressing one's personality upon history. And so on.

It is not only Eliot's critical stance against which Bloom has reacted so severely. Even more severe has been his re-

action to Eliot's cultural stance, which Eliot summed up in his famous description of himself as "classicist in literature, royalist in politics, and anglo-catholic in religion." One could pick virtually any passage from Eliot's work to exemplify this identity, but the particular expression to which Bloom has probably taken greatest offense is found in the eerily abstracted and ethereal lectures that Eliot delivered on German radio shortly after World War II, which he later published under the title "The Unity of European Culture" in *Notes Toward the Definition of Culture.* The unity of European culture, he announced, was Christian culture, and so it remains:

> It is in Christianity that our arts have developed;
> it is in Christianity that the laws of Europe
> have—until recently—been rooted. It is against
> a background of Christianity that all our
> thought has significance. . . . If Christianity
> goes, the whole of our culture goes.

In an essay published two years ago on the centenary of Eliot's birth, Bloom quoted these lines, reflecting on how little Eliot's idea of Christian culture relates to what we, some forty years later, define as culture. Exactly what Bloom might have had in mind, his own idea of Western culture, can be better glimpsed in *Ruin the Sacred Truths: Poetry and Belief from the Bible to the Present,* the book he published that same year. Based on the Norton Lectures delivered at Harvard, the book is a rather disjointed series of six essays that journey through Western literature, making stops at the Bible, Homer, and Dante (with a short detour to Virgil), Shakespeare, Milton, and the Romantics (mainly Blake and Wordsworth), and ending up, predictably enough, with Freud, Kafka, and (briefly) Beckett. The book lacks a single sustained argument, except perhaps the unexceptionable idea that great poetry never accords with conventional religious belief. Mainly, it is an attempt to apply Bloomian categories of misreading to the classics of Western literature.

The point of this effort, however, is not so much to identify the anxieties behind these works as to locate in them the origins of influence itself, of what Bloom elsewhere has called "facticity." A somewhat confusing but suggestive neologism, "facticity" connotes for Bloom the overpowering hold that certain classic texts—the Bible, Kafka, Freud—have on our collective cultural mind, by virtue of having created the very categories in which we conceive of culture. These are texts that "read us more fully and vividly than we can ever hope to read" them. More than being simply "classics," these books are the authors of our very selves. They constitute the essence of the Bloomian canon.

Read this way, *Ruin the Sacred Truths* is Bloom's rejoinder to Eliot's Christian culture, Bloom's own elaboration of the Western literary tradition, which he wittily nicknames "J to K." K stands, of course, for Kafka, whose presence, like a hovering spirit, broods over the entire argument. J refers rather more recondite to the Yahwist, the name given to one of the four hypothetical source-documents that biblical scholars since the nineteenth century have believed underlie the present text of the Pentateuch, the five books of Moses in the Hebrew Bible. (pp. 34-6)

As for what "J to K" represents, Bloom is disarmingly vague, except to imply that it designates a kind of biblical or Yahwistic sensibility toward things. We are told, for example, that Hamlet's way of negation "is biblical in origin, which is why it seems so Freudian to us, because Freudian negation is biblical and not Hegelian, as it were." But what is biblical about Freudian negation, or biblical about any kind of negation? We are never told. What is clear to a reader of *Ruin the Sacred Truths,* however, is that the spirit of the Yahwist, whether or not it animates the classics of Western literature, definitely animates Bloom. The best sections in the book, the only ones in which he seems truly engaged with his material, are those dealing with the Bible, or with other Jewish topics, such as Freud's implicit Jewishness, or Kafka's.

The Jewish element in Bloom is not new. In his first book, *Shelley's Mythmaking,* Bloom used Martin Buber's philosophy of I and Thou as a foil for discussing Romanticism. And most famously of all, in *Kabbalah and Criticism,* in a juxtaposition that he himself confided might seem "lunatic," Jewish mystical traditions were invoked and explored as paradigms for the anxieties of influence. Yet reading through the selections in *The Poetics of Influence,* through these essays spanning Bloom's entire career, one is struck by how continuously Jewish elements recur in his writings, and only more so in recent years, when his freshest and most powerful writing has been about the Bible. Now, in **The Book of J,** he has finally produced a book-length study of the Yahwist, in which his stated objective is nothing less than to recover this writer as "one of the small group of Western authors we identify with the Sublime."

The Book of J consists of a translation of the Yahwist's document by the poet and editor David Rosenberg, accompanied by a series of introductory essays, commentaries, and conclusions by Bloom. The first thing to be said about this book is that the idea of printing the Yahwist document on its own, as a separate text, was brilliant. Seeing J's narrative apart from its context, even if in fragments, one gets a vivid picture of what the Bible's early sources might have been like. Alas, Rosenberg's translation of the document is not successful. Seeking to capture the "poetic" individuality of J's voice, he has managed to escape the faceless banality and committee-ish impersonality that plague most contemporary Bible translations. But in straining to reproduce the dense verbal art of the Yahwist's "original narrative voice and flow," his rendition is full of awkward locutions in English ("It is not good the man be alone"; "Judah was his name, the finish to her having of children"; "It was scalding to Yahweh; to Moses, his heart was singed"); odd and incorrect translations ("holocaust" for *minhah,* a gift or tribute offering; "contempt" for *ra'ah,* "evil"); forced, almost silly puns ("Jacob" because "he might jaywalk behind me"); and the unnecessary insertion of phrases and similes not present in the original Hebrew (the Dylanesque "blown in the wind," gratuitously added to Cain's curse in Genesis 4:12).

Some have suggested that Bloom, whose control of Hebrew seems from several indications to be less than perfect, was misled by Rosenberg's translations into committing some of his more egregious misinterpretations. My impression is the opposite: that Rosenberg's translation was produced with Bloom's reading in mind. A brief example of a subtle distortion that is typical of both Rosenberg's translation and Bloom's interpretation of J's meaning will illustrate what I mean. In Genesis 4:4, after giving birth to Cain, Eve declares, *"kaniti ish et adonai,"* a line usually translated as "I have gained [or "gotten" or "acquired"] a man with the help of the Lord." Rosenberg translates it as "I have created a man as Yahweh has."

In context, Eve's statement is a kind of punning pseudo-etymology on *Kayin,* as Cain's name is pronounced in Hebrew, and the verb *kaniti.* Rosenberg's translation of the latter, "I have created," is a rather inspired rendition of a difficult verb, and it draws, I suppose, upon a similar Ugaritic root with that meaning recently noted by Bible scholars, notably Nahum Sarna. It is not this part of Rosenberg's translation that is suspicious, however, but its conclusion: "as Yahweh has." Here again, the meaning of the Hebrew particle *et,* as it appears in the Bible, is problematic, but there is little justification for taking the words *et adonai* to mean "just like God," a translation that turns Eve's etiological statement into a boasting challenge, into a kind of Promethean, Byronesque vaunting of creative power.

Rosenberg's distorted rendition, however, is perfectly consonant with Bloom's reading of J, an interpretation that sees the Yahwist document as being about the same thing that Bloom sees as the theme of all strong literature: the agonistic struggle for the Sublime, or what in this book Bloom calls "the Blessing"—the promise of immortality, "more life, and the promise of yet more life, into a time without boundaries." All strong writers face this struggle, and Bloom's J, one of the strongest, is no different.

The interest of the literary endeavor, for Bloom, has always lain in the expression of personality—the personality of the poet, the personality of the critic—and so it is no surprise that he should instinctively believe that the Yahwist, or J, was a recognizable person, not a mere editor, let alone a document or a hypothetical source. Now, in this book, Bloom reveals to us the Yahwist's precise identity. J was a woman, living in the early tenth century, a member of the royal court of Solomon's son and successor Rehoboam of Judah, probably a princess herself, perhaps even David's granddaughter.

Whether or not she was of royal blood, this J, according to Bloom, lived with the memory of David's achievements, in the long shadow of his glory. She knew firsthand the intellectual and material splendor of the Solomonic court and its enlightened secularism. But she also had the unlucky fate of outliving Solomon, of having to witness the inglorious and indifferent reign of Rehoboam, whose petty history is narrated in 2 Samuel by the writer known as the Court Historian, a figure who was, in Bloom's surmise, J's contemporary and friendly literary rival.

Virtually all the critical and journalistic ballyhoo surrounding the appearance of this book has revolved around Bloom's insistence on J's gender, and so it is worth saying at the outset that this is the book's least interesting idea. Bloom in no way intends his proposal to be an endorsement of a feminist approach to the Bible, nor is it his intention to add a chapter to the history of forgotten women writers. His strongest reason for supposing that J was a female is his "increasing sense of the astonishing difference between J and every other biblical writer," along with his feeling that J's most sympathetic and complex characters, such as Tamar, Rebecca, and Zipporah, are all females—a feeling that is at least corroborated by Bloom's treatments of these characters' stories in the Bible, which do happen to be among the best parts of *his* commentary. Still, this is hardly proof of J's gender. The same logic would lead us to conclude that the author of *Madame Bovary* was a woman.

The real problem with Bloom's speculation about J's gender is that he himself is unclear as to how seriously he wishes it to be taken, or whether he intends it mainly as a provocation. "Since I am aware that my vision of J will be condemned as a fancy or fiction, I will begin by pointing out that all our accounts of the Bible are scholarly fictions or religious fantasies," he writes disingenuously. Yes, in some ultimate sense, all scholarship, all religious beliefs, are fictions or fantasies. Some are more fictitious, more fantastic. Or less fantastic. In fact, most of Bloom's historical arguments in the book, not only the ones about J's gender, are extremely conjectural, even though most (including the gender question) have been broached in the past by one biblical scholar or another. These include Bloom's dating of J; his claim that she lived in Rehoboam's court; the suggestion that she was of royal stock; the allusions to Rehoboam's name buried in a number of Hebrew words; the close relationship that supposedly existed between J and the Court Historian. All these factual assertions are much less certain than Bloom pronounces them to be.

Still, this is not a book aiming to persuade Bible scholars. It is directed to another audience, to the reader disaffected from the Bible in its canonized form as either Torah (in Judaism) or Old Testament (in Christianity), as a document of sacred law and divine history. J is a Bible with virtually no law or history. It is, instead, a surpassing narrative, one lying beyond all the familiar genres of Western literature. And above all it is the work of a writer of astonishing originality whose cognitive power is "unmatched among Western writers until Shakespeare," and who, Bloom claims, was literally buried by her successors, that is, by the founders of Judaism and Christianity—revised, censored, and mutilated by them, until she and her narrative alike have become virtually unrecognizable.

The real J, whom Bloom seeks to rescue from oblivion, was neither a historian nor a theologian, nor even a religiously inclined writer. She was, he insists, a teller of tales, surpassingly ironic and sophisticated, essentially "a comic writer . . . in the difficult mode of Kafka" who brought her imaginative vision to bear upon telling, or retelling, the early history of her nation, the people of Israel, and their God, Yahweh. Although J's narrative, Bloom ac-

knowledges, must inevitably testify to an "archaic Judaism," to more ancient traditions that J received, she herself did not write out of pious motives or religious belief. She wrote for the same Bloomian reason that anyone of immense literary power writes, now or then: to gain "the Blessing."

"The Blessing," immortality, fame, the spreading of one's name, "more life," the uninhibited "expression of personality"—these are the main themes of J's narrative. The patriarchs and the ancestors of Israel, all "theomorphic" men who share Yahweh's best features and his worst, incessantly strive to gain the Blessing. J's real protagonist, though, is Yahweh himself, and he is as different from the God of "normative" Judaism and Christianity as J is from the rest of the Bible. "Impish," a "sublime mischief-maker," Yahweh is a literary character, nothing more or less. His main attributes are not holiness or righteousness or justice, the features usually associated with God, but "vitalism" and "uncanniness." A kind of unpredictable life force, J's Yahweh is a God who can eat roasted calf with Abraham yet seek to kill Moses. He is a God to beware; and J's own attitude toward him resembled, Bloom tells us, that of "a mother's somewhat wary but still proudly amused stance toward a favorite son who has grown up to be benignly powerful but also eccentrically irascible."

J's narrative, in Bloom's account, consists of Yahweh's repeated efforts at "trying on" the Blessing—on the patriarchs, on Moses, finally on the people of Israel in their entirety—while he awaits the arrival of King David, the only figure in history who will prove himself truly capable of carrying the promise of the Blessing to fruition. For J, however, David is "always in the future," beyond the compass of her book. Within her narrative's confines, no one, except for a few women, is truly able to bear the Blessing.

Even Yahweh finds his moment of truth. It occurs at Mount Sinai, when he seeks to extend the Blessing from a few chosen theomorphic individuals to an entire people, the nation of Israel. Caught up in a "crisis of representation," not knowing whether to let himself be seen or not, Yahweh is overcome with anxiety; at one moment he invites the Israelites to approach him, at the next he warns them not to come too close. Nor does Yahweh ever quite recover from this crisis. After Sinai, he loses his early dialectical, crafty self, his freedom from all inhibitions. While the Israelites wander through the desert for the subsequent forty years, he becomes increasingly anxious, "an intensely nervous leader of an unruly rabble," prone to uncontrollable fury whenever his creatures manifest what he regards as the least disrespect.

This Blakean portrait of Yahweh, which Bloom gleefully pronounces both "scandalous" and "blasphemous," is the heart of his reading of J. As a piece of Bloomian misreading, it is utterly compelling. This is partly because his handling of the text is so deft, and partly because his Yahweh is so entirely disturbing—I was about to say, unpleasant—a being. A kind of unchecked Nietzschean will to power let loose on the world, Yahweh is "in no way morally or spiritually superior to the builders of Babel. . . . We seek fame and Yahweh scatters us, that every name be scattered also, except his own." It does no good to object that this thoroughly amoral Yahweh, beyond all good and evil, is antithetical to every conception of God in Judaism, and in nearly any other religion, since that is precisely Bloom's argument. So, too, it is entirely beside the point to note that theomorphism, the all-consuming desire to be a god that Bloom sees as the main ambition of virtually all the patriarchs and revered ancestors of Israel, is fundamentally opposed to the deepest values in Jewish tradition.

It does make one wonder, though, why Bloom should find this disturbed figure of Yahweh so attractive, why he should so enthusiastically embrace the theomorphic Sublime as his own ideal. A good part of the answer to both questions lies in Bloom's attitude to J's later successors and readers, all those who make up what he repeatedly refers to as the "normative" tradition—first E, P, D, and R, then the clerics of Judaism and Christianity, even most modern Bible scholars. All these religious types, he argues, have been unable to abide J's anthropomorphic portrait of Yahweh: they have preferred Yahweh to be a concept rather than a personality, and have sought to press him into their respective clerical services rather than appreciate his uncanny vitalism. And so, Bloom argues, J has consistently been misread; her Yahweh has been theologized into a holy abstraction, her deep ironies turned into flat moralizations, the originality of her imagination all but effaced.

On all these points, Bloom is at best only partly correct, at least factually. The early rabbis, for example, often imagined God in even more anthropomorphic terms than J does, and none more so than the disciples of Akiba, the famous sage of the second century C.E., whom Bloom singles out as the foremost exemplar of the religion of the rabbis. On the other hand, when Jewish philosophers like Philo or Maimonides felt the need to allegorize or to explain away J's anthropomorphisms, it was hardly out of a failure of imagination, as Bloom implies, but for good philosophical reason. Even today, there are those among us who would find repugnant the thought of God burning with anger through his nostrils, let alone feasting on roasted calf.

To be sure, Bloom is correct in asserting that J's Yahweh is not identical to the God of the rabbis, just as J's Judaism, if one can even use that word to describe her religious beliefs, must have been very different from the religion of the rabbis living a millennium later. Still, for all but the most religiously orthodox readers of the Bible, such an assertion is merely a truism. And Bloom's parallel claim that while J's successors worshiped Yahweh, J herself did not, is more questionable on its own terms. Even if Yahweh was a personality rather than a concept, why could J have not worshiped him? J's religion was assuredly different than the rabbis', but how do we know that it was any less "normative" for her time?

The "normative" is the least examined idea in Bloom's book. As he uses it, the term sounds like nothing more than a depressing "religious establishment," a platitudinous authoritarian image that may have been born of endless afternoons passed unhappily in Hebrew school. In fact, the notion of normativity in Judaism, as in any religious tradition with a long history, is deeply problematic, and Bloom should know this from his studies in the history of the Kabbalah. There is not, in Jewish history, a single "normative" Judaism, not even within a single historical period. And there is no better evidence for the problematic nature of the normative in Judaism than the Bible itself: in its final canonized form this single text preserved, side by side, without discrimination or comment, at least four sources with wholly different ideologies and programs. Nor did the discrepancies in the biblical text go unnoticed by its later exegetes in the "normative" tradition. But these commentators did not deny or suppress them. Instead, they turned the Bible's lacunae and inconsistencies into occasions for interpretation, into spurs for meditation on the Bible's "deeper" meaning, for the discovery of the hidden unity of the divine will.

Bloom's suggestion that the "normative tradition" was a conspiratorial force that continuously has sought to bury and to repress his hapless J is pretty much a chimera, a straw man. But it is Bloom's sense of himself as outside the normative, wherever that may be, that is the key to his project of recovery. Although he appears to ground his reading of J on the Documentary Hypothesis, a scholarly theory with established credentials, its inspiration is really beyond scholarship. To recover J's originality, Bloom tells us, he requires a method of reading that is "partly outside every normative tradition whatsoever, or if inevitably inside, however unwittingly, then inside with a considerable difference."

Here, again, exactly what Bloom means by "outside every normative tradition" is ambiguous. At times it seems to amount simply to "literary." All he wishes, Bloom modestly disclaims, is to restore J as a writer, albeit a writer with the talent of Shakespeare. At other times, though, Bloom's claim to being outside every "normative" tradition means something more substantive, more subversive. And indeed, the real model for Bloom's antithetical criticism is an ancient interpretive tradition that has been customarily considered outside "normative" tradition. I refer to gnostic exegesis.

Like Bloom, the early Gnostics, who were later branded as "heretical" by the "normative" Christian church, read the Bible against its grain, in the light of their own dualistic religious beliefs. Their goal, though, was expressly to reveal the real identity of the Old Testament God, who, they tried to show, was the evil demiurge, a false world-creator, rather than the true and unknowable divinity, the object of all authentic Gnosis. Bloom has frequently cited the Gnostics admiringly, and though he seeks in his new book to distance his readings from theirs, along with those of "normative" Judaism and Christianity, the Gnostics are his unacknowledged methodological precursors. Like the Gnostics, Bloom's goal is to retrieve an all-but-hidden divinity.

That divinity, however, is not Yahweh, but *his* creator, J. Like Yahweh, J is "uncanny," "ironic," "a visionary of incommensurates." Indeed, J happens to be the single wholly theomorphic character in *The Book of J.* She is Yahweh's sole rival. J's very Bloomian "divinity" is her originality, her "facticity." Because she has discovered the very ways in which we represent ourselves to others, our notions of personality and human behavior, J's influence on us is, with Shakespeare's, so overwhelming that we are "contained" by her. She defies all representation, since she defined the very modes of representation that we must employ to represent her. She is, quite literally, our creator.

Early in the book, after Bloom makes his point that J's Yahweh is a literary character, he notes (with a little too much pleasure) that this fact makes all subsequent Western religion into the worship of a literary character. Unfortunately Bloom is himself not exempt from this charge. He has simply exchanged the Supreme Being for the Supreme Fiction—or the Supreme Fictionalist. Behind this adulation of the writer, students of literature will easily recognize a late version of the Romantic belief in poetry as personal religion, the worship of the imagination as an inner divinity. Yahweh is J's "awakened imagination," Bloom writes in a happy line. Well, J is Bloom's awakened imagination.

There is more at stake here than belated Romanticism. Cynthia Ozick once attacked Bloom for "idol-making," for positing a view of literature that effectively (and, according to Ozick, correctly) showed it to be an idol; and by "idol" she meant not just an object of false or deluded worship, but a Moloch-idol, a fiery consumer of helpless children, a usurper of divinity by violence. And worst of all, Ozick argued, Bloom knows that he is an idol-maker. He is, she wrote, "a system-builder who is aware that a closed, internalized system is an idol, and that an idol, without power in itself, is nevertheless a perilous, indeed a sinister, taint in the world."

The one mistake in Ozick's characterization of Bloom is the assertion that his idol is literature. It is not. Bloom's idol is the poet, the strong writer, the writer possessed of "facticity," that stranglehold on our cultural imagination that we must all struggle to escape, Bloom claims, just as Jacob wrestled with the angel of God. For Bloom, these strong writers, "J to K," are both our gods and our adversaries. However ambivalently, they possess authority. They speak to him. They share in "the strong light of the canonical, of that perfection which destroys."

Bloom has borrowed this evocative, haunting phrase from Gershom Scholem, the great modern scholar of Jewish mysticism, who coined it to describe Kafka. "The Strong Light of the Canonical" is also the title of a series of three lectures that Bloom delivered in New York in 1985, which were later printed privately as a small pamphlet. Subtitled "Kafka, Freud and Scholem as Revisionists of Jewish Culture and Thought," the first two lectures in the pamphlet, on Kafka and Freud respectively, are identical with the sections on these writers in *Ruin the Sacred Truths.* The third lecture, however, has not (to the best of my knowledge) been reprinted. Dealing with Scholem, it is a kind of key to the secret of "J to K," but it is most important for what it reveals about Bloom's own ambitions.

For Bloom, Scholem is "Miltonic," a titanic figure. By having single-handedly restored Jewish mysticism to its rightful place in the history of Judaism, and by having re-

vealed a mythical presence at the very heart of "normative" Jewish tradition, Scholem epitomizes for Bloom the scholar as strong misreader. The historian of Kabbalah, Bloom rhapsodizes, is its "epic poet." Scholem is "a philological equivalent of Kafka." Although his writing was cloaked in the guise of traditional philology, Scholem was in Bloom's view the bearer of a new Kabbalah, a new Gnosis. Its message is precisely our alienation from the normative.

Bloom's understanding of Scholem is a misreading, in both the literal and the Bloomian sense. Scholem's greatness, in Bloom's eyes, lay not in his scholarly achievements, in his massive reconstruction of an entire tradition of esoteric Jewish speculation, but in the profoundly revisionist impact of his researches. These entirely transformed our conception of Jewish existence in its historical totality. Scholem proved, Bloom writes, "that the normative tradition, rather like any normative personality, is largely a shifting series of masks." And all that remains of Judaism are the shifting masks: "The indubitable effect [of Scholem's work, along with Kafka's and Freud's] upon all subsequent Jewish writing is to remind us that there is only interpretation."

If Eliot is Bloom's authentic precursor, Scholem may be said to represent his true ideal. "J to K," which is Bloom's answer to Eliot's "Christian culture," is also Bloom's attempt to discover an equivalent to the Kabbalistic tradition that Scholem located at the center of Judaism. "J to K" is Bloom's Jewish counter tradition, the antithetical presence suppressed by the Jewish "normative." And Scholem, with Freud and Kafka, is himself part of the antithetical tradition. Indeed, as Bloom tells us at the end of his essay, Scholem, with Kafka and Freud, constitutes nothing less than the essence of Jewishness today.

But there is a significant difference, alas, between Scholem's Kabbalah and Bloom's "J to K." For all its mystical craziness, Kabbalah possessed a genuine spiritual power that responded to deep religious needs. What attracts Bloom to Kabbalah, by contrast, is not its spirituality, but the anarchism implied in Scholem's history of it. "J to K" itself is spiritually empty. Its only teaching is that all meaning is wandering meaning. At best, "J to K" is a Jewish High Culture ("an amalgam of imaginative literature, psychoanalysis, and a kind of Kabbalah"), but it lacks a Judaism.

How might a Jewish High Culture exist without a Judaism? Bloom himself is aware of the question; he calls it "most curious." And yet, he insists, what offers itself as normative Judaism—Torah, Talmud, midrash, and so on—does not speak to him, whereas "Kafka, Freud, and Scholem, unlikely but inevitable triad, do." What Bloom fails to recognize is that there exists in modern Jewish intellectual life a strong precedent of disaffected intellectuals not unlike himself, who, for all their alienation from the religious tradition, have found a Jewish life for themselves in studying it. Scholem himself was of this type. However unobservant he was in his religious practice, however enlightened and secularized were his scholarly methods, and unorthodox his historicizing conclusions, in his devotion to textual study as a path to perfection Scholem was wholly within the bounds of "normative" Jewish tradition. In fact, it is hard to conceive of anything more normative in Judaism than this kind of devotion, the "piety" of the intellect.

To Bloom, however, such study does not offer itself as a path to anything. The normative tradition does not warrant intellectual interest. It is there only to be overcome, to be escaped from. One must admire him for his honesty about all this, for his forthrightness in standing by his estrangement from Jewish tradition, for his refusal to settle for any traditional palliative. And judging from **The Book of J**'s success in the bookstores, it would seem that his adversary stance has struck a powerful chord among many readers. There appears to be an audience for a Jewish High Culture without Judaism. Still, for all its literary energy, its fresh insights, its seductive surprises, **The Book of J** represents a tradition that preserves and transmits nothing. Scholem would not have been impressed. (pp. 36-40)

David Stern, "The Supreme Fictionalist," in The New Republic, *Vol. 204, No. 5, February 4, 1991, pp. 34-40.*

FURTHER READING

Bloom, Harold. *The Anxiety of Influence: A Theory of Poetry.* New York: Oxford University Press, 1973, 157 p.
    Introduces Bloom's theory of willful misreading.

———. *The Breaking of the Vessels.* Chicago: University of Chicago Press, 1982, 107 p.
    Presents the Yahwist as one of Bloom's three paradigms for poetic originality.

———. *Ruin the Sacred Truths: Poetry and Belief from the Bible to the Present.* Cambridge, Mass: Harvard University Press, 1989, 204 p.
    Elaboration of the Western literary tradition in which Bloom identifies J as the first great writer.

Ellis, Peter F. *The Yahwist: The Bible's First Theologian.* Notre Dame, Ind.: Fides, 1986, 308 p.
    Includes a translation of the J segments of the Pentateuch and historical commentary on the identity of J.

Friedman, Richard Elliott. *Who Wrote the Bible?* New York: Summit Books, 1987, 299 p.
    Identifies J's sympathy toward women and suggests that J may have been a woman.

Frye, Northrop. *The Great Code: The Bible and Literature.* New York: Harcourt Brace Jovanovich, 1982, 261 p.
    Argues for individual authorship of the Pentateuch.

Josipovici, Gabriel. "By divers hands: The Problems of Parcelling out the Pentateuch." *Times Literary Supplement* 4,594 (19 April 1991): 3-5.
    A review of *The Book of J* that takes issue with Rosenberg's translation and, particularly, with Bloom's theses. Josipivici accuses Bloom of willful misreading and one-dimensional arguments.

Rosenberg, Joel. *King and Kin: Political Allegory in the Hebrew Bible.* Bloomington: Indiana University Press, 1986, 255 p.
    Examines the possible collaboration between the Yahwist, J, and the Court Historian, E.

Feminist Literary Criticism
in 1990

A dynamic alternative to traditional critical approaches, feminist literary criticism is a method of interpreting texts that includes a heightened awareness of such issues as gender stereotypes, the author's economic situation, overt or tacit discrimination by publishers and reviewers, and the relationship between the author's gender and the nature of his or her text. During its evolution as a discipline within university literature departments since the 1970s, feminist criticism has proven capable of accomodating deconstructionist and other post-structuralist critical strategies as well as methods and terminology from such diverse fields of inquiry as psychology, sociology, and Marxism.

Ongoing concerns among feminist critics include the conservative backlash against feminism in the 1980s, the effect of both fiction and non-fiction texts—particularly of the "self-help" variety—aimed specifically at women, and the relationship between criticism and political action. Additionally, one of the most pressing issues in 1990 was the subject of multiculturalism. Many feminist critics and educators are scrutinizing their work for evidence of classism, racism, heterosexism, and xenophobia, and exploring ways to contravene the traditional view that knowledge of middle-class white women is applicable to all women.

As feminist literary criticism advances into the 1990s, one of its primary goals is ensuring that the perspectives of all women, regardless of class, race, ethnicity, religion, or sexual preference, are legitimized.

PRINCIPAL WORKS DISCUSSED BELOW

POETRY AND FICTION

Adams, Alice
  After You've Gone
Emecheta, Buchi
  The Joys of Motherhood
Gilchrist, Ellen
  Light Can Be Both Wave and Particle
Greer, Germaine, et al, eds.
  Kissing the Rod: An Anthology of Seventeenth-Century Women's Verse
Kauffman, Janet
  Obscene Gestures for Women
Lonsdale, Roger, ed.
  Eighteenth-Century Women Poets: An Oxford Anthology
Nwapa, Flora
  Efuru
Packer, Nancy Huddleston
  The Women Who Walk

Pesetsky, Bette
  Confessions of a Bad Girl
Rotter, Pat, ed.
  Bitches and Sad Ladies: An Anthology of Fiction By and About Women
Sullivan, Rosemary, (editor)
  Poetry by Canadian Women
Wilson, Katharina, and Warnke, Frank J., (editors)
  Women Writers of the Seventeenth Century

CRITICISM

Alloula, Malek
  The Colonial Harem
Banta, Martha
  Imaging American Women: Ideas and Ideals in Cultural History
Brodzki, Bella, and Schenck, Celeste
  Life/Lines: Theorizing Women's Autobiography
Cixous, Hélène, and Clement, Catharine
  Newly Born Woman
Doane, Janice, and Hodges, Devon
  Nostalgia and Sexual Difference: Resistance to Contemporary Feminism
Duchen, Claire
  French Connections: Voices from the Women's Movement in France
Epstein, Cynthia Fuchs
  Deceptive Distinctions
Felski, Rita
  Beyond Feminist Aesthetics: Feminist Literature and Social Change
Gilbert, Sandra, and Gubar, Susan
  No Man's Land: The Place of the Woman Writer in the Twentieth Century 2 vols.
Hansen, Karen V., and Philipson, Ilene J. (editors)
  Women, Class, and the Feminist Imagination: A Socialist-Feminist Reader
Heilbrun, Carolyn G.
  Hamlet's Mother and Other Women———.
  Writing a Woman's Life
Higgonet, Margaret R., et al, eds.
  Behind the Lines: Gender and the Two World Wars
Kristeva, Julia
  About Chinese Women
Leidholdt, Dorchen, and Raymond, Janice
  The Sexual Liberals and the Attack on Feminism
Loraux, Nichol
  Tragic Ways of Killing a Woman
MacKinnon, Catharine A.
  Feminism Unmodified: Discourses on Life and Law
Meese, Elizabeth, and Parker, Alice

Linda Simon

[*In the following excerpt, Simon reviews three books concerning women's autobiography, and argues against essentializing gender in feminist criticism.*]

Biography and autobiography present quite enough problems for critics and scholars even when we do not consider the gender of the subject. What, after all, happens in the process of distilling a life into the pages of a book? How do we perceive the theme and plot of an individual's life? What questions do biographers ask of sources to help them understand a life as it was lived? What criteria should we apply when evaluating a biography or autobiography as a work of literature or history?

These problems are compounded when we decide to compare the biographies and autobiographies of women with those of men; and, inevitably, the lives of women with the lives of men. What is the difference—is there a difference—in the shape of women's and men's life stories?

It is this last question that complicates the whole enterprise of feminist literary criticism, whether focused on fiction, poetry, or such non-fiction as biography and autobiography. There are many reasons for differences in texts: cultural, historical, sociological, psychological reasons, that have nothing to do with gender. But examining textual differences according to gender presupposes an assumption that not all feminist critics share: that there is an essential definition of maleness and womanness that transcends historical and cultural context.

Those who subscribe to such a definition would have us seek patterns of behavior that distinguish all men from all women. Whether women are artists, journalists, scientists, social activists, entertainers, mystics, mothers, pioneers, socialites, gymnasts—it does not matter how a woman defines her identity, these critics say, in order to examine the text of her life; it only matters whether the individual is a woman. A middle eastern woman, veiled and shrouded, therefore, has more in common with Emma Goldman, say, than does John Reed. A fifteenth century British noblewoman has more in common with Grace Paley, for example, than with Henry VI. And, these critics assert, ways that women choose to relate their lives have some consistency throughout female experience.

As improbable as these assertions may seem, they have formed the basis for some past work on women's biography and autobiography, and they have been revived by Carolyn Heilbrun in her latest reflection on the subject, ***Writing a Woman's Life.***

The title itself is confusing. A woman's life story, after all, may be written by a biographer (male or female) or by the woman herself. Those projects are distinct from their conception, and the resulting texts cannot be discussed as if they were interchangeable. One, biography, is a work of history; the other, a primary source upon which histories may be based. One, biography, bears the burden of recording verifiable evidence; the other, of inventing a text that translates felt experience into a work of literature.

The biographer aligns with the reader in examining a life as a text. She "reads" a life for them, patterns, and plot. She serves as mediator between sources about her subject and the reader, allowing the reader to enter the subject's historical context. A biographer draws her conclusions from a legacy of words: diaries, letters, legal documents, memoirs of friends or lovers or enemies, transcripts of interviews. She cannot be certain of anything that has not been documented as some form of text.

The autobiographer, on the other hand, is both subject and source, I and eye. Her task is to assert a consistent identity, much as the novelist does in creating the protagonist of a tale. Whatever the autobiographer's motivation—to be remembered, to set the record straight, to give testimony to an existence that would otherwise be obliterated by death, to fulfill public expectations for juicy gossip—she creates a text that the biographer may one day read as one source, among many, in examining a life. The autobiographer is able to draw upon undocumented sources—feelings and memories—and select from them. She is not constrained to place herself within a context, to explain anything, to defend her behavior.

Biographers have pressures from the marketplace that place constraints on the shape of their work. They are, as a rule, never so famous as their subject. But biographers do gain status in the literary community according to their subject. If I am writing about T.S. Eliot, I am more important, as a biographer, than if I am writing about the American poets Louis Zukofsky or Lorine Niedecker. I will have an easier job finding a publisher. My book will be reviewed in more journals. I will be invited to speak at more author's hours at local libraries.

If I am compelled, out of sympathy with their lives, to write about Zukofsky or Niedecker, I need to justify to potential publishers why that person's life will result in a marketable book. I will have to persuade an editor that my subject had alliances with interesting people; led a life filled with action and tension; travelled to colorful places;

produced work that was defined by others (recognizable critics, for example) as successful. If I can find instances of insanity, alcoholism, disease (preferably venereal), and adultery, so much the better.

If I am fortunate enough to find a publisher who will commission a biography of Niedecker, I will be fulfilling expectations about biography in general, not about women's biography in particular, when I set out to write. (pp. 133-35)

Autobiography has different constraints from the marketplace. An autobiography may be poetic and impressionistic and still be taken seriously. The autobiographer does not have to sell veracity or thorough documentation to find a publisher. She merely has to present a good story, with the same requirements that might make a good novel. She does not have to be famous—in the past year we have seen autobiographies by such women as Eva Hoffman, Mary Morris, Mary Kay Blakely, Nancy Mairs—women who are not likely subjects of a biography, but are published because they have created, in their text, an interesting character.

I take this time to distinguish between biography and autobiography because if we want to consider seriously the issue of life plots, it is autobiography that is our primary source; it is autobiography that is free of the constraints of publishing and marketing that shape most biography; it is autobiography that defines itself as invented life.

Heilbrun's reading of autobiographies leads her to conclude that women are bereft of a story of their own. But her reading is curiously selective. She cites the autobiography of Ida Tarbell, for example, to prove that women refuse to disclose their feelings of aggression and anger when they tell about their lives, but she fails to cite others, such as the autobiography of Elizabeth Gurley Flynn, a contemporary of Tarbell, and like her involved in social activism and reform, whose book bristles with the indignation one would expect from its inflammatory title, *The Rebel Girl.* Nor does Heilbrun compare Tarbell's work with other such "public" autobiographies as Ray Stannard Baker's *American Chronicle.* Baker, a colleague of Tarbell, was also a muckraker, but not so well-known as she, then or now. When Heilbrun complains that Tarbell's book is what it is because she had no model for a woman's story, I wonder why Tarbell, who forged her own career aggressively, who began as a biographer, who invented, with a handful of other writers, the "literature of exposure," would suddenly, at the end of her life, have needed to emulate other writers' work.

I would argue, instead, that Tarbell, who wrote her life story because she needed money, was responding to her readers' expectations for a book that focused on her work as a journalist and her central role as a major force in the country's political history. Heilbrun would like us to believe that the same criteria apply to Tarbell and Flynn, but not to Baker; but the *kind* of autobiography a writer chooses affects the telling of the tale, and that choice is not necessarily gender-based.

Take Gertrude Stein, for example, whose *Autobiography of Alice B. Toklas* has been examined by feminist critics as if it were an authentic effort to explore her identity, and lamented as a work that bows to patriarchal conventions. But Stein was writing for fame and fortune, at the suggestion of friends with publishing connections, to perpetuate the legend of herself as the center of a Parisian community of writers and artists. All the time she was writing, she complained in her *real* work—those serious, hermetic volumes that Yale University published after her death—about the whole enterprise of commercial publishing. She did not mean *The Autobiography* to reflect the reality of her life plot. That plot was explored, in all its tortuous circumlocutions, in the hermetic works.

Yet critics such as Heilbrun do not allow for different aims and motivations in writing one's life story. Instead, they recall the lives of a small circle of unhappy women—Sylvia Plath, of course, and Virginia Woolf—to generate criteria about the telling of lives for the rest of women, in all cultures, through all time. It is as if sweeping theories about the telling of men's lives were constructed from the life stories of Gerard de Nerval (who, the story goes, walked his lobster through the streets of Paris) or Wittgenstein, who seems to have been a trifle rigid.

Heilbrun veers from criticizing the writing of a life to evaluation of the life as it was lived. She complains about Eudora Welty because she is a proud southern lady whose memoir, *One Writer's Beginnings,* is to Heilbrun's taste too sentimental and nostalgic. "I do not believe in the bittersweet quality" of the book, Heilbrun tells us. "Nostalgia, particularly for childhood, is likely to be a mask for unrecognized anger." I think such an assessment is irresponsible, but Heilbrun insists that all women are restively squirming to lace themselves into ill-fitting corsets of life. (pp. 135-37)

Heilbrun, in her effort to help forge a new direction in feminist criticism, ignores the complexities that distinguish each life from every other, male or female. Her approach, based as it is on the belief in a generalized female experience, is shared by many other feminist critics. But this belief is being questioned publicly now in such works as *Inessential Woman: Problems of Exclusion in Feminist Thought,* by Smith College philosophy professor Elizabeth Spelman.

Feminist theory, Spelman sees, has evolved from many disciplines, most significantly from psychology, sociology, literature, and history. Yet the women on whom writers have based their work have been, for the most part, white and middle-class. They have been educated far beyond most women in the world. They have access—unusual for other cultures and other times—to goods, services, support systems, and one another.

This homogeneity disturbs Spelman. "Is it really possible," she asks, "for us to think of a woman's 'womanness' in abstraction from the fact that she is a particular woman, whether she is a middle-class black woman living in North America in the twentieth century or a poor white woman living in France in the seventeenth century?"

To explore this issue, Spelman takes a close look at two seminal works in feminist theory: Simone de Beauvoir's *The Second Sex* and Nancy Chodorow's *The Reproduction of Mothering.* In both works, she finds that a lack of recognition of the differences in race and class weakens each author's generalizations about consistencies in the behavior of women, about sexism, and about alternatives possible in women's lives. De Beauvoir, she notes, resists the idea that there is some "essence" of womanhood common to all females and urges her readers to look at the lives that women lead in order to draw conclusions about gender. But at the same time, de Beauvoir insists that "woman"—no matter who or where—"lacks the sense of the universal," and instead sees the world as "a confused conglomeration of special cases."

When describing relationships between men and women, de Beauvoir ignores the influence of race or class. Spelman cautions us to remember that power is based not only on gender. "To refer to the power 'all men have over all women,' " she writes, "makes it look as if my relationship to the bank vice president I am asking for a loan is just like my relationship to the man who empties my wastebasket at the office each night."

Unlike de Beauvoir, Nancy Chodorow evolves theory from a universal human experience: parenting, and she claims that the relationship between mother and child is therefore universally consistent. Drawing upon Freud (who himself based his theories on women of a particular Viennese class), she concludes that girls see their mothers as extensions of themselves, while boys see her as the "Other" with whom they can never identify. This early relationship then sets a pattern that establishes all future relationships, causing women to invest themselves in their connections with others, and men to seek power over others.

Besides raising questions about the connections men do make in their public and private lives, Spelman also questions Chodorow's assumption that women necessarily identify with one another and value a strong sense of community with other women. How, then, Spelman asks, do some women become racist?

"There are no short cuts through women's lives," Spelman concludes. It is very good advice for feminist critics, and Bella Brodzki and Celeste Schenck would agree. Their collection of essays, *Life/Lines: Theorizing Women's Autobiography* breaks new ground in our understanding of the range of life plots available to women as they transform their experiences into literature.

Although Heilbrun herself defends her interest in "privileged" women in one of these essays, other contributors examine the life stories of women from a variety of backgrounds and cultures. There are essays on blacks, native Americans, Latin Americans, lesbians, medieval and Renaissance women, and a turn-of-the-century Egyptian feminist. Autobiography as genre is defined broadly to include poetry, fiction, and film. And other contextual considerations, besides gender, are explored. So, in discussing Native American autobiographies, British writer Helen Carr pays close attention to the motivations and assumptions of the anthropologists who collected the testimonies. Nellie McKay, writing about Zora Neale Hurston, does not exclude race and cultural context from her study; to

illuminate Hurston's work, she even compares it to the autobiography of Frederick Douglass. It is rare, indeed, to set male autobiography beside female and to question differences; but *Life/Lines* is an unusual book in its scope and aim.

What makes the collection so refreshing, when set against Heilbrun's book or Estelle Jelinek's *Women's Autobiography,* is the editors' uncompromising commitment to diversity and their recognition that gender "is no longer the only situating category of interest" for many feminist critics. "As we see it," Brodzki and Schenck tell us, "this vigilant stance can help us to push beyond the mere overturning of binary oppositions, the implications of which are as crucial for male as for female readers and critics of autobiography. The establishment of a separatist female tradition, even feminist critics have warned, carries the danger of reverse reification. Autobiography can thus provide male and female readers with fertile ground for reseeding, along newly drawn feminist lines, contemporary ideas about selfhood." (pp. 137-39)

> *Linda Simon, "The Shape of Women's Lives,"*
> *in* Michigan Quarterly Review, *Vol. XXIX,*
> *No. 1, Winter, 1990, pp. 133-39.*

Carol Barash

[*The following excerpt reviews two recent anthologies of women's poetry from previous centuries and highlights the political issues invoked by reprinting early women authors.*]

When I was in college, almost no women writers were included in seventeenth- and eighteenth-century English literature courses. That was ten years ago. Now, after a decade which has seen the reprinting of at least a dozen major novels by women before Jane Austen, as well as the production of new biographies of seventeenth- and eighteenth-century women's lives and groundbreaking anthologies of seventeenth- and eighteenth-century women's poetry, no one can use a lack of material as the excuse for leaving women out. And the possibility of using computers to provide access to works which have been unavailable for at least 200 years is likely to change the way we teach women's writing even more in the 1990s.

Amidst this wealth of new material serious problems arise. Battles are constantly waged not only between feminists and the old guard, who still would like to keep women out of the Augustan canon altogether, but also among feminists themselves, who are deeply divided about the aims and the politics of reprinting "lost" or "neglected" works by women writers. With what political motives are we attempting to introduce these women into a canon which has so fiercely resisted them for nearly 200 years? Are we looking for "great books" which happen to be written by women? Attempting to trace the tumultuous "careers" of those women who fought for acceptance and acclaim as published writers? Or reconstructing the "culture" out of which these women's writings arise and the problematic relationship(s) their gender, race and class give them to that culture?

Consider for a moment the career of Ann Yearsley (1752-1806). A dairy-maid by profession, Yearsley published four volumes of poetry, a historical tragedy and a novel. She was "discovered" by Hannah More, Bluestocking and poet, who published and marketed Yearsley's early writings and—not surprisingly—gained considerably more than Yearsley from the arrangement. More later set up a school for Yearsley and her family to run, with More herself as trustee; she was outraged when Yearsley used the school's profits for "Gauze Bonnets, long lappets, gold Pins etc." Yearsley resisted More's attempts to keep her financially dependent, breaking off ties with More, eventually telling her own version of their relationship in the fourth edition of her *Poems* (1786) and writing a *Poem on the Inhumanity of the Slave Trade* to compete with More's famous *Slavery, A Poem*.

To teach the poetry of either Yearsley or More without attending to the class relationship between them is to assume a kind of women's community, a kind of transpolitical female situation which, at least in the eighteenth century, clearly does not exist. And to teach either woman's anti-slavery poem without suggesting the ways in which white women colonized black women's political discourse even as they fought against slavery is to rip these women out of their historical context, to show them as "politically correct" (in twentieth-century terms) but fail to tell the complicated stories of how their political identifications and alliances were actually formed.

But there are also dangers in exposing the implicit prejudices of early women's writing, even with the best political intentions. It is all too easy to rummage through our foremothers' attics looking for choice snippets of "feminist" writing (or, alternately, for the places where they were racist, class-biased, homophobic), far more difficult to discuss their political conflicts in ways that keep the pulse of those conflicts alive for ourselves and our students. While it is clear that seventeenth- and eighteenth-century (white, middle-class) feminists used black and poor peoples' oppressions to figure for their own—as in the narrator's complicated identification with Oroonoko and Imoinda, the slave hero and heroine, in Aphra Behn's *Oroonoko, Or the Royal Slave* (1689)—do we perhaps threaten to analyze feminism out of existence when we show the ways in which the rise of modern feminism, in the later eighteenth century, is riddled with conflicts among women themselves? What do we gain and lose by using twentieth-century feminist (or Marxist or post-structuralist) theory to politicize early women's writing?

I raise these questions not so much because I feel confident of my own answers, but because these are the questions which link a local problem in Women's Studies—reprinting works by early women writers—with larger problems in contemporary feminist politics. If the current wealth of editions and anthologies is to be more than a temporary form of self-promotion by and for white Anglophone women, we must seek to situate these reprints in the complicated political and economic matrix out of which they arise.

While for publishers these anthologies are big business—virtually every publishing house that competes in the aca-demic market has produced or commissioned an anthology of women's writing before 1800—editing such an anthology (or a scholarly edition of an eighteenth-century woman's novel, or the works of a seventeenth-century woman poet) is likely neither to get an assistant professor tenure nor move a feminist editor up the corporate ladder. Perhaps it is because the stakes are actually so small that we attempt to possess the women whose works we're editing, as if there can be only one legitimate edition of a given work, or one serious anthology of a given century's women writers. While I don't think we should be at one another's throats, a wide range of editions and anthologies of women's writing seems to me a good thing, especially if each is precise about its own political and historical frame of reference.

I have in front of me two very different books: ***Kissing the Rod: An Anthology of Seventeenth-Century Women's Verse,*** edited by Germaine Greer, Susan Hastings, Jeslyn Medoff and Melinda Sansone (1988), and ***Eighteenth-Century Women Poets,*** edited by Roger Lonsdale (1989). The production of anthologies is particularly difficult, since one inevitably emphasizes some writers, neglects others and shapes the readers' sense of individual authors with the works selected. In addition, an anthology creates implicit relationships among writers and highlights certain political issues while giving less emphasis to others. (For instance, while many women wrote poems in praise of Anne, Queen from 1702 to 1714, ***Eighteenth-Century Women Poets*** includes "racism" in the Index but not "monarchy.") Taken together, these two anthologies offer a vast range of poetry formerly available only in rare book libraries. As a pair they also raise important questions about the relationship between feminist theory and the construction of the category "woman writer" in the later twentieth century.

Though I've been reading and writing about seventeenth- and eighteenth-century women's poetry for over five years, both anthologies include works I'd never read before. And while each has minor errors here and there, both editorial teams are to be commended for their archival sleuthwork, their commitment to finding new facts about as well as new poems by these women, and their inclusion of bibliographical material to aid the reader who seeks additional information.

A century is a good scope for such an anthology, not only as it dovetails with the way English literature is carved up at many universities, but also in terms of political and historical coherence. It is often possible to see the changes in the cultural construction of gender and language operating for a group of women over 100 years' time. The eighteenth century in England, for instance, sees the rise of both the professional writer and the cult of domesticity. Together, these two ideological shifts tend to position the eighteenth-century woman writer as teacher and moralist, creating hierarchies among women and suggesting that some women's writing has more authority than others'.

The vast differences between ***Kissing the Rod*** and ***Eighteenth-Century Women Poets*** suggest both the impact of this professionalization of the woman writer on what women actually wrote, and the ways in which it continues to shape the way we talk about women writers before and after, say, 1700. While Lonsdale calls women who write poetry "women poets" and describes women's increasing confidence in a range of verse forms throughout the century, Greer and her co-editors announce women's subservience in the phrase "kissing the rod" as well as in the trivializing subtitle of "women's verse."

Greer takes the title from Torriano's *Proverbial Phrases* (1666), which explains that the term is "taken from Children, who when they do amiss, and are punish'd, they are made to vent their vexation no otherwise than by kissing that rod with which they were punish'd." She defends the peculiar choice of title thus:

> Whether the rod is wielded by paternal authority . . . a husband, the king . . . or God himself, women have always been obliged for their own survival to humble themselves before it, and to flatter it. Such contradictions constitute the peculiarly insidious and destructive character of sex oppression.

But Greer and her co-editors have, in large part, constructed this myth of women's humility by omitting important poems which defy this generalization. They have included Amelia Lanyer's "Description of Cookeham" but not her poems about women, Aphra Behn's poems to other poets but none of her erotic or political poems. And in an attempt to create a sense of community among women poets, they often include anonymous poems in female voices—such as the poem by "Philo-Philippa" to Katherine Philips—which may not have been written by women at all.

In contrast, *Eighteenth-Century Women Poets* has no feminist political agenda. Lonsdale, who also edited the *Oxford Anthology of Eighteenth-Century Verse,* is careful not to generalize about the range of women who wrote poetry in the eighteenth century, or about their subject-matter. His introduction discusses changing literary tastes over the course of the century, particularly the rise of what he calls the "idiom" of sensibility, which seemed to encourage greater numbers of women to write poetry, but also to limit those things they actually wrote about. Unlike *Kissing the Rod,* which has a rather awkward critical apparatus, with poems often beginning at the bottoms of pages and footnotes at the top, *Eighteenth-Century Women Poets* is consummately readable.

My only real complaint is that in Lonsdale's enthusiasm to include as many women poets as possible he often chooses extracts from longer poems which turn them into entirely different works from their originals. For instance, he begins Anne Finch's "The Spleen" with the passage in which the poet discusses her own experience of melancholy and depression. This is certainly the most moving and poetically powerful section of the poem, but to read it in isolation turns a poem of satire and social commentary into, essentially, a poem about an individual woman's experience.

If the editors of anthologies inevitably shape myths of literary (or feminist) history out of a range of unwieldy primary sources, the editors of new editions of eighteenth-century novels attempt to make earlier works "accessible" to the modern reader. Pandora Press and Virago Press, feminist publishing houses in London which have now become part of larger conglomerates, were the first to reprint early novels by women. While one delights in editions of Eliza Haywood's *The History of Miss Betsy Thoughtless* (1751; 1986) or Sarah Scott's *Millenium Hall* (1762; 1986) that can be taken to bed, the Pandora editions in particular are often unforgivably sloppy, with dozens of typos that any proofreader should have caught. And (as Margaret Anne Doody recently pointed out in *Frances Burney, The Life in the Works*) Virago's edition of Frances Burney's *Cecilia* is essentially stolen from a Victorian editor, Annie Raine Ellis, whose notes are included but whose feminist scholarship goes unacknowledged.

Virago's "Modern Classics" and Pandora's "Mothers of the Novel" reprints are aimed at what Virginia Woolf called the "common reader," the person who still reads good fiction. In an attempt to attract this audience, Pandora's reprints are introduced by contemporary British novelists. In the best cases—such as Margaret Drabble's introduction to Frances Burney's *The Wanderer; or, Female Difficulties* (1814; 1988)—there is a solid match between eighteenth- and twentieth-century sensibilities. In the worst cases, the introductions either repackage clichés about women in the eighteenth century or confess to not having liked the novel at all!

But even if their editions are sloppy and not apt to outlast the current boom in the Women's Lit biz, Pandora's and Virago's pioneering example has forced major publishers to commission scholarly editions of these same works, editions based on primary research and aimed at teaching all of us new things about the eighteenth century and the writing—and the women—it produced. (pp. 11-12)

> *Carol Barash, "Reprint Rights, Reprint Wrongs," in* The Women's Review of Books, *Vol. VII, No. 5, February, 1990, pp. 11-12.*

Victoria Kahn

[In the following excerpt, Kahn discusses the variety of viewpoints on pornography within the feminist community.]

[*The Sexual Liberals and the Attack on Feminism*] takes its title from a conference held at New York University Law School in 1987, where the 25 papers it includes were presented. The papers address a variety of topics of concern to the anti-pornography movement. Their authors share the view that the erotic portrayal of male dominance and female subordination in pornography characterizes relations between the sexes throughout society; so while some of them attack the pornography industry, others consider related issues such as abortion, the sexual abuse of women and children, and reproductive technologies.

Central to the volume, as the title announces, is its critique of "sexual liberalism." This is defined by Dorchen Leidholdt in the Introduction as "a set of political beliefs and practices rooted in the assumption that sexual expression is inherently liberating and must be permitted to flourish unchecked, even when it entails the exploitation or brutalization of others." The authors attribute this view of sexuality partly to liberal political theory, whose "gender-neutral" definition of political equality and individual rights cannot explain the existence of—and in fact systematically ignores—actual gender inequality. Of particular concern to the anti-pornography feminists is their critics' contention that pornography is a constitutional, free speech issue. In fact, the anti-porn feminists argue, the exercising of this right is a zero-sum game when men have more power than women: in our society the "right" only protects those who already have it in the first place.

The contributors contend that in defending the right to privacy, the "liberals" assume that equality already exists in individual, private relations and that the state doesn't need to intervene to guarantee it. But, their objection to this runs, by requiring that the state not interfere with the right to privacy, the "liberals" are preserving the status quo and protecting only those individuals—men—who don't need its protection in the first place. . . .

A number of the contributors convincingly show how the pro-sex camp's unwitting liberal assumptions limit their ability to recognize systematic harm to women. For example, Louise Armstrong indicts the feminist community for forgetting that incest is an important political issue. "The nominally liberal ideology of illness and cure," she argues, "rather than crime and accountability . . . is providing a new shield of protection against offenders." While there has been much talk about incest, Armstrong feels it has focused on individual psychology rather than power relations. She particularly takes to task mental health professionals (including some feminist therapists), the legal system and the media for promoting the attitude that sexual violence is an illness. In assailing this view, Armstrong reminds us that incest is not simply the result of "illness" but of an abuse of power which informs all gender relations.

Twiss Butler attacks the public/private distinction that informs the liberals' defense of abortion as well as of pornography. The more vigorously liberals and civil libertarians "defend the 'right of privacy' for abortion, the more legitimacy accrues to such other 'privacy rights' as unlimited access to pornography and other behavior characterized, however harmful to women, as 'sex' and therefore as 'private.' "

John Stoltenberg similarly observes that critics of the Supreme Court's recent decision to uphold a Georgia statute outlawing homosexual sex between consenting adults undermined their own position. By resting their case on the right to privacy, Stoltenberg claims, the critics of this decision actually reinforced the status quo, thereby harming not only gay men but also women. . . .

Janice Raymond examines the question of power somewhat more obliquely by noting that the pornography debate is represented in the feminist and establishment press as a conflict between feminists rather than an issue that affects men as well. This reporting

> sentimentalize[s] dissension, and [it sentimentalizes] unity among women. It is as if to hold a

strong position on feminist issues any more is tantamount to dividing women. If you're not a moral relativist, you're an extremist or, in some circles, a fascist. Enter the liberal notion of unity—a unity that is achieved only by ceding the capacity for making moral and political judgments.

In spite of its flaws, [*The Sexual Liberals and the Attack on Feminism*] does make one think about whether pornography is merely a form of representation (as critics of the collection would claim) or the actual practice of violence against women. The anti-pornography feminists argue that pornography is not just representation but the exploitation of real women. And because pornography *is* violence, it is not open to interpretation as images are. Pornography only superficially allows for a variety of responses on the viewer's part: women who claim to find certain forms of pornography liberating have simply internalized the male ideology of sexual pleasure.

For their part, the pro-sex feminists do see in the anti-pornography critique a view of representation, a simplistic one according to which images monolithically influence and victimize the hapless viewer. From this perspective, the anti-pornography feminists' view that ideology is seamless and all-powerful backfires: for when they assert that dominant ideas are all-powerful they simply reproduce that ideology and close the door to dissent. If pornography *is* a kind of representation, however, the interpretation of its images is not simply determined by the dominant ideology. Images are inherently ambiguous and individuals will supply their own interpretations.

> Of particular concern to the anti-pornography feminists is their critics' contention that pornography is a constitutional, free-speech issue. In fact, the anti-porn feminists argue, the exercising of this right is a zero-sum game when men have more power than women: in our society the "right" only protects those who already have it in the first place.

Each camp's concept of representation is tied to its account of how to resist the status quo. The pro-sex movement emphasizes the fissures in ideology and the consequent possibilities for dissent. Many anti-pornography feminists see male dominance as systematic, and therefore invulnerable to challenges from within; only "re-presentation" from without will weaken it. Anti-pornography feminists are not united on this point, though; Catharine MacKinnon, for example, talks about the need to find "a vulnerable place in the system" in her paper, "Liberalism and the Death of Feminism." But MacKinnon does share the anti-porn feminists' belief that by *describing* the dominant ideology of Western liberalism, they are also *exposing* the systematic contradictions which make up the system.

Representation is the locus of dissent for both camps—but in the pro-sex case everything is already representation, whereas in the anti-porn case it is only in the critique of pornography and of all other forms of male dominance that representation occurs.

The contradictions inherent in both arguments become apparent when we examine the pro-sex and anti-pornography views of the legal treatment of pornography. While the pro-sex camp sees images and symbols as inherently open to various interpretations, it does not feel the law is similarly open: one can be a "resisting reader" of images, but not of legal institutions. A selective view of resistance afflicts the anti-pornography movement as well: one can't resist images but one can resist the dominant legal ideology by working through the legal system itself. Many of the contributors to the book defend or rely on the Minneapolis anti-pornography ordinance drafted by MacKinnon and Andrea Dworkin, which defines pornography as "the graphic sexually explicit subordination of women through pictures and/or words," and makes it actionable as an abuse of civil rights. But working within the legal system like this is at odds with the assumption that "re-presentation" or critique of society can only take place "from without."

The pornography debate raises more questions about tolerance and the state's role in furthering women's interests. In defending tolerance of a wide range of sexual practices, the pro-sex feminist argues that the subjective experience of sexuality is richly complicated. While women's experience may be shaped by a male ideology of sexual pleasure, repression or censorship of that ideology won't make their experience truer or more authentic. In the pro-sex camp's view, the anti-porn feminist can't afford to recognize positive sexual possibilities, for if she did she would have to admit that there was something to be lost in having the state regulate pornography. It isn't just that the pro-sex camp believes in suspending judgment on whether any sexual practices are exploitative; it is actively against regulation by the state as contrary to women's interests.

For the anti-porn feminist, such suspicion of the state is based on a dangerous fallacy. The danger they see is that this suspicion, which rests on the view that there is a private realm of experience which the state should not interfere with, may reinforce the myth that sexuality is private. In fact the state is always present in the bedroom, as MacKinnon, Dworkin, Susan Kappeler, Twiss Butler, Dorchen Leidholdt, and others in this collection argue. In their view, to refuse to pass legal as well as personal judgment on individuals' sexual practices is to adopt a false neutrality; and by abdicating judgment and by insisting on the authority of subjective experience, the pro-sex camp gives up the ability to criticize society in other areas. If everyone has the right to their own opinion, then every opinion is equally right. This is what Marcuse called repressive tolerance: by refusing to take sides, he pointed out, it "actually protects the already established machinery of discrimination."

In reading *The Sexual Liberals and the Attack on Feminism* I was struck, finally, by the way the effort to "do justice" to both positions in the pornography debate drama-tizes the very problems at issue. Does anyone who tries to give a fair account of each position automatically side with the pro-sex camp, or with the view that more discussion or expression is better than less, or with the claim that all positions deserve equally to be heard? Andrea Dworkin's call in this collection for "proselytizing dialogue" strikes me as somewhat of an oxymoron; yet I am also sympathetic to MacKinnon's argument (made elsewhere) that the First Amendment protects the freedom of speech of those who already have it. Or, as A.J. Liebling said, freedom of the press belongs to those who own the press. Where you come down in this debate will finally depend not only on how you read images but on how much confidence you have in the ability of feminist lawyers and activists to change the legal system from within.

> *Victoria Kahn, "Lambasting the Liberals," in* The Women's Review of Books, *Vol. VII, No. 5, February, 1990, p. 16.*

Sandra Harding

[*In the excerpt below, Harding encourages a greater awareness of such issues as race, class, sexual orientation, and ethnicity, along with gender, in Women's Studies courses.*]

I began teaching Women's Studies in 1973, the year I emerged from graduate school after five years as a returning student. In those early days, two dangers were constantly on the minds of those of us—overwhelmingly white, heterosexual and economically more advantaged than most women—who were struggling to establish Women's Studies programs. Would the politics of feminist teaching, research and organizational forms get us ejected from campus? Or would the accommodations we made in order to conduct feminist projects on campuses lose us the politics of the women's movement and, with it, feminism?

"Revolution, or merely reform? Purity or co-optation?"— so the choices appeared. For most of our colleagues, the very idea of the purportedly "special" concerns that a Women's Studies course or program represented was beyond the pale—as it still remains for a dwindling few today. For a few others, Women's Studies was already too conservative—we were part of *their* problem.

If the path Women's Studies travels is often smoother today than it was two decades ago, it is at least in part because almost everyone can see that Women's Studies excels at just what higher education is supposed to do: educate the young and not so young to lead more rewarding lives in ways that contribute to democratic societies; conduct and inspire research and scholarship that expand the forefronts of knowledge by existing standards, as well as through progressive questioning of those standards; maintain organizational practices that help faculty and students work toward those goals.

From the beginning a locus of tension within Women's Studies as well as between it and the rest of higher education was the issue of what role would be given to the voices of the Other women—poor women, lesbians and women of color most notably. (That was how "we" thought about the issues: what role would "we" give Other women?!) Just what should count as revolution or mere reform, purity or co-optation, was itself a terrain of feminist struggle. . . .

Now "revolution vs. reform" and "purity vs. co-optation" no longer seem to be useful ways to formulate our options, if they ever were. But what should count as progressive in Women's Studies is no less contentious now than it was two decades ago and—my point here—it should remain so. Perhaps we should conceptualize Women's Studies as a permanent revolution in order to do justice to its continuing exploration of new "disloyalties to civilization."

Consider this point in terms of recent tendencies to think anew about Women's Studies' responsibilities to advance the lives of marginalized women. The old issue about Other women was usually phrased as one about inclusion: would Women's Studies advance only the voices and perspectives of white, Western, straight, relatively economically advantaged women, or would it also include the voices and perspectives of the Others?

What was up for inclusion were both persons and texts. Marginalized women should be hired and promoted; their voices and writings should be an important part of the Women's Studies presence. This old agenda is far from completed; the bodies and texts of marginalized women are still far too underrepresented on our campuses. But at the same time, the challenge to women of the dominant groups has gone beyond inclusiveness. How can those of us from those dominant groups distinguish between our feminist agendas and a culturally narrow self-interest if we do not try to understand where *we* are located in the social networks of institutionalized marginalization, oppression and exploitation? How can we understand our own lives if we cannot understand what consequences the beliefs and actions of "our group"—including us feminists—have for women in marginalized groups, around the world as well as locally?

In short, what standards would make Women's Studies research, courses and curricula into part of the solution rather than part of the problem? One stage of this agenda could be to insist that every Women's Studies project be able to answer appropriately the question "For whom?" Whose problems generate research, teaching and administrative projects? . . .

Another way to put the question is: With whom should Women's Studies faculty and programs be making alliances? Obviously, with progressive elements in our administrations and disciplines. But certainly with Afro-American and ethnic studies programs, with the Left, and with the first whisperings of attempts to found lesbian and gay studies programs. This is where the issue moves beyond the inclusion of persons and texts. What should we be doing in order to become desirable allies from *their* perspectives? In what ways are Women's Studies courses, scholarship and curricula still part of the problem that their programs are designed to solve?

As long as inclusive tendencies in Women's Studies stay at the level of studying Others, Women's Studies remains part of their problem. Here is where the determination to take responsibility for who we are becomes crucial. What would it mean, for instance, for white feminists to develop their scientific and political programs to take responsibility for who we are *as whites,* beyond merely being the friend or ally of women of color by supporting the advancement of their persons and texts? For one thing, it would require providing less partial and distorting descriptions and explanations of the racial conditions of white women's lives and how these conditions affect the lives of women of color here and around the world. (Analogous agendas can be constructed for the conditions of heterosexual and economically privileged lives.)

In *The Invention of Africa* (1988), the Zairean philosopher Valentine Y. Mudimbe argues that just as European and American imperialists invented an Africa that would serve their purposes (they said that they discovered it), so must Africans now invent a West that serves Africans' purposes. The imperialists claimed to discover in Africa a primitiveness, a pre-logicality, an immorality that could serve as the mirror for the purportedly civilized West that they were simultaneously inventing. But this kind of project can usefully be developed by the other side, Mudimbe points out. For Africans today, a "critical reading of the Western experience is simultaneously a way of 'inventing' a foreign tradition in order to master its techniques, and an ambiguous strategy for implementing alterity."

Can Westerners too join in this critical reading, adapt it to our situations and use it as a tool for liberation? Feminists have already begun, in their reinvention of contemporary gender relations in the West as a bizarre set of beliefs and practices performed by the indigenous people who rule our societies. Can we continue to master the "folk wisdom" of these "natives" as we "discover" further dimensions of the incompatibility between their racist, class-exploitative and homophobic projects and those of Women's Studies?

> *Sandra Harding, "The Permanent Revolution," in* The Women's Review of Books, *Vol. VII, No. 5, February, 1990, p. 17.*

Peggy Pascoe

[In the following excerpt, Pascoe explicates a multicultural approach to Women's Studies courses as the most effective way to illuminate a variety of power relations without normalizing white, middle-class experience.]

As Women's Studies enters the 1990s, the challenge of developing its multi-cultural potential looms larger than ever. The central questions are familiar ones: How do we teach students about women of diverse backgrounds? How do we devise a feminist theory that takes adequate account of race, class and cultural relations?

These questions may be familiar, but the context in which we answer them is changing. Feminist scholars once saw answers in assigning autobiographies of racial ethnic women. (I follow Evelyn Nakano Glenn's lead in using this term instead of "ethnic minority women," "Third World women" or "women of color.") Now these scholars are beginning to see how much more than superficial inclusion is needed for a deeply multi-cultural analysis.

Working out that analysis is challenging enough in places like California, where the majority of students entering college today are from groups usually designated as ethnic "minorities." At the University of Utah, where I teach, it is even more so. Because racial ethnic student enrollment (black, American Indian, Asian/Pacific Island, and Hispanic males and females) is a tiny five percent of the student population—women's total enrollment is only 43 percent, and these figures seem never to have been broken down for race and gender, only for race *or* gender—it is unusual for me to have more than one or two racial ethnic women in any class I teach.

Although Utah may be an extreme case (it certainly exhibits some distinct peculiarities), I suspect that my situation—I am a white woman trying to teach material about racial ethnic women to an almost entirely white audience—is all too common. It was the challenge of facing this audience that spurred me to make racial ethnic women even more central in my American women's history survey course. If that course turned out to be an eye-opener for my students, it was also one for me.

Women's Studies teachers are proud of the increased attention they have paid to race, class and culture. Yet much of the progress consists of adding classes devoted to specific groups—a separate course on Chicanas, for example. As Johnetta Butler noted last year in this publication, it is when the issue becomes one of omitting material on white women in order to incorporate material on racial ethnic women—the kind of question most clearly posed in survey courses—that resistance is greatest. Even teachers who declare their eagerness to take advantage of the recent outpouring of materials on racial ethnic women debate "how much" of it to use in survey classes.

In my situation, however, this consideration paled before the resistance of students to my initial attempts to increase classroom coverage of racial ethnic women. Some found the material exotically interesting but not really significant. Others complained that it was just "too difficult." The boldest simply asked, "Why do we study so much about ethnic minority women?"

The need to bring the history of racial ethnic women front and center seemed paramount. To meet it, I sought out materials that would immerse my culture-blind students in racial ethnic women's experiences. I assigned such a quantity of material, I felt sure I was making my course truly multi-cultural. In the first half of my survey, for example, I taught Harriet Wilson's *Our Nig; or, Sketches from the Life of a Free Black,* the poems of Phillis Wheatley, the speeches of Sojourner Truth and a whole host of slave documents as well as Jacqueline Jones' *Labor of Love, Labor of Sorrow: Black Women, Work, and the Family from Slavery to the Present.* I started the course with a lecture on Iroquois Indian women and ended with one on Plains Indian women; I talked about Hispanic women

in colonial New Mexico and invited a guest lecturer to speak on Hispanic women after the American conquest.

As a result, my students learned a great deal about the experiences of diverse groups of women. Yet the way they used this knowledge raised disturbing questions about how students in mostly white classrooms interpret multi-cultural comparisons. I urged students to refine their skills at analyzing gender by making cross-cultural comparisons: for example, to compare Iroquois women's economic status with that of colonial white women. My students quickly arranged their comparisons into neat polarities. Iroquois Indian women provided a vision of freedom; Chinese immigrant women exemplified victimization. In both cases, racial ethnic cultures fell into "good" or "bad" categories along a continuum in which white women were always at the center. I had placed a lot of emphasis on ethnic minority women in order to make the term "minority" ridiculous, but I had not managed to overcome the tendency, strong in the predominantly white classroom, for students to see white women as the norm and racial ethnic women as deviations.

Consider, for example, the way students understood the situation of Chinese immigrant prostitutes, who for a short time in the nineteenth century constituted a majority of the Chinese immigrant women in California. Chinese immigrant prostitutes were extremely vulnerable to male domination—they were held as indentured servants in circumstances usually little better than slavery. Much impressed by the details of their oppression, my students discussed (in tones of horror) how the history of Chinese immigrant prostitutes differed from that of white, middle-class Victorian women. They placed the blame for the Chinese immigrants' plight at the door of Chinese culture. To do so, they had to overlook a significant fact: Chinese prostitutes in China were far less vulnerable than Chinese prostitutes in the United States, and the reasons had as much to do with the racial attitudes of American citizens as they did with the gender dynamics of Chinese culture.

My students' inability to see this forced me to do some hard thinking about the theoretical underpinnings of my course. The problem was not that students had learned the wrong things about Chinese culture. On the contrary, understanding gender dynamics within cultural groups is not only necessary grounding for the study of women's history, it is also one of the central benefits of multi-cultural courses. The problem was that studying the different forms of male dominance *within* cultural groups yields inadequate explanations for relations *between* cultural groups. In the late nineteenth-century Southwest, for example, the status of Hispanic women was shaped by at least two forces: traditional notions of Hispanic male authority and the white, middle-class gender prescriptions that accompanied Anglo economic conquest of the region. In a society as culturally diverse as the United States, relations between cultural groups have been—and continue to be—critical in women's history.

Both my students and my course were stumbling over the theoretical notion, still widespread in Women's Studies circles, that the power relations of gender are most visible when other power relations—race, class, culture, ethnicity—are least visible. That notion was inherent in the organization of my course. As a result, the nineteenth-century Cult of True Womanhood seemed to be a clear illustration of feminist theories about gender dynamics. But the relations between slave women, slave men and slaveholders appeared to be "complicated" by factors of race, class and culture that muddied the theoretical waters.

As long as Women's Studies courses focused most of their attention on immersing students in the experiences of women, these theoretical difficulties were muted. The goal of multi-culturalism was met, in the main, by the simple inclusion of personal narratives by racial ethnic women. Teachers concentrating on giving voice to diverse cultural constituencies could—and often did—ignore warnings by racial ethnic scholars about the deficiencies of this approach.

But we who teach in universities are now trying to keep pace with what Barbara Christian has eloquently titled "the race for theory." We feel with increasing urgency the need to think carefully about the theoretical underpinnings of Women's Studies courses. Put most cynically, it appears that feminist scholars are giving the long-neglected experience of racial ethnic women its due just at the point at which "experience" is being subordinated to "theory" in Women's Studies parlance. As a result, an increasing number of pioneering racial ethnic women scholars are faced with the devastating charge that their work isn't "theoretical" enough.

The new feminist theories demonstrate a level of complexity so daunting as to make many of the central concepts of Women's Studies—identity, experience, race, class, culture, even gender—seem unfashionably simplistic. But for all their sophistication, they have yet to show a good record of making racial ethnic women central in feminist analysis. When faced with feminists who argue for the importance of theory by downgrading experience, it is more than a little tempting to stand firm in defense of experience. But a better solution, as racial ethnic scholars have pointed out time and again, is to challenge the identification of feminist theory based on white, middle-class women with feminist theory in general.

To learn this lesson, I had to revise my own understanding of the simple and the complicated. Rather than focusing my course on those seemingly simple cases in which power differences could be pared down to gender relations within a given culture (Victorian husbands' legal authority over Victorian wives; the relative "equality" between slave women and slave men), I began to seek out cases in which a whole range of power relations based on race, class, ethnicity and gender was visible. For this purpose, it was the points at which two or more cultures came into contact with each other that seemed significant, for it was at such cultural crossroads that the power relations between groups were most apparent (and, perhaps, most subject to change).

> Women's Studies teachers are proud of the increased attention they have paid to race, class and culture. Yet much of the progress consists of adding classes devoted to specific groups—a separate course on Chicanas, for example. . . . [It] is when the issue becomes one of omitting material on white women in order to incorporate material on racial ethnic women—the kind of question most clearly posed in survey courses—that resistance is greatest.

I took the first steps toward teaching about cultural crossroads hesitantly and experimentally, worried that my students wouldn't be able to handle the complexity of the issues. I could not have been more wrong. My first lecture of this kind focused on two women—one white, one Indian—caught in the conflicts between cultures in colonial America.

Mary Jemison, the white woman, was an Indian captive who, choosing to retain Indian customs, pointed out that the lot of Seneca women seemed to her preferable to that of white women. She is known to history because her choice made her a racial curiosity in the eyes of white readers. Mary Musgrove, the Indian woman, was a half-blood Creek whose Indian lineage combined with her training in English to put her in a position to call herself "the empress of the Creeks." Yet she found that the same Georgia colonists who benefited from her language skills and land negotiations tried to convince her white husband to make her behave like a white colonial woman should, meaning that she should drop her claim for payment for her services.

My next lecture was a rereading of Phillis Wheatley. Earlier, I had found the style of her religious writing troublingly atypical for black women of her day. Now it seemed full of clues to the entire range of power relations in the colonial period. Both these lectures fascinated the students, who clearly wanted more.

Trying to oblige, I stayed up late one night putting together a lecture on Ida Wells-Barnett. Too exhausted to finish it, I contented myself with getting the biographical details straight and emphasizing Wells-Barnett's significance as a leader of the black community. I promised myself that I would do better next time. But when I gave the lecture in class the next day, one of the students raised her hand to point out exactly how Wells-Barnett's fight against lynching led her to formulate a wide-ranging critique of the gender system of white Victorian America. As I listened to this student finish my lecture for me, I learned what I should already have known; that the clearest understanding of gender comes from studying it in relation to a variety of other forms of dominance, not from studying it in artificial isolation. (pp. 22-3)

Peggy Pascoe, "At the Crossroads of Culture,"

in The Women's Review of Books, *Vol. VII, No. 5, February, 1990, pp. 22-3.*

Jean Bethke Elshtain

[*In the excerpt below, Elshtain surveys the various moral, philosophical, and legal arguments presented historically in support of feminism, and reviews several recent works on this subject.*]

Understood historically, feminism is a concern with the social role and identity of women in relation to men in societies past and present, animated by a conviction that women suffer and have suffered injustices because of their sex. The political language and aims of modern feminism emerged from the French Revolution and the Enlightenment. Associated historically with forces combatting orthodoxy and autocracy, feminism defined itself as a struggle for recognition of the rights of women, for equality between the sexes, and for redefinitions of womanhood. Drawing upon liberal and rationalist as well as utopian and romantic ideas in Western Europe and America, feminism has long resisted easy definition, and its implications for moral life are ongoingly contested and contestable.

Moral feminism is most often traced to the publication of Mary Wollstonecraft's **Vindication of the Rights of Women** in 1792. Wollstonecraft adumbrated what were to become inescapable feminist preoccupations including, but not limited to, the defense of political and natural rights. She challenged received notions of the distinctive virtues of the two sexes; argued for a transformed education for male and female; attacked martial images of citizenship; and celebrated an androgynous notion of the rational self.

Reason became a weapon for women's emancipation, deployed against the exclusive identification of women with 'nature' and their sexual function and capacity. Faith in reason was then coupled with a strong belief in progress. These convictions, refined in and through an already deeply rooted tradition of liberal contractarianism and commitment to formal legalistic equality, are most manifest in John Stuart Mill's classic nineteenth-century tract, **The Subjection of Women** (1869). Counterposing 'Reason' and 'Instinct', Mill looks forward to a society based on rational principles. Reason, he contends, requires nullifying differences of treatment based on considerations of sex, among other 'accidents of birth'. Granting women equality of citizenship and civil liberty in the public realm will help to bring about a deeper transformation in the social relations of the sexes.

Liberalism has been attractive to feminist thinkers. The language of rights is a potent weapon against traditional obligations, particularly those of family duty or any social status declared 'natural' on the basis of ascriptive characteristics. To be 'free' and 'equal' to men became a central aim of feminist reform. The political strategy that follows from this dominant feminism is one of inclusion: women, as well as men, are rational beings. It follows that women as well as men are bearers of inalienable rights. Leading proponents of women's suffrage in Britain and the United States undermined arguments which justified formal legal-istic inequality on the basis of sex differences. Such feminists claimed that denying a group of persons basic rights on the grounds of some presumed difference could not be justified unless it could be shown that the difference was relevant to the distinction being made. Whatever differences might exist between the sexes, none, based on this view, justified legal inequality and denial of the rights and privileges of citizenship.

Few early feminists pushed liberal universalism to its most radical conclusion by arguing that there were *no* justifiable bases for exclusion of adult human beings from legal equality and citizenship. Proponents of women's suffrage were also heirs to a tradition that stressed the need for social order and shared values, emphasized civic education, and pressed the importance of having a propertied stake in society. Demands for the inclusion of women did not often extend to *all* women. Some women, and men, would be excluded by criteria of literacy, property-ownership, disability, or, in the United States, race.

At times, feminist discourse turned liberal egalitarianism on its head by arguing *for* women's civic equality on grounds that served historically to guarantee women's exclusion from politics. One finds the case for greater female political participation argued in terms of women's moral supremacy or characteristic forms of virtue. These appeals, strategic though they have been, were never *merely* strategic. They spoke to and from women's social identity. At various times, radical, liberal, democratic and socialist feminists have paid homage to women as exemplars of particular forms of social virtue.

From the vantage point of rights-based feminism, the emphasis on civic-based motherhood was a trap. But the historic discourse that evoked images of maternal virtue was one feminist response to a complex, rapidly changing political culture. That political culture, in the Western democracies, was committed to liberalism but included as well civic republican themes of social solidarity and national identity. Women made their case within a male-dominated political order from *their* own sphere, a world of female-structured sensibility and imperatives that signified doubly their exclusion from political life and their cultural strength and importance. Less able than men to embrace the identity of a wholly autonomous social atom, often rejecting explicitly the individualist ideal, many feminists endorsed expanded familial values, stripped of patriarchal privilege, as the basis for a new social world.

Feminists also turned variously to socialism, in its utopian and 'scientific' aspects, and to romanticism. Finding in notions of class oppression an analogue to women's social position vis-à-vis men, socialist feminists promoted notions of sex-class struggle and revolt. Feminists indebted to romanticism embraced a robust notion of a passionate, feeling self breaking the encrustations of social custom. Pressing a notion that women suffered as much from *repression*, or internalized notions of their own incapacities, as from *oppression*, or systematically imposed rules and customs that guaranteed sex inequality, feminist romantics stressed women's 'especial genius' (in the worlds of the American transcendentalist, Margaret Fuller) and hoped to see a social transformation that would free women's 'difference' and allow it to flourish, even to dominate.

The diverse history of feminisms in the plural forms the basis of current feminist discourse and debate. These debates secrete ethical imperatives and trail in their wake moral implications whether or not the thinkers involved articulate fully such imperatives or implications. Varieties of liberal, socialist, Marxist, and utopian feminism abound. Sexuality and sexual identity have become highly charged arenas of political redefinition. Some feminists see women as universal victims; others as a transhistorical sex-class; others as oppressed 'nature'. A minority urge women to separate entirely from male-dominated society. Some want full integration into that society, hence its transformation towards liberal equality. Others insist that the feminist project will not be complete until 'women's values', correctly understood, triumph. There are feminists who embrace a strong notion of women's difference, ontologically grounded, and others who reject any such idea as itself sexist. It's hard to wend one's way through the thicket of contemporary feminist discourse without some sort of map. But even with various categorical markers at hand, it is tricky at times to figure out what game is being played.

Is feminist scholarship primarily or exclusively the ideological arm of the feminist movement? There are feminist analysts who make this argument and insist that unless a text helps feminist doctrine, as they understand it, to triumph, it does not deserve the name 'feminism' and must, instead, be condemned as suspect if not downright heretical. There are other feminists who make a distinction between feminism as politics and feminism as the inspiration and occasion for scholarly endeavor. Anthropologist Judith Shapiro, for example, insists that the time has come for scholars to loosen the tie between their endeavors and the political rhetoric and ideological claims of feminism. "The danger," she wrote in an essay, "Anthropology and the Study of Gender," "in too close an association between scholarship and social reformism is not only in the limits it places on intellectual inquiry, but also in the implication that our lives as social, moral, and political beings are dependent on what we are able to discover in our scientific research. Loosening the tie would have liberating consequences . . . for anthropological investigation and for feminism as a social movement." But the hard-liners counter that a feminist text must exemplify and elaborate a "shared commitment to certain political aims and objectives" (in Rosalind Cloward's words) and that books are properly read and measured against a clear set of ideological criteria.

A will to power and truth as anathematizing the heretical and embracing the politically correct is painfully evident in a number of the texts under review. The *primary* aim of several of these works is to round up and to isolate the usual suspects and to form the friends into one of Milan Kundera's circle dances. Thus Janice Doane and Devon Hodges, in *Nostalgia and Sexual Difference,* attribute a terrible anxiety to those they deem foes, a deep fear of the feminist project as they understand it. The suspect roster includes Thomas Berger, George Stade, Dan Greenburg,

Ishmael Reed, John Irving, Christopher Lasch, and Brigitte and Peter Berger. Several "political reactionary" feminists are also indicted as co-conspirators, including Betty Friedan, Germaine Greer, and Jean Elshtain, because they have "expressed concern about feminism's effect on founding structures, life forces, and of course, the family as the home of natural truths about men and women." The circle dance is enfolded by repeated use of the encomium "fine," to endorse articles and arguments the authors embrace. The text is peppered with "in a fine article" or "in her fine article," a locution that makes its way even into the footnotes in a fervor of approval.

What is odd about the authors' rogues' gallery is how little its members share with one another. Lasch and the Bergers, for example, are at odds in their assessment of the baneful or beneficial effects of capitalism. Because their views about feminism are integrally related to their general analyses of liberal capitalist society, they vary dramatically. Never mind; in drawing up a hit list, fine distinctions simply get in the way. (pp. 181-84)

Similarly, the trio Friedan, Greer, Elshtain is very odd, as each of our understandings of feminism and its politics differs in important, not trivial ways. None, to my knowledge, have ever fretted about "life forces." Indeed, I have no idea what Doane and Hodges are talking about, and I doubt Friedan and Greer do either. And in light of the fact that each of us, in her own way, has denied explicitly that the family is a home for *natural* truths *simpliciter,* it becomes clear that Doane and Hodges are practicing the dogmatizing, not the expansive and exploratory, sort of feminist scholarship. One telltale sign is this: at least one of the three "reactionary feminists" condemned was not even read by the authors, or at least there is no evidence of this; rather, a debunking essay by a socialist feminist entitled, "The New Conservative Feminism," which indicts the same crew, is used as the sole source for Doane's and Hodges's matter-of-fact, unexplored repudiations. This is not the way scholarship works, but it is the way ideology functions and reproduces itself.

In a like way, Catharine A. MacKinnon, best known for her efforts (together with Andrea Dworkin) to ban pornography as a form of discrimination on the basis of sex (hence a violation of the civil rights of women lodged in the conviction that civil liberties, most of the time, are "bourgeois hypocrisy," to be overridden when, in Dworkin's words, "We're talking about the oppression of a class of people"), does not shy away in the least from condemnations of political opponents as enemies. In *Feminism Unmodified: Discourses on Life and Law,* MacKinnon sees the First Amendment as the self-interested expression of "white men from the point of view of their own social position. Some of them owned slaves; most of them owned women." The First Amendment was written to guarantee their freedom to perpetuate such ownership. Dubious as legal scholarship, this is impossible as political history. It cannot explain why there should have been any debate about the passage of the First Amendment at all, unless MacKinnon further assumes that some of the writers and amenders of the Constitution didn't know their own true interests and hence failed to push unambiguously for a measure that was to their "sex-class" advantage.

MacKinnon's approach to feminist discourse is relentlessly exclusionary. There is "the feminist theory of power" and "the feminist theory of knowledge"—no room for debate; one need only separate the correct from the incorrect. Her work aims at closure, not conversation, and its political implications are deeply troubling. By spreading oppression, victimization and patriarchal horror around so universally and uniformly, women emerge as "abject victims," not historic agents. (pp. 184-85)

Understood historically, feminism is a concern with the social role and identity of women in relation to men in societies past and present, animated by a conviction that women suffer and have suffered injustices because of their sex.

Another writer is Cynthia Fuchs Epstein, whose latest work is **Deceptive Distinctions.** As in her earlier work, *Woman's Place,* published in 1971, Epstein laments the fact that women were a resource not being properly exploited to the wider benefit of society as a whole. Epstein believes in 'reality' and criticizes claims that differences between males and females other than utterly trivial ones exist or, if they do exist, that they matter. For Epstein the body, that extraordinary container for identity and being, is seen as "raw physiology."

Her treatment of embodiment positions Epstein squarely on the so-called 'equality' side of the current "difference versus equality" debate, as it has been unfortunately cast. Epstein, however, does not consider the class dimension to this debate historically. Middle-class women have been more likely to push formal-legalistic equality and to challenge exclusion from public life, by which they mean the positions of official power wielded by men. Working-class women, on the other hand, have been less concerned with abstract rights than with concrete socio-economic matters, many of them lodged in recognition of biological difference, primarily the fact that it is women who get pregnant and give birth. Using the findings of science (which is, however, divided on this score, with recent scholarship, much of it carried out by women, emphasizing differences), Epstein insists that in an ideal world gender distinctions would be a matter of complete indifference. Epstein makes judgements about the works of a whole crew of feminist analysts based, not upon their own work, but upon polemical secondary sources. Here are a few examples. I get yet another walk-on role, this time as a "self-identified feminist," in fact a "conservative" who "regards the family in universal terms." As proof, from my book, *Public Man, Private Woman,* she cites a few words *as quot-*

ed by the author of "The New Conservative Feminism," the same source Doane and Hodges accept as Holy Writ. In fact, my treatment of the family in *Public Man, Private Woman* is framed with these words: "I recognize that there is no such thing as 'the family' but that there are multiple variations on this theme." Similarly, three feminist writers on motherhood—Alice Rossi, Dorothy Dinnerstein, and "June Flax," (whose name Epstein has wrong as it is 'Jane', not 'June')—are excoriated based upon the blasts of others rather than upon a direct engagement with their work. Alice Rossi's "biosocial perspective" is sidebunked, but none of Rossi's own work appears in the bibliography. Such lapses are disappointing coming, as they do, from a serious sociologist.

Moving from Epstein's report to Claire Duchen's very helpful collection, **French Connections,** a slice of life from the recent past that introduces the French MLF (*mouvement de libération des femmes*) through "certain key debates," is a dizzying experience. Duchen's selections detail the contentiousness, the internecine ideological warfare, and the remarkable fact that what emerged as the most "telling questions" included: "Can you be feminist and heterosexual? Can men be political allies or are all men always the enemy?" Clearly there is real sectarian battiness at work if those are *the* questions. There are a number of dissenting voices. François Picq, for example, characterizes what the MLF became as a "Parisian, intellectual, narcissistic group." Annie Leclerc also distances herself from the most egregious examples of rhetorical overkill, but she goes on to issue a remarkable utopian plaint: "We have to invent everything anew." This is a recipe for both arrogance and defeat. (pp. 185-86)

The contrast between the narrowly ideologizing and the more expansive instances of feminist and women's studies scholarship grows more and more apparent with each passing day. Even works under review here that are neither particularly expansive nor gripping, for example, Demaris Wehr's **Jung and Feminism** and Donald Meyer's **Sex and Power,** which is less than the sum of its 721 pages, offer *something* to the reader beyond categorical rigidities or rhetorical overkill. Wehr's effort is marred by overgeneralizations about androcentrism, sexism, and misogyny—they are not one and the same—and underlaboring in her attempt to convince the reader that Jung's psychology of types, with its essentializing categories, has something to offer modern feminism. I doubt it, and merely intoning the virtues of "holism" doesn't do the trick. Jung's Manicheanism, which identifies "the feminine principle" with matter and the "masculine principle" with spirit, has in the past and will in the future work great mischief; moreover, Wehr's definition of "internalized oppression" as something that "feels a certain way inside a woman, it speaks with a certain voice, and it has a certain effect on her" evaporates as soon as one focuses on it for more than a fleeting moment.

Meyer's troubles, on the other hand, are reminiscent of the story Abraham Lincoln once told a group of interlocutors who were pushing a particular author upon him, and he replied that no one had ever delved deeper into the well of knowledge or come up drier. Meyer tells four stories of the rise of women in the United States, Russia, Sweden, and Italy from the mid-nineteenth century to 1987. He makes the solid and welcome point that women are not to be construed as history's victims but as active persons confronting concrete dilemmas in particular times and places, and he notes that many formidable early historians of women, Mary Beard among them, mocked "relapses into the pathos of victimonology, when their own data showed strong effective women." He assumes a 5,000-year-old conflict between men and women that takes particular forms in diverse societies. But his work is too atheoretical, missing an animating vision, and by its conclusion one is caught muttering, as political scientist Jane Jaquette has pointed out, "A woman's work is never done."

By contrast, the texts by Thurston, Banta, Scott, and Loraux, and those edited by Haus and Higgonet and associates, offer solid food for thought, many pleasures to the reader, a plethora of challenges to received wisdom, and as they do so display feminist scholarship at its most engaged yet thoughtful best. Their subjects range from the popular romance novel to classic Greek tragedy; from the construction of bodily imagery to war as a "gendering activity"; from Foucaultian insights to culture-constituting imagery. Feminism serves, for these scholars, as inspiration, as challenge, as focus, as organizing theme. The political commitments of the writers involved, insofar as these are made explicit, range from Marxist to vaguely liberal. I note this to allay any suspicion that one particular brand of feminism is more susceptible than some other to the dogmatics of the circle dance. This is not necessarily so. Liberals as well as radicals and socialists of many stripes can and have formed the circle and narrowed the boundaries of discourse by eliminating, or seeking to eliminate, undesirable elements.

To happy specifics, then. Thurston writes in a generous, populist spirit [in *The Romance Revolution: Erotic Novels for Women and the Quest for a New Sexual Identity*]. She notes the extraordinary number of adult women reading romances (more than twenty million by her estimate), not so that she can then throw up her hands in horror and condemn their mindlessness but in order to take seriously the literary genre that engages them. And what she finds is fascinating. The new paperback romance novel came to full bloom during the same years that saw the rise of feminist politics and writing. While those who have bought into the notion that the "masses" are "overwhelmingly passive, manipulated, and dominated from above" see in the romances a reaction to feminism, Thurston finds feminist themes running through many of the texts. The heroine is an individual in her own right. She "possesses a passionate drive for self-determination and autonomy." The romance narrative is one of "reciprocal sexual satisfaction." Male heroes shed tears. In three-fourths of the texts in which a rape occurs, the point that it was not the woman's fault is made explicitly by the male hero. And so on.

Rather than being the "opiate of the female masses," these tales that reach millions are reflective of an upsurge in female assertiveness, especially of the erotic sort. The romances, Thurston claims, "constitute the first large and autonomous body of sexual writing by women addressed to feminine experiences," and she worries that feminist antipornographers would drum this literature out of business if they succeed in their efforts. This may, in fact, be an explicit intent of one segment of the antipornography ranks, since the sexuality elaborated in the romances is normatively heterosexual—or so Thurston hints. She writes, "To suggest that heterosexual bonding is in itself inherently conservative and inimical to women, as some feminists have done, is to both deny human needs and turn a blind eye to where grassroots social change has and is taking place."

Similarly, and from a very different vantage point, the German Marxist-feminist project outlined in *Female Sexualization* speaks to the politics of everyday human life as reconstructed from personal memories of the socialization and "sexualization" of the female body: "Frauenformen," the writers call it. Borrowing heavily if critically from the work of Foucault, Haus and the other members of her "collective" aim to "denaturalize the body," to extricate the social and historical body from various "naturalistic and ahistorical conceptions." They are tuned in to a politics of identity that is bodily-based. Countering Epstein's "raw physiology" reductionism, the participants in this project understand that the body is a site in and through which complex formations of identity occur and that human beings do not conform to social norms concerning the body in ways that are uncomplicated. Although I grew a bit weary of the lengthy, detailed reconstructions of memories concerning body hair, legs, postures, tummies, and all the rest, I was impressed by the thoughtfulness brought to bear and the theoretical acumen that facilitated this reflective effort.

The most interesting feature of the book is its coming to grips with the thinking of Karol Wojtyla (Pope John Paul II), specifically his lectures on the "theology of the body" written before he became Pope. These socialist feminists describe Wojtyla's procedure as "remarkably modern . . . quite sophisticated." As they sum it up, Wojtyla privileges the dignity of the human person who is never to be treated as a means to another's end, whether in work or love. He rejects utilitarianism and egoism. He refutes the notion that human beings are slaves to the sexual drive and repudiates the view that this drive is evil. "Wojtyla does not consider desire to be morally wrong in itself; what would be wrong would be the subordination of the will to desire." Because, on Wojtyla's view, humans are social and sexual beings, the sex drive must be integrated into morality—into personhood, self-determination, free will, an inner life, and responsibility to others. This is a sexual ethic based, in Wojtyla's words, on pleasure "without treating the person as an object of pleasure," whose ultimate goal is "integrated love, which incorporates all human impulses" and involves "full and deep appreciation of the beauty of the [other] person." (pp. 187-89)

Some feminists see women as universal victims; others as a transhistorical sex-class; others as oppressed "nature." A minority urge women to separate entirely from male-dominated society. Some want full integration into that society, hence its transformation towards liberal equality. . . . It's hard to wend one's way through the thicket of contemporary feminist discourse without some sort of map.

Anyone interested in culture, politics, history, and literature will profit from reading the remaining four books under review. First, the collection edited by Higgonet, Jenson, Michel, and Weitz, *Behind the Lines: Gender and the Two World Wars,* is a vital entry in the new feminist scholarship on war and war-making, on the construction of motherhood as a feature of national security, for example, and whether and, if so, how nations traffic in gendered representations in their war/peace politics. The multiple authors of this text refuse to traffic in banalities and overwrought analogies. They teach us much that we might not even want to know. For example, Sandra Gilbert's pathbreaking essay, "Soldier's Heart: Literary Men, Literary Women, and the Great War," supplies us with startling examples of the upbeat prowar literature of many women writers and feminist activists in the World War One period. My favorite is Rose Macaulay who, in her poem, "Many Sisters to Many Brothers," expressed envy of the soldier's liberation from the dreariness of the home front in these words: "Oh it's you that have the luck, out there in blood and muck." Concludes Gilbert: "In the words of women propagandists as well as in the deeds of feather-carrying girls, the classical Roman's noble *patria* seemed to have become a sinister, death-dealing *matria.*"

Second, Joan Scott's essays in *Gender and the Politics of History* compel us to recognize that any "unitary concept," including, of course, male, female, power, oppression, equality, "rests on—contains—repressed or negated material and so is unstable, not unified." She offers, among her many insights, a sophisticated discussion of the "difference" question. Scott rejects the idea, following Martha Minow, that equality versus difference constitutes an opposition. "Instead of framing analyses and strategies as if such binary pairs were timeless and true, we need to ask how the dichotomous pairing of equality and difference itself works. Instead of remaining within the terms of existing political discourse, we need to subject those terms to critical examination." Within their very different frameworks and projects, and without heavy theoretical thematizing of the issues at stake, Loraux's *Tragic Ways of Killing a Woman* and Banta's *Imaging American Women* carry out Scott's call to subject existing terms to critical examination.

Third, Loraux's ninety pages are a marvel of condensa-tion. Homing in on one question—how women in the tragedies are done to death—she shows us that Greek tragedy "as a civic institution, delighted in blurring the formal frontier between masculine and feminine and freed women's deaths from the banalities to which they were restricted by private mourning." The suicide of wives and the sacrifices of virgins are, of course, most important. Suicide is the "woman's solution." A man "worthy of the name could die only by the sword or the spear of another, on the field of battle." Importantly, "the woman in tragedy is more entitled to play the man in her death than the man is to assume any aspect of woman's conduct, even in his manner of death." Chillingly and powerfully, there is, for women, "liberty in tragedy—liberty in death." By resisting any temptation to dogmatize, to take the Greeks to task one more time for, in Epstein's words, suppressing "women's rights," a remarkable achievement indeed as there were no "rights" of any sort to suppress, the concept of rights being entirely foreign to the Greeks, Loraux opens a window into the world of Greek tragedy that was, at least for me, and I assume for many others, previously closed.

Finally, Banta's enormous work is wonderfully evocative. She begins with some rather loose definitions of imaging as "the making of visual and verbal representations . . . and responses to these artifacts at every level of society." There is, she notes in line with Scott's theoretical discussion, "no unity, no access to interpretive certainties, no absolutes, no guaranteed rapport between seeing and knowing in a society struggling with conventions that were in the process of creating still newer conventions." If Banta had been in the room as I read these words, I would have kissed her. Without in any way backing off political implications; without in any way diluting awareness of and concern with gender; without in any way muting the feminist energy at work in her text, Banta offers up ideals and images that have simultaneously differentiated and "nationalized," constructed unities and marked separateness.

She discovered that between 1876 and 1918 the images being offered about the American female to the public at large were "not only varied to the point of potential self-contradiction, they were all pervasive." She finds the Beautiful Charmers, the New England Woman, the Outdoors Girl, even the Feminine Charms of the Woman Militant. Changes in "feminine ideals" were responses to "wider social forces, idealizations and discontents," and themselves helped to deepen or to soften these contradictory forces. . . . Banta expands upon the contributions of several authors of *Behind the Lines,* when she elaborates the many feminized ways in which America herself is and has been represented—as Columbia, as Iron Amazon, as Sacred Mother, as the Girl He Left Behind. This is a splendid effort.

Towards the end of her remarkable career, Hannah Arendt and her colleague, the political scientist Hans Morgenthau, had the following exchange, reported in Elisabeth Young-Bruehl's biography of Arendt. Morgenthau queried: "What are you? Are you a conservative? Are you a liberal? Where is your position within contemporary possibilities?" And Arendt responded: "I don't know. I really don't know and I've never known. And I suppose I never had any such position . . . And I must say I couldn't care less. I don't think the real questions of this century will get any kind of illumination by this sort of thing." Arendt was right. Those feminist texts that proclaim, in effect, "shut up and fight" or "shut *them* up in order to better fight" offer illumination into nothing except the workings of dogmatic minds and ideological projects. Contrastingly, those feminist writers and scholars who refuse to join the circle, who retain their independence of mind and thought, in the long run better serve any feminism worth its salt. By that I mean a feminist position open to debate, committed to democracy, prepared to pursue politics as the art of the possible. (pp. 190-92)

Jean Bethke Elshtain, "Feminism and Politics," in Partisan Review, *Vol. LVII, No. 2, Spring, 1990, pp. 181-92.*

Susan Z. Andrade

[*In the excerpt below, Andrade offers a comparative reading of Flora Nwapa's* Efuru *and Buchi Emecheta's* The Joys of Motherhood *in an attempt to constitute an African feminist literary criticism.*]

> What we properly understand by Africa, is the Unhistorical, Undeveloped Spirit, still involved in the conditions of mere nature, and which had to be presented here only as on the threshold of the World's History. —G. W. Hegel

> Traditions are not born. They are made. We would add that they are not, like objects of nature, here to stay, but survive as *created social events* only to the extent that an audience cares to intersect them. —Hortense Spillers

Hegel's racist representation of Africa as outside history reflects only the archival gaps that imperialism produces. Although Africa's silence in hegemonic European historical discourse should be acknowledged, its absence from world history must of course be rejected. While Africa is explicitly named by Hegel as an epistemic void, the (literary) history of African women has gone unnamed, its absence unnoticed. Hortense Spillers' work functions as a response to Hegel by noting historical constraints upon and present opportunities for the creation of new traditions. African feminist criticism now confronts the questions implicit in Spillers's view of history as narrative: whose tradition is being made, and how should it be represented? African feminist criticism will rely on its historical links to white feminist and male cultural critics, but ultimately, because it speaks from the margins of both fields, it must not only "care to intersect" but build beyond them.

Much contemporary white feminist criticism typically represents itself as the outermost possible frame for understanding the place of women as they function within cultural systems. By representing itself as color-blind and universal, however, such feminist theory neglects to examine its own inscription within a European system of thought which is saturated by imperialism. "Third World" feminist critics from various disciplinary contexts have launched this critique. While "Western" feminist discourse is not monolithic, there is, in Chandra Mohanty's words, "a coherence of effects" resulting from the assumption of Europe/Euro-America as "a primary referent in theory and praxis." This, for example, is the gist of Gayatri Spivak's searing critique of a classic of feminist poetics, Sandra Gilbert and Susan Gubar's *The Madwoman in the Attic,* a text that takes for its radical trope the figure of a white Caribbean woman whose insanity results from geographic/racial contamination.

Julia Kristeva's *About Chinese Women,* a travel narrative written after a three-week stay in the People's Republic of China, offers another example of how the "Third World" is reduced to a metonymic function. The *sémiotique,* her category of opposition to the phallogocentric *symbolique,* is strategically fragmented, locatable only in the interstices of European hysterical and avant-garde discourse, but appears to permeate all aspects of Chinese culture, which she describes as monolithic. Represented as the site that managed to evade the Law of the Father, China thus serves as the transparent passageway through which white women can locate the feminine pre-Oedipal.

Similarly, while Hélène Cixous's deconstructive manoeuvres in *Newly Born Woman* strive to subvert all ontologically grounded identity, they are undermined by her use of such imperialist tropes of woman as the "dark continent" and the metaphoric unknowability inscribed there. Uzo Esonwanne, calling into question Cixous's celebration of "writing as an emancipatory act," argues [in "Feminist Theory and the Discourse of Colonialism"] that any such strategy which does not take into account "the material dimension of imperialism or the manifest heterogeneity of women is doomed to reproducing imperialist and patriarchal violence."

To be sure, gross generalizations about feminism (constructed as white) and the "Third World" (constructed as male) are not restricted to theorists who focus on Europe or Euro-America. [In "Feminist Criticism and the African Novel"] Africanist Katherine Frank is unable to reconcile feminism with a monolithic Africa:

> Feminism, by definition, is a profoundly individualistic philosophy: it values personal growth and individual fulfillment over any larger communal needs or goods. African society, of course, even in its most westernized modern forms, places the values of the group over those of the individual with the result that the notion of an African feminism almost seems a contradiction in terms.

Carole Boyce Davies has criticized Frank's facile reading of an Africa unable to generate independent African feminism. Moreover, Frank's argument, both here and in a later essay, characterizes communalism in all African societies as patriarchal and all feminism as European and individualistic. In so doing, she upholds the logic of the argument implied above: that of an irreconcilable difference between feminist criticism (which must be Eurocentric) and cultural criticism (which must be masculinist). Frank is simply more blunt than Gilbert and Gubar, Kristeva, or Cixous in her assumption that feminism is necessarily a metaphor for individualism.

While these feminist critics gloss over race, many critics of colonial texts ignore the category of gender. Using a logic parallel to Eurocentric feminists, these theorists read texts exclusively through the privileged category of race. In the tradition of Frantz Fanon, Abdul JanMohamed posits the revolving figure of the manichean allegory as, "a field of diverse yet interchangeable oppositions between white and black, good and evil, superiority and inferiority, civilization and savagery." The versatility of this trope always assures a favorable representation for the hegemonic power. To this end, this allegorical model is useful in deciphering race relations. However, the model seems capable of addressing only one category of analysis at a time, which requires that marginalized categories be assimilated into, rather than accommodated by, the model, which remains fixed. Categories such as gender or sexual identity must be reconstructed to fit the requirements of the model or be ignored, since the model cannot adjust to them. There is no room for the necessary heterogeneity of the many facets of subject constitution. And because, in the colonial or neo-colonial context, race is generally the most salient category, gender is subsumed under its rubric. For example, JanMohamed's readings of the works of Isak Dinesen and Nadine Gordimer focus exclusively on European subjectivity and inevitably elide the complex set of relations their white *female* characters bring into play. This kind of analysis also encourages the conflation of categories; the violence of colonialism is translated into the emasculation (read: feminization) of male natives, a gesture that codes femininity pejoratively. Such analyses inevitably elide the gendered and racial violence to which female natives are subjected.

This subsuming of gender into race underlies Malek Alloula's *The Colonial Harem,* a text that seeks to demystify the visual construction of the Algerian woman by juxtaposing the author's (re)reading against frequently pornographic photographs taken at about the turn of this century. Alloula interprets the disrobing of the women as unveiling, and the subsequent "penetration" of the harem as an imperialist gesture. The lack of any analysis of gender, however, allows Alloula to fetishize the veil as a screen behind which Algerian women could hide from the camera. For him, the veiled woman has almost as much power as the camera itself: "concentrated by the tiny orifice for the eye, this womanly gaze is a little like the eye of the camera, like the photographic lens that takes aim at everything." Reading the veil as metaphor for the frustration that the native woman can cause the imperialist camera is a useful form of cultural analysis. Its unquestioning valorization, however, must ignore the problematic reasons for obscuring women's bodies from men's view.

Too often, masculinist cultural critics and Eurocentric feminist critics each read their valorized category allegorically, and then use it to displace and replace gender or race respectively. That is to say, for Eurocentric feminists, race is merely a trope for gender, another way to understand the larger oppression of women. For masculinist cultural critics, the privileged category of race subsumes all others; gender serves as a lens through which the greater oppression of Non-Europeans can be understood. Neither of the above theoretical positions offers a space from which an

African feminist criticism can be articulated, for neither is able to address the heterogeneity that analysis of African women's texts must foreground: to respect the cultural heterogeneity of Africa as well as that of African women. Taking seriously Mohanty's admonitions against sweeping generalizations about "Third World" women and Chinua Achebe's suggestion that critics should read national or ethnic literatures within Africa, I focus my analysis on women's texts and the history of Igbo culture in southeastern Nigeria.

My provisional approach to African women's literary history concentrates on an intertextual reading of women's narratives but also involves "real" history—what Carole Boyce Davies has called the text and context necessary to reading African women's literature. This reading of an Igbo women's literary tradition, one of the first novelistic African female literary traditions, focuses on the dialogic relation between Flora Nwapa's *Efuru* (1966) and Buchi Emecheta's *The Joys of Motherhood* (1979). (pp. 91-4)

> Reading against the canon, intruding into it a configuration of symbolic values with which critics and audiences must contend, the work of black women's writing not only redefines tradition, but also disarms it by suggesting that the term itself is a critical fable intended to encode and circumscribe an inner circle of empowered texts. —Hortense Spillers

Spillers's contention that black women's writing "not only redefines tradition but also disarms it," helps simultaneously to address the absence/presence of literary precursors in African women's literary history and to confront the ways in which women have been written out of history. Similarly, while disagreeing with Paul de Man's notion of a purely textual history, [Anne] Herrmann asserts [in *The Dialogic and Difference: "An/Other Woman" in Virginia Woolf and Christa Wolf*] that the interplay within a female literary history is "between history in which it has been virtually impossible for women to write and be read and the texts produced as a form of resistance against particular historical conditions. The construction of the latter requires both the retrieval of an inaccessible past and its inscription in a narrative which has never been told before; that is, a novel fiction." Therefore, if the act of writing is one of the most powerful ways by means of which women inscribe themselves into history, then the acts of African women writers inscribing themselves and (re)inscribing their precursors into a literary history functions as a powerful response to Hegel's dictum on the exclusion of Africans from history. Reading Nwapa's *Efuru* and Emecheta's revision of that narrative in *The Joys of Motherhood* reveals one such example of a female literary history, illustrating the bridges between texts as well as the discursive chasms within history. The historical inter-text to *Efuru* and *The Joys of Motherhood* is the 1929 Igbo Women's War, in Igbo, *Ogu Umunwanyi,* which is archivally recorded by the British as the "Aba Riots." The Women's War was the violent culmination of traditional manifestations of Igbo women's power, called "making war on" or "sitting on" a man. Such power usually took the form of raucous and destructive behavior by women and was directed at men who were perceived to threaten their personal or economic security. (pp. 95-6)

Of the archival (mis)representation of the Women's War as the "Aba Riots," a name which limits the scope and de-politicizes its feminist impetus, [historian Judith] Van Allen notes that the control of language means the control of history. Her reading illustrates how certain discursive formations constrain and silence others and offers an example of how the British replicated Hegel's gesture of writing Africans out of history. Dialogism offers a strategy which combats the monologic power of this type of hegemonic discourse. In the glossary to the English translation of *The Dialogic Imagination,* editor/translator Michael Holquist defines authorial or hegemonic discourse as: "privileged language that approaches us from without; it is distanced, taboo, and permits no play with its framing context. . . . It has great power over us, but only while in power; if ever dethroned, it immediately becomes a dead thing, a relic." (Re)reading the Women's War, therefore, is one manner of dethroning the authority of the "Aba Riots." Another involves reading the literary production of African women as their self-inscription into history. *Efuru,* the first published novel by an African woman and the text that inaugurates an African women's literary history, thus interrogates the imperialist authority that Hegel symbolizes.

Much contemporary white feminist criticism typically represents itself as the outermost possible frame for understanding the place of women as they function within cultural systems. By representing itself as color-blind and universal, however, such feminist theory neglects to examine its own inscription within a European system of thought which is saturated by imperialism.

Despite its paradigmatic status, relatively little critical attention has been paid to *Efuru.* Critics have dismissed Nwapa's writing as trivial, useful only for an understanding of domestic Igbo village life. Curiously, many defenders of Nwapa argue that it is precisely *because* she offers such a narrative of domesticity that she deserves her place in the African canon. My interest here is neither in the authenticity nor the importance of Nwapa's representation of village life, but rather, on the tensions that the first woman-authored novel must confront when written in a colonial/neo-colonial situation. On the one hand, she manipulates the language and narrative form of the colonizer; on the other, she representes a dignified African female character against the backdrop of frequently perjorative representations of female characters by male authors. This (dialogic) tension is symptomatic of the choice between "tradition" and "modernity" that a first novel in a colonial context must make. *Efuru*'s insistence on the virtue of its protagonist and on the importance of Igbo custom

indicates Nwapa's privileging of the discourse of tradition over that of modernity. Though published only thirteen years later, *The Joys of Motherhood* emerges into an already existing female literary tradition. Emecheta does not need to assert the importance of a woman's literary community, since one already exists. While acknowledging her debt to *Efuru* through the similarity of the protagonist's stories, Emecheta nevertheless goes on to revise it through her critique of indigenous patriarchy and colonialism.

This reading begins with the fact that one of the last lines in *Efuru* serves as the title of *The Joys of Motherhood.* For much of their stories, the female protagonists share a similar personal and family history. Both Efuru and Nnu Ego are from Igbo villages. They are both attractive only daughters of important men who are wealthy warrior/athletes. Each is the favorite child of her father, the daughter of a favorite woman. The mothers of both protagonists are dead at the time of the narratives, leaving the daughters with no female model on which to pattern their search for independence. For this reason they are entirely dependent on the fathers. Indeed, Efuru and Nnu Ego are invested in attaining the respect that adherence to traditional mores offers; perhaps because of their priviledged backgrounds, neither is a true rebel. Both women are married twice. In each case, the first marriage is terminated because the husband rejects the young wife. And for a time in both marriages, both are stigmatized by their inability to bear children. Lastly, both are skilled market women who attain economic independence through successful trading. The novels' similarities end there. (pp. 96-8)

Nwapa's insight lies in her representation of an (economically) independent female character who determines her own life without denying her Igbo identity. Efuru's status as a "genuine" African female subject inserted into the male dominated discursive system of literature is established by the text's implicit rejection of the corruption that the city signifies and by its nostalgic resurrection of Igbo history. Nwapa locates her ideal representation of Igbo female power and independence at the turn of the century. This narrative strategy is especially telling when historically contextualized; at the time Nwapa was writing, Europe and the United States were witnessing the birth of the second wave of European feminism. That Efuru's life appears to have no contact with Europe, certainly none with European-style feminism, means that the narrative's prototype of female power is Igbo—a powerful statement in the face of a post-second-world-war feminism that implied the global liberation of women would begin in the "West." Efuru's life, that of a noble and dignified village woman, is the prototype of an idealized "traditional" woman under duress. She adheres to the role of the dutiful daughter and wife: she works hard, cooks well, respects her elders, behaves without condescension to the other inhabitants of Ogwuta, helps those in need—and eventually becomes a devout follower of the female/feminist deity, Uhamiri. Efuru's adherence to indigenous practices such as polygamy and cliterodectomy can be interpreted, among other ways, as a valorization of traditional Igbo custom.

Female solidarity and strong women's friendships arise from the practices of Igbo life, and Nwapa makes her strongest feminist statement through the affirmation of a traditional women's community. Although she is generally considered an exceptional woman, no one appears to envy Efuru. Only one woman, the village gossip Omirima, speaks ill of her when she comments spitefully on Efuru's childlessness. Toward the end of the narrative, she is the one who initiates the rumor that Efuru is an adulterer. In both instances, however, Efuru's reputation is rescued by the efforts of the other women of the village.

One of *Efuru*'s examples of indigenous feminism is to be found in an embedded folktale. The tale's only male character is the villain. Of the four sisters, whose names correspond to the days of the Igbo week, Nkwo, the youngest, is extremely beautiful and "the kindest of them all." When Nkwo is desired as a wife by a maggot-eating blue spirit so strong that their mother cannot protect her, she turns to her sisters for help. Eke and Afo refuse her, but Orie takes in both her sister and her sister's new husband, helping Nkwo negotiate around a dinner of maggots. At night, the two sisters trick the sleeping spirit, run out of the house and burn it (and him) down. The narrative later reveals that Orie day is Uhamiri's special day, when, in addition to other taboos, women worshippers cannot sleep with their husbands. Recounted directly before Efuru's wedding to Gilbert, the tale serves to foreshadow the end of their marriage. Efuru, like Nkwo, is represented as both beautiful and kind. Through Orie, the tale points to the rescuing function that the deity, Uhamiri, will have in Efuru's life. (pp. 98-9)

Nwapa's tribute to women's independence notwithstanding, the narrative manifests a blindspot about the ideology of motherhood. Although the novel moves toward a celebration of Efuru's independence, economic success and goodness, there is a constant undercurrent of doubt about the ability of a woman without children to be happy. In the Bakhtinian sense, *Efuru*'s dialogism is comprised of the competing discourses of economic independence and maternal satisfaction. Repeatedly, the text offers advice on what a woman should do in order to conceive, how she should conduct herself during pregnancy, childbirth, and the upbringing of the child. In fact, Oladele Taiwo calls the narrative, "almost a manual of mothercare." But motherhood is the one condition that the otherwise perfect Efuru cannot satisfy. The closing lines of the text have been read by several critics as key to an understanding of the text. Although Uhamiri appears to have everything she needs, the narrative suggests that motherhood is necessary to completely fulfill her—and, by extension, her disciple, Efuru.

> Efuru slept soundly that night. She dreamt of the woman of the lake, her beauty, her long hair and her riches. She had lived for ages at the bottom of the lake. She was as old as the lake itself. She was happy, she was wealthy. She was beautiful. She gave women beauty and wealth but she had no child. She had never experienced the joy of motherhood. Why then did the women worship her?

The Joys of Motherhood literally (and literarily) begins where *Efuru* ends, for it is from this paragraph that Emecheta derives her title. With regard to the slight semantic modification from Nwapa's text to the title of Emecheta's, Henry Louis Gates might say that the later writer was engaged in an act of signifyin(g), of renaming and revisioning the earlier text. Of greater significance is *The Joys of Motherhood*'s recognition of its precursor's ambivalence about happiness without children. The later narrative revises its forebear by giving *its* protagonist, Nnu Ego, Efuru's primary unfulfilled wish—many times over. By (re)writing Nnu Ego's "barrenness/fecundity" to coincide with her change of husbands, *The Joys of Motherhood* dialogizes *Efuru*'s "tragic flaw" and shifts responsibility for conception onto the man. More importantly, Emecheta's act of writing this narrative draws attention to the ironic status of *Efuru* as the "mother" text of (anglophone) African women's literature, thereby signifying on Nwapa again. By so doing, *The Joys of Motherhood* appropriates the male purview of the production of texts by conflating it with the female production of children.

Through the character of Nnu Ego, *The Joys of Motherhood* also interrogates Nwapa's idealistic portrayal of a female struggle and of Efuru as the perfect woman. As Rachel Blau Du Plessis says in another context [in *Writing Beyond the Ending: Narrative Strategies of Twentieth-Century Women Writers*], the glorification of a female character as exceptional serves to reinforce the norm of prescribed behavior for other women; it "sets in motion not only conventional notions of womanhood but also conventional romantic notions of the genius, the person apart, who, because unique and gifted, could be released from social ties and expectations." In contrast to the noble, talented, and indomitable Efuru, who overcomes her life's problems and eventually determines her own destiny, Nnu Ego is weaker, more petty in her dealings with others; her life is overwhelmed by both colonialism and indigenous patriarchy, and she dies an ignoble death, alone.

Emecheta's response to Nwapa's treatment of Igbo history is to represent two less idealized images of Igbo women through the pre-colonial Ona and her colonial daughter, Nnu Ego. Reading *Efuru* dialogically through *The Joys of Motherhood* highlights the absence of specific dates or historical events in the precursor text. In contrast, *The Joys of Motherhood* opens by giving dates and ages, encouraging the reader to locate the text in a specific time and place: "The year was 1934 and the place was Lagos, then a British colony." This historical specificity indicates that Efuru's contemporary is not Nnu Ego, but her mother, Ona. Thus, the later text comments both chronologically and tropologically on its predecessor's protagonist, for while the events of Efuru's life parallel Nnu Ego's, it is with Ona that Efuru shares a certain pre-colonial, culturally sanctioned independence in village life. *The Joys of Motherhood* affirms *Efuru*'s claim that pre-colonial Igbo women had more independence than their colonized descendants. Of the difference between the two generations, its narrator says: "To regard a woman who is quiet and timid as desirable was something that came after his [Agbadi's] time, with Christianity and other changes." Acknowledging that under colonialism Igbo women enjoyed far less freedom, however, does not blind Emecheta to women's subjection under indigenous patriarchy. Ona's willful struggles with her lover, Agbadi, occasionally result in her public humiliation. And while her status as "male daughter" permits her to contribute sons to her father's diminishing line, it also means that she is unable to marry.

Reading *The Joys of Motherhood* from the vantage of *Efuru,* however, offers a different dialogic perspective. While the later narrative depicts the misery of colonialism, it represents the phenomenon itself as an act committed *on* Africans. No suggestion of their complicity with or resistance against the process is offered. And while it does not depict the pre-colonial period as paradisaical, *The Joys of Motherhood* barely examines relations of power within the Igbo hierarchy. In contrast, *Efuru* offers a perceptive, albeit marginalized, account of the historical events that preceded colonialism and aided greatly in its acceleration. In this way, it offers a critique of the protagonist and her entire family, their personal stature and longstanding wealth: "her family was not among the newly rich, the wealth had been in it for years." Toward the end, however, the narrative undermines that family stature by revealing at his death the manner in which Efuru's father obtained his riches:

> It was the death of a great man. No poor man could afford to fire seven rounds of a cannon in a day. . . . The cannons were owned by very distinguished families who themselves took part actively in slave dealing. . . . Now the shooting of the cannon did not only announce the death of a great man, but also announced that the great man's ancestors had dealings with the white men, who dealt in slaves.

Not only is Efuru's personal prestige put into question, but the narrative implicitly suggests that the construction of Igbo history is determined by the interests of the hegemonic power. Because of Nwashike Ogene's stature and because of the chronological remove of their fathers' histories, Nwosu and the fishermen do not connect the death of this great man to the cannon that celebrates his greatness. His family's role in the slave trade will probably slip through the cracks of historical discourse; only his wealth and stature will be remembered. Thus *Efuru* specifically rejects the nostalgic approach to Ogwuta's past, pointing instead to traces of colonial violence evident in the structures of the current village hierarchy. (pp. 100-02)

Although the pre-colonial period is not represented as paradisaical, *Efuru* is idealistic in its representation of a supportive women's community. Emecheta interrogates this idealism through the textual representation of the great desire for—and constant frustration of—a female community. She also addresses Nwapa's idyllic depiction of turn of the century Igbo life as well as the mid-century oppressive conditions of colonialism. For Nnu Ego, this lack of community partly results from the absence of other, older, women. The cross-generational protection from male power which Ajanapu offers Efuru is reinscribed as Ona's unsuccessful attempt to secure greater freedom in Nnu Ego's life. Her deathbed wish of Agbadi is "to allow [their daughter] to have a life of her own, a husband if she wants one"; nevertheless, he arranges two marriages for their

compliant daughter. Later, Nnu Ego's friendship with Cordelia is cut short when the latter's husband finds work far away. Since Cordelia had helped her survive the loss of her first baby and had explained gender and race relations of power in Lagos, the loss of this friendship is especially missed. Nnu Ego's friendship with the Yoruba woman, Iyawo, who saves Nnu Ego and her son from starvation, is always tenuous because of the economic inequality of their situations.

The Joys of Motherhood most thoroughly explores the possibility of an Igbo women's community and illustrates its failure through the figure of Adaku. The tension between Nnu Ego and Adaku is due partly to their competition for limited resources in the urban colonial context. The cramped single room in which the Owulum family lives in poverty contrasts with the clearly delineated women's living space, greater autonomy over their economic resources, and more control over their sexual activity described in the rural context of *Efuru.* Through the women's failed cooking strike, *The Joys of Motherhood* problematizes *Efuru*'s assumption that tradition is the only appropriate avenue to power. In an attempt to force Nnaife to give over all of his money to his hungry family, Adaku instigates a cooking strike and Nnu Ego joins her. Within a village economy, men would have no recourse other than to capitulate or do their own cooking; here Nnaife's male co-workers share their lunches with him. The strike is soon abandoned.

Traditional forms of women's resistance are ineffective in this new context, and *The Joys of Motherhood* suggests that different forms of power have to be adopted. Adaku's departure from the Owulum family and her brief period of prostitution may be read as such a strategy. She is able to accumulate enough capital to begin a more prosperous cloth vending business, and move out of the room, happier in her new living arrangement. Her greater economic security signifies a certain success in the context of Igbo valorization of women as good traders and contrasts sharply with Nnu Ego's poverty. Through Adaku, *The Joys of Motherhood* responds to and subverts the authority of Jagua, the "naughty" Igbo prostitute. . . . Emecheta's text does not linger over the details of Adaku's prostitution, offering only her decision and the consequent horror of the Ibuza community in Lagos. By emptying prostitution of glamour, the feminist narrative thus refigures the topos of the prostitute. Most importantly, unlike Jagua (*Efuru* or Nnu Ego), Adaku is not interested in (re)marriage, choosing to live outside the boundaries of patriarchal protection: " 'I want to be a dignified single woman. I shall work to educate my daughters, though I shall not do so without male companionship.' She laughed again. 'They do have their uses'."

The Joys of Motherhood dialogizes *Efuru*'s easy success and blind adherence to Igbo tradition by separating the discourse of tradition from that of power and locating them in rival characters, privileging the latter over the former. The discourse of tradition is represented by Nnu Ego (who bears the children Efuru desires), that of rebellion by Adaku (who controls her destiny and achieves Efuru's economic independence). In this light, the final passages of *The Joys of Motherhood* constitute a response to the infamous last paragraph of *Efuru.* Du Plessis says that "one of the moments of ideological negotiation in any work occurs in the choice of a resolution." Nwapa negotiates the closure by so elevating the discourse of motherhood that the success of Uhamiri, and by extension, that of Efuru is undermined. In response, Emecheta blatantly criticizes her precursor's privileging of motherhood through *her* last lines. The poignant depiction of Nnu Ego's death represents the final undermining of *Efuru*'s maternal discourse:

> After such wandering on one night, Nnu Ego lay down by the roadside, thinking that she had arrived home. She died quietly there, with no child to hold her hand and no friend to talk to her. She had never made many friends, so busy had she been building up her joys as a mother. . . .

> Stories afterwards, however, said that Nnu Ego was a wicked woman even in death because, however many people appealed to her to make women fertile, she never did. . . .

> Nnu Ego had it all, yet still did not answer prayers for children.

By foregrounding Nnu Ego's self-abnegation in favor of children, *The Joys of Motherhood* responds to its precursor's last line ("Why then did the women worship her?"); it thereby signals a dialogic return to the discourse of economic independence that the childless Uhamiri represents in *Efuru.* (pp. 102-04)

The topos of rebellion links these texts. Nwapa's creation of a feminist protagonist is an act of rebellion against an Igbo literary tradition dominated by male writers and by the figure of Jagua Nana. Yet her assertion of an authentic and independent Igbo feminist marginalizes the day-to-day struggles that such a character must confront. More importantly, Efuru's desire to be traditional (here inscribed as motherhood) threatens to subvert the text's manifest assertion of female independence. Emecheta interrogates Nwapa's elision of indigenous patriarchy and the colonial oppression of Igbo women, an oppression that the precursor's insistence on the valorization of tradition demands. Despite the heteroglossic critique of *Efuru* by *The Joys of Motherhood,* the relation of the second text to the first is not a violent rewriting. Rather, their intertextual relation is one that ultimately emphasizes the affinities that marginalized women writing in a shared tradition must acknowledge. As Michael Awkward has written in his study of African-American women writers, the later work (re)presents its precursor as "a literary forebear whose texts are celebrated even as they are revised, praised for their insights even when these insights are deemed inadequate to describe more contemporary manifestations of Afro-American women's peculiar challenges in a racist and sexist society." In its rebellion against the "mother text," *The Joys of Motherhood* inscribes the conservatism of its precursor into the text through Nnu Ego and its rebelliousness out of it through Adaku. The silencing of Adaku's radicalism need not be equated with absence, however. Instead it can be read as an evasion of textual compromise. The near silent presence of Adaku, like that

of the historical phenomenon of the Women's War, resists narrative closure, and thereby marks a rebellious potential.

The "real" Igbo Women's War—so important to a consideration of African women's rebellion—is sometimes absent from these texts, sometimes merely silent. The radical potential of Igbo women can thus be read into, and out of, these narratives. What should be clear by now is that this dialogue between authors on the rightful place of tradition and rebellion in every way constitutes a sophisticated, intertextually rich literary history. Like Adaku (and the Igbo Women's War), the tradition itself is not absent but silenced. It requires not *construction,* only recognition. (p. 105)

> *Susan Z. Andrade, "Rewriting History, Motherhood, and Rebellion: Naming An African Women's Literary Tradition," in* Research in African Literatures, *Vol. 21, No. 1, Spring, 1990, pp. 91-110.*

Robert Lerner and Stanley Rothman

[*In the following excerpt, the authors posit a conspiracy of feminists in the political and publishing worlds that has forced schools into using textbooks that advocate equality between the sexes.*]

In the spring of 1974, the local Board of Education in Kanawha County, West Virginia, began the process of selecting new readers for the following school year, as required by state law. One member of the Board of Education, the wife of a fundamentalist minister, examined the new books under consideration and concluded that many were morally flawed and anti-Christian. After she showed them to others of similar persuasion and word got around, 1,000 people attended the board meeting at which the decision was to be made whether or not to adopt the books. Many of the citizens at the meeting wanted to reject the new books, and these protesters took the board's decision to adopt as a direct insult. In September a massive school boycott began. Events soon got out of hand, and protesters fire-bombed classrooms. Finally, the local Board of Education, while retaining the controversial books, agreed to allow parents to decide whether their children had to read them, and things quieted down.

This account of the Kanawha County dispute fits comfortably into a tradition of thinking about assaults on the curriculum. We can date this tradition from at least as early as H. L. Mencken's famous dispatches on the Scopes "monkey" trial in 1925. In this view, challenges to public education invariably originate with conservatives, who are motivated by Christian dogma or jingoism. Those who oppose them, like Scopes's lawyer Clarence Darrow, base their arguments on the liberal ideals of free speech and free inquiry.

Yet during the last thirty years, a different kind of effort has been mounted to censor and reshape elementary- and secondary-school textbooks. This effort, led by liberal feminists, has centered on the charge that most textbooks are "sexist," and so successful has it been that in a study of readers designed for elementary- and junior-high-school use, Paul Vitz could unearth no positive portrayals of motherhood or marriage for women. Moreover, in romantic fairy tales, women often save men, but not one man even attempts to save a woman, while stories about physical competition between girls and boys mostly show the girls winning. Vitz characterizes other competitive stories as variations on the theme, "Wonder Woman and the Wimp."

Although professionals in the field of education have fought ferociously against efforts by conservatives or traditionalists to censor textbooks and other curricular materials, their response to similar campaigns by feminists has generally been one of eager acquiescence.

Such changes are not limited to early-grade readers alone. Although the results of our own study of forty years of high-school history textbooks are not all in, our findings are comparable to those of Vitz. For example, in the 1966 edition of a widely used textbook, *Rise of the American Nation,* there are 12 index entries under the heading "women" as compared with 38 in the 1982 revision of the same book. The latter include entries like "women at Jamestown," "Indian women," "women in colonial times," "women in the revolution," "problems of women workers," "expanding roles for women," etc., all of which are absent from the earlier volume, and some of which say little more than that women were present or could not vote.

The process by which feminists have achieved a success conservatives could only dream about in reshaping elementary- and secondary-school textbooks to conform to their political agenda can be separated into four different but interrelated parts. First came pressure from the women's movement. Second, the federal government responded to this by funding the development of an alternative feminist curriculum through a relatively obscure piece of legislation, the Women's Educational Equity Act of 1974 (WEEA), which remains law today. Third, members of the education professions, many of them women and many of them politically liberal, provided institutional support in transforming textbook material and teaching techniques. Finally, the publishing industry, which contained a substantial minority, or possibly even a majority, of persons who sympathized with the feminist movement, was only too willing to incorporate the desired changes into new editions of their books. (p. 54)

[In] the early 1970's, women's groups launched a number of specific task forces to combat what they regard as sexism in the curriculum. These included Women on Words and Images, a task force of NOW, which helped to persuade the publishing firm of Scott, Foresman to develop "anti-sexist" guidelines for textbooks, and Feminists on

Children's Media, which agitated for, and circulated, lists of "non-sexist" children's books. The problem, as one publisher was quoted as saying, was not that there were no women in the textbooks, but that they were portrayed there as mothers and sisters rather than as "individuals."

If traditional curricular material was sexist because boys and men outnumbered girls and women, and, most importantly, because women appeared in nurturing roles while men appeared in achieving roles, then non-sexist books would have to show equal numbers of men and women in nurturing and achieving roles. In the new model, masculine and feminine traits would temper each other and combine (as one contributor to a U.S. government pamphlet put it) in "a balanced, more fully human, truly androgynous personality."

It is important to point out here that there were no federal guidelines in place to which these groups were objecting and which they wanted to revise. Rather, their objections were to generally accepted portrayals, which they wanted to make unacceptable and to replace through law or political pressure.

Since decisions about curricula usually occur at the local level, most textbook controversies are not federal issues. Nevertheless, it has often been federal funding that has assisted in the creation and dissemination of feminist curriculum materials, in the establishment of magazines and other media networks, and in the publication of alternatives to traditional curricula. (pp. 54-5)

As far as feminist groups were concerned, the survival of [WEEA], despite low-level funding, ensured a continued impact on curriculum. Testimony for the 1984 reauthorization included support for disseminating "non-sexist" curricula by sponsoring a quarterly magazine for that purpose and a teacher handbook on "sex equity." The materials were then to be published and distributed with the help of the WEEA staff, again with funding provided by the federal government. Reagan signed the reauthorization of the act without comment.

The role of states and localities in condoning or condemning textbooks according to their adherence to ideological guidelines has also changed at least as much as the role of the federal government. In fact, in recent years the 22 states that have statewide textbook-adoption policies have played a major part in restructuring the entire textbook market, because of the volume of sales they control.

In one of those states, California, the law, in addition to the well-known sexually-neutral language requirements, establishes the following guidelines: (1) illustrations must contain approximately equal proportions of men and women; (2) in the representation of each profession, including parent, men and women must be shown in equal numbers; (3) the contributions of men and women to developments in history or achievements in art or science must appear in equal numbers; (4) mentally and physically active, creative, problem-solving roles, and success or failure in these roles, must be divided evenly between males and females; (5) the number of traditional and non-traditional activities engaged in by characters of both sexes must be approximately even; (6) the gamut of emotions must occur randomly among characters, regardless of gender; and (7) both sexes must be portrayed in nurturing roles with their families.

The process of screening that accompanies these rules specifies that a textbook must pass muster at open hearings around the state. NOW has participated extensively in such hearings and helped to influence the choice of textbooks. Publishers are held to very stringent standards of "sexism" and must respond to *any* criticism in order for a text to be accepted. The result, of course, is that only texts which satisfy these criteria for historical and thematic representation become part of the official curriculum.

Although professionals in the field of education have fought ferociously against efforts by conservatives or traditionalists to censor textbooks and other curricular materials, their response to similar campaigns by feminists has generally been one of eager acquiescence. To cite only two representative instances. In 1972, no sooner did feminist groups demand the elimination of "sex-role stereotypes" from the curriculum and the textbooks than the New York State Teachers Association endorsed their demand. Similarly, in 1973, a feminist group in Kalamazoo, Michigan, complained that the Houghton Mifflin readers then being used in the local schools presented an "unbalanced" picture of women. The director of elementary education remarked that "while we could have resisted the demands of the committee, we didn't." With the support of school officials, the protesters spent the summer devising supplementary materials which were used to "correct" the original readers. (pp. 55-6)

One survey of editors found that only 20 percent characterized themselves as conservatives, while 47 percent characterized themselves as liberals, and 33 percent as strong liberals or radicals. Moreover, 70 percent of the men and 90 percent of the women identified themselves as Democrats. No wonder, then, that Scott, Foresman, working with the feminist group Women on Words and Images, developed the first guidelines on sexual content for textbooks in 1972, and that representatives of the same firm testified in favor of the WEEA at a hearing held in the House. There, it was made clear that a group of women had formed within the company, specifically for the purpose of rewriting textbooks. The person testifying also noted that 80 percent of the editors at the firm were women.

At the same time as these changes from above were taking place, pressure from the state of California, which instituted stringent requirements concerning the proper representation of women in textbooks adopted for the entire state, prompted such other publishers as Holt, Rinehart & Winston, Houghton Mifflin, and Macmillan to follow suit. (Not that they necessarily needed to be pressured, given the fact that they, like Scott, Foresman, were only too ready to go along with the feminist agenda.)

Are the changes feminists have made in the textbooks overdue reforms of a system that denied a significant segment of the population fair representation, or are they a nonfictional example of what George Orwell in *1984* referred to as Newspeak? Surely the latter. Equal numbers of men and women performing the same roles in equal proportion may represent an ideal for the future—though that is itself, to put it mildly, debatable. What is not debatable, however, is that such a picture distorts the simple truth both about the present and the past. To bolster it with law and public funds is to use the power of government to spread a blatant lie. As such, it is indeed a form of Newspeak—and so is the fact that it justifies itself in the name of liberal values. (p. 56)

> *Robert Lerner and Stanley Rothman, "Newspeak, Feminist-Style," in* Commentary, *Vol. 89, No. 4, April, 1990, pp. 54-6.*

Harriet Goldhor Lerner

[In the excerpt below, Lerner offers a feminist perspective on self-help books aimed predominantly at women.]

The first self-help book I ever read was called *Always Ask a Man,* by Arlene Dahl. It was written before the second wave of feminism at a time when girls and women were explicitly encouraged to offer men narcissistic protection by feigning weakness, dependency and incompetence when we were not fortunate enough to possess these traits naturally. Dahl's advice typifies the majority of guidebooks for women written before the 1970s, explicitly prescribing male dominance while implicitly warning women that men were weak:

> the successful female never lets her competence compete with her femininity. Never upstage a man. Don't top his jokes even if you have to bite your tongue to keep from doing it. Never launch loudly into your own opinions on the subject . . . Instead draw out his ideas to which you can gracefully add your footnotes from time to time. If you smoke, don't carry matches. In a restaurant let your mate or date do the ordering. You may know more about vintage wine than the wine steward but if you are smart you'll let your man do the choosing and be ecstatic over his selection even if it tastes like shampoo.

Biting our tongues (one can glimpse here the excruciating activity behind female "passivity") and reflecting men "at twice their natural size" has been the hallmark of successful femininity throughout the ages. But beyond providing these and other tips, the advice-giving industry that I was raised on drove home the paradoxical notion that women should strengthen men by relinquishing our own strength. To do otherwise, or simply to be ourselves, was unfeminine, unlovable, castrating, destructive and yes, even life-threatening to men.

Around the time of the *Cinderella Complex,* the self-help industry changed directions. Dependency, we were told in the eighties, was a bad thing that women presumably possessed more of than men. From my perspective, this was a questionable assumption at best. First, emotional dependency (in contrast to economic dependency) is not a bad thing but rather a universal aspect of human experience. Second, the generalization that women are more dependent than men is false, although male dependency needs are more hidden and better taken care of *by* women. Although developing competence and self-reliance is admittedly not a bad idea, female self-esteem plummeted further as women were admonished for the very "passive-dependent" behaviors we were raised to cultivate.

> I confess to an initial (although short-lived) fondness for the word "codependence," a relational term that is nicer than, say, "masochism." For women, being codependent means simply that we have learned what the culture has taught.

It is in the role of mother that women have been hardest hit by the self-help world. Until the recent entrance of the "dysfunctional family system" into our collective vocabulary (a term reminiscent of broken stereo components), it had been assumed that the mother *is* the child's environment and that her offspring will flourish if she only does her job well enough. Since children are so frequently imperfect, a mother's crimesheet has been endless, as are the contradictory, anxiety-provoking, guilt-inducing messages that have for so long been aimed in her direction. (p. 15)

Although the content of the advice-giving industry changes with the socio-economic climate of the times, what does not change is the relentless, unabashed focus on improving and perfecting women. If only women would do more (Enter Superwoman!), or want less (Mother stay home!), or solve our personal problems—then men and their institutions would not have to change.

The advice-giving industry, a multi-billion-dollar business, teaches us to privatize, individualize and pathologize "women's problems," rather than to understand these difficulties as a natural and shared outgrowth of inequality and the socially constructed fabric of work and family roles. Of course, personal change can reinforce rather than obscure the necessity for social change; women do want to acquire skills to get beyond conflict, distance and pain, and because the personal *is* political, we can work for change at all systems levels. But self-help books keep us narrowly focused on the question "What's wrong with me?" or, more popularly today, "What's wrong with my dysfunctional/toxic parents?" (an improvement, I suppose, on the earlier exclusive focus on bad mothers). Larger contextual issues are obscured from view, detouring us from challenging the class, gender and racially stratified systems in which we live and work and in which our family history has evolved.

The books in the psychology/self-help (and now recovery) sections of bookstores have virtually nothing in common with other kinds of how-to/fix-it guides. They are unique partly because more remains unknown than known about human emotional functioning. There are countless ways to name, frame or tackle a particular problem, and at a time when everyone is jumping on the profitable advice-giving bandwagon, it is difficult for consumers to separate the wheat from the chaff. Luckily, feminism can provide us with a few guidelines: for example, beware of books telling us that women are sick.

This brings me to recovery books, the recent proliferation of which might embarrass any good feminist. Yet feminist criticism is relatively rare and recovery books are best-sellers in bookstores nationwide, feminist bookstores included. A recent issue of *Feminist Bookstore News* lauds recovery as a feminist issue; the contents of the entire issue bear uncritical testimony to this viewpoint. I fear, however, that the recovery movement (and it is indeed a movement, if not an epidemic) is lulling us back into sleepiness, back into self-blaming and parent-blaming, back into diagnostic labels and a narrow disease model of our problems and pain. The advice-giving industry would have us all 12-stepping our way out of codependence and multiple addictions.

Codependence (sometimes written "codependency") is a label of such vast inclusiveness that we are all "it." If one surveys the literature one finds that codependence is anything that interferes with our capacity for healthy autonomy and intimacy, any under-responsibility for self and over-focus on others, any neglect or abuse of our own person. Codependence thus embraces everyone and everything—a fact that seems to bother enthusiasts not at all.

I confess to an initial (although short-lived) fondness for the word "codependence," a relational term that is nicer than, say, "masochism." For women, being codependent means simply that we have learned what the culture has taught. Yet codependence is labeled a progressive, fatal (albeit treatable) disease by some and an incurable condition by others. *Breaking Free,* a recent "recovery workbook" on codependence, notes: "This is a chronic condition that can return any moment. You're only in remission from codependence when you are practicing recovery."

The term "addiction" is similarly all-inclusive. As the concept has been globalized from chemical to "process" addictions, it has embraced all the predictable, patterned behaviors that human beings use reflexively to lower anxiety. The recovery literature documents our additions to sex, food, caretaking, relationships, romance, fantasies, drama, work, crises, shopping and laziness. Women who are so addicted, or who are co-addicts—that is, addicted to partners who are addicted to something—are encouraged to join a 12-step recovery group of the similarly afflicted. The "Adult Child" movement has also been globalized from "Adult Children of Alcoholics" to "Adult Children of Dysfunctional Families," a diagnostic label from which none of us is exempt.

Recovery literature, programs and products are purportedly grounded in the 12-step principles of Alcoholics Anonymous, the fastest-growing spiritual movement in the country. The concept of a Higher Power ("turning our will and lives over to Him") is central to 12-step spirituality, although feminist recovery groups reframe "Him" as "the goddess within," "a guiding white feminine light," "one's higher self" and so forth. Sonia Johnson criticizes the Twelve Steps in her latest book, *Wildfire* (1989), voicing negative sentiments more boldly than most feminists would dare to articulate them. Feminist experts in addiction have voiced equally strong praise for 12-step spirituality, which has quite literally saved the lives of countless women and men who would otherwise have died from drinking.

My own concerns center on the exploitation and misuse of 12-step language and spirituality now that "recovery" has become big business. When I telephoned the largest American publisher of 12-step self-help material (their catalogue is 152 pages long!), I was put on hold and subjected to affirmations and inspirational meditations read in hollow voices that left me feeling like I had just stepped into the world of Margaret Atwood's *The Handmaid's Tale.* I have a similarly creepy feeling in response to the new market of self-help music tapes "created especially for Twelve Steppers," with subliminal affirmations and 12-step wisdom for recovering people. And I agree entirely with Sonia Johnson, who finds the ubiquitous labeling of primarily white, middle-class problems as "addictions" to be both preemptive and callous:

> In the face of the grief and confusion, the unspeakable anguish of families of color who have one or more members with brains permanently scrambled by PCP or horribly dead from physiological addiction, of desperate human beings whose neighborhoods are occupied by foreign armies of drug dealers waging war against their children . . . in the face of this nightmare, to lump all societal problems together as "addictions" is to make a mockery of those who are suffering lives shattered by addiction and carelessly to erase their experience.

Recovery is fast moving from a grassroots to an entrepreneurial phenomenon, which, as social worker Lorie Dwinell observed at the plenary session of the 1989 American Family Therapy Association conference, is inevitable in problems-for-profit capitalism. Dwinell, herself an advocate of Adult Child and recovery work, reminds us that all movements will overstate their case, that anything that can be used can also be abused, and that we should not discredit a movement because of the inevitably stupid remarks made by some of its proponents. Obviously, there is both good and bad here, even Very Good and Very Bad.

In the Very Bad category, recovery books purport to embrace feminist and family systems theory, while distorting and simplifying both, promoting the shaming and blaming of the self and one's family. In the Very Good category, recovery books have given women permission and skills to take better care of themselves, both in and out of relationships. In contrast to the advice-to-women books that I was raised on, the recovery literature focuses on both authenticity and the self. There is no sacrificing the "I" for the relational "We."

The recovery movement has also provided women with a strong sense of female community and has paid respectful attention to lesbian relationships rendered invisible by the earlier self-help industry. The literature has encouraged women to speak openly about how experiences such as alcoholism, sexual abuse and incest have affected our lives, and in so doing to recognize private experience as validat-

ed and shared. These large achievements tempt one to say, "If it works, don't knock it." I've heard enough "It-saved-my-life" stories from the women's community to feel almost apologetic for my own deep misgivings.

The recovery literature is inspirational and prescriptive, but more important, it confers identity, which has me pondering the following question: Why do so many women I meet in my professional travels use recovery labels to identify themselves with perfect ease and comfort (as in, "Hi, I'm Sue. I'm an Adult Child, and I'm in recovery from relationship addiction")? Why are so comparatively few women comfortable using the "F" word (as in, "Hi, I'm Jane, I'm a feminist")? Why is it easier, more permissible, reassuring, or simply just possible, to move forward by defining oneself as a recovering person?

And here we do come full circle back to Arlene Dahl, to the advice-giving industry I was raised on, to the culturally ingrained belief that women who put their primary energy into their own growth are hurtful and destructive to others. Women tend to feel so guilty and anxious about any joyful assertion of self in the face of patriarchal injunctions that each small move out from under is invariably accompanied by some unconscious act of apology and penance. I believe that it is an act of deep apology, especially to the dominant group culture, for women to move forward in the name of recovery, addiction and disease.

The feminist movement, like the civil rights movement, is a profoundly transforming, enlivening and empowering social revolution. Because we have been *so* effective, the backlash against feminism has been *so* virulent. In the face of such resistance we might all shuffle back to the broom closet, which we have not done. But it hardly requires explanation that many women are hesitant to become feminist activists, even when they support feminist goals. Recovery, to my mind, is a sort of compromise solution. It teaches women to move in the direction of "more self" while it sanitizes and makes change safe, because the dominant group culture (never fond of "those angry women") is not threatened by sick women meeting together to get well. . . .

Whatever its drawbacks, the recovery movement does demonstrate the power of women as organizers. That excites me. The leaders of the codependency movement are women, mostly "ordinary" white women who started a grassroots movement that has spread like wildfire throughout our nation.

And so I keep my faith in women's wisdom. I trust we will ultimately take what is useful from the self-help world while resisting the lure of negative self-definitions and the depoliticizing of our lives. My work as a feminist and a clinical psychologist teaches me daily that nothing shapes our experience as powerfully as the language we frame it in. Surely, we can take the best of what the advice-givers offer without de-contextualizing our problems and without sifting them through negative, dispiriting, pathologizing filters. It is *my* expert opinion that women are *not* sick. (pp. 15-16)

Harriet Goldhor Lerner, "Problems for Prof-

it?" in The Women's Review of Books, *Vol. VII, No. 7, April, 1990, pp. 15-16.*

Amanda Leslie-Spinks

[*In the following excerpt, Leslie–Spinks reviews* The Difference Within: Feminism and Critical Theory *by Elizabeth Meese and Alice Parker, which collects essays concerning the differences among and within feminists and the feminist movement.*]

A few years ago, some feminists began to worry about the "a-word," that ubiquitous "and" that appeared with dreary regularity in the titles of books and courses and in the names of women's groups. "Additive feminism" was a kind of plague, but no one could think what to do about it. Surely it was necessary to reconsider almost everything from a gender-sensitive point of view. We did need to know about Women and Society, and the State, and Sex, and . . . so on. Yet those of us who fell back on the "Women and . . . " formula knew a twinge of guilt. Did we really mean that women stood apart with their own special perspective on the world, as the compound titles suggested? If so, how were they affected or effective? Did we mean all women? How did we choose our topics? There was a feeling of work deferred, doubts left unformulated.

Now, largely as a result of events in the women's movement, those repressed questions have resurfaced. Women of color first articulated the imperative to deal with them, insisting that their goals could not be collapsed into those of the white feminist establishment. No one—neither men nor feminists—could speak "for women" without silencing key differences between women. Since then many other voices have been heard—celibates, rural women, retirees, children, environmentalists, neo-conservatives, S/M practitioners, sex industry workers . . . an open-ended list. What they share, however, is the insight that marginalization and cooptation of differences (any kind of difference from some usually tacitly-held norm) is the main business of the powerful.

In a sense this is familiar territory. Feminists have long understood that male power relies on devaluing the ways in which women differ from a silent male standard. What remains to be explored is how those same processes of getting and keeping a hegemonic position (that is, claiming one's own identity as the norm) are played out between women, and are even practiced by individuals on themselves—when, for instance, the "mother" in us attempts to stifle the "professional."

This new suspicion that "identities" are linked to suppression has given rise to thorny political and epistemological problems for feminists. These are only now beginning to be corraled into the more or less coherent project of "thinking difference." That, of course, is a typically abstract, "post-structuralist" sort of label. But it does make clear that there is no reason to stop with any particular differences—say race, class and gender differences from the white, bourgeois male standard. There is no justification for ignoring other norms (for instance, heterosexuality, physical ability, or the scientific method) in trying to understand the functioning of power on the "micro" level of our personal biographies.

This fruitful but complex vision of political reality is a challenge as well as an opportunity for feminist thinkers: they have to trace out that shaky ground between feminism and post-structuralism without ending up at post-feminism. It is this task that is begun in Elizabeth Meese and Alice Parker's extremely useful collection of essays [*The Difference Within: Feminism and Critical Theory*].

The title was, I think, carefully chosen to distance this work from that tempting search for a substantive female difference, a difference *from* men. "Difference" in this sense has really itself become an "identity." In so doing, it has lost its critical edge and gained an interest in maintaining itself, maintaining the status quo.

The editors want to suggest that we should not be looking for an "identity within," for an uncontested feminist consciousness, for a center which, by definition, would maintain itself by controlling the margins. We should be looking for difference understood as a continual resistance to the conservative forces of "identity." Even to raise this possibility makes clear how much we have counted on "identity" as the authentic starting-point for writing and thinking and political organizing, and how difficult it is to start instead from resistance to identity—in other words, from difference.

"How do we articulate 'the difference within'," Meese and Parker ask in the introduction, "knowing full well the shifting ground on which we/you stand? Certainly we must abandon the dream of an outside or an inside that would provide firm footing, whether we call it 'reality,' 'experience' or 'consciousness'." These are fighting words to many North American feminists who are unsympathetic to the idea that reality isn't "real," and who have tended to see experience as a kind of touchstone of honesty in a sea of false images. But in fact, much of our recent work on the problems raised by essentialism, separatism and solidarity has also brought into focus the unintentional reproductions of oppression by women of women. So although the language may be unfamiliar, Meese and Parker's demand that we abandon firm footing—because it is almost certainly on someone else's head—is not an unthinkable next step. The question, of course, is how to take that step without abandoning concrete struggles against the physical, psychological and economic abuse of women.

The reader should not expect a single answer, but what she might expect, and what this volume actually delivers, is a number of suggestions about how to see and resist the destructive powers of naming that set us in oppositions. There is no question, however, that working with difference is and will be a lot of work.

> Feminists have long understood that male power relies on devaluing the ways in which women differ from a silent male standard. What remains to be explored is how those same processes of getting and keeping a hegemonic position (that is, claiming one's own identity as the norm) are played out between women. . . .

The collection begins with an amusing essay by Catharine Stimpson, **"Nancy Reagan wears a hat: Feminism and its cultural consensus."** It was a good choice as a starter because Stimpson really sets the stage for the "Feminism meets Godzilla" scenario of our encounter with continental, post-structuralist ideas. Her subject, in other words, is where we came from in order to get to "the problematic of difference."

She begins her account in the late sixties, when, broadly speaking, feminists shared the view that one of the chief features of our society was the constant and cunning misrepresentation of women—in ads, in art, in scholarly work. The underlying expectation and the basis for what Stimpson refers to as the cultural consensus of feminism was that we could cut through the misrepresentations to the real thing—expose the distortions, restore the past, generate more accurate representations. On the political front, that "misrepresentation" could be beaten by overcoming women's exclusion from the political arena, by being represented.

During the seventies, however, groups emerged who found it very difficult to share the same umbrella of discourse about women—among them radical conservatives, neo-liberals, neo-conservatives and (the odd women out) feminist post-modernists. Extremely divisive confrontations began over competing representations of women; Stimpson mentions the defeat of the ERA, the pornography debate, the Ginny Foat trial. In the fragmentation that has followed, Stimpson suggests, we might be well advised to listen to the one group that has been saying for some time that it is not any particular representation that is wrong, but the notion of representation altogether and our faith in it. (p. 15)

In her contribution, **"Some different meanings of the concept of 'difference',"** Michele Barrett sounds a note of warning. "Difference" is an ambiguous concept because it has emerged from competing intellectual traditions. There is, for instance, a psychoanalytic version of difference that is essentially connected to processes of sexual differentiation—a meaning that is close to the traditional feminist concern with differences between men and women. Then there is a concept of difference that has grown out of Saussurian linguistics:

> "Difference" in this sense is shorthand for a theory of meaning as positional or relational: an approach that offers a fundamental challenge to the "realist" epistemological certainties of much

of Western social thought as well as to what we could call "classical theories of representation."

Finally, there is a third meaning of difference that is really a celebration of the plurality of experience possible in modern life.

Unless we can untangle these, Barrett claims, we are probably in for some confused and rancorous debates on important theoretical and strategic issues. "Difference II rejects the human subject on which Difference III is predicated . . . Differences I and III incline towards essentialism; Difference II is deconstructive in its approach to gendered subjectivity." You see the problem.

One of the great strengths of this collection is that it exemplifies the concern with difference that is the book's subject. The authors are not all women, all white, or all anything; they do not reflect any subtle norm of political correctness, or any kind of "party line." The editors report that they intentionally avoided any unison of voices, choosing instead "Afro-American, Jew, WASP, Indian, male, female, Chilean exile, British Marxist, poet, critic, United States citizen, homeowner, renter." The reader finds helpful reflections about the suppression of difference in all sorts of arenas—in literature, in propaganda, in political organizing, in representations of cultures and histories and even in those private examinations of conscience that engage the well-heeled, property-owning feminist as she steps to the conference podium to speak about inequalities.

In **"The Power of Division,"** Jonathan Culler suggests that a commitment to maintaining a diversity of voices (as the editors have done) is actually of strategic importance in struggling against those in control. Culler reflects on the rather irritable reaction of tenured male faculty towards the proliferating debates among feminist literary critics. Their response has been, he says, to profess openness to a feminist position but to ask that women come to some agreement among themselves about what they want. Culler suspects, however, that asking "What does woman want?" is really a way of finding out what she is prepared to leave out of account.

> Historically, that question has been a way of deflecting attention from the multifarious requests and projects women might be pursuing by positing a deeper, hidden and unifying desire that would make all clear, if only sustained and theoretical enquiry could reveal it to us.

His advice is not to comply, but to insist on being of two minds, or many minds. By not collapsing their differences, women are refusing to become one pole, the weaker pole, in a force field dominated by men. They gain thereby the possibility of stretching the field of debate beyond polarized oppositions. "The power of division," Culler writes, "is the power of ongoing argument, in which incompatible positions work to focus attention on a set of issues, set the terms of an entire field, articulating a space of exploration and debate." . . .

The "difference within" is not a soothing subject, and pursuing it raises many justified fears that the divided are also the conquered. But on the other hand, the analysis of "difference" suggests for the first time the possibility of displacing the old dualisms, which seem somehow always to impede the possibility of radical change. This work is now well begun, and it would be a failure of nerve not to take it as far and as fast as possible. (p. 16)

Amanda Leslie-Spinks, "Different Differences," in The Women's Review of Books, *Vol. VII, No. 8, May, 1990, pp. 15-16.*

Helen Vendler

[*In the following excerpt, Vendler reviews several recent volumes of feminist cultural analysis, including Camille Paglia's* Sexual Personae: Art and Decadence from Nefertiti to Emily Dickinson *and Sandra Gilbert and Susan Gubar's* No Man's Land: The Place of the Woman Writer in the Twentieth Century. *For a response by Gilbert and Gubar and a final defense by Vendler, see excerpts below.*]

The political, social, medical, and personal struggle for women's equality has had many heroines in the practical world, but its ventures in the intellectual sphere have had uneven results. Of these the clearest successes seem to be in the fields of history and sociology, where newly retrieved information about women's lives, interesting in itself, also has explanatory power. Explorations in my own subject, literary criticism, have seemed to me more dubious. It is not from any lack of sympathy for the practical and legal goals of the women's movement that I have often felt disquiet in reading what used to be called "feminist criticism" or "feminist literary theory," and is now sometimes called "feminist cultural analysis." A number of new books in this vein, both good and bad, suggest some of the pitfalls and possible benefits of this work. I shall also look at a book diametrically opposed to feminist positions, but unsuccessful in its own counterclaims.

The feminist literary criticism that appeared in the Sixties and Seventies was frequently naive. It spent most of its energy describing how women were represented in literary works by both men and women writers. The male writers came off badly. Feminist literary critics wrote about literary characters as if they were real people (though sophisticated ideas about narrative since Aristotle would have suggested otherwise) and they predictably found women characters treated less sympathetically by men than they would like. They also wrote as though authors had a public duty to be ideologically correct on sex, race, and class (correctness being defined in contemporary terms), and could be criticized and patronized when they were not. This early school of feminist thought is still in full cry, and Milton remains the chief sinner among the poets, and Dickens perhaps the worst offender among nineteenth-century novelists. It is common, for instance, for feminists to refer to Milton's "misogyny," although in fact Milton was far ahead of his time in the respect, both spiritual and intellectual, he showed for woman as a moral agent (as in his treatment of Eve).

It did not seem to occur to feminists who complained about Dickens's or Hardy's or Lawrence's fictional women to deplore the stiff, idealized, antagonistic, or

calumniatory portraits of men by female novelists from Jane Austen to, say, Fay Weldon. What might twentieth-century men think of Mr. Darcy, Mr. Rochester, Casaubon, or Ladislaw as portraits of marriageable members of their sex? In truth, both men and women novelists give fictional embodiment to their own sexual fantasies when they sketch the opposite sex, and both tend to be more believable when portraying their own sex. "Masculinists" (were there any) would have a lot to complain about if they looked into the taxonomy of the male sex as depicted by women novelists, starting perhaps with Mrs. Stowe's Simon Legree and Uncle Tom, and ending with Mary Gordon's fathers and priests.

Early feminist critics also (vainly) attempted to prove that there was a special female way of writing or "women's language." For a while, this investigation drew theoretically on Erik Erikson's model of female "inner space," and we heard a lot about nests, sanctuaries, and wombs as images recurring in writing by women. More recently, this romantic view of women's writing has appeared in France, where attention is paid less to matter than to manner; we are told that women's writing should avoid the law-giving patriarchal manner by being "writerly," disruptive, playful, subversive, or avant-garde; or we are urged to direct our attention to a maternal preverbal "semiotic" realm, the *chora,* which is, so to speak, the id of language before the superego of the symbolic puts its repressive (and therefore masculine) stamp upon it. (p. 19)

It is not from any lack of sympathy for the practical and legal goals of the women's movement that I have often felt disquiet in reading what used to be called "feminist criticism" or "feminist literary theory," and is now sometimes called "feminist cultural analysis."

A recent theorist of feminist aesthetics, Rita Felski, has given up on both crude feminist socialist realism (which treats fictional creations as though they were real people) and the theory of *écriture féminine.* This leaves her with very little to hang on to that can be called feminist aesthetics. Nevertheless, her arguments against the mistaken formulations of her predecessors [as put forth in her ***Beyond Feminist Aesthetics: Feminist Literature and Social Change***] may help to refine feminist theory. Felski's formulations are, generally speaking, Marxist ones, but she is prevented from taking a position based entirely on the ideological treatment of male and female characters by her reading of Adorno (that huge stumbling block in the way of socialist realist thinking). Because Adorno's fundamental aesthetic medium was music, he faced squarely the definition of art as a syntactic system of formal relations. This is the definition of what all the arts (including the verbal arts of prose and poetry) have in common, what distinguishes them from exposition. Adorno recognized that about all you could say concerning the systems of relations set in motion by genuine artists was that they weren't ready-made reproductions of social reality—these are the specialty of propaganda and advertising. To Adorno, art represents a "negative" oppositional sphere to the capitalist processing of all social information into commodity status.

Felski is not satisfied to have art be seen as a private negation of the commodities that are brokered to a wider public. She wants women's art to reside in the "public sphere" (she borrows the phrase from Habermas), to be part of a public discourse in opposition to the status quo. This is to insist on the possibility of a common discourse perceived as expressing the interests of an entire community rather than isolated, "private," persons. Felski is impatient with feminist theorists who scrutinize a novel or a poem in isolation, examining its themes for ideological correctness, or its surface for a disruptive style. She is more interested (predictably, but also sanely) in the conditions in which literature by women is produced, distributed, and read. How do women get to make and publish whatever they do, and what purposes do their works serve for women readers?

The only thing wrong with all this, from my point of view, is calling it "aesthetics," when it should properly be called the sociology of literature. Marxist theory, with its apparently inevitable bias against art produced by and for an educated group, is unable to deal with the question of aesthetic power except by counting heads: if a lot of people have liked something, then it has "aesthetic power," and its "reception" deserves to be studied. A more sophisticated Marxism attempts to see richness and complexity of representation as a criterion of aesthetic power, but this theory collapses when faced with works of art that are less concerned with representation (as the word is normally understood) than with something else—that syntax of internal relations I have mentioned above, for instance, or volatility of tone, or play of color. Adorno, biting the bullet, thought that the artist who developed a new technique should be considered the most progressive artist, since new techniques widen the possibilities of articulation within a given medium. But I have not seen many Marxist literary critics following his lead.

Felski sees, quite correctly, that much recent writing by women has been confessional—she mentions books by Kate Millett, Marilyn French, and Ann Oakley—and she wants to preserve this (essentially realist) writing from the argument of some feminists that realism (in its acceptance of fictional illusion and its non-"writerly" quality) is a sign of complicity with the ideological status quo. Felski admits that even the more adventurous forms of feminist confession, such as Kate Millett's *Flying,* show "a conspicuous lack of interest in irony, indeterminacy, and linguistic play." Felski then makes the intelligent point that irony need not be found only in the surface of a work; irony is found in the infinitely extendable nature of writing itself with respect to its material. Writing is

> an endless chain of signifiers. . . . This lack of identity between the text and the life, experience and its representation, is of course a central

problem of autobiography, and, in a broader sense, of literature itself.

Though the self, as Felski sees it, is always a social construction, she reminds us that we do part of the constructing:

> Oppositional identities are often asserted only painfully and with difficulty and serve to articulate experiences of alienation, exclusion, and suffering in people's lives. The fact that they are socially constructed does not mean that they are any less "real," or that their political function can be reduced to one of complicity with ruling ideologies.

Here, however, she seems to be confusing the actual self constructed in life with the fictional self articulated in confessional memoirs or novels.

Often, as in the passage I have just quoted, Felski is more certain about what she dislikes in previous literary criticism (in this passage, French feminist dismissal of realist writing by women) than about a new direction she hopes to point to. She is ambivalent about what has come to be called "the autonomy of the work of art"—that is, its independence of any social ideology, its aims beyond the limited one of representation. She repeats the old accusation—that emphasis on the autonomy of the work of art "has helped to encourage a mystification of art as a quasi-transcendental sphere . . . perpetuating the myth of the great artist as solitary genius." Does she mean that there are no great artists? Or that they were not geniuses? Or that they were great geniuses but not solitary? Or what? Simply to say that Beethoven came out of the German musical tradition and was supported by patrons ("the historical and ideological determinants affecting the production of art and the dissemination of aesthetic values") does not mean that he was not also a great artist and a solitary genius. The absence of female Beethovens may perhaps be explained by the absence of instruction and patronage for women, but instruction and patronage alone do not explain why one instructed and supported artist turns out to be Beethoven and another does not.

The "myth of the great artist as solitary genius" has enough truth in it to survive. To suspect the existence of many mute inglorious Miltons, male and female, should not lead to the conclusion that instruction and patronage play anything but a subordinate part in the creation of great art. Even given a wage, a teacher, a study, and a publishing house, the genius still does the work all alone. To note the uniqueness and unpredictability of great art is not to "mystify" it.

Felski adds that there is something to be said for acknowledging the autonomy of art:

> The formal complexity of the text is perceived to serve a potentially critical function by distancing and defamiliarizing the ideological frameworks within which it operates.

To which I can only say, "Whither away, Delight?" But then, socialist criticism has never been strong on delight, while art is. And in attempting to bridge high and low culture (saying that works of both kinds can be useful in her "oppositional public sphere") Felski evades a more central issue: Can a work's instrumental value be used as an aesthetic criterion at all? (By instrumental value I mean the good—political, moral, religious—that it does; in this view, the banal Catholic holy card is as efficacious as a Piero della Francesca.) Felski backs away from an absolutely instrumental feminist valuation—"a position that taken to its logical conclusion would rate *The Women's Room* [by Marilyn French] as a better work of art than the writing of Kafka." But she assumes that bad works can be important during the time that they generate political excitement:

> [Some] examples of feminist fiction that served an important purpose at the time of publication by articulating women's discovery of their oppression may appear aesthetically naive or excessively didactic *at a historical distance* [italics mine].

Is she implying that, as new converts, we like the holy cards and then we graduate to the paintings? But surely it is the function of a feminist literary critic, as of any other literary critic, not to overlook aesthetic naiveté or excessive didacticism (or other aesthetic embarrassments) whether the work is new or not. These are crippling deficiencies in a work of art. What good artist has been aesthetically naive or excessively didactic? It is not only "at a historical distance" that a reader who is a feminist critic should not be swept up in ideological approval of third-rate work. It is always and everywhere.

The absence of female Beethovens may perhaps be explained by the absence of instruction and patronage for women, but instruction and patronage alone do not explain why one instructed and supported artist turns out to be Beethoven and another does not.

Felski's conception of art ends up where political criticism usually ends up—valuing a naive and didactic "articulation of oppression" because it has awakened certain members of an oppressed class. It seems of no use to tell such critics that propaganda is not valuable except as you value propaganda. If you value art, you cannot value propaganda as art. The "aesthetically naive" and the "excessively didactic" are corrupt when their naiveté and didacticism have an ideological purpose. And corruption cannot serve an "important purpose," at least not any important purpose one would call aesthetic. A political function, of course, is something else.

The female writer, the female audience—Felski writes as if both these concepts stood for clearly identifiable entities, without questioning them. But as social constructs they are as open to questioning as any other social construct. (pp. 19-21)

Any writer knows that the word "woman" probably has as many meanings as it has users, once you get past the fact of biological difference. The word "woman" seems to mean, for many feminists, "person oppressed by a male power system." But this definition can be widened beyond women, since the poor and other marginal people can also be said to be oppressed by that system (if indeed it is possible to ascribe agency to a system at all, and if you accept the idea that maleness is a quality of the system).

Many people have found it difficult to understand why those women who support freeing the oppressed do not turn their attention to the larger world of the oppressed, rather than to themselves alone. This has always been the source of tension between socialism, with its concept of class oppression, and feminism, with its concept of gender oppression. The splitting of discontented socialist women from socialist groups where they felt themselves sidelined by the men of the movement is retold in some of the essays in [Karen V.] Hansen and [Ilene J.] Philipson's collection, *Women, Class, and the Feminist Imagination: A Socialist-Feminist Reader.* Soon enough, the socialist feminists were at war with both the radical (often lesbian) feminists, and equally with the liberal middle-class (often academic) feminists, a still-unsolved tragicomic conflict rich in human implication.

It is a relief to pass from the literary unease of Felski's book to straight political history, to read about the founding of unions and women's organizations, the struggle for reproductive rights, and so on. With the collapse of Eastern bloc communism, socialists have been retheorizing with a vengeance. The most utopian hope in *Women, Class, and the Feminist Imagination* is that socialist feminism can "direct Marxist theorizing toward questions of feeling, consciousness, and an appreciation of emotional life," the very psychological questions that are the concerns of literature. Such a hope seems unlikely to be realized by neo-Marxist literary critics.

The "postfeminist" results of feminist demands for reform described in some of the essays collected in *Women, Class, and the Feminist Imagination* make sad reading, especially if one thinks of Felski's wish for better conditions in the production and reception of women's art. Very little "shared parenting" really goes on; wage-earning mothers feel increasing pressure to find time for their children and their work; black teen-age women are often single parents; the promises and premises of the women's movement are largely empty, or at best transient, for women who are not middle-class. These socialist essays, while concentrating on women, still see them subsumed in the class of the poor or the overworked. They do not make gender an overriding concept, as feminist literary criticism has done.

Feminism's own self-criticism is represented not only in Hansen's socialist reader but in another new collection, *Feminism/Postmodernism,* edited by Linda Nicholson. Again and again in this book some of the simplistic concepts of the "second wave" feminism of the Sixties are scrutinized, from the concept "woman" itself (by Judith Butler of Johns Hopkins University) to the concept of "community" (by Iris Marion Young of Worcester Polytechnic Institute). This attempt to refine feminist concepts is more than welcome. The sheer diversity among women,

and the insufficiency of any one definition of them (whether psychoanalytic, sociological, or political) has often led
the women's movement to react purely strategically, and
to adopt a set of narrowly political definitions of women
(such as "those oppressed by men") which have alienated
those women who think of themselves differently. Similarly, the utopian and "touchy-feely" use of the word "community" (deriving from the intimacy of small groups
meeting for discussion or living together) can give an outsider the creeps. (p. 21)

**Feminism's unacknowledged problem,
visible from its inception, has been its
ascription of special virtue to women.**

In their questioning of separatism some women critics are
repudiating the privileged status of gender itself. Christine
Di Stefano (University of Washington) writes,

> For some writers, gender is no more and perhaps
> not even as basic as poverty, class, ethnicity,
> race, sexual identity, and age, in the lives of
> women who feel less divided from men as a
> group than, for example, from white or bour-
> geois or Anglo or heterosexual men *and* women.

According to *Feminism/Postmodernism,* the "essentialism" of a notion of "woman" that transcends history and
culture is currently perplexing the women's movement.
Claims that there are universal models of "the reproduction of mothering" (as in the work of Nancy Chodorow)
or that women in general have "a different voice" (as
Carol Gilligan has put it) can be and have been plausibly
accused of drawing wide conclusions about "women"
from samples drawn from a single culture or social class
or historical moment. The revisionist critics in Nicholson's collection can be seen as taking part in one of the perpetual outbreaks of nominalist skepticism against Aristo-
telian universalism. The "sect of one" is the logical reduction of the nominalist position, while the party line is the
logical end of the universalist position. The most cheering
thing, finally, about all political movements is their unsuppressible tendency to splinter, as their broad original manifestoes are more and more rigorously scrutinized.

The trouble lies not in feminist theory, which seems to be
questioning itself rather energetically, nor in the exploration of women's past, which is proceeding with both instructive and entertaining findings. Rather, as I have said,
the trouble lies in the actual practice of literary and cultural criticism. Before getting to my critical examples, I want
to mention briefly two typical exhumations of literary evidence, one disappointing, the other distinctly exhilarating.
The collection of excerpts [in *Women Writers of the Seventeenth Century*] by Katharina Wilson and the late
Frank Warnke offers little of interest to the modern English-speaking reader. These are not uninteresting women,
but the excerpts are short, the headnotes are long, and the
translations of poetry are ludicrous. . . . It is hard to

imagine a literature course based even in part on this collection of feeble writings, mostly in translation. Some of
them of are of evident biographical or historical interest,
but none has any literary distinction.

On the other hand, Roger Lonsdale's [*Eighteenth-
Century Women Poets: An Oxford Anthology*] is a pleasure to leaf through. Aside from a gratuitous comment
(seemingly borrowed from the English critic John Bar-
rell's *Politics, Language and Poetry*) disparaging Wordsworth's attitude toward his sister in "Tintern Abbey," the
collection is ably introduced and splendidly chosen. If one
discovers no major talents in it (nor does Lonsdale claim
that there are any), the book provides much evidence (especially by comparison with the volume of seventeenth-
century poetry) of the rise in the number of literate and
literary women in England between the seventeenth and
eighteenth centuries. The women were of course largely
self-educated, and most of them had fathers with large libraries (as, later, did Emily Dickinson and Virginia
Woolf); they were tutored or sent to school, were sponsored into print by male clergymen, teachers, relatives, or
fellow writers, and were financially supported either by
husbands, families, or subscribers to their books. Lonsdale
has passed over the unreadable epics, plays, and novels
composed by his authors in favor of their lyrics—evidence
of how leaden the weight of cultural topicality can be, and
of the superior survival value of the less topical lyric.

The light verse of the women tends to be better than their
"serious" verse, the domestic verse better than the public
verse. One comes across a good deal of reflection on the
lot of women, all sociologically interesting, and some revealing sidelights on women as oppressors of children and
servants. There is at least one nice specimen of woman-as-
bigot, Mary Alcock's criticism of Catholic Ireland: "How
blest would be Iërne's isle, / Were bigotry and all its guile
/ Chased as a cloud away." Social satire and self-irony
(typical properties, feminist criticism reminds us, of marginal people) are present in varieties ranging from the
mordant to the mocking. (pp. 21-2)

Feminism's unacknowledged problem, visible from its inception, has been its ascription of special virtue to women.
In its most sentimental form, feminism assumes that men,
as a class, are base and women are moral; in its angry version, that men are oppressors and women the oppressed.
This is to ignore what some cooler feminist minds have
suspected, that the possession of power, rather than
whether one is a woman or a man, is what determines the
act of oppression. Nina Auerbach lately quoted Florence
Nightingale: "I am sick with indignation at what wives
and mothers will do, the most egregious selfishness. And
people call it all maternal or conjugal affection and think
it pretty to say so." Some maternal cruelty may be explained on the grounds that the oppressed will oppress,
but a structural analysis of that sort ignores the contribution of temperament: there are choleric, sadistic, indifferent, and cold women just as there are such men. The home
is an almost wholly unsupervised theater of operations;
and the oppressions carried out by schoolmasters and prison guards are not incomparable with those carried out on

some children by their mothers during those long days when they are alone together.

That the violent physical abuse of children comes more frequently from men does not make any less reprehensible the character-destroying behavior—harshness, hatred, silence, and neglect—of some mothers. The abuse of power by both sexes, and the deficient moral behavior of both men and women to each other and to children, is the truth concealed by feminism; and feminism cannot represent itself as a movement with a redemptive purpose unless it acknowledges its own sentimentalizing of women. Feminism must bring itself to see women as victimizers as well as victims, as persons who are bigoted against men just as men are bigoted against them, as people oppressive to children in the way men can be oppressive to women or to children. To the extent that truth is preferable to cant, a de-idealizing of women is necessary for the women's movement. This in no way precludes protest of ill-treatment of women. But idealizing women falsifies one's tone toward them.

No matter how unintended, this falsity of tone pervades Carolyn Heilbrun's 1981 essay, **"Women, Men, Theories, and Literature,"** included in her recent collection of essays, *Hamlet's Mother and Other Women.* The essay ends with giddy praise of two courses Heilbrun and her colleague Nancy Miller gave together:

> In the (to me, at least) extraordinary dialogue that took place in the seminars between Miller and me and between us and our students, the dazzling Riffaterrian skills [of Miller] and the Trillingesque moral choices [on Heilbrun's part] illuminated one another. Each of us . . . became literally, and literarily, inspired to new and exciting work. Our excitement was increased by the knowledge that the economy of male domination, when deconstructed, when submitted to post-structuralist decodings by the most dazzling practitioners [presumably the dazzling Miller], reveals woman as the vital key. . . . We are dropping a bomb into the stable world of literary masterpieces.

Earlier, Heilbrun had said that "language has been a powerful social force, male, that undermines the autonomy of the individual, female." This may have been heady stuff for the seminar students, but it is not true. Language is certainly a powerful force in the hands of anyone who uses it well, whether Jane Austen or Shakespeare, but it is of itself neither male nor female, and it can as well affirm the autonomy of the female subject (think of Emily Brontë's "No Coward Soul is Mine") as deny it.

The description of "feminist teaching," as Heilbrun gives it, is just another version of the teaching of literature as moral propaganda—a method used earlier by other ideologues, on the right and left, for religious or political ends. Of course, students can be stirred by the univocal moral rhetoric of liberation, but is that what a literature class exists to purvey? What would Jane Austen and George Eliot, those skeptical intelligences, make of the rhetoric used by feminist critics on their behalf?

Nor do Heilbrun's other essays collected here suggest that

her students were being exposed to literary (rather than moral) judgments. I offer as evidence her comparisons of Woolf and Joyce. She makes bizarre remarks: had Leonard Woolf, she says, taken Virginia to a Freudian psychiatrist she would not have written her novels. The view of Woolf offered here depends on dubious statements, e.g., that the "great art of the patriarchy" taught "that anger is inimical to creation." One wonders what the creators of Lear, Sporus, and Satan might think of this idea.

Heilbrun opens her essay on Woolf and Joyce with Lionel Trilling's characterization of Joyce as "a man of the century into which he was born." She comments, "With Victorian patriarchs as with thieves, it takes one to know one." This was meant, perhaps, to be funny. Heilbrun then quotes Woolf showing diffidence about her powers, and calls Woolf's sentiment "that female diffidence, that lack of confidence which male writers do not experience." Has she read Keats's letters or his preface to *Endymion?* Wallace Stevens's journals? Hopkins's retreat notes? Herbert's poems?

Heilbrun continues, "But however modern Joyce's technique, his art was profoundly conservative" (as though to invent a radical new style were not to invent a radical new way of seeing). "The old cosmology" was all Joyce had to offer by way of substance, and he was therefore no threat to the established order:

> Academics could exercise upon him all their ingenuity and talent without having their central conventions or perceptions disturbed. As one critic [S. L. Goldberg, in 1961], admiring *Ulysses* but tired of all these technical interpretations, was to write: "He has nothing especially new to say about social or ethical or religious values; in many ways he seems old-fashioned."

Heilbrun adds, "In 1977, Philippe Sollers wrote that 'Not enough attention has been given to the fact that throughout his life Joyce wrote with money provided by women.'" (No mention is made of the fact that Virginia Woolf wrote with money partly provided by Leonard.) The essay closes with Woolf "raiding the inarticulate" because she has found new things to say, while "Joyce, in the same years, wanted a new way to say the same things, being no longer disposed to say them in the old way." If this is what a conversion to feminism does to the truth of Joyce's subversive anti-imperial reimagining of the English novel, then such conversions are, for literary criticism, lamentable.

Animus is not new in literary criticism, and perhaps it is natural for converts to be enthusiasts, both for and against. Yet the vulgarity of some of the recent literary criticism by feminists seems to me a new ingredient in critical writing. Perhaps it is meant as a sign of populist credentials ("We're not mandarins, we tell jokes and make low puns.") The prose style of the team of Sandra Gilbert and Susan Gubar, in their two-volume *No Man's Land: The Place of the Woman Writer in the Twentieth Century* (a third volume is to come) is the most serious obstacle to taking them seriously as writers on literature.

Consider the following deplorable passage, which begins with one of the all-purpose adjectival phrases the authors frequently use to cram information into a sentence, and which concludes with a repellent pun that directs us to a footnote:

> In practice, moreover, as the masterful mistress of a Paris salon comparable to the ones hostessed by such other literary Amazons as Edith Wharton and Natalie Barney, Stein set the scene and directed the action of just the (male) modernist experimentation that was to create the "twentieth century" as we know it. . . . From Freud's point of view, the "masculinity complex" could be carried no further. The father had been turned into a fat-her.

The appalled reader, turning to footnote 32, will read, "We are grateful to Molly Gubar for calling this linguistic possibility to our attention at the age of six." It is not hard to imagine what feminists would make of this remark about Gertrude Stein had it been made by a man. If "to hostess" is a new talk-show verb, I hope it has a short life. Moreover, to call Edith Wharton a "literary Amazon" is to forget that refinement, delicacy, and sorrow accompanied her energy and satiric force. And to pick up Shakespeare's bewildered but urbane self-defense from his angelic boy—"A woman's face . . . / Hast thou, the master-mistress of my passion"—and apply it to Stein "hostessing" her salon is to make a pointless and distracting allusion (a persistent and annoying tactic in the overstuffed sentences of *No Man's Land*).

Fat-her is not alone. "Da, ma, dada, mama, . . . one wonders whether even Derrida would like to be a Derri-ma"; "The sapphistries of artists were perquisites of aristocracy" (the pun seems to be borrowed from a book called *Sapphistry* by one Pat Califia). Because Rojack, the hero of Mailer's *An American Dream,* "sodomizes a German maid who has the suggestive name of *Ruta,*" Gilbert and Gubar pursue the matter further, saying, "Moreover, when this Ruta-rooter does find [another woman]," etc.

These few sentences from *No Man's Land* reveal on a small scale what the current two volumes demonstrate on a large one: Gilbert and Gubar have no clear idea what literary history can do, what it should do, how it should be written. This is a subject that has been commented on a good deal lately, by Hayden White and Geoffrey Hartman, among others. The amateurishness and slapdash quality of the literary history in *No Man's Land* is evident particularly in its lack of proportion. Literary historians of a century's writing by women in England and America cannot, without losing narrative momentum, insert mini-books on particular writers: forty pages on Kate Chopin, forty-five on Edith Wharton, forty-five on Willa Cather, twenty on Gertrude Stein. These leisurely and often boring chapter-long discussions on single writers sit ill with the attempt to gobble up entire eras in a single indigestible paragraph:

> The plot of sensual battle is of course as old as literature itself. From the legendary Lilith, who resists Adam's (and God's) wish to control both her body and her language, to the rebellious women of Aristophanes' *Lysistrata* and the mythical Amazons, . . . women have often been depicted as militants. . . . A long poem by the fourth-century Greek poet Quintus Smyrnaeus gives a characteristic account of the defeat of the Amazon Penthesilea. . . . Again, in Tasso's *Gerusalemme Liberata* (1580) the Christian hero Tancred unknowingly fights and kills Clorinda, an Islamic woman whom he loves.

The inclusiveness desired by the historian, and made possible by "research assistants" such as those amply thanked by Gilbert and Gubar in their preface, might excuse these summary paragraphs, were it not that the writing in the "leisurely" chapters is just as unreadable. Gilbert and Gubar are addicted to plot summary (issuing in a literary boredom second only to hearing dreams retold); but they are peculiarly incoherent when they summarize, having themselves no gift for narrative. (pp. 22-4)

Northrop Frye once said that he didn't believe in any of the ways of dividing up literature under thematic titles—women's writing, gay writing, black writing, and so on. Literature makes its own verbal universe, and its fundamental organizing structures are not documentary, thematic, or ideological ones.

Gilbert and Gubar necessarily come up against the well-documented fact that woman writers of talent tend to dislike second-rate work. Perhaps because every serious writer is afraid of slipping back into the easier word, the sentimental rendition, the cliché of convention, there is a strong reaction to that fear; many writers are vehement in their attacks on forms of literary corruption. But instead of seeing the repudiation of trash as a mark of literary integrity, Gilbert and Gubar invariably interpret it in their authors as "scorn," "contempt," "disdain," "hostility," or distrust toward other women. With respect to Willa Cather, they say, "Cather's critical statements raise interesting questions about the concept of female misogyny, for the intensity of her hostility implies that—as the old saying goes—it takes one to know one." They quote her (apparently just) criticism of Elizabeth Cady Stanton who, with an editorial committee, produced the "Women's Bible." Cather remarks on

> the temerity of these estimable ladies who, without scholarship, without linguistic attainments, without theological training, not even able to read the Bible in the original tongues, set themselves upon a task which has baffled the ripest scholarship.

To find this reasonable criticism repudiated by Gilbert and Gubar as misogyny is to confirm one's sense that truth-telling is endangered by the feminist imperative that "sisterhood" should make women "supportive" of the work of other women, no matter how shoddily done. Preferring psychological "supportiveness" or strategic political solidarity to truth, competence, and literary honesty is something that writers like Cather or Wharton cannot accede to without being false to themselves. Gilbert and Gubar's easy acceptance of banal and inept work puts them in a different category from Cather or Wharton. (p. 24)

Gilbert and Gubar exhibit the depressing refusal of judgment, or incapacity for judgment, that marks most political criticism when it trains its glance on its own partisans. Feminist critics have disparaged male historians for their "exclusions"; it is possible to blame feminist literary historians for their inclusions, and for their own misogyny toward women writers who recognize twaddle as twaddle and are not afraid to say so. . . .

Certainly any book on women's writing in the twentieth century should deal with the historical developments that interest Gilbert and Gubar—the rise of substantial numbers of women writers and the consequent representation of the sex war from both sides; a conspicuous literary lesbian subculture; the expansion of opportunities for women by women's suffrage and female work during World War I. But Gilbert and Gubar describe all this so chaotically, so vulgarly, and with so little sense of proportion, that these two volumes must seem, even to feminists, "aesthetically naive and excessively didactic" (to return to Felski's categories). We still lack a critical history of women's literary work in the twentieth century that is historically informed and has a plausible theory of art as well as an unsentimental view of women.

Perhaps the perspective of an untrodden field gives women literary historians their epic ambitions to cover everything. Camille Paglia's *Sexual Personae: Art and Decadence from Nefertiti to Dickinson* is an attempt (nonfeminist) at telling the story of the androgyne from ancient Egypt to the *fin de siècle*; this book bears an enthusiastic comment from Harold Bloom, once Paglia's dissertation adviser at Yale. Paglia's tour takes us from Spenser's Belphoebe and Britomart to Wilde's Cecily and Gwendolyn, with stops along the way for various writers and painters, and many examples of the beautiful boy syndrome. Paglia's conception of the androgyne in history is broad enough to produce the present subtitle: *Art and Decadence from Nefertiti to Emily Dickinson.* This would be a joke if it were not seriously intended.

Paglia's book raises the question of what counts as evidence in literary argument. The value of evidence has been called into question by the assumption, shared by both Marxist and postmodernist critics, that values are masks for vested interests, and that "taste" and "judgment" are coercive elitist gestures. The asserted relativism of literary value, bolstered by well-worn examples of historically fallible critical taste (actually minor in comparison to the sustained historical agreement on the talent of canonical authors) relieves such critics from the burden of evidence. Their conclusions are simply naked claims for their own interests—made, in Paglia's case, for seven hundred pages. "My method," says Paglia, "is a form of sensationalism," and her argument is that "Judeo-Christianity never did defeat paganism, which still flourishes in art, eroticism, astrology, and pop culture" (on which a second volume is promised). Cruelty (as in Sade) is a running theme through the book: Paglia asserts the necessity of cruelty (an intensified form of Apollonian art-order) to

hold back the "chthonian" forces embodied in Nature and "her" surrogate, woman. (pp. 24-5)

Paglia's impatience with the sentimentality of feminism blinds her to her own sentimentality toward the masculine, Jack the Ripper and all. Men have, she says, "concentration and projection," symbolized by their splendid capacity for projectile urination:

> Male urination really *is* a kind of accomplishment, an arc of transcendance [*sic*]. A woman merely waters the ground she stands on. . . . To piss is to criticize. John Wayne urinated on the shoes of a grouchy director in full view of cast and crew. This is one genre of self-expression women will never master. A male dog marking every bush on the block is a graffiti artist, leaving his rude signature with each lift of the leg. Women, like female dogs, are earthbound squatters.

The question begging of such a passage (What is transcendent about pissing? How is a dog an artist?) apparently does not bother Paglia; she goes on as if assertion were its own evidence. The most telling clue to Paglia's mind is her paragraph style: the sentences lack connection and syntactic subordination; they lie on the page like so many mutually repellent atoms, incapable of forming a molecular structure.

Northrop Frye once said that he didn't believe in any of the ways of dividing up literature under thematic titles—women's writing, gay writing, black writing, and so on. Literature makes its own verbal universe, and its fundamental organizing structures are not documentary, thematic, or ideological ones. The lifting of the documentary into the symbolic, of the thematic into the syntactic, is the task of art. Disregarding its most fundamental transformations does it poor service. Perhaps that is why books that round up literature behind thematic fences—religion, politics, women, sexual personae—are usually reductive of the genres they treat.

The skittish imagination mocks these attempts to bind it down; language's fertile misrule mocks such feeble taxonomies. The imp of the perverse, the Muse of the unpredictable next line, laughs, of course, at us all. But while criticism tags her footsteps, it needs to follow her with at least some respect for accuracy and evidence and considered judgment. It needs to understand the re-working of (and disregard for) the documentary that is necessary to literature's symbolic intent. Criticism might also aim for concepts and language that do not violate the supple aims of imaginative work. More highly evolved feminist criticism may be on the way, but it will have to go beyond its current practitioners' innocence about how the imagination works, and what it does. (p. 25)

Helen Vendler, "Feminism and Literature," in The New York Review of Books, *Vol. XXXVII, No. 9, May 31, 1990, pp. 19-25.*

Greg Johnson

[*The following review essay surveys several recent vol-*

umes of short stories by female authors as exemplary of feminist fiction in the 1980s.]

An anthology of short stories published in 1974, one intended to represent the best of women's writing in the late 1960's and early 1970's, bore an arresting but repellent title: ***Bitches and Sad Ladies: An Anthology of Fiction By and About Women.*** The book's editor, Pat Rotter, claimed in her introduction that the stories, written during a tremendous surge of progress for the women's movement, revealed a Janus-like dual identity for the contemporary woman: "They are two sides of the same coin, but when you spin the coin on its edge one side blurs into the other, just as . . . the bitch and sad lady blend into a multidimensional character. Woman." Yet this "multidimensional" woman is defined by her self-conscious reaction to inherited roles. The bitch claims autonomy and angrily rejects the subservient status of wife and mother, while the sad lady allows herself to be abused by men, accepting her masochistic embrace of subjugation as a normative version of conventional female dependency. Rotter's formulation is equivalent, of course, to the classic "double bind" to which feminist critics refer so often: a woman who capitulates to patriarchal suasion is lost, but one who refuses definition by others is immediately and harshly defined by that very refusal. She becomes the monstrous archetype of male fantasy, the castrating bitch, whose manifestations are as old as Western culture: the Siren with her irresistible beauty and murderous intentions, the Medusa with her paralyzing ugliness and phallic hair. Again, two sides of the same coin. Again, one multidimensional character known as Woman.

As feminist research has demonstrated, this double bind has been felt acutely by women daring to wield the phallic pen for the purpose of creating art, surely the most audacious—and thus conventionally masculine—of all human enterprises. Our country's most prominent feminist critics, Sandra Gilbert and Susan Gubar, have appended to the title of ***No Man's Land*** (their ongoing multivolume study of this century's English and American women writers) a telling subtitle: *The Place of the Woman Writer in the Twentieth Century.* The subtitle recalls old adages about "a woman's place," implies that women's writing necessarily has a distinct social and political identity in the literary history of this century, and suggests that the place for woman's writing must be brought—that is, forced—into being. In the twentieth century, Gilbert and Gubar write, "both women and men engendered words and works which continually sought to come to terms with, and find terms for, an ongoing battle of the sexes that was set in motion by the late nineteenth-century rise of feminism and the fall of Victorian concepts of 'femininity.' " Like such words and works, contemporary feminist theory is still in a searching, even primitive stage, defining terms and seeking an appropriate language by which to ask not-quite-formulated questions.

In times of explosive social change, which is mirrored by tremendous flux in aesthetic-literary theory, there will be heated disagreement even over which questions should be asked, and contemporary feminists have developed few common assumptions about the nature of the "woman writer," the characteristics of her art, or her political, so-

cial, and aesthetic goals. If Gilbert and Gubar's 1979 study, *The Madwoman in the Attic: The Woman Writer and the Nineteenth-Century Literary Imagination,* was widely acclaimed as a groundbreaking investigation, a major controversy arose over their *Norton Anthology of Literature by Women* (1985), which some critics (not all of them men) saw as a regressive ghettoization of women writers rather than as a needed incorporation of their work into the genderless ideal of "Literature by Writers."

Clearly, women who are both critics and accomplished fiction writers have tended to be skeptical of gender-specific responses to literature by women. Although Virginia Woolf apparently believed in (but never clearly defined) a basic difference between male and female sentence structure—discussed by Gilbert and Gubar under the rubric of "Sexual Linguistics"—Woolf also insisted in a 1924 essay, "Indiscretions," that the gender of great writers is "quite immaterial. They are not men when they write, nor are they women. They appeal to the large tract of the soul which is sexless . . . and man and woman can profit equally by their pages, without indulging in the folly of affection or the fury of partisanship." Similarly, in her recent (*Woman*) *Writer: Occasions and Opportunities,* Joyce Carol Oates considers the issue without lapsing into theoretical jargon or polemical fanfare: "When the writer is alone with language and with the challenging discipline of creating an art by way of language alone, she is not defined to herself as 'she'. . . . A woman who writes is a writer by her own definition; but she is a *woman* writer by others' definitions." Yet Oates adroitly notes that many male critics still ignore the bulk of literary achievements by women, and that women writers who themselves ignore the gender issue do so at their peril: "Better to be despised . . . than to be ignored; or damned with condescending praise." Or, in Pat Rotter's terms, better the angry militance of the bitch than the featureless ignominy and depression of the subservient sad lady.

Until the still-undefined "place" of the woman writer becomes a condition of autonomy unrelated to her gender and its predicaments, the continuing relevance of feminist criticism (including its anthologies and other manifestations) can hardly be questioned. To consider five volumes of short stories by women, then, is not to relegate several very different writers to a sexual ghetto, nor is it to assume that they write out of common experiences or for similar reasons. To discover what points of comparison do exist, however, can help to calibrate our cultural progress—or lack thereof—toward a time when "normative" will not mean "white, Christian, heterosexual male," but will simply mean "human." At that point, of course, the current fragmentation of literature into women's writing, black writing, gay writing, *et al.,* will seem a curious aberration in our cultural development.

For the present, we are in the midst of exciting change but also, depressingly often, mired in the inflated, self-conscious jargon that perhaps inevitably attends any "movement." Although dust-jacket copy is normally to be ignored when reviewing a book's contents, the bombastic hyperbole which Knopf has inflicted upon Janet Kauffman's slender collection, ***Obscene Gestures for Women,*** illustrates the problem so conspicuously that it cannot be overlooked. This jacket blurb warms up by reminding us of Kauffman's "now-fabled" first collection, *Places in the World a Woman Could Walk,* which "thrust this Michigan farmer to the forefront of her generation's concern with the business of restating the terms of literature and with discourse on feminist issues." We learn that this same Michigan farmer has also written a novel ("wherein the ancient debate between mother and daughter plays itself out to the end of speech") and that Kauffman, in this new gathering, presents "her heroic vision of a woman's lot as a succession of inexorable struggles to guarantee life to the self," a vision achieved by drawing "on the vocabulary that is ceaselessly delivered to her by her authentic experience with the land." (pp. 278-80)

It was only a matter of time, of course, before the jargon-riddled prose of current literary theory intersected with the old-fashioned American hard sell; in any case, it is difficult to imagine a more egregious—or more misleading—advertisement for Kauffman's book. This preliminary foolishness appears even more regrettable when one has read the stories, for Kauffman is a writer of modest but genuine talent who was probably embarrassed to find herself hurled toward "the end of speech." Originally published in magazines as various as *The New Yorker, The Paris Review,* and *Forehead,* these brief pieces show Kauffman as a wily experimenter in technique and form who nonetheless writes within a consistently narrow emotional range. Her better efforts, such as **"Machinery,"** "The Easter We Lived in Detroit," and **"Where I'd Quit,"** are powerful short takes on the survival of erotic and family life within a technocratic culture. Others, however, are simply too brief, and too self-conscious in their technical sleight of hand, to have much emotional resonance or staying power.

Kauffman's elliptical prose style is often appropriate to her knowing, weary characters and to her finely described settings in the rural Midwest. In **"Machinery,"** whose narrator begins by stating flatly, "I don't have a heart of steel," Kauffman shows that the steely determination of her women is only a surface hardness. The narrator is concerned about her teenage son, who expresses his rebellious nature by shoplifting. She disapproves of his interest in music, finding a more appropriate metaphor for life in the farm machinery she operates daily: "If he knew one machine, knew it backwards and forwards, he'd at least know more than himself." In **"Where I'd Quit,"** a machine-shop worker conducts an affair with a married woman, whom he meets near a large gully called "Eight Mile Drain." The story poignantly suggests the persistence of romance in even the unlikeliest settings, evoking the grace of temporary but genuine human connections. **"Marguerite Landmine"** also displays Kauffman's unique view of erotic relations, as in this description of Marguerite, an enigmatic performance artist, and her brief liaison with a young traffic cop. . . . In the final scene Marguerite, one of whose nicknames is "Marguerite Origami" because her favorite medium is paper, serves as an allegory of a woman fiction writer, triumphant in her autonomy but sadly detached from her own romantic art. (pp. 280-81)

Clearly, anger and stridency are out of fashion; but the muted, technically skillful prose found in the books under review suggests that aesthetic subtlety has effectively compensated for any lessened intensity in women's writing.

If this author would concern herself less with flashy technique than with her true strengths as a writer—especially her oblique studies of sexual and domestic relationships in the Midwest—she would do far more justice to her considerable talent.

In *After You've Gone,* Alice Adams' tenth book of fiction, the typical character is an intelligent, career-minded woman whose personal history includes a series of failed relationships with men. Her heroines tend to hold feminist ideals—generally they are self-supporting, intellectually autonomous, and politically liberal—but fail to practice these ideals when choosing and relating to their male partners. As the title of a recent bestselling self-help book would have it, they're smart women who make foolish choices. (The first clue to their emotional dependency, at times verging on desperation, is in the volume's title, which suggests wistful melancholy rather than jubilant independence.) The title story is representative: a successful lawyer has been abandoned by her handsome lover (a charismatic poet whom she has supported financially) in favor of a younger woman. An epistolary letter addressed to the poet but probably never mailed, **"After You've Gone"** is both sarcastic and affectionate, embittered and fair-minded. But if the woman's recollections and present resolve to do better suggest her intelligence and renewed self-esteem (she has since become involved with another man—"a more known quality than you were," she tells her former lover), they also betray her lingering investment in the past relationship.

Similarly, the heroine of **"On the Road,"** Brendan Hollowel, is a renowned scholar trapped in a loveless marriage to a Washington attorney. The story follows Brendan through one of her lecture tours, during which she is approached by a handsome stranger. She rebuffs him, but then finds herself "headed for the elevator, hurrying like a schoolgirl, or some classically frustrated, quite deranged spinster lady." Seeking solace in sisterhood, she discovers that her friendships with women are charged with negative rather than positive energy. "Aren't women supposed to be nicer to each other these days?" she asks herself in despair. "To be less rather than more competitive? In a discouraged way she decides that in some instances, at least, the grounds for competition have simply shifted, if ever so slightly." Like several others in this volume, this story seems to stop rather than end, with Brendan's conflicts still unresolved, her life quite likely to continue in the same melancholy groove. (pp. 282-83)

Although love generally brings to Adams' women the "Deep, irremediable scars" mentioned on the last page of

"A Sixties Romance," it also deepens their self-awareness and leads to a self-sufficient, if emotionally brittle, maturity. These women combine fragility and strength, and their emotional hesitations are effectively suggested by the author's prose style, which is both deft and delicate, ironic and questioning. With its numerous intelligent but melancholy ladies, and its equally numerous handsome heels to whom they seem in thrall, *After You've Gone* might well displease the most militant fringes of feminist criticism; but it's an honest, wise, and finely written book. (p. 283)

Two of the better stories in *Light Can Be Both Wave and Particle* [by Ellen Gilchrist] deal with childhood. In **"The Tree Fort"** and **"The Time Capsule,"** both set in the 1940's and featuring Rhoda Manning, Gilchrist evokes the mingled vulnerability and wayward vitality of children, as well as their capacity for wonder. **"The Tree Fort"** ends by emphasizing Rhoda's almost painfully intense physicality: "I was pure energy, clear light, morally neutral, soft and violent and almost perfect. I had two good eyes and two good ears and two arms and two legs. If bugs got inside of me, my blood boiled and ate them up. If I cut myself, my blood rushed in and sewed me back together." Another linked pair, **"The Starlight Express"** and the title story, are longer and more diffuse than the childhood reminiscences, but Gilchrist's intriguing plots and vivid characterizations help compensate for flaws in structure and narrative viewpoint. In **"The Starlight Express,"** a woman abandoned by her husband gives birth prematurely to twins in an isolated house, helped through the ordeal by Freddy, the man who genuinely loves her. On the way to meet Freddy, the woman has met a young Chinese-American medical student, Lin Tan Sing, who becomes in turn the hero of the volume's title story. The most likable and original character in the volume, Lin Tan falls in love with the daughter of a formidable American poet. Their romance is winsome, touching, and completely convincing; the two meet on a bridge overlooking Puget Sound, and the story finally suggests a harmonious marriage between East and West, between careful reason and honest emotion.

There is one other intriguing piece—"Traceleen Turns East," a briskly paced Southern Gothic tale of an armed kidnapper holding several New Orleans matrons at bay— but the volume is weakened by stories that are either too brief or too haphazardly written to have significant impact. In "The Song of Songs," for instance, a wealthy New Orleans woman meets the mother who had given her up for adoption as a child, but their reunion is presented matter-of-factly, with little sense of the emotional experience of either woman. "The Man Who Kicked Cancer's Ass" is a woeful example of "redneck chic," its male narrator a stereotypical Southern vulgarian who is enraged by his cancer diagnosis. But most disappointing is the novella-length **"Mexico,"** which concludes the volume. Another story dealing with Rhoda and her brother Dudley, "Mexico" presents her at age fifty-three, dissatisfied with her life and yearning for adventure and sexual intrigue. She, Dudley, and their cousin Saint John travel to Mexico, where Rhoda attends a bullfight and decides on the spot that she must sleep with the handsome young bullfighter. Although Rhoda is a potentially sympathetic character, a

woman whose hard-boiled exterior conceals a romantic longing to live her life to the hilt, Gilchrist has her heroine curse like a sailor, indulge in maudlin self-pity, and discuss her sex life in graphic terms with her brother and cousin. (pp. 283-84)

This is a perplexing volume, then, from a talented writer. In **"Mexico,"** and even in some of the more successful stories, Gilchrist seems to get carried away with her own breezy style and verbal facility. The stories read quickly and are often enjoyable, but they lack the meticulous thought and craft that make for the most memorable fiction.

Like Gilchrist, Bette Pesetsky has won critical praise for much of her early work, which includes three novels and a 1982 collection, *Stories Up to a Point*. Her new book, ***Confessions of a Bad Girl,*** bears comparison with Gilchrist's in a number of ways. Pesetsky's volume also includes several linked stories: the first half of the book, entitled "Confessions," portrays Cissie and Sylvester, a brother and sister who are coping with a chaotic family life in Milwaukee; and another family called the Spacedons, a strange household which includes four adult children, all of whom are adopted. The volume's second and shorter half, "Bad Girl," offers a miscellany of outwardly successful women whose tough exteriors belie their emotional bewilderment and lack of self-understanding. Although Pesetsky's prose is much sparer than Gilchrist's, lacking in lyricism or introspection of any kind, these pieces also seem, at times, glibly and haphazardly written. Two or three of the stories are impressive, but most of them fail because Pesetsky's disjointed narrative structures preclude the reader's involvement with her characters and because the emotional tactics of her typical women are off-putting rather than poignant. Pesetsky often seems on the verge of going beneath the tough, knowing exterior of her characters, but for some reason she seldom takes the plunge.

In **"The Prince of Wales,"** a coming-of-age story focused on Cissie, Pesetsky's emotionally oblique manner works fairly well. The teenaged Cissie is invited to a wedding reception for a young woman who has scandalized her Milwaukee neighborhood by marrying an "old butcher—an ancient, withered man." The climactic scene echoes Katherine Mansfield's famous story, "Her First Ball," as the butcher dances Cissie wildly around the room: "He had worn me out. I found an empty chair, my chest heaving and the sound of seashore waves in my ears. I focused on old landmarks—the blistering paint, the ceiling-crack, the striations in the third glass globe that swayed from its chain." Like Mansfield's protagonist, Cissie refuses to see anything but romantic excitement in this dance, even though it is clearly based on an old man's lechery. The ironic contrast between what Cissie sees and what the author shows the reader is effectively chilling. But in subsequent stories Pesetsky narrates much of Cissie's life in a deliberately offhand, casual style that serves only to alienate the reader. (pp. 281-85)

One of the few stories that delves into a character's emotional life is focused not upon Cissie but upon her brother. In **"Penny and Willie,"** Pesetsky shows Sylvester mired in the confusions of family life, becoming increasingly alien-ated from his daughter and wife. In a touching effort to bring the family together he buys a dog, but the tactic fails: Penny drops out of college to marry a boyfriend and move to California, and soon afterward Joyce asks Sylvester to move out. As the years pass and he drifts in and out of var-ious affairs, the one stable element in his life is the dog Wil-lie. The final scene focuses poignantly upon "Willie, a constant of love," and in a final wrenching twist suggests the future loneliness of Sylvester's life. (p. 286)

Like Ellen Gilchrist, Bette Pesetsky is clearly a talented writer: she has a fine comic sense, a remarkable feel for the discontinuities of family relationships, and an ability to focus on seemingly small but pivotal moments in her char-acters' lives. Yet these virtues work fitfully in *Confessions of a Bad Girl.* Pesetsky's quick-moving, restless style com-bines with her formal experimentation (the very brief, truncated scenes, the swift hurtling through time) to put her characters at a distance; the reader often feels that he is viewing them through a telescope, and hopes in vain that the author will bring them closer.

There is no such frustration in reading Nancy Huddleston Packer's *The Women Who Walk,* in which lucid, adroitly controlled narratives soon bring the reader into intimate contact with the emotional quandaries of the characters. Like Alice Adams' protagonists, Packer's tend to be aban-doned or otherwise mistreated women; their angry resent-ment often has a savage intensity. In **"Saturday People,"** a divorced woman's rage at her ex-husband keeps her life in constant turmoil. After indulging in a sarcastic tirade during one of their phone conversations (they have ongo-ing arguments over his custodial visits with their young daughter), the woman hears herself: "The whiney shrill-ness of my voice seemed to echo from every corner of the room. I stood holding the phone, trembling, suddenly ashamed at how my self-pity, my self-righteousness, domi-nated me." (pp. 286-87)

Although Packer's material may be the stuff of melodra-ma, her crisp, straightforward prose and her deft explora-tion of emotional conflict give this volume its luster of hard-won objectivity and wisdom. Even her most desper-ate women recognize their self-destructive behavior as ir-rational and temporary, and many are too intelligent not to glimpse a way out. The most common route is through sympathetic communion with others: the mother's affec-tion for her daughter in "Saturday People"; Marian's identification in "The Women Who Walk" with a mysteri-ous woman she sees wandering the streets of her neighbor-hood. The excellent "Breathing Space" also makes use of a doppelgänger figure as another divorced woman at-tempts to cope with her emotionally disturbed young daughter, whose irrationally mocking and sarcastic atti-tude toward her mother comes to represent the latter's own repressed anger and sense of futility.

The only major weakness in Packer's stories is that they often follow a somewhat predictable track: in "The Day the Tree Fell Down," a bickering couple's argument over a fallen tree adroitly reveals the conflicts in their marriage, but it concludes with a reconciliation scene that will sur-prise few readers; "Lousy Moments," an otherwise excel-

lent and darkly funny story about the travails of a creative-writing professor, simply stops rather than ends. Even in "Breathing Space," the closing exchange between the mother and her institutionalized daughter has been tele-graphed several pages in advance. However, there are no-table exceptions to this problem of endings. **"Making Amends,"** perhaps the volume's finest story, dramatizes a brief reunion—a dinner meeting in a dimly lit restau-rant—between a woman and the charismatic lover who had abandoned her many years earlier. Though the lover was (and still is) little more than a gigolo, Packer skillfully conveys his considerable charm and the woman's emo-tional vulnerability. Although the man is ostensibly just "making amends" for caddish behavior in the past, it's soon clear that he is attempting to seduce the woman once again, and that she may well succumb. Despite its simple plot, the story develops an extraordinary suspense as it dramatizes the subtle interplay between these former lov-ers, focusing on the woman's internal conflicts between anger and longing, autonomy and desire. The final scene more than fulfills a generally accepted criterion for the short-story form: it is both surprising and exactly right.

Considering these five volumes of stories as a whole, one might complain that this element of surprise is generally lacking; but this is only to say that these books are prod-ucts of the 1980's, a time when conservatism and retrench-ment characterized even a genre previously known for boldness and idiosyncrasy. These volumes suggest that the accelerated progress of the women's movement in the 1960's and 1970's—like the fictional experimentation tak-ing place during those same years—has perhaps required a slow-down, a time for processing and self-examination. Clearly, anger and stridency are out of fashion; but the muted, technically skillful prose found in the books under review suggests that aesthetic subtlety has effectively com-pensated for any lessened intensity in women's writing. A current anthology of stories by women could hardly be called *Bitches and Sad Ladies*: increased political and eco-nomic power have channeled the rage, while heightened self-esteem and awareness of gender bias has dissipated the sadness. Thus, today's best women writers tend to be master ironists rather than shrill polemicists or unhappy complainers. Fortunately, the current mood of thoughtful reassessment has fostered the recognition that the virtues of good writing are constant, whether or not a particular work is fueled by a distinct ideology or a collective anger. At their best moments, these five very different writers show clearly that writing well is still the best revenge. (pp. 287-88)

Greg Johnson, "Some Recent Herstories," in The Georgia Review, *Vol. XLIV, Nos. 1 & 2, Spring-Summer, 1990, pp. 278-88.*

Janice Williamson

[*In the essay excerpted below, Williamson offers a Cana-dian academic's perspective on the progress of feminism and the role of feminist critics in Canadian universities.*]

The University of Calgary English Department poster which announced my exchange scholar talk was tacked to my office door for a single day when someone inscribed a provocative 'x' through the word 'nice'. With the qualifier 'nice' x-ed out, the feminist subject was *sous rature*. The writing was on the wall, but how was I to decode the signature? Was this feminist or anti-feminist écriture? Could it be the initiation of a sacred holiday—a western feminist passover? Perhaps it was merely the sign of a theoretically inclined student or colleague? I concluded Jacques Derrida was on a clandestine western Canadian tour since the Derridean notion of 'erasure' draws attention to the 'other' in the sign 'nice,' that which is 'not-nice' in feminism. My thesaurus reorients me to this concept—the entry for 'not-nice' reads:

> . . . bad, ill, arrant, as bad as bad can be, dreadful; horrid, horrible; rank, peccant, foul, fulsome; rotten,—at the core,. . . . hateful,—as a toad; abominable, detestable, execrable, cursed, accursed, confounded; damned, infernal; diabolic, unprofitable, incompetent, and irremediable.

In light of this 'bad as bad can be,' how is the concept 'feminist' destabilized by this nixed 'nice'? Questions about the feminist come to mind:

Is she nice? Furious? White? A woman of colour? Middle class? Lesbian? Working Class? Theoretical? Action-oriented? Political? Cooperative? Difficult? Heterosexual? Serious? Amusing? Soft-spoken? Furious? Well-suited? Bisexual? Dressed like a feminist? Privileged? Struggling? Disciplined? Interdisciplinary? Different? Like me? Defensive? On the offensive? Offensive? Authoritarian? Democratic? Well balanced? In process? In the movement? On the move? Well put together? Natural? Made up? Furious? Feared? Derided? Masculine? A real woman?

Feminist voices are in contra-diction, they 'speak against' each other and often lead to angst or irony, the latter inspiring the title of my paper, an interrogative restatement of American feminist Pauline B. Bart's autobiographical title, 'Being a Feminist Academic: What a Nice Feminist like Me is Doing in a Place like This.' Some of the contradictions the feminist turns inside, she shares with others. German critical theorist Theodor Adorno's offered recognizable 'reflections from damaged life':

> When oppositional intellectuals endeavour [. . .] to imagine a new content for society, they are paralysed by the form of their own consciousness, which is modelled in advance to suit the needs of this society.

For the feminist critic/teacher/writer, the contradictions involve an interior splitting when 'the form of [. . .] our own consciousness becomes an aspect of our inquiry.' The editors of the feminist journal *Signs* describe 'the curious doubleness of gender' in feminist scholarship:

> We are our own subject matter as, and because, women or Woman is our subject matter; we live and think and write within the gender constructs about which we think and on which we work.

This implicated terrain of intellectual inquiry and self-analysis has helped feminists develop complex critiques of gender and subjectivity which privilege contradiction. However the feminist professor herself is supposed to be preeminently a non-contradictory subject. On the one hand, feminist critics can be dismissed by non-feminists as one-dimensional—too narrow in interest and expertise. Alternatively, politically sympathetic students and colleagues demand congruence between theory and practice. We ask ourselves how we measure up to feminist ethical standards, standards which are often non-specific, unspoken, and certainly ideal. There are pre-conceived notions about what feminists are supposed to look like, how we are supposed to behave or dress, and what kind of language we should speak.

Academic feminists function within professional economics which encourage, support and privilege individualist initiatives over collective intellectual work. The liberal humanist tradition tends to glorify the solitary scholar and artist over a more communitarian model of intellectual and creative life. Structurally, the institutional procedures for rewarding productivity and organizing curriculum make it difficult for colleagues to collaborate together. In this already atomized setting, the feminist is often isolated in a department where she stands out as an exception to the rule rather than someone connected to a social movement and the collective action which marks part of the feminist difference.

Ideally, the academic feminist develops a double discourse which allows her to address critical issues within and outside her field of study while she also translates and participates in conversations between feminists who may or may not have access to her critical vocabulary.

When there are groups of self-identified feminists, other tensions can come into play. In a review, Margaret Atwood described Ontario poet Bronwen Wallace as a 'second-generation' feminist [who assumes] . . . unselfconsciously and as something given or known by the reader, positions that earlier poets had to hammer into shape in a much more step-by-step, laborious and sweaty manner.' A similar intergenerational diversity has developed within the academy. A new generation of women whose feminism developed within the activist second wave of the women's movement is taking its place alongside solitary trailblazing feminists who were politicized and made their mark within the male-dominated academy. These diverse feminist histories sometimes lead to painful revelations about different priorities and strategies. A hierarchy of interests can develop between various feminist positions, interests which often privilege less radical reform-minded solutions to problems. [In a footnote, the critic states that "Catherine Heilbrun represents one of the critical differences in feminist approaches. Her liberal vision of feminist activism includes moderating notes on institutional decorum: 'without acting or feeling like revolutionaries determined to overthrow the establishment, we can propose a new view of the world.' 'Women, Men, Theories, and Literature,' *The Impact of Feminist Research in the Academy,* 1987. More alarmingly, K. K. Ruthven's book *Feminist Literary Studies: An Introduction,* 1984, suggests that feminist criticism emerges out of a critical space inhabited at times by feminist 'vigilantes' like Monique Wittig."] On the other hand, a vanguardist notion of change within the academy doesn't necessarily take into account the painful lessons learned by those women with institutional experience. As our feminist students assume their places alongside us in the universities, the potential polarization of generations will undoubtedly be diluted by more varied approaches marking new intellectual and political formations. (Implicit in these observations is an optimism that feminists will become more rather than less numerous in the academy.)

Feminist scholarship and pedagogy are part of a continual process of self-consciousness raising, a process whereby the demands of feminist praxis—a collective, caring and politicized activity—are challenged not only in the institutional structures of the academy but through the workplace socialization which the feminist critic has undergone during her own academic disciplining. [Williamson adds in a footnote that this "disciplining has been analyzed by Dorothy Smith in terms of professionalization. 'The professional discourse [develops] . . . a momentum of its own. The structures which have been developed have become the criteria and standards of proper professional performance. Being a professional involves knowing how to do it this way and doing it this way is how we recognize ourselves as professionals. The perspective of men is not apparent as such for it has become institutionalized as the "field" or the "discipline" '. 'An analysis of ideological structures and how women are excluded: consideration for academic women,' *Canadian Review of Sociology and Anthropology,* 1975."] The tension between feminist theory and embodied practice continues throughout one's academic career. In offering 'some suggestions about how to do theory that is not imperialistic, ethnocentric, [or] disrespectful,' Maria C. Lugones and Elizabeth V. Spelman ask:

> When we speak, write, and publish our theories, to whom do we think we are accountable? Are the concerns we have in being accountable to 'the profession' at odds with the concerns we have in being accountable to those about whom we theorize? Do commitments to 'the profession,' method, getting something published, getting tenure, lead us to talk and act in ways at odds with what we ourselves (let alone others) would regard as ordinary, decent behaviour?

Since systemic racism effectively replicates white privilege within the academy, most women academics are white and authorized to speak from their dominant racial position. While marked by these and other exclusions, feminism within the university has opened a discursive space, an ongoing conversation between women about Woman and women. These conversations enable us to discuss our diverse politics, our differing experiences—to agree and to disagree. According to Columbia University's Nancy Miller, this conversation 'acknowledges our ongoing contradictions, the gap, and the (perhaps permanent) internal split that makes a collective identity or integrity only a ho-

rizon, but a necessary one.' In Alberta, horizons have serious perceptual implications. In response to Miller's scepticism, I'm more optimistic about the development of a sense of collectivity, however situational and provisional. Conversations between women illuminate different relationships to feminism itself. Many feminists have theorized their politics and practice within different feminist ideological paradigms. We call ourselves liberal feminist, radical feminist, psychoanalytic or socialist feminist; or we imagine the unimaginable, a feminism outside of ideology. [Williamson adds in a footnote that some "feminist theorists abandon these ideological categories in favour of a serenely critical vocabulary, i.e. a 'feminist semiotician,' or a 'psychoanalytic feminist.' However, this tendency can simply void feminist critical theory of any political agenda, an avoidance which ignores the engaged historical genealogy of feminism. On the other hand, a competitive hierarchy of feminisms has its own limitations. Rosalind Delmar describes the tendency of one feminist ideological framework, i.e. liberal, socialist, or radical, to vilify others as a 'sort of sclerosis of feminism.' 'What is Feminism?', *What is Feminism?,* eds. Juliet Mitchell and Ann Oakley, 1975."] Borders blur and realign. Categories continually multiply indicating the critical engagement and energy of feminist theorizing and its interdisciplinary roots in political theory, philosophy and cultural studies.

> Since feminism begins at home, so to speak, as a collective reflection on practice, on experience, on the personal as political, and on the politics of subjectivity, a feminist theory exists as such only insofar as it refers and constantly comes back to these issues. [Teresa de Louretis]

In an early critique, socialist feminist Lillian Robinson asked whether feminist criticism was politically 'engaged' or 'merely engaged to be married, . . . simply bourgeois criticism in drag.' To be effective, Robinson argued, feminist criticism 'must be ideological and moral criticism; it must be revolutionary.' The consequences of this commentary become more serious when one considers the potential deradicalization of feminism within the academy. This is not to suggest that intellectual critical work and theory are necessarily disconnected from some primary ground of feminist activity. Feminist theorists along with 'other postmodern philosophers . . . [raise] important metatheoretical questions about the possible nature and status of theorizing itself.' With its commitment to social transformation, feminist interventions make changes in the social organization of knowledge and (ideally) the way institutions work. In a parallel universe, feminist praxis in the streets develops through its own active thinking and redefinition of issues. One of the early signs of this theorizing in action was the development of two apparently contradictory discourses about women's liberation. On the one hand, equal rights arguments provided a basis for thinking through issues like pay equity; on the other hand, an insistance on gendered specificity provided the critical difference to argue for free-standing abortion clinics.

Feminist work tends to address different constituencies or communities. We write for fellow travellers, specialists in the field. As well, we address feminists who work in other disciplines or in non-academic settings. While there are many feminists outside the academy who debate theoretical questions, the feminist within the academy is identified as split off from others in a false dichotomy between academy and community. Ideally, the academic feminist develops a double discourse which allows her to address critical issues within and outside her field of study while she also translates and participates in conversations between feminists who may or may not have access to her critical vocabulary. The complexity of contemporary Canadian cultural politics has meant voices perceived to be speaking 'from the margins' have recently demanded self-critique and analysis from those at the 'centre.' Significant feminist issues have thus emerged as public discussions about writing and representation, cultural appropriation, and the politics of racism. (pp. 35-40)

There is a generalized perception of feminism in English Studies as a limited field rather than a series of widely varying critical practices. There remains a 'fear of the f word feminism,' a fear which sometimes leads to trivialization and dismissal. Unless English Studies attends seriously to its own critical gaps, nothing more substantial than stopgap tokenism will be possible when it comes to both female and feminist colleagues. The sorry statistics of the representation of women in the academy are magnified when we consider the absence of visible minorities and aboriginal peoples in our intellectual communities. In the familiar hierarchy of interests, there is a pyramid of gender and race narrowing to little representation of non-white non-males at the top. In the University of Alberta Department of English, more than twice as many overworked, underpaid, short-term contracted sessionals are women. While the discipline is dominated by female students, one-quarter of the tenured and tenurable faculty are women, and this ratio is far better than in many other institutions. Studies suggest that women's position is worsening rather than improving in Canadian universities. In spite of this, efforts to improve the status of women in the academy are often met by a violent rhetoric of resistance. (p. 40)

The entrance of more feminists into the academy and the growth of feminist intellectual work lead to unsettling insights. Embedded in the work of academic feminists is an affirming commitment to struggle as a feminist in a recalcitrant patriarchal institution. This requires a necessary scepticism about the position of feminism(s) within such an institutional context. In addition, feminist academics belong to the professional class. Most full-time university professors' earnings are in the top 4 per cent of Canadian women's income. Thus, there is a split between the working middle-class of women (translate this into upper class on a comparable male wage scale) and the often impoverished and sometimes dependent economy of most women. Other doubts have been raised by feminist scholars. Keith Louise Fulton comments that 'we have learned from experience that it is far easier for our goals to be subsumed and changed by the institutions than for the institutions to be redirected and changed by our goals.' Constance Penley observes that many feminists

> believe that the university can greatly benefit from incorporating feminism into the curriculum . . . [but] are more dubious about what feminism receives in turn from its new-found ac-

ademization. [These doubts] . . . include the debilitating effects of the continuing entrenched sexism of the university, the loss of feminist theory's political radicalness through the attempt to ensure its academic respectability, and the creation of an 'elite' of feminist scholars who take their research cues from the university rather than the movement.

Unchanging sexist structures underpin concerns about the appropriation of feminist politics and provide enabling ground for self-criticism. But what would be lost were feminists to simply abandon the academic workplace?

Students develop their feminist critique along a variety of paths: through painful revelations about their own lived experience of the violence or exclusionary tactics of patriarchal institutions; through enabling feminist sisters or mothers or friends who provide alternate female identities and perspectives; or through the insights gained in feminist activism, cultural production and classrooms. The process of 'consciousness raising' can be temporarily immobilizing as the woman recognizes over and over and over again the patterns of inequity and discrimination which extend across gender, race, class, sexuality and ability lines. The feminist professor can provide experienced support and a space for thinking through feminism as an 'old age' practice. (pp. 41-2)

Literary historians like Chris Baldick [in his *The Social Mission of English Criticism 1843–1932*, 1983] have noted how literary studies developed in the nineteenth century in response to the

> needs of the British empire expressed in the regulations for admission to the India Civil Service; . . . the various movements for adult education [for the working class; and] within this general movement, the specific provisions made for women's education.

It would thus seem ironic that the colonized, the working class and women have been so ill-served by traditional English Studies. According to Baldick's research, English Studies was 'not designed to emancipate but to confirm women in their established roles.' F. D. Mauris in his 1855 Lectures to Ladies on Practical Subjects (1855) announced that '[Women] need education, not only to show them what they can do, but what they cannot do and should not attempt.' The leap from this nineteenth-century cautionary advice to a contemporary feminist's classroom in the English Department at the University of Alberta is a long one, but one which may elaborate some critical gaps.

Until recently, feminist critics, theorists, teachers and writers were told that their work was unscholarly and not worth pursuing. Now that trading in the literary marketplace has announced a bull-market in feminism's stock, we might reflect on this change of institutional heart and ask how this affects pedagogy and scholarly practice. According to an analysis of the publication history of articles on women and women's issues in fifty 'central disciplinary journals' of history, literature, education, philosophy and anthropology between 1966 and 1980, the number of articles on women rose from an average of 2.05 of the total number of articles published 1966-70 to an average of 5.31 between 1976-80. The authors commented that 'while one can see the marks of a feminist consciousness working within the field of literary studies, we are surprised by the weakness of the trends we have discerned in literature.' In literary studies the percentage of articles on women rose an average of 2.72 percent from 1966-80 to 7.49 percent of the total number of articles published.

While curriculum development might restrict the number of women writers taught in an english department, students are demanding more feminist studies. In the University of Alberta English Department, more than half of the Honours tutorials requested by students in 1989 were on women authors and feminist theory. Feminist libraries are in circulation among female and male colleagues whose work now necessitates a familiarization with feminist literary criticism.

Male colleagues whose courses until recently have been restricted to male-dominated literary canons are now proposing courses on feminist topics. This recent positive development has its limitations. The confusion of 'style' with 'gender' issues in the appropriation of 'woman' in poststructuralist theory can be read as a symptom of uninformed masculist readings of feminist topics. In addition, there is the potential for feminist analysis to be peripheral rather than developed as part of the elaborate and substantial history of engaged feminist thinking. In some cases, male academics teach these courses because there are not enough tenured or tenurable feminist women available to direct them, unwittingly participating in the perpetuation of gender inequity in hiring. In other cases, feminist faculty are deliberately overlooked and non-feminist faculty are assigned 'women's' courses in an attempt to diffuse the transformative implications of feminist critique. This development is particularly disturbing in the current classroom situation where feminist students are subject to harrassment by non-feminist faculty. Our culture's hysterical response to and 'demonology' of feminism, which [in 1989] informed the brutal slaying of 14 University of Montreal women engineering students identified as 'a bunch of feminists,' is part of an anti-feminist zeitgeist which demands the instructor make a safe place for feminist discourse within the classroom.

What is the critical gap that emerges when women do not have the opportunity to teach in the classroom? First, for the feminist, social justice issues are significant. Why should we participate in perpetuating institutional practices which replicate the structural inequities of society in general and deny eligible women work? Second, affirmative action in the university has implications which reach far beyond the corporate employment model. Our role includes producing knowledge and helping to develop critical thinking in our students. Public discourse is shaped all too often in the narrow corridors of a blinkered singular perspective. Male-based research and attitudes do not provide an adequate knowledge base for critically thinking citizens of both genders. When we look inside the classroom, it matters which gender or race is leading the discussion. Studies have shown that conversational dynamics virtually depend upon the gender of the instructor: female

students speak more often when their instructor is female. We also know that the presence of visible minority teachers determines the length of time visible minorities continue their studies. Feminist criticism and theory has translated feminist politics into new and different conversations between English Studies colleagues, between disciplines, between academic and non-academic communities, and between professor and student. Within this context feminist pedagogy becomes a site of transformation. (pp. 44-6)

> Students develop their feminist critique along a variety of paths: through painful revelations about their own lived experience of the violence or exclusionary tactics of patriarchal institutions; through enabling feminist sisters or mothers or friends who provide alternate female identities and perspectives; or through the insights gained in feminist activism, cultural production and classrooms.

Social and political theorist Patricia Elliot 'remodels' our conception of the feminist professor proposing that we are 'a friendly guide in a foreign country.' Like guides we have special 'knowledge the student does not (yet) possess. Although [our] power of judgement is considerable and the relationship between student and teacher is necessarily unequal, it is also a relationship which has as its goal the sharing of knowledge and the empowerment of the student.' In order to avoid the colonizing gaze of the tourist, this useful model can be revised to include a reciprocal process whereby the feminist teacher is also 'a strange guide in familiar territory.' For we rewrite the familiar as unfamiliar, making temporarily strange what students have come to accept as common sense.

For instance, students have conceptual models which organize how they approach literature, models which have been tidily constructed in their schooling. Patrocinio Schweickart notes the narrow conceptual field of traditional English Studies and points to 'the challenge of diversity.' She writes about how 'hostile' students of literature become when confronted with feminist issues. Her students felt 'cheated because the discussion of the issues of race and gender interfered with the 'larger issues'—the critical approaches to literature—that [they] had come to the course to learn.' This hierarchy of interests reflects a learned disciplined response predicated on erasing difference, minimizing specificity and silencing contextual issues. Feminist pedagogy means that qualitatively different conversations develop within the class. Structurally, the passive mode of knowledge production based on the parenting model of teacher as authority can be interrupted by small group discussion, a process which requires intricate interpersonal choreography in order to affect a genuine exchange of ideas from as many students as possible. Curriculum changes which introduce courses like 'Writing by Native and Black Women Writers' call into question traditional canonical structures, even those mobilized in alternative courses on a 'women's literary tradition' which may encode ethnocentric exclusions. Alternative writing assignments such as journals create different relationships to the sharp division between personal experience and intellectual work. As well, integrating women's texts and feminist critical readings into general English Studies courses is part of the process of 'feminizing' the discipline.

In analysing feminist texts, a different mode of reading is necessary in order to apprehend how it tends to transgress and exceed traditional boundaries. Within many traditional English Departments, outmoded genre hierarchies tend to undervalue writing which blurs genre distinctions between academic and 'creative' work even though these boundaries have been challenged by major contemporary critical practitioners. Linda Hutcheon writes that

> it is a truism of contemporary criticism that the seriously playful textuality of the writing of Derrida or the fanciful fragments of the later works of Barthes, for instance, are as literary as they are theoretical. . . . Postmodern representational practices that refuse to stay neatly within accepted conventions and traditions and that deploy hybrid forms and seemingly mutually contradictory strategies frustrate critical attempts . . . to systematize them, to order them with an eye to control and mastery—that is, to totalize.

For many feminists, the apparent seamlessness of the literary genre, the traditional object of study, splits and unravels. Louise Dupré insists on a different mode of reading feminist texts forcing us to 'think further.' . . . The 'fiction-theory' of Nicole Brossard, the 'gynanthropic' texts of Louky Bersianik, the 'essay in process' of Gail Scott, the 'ficto-criticism' of Aritha van Herk, and the 'theograms' of Betsy Warland provide some indication of the contemporary Canadian women writer's desire to push the reader and writing 'plus loin.' In refusing distinctions between abstract theorizing, fiction or autobiography, they offer embodied textual alternatives which derive from theoretical issues and remake theory.

For many women writers, the distinction between oral testimony and literary work can be particularly vexing. Different topics of conversation emerge. The study of the 'aesthetic' and 'literary' tends to isolate literature from other forms of cultural production like popular writing or government documents where rhetorical flourishes and structural conventions encode ideology about our culture's constructions of gender, race, class and sexuality. In order to read many women's texts, the literary gives way to 'writing' or expands from the written to oral testimony by non-artists. The double-voiced poem 'Where the Sky is a Pitiful Tent' by Claire Harris is a textual dialogue between Harris' poetic discourse and the oral testimony of Guatamalan revolutionary Rigoberto Menchu provides a powerful reminder of the politics and powers of difference. The literary canon may also expand into a reading of 'nonliterary' texts, such as Makeda Silvera's *Silenced Talks with Working Class West Indian Women About Their Lives and Struggles as Domestic Workers in Canada.* In *Rivers Have Sources, Trees Have Roots: Speaking of Rac-*

ism, Dionne Brand and Krisantha Sri Bhaggayadatta analyse Canadian racism through oral testimonies of those who have restricted access to the cultural production privileged in Canadian literary studies. By listening to diverse stories, we can begin to understand the relation between a white Anglo-Celt culture and the native cultural heritage whose storytelling can shift with exquisite dexterity from stories about women's actual and mythological role in the traditional Sundance to contemporary accounts of Alberta's racism or the status of women within native communities. However, a cautionary note [in Nancy Armstrong and Leonard Tennenhouse's *The Violence of Representation: Literature and the History of Violence*] reminds the critic of what is at stake in contemporary critical readings of non-canonical texts:

> Whatever happens to cultural information when it becomes literature is happening with alarming reach and speed across vast territories of cultural space and time, thanks in part to the new interest in culture criticism and the institutional encouragement it has been receiving. In the name of doing non-canonical work, scholars throughout the humanities and social sciences have been extending literary critical methods into new areas which have never been read that way before. . . . They have brought new understanding of the heterogeneity of any culture, including our own, and have clearly done much to revise traditional categories of period, style and genre. But they have also scooped out these materials and incorporated them within contemporary academic discourse. We should be concerned, then, to ensure that our political self-consciousness keeps pace with the rapidly increasing use of certain interpretive procedures for reading other areas of our culture and cultures other than ours.

How do we maintain this critical self-consciousness? How do we read the cross-cultural social text? In a front-page cutline and photograph of Iranian women, the issues which circulated around Salman Rushdie's self-exile surface. This international crisis revealed racist ideology and unmasked other relations of power and domination. Censorship laws administered by the state were acknowledged as dangerous when Brian Mulroney announced that Canada had been internationally disgraced for appearing to 'ban' Rushdie's *The Satanic Verses.* This reading of the Rushdie crisis orients us to the relationship between the state and censorship and the tendency for a liberal political agenda about equal rights to overtake any critique of racism.

The cutline under the photograph of the Iranian women helps to make sense of the photograph and its relation to racism, but neglects to note that these "students" are women. It simply orients our attention to 'the other' of Iran and the exotic mysteries of women in the chador. To point to feminist criticism as a definitive anti-racist anti-colonialist discourse is to mythologize feminism's history. Like other western scholarship, feminist critical writings can [according to Chandra Mohanty in "Under Western Eyes: Feminist Scholarship and Colonial Discourses"]

> discursively colonize the material and historical

heterogeneities of the lives of women in the third world, thereby producing / re-presenting a composite, singular 'Third World Woman'—an image which appears arbitrarily constructed, but nevertheless carries with it the authorizing signature of Western humanist discourse [a discourse which assumes . . .] privilege and ethnocentric universality.'

How do we read these women beyond this 'privilege and ethnocentric universality'? What repertoire of tourist images and associations do we deploy in our thinking about women wearing chadors? Do we imagine unanimity among Iranian women? Would all Iranian women x out the face of Rushdie's photographs? Where are the representations of those women who oppose the Ayatollah's political exploitation of Rushdie? Are we aware that during the Algerian revolution, the chador indicated dissent and revolution? How do we read the history of Arab women in their own terms? For example, a 1930's program in Iran advised Iranian women to remove their veils and wear European hats. These women were forced to wear their 'western' hats at their husband's workplace or their husbands risked losing their pay. Is this memory of 'westernization' one that enables us to read the sign of the chador with assurance? Chandra Mohanty would insist that 'first world' feminists avoid theorizations of women as 'victims' or 'dependents' in the 'third world' noting that 'sisterhood cannot be assumed on the basis of gender; it must be forged in concrete, historical and political practice and analysis.' We are thus cautioned to avoid a singular reading of Iran, or Iranian women, or 'students' in this photograph and instead to develop an understanding of the sign systems which elaborate 'their' world as represented through our own.

Our culture's hysterical response to and "demonology" of feminism, which informed the brutal slaying of 14 University of Montreal women engineering students identified as "a bunch of feminists," is part of an anti-feminist zeitgeist which demands the instructor make a safe place for feminist discourse within the classroom.

In order to accomplish adequate feminist readings of texts, a critical self-consciousness about sexuality is also essential. Indeed, because analyses of gender and women are so frequently reduced to sexual signs, questions of sexuality are central to feminist theorizing. However, foregrounding non-heterosexual cultural issues is for the most part prohibited within a heterosexist economy in English Studies. While all lesbians are not feminist and all feminists are not lesbian, feminist pedagogy explores lesbian alternative textual strategies and alternative female identities. This process opens up a discursive space for hypotheses about how homophobia and heterosexism are inscribed

in texts and critical readings. The pedagogic implications of this process are illuminating. In a freshman English course, I made a point of noting each writer's sexual preference, information often ignored in the classroom. Near the end of the course, students were informed of Virginia Woolf's bisexuality. A voice from the back of the room groaned, 'Oh no not another one. Aren't any of these writers normal?' Behind this appeal to the 'normal' was an opportunity to open up discussion about the modes of violent rhetoric which inscribes the different as 'perverse.'

Outside the classroom, homophobia informs our reading and writing. A telling absence and silence in a contemporary Canadian literary anthology, Oxford's welcome first anthology of *Poetry By Canadian Women,* suggests the systemic implications of homophobia. On the cover is a portrait of a modernist woman with a Nancy Cunard haircut and earrings who poses on an ornate chair in front of an exotic tapestry which provides a partial decorative frame. The figure's skin is just one shade off the whiteness of the painting's background. Class and cultural markers of this Canadian woman reader/poet are clearly identified.

Within the anthology, editor Rosemary Sullivan has selected exciting new work by Canadian women, including contemporary women of colour like Dionne Brand, Claire Harris and Marlene Nourbese Philip who have been absent in other contemporary Canadian anthologies. However, there is a trace of another critical blindness in the text—a moment in the introduction where the construction of sexuality and the suppression of lesbianism are telling. Here Sullivan comments that

> we write best when we learn to draw on our comprehensive identity, the creative self that Virginia Woolf called hermaphroditic, is, I think, demonstrated by the work of the poets in this anthology.

> Furthermore, the profound impact that women's writing—for instance, the creative dialogue between George Bowering and Daphne Marlatt, Patrick Lane and Lorna Crozier—make it clear that when the artificial barriers are down, we are all the beneficiaries.

In this passage, Sullivan's curious pairing and faulty parallelism creates its own 'artificial barriers.' George Bowering and Daphne Marlatt are writers from the same cultural community who have corresponded through creative texts and interviews. The other pair, Patrick Lane and Lorna Crozier not only correspond but live with each other. Missing from the Bowering/Marlatt duo is a third term: Daphne Marlatt's latest books have been responses to and in one case a collaboration with the work of Betsy Warland, her lesbian lover. Omitted from this introduction and from the anthology itself is the writing of Betsy Warland whose active organization of women writers in Canada and innovative poetry directly concerns the critical consequences of 'poetry by Canadian women.' My commentary is not intended to argue the selection of writers in the anthology itself but to expose the critical implications of a rhetorical silence about lesbian sexuality. In the dazzling asymmetric leap between these two pair of writers, husband and wife, Lane and Crozier, and fellow travellers Marlatt and Bowering, the 'hermaphroditic' masquerades as 'artificial barrier.' For the unconscious heterosexist exclusionary politic rewrites the lesbian lover's signature and conjures up the transvestite spectacle of Betsy Warland costumed in drag as George Bowering.

This masquerade returns us to the poster announcing my talk at the University of Calgary. There is a coincidental but uncanny resemblance between the poster dreamed up by Eric Savoy, the University of Calgary Speaker's Committee Chair, and the cover of former Calgarian Erin Mouré's collection of poetry *Furious.* Is the resemblance merely an atmospheric accident? In the cover design, Mouré calls attention to her western roots. The book jacket notes 'The cover photo is from a 1983 wilderness equipment catalogue of Taiga Works.' Well protected against a hostile environment, this cover girl introduces us to Mouré's 'furious' poems. In *Furious,* the 'Kindly Ones,' the hideous hags, the furies, are given voice in a section of the book called 'Visible Affection' and concerned with the language and community of lesbian affections.

This book was part of my syllabus for a Canadian poetry course in an English Department in 'a place like this.' What is at risk 'in a place like this' for the professor who publicly addresses the issue of homophobia and heterosexism? Recently I gave a lecture on Mouré's lesbian writing. Twelve hours later, in the middle of the night, someone tied ropes between my backyard fence and a truck and ripped apart the fenced border between the privacy of my own backyard and public space. After an investigation, the police documented the incident as an act of public mischief and concluded that the lecture had incited the vandalism. They then urged me to continue the 'creative' lectures in spite of what they identified as violent harassment.

What is a nice feminist? Probably 'furious.'

What is 'a place like this?' That's for us to read, write and transform. (pp. 46-54)

> *Janice Williamson, "What Is a ~~Nice~~ Feminist Like Me Doing in a Place Like This?" in* Open Letter, *Seventh Series, No. 8, Summer, 1990, pp. 34-59.*

Felicia Bonaparte

[*In the following letter to* The New York Review of Books, *Bonaparte supports Vendler's opposition to feminist criticism that emphasizes the differences between men and women (see excerpt above).*]

To the Editors:

Thank you for publishing Helen Vendler's splendid essay "Feminism and Literature." It is not only a welcome correction to some of what passes as feminist thought but itself a feminist document. I consider it feminist because I believe that to maintain women write and read differently, think and feel in some unique way, and that they are interested in questions only that pertain to themselves is to confine them to what, in essence, is an intellectual kitchen as narrow, as limiting, as unacceptable as was the domestic

kitchen to which they were confined in the past. When I began teaching, thirty years ago, it was only the most bigoted men who argued that women's minds worked differently. Now, with the best intentions undoubtedly (although, as far as I can see, on the basis of no evidence and with devastating consequences, for division of nature surely argues for division of labor, thus unequal opportunity), it is women supposedly liberated. My idea of liberation is to be allowed to do anything I have a mind to and in whatever way I choose. And I should like to be taken seriously enough in my efforts to be judged and interpreted not by my sex but by the quality of the work I produce.

This is what Helen Vendler has done and what she recommends we all do. I think that novelists like Jane Austen and George Eliot would have agreed. I know that Charlotte Brontë would have. When she learned that George Henry Lewes would be reviewing her novel *Shirley,* she wrote to beg him to consider it independently of her sex. When he did not, she wrote again in frustration and disappointment: "after I had said earnestly that I wished critics would judge me as an *author,* not as a woman, you so roughly—I even thought so cruelly—handled the question of sex. I dare say you meant no harm, and perhaps you will not now be able to understand why I was so grieved at what you will probably deem such a trifle, but grieved I was, and indignant too."

> *Felicia Bonaparte, in a letter to the editor in* The New York Review of Books, *Vol. XXXVII, No. 13, August 16, 1990, p. 59.*

Sandra M. Gilbert and Susan Gubar

[*In the following excerpt, Gilbert and Gubar respond to Vendler's attack on their two-volume literary-historical survey* No Man's Land: The Place of the Woman Writer in the Twentieth Century *(see excerpt above).*]

To the Editors:

Sweetness *versus* Light?

Helen Vendler's review-essay "Feminism and Literature" is so vitriolic, so contradictory, and so undocumented in its representation of feminist literary criticism that even a disinterested reader would be surprised at its intellectual and rhetorical lapses. As targets of Vendler's most hectic attack, therefore, we were at first horrified by the piece.

We hardly knew how to reconcile the scrupulously cool and scholarly author of appreciative books on Yeats, Stevens, Herbert, and Keats with the rancorous name-caller who labeled our work "vulgar," "repellent," "slap-dash," "amateurish," "boring," "incoherent," "chaotic," "naive," and "didactic" without ever bothering to outline the ideas we explore throughout two volumes on the situation of women writers in England and America from the late nineteenth century to the present. Nor could we relate to the famous Harvard professor, *New Yorker* critic, and former MLA president who supposedly stood for the humanistic values of reason and tolerance to the feverish polemicist who—in discussions of other books treated in the same review—confessed that the idea of community gives her "the creeps," charged that "the oppressions carried out by schoolmasters and prison guards are not incomparable with those carried out on some children by their mothers during those long days when they are alone together," and gloated, with no evident irony, that the "most cheering thing, finally, about all political movements is their unsuppressible tendency to splinter." . . .

"[S]he goes on as if assertion were its own evidence," Vendler writes of Camille Paglia, one of the authors under review, but such a statement actually, if somewhat surprisingly, characterizes her own method in this essay. What might explain such a disintegration of Vendler's reputed intellectual poise? After studying the piece more than we would like to, we think we have finally found one clue. At a curious juncture, commenting on Rita Felski's analysis of the connection between "formal complexity" and "ideological frameworks," the critic bursts into a complaint that is clearly heartfelt: "To which I can only say, 'Whither away, Delight?' " (sic; Vendler is evidently alluding to the first line of Herbert's "The Glimpse"— "Whither away delight?"). Apparently Vendler fears that the aesthetic delight of literary texts (what Horace called *dulce* and what Matthew Arnold, echoing Swift, interpreted as "sweetness") has been hideously endangered by critics who seek to illuminate the moral or sociocultural significance of such texts (what Horace called *utile* and what Swift, then Arnold, interpreted as "light").

How strange, though, to find a thinker whom most of us would have defined as Arnoldian quarreling with western culture's traditional coupling of *dulce* and *utile,* "sweetness" and "light." What could account for such an obstinate, even distraught clinging to the notion that under the aegis of feminism aesthetic delight will (to risk a "repellent" pun) wither away? As unregenerate cultural critics and feminists, we venture an "impertinent" guess that Vendler's problem is a generational one which we understand all too well. For those of us educated by New Critical teachers who sermonized that literature's monuments of unaging intellect were and should be ideologically neutral, it was shocking to encounter the suggestions (put forward by reader-response critics and marxist theorists as well as feminists) that no text is above the political/ideological fray. This meant not just that works of art were never merely "sweet" but also that the "light" they shed might be experienced by some as deadly or at least as inimical either to the delight of the audience or to the audience itself.

Readers of our generation had to unlearn the children's saw "Sticks and stones can break my bones but words can never hurt me." Words—stories, poems, images—can, we discovered, be painful. When the wolf gobbles up Little Red Riding Hood's grandmother, the sentences of the fairytale can wound an attentive five-year-old. When Milton, despite what Vendler sees as the nobility of his intentions, puts Eve to sleep while the angel prophesies destiny to Adam, or when he defines woman as secondary ("Hee for God onlie, shee for God in him"), the nineteen-year-old sophomore may be distressed. When Wagner reveals that to be an *Ur* artist, a *Meistersinger* (Walter), is to be male, and to be female is to be his prize (Eva), the thirty-year-old opera-goer may be disconcerted. These are per-

haps epiphanies of such pain that in order to cope with them Vendler must repress them. For her, retaining delight (sweetness) necessitates a self-induced blindness, a turning-away from ideological content (light).

Traces of such repression are everywhere apparent in Vendler's discussion of "Feminism and Literature," manifested in the logical inconsistencies and rhetorical peculiarities we've already noted. But most striking is the disjunction between this critic's declared espousal of "the practical and legal goals of the women's movement" and her vehement distaste for feminist criticism. "[I]n the fields of history and sociology," she admits, "newly retrieved information about women's lives . . . has explanatory power." Yet at the same time, she confesses to "disquiet in reading" works which attempt to relate such "information about women's lives" to male- or female-authored literary texts. Disingenuously arguing that " 'Masculinists' (were there any)" would have as much to complain about as feminists do, she posits a historically unfounded sexual symmetry which eventually leads her not only to compare (some) mothers to prison guards but also completely to ignore the literary implications of social facts that she herself adduces—i.e., that many women of letters were "largely self-educated, and most of them had *fathers* with large libraries" (emphasis ours).

"[T]he genius," Vendler insists, articulating what is plainly one of her central aesthetic assumptions, "still does the work all alone." Material conditions ("a wage, a teacher, a study, and a publishing house") may be necessary to, but are not sufficient for, the artist's *Bildung.* As for family history, gender definitions, political changes, ideological imperatives, cultural presuppositions, literary influences, audience expectations—these have little or nothing to do with the transcendent (and virtually inexplicable) achievements of the "solitary genius." Nor, evidently, have they much to do with the suppression of "mute inglorious Miltons." Theologizing the aesthetic, sanctifying pure sweetness, Vendler celebrates the mystical inspiration of the artist as if he or she invariably inhabited a kind of sacred cloister. But the "genius" then becomes a saint or god whose words can never be illuminated or interpreted, only worshipped.

Is literary history, therefore, no more than a hermetically hagiographical project for Vendler? If so, it is not surprising that feminist criticism "disquiets" her, since, no matter what methodology individual scholars adopt, our enterprise consistently assumes a crucial relationship between literature and life. But of course if such a relationship frequently reveals pain, a zealous acolyte of sweetness might prefer not to shed light on it. Alas, though, as Vendler's piece demonstrates, zealotry turns into bigotry when a blindness to such disturbing categories of analysis as gender (or race or class) replaces insight into what might be the function of criticism at the present time. (p. 58)

No doubt because sex battles and sex-changes might sour the aesthetic taste buds, Vendler obliterates our account of them. Certainly readers of *The New York Review of Books* would never have a clue that we discuss these matters—and (to turn to other portions of Vendler's "review"), they would be left supposing that serious critics of the stature of Carolyn Heilbrun and Nancy K. Miller are somehow girlishly "giddy" while the exhilaratingly frank and inventive contemporary poet Sharon Olds is a "pornographic" author of "dull twaddle." "Animus," as Vendler herself remarks, "is not new in literary criticism." But her sort of animosity seems to us to be impelled not only by a stubborn aversion to critical "light" but also by a deep alienation from a female community which gives her the "creeps." As we noted in a chapter of *The War of the Words* entitled " 'Forward into the Past': The Female Affiliation Complex," rivalry between women is fostered both by a need for (exclusive) male approval and, more importantly, by an anxiety about the contamination associated with a shared oppression. Vendler seems to be involved in such a syndrome.

Conscious as we may be, however, of historical tensions and in particular of the painful light some texts emit, we—along with a number of other feminist critics—find works of art all the more fascinating when interpretation supplements appreciation. Indeed, such diverse cultural artifacts as "Little Red Riding Hood," *Paradise Lost,* and *Die Meistersinger* nurture us not just with some sort of aesthetic NutraSweet, but with precisely the intellectual "meat" of "delight" for which Herbert called in "The Glimpse."

When we understand why what we love does what it does to us, we understand our lives. And what we love is not Sweet 'n Low, it is sweet and *light.* To revert to Swift's parable of the bees and to proffer a final set of "vulgar" witticisms, we want to say that we are as capable as you are, Helen Vendler, of waxing enthusiastic about Herbert and Milton and Keats—as well as about the Brontës, Dickinson, and Woolf. But our advice to you, intended seriously as well as sardonically, would be *Helen, honey, lighten up.* (pp. 58-9)

> *Sandra M. Gilbert and Susan Gubar, in a letter to the editor in* The New York Review of Books, *Vol. XXXVII, No. 13, August 16, 1990, pp. 58-9.*

Helen Vendler

[*Vendler, in defending her original essay above, asserts that her criticism of Gilbert and Gubar lies in their attachment to ideological correctness rather than more aesthetic critieria when reviewing literature.*]

Gilbert and Gubar [see excerpt above] write as though the use of literature could be separated from its delight. This is the error of morally didactic critics, against whom (calling them apostles of the Hebraic emphasis on morality, and urging on them a Hellenic emphasis on sweetness and light) Arnold made his criticisms. Our new Puritans, who wish art to be ideologically correct, and reproach everything from fairy tales to opera (with the wisdom of self-righteous hindsight) when artworks do not conform to their twentieth-century rules of ideological correctness, seem incapable of "reading" Eve in *Paradise Lost* or Eva in *Die Meistersinger* as anything but a real oppressed woman done ill to by some man (whether God, Milton, Wagner, Walther, or a wolf—it makes no difference).

Whether or not this view is maintained by a five-year-old or a sophomore, it cannot be maintained by literary critics, who must understand the role of archetype and convention in narrative (not to mention the need for a soprano part and comic closure in opera).

In fact, artworks perform their moral instruction through their aesthetic totality (and not by any single, isolatable strand such as the novelistic fate of any single character, male or female). This does not make them "ideologically neutral"; it means that the ideological character of a work of art is determined by the system of relations in which all its parts—from "ideas" to "characters" to "temporality" to "tone" to "plot"—participate. No New Critic that I know of ever taught (or as Gilbert and Gubar would put it, "sermonized") that literary works "were and should be ideologically neutral." On the contrary. New Critics, from Richards to Tate, regarded works of art, including their own, as unarguably ideologically powerful. They investigated literature (from the Bible to contemporary poetry) to discover how literature produced its undeniable moral effects. But they investigated these questions with a learned, historically based, and profound sense of literature; they understood literary means less crudely than those who would regard a fairy-tale godmother, a mythological Eve, a fictional soprano, and living women as interchangeable characters.

I am amused by the *ad feminam* remarks in Gilbert and Gubar's letter, accusing me personally of various hysterias, repressions, disintegrations, and bigotries; finally, they diagnose me as "involved in a syndrome" of fear of contamination by association with women. These are merely the demagogic responses of authors who have neither the personal acquaintance nor the professional competence to make such diagnoses. Nor will it do to say, in matters of such consequence, that "Vendler's problem is a generational one"; after all, Sandra Gilbert and I are only three years apart in age. No: it is a question of judging the means and the effects of art—which deserves better than the simple litmus test of ideological "correctness."

> *Helen Vendler, in a letter to the editor in* The New York Review of Books, *Vol. XXXVII, No. 13, August 16, 1990, p. 59.*

FURTHER READING

French, Marilyn. "World Class Pleasures." *Ms.* No. 1 (July-August 1990): 66-7.
> Surveys recent reprints and English translations of works of fiction and scholarship by European and Third World women.

The Georgia Review, Special Issue: "Women and the Arts" XLIV, Nos. 1-2 (Spring-Summer 1990).
> This special double-issue offers an assortment of fiction, essays, poetry, and criticism by both unknown and famous women authors.

Greene, Sue N. "Report on the Second International Conference of Caribbean Women Writers." *Callaloo* 13, No. 3 (Summer 1990): 532-38.

>Introduces critical issues discussed at a conference held in Trinidad in April 1990.

Herman, Ellen. "Radical Feminism: The Early Years." *Sojourner: The Women's Forum* 15, No. 12 (August 1990): 1b-2b.

>Reviews *Daring to Be Bad: Radical Feminism in America, 1967-1975,* a history of feminism from its roots in the Civil Rights movement of the 1950s to the present.

Kamboureli, Smaro. "Theory: Beauty or Beast? Resistance to Theory in the Feminine." *Open Letter: A Canadian Journal of Writing and Theory* 7th series, No. 8 (Summer 1990): 5-26.

>Kamboureli briefly examines the 18th-century novel *La Belle et la Bête* by Mme. Leprince de Beaumont as a fabular construct that illuminates the resistance to feminist literary theory in contemporary Canada.

Lakritz, Andrew. "The Equalizer and the Essentializers, or Man-Handling Feminism on the Academic Left." *Arizona Quarterly* 46, No. 1 (Spring 1990): 77-103.

>Examines evidence of attempts to reassert patriarchal power structures in both academic literary criticism and popular culture.

Michigan Quarterly Review, Special Issue: "The Female Body" XXIX and XXX, Nos. 4 and 5 (Fall 1990–Winter 1991).

>Special two-part series, containing poetry, fiction, essays, and art-work exploring the nature, status, or interpretations of the female body. Includes works by Margaret Atwood, Marge Piercy, John Updike, Andrea Dworkin, Carol Gilligan, Catharine A. MacKinnon, and others.

Minnich, Elizabeth Kamarck. *Transforming Knowledge.* Philadelphia: Temple University Press, 1990, 210 p.

>Examines and refutes a variety of forms of patriarchy invested in the academy.

Owusu, Kofi. "Canons under Siege: Blackness, Femaleness, and Ama Ata Aidoo's *Our Sister Killjoy.*" *Callaloo* 13, No. 2 (Spring 1990): 341-63.

>Combines race- and gender-oriented methods of analysis in an attempt to model a "womanist" critique of culture and literature.

Price, Deborah. "Book Review Editors." *Belles Lettres: A Review of Books by Women* 5, No. 3 (Spring 1990): 26-7.

>Discusses book reviewing policies with regard to female authors and editors in the country's major reviewing journals.

Walker, Cheryl. "Feminist Literary Criticism and the Author." *Critical Inquiry* 16, No. 3 (Spring 1990): 551-71.

>Surveys recent feminist criticism concerning the implications of Roland Barthes's theory of "the death of the author."

Ward, Cynthia. "What They Told Buchi Emecheta: Oral Subjectivity and the Joys of 'Otherhood'." *Publications of the Modern Language Association of America* 105, No. 1 (January 1990): 83-97.

>Examines critical response to the novels of Emecheta as paradigmatic of the struggle for an authentic African feminist literature.

Henry Louis Gates, Jr.
and Current Debate in African-American Literary Criticism

Henry Louis Gates, Jr., whom Wahneema Lubiano dubbed "one of the most read and misread figures within African-American literary discourse in this century," is at the center of a current debate on the directions of African-American literary criticism. A prominent figure in the academic world, Gates has developed the theory of "Signifyin(g)," based concurrently on traditional Western post-structuralist thought and on the black vernacular and literary tradition, as elaborated in his text, *The Signifying Monkey*. Signifying, a term developed by structural linguist Ferdinand de Saussure, refers to the often tentative association between words and the ideas they indicate. Post-structuralists such as Jacques Lacan expanded on Saussure's definition, using "signification" to point to relations between objects or ideas. Gates has taken signifying one step further, tracing the word's use in African-American vernacular to indicate a complex system of parody. Enclosing in parentheses the "g" that is not pronounced in vernacular speech, Signifyin(g) is, for Gates, black writers' use of pun, pastiche, repetition, parody, and playing "The Dozens" (a verbal game of exchanging insults) to respond to previous works in their tradition. While Gates considers Signifyin(g) an effective method of fusing contemporary criticism and black literature, many critics have questioned his use of post-structuralism, a predominantly Western and academic theory they consider inappropriate for criticism of texts by black authors.

Many of Gates's detractors point out the irony of a specifically black literary theory based upon Western critical thought. Andrew Delbanco stated: "Gates' problem, the problem with Afro-American literary criticism today, is that he wishes to combine a critical advocacy of certain literary works with a spirit of opposition toward the culture that produced them." Until recently, criticism of African-American literature emphasized political, historical, and social interpretations. The Black Arts Movement of the 1960s, led by such writers as Amiri Baraka and Larry Neal, was a pivotal group that extolled literature and critical works that could speak to the entire black community, and stressed the importance of representing common black experience. Later critics, most notably Gates and Houston A. Baker, Jr., argued for text-specific readings of black literature that explore works in relation to themselves and each other rather than viewing them as literal reflections of historical or social aspects of African-American society. Gates has argued that, with Signifyin(g), he is not merely applying post-structuralist theories to black texts, but is transforming and adapting these ideas, creating an original tool for reading African-American literature.

Henry Louis Gates, Jr.

This departure from the political reading of black literature has prompted some to read Gates's critical work as consciously apolitical and entirely separate from the black experience. Joyce A. Joyce opined: "Black creative art is an act of love which attempts to destroy estrangement and elitism by demonstrating a strong fondness or enthusiasm for freedom and an affectionate concern for the lives of people, especially Black people. . . . It should be the job of the Black literary critic to force ideas to the surface, to give them force in order to affect, to guide, to animate, and to arouse the minds and emotions of Black people." Other commentators, however, consider Signifyin(g) an insightful political theory that highlights a subversive use of language to undermine existing power structures in America.

Although critical theory has become a significant focus for students of African-American literature, one of the most common censures of current critical works is their inaccessibility: such critics as Gates and Robert Stepto are often faulted for their use of enigmatic language. Charles Larson noted: "If there is any limitation [in Gates's *The Signifying Monkey*] it is that the style of the book itself—primarily aimed at the academic reader—is often ponderous." While Gates contends that he writes for an academic audience, many of his peers claim that the critic of black literature bears a primary responsibility to the African-American community. Alienating many readers, Gates's detractors claim, has led to a distinct rift between academics and the general population. Barbara Christian commented: "I feel that the new emphasis on literary critical theory is as hegemonic as the world which it attacks. I see the language it creates as one which mystifies rather than clarifies our condition, making it possible for a few people who know that particular language to control the critical scene."

The intensive debate regarding his work reflects Gates's status as one of the most influential figures in contemporary African-American literary criticism. Robert Elliot Fox claimed: "I believe that when the history of Afro-American literary criticism in the twentieth century is written, it will show that Henry Louis Gates, Jr.—along with Houston A. Baker, Jr., with whom he has an occasionally combative but always mutually enriching dialogue—produced the meta-work, the master enterprise in the effort to discover, re-evaluate, and interpret black texts; to, more broadly, enable in its speaking the 'text' of blackness itself."

PRINCIPAL WORKS DISCUSSED BELOW

Gates, Henry Louis, Jr.
   Black Literature and Literary Theory (editor) 1984
   Figures in Black: Words, Signs and the "Racial" Self 1987
   The Signifying Monkey: A Theory of Afro-American Literary Criticism 1988

OTHER WORKS DISCUSSED BELOW

Baker, Houston A., Jr.
   Blues, Ideology, and Afro-American Literature: A Vernacular Theory 1984
   Modernism and the Harlem Renaissance 1987
Dixon, Melvin
   Ride Out the Wilderness: Geography and Identity in Afro-American Literature 1987
Fisher, Dexter, and Stepto, Robert (editors)
   Afro-American Literature: The Reconstruction of Instruction 1978
Gayle, Addison, Jr.
   The Black Aesthetic 1972
Harper, Michael, and Stepto, Robert (editors)
   Chant of Saints: A Gathering of Afro-American Literature, Art, and Scholarship 1979
Harris, Norman
   Connecting Times: The Sixties in Afro-American Fiction 1988
Jones, LeRoi, and Neal, Larry
   Black Fire 1969

Lenz, Gunter H. (editor)
   History and Tradition in Afro-American Culture 1984
Stepto, Robert
   From Behind the Veil: A Study of Afro-American Narrative 1979

Henry Louis Gates, Jr.

[*In an essay entitled " 'Race,' Writing, and Culture"* (Critical Inquiry, *Autumn, 1986), Tzvetan Todorov responded to an earlier issue of* Critical Inquiry *(see Further Reading) edited by Gates. Addressing Gates's introduction, Todorov noted that the author contradicts himself by supporting Anthony Appiah's statement that it "is not necessary to show that African literature is fundamentally the same as European literature in order to show that it can be treated with the same tools," yet also asserting: "I believe that we must turn to the black tradition itself to develop theories of criticism indigenous to our literature." Gates defends his proposition of a black-specific theory of literary criticism in the excerpt below.*]

[Tzvetan] Todorov questions my belief that "we must turn to the black tradition itself to develop theories of criticism indigenous to our literatures." He accuses me of presupposing, thereby, that "the content of a thought depends on the color of the thinker's skin." If so, he continues, then I am at fault for saying implicitly that "only birds of a feather can think together," and thereby I "practice the very racialism one was supposed to be combatting." This, he concludes, "can only be described as cultural apartheid: in order to analyze black literature, one must use concepts formulated by black authors." Todorov's reasoning here seems to me specious. It is intended, it seems, to show that I am unwittingly guilty of the very "racialism" that I condemn: "if 'racial differences' do not exist," he asks, then "how can they possibly influence literary texts?" Todorov is being disingenuous here, and is guilty of shallow thinking about a serious problem for all theorists of so-called "noncanonical" literatures. Todorov attempts nothing less than a neocolonial recuperation of the sense of difference upon which a truly *new* criticism of world literature must be granted.

The term that I use to qualify my assertion is *attitudes*: "how attitudes toward [pointed or purported] racial differences generate and structure texts by us *and* about us" [Gates, "Writing 'Race' and the Difference It Makes," *Critical Inquiry*, 1985, see Further Reading]. There is no question that representations of black character-types in European and American literature have a history—and a life—of their own, generating repetitions, revisions, and refutations. Within African and Afro-American literature, there can be no question that the *texts* that comprise these traditions repeat, refute, and revise key, canonical tropes and topoi peculiar to those *literary* traditions.

The term that is unstated in my sentence is "textual": we must turn to the black *textual* tradition itself to develop theories of criticism indigenous to our literatures. I believed that when I wrote that sentence; I believe it even more firmly now, especially since confronted with this remark of Todorov's: "In order to analyze football players, should we use only 'indigenous' concepts and theories?"

It is naive to think that the theorists of Afro-American or African literature can utilize theories of criticism generated by critics of European or American literature without regard for the textual *specificity* of those theories. Since Todorov has learned something from Anthony Appiah's essay ["The Uncompleted Argument: Du Bois and the Illusion of Race," *Critical Inquiry,* 1985, see Further Reading], I can do no better than to cite Appiah . . . on what he rather cleverly has called "the Naipaul fallacy," a passage which Todorov for some reason conveniently ignores: "nor should we endorse a *more sinister line* . . . : the post-colonial legacy which requires us to show that African literature is worthy of study precisely (but only) because it is fundamentally the same as European literature." Appiah then concludes with devastating impact that we must not ask "the reader to understand Africa by embedding it in European culture." (pp. 205-06)

[Todorov] has failed to understand the necessity of a task which Appiah, Houston Baker, Wole Soyinka, and I (among others) believe to be absolutely essential if there is to be created something that is validly "African" in contemporary literary theory. To deny us the right even to make the attempt is either for Todorov to be engaged in bad faith, or to be implicated in one more instance of what Appiah calls the "post-colonial legacy." (p. 206)

Theories of criticism are text-specific: the New Critics tended to explicate the metaphysical poets, the structuralists certain forms of narrative, and deconstructionists found their ideal field of texts among the Romantics. While each school of criticism claims for itself what Todorov calls "a universal aspiration," in practice European and American critics tend to write about European and American writers of one specific sort or another. (Todorov, to his credit, mentions Chester Himes' *For Love of Imabelle* as an example of the thriller in *The Poetics of Prose,* but only in passing. Sartre's fantasies of "the being" of "the" African in *Black Orpheus* are racialist, as is his consideration of Richard Wright's "split" audience in *What Is Literature?* A passing nod, and racialist musings, however, are at least *something;* Todorov and Sartre are among the very few [white] critics in this century who have even *read* the works of the black traditions.) This observation has been made so many times before that it is a commonplace of the history of criticism. Why does Todorov choose to parody this point? So that he can claim that I am a racialist.

My position is clear: to theorize about black literatures, we must do what all theorists do. And that is to read the texts that comprise our literary tradition, formulate (by reasoning from observed facts) useful principles of criticism from within that textual tradition, then draw upon these to read the texts that make up that tradition. *All* theorists do this, and we must as well. Todorov's position— let me call it the neocolonial position—pretends that "where [analytical concepts] come from" is irrelevant to the literary critic. My position is that for a critic of black literature to borrow European or American theories of literature regardless of "*where they come from*" is for that critic to be trapped in a relation of intellectual indenture or colonialism. (Please note, M. Todorov, that I wrote

"critic of black literature," and not "black critic.") One must *know* one's textual terrain before it can be explored; one must know one's literary tradition before it can be theorized about.

What can be at all controversial—or "racialist"—about my position? I believe that Todorov finds it problematic because it implies that what European or American critics pretend or claim to be their subject—the wondrous institution of "literature"—in practice means only the branch of that vast institution occupied by "white" authors. To discourage us from reading our own texts in ways suggested by those very texts is to encourage new forms of neocolonialism. To attempt such readings is neither to suggest that "black" texts have no "white" antecedents nor that the Western literary and critical traditions have no relevance for critics of "other" literatures. Several aspects of formal literary language-use seem to be common to all formal literatures: for instance, the structure of a metaphor, *style indirect libre,* even the *skaz* of the Russian Formalists, it seems obvious to me, are the same in "noncanonical" literatures. My method does not mean that we have to reinvent the wheel. No, we turn to our literary tradition to define its specificity, to locate what I call its *signifying black difference.* The critic of black literature who does not do this is the critic destined to recapitulate unwittingly the racist stereotype of Minstrel Man, a Tzvetan Todorov in black face. And who would want to look so foolish? (pp. 207-08)

Henry Louis Gates, Jr., "Talkin' That Talk," in Critical Inquiry, *Vol. 13, No. 1, Autumn, 1986, pp. 203-10.*

Joyce A. Joyce

[In the following excerpt Joyce claims that the critic's role is to mediate between the creative writer and the reader; post-structuralists such as Gates, she argues, alienate rather than enlighten readers.]

In April 1984 a former student of mine came to my office specifically to discuss James Baldwin's essay "On Being 'White' . . . And Other Lies," which appeared in the April 1984 issue of *Essence* magazine. This very bright young woman was bothered because she knew that if she only marginally understood the essay, then many of "our people"—to use her phraseology—the ones who read *Essence* but who have not read some of Baldwin's other works, would not understand the essay. I still have trouble believing that the response I gave this young woman came from my mouth as I heard myself say that James Baldwin writes like James Baldin. "How is he supposed to write?" I asked the student, whom my emotions told me I was failing. Her response was simple. She said, "He is supposed to be clear."

I realized that I was trapped by my own contradictions and elitism, while I agreed that if a reader is familiar with Baldwin's previous essays, particularly his "Down at the Cross: Letter from a Region in My Mind," the major piece in *The Fire Next Time,* he or she would better understand how Baldwin thinks, how he shapes his ideas, his thought and feeling patterns—his Baldwinian sensibility. As the student stared at me, I realized that she and I—the student and the teacher—had exchanged places. For she was teaching me—implicitly reminding me of all those times when I cajoled and coerced her away from narrow and provincial interpretations of the literary work and preached of the responsibility of the writer to his or her audience.

As we discussed the contents of Baldwin's essay, I was intellectually paralyzed by thoughts of the intricacies of the relationship of the writer to the audience, by the historical interrelationship between literature, class, values and the literary canon, and finally by my frustration as to how all these complexities augment ad finitum when the writer is a Black American. For in the first works of Black American literature the responsibility of the writers to their audience was as easy to deduce as it was to identify their audience. The slave narratives, most of the poetry, *Clotel,* and *Our Nig* were all addressed to white audiences with the explicit aim of denouncing slavery. This concentration on the relationship of Black Americans to the hegemony, to mainstream society, continues to this day to be the predominant issue in Black American literature, despite the change in focus we find in some of the works of Black women writers.

With Black American literature particularly, the issue of the responsibility of the creative writer is directly related to the responsibility of the literary critic. As is the case with James Baldwin, the most influential critics of Black literature have been the creative writers themselves, as evidenced also by W. E. B. Du Bois, Langston Hughes, Richard Wright, Ralph Ellison, Amiri Baraka, and Ishmael Reed. In his essay "Afro-American Literary Critics: An Introduction," found in Addison Gayle's landmark edition of *The Black Aesthetic,* Darwin Turner pinpoints why up to the 1960s a number of Black literary artists were also critics. Turner explains, "When a white publisher has wanted a black man to write about Afro-American literature, the publisher generally has turned to a famous creative writer. The reason is obvious. White publishers and readers have not been, and are not, familiar with the names and work of black scholars—the academic critics. Therefore, publishers have called upon the only blacks they have known—the famous writers." After the 1960s, however, a group of literary scholars who had not begun their careers as creative artists emerged.

The 1960s mark a subtly contradictory change in Black academia reflective of the same contradictions inherent in the social, economic, and political strife that affected the lives of all Black Americans. Organizations like SNCC [Student Nonviolent Coordinating Committee] and CORE [Congress of Racial Equality]; the work of political figures like Stokely Carmichael, H. Rap Brown, Julian Bond, Huey Newton, Medger Evers, Martin Luther King, Malcolm X, and Elijah Muhammad; the intense activity of voter registration drives, sit-ins, boycotts, and riots, the Black Arts Movement; and the work of Black innovative jazz musicians together constituted a Black social force that elicited affirmative action programs and the merger of a select number of Blacks into American mainstream society. This merger embodies the same shift in Black con-

sciousness that Alain Locke described in 1925 in *The New Negro* where he suggested that the mass movement of Blacks from a rural to an urban environment thrust a large number of Blacks into contact with mainstream values. He wrote:

> A main change has been, of course, that shifting of the Negro population which has made the Negro problem no longer exclusively or even predominately Southern. . . . Then the trend of migration has not only been toward the North and the Central Midwest, but cityward and to the great centers of industry—the problems of adjustment are new, practical, local and not peculiarly racial. Rather they are an integral part of the large industrial and social problems of our present-day democracy. And finally, with the Negro rapidly in process of class differentiation, if it ever was warrantable to regard and treat the Negro *en masse* it is becoming with every day less possible, more unjust and more ridiculous.

Professor Locke's comments here manifest the same social and ideological paradoxes that describe the relationship between the contemporary Black literary critic and his exogamic, elitist, epistemological adaptations.

For Professor Locke's assertion that to regard and treat the Negro en masse is becoming "every day less possible, more unjust and more ridiculous" is the historical prototype for Henry Louis Gates, Jr.'s denial of blackness or race as an important element of literary analysis of Black literature. Immersed in poststructuralist critical theory, Gates writes:

> Ultimately, black literature is a verbal art like other verbal arts. "Blackness" is not a material object or an event but a metaphor; it does not have an "essence" as such but is defined by a network of relations that form a particular aesthetic unity. . . . The black writer is the point of consciousness of his language. If he does embody a "Black Aesthetic," then it can be measured not by "content," but by a complex structure of meanings. The correspondence of content between a writer and his world is less significant to literary criticism than is a correspondence of organization or structure, for a relation of content may be a mere reflection of prescriptive, scriptural canon, such as those argued for by Baker, Gayle, and Henderson. . . .

Interestingly enough, Locke's attenuation of race as a dominant issue in the lives of Blacks in the 1920s and Gates's rejection of race, reflecting periods of intense critical change for Black Americans, point to their own class orientation that ironically results from social changes provoked by racial issues. (pp. 335-37)

Up to the appearance of Dexter Fisher and Robert Stepto's *Afro-American Literature: The Reconstruction of Instruction* in 1979 and Michael Harper and Robert Stepto's edition of *Chant of Saints: A Gathering of Afro-American Literature, Art, and Scholarship,* also in 1979, the Black American literary critic saw his role not as a "point of consciousness of his language," as Gates asserts, but as a point of consciousness for his or her people. This role was not one the critic had to contrive. A mere glance at the representative works from the Black literary canon chosen by any means of selection reveals that the most predominant, recurring, persistent, and obvious theme in Black American literature is that of liberation from the oppressive economic, social, political, and psychological strictures imposed on the Black man by white America. As characteristic, then, of the relationship between the critic and the work he or she analyzes, the critic takes his or her cues from the literary work itself as well as from the historical context of which that work is a part.

Consequently, Black American literary critics, like Black creative writers, saw a direct relationship between Black lives—Black realities—and Black literature. The function of the creative writer and the literary scholar was to guide, to serve as an intermediary in explaining the relationship between Black people and those forces that attempt to subdue them. The denial or rejection of this role as go-between in some contemporary Black literary criticism reflects the paradoxical elements of Alain Locke's assertions and the implicit paradoxes inherent in Black poststructuralist criticism: for the problem is that no matter how the Black man merges into American mainstream society, he or she looks at himself from an individualistic perspective that enables him or her to accept elitist American values and thus widen the chasm between his or her worldview and that of those masses of Blacks whose lives are still stifled by oppressive environmental, intellectual phenomena. When Professor Gates denies that consciousness is predetermined by culture and color, he manifests a sharp break with traditional Black literary criticism and strikingly bears out another of Wright's prophetic pronouncements made in 1957 when he said,

> . . . the Negro, as he learns to stand on his own feet and expresses himself not in purely racial, but human terms, will launch criticism upon his native land which made him feel a sense of estrangement that he never wanted. This new attitude could have a healthy effect upon the culture of the United States. At long last, maybe a merging of Negro expression with American expression will take place.

If we look at the most recently published works of Black literary criticism and theory—Joe Weixlmann and Chester Fontenot's edition of *Studies in Black American Literature: Black American Prose Theory, Volume 1* (1984), Henry Louis Gates, Jr.'s edition of *Black Literature & Literary Theory* (1984), Houston A. Baker, Jr.'s *Blues, Ideology, and Afro-American Literature: A Vernacular Theory* (1984), and even Michael Cooke's most recent *Afro-American Literature in the Twentieth Century: The Achievement of Intimacy* (1984)—we witness the merger of Negro expression with Euro-American expression. (pp. 338-39)

Following the same methodological strategies characteristic of the works of Northrop Frye and poststructuralist critics like Roland Barthes, Paul de Man, Jacques Derrida, and Geoffrey Hartman, Black poststructuralist critics have adopted a linguistic system and an accompanying world view that communicate to a small, isolated audience. Their pseudoscientific langauge is distant and sterile. These writers evince their powers of ratiocination with an overwhelming denial of most, if not all, the senses. Ironically, they challenge the intellect, "dulling" themselves to the realities of the sensual, communicative function of language. As Wright predicted, this merger of Black expression into the mainstream estranges the Black poststructuralist in a manner that he perhaps "never wanted," in a way which contradicts his primary goal in adopting poststructuralist methodology.

Although the paradox embodied in this estrangement holds quite true for the white poststructuralist critic as well, its negative effects are more severe for the Black scholar. Structuralism in mainstream culture is a reaction to the alienation and despair of late nineteenth- and early twentieth-century existentialism which [according to Robert E. Scholes in his *Structuralism in Literature: An Introduction*] "spoke of isolated man, cut off from objects and even from other men, in an absurd condition of being." In order to demonstrate the common bond that unites all human beings, structuralist thinkers—philosophers, linguists, psychoanalysts, anthropologists, and literary critics—use a complex linguistic system to illuminate "the configurations of human mentality itself." Structuralism, then, "is a way of looking for reality not in individual things [in man isolated] but in the relationships among them," that is, in the linguistic patterns that bind men together. Yet, ironically, the idea that the words on the page have no relationship to an external world and the language used—the unique meanings of words like *code, encode, sign, signifier, signified, difference, discourse, narratology,* and *text*—create the very alienation and estrangement that structuralists and poststructuralists attempt to defeat. Hence I see an inherent contradiction between those values postmodernists intend to transmit and those perceived by many readers.

In the September 1983 special issue of *Critical Inquiry,* Professor Barbara H. Smith's comments on the classic canonical author can analogously illuminate how values are transmitted through literary theory as well. She says simply, "The endurance of a classic canonical author such as Homer . . . owes not to the alleged transcultural or universal value of his works but, on the contrary, to the continuity of their circulation in a particular culture." Thus, in adopting a critical methodology, the Black literary critic must ask himself or herself "How does a Black literary theorist/critic gain a voice in the white literary establishment?" Moreover, despite Professor Smith's and the poststructuralists' attenuation of values, the Black literary critic should question the values that will be transmitted through his or her work. The Black critic must be ever cognizant of the fact that not only what he or she says, but also how he or she writes will determine the values to be circulated and preserved over time once he or she is accepted by mainstream society, if this acceptance is his or her primary goal. Despite writers like John Oliver Killens, John Williams, Gayle Jones, Naomi Long Madgett, and Ann Petry, who are seriously overlooked by the white mainstream, the most neglected aspect of Black American literature concerns the issue of form or structure. I agree fully with Professor Gates when he says that social and polemical functions of Black literature have overwhelmingly superseded or, to use his word, "repressed" the structure of Black literature. But I must part ways with him when he outlines the methodology he uses to call attention to what he refers to as "the language of the black text." He says [in **"Criticism in the Jungle"**], "A study of the so-called arbitrariness, and of the relation between a sign, of the ways in which *concepts* divide reality arbitrarily, and of the relation between a sign, such as blackness, and its referent, such as absence, can help us to engage in more sophisticated readings of black texts." It is insidious for the Black literary critic to adopt any kind of strategy that diminishes or in this case—through an allusion to binary oppositions—negates his blackness. It is not a fortuitous occurrence that Black creative writers for nearly two-hundred years have consistently addressed the ramifications of slavery and racism. One such ramification that underpins W. E. B. Du Bois's essays and Langston Hughes's poetry and that emerged undisguised in the 1960s is the issue of Black pride, self-respect as opposed to self-abnegation or even self-veiling.

The Black creative writer has continuously struggled to assert his or her real self and to establish a connection between the self and the people outside that self. The Black creative writer understands that it is not yet time—and it might not ever be possible—for a people with hundreds of years of disenfranchisement and who since slavery have venerated the intellect and the written word to view language as merely a system of codes or as mere play. Language has been an essential medium for the evolution of Black pride and the dissolution of the double consciousness. For as evidenced by David Walker's *Appeal,* Claude McKay's "If We Must Die," Richard Wright's *Native Son,* the poetry of Sonia Sanchez and Amiri Baraka, and most recently by Toni Morrison's *Tar Baby,* the Black writer recognizes that the way in which we interpret our world is more than a function of the languages we have at our disposal, as Terry Eagleton asserts [in *Literary Theory: An Introduction*]. Even though Innis Brown in Margaret Walker's *Jubilee* cannot read or write, he understands clearly—he interprets quite accurately—that he has been wronged when his white landlord attempts to collect from Innis money for services Innis has not received. And though he too cannot read or write, Jake, Milkman's grandfather in Morrison's *Song of Solomon,* dies rather than surrender his land to the whites who shoot him. Shared experiences like these can bond a people together in ways that far exceed language. Hence what I refer to as the "post-structuralist sensibility" does not aptly apply to Black American literary works. In explaining that an essential difference between structuralism and poststructuralism is the radical separation of the signifier from the signified, Terry Eagleton presents what I see as the "poststructuralist sensibility." He writes, ". . . nothing is ever fully present in signs: it is an illusion for me to believe that I can ever be fully present to you in what I say or write, because to use signs at all entails that my meaning is always somehow dispersed, divided and never quite at one with itself. Not only my meaning, indeed, but me; since language is something I am made out of, rather than merely a convenient tool I use, the whole idea that I am a stable, unified entity must also be a fiction." For the Black American—even the Black intellectual—to maintain that meaningful or real communication between

human beings is impossible because we cannot know each other through language would be to erase or ignore the continuity embodied in Black American history. Pushed to its extreme, poststructuralist thinking perhaps helps to explain why it has become increasingly difficult for members of contemporary society to sustain commitments, to assume responsibility, to admit to a clear right and an obvious wrong.

Yet we can only reluctantly find fault with any ideology or critical methodology that seeks to heighten our awareness and cure us of the political, elitist, and narrow pedagogical and intellectual biases that have long dictated what we teach as well as how we teach. (pp. 339-42)

It is no accident that the Black poststructuralist methodology has so far been applied to fiction, the trickster tale, and the slave narrative, Black poetry—particularly that written during and after the 1960s—defies both linguistically and ideologically the "poststructuralist sensibility." According to Terry Eagleton, "most literary theories . . . unconsciously 'foreground' a particular literary genre, and derive their general pronouncements from this." Equally as telling as their avoidance of Black poetry is the unsettling fact that Black American literary criticism has skipped a whole phase in the evolution of literary theory. The natural cycle organically requires that one school of literary thought be created from the one that goes before. For just as structuralism is a reaction to the despair of existentialism, poststructuralism is a reaction to the limitations of the concepts of the sign. [According to Josué V. Harari in "Critical Factions/Critical Fictions"], "The post-structuralist attitude is therefore literally unthinkable without structuralism." Consequently, the move in Black American literature from polemical, biographical criticism to poststructuralist theories means that these principles are being applied in a historical vacuum.

Since the Black creative writer has always used language as a means of communication to bind people together, the job of the Black literary critic should be to find a point of merger between the communal, utilitarian, phenomenal nature of Black literature and the aesthetic or linguistic—if you will—analyses that illuminate the "universality" of a literary text. Rather than being a "linguistic event" or a complex network of linguistic systems that embody the union of the signified and the signifier independent of phenomenal reality, Black creative art is an act of love which attempts to destroy estrangement and elitism by demonstrating a strong fondness or enthusiasm for freedom and an affectionate concern for the lives of people, especially Black people. Black creative art addresses the benevolence, kindness, and brotherhood that men should feel toward each other. Just as language has no function without man, the Black literary critic is free to go beyond the bonds of the creative writer. For we have many thoughts that we have yet no words for, particularly those thoughts that remain in an inchoate state. It should be the job of the Black literary critic to force ideas to the surface, to give them force in order to affect, to guide, to animate, and to arouse the minds and emotions of Black people. (pp. 342-43)

Joyce A. Joyce, "The Black Canon: Recon-

structing Black American Literary Criticism," in New Literary History, *Vol. 18, No. 2, Winter, 1987, pp. 335-45.*

Henry Louis Gates, Jr.

[*In the following response to Joyce's essay, "The Black Canon: Reconstructing Black American Literary Criticism," Gates argues that the reader has a responsibility to the writer and that he, as a critic, writes for an academic readership.*]

I have structured my response to Joyce Joyce's "The Black Canon" [see excerpt above] in two parts. The first section of this essay attempts to account for the prevalence among Afro-Americans of what Paul de Man called the "resistance to theory." The second section of this essay attempts to respond directly to the salient parts of Professor Joyce's argument. While the first part of my essay is historical, it also explains why literary theory has been useful in my work, in an attempt to defamiliarize a black text from this black reader's experiences as an African-American. This section of my essay, then, is something of an auto-critography, generated by what I take to be the curiously *personal* terms of Joyce Joyce's critique of the remarkably vague, yet allegedly antiblack, thing that she calls, variously, "structuralism" or "poststructuralism." Apparently for Joyce Joyce, and for several other critics, my name and my work have become metonyms for "structuralism," "poststructuralism," and/or "deconstructionism" in the black tradition, even when these terms are not defined at all or, perhaps worse, not adequately understood. . . . These terms become epithets where used as in Joyce Joyce's essay, and mostly opprobrious epithets at that. Just imagine: if Richard Pryor (and his all-too-eager convert Michael Cooke) have their way and abolish the use of the word *nigger* even among ourselves, and black feminists abolish m—, perhaps the worse thing a black person will be able to call another black person will be: "You black poststructuralist, you!" What would Du Bois have said?!

Unlike almost every other literary tradition, the Afro-American literary tradition was generated as a response to allegations that its authors did not, and *could not,* create "literature."

I must confess that I am bewildered by Joyce Joyce's implied claim that to engage in black critical theory is to be, somehow, antiblack. In fact, I find this sort of claim to be both false and a potentially dangerous—and dishonest—form of witch-hunting or nigger-baiting. While it is one thing to say that someone is *wrong* in their premises or their conclusions, it is quite another to ascertain (on that person's behalf) their motivations, their intentions, their *affect;* and then to imply that they do not love their culture, or that they seek to deny their heritage, or that they

are alienated from their "race," appealing all the while to an undefined transcendent essence called "the Black Experience," from which Houston Baker and I have somehow strayed. This is silliness.

Who can disagree that there is more *energy* being manifested and good work being brought to bear on black texts by black critics today than at any other time in our history, and that a large part of the explanation for this wonderful phenomenon is the growing critical sophistication of black readers of literature? Or that this sophistication is not directly related to the fact that we are taking our work—the close reading, interpretation, and *preservation* of the texts and authors of our tradition—with the utmost *seriousness?* What else is there for a critic to do? *What's love got to do with it,* Joyce Joyce? Precisely this: it is an act of love of the tradition—by which I mean *our* tradition—to bring to bear upon it honesty, insight, and skepticism, as well as praise, enthusiasm, and dedication; all values fundamental to the blues and to signifying, those two canonical black discourses in which Houston and I locate the black critical difference. It is merely a mode of critical masturbation to praise a black text simply because it is somehow "black," and it is irresponsible to act as if we are not all fellow citizens of literature for whom developments in other sections of the republic of letters have no bearing or relevance. To do either is most certainly *not* to manifest "love" for our tradition.

Before I can respond more directly to Joyce Joyce's essay, however, I want to examine the larger resistance to (white) theory in the (black) tradition.

Unlike almost every other literary tradition, the Afro-American literary tradition was generated as a response to allegations that its authors did not, and *could not,* create "literature." Philosophers and literary critics, such as [David] Hume, [Immanuel] Kant, [Thomas] Jefferson, and [George] Hegel, seemed to decide that the presence of a written literature was the signal measure of the potential, innate "humanity" of a race. The African living in Europe or in the New World seems to have felt compelled to create a literature both to demonstrate, implicitly, that blacks did indeed possess the intellectual ability to create a written art, but also to indict the several social and economic institutions that delimited the "humanity" of all black people in Western cultures.

So insistent did these racist allegations prove to be, at least from the eighteenth to the early twentieth centuries, that it is fair to describe the subtext of the history of black letters as this urge to refute the claim that because blacks had no written traditions, they were bearers of an "inferior" culture. The relation between European and American critical theory, then, and the development of the African and Afro-American literary traditions, can readily be seen to have been ironic, indeed. (pp. 345-47)

Black literature and its criticism, then, have been put to uses that were not primarily aesthetic; rather, they have formed part of a larger discourse on the nature of the black and his or her role in the order of things. The integral relation between theory and a literary text, therefore, which so very often in other traditions has been a sustaining relation, in our tradition has been an extraordinarily problematical one. The relation among theory, tradition, and integrity within the black literary tradition has not been, and perhaps cannot be, a straightforward matter.

Let us consider the etymology of the word *integrity,* which I take to be the keyword implied in Dr. Joyce's essay. *Integrity* is a curious keyword to address in a period of bold and sometimes exhilarating speculation and experimentation, two other words which aptly characterize literary criticism, generally, and Afro-American criticism, specifically, at the present time. The Latin origin of the English word *integritas* connotes wholeness, entireness, completeness, chastity, and purity; most of which are descriptive terms that made their way frequently into the writings of the American New Critics, critics who seem not to have cared particularly for, or about, the literature of Afro-Americans. Two of the most common definitions of *integrity* elaborate upon the sense of wholeness derived from the Latin original. Let me cite these here, as taken from the *Oxford English Dictionary:* "1. The condition of having no part or element taken away or wanting; undivided or unbroken state; material wholeness, completeness, entirety; something undivided; an integral whole; 2. The condition of not being marred or violated; unimpaired or uncorrupted condition; original perfect state; soundness." It is the second definition of *integrity*—that is to say, the one connoting the absence of violation and corruption, the preservation of an initial wholeness or soundness—which I would like to consider in this deliberation upon "Theory and Integrity," or more precisely upon that relationship which ideally should obtain between African or Afro-American literature and the theories we borrow, revise, or fabricate to account for the precise nature and shape of our literature and its "being" in the world.

It is probably true that critics of Afro-American literature (which, by the way, I employ as a less ethnocentric designation than "the Black Critic") are more concerned with the complex relation between literature and literary theory than we have ever been before. There are many reasons for this, not the least of which is our increasingly central role in "the profession," precisely when our colleagues in other literatures are engulfed in their own extensive debates about the intellectual merit of so very much theorizing. Theory, as a second-order reflection upon a primary gesture such as "literature," has *always* been viewed with deep mistrust and suspicion by those scholars who find it presumptuous and perhaps even decadent when criticism claims the right to stand, as discourse, on its own, as a parallel textual universe to literature. Theoretical texts breed other, equally "decadent," theoretical responses in a creative process that can be remarkably far removed from a poem or a novel.

For the critic of Afro-American literature, this process is even more perilous precisely because the largest part of contemporary literary theory derives from critics of Western European languages and literatures. Is the use of theory to write about Afro-American literature, we might ask rhetorically, merely another form of intellectual indenture, a form of servitude of the mind as pernicious in its intellectual implications as any other form of enslave-

ment? This is the issue raised, for me at least, by the implied presence of the word *integrity* in Joyce Joyce's essay, but also by my own work over the past decade. Does the propensity to theorize about a text or a literary tradition "mar," "violate," "impair," or "corrupt" the "soundness" of a purported "original perfect state" of a black text or of the black tradition? To argue the affirmative is to align one's position with the New Critical position that texts are "wholes" in the first place.

To be sure, this matter of criticism and integrity has a long and rather tortured history in black letters. It was David Hume, after all, who called the Jamaican poet of Latin verse, Francis Williams, "a parrot who merely speaks a few words plainly"; and Phillis Wheatley has for far too long suffered from the spurious attacks of black and white critics alike for being the original *rara avis* of a school of so-called "mockingbird poets," whose use and imitation of received European and American literary conventions have been regarded, simply put, as a corruption itself of a "purer" black expression, privileged somehow in black artistic forms such as the blues, signifying, the spirituals, and the Afro-American dance. Can we, as critics, escape a "mockingbird" relation to theory, one destined to be derivative, often to the point of parody? Can we, moreover, escape the racism of so many critical theorists, from Hume and Kant through the Southern Agrarians and the Frankfurt School?

As I have argued elsewhere, there are complex historical reasons for the resistance to theory among critics of comparative black literature, which stem in part from healthy reactions against the marriage of logocentrism and ethnocentrism in much of post-Renaissance Western aesthetic discourse. Although there have been a few notable exceptions, theory as a subject of inquiry has only in the past decade begun to sneak into the discourse of Afro-American literature. The implicit racism of some of the Southern Agrarians who became the New Critics and Adorno's bizarre thoughts about something he calls "jazz" did not serve to speed this process along at all. Sterling A. Brown has summed up the relation of the black tradition to the Western critical tradition. In response to Robert Penn Warren's line from "Pondy Woods" (1945), "Nigger, your breed ain't metaphysical," Brown replies, "Cracker, your breed ain't exegetical." No tradition is "naturally" metaphysical or exegetical, of course. Only recently have some scholars attempted to convince critics of black literature that the racism of the Western critical tradition was not a sufficient reason for us to fail to theorize about our own endeavor, or even to make use of contemporary theoretical innovations when this seemed either useful or appropriate. Perhaps predictably, a number of these attempts share a concern with that which, in the received tradition of Afro-American criticism, has been most repressed: that is, with close readings of the text itself. This return of the repressed—the very language of the black text—has generated a new interest among our critics in theory. My charged advocacy of the relevance of contemporary theory to reading Afro-American and African literature closely has been designed as the prelude to the definition of principles of literary criticism peculiar to the black literary traditions themselves, related to and compatible with contemporary critical theory generally, yet "indelibly black," as Robert Farris Thompson puts it. All theory is text-specific, and ours must be as well. Lest I be misunderstood, I have tried to work through contemporary theories of literature *not* to "apply" them to black texts, but rather to *transform* by *translating* them into a new rhetorical realm. These attempts have been successful in varying degrees; nevertheless, I have tried to make them at all times interesting episodes in one critic's reflection on the black "text-milieu," what he means by "the tradition," and from which he extracts his "canon."

It is only through this critical activity that the profession, in a world of dramatically fluid relations of knowledge and power, and of the reemerging presence of the tongues of Babel, can redefine itself away from a Eurocentric notion of a hierarchical canon of texts, mostly white, Western, and male, and encourage and sustain a truly comparative and pluralistic notion of the institution of literature. What all students of literature share in common is the art of interpretation, even where we do not share in common the same texts. The hegemony implicit in the phrase "the Western tradition" reflects material relationships primarily, and not so-called universal, transcendent normative judgments. Judgment is specific, both culturally and temporally. The sometimes vulgar nationalism implicit in would-be literary categories such as "American Literature," or the not-so-latent imperialism implied by the vulgar phrase "Commonwealth literature," are extraliterary designations of control, symbolic of material and concomitant political relations, rather than literary ones. We, the scholars of our profession, must eschew these categories of domination and ideology and insist upon the fundamental redefinition of what it is to speak of "the canon."

Whether we realize it or not, each of us brings to a text an *implicit* theory of literature, or even an unwitting hybrid of theories, a critical gumbo as it were. To become aware of contemporary theory is to become aware of one's presuppositions, those ideological and aesthetic assumptions which we bring to a text unwittingly. It is incumbent upon us, those of us who respect the sheer integrity of the black tradition, to turn to this very tradition to create self-generated theories about the *black* literary endeavor. We must, above all, respect the integrity, the wholeness, of the black work of art, by bringing to bear upon the explication of its meanings all of the attention to language that we may learn from several developments in contemporary theory. By the very process of "application," as it were, we recreate, through revision, the critical theory at hand. As our familiarity with the black tradition and with literary theory expands, we shall invent our own theories, as some of us have begun to do—black, text-specific theories.

I have tried to utilize contemporary theory to *defamiliarize* the texts of the black tradition, to create a distance between this black reader and our black texts, so that I may more readily *see* the formal workings of those texts. Wilhelm von Humboldt describes this phenomenon in the following way:

> Man lives with things mainly, even exclusively—since sentiment and action in him depend upon his mental representations—as they are

conveyed to him by language. Through the same act by which he spins language out of himself he weaves himself into it, and every language draws a circle around the people to which it belongs, a circle that can only be transcended in so far as one at the same time enters another one. I have turned to literary theory as a "second circle."

I have done this to preserve the integrity of these texts, by trying to avoid confusing my experience as an Afro-American with the black act of language which defines a text. On the other hand, by learning to read a black text within a black formal cultural matrix, and explicating it with the principles of criticism at work in *both* the Euro-American and Afro-American traditions, I believe that we critics can produce richer structures of meaning than are possible otherwise.

This is the challenge of the critic of black literature in the 1980s: not to shy away from literary theory; rather, to translate it into the black idiom, *renaming* principles of criticism where appropriate, but especially *naming* indigenous black principles of criticism and applying these to explicate our own texts. It is incumbent upon us to protect the integrity of our tradition by bringing to bear upon its criticism any tool of sensitivity to language that is appropriate. And what do I mean by "appropriate"? Simply this: *any* tool that enables the critic to explain the complex workings of the language of a text is an "appropriate" tool. For it is language, the black language of black texts, which expresses the distinctive quality of our literary tradition. A literary tradition, like an individual, is to a large extent defined by its past, its received traditions. We critics in the 1980s have the especial privilege of explicating the black tradition in ever closer detail. We shall not meet this challenge by remaining afraid of, or naive about, literary theory; rather, we will only inflict upon our literary tradition the violation of the uninformed reading. We are the keepers of the black literary tradition. No matter what theories we seem to embrace, we have more in common with each other than we do with any other critic of any other literature. We write for each other, and for our own contemporary writers. This relation is a sacred trust.

Let me end this section of my essay with a historical anecdote. In 1915, Edmond Laforest, a prominent member of the Haitian literary movement called "La Ronde," made of his death a symbolic, if ironic, statement of the curious relation of the "non-Western" writer to the act of writing in a modern language. M. Laforest, with an inimitable, if fatal, flair for the grand gesture, calmly tied a Larousse dictionary around his neck, then proceeded to commit suicide by drowning. While other black writers, before and after M. Laforest, have suffocated as artists beneath the weight of various modern languages, Laforest chose to make his death an emblem of this relation of indenture. We commit intellectual suicide by binding ourselves too tightly to nonblack theory; but we drown just as surely as did Laforest if we pretend that "theory" is "white," or worse—that it is "antiblack." Let scores of black theories proliferate, and let us encourage speculation among ourselves about our own literature. And let us, finally, realize that we must be each other's allies, even when we most disagree, because those who would dismiss both black literature and black criticism will no doubt increase in numbers in this period of profound economic fear and scarcity unless we meet their challenge head-on.

That said, let me respond to the salient points in Joyce Joyce's essay. Joyce Joyce's anecdote about the student who could not understand Jimmy Baldwin's essay "On Being 'White' . . . and Other Lies" is only remarkable for what it reveals about her student's lack of reading skills and/or training. Let me cite a typical paragraph of Baldwin's text, since so very much of Joyce Joyce's argument turns upon the idea of *critical language as a barrier of alienation between black critics and "our people"*:

> . . . Without further pursuing the implication of this mutual act of faith, one is nevertheless aware that the Jewish translation into a white American can sustain the state of Israel in a way that the Black presence, here, can scarcely hope—at least, not yet—to halt the slaughter in South Africa.
>
> And there is a reason for that.
>
> America became white—the people who, as they claim, "settled" in the country became white—because of the necessity of denying the Black presence, and justifying the Black subjugation. No community can be based on such a principle—or, in other words, no community can be established on so genocidal a lie. White men—from Norway, for example, where they were *Norwegians*—became white: by slaughtering the cattle, poisoning the wells, torching the houses, massacring Native Americans, raping Black women.

We are not exactly talking about the obscure or difficult language of Fanon or Hegel or Heidegger or Wittgenstein here, now are we? Rather than being "trapped by [her] own contradiction and elitism," as Joyce Joyce claims she was, and granting this student her point, Joyce Joyce *should* have done what Anna Julia Cooper or Du Bois would have done: sent the student back to the text and told her to read it again—and again, until she got it *right*. Then, she, a teacher in training, I presume, must serve as an interpreter, as mediator, between Baldwin's text and "our people" out there. (Would the superb and thoughtful editors of *Essence,* by the way, publish an essay their readers could not understand? Perhaps the anecdote is merely apocryphal, after all.) Next time, give the child a dictionary, Joyce, and make her come back in a week.

To use this anecdote to conclude that Baldwin (and, of course, we blankety-blank poststructuralists) has abnegated "the responsibility of the writer to his or her audience" is for a university professor to fail to understand or satisfy our most fundamental charge as teachers of literature: to preach the responsibility of *the reader* to his or her *writers.* Joyce Joyce, rather regrettably, has forgotten that the two propositions are inseparable and that the latter is the basic charge that *any* professor of literature accepts when he or she walks into a classroom or opens a text. *That's* what love's got to do, got to do with it, Joyce Joyce. How hard are we willing to work to meet our responsibilities to our *writers?* What would you have Jimmy Baldwin *do:* rewrite that paragraph, reduce his level of diction to a lower com-

mon denominator, then poll the readers of *Essence* to see if they understood the essay? What insolence; what arrogance! What's love got to do with your student's relation to Baldwin and his text? We should *beg* our writers to publish in *Essence* and in every other black publication, from *Ebony* and *Jet* to the *Black American Literature Forum* and the *CLA Journal.*

The relationship between writer and reader is a reciprocal relationship, and one sells our authors short if one insists that their "responsibility," as you put it, is "to be clear." Clear to whom, or to what? Their "responsibility" is to write. Our responsibility, as critics, to our writers, is to work at understanding *them,* not to demand that they write at such a level that every one of "our people" understands every word of every black writer without working at it. Your assertion that "the first works of black American literature" were "addressed to white audiences" is not strictly true. The author of *Our Nig* [Harriet Wilson], for example, writes that "I appeal to my colored brethren universally for patronage, hoping they will not condemn this attempt of their sister to be erudite, but rally around me a faithful band of supporters and defenders." How much "blacker" can an author get? No, even at the beginning of the tradition, black writers wrote for a double or mulatto audience, one black *and* white. Even Phillis Wheatley, whose poetry was the object of severe scrutiny for those who would deny us membership in the human community, wrote "for" Arbour Tanner, Scipio Moorehead, and Jupiter Hammon, just as black critics today write "for" each other and "for" our writers, and not "for" [Jacques] Derrida, [Fredric] Jameson, [Edward] Said, or [Harold] Bloom.

It is just not true that "the most influential critics of black literature have been the creative writers themselves." Rather, I believe that our "most influential critics" have been academic critics, such as W. S. Scarborough, Alain Locke, Sterling A. Brown, [W. E. B.] Du Bois (a mediocre poet and *terrible* novelist), J. Saunders Redding, Darwin T. Turner, and Houston A. Baker, among others (though both Brown and Baker are also poets). "Most influential" does not necessarily mean whom a white publisher publishes; most influential, to me, means who has generated a critical *legacy,* a critical *tradition* upon which other critics have built or can build. Among the writers that Joyce Joyce lists, Ralph Ellison has been "most influential" in the sense that I am defining it, while [Langston] Hughes is cited mainly for "The Negro Artist and the Racial Mountain," Wright mostly for his two major pieces, "The Literature of the Negro in the United States" and "Blueprint for Negro Literature," while almost none of us cites Du Bois at all, despite the fact that Du Bois was probably the very first systematic literary and cultural theorist in the tradition. Rather, we *genuflect* to Du Bois.

I am not attempting to deny that creative writers such as Amiri Baraka and Ishmael Reed have been remarkably important. Rather, I deny Joyce Joyce's claim that a new generation of academic critics has usurped the place of influence in the black tradition which creative writers occupied before "the 1960s." The matter is just not as simple as a "shift in black consciousness" in the 1960s, similar to that caused by migration in the 1920s, which Joyce Joyce maintains led to "the merger of a select number of blacks into American mainstream society" and, accordingly, to our "exogamic, elitist, epistemological adaptations." No, I learned my trade as a critic of black literature from a black academic critic, Charles Davis, who made me read Scarborough, Locke, Redding, Ellison, Turner, and Houston Baker as a matter of course.

This is a crucial matter in Joyce Joyce's argument, though it is muddled. For she implies (1) that larger sociopolitical changes in the 1960s led to the crossover of blacks into white institutions (true), and (2) that the critical language that I use, and my firm belief that "race" is not an essence but a trope for ethnicity or culture, both result from being trained into a "class orientation that ironically result[s] from social changes provoked by racial issues."

There are several false leaps being made here. In the first place, what Joyce Joyce erroneously thinks of as our "race" is our *culture*. Of course I "believe in" Afro-American culture; indeed, I celebrate it every day. But I also believe that to know it, to find it, to touch it, one must locate it in its *manifestations* (texts, expressive culture, music, the dance, language, and so forth) and not in the realm of the abstract or the a priori. Who can argue with that? The point of my passage about our language with which Joyce Joyce takes such issue is that for a literary critic to discuss "the black aesthetic," he or she must "find" it in language use. What is so controversial, or aristocratic, about that? As for my "class orientation," the history of my family, whether or not we were slaves or free, black or mulatto, property owners or sharecroppers, Howard M.D.s or janitors, is really none of Joyce Joyce's business. To say, moreover, that because I matriculated at Yale (when Arna Bontemps and Houston Baker taught black literature there, by the way) and at the University of Cambridge, I became a "poststructuralist" is simply illogical.

This claim is crucial to Joyce Joyce's argument, however, because of her assertion that "middle-class black men" adopted "mainstream [white] lifestyles and ideology" with great intensity after the "integration" of the 1960s. This dangerous tendency, her argument runs, culminated in 1979 with my oft-cited statement about a black writer or critic being the point of consciousness of our *language*. I am delighted that Joyce Joyce points to the significance of this statement, because I think that it is of crucial importance to the black critical activity, and especially to the subsequent attention to actual black language use that is apparent in much of our criticism since 1979.

Why has that statement been such an important one in the development of Afro-American literary criticism? Precisely because if our literary critics saw her or his central function as that of a "guide," as Joyce Joyce puts it, or as "an intermediary in explaining the relationship between black people and those forces that attempt to subdue them," she or he tended to fail at both tasks: neither were we as critics in a position to "lead" our people to "freedom," nor did we do justice to the texts created by our writers. Since *when* have black people turned to our critics to lead us out of the wilderness of Western racism into the promised land of freedom? If black readers turn to black critics, I would imagine they do so to learn about the wondrous workings of *literature,* our literature, of how our artists have represented the complex encounter of every aspect of black culture with itself and with the Other in formal literary language. Who reads our books anyway? Who can doubt that **Black Fire,** the splendid anthology of the Black Arts edited by Larry Neal and LeRoi Jones, has sold *vastly* more copies to black intellectuals than to "our people"? Let us not deceive ourselves about our readership.

Joyce Joyce makes a monumental error here, when she offers the following "syllogism":

> 1. The sixties led to the "integration" of a few black people into historically white institutions.
>
> 2. Such exposure to mainstream culture led to the imitation by blacks of white values, habits, and so on.
>
> 3. Therefore, black people so educated or exposed suffer from "an individualistic perspective that enables him or her to accept elitist American values and thus widen the chasm between his or her worldview and that of those masses of Blacks whose lives are still stifled by oppressive environmental, intellectual phenomena."

Joyce Joyce arrives at this syllogism all because, I think, we can see important structures of meaning in black texts using sophisticated tools of literary analysis! As my friend Ernie Wilson used to say in the late sixties, "Yeah, but compared to *what?*"!

Let me state clearly that I have no fantasy about my readership: I write for our writers and for our critics. If I write a book review, say, for a popular Afro-American newspaper, I write in one voice; if I write a close analysis of a black text and publish it in a specialist journal, I choose another voice, or voices. Is not that my "responsibility," to use Joyce Joyce's word, and my privilege as a writer? But no, I do not think that my task as a critic is to lead black people to "freedom." My task is to explicate black texts. That's why *I* became a critic. (pp. 348-57)

And who is to say that Baker's work or mine is not implicitly political because it is "poststructuralist"? How can the demonstration that our texts sustain ever closer and sophisticated readings *not* be political, at a time in the academy when all sorts of so-called canonical critics mediate their racism through calls for "purity" of "the tradition," demands as implicitly racist as anything the Southern Agrarians said? How can the deconstruction, as it were, of the forms of racism itself (as carried out, for example, in a recent issue of *Critical Inquiry* by black and nonblack poststructuralists) not be political? How can the use of literary analysis to explicate the racist social text in which we still find ourselves be anything *but* political? To be political, however, does not mean that I have to write at the level of diction of a Marvel comic book. No, my task—as I see it—is to train university graduate and undergraduate students to think, to read, and, yes Joyce, even to *write* clearly, helping them to expose false uses of language, fraudulent claims and muddled argument, propaganda and vicious lies from all of which our people have suffered just as surely as we have from an economic order in which we were zeroes and a metaphysical order in which we were absences. These are the "values," as Joyce Joyce puts it, which I hope "will be transmitted through [my] work."

Does my work "negate [my] blackness," as Joyce Joyce claims? I would challenge Joyce Joyce to *demonstrate* anywhere in my entire work how I have, even once, negated my blackness. Simply because I have attacked an error in logic in the work of certain Black Aestheticians does not mean that I am antiblack, or that I do not love black art or music, or that I feel alienated from black people, or that I am trying to pass like some poststructural ex-colored man. My feelings about black culture and black people are everywhere manifested in my work and in the way that I define my role in the profession, which is as a critic who would like to think that history will regard him as having been a solid "race man," as we put it. My association with Black Studies departments is by choice, just as is my choice of subject matter. (Believe me, Joyce, almost no one at Cambridge wanted me to write about black literature!)

Sterling A. Brown has summed up the relation of the black tradition to the Western critical tradition. In response to Robert Penn Warren's line from "Pondy Woods" (1945), "Nigger, your breed ain't metaphysical," Brown replies, "Cracker, your breed ain't exegetical."

No, Joyce Joyce, I am as black as I ever was, which is just as black as I ever want to be. And I am asserting my "real self," as you put it so glibly, and whatever influence that my work has had or might have on readers of black literature *establishes a connection between the self and the people outside the self,* as you put it. And for the record, let me add here that only a black person alienated from black language use could fail to understand that we have been deconstructing white people's languages—as "a system of codes or as mere play"—since 1619. That's what signifying is all about. (If you don't believe me, by the way, ask your grandparents, or your parents, especially your mother.)

But enough, Joyce Joyce. Let me respond to your two final points: first, your claim that "the poststructuralist sensibility" does not "aptly apply to black American literary work." I challenge you to refute any of Houston Baker's readings, or my own, to justify such a strange claim. Argue with our readings, not with *your* idea of who or what we are as black people, or with *your* idea of how so very many social ills can be traced, by fits and starts, to "poststructuralist thinking."

Finally, to your curious claims that "black American literary criticism has skipped a whole phase in the evolution of literary theory," that "one school of literary thought [must] be created from the one that goes before," and that "the move in black American literature from polemical,

biographical criticism to poststructuralist theories mean[s] that these principles are being applied in a historical vacuum," let me respond by saying that my work arose as a direct response to the theories of the Black Arts Movement, as Houston Baker demonstrates so very well in the essay that you cite. Let me also point out politely that my work with binary oppositions which you cite (such as my earlier Frederick Douglass essay) *is* structuralist as is the work of several other critics of black literature in the seventies (Sunday Anozie, O. A. Ladimeji, Jay Edwards, and the essays in the black journal *The Conch*) and that my work as a poststructuralist emerged directly from my experiments as a structuralist, as Houston Baker also makes clear. No vacuum here; I am acutely aware of the tradition in which I write.

Was it [John Maynard] Keynes who said that those who are "against theory" and believe in common sense are merely in the grip of another theory? Joyce Joyce makes a false opposition between theory and humanism, or theory and black men. She also has failed to realize that lucidity through oversimplification is easy enough to achieve; however, it is the lucidity of *command* which is the challenge posed before any critic of any literature. The use of fashionable critical language without the *pressure* of that language is as foolish as is the implied allegation that Houston and I are nouveau ideological Uncle Toms because we read and write theory. (pp. 358-59)

Henry Louis Gates, Jr., " 'What's Love Got To Do with It?': Critical Theory, Integrity, and the Black Idiom," in New Literary History, *Vol. 18, No. 2, Winter, 1987, pp. 345-62.*

Barbara Christian

[*Christian is a critic and educator born in the U.S. Virgin Islands. In the following excerpt, she faults current literary theorists for disassociating their works from their primary texts and suggests the Black Arts Movement generated prescriptive theory that restricts the creative writer.*]

I have seized this occasion to break the silence among those of us, critics, as we are now called, who have been intimidated, devalued by what I call the race for theory. I have become convinced that there has been a takeover in the literary world by Western philosophers from the old literary élite, the neutral humanists. Philosophers have been able to effect such a takeover because so much of the literature of the West has become pallid, laden with despair, self-indulgent, and disconnected. The New Philosophers, eager to understand a world that is today fast escaping their political control, have redefined literature so that the distinctions implied by that term, that is, the distinctions between everything written and those things written to evoke feeling as well as to express thought, have been blurred. They have changed literary critical language to suit their own purposes as philosophers, and they have reinvented the meaning of theory.

My first response to this realization was to ignore it. Perhaps, in spite of the egocentrism of this trend, some good might come of it. I had, I felt, more pressing and interesting things to do, such as reading and studying the history and literature of black women, a history that had been totally ignored, a contemporary literature bursting with originality, passion, insight, and beauty. But unfortunately it is difficult to ignore this new takeover, since theory has become a commodity which helps determine whether we are hired or promoted in academic institutions— worse, whether we are heard at all. Due to this new orientation, works (a word which evokes labor) have become texts. Critics are no longer concerned with literature, but with other critics' texts, for the critic yearning for attention has displaced the writer and has conceived of himself as the center. Interestingly in the first part of this century, at least in England and America, the critic was usually also a writer of poetry, plays, or novels. But today, as a new generation of professionals develops, he or she is increasingly an academic. Activities such as teaching or writing one's response to specific works of literature have, among this group, become subordinated to one primary thrust, that moment whenone creates a theory, thus fixing a constellation of ideas for a time at least, a fixing which no doubt will be replaced in another month or so by somebody else's competing theory as the race accelerates. Perhaps because those who have effected the takeover have the power (although they deny it) first of all to be published, and thereby to determine the ideas which are deemed valuable, some of our most daring and potentially radical critics (and by *our* I mean black, women, third world) have been influenced, even coopted, into speaking a language and defining their discussion in terms alien to and opposed to our needs and orientation. At least so far, the creative writers I study have resisted this language.

For people of color have always theorized—but in forms quite different from the Western form of abstract logic. And I am inclined to say that our theorizing (and I intentionally use the verb rather than the noun) is often in narrative forms, in the stories we create, in riddles and proverbs, in the play with language, since dynamic rather than fixed ideas seem more to our liking. How else have we managed to survive with such spiritedness the assault on our bodies, social institutions, countries, our very humanity? And women, at least the women I grew up around, continuously speculated about the nature of life through pithy language that unmasked the power relations of their world. It is this language, and the grace and pleasure with which they played with it, that I find celebrated, refined, critiqued in the works of writers like Morrison and Walker. My folk, in other words, have always been a race for theory—though more in the form of the hieroglyph, a written figure which is both sensual and abstract, both beautiful and communicative. In my own work I try to illuminate and explain these hieroglyphs, which is, I think, an activity quite different from the creating of the hieroglyphs themselves. As the Buddhists would say, the finger pointing at the moon is not the moon.

In this discussion, however, I am more concerned with the issue raised by my first use of the term, *the race for theory,* in relation to its academic hegemony, and possibly of its inappropriateness to the energetic emerging literatures in the world today. The pervasiveness of this academic hegemony is an issue continually spoken about—but usually in hidden groups, lest we, who are disturbed by it, appear ignorant to the reigning academic élite. Among the folk who speak in muted tones are people of color, feminists, radical critics, creative writers, who have struggled for much longer than a decade to make their voices, their various voices, heard, and for whom literature is not an occasion for discourse among critics but is necessary nourishment for their people and one way by which they come to understand their lives better. Clichéd though this may be, it bears, I think, repeating here.

The race for theory, with its linguistic jargon, its emphasis on quoting its prophets, its tendency towards "Biblical" exegesis, its refusal even to mention specific works of creative writers, far less contemporary ones, its preoccupations with mechanical analyses of language, graphs, algebraic equations, its gross generalizations about culture, has silenced many of us to the extent that some of us feel we can no longer discuss our own literature, while others have developed intense writing blocks and are puzzled by the incomprehensibility of the language set adrift in literary circles. There have been, in the last year, any number of occasions on which I had to convince literary critics who have pioneered entire new areas of critical inquiry that they did have something to say. Some of us are continually harassed to invent wholesale theories regardless of the complexity of the literature we study. I, for one, am tired of being asked to produce a black feminist literary theory as if I were a mechanical man. For I believe such theory is prescriptive—it ought to have some relationship to practice. Since I can count on one hand the number of people attempting to be black feminist literary critics in the world today, I consider it presumptuous of me to invent a theory of how we *ought* to read. Instead, I think we need to read the works of our writers in our various ways and remain open to the intricacies of the intersection of language, class, race, and gender in the literature. And it would help if we share our process, that is, our practice, as much as possible since, finally, our work *is* a collective endeavor.

The insidious quality of this race for theory is symbolized for me by the very nature of this special issue—Minority Discourse—a label which is borrowed from the reigning theory of the day and is untrue to the literatures being produced by our writers, for many of our literatures (certainly Afro-American literature) are central, not minor, and by the titles of many of the articles, which illuminate language as an assault on the other, rather than as possible communication, and play with, or even affirmation of another. I have used the passive voice in my last sentence construction, contrary to the rules of Black English, which like all languages has a particular value system, since I have not placed responsibility on any particular person or group. But that is precisely because this new ideology has become so prevalent among us that it behaves like so many of the other ideologies with which we have had to contend. It appears to have neither head nor center. At the least, though, we can say that the terms "minority" and "discourse" are located firmly in a Western dualistic or "binary" frame which sees the rest of the world as minor, and tries to convince the rest of the world that it *is* major, usually through force and then through language, even as it claims many of the ideas that we, its "historical" other, have known and spoken about for so long. For many of us have never conceived of ourselves only as somebody's *other*.

Let me not give the impression that by objecting to the race for theory I ally myself with or agree with the neutral humanists who see literature as pure expression and will not admit to the obvious control of its production, value, and distribution by those who have power, who deny, in other words, that literature is, of necessity, political. I am studying an entire body of literature that has been denigrated for centuries by such terms as *political.* For an entire century Afro-American writers, from Charles Chesnutt in the nineteenth century through Richard Wright in the 1930s, Imamu Baraka in the 1960s, Alice Walker in the 1970s, have protested the literary hierarchy of dominance which declares when literature is literature, when literature is great, depending on what it thinks is to its advantage. The Black Arts Movement of the 1960s, out of which Black Studies, the Feminist Literary Movement of the 1970s, and Women's Studies grew, articulated precisely those issues, which came *not* from the declarations of the New Western philosophers but from these groups' reflections on their own lives. That Western Scholars have long believed their ideas to be universal has been strongly opposed by many such groups. Some of my colleagues do not see black critical writers of previous decades as eloquent enough. Clearly they have not read Wright's "Blueprint for Negro Writing," Ellison's *Shadow and Act,* Chesnutt's resignation from being a writer, or Alice Walker's "Search for Zora Neale Hurston." There are two reasons for this general ignorance of what our writer-critics have said. One is that black writing has been generally ignored in this country. Since we, as Toni Morrison has put it, are seen as a discredited people, it is no surprise, then, that our creations are also discredited, but this is also due to the fact that until recently dominant critics in the Western World have also been creative writers who have had access to the upper middle class institutions of education and until recently our writers have decidedly been excluded from these institutions and in fact have often been opposed to them. Because of the academic world's general ignorance about the literature of black people and of women, whose work too has been discredited, it is not surprising that so many of our critics think that the position arguing that literature is political begins with these New Philosophers. Unfortunately, many of our young critics do not investigate the reasons *why* that statement—literature is political—is now acceptable when before it was not; nor do we look to our own antecedents for the sophisticated arguments upon which we can build in order to change the tendency of any established Western idea to become hegemonic.

For I feel that the new emphasis on literary critical theory is as hegemonic as the world which it attacks. I see the language it creates as one which mystifies rather than clarifies our condition, making it possible for a few people who know that particular language to control the critical scene—that language surfaced, interestingly enough, just when the literature of peoples of color, of black women, of Latin Americans, of Africans began to move to "the

center." Such words as *center* and *periphery* are themselves instructive. (pp. 51-5)

Now I am being told that philosophers are the ones who write literature, that authors are dead, irrelevant, mere vessels through which their narratives ooze, that they do not work nor have they the faintest idea what they are doing; rather they produce texts as disembodied as the angels. I am frankly antonished that scholars who call themselves Marxists or post-Marxists could seriously use such metaphysical language even as they attempt to deconstruct the philosophical tradition from which their language comes. And as a student of literature, I am appalled by the sheer ugliness of the language, its lack of clarity, its unnecessarily complicated sentence constructions, its lack of pleasurableness, its alienating quality. It is the kind of writing for which composition teachers would give a freshman a resounding F.

Because I am a curious person, however, I postponed readings of black women writers I was working on and read some of the prophets of this new literary orientation. These writers did announce their dissatisfaction with some of the cornerstone ideas of their own tradition, a dissatisfaction with which I was born. But in their attempt to change the orientation of Western scholarship, they, as usual, concentrated on themselves and were not in the slightest interested in the worlds they had ignored or controlled. Again I was supposed to know *them,* while they were not at all interested in knowing *me.* Instead they sought to "deconstruct" the tradition to which they belonged even as they used the same forms, style, language of that tradition, forms which necessarily embody its values. And increasingly as I read them and saw their substitution of their philosophical writings for literary ones, I began to have the uneasy feeling that their folk were not producing any literature worth mentioning. For they always harkened back to the masterpieces of the past, again reifying the very texts they said they were deconstructing. Increasingly, as *their* way, *their* terms, *their* approaches remained central and became the means by which one defined literary critics, many of my own peers who had previously been concentrating on dealing with the other side of the equation, the reclamation and discussion of past and *present* third world literatures, were diverted into continually discussing the new literary theory.

From my point of view as a critic of contemporary Afro-American women's writing, this orientation is extremely problematic. In attempting to find the deep structures in the literary tradition, a major preoccupation of the new New Criticism, many of us have become obsessed with the nature of reading itself to the extent that we have stopped writing about literature being written today. Since I am slightly paranoid, it has begun to occur to me that the literature being produced *is* precisely one of the reasons why this new philosophical-literary-critical theory of relativity is so prominent. In other words, the literature of blacks, women of South America and Africa, etc., as overtly "political" literature was being preempted by a new Western concept which proclaimed that reality does not exist, that everything is relative, and that every text is silent about something—which indeed it must necessarily be.

There is, of course, much to be learned from exploring how we know what we know, how we read what we read, an exploration which, of necessity, can have no end. But there also has to be a "what," and that "what," when it is even mentioned by the new philosophers, are texts of the past, primarily Western male texts, whose norms are again being transferred onto third world, female texts as theories of reading proliferate. Inevitably a hierarchy has now developed between what is called theoretical criticism and practical criticism, as mind is deemed superior to matter. I have no quarrel with those who wish to philosophize about how we know what we know. But I do resent the fact that this particular orientation is so privileged and has diverted so many of us from doing the first readings of the literature being written today as well as of past works about which nothing has been written. (pp. 56-7)

I am particularly perturbed by the movement to exalt theory, as well, because of my own adult history. I was an active member of the Black Arts Movement of the sixties and know how dangerous theory can become. Many today may not be aware of this, but the Black Arts Movement tried to create Black Literary Theory and in doing so became prescriptive. My fear is that when Theory is not rooted in practice, it becomes prescriptive, exclusive, élitish.

An example of this prescriptiveness is the approach the Black Arts Movement took towards language. For it, blackness resided in the use of black talk which they defined as hip urban language. So that when Nikki Giovanni reviewed Paule Marshall's *Chosen Place, Timeless People,* she criticized the novel on the grounds that it was not black, for the language was too elegant, too white. Blacks, she said, did not speak that way. Having come from the West Indies where we do, some of the time, speak that way, I was amazed by the narrowness of her vision. The emphasis on *one way* to be black resulted in the works of Southern writers being seen as non-black since the black talk of Georgia does not sound like the black talk of Philadelphia. Because the ideologues, like Baraka, come from the urban centers they tended to privilege their way of speaking, thinking, writing, and to condemn other kinds of writing as not being black enough. Whole areas of the canon were assessed according to the dictum of the Black Arts Nationalist point of view, as in Addison Gayle's *The Way of the New World,* while other works were ignored because they did not fit the scheme of cultural nationalism. Older writers like Ellison and Baldwin were condemned because they saw that the intersection of Western and African influences resulted in a new Afro-American culture, a position with which many of the Black Nationalist idealogues disagreed. Writers were told that writing love poems was not being black. Further examples abound.

It is true that the Black Arts Movements resulted in a necessary and important critique both of previous Afro-American literature and of the white-established literary world. But in attempting to take over power, it, as Ishmael Reed satirizes so well in *Mumbo Jumbo,* became much like its opponent, monolithic and downright repressive.

It is this tendency towards the monolithic, monotheistic, etc., which worries me about the race for theory. Constructs like the *center* and the *periphery* reveal that tendency to want to make the world less complex by organizing it according to one principle, to fix it through an idea which is really an ideal. Many of us are particularly sensitive to monolithism since one major element of ideologies of dominance, such as sexism and racism, is to dehumanize people by stereotyping them, by denying them their variousness and complexity. Inevitably, monolithism becomes a metasystem, in which there is a controlling ideal, especially in relation to pleasure. Language as one form of pleasure is immediately restricted, and becomes heavy, abstract, prescriptive, monotonous.

Variety, multiplicity, eroticism are difficult to control. And it may very well be that these are the reasons why writers are often seen as *persona non grata* by political states, whatever form they take, since writers/artists have a tendency to refuse to give up their way of seeing the world and of playing with possibilities; in fact, their very expression relies on that insistence. Perhaps that is why creative literature, even when written by politically reactionary people, can be so freeing, for in having to embody ideas and recreate the world, writers cannot merely produce "one way." (pp. 58-9)

There is at least one other lesson I learned from the Black Arts Movement. One reason for its monolithic approach had to do with its desire to destroy the power which controlled black people, but it was a power which many of its ideologues wished to achieve. The nature of our context today is such that an approach which desires power singlemindedly must of necessity become like that which it wishes to destroy. Rather than wanting to change the whole model, many of us want to be at the center. It is this point of view that writers like June Jordan and Audre Lorde continually critique even as they call for empowerment, as they emphasize the fear of difference among us and our need for leaders rather than a reliance on ourselves.

For one must distinguish the desire for power from the need to become empowered—that is, seeing oneself as capable of and having the right to determine one's life. Such empowerment is partially derived from a knowledge of history. The Black Arts Movement did result in the creation of Afro-American Studies as a concept, thus giving it a place in the university where one might engage in the reclamation of Afro-American history and culture and pass it on to others. I am particularly concerned that institutions such as Black Studies and Women's Studies, fought for with such vigor and at some sacrifice, are not often seen as important by many of our black or women scholars precisely because the old hierarchy of traditional departments is seen as superior to these "marginal" groups. Yet, it is in this context that many others of us are discovering the extent of our complexity, the interrelationships of different areas of knowledge in relation to a distinctly Afro-American or female experience. Rather than having to view our world as subordinate to others, or rather than having to work as if we were hybrids, we can pursue ourselves as subjects.

My major objection to the race for theory, as some readers

have probably guessed by now, really hinges on the question, "for whom are we doing what we are doing when we do literary criticism?" It is, I think, the central question today especially for the few of us who have infiltrated the academy enough to be wooed by it. The answer to that question determines what orientation we take in our work, the language we use, the purposes for which it is intended.

I can only speak for myself. But what I write and how I write is done in order to save my own life. And I mean that literally. For me literature is a way of knowing that I am not hallucinating, that whatever I feel/know *is.* It is an affirmation that sensuality is intelligence, that sensual language is language that makes sense. My response, then, is directed to those who write what I read and to those who read what I read—put concretely—to Toni Morrison and to people who read Toni Morrison (among whom I would count few academics). That number is increasing, as is the readership of Walker and Marshall. But in no way is the literature Morrison, Marshall, or Walker create supported by the academic world. Nor given the political context of our society, do I expect that to change soon. For there is no reason, given who controls these institutions, for them to be anything other than threatened by these writers.

My readings do presuppose a need, a desire among folk who like me also want to save their own lives. My concern then is a passionate one, for the literature of people who are not in power has always been in danger of extinction or of cooptation, not because we do not theorize, but because what we can even imagine, far less who we can reach, is constantly limited by societal structures. For me, literary criticism is promotion as well as understanding, a response to the writer to whom there is often no response, to folk who need the writing as much as they need anything. I know, from literary history, that writing disappears unless there is a response to it. Because I write about writers who are now writing, I hope to help ensure that their tradition has continuity and survives.

So my "method," to use a new "lit. crit." word, is not fixed but relates to what I read and to the historical context of the writers I read *and* to the many critical activities in which I am engaged, which may or may not involve writing. It is a learning from the language of creative writers, which is one of surprise, so that I might discover what language I might use. For my language is very much based on what I read and how it affects me, that is, on the surprise that comes from reading something that compels you to read differently, as I believe literature does. I, therefore, have no set method, another prerequisite of the new theory, since for me every work suggests a new approach. As risky as that might seem, it is, I believe, what intelligence means—a tuned sensitivity to that which is alive and therefore cannot be known until it is known. (p. 62)

> *Barbara Christian, "The Race for Theory," in* Cultural Critique, *No. 6, Spring, 1987, pp. 51-63.*

William E. Cain

[*Cain is an American critic and educator and the author of* The Crisis in Criticism: Theory, Literature, and Re-*form in English Studies (1984). In the following excerpt, he explores the role of history in African-American studies.*]

One of the most remarkable aspects of literary studies at the present time is the rapt absorption in "history," and this trend is especially evident in scholarship devoted to Afro-American literature. Many fine critics are now publishing in this field, and they are accomplishing much important, exciting work. Not only are they enriching their literary analyses with ample historical details, citations, and references, but they are also seeing how historical texts, documents, and other written records might themselves be profitably interpreted and their verbal complexity explored.

It might at first seem obvious that a critic interested in Afro-American literature would find himself or herself led to consider history carefully. The major Afro-American literary texts by Frederick Douglass, W. E. B. Du Bois, Richard Wright, Ralph Ellison, and others are clearly bound up with the history of race relations in America. One could not hope to speak and write well about these texts without focusing on their relation to, and place within, the struggles of the Afro-American people. Indeed, this literature would seem to possess its greatest meaning and relevance within the drama and movement of American and Afro-American history. Yet when critics examined these texts in the past—Ellison's *Invisible Man* is a notable case in point—they usually highlighted formal properties such as tone, symbolism, imagery, narrative structure, characterization. They rarely sought to connect the novel to Ellison's biography, the involvement of blacks in Communist and left-wing political organizations, the ideology of the Cold War, the emergence in the late 1940s and early 1950s of the Civil Rights campaigns, and the dynamics of black protest and leadership. Critics valued Ellison's novel for its literary distinction, for its coherence and power as a work of art.

In large measure this formalist approach, which today's historically-minded critics are seeking to counter, attests to the pervasive influence of the New Criticism. It was, after all, a central achievement of the New Criticism, in the 1930s and 1940s, to demonstrate the perils of an overinvestment in history and to hone methods for the intensive reading of specific texts, texts whose literary interest had been seemingly lost amid historical and philological facts. Of course many did, during this period, argue fervently against the New Critics' devaluation of history. A. S. P. Woodhouse, Douglas Bush, and Rosemond Tuve were particularly vocal in contesting the New Critical isolation of the text from its contexts and in assailing its apparent determination to transform all good poems into versions of the seventeenth-century lyric. The New Critics and their followers parried these challenges effectively, however. They were able to invoke the "literary history" which T. S. Eliot and F. R. Leavis had sketched in a number of important essays and books, and which the New Critics themselves, in works such as Cleanth Brooks' *Modern Poetry and the Tradition* (1939) and *The Well-Wrought Urn* (1947), had cogently elaborated. These were histories, it was said, that truly featured literature, refusing to surround it with non-literary matter. Even more importantly perhaps, the New Criticism made pedagogical sense; it turned students directly to the text itself, and it identified skills for the teacher to foster and the students to learn. It also provided a means through which to bond teaching to scholarly publication, as the insights gleaned from close readings in the classroom laid the groundwork for explicative studies of style and structure that quickly filled the academic journals.

As is well-known, the reaction set in during the mid-1960s when Roland Barthes, Jacques Derrida, Jacques Lacan, and the associated avatars of structuralism descended upon the United States. Extraordinary in its brilliance and impact, their writing provoked major changes in critical assumptions and technique. Eventually it would help kindle the emphasis on history we are witnessing today in the field of Afro-American literature and in other fields as well; but initially, it served primarily to dramatize limits to the interpretive methods of the New Criticism. Few in America stressed how Barthes and his Continental confrères might aid in returning us to history. For American critics, structuralism was valuable because it zeroed in on readers and the reading process, skeptically noted and sought to undermine the unduly neat New Critical stress on "poetic ambiguity" and "organic unity," and keyed literary and cultural studies to the "sign" and its systems.

The situation began to alter in the early to mid-1970s as literary theory continued to expand and as theorists started briskly to criticize the shortcomings of structuralism. More than anyone else, Michel Foucault inspired the many counter-statements to structuralism and, later, to post-structuralist deconstruction that resounded during these years. Whereas Barthes and Derrida had enabled American critics to refine, if not wholly break with, New Critical explication, Foucault, in his turn, revealed the absence of social, historical, and political contexts in the work which the newer "new criticism" had spawned.

Obviously I am writing in a kind of shorthand here. The story has curious complexities that I do not have room to trace, among them the manner in which defenders of structuralism, like the New Critics before them, professed that they had been historically inclined all along. Nevertheless it is basically true, I think, that by the mid-1970s literary theory had split into two main camps: deconstruction—headed up by Derrida and Paul de Man—and "archaeology of knowledge"—resourcefully practiced and described by Foucault. Many extolled the adroit textual studies of the deconstructionists, but a good many others deemed deconstruction to be narrow and complacent, too far removed from the pain and clash of history and the affiliations between knowledge and real-world power. Foucault re-legitimated history for men and women in literary studies and made it exciting. He bracingly appealed for "relentless erudition" and counseled critics to delve intrepidly into unread (or under-read) texts and to knock down the barriers separating the traditional academic departments.

Foucault and the scholars he influenced not only renewed the study of history, but also triggered the "opening up" of the canon to include texts by blacks and women and launched the movement toward "inter-disciplinary" approaches. Marxism and, especially, feminism, also contributed greatly to these trends. Intriguingly, deconstruction itself came to seem something of a friend rather than a foe; in fastening upon the "intertextuality" of texts, it brought notice to the manifold crossings that link one text to the next and that make notions of a discrete text and a tightly bound canon therefore seem highly misleading.

This account seems persuasive to me in accounting for the relative neglect of history in the literary/critical past, its return in the present, and its considerable appeal for scholars who are examining Afro-American texts. It is tempting to add that many academics' discontent with the Reagan administration has also boosted the increasingly animated investigation of history, power, politics. Reaganism, one could conceivably contend, has made the quest for "the real" and the commitment to historical reality into a scholarly imperative. But it must be admitted that it is difficult to determine exact relationships between what transpires in the academic disciplines and what is happening in the society as a whole. It is difficult, in a word, to know just how to connect the history of the various disciplines with general—sometimes called "big"—history.

Clearly there are links between the two histories—the academy is not a "world elsewhere"—yet the fit between them may be rougher than we ordinarily assume. Commentators on the critical and theoretical scene often take as a given, for example, that the political upheavals of the 1960s—Vietnam, feminism, Civil Rights—prompted the boom in literary theory, as though the structuralist and post-structuralist dynamic mirrored the marches on the street. To an extent, however, the changes within literary study have occurred "within" the discipline and show an internal logic. Again, this observation does not imply that academic history and Big history are unrelated, but, rather, recognizes that the current concern in literary studies for opening up the canon, feminist theory and practice, writing by minorities, and historical research with a political bent represents, if anything, a kind of belated "catching up" with the political energies and struggles of the 1960s. When structuralism and post-structuralism first appeared on the American shores, they were welcomed because they furnished models for interpreting classic texts, and decidedly not because they reflected campus and national politics.

At a certain, later point, critics and theorists attuned to the new theories and practices did take the important next step: they asked why *these* literary and theoretical texts and not others, why *these* methods (which seemed another type of formalism writ large) and not others more historically and politically astute. Let's disavow the rigidities of the canon and aim instead for greater pluralism, it was declared; let's cease trafficking in non-historical criticism, whether it be Brooks' or Derrida's. "History" then became a compelling interest for many scholars.

The abundant new "historical" work in literary studies today thus needs to be carefully considered in relation both to the history of the discipline and the history of American society and culture. We cannot assume that these different histories readily accord with one another, and we need to be cautious as we calibrate their affinities. How much does the new work flow from the historical currents of the discipline and academy in their own right? How much or how little does it develop from, and answer to, the general political situation? In the long run, will it minister more effectively to democratic values than did the kinds of work it has displaced and with which it currently competes? Such questions point to the necessity for ongoing inquiry into the nature and implications of academic labor. They make clear the need for regular stock-taking and revaluation, which is one of the functions of "theory" and which most, except for a few antitheoretical holdouts, now acknowledge as essential to work well done. (pp. 190-93)

During the 1960s and 1970s, literary criticism confronted some of the same troubles which unsettled the study of history. Students and faculty complained about the absence of black teachers in English departments, and also indignantly drew attention to the white male authors dominating the reading lists. Since that time, there have been changes for the better. The number of black men and women teaching literature is still smaller than it should be, but it has begun to grow somewhat. The canon, too, is certainly more inclusive than ever before. Long gone are the days when scholars could assemble an exhaustive history of American literature—as did the compilers of the *Literary History of the United States* (1948; 3rd. ed., 1963)—and not refer even once to Frederick Douglass. Literary critics now bring a keener historical consciousness to teaching and research. They are more interested in, and sensitive to, the place of history in literary study and the variety of writers and texts that literary history should embrace.

This is a welcome development, of course, but some of the self-proclaimed historical work in Afro-American literature and criticism has taken a disconcerting direction. On the one hand, it advances new claims for the historical importance of its authors, texts, organizing tropes, and linguistic practices. Yet, on the other, it occasionally seems riskily distant from the historical past of these literary materials, and nettlingly fails to place this grand textual repertoire at the service of the historical present. Such work also appears so intent upon considering how vanguard criticism changes perceptions of Afro-American literature that it misses opportunities to ask whether the literature might itself prompt adjustments in the procedures, values, and institutional networks of criticism.

I am led to these observations by my reading of Henry Louis Gates' collection, *Black Literature and Literary Theory,* a book which I simultaneously find admirable and distressing. *Black Literature and Literary Theory* represents an attempt to query and employ post-structuralist methods. Its dauntingly high-powered contributors wield an array of sophisticated, mostly deconstructionist, implements; and they write with a steely insistence upon each and every tropological and signifying turn, however much this might endanger the clarity of their prose. Many of the essays in Part I of the book, which is keyed to "theory," and in part II, pledged to "practice," are indeed smartly galvanizing. Gates himself provides a lively introduction,

"Criticism in the Jungle," and a dense but rewarding essay that stalks the signifying systems of Ishmael Reed's dazzling *Mumbo Jumbo.* (pp. 198-99)

[A] dismaying, and . . . representative sign of the methodological fault-lines of *Black Literature and Literary Theory* appears in Gates' Introduction when he opines that "we write, it seems to me, primarily for other critics of literature." This may well be correct, but it's surprising that Gates does not even balk at this situation, let alone grapple with it. Is it desirable that critics write for other critics? Is this the fate one wishes for Afro-American literature, whose texts are grafted to protest and struggle and have manifest political interest and resonant implications for American society? Might there be ways of reading and writing about Afro-American literature that enable us to break down the partition between professional critics and everybody else? One would think that post-structuralism, which vaunts its willingness to detonate entrenched assumptions, would generate at least a little skepticism on Gates' part about the conditions of criticism.

In many ways it is obviously desirable that Afro-American literature should become a field for the salaried intelligentsia to write about. We academics should care as much, and maybe more, about the texts in this domain as we do about the novels of Henry James and the poetry of T. S. Eliot; and, if doubts linger about their literary power and subtlety, we should be equipped to show that Douglass, Wright, and Hurston can stand up to jargon and stringent technical scrutiny as stoutly as do James and Eliot. But the risk that accompanies certain post-structuralist readings of Afro-American literature—a risk apparent in Gates' book—is that these readings may make the text *less* historically grounded and *less* socially significant even as they seek to enliven it with methodologically up-to-date, and seemingly historicized, terms. (pp. 200-01)

> *William E. Cain, "Literature, History, and Afro-American Studies," in* College English, *Vol. 50, No. 2, February, 1988, pp. 190-205.*

Craig Werner

[In the following excerpt, Werner discusses critical attacks on Gates and Robert Stepto.]

An unnecessary and wasteful internecine battle is being waged by critics of Afro-American literature. As the critical tradition—which can trace its lineage from W. E. B. DuBois and Sterling Brown through Larry Neal and Audre Lorde—reaches a professional maturity of ambiguous value, a substantial number of significant critics have found it necessary to align themselves with camps defined by their support of, or dismay over, "critical theory." Recent essays by Barbara Christian ("The Race for Theory," *Cultural Critique*) [see excerpt above], Norman Harris ("'Who's Zoomin' Who': The New Black Formalism," *MMLA*), and Joyce A. Joyce ("The Black Canon: Reconstructing Black American Literary Criticism," *New Literary History*) [see excerpt above] assail the "theoretical" criticism of Houston Baker, Robert Stepto, and Henry Louis Gates, Jr. Based in part on substance and in part on style—to accept, momentarily, a distinction ultimately irrelevant to Afro-American discourse—the battle threatens to create a situation in which critics on both sides fail to exploit useful insights generated within the other camp. If we are to remain or to become an actual community—a vision basic to the tradition on which all critics of Afro-American literature draw and to which many belong—we must now confront several basic questions: will we generate an alternative to the petty, hierarchical, and ultimately irrelevant disputes all too common in mainstream criticism? Will we succeed in constructing a discourse—consistent with the basic values of Afro-American writers from Frederick Douglass and Harriet Jacobs through Ralph Ellison and Toni Morrison—that can acknowledge diversity by accepting, nurturing, and *using* the insights of poststructuralists and black nationalists, pluralists and feminists, close readers and cultural historians?

The essays cited above did not instigate the current battle, which has roots both in nationalist attacks on integrationist poetics during the Black Aesthetic movement of the 1960s and in several theoretical essays published in Stepto's anthology *Afro-American Literature: The Reconstruction of Instruction* that attack modes of criticism focusing on "extra-literary" concerns. The success of these attacks, originally intended as correctives for the excess of the Black Aesthetic movement, can be measured by the defensive postures assumed by Harris, Joyce, and Christian, all of whom (rightly) perceive that Gates, Stepto, and Baker occupy positions closer to the center of literary power in the United States. Although the differences between individual positions should not be underestimated, Harris, Joyce, and Christian all criticize the theorists for imposing an inappropriate (continental, academic, Euro-American, abstract) vocabulary on Afro-American materials, for ignoring the political circumstances conditioning Afro-American literature, and (although Christian would probably not endorse this extension) for failing to accept "blackness" as an essence. Related to these substantial issues are a cluster of criticisms focusing on the theorists' styles, which are widely perceived as expressions of indifference to or contempt for the largely nonacademic Afro-American community. Although it frequently remains implicit—at least in print—this criticism is often accompanied by a corollary belief that the theorists, the most influential of whom are based at Ivy League institutions, have created a kind of literary Tuskegee Machine. Supported by the power of mainstream literary institutions such as *Critical Inquiry* and *The New York Times Book Review* (which selected Gates rather than a black woman critic to write a major essay celebrating black women's literary self-determination), this theoretical machine is seen as excluding or marginalizing critics—especially those based in the Midwest or South—who choose not to employ an acceptably academic vocabulary.

The publication of Gates's first critical book, *Figures in Black: Words, Signs and the "Racial" Self,* and of Stepto's essay on Charles Chesnutt (to be included in *Write Me A Tale: Storytelling in the Afro-American Narrative*) in Gunter Lenz's fine anthology *History and Tradition in Afro-American Culture* provides an ideal occasion for reconsidering the antitheoretical positions. An attentive reading of the new work suggests that the antitheorists have a tendency to create "straw men" whose positions are only distantly related to those actually professed by Gates or Stepto. For example, the oft-reiterated idea that Stepto and Gates seek to uproot literature from its social/cultural/political grounding clashes sharply with their actual practice. Both Gates and Stepto emphasize that the rhetorical and linguistic structures that characterize "black texts" derive from the specific historical circumstances of Afro-Americans in a world shaped by racist discourses. Far from denying the relationship between literary and political discourses, both Stepto and Gates understand linguistic structures as part of a larger context grounded in actively oppressive political structures. When Gates identifies "signifying" as the crucial Afro-American rhetorical strategy, he does so with an awareness that this masked, but still subversive, form of parody reflects the practical, highly political experience of slaves forced to hide their "real" thoughts from masters who could well punish open expression with death. Gates's emphasis on the continued viability of "signifying," then, can justifiably be interpreted as a highly political, although appropriately masked, comment on the continuing presence of the slave-master power structure in contemporary American society. Similarly, Stepto's dialectic of *ascent*—the journey from symbolic South (slavery, the projects) to symbolic North (Canada, a good job) and a freedom requiring Euro-American "literacy" (writing, the ability to negotiate economic and social conventions)—and *immersion*—the reverse journey to communal roots and Afro-American literacy (orality, music, the ability to negotiate the rituals of the black community) motivated by the isolation attendant on a successful ascent—is inextricably intertwined with the political contexts connecting the experiences of fugitive slaves and contemporary black professionals. As Norman Harris' . . . study *Connecting Times: The Sixties in Afro-American Fiction* demonstrates, Stepto's paradigm can be profitably applied to much more explicitly political readings of Afro-American literature.

Part of the misapprehension of Gates's and Stepto's political positions results from an unfortunate overemphasis on *Afro-American Literature: The Reconstruction of Instruction,* a somewhat polemical anthology reacting against the late—and perhaps decadent—phase of the Black Aesthetic movement. Too often taken as the theorists' canonical text, the anthology includes early versions (Stepto's partial articulation of ideas developed fully in *From Behind the Veil*) or experiments with methodologies later modified or abandoned (Gates's structuralist reading of Frederick Douglass). Any cogent critique of the theoretical positions must, at a minimum, acknowledge the early work as part of an ongoing process. This is not to suggest that past statements be placed beyond criticism, particularly when the critic chooses to reprint the early statements in contemporary contexts, as does Gates in *Figures in Black.* Given the existing confusion over the theorists' actual positions, it seems particularly unfortunate that Gates uses process—in itself a legitimate and necessary concept—as a way of avoiding commitment. Stressing that he has experimented with various voices (using structuralist and poststructuralist along with more traditional literary-historical methodologies), Gates collects essays written over the last decade without indicating those he would now endorse and those he recognizes as dead-ends. As a result, his germinal work on Ishmael Reed and Harriet Wilson is presented with the same "authority" as his extremely problematical attack on James Weldon Johnson's views of dialect writing or his somewhat programmatic structuralist reading of Douglass. Particularly in light of his willingness to attack the well-defined positions of the Black Aestheticians, it seems unfair for Gates to avoid an analogous clarity. It is to be hoped that his forthcoming theoretical study *The Signifying Monkey* will rectify this problem.

Ironically, the attack on the theorists' refusal to accept "blackness" as an "essential" reality—a characteristic, or complex of characteristics, existing in some sense beyond the mediating/distorting influence of Euro-American culture—highlights the single most important contribution of poststructuralist theory to Afro-American literary criticism. Articulating a perception shared with black feminist critics such as Christian and Lorde, Gates argues that the problem with the essentialist position lies *not* in its nationalist politics but in its denial of Afro-American diversity. To assert a single core of Afro-American identity is to reenforce, however unintentionally, the binary, hierarchical, substructure of Euro-American racist thought. Whether accorded positive or negative value, the "black essence" remains a minor function of a discourse that denies all value to difference, to "otherness." Accepting the oppressors' premises offers very little hope for successfully resisting the oppressors' power. In pursuing my own work on pluralist aesthetics, I have found Gates and Stepto compatible with the influence of such highly political "separatist" theorists as Malcolm X and Adrienne Rich. My "political" criticism of Gates would be precisely that he does not push the implications of poststructuralist theory far enough. By elevating the concept of "repetition and inversion" as the core of Afro-American aesthetics, he gives too little play to truly *different* elements of the Afro-American tradition, particularly the communal call-and-response dynamic (emphasized by Stepto) that subverts Euro-American ideas of individual performance as power.

The preceding defense should not be mistaken for uncritical acceptance of the theorists' positions. For if their work makes substantial contributions to Afro-American literary studies, it also raises serious issues concerning literary and professional style. Like the Euro-American theorists on whose work they draw, Gates, Stepto, and Baker have all drawn repeated criticism for the density and technical vocabulary of their writing. Even though diverse vocabularies are a real, inevitable, and ultimately desirable aspect of any pluralistic discourse, a curious tension would seem to exist between the professed principles of the theorists' work and their mode of expression. Given their laudable desire to derive critical principles from the Afro-American tradition—to signify on the Euro-American theorists whose work they revise—it seems strange that the theorists choose to speak in such undeniably difficult voices. The theorists are by no means unaware of the problem. In his somewhat intemperate response to Joyce's *New Literary History* essay, Gates emphasizes that he writes primarily for other writers and critics. Responding to my

review of *From Behind the Veil,* Stepto quite justifiably cautioned me against condescending to nonspecialist readers by insisting on a simplified vocabulary. Granting the legitimacy of both positions, it nonetheless seems clear that whatever the theoretical justification for the technical voice, it does not, in fact, communicate particularly well with *either* the general body of Afro-American literary critics (witness the Joyce, Harris, and Christian essays) *or* with the intelligent nonspecialist audience. It seems reasonable to suggest that Gates's, Baker's, and Stepto's stylistic choices reflect their immediate focus on the community of relatively sophisticated readers at Ivy League institutions where they teach. Without claiming access to any moral or political imperative, I would urge these critics to give deeper consideration to the realistic situations of potential readers in idiosyncratic positions throughout the diverse community of readers interested in Afro-American literature. . . . The beauty of the styles Gates, Stepto, and Baker invoke in constructing their critical heritage—DuBois and Hurston, the folktales, and the blues—lies largely in the subtlety with which they negotiate a variety of audiences. As Toni Morrison, Audre Lorde, and countless Afro-American musicians continue to demonstrate, such negotiation remains possible. As Duke Ellington and Julius Erving clearly know—to subvert the distinction offered near the beginning of this essay—in the Afro-American tradition style is substance, and substance is style.

Behind the question of literary style, however, lurks a more insidious issue concerning the professional style attributed to the theoretical critics. Based on a complicated tangle of half-truths, misperceptions, and a few troublesome facts, the theorists are frequently perceived as a function of a larger (and somewhat amorphously defined) American literary/academic power structure. My own populist paranoia—grounded in my Euro-American, Rocky Mountain upbringing and reenforced by four years teaching in the excellent Southern Studies program at the University of Mississippi—at times leads me to hallucinate elitist demons upon any mention of Yale, Harvard, New York City, or the Eastern Time Zone. Neither my professional experience nor my limited personal contact with the theorists has supported the demonic interpretation of their characters. Nonetheless, if Harris' and Joyce's essays suggest that they do not read the theorists' work with sufficient attention, there is a nagging suspicion—reenforced by Gates's editorial work on the anthologies *Black Literature and Literary Theory* and *"Race," Writing and Difference*—that the theorists do not read or value the work of those outside the theoretical elite at all. Certainly, as Christian's cogent essay emphasizes, many well-established critics feel that the theorists fail to understand or honor choices of voice and audience that differ from their own.

What seems clear in relation to the future development of Afro-American literary criticism is that *all* perspectives—theoretical or practical, political or textual—deserve, at a minimum, careful consideration. It has become increasingly necessary that we read one another's work openly and well, and that, where possible, we attempt to construct bridges between diverse vocabularies. Most basically, it is imperative that we not indulge ourselves in power-tripping or rhetorical posturing, both dangerous illusions in a depressing political context where the symbiotic relationship between exclusive discourses and oppressive institutions seems ever more clear. This is not to say we should not criticize one another's work. Indeed, we have reached the point where we can—and, out of respect for our writers, must—insist on *serious* work. We should not, out of respect for the diversity of our communities, insist upon a unified approach. (pp. 125-30)

> *Craig Werner, "Recent Books on Modern Black Fiction: An Essay-Review," in* Modern Fiction Studies, *Vol. 34, No. 1, Spring, 1988, pp. 125-35.*

Marcellus Blount

[*In the following excerpt, Blount provides an overview of recent theoretical approaches to African-American literary criticism.*]

As authors of three recent studies of Afro-American literature, Houston Baker, Melvin Dixon, and Henry Louis Gates respond in distinctive, yet complementary ways to the basic questions about the nature of Afro-Americanist criticism. What is its most appropriate language? What does it seek to accomplish? For whom is it written? These questions initiate our present quest for useful theories for reading Afro-American texts, and each in its own way problematizes the critic's access to clarity and authority. As a way of coming to terms with our various discourses, we should begin to acknowledge that Afro-Americanists publish for a multiplicity of reasons both personal and professional, scholarly and political, and that our work participates in diverse intellectual and cultural traditions that share and discriminate among various conventions of address and audience. The post-structuralist "discovery" that no theory of representation is free of its own devious agenda seems less shocking to Afro-Americanists, who know through experience and education, formal or otherwise, that while language is seldom fatal it does pose a constant threat to black subjectivity. The realization, both eager and wary, that language is a tool of liberation *and* oppression seems to be the always-given of the Afro-American experience. Black folks have already been there, and as Baker and [Amiri] Baraka would put it, this contemporary business and all is just the "changing same."

Indeed, the dilemma of the critic of Afro-American literature recalls in many ways the difficult decisions that have enabled Afro-Americans to develop and sustain a viable literary tradition. Historically, blacks have negotiated their identities within various Euro-American markets of society and culture, often by bartering their artistic sense of self for the right to speak, sometimes by subverting those economies of ideological and rhetorical oppression as a means of social and cultural self-determination. The choices that face Afro-Americans today have not changed, and the most perceptive recent critics of Afro-American literature have mastered rather easily the contradictory conventions of their trade in part, I suspect, through their brisk familiarity with the artistic quandaries

of Afro-American creative writers. Blacks have always found renewal out of the clash of disparate languages of the self, and cultural critic Albert Murray puts it best in his dialectic of "antagonistic cooperation." The social and political dynamics that both shape and disfigure Afro-American art, much as the institutions that permit and discourage Afro-Americanist scholarship, are engaged in perpetual and creative battle. Whatever our given names, our professional identities are inscribed within a history of continuing struggle.

Our present task of writing (and righting) Afro-American literary history participates in these efforts of black Americans, male and female, "free" and "enslaved," to sing, to speak, and to write themselves into artistic and political being. Resounding in Baker's **Modernism and the Harlem Renaissance,** Dixon's **Ride Out the Wilderness,** and Gates's **Figures in Black** are the voices of the Afro-American creative artists whose promise we are now fulfilling. By renewing the cultural aesthetics of Afro-American writers, these three critics offer compelling solutions to the problem which James Weldon Johnson depicted in his 1928 essay "The Dilemma of the Negro Author" as the double and racially divided audience, but which is as well the problem of our multiple and culturally divided discursive desire. Even if it were possible to select our intended audience, the relevant issues of language and power and authority would remain. Regardless of whether we would write primarily for blacks or whites, Afro-Americanists or non-Afro-Americanists, other scholars or general readers, the fact remains that we must strive to make our critical language our own, even if we, like our nineteenth-century spiritual ancestors, must be ruthless in exploiting whatever mode of discourse will help us either to clarify or to conceal our critical intentions. As critic Robert Stepto argues in **From Behind the Veil,** the nineteenth-century black writer's search for artistic voice, although variously structured, almost always involved the quest for freedom and literacy. While these writers, more often than not, could merely register the need or "their call" for freedom and literacy, twentieth-century black artists have formulated "their response" in a variety of ways richly emblematic of their shared creativity. While the terms of oppression have changed since the nineteenth century, the fundamental issues remain even today. How can Afro-Americans operate within Euro-American political and economic institutions such as the research-oriented university without forgetting or denying or losing the strength of their sustaining cultural heritage? The three black male critics under review have developed distinctive strategies for negotiating the terms of their *self*-possession, and I should like to discuss their recovery of Afro-American culture within and against the rhetoric of post-structuralist scholarship. By appropriating Stepto's model for reading Afro-American literary history, I will address briefly my notions of the Afro-American*ist* quest for freedom *beyond* literacy.

Although the periodization of literary and critical trends often can be misleading, we knew that the "contemporary" phase of Afro-American literary criticism had arrived with the editorial collaboration of Stepto and Dexter Fisher in **Afro-American Literature: The Reconstruction** *of Instruction* (1979). As a reaction against the explicitly political and sociologically-minded pronouncements of the lingering Black Arts Movement, the collected authors, including both Dixon and Gates, began to implore others to read Afro-American literature *as* literature, to view the political and cultural relations of Afro-American works as textual and rhetorical strategies, and to cease reading these texts as though all black writers stood before the judge of American race relations with either their hats or their guns in their hands. Among others, Baker attempts to demonstrate in an essay later to become a chapter in his *Blues, Ideology, and Afro-American Literature* (1984) that these "newest" critics, especially Gates and Stepto, were working to sever the lines that tie Afro-American literature to the political concerns of the Black Aesthetic spokesmen. Baker takes these "reconstructionists" to task for adopting the language of Euro-American literary theorists of the Yale persuasion, and while he is correct in reading Robert O'Meally's essay "Frederick Douglass's 1945 *Narrative*: This Text Was Meant To Be Preached" as a model for the study of the relations between the vernacular and written discourse, he undervalues the usefulness of Stepto's treatment of the rhetorical strategies of self-discovery and external authentication that shape the basic texts of the slave narrative tradition. Still Baker is essentially correct: ultimately one's sense of identity is inevitably political, whether or not we should want to read the material bases of the production of Afro-American literature.

Three of the pieces in Gates's collection of essays, *Figures in Black,* first appeared in *Afro-American Literature,* and within his own critical typology, he quite correctly categorizes them as examples of his "repetition and imitation" phase. These essays demonstrate his remarkable erudition and mastery of European and American history and philosophy, yet by enlisting the assistance of the very traditions that negate his own culture's subjectivity, Gates risks rhetorical subservience to the critical ideologies that have silenced and ignored his racial ancestors. His radical "liberation" from the bonds of the sociological imagination (as announced in *Afro-American Literature*) seems rather fettered, and if Gates's later criticism did not work to rescue him from the binary oppositions of his structuralist literacy, he might have provided us merely with yet another example of yet another brother gone.

Fortunately, Gates collects these early essays as markers for his later progress, as *Figures in Black* evolves into a compelling metaphor of his maturing critical self. Inscribed within the rhetoric of Douglass's narratives of slavery and freedom, Gates's essays move toward the critical autobiography of a brilliant ex-Europeanist. He presents his early critical confusion to heighten the clarity of his present voice, even as he revises his point of view in the earlier essays to emphasize the lines of continuity throughout his critical project. His essays take us up from the intellectual constraints of his earliest theoretical pieces, through his less ambitious and therefore more successful readings of individual authors, and finally toward the ground-breaking revelations of his rather ubiquitous article, **"The Blackness of Blackness: A Critique on the Sign and the Signifying Monkey."** By the end of the col-

lection, we are convinced that the Black Arts Movement continues still, albeit with Gates's decidedly new political agenda.

Throughout his career, Gates has been working in two different directions: he wants us to use contemporary theory to augment our understanding of Afro-American literature and to use Afro-American literature to influence our formulations of contemporary theory. In **"Signifying Monkey,"** he battles on both fronts, waging a full-scale war against cultural hegemony and critical ignorance, as various anxieties, subversions and parodies of influence, all conceptualized within the Europeanist deconstructions of [Paul] De Man, [Jacques] Derrida, [Jacques] Lacan, and others, are cast in the languages of African mythology and the Afro-American vernacular. For Gates, the basic instability of literary relations becomes a complicated system of reading and rereading, projection and displacement, as he attempts to theorize about a range of literary antagonisms as useful acts of cultural cooperation, even as he redefines such intertextual relations as instances of "signifying" and "signification."

We recognize the latter term as the albatross of various structuralisms, yet fortunately Gates invokes it only to replace it with Afro-American notions of signifying: that arena of cultural performance available to some of us when we grow tired of emulating Europeanist discourse. Most of us would not think of signifying as the "trope of tropes," but we do anticipate its eagerness to indulge our delight in verbal play, as well as its usefulness for parodying the things and people closest to us. The Signifying Monkey, like his Yoruba relations, is a master of wit and narrative performance; within black communities, "signifying," his lifelong occupation, is a distinctive style of narrative parody and reinterpretation. In Gates's theory, we see the relationships among [Jean] Toomer, [Sterling A.] Brown, [Zora Neale] Hurston, [Ralph] Ellison, [Richard] Wright, and [Ishmael] Reed as ones of repeated signifying, as these classic Afro-American writers emerge in a cultural tradition of repetition and revision. As Gates's work has developed, he has discovered that by translating critical theory into vernacular practice he can speak with equal authority to audiences of both Europeanists and Afro-Americanists. In **"Signifying Monkey,"** he transforms his earlier imitations into parody, as he exploits present conventions of jargon-ridden diction, willful misreading, and theoretical solipsism in order to undermine and to disrupt the tendencies of contemporary critical theory. Like the prescient grandfather in Ellison's *Invisible Man,* he seems to have overcome contemporary theorists with his "yeses," and with the bristling ironies of his endeavor, he signifies upon the theorist camp. Needless to say, the Signifying Monkey knows that Afro-Americanist freedom lies *beyond* Euro-American critical literacy. (pp. 462-66)

Marcellus Blount, "Written by Ourselves," in The Southern Review, *Louisiana State University, Vol. 24, No. 2, Spring, 1988, pp. 462-72.*

Theodore O. Mason, Jr.

[*In the following essay, Mason discusses the positions of Gates, Joyce A. Joyce, and Houston A. Baker, Jr. on the role of the literary critic.*]

In its Winter 1987 issue, *New Literary History* published a series of brief articles by three prominent Afro-American literary critics concerning the issue of canon formation and the current state of black literature and literary criticism. At first glance, the vehemence of the exchange between Joyce A. Joyce, Henry Louis Gates, Jr., and Houston Baker, strikes the reader as remarkable. This heat is more than the result of the usual academic disagreements concerning the interpretation, significance, or value of particular events or texts. Though we find these disagreements in the pages of this issue of *New Literary History,* I believe we find much more. Even the casual reader discovers what appears to be the extraordinarily personal nature of the remarks made by all three critics. To be sure, one might attribute the intransigence, and occasionally the truculence, of each critic to some barely concealed personal animus. But closer inspection reveals that all three—Joyce, Gates, and Baker—conceive of themselves as players in a game for exceedingly high stakes (personal issues aside). They are probably correct in this belief, since canon-formation remains a fascination among many critics of Afro-American literature. And those same critics—including Gates, Baker, and Robert Stepto, among others—hold that a good deal of the future of Afro-American literary study depends upon how the issue of canon-formation gets resolved with respect to black literature.

Certainly, it would be a mistake to ignore the specifics of the exchange between Joyce, Gates, and Baker, even if our interests lie more in the underpinnings of those arguments and their subsequent implications. If we are to believe Joyce, her two male antagonists hide the most unscrupulous of intentions behind the veil of post-structuralist criticism. Their attention to language use, expressed in near-scientific terminology, masks a virulent misogyny, a fundamental betrayal of their race, and a mean and narrow self-aggrandizement. The sycophantic dependence upon European modes of criticism leads Gates and Baker, argues Professor Joyce, to an almost willed submission to racist oppression. In this view, black post-structuralism (as advanced by Gates in an earlier work, **"Preface to Blackness: Text and Pretext"**) denies the significance of "blackness or race as an important element of [the] literary analysis of black literature." This deemphasis on race as a significant determinant derives from a view of culture and literary production predominantly, if not exclusively "elitist" and "exogamic."

On the other hand, if we are to believe Baker and Gates, Professor Joyce's objections to Afro-American post-structuralism stem from a faulty understanding of culture, a general intellectual "laziness and complacency," the persistent ethos of "minstrelsy," and a fundamental ignorance of recent modes of criticism. Says Baker, "There is no evidence in [her article] that Professor Joyce has read either European or American post-structuralists, or Afro-American post-structuralists." Her desire to rededicate

criticism to the service of black people and black culture then is nothing more than a naive and fuzzy-headed populism. In fact, this populism works in the service of a general intellectual and ideological conservatism that reflexively criticizes the innovative because it fears the instability of change and the challenge of the new.

The ideological implications raised by these respective remarks, as well as those raised by the larger issue of canon-formation itself, reveal much more than these particular arguments, which can only be summarized briefly here. Though there is much to admire in Professor Joyce's argument, I find room there for sympathetic disagreement, too. In her analysis, authority should reside generally in the writer's or the critic's projected audience—in this instance the black audience. As she makes clear in an opening anecdote concerning a student's inability to understand a James Baldwin essay, the writer has a responsibility to make his ideas clear, presumably to the broadest possible audience. But this unexceptionable requirement upon the writer quickly becomes politically and ideologically charged. In Arnoldian accents, Professor Joyce indicates the nature of the relationship among black writers, black critics, and black audiences. Traditionally (according to Joyce), "Black American literary critics, like Black creative writers, saw a direct relationship between Black lives—Black realities—and Black literature. The function of the creative writer and the literary scholar was to guide, to serve as an intermediary in explaining the relationship between Black people and those forces that attempt to subdue them." The black critic, then, ought to reassume this mantle, apparently discarded by black post-structuralists in the pursuit of approval by the white critical establishment. "It should be the job of Black literary critics to force ideas to the surface, to give them force in order to affect, to guide, to animate, and to arouse the minds and emotions of Black people." Acting as a mediator searching for the points of contact between the utilitarian political interests of the black community and the aesthetic and linguistic aspects of literary analysis, the critic facilitates the creation of a black counter-hegemony based on the overarching principle of familial love and loyalty.

While this vision of ethnic solidarity has its laudable aspects, its foundations likely will not stand up to anything like close analysis. For one thing, Professor Joyce neglects an examination of the manifest class basis of literary production and consumption in the United States. Most of the teaching of literature in this country takes place in the academies of the Empire (to borrow from Bruce Franklin), a condition which makes the writer's or the critic's reaching "The People" a problematic undertaking at best. At the very least, a reader's access to the forum wherein he or she might receive the kind of invigorating guidance Joyce recommends is absolutely controlled by brute economic and class considerations. College education is a middle- and upper-class privilege, generally unavailable to members of the under classes. Financial conditions determine completely one's capacity to benefit from the collective wisdom of writers and critics. Although Joyce suggests in her rejoinder to Gates and Baker that the minds she instructs in college courses will themselves affect other minds in a kind of ripple effect, such a process will not meet the powerful demands she places on the critic, especially given the class basis of higher education in America. If we step outside the upper-class circle of higher education and ask the question, who reads any serious literature or literary comment (even a Baldwin essay in *Essence*), the frightening answer to that question should be enough to damage the position which advocates conferring authority on a populist audience.

If it were not enough that the audience upon which Joyce's argument depends is fundamentally an illusion and its access to literature hardly comprehensive, the kinds of arguments articulated in this issue of *New Literary History* seem even further removed from the condition and—in their more esoteric form—the understanding of the People. Literary production in the United States is ridden with class distinctions of its own, mirroring in roughly congruent fashion the class basis of everyday life—from "lay" readers up through the varying professional ranks, in the process of professional advancement, and in the acknowledgment that certain journals are superior to others. This form of elitism constitutes a fundamental part of the industry that is literary production and comment. A critic leveling the charge of elitism at a colleague either states the obvious or ignores his or her own involvement in a highly stratified profession, where making serious valuative judgments about the writer's work and other critics' work, too, is part of the job.

Yet, if the foundations of Professor Joyce's arguments betray certain hindering limitations, the arguments of Professors Gates and Baker assuredly fare no better. Their strategy in response to Professor Joyce's attack is to take the intellectual high ground. Gates acknowledges the fundamental class basis of literary production by way of an admission that criticism is written for an educated audience of writers and critics. He defends that position on the grounds that literary theory is necessarily a professional pursuit with a long and complicated tradition *generally* beyond the understanding of "the People" whom Professor Joyce sees as so central to the enterprise. In this model, all power goes not to the People but to the intellectual superiority of theory as a pursuit and to the professionalization of Afro-American literary criticism as an enterprise. The critic of Afro-American literature is more correctly seen, in Gates's view, not as a cultural commentator or ideological priest, so much as a scientist who deals in the aesthetic permutations of language. Taking the scientific approach presumably makes for better criticism and theory in part because the scientist develops his or her skill by an insistent immersion in a community of like-minded readers and writers. Over time this community develops special terminology and methods that give rise to professional literature (criticism and theory) of greater accuracy, insightfulness, and truth. Yet . . . the black poststructuralist position operates out of a naive understanding of science as a pursuit, seeing in literary versions of mathematical accuracy and theoretical consistency (fictions in themselves) some claim to objectivity and overarching truth.

Gates's implicit sensitivity to the issue of class does not lead him to "deconstruct" the business of literary production and comment, but rather to a generalized, if slightly uneasy, acceptance of the status quo. To be sure, both he and Professor Baker envision the critic of Afro-American literature combatting the racism inherent in previous versions of Western criticism. Gates devotes a significant part of his rebuttal to recapitulating the self-evident value of the theoretical tradition—a tradition bearing a huge responsibility.

> A literary tradition, like an individual, is to a large extent defined by its past, its received traditions. We critics in the 1980s have the especial privilege of explicating the black tradition in ever closer detail. We shall not meet this challenge by remaining afraid of, or naive about, literary theory; rather, we will only inflict upon our literary tradition the violation of the uniformed reading. We are the keepers of the black literary tradition. No matter what theories we seem to embrace, we have more in common with each other than we do with any other critic of any other literature. We write for each other, and for our own contemporary writers. This relation is a sacred trust.

Any astute reader will recognize that in this passage Gates has exchanged the scientist's smock for clerical vestments. The black critic is now a priest, carefully guarding the collective tribal wisdom from violation by the vulgar and the uninitiated. Yet even though Gates severely limits membership in this fraternity and explicitly denies that the black critic plays any significant role in the political and economic liberation of black people, it is hard not to discover that both Joyce and Gates see the black critic as performing generally the same role. Although Gates might deny the connection, if we ask "For whom is this tradition kept?" the answer will not be simply "for the clerical class," even though Gates asserts that this is his audience. Rather the answer will inevitably invoke larger spheres such as *black people,* or more abstractly *black culture.* For her part, if Professor Joyce finds this connection disquieting, she can hardly escape a recognition of her membership in the priest class. Joyce, Gates, and Baker all emphasize the need for a protective solidarity to defend black culture and the black critical tradition from the depredations of the surrounding racist environment. Even if Joyce phrases this need in terms of familial love and Gates by distinction in the accents of the scientist or the cleric, little, finally seems to separate them.

Clearly, then, *both* sides in this debate try to take the high ground by assuming the mantle of liberator and custodian. Aside from the more general and explicit reasons for adopting this perspective, assuming the guise of liberationist is a response to the problematic of being black in the Academy (and in Joyce's case black and female). It is easy to slip into a sense of profound complicity in the "distribution" of hegemonic values when one works as an academic. When one's critical and pedagogical stance is avowedly antagonistic to dominant values (such as those skeptical methodologies which unmask hidden oppressive structures), the same yet holds true: the most radical postures—perhaps especially the most radical ones—promote the interests of the institution and the industry at large.

The very organization of labor within the university tends to limit radically the possibility of ideological change within the walls of the academy. Literary study is organized into departments where critical and ideological debate is frequently rendered ineffective or irrelevant, frustrated by the compartmentalization of interests and approaches. The critic who wishes to revise canons by way of a revised evaluation of black literature frequently finds himself or herself the lone voice that "does" Afro-American literature, his or her effectiveness repressed by the very "liberality" that occasioned his or her appointment in the first place.

The "intramural" struggle voiced in the pages of *New Literary History* reflects precisely the problem of being a black academic in a racist environment on two grounds. In truth, the conflict between the two parties is not about methods or goals (since the differences between the two on these grounds are radically overestimated and overstated), but really about apostolic succession, "generational" conflict, gender, and power. Baker is likely aware of the possible "generational" aspects of this exchange, especially in view of his persuasive and influential second chapter in **Blues, Ideology, and Afro-American Literature: A Vernacular Theory** ["Discovering America: Generational Shifts, Afro-American Literary Criticism, and the Study of Expressive Culture"]. Baker and Gates represent the class of well-established, older, and generally male, academic critics, who take as their project the reconstruction of Afro-American literary criticism, even if they disagree about the appropriate methods to effect this reconstruction. Gates sees greater possibilities in rhetorical and formal criticism, Baker in a reinvigorated use of the social and the vernacular aspects of Afro-American expressive culture. Joyce, on the other hand, belongs to the following generation—a group comprising a significant number of immensely talented women.

Within an environment perceived to be hostile and racist, this debate between generations becomes an argument about credentials: who's black and who's not, who has the greater interests of black people at heart, and so on. Aside from the manifest unsubstantiability of these assertions (and perhaps even their irrelevance, given the conditions under which we work), one clearly sees in the accents of their discussion the signs of an uneasy defensiveness, particularly in the need to invoke a shielding authority (the People or Science) in various guises. The point here is not that able critics such as Joyce, Gates, and Baker have no need to feel defensive; the opposite is more likely true. The point *is* that a submission to the very forces they wish to combat occasions the dismaying spectacle seen in the pages of *New Literary History:* the "Dozens" meets the Academy.

Another way of thinking about this issue is to recognize the similarities between this published disagreement and the Battle Royal in Ellison's *Invisible Man,* where young black men are blindfolded and made to fight each other for the amusement of whites. And while it is difficult to know what motivated the editors of *New Literary History* to publish this argument (whose contributors saved their best work for other places), perceiving the similarities be-

tween the Battle Royal and this discussion proves difficult to avoid. At least the Invisible Man got a scholarship out of his fight.

Those of us sitting in the balcony with both a professional and personal interest in the issues raised by Joyce, Gates, and Baker have good reason to feel confronted with Hobson's choice. Neither of these positions outlined in the pages of *New Literary History* seems especially fruitful. One way out of this dilemma is to realize that we labor in a field remarkably absent of authority. We discover more and more that Afro-American literary criticism is an area of pursuit remarkably open and fruitfully unstable, the hegemonic claims made on behalf of Afro-American post-structuralism and other theoretical positions notwithstanding.

This instability is occasioned by the constant "appearance" of new works, for one thing. The "rediscovery" of heretofore undervalued texts (Gates's resuscitation of Harriet Wilson's *Our Nig,* for instance) can do nothing but make dubious relatively fixed notions of the nature, methods, results, and goals of Afro-American literary criticism. The redefinition of "literary culture" to include previously excluded expressive forms also facilitates this necessary process of liberalization. The newness of the "tradition" makes scholarship in this area usefully tentative and provisional. This provisionality means that critical pluralism has a higher value than critical monism and that the primary works themselves that receive our attention take on a reinvigorated authority.

Yet more importantly, we need to place our critical and theoretical efforts even more persistently within the perimeter of a rejuvenated cultural and ideological context. While the recent developments in theoretical criticism mark an advance over vulgarized "race and superstructure" criticism, no significant argument has been advanced that challenges the value of "reading" literary production and comment within the context of cultural formations.

It is easy to understand that the "avant-garde" in current Afro-American literary criticism arose in response to the crudities, real and perceived, of literature and literary comment produced in the late sixties and early seventies. Too often, that form of writing reflexively emphasized directness, simplicity, and an essential nonliterariness in response to domination by white upper-class literary models and values. The emphasis on "blackness" and liberationist pyrotechnics frequently masked a poverty of aesthetic vision. Yet the aesthetics of the sixties produced at least one benefit of incalculable value—the persistent linkage of rhetoric and ideology—even if in these earlier versions such a connection was frequently monolithic and underdeveloped.

If indeed the most pressing project confronting us is to *begin* work in sorting out the boundaries, quality, and variety of the Afro-American literary tradition, then to do so without recourse to culture seems silly and short-sighted at best. The "blackness" that concerns us may be more rhetorical and tropological than transcendent, and our interests may lie more in aesthetics than anything else, yet it remains that the *aesthetic* is an ineluctably cultural and ideological category. Gates himself provides a useful example of the cultural basis of aesthetics, despite his criticisms of critical approaches more cultural than aesthetic.

One of the central concepts in Gates's critical lexicon is *integrity*. In his description of integrity, Gates invokes the now familiar NEH symposium [a seminar on redefining black literature held at Yale University in June, 1977] that gave rise to ***Afro-American Literature: The Reconstruction of Instruction.*** He outlines the standard argument of that symposium's intentions, i.e., that it sought to rescue Afro-American literature from the hands of vulgar sociologists who wanted to treat literature as raw data that when analyzed would chronicle the history of black degradation caused by white racism. *Integrity* I take to refer to the treatment of literature as literature and not as something else, as aesthetic rather than "cultural," revealing an interest in rhetoric and form, rather than paraphrasable content. Parts of this critical perspective are certainly unexceptional. But Gates causes himself a problem when he argues, "Further, and most crucially, the conference seemed to argue, just as we read and reread Joyce's *Ulysses* more to discover the art of the novel than to remark at the manners and morals of a Dublin Jew, we must read the works of black authors as discrete manifestations of form and genre and as implicit commentaries on the white literature of similar structure. The conference itself, in short, represented an attempt to take the 'mau-mauing' out of the black literary criticism that defined the 'Black Aesthetic Movement' of the sixties and transform it into a valid field of intellectual inquiry once again." The confusions in this particular argument are manifold and problematic. The avowed motivation in Gates's representation of this symposium's motives is intellectual—i.e., to restore intellectual rigor and validity to a deteriorating field of criticism. To do so, one must evidently depoliticize criticism, returning its *integrity* by closer (if not exclusive) scrutiny to matters of form and rhetoric. Yet Gates's reference to James Joyce complicates and vexes his essay's insistence on the depoliticization of criticism. I can think of no more profoundly political or ideologically-based consideration than "implicit commentaries on the white literature of similar structure," a kind of literary practice that has as its heart an interest in the relation between hegemonic discourse and dominated discourse. Gates's reluctance to enter the realm of ideology is even more puzzling given his clear understanding of the fashion in which past critical practices have excluded blacks from any consideration as artists. (After all, this issue did form the subject of his doctoral dissertation.) In the light of this obvious contradiction indicated by the reference to Joyce and similar instances elsewhere, we have to view the concept of *integrity* in one of two ways. Either literary study (even in this proper idealized form) is not nearly so *integral* as it seems, or Gates is actually making an argument not against politics and ideology as general concerns, but rather is mounting an attack on a specific political ideology, the liberationist movement of the sixties. Presumably, he could also hold both views. In any case, as an argument for methodological rigor and purity, *integrity* can hardly be said to be minimally successful, much less compelling.

Even though Gates characterizes his critical approach as fundamentally rhetorical and formal, his work is more culturally based than he would prefer to admit. In fact, where Gates imagines himself to be most ideologically "free," he finds himself most ideologically bound. The latter stages of **"Literary Theory and the Black Tradition,"** the first chapter in *Figures in Black,* demonstrate this condition especially well. In a discussion of Houston Baker's "repudiation" and Robert Stepto's "authentication," Gates writes, "I have tried to supplement these creative theories by locating a metaphor for literary history that arises from within the black idiom exclusively, that is not dependent upon black-white power or racial relations, and that is essentially rhetorical. I call it critical signification, and I take it from the black rhetorical strategy called Signifyin(g)." While Gates is right to save the useful things from Baker and Stepto, and while his repudiation of vulgar Marxist or nationalist criticism is also appropriate, this defense of signifyin(g) proves hard to sustain. Suppose for a moment that the origins of signifyin(g) actually have nothing to do with black-white power or racial relations and are essentially rhetorical and literary (a dubious proposition at best). I would argue that even exclusively "intertextual" relations are about power and hardly divorced from the larger ideological considerations that condition literary production, even if those considerations are far more vexed and involved than vulgarized discourse would have them. If I "trope off" or "riff off" of another artist's or critic's work (or if I use *signifyin(g)* as part of a literary analysis, for instance), I am using his or her power in some significant fashion. I channel it, funnel it, emend it to my own purposes. This usage cannot be said to take place outside of the realm of cultural relations in any sense of the word. This "troping" is inevitably an implicit, if not explicit, comment on the source I'm using.

Now, when a black writer takes a trope used by writers of other races and cultures, which happens frequently, that exchange has immediate cultural and historical implications that no critic or theorist can justifiably ignore. Ellison's use of the underground man, or Wright's for that matter, or Reed's use of the Western or the radio-play, or his parody of the *Bildungsroman* (in *Free-Lance Pallbearers*), or Morrison's borrowing from classical epic in *Song of Solomon*—by their very use, all of these rhetorical practices borrowed from Western tradition make a comment on a particular rhetorical relation, but also on a cultural and ideological one.

What surprises me is that Gates *should* be aware of this. I cite only two instances from the first chapter of *Figures in Black.* When Gates criticizes Baker's *repudiation,* he cites Baker's rejection of the importance of the frontier in Afro-American literature. By refuting Baker's assertion that the frontier is of no importance in Afro-American literature, Gates acknowledges an intercultural relation between white and black American literature that conditions literary production and study. In addition, when he argues in a number of places that his entire critical project concerns the eclectic use of European modes of criticism and their transformation by application to Afro-American literary texts, it's hard to imagine that he believes such a transformation will be complete, or that even if complete, that the ideological issues conditioning that transformation (some of which are "extra-literary") will somehow disappear. The only reason why Paul de Man, for instance, has to be "transformed" is that he was a white European of a particular class who considered primarily European literature.

When Gates uses *intertextuality* or some variant of that word in conjunction with this critical transformation, he implicitly establishes a relationship between himself and a source for that critical terminology that is not merely rhetorical, since at base that relationship concerns the connections between marginalized discourse and dominant discourse, between marginalized and dominant classes. In fact, such a transformation, or even the attempt at transformation, constitutes both a profoundly rhetorical and explicitly ideological act. Perhaps most succinctly stated, formal and rhetorical practices *are,* in some significant fashion, always culturally grounded and, hence, ideological.

Like the exchange between Joyce, Gates, and Baker in *New Literary History,* the attempt to divorce the literary consideration of Afro-American literature from the cultural consideration of Afro-American literature is overburdened with a language and a tone disproportionate with its real effects on the practice of critics of Afro-American literature or its general intellectual significance. This excessive burden results from a covert privileging of literary theory generally (protests to the contrary notwithstanding), and perhaps more specifically the fetishizing of canon-formation as a practice.

The field of Afro-American letters is as yet only minimally explored, despite the publication of a vast number of worthy books and articles, including those mentioned here. As the first step toward a fuller recognition of the useful fluidity and uncertainty occasioned by this condition, I suggest that canon-formation as an enterprise be junked, in favor of more persistent textual and cultural analysis. This type of analysis needs to be conditioned by an appreciation of the advances of theory, but not overawed by theory. At this point, canon-formation is a reflexive trope too dependent on the dominant mainstream academic tradition, and likely a step or two behind. In its place should come a greater commitment to an ideological, critical, and intellectual independence. And with that independence should come a recognition that in general, dominant modes of analysis and the dominant literary tradition itself can either aid or hinder what we do, but that finally they lack authoritative power. (pp. 606-14)

> *Theodore O. Mason, Jr., "Between the Populist and the Scientist: Ideology and Power in Recent Afro-American Literary Criticism or 'The Dozens' as Scholarship," in* Callaloo, *Vol. 11, No. 3, Summer, 1988, pp. 606-15.*

John Wideman

If you look up "signifying" in a dictionary, you'll find a set of definitions. If you hear the word used by a black person, chances are you'll need something more than a dictionary to understand what the speaker means. The word "signifying" is situated where Henry Louis Gates Jr. in [*The Signifying Monkey: A Theory of Afro-American Literary Criticism*] situates the critic of comparative black literature, "at a sort of crossroads, a discursive crossroads at which two languages meet, be these languages Yoruba and English, or Spanish and French, or even (perhaps especially) the black vernacular and standard English."

To identify the concept of signifying drawn from Afro-American oral tradition and signal its difference from, as well as convergence with, another universe of discourse, Mr. Gates employs a capital letter to distinguish black usage: Signifying. Since this seemingly innocent naming—assigning upper case to black, lower case to white—also implies hierarchy and pecking order, it is itself an example of Signifying. Signifying is verbal play—serious play that serves as instruction, entertainment, mental exercise, preparation for interacting with friend and foe in the social arena. In black vernacular, Signifying is a sign that words cannot be trusted, that even the most literal utterance allows room for interpretation, that language is both carnival and minefield.

It is not difficult to understand why Africans forcibly transported across an ocean would be suspicious of a language that gave them the status of chattel slaves and defined them as less than human. Mastery of that language entailed internalization of the master's values, paying lip service, at the very least, to the notion of white superiority. Slaves learned to resist this literal process of self-destruction by saying little, saying no, saying to themselves and each other a different version of the new tongue, a version that slipped the yoke and turned the joke back upon those who would destroy them.

Double-voiced, double-edged, intricately, intimately relating African languages with European languages in a fashion that transforms both, black vernacular records a culture coming into being. The Signifying Monkey—one ear trained on his African mentor, the Yoruba trickster god Esu-Elegbara, the other taking in the polyvoiced babble of the New World, mischievous eyes and mouth never still—is the figure brilliantly drawn by Mr. Gates to evoke the chain of Signifiers that articulate a black literary heritage. Mr. Gates divides his study into two parts. The first is theoretical, demonstrating how Esu-Elegbara and the Signifying Monkey "serve in their respective traditions as points of conscious articulation of language traditions, aware of themselves as traditions, complete with a history, patterns of development and revision, and internal principles of patterning and organization. Theirs is a metadiscourse, a discourse about itself."

Part Two consists of close readings of individual texts. Mr. Gates focuses first on a group of ex-slave narratives from the late 18th century, and follows that with a section each on Zora Neale Hurston's *Their Eyes Were Watching God,* Ishmael Reed's *Mumbo Jumbo* and Alice Walker's *The Color Purple.* These critiques are erudite, imaginative, instructive, even though *The Color Purple* receives by far the least effective treatment; Mr. Gates is surprisingly unaggressive as he discusses the conventions embodied in epistolary novels, skipping over matters, such as the function of comic spelling in Celie's letters, that have direct bearing on his argument.

As the Signifying Monkey goes on about the business of proving that "a truly indigenous black literary criticism is to be found in the vernacular," the reader is treated to fascinating insights into West African divining rituals, the myths and philosophy that drive them, a comprehensive survey of the literature on Signifying, evidence of how cursorily the works of Afro-American writers have been read, visitations from luminaries of post-modernist criticism. Mr. Gates engages in a kind of literary archeological expedition that reminds us that the author, the W. E. B. Du Bois Professor of Literature at Cornell University, is a collector of books, one who already has to his credit a discovery, *Our Nig,* that has forced historians to push back the starting date of black novel-writing in America to 1859. In other words, this somewhat intimidating, quite serious essay in literary criticism can be enjoyed by a variety of readers.

Mr. Gates is strongest when he renders the spirit of the tradition while he interprets it, sustaining an illusion of spontaneous invention and discovery. The opposite of this improvisatory mode is a highly determined, premeditated, sometimes assaultive prose when the text has something to prove, no matter how evidence is stretched or fast-shuffled. Esu-Elegbara's high-spirited presence is forgotten. The author's gift for mimicry and signifying revision occasionally leads him astray—to reproducing the double talk of those critics bemused by the self-reflexive, self-referential dimensions of language. Even the Signifying Monkey can't make that dead horse go.

The trope of the "Talking Book" (scenes in which books *speak* to the literate but remain silent to the entreaties of the unlettered) that Mr. Gates employs to connect four ex-slave narratives is an example of how the author pushes too hard. Though each narrative contains a Talking Book scene, correspondences among the scenes appear arbitrary, strained. To demonstrate relationships among tropes, is it important or not to establish that artists knew each other's work? Mr. Gates's description of Jelly Roll Morton's recording "Maple Leaf Rag" makes it clear that Morton possessed intimate acquaintance with the music he revised, extended, Signified upon. Ishmael Reed's parodies and pastiches depend on knowledge of the sources he sends up. For earlier writers is it enough to point out that certain things were in the air, whether or not specific links can be proved? What about the Talking Book trope in literature not written by blacks? Was it a common way of "figuring" literacy versus illiteracy? Is it important or not to establish the blackness of this trope?

In his close readings of individual books, Mr. Gates shines, teaching us how to read better and also justifying the complexity of his theoretical approach. He demonstrates conclusively how the narrator of *Their Eyes Were Watching God* achieves a synthesis of oral and written language, standing inside and outside of the character of Janie, controlling Janie's voice in order to free it. Russian Formalists and the writer and critic Tzvetan Todorov are pushed into service, and his detective fiction typology helps unscramble the multiple plots that structure *Mumbo*

Jumbo. Eclectic, exciting, convincing, provocative, challenging even when he's not altogether convincing, Mr. Gates gives black literature room to breathe, invents interpretive frameworks that enable us to experience black writing rather than label it in terms of theme or ideology. From this perspective his book is a generous, long-awaited gift.

At least three times in his preface, Mr. Gates remarks that the language of his book is different from the language he writes about, so different it finally may be opaque to the very folks whose traditions he's celebrating. The knowledge that he is writing himself away from his people bothers him enough to offer an apology: "If I have once again failed to do so [write a book his parents and brother can understand], then once again I apologize."

In spite of the playful banter in which this apology is embedded, there is an irony here that is sharp and possibly painful. Rather than growing closer, standard English and black vernacular seem to be splitting farther apart. Blacks and whites find it increasingly difficult to understand one another. As a man in the middle, Mr. Gates asks questions all of us who write and teach should be asking ourselves. Are we part of the problem? Why is it that the more we learn, the more difficult it is to share it without retreating to arcane, specialist vocabularies? At what point do our words become an irrelevance to the people who nurtured us, whose lives we sought to touch and celebrate when we embarked on a quest for knowledge?

One goal of Mr. Gates's book is to illuminate the power of black vernacular tradition, its consciousness of itself at extremely complex, sophisticated levels. Is it necessary or appropriate that the language of that book be foreign to the majority of the tradition's carriers? What's being lost and gained? Maybe the best news about *The Signifying Monkey* is its willingness to struggle with such issues. Like great novels that force us to view the world differently, Mr. Gates's compelling study suggests new ways of seeing. When racist assumptions are replaced by multicultural awareness, literary debate can be enlivened, enriched. Mastering the master tongue remains a perilous enterprise for the minority writer. How far we've come, how far still to go.

> *John Wideman, "Playing, Not Joking, with Language," in* The New York Times Book Review, *August 14, 1988, p. 3.*

Andrew Delbanco

[*Delbanco is an American critic and educator. In the following review of* The Signifying Monkey: A Theory of Afro-American Literary Criticism *and* Figures in Black: Words, Signs, and the "Racial Self," *Delbanco examines Gates's theory of "Signifyin(g)."*]

In the late 1930s a young writer named Richard Wright charged that virtually all black American writers before him had approached "the Court of American Public Opinion dressed in the knee-pants of servility." Having addressed themselves for too long with a schoolboy's eagerness to impress "a small white audience rather than . . . a Negro one," black writers, Wright declared, should henceforth stop catering to white tastes, and turn instead to their own religious and folk traditions in America:

> There is . . . a culture of the Negro which is his and has been addressed to him; a culture which has, for good or ill, helped to clarify his consciousness and create emotional attitudes which are conducive to action. This culture has stemmed mainly from two sources: (1) the Negro church; (2) and the folklore of the Negro people.

Wright issued this manifesto as a Marxist who believed that "a Negro writer must create in his readers' minds a relationship between a Negro woman hoeing cotton in the South and the men who loll in swivel chairs in Wall Street and take the fruits of their toil." He was committed to the urgent project of raising his people's political consciousness, and he believed that the black religious and folk heritage in America could become instruments toward that purpose.

Now, more than a half century later, Henry Louis Gates Jr., in a series of loosely connected essays on topics ranging from the West African god Esu-Elgebara, a deity of fertility and knowledge "who interprets the will of the gods to man," to the fiction of Alice Walker, has set out to expose the common roots of black consciousness in Africa and America, and thereby to "identify a theory of criticism that is inscribed within the black vernacular tradition" from its beginnings in tribal myth. Gates . . . [in *The Signifying Monkey: A Theory of Afro-American Literary Criticism*], is concerned with some of the same issues as was Wright: with the pain of self-recognition for black children; with the continuing struggle (even after the emergence of a black middle class) against the subhuman black image in the white mind; with the restorative power of humor in the face of degradation. Wright, of course, believed in Soviet socialism as the best model for social justice in America; those were the heady days before the Molotov-Ribbentrop pact and Stalin's show trials. Gates, by contrast, is writing from within the American academy at a time when the idea of revolution seems mainly an abstraction to be debated in arcane journals by tenured literati.

It is unfair, perhaps, to hold a critic accountable to a rhetorical standard set by a great writer. Wright was looking for the language that would most effectively represent intolerable experience, while Gates is trying to represent the ways in which blacks in America have written about that experience. But Gates is also working within a tradition that tends to doubt the distinction between critical work and creative work, that endows both with comparable homiletic power. In confronting the delicate and highly charged question of cultural continuity between Africa and America, Gates believes that what is needed now are "black, text-specific theories" whose genealogies lie in African and Afro-American folk culture, where they are waiting to be discovered. He is committed to "the authority of the black vernacular tradition, a nameless, selfless tradition, at once collective and compelling, true somehow to the unwritten text of a common blackness," which, if

traced back to its origins, serves as a "signpost at that liminal crossroads of culture contact and ensuing difference at which Africa meets Afro-America."

Beginning with a long chapter ambiguously titled "A Myth of Origins: Esu-Elegbara and the Signifying Monkey," Gates surveys some of the forms in which this "one specific trickster figure . . . recurs with startling frequency in black mythology in Africa, the Caribbean, and South America." Gates approaches the works of Afro-American literature, too, with this premise of its continuity with the African past. He is committed, moreover, to the idea of a natural linkage between texts and the exegetical method by which their inner spirit can be revealed. This is an attractive, if anachronistic, notion. It implies that the responsible critic ought to honor the spirit of his subject by emulating it—a worthy imperative that seems to have a certain urgency for Gates, since he goes so far as to apologize, in the preface to *The Signifying Monkey,* for having written a book that his parents and brother are unlikely to understand. What he apparently means by this disclaimer is that, despite his inclination to meet the texts on their own terms, he has written his study largely in the hermetic language of contemporary literary theory, and wishes it could be otherwise. Many of his readers will wish so, too.

By "signifying," Gates most often means something close to the idea, made familiar by Walter Jackson Bate and Harold Bloom, that writers throw off the oppressive weight of their predecessors by first incorporating, then transforming, them. Although black writers have performed this revisionary activity on both black and white texts, Gates is mainly interested in defining an Afro-American tradition by showing the ways in which (as Bloom might say) it willfully misquotes itself.

For Gates, this collapse of the past and the future into a continuous literary present takes place within the familial boundaries of Afro-American writing itself. Thus (although she is not one of Gates's examples) Toni Morrison, in *Beloved,* may be said to have in mind certain excruciating precedents in the slave-literature for her tale of infanticide, or perhaps the terrible moment in a novel by Chester Himes when the narrator reflects that it might be better for a screaming baby if "they'd cut his throat and bury him in the backyard before he got old enough to know he was a nigger." Morrison, of course, also "signifies" the texts of Faulkner; but Gates applies his literary-historical definition of "Signifyin(g)" mainly to the relations between blank texts and other black texts.

The "Signifying" of Gates's title is what is nowadays called "multivalent." Its primary meaning is simply "denoting," or "representing." But its concurrent meaning (as suggested by an alternate spelling that capitalizes "S" and brackets "g" to indicate the consonant that tends to get dropped in colloquial black speech) is quite different. As Gates explains, with a monologue from H. Rap Brown:

> A session [of Signifyin(g)] would start maybe by
>   a brother
> saying, "Man, before you mess with me
> you'd rather run rabbits, eat shit and
> bark at the moon." Then, if he was talking

to me, I'd tell him:

Man, you must don't know who I am.
I'm sweet peeter jeeter the womb beater
The baby maker the cradle shaker
The deerslayer the buckbinder the women finder

• • • • •

I'm the man who walked the water and tied
the whale's tail in a knot
Taught the little fishes how to swim

• • • • •

I might not be the best in the world, but I'm in
the top two and my
brother's getting old.
Ain't nothing bad 'bout you but your breath.

This catalog of extravagances is assembled (by H. Rap
Brown) with an exhilarating inventiveness and a boastful
joy. It is an inner-city version of verbal one-upmanship
that is both cruel and respectful toward its audience, in the
way that only certain forms of antagonistic performance
can be. The word "bad" in the final line is perhaps the purest example of what Gates means by "Signifyin(g)"—it is
simultaneously an endorsement and a reversal of the conventional meaning of the word in white usage. Both meanings, white and black, are present. The word is thereby enriched.

There are many other entertaining examples of "Signify-
in(g)" in Gates's book. Here is a brief one that is closer in
its diction to the norms of academic discourse: "Nigger,
your breed ain't metaphysical," says Robert Penn Warren
in his poem "Pondy Woods." "Cracker," Sterling A.
Brown replies some years later, "your breed ain't exegetical." In this case, the repetitive and parodic energy of
"Signifyin(g)" is paramount, which is what Gates has
chiefly in mind when he explains that "Signifyin(g) is my
metaphor for literary history." Gates means that repetition, revision, and usurpation are as integral to black
street talk as they are to the history of Western poetry.
Thus he establishes a connection between what is now
called "intertextuality" (it was formerly known as allusion) and a particular black folk tradition that involves parodic mimicry.

As Gates recognizes, "Signifyin(g)," whether verbal or
wordlessly dramatic, is a human activity, not a black one.
Rap Brown's banter, for instance, in its hyperbolic appropriation to the self of fertility myths and creation myths
borrowed from the dominant culture, is remarkably akin
to the tradition of Southwestern humor that culminated
in Twain, and to the poetry of Whitman. As a form of creative play somewhere between sadism and ceremony, it is
also close to the old vaudeville routine of stepped retalia-
tion: one thinks of the Laurel and Hardy skit in which, as
traveling salesmen, they break a prospective customer's
flower pot after he slams the door on them. What follows
is a stately sequence of symmetrical reprisals: headlights,
then houselights smashed; bumpers, then trellises ripped
out—until, after a crescendo of mutual destruction, car
and house lie in ruins.

When Gates uses "Signifyin(g)" to mean something like

the ferocious language-game of Rap Brown, he is intent
on establishing an indigenous black tradition. He is a lively observer of its manifestations in various forms of black
expression, from the Yoruba myths of the trickster god
Esu to the Afro-American folktales of the "Signifyin(g)"
monkey, who taunts the proud lion and the obtuse elephant with his wit. But Gates is aware, I think, that neither his observations on literary influence nor his explorations of folk traditions finally constitute an inductive inquiry into the roots of Afro-American literature. "Each of
us," he concedes, "brings to a text an implicit theory of
literature," rather than finding it there. *The Signifying
Monkey* is really about the search for legitimizing precedents in black culture for a literary theory that Gates
learned mainly at Yale.

Gates is au courant in his deployment of the latest literary
technologies. But he is somewhat out of step with the his-
toricism that has come to inform literary criticism in the
last decade or so. His sense of the relations between texts
is oddly ethereal. They seem to exist for him in some kind
of timeless continuum, in which they exert mutual attraction and repulsion. He talks about the slave narrative, for
example, as a "countergenre, a mediation between the
novel of sentiment and the picaresque, oscillating somewhere between the two in a bipolar moment." This is a
way of saying that the slave narrative combines elements
of piety, the deliverance plot, swashbuckling, and even de-
flating humor at the master's expense. But the remark attends very little to the complex genealogy of the texts.

Gates's framework for understanding black texts is essentially that of European romantic fiction. That is arguably
one universe in which the slave narrative can be placed.
But surely one must ask whether those narratives were
forced into that mold by the abolitionist editors who in
many cases supervised their transcription and publication,
and may have, in the process, imposed a known form upon
unknown experience. Were the generic conventions of European fiction imposed upon the minds of barely literate
ex-slaves? Or is Gates talking about structural resemblances that cannot be causally explained? These fundamentally historical questions do not arise much in Gates's
work.

Similarly, Gates wants not to stress the roots of certain
black texts in white traditions (the slave narratives are rich
in biblical, especially Old Testament elements), but he sees
them resolutely through European literary perspective.
There is within this new-style critic an old New Critic,
who values in a text the qualities of ambiguity, irony, allu-
siveness, structural intricacy—the very features emphasized by T. S. Eliot, John Crowe Ransom, Cleanth Brooks,
and Allen Tate, but nowadays condemned as expressions
of the withdrawal of literary modernism from the scene of
progressive political struggle. Gates is in the singular position of sharing the vocabulary, the style, and the political
disposition of his critical contemporaries while facing a literature that he wants to celebrate rather than debunk.

This, I think, is the central problem for Afro-American literary criticism, of which Gates's work is the most ambitious example to date. Despite the bad reputation that
close formal analysis has acquired among critics who con-

sider it an evasion of political analysis, it can still claim to be in the service of a radical social criticism when applied to texts that can be shown to be fundamentally at odds with the social order. Thus it is possible for Gates to gloss Frederick Douglass's statement to his readers that "you have seen how a man became a slave, you will see how a slave became a man" with the rather professorial remark that Douglass's "major contribution to the slave's narrative was to make chiasmus the central trope."

Here is my favorite example from the slave literature of the subversive force within an apparently deferential text. It is an apparently benign dialogue between a slave named Pompey and his master, who is preparing for a duel:

> Pompey, how do I look?
> O, massa, mighty.
> What do you mean "mighty," Pompey?
> Why, massa, you look noble.
> What do you mean by "noble"?
> Why, sar, you just look like one *lion.*
> Why, Pompey, where have you ever seen a lion?
> I see one down in yonder field the other day, massa.
> Pompey, you foolish fellow, that was a *jackass.*
> Was it, massa? Well, you look just like him.

These slave texts, in other words, are simultaneously dependent on, and free of, white models; and despite the many wonderful instances of sly "Signifyin(g)," their paradoxical relationship to white texts is not easy to resolve.

Gates writes of Frederick Douglass, for example, with a reverential passion that is as moving as it is virtually unknown in contemporary writing about other 19th-century American figures. (Andrew Jackson, once treated by mainstream scholars as a populist hero, is now chiefly represented as an Indian-killing demagogue; Herman Melville, once thought of as the epic poet of democracy, is now often described as a witting apologist for corporate expediency.) And yet Gates, even as he wants to represent Douglass as a liberator who escaped the racist categories in which he was imprisoned, must recognize Douglass's assent to other crippling assumptions imposed on him by the same culture that enslaved him: the Enlightenment premise, for instance, that only literacy denotes civilization. (pp. 28-31)

Gates's problem, the problem of Afro-American literary criticism today, is that he wishes to combine a critical advocacy of certain literary works with a spirit of opposition toward the culture that produced them. The problem has been resolved by other black critics through the practice of literary biography, which has the capacity to describe the inhibiting context within which the dissenting imagination in America has managed to flourish. Others, such as Houston Baker Jr., have pointed out that the difference between the spirit of the Harlem Renaissance (which remains the authorizing moment for Afro-American letters) and the larger modernist movement of which it was a part has to do with this same distinction between attacking the regnant culture and generating an alternative: "Rather than bashing the bourgeoisie," Baker has written, as the Anglo-American modernists were doing, black writers in the 1920s and '30s "were attempting to create one."

In the 1980s, rather than dismantling the received literary canon (as many of their white counterparts are doing), many black critics are attempting to build one. Despite the delicacy and the constructive nature of this task, however, Gates tends to fall back into the portentous jargon of a literary criticism that is ill-suited to it. His analysis is murderously dissecting, a reductive translation of the living language of Ralph Ellison and Zora Neale Hurston into the taxonomies of Mikhail Bakhtin and Jacques Lacan.

It is also frequently downright silly. After noting, for example, the distinction between white and black uses of "signifying," Gates generalizes his observation into the statement that "all homonyms depend on the absent presence of received concepts associated with a signifier." Now, it is true that the force of the word "Signifyin(g)" derives in part from the differences between its familiar linguistic sense (to denote) and the more playful sense (to make parodic fun) that Gates is interested in. Still, Gates's generalization about "absent presence" is somewhere between rhetorical exaggeration and sheer nonsense. Does the word "squash," when used to signify an indoor racquet game, always carry with it the subliminal suggestion of a yellow vegetable?

Once one gets used to this sort of thing, *The Signifying Monkey* turns out at heart to be a poignant book. It is continuous with an important discussion that has always been central to black intellectual life—Alain Locke's suggestion, for instance, that a "New Negro" was emerging in the 1920s, whose cultural identity, fostered by the rediscovery of the African past, was now secure, and that "our poets have now stopped speaking for the Negro—they speak *as* Negroes." Gates is reentering territory that was fought over by black intellectuals a half century ago. There is a certain horror in the fact that, more than 60 years later, he must still press this same case.

Of course, not all black intellectuals granted the premise that a prehistorical black identity could or should be recouped. Some thought that, by insisting on their African identity, blacks were merely confirming the image of a titillating savage that lurked in the white mind. (p. 32)

The trouble with the Harlem Renaissance was that it became, at least for some of its white enthusiasts, a kind of anthropological festival. It partook of the same spirit that allowed for a long time in America that the only breasts permitted to be bared publicly were black breasts in the pages of *National Geographic,* the same spirit that lured white men north on "safari" into Harlem in search of "specialty sex." Embarrassment and prudery can only exist as a relation between two human consciousnesses: if one is judged subhuman by the other, then all is permitted. There is no such thing as a naked animal.

The willed connection of black Americans to the African past, in other words, has remained not only tenuous, but also suspect in its effects. Gates sees the difficulties, but he puts them mildly: "The degree to which the [Afro-American] figure of the Monkey is anthropologically related to the figure of the Pan-African trickster, Esu-Elgebara, shall most probably remain a matter of speculation." He acknowledges the fragility of the oral tradition with which he is working, but he pays little attention to the brutal deformation that African culture suffered in its forced translation to the New World.

Still, whatever the pitfalls of pursuing that past, or the obstacles to furnishing the sense of that past with an empirical basis, it has never been far from the center of black intellectual life. It was the occasion for James Baldwin's eloquent insistence that the effacement of the slave experience by substituting "X" for the slavemaster's name was as much a mutilation of memory as a gesture toward freedom. It has since been the cause of a number of powerful anthropologists and historians to show the tenacity of tribal and familial identities, even under the corrosive effect of the black diaspora, even under slavery itself.

The African past may have been an ungraspable phantom, but the idea of it was not. The idea of a retrievable black history that predates slavery has been an inescapable force in the lives of black Americans. It is everywhere attested by the extraordinary literature they have produced. In this sense, Gates's books, like the prolific output of young black fiction writers in the last decade, are alive to contemporary experience, certainly more so than most academic criticism. The stakes are real for Gates, as real as they once were for those who believed that critical writing could actually further social reform or political change. This may explain his ambivalence toward the exclusionary language in which he feels compelled to write. He understands that it is not much of a political or affective instrument.

Gates is contending with one of the fundamental problems that have engaged Afro-American writers for a long time. Like the literature of other immigrant peoples, black writing in America has never strayed far from the problem of assimilation. It is important to remember that assimilation has been more painful for blacks than for other immigrants, because the sense of loss can never be quite attached to a recoverable past, and the sense of gain in consenting to the new American identity can never be complete.

At the end of his *Autobiography of an Ex-Coloured Man* (1912), which tells the story of a light-skinned black who marries a white woman, James Weldon Johnson writes that "I cannot repress the thought that I have sold my birthright for a mess of pottage." This fear, imprecise but visceral, is present from the earliest black texts, such as William Wells Brown's account, written in 1865, of his being "scraped, scrubbed, soaked, washed" on his way from fieldwork to service in the plantation house, to Malcolm X's harrowing tale of his burning the kinks out of his hair by soaking it in lye. Anguish over the racial self-hatred of American blacks must have reached a peak 20 years ago, when Eldridge Cleaver accused James Baldwin of "shameful, fanatical, fawning, sycophantic love of the whites."

Yet once the scrubdown has been refused and the hair "relaxer" thrown away, the great problem for the black intellectual remains the forging of an independent identity within a white culture that is hostile *and* seductive. Black reformation of white language has been one means toward

that end. In the '30s the young anthropologist (and incipient novelist) Zora Neale Hurston recorded with delight the variations on standard English that she found among rural Southern blacks, who made old words like "feature" and "ugly" and "confidence" and "beaucoup" into new verbs. Forty years later, Malcolm reported the bewilderment of a downtown Negro when a hustler walks by on a Harlem street and announces his intention to pawn some clothes: "I'm going to lay a vine under the Jew's balls for a dime." The man from downtown, Malcolm remarks, looked "as if he's just heard Sanskrit."

It was not Sanskrit. Gates would call it "Signifyin(g)." However one names such reformulations of the coercive white language, they are expressions of the impulse toward black freedom. It is an impulse given impetus, as Baldwin once put it, by the fact that "the American Negro has the great advantage of never having believed that collection of myths to which white Americans cling." If this has been an advantage, however, it has also been a great deprivation. It was because of this suspension between worlds—the one ungrounded and inchoate, the other forbidding and closed—that the black novel was stalled, even as it emerged as a mature genre after the Civil War. It was blocked by its contradictory impulses to conserve the memory of apartness for the former slave while helping to lift him into the civic life of his country.

That is why the first black novelists were obsessed with the figure of the mulatto, who embodied the condition of suspension between worlds. When Malcolm, a hundred years later, repudiated his Stepin Fetchit self and asserted the vigor of his blackness, he came back to the sanctification of the individual and the colorblind vocabulary of human rights. Even these angriest of black writers came to doubt that "Signifyin(g)" on Mister Charlie is ultimately the best means toward real freedom. They have looked instead for a transcendent language into which race might disappear.

Gates is caught, I think, in something like the same pincer. His own language, to borrow a term from his preferred lexicon, tends to deconstruct itself. He is talking about universal habits of mind that operate within all literary texts; but he is also intent on identifying a unique black tradition that he believes has been slighted by (mainly white) critics. At one point he declares that "a vernacular tradition's relation to a formal literary tradition is that of a parallel discursive universe." Parallel lines, however, never meet; and most of Gates's work is devoted to showing, with valuable results, the many points of collision between black folk traditions and the "high" texts of Afro-American literature. Gates pays little attention to the points of intersection between white and black texts, but could just as well attend, say, to Ralph Ellison's allusive use of Emerson and Whitman as to his reprise of Booker T. Washington.

Eventually Gates concedes that "parallel universes . . . is an inappropriate metaphor; *perpendicular* universes is perhaps a more accurate visual description." The correction is apt. Perpendicular lines, if they are sufficiently extended, do meet. Black folk tales meet black fiction; but black texts, oral and written, also meet white texts. When Gates keeps these interracial transactions out of view, one recalls

Ellison's infuriated response to Irving Howe's essay "Black Boys and Native Sons" in 1963, in which Howe argued Ellison's indebtedness to Richard Wright:

> It requires real poverty of the imagination to think that [a sense of life and possibility] can come to a Negro *only* through the example of *other Negroes,* especially after the performance of the slaves in re-creating themselves, in good part, out of the images and myths of the Old Testament Jews.

Ellison had insisted in *Invisible Man* that blacks must find and keep their history in America, that to obliterate the slave-memory would be to duplicate one of the crimes of slavery itself: the destruction of a people's past. The terrible fact is that the predominantly oral traditions of West Africa *did* almost completely disappear in the decades after the Middle Passage. Gates's work, like the work of all serious black writers in America, is raised against the debilitating knowledge of this loss. It also flirts with the compensatory, but potentially insidious, idea of a residual race-consciousness that somehow survives in the blood.

In one of his more affecting sentences, Gates remarks, about the sometimes unbridgeable space between black and white expression, that "to learn to manipulate language in such a way as to facilitate the smooth navigation between [the white linguistic realm and the black] has been the challenge of black parenthood and remains so even today." Such is the crossing that we witness when W. E. B. DuBois, having written with immense respect about the black "sorrow songs" to which he was introduced in the post-Reconstruction South, nevertheless comes back to an oratorio of Handel as equally "real" music that moved him in the chapel of Fisk University. (pp. 32-4)

> Andrew Delbanco, "Talking Texts," in The New Republic, *Vol. 200, Nos. 2 & 3, January 9 & 16, 1989, pp. 28-34.*

Wahneema Lubiano

[*In the following excerpt, Lubiano examines the political implications of Gates's theory of "Signifyin(g)."*]

Henry Louis Gates, Jr., is both one of the most read and misread figures within African-American literary discourse in this century. To some extent his work has generated more heat than light, the ubiquitousness of his written and public presence having rendered him and his work phenomena more talked about than read, more excoriated than understood, more inveighed against than engaged. The terrain of his work has been largely literary history; his sorties into literary criticism and theory, however, also provide a basis for much productive critical work in the future. The implications of *The Signifying Monkey*—in "blue-print" form ("The Blackness of Blackness: A Critique of the Sign and the Signifying Monkey") widely disseminated in manuscript form over the past five or six years and periodically in lectures given around the country—have already transformed discussions and work within the field.

Being awarded a MacArthur Foundation Fellowship thrust Gates into the public arena at a time when debates over deconstruction and other forms of post-structuralist theories, as well as post-colonialist critiques and a reenergized Marxist literary discourse, were generating interest in texts by writers from marginalized groups. Tracing the influence of Gates on African-American literary discourse as well as its influences on him, however, extends beyond the confines of the present project. What I intend to do here, rather, is to delineate the agendas Gates sets himself in *Figures in Black* and *The Signifying Monkey* in order to underscore something of the importance and open-endedness of the two studies.

Gates has put together a spectacular piece of "native informacy" which is even more useful because it is addressed to both "natives" (practitioners of African-American literary criticism) and those on the "outside" (who know nothing of the field). He covers the terrain of African-American literary history with his own formalist and historical interests very much uppermost, but in neither book does he close down discussion in order to raise a monolithic African-American point of view, either of criticism or of literature. His work is, rather, part of the reclamation project about which Frantz Fanon theorizes [in *The Wretched of the Earth*]. (pp. 561-62)

The first two chapters of *Figures in Black* historicize the confrontation of the first writings of African-Americans with Euro-American dominance. Gates intervenes in that history by re-narrating the paradigms of that discourse. He explains the writings' position as political cannon fodder in the context of North American ideology and its support of slavery. Further, Gates describes the complexities of the position that he and other critics of African-American literature occupy—the difficulty and demands of speaking to a split audience.

From the beginning Gates has asserted that he wants to change the perception, held by critics of both Euro-American texts and African-American texts, that African-American texts are transparent reflections of the history, sociology, and psychology of African-Americans. He argues that "Blackness" as a Western Enlightenment formulation was and is a metaphor for the metaphysical anomaly or non-metaphysicality of African-Americans. By the late 1960s, Black militants set out to dethrone the Euro-American hegemonic aesthetic and to crack its hold on African-American literary production. The Black Aesthetic critics who took responsibility for the initiative, reclaimed "Blackness" as a privileged "essence" for Black art. Each time it is reenacted, however, this reclamation project begins as a defensive position and all too often proceeds to exhaust itself in critical, often ahistorical, tautologies. Nonetheless, Gates recognizes that the work of the Black Aesthetic critics "determined the nature and shape" of his own critical response, and he understands that his insistence on the primacy of a "repressed" African-American formalism has been "somewhat excessive and too polemical" when he meant it to be *corrective* and polemical."

Gates's work has been read as consciously apolitical, as an attempt to divorce texts from their historical and political contexts, the politics of their production and reception, and the politics—both implicit and explicit—of their content. Surely such a criticism is unwarranted, however, as evidenced by his reading of the Harlem Renaissance, which concerns itself with the short-sighted (and middle-class-centered) dismissal of dialect, and by his reading of Wright's reactionary race and art politics. In such cases, and others, Gates demonstrates his commitment to reading African-American texts vis à vis historically specific cultural practices. Nonetheless, I do have a problem with his assertion that "a poem is above all atemporal" and "must cohere at a symbolic level if it coheres at all," for logic as well as Bakhtin—"it is not, after all, out of a dictionary that the speaker gets his words!"—tells us that symbols evoke different meanings in different circumstances. Moreover, one can agree with Gates's use of Wittgenstein's admonishment "not to forget that a poem, even though it is composed in the language of information, is not used in the language of giving information" without necessarily supporting or giving comfort to the idea that poetry exists apart from its times—especially when one is armed from the arsenal of historicity that Gates puts in the services of one's reasoning.

In fact, Gates's concern that a historicized formalism has been neglected in past epochs prompts his criticism that African-American literature has been put to uses not primarily aesthetic. It is crucial to understand the distinction, however, between Gates's recognition that African-American texts weren't being read for aesthetic features and some spurious admonition that the terms of the Euro-American aesthetic be adopted by the marginalized group. Gates is not so naive. He realizes that it is possible, rather, to rethink a marginalized group's project to eschew "aesthetics" as a basis for privileging cultural production; that is to say, one can re-create the grounds for "aesthetic" judgment from *within* a marginalized group in order to do justice to, to appreciate, "intentionality" or "craft" among members of that group. It is this project that Gates and the Black Aesthetic critics have in common.

On the other hand, viewing African-American literature as simple sociological and historical reflection *is* a reductionist exercise whether it is practiced by Euro-Americans dismissing the writing of African-Americans or by Black Aesthetic critics privileging it. It is precisely at this point that Gates sees his agenda diverging from the Black Aesthetic critics'. Whether from the comfortably racist Thomas Jefferson, who would have it believed that African-Americans could not produce anything of cultural value, or the friendly American Marxist critic Max Eastman, who praised Claude McKay's *Harlem Shadows* because it was the work of a "pure-blooded negro," Gates recognizes the damage that "essentialist" theory inflicts on African-American cultural production. While Black Nationalist and Aesthetic critics of African-American literature *and* Black Marxist writers and critics—preeminent among them Richard Wright—privileged the "treatment" of the African-American proletariat and street caste, they did so generally within terms only of content, not of form: the African-American "lumpen" were the shapeless "stuff" of the art of the literary worker and were the site of politically engaged art and work. Such

critics did not theorize about the possibility of the lumpen (rural or urban) being themselves engaged in art-making except in their unconsciously lived lives. Wright could not even give a name to the artistic production of those people; for him, what they did was "the form of things unknown."

Another of Gates's reservations about the Black Aesthetic critics is that they treat "Blackness" as an entity rather than a metaphor. But since the Western discourse on race postulates biology as a signifier of metaphysical being, the "race" critics may be privileging biology in a manner more complicated than Gates has acknowledged: What if "Blackness" as a positive essentialist biological category is evoked not only as a corrective to racist essentialist formulations but also as a corrective to a racist metaphorical confusion of race and being? If such is the case, Addison Gayle, Stephen Henderson, and the other Black Aesthetic critics have been using "Blackness" as their site for rhetorically subverting the racist metaphor with full knowledge that such an act is fraught with danger. In other words, while Gates states, accurately, that "Blackness" is not a material object but a metaphor, within a racist discourse "Blackness" has been treated as a material presence subsumed by its negative force as a metaphor for debasement. (pp. 563-66)

According to Gates *The Signifying Monkey* is "more precisely a theory of literary history." I would add that, in common with other seminal historical and interpretive studies, it also provides an extremely valuable critical apparatus useful in approaching all kinds of texts. In his study, Gates discusses "explicitly that which is implicit in what we might think of as the logic of the tradition", in other words, he makes visible what was previously invisible both within the marginalized group and to the dominant group outside. This theory of African-American literature has its genesis in the first two chapters of *Figures in Black* and the manifesto apparent therein, a manifesto that stresses the importance of attending to form, which, according to Gates, is the neglected "other" of African-American literary discourse. The program Gates called for in *Figures in Black*—to connect the fictiveness and literariness of African-American literature to its own culture—is made manifest in this study. In the first three chapters of *Signifying Monkey* Gates gathers together a vast amount of material across a wide spectrum of scholarly domains. He assembles a cast of hundreds. He brings into African-American literary discourse the work of anthropologists, historians, and linguists of the New and Old World. As he molds this material, Gates re-historicizes the African literary presence in the New World and broadens our appreciation of the cultural practices that survived the diaspora.

Gates's insights owe much to the work done during the 1960s and 1970s by Black Nationalist scholars, many of whom were in graduate school during the period of the Black militancy upheavals, and to other scholars who served as fellow travelers with the Black Nationalist cultural workers. That time marked the biggest outpouring of cultural production and revisionist scholarship since the other great revisionist period that began right before, and continued during, the Harlem Renaissance (generally considered to be the decade between 1919 and 1929).

Gates outlines the historical and geographical evolution of the Signifying Monkey, the New World descendant of the Old World god/goddess Esu-Elegbara, the trickster of Yoruba, Fon, and Dahomey cultures, and that figure's place in African and African-American cultures. While the name and specific descriptions of the figure vary from culture to culture, similarities are numerous and distinct enough that anthropologists, linguists, and historians have developed an incredibly large body of work to which Gates lays claim in his argument that within African, Caribbean, and South American cultures the figure embodies the principle of indeterminacy and interpretation; in other words, Esu embodies "the uncertainties of explication." The divine trickster Esu-Elegbara, tied to the Ifa system of divination, does not survive the journey to North America intact, primarily because African religious and cultural practices were proscribed there, but an important representative of his attributes, the Signifying Monkey, does. The Signifying Monkey, a key player in a group of animal tales and, therefore, in folklore, would certainly have been less threatening than a divine trickster and, as a result, could have escaped the repressive apparatus of the slave system's otherwise quite stringent and comprehensive policing.

In exploring the value of the Signifying Monkey for theorizing about African-American cultural production, Gates must analyze how "signifying" functions in the vernacular. Whereas in standard English, "signification" refers to *meaning,* by contrast, in the vernacular it refers to engagement in rhetorical games; in other words, that which standard English refers to as figuration or figurative language corresponds to signifying in the vernacular. The difference, however, is both more powerful and more subtle than the instrumental difference between the denotative meanings generated by the two practices of language suggests. Although figurative language in standard English is tied to particular kinds of extra-normal usage—such as occasion or other clearly understood and demarcated organized usages as poetry, lyrical prose, or dramatic license—within the dynamic of the vernacular, figurativeness is a mode of speech or conversation as well as a mode of "reading" that speech and "capping" or "revising" it. Vernacular signifying, according to folklorist Roger Abrahams, "emphasizes 're-figuration,' " or "repetition and difference," or "troping" as a matter of *conversational* interplay. So while "signification" refers to "meaning" in standard English, in the vernacular it means "ways of meaning."

Vernacular signifying concerns itself with the *suspension* of meaning and the chaos that ensues. It is a playful mode, full of puns and substitutions that are humorous or functional in a "telling manner." It "luxuriates in the *inclusion* of the free play of associative rhetorical and semantic relations"; in short, "everything that must be excluded for meaning to remain coherent and linear comes to bear with the process of signifying." By contrast, standard English "signification" depends for order and coherence upon *some* attempt at a restraint of "unconscious" associations.

Vernacular signifying always deliberately replaces what is being said, asked, understood with something else—as though the utterance itself were only the departure point for an artistic rearrangement of signs. That the vernacular exists as a discourse parallel to standard English is important, but equally important is the *manner* in which it exists. Vernacular language moves along lines of alteration, maintaining contradictory, ironic, oblique stances vis à vis experience, narration, or even assumptions about reality. Thus, as Claudia Mitchell-Kernan points out [in "Signifying," in *Mother Wit from the Laughing Barrel,* edited by Alan Dundes], one can "signify on" something or someone and redress a power imbalance.

Vernacular signifying is to me an *attitude toward* language fully as much as it is a use of language; as much a reminder of possibilities of meaning as it is a vehicle of meaning. As such, the vernacular is perfectly constituted to undermine ironically whatever dominant language form it employs. In other words, it stands in deconstructive relation to the dominant language whether by using the dialect and syntactical structure of the African-American "other" or by subverting standard English. In this way, the vernacular reflects the defensive status and indirect stance of its users.

While explorations of the vernacular and of signifying as the dominant mode within that system have occupied numerous linguists and anthropologists for at least two decades, Gates draws together their findings and its implications for literary discourse. Following the work of Mitchell-Kernan, Geneva Smitherman, and others, he further elucidates the varieties of rhetorical strategies available in order to put to rest the notion that verbal signifying is only the rhetorical victimage of one powerless person by another equally powerless person in the form of either ritualized insult exchanges—such as the "dozens"—or more specific and momentary insults and verbal manipulations.

The political implications for discussions of race and culture are tremendous. Signifying is equivalent to both form and content and serves to mark their relationship to historical context. When one signifies in the public domain—with an owner, employer, or Euro-American readership (within the pages of a text)—one intervenes politically as well as artistically. As the basis of a critical apparatus, signifying allows us to debunk the fallacy that it is only the "stuff" of African-American lies that is art; signifying is a mode of vernacular artistic production as well as a mechanism for "on-site" meta-commentary. As the linchpin of a critical theory, signifying restores the fictiveness and politicalness of verbal indirection, a holdover not just from slavery but from African cultural practice.

Furthermore, signifying is a collectivist mode of artistic production. Within its dynamic, revision is not necessarily always and only an act of individual competition. Gates describes the activity of signifying revision by means of an analogy to jazz: "The most salient analogue for this unmotivated mode of revision in the broader black cultural tradition might be that between black jazz musicians who perform each other's standards on a joint album, not to critique these but to engage in refiguration as an act of homage. . . . This form of the double-voiced implies unity and resemblance rather than critique and difference." Mitchell-Kernan provides another interesting example with her account of her interaction with some of her male signifying respondents, a highly orchestrated exchange with a bit of a bite on her part that keeps the gendered power differential destabilized.

[What] Gates is signaling "within the group" is that our tradition is much more varied than our critical apparatuses have been able to account for; but, more important, he is signifying, in the presence of Euro-America, that we do not have to repeat its mistakes about us.

Signifying is both practice and theory since each speaker takes as his/her raw material the previous utterance, then decodes it across a wide spectrum of possibilities, and in finally "capping" it remaps the rhetorical strategy. Signifying also embodies the refusal to be defined, the refusal constantly and consistently to identify oneself and one's position. In short, it marks the refusal—as Du Bois articulates in the epigraph above—to answer as if a problem, to be defined in terms of the categorical imperative, to be "policed" in language.

Finally, signifying reinscribes racial difference as cultural difference, with all of the complexities entailed in such a categorization. Even more significant, racial difference played out in language also marks an interesting nexus of class difference, for while signifying is a "game" activity that cuts across class lines within the African-American group, it was supported in the New World first by the manner in which slavery enforced illiteracy which in turn bolstered an oral tradition, and later by political and economic segregation and continued power differentials. African-Americans have been uni-class for most of their history in the United States, and even now in the late twentieth century, when class divisions are more apparent, not only do class differences among African-Americans continue to be less salient than class and other differences between Euro-Americans and African-Americans, but African-American cultural structures, which have to a great degree survived the Black diaspora, remain steadfast and uniform.

The implications of signifying criticism include the possibility of transforming dominant Euro-American theorizing about African-American culture and the African diaspora, discussing the relationship of language to a political world, and understanding the relationship of an African-American working-class and street people to self-intentioned literariness and self-consciousness within the field of language—a project to which Zora Neale Hurston addressed herself in "Characteristics of Negro Expression" (reprinted in *Voices from the Harlem Renaissance* [1976]).

Gates's contribution to our appreciation of the extent of African "holdovers" in the New World is profound. . . .

African-Americans were not a blank slate, despite the intention and efforts of the slave system to make them so. (pp. 566-71)

Gates's vernacular signifying theory provides at once a way into particular texts, a way to rethink the relationship between African-American texts and other discourses, and a way to chart the political possibilities tied into writers' uses of the vernacular. On a broader field, what Gates is signaling "within the group" is that our tradition is much more varied than our critical apparatuses have been able to account for; but, more important, he is signifying, in the presence of Euro-America, that we do not have to repeat its mistakes about us. (p. 572)

> *Wahneema Lubiano, "Henry Louis Gates, Jr., and African-American Literary Discourse," in* The New England Quarterly, *Vol. 62, No. 4, December, 1989, pp. 561-72.*

Brad Bucknell

[In the following excerpt, Bucknell addresses the reconciliation of literary theory and history in Gates's work.]

Recent criticisms of the English canon continue to challenge deeply held notions about literature: its worth, its history, indeed perhaps its very "literariness." But it is especially the dissenting voices of feminists and people of colour (and those who cross the boundaries between these two diverse groups) who raise old questions about literary history, questions which traditional scholarship has never really been able to answer. I speak here of the difficulty in reconciling what could loosely be called "formalist" or text-centred theories of literature (Russian formalism, New Criticism, mythic criticism, and most recently in North America, various forms of post-structuralism) with those branches of research which maintain that the "world" (of nature, of the "self," of class) can be, and is, represented in literary works. Jerome J. McGann points out that the conflict between text-centred criticism and more sociohistorical kinds of studies is focused upon issues of language and the problematics of reference. From a sociohistorical perspective, text-centred critics may be taken to task for their lack of attention to matters of reference. As McGann puts it (perhaps a bit in the extreme),

> referentiality appears as "a problem" in formalist and text-centered studies precisely by its absence. Though everyone knows and agrees that literary works have sociohistorical dimensions, theories and practices generated in text-centered critical traditions bracket out these matters from consideration. . . .

On the other hand, sociohistorical research has been unable to counter effectively the criticism which suggests

> that language and language structures (including perforce, literary works) are modeling rather than mirroring forms. They do not point to a prior authorizing reality (whether "realist" or "idealist"), they themselves *constitute*—in both the active and passive sense—what must be considered reality. . . .

Each "side" of the critical debate lacks what the other could supply. But those who are critical of the techniques of making and sustaining the canon of English literature might take umbrage with either camp, especially on issues concerning power and evaluation.

Barbara Herrnstein Smith, in a gesture similar to McGann's, defines a polarization in the Anglo-American critical tradition between "scholarship," which assembles the philological and historical facts necessary for editing and annotating works, and "criticism," which assigns literary merit or value to works. She points out that the emphasis in Anglo-American studies has for the last fifty years been upon criticism. Using I. A. Richards and Northrop Frye as her examples, Smith states that the criticism of the greater part of the century has been

> [b]eguiled by the humanist's fantasy of transcendence, endurance and universality . . . [a]nd at the same time, magnetized by the goals and ideology of a naive scientism . . . [and] has foreclosed from its own domain the possibility of investigating the dynamics of [literary] mutability and understanding the nature of [literary] diversity.

It seems to me that her words about the essential evaluative narrowness of this dominant trend could apply to traditional methods of sociohistorical scholarship as well. The collecting and organizing of facts may be no less subject to "invisible" cultural standards of the " 'natural,' 'objective,' and 'real' " than are the less palpable criteria of the critics. The giveness of the texts of the tradition implies that the fact-finders and the critics both have had a hidden, if also at times unconscious, agenda which has ensured that the English canon has continued to be predominantly white and male.

Those who challenge "the" tradition are themselves by no means unified on issues concerning language, history, and methods of critical evaluation. But many agree that any critique of the canon must be both political and historical. It must question the implicit and explicit ideological presuppositions that have gone into the founding of that order. Even revisionary critiques which might be more "text-centered" than specifically historical must be aware of the exclusivity that is part of the normative premises of the literary institution's formation. Thus, a unique and complex sense of history and especially literary history often pervades critiques of the canon, even among those who might be considered "text-centered" critics.

Henry Louis Gates, Jr. could probably be considered a "text-centered" Afro-American critic, and what I want to explore in this paper are some of the complexities of his thought as he re-addresses problems, not only of the canon, but of reconciling theory and history as well. Gates is well known in the Afro-American critical world as both a critic and an editor, and I will focus first upon one of his earliest editorial endeavours, a collection of essays by the black American critic, Charles T. Davis. A discussion of Davis will, in a sense, historicize Gates, and also help to expose some of the problems Afro-American critics face in general as they struggle to make a place for their own literary and critical past(s) in the face of the dominant cul-

ture's ideals of literary art. With this as background, I will then attempt to explicate Gates's notion of "signifyin(g)" which is his critical metaphor intended to bear the mark of the potential exploration of language and history, not from a place of irreconcilability, but rather from one of necessary relationship. . . . [For] the purposes of this paper I will focus on the earlier, concise essay version of "signifyin(g)" found in **"The blackness of blackness: a critique of the sign and the Signifying Monkey."** For Gates, "signifyin(g)" is an attempt to find a distinctively black method of reconciling history and form, textuality and experience, at least in part through a reappropriation of contemporary critical theory. The issues that such an endeavour raise are complex, not least because of the problems in finding a distinctive critical method that is not already inhabited by dominant Western values. Some Afro-American critics disagree with Gates's methods, and later in the paper I will bring some of their concerns into the discussion. The interplay between Gates and his critics will help to illustrate further the difficulties faced by those who attempt to come to terms with their literary and historical marginalization.

Henry Louis Gates's editing of *Black is the Color of the Cosmos: Essays on Afro-American Literature and Culture, 1942-1981,* a collection of essays by one of his former teachers, the critic Charles T. Davis, is significant in a couple of ways: as a gesture of respect and elucidative evaluation, the book is a kind of historical document, consolidating and giving shape to the work of an eminent black critic. This historical gesture of preservation and acknowledgement is, however, given to one who, in Gates's words, "trained a generation of critics and scholars of Afro-American literature whose central concerns are matters of language." The preservation of one who was so interested in criticism from the point of view of language serves to emphasize how important a connection between language and history can be for the Afro-American critic, since however much Davis and indeed Gates choose to focus upon language, the shadow of history remains ever present.

History for the black critic, male or female, is a kind of nightmare from which it is difficult to awaken; and it is so for some very complex reasons. The reality of hundreds of years of overt and covert enslavement, exploitation, and degradation of black people does not necessarily—at least for Davis and Gates—establish a unified Afro-American "experience" that can be straightforwardly discerned in Afro-American literature. Gates points out that Davis taught his students to "eschew the expressive realism of literary theories which see the text essentially as a complex vehicle by which the critic arrives at some place *anterior* to the text . . . [such as] at his or her sense of a supposedly transcendent 'racial conscious,' a literary sense of blackness in Western culture . . . " It is true that Davis does describe a shifting sense of the idea of "blackness." The history that he outlines in "Black is the Color of the Cosmos" is one of the changing nature of the concept of blackness in Afro-American writing, a consideration which, ironically (for Davis) changes from being "regarded as a handicap socially and culturally" into "an artistic strength." The central figure in the twentieth century who marks the most profound change in the conception of blackness is Richard Wright, whom Davis claimed "made blackness a metaphysical state, a condition of alienation so profound that old values no longer applied."

But at the same time, Davis also states that all "writers arrive at a reconciliation of a sense of tradition and a sense of difference. For nearly all black writers in America that sense of difference was the recognition of blackness." If blackness is something that changes in definition and importance over time, it is also something that remains a constant and significant difference for the Afro-American writer. This complex sense of blackness is an important element in the "double-history" of "every black work." Davis sees this double history as consisting of the "tradition of American letters," apparently meaning predominantly white letters, and beyond this,

> the rich and changing store of folk forms and folk materials, the advantages of a dialectical tongue, with a separate music of its own . . . that grew from a community given an amount of homogeneity through isolation and oppression.

These comments occur in the first section of the book which Gates organizes under the heading "Theories of Black Literature and Culture," a section in which Davis, in an essay called "The American Scholar, the Black Arts, and/or Black Power," takes aim at the Black Arts movement that had developed in the late sixties. Davis takes particular issue with such writers as Larry Neal who proclaimed that the "dead forms taught most writers in the white man's schools will have to be destroyed, or at best, radically altered. We can learn more about what poetry is by listening to the cadences in Malcolm's speeches, than from most of Western poetics." For Davis, who had no wish to lose Aristotle, such comments showed a profound lack of historical sensibility: "It is as if history and aesthetic criticism were erased by the sweep of a damp rag across a blackboard." But for Neal and others, these sentiments were the only way of overcoming the "double consciousness" of the American black that W. E. B. Dubois had elaborated much earlier in the century: "One ever feels this twoness,—an American, a Negro; two souls, two thoughts, two unreconciled strivings; two warring ideals in one dark body . . . "

The conflict between those who feel the need to establish a more definitive black tradition in history and writing and those who desire to take into consideration the influence of white literature and history does not begin or end with Davis and Neal. But this issue, along with several others I have raised in this discussion of Davis are very pertinent to a reading of Gates. Gates will speak of a "double-voiced" or "two-toned" *critical* method; he will go further than Davis in working against the idea of a unified pretextual "racial identity"; and, as we will see somewhat later, he will suffer criticism for his use of white critical techniques. But it is also important to note that in editing the book on Davis, Gates, a critic with definite text-centred predilections, has historicized himself, located himself, and his critical concerns within the context of the conflict of the difficult historical/critical/social conditions

that confront the Afro-American scholar. Admittedly, his method is "text-centered," and much of it is influenced by contemporary white, male theorists. But, at the same time, his concern is to construct a history of black literature upon the "difference" of being black, though not upon a transcendent evaluation of "blackness." History and what this means to issues of black language are central to his concerns.

Gates is by no means unaware of the problem of "two-ness." The issue arises most crucially when Gates is attempting to elaborate his own critical approach. In **"Criticism in the Jungle,"** his introductory essay to **Black Literature and Literary Theory,** Gates asks, among other things:

> Can the methods of explication developed in Western criticism be "translated" into the black idiom? How "text-specific" is literary theory, and how "universal" are rhetorical strategies? If every black canonical text is, as I shall argue, "two-toned" or "double-voiced", how do we explicate the signifyin(g) black difference that makes black literature "black"?

And in the Introduction to his **Figures in Black: Words, Signs, and the "Racial" Self,** he puts it even more baldly: "Can it be a legitimate exercise to translate theories drawn from a literary tradition that has often been perpetuated by white males who represent blacks in their fictions as barely human, if they deem it necessary to figure blacks at all?"

Gates's answer to the last question is both simple and complex. On the one hand, he says that "*any* tool that enables the critic to explain the language of a text is an appropriate tool. For it is language, the black language of the black text, that expresses the distinctive quality of our literary tradition." This is his straightforward answer. More complex motivations stem from his feeling that "the structure of the black text has been *repressed* and treated as if it were transparent . . . as if it were invisible, or literal, or a one-dimensional document." The reasons for this repression are also complex. Gates sees the problem as being in part the result of what he calls the " 'anthropology' fallacy" which, as a kind of grid for viewing black art, "include[s] all sorts of concerns with the possible *functions* of black texts in 'non-literary' arenas . . . " This kind of attitude marks the reception of the first slave narratives that appeared in the eighteenth century. Joined with this fallacy are the " 'perfectibility' fallacy" and the " 'sociology' fallacy": that is, "that blacks create literature primarily to demonstrate their intellectual equality with whites, or else to repudiate racism . . . ". The complexities here are immense since, according to Gates, "the black tradition's own concern with winning the war against racism" has in the past led it to accept "black literature as evidence of the humanity of blacks. . . . " Concomitant with these "arbitrary suppositions' comes the belief that Afro-American literature existed primarily " 'to contain Black experience,' " which also meant that "a myth of familiarity obtained when the black critic read a black text." Hence, in the tradition of Afro-American criticism since the early nineteenth century, texts were analyzed in terms of content, "as if a literary form were a vacant enclosure that could be filled with this or that matter," this "matter" being some more or less creditable version of the " 'Black Experience.' "

Gates suggests that a kind of formal history is requisite for critics of black texts. His emphasis is on the black tradition of figuration, the ability of "saying one thing to mean something quite other," which has been essential "to black survival in oppressive Western cultures." In this way Gates hopes to resist the irony of positing "a 'black self' in the very Western languages in which blackness itself is a figure of absence, a negation." Thus, while claims to an "essence called 'blackness' " may be in ways politically healthy, they also raise the ideal of "a transcendent signified, of a full and sufficient presence," which is to "take the terms of one's assertion [of a free 'self'] from a discourse determined by an Other. Even the terms of one's so-called 'spontaneous' desire have been presupposed by the Other."

"Twoness," it is clear, is a difficult business. One can understand Gates's resistance to a literary criticism based on content, where the creator of a black text or a black criticism immediately "buys in" to the racist metaphysical presuppositions implicit in the images of the oppressor—whether the images are meant to be "good" or "bad." Yet, the move toward the study of a black tradition of figuration, and Gates's concomitant challenge to the notion of a transcendent "black" experiencing self, raises the dilemma of defining one's resistance to transcendent signifieds on the basis of the Other's critique of transcendent signifieds—the Other in the second case being (at least) Derrida and Lacan. Gates is aware of the problem and attempts to resist colonization by contemporary theory through reappropriation, a playing off of contemporary critiques of language, the intertext, and the self against the "difference" of the black tradition of "signifyin(g)."

Gates feels the need to resist the unifying *trope* of "the Black Experience," and instead

> to derive principles of literary criticism from the black tradition itself, as defined in the idiom of critical theory but also in the idiom which constitutes the "language of blackness", the signifyin(g) difference which makes the black tradition our very own.

The "signifyin(g) difference" is then not merely the repetition of contemporary critical theory, but rather a means of "explicat[ing] a black text [which] changes both the received theory and received ideas about the text."

"Signifyin(g)," in the sense that Gates uses the term, is crucial to the method of "critical bricolage" he applies in revising the method of formal examination of black literature. In **"The blackness of blackness: a critique of the sign and the Signifying Monkey,"** Gates offers his most extensive revision of contemporary theory in the service of black texts. His first move is to reappropriate the Saussurean neologism of "signifying" by pointing out that it is (curiously) "a homonym of a term in the black vernacular tradition that is approximately two centuries old.". . . "Signifyin(g)" in Gates's sense, is a theory of interpretation which is culled from the "black cultural matrix;" it

is "a theory of formal revision; it is tropological; it is often characterized by pastiche; and, most crucially, it turns on repetition of formal structures, and their difference." Similar to the notion of the "master trope" as variously outlined by [Giovanni Battista] Vico, [Friedrich] Nietzsche, [Paul] de Man, [Harold] Bloom, and [Kenneth] Burke, signifying is the "slave's trope of tropes," which can be seen to subsume the traditional Western rhetorical categories: metaphor, metonymy, synecdoche, irony, and several others. It is actually composed of a collection of black rhetorical tropes of its own, such as " 'marking', 'loud-talking', 'specifying', 'testifying', 'calling out' (of one's name), 'sounding', 'rapping', and 'playing the dozens'." Gates is of course "signifying" on the Western critical tradition here, repeating and revising, if not attempting, through inverting historical precedent, to out-do Western tropological history by showing the difference between it and the black cultural matrix he is trying to explicate.

He continues the revision with a history of the mythic figure of the Signifying Monkey itself, a figure which populates, in different forms, the mythology of Africa, the Caribbean, and both South and North America. The various figures are "mediators, and their mediations are tricks." The monkey "invariably 'repeats' to his friend the Lion, some insult generated by their mutual friend, the Elephant." The Lion's mistake is to take the monkey literally, and he goes off to address the puzzled Elephant, who "invariably" trounces him. The rhetorical practice of the Monkey, like all "signifying," is "unengaged in information-giving," and instead, focuses (if that is the right term) on "the chain of signifiers, and not on some transcendent signified." As such, the Monkey is not just " 'a master of technique', . . . he *is* technique, or style, or the *literariness* of literary language" itself.

In more recent black vernacular, signifying plays upon the ironic variability of language, the play between definition and contextual variation. Gates cites a passage from Claudia Mitchell-Kernan which he considers a particularly accurate version of the nature of signifying. Mitchell-Kernan suggests that in signifying, dictionary definitions are not always sufficient because meaning may go "beyond such interpretation."

> Complimentary remarks may be delivered in a left-hand fashion. A particular utterance may be an insult in one context and not another. . . . The hearer is thus constrained to attend to all potential meaning-carrying symbolic systems— the total universe of discourse.

Gates sees this indirect means of rhetorical play as the foundation of the black tradition: "Our literary tradition exists because of these precisely chartable formal literary relationships, relationships of signifying."

Gates wishes to adopt this vernacular rhetorical procedure to create a kind of black intertextual literary history. But this is not the intertext of [Roland] Barthes and [Julia] Kristeva which can never be "reduced to a problem of sources or influences." Rather, Gates seems to desire a very precise method of intertextual relationship, one in which the signifying connections between black texts may be clearly delineated. . . . For Gates, "parodic narration and the hidden or internal polemic" are the two double-voiced components of "critical parody" which he calls "critical" and/or "formal signifying." And formal signifying is Gates's metaphor for literary history.

Critical parody is a process whereby one author repeats and revises the formal structures of another author. Gates points, for example, to Ralph Ellison's signifying on the titles of Richard Wright's *Native Son* and *Black Boy* with his own *Invisible Man*. Wright's titles suggest "race, self and presence," to which Ellison answers with an "ironic response . . . of absence" in the suggestion of invisibility, and also with a stronger sense of mature status with "man," as opposed to "son" or "boy." This is all part of Ellison's complex method of signifying on Wright through the use of "a complex rendering of modernism" as opposed to Wright's "distinctive version of naturalism."

The idea of critical parody is, of course, not unknown outside of the black tradition. Jean Rhys's *Wide Sargasso Sea* is a kind of critical parody of *Jane Eyre*; [Gilbert] Sorrentino's *Mulligan Stew* parodies *Ulysses* which is itself a compendium of critical parodic inversions. But Gates's idea of critical parody in Afro-American writing has to do with the particular way that writers in the black tradition read and critique each other, not just formally, but also in terms of the specific "hidden polemic" of "blackness." The "hidden polemic" focuses on the concerns that successive writers have had in attempting to represent the "recurring referent of Afro-American literature—the so-called black experience." Here, however, Gates is less precise than we might hope, saying only that the hidden polemic may be seen in reading "the relation of Sterling Brown's regionalism to Toomer's lyricism, Hurston's lyricism to Wright's naturalism, and, equally, Ellison's modernism to Wright's naturalism." These relations are not as completely elaborated as is the book that signifies on all of these others: Ishmael Reed's *Mumbo Jumbo*.

Gates's explication of *Mumbo Jumbo* is lengthy and detailed. He sees Reed's work generally, and *Mumbo Jumbo* specifically, as being concerned with the preceding texts of Ellison, Hurston, Wright, Baldwin, and others. More important, however, is Reed's concern with "the process of willing into being a rhetorical structure, a literary language" which allows him to "posit a structure of feeling that simultaneously critiques both the metaphysical presuppositions inherent in Western ideas and forms of writing, and the metaphorical system" in which " 'blackness' " is a figure of " 'natural' absence." At the same time, Reed also takes on the "Afro-American idealism of a transcendent black subject, integral and whole." (pp. 65-76)

One of the difficulties I have with Gates's lengthy discussion of Reed is part of a problem that occurs in much criticism of post-modern texts. Phrases about the "indeterminacy of interpretation *itself*" or "a discourse on the history and nature of writing *itself*" begin to sound too much like rather standard generalizing critical terminology. No doubt *Mumbo Jumbo* and much other postmodern literature involves the critique of writing and its various claims to some kind of authenticity or "truth," and critics are right to describe the nature of such literary analyses. Often, however, it seems that another kind of essentialism

is unwittingly implied when critics say that history, or writing, or anything "itself " is critiqued or exposed or undone. Surely what they mean—and it is clearer in Gates than in most—is that the *ideology* of history or writing is called into question, that the relationship between ideas, words, and things is shown to be difficult, untrustworthy, and yet powerful, and in some sense, even real.

There is also the problem of a certain vagueness in some of Gates's terminology. I have already mentioned the way Gates marks the relations between authors using such terms as "modernism," "lyricism," "naturalism," and "regionalism." But though the connections Gates demonstrates between texts are convincing, it is difficult to know precisely what "lyricism" or "modernism" might mean in terms of these relationships. For instance, in another example of how Ellison's "modernism" signifies upon Wright's "naturalism," Gates compares each author's symbolic treatment of a descent into the underworld of the city sewer system. He points to the "heavy-handed" symbolism of Wright's "The Man Who Lived Underground," saying that the moment at which Fred Daniel stumbles upon a dead baby as he flees through the sewer "is precisely [the] point in the narrative that we know Fred Daniels to be 'dead, baby'." In contrast to this supposedly awkward symbolism, Gates notes Ellison's play upon this underground scene in *Invisible Man*. In Ellison's book, the narrator/protagonist burns "the bits of paper [high school diploma, a doll, letters, etc.] through which he ha[s] allowed himself to be defined by others." According to Gates, Ellison, by "explicitly repeating and reversing key figures of Wright's fictions . . . exposed naturalism as merely a hardened convention of representation of 'the Negro problem', and perhaps part of 'the Negro problem' itself."

The connection Gates is drawing between the two texts is undeniable, and one could probably agree on Gates's general point about Wright's "naturalism" and Ellison's "modernism." But to do so, more context is necessary in order to bring the point more fully to light. What, one might ask, is the precise nature of the "reversal" that Ellison is performing that makes it "modernist" as opposed to simply parodic or revisionary? Taken as incidents in themselves, and without a broader idea of what "modernism" or "naturalism" might mean in Ellison and Wright generally, or in the Afro-American tradition as a whole, there is no particular reason that either descent should be seen as more or less "naturalistic" or "modernist" than the other. Of course, Gates can hardly be expected to explicate completely terms which perhaps no one in any critical community has satisfactorily defined. But it seems likely, or at least possible, that Afro-American "regionalism" or "modernism" would have similarities to, and differences from, other such classifications outside the Afro-American community. Some elaboration on these similarities and differences, and perhaps some provisional definitions of these terms would be very useful.

Some in the Afro-American critical community take more serious issue with the potential narrowness of Gates's theory. Deborah E. McDowell is one who suggests that Gates's analysis of the black intertext "characterizes the formal relations between [Wright, Ellison, and Reed] as largely adversarial and parodic." McDowell's own concern is with comparing representations of the black female "self" in the nineteenth-century novel *Iola Leroy* by Frances E. W. Harper to those found in Alice Walker's *The Color Purple*. Despite "current critical fashion," she maintains that for black women writers "imaging the black woman as a 'whole' character or 'self' has been a consistent preoccupation." Thus, while there is much to parody in Harper's earlier and more "outwardly" determined Iola Leroy, Walker does not take advantage of this with her "inwardly" directed Celie. McDowell maintains that this sort of lack of intertextual aggression is the "fundamental distinction between Afro-American male and female literary relations."

McDowell's criticism raises the problem that Gates, perhaps unintentionally, has made a particularly *male* theory of Afro-American intertextuality. He does credit Zora Neale Hurston with being the "first author of the tradition to represent signifying itself" as a means of female liberation, and as "a rhetorical strategy in the narration of fiction." He also points out that both Hurston and Reed seem to "relish the play of the tradition." But it is clear from the amount of space given to Reed that for Gates, what is more important is Reed's "magnificently conceived play *on* the tradition." The sense of who is "stronger," to borrow from Harold Bloom, is quite clear.

Joyce A. Joyce goes even further than McDowell in criticizing Gates [see excerpt above]. Like McDowell, she also feels that the idea of a black "self" cannot be done away with. She says that the "Black creative writer has continuously struggled to assert his or her real self and to establish a connection between the self and the people outside that self." For Joyce, the move in Afro-American criticism away from "polemical, biographical criticism" and toward post-structuralism is a movement towards operating in a "historical vacuum." Black post-structuralism is an acceptance of "elitist American values," which widen the gap between intellectuals and "those masses of Blacks whose lives are still stifled by oppressive environmental, intellectual phenomena." Worst of all is that for the critic to conceive of blackness as an arbitrary "sign" as Gates does is to negate "his [Gates's] blackness."

It is probably true that Gates has not closed any "gaps" between the tower and the street. But it is also true that he has been consistently aware of the dangers in trying to make the experience of Afro-Americans in either place a mere given. Gates has not been co-opted by the white contemporary critical world; rather, he has used some of its tools to point out that "blackness"—Gates's own, or that of others in the Afro-American community—is a complex issue. He has not tried to deny blackness, but instead, he has attempted to point out that to consider the experience of blackness as any *one* thing is to accept a kind of unifying principle which Gates sees as being *historically* used against Afro-Americans. To make blackness a "unity" (a "presence" of "self" or community) is to risk a "oneness" which immediately posits an "other," thus repeating a divisive and dangerous set of metaphysical presuppositions. As Gates says in his response to Joyce: "Who can doubt

that *Black Fire,* the splendid anthology of the Black Arts . . . has sold *vastly* more copies to black intellectuals than to 'our people'?" The assumption that "our people" are "one" is a dismissal of the diversity of experience that cannot and, for Gates, must not be subsumed under any easy sign of categorical completeness.

Gates has pointed out in [**"Authority, (White) Power, and the (Black) Critic; or, It's All Greek to Me"**] that issues of "theory, tradition, and integrity within the black literary tradition [have] not been, and perhaps cannot be . . . straightforward matter[s]." But with the theory of "signifyin(g)," Gates has begun the difficult work of reconciling the opposing voices and influences that affect the Afro-American critic. His work is not mere mimicry of white critical theory, but instead a subtle and insightful revision and reappropriation of many aspects of many theories brought together in order to acknowledge and help in the establishment of an Afro-American literary and critical tradition. As such, Gates alerts us to the possibility of a theory in the black idiom in which "*black people theorize about their art and their lives in the black vernacular.*" As one gesture of resistance to the silence which has historically been imposed upon non-canonical literatures and theories of those literatures, "signifyin(g)" stands as a complex and important theoretical model. (pp. 77-81)

> *Brad Bucknell, "Henry Louis Gates, Jr. and the Theory of 'Signifyin(g)',"* in Ariel: A Review of International English Literature, *Vol. 21, No. 1, January, 1990, pp. 65-84.*

JoAnne Cornwell-Giles

[*In the following excerpt, Cornwell-Giles provides an overview of the origins of and trends in African-American literary criticism.*]

The development of Afro-American criticism has followed conservative lines. When compared to that of Europe and mainstream America, this criticism has consistently favored the nurturing of a dialogue—both actual and symbolic—between the artist and the critic, with a demand for accountability to the intended audience. Because of this conservatism, the criticism has tended to be sanctioned only when it has maintained dialogue. Within the last decade or so, however, there has been a perceptible breakdown in the dialogue, due primarily to the altered trajectory of critical theory and the necessity (or desire) of many critics to follow new departures. These departures are reflected in the language of "new" black critical works. References by Houston Baker, for example, to the archaeology of knowledge or his use of expressions like "language . . . 'speaking' the subject" reflects the character of this new critical language and suggests the inclusion into the Afro-American domain of perspectives previously unrelated to the study of Black literatures. Additionally, there has been a shift in criticism toward the study of discourse in its broader sense, which is perceived as having resulted primarily from the influence of Western criticism, particularly French deconstructionism. A look at the works of critics such as Barbara Christian, however, reveals a vital sector of contemporary Afro-American criticism which remains leery of the jargon which belies hallowed traditions. Christian looks specifically to history to discover the cultural imperatives which have framed Black literary production and critical response. Nonetheless, her work, much like Baker's, is as concerned with the discourse on literature (how is it framed? by whom? and to what ends?) as it is with specific literary texts and contexts.

The development of Afro-American criticism, by virtue of the "centricity" created by its conservatism, culminated two decades ago in the Black Aesthetic movement. Ironically, a bifurcation resulted in that critical discourse—in which uniformity of technique and purpose were valued aesthetic criteria—, and new possibilities were created which explain the expanded nature of Afro-American criticism today. The works of Houston Baker and Barbara Christian embody these new horizons and attest to the fact that these recent developments in critical theory are not solely the response to historical factors or reflections of some faddist eclecticism. Rather, the developments relate to the internal logic of critics' own discourse. The goal of this essay, in formulating an *état present* of Afro-American criticism, will be to explore the relationship between its historical and etiological dimensions. (pp. 85-6)

Knowledge is incremental: We build upon what has gone before, if only to discard or reform this knowledge or to use it against itself. This becomes evident when one traces the history of any intellectual discipline within our culture. It also happens, however, that the accumulation of knowledge in one area contributes to the ability to know across disciplinary lines: Thus, literary histories reflect political or religious ideologies of the period, and the scientific inquiry which leads to technological advances is related to the metaphysics of the culture. The work of Michel Foucault, in particular his *Madness and Civilization,* is largely responsible for establishing the very widely used conceptual framework for this kind of investigation into Western institutions. These relationships notwithstanding, a growing number of disciplines are present in our culture, and these disciplines are continually warring with each other for autonomy, or jealously guarding their prized (perceived) separate identities. The curricula of our universities demonstrate this phenomenon very clearly. For example, philosophy departments generally choose to distance themselves from departments of religious studies, though historically these fields have overlapped. In a similar fashion, critical theory—alias literary criticism—is progressively distancing itself from the study of literature proper and aligning with other disciplines to make "discourse" in the broader sense the focus of its energy.

There exists, then, a model on the broader cultural level for the shift of Afro-American criticism away from its originally intended object within Black literary traditions. Disciplines grow out of each other, or split from a parent body of knowledge for a variety of reasons, not the least important of which is the need for specialization. This is certainly the case with the literature of Black Americans—a literature whose breadth has increased dramatically over the last half-century. There are also other reasons which seem to be more idiosyncratic in their intent

and demonstrate that knowledge of the world cannot ultimately be separated from self-knowledge. Whatever the reasons for the changing horizon of disciplines through time (and the changing horizon of criticism), these changes are always related in a fundamental way to the ongoing process of framing a concept of the "self"—a process which has had particular significance for Afro-Americans. This process is seen to be both necessary and empowering.

I will refer here to disciplines in their dynamic interrelationships as "isms," since, as the foregoing discussion already suggests, they are propelled not simply by necessity, but also by questions of identity and the desire for power. It is the ism, then, that mediates past knowledge, filters it through its own specific lens, purges it of what is perceived as otherness, and uses this new "raw material" in innovative ways. Ironically, the process of appropriating knowledge through an ism, though necessary and empowering, can inhibit our understanding that as humans, particularly within the framework of a given culture, we come to know in much the same ways.

Our propensity for self-definition by virtue of the marginalization or exclusion of perceived otherness is a feature which, while seeking to make us distinct, demonstrates our sameness. It should be evident that this paradox of sameness in our approach to knowing is fundamental to the tensions which exist among isms. This paradox is central to the fact that interdisciplinary studies programs at universities are rarely more than strategic concessions on the part of the dominant order. It is central as well to the fact that Black studies, women's studies, and other marginalized disciplines can and sometimes must be ghettoized for the sake of the supposed preservation of the dominant ism. In short, our way of knowing invariably has power implications which are a function of that very process of appropriating knowledge. As we shall see, this also relates to the shift and direction of criticism within the Afro-American tradition.

The fact of marginalization is itself a powerful incentive for seeking radically to restructure the order which is responsible for one's exclusion. Viewed from this perspective, the isms which occupy the margins of our society (and here I would place Afro-American cultural orientations within the broader context of Western civilization) take on a new potential significance: They are more than just examples, further out, of the ongoing process of appropriating knowledge within a culture which must by nature create a center and a margin. This might be adequate to assume, were it not for the fact that they also *symbolize* otherness for that culture; and so, to some degree, they symbolize otherness for themselves. By understanding the dynamics of this marginalization, then, we come to understand the potential housed in these marginalized spaces for revolutionizing in a fundamental way the manner in which all disciplines come to knowledge.

As we move into an investigation of some aspects of Afro-American literary criticism, which has emerged through a medium of strategic and symbolic marginalization, it becomes clear that the very process of appropriating knowledge is inherently revolution-generating. The expressive forms, including the literature involving Black Americans, share in a network of intellectual traditions which historically have viewed African peoples first and foremost in terms of their otherness and their symbolic or metaphorical significance for the dominant group. Examples in the American tradition are numerous, ranging from the tradition of minstrelsy to race records to media advertising. In the literature focusing on Black people over the last 150 years, we find a large body of plantation literature which consisted primarily of fictional writing by non-Blacks who caricatured Southern slave culture. The works of Joel Chandler Harris and Thomas Nelson Page are particularly well known. This phenomenon was countered to some extent by the abolitionist press, whose primary mission was to sensitize the influential Northern reading public to the atrocities of that same slave culture, but had its own agenda for how this was to be done.

It should not be surprising, given this climate, that the literature written by people of African descent has fostered the growth of a brand of literary criticism which, while not ignoring major developments in Western critical theory, has responded to the specific realities of the marginalized space and to the appropriation of knowledge therein. What emerges as outstanding about the recent approaches of Afro-American critics has preeminently to do with the resonances being uncovered between the most avant-garde mainstream theories, on the one hand, and what might be referred to as folk or vernacular traditions within these heretofore marginalized cultures, on the other. This emphasis on resonances has the potential for restructuring the approaches to canonization which have previously allowed the ism to go unchallenged as the determiner of quality and the purveyor of value in literature. Also, as critics begin to acknowledge the interdisciplinary imperatives at work in our culture, constructs from disciplines as seemingly remote as physics and mathematics are now allowing discourse to be structured in new ways.

Throughout the development of their discipline, Afro-American critics have responded to a common challenge insofar as theirs has been the study of a literature born out of the central philosophical dilemma of how one comes to self-knowledge without adopting the point of view of a dominant, marginalizing discourse. This philosophical question has also clearly been a political one within the context of slavery and racial domination. Within the language controlled by the dominant culture, the examination of the self was necessarily also the examination of otherness.

Literature and the criticism which would extend from it emerged, then, with a particular centricity—that of keenly observing and commenting on the movements of the *cultural* self within the confines of this dilemma. Indeed, the importance of commitment to the struggle as an aesthetic criterion for Afro-American literature and criticism derives from this centricity, as does the demand that criticism remain in touch with the literature and not develop into an esoteric literature of its own. That this "self-centered" literature has also been heavily autobiographical seems logical from this perspective as well, since "saying" oneself has strong implications for self-creation and empowerment. An important role of criticism, then, has been to second the literature in its emphasis on the reconciliation of outside and inside within the self of discourse.

As the Black press developed during the nineteenth century, and later with the buildup of creative horsepower during the Harlem Renaissance in the 1920s, critics in the United States could begin furthering this reconciliation in earnest. Widening options would foster a process of cultural self-examination through criticism that plantation literature and the abolitionist press had previously been unable to accommodate. From that point forward, Afro-American criticism, like the literature, would be propelled by the ongoing demand for cultural self-examination. By watching itself watching the literature, criticism has worked to keep the two linked. A by-product of this linkage is apparent in the large proportion of modern Afro-American writers who view their writing as a manifestation or reflection of, or in some way a commentary on, the struggle. Another is to be seen in the proportion of writers of note who have also been involved in criticism, from W. E. B. Du Bois at the turn of the century to Claude McKay during the Harlem Renaissance era to Richard Wright and James Baldwin in the '50s and '60s. The characteristic closeness of the creative and critical functions in the Afro-American tradition finds its fullest expression, however, during the Black Arts movement of the '60s and '70s.

Critics of the Black Aesthetic who were a part of this movement contributed significantly to the refinement of a perspective on Black literature through the strategies they used to observe Black culture expressing itself. The negation of the legacies of abolitionist and plantation literary traditions was essential if critics were to carve a space for themselves and claim their own voice. During this phase critics actually pursued the centrism of both literature and criticism to an extreme degree, thereby causing a bifurcation in the critical orientation of such importance that Black criticism would never be the same. In this way, Black Aesthetic criticism actually proved to be a catalyst for the more recent developments in critical theory by Black critics.

As we know, many writers of the Black Aesthetic period were also critics of literature—some if only by the strong implications of their own creative writing. Barbara Christian, in her insightful article "A Race for Theory" [see excerpt above], speaks of this phenomenon in which the creative and critical functions are so fully merged that theorizing came to be expressed through narrative forms. This merger is fascinating from a critical standpoint, in that it is at once traditional (in the historical sense) and extremely innovative. This is a characteristic of Afro-American creative expression which probably would have emerged more visibly during the Black Aesthetic movement were it not for the fact that this movement gave priority to the political aspects of literary expression already implicit in the linkage between creation and criticism. The politics of Afro-American literature and criticism moved for a time to the forefront, circumscribing limitations for critical theory. Benchmark works like *From Plan to Planet* by Haki Madhubuti informed creative people that they were only secondarily writers, but first and foremost Black; members of a community before individuals; owing allegiance to the black media more than publishers. In order to demonstrate correct politics, the writer/critic was expected to be concerned with the preservation of a specifically perceived authenticity. The fundamental irony of this approach, as we know, was that, while carrying out a very effective indictment of the politics of knowing within the dominant and marginalizing culture, critics of the Black Aesthetic were engaging in a process which effectively sought to marginalize those Afro-Americans whose works or whose criticism did not reflect their Black Aesthetic creed.

It bears emphasizing at this point that the development of Afro-American criticism along the lines described here, culminating in the expression of a Black Aesthetic creed, marks a very logical progression. This body of criticism, although considered radical by some, clearly represents the intersection of at least two identifiable trajectories. The first emerges from the process referred to earlier by which we all appropriate knowledge based on principles of the exclusion of perceived otherness, with all its political implications. The other trajectory stems from the fact that, within the marginalized space which has also become the *symbol* of otherness, the ideas of otherness and the self can merge. When this happens, a radical recentering of discourse becomes an imperative.

Thus, a dominant characteristic of Black Aesthetic criticism was fated to expose the limitations of Black Aesthetic discourse. As the boundary between the self and that defined as other moved closer to the center of that cultural space, an epistemological breakdown became imminent, since the cultural space was being defined in terms of a concept of Blackness that was being used to marginalize other Blacks. It is important to point out here that this extreme degree of centricity is not an isolated phenomenon, nor is it culture-specific. Rather, it is systemic, as demonstrated by the fact that an analogous set of circumstances in the African world produced a similar kind of extreme centricity in modern African criticism. (pp. 86-91)

> *JoAnne Cornwell-Giles, "Afro-American Criticism and Western Consciousness: The Politics of Knowing," in* Black American Literature Forum, *Vol. 24, No. 1, Spring, 1990, pp. 85-98.*

Kenneth Warren

In order to appreciate the drama enacted in Henry Louis Gates, Jr.'s *The Signifying Monkey* one must keep in mind the characterizations of the text's two central antagonists. On the one hand is a figure emerging from the Black Arts movement preaching a gospel of a black cultural essence that is necessarily incompatible with white literary standards; and on the other is an avatar of Euroamerican post-structuralist theory with its attendant attack on referentiality and its valorization of intertextuality and indeterminacy. These two figures have crossed words if not swords in much of Gates's work, for *The Signifying Monkey* is a pastiche of new and previously published material as well as the second part of a projected trilogy on African-American literature. Gates's task in this conflict

has been to stage his drama so that the hero does not end up either uttering a mealy-mouthed cultural nationalism—convinced of the reality of black difference but too steeped in deconstructive thought to say so plainly—or expounding an eviscerated deconstructive critique that debunks everything except the sanctity of the black textual space.

So enter Ishmael Reed's freewheeling, satiric fiction, *Mumbo Jumbo,* which Gates points to as "the text-specific element from which my theory arose." Readily acknowledging that his efforts to explicate *Mumbo Jumbo* both prompted and shaped *The Signifying Monkey* (indeed the acknowledgment of black textual antecedents is the key refrain of Gates's text), Gates uses Reed's parodic novel as a means of sidestepping the binary opposition of "white" critical theory and "black" fictional text. *Mumbo Jumbo*'s parody of other African-American texts, its critique of the Black Arts Movement, and its linguistic playfulness underscore for Gates that one need not import self-reflexiveness and theorizing into the black tradition, because all of these features are always already there.

Then taking his cue from Reed, Gates argues in the first section of *The Signifying Monkey* that theorizing and critique are not merely indigenous to but come to define the black tradition in letters. Constructing a myth of origins around the trickster figures of Esu-Elegbara from Yoruban mythology and the signifying monkey from New World black vernacular traditions, Gates maintains that the black vernacular celebrates figurative language and ambiguity rather than literal interpretations and determinate meanings. To buttress this claim he draws upon a body of mythic literature—folk tales and lyrics—as well as the studies of linguists and anthropologists.

The vernacular term that comes to stand for figurative language use is "Signifyin(g)"—a word encompassing a variety of rhetorical practices, including lying, speaking indirectly, and playing the verbal game of exchanging insults, called "The Dozens." Gates parenthesizes the *g* at the end of the term to indicate that in the spoken vernacular the final consonant is usually not pronounced. Most significant for Gates is that Signifyin(g), in black vernacular usage, revises and critiques both the standard English usage of signification and the structuralist conception of the sign, as represented by the work of Ferdinand de Saussure. In the first case, Signifyin(g), rather than denoting the meaning of the word, replaces meaning with rhetorical figures; rhetoric ousts semantics. Second, Gates claims that in marking its critique of standard meanings by punning on "signification," the black vernacular stands in analogous relation to the critiques of Saussure offered by Jacques Derrida and Mikhail Bakhtin. The vernacular term corresponds with Derrida's coinage of *différance* to signal his revision of structuralism's "difference." More important for Gates, where structuralism had denied the human subject a role in determining the relationship between signifier and signified, Signifyin(g) arises from a vernacular origin. Like Bakhtin's location of novelistic discourse within an interplay of social languages that produces "double-voiced" utterances, Gates's identification of the vernacular origin of Signifyin(g) restores to literary analysis the social text that structuralism had expunged from its linguistic universe.

However, unlike the broad range of languages, dialects, and jargons included by Bakhtin, the "social" for Gates centers chiefly on the fact that black writers read and revise the works of other black writers. This focus on a literary tradition creates in Gates's work a style of critique that moves abruptly from claims based on the determinations of linguistic structure, tradition, or literary form to those based on authorial intention. For example, Gates readily employs a logic of cultural necessity to argue that theories of narrative held by Zora Neale Hurston, Richard Wright, and Ralph Ellison "comprise a matrix of issues to which subsequent black fictions, by definition, must respond." At other times, however, Gates's language seems to grant individual writers the discretion to define their relationship to other authors: "While most, if not all, black writers seek to place their works in the larger tradition of their genre, many also revise tropes from substantive antecedent texts in the Afro-American tradition." The oscillation between structural and/or cultural determinations on the one hand and assertions of authorial autonomy on the other suggests that Derrida and Bakhtin are overshadowed by the figure of Harold Bloom, who appears only briefly on the set of *Signifying Monkey* to provide some key rhetorical terms. These brief appearances notwithstanding, one can read *The Signifying Monkey* as Gates's rewriting of Bloom's oedipal drama for the black tradition in which psychology gives way, once again, to rhetoric, and "Signifyin(g)" replaces "anxiety." Thus, while for Bloom "strong poets make [poetic] history by misreading one another, so as to clear imaginative space for themselves," for Gates "Signifyin(g) revision serves, if successful, to create a space for the revising text." Bloom's allegory of textual revision functions for Gates as a means of bending Derrida and Bakhtin to his own ends.

Clearly, the revisions here are intended to clear a space for Gates's text in the firmament of theory. The rapid movements from theory to theory are intended less to work through the problems created by such juxtapositions than to suggest a means of negotiating among the gaps and fissures separating theoretical universes. By using the terminology of one theory to revise and redeploy the terms of another, Gates occasionally overlooks apparent contradictions in methodology and implications in order to proclaim (quite provocatively) that theory is nothing more than strategies of language use inferred from the texts that one attends to. Writers of theory, like their counterparts in fiction, simply produce ways of Signifyin(g) on other writers.

By rewriting theorizing as Signifyin(g), Gates articulates

in the first section of his book an intriguing counterargument to the claim that theory is somehow foreign to the black tradition: to theorize is to do nothing that black writers have not done for centuries. And even if one does not assent fully to this argument, Gates's demonstrated ability to suggest relations among black-authored fictions may help lay to rest the tiresome charges that attention to figurative language and literary form is inherently at odds with African-American literary practice. (pp. 224-26)

> *Kenneth Warren, in a review of "The Signifying Monkey: A Theory of Afro-American Literary Criticism," in* Modern Philology, *Vol. 88, No. 2, November, 1990, pp. 224-26.*

FURTHER READING

Baker, Houston A., Jr. "In Dubious Battle." *New Literary History* 18, No. 2 (Winter 1987): 363-69.

> Response to Joyce A. Joyce's essay "The Black Canon: Reconstructing Black American Literary Criticism."

Bhabha, Homi K. "Opening the Floodgates." *Poetics Today* 8, No. 1 (1987): 181-87.

> Review of *Black Literature and Literary Theory,* a collection of essays edited by Gates. Questions the validity and purpose of reading African-American literature through structuralism and post-structuralism.

Critical Inquiry, Special Issue: " 'Race,' Writing, and Difference" 12, No. 1 (Autumn 1985).

> Special issue, edited by Gates, devoted to literature and the perception of race, including essays by Edward W. Said, Anthony Appiah, and Jacques Derrida.

Joyce, Joyce A. " 'Who the Cap Fit': Unconsciousness and Unconscionableness in the Criticism of Houston A. Baker, Jr., and Henry Louis Gates, Jr." *New Literary History* 18, No. 2 (Winter 1987): 371-84.

> Joyce's response to Gates's essay " 'What's Love Got To Do with It?': Critical Theory, Integrity, and the Black Idiom" and Baker's essay "In Dubious Battle."

Martin, Reginald. "The New Black Aesthetic Critics and Their Exclusion from American 'Mainstream' Criticism." *College English* 50, No. 4 (April 1988): 373-82.

> Discusses the significance of the Black Arts Movement of the 1960s and its current status in critical discourse.

Václav Havel:
Playwright and President

Václav Havel, a Czechoslovakian playwright and nonfiction writer, was born in 1936.

The entry below contains criticism on Havel's literary works, focusing upon *Letters to Olga* and *Disturbing the Peace* as well as his important contributions to contemporary drama. For further commentary on Havel's life and works, see *CLC,* Vols. 25 and 58; *Contemporary Authors,* Vol. 104; and *Newsmakers 1990.*

This entry also features discussion of Havel's role in political events in Czechoslovakia that culminated with the "Velvet Revolution" of late 1989, when a relatively peaceful transition of power included Havel's election to the presidency.

From Dissident to President:
A Chronology

Background information: The Republic of Czechoslovakia was formed immediately after World War I, and Tomas Masaryk, a principal conceptualist of the nation, served as its first president. The Republic comprised the former Habsburg "crownlands" of Bohemia, Moravia, and Silesia as well as former Hungarian territories, including Slovakia. During the 1930s, tensions between various ethnic groups within the country escalated, and a German minority sought affiliation with Nazi Germany. The Munich Pact of 1938 partitioned the nation and ostensibly dissolved the Republic. Following the Allied victory in World War II, a coalition government ruled the reestablished Republic until 1949, when communist leaders gained control and Czechoslovakia became one of the Eastern Bloc countries modeled on the Soviet style of government. A period of reform occurred during the 1960s, culminating with the rise of Alexander Dubček to communist party leadership. In 1968, however, the Soviet army invaded Czechoslovakia, and firm government control of society, culture, and the economy was reinstituted under the leadership of Gustáv Husák. In 1989, Czechoslovakia, like other Eastern bloc countries, renounced exclusive communist leadership in favor of more democratic forms of government. A new coalition government was formed in Czechoslovakia in December of 1989 with Václav Havel serving as president.

1951: Havel is denied access to higher education for rea-

Václav Havel after completing his address to the U.S. Congress.

sons related to "class" and "political profile." He works as an apprentice and a laboratory technician through 1955.

1955: He begins publishing articles, mainly on literary topics.

Autumn 1956: At a meeting of young authors at the Dobřís Writers' Home near Prague, Havel makes his first public speech, in which he chastises dominant literary figures and trends in Czechoslovakia.

1957-1959: Havel completes his mandatory, two-year military service.

1960: After having been turned down repeatedly for positions in higher education, Havel joins the avant-garde Na zábradí Theatre (The Theatre on the Balustrade); he originally serves as a stage hand, then as a contributor of scripts, and eventually as literary advisor. His early plays

Zahradní slavnost (1963; *The Garden Party*) and *Vyrozumění* (1965; *The Memorandum*) are produced here and establish Havel's reputation as an absurdist playwright concerned with bureaucracy, conformity, language, and identity.

July 9, 1964: Marries Olga Šplíchalová.

1965: Joins editorial staff of *Tvář*, a monthly political journal that is soon closed by staff who refuse to follow the dictates of the Communist Party and the Writers' Association. // Havel becomes chairman of a group of young writers in the Czechoslovak Writers' Association. At a conference of the Association held in May on the twentieth anniversary of the liberation of Czechoslovakia from Nazi occupation, Havel disparages activities of the Association, citing unfair treatment of unconventional writers.

June 1967: In a speech at the Fourth Congress of the Writers' Association, Havel attacks undemocratic procedures of the group; following pressure by Communist Party officials, Havel, Ivan Klíma, Pavel Kohout, and Ludvík Vaculík are removed from a list of candidates for the Association's Central Committee.

March-April 1968: A period often referred to as the "Prague Spring," in which an artistic community flourishes and gradual easing of social and cultural restrictions seems imminent, is underway and lasts until August. // Havel signs a proclamation by twenty writers on the establishment of an Independent Writers' Circle within the Writers' Association. He is elected chairman of a seven member committee of the Circle, and holds this position until the dissolution of the Writers' Association in 1970. // Havel is among 150 cultural figures who sign an open letter to the Communist Party Central Committee commenting upon the progress of democratization under the Dubček regime. "Na téma opozice" ("On the Subject of Opposition"), an article advocating a two-party system and the creation of a democratic party based on Czechoslovak "humanitarian traditions," is published in the weekly *Literární listy*.

May-June 1968: Havel spends six weeks in the United States while his play, *The Memorandum,* is staged at the New York Shakespeare Festival. The play earns Havel his first Obie prize.

August 1968: The Soviet army invades Czechoslovakia. Alexander Dubček is replaced as prime minister by Gustáv Husák. // Havel takes part in Free Czechoslovakia radio broadcasts, contributing daily commentary. He also chairs the editorial staff of *Tvář*, a revived monthly that publishes until June 1969.

August 1969: Havel is one of ten signatories of a declaration, "Deset bodů" ("Ten Points"), condemning the post-Dubček policy of "normalization." He is consequently interrogated and charged with subverting the republic. All ten signatories were to be tried in October, but the trial was postponed indefinitely.

1971-1972: Confidential official circulars list Havel among authors whose works are barred in schools and libraries in Czechoslovakia.

May 1972: Havel and other banned authors are denounced at the founding congress of the new, "normalized," Writers' Association.

April 1975: Copies of "Dopis Dr Gustávu Husákovi" ("Letter to Dr. Gustáv Husák"), in which Havel addresses a discussion of his country's problems to its leader, circulate in Czechoslovakia.

September 1976: The arrest of members and followers of the rock band Plastic People of the Universe as an "offense to culture" and for disturbing the peace prompts Havel and six other writers to arrange protests and international appeals against persecution of the band. Amnesty International and such noted authors as Heinrich Böll, Allen Ginsberg, and Kurt Vonnegut were among those who lodged formal protests. This incident deeply influenced Havel's opposition to the Czechoslovakian government. In his essay "Proces" ("The Trial") Havel wrote that the event inspired

> an urgent questioning of what one should actually expect from life; whether one should silently accept one's place in the world as it is presented to one and slip obediently into one's preassigned place in it, or whether one should be "reasonable" and take one's place—or whether one has the right to resist in the name of one's own human condition.

Havel is invited later in the month by the Austrian Minister of Education to the première of his plays *Audience* and *Private View,* but is denied a travel permit by his country's Foreign Ministry because he "is not representative of Czech culture."

Late 1976: Havel takes part in discussions leading to the foundation of Charter 77 (a human rights group) and to the composition of its 'Declaration' released on January 1, 1977 [a portion of the Charter 77 Declaration is printed below]. Havel, philosopher Jan Patocka, and former Foreign Minister Jiri Hajek are designated as Charter spokesmen.

January 1977: Havel, actor Pavel Landovský, and author Ludvík Vaculík are detained while attempting to deliver the 'Declaration' and its list of signatories to Prime Minister Husák, the Federal Assembly, and the Czechoslovak News Agency. Repressive action is taken against most of the signatories. Havel is arrested and interrogated, held until May 20, and charged with subversion of the Republic as the author of "Letter to Dr. Gustáv Husák" and as the principal organizer of Charter 77.

October 1977: Criminal proceedings commence against Havel and three others; Havel is sentenced to fourteen months' imprisonment, conditionally deferred for three years, for attempting to damage the interests of the Republic.

January 1978: Havel is detained by police upon arriving at the Railwayman's Ball; he is held for investigation until March 13, accused of obstructing and assaulting an official. Criminal proceedings are halted in April.

April 1978: VONS (Výbor na obranu nespravedlivě stíhaných; The Committee for the Defense of the Unjustly

Prosecuted) is established, with Havel among its members. Havel is active with VONS until his arrest in May 1979.

November 1978: Havel is kept under constant surveillance; he reports this experience in a two-part essay "Zprávy o mém domácím vězení a jevech s ním souviseejících" ("Reports on my House Arrest and Attendant Circumstances"), and protests this illegal restriction in a letter to the Federal Ministry of the Interior.

May 1979: A large-scale drive against VONS by security police results in a number of house searches and the arrest of fifteen committee members. Ten, including Havel, are taken into custody and charged with criminal subversion of the Republic; four of the ten are released.

October 1979: Six people, including Havel, are put to trial for criminal subversion of the Republic for their activities with VONS. Havel is sentenced to four and a half years in prison.

June 1981: The European Parliament passes a resolution calling for the release of Havel and others arrested and imprisoned for political reasons in Czechoslovakia.

February 1982: The International Committee for the Defense of Charter 77 confers the Jan Palach Peace Prize on Havel for his literary works and his selfless defense of human rights.

July 1982: The International Theatre Festival at Avignon, France, includes a "Night for Václav Havel," featuring Samuel Beckett's play *Catastrophe* (reprinted in *CLC*, Vol. 25, pp. 230-31) and Arthur Miller's monologue *I think about you a great deal* (reprinted below).

February-March 1983: Havel develops pneumonia and is transferred to a prison hospital in Prague. On February 7, his sentence is suspended for health reasons and he is moved to a public hospital; in March he is released from the hospital and shortly thereafter resumes his activities with Charter 77.

January 1985: Havel is arrested for forty-eight hours in connection with the nomination of new Charter 77 spokesmen.

August 1985: Havel is twice taken into custody in connection with the drafting of a Charter 77 statement on the anniversary of the 1968 Soviet invasion of Czechoslovakia.

April 1987: Thousands cheer Soviet Premier Mikhail Gorbachev, who has been actively promoting *Glasnost,* or "openness"—a policy that promises greater cultural freedoms in Communist nations—during his visit to Prague in April. // Havel claims that Gorbachev refrained from attending press conferences in Prague in order to avoid questions concerning the 1968 Soviet invasion of Czechoslovakia.

August 1988: Thousands demonstrate in Prague on the twentieth anniversary of the Soviet invasion. Police respond violently, making numerous arrests.

October 1988: Some five-thousand people gather in Wenceslas Square in Prague to celebrate the seventieth anniversary of the founding of the Czechoslovak Republic.

Police attack the crowd with water cannons, tear gas, and other means, and make nearly one hundred arrests.

November 1988: An international symposium on seventy years of Czech history is scheduled in Prague; the night before the symposium is to begin, several activists are arrested, and, the next day, Havel is apprehended by police within seconds after opening the conference; he is released shortly thereafter.

January 1989: In radio broadcasts, Havel discusses the upcoming anniversary of the death of Jan Palach, who set himself on fire twenty years before in Wenceslas Square to protest the Soviet invasion. Havel is arrested on January 16 while observing a memorial service in the Square, charged with inciting this illegal event, and sentenced to nine months in prison. The next day further arrests are made of people who attempt to lay flowers in the Square; on January 19, police aggressively disrupt a spontaneous demonstration.

May 1989: Pressured by an appeal from over 3000 people from the arts and sciences in Czechoslovakia, and preceding Helsinki Accord meetings (where human rights will be discussed), the government releases Havel from prison.

November 17, 1989: A gathering of students marking the fiftieth anniversary of a student murdered by Nazis becomes a demonstration that marches toward Wenceslas Square and demands reforms similar to those recently adopted in East Germany and Poland. Police launch a brutal attack on the students.

November 18: Student and theater groups call for a nationwide, general strike.

November 19: Obcanske Forum (Civic Forum) is founded and serves as the major group negotiating with the Communist party on a new government. // A crowd in Wenceslas Square continues to swell, chanting slogans demanding freedom and the resignation of the government.

November 21: A number of leaders from various opposition groups address the crowd in Wenceslas Square. Havel states the demands of Civic Forum (sweeping resignations within the existing government and formation of a new government).

November 22 and 23: Demonstrations continue. Prime Minister Ladislav Adamic meets with representatives of Civic Forum; at Adamic's request, Havel is not present.

November 24: Dubček and Havel address a wildly cheering crowd. Official resignations of the Politburo and the Communist Central Committee secretariat are announced.

November 26: Official negotiations between The National Front, which consists of Communist Party members and various satellite parties, and Civic Forum begin on the composition of a new government. Timothy Garton Ash reported the encounter in *The New York Review of Books:*

> "We don't know each other," says [Prime Minister Adamic], extending his hand across the table. "I'm Havel," says Havel. Just in case you didn't guess. It's a short getting-to-know-you session, but they agree to meet on [November

28]. The Prime Minister promises the release of political prisoners. [Civic Forum had demanded that political prisoners be released by December 12—United Nations Human Rights Day.]

November 28: Civic Forum sets December 2 as the deadline for the establishment of a new government.

December 1: A provision guaranteeing that the Communist Party will have a leading role in the government is deleted from the Constitution. Negotiations continue as Civic Forum expresses opposition to a new government in which sixteen of twenty-one cabinet posts are held by Communists.

December 4: At the Malta Summit, Warsaw Pact member nations formally renounce the Soviet invasion of Czechoslovakia in 1968 as an intervention in Czech affairs. // As negotiations continue, both groups announce that the first free elections in Czechoslovakia since World War II will be held in early summer 1990.

December 12: Failing to form a new government, Adamic resigns. Marían Calfa is designated by President Gustáv Husák to form a new government, which is established shortly and dominated by members of Civic Forum.

December 29: The Czechoslovak Parliament unanimously elects Havel Interim President.

July 5, 1990: Havel is elected to a two-year term as President of Czechoslovakia.

> Information in this listing was gathered from various issues of the *New York Review of Books, The New York Times, The New Republic, The Nation, Time Magazine,* and *Newsweek;* Vilem Precan's chronology printed in Václav Havel's *In Search of Human Identity* (London: Rozmluvy, 1984); and "A Short Bio-Bibliography of Václav Havel" in *Václav Havel or Living in Truth,* edited by Jan Vladislav (London: Faber, 1987).

PRINCIPAL WORKS

PLAYS

*Zahradní slavnost   1963
  [*The Garden Party* (first publication), 1969]
*Vyrozumění   1965
  [*The Memorandum*   (first publication), 1967]
Ztížená možnost soustředění   1968
  [*The Increased Difficulty of Concentration*   (first publication), 1969]
**Spiklenci   1970
**Zebracka opera [adaptor; from the play of the same title by John Gay] 1975
**Audience   1975
**Vernisáž   1975
**Horsky hotel   1976
Protest   1978
Omyl   1983
Largo desolato   1984
  [*Largo desolato*   (first publication), 1987]

Pokouseni   1985
  [*Temptation*   (first publication), 1988]
Hostina   1985

NONFICTION

Dopisy Olze   1983
  [*Letters to Olga: June 1979 to September 1982,* 1988]
O lidskou identitu   1984
Dálkový výslech   1986
  [*Disturbing the Peace: A Conversation with Karel Hvížďala,*   1990]

*Collected with various nonfiction pieces in *Protokoly,* 1966.

**Collected in *Hry 1970-1976,* 1977.

Maius Bergman

In December 242 Czechoslovak citizens, among them participants in the ill-fated "Spring of 1968," affixed their signatures to a document "regretfully" detailing their government's failure to honor the human rights provisions of the Czechoslovak Constitution, the International Covenant on Civil and Political Rights, the International Covenant on Economic, Social and Cultural Rights, and the Final Act of the Helsinki Conference on European Security. The document, titled "Charter 77," was ready on January 1, and on January 6 some of its signatories attempted to present it to the Czechoslovak Premier, the Chairman of the Federal Assembly, and the Czechoslovak News Agency. Copies of the document were confiscated, and some of its authors detained. "Charter 77" then was sent to the same officials through the mails, but it remained unacknowledged. So the signatories sent it to the Western (including Communist) press. At this point the Czech media swung into action. The document, said *Rude Pravo,* was nothing but a call for "the dismantling of socialist democracy" and for the "restoration of bourgeois capitalism." Its authors were "standard bearers of subversion," "renegades," "venal tricksters," "pharisees," "political shipwrecks" taking their orders from "anti-communist and Zionist centers" abroad. These ringing words were instantaneously endorsed by all other newspapers, by Prague Radio and TV, and by "the working people of Czechoslovakia," meeting "spontaneously" (so it was reported) throughout the country. And so yet another witchhunt was on.

That a document of this sort should have been signed by so many people (soon to exceed 300) might have come as a surprise to Czechoslovakia's leaders. But the existence of restiveness and courage within the country is something they have been acutely aware of. As Alan Levy pointed out in a perceptive article in *Index on Censorship* (London, Autumn 1976), "Czechoslovakia is the only country in Eastern Europe where a real opposition exists. The surviving leaders of the Prague Spring and the half-million members expelled from the Communist Party comprise a shadow Cabinet and a shadow Party with more support and experience than those who hold the cards and the titles today." During the past few years, a number of former political leaders and prominent intellectuals—among them Alexander Dubček, the philosopher Karel Kosik, the historian Vilem Precan, the novelists Ludvik Vaculik and Ivan Klima and the playwright Vaclav Havel—have addressed open letters to the authorities, given interviews to foreign newsmen, and published articles in foreign newspapers and journals. In addition, there is a lively samizdat network within the country, known as Padlock Press, which has circulated more than fifty books by well-known authors proscribed by the censors. All this activity has survived the various efforts to suppress it.

Yet Czechoslovak dissidents, while eloquent and outspoken, have scrupulously refrained from formulating their complaints in overtly political terms. Czechoslovak intellectuals have not asked their government to carry out social and economic reforms or to institute political pluralism, but to respect human rights and individual dignity, to put an end to witless prosecutions, and to enter into a dialogue with those for whom the moral health of the country is more important than a political program or ideological slogans.

"Charter 77" carries on the same tradition. It documents and asks for an end to violations of freedom of expression and religion, to denials of the right to emigrate, and to politically motivated prosecutions. At the same time, "Charter 77" goes out of its way to deny any intention of engaging in political activity, of "raising its own program for political or social reforms or changes." Its proclaimed aim is to enter into "a constructive dialogue with the political and state authorities."

Verbal violence is as traditional in countries under Soviet-style regimes as is cherry *pirog*. Yet the Czechoslovak leaders *do* have some cause for alarm this time: despite the efforts of the "Charter" signatories to avoid being charged with "conspiracy," their very number raises the specter of an "organization"; and although the rejection of political aims is unquestionably genuine, Husak and his allies cannot but recall (as indeed *Rude Pravo* has already pointed out) that the "Prague Spring" also began with a seemingly apolitical revolt by intellectuals, particularly writers, in 1967. The fact that the signers have appealed directly to the "Euro-Communists" is not exactly good news either. The Italian and British Communists already have rebuked the Czech government. Even the French Communists, who only a few years ago denounced Artur London's *Confession* as "anti-socialist propaganda," now have joined in the chorus.

Finally, it has not escaped the Prague authorities that "Charter 77" came out on the eve of the Belgrade conference on European security, which in June is to review the results of the Helsinki Final Act; and that it coincided, too, with the advent of a new American administration, more forcefully committed to a defense of human rights than its predecessor. Both Washington and Moscow have expressed their concern about the developments in Prague: the first by publishing a formal statement criticizing the Czech government for its repressive actions against the signatories of the "Charter," and the latter by quietly cautioning its allies not to get carried away by their heady

rhetoric. The Soviets, of course, have their own (and familiar) problems: on the one hand, they are anxious not to spoil their "case" against US violations of the Helsinki agreements, which they hope to present in Belgrade. On the other, they cannot easily tolerate the burgeoning activities of their own dissidents, especially those of the various groups that have made it their business to monitor their government's record on Helsinki. Hence the latest arrests, detainments and searches in Moscow and the Ukraine, and the expulsion of George Krimsky, an AP correspondent with a discomfiting command of the Russian language and an equally discomfiting knowledge of the dissident scene. Mass arrests and trials, however, coupled with murmurs of discontent among the still faithful in Rome and Paris, are hardly in Moscow's interest right now.

Probably because of all these diverse pressures, the Czech authorities apparently decided to refrain from taking drastic measures against the dissidents. In recent weeks, the official press have been at pains to stress that while "violations of legality" will be punished, "nobody in Czechoslovakia has been penally persecuted or punished for their political or philosophic opinions." This is palpable nonsense, of course, as are claims that some of the signatories, such as the writer Pavel Kohout, fearing deportation, have now declared that they are "happy in Czechoslovakia and are not afraid of persecution." And although the campaign is still on, the Czech press has now taken to referring to the "Charter 77" in the past tense, a "failure" and a decisive "defeat" at the hands of the party and the entire nation, more closely "rallied" around the party than ever before. It is likely, therefore, that Prague would like to see the dust settle, at least for the time being.

Yet a respite, if it comes, is not apt to endure. The spokesmen of "Charter 77" continue to speak out and to give interviews to Western correspondents, and more people have now signed the document, too: there are over 500 by now, among them a large number of industrial workers. All told, the recent events in Czechoslovakia—as well as, for that matter, in Poland, Hungary and East Germany—provide a striking illustration of how fragile is Communist legitimacy in Eastern Europe. Mr. Gierek (as he recently made it known) may be prepared to pardon the protesting workers in his country, and Dr. Husak may try to call off the dogs, but both will continue to preside over empires which, like extant volcanoes, are bound to rumble and erupt. (pp. 12-13)

Maius Bergman, "Dissent in Czechoslovakia," in The New Republic, *Vol. 176, No. 9, February 26, 1977, pp. 12-13.*

Arthur Miller

[*The author of such plays as* Death of a Salesman *and* The Crucible, *Miller is considered a major twentieth-century American dramatist. The monologue reprinted below was written as an expression of solidarity with Havel for a performance on July 21, 1982, at the International Theatre Festival in Avignon, France.*]

I think about you a great deal

The WRITER *enters. Wears shirt and trousers. Carrying a bundle of mail. Sits, goes through letter after letter; of a dozen he removes two of importance, the rest he—after an instant of hesitation—drops into his wastebasket. Instantly, the* IMPRISONED ONE *enters, in his forties, wearing rumpled gray clothing. He sits. The* WRITER *does not face him directly.*

WRITER: Yes.
[Slight pause]
Amazing, how often I think of you even though we've barely met. And that was so long ago.
[Reaches into the waste basket, retrieves the letters he dropped in.]
I suppose it happens whenever I get a load of this kind of stuff. Must get fifty pounds of it a month. I'm on the master list, obviously. Look at this . . . *[Reads off the senders' names.]* 'Ban the Bomb', 'Planned Parenthood', 'Save the Children', 'American Indian Fund', 'Friends of the Arts', 'National Organization for Women', 'Fight the Klu Klux Klan', 'Amnesty International', 'Central Park Conservancy',—whatever that is, 'Save the Animals', 'Save Africa', 'Save the Rain Forests', save, save, save, save. The mind simply cannot take all this seriously. Things just can't be this bad.
[Slight pause]
I must say, though—it does remind me of you. Your situation seems worse than all the others, though . . . I'm not sure why. Maybe it's the immense investment so many of us have made in socialism. That people who even call themselves socialist should imprison the imagination . . . That's really what it is, isn't it—the war on the imagination. And maybe, too, because your prison is probably further west than Vienna. You are almost within range of the sound of our voices. You can almost hear us. I suppose. In effect. Whatever the reason, I really do think about you a great deal.
[Slight pause]
Reminds me of another writer I knew many years ago in New York. Quite talented, we all thought. Poet and playwright. Lot of promise. But he had an active case of claustrophobia. Couldn't bear to enter an elevator. And they had no money so he and his wife lived in this tiny room which drove him crazy—used to walk the streets half the night. (It was a lot safer to walk the streets at night in those days.) Anyway . . . in desperation he took a job writing advertising copy for . . . I think it was General Motors. Which allowed him to move into a larger apartment, and eased his anxieties. Years passed and I met him again and naturally I was curious about what he was working on. But the poetry had died, the plays too; what he wanted to show me was this thick file of ads he had written. In fact, he was such a favourite, the company had given him a special office on the ground floor of their skyscraper so he could avoid the elevator. He was middle-aged by this time, and it was quite . . . moving, actually . . . to see how proud he had become of these works in praise of General Motors. In fact, he showed me his different drafts, and pointed out how he had shifted various ideas around until the whole conception was perfected. And I kept watching the look of triumph on his

An excerpt from Charter 77

The responsibility for the preservation of civil rights naturally rests with the State power. But not on it alone. Every individual bears a share of responsibility for the general conditions in the country, and therefore also for compliance with the enacted pacts, which are as binding for the people as for the government.

The feeling of this coresponsibility, the belief in the value of civic engagement and the readiness to be engaged, together with the need to seek a new and more effective expression, gave us the idea of creating Charter 77, whose existence we publicly announce.

Charter 77 is a free and informal and open association of people of various convictions, religions and professions, linked by the desire to work individually and collectively for respect for human and civil rights in Czechoslovakia and the world—the rights provided for in the enacted international pacts, in the Final Act of the Helsinki Conference, and in numerous other international documents against wars, violence and social and mental oppression. It represents a general declaration of human rights.

Charter 77 is founded on the concepts of solidarity and friendship of people who share a concern for the fate of ideals to which they have linked their lives and work.

Charter 77 is not an organization; it has no statutes, permanent organs or registered membership. Everyone who agrees with its idea and participates in its work and supports it, belongs to it.

Charter 77 is not intended to be a basis for opposition political activity. Its desire is to serve the common interest, as have numerous similar organizations of civic initiative East and West. It has no intention of initiating its own programs for political or social reforms or changes, but it wants to lead in the sphere of its activity by means of a constructive dialogue with the political and State authorities—and particularly by drawing attention to various specific violations of civil and human rights, by preparing their documentation, by suggesting solutions, by submitting various more general proposals aimed at furthering these rights and their guarantees, by acting as a mediator in the event of conflict situations which might result in wrongdoings, etc.

By its symbolic name, Charter 77 stresses that it has been established on the threshold of what has been declared the year of political prisoners, in the course of which a meeting in Belgrade is to review the progress—or lack of it—achieved since the Helsinki Conference.

As signatories of this declaration, we designate Dr. Jan Patocka, Dr. Vaclav Havel and Professor Jiri Hajek to act as spokesmen for Charter 77. These spokesmen are authorized to represent Charter 77 before the State and other organizations, as well as before the public at home and throughout the world, and they guarantee the authenticity of its documents by their signatures. In us and other citizens who will join Charter 77, they will find their collaborators who will participate in the necessary negotiations, who will accept partial tasks, and will share the entire responsibility.

We trust that Charter 77 will contribute to making it possible for all citizens of Czechoslovakia to live and work as free people.

face. And you couldn't help being happy for him—that he had earned so much space around himself. He obviously no longer lived in his old anxiety. Seemed really satisfied with life now, with a solid feeling of accomplishment. His was clearly a successful life . . . that had substituted itself for a poet.

[*Slight pause*]
I thought about you, then. They have taken away your space, haven't they—because you have refused to write their ads. Amazing how, more than anything, power loves praise. But there are fifty other conclusions one could draw from this and none of them change anything for you. So I suppose we must raise it all to the moral level. The moral level is where nothing gets changed. Yet it exists, doesn't it; just as my thinking so often of you exists. In fact, it joins us together, in a way. In some indescribable way we are each other's continuation . . . you in that darkness where they claw and pound at your imagination, and I out here in this space where I think about you . . . a great deal.
[*He drops the clump of appeals into the basket.*]
There will be another clump tomorrow. And the next day and the next. [*Slight pause*] Imagine . . . if they stopped! Is that possible? Of course not. As long as mornings continue to arrive, the mail will bring these acts of goodness demanding to be done. And they will be done. Somehow. And so we hold your space open for you, dear friend.

The WRITER *goes to his typewriter and writes. The* IMPRISONED ONE, *after a moment, rises and walks out. The* WRITER *continues to write.* (pp. 263-65)

> Arthur Miller, "I think about you a great
> deal," in Václav Havel or Living In Truth.
> Edited by Jan Vladislav, Faber & Faber Limit-
> ed, 1987, pp. 263-65.

Pavel Kohout   (translated by M. Pomichalek and A. Mozga)

[*Kohout, like Havel, is a signatory of Charter 77 and a playwright whose works were banned in Czechoslovakia. When Kohout left his native country in the late 1970s, to visit Vienna, Austria, he was stripped of his citizenship. The piece reprinted below was written in 1986 in Vienna.*]

Investigating world drama, a theatre criminologist would be bound to discover a great many instances of theft of character, some of which have even had to be settled in court as plagiarism. To list all the appropriations from authors who, long dead, left their characters to be dealt with at will by their heirs, would prove a nigh impossible task. Except for Ferdinand Vaněk, however, I do not know of any figure playwrights have borrowed with the kind approval of the hero's original father.

I was sitting in Václav Havel's hillside cottage that summer day when, for the 'entertainment of friends', as he remarked with characteristic modesty, he read his one-act play, *Audience.* In it he used the character of Vaněk as a means of describing to us the lot of a brewery worker—his own. With characteristic immodesty, I note that it was I

who, after the reading, drew his attention to the fact that he had discovered a vehicle for translating concrete information about concrete people and problems in a concrete period into a dramatic form capable of sustaining life on stage.

The worldwide acclaim received by the play soon proved right both author and listener, the latter—by the same twist of fate that expelled both men from the Czech theatre—also a playwright. And when Vaněk performed equally successfully in a second play, *Private View,* I tentatively asked his creator for permission to use him in recording my own experiences. He agreed not only willingly but actively endorsed the proposal. Out of this conversation grew the idea for a jointly composed evening of theatrical entertainment. In the autumn of 1979 the world première of his *Protest* and my *Permit,* collectively named *Tests,* took place in the Akademietheater in Vienna.

By that time Václav Havel was already in jail. As a homage to him I wrote another Vaněk-play, *Morass,* and persuaded our mutual friend, Pavel Landovský, to contribute *Arrest,* yet another play structured around the hero whom we three have come to pass back and forth among us like a challenge cup. This pair we provisionally named *Rests.* Five years later still when, for the first time, I felt the need to reflect in dramatic form the experience of my involuntary stay in the West—a consequence of a trip to Vienna—I added to the sequence my third work, *Safari.*

How can one explain the fact that a writer who has never lacked his own ideas uses a colleague as the basis of a drama—and does so three times? If we disregard my affiliation with a group of authors ruled by the great William and, in our century, presided over by Brecht—both of whom considered the scenic adaptation of the works of others as no less a creative adventure than the treatment of an original theme—I personally see two causes.

Distance in time has confirmed my belief that the initial impulse was generated jointly by the state of society and that of my own life. I was—and feel I still am today, in this other world—a member of a small but amazingly vital community, one forged by far more than the voluntarily chosen and collectively borne lot of exiles in their own country. In this extreme situation people with entirely different personal histories and ideas discovered themselves as well as each other. Without surrendering their own convictions they learned to understand others; without losing the traits of their individuality they found what they have in common.

Although, taken superficially, Václav Havel and I seem almost polar opposites in terms of personality and political inclinations, our friendship has become one of the dominant factors in my life. The nature of our understanding is a topic for another and more important essay, one reflecting on the possibility of a consensus among the whole of Czech society. The two of us have clearly answered this question in the affirmative, and it appears to me that talking over the character of Ferdinand Vaněk was an expression of my need to meet Václav Havel also in the writer's most intimate sphere—in creation. A Freudian philosopher would probably delight in calling this a manifestation of abnormal sexuality. In fact, through the psychology of his/my hero and with my typewriter as the only tool, I established a much closer and more permanent relationship with my friend than anyone could possibly achieve in bed.

That is why I am certain of the second cause of my attraction to and as yet undiminished relations with the dramatic principle of *Audience,* which has held firm under the threefold pressure added by me. After all, what is the essence of its aesthetics? Vaněk. And what is the essence of Vaněk? Havel. And the essence of Havel?

During the eight long years I have not seen him, half of which he has spent behind bars, the original has surely changed; but the essence is bound to have endured. To describe it as accurately as possible, I must once again resort to intimate vocabulary: chastity. At first, this may sound ridiculous—considering my familiarity with my friend's renaissance personality, his eager penchant for every joy life has to offer. But for a long time I have also known that there is a chastity of a higher order. Both Havel and his fictional twin brother Vaněk have everything that makes a man a man, but they have retained the soul of a child.

Even a child knows how to do wrong, how to hurt, pretend and lie, but to the child these actions are dictated by instant need or emotion, not moral corruption, which is acquired only later. When a child tries to deceive or, more still, to harm, it usually does so with guileless awkwardness, eliciting compassion. A man with the soul of a child does not always elicit compassion in human conflicts, but neither does he forfeit the sympathy of others. Furthermore, in key confrontations such as the one presently taking place in Czechoslovakia, he unconsciously irritates both the bureaucratic (equals police) apparatus as well as the mass of his fellow citizens.

Omnipotent authority is faced with a shy, polite, even obliging intellectual of a visibly non-athletic cast, the like of which it has come to deal with expeditiously, if he be furnished with the soul of an ordinary man—commonly a mixture of cowardice and cynicism—and therefore amenable to a bargain. But when authority enters, this man does not rant and rave; he neither quarrels nor exchanges blows; he doesn't even lie. At the most, he is silent, if the truth might hurt someone other than himself. When authority displays its candies of all flavours and whips of all sizes, it at first misses his quiet 'No', and when it finally hears it, it does not believe. It shows him its instruments; it uses them.

Before his trial ever began, Václav Havel was offered *laissez passer* to New York. The fury he unleashed by his persistence in saying No brought down on him a (for such a delicate man astronomical) term of four and a half years in prison. Only slightly before the term expired was he released, a seriously ill man they feared might die in prison. Ferdinand Vaněk has inherited his disposition.

To once critical intellectuals, the overwhelming majority of whom have by now come to an arrangement with authority, he poses no less of a problem. To them he is an inconvenience greater than authority itself, since he proves them guilty of a life-sized lie: guilty in front of the world, their families and even themselves. Whereas au-

thority knows his momentary powerlessness, to this group of despondents Václav Havel is a very real danger, because the future threatens to prove him right, and that will necessarily mean a condemnation of them. They hate him but at the same time, just to be sure, they obsequiously curry favour with him, only to slander and denounce him the next moment.

As Havel at times in real life, Vaněk is a 'reagent' on stage. His mere appearance whips them on to fervent activity and elicits cascades of words that are supposed to habilitate or rehabilitate them, to convince or convict him. The less they tolerate him, the more they invite him; the fewer questions he asks, the more answers they provide; the less he blames them, the more stubbornly they defend themselves; the more he calms them, the more agitated they get; the more magnanimous he is, the more aggressive they become, and yet—the more they try to hold him back when at last he wants to remove his irritant self from their presence. It is precisely his departure they obviously fear most, the maltster in *Audience,* the couple in *Private View,* and the writer Staněk in *Protest* as well. As if departing together with him were their secret hope—that through him the world might once again become a more decent place, and they more decent people.

No matter how different the life and style of the authors who have appropriated Vaněk so far, each of their Ferdinands preserves symptomatic traits of his spiritual father. Invariably, each and every one of them is in essence Havel portrayed by different painters, including himself.

A good portrait or self-portrait is never as descriptive as a photograph but can present a more truthful depiction and, by eliminating secondary ornaments and focusing only on essentials, reveal the immutable centre of the subject's personality. It is in this sense that Ferdinand Vaněk is an artistic artefact, a skilfully crafted *dramatis persona* escaping the fluidity of life and functioning in accordance with the laws of the theatre. The transposition of Havel's chastity from life to drama via this prototype in all three original plays is proof of an artistic blessing of the highest degree. This is precisely where Havel—Vaněk is the most truthful embodiment of Vaněk-Havel, something of a popular reincarnation of the centaur, Cheiron.

My last piece, *Safari,* summons him on a first investigation of Western society. At the end of the play I, honest debtor that I am, return him to the country of his original owner. He cannot cross over to me a second time, I can only rejoin him. This I hope for; but I also believe that he will not wait, that he will, shyly yet without hesitation, enter into further plays which, in turn, will chart the features of our time on the blank map of contemporary Czech theatre. (pp. 245-49)

Pavel Kohout, "The Chaste Centaur," translated by M. Pomichalek and A. Mozga, in Václav Havel or Living In Truth, edited by Jan Vladislav, Faber & Faber Limited, 1987, pp. 245-49.

Mark Fisher

[While serving a four-and-a-half-year prison term, Havel] was allowed to write one four-page letter every week to his wife, Olga, under bizarre restrictions. No crossings out or corrections were allowed; no quotation marks, no underlining or foreign expressions. 'We could only write about "family matters". Humour was banned as well: punishment is a serious business, after all, and jokes would have undermined the gravity.'

In spite of this, and the absence of any replies from Olga, the 142 letters [collected in *Letters to Olga: June 1979 to September 1982*] build up a remarkable view of a marriage of complementary opposites. Havel is a middle-class intellectual; Olga is working-class, 'very much her own person, sober, unsentimental, and she can even be somewhat mouthy and obnoxious; in other words, as we say, you can't get her drunk on a bun.' The declarations of love are clipped—'I kiss you' at the end of most letters—but the level, steady concentration on each other is rock solid: 'Your recommendation to eat a lot of cheese brought a tender smile to my face.'

The main text of the book, however, charts the journey into himself. Trapped in prison camp life, making heavy steel mesh with a spot welder, he sets himself targets to survive. He aims to improve his English, write 'at least two plays' and 'study the entire Bible thoroughly.' He wryly reads Saul Bellow's *Herzog*: 'It's about a crisis of intellectuality in conditions of complete intellectual freedom.'

But as he beats these targets and learns to circumvent the mindless lack of logic in prison routine, he's faced by a worse struggle, to make sense of his life.

He returns again and again to the nature of responsibility, seeing it as a personal duty to be assumed by each of us. 'Why do we do good at all,' he wonders, 'even when there is clearly no personal advantage in doing so (for instance, when no one knows about it and never will)? And if we fail to do good, why do we apologise to ourselves?'

The last 16 letters bring these themes to a climax. He ends by criticising himself for failing to discover new philosophical truths, but he has at least come through. 'It's strange, but I may well be happier now than at any time in recent years. In short, I feel fine and I love you.'

In 1983 he became acutely ill and, thinking he was dying, the Czech government responded to international pressure and moved him into a civilian hospital. For a glorious month he was allowed friends and books and gossip, 'released from the burden of prison but not yet encumbered by the burden of freedom. But the beautiful dream had to end. The day came when I had to step back into the world as it really was . . . and I've been moving along its uncertain surface ever since.' Until this week [in February, 1989, when Havel was sentenced to nine months imprisonment for "incitement" and "obstruction"].

Mark Fisher, "Between Bars," in The Observer, *February 26, 1989, p. 46.*

Carole Angier

[These *Letters to Olga: June 1979 to September 1982*] are fascinating, as much for what they leave out as for what they put in. They were all, of course, subject to prison censorship and rules, and most to further arbitrary control by Havel's sadistic first jailer. As a result there is nothing in them about his daily life in prison—his regular punishments, harsh labour, battles with informers. He wasn't allowed to joke. He often had to write in evasions, or on subjects he was ordered to—though here he smuggled in humour after all, distinguishing 15 separate moods when told to write about himself, and numbering them carefully. These constraints on the letters added to their role—as his one escape from the horrors of prison, his one link to his life of writing—and the result is contemplation, introspection, increasing abstraction. It's not easy; but it's extraordinarily worthwhile.

The letters do start off more mundanely, with long lists of things for his wife to bring, and repeated pleas for her to write more often and more fully. Some readers dislike this nagging, Havel's translator says: and defends him, arguing that the letters show growing acceptance of her independence, even growing love. I don't think this is true; as usual, the truth is harsher. Havel clearly loves his wife, but she wasn't his ideal correspondent. She didn't write easily herself, and couldn't send him the detailed, chatty news he wanted. So that too drove him into abstraction. By the end, in his last 16 letters, he was writing pure phenomenological philosophy, and the salutation to "Dear Olga" is the only trace of her left. He wasn't writing to *her* any more, he was just writing.

But he writes, despite all the handicaps, so well. He writes about the theatre, what he despises about it and what he loves; he writes about his own plays, their obsession with the theme of human identity, the importance of their structures. He writes about prison: about how the small pleasures and pains are what occupy him; about how he isn't bored, as he thought he would be, but always chasing after something; about how the world recedes in concreteness, but grows in value; about the difficulties of meetings and the importance of tea. But above all he writes about his two great subjects: himself, and the meaning of life.

He writes about himself openly and lucidly: about his body, especially his haemorrhoids, but more especially about his psyche. He is obsessive, anxious, submissive, overpolite, but underneath unswayable. He is still the fat boy of his childhood, always a little outside the world, needing both to please and yet to prove himself again and again. He is, in fact, Vaněk, the chaste hero of his three most famous one-act plays. He is not a natural resister; but true to his dialectic, the first thing he resists is his own nature. That makes him, I feel, a true hero.

He writes most and best about the meaning of life, about responsibility and identity, about philosophy. His thinking is deeply European: phenomenological and dialectical. In everything—in argument, in his plays, in these letters as a whole—he works in cycles: thesis, antithesis, synthesis, then back to the synthesis and start again. He distrusts answers and prefers questions; open-endedness is his ideal.

He insists on an experienced absolute standard behind everything we encounter and do in the world; but he is wonderful on the ways in which those who harden this experience into a closed ideology become even more dangerous than those who deny it altogether. He is a scourge to pessimists, writing—very beautifully—that hope and faith are inner, of the spirit, and do not come from objects or events: the meaningfulness of life comes from our hope and faith in it, and nothingness and despair from our giving up, not the other way around ("it was not the evil of the world that ultimately led the person to give up, but rather his own resignation that led him to the theory about the evil of the world"). And the letters are full, through and despite everything, of his own faith and hope.

Carole Angier, "A True Hero," in New Statesman & Society, *Vol. 2, No. 39, March 3, 1989, p. 43.*

William Scammell

These prison letters [*Letters to Olga*] of the distinguished Czech playwright and so-called dissident take on an added poignancy—as though they were not poignant enough already—from the fact that their author has just been rearrested for 'incitement' in the recent gatherings to mark the twentieth anniversary of the self-immolation of Jan Palach. Havel's only crime, of course, has been to act as witness to his country's sorry history, and to insist that the truth be told. Fifty years ago, the Russian poet Marina Tsvetayeva wrote a group of poems 'To Czechia', her adoptive country for a period, in which she says 'The Czechs don't have a sea. / Their sea's a sea of tears.' The lines ring as true today, alas, as on the day they were written. . . .

These piercing letters, censored of course, and written once a week under various difficulties to his wife Olga, are testimony to a capacious mind and a lively, indomitable spirit which refuses to be deflected from its quest for self-knowledge and social equity. Bonhoeffer's 'perspective from below' is his chosen epigraph: 'We have to learn that personal suffering is a more effective key, a more rewarding principle for exploring the world in thought and action, than personal good fortune.' There's nothing grandiose, inflated or martyrish, however, about Havel's stream of thoughts and reflections. Prison conditions are onerous, with deliberately high work quotas, but less harsh, one guesses, than in the Russian Gulag—though 'less' is a strictly relative word in this context. Any Western reader sat in his easy chair is bound to feel uncomfortable about hazarding such guesses, and in endorsing the spiritual value of suffering, which he can only experience by proxy. Nonetheless such human greatness shines out of the pages of this and other memoirs, by such diverse witnesses as Marchenko, Ginzburg, Kuznetsov, and Mrs Mandelstam, that one can only assent to the evidence, while remaining eternally scornful of the cliché.

Havel sets himself a series of tasks in order to survive, some menial, some huge: to create 'a new concept of time . . . a new concept of life' which will result in 'self-consolidation . . . inner freedom . . . I don't want

to change myself, but to be myself in a better way . . . the only way for someone like me to survive here is to breathe his own meaning into the experience.' That last prescription, which is almost a definition of what art is, or at any rate of its authenticity, is one he nobly lives up to in the midst of prison squalor and tedium.

'The spirit needs the WORLD,' he cries at one point. 'Without it, it's running on empty.' For him a large part of that world consists of Olga, to whom he issues a stream of instructions and requests, sometimes contradictory. First he begs her to write more often and 'be herself', not worrying about grammar, logic, deep thoughts, etc; then he chides her for her mental sloppiness. She is to take care of herself and look pretty, learn how to cope with all the practical and bureaucratic difficulties of Czech life (lighting the boiler, battling with the planning authorities), represent his interests, supply him with practical and cognitive necessities, be cheerful and courageous, not spike her hair . . . Behind the nagging, as Paul Wilson points out in his excellent Introduction, one feels the awful constraints and anxieties of Havel's situation, and also senses the love he bears her, together with the dependence of a strong man on an equally strong woman with her own complementary role in their personal and public drama. . . .

Olga's few permitted visits are immensely looked forward to, then agonised over in analytical post-mortems. Paradoxically, that which is most desired becomes that which is most feared. His identification with other 'outsiders' and spiritual mentors such as Kafka and Camus is of practical as well as metaphysical use, for they too are concerned with 'ridding phenomena of false meaning' in order to 'inquire after the nature of Being' (the function, Havel says, of all his plays). Writing is a 'biological necessity', creation and freedom are indivisible—and yet their loss is both more and less painful than he had expected. Within a sentence or two of such meditations, he switches to the 'prospect of a life sentence with that middle-class furniture' in their Prague flat.

This is a brave and penetrating book, which should be placed not only alongside other classics of prison literature but also next to Kundera and Brodsky, at the centre of that crucial debate on the rival tyrannies of social and aesthetic commitment. Havel's hard-won traditional wisdom, that with luck we may be 'victorious . . . by virtue of [our] defeats', might prove to be as true of art as of life itself.

William Scammell, "Bearing Witness," in The Listener, *Vol. 121, No. 3104, March 9, 1989, p. 33.*

Václav Havel

[*Havel made the statement below in February 1989 in court in his own defense while on trial for allegedly inciting people to hold an illegal memorial service for Jan Palach, who set himself on fire in January 1969 to protest the Soviet invasion of Czechoslovakia.*]

I have said all I can to the individual arguments of the prosecution during the course of the trial and the interrogation. I shall not repeat myself, therefore, but I will summarize my point of view: I believe that the charges against me of incitement and obstruction of the exercise of duty of a public official have not been proven. I consider myself to be innocent and ask to be released.

In conclusion, however, I would like to speak out on one aspect of the whole case, which has not as yet been mentioned. During the prosecution, it was claimed that I attempted to conceal the real antistate and the antisocialist nature of an organized gathering of people. This claim, which, by the way, is not and cannot be substantiated, suggests that I acted with a political goal in mind. That surely entitles me to deal for a moment with the political side of the whole case.

Firstly, I must say that the words "antistate" and "antisocialist" lost any semantic meaning long ago, since during their long years of quite wanton use, they became a pejorative label for all citizens who, for various reasons, made the government feel uncomfortable. By that, I am not referring to their political thinking. In fact, three general secretaries of the Communist party of Czechoslovakia—Slánský, Husák, and Dubček—have at various stages in their lives been labeled with these words. Today it is Charter 77 and other independent groups that are marked by these epithets, naturally only because the government does not like the influence they wield and because it feels the need to somehow get rid of them. As has been seen, not even my indictment has avoided this purely linguistic means of political defamation.

What then is the real political significance of what we do? Charter 77 came into being and functions as an informal society that tries to monitor Czechoslovakia's safeguarding of human rights and the government's adherence to international treaties and the Czechoslovak constitution. For twelve years now, Charter 77 has been drawing the government's attention to the serious discrepancies between their obligations and social practice; for twelve years we have been pointing out various unsalutary occurrences and crises, violations of constitutional rights, arbitrariness, disorder, and incompetence. The work that Charter 77 carries out corresponds to the opinions of a considerable section of our society; I am convinced of this daily. For twelve years now, we have been offering the government dialogue on these matters. For twelve years, the government has not reacted to our initiative; it has merely imprisoned and persecuted us for it. In fact, the government itself today admits to numerous problems that Charter 77 has been indicating for a number of years and that could have been solved long ago if it had paid heed to what was said. Charter 77 has always stressed its policy of nonviolence and the lawfulness of its work. Its policy has never been to organize disturbances on the streets, and this still applies.

More than once I have publicly drawn attention to the fact that the measure of respect shown to nonconformist and critical citizens is an indicator of the measure of respect toward public opinion in general. Many times I have said that the continuing lack of respect for peaceful expressions of public opinion may in the end arouse increasingly more perceptible and emphatic protests by society. Many times

I have said that it will be of help to no one if the government continues to wait until the people begin to demonstrate and go on strike; that can easily be prevented by a businesslike dialogue and the good will to listen to even those voices that are critical.

These warnings were ignored. As a result, the current rulers are now reaping the rewards of their own arrogant attitude.

I must confess to one thing. On Monday January 16 I wanted to leave Wenceslas Square immediately after the flowers had been placed by the statue of St. Wenceslas in remembrance of Jan Palach. In the end, I stayed at the Square for over an hour mostly because I simply could not believe my eyes. Something that I could not have imagined in my wildest dreams had happened. The totally unwarranted action by the police against those who wished, quietly and without any publicity, to lay flowers at the statue, immediately transformed quite coincidental passers-by into a protesting crowd. I suddenly realized the depth of civic discontent if such a thing could come to pass.

The council for the prosecution has quoted my statement, addressed to the authorities, saying that the situation is serious. I even told our representatives that the situation is more serious than they think. On January 16 I suddenly realized that the situation was more serious than I myself had thought.

As a citizen interested in seeing this country prosper in peace, I firmly believe the authorities will finally draw a lesson from what has happened and initiate a dignified dialogue with all sections of society, without excluding anybody from participating in this dialogue by labeling him/her "antisocialist." I firmly believe the authorities will finally cease treating the *independent groups* as though they were an ugly girl smashing the mirror because she thinks it is to blame for her appearance. This is why I also firmly believe I will not be unjustifiably sentenced again.

I do not consider myself guilty. There is therefore nothing to be sorry for. If I am punished, I will accept my punishment in a spirit of sacrifice for the benefit of a good cause. Such a sacrifice however is negligible in light of the absolute sacrifice of Jan Palach, whose anniversary we wished to commemorate.

> *Václav Havel, "A Statement to the Court," in* The New York Review of Books, *Vol. XXXVI, No. 7, April 27, 1989, p. 41.*

Herman Schwartz

[*Schwartz is a contributing editor to* The Nation *and a professor of law at American University. He was asked to attend Havel's trial by Helsinki Watch but was not admitted into the courtroom.*]

The gusts of *glasnost* and *perestroika* blowing out of Mikhail Gorbachev's Moscow have reached Czechoslovakia and made its rulers shiver. Like true Brezhnevites, they have reacted with a dose of repression, but this time with a difference. The crackdown has been accompanied by a series of liberalizing moves, revealing conflict and confusion within the regime over how to deal with this new reality.

The most notorious action was the conviction of the noted playwright and human rights activist Vaclav Havel in February, just after Czechoslovakia had initialed the Vienna Concluding Agreement, refining and expanding the 1975 Helsinki Accords on basic human rights. Havel was prosecuted for some January radio broadcasts in which he allegedly incited people to hold an illegal memorial for Jan Palach, who burned himself to death twenty years ago in protest over the Soviet invasion of his country, and for interference with the police at a memorial rally a week later.

The case against Havel was so contrived and flimsy that even the judge remarked on its weakness. As Havel said in his appeal a month later, "The verdict would have been far more honest had it merely stated, 'Vaclav Havel, you are getting on our nerves, and so you will go to prison for nine months.' "

The outrage at Havel's conviction spilled far beyond the usual circles. Approximately 3,000 members of Czechoslovakia's official artistic and scientific community signed a petition in support of Havel, the first time those establishment types have made such a protest. Charter 77 has learned of government instructions to harass those who signed. Poland allowed two of Havel's plays to be staged the week of his trial, the first performances of his work there since 1981, when martial law was imposed; Premier Mieczyslaw Rakowski attended.

On appeal, Havel's sentence was reduced from nine months to eight and he was given a milder prison regimen, making him eligible for release on May 15, two weeks before a session of the Helsinki Accord signatories in Paris. Czechoslovakia will thus be able to avoid the embarrassment of having a Nobel Peace Prize nominee in prison for an innocuous broadcast when it discusses human rights.

In the international focus on Havel, however, many others whom the regime has persecuted, in some cases more harshly, have been overlooked:

> Jana Petrova, 22, of the Independent Peace Association, and Ota Veverka, 32, of the John Lennon Peace Club, were tried with five others on charges growing out of the Palach memorial in January. The seven had gone to place flowers at the spot where Palach killed himself, and for this they were charged with "hooliganism." Even though the prosecutor admitted his witnesses were weak, all seven defendants were convicted on February 22. Petrova got nine months in prison and Veverka twelve; the others received suspended sentences and fines.

> Ivan Jirous, 45, a revered poet, philosopher and publisher of *samizdat,* was sentenced on March 9 to sixteen months' imprisonment for "attacking a state organ" and "harming the interest of the Republic abroad" by circulating a petition that blamed the authorities for the April 1988 death in prison of activist Pavel Wonka and called for reform of the Czechoslovak penal code and release of political prisoners. His co-defendant, Jiri Tichy, received six months.

> Hana Marvanovna and Tomas Dvorak, members of the Independent Peace Association, were convicted of "preparation for incitement" on March 17 in connection with rallies last year. They have been in jail since last October, despite being given suspended sentences, because the prosecutor appealed and asked for their continued detention pending the outcome of the appeal.

There have been also innumerable detentions ranging from a few hours to almost five days; beatings; house searches; confiscation of writings, typewriters and books; and hugely increased penalties for ignoring police orders to move—up to 20,000 crowns, the equivalent of almost seven months' average wages. (pp. 660-61)

When I was in Czechoslovakia a year ago, there were few signs of protest beyond some demands for religious freedom and the activities of some courageous individuals, including the 1,200 to 1,300 signatories of Charter 77. Something happened during the next few months, however, and particularly to young people. It has often been noted that 1988 was the year of the "double eights." Many of the great events in Czechoslovak history occurred in years ending with "8": the creation of the modern democratic state in 1918; Munich in 1938; the Communist takeover in 1948; and the bloom and demise of the Prague Spring in 1968. The authorities were nervous, I was told last year, and as the second half of 1988 got under way, it turned out that they had good reason to be.

The twentieth anniversary of the Soviet invasion on August 21 provided the flashpoint. To everyone's amazement, thousands demonstrated in Prague. Many were young people, whom Alexander Dubcek, Communist Party General Secretary at the time of the invasion, called "the children of 1968": One 21-year-old demonstrator had been in a protest against the invasion when she was only three weeks old. The police responded to the August 21 events with brutality and numerous house searches and arrests.

That did not stop the aroused Czechoslovaks, however. Two relatively new groups, the Independent Peace Association and the Czech Children, announced a meeting shortly thereafter, on September 23 at the foot of the statue of Saint Wenceslas, to discuss the current problems. When several hundred people showed up, the police arrested many and forcibly removed them to the police station for interrogation.

On October 13 the Movement for Civil Liberties was formed. Its manifesto, signed by 120 of Czechoslovakia's most prominent human rights activists, called for political action to reshape the legal system, protect the rights to speech and belief, foster political and economic pluralism and save the environment. It also demanded the removal of Soviet troops. The police reacted by arresting many of the signatories in the early hours of October 27 and holding them for up to ninety-six hours while searching their homes and confiscating books, typewriters and other personal property. The following day some 5,000 people gathered at Wenceslas Square to celebrate the seventieth anniversary of the founding of the Czechoslovak Republic. Police attacked them with water cannons, tear gas, truncheons and dogs and arrested nearly a hundred people.

A number of groups, including Charter 77, then planned an international symposium for November 11 to discuss how events in Czechoslovakia during the past seventy years have affected European history. Many distinguished foreign visitors came to Prague for the conference. But beginning November 10 some thirty-eight activists were put under house arrest to prevent the seminar from taking place. It was nevertheless hastily opened by Vaclav Havel—who was grabbed by the police within seconds.

A series of incidents [in January 1989] was the most extended and spontaneous, and drew the harshest responses. On January 15, twenty-six people ventured to Wenceslas Square to lay flowers at the site of Jan Palach's self-immolation. They were intercepted by the police on their way to the subway and forced to turn back. The next day eight of them returned to place the flowers and were promptly arrested; a policeman later admitted in court that his orders were to arrest anyone who laid flowers, even peacefully. Havel was also arrested, though only a bystander.

That set off a week of daily spontaneous demonstrations during which police again used water cannons, truncheons and dogs, and made numerous arrests. (pp. 661-62)

Repression has not been the regime's only response, however. Obviously perplexed, Czechoslovakia's rulers have tried a few liberalizing measures. They have allowed some public meetings to be held, including one on Human Rights Day, December 10. They have stopped jamming Radio Free Europe. The Independent Peace Association is being permitted to meet publicly. The Czechoslovak press was allowed to publish the full text of the Polish agreements legalizing Solidarity. Some of the priests who were denied permits to practice because of their association with Charter 77 have had the permits temporarily restored. A few dissidents have actually been acquitted by the courts, and the sentencing seems more lenient.

The Havel case is perhaps the best example of the regime's floundering. There was plainly no basis for charging him, for Havel had done nothing remotely illegal, even by the elastic standards of the Czechoslovak penal law. The purpose of the prosecution, according to several observers, was to make it clear that no matter what happens in the Soviet Union, Poland or Hungary, the old bosses are still in charge in Czechoslovakia. Instead, the case set off an avalanche of criticism both at home and abroad, which probably forced the government to reduce Havel's sentence. (pp. 662-63)

"An electric tension has struck the society," said Vaclav Havel in an interview last October. "It is becoming more restless, it is becoming more interested in everything; people are more daring, they are overcoming their fear, as if they were awakening from that long apathy, which lasted so many years." One of the defendants in the flower trial said to me, "The police brutality hasn't intimidated anyone. During that week [in January] our self-confidence rose steadily."

Czechoslovakia's Communist Party leaders know this and are frightened. They hold office only because of the Soviet rape of their country in 1968 and fear—rightly—that any significant loosening will dump them all into history's garbage can, for their unpopularity is monumental. Whether they will be able to hold off an upsurge of resentment and a yearning for democracy and freedom no one can comfortably predict. (p. 663)

> *Herman Schwartz, "Fueling Demands for Czech Reform," in* The Nation, *New York, Vol. 248, No. 19, May 15, 1989, pp. 660-63.*

Michael Heim

[Heim teaches Czech and Russian literature at the University of California, Los Angeles, and has translated works by such authors as Milan Kundera, Pavel Kohout, and Bohumil Hrabal.]

After 20 years of enforced obscurity Václav Havel, Czech playwright extraordinary, has exploded onto the television screens of his country and ours. No one looks more uncomfortable in the political arena than Havel; he would clearly be happier back in the theater, rehearsing one of the dozen or so plays he has written since the 1968 Soviet invasion. There are those who feel that the production of Havel's plays—none, new or old, has been allowed on the Czech stage for 20 years—would mean more than all the recent shuffling in the political stratosphere.

A few weeks before the shuffling began, Havel received another in his growing collection of literary awards. The award, given yearly by the Assn. of German Writers to the author who has contributed most to world peace, is traditionally presented at the Frankfurt Book Fair, the annual clearing house for world publishing (it exhibited 378,699 titles this October). For the first time in the history of the award, the recipient could not attend the ceremony: Havel has declined all invitations to leave Czechoslovakia because while the regime has been known to let dissidents out, it has never been known to let them back in. . . .

The 53-year-old Havel has spent a number of the post-invasion years in prison for his efforts to set words right, and the German writers were honoring him for his "exemplary and persuasive attempt to live in truth." On this occasion he chose to discuss a word that has come to be used lightly in our century, especially in Eastern Europe. "Words have their history," he said.

> There was a time, for instance, when entire generations of the humiliated and oppressed considered the word *socialism* a magnetic synonym for a more righteous world, and when the ideals expressed by the word led people to sacrifice many years of their lives and even life itself for it. I don't know how things stand in your country, but in mine the very word *socialism* has long since turned into a rubber truncheon that *nouveau riche* bureaucrats who believe in nothing use to beat their free-thinking fellow-citizens while calling them 'enemies of socialism' and 'anti-socialist forces'.

Another of Havel's words with a history is the word *histo-*

ry itself. The communist regimes claim to represent a science of history governed by the laws of dialectical materialism. For them history is moving inexorably forward to the utopia that is communism. In his 1975 **"Open Letter to President Husák"** (Husák took over after the Soviet invasion and still holds certain honorary positions), Havel accused the regime of calling history to a halt. "True, the country is calm," he wrote, "calm as a morgue." The regime fostered entropy, order without life, and dressed it up as history. Since the regime had absolute power, it could do what it pleased to language as easily and surely as it could do what it pleased to people.

Not surprisingly, Havel is obsessed with history much as he is obsessed with words, and he combines his two magnificent obsessions in several plays by returning to works with a past. Like Brecht, he has reworked John Gay's *Beggar's Opera,'* and his *Temptation* . . . represents a stunningly topical yet non-reductionist extension of the Faust legend: The devil can't hold a candle to the bureaucrats. In works like these the present resonates with history, and history is something Havel takes seriously. If he rejects the Communist march of history toward a radiant future, he is nonetheless wary of the tendency to dismiss history as absurd and therefore worthless. He would certainly agree with Santayana's oft-quoted adage: "Those who cannot remember the past are condemned to repeat it."

On the other hand, Havel has been through too much to assume that merely remembering history will repeal the sentence. So back we come to words and, more specifically, to the debasement of language that Havel bemoans as much as he does the distortion of history. Take *The Memorandum,* one of the few Havel plays currently available in paperback here. The action begins with a series of nonsense syllables. They turn out to be a new language. One bureaucratic agency has required another bureaucratic agency to introduce a language with no ambiguity; that is, a language with a single word for a single concept. "And now I shall name some of the most common interjections," says the teacher engaged to teach the language. "Our *ah* becomes *zukybaj;* our *ouch, bykur;* our *oh* becomes *hajf dy doretop, pish* is *bolypak juz,* and the interjection of surprise *well!—zyk!* However, *well, well!* is not *zyk-zyk!,* as some have concluded, but *zyk-zym.*" By choosing interjections, Havel reduces an already ridiculous idea to total absurdity (what document will need the word *pish?*) and makes a point about language that holds by analogy for history: It cannot be transformed into a set of positivist, absolute, right-or-wrong principles.

Because *The Memorandum* opened in 1965, it could open in Prague, and clearly Havel would have preferred to go on communicating with his audience from the stage. (The above excerpt gives only a faint idea of how hilariously stageworthy that play truly is.) When the "events" and "normalization" closed his country's theaters to him, he continued writing plays—he was constitutionally unable to do otherwise. But the plays could only be staged abroad; they could not reach their primary public. To reach that public, Havel resorted to another genre.

Plays are best read in conjunction with performance, but essays are self-contained and thought-provoking and can

circulate with relative ease in clandestine carbons. Havel became an essayist in spite of himself as he became an activist in spite of himself. Both aspects of this new life came to a head with the formation of Charter 77, the Czechoslovak opposition's response to the Helsinki Agreements and by now the longest-lived human rights organization in the East bloc.

As Charter 77's first spokesman, Havel often found himself exhorting his fellow-countrymen to do more or less what he was recently praised for in Frankfurt, that is, to "live in truth," stand behind what they think and do, vouch for themselves, take responsibility for their own acts. His fellow-countrymen soon watched him go to jail for his principles. He did not convert large numbers of them. As he points out to his wife in the edifying and moving prison diary **Letters to Olga,** he realized that his stand made him seem a martyr to some and a goody-goody to others; it may even have diminished his influence. Again he was constitutionally unable to do otherwise.

Perhaps that is why he has emerged from it all with his faith in humanity intact. "I am not interested in why man commits evil," he writes in the **Letters;** "I want to know why he does good (here and there) or at least feels he ought to." Once the political situation in Czechoslovakia is on an even keel, Havel will doubtless abandon the political platform for the stage; he will go back to writing plays that explore why man does good. Let us do what we can to keep them on our stages, and let us hope audiences in his own country will soon be able to see his repertory in its entirety. The amazing events of the past few weeks can have left only the most cynical unconvinced of the possibility of change. To them I say, with Havel: "Half dy doretop, bolypak juz!"

Michael Heim, "Turning the Words Loose in Prague," in Los Angeles Times Book Review, *December 10, 1989, p. 15.*

William A. Henry III

A few months after the 1968 Soviet invasion ended the Prague Spring of intellectual freedom in his homeland, Czech playwright Václav Havel joined many of his countrymen lining up at the U.S. embassy in quest of a visa. Like most of those in the queue, he had something to flee from: the hard-line new government wanted him out and had banned his works from production or publication. Unlike most of the others, Havel had someplace to go: three of his plays had won acclaim in the West, and he had been offered both a job at New York City's prestigious Public Theater and a foundation grant to underwrite him in the U.S. for a year. But when a friend in the queue asked Havel if he really intended to leave, he said, "No, I don't think so. I think things will get very interesting here."

Interesting the past two decades have been. Also turbulent, irritating, at times humiliating and occasionally frightening. As one of a handful of prominent Prague intellectuals who chose neither to flee nor to fall silent but to fight back, Havel was jailed three times for a total of almost five years on the flimsiest of charges. One four-month stretch was served in a cell 12 ft. by 7 ft., which he shared with a burglar. A second imprisonment ended when he nearly died of pneumonia that was neglected, perhaps deliberately, by prison doctors. His last internment, four months of a scheduled eight, was in 1989 for participating in a flower-laying ceremony in memory of a student who set himself afire to protest the 1968 invasion.

When nominally free, Havel endured nonstop surveillance; friends who came to visit were sometimes turned away and harassed for the attempt. His homes and car were repeatedly and imaginatively vandalized, doubtless by ever present security forces; repair workers whom he hired were threatened with police reprisals. The country cottage where he celebrated his 40th birthday was officially ordered vacated, one day later, as unfit for human habitation. Havel was never physically tortured, although on at least one occasion a policeman threatened, "Today you're going to get so beat up that you'll have your trousers full."

Through it all, Havel kept writing, kept publishing, kept denouncing the communist system as a concatenation of lies, no less corrupting for being universally recognized as lies. He spurned every chance to redeem his fortunes by recantation or silence. When the system made him suffer, his suffering became the subject of his art. Forced for a time to work stacking empty beer barrels, he turned even that into two brief satires. Although the obvious villains in his writings were communist leaders, whom he sometimes denounced by name, his ultimate targets were fellow citizens, whose crime lay in getting along by going along. His moral courage was accompanied, as is often the case with self-selected martyrs, by flashes of stiff-necked arrogance. He seemed to mirror himself in the descriptive name of his most autobiographical character, Nettle, pricking the complacency of what he saw as a materialistic nation.

Zealous idealists rarely get a chance to lead, and when they do, they rarely show much aptitude for the give-and-take of politics, the careful timing, the restraint. Yet in an irony more exquisite than any he ever envisioned for the stage, Vaclav Havel became not only the conscience but also the commonsense leader of the mass movement that led to Czechoslovakia's orderly ouster of its communist leaders. Having inspired fellow citizens by his rhetoric and unrelenting example, he heard them demand that he take over as head of state. That was not for him, he said. He was a writer. In fact, his work so depended on being an outsider that he joked about asking the new government to put him back in jail two days a week. But the more he denied interest in the presidency, the more insistently his fellow citizens marched and sloganeered on his behalf.

Last Thursday the Parliament amended the presidential oath of office to eliminate the customary pledge of loyalty to socialism, a vow that the nonsocialist Havel likely would have refused to take. In the same session, Parliament honored Havel's determination to have "close by my side" another revered ghost from 1968. Alexander Dubcek, the former leader who launched the Prague Spring, was restored to a post of power, after two decades of internal exile, by being elected the legislature's new presiding officer. The stately transition was completed on Friday,

when Prime Minister Marian Calfa, whose Communist Party colleagues so long denounced Havel as a slanderer of the state, praised him as "a man who is faithful to his beliefs despite persecution." After Havel was unanimously elected, he emerged to tell supporters, "I will not disappoint you, but will lead this country to free elections. This must happen in a decent and peaceful way so the clean face of our revolution is not sullied. It is a task for us all." (p. 62)

As an artist, Havel has always been a political prophet, prone to jeremiads. In *Largo Desolato,* the hero faces unspecified tortures, which he can avert if he changes his name and declares himself not to be the author of his works. Although he ultimately says no, he wavers for a moment, and that is enough to satisfy the state. In *Temptation,* Havel retells the Faust myth in terms of the ego-driven distortions of truth committed by his compatriots. In the essay **"The Power of the Powerless,"** he lambastes an archetypal grocer who places a poster saying WORKERS OF THE WORLD UNITE in his shopwindow to prove himself orthodox and ensure his comfort. Dissecting the web of hypocrisies and self-deceptions that formed the social fabric of communist life, Havel argues for "living within the truth." He writes, "You do not become a 'dissident' just because you decide one day to take up this most unusual career. You are thrown into it by your personal sense of responsibility, combined with a complex set of external circumstances. You are cast out of the existing structures and placed in a position of conflict with them. It begins as an attempt to do your work well, and ends with being branded an enemy of society."

If Havel, 53, actually were an enemy of the society in which he grew up, it would be understandable. Long before he was singled out for his outspoken politics and insurrectionist art, he was subjected to discrimination because he was born to wealth. His father was a real estate developer. An even richer uncle owned hotels and the Barrandov movie studios, which remain the center of Czechoslovak filmmaking. One of his English-language translators, Czech émigré Vera Blackwell, has said, "If Czechoslovakia had remained primarily a capitalist society, Vaclav Havel would be just about the richest man in the country." Instead, by the time Havel was a teenager, the communists had dispossessed the family. More painful still, Stalinist rules barred youths of upper-class descent from full-time education beyond early adolescence. Undaunted, Havel took a menial job in a chemical laboratory and went to night school in an attempt to qualify for university study, but his application was rejected time and again. Intrigued by the theater, he signed on as a stagehand.

Finally, talent won out over bureaucracy. Within a few years he worked his way up to literary manager of the Theater on the Balustrade, Prague's principal showcase for the avant-garde. That made him a prominent part of the Prague Spring, which was not just a fleeting season but several years of increasing freedom, ferment and hope. Havel's first script, *The Garden Party,* a surreal satire of communist pedanticism, was produced at home in 1963 and in at least seven other nations—in 18 separate theaters in West Germany. British critic Kenneth Tynan lauded the play as "absurdism with deep roots in contemporary anxieties." The perspective in that and subsequent plays often reminded critics of Samuel Beckett, the Irish-born playwright of diminution and despair whose death was announced last week. Havel considered himself a disciple of Beckett's, although his work rarely shared the older writer's paralyzing hopelessness, and Beckett returned the compliment: his 1984 one-act *Catastrophe,* portraying the inquisition of a dissident, was an explicit tribute.

Havel's English-language reputation was secured with his second play, **The Memorandum,** in which a society's leaders imposed an artificial language, incomprehensible to everyone but nonetheless required for all transactions. It debuted in Prague in 1965 and reached the U.S. in May 1968 in an award-winning production by Joseph Papp's prestigious Public Theater in New York City. Havel attended the premiere. Three months later, Soviet tanks rolled through the streets of Prague. The political and artistic blossoming withered and died. The bureaucrats Havel had mocked were firmly back in charge.

He was soon out of a job at Balustrade. Although he continued to write for publication or production in the West, his public role in Prague shifted to politics. He became a principal organizer of Charter 77, a human rights organization designed to compel Czechoslovakia to honor the commitments in existing treaties and its own constitution. As Havel argued, "If an outside observer who knew nothing at all about life in Czechoslovakia were to study only its laws, he or she would be utterly incapable of understanding what we were complaining about." Havel was first jailed in 1977. By August 1978, he was "free" under house arrest behind a barricade that said, ENTRANCE FORBIDDEN. When Havel asked police what offense he was charged with, he reported in **"Technical Notes on My House-Arrest,"** he "was only told that they had no instructions to pass such information on to me."

Even at low ebb, Havel was protected in some measure by his prominence abroad. Authorities made no effort to uproot him from the handsome granite apartment block built by his father and also tenanted by his brother, where Havel has room after room lined with books and videotapes, the elegance tempered by big beer-hall ashtrays, overflowing with butts, on seemingly every table. The car that the police most often vandalized was a white Mercedes. Although his manner is earthy and direct and his short, dumpy frame and mustache bring to mind a small, playful walrus, Havel still has a touch of the patrician. He is accustomed to center stage and rarely brooks disagreement, even from friends. His marriage has endured a quarter-century and produced one of the century's most touching prison volumes, **Letters to Olga,** but friends say Havel can be as overbearing to her as to anyone else—which is very overbearing indeed. If Havel is the embodiment of moral rectitude to his nation, that is even more strongly the way he sees himself. His true passion is not for possessions or power but for giving life a purpose. That is why the people of Czechoslovakia were able to do last week what the government never could: persuade him to move out of the flat built by his father, with its sweeping views

of the Vltava River and the Hradcany castle complex, across the river into the castle itself. It is Prague's presidential palace. And it is now, in an era of electric change, the dissident's home. (p. 64)

William A. Henry III, "Dissident to President," in Time, *New York, Vol. 135, No. 2, January 8, 1990, pp. 62, 64.*

Stephen Cohen

On December 9 [1989] a van carrying a gift of 50,000 roses from Portugal to the Czech people was greeted by a huge crowd on Norodni Avenue. Standing on the van's roof, a Portuguese student expressed his country's support for Czech freedom. As a heavy snow began to fall, the roses were handed out to the people. It seemed a fitting metaphor for the Czechs' peaceful revolution, the cold snow symbolizing 40 years of Communist dictatorship, and the roses, Czech hopes for freedom and democracy. It also seemed appropriate that the gift came from Portugal, another small, vulnerable European nation that had suffered decades of oppressive rule.

The next day a new Czechoslovak Cabinet took office, the first since 1948 without a Communist majority. The opposition Civic Forum, which negotiated for the new Cabinet, was itself barely three weeks old, founded on November 19 by Czech dissidents and human rights activists who had been in and out of prison for 20 years. (p. 13)

One reason for Civic Forum's success is the moral authority of its principal leader, Vaclav Havel, a playwright who spent five years in prison, whose plays could not be performed, and whose banned writings circulated widely in samizdat form. When asked what he had learned from his rise from persecuted dissident to popular leader, Havel replied, "When a person behaves in keeping with his conscience, when he tries to speak the truth, and when he tries to behave as a citizen, even under conditions where citizenship is degraded, it may not lead to anything, yet it might. But what surely will not lead to anything is when a person calculates whether it will lead to anything or not."

Civic Forum leaders, however, were not just ivory tower moralists. Using modern political technology and old-fashioned grass-roots politics, they bypassed the Communist-controlled newspapers, radio, and television. At different locations in Prague, TV sets were mounted high inside store windows, with speakers attached by bailing wire to outside walls. A videotape of the November 17 marchers, holding candles, singing "We Shall Overcome" in Czech, and being beaten by police, was played and replayed. From early morning until late at night, crowds of shoppers and commuters stood watching, mesmerized. Students distributed copies of the tape all over Czechoslovakia. An entire museum was turned over to an exhibition of photographs of the November 17 march. Hundreds of thousands of Czechs passed through the gallery to see pictures of police beating peaceful marchers.

Writers and artists produced leaflets and posters bearing messages from Civic Forum. Copies were taped to nearly every wall and store window in downtown Prague. At night teams of high school students, organized by Civic Forum and wearing its improvised credentials, removed older leaflets and posters to make room for new ones the next morning.

Civic Forum also showed considerable political sophistication by emphasizing that it did not condemn all Communists and would not threaten Soviet interests. In a December 2 interview in the Communist paper, *Rude Pravo*, Havel stated, "There is no doubt that among the Communists there are endless numbers of clever, talented, productive people who for decades had to keep silent the way all non-Communists had to keep silent." (pp. 13-14)

Civic Forum's office could have been mistaken for the headquarters of the American anti-Vietnam War movement in the late 1960s. Dozens of university students worked day and night, on little sleep and infrequent meals. Meanwhile their elders, the dissidents and human rights activists who organized Civic Forum, met interminably to ensure that decisions were made only by consensus. Periodically the leadership would emerge to negotiate with the government or to hold press conferences for the international reporters assembled in Prague.

At Civic Forum press conferences, held in Prague's Magic Lantern Theater, nearly all questions were posed in English and answered in Czech, with instant translation by Rita Klimova, a Czech human rights activist who grew up in the United States during World War II and speaks idiomatic English with a perfect New York accent. Usually a half-dozen members of Civic Forum's collective leadership sat on the theater's stage, taking turns providing answers. On December 7, however, following the regular press conference, Havel was interviewed alone. Dressed in blue jeans and sweater, slouching in his chair, and chain-smoking, Havel explained, "I have called this conference because of the many requests from the press for interviews which I have been unable to grant. If I did so, I would be spending all my time commenting on the revolution and have no time for participating in the revolution."

One journalist kept wanting to know whether Havel was a candidate for Czechoslovakia's presidency. "Many Civic Forum supporters are wearing Havel for President buttons today," he asked. "Are you running for president?" Havel replied, "My profession is that of playwright. The more democracy and normal conditions come to the country, the less will be my role in political life."

"Do you support those who produced the Havel for President buttons?"

"I understand the buttons come from Hungary. My influence does not yet extend that far."

Frustrated, the reporter shouted at Havel, "You are ducking my question. I asked whether you support those who produced the buttons. Answer my question."

"I've answered your question in a roundabout way, which it seems to me is very presidential. I've watched President Bush's press conferences on television, and he answers questions in the same fashion."

Three days later, on December 10, Havel formally declared his candidacy. On December 19, the new prime minister, Marian Calfa, told Parliament it had "no alternative" but to elect Havel president of Czechoslovakia. (p. 14)

Stephen Cohen, "Roses in the Snow," in The New Republic, *Vol. 202, Nos. 2 & 3, January 8 & 15, 1990, pp. 13-14.*

From a New Year's Day Speech:

[Tomas Masaryk, who established the first Czechoslovak Republic in 1918], founded his politics on morality. Let us try, in a new time and in a new way, to revive this concept of politics. Let us teach both ourselves and others that politics ought to be a reflection of the aspiration to contribute to the happiness of the community and not of the need to deceive or pillage the community. Let us teach both ourselves and others that politics does not have to be the art of the possible, especially if this means the art of speculating, calculating, intrigues, secret agreements, and pragmatic maneuvering, but that it also can be the art of the impossible, that is the art of making both ourselves and the world better.

We are a small country, but nonetheless we were once the spiritual crossroads of Europe. Is there any reason why we should not be so again? Would this not be another contribution through which we could pay others back for the help we will need from them?

The home Mafia—those who do not look out of their airplane windows and eat specially fed pigs—are still alive, true, and make trouble from time to time, but they are no longer our main enemy, and international Mafias are even less of an enemy. Our worst enemy today is our own bad qualities—indifference to public affairs, conceit, ambition, selfishness, the pursuit of personal advancement, and rivalry—and that is the main struggle we are faced with.

We are going into free elections, and an election battle. Let us not allow that battle to sully the still clean face of our gentle revolution. . . .

—*Václav Havel*

Timothy Garton Ash

[*Ash is an historian and a political commentator on Central and Eastern Europe who frequently contributes essays to the* New York Review of Books. *Excerpted below are his observations on the revolution in Czechoslovakia in 1989 and Havel's role in the historic events.*]

My modest contribution to the revolution was a quip. Arriving in Prague on Day Seven (November 23), when the pace of change was already breathtaking, I met Václav Havel in the back room of his favored basement pub. I said: "In Poland it took ten years, in Hungary ten months, in East Germany ten weeks: perhaps in Czechoslovakia it will take ten days!" Grasping my hands, and fixing me with his winning smile, he immediately summoned over a videocamera team from the samizdat *Video-journál,* who just happened to be waiting in the corner. I was politely compelled to repeat my quip to camera, over a glass of beer, and then Havel gave his reaction: "It would be fabulous if it could be so. . . . " Revolution, he said, is too exhausting.

The camera team dashed off to copy the tape, so that it could be shown on television sets in public places. Havel subsequently used the conceit in several interviews. And because he used it, it had a fantastic career. It was repeated in the Czechoslovak papers. An opposition spokesman recalled it in a television broadcast just before the general strike—on Day Eleven. It was on the front page of the Polish opposition daily, *Gazeta Wyborcza.* It popped up in the Western press. And when I finally had to leave Prague on Day Nineteen, with the revolution by no means over people were still saying, "You see, with us—ten days!" Such is the magic of round numbers.

I tell this story not just from author's vanity, but also because it illustrates several qualities of the most delightful of all this year's Central European revolutions: the speed, the improvisation, the merriness, and the absolutely central role of Václav Havel, who was at once director, playwright, stage manager, and leading actor in this, his greatest play. I was only one of many—indeed of millions—to feed him some lines.

Next morning I got a complimentary theater ticket. A ticket to the Magic Lantern theater, whose subterannean stage, auditorium, foyers, and dressing rooms had become the headquarters of the main opposition coalition in the Czech lands, the Civic Forum, and thus, in effect, the headquarters of the revolution. The ticket changed. At first it was just a small note with the words "Please let in and out" written in purple ink, signed by Václav Havel's brother, Ivan, and authenticated by the playwright's rubber stamp. This shows a beaming pussycat with the word "Smile!" across his chest. Then it was a green card worn around the neck, with my name typed as "Timothy Gordon Ash," and the smiling cat again. Then it was a xeroxed and initialed paper slip saying "Civic Forum Building," this time with two smiling cats (one red, one black) and a beaming green frog. I have it before me as I write. Beneath the frog it says *"très bien."*

In any case, the tickets worked wonders. For nearly two weeks I, as an historian, was privileged to watch history being made inside the Magic Lantern. For most of that time, I was the only foreigner to sit in on the hectic deliberations of what most people called simply "the Forum." But before I describe what I saw, we must briefly recall—or reconstruct—the beginning of the revolution.

Students started it. Small groups of them had been active for at least a year before. They edited faculty magazines. They organized discussion clubs. They worked on the borderline between official and unofficial life. Many had contacts with the opposition, all read samizdat. Some say they had a conspiratorial group called "The Ribbon"—the Czech "White Rose," as it were. But they also worked through the official youth organization, the SSM. It was through the SSM that they got permission to hold a dem-

onstration in Prague on November 17, to mark the fiftieth anniversary of the martyrdom of Jan Opletal, a Czech student murdered by the Nazis. This began as officially scheduled in Prague's second district, with speeches and tributes at the cemetery.

But the numbers grew, and the chants turned increasingly against the present dictators in the castle. The demonstrators decided—perhaps some had planned all along—to march to Wenceslas Square, the stage for all the historic moments of Czech history, whether in 1918, 1948, or 1968. Down the hill they wound, along the embankment of the River Vltava, and then, turning right at the National Theater, up Národní Street into Wenceslas Square. Here they were met by riot police, with white helmets, shields, and truncheons, and by special antiterrorist squads, in red berets. Large numbers of demonstrators were cut off and surrounded, both along Národní and in the square. They went on chanting "freedom" and singing the Czech version of "We Shall Overcome." Those in the front line tried to hand flowers to the police. They placed lighted candles on the ground and raised their arms, chanting, "We have bare hands." But the police, and especially the red berets, beat men, women, and children with their truncheons.

This was the spark that set Czechoslovakia alight. During the night from Friday to Saturday—with reports of one dead and many certainly in hospital—some students determined to go on strike. On Saturday morning they managed to spread the word to most of Charles University, and to several other institutions of higher learning, which immediately entered the occupation strike. (Patient research will be needed to reconstruct the precise details of this crucial moment.) On Saturday afternoon they were joined by actors, already politicized by earlier petitions in defense of Václav Havel, and drawn in directly by the very active students from the drama and film academies. They met in the Realistic Theater. Students described the "massacre," as it was now called. The theater people responded with a declaration of support. This not only brought the theaters out on strike—that is, turned their auditoriums into political debating chambers—but also, and, as far as I could establish, for the first time, made the proposal for a general strike on Monday, November 27, between noon and 2 PM. The audience responded with a standing ovation.

On Sunday morning the students of the film and drama academies came out with an appropriately dramatic declaration. Entitled "Don't Wait—Act!" it began by saying that 1989 in Czechoslovakia might sadly be proclaimed the "year of the truncheon." "That truncheon," it continued, "on Friday, November 17 spilled the blood of students." And then, after appealing "especially to European states in the year of the two hundredth anniversary of the French Revolution," they went on to list demands which ranged from the legal registration of the underground monthly *Lidové Noviny* to removing the leading role of the Communist party from the constitution, but also crucially repeated the call for a general strike. (Incidentally, within a few days the students had all their proclamations neatly stored in personal computers, and many of the flysheets on the streets were actually computer printouts.)

It was only at ten o'clock on Sunday evening (Day Three), after the students and actors had taken the lead, proclaiming both their own and the general strike, that the previously existing opposition groups, led by Charter 77, met in another Prague theater. The effective convener of this meeting was Václav Havel, who had hurried back from his farmhouse in Northern Bohemia when he heard the news of the "massacre." The meeting included not only the very diverse opposition groups, such as the Committee for the Defense of the Unjustly Prosecuted (VONS), the Movement for Civic Freedoms, and *Obroda* (Rebirth), the club of excommunicated Communists, but also individual members of the previously puppet People's and Socialist parties. The latter was represented by its general secretary, one Jan Skoda, who was once a schoolmate and close friend of Havel's, but who had carefully avoided him throughout the long, dark years of so-called normalization.

This miscellaneous late-night gathering agreed to establish an *Občanské Forum,* a Civic Forum, "as a spokesman on behalf of that part of the Czechoslovak public which is increasingly critical of the existing Czechoslovak leadership and which in recent days has been profoundly shaken by the brutal massacre of peacefully demonstrating students." It made four demands: the immediate resignation of the Communist leaders responsible for preparing the Warsaw Pact intervention in 1968 and the subsequent devastation of the country's life, starting with the President Gustav Husák and the Party leader Miloš Jakeš; the immediate resignation of the Federal interior minister, František Kincl, and the Prague first secretary, Miroslav Stěpán, held responsible for violent repression of peaceful demonstrations; the establishment of a special commission to investigate these police actions; and the immediate release of all prisoners of conscience. The Civic Forum, it added, supports "with all its authority" the call for a general strike. From this time forward, the Forum assumed the leadership of the revolution in the Czech lands. (pp. 42-3)

On Wednesday and Thursday, Days Six and Seven, there were yet larger demonstrations, while first talks were held between Prime Minister Adamec and a Forum delegation, which, however, at the prime minister's earnest request, was not led by Václav Havel. The prime minister, Havel told me, sent word through an aide that he did not yet want to "play his trump card." At the same time, however, Havel had direct communication with Adamec through a self-constituted group of mediators, calling itself "the bridge." "The bridge" had two struts: Michal Horáček, a journalist on a youth paper, and Michael Kocáb, a rock singer.

The revolution was thus well under way, indeed rocking around the clock. And its headquarters was just a hundred yards from the bottom of Wenceslas Square, in the theater called the Magic Lantern. (p. 43)

A political scientist would be hard pressed to find terms to describe the Forum's structure of decision making, let alone the hierarchy of authority within it. Yet the structure and hierarchy certainly exist, like a chemist's instant crystals. The "four-day-old baby," as Havel calls it, is, at first glance, rather like a club. Individual membership is acquired by personal recommendation. You could draw a tree diagram starting from the founding meeting in the appropriately named Players' Club theater: X introduced Y, who introduced Z. Most of those present have been active in opposition before, the biggest single group being signatories of Charter 77. Twenty years ago they were journalists, academics, politicians, lawyers, but now they come here from their jobs as stokers, window cleaners, clerks, or, at best, banned writers. Sometimes they have to leave a meeting to go and stoke up their boilers. A few of them come straight from prison, from which they have been released under the pressure of popular protest. Politically, they range from the neo-Trotskyist Petr Uhl to the deeply conservative Catholic Václav Benda.

In addition, there are representatives of significant groups. There are The Students, brightly dressed, radical, and politely deferred to by their elders. For, after all, they started it. Occasionally there are The Actors—although we are all actors now. Then there are The Workers, mainly represented by Petr Miller, an athletic and decisive technician from Prague's huge CKD heavy machinery conglomerate. All intellectual voices are stilled when The Worker rises to speak. Sometimes there are The Slovaks—demonstratively honored guests. And then there are those whom I christened The Prognostics, that is, members of the Institute for Forecasting (*Prognostický Ustav*) of the Czechoslovak Academy of Sciences, one of the very few genuinely independent institutes in the whole country's official academic life.

The Prognostics are, in fact, economists. Their particular mystique comes from knowing, or believing they know, or, at least, being believed to know, what to do about the economy—a subject clearly high in the minds of the people on the streets, and one on which most of the philosophers, poets, actors, historians, assembled here have slightly less expertise than the ordinary worker on the Vysočany tram. The Prognostics are not, of course, unanimous. Dr. Václav Klaus, a silver-gray-haired man with glinting metal spectacles, as arrogant as he is clever, favors the solutions of Milton Friedman. His more modest colleague, Dr. Tomáš Ježek, by contrast, is a disciple (and translator) of Friedrich von Hayek. But you get the general drift.

All these tendencies and groups are represented in the full meetings of the Forum, which move, as the numbers grow from tens to hundreds, out of the smoking room into the main auditorium. This "plenum"—like Solidarity in Poland, the Forum finds itself inadvertently adopting the Communist terminology of the last forty years—then appoints a series of "commissions." By the time I arrive there are, so far as I can gather, four: Organizational, Technical, Informational, and Conceptional—the last "to handle the political science aspect," as one Forum spokesperson-interpreter rather quaintly puts it. By the time I leave there seem to be about ten, each with its "in tray"—a white cardboard box lying on the foyer floor. For example, in addition to "Conceptional" there is also "Programmatic" and "Strategic."

As well as voting people onto these commissions, the plenum also sometimes selects ad hoc "crisis staffs," and the groups or individuals to speak on television, negotiate with the government, or whatever. I say "voting," but what actually happens is that the chairman chooses some names, and then others propose other names—or themselves. There is no vote. The lists are, so to speak, open, and therefore long. Thus "for the Conceptional commission I propose Ivan Klíma," says Havel, adding: "Ivan, you don't want to write any more novels, do you?" Generally the principle of selection is crudely representative: there must be The Student, The Worker, The Prognostic, etc. Sometimes this produces marvelous comments to a Western ear.

"Shouldn't we have a liberal?" says someone, in discussing the Conceptional. "But we've already got two Catholics!" comes the reply. Thus Catholic means liberal—which here actually means conservative.

To watch all this was to watch politics in a primary, spontaneous, I almost said "pure" form. All men (and women) may be political animals, but some are more political than others. It was fascinating to see people responding instantly to the scent that wafted down into the Magic Lantern as the days went by. The scent of power. Some who had never before been politically active suddenly sat up, edged their way on stage, proposed themselves for a television slot; and you could already see them in a government minister's chair. Others, long active in the democratic opposition, remain seated in the audience. Not for them the real politics of power. (pp. 43-4)

If one had to describe Havel's leadership, Max Weber's often misused term "charismatic" would for once be apt. It was extraordinary the degree to which everything ultimately revolved around this one man. In almost all the Forum's major decisions and statements he was the final arbiter, the one person who could somehow balance the very different tendencies and interests in the movement. In this sense, as in Solidarity, many decisions were not made democratically. Yet a less authoritarian personality than Havel it would be hard to imagine. (The contrast with Lech Walesa is striking.) And the meetings of the plenum were almost absurdly democratic. The avuncular Radim Palouš was an exemplary chairman. Everyone had his or her say. Important issues were decided by vote. At one point, an assembly of perhaps two hundred people was editing the latest Forum communiqué, line by line.

So all this—the plenums, the commissions, the ad hoc groups, Havel, John Bok, the *Minotaurus* set, the smoking room, the dressing rooms, the hasty conversations in the corridors, the heat, the smoke, the laughter, and the exhaustion—made up that unique political thing, "the Magic Lantern." The story of the revolution, in the days I witnessed it, is that of the interaction of "the Magic Lantern" with three other compound forces, or theaters. These may be called, with similar poetic license, "the people," "the powers that be," and "the world." (p. 44)

Day Eight (Friday, November 24). In the morning, a ple-

num in the smoking room. Appointing people to the commissions. The agenda for this afternoon's demonstration. The proposed slogans, someone says, are "objectivity, truth, productivity, freedom." It is no surprise that two out of four have to do with truth. But "productivity" is interesting. From several conversations outside I gather that the "Polish example" is widely seen here as a negative one. If economic misery were to be the price for political emancipation, many people might not want to pay it. So the Forum places a premium on economic credibility. Demos only after working hours. The lunchtime general strike on Monday as a one-time necessity.

In the early afternoon comes Dubček. He looks as if he has stepped straight out of a black-and-white photograph from 1968. The face is older, more lined, of course, but he has the same gray coat and paisley scarf, the same tentative, touching smile, the same functionary's hat. Everything contributes to the feeling that we have just stepped out of a time warp, the clocks that stopped in 1969 starting again in 1989. Protected by Havel's bodyguards—lead on, John Bok—we emerge from the belly of the Lantern, Dubček and Havel side by side, and scuttle through covered shopping arcades and tortuous back passages to reach the balcony of the Socialist Party publishing house and *Svobodné Slovo:* the balcony of the free word. Along the arcades people simply gape. They can't believe it. Dubček! It is as if the ghost of Winston Churchill were to be seen striding down the Burlington Arcade.

But when he steps out onto the balcony in the frosty evening air, illuminated by television spotlights, the crowds give such a roar as I have never heard. "DUBCEK! DUBCEK!" echoes off the tall houses up and down the long, narrow square. Many people mourn his ambiguous role after the Soviet invasion, and his failure to use the magic of his name to support the democratic opposition. He has changed little with the times. His speech still contains those wooden, prefabricated newspeak phrases, the *langue de bois*. (At one point he refers to "confrontationist extremist tendencies.") He still believes in socialism—that is, reformed communism—with a human face. The true leader of this movement, in Prague at least, is Havel, not Dubček. But for the moment none of this matters.

For the moment all that matters is that the legendary hero is really standing here, addressing a huge crowd on Wenceslas Square, while the emergency session of the Central Committee has, we are told, been removed to a distant suburb. "Dubček to the castle!" roars the crowd— that is, Dubček for president. The old man must believe he will wake up in a moment and find he is dreaming. For the man who supplanted him and now sits in the castle, Gustav Husák, it is the nightmare come true.

After Dubček comes Havel. "Dubček-Havel" they chant, the name of '68 and the name of '89. (People point out with delight that 89 is 68 turned upside down.) Then Václav Malý, the banned padre, reads a message from the man he calls "the third great symbol" of this movement, the ninety-year-old František Cardinal Tomášek. "The Catholic Church stands entirely on the side of the people in their present struggle," says the message. "I thank all those who are fighting for the good of us all and I trust completely the Civic Forum which has become a spokesman for the nation." "Long live Tomášek," they cry, but I notice that when Malý later strikes up the old Czech Wenceslas hymn, much of the crowd either do not know the words or are reluctant to sing them. A striking contrast with Poland.

7:30 PM. The press conference. Havel and Dubček together on stage. They are just starting to field questions about their different ideas on socialism when someone brings the news—from television—that the whole politburo and Central Committee secretariat has resigned. The theater erupts in applause. Havel leaps to his feet, makes the V for Victory sign, and embraces Dubček. Someone brings them champagne. Havel raises his glass and says "to a free Czechoslovakia!" (p. 45)

After midnight. Back in Havel's basement pub, with a wall painting of a ship in stormy seas. Beer and *becherovka.* What do you talk about on the night of such a tremendous victory, when, in just over a week, you have removed the gibbering thugs who have ruined the country for twenty years? In the first instant, on the stage of the Magic Lantern, you may cry, "To a free Czechoslovakia!" But you can't go on talking like characters in a nineteenth-century play. So you suddenly find yourself talking about cats. Yes, cats. Two cats called "Yin" and "Yang," whom their owner has not seen for more than a week. Poor things. Victims of the revolution. (pp. 45-6)

Day Ten (Sunday, November 26). 11 AM. A delegation led by Prime Minister Adamec, and formally described as representing the government and National Front (uniting the Communist with the formerly puppet parties), meets with a Forum delegation led by Havel. "We don't know each other," says the prime minister, extending his hand across the table. "I'm Havel," says Havel. Just in case you didn't guess. It's a short getting-to-know-you session, but they agree to meet again on Tuesday. The prime minister promises the release of political prisoners (several of whom do indeed appear in the Magic Lantern in the course of the day), and also to come to this afternoon's rally.

2 PM at the Letná stadium again. Adamec arrives before the Forum leaders, and stands around stamping his feet in the cold. How do you feel? someone asks him. "Very nice," he says, "I think this was necessary," as the crowd roars, "Dubček! Dubček!" I notice his aide trying to suppress a broad grin. Havel delivers a brief speech, describing the Forum as a bridge from totalitarianism to democracy, and saying that it must exist until free elections. Then they give Adamec his chance. But he blows it, talking about the need for discipline, for no more strikes, for economic rather than political change. You feel he is talking as much to the emergency Central Committee meeting that will take place this evening as to the people in front of him. And they feel it too. They boo and jeer.

The crowd again displays an extraordinary capacity to converse with the speakers in rhythmic chant. "Make way for the ambulance," they cry, or "Turn up the volume." When a long list of political prisoners is read out they chant, "Štěpán to prison." "Perhaps we should give him

a spade," says Václav Malý from the platform. "He'd steal it!" comes the almost instantaneous response, half a million speaking as one. And then "Here it comes!" Sure enough, there is a spade held aloft at the front of the crowd. "Štěpán, Štěpán," they cry as in a funeral chant, and once again they ring their keys, as for the last rites. (Next morning we have the news that Štěpán, along with other discredited members of the leadership, has resigned at the emergency meeting of the Central Committee.)

6 PM. An important plenum at the Magic Lantern. Havel poses the "fundamental question" of the future of the Forum. He personally doesn't want to be a "chief," he says, or a professional politician. He wants to be a writer. Václav Malý says much the same thing, except that he wants to be—he is—a priest. Yet it is clear to everyone that Havel must carry on at least until the elections—and "in the elections," Dienstbier jokes, "I don't give you any chance!"

Someone else reports telephone calls complaining about undemocratic methods. Here is the familiar conflict between politics and morality, between the requirements of unity and democracy. The students insist on the need for unity, continuity, and Havel's leadership. But other voices are raised in favor of immediately founding political parties. A social democratic party will announce itself within the next few days. The Forum, everyone agrees, must not be a centralized, partylike organization. What is it then? How do you describe a civic crusade for national renewal? (p. 46)

[Day Fifteen (Friday, December 1)]. 5 PM. Plenum. Several people have been nominated already for the "crisis staffs" over the weekend. Are there any more volunteers? This is a critical weekend, since Sunday is the deadline set by the Forum for the announcement of the new government, and they will then have to react to Adamec's list. Effectively, almost anyone from among this miscellaneous group could appoint himself to participate in the crucial decision. But everyone is simply exhausted after a fortnight of revolution. Their wives and children are complaining. And damn it, it is the weekend. So the list of volunteers grows only slowly.

The meeting wakes up when a burly farmer arrives, having just successfully disrupted an official congress of agricultural cooperatives. He reads out—no, he elocutes—a rousing statement, beginning, "We the citizens . . . ," and calling for everything from freedom to fertilizers. Then he asks for speakers from the Forum to come out into the countryside. People in the country, he says, think Charter 77 is a group of former prisoners.

After seven, Havel and Petr Pithart return, also exhausted, from their five-hour-long negotiations with the Czech (as opposed to the federal) prime minister, František Pitra. Here, too, the central issue was the composition of a new government, and changes in those arrangements (e.g., for education) which are within the competence of this body. Finally they have agreed to a joint communiqué, after arguing for an hour over one word—"resignation." Havel says: You must understand what it means for these people to sign a joint communiqué with us, whom for twenty years they have regarded—or at least treated—as dangerous criminals.

The early hours. The king of Bohemia arrives back in his basement pub. "Ah, *pane* Havel!" cries a girl at a neighboring table, and sends over her boyfriend to get an autograph on a cigarette packet. Havel is a Bohemian in both senses of the word. He is a Czech intellectual from Bohemia, with a deep feeling for his native land. But he is also an artist, nowhere happier than in a tavern with a glass of beer and the company of pretty and amusing friends. Short, with light hair and moustache, and a thick body perched on small feet, he looks younger than his fifty-three years. Even in quieter times, he is a bundle of nervous energy, with hands waving like twin propellers, and a quite distinctive, almost Chaplinesque walk: short steps, slightly stooping, a kind of racing shuffle. He wears jeans, open shirts, perhaps a corduroy jacket, only putting on a suit and tie under extreme duress: for example, when receiving one of those international prizes. Negotiations with the government, by contrast, do not qualify for a suit and tie. His lined yet boyish face is constantly breaking into a winning smile, while from inside this small frame a surprisingly deep voice rumbles out some wry remark. Despite appearances, he has enormous stamina. Few men could have done half of what he has done in the last fortnight and come out walking, let alone talking. Yet here he is, at one o'clock in the morning, laughing as if he made revolutions every week.

Day Sixteen (Saturday, December 2). A shabby back

Caricature of Havel by David Levine.

room, with a broken-down bed and a girlie calendar on the wall. On one side, the editors of a samizdat—but soon to be legal—paper. On the other side, Havel, the head of the Stockholm-based Charter 77 Foundation, František Janouch, and, from Vienna, the chairman of the International Helsinki Federation, Prince Karl von Schwarzenberg, with tweed jacket and Sherlock Holmes pipe. Arrangements are to be made for the newly legal paper. The Prince takes note of their needs. At one point, there is talk of some fiscal permission required. Havel takes a typewritten list of names out of his bag, and finds the name of the finance minister. "Does anyone know him?" he jokes. Silence. Schwarzenberg says: "What kind of country is this, where one doesn't know the minister?"

Suddenly people have red, white, and blue badges saying "Havel for President." They are made, I am told, in Hungary. Havel shyly says, "May I have one?" and pops it into his pocket.

In the evening there is a ceremony on the stage of the Magic Lantern to thank the staff for their help, since on Monday they are to resume more normal performances. After short speeches, the lights go down, a fireworks display is projected onto the backdrop, and everyone joins in signing the Czech version of "We Shall Overcome," swaying from side to side with hands raised in the V-for-Victory sign. Then we drink pink champagne. Emerging from the auditorium, I see a solitary figure standing in the foyer, with half-raised glass, indecisively, as if pulled in four directions at once by invisible arms. It is Havel. (pp. 49-50)

On Tuesday [December 12] there were further, inconclusive talks with Adamec. On Wednesday he threatened to resign, and on Thursday he did so. His former deputy, Marián Calfa, a Slovak, was asked by President Husák to form a new government. The Forum said they might be able to come to an agreement with him, and made some "suggestions" for the new cabinet.

There followed "round table" talks between representatives of all the official parties—crucially, of course, the Communists, headed here by Vasil Mohorita—and those of the Forum, headed by Havel, and of the Public Against Violence, headed by Jan Carnogurský. As in Poland, the "round table" really had just two sides. But in Poland, the round table took two months; in Czechoslovakia, two days. Precisely meeting the Forum's deadline, on Sunday, December 10, UN Human Rights Day, Gustav Husák swore in the new government, and then resigned as president.

Václav Havel read out the names of the new cabinet to a jubilant crowd on Wenceslas Square. Virtually all the Forum's "suggestions" were reflected in the agreed list. (p. 50)

It was an extraordinary triumph at incredible speed. The "ten days" actually took just twenty-four. Well might the factory sirens blow and church bells ring on the morrow, instead of the threatened general strike. Within the next week, Klaus and Carnogurský were already announcing fiscal and legal changes to start the country down the road to a market economy and the rule of law: the road conjured up seemingly out of nothingness in those steamy dressing rooms and corridors of the Magic Lantern just a fortnight before. The next Sunday, Jiří Dienstbier was cutting the barbed wire of the iron curtain on the Czechoslovak-Austrian frontier, holding the giant wire cutters with his colleague, the Austrian foreign minister, Aloïs Mock. The students held another demonstration, taking exactly the same route that they had on Day One, just a month before: along the embankment, right at the National Theater, up Národní Street into Wenceslas Square. This time they were not met by truncheon-wielding police, by white helmets or red berets, for this time the police were, in a real sense, under their control. (pp. 50-1)

Timothy Garton Ash, "The Revolution of the Magic Lantern," in The New York Review of Books, *Vol. XXXVI, Nos. 21 & 22, January 18, 1990, pp. 42-51.*

Martin Garbus

[*Garbus, a lawyer and human rights activist, served as advisor to the post-Communist Czechoslovak government on drafting its Constitution and new laws.*]

On December 20, 1989, two days before Samuel Beckett's death, I delivered to Vaclav Havel in Prague a signed manuscript copy of Beckett's *Catastrophe.* In 1982 Beckett dedicated the play to Havel, then serving a four-and-a-half-year prison sentence. Beckett, whose plays were banned in Czechoslovakia by the Communist regime, became a hero to the opposition there. A poster circulated depicting a gagged Beckett and bearing the legend, "If Samuel Beckett had been born in Czechoslovakia, we'd still be waiting for Godot." Now, outside the Civic Forum office in Wenceslas Square, there were posters proclaiming "Godot Is Here." Havel, whose works expose the absurdities of the totalitarian state, regards Beckett and Harold Pinter as his masters. And never has absurdism seemed more real than in Kafka's Prague after the revolution. Only nine days after I delivered the manuscript to him, Havel became President of Czechoslovakia.

Upon receiving the manuscript, Havel commented, "After Samuel Beckett, we live in a different world than we did before him." He called Beckett "a man who was the most important playwright in the twentieth century and who influenced all other important playwrights of our century."

Havel had not read *Catastrophe* until after his release from prison in 1983, and immediately he wrote a play in response, *The Mistake.* "The two plays together added to each other and were supportive of each other," Havel told me. "I hope by saying that, I am not suggesting that I am equal as a playwright to Samuel Beckett."

The Mistake is the only dramatic work Havel has written that is based on his prison experience. In it a gang of convicted criminals tries to establish its dominance over a new arrival, who does not respond to flattery, threats or violence. They conclude he is "some kind of a bloody foreigner" and hasn't the slightest idea what is demanded of him. There is no communication whatsoever.

When I informed Havel that Beckett was dying in Paris, he was deeply moved and spoke of visiting him after the question of the presidency was resolved. That was not to be. A personal message he sent to Beckett was never delivered.

The day Beckett died I was again in Havel's office. Outside, students (who did not know of the death) chanted "Godot has arrived" and "Havel to Kafka's castle." We talked of revolution and theater, and Havel said, "This revolution had strange and dramatic aspects. It was classic drama, absurd antidrama."

Sitting there with Havel, I was reminded of the December day, thirteen years before, when I sat with Andrei Sakharov in the kitchen of his Moscow flat. Sakharov, who was then writing the letter on human rights that had such a profound influence on Jimmy Carter, told me, "A man may hope for nothing yet nonetheless must speak because he cannot remain silent." Havel put it differently: "When a person behaves in keeping with his conscience, when he tries to speak the truth and when he tries to behave as a citizen even under conditions where citizenship is degraded, it may not lead to anything, yet it might. But what surely will not lead to anything is when a person calculates whether it will lead to something or not."

Both men would have agreed with what Beckett said in his play *Worstward Ho*: "Try again, fail again, fail better." And now, in their separate ways, they have succeeded.

Martin Garbus, "Godot is Here," in The Nation, *New York, Vol. 250, No. 4, January 29, 1990, p. 124.*

Milan Kundera

I have always been especially allergic to the remark attributed (wrongly, I think) to Goethe: "a life should resemble a work of art." It is because life is formless and does not resemble a work of art that man needs art. Yet in these great days for my old homeland, Central Europe, I learned with enormous joy that Vaclav Havel would soon become president of the Czechoslovak Republic. I think about him and say to myself: there are cases (very rare) where comparing a life to a work of art is justified.

Havel's entire life is in fact built on a single great theme; there is nothing random about it, there are no shifts in direction (Havel was never touched by the lyrical illusions of communism and thus had no need to rid himself of them, as have many of his elders); this life is one gradual, continuous process, and it gives the impression of a perfect compositional unity. Moreover, it seems to me that Havel himself shapes his life with an artist's pleasure, as a sculptor does his stone, progressively giving it an ever greater clarity of meaning and form. The way he led the struggle of the past weeks ("a kind of peaceable revolution," he told me in a letter) was fascinating not only from the political standpoint but also from the aesthetic. It was like the *prestissimo* finale of a sonata by a very great master.

A work of art is meant to be perceived by others. Making one's life a work of art immediately exposes it to scrutiny, to the flood of light. It is unavoidable. But if the man thus illuminated is an artist as well, he takes a risk: his life become work of art can cause his works of art to be forgotten. In Havel's case, this would be a pity. He was under thirty when his first plays were performed in Prague: *The Garden Party* and *The Memorandum.* They were intelligent, provocative, unlike anything else (I once discussed this in the preface to a volume of his plays: they could be placed if need be, but only approximately, within the context of the theater of the absurd), and had an irresistible humor. In fact, if these two plays are my favorites among all his work, it is because I was still able to see them in Prague, in superb productions that were entirely faithful to the author's spirit. And because I was able to see them at the Theater on the Balustrade, where Havel was working at the time and which, for Czech intellectuals, will always remain the symbol of the sixties and of their impudently free spirit. The later works (for instance, the excellent one-act *Audience*) are no less fine; if there still existed in the world companies that consider an author's text to be the foundation of theater art, these plays would be in the repertory everywhere.

Even though Havel is known to the world primarily (and justly) as a founder of Charter 77, as a dissident who has spent years in prison, as the prime moral representative of his country, at heart he will always be a dramatist, a poet of the theater. To ignore this is to fail to understand him. It means failing to understand, first of all, how deeply he is rooted in the specificity of the national tradition: the nineteenth-century movement of Czech renewal was organized not around the Church, not around an army, not around a political party, but around culture in general and the theaters in particular. The greatest Czech political figures of the time were writers: Frantisek Palacky, a historian; Karel Havlicek (curiously, his name is the diminutive form of Havel), a satiric poet; and then Tomas Masaryk, a philosopher.

His dimension as an artist will make Havel different from today's other great political personages. We should not forget that his earliest plays put his audiences into a state of perpetual laughter. Yes, at the start of Havel's career, there was laughter. Humor. And humor means skepticism. And skepticism in turn means self-irony. Two years ago, in Paris, I saw his play *Largo Desolato.* In it, Havel ironically considers his own situation: that of a man who devotes himself to political struggle and thus is no longer master of a life—his own—that everyone else seeks to appropriate. When, in the last act, the police come to arrest the protagonist, he is almost happy with the opportunity finally to be alone, to belong to no one but himself. The dissident, this modern hero, bears his fate not as an exhilarating glory but rather as a burden that is almost absurd. He would prefer to do other things (write plays, for instance, or poetry), to be rid of his destiny, but he cannot. For meanwhile, something mightier than he has seized hold of him, something that goes beyond him, something that Havel calls *responsibility.*

To him this is the ethic of dissidence. Havel discusses it in an essay (on *A Czech Dreambook* by Ludvik Vaculik, a magnificent work that springs from the same "skeptical dissidence"). Underlying this ethic is the skeptical certain-

ty (which only a dramatic author or a novelist can arrive at) that there is no unity between a man's character and his destiny, that the one is always victim of the other. (The work of art that a life becomes is not identical with that life; it may even be hostile to it.) This capacity to take an ironic view of one's own situation, to guard one's life against any melodramatic interpretation (kitsch interpretation, we would say in Central Europe), can be called a kind of wisdom. Among the great political figures of our time, I see no other who possesses that wisdom. For it is the wisdom of a poet. (pp. 16-17)

> *Milan Kundera, "A Life Like a Work of Art,"* translated by Linda Asher in The New Republic, *Vol. 202, No. 5, January 29, 1990, pp. 16-17.*

Marketa Goetz-Stankiewicz

[*Ms. Goetz-Stankiewicz is a critic who specializes in European drama. She also edited* The Vaněk Plays: Four Authors, One Character, *which contains plays by Havel, Pavel Kohout, Pavel Landovský, and Jiří Dienstbier based on a character introduced in Havel's play* Audience.]

When approaching a play by Václav Havel, a critic or commentator is bound to have certain preconceptions. He knows that Havel is one of the most famous "dissidents" of the Communist regime in Czechoslovakia, that none of his plays has been performed in official theatres there, that he has been harassed and imprisoned several times during the last dozen years. . . . Despite all this (or is it *because* of it?), his eloquent politico-philosophical essays as well as his plays have been translated into and performed in many languages. Here, critics are bound to argue, we obviously have a literary figure whose life and writings are so closely interwoven with the political situation in his country that we have a ready-made package-deal guide to the interpretation of his works. Journalists, reviewers, and academic commentators have seemed to follow this obvious approach and discussed Havel's writings largely as the direct outcome of what he has been observing in his own society. The "dissident playwright" label has stuck hard and fast to Havel's image. But does it do him justice? In this essay I propose to peel off the label and let the reader decide whether he wishes to stick it back on again after—and if—he or she has read my remarks.

In true Havelesque spirit we must first clarify some assumptions: What *is* "political theatre"? Is not drama, dealing mostly with human conflicts and tensions, "political" by its very nature? However, as we wisely put aside this vast question, other related questions begin to sprout like mushrooms after a warm rain. (p. 93)

In the afterword to a selection of his plays written in 1976 Havel ironically defines the obliquely "political" roots of his writings. He tells us that the "seemingly unfortunate combination of a bourgeois origin and life in a communist state," though burdening his life with disadvantages, was in fact beneficial in the sense that it allowed him "to see that world, so to speak, from 'below,' " whence "the absurd and grotesque dimensions of the world are most apparent." This wry remark seems to reduce any attempt to argue that Havel is or is not a "political" playwright to an academic game of pigeon-holing or else it shows that the question is simply pointless. In this spirit I turn to his play *Temptation.*

"The first impulse to write a Faust play," Havel told his friends in 1986 during an evening of discussions about *Temptation,* "came in the year 1977 when I was in prison for the first time." Being subjected to lengthy interrogations and particularly harassing pressures during that time, he felt he was "almost physically tempted by the devil." Moreover, by some strange coincidence, the prison authorities handed him Goethe's *Faust* and Thomas Mann's *Dr. Faustus* as reading matter. Gradually he began to feel that he would like to "grasp this material in my own way," but he had no idea how. During the following years, interrupted by a four-year prison term, he made two attempts to write a Faust play but each time destroyed what he had written. In 1985 he began to read magic literature, assembled for him by his friend, the writer and literary scholar Zdeněk Urbanek (to whom *Temptation* was later dedicated). Still, he tells us, he had no idea how to tackle the theme. Then one day he began "to draw sketches and graphics, schemes of entrances and exits, envisage the structure of the play." This is important in the sense that he did not begin, as Western critics imply, with a political idea but with an artifact for the stage. When Havel began writing he completed the play within ten days—unusually fast for an author who was used to spending two or three years on a play. Exhausted after its completion, he needed weeks to calm down and let the play go on to "lead its own life," as a text radiating meanings "about which the author cannot know in advance where they will lead and where they will end."

Temptation had its première in German in 1986 at the Akademietheater in Vienna, and in 1987 was performed by the Royal Shakespeare Company in Stratford-upon-Avon; during the Fall of that year it was performed in London, and in Spring 1989 it had its North American première at the Public Theatre in New York. The critical reactions to the play are revealing. They vary considerably according to the places from which they come, and tell us as much about the assumptions and the receptive climate of these places [as] about the play itself. The Viennese papers, for example, were mostly concerned with its allegedly unsatisfactory treatment of Goethe and the venerable Faust tradition. Goethe, it was claimed with variations, was put at the service of anti-totalitarian criticism. (pp. 94-5)

The reaction of the British papers and other media to Roger Michell's production of *Temptation* was remarkably different. Brought up on Shakespeare, Wilde, Beckett, and Stoppard, the British critics, shrewdly aware that "the play's the thing," comment on the drama as "an intoxicatingly theatrical piece" [Michael Billington, *The Guardian,* May 2, 1987]. Although the workings of evil shown are acknowledged to "spring from a totalitarian system," the point is made repeatedly that the play is "not confined to that system" [Zina Rohan, BBC World Service Broadcast, May 4, 1987]; rather it is regarded as "one of the great artistic adventures of our day" [Michael Coveney, *The Financial Times,* May 1, 1987].

Responding to a flashy but shallower production of *Temptation,* New York critics retired into the safe niche of isolationism and regarded the play largely as sailing under the flag of one who opposes an oppressive political regime. This reaction, as was said before, is to be expected. The playwright himself is acutely aware of the problem, and has repeatedly mentioned his dissatisfaction with being labelled a "dissident"—"the term . . . implies a special profession." (pp. 95-6)

[Czechoslovakian reactions] are based, of course, only on a reading of the text or listening to a tape recording. In 1986 there appeared (in the Czech samizdat series *Nové cesty myšlení* [New Ways of thinking]) a volume entitled *Faustování Havlem* (something like Fausticizing with Havel). It was published on the playwright's fiftieth birthday, which coincided with his being awarded the prestigious Erasmus Prize of the Netherlands. The volume comprises six essays by philosophers, scientists and literary critics none of which discusses what the West has been variously interpreting as the "political" (meaning anti-totalitarian) thrust of the play. They discuss the philosophical, dramatic, literary or metaphysical aspects of *Temptation* to remarkable effect. One of the most interesting essays from the standpoint of our present context is the philosopher Radim Palouš's contribution "The Temptation of Speech". Here Palouš seems to touch on the tantalizing quality of Havel's work as a contemporary playwright. Havel reveals the vastly different ways in which language may be used: on the one hand to express the highest flights of man's intellect—his ability to reason and analyse the complexities of his physical and spiritual existence, to define his perception of truth; on the other hand the ability to conceal and blur the reasoning process, jumble analysis, bury what he knows to be the truth, and mask the putrid lie with the make-up of smooth rhetoric. One might say that Havel's plays are finely choreographed wrestling matches between two types of rhetoric. Although every single one of his plays deals with a critique of language in one way or another, the playwright seems to have given it the most challenging treatment it has yet had in his Faust play, *Temptation.* This, as I hope to show, is "political" theatre in its oldest and widest sense.

But first a note on what the play is about. A scientist named Foustka (a Czechified diminutive of Faust) employed in a scientific Institute gets secretly involved with black magic. He is found out because his tempter, a seedy Mephistophelian figure who is working for the Institute as a sort of agent provocateur, betrays his secret activities. Foustka tries to explain what the Institute's authorities consider a breach of loyalty to the profession. While all this is going on, Foustka finds himself between two women: his steady woman friend Vilma whose bed he shares once or twice a week, and Maggie, the Institute's secretary who falls in love with him, begins to defend his way of thinking, and as a result loses her job as well as her sanity. At a costume ball held in the Institute's garden things come to a head, Foustka's coat catches fire and everything goes up in smoke. (pp. 96-7)

We are never told explicitly what kind of scientific research is being carried on in the Institute where Dr. Foustka is employed. However, we do get plenty of information about its general nature: its progressive programmes which initiate an "extensive educational, popular-scientific and individually therapeutic activity. . . . " These and other vast and obviously laudatory generalizations are spouted by the Institute's Director and his devoted parrot—the Deputy. Nowhere is there mention of any concrete issue or problem; the language keeps us, as it were, at bay. In fact, while seeming to inform, it mystifies; while apparently communicating, it sets up a barrier totally preventing communication. The only times when a specific task or item peeks over this barrier of abstractions is when the Director enquires whether certain things have been attended to. These things turn out to have nothing whatsoever to do with the Institute's nature but rather with irrelevant—in this context surprisingly strange, though for the audience highly amusing—issues like whether the falcons have been fed or whether the soap has been distributed. (p. 97)

After his initial talk with his seducer Fistula, [Foustka] seems to have graduated into the master class of rhetoric. Before Fistula's appearance Foustka was a monosyllabic office colleague who stuttered even as he asked the Institute's secretary Maggie for a cup of coffee. At the office party the same evening (after Fistula's first visit) he emerges as an eloquent speaker who winds his way through complex philosophical arguments like a fish through water. What has happened? Fistula, a smelly, shabby latter-day devil to Foustka's nervous and hectic Faust, seems to know his client . . . better than the latter knows himself, has awakened in him talents he did not know he possessed. Goethe's Faust had first to attain youth and vigour before he could seduce Margaret. Two centuries later Havel's Foustka manages to seduce the secretary Maggie with merely an agile tongue. "Have you ever thought," he asks her over a drink at an office party, "that we would be quite unable to understand even the most simple moral action which is not motivated by self-interest, that in fact it would appear to be quite absurd, if we did not admit to ourselves that somewhere within it there is concealed the prerequisite of something higher, some absolute, omniscient and infinitely just moral authority, through which and in which all our actions gain a mysterious worth and through which each and every one of us constantly touches eternity?"

The strategic vocabulary of the passage and its implied progression is obvious. Consider this table:

NOUNS	VERBS
action	think
authority	understand
worth	touch
eternity	gain
ADJECTIVES	OTHER
moral (twice)	something
concealed	higher within us
absolute	
just	

In one grand linguistic swoop we are whirled from action and thought and, by means of our own "higher" qualities, to eternity and justice. It is not surprising that Maggie falls for this. After all, she is only one of a long line of female characters who have fallen for the rhetorical feats of Havel's protagonists. The playwright himself likes to remember the shrewd words of a Czech critic who said of his first play *The Garden Party* that "its hero was the phrase." The ability (or temptation?) to let the phrase perform, to play the pliable instrument of language, trying out all its registers while monitoring the listener's reaction, has seized nearly all the figures that populate Havel's dramatic universe. For the most part these figures are slaves to the phrase, they are entirely integrated into the social system, spout prepackaged comments and become interchangeable mouthpieces of a certain type of language. A few central characters, however, not quite integrated, troubled, insecure and system-shy, provide us with a fascinating gallery of strategic language acrobats which culminates in Foustka, the scientist/magician whom the devil taught the use of language.

It is obvious that much of this sharp critique of language is directed against a totalitarian system—the one under which the playwright was until recently living. The Czech scholar and essayist Petr Fidelius has written eloquently about the "semantic inflation" which, though an innocuous research subject for linguists under certain circumstances, can become a powerful political tool, if used by centrally controlled media. People exposed to the constant onslaught of this tool, namely the language of propaganda, Fidelius argues, gradually begin to live in a lie; a lie not in the moral but in the existential sense: "Life in a lie does not necessarily manifest itself by asserting something that is not true. . . . life in a lie mostly cannot be measured by an average moral yardstick, indeed it frequently gives the impression of being entirely honourable and irreproachable." The horrific result of this is that people, without wanting to, contribute to the general attitude "that it no longer makes any sense to speak about the truth." In the universe of Havel's plays it certainly does not make any sense to speak the truth. It is no longer recognizable, having been atomized by false language—a language that no longer has the task of seizing and formulating reality.

Without explicitly mentioning political issues Havel has provided us with a playwright's version of models of "semantic inflation"—of language which has gone dead under the leaden weight of an ideologically controlled bureaucracy. That he can do this while combining intellectual content with tension-filled theatre, as well as rollicking comedy, is indeed a feat. (pp. 98-9)

We in the West respect . . . bold attempts to get answers to questions, regardless of the cost. It is here that Havel's label as "dissident" playwright peels off. For what he has done is provide us with a variety of language models for this quest-pose which he reveals to be an empty shell. By having his most innocent, humane, and brave characters (it is interesting that they are all women, but that is another story) fall for this pose, Havel has tapped a deep source in Western social consciousness. With surprising consistency and in harmony with his own expanding and maturing perception of today's world, Havel is exploring the secret patterns of strategic linguistic behaviour which we all face in many walks of life.

What is the implied motivation behind the inevitable rhetorical outbursts of his main characters? They all talk well, indeed convincingly, if we do not listen too closely. If we do, however, their web of words becomes transparent and another reality appears behind it. In *The Garden Party,* the eager beaver Hugo Pludek's pseudo-philosophic ramblings about the complexity of man and his truths are linked to his desire for a career in the government (the temptation of gaining power). When the hapless would-be-integrated bureaucrat Gross in *The Memorandum* muses about the marvels of technology and the stresses of modern man, he is trying to convince others (and perhaps himself) that a yes-man in society can still preserve his own private vision of values (this is the temptation to combine toeing the line—any line!—with remaining a "thinking man.") Similarly, Eduard Huml, who has "increased difficulties of concentration," delves into abstract issues of moral philosophy when his private life is in a mess (this is the temptation of trying to have your cake—erotic embraces wherever available—and eat it too—thus remaining a sage).

Returning to *Temptation* we find that this theme, which has been appearing with increasing insistence in Havel's plays since he began to write, reaches a peak. Double play, the unwillingness to give up one thing for another, the refusal to adhere to a hierarchy of values, the constantly perfected construction of strategic arguments in order to rationalize this form of duplicity—all these are based here on the time-honoured, well-known pattern of the Faust story. Although the devil in Havel's play is a shabby informer, Faust has become a mediocre corporation scientist, and evil has, in Havel's own words, become banal and "domesticated"; the subtle process of temptation, albeit by less "traditional" means, continues.

Foustka's linguistic seduction of Maggie during the Institute's party—a tension-filled dramatic event for the audience—is interrupted four times. Twice colleagues ask Maggie to dance; twice Vilma, Foustka's steady woman friend, comments on the growing intensity of the couple's involvement with a cool "Having a good time?" The first time, Foustka can answer self-assuredly: "Maggie and I have been discussing some philosophical questions". The second time, Vilma's identical question finds the two in a passionate embrace. Now Foustka's response is silence. He has achieved his (or Fistula's?) aim. His elegant, passionate speeches about man and the universe have produced the result promised by Fistula (and secretly wished for by himself?): Maggie has indeed fallen in love with him. However, the stages of this process merit a closer look. Maggie's reactions move first from the awkward admission that she has never really thought about things "in this way" and shy admiration, "you know how to put it so nicely"; then to fervent agreement, "Yes, yes, that's exactly how I've always felt it to be"' next, to acknowledging a marvellous discovery in herself, "I've never felt anything like this before"; finally to complete emotional abandon,

"I love you. . . . Yes, and I'll go on loving you till the day I die". The successful strategy of the rhetorical process can be gauged from the listener's reactions: first, the speaker makes it clear that he is worthy of being listened to; secondly, he shows that he deserves admiration; thirdly, he finds and stresses a point of recognition, a moment of mimesis; fourthly, he causes the listener to experience the uniqueness of this moment in her life; fifthly, he makes her the sole accomplice of his thoughts (his last comment is: "who else should I confide in but you?" Now he has won her entirely.

Yet here we realize with renewed intensity that Havel never permits us to formulate a comfortably assured answer; rather, like Kafka or Beckett, he opens up myriad questions which seem to extend out of sight. Shades of implied shades of meaning mock and tempt the reader. As an example I would like to consider the argument of the Czech philosopher Radim Palouš, mentioned earlier in these pages. With an eloquence that stems from intellectual passion Palouš sets out to throw a different light on Havel's disturbing graphics of human language. During the successful attempt at seduction by language, Palouš argues, something entirely different gradually happens. Although Maggie, in the tradition of Goethe's Gretchen, falls into Faustka's arms and declares her eternal love for him, behind the mask of victorious Eros another process is initiated: the strategic argument designed to win the listener for the speaker has somehow released a "good force," the only truly honest response in the general jumble of lies, masks, and forms of pretense which rule the rest of Havel's play. Thus the weapon handed to Foustka by the evil power has turned out to be a boomerang—it endangers the originator, the devil himself. Maggie perceives only those aspects in Faust's reasoning which awaken her notions of goodness. Intuitively she gravitates to meanings which appeal to her pure spirit, but which she had not been able to formulate herself. Now she recognizes the mute stirrings of her soul in the words expressed (for whatever reason) by someone else. She returns Foustka's talk, in Radim Palouš words, to "the first and true level of language celebrating the amazing working of the universe as such." So, despite the fact that Foustka achieves his purpose—Maggie falls in love with him—he has won a Pyrrhic victory in the sense that he has got more than he bargained for: she loves him forever. Also, and more significantly, despite the fact that she fell for the tool provided by evil, this fall inadvertently provided her with a weapon against the falsehood around her. Out of temptation through language there emerged language as the carrier and formulator of notions of truth and goodness. No matter how resourceful and, under the circumstances, reassuringly noble the argument is, it does push a point. True, Maggie remains a character untouched by evil, an unblemished carrier of truth. However, when Palouš speaks of "the first and true level of language," he himself takes a quasi-metaphysical leap which would convince neither the literary theorist nor the moral philosopher. As for the reader concerned with political issues, Maggie's "positive" stance has little value. After all, she has ended up in the asylum.

Nevertheless Palouš argument shows what intellectual adventures the play has in store for us. Several other essays from *Faustování's Havlem,* though pursuing entirely different lines of thought, testify similarly to the play's challenging wealth. It is due, I would argue, to the mysterious quality of Havel's plays, revealing a deep kinship, as I said earlier, with Kafka and Beckett. In the case of the latter, crowds of interpreters finished up in a similar cul de sac. But there is something else in *Temptation* which is likely to give future critics much food for discussion. Embedded in the play is a textbook on the complexities of temptation or—on the other side of the coin—seduction. There are three key scenes of dialogue between Fistula, the tempter, and Foustka, the tempted. Or is this the wrong way of putting it? Should one say Fistula, the stimulator, and Foustka, the stimulated? After all, the former tells us that he is not much of a tempter but that at most he "occasionally provide[s] . . . a stimulus". These three debates are like sparkling linguistic fencing, in which, although the stimulator at first clearly has the upper hand, the stimulated gradually rises to the occasion and finally outdoes his opponent (or does the latter merely let him score a point because he has already taught his lesson and thereby achieved his purpose?). With an intellectual playfulness and unerring sense for the histrionic that might deceive us about the seriousness of the topic discussed, the playwright takes us through a spectrum of philosophical questions about truth and falsehood, reason and rationalisation, good and evil. These debates, it seems to me, represent something unique in contemporary theatre in the sense that they provide what Havel himself thinks good theatre should be, namely "an adventurous journey," which playwright and audience experience simultaneously and which is "equally surprising, tantalizing and disturbing for us all."

But we must return to our initial question: Is Havel to be regarded as a "political" playwright in the sense that he is an eloquent critic of totalitarianism? Yes, because he defines, with intellectual and dramatic energy, the rigid social structures dictated by a totalitarian ideology which pulverize and absorb personal identity. This in itself is no mean accomplishment. However, as I have tried to show, there is much more. By showing us how disturbingly close our most cherished linguistic formulations are to the dark realm of confusion and danger, Havel casts a giant question mark over the assumptions underlying the time-honoured patterns by which we are accustomed to live. If we find that he formulates his own thoughts on this matter in a possibly rather utopian manner, we might remember that he wrote them from prison, half-way through his long incarceration: "I would say that it is precisely this joint participation in an unusual journey, this collective uncertainty about where the journey is leading, this delight in discovering it together and finding the courage and the ability to negotiate . . . new vistas together—it is all this that creates a remarkable and rare sense of community among the participants, this exciting sense of mutual understanding, of a 'new brotherhood'." It is, I would argue, a welcome and rare challenge for any theatregoers in the West today to let themselves be taken on an exploratory adventure of this kind offered by a contemporary playwright. (pp. 100-03)

Marketa Goetz-Stankiewicz, "Variations of Temptation—Václav Havel's Politics of Language," in Modern Drama, *Vol. XXXIII, No. 1, March, 1990, pp. 93-105.*

H. Stuart Hughes

[*Hughes is the author of* Sophisticated Rebels: The Political Culture of European Dissent, 1968-1987, *which includes passages on Havel's political activities.*]

Of all the wonders of [1989], the most wondrous has been the rise of the playwright and dissident Václav Havel from prison to the presidency of Czechoslovakia. ***Disturbing the Peace: A Conversation With Karel Hvízdala*** explains how this transformation could have come about.

Rather more than a "conversation," as the subtitle describes it, the book consists of a set of scrupulous and sensitive answers to questions posed through underground mail by a Czech writer in exile, recorded and reworked over the year 1985-1986, when Havel was turning 50.

Basically, it is an autobiography, informal, understated, tentative in judgment—the only sort of memoir the future president could have allowed himself to compose. As such, it was put together at the optimum point in time, when rays of hope were beginning to penetrate the gloom of life under a tyranny and when the future leaders of a free Czechoslovakia had established a network of personal associations ready for quick mobilization if the hour of liberation should strike.

The translator, Paul Wilson, who knows Havel's country at first hand and whose text reflects his colloquial command of the language, had originally hoped to bring ***Disturbing the Peace*** up to date by extracting from the author a few reflections on the events of last autumn. Havel refused: "The book has its own architecture . . . and if we were to start adding material . . . it would just keep rising like some strange loaf of Christmas bread." He was quite right.

Jogging easily from topic to topic, ***Disturbing the Peace*** pinpoints three formative phases: a privileged childhood, a hands-on start in the theater, and a groping, half-reluctant passage into open dissent.

Young Václav's parents were prosperous—apparently even under the Nazi occupation—but their son "understood . . . as a handicap" the "perks" he enjoyed; he felt cut off from those around him by "an invisible wall"; he felt "alone, inferior, lost, ridiculed." As a result, he developed "an antagonism toward undeserved privileges, toward unjust social barriers."

This conviction may have eased the shock when at age 15 his real handicapping began. Denied access to higher education because of his "bourgeois" origin, he went to work, first as a carpenter, then as a laboratory assistant, all the while attending night school and reading voraciously. Eventually he was called up for military service.

Here he found his vocation. He and a friend "decided to do something that required a lot of bravado"; they decided to write a play and, along with other friends, to perform it. On his return to civilian life, Havel signed up as a stage-hand in a "liberated" theater, shifting from one odd job to another until he emerged as a playwright who both made people laugh and won their respect.

For him, the theater "became a place for social self-awareness, a vanishing point where all the lines of force of the age" met, "a seismograph of the times, a space, an area of freedom, an instrument of human liberation." At the same time, "the delight in performance, the rhythm, the pure fun . . . seemed to make . . . learned ideological debates . . . fundamentally inappropriate." Trapped in the Kafkaesque world of despotism, threatened with "loss of self," Havel enrolled as a "faithful" heir of the theater of the absurd.

From this point on, struggle against it as he might, his evolution from a mere "curious observer" of Czechoslovakia's fate toward active participation in—and eventually leadership of—dissent appears in retrospect as virtually inevitable. (pp. 3, 10)

[In the mid-1970s he wrote] an open and explosive letter to his country's Communist president and to play a decisive role in the drafting and circulation of Charter 77. This document, whose signatories included the elite of Czech dissidence, initiated a slow awakening from public torpor; its chaotic but astonishingly efficient working methods prefigured the spectacular success of Civic Forum in the last months of 1989. Charter 77 landed Havel in jail. It also made him famous.

He bore up well under the ordeal of imprisonment, particularly during a subsequent four-year stay. The experience both hardened him and made him more reflective. By the time of his triumphal release in 1983, he had discovered who he was; that discovery constitutes the core of *Disturbing the Peace.*

He belongs, Havel tells us, "to the generation of the Beatles," heartily endorsing John Lennon's verdict on the 1970s as not "worth a shit." By temperament no revolutionary, wary of "diffuse . . . ideological polemics," he believes in supporting "concrete causes" and in being "prepared to fight for them unswervingly, to the end." In consequence, he chides the Czech reformers of 1968 for dithering in the face of Soviet threats, and his fellow writer, Milan Kundera, for his "skepticism regarding civic actions that have no immediate hope of being effective" and for refusing "to admit that it occasionally makes sense to risk appearing ridiculous and act bravely." As for himself, he has "never been a politician"; he has never possessed "the necessary qualities for it." The events of 1989 were to prove him wrong.

What sort of man emerges from this scattering of judgments? What are we to make of Havel's oscillation between seriousness and humor, between sense and nonsense? How can we reconcile his playfulness with his profound moral commitment?

Havel's reply is to tell us that these apparent contradictions "are only two sides of the same coin." Granting that "it's difficult to explain," he argues that "Without the laughter we would simply be unable to do the serious

things." The dramatist of the absurd, we learn, and the steadfast leader in tight situations are one and the same person. . . .

Havel exudes vitality and love of life; he exudes good will: In short, he is a thoroughly admirable person. *Disturbing the Peace* documents with disarming self-irony the path of a man who kept learning on the job until the moment when he had greatness thrust upon him.

In the new perspective opened up by Czechoslovakia's liberation, portions of *Disturbing the Peace* may strike today's readers as irrelevant. Despite a helpful glossary, they may get lost in Havel's account of his relations with literati unknown outside their own country. The interview form entails repetition and an unevenness in presentation. But these are minor cavils. *Disturbing the Peace* is a gem of modest self-revelation by a man skeptical about heroes who in fact became "the conscience of his nation."

Havel applies the expression not so much to himself as to the traditional role of Czech writers. The exemplar that springs to mind is, of course, Thomas Garrigue Masaryk, the founder and "philosopher-king" of Czechoslovakia. But Havel is no Masaryk: He lacks his predecessor's solemnity; he prefers blue jeans to the trappings of a royal sage.

He is, rather, a complex creature who fascinates his more stolid countrymen. Hence his apparently unshakable popularity. Who but he could have gotten away with condemning the 1945 expulsion of the Sudeten Germans as an act of revenge? Who but he possesses the combination of imagination and statesmanship to launch Czechoslovakia on a course of mediation between East and West? Prague, after all, lies at the very center of Europe, and its unconventional president figures as the first leader from a former satellite nation to speak out—and to be heard—in behalf of a united Europe.

Present reports indicate that after the current elections, he will consent to stay on for another couple of years. Let's hope so. (p. 10)

> *H. Stuart Hughes, "Conscience in Blue Jeans," in* Los Angeles Times Book Review, *May 20, 1990, pp. 1, 10.*

Robert Brustein

[Brustein is artistic director of the American Repertory Theater and theater critic for The New Republic.*]*

In 1986, Vaclav Havel tape-recorded his answers to 50 questions mailed to him by a friendly interrogator, the émigré Czechoslovak journalist and playwright Karel Hvizdala. The result is *Disturbing the Peace,* and it unquestionably is the finest work this Czechoslovak artist has yet produced—ably translated by Paul Wilson. Part autobiography, part political philosophy, part history, part esthetics, the book finds its unity in the personal qualities that catapulted a lonely dissenter, ostracized as an enemy of the people, into prominence as the reluctant President of his country; modesty, tolerance, inner grace, courage, discriminating intelligence and, above all, strength of principle. There may be disagreement about Mr. Havel's powers as a dramatist—Mr. Havel himself expresses doubts about his theatrical talents. But *Disturbing the Peace* leaves no room for controversy about his place in the moral pantheon of our century.

The career of this heroic literary figure runs counter to the common wisdom about the individual in mass society—a fate that Mr. Havel continually warned about in his writings. Instead of being crushed by the state juggernaut, Mr. Havel eventually triumphed over a mechanism that controlled the press and other media and the reins of government, despite unceasing harassment, the banning of his books and a long imprisonment. Mr. Havel has no ordered political program. His mission, as he defines it, is "to be a Cassandra who tells us what is going on outside the walls of the city" and "to speak the truth about the world I live in, to bear witness to its terrors and miseries—in other words, to warn rather than hand out prescriptions for change."

Mr. Havel is obsessed with the erosion of the spirit in the modern world, continually enjoining humankind to extricate itself from "the obvious and hidden mechanisms of totality." It is a prescription that informs his plays, his manifestoes, his appeals to the former Czechoslovak leaders Alexander Dubcek and Gustav Husak, even his prison-composed (and self-censored) *Letters to Olga,* his wife. (pp. 1, 30)

[His willingness to take risks without fear of ridicule] may very well be Mr. Havel's animating impulse. It also explains his affection for hippies and rock musicians, as well as why he called John Lennon (to the irritation of a few American intellectuals) one of the major figures of the century. Mr. Havel considers rock-and-roll the expression of a haunted, battered humanity. In a repressive climate, it carries the force of political action. Therefore his spirited support of the Plastic People of the Universe, a rock group arrested and tried by the Husak regime, simply reinforced his defense of besieged artists everywhere from totalitarian attacks "on life itself, on the very essence of human freedom and integrity." May his words be heard on Capital Hill during the debates on the National Endowment for the Arts and its support of controversial artists.

Mr. Havel describes his playwriting in much the same terms—defending what is human against repressive social mechanisms. He openly identifies his work as theater of the absurd, unlike other writers (Samuel Beckett, Eugene Ionesco, Jean Genet) who disliked such generic descriptions. But the absurd for Mr. Havel is as much a political and philosophical concept as an esthetic one. He believes, along with the best 20th-century playwrights, that illusionistic theater is a sham, that realism is inadequate to the obscurity and unpredictability of modern life, that the role of the theater is not to be positive or instructive, soothing or explanatory, but rather to remind people that "the time is getting late, that the situation is grave."

This sounds like a civil-defense alarm, and Mr. Havel's view of the absurd has a lot to do with a sense of social crisis, collapsing worlds, language abuse, robotic structures, entropic rule, metaphysical uncertainty—which is

to say, with his experience of life in Czechoslovakia (no wonder he adds that if the theater of the absurd had not existed, he would have been forced to invent it). Still, Mr. Havel's relationship to political theater is as ambiguous as that of Chekhov, who wrote, "Writers must occupy themselves with politics only in order to put up a defense against politics." The absurd for Mr. Havel is another form of artistic resistance.

He has a similar sense of his own absurdity, and one of the most endearing things about *Disturbing the Peace* is its self-mocking tone. Mr. Havel expresses real doubts about whether he is worth all the attention he is getting; he is unusually honest about assessing his marriage, his talents and his neuroses, particularly the despondency that followed his release from prison. Completed three years before history endorsed Mr. Havel's sense of the absurd by rearranging his destiny, the book finds him already admitting that he is "tired of playing the builder's role, I just want to do what every writer should do, to tell the truth!" As joyous as it is dangerous, truth-telling is recommended for every intellectual because "even the toughest truth expressed publicly . . . suddenly becomes liberating." At all events, it defines the intellectual's essential role—to act as outsider and irritant, "chief doubter of systems, of power and its incantations."

Those systems, powers and incantations are not just to be found behind what used to be called the Iron Curtain. Mr. Havel's sense of crisis is global and embraces Western civilization, too—the people of London and New York as well as Prague and Moscow, the workers at America's I. B. M. as well as Czechoslovakia's Skoda automobile plant. For the "totality" that Mr. Havel perceives is spreading throughout the world, in every form of confining system, "from consumption to repression, from advertising to manipulation through television." To combat and resist it, Mr. Havel enjoins us to rediscover and reaffirm the old-fashioned values that represent our truly human qualities: to speak difficult truths without fear, to adopt strong principles and stick to them, to expose all forms of hypocritical cant, to resist encroaching tryannies—and never to lose a sense of absurdity even at the risk of ostracism or ridicule. The exemplary witness of his bad time, he inspires us with the courage and confidence to bear witness to our own. (p. 30)

> *Robert Brustein, in a review of "Disturbing the Peace," in* The New York Times Book Review, *June 17, 1990, pp. 1, 30.*

Herbert Mitgang

Because of his involvement in the human rights movement, Mr. Havel was jailed several times and his plays, including *The Garden Party, The Memorandum* and *Largo Desolato,* were banned in his own country. [In 1988], a book of his censored prison letters to his wife, *Letters to Olga,* was published in the United States. In *Disturbing the Peace,* he opens up even more about his feelings as a victim of a totalitarian government.

Mr. Havel proves to have a remarkable ability to stand back and look at himself almost as another person: a character in a cruel charade where the government could drop the curtain on him any time it wanted to.

Even after being released from prison, he says, "I felt boundless despair mingled with a sort of madcap euphoria." He was constantly shadowed, interrogated and placed under house arrest. Still: "It was an exciting time, what with attacks by the police, escaping from shadows, crawling through the woods, hiding out in the flats of co-conspirators, house searches, and dramatic moments when important documents were eaten."

What better preparation could there be for a future President to learn to respect freedom of expression for others than to be forced by the state literally to swallow his own words?

In the strongest sections of *Disturbing the Peace,* Mr. Havel discusses playwriting and the international theater. Speaking like an homme engagé, he says that the theater must be more than a factory for producing plays. Ideally, he continues, it should be "a living spiritual and intellectual focus, a place for social self-awareness, a vanishing point where all the lines of force of the age meet, a seismograph of the times, a space, an area of freedom, an instrument of human liberation."

Mr. Havel believes that the theater of the absurd is the most significant phenomenon of the 20th century because it demonstrates modern humanity in a state of crisis. Interpreting Samuel Beckett's *Waiting for Godot,* Eugene Ionesco's *Chairs* and Harold Pinter's *Caretaker,* he says that they use banality as a weapon: "The plays are not—and this is important—nihilistic. They are merely a warning."

Speaking of the devolution of power in the Soviet Union, Mr. Havel finds modest grounds for hope because of President Mikhail S. Gorbachev's activities. But he believes that the real changes must come from below. He was prescient about developments in his own country:

> Something is happening in the social awareness, though it is still an undercurrent as yet, rather than something visible. And all of this brings subtle pressure to bear on the powers that govern society. I'm not thinking now of the obvious pressure of public criticism coming from dissidents, but of the invisible kinds of pressure brought on by this general state of mind and its various forms of expression, to which power unintentionally adapts, even in the act of opposing it.

The book, ably translated by Paul Wilson, a Canadian editor, is derived from tape recordings made in 1986 between the playwright and Karel Hvizdala, a Czechoslovak journalist living in West Germany. The American reader should be forewarned that there are prolix passages about obscure Czechoslovak personalities and dated events. These are easy to skip because the book is constructed in question-and-answer form.

Disturbing the Peace works, for the most part, because Mr. Havel gave his responses during a more relaxed time in his life, before he could possibly have dreamed that a playwright, let alone a former convict, would one day become President of Czechoslovakia.

Herbert Mitgang, "Havel Discusses Writers and Politics," in The New York Times, *June 27, 1990, p. C17.*

Jerzy Kosinski

[*Kosinski, author of such novels as* The Painted Bird *and* Being There, *was a past president of the American PEN Center.*]

As the 20th century veers into its last decade, it seems only natural that intellectuals stand at the helm of Central and Eastern Europe. After all, aren't they best equipped to articulate the notion of human beings as nature's most artful creation—and as its most endangered species?

In Hungary the interim president is Arpad Goncz, an insightful novelist, essayist and translator who was jailed for six years in the aftermath of the 1956 uprising. In Poland Prime Minister Tadeusz Mazowiecki is a former Catholic publisher and Bronislaw Geremek, Solidarity parliamentary caucus leader, is a professor of medieval history. . . . And in Czechoslovakia, Vaclav Havel—the innovative master of the absurdist stage, to whom, in tribute, Samuel Beckett dedicated *Catastrophe,* a play inspired by Havel's political stance and imprisonment—is president.

Disturbing the Peace is a collection of Havel's spontaneous and frank conversations with Karel Hvizdala, a Czechoslovak journalist. It was completed in 1986 and issued by Edice Expedice, Havel's own samizdat, then published in Czechoslovakia in 1989 as the first samizdat to appear there legally. Whether talking about his family background or himself in real life, the dramatis personae of his plays or the harsh impact of his imprisonments, Havel comes across as an intellectual par excellence, a parliamentarian of the politics of hope. Elected president in December, today Vaclav Havel charts a new chapter in Czechoslovak history. It is fitting tribute to a man who was one of the prime pensadores of Charter 77, the unprecedented political initiative that aimed, in Havel's words, at "saying goodby forever to the principle of 'the leading role of the party.' " Charter 77 also, remarkably, united in a nonviolent, nonpartisan and ultimately open and tolerant manner masses of people of diverse backgrounds, views and occupations.

Founded in 1977 and incorporating the lesson of the 1968 Prague Spring of "what is permitted and not permitted," the Manifesto of Charter 77 culminated in the Civic Forum, the nonviolent and nonpartisan alliance that Havel brought about in November. As he relates here, the manifesto sought the humanist tradition of a midpoint between protest and consensus, conformism and idiosyncrasy, participation and withdrawal. It was as grounded in the spiritual defiance of Jan Hus, the Czech religious reformer who was the antecedent of the Protestant Reformation, as in the Jeffersonian tenet that "all men are created equal." It drew intellectual sustenance from Tomas Garrigue Masaryk, the philosopher and educator who was the first president of Czechoslovakia, and from the wisdom of Eduard Benes, sociologist and economist and Masaryk's enlightened foreign minister, who succeeded him as president of Czechoslovakia.

Motivated by Havel, who in these conversations acknowledges the role of many activists in its development, Charter 77 called for the creation of a brand-new direct counterpart to the hierarchical autocracy of communism and fascism. It was a new type of participatory democracy, "a free, informal, open community of people of different convictions, different faiths and different professions united by the will to strive individually and collectively for the respect of civil and human rights in our own country and through the world. Charter 77 is not an organization; it has no rules, permanent bodies or formal membership. It does not form the basis for any oppositional political activity." (pp. 3, 9)

If *Disturbing the Peace* merits our utmost attention, it is because these auto-reflective conversations conducted four years before Havel's unexpected presidency contain a truly Jeffersonian vision of massive social reforms. That vision, so respectful of human rights in Czechoslovakia today, could affect social change in any country that, putting up with a totalitarian establishment, is still more put off by the prospect of civil war. (p. 9)

> Jerzy Kosinski, *"Václav Havel and the Politics of Hope,"* in Book World—The Washington Post, *July 1, 1990, pp. 3, 9.*

Stanislaw Baranczak

Not long ago, there was just one world leader whose résumé included a few plays actually written by him and performed on stage (though their production anywhere near Broadway seems a rather remote possibility). Now there are two: the pope has been joined by the president of Czechoslovakia. Who's next? Hasn't a recent article published in a Solidarity newspaper proposed Leszek Kolakowski for the presidency of Poland? Kolakowski, let's not forget, is the author not just of works of philosophy, but also of a comedy he wrote in his spare time. The trend seems to be on the rise. You don't have to be royalty to collect royalties; being the president of a small nation will suffice.

Our amusement at the sight of a playwright becoming his country's president speaks volumes about the declining standards in the West's political life. What's so strange about the election of an outstanding writer from Bohemia? Is it any more consistent with the natural order of things if a much less outstanding golf player from Indiana gets elected to do the same? Weren't Lincoln and Churchill gifted writers? Wouldn't we all be slightly better off if our leaders knew how to select a proper word, put together a precise sentence, plant a stirring idea in a well-constructed paragraph?

Admittedly, even though there might be some truth in the tired Shelley line (you know, the one about poets being the unacknowledged legislators of the world), things get a little complicated when a poet, or a playwright, becomes acknowledged as a legislator, a minister, or a president. First of all, the sort of parliament or government he serves is not entirely inconsequential. The sad case of the talented poet Ernesto Cardenál, who lent support to Daniel Ortega's regime by accepting the position of its minister of cul-

ture, is just one example of the incompatibility between literature's natural thirst for freedom and despotism's natural desire to suppress freedom. That is a conflict in which something has to give, and all too often it has been the writer's conscience that has given.

Moreover, history provides us with a hair-raising number of examples of humanity's worst enemies, from Nero to Hitler, Goebbels, Stalin, and Mao, who considered themselves, at least before their ascent to power but sometimes also a long time after it, artists or writers. A failed artist or a graphomaniac seems to be particularly good material for the making of a ruthless oppressor; he need only apply his crude aesthetic principle of mechanical symmetry to the unruly and formless human mass.

And even if the political system is a democratic one, and the "acknowledged legislator" or leader happens to be an artist or a writer wise enough to be profoundly aware of human diversity, his success in the world of politics is far from assured. As a writer, his chief strength—the force that made him a "legislator," however "unacknowledged," in the first place—was his steadfast rejection of compromise. As a politician, however, he soon finds out that politics in a democratic society is nothing but the art of compromise.

If it so happened one day that destiny wanted the first president of post-Communist Czechoslovakia to be a writer, what kind of writer should he ideally be? Let us imagine a group of Czechoslovak citizens gathered secretly in a private apartment in the middle of 1989, taking refuge from their depressing reality by discussing this preposterous question, a question as thoroughly outlandish to them as the seashore that Shakespeare gave Bohemia in *A Winter's Tale.* Any answer would certainly have included the reverse of the qualities we have just mentioned.

First, the literary president should be a writer with an extraordinarily strong moral backbone, someone whose life, like his work, has been dedicated to searching for the untraversable borderline between good and evil; someone, therefore, who would be able to bring the spirit of ethics into his country's national and international politics. Second, the literary president should be a good writer, endowed with the sense of measure and balance that in the sphere of aesthetics is called good taste or artistic skill, and in the sphere of politics translates into a pluralistic tolerance for the natural diversity of people and their opinions. A playwright—someone who shows the world through dialogue—would be a particularly well-qualified candidate: the spectacle of conflicting human perspectives forms the lifeblood of his art.

And third, the literary president should be a writer blessed with a tremendous sense of humor, preferably of the self-mocking, ironic, absurdist sort. For it is only with such a sense of humor that a writer-turned-president would be able to think seriously of making his nation ascend from the depths of the totalitarian absurd toward a more or less rational social organization, while at the same time never taking himself and the miracle of his own ascension too seriously. In short, the ideal president of Czechoslovakia that our depressed friends would have likely dreamed up is this: a genuinely good playwright with a genuinely strong set of moral convictions balanced by a genuine sense of pluralistic tolerance and a genuine sense of humor.

In the middle of 1989, there happened to be one living and breathing candidate who matched this impossibly exacting description. His name was Václav Havel.

"The real test of a man is not how well he plays the role he has invented for himself, but how well he plays the role that destiny assigned to him." This is how Havel himself, quoting the dictum of his friend and mentor, the late philosopher Jan Patočka, reflects on all the twists of fate that made him first Czechoslovakia's most vilified dissident and then its most venerated president. The issue of the "role" (a fitting term in the mouth of a playwright) is crucial in Havel's philosophical system. What he means by that is the responsibility that man, "thrown into the world," accepts by relating his life to the Absolute Horizon of transcendence (which is defined by Havel, who is reluctant to resort to the vocabulary of theology, as the "Memory of Being").

This kind of outlook, in Havel's case, owes as much to the inspiration drawn from the works of existentialists and phenomenologists as to the inspiration provided by life. *Letters to Olga,* Havel's most detailed and extensive exposition of his philosophy of existence, was written, symbolically enough, in a prison cell—a place to which his "role" consistently led him. It was a place that he converted, ironically, into a stage on which to play, even more eloquently, the same role he had played outside the prison walls. *Letters to Olga* focused on the final outcome of a life, on its complete philosophy. The life that produced this outcome has now, in turn, become the focus of *Disturbing the Peace,* a highly engaging autobiographical sketch in the form of a book-length interview. This much-needed book explains how the events of the unbelievable fall of 1989 can be seen as an almost inevitable phase in Havel's lifelong "role," which was both "assigned to him" by destiny and "invented" by himself.

The facts of Havel's life were more or less known in the West even before 1989, mostly thanks to the publicity generated by his trials and his prison sentences. Havel's life was marked by absurd paradoxes early. Born in 1936 into the wealthy family of a civil engineer, he was suddenly a social pariah—the child of a class enemy—in 1948, when Czechoslovakia turned Communist. He was denied access to a higher education, worked for a while as a laboratory technician, and went through a two-year military service. Throughout that ordeal, he wrote (his first article was published in 1955), and made his presence known in public appearances, such as his speech at an official symposium of young writers in 1956, shockingly critical of the official hierarchy of literary values.

From 1959 on, his life was inextricably linked to theater. He joined Prague's unorthodox Theater on the Balustrade, initially as a stage hand, and ended up as its literary adviser. *Garden Party,* his first play, premiered in 1963. In 1965 he joined the editorial staff of the monthly *Tvář,* a tribune of rebellious young writers.

Those were heady times of growing ferment and hope, but change was yet to come. *Tvář* was soon closed down by its own editors, unable to continue publishing under the watchful eye of the Party. Between 1956 and 1968, Havel used consecutive congresses of the Czechoslovak Writers' Association as forums for his increasingly critical speeches, but his ideas were staunchly resisted by the well-entrenched camp of Communist writers. In March 1968 he helped establish the Circle of Independent Writers, thus creating a cultural alternative of major importance. Meanwhile his next plays had their Czech and Western premieres, and his name became internationally known.

Havel became even better known after the Prague Spring and the Soviet invasion, when he emerged as one of the most eloquent champions of human rights in Husák's police state. His participation in actions of protest and his own analyses of the social apathy induced by Brezhnev's Czechoslovak puppets (such as his famous **"Letter to Dr. Gustáv Husák,"** which was written in 1975) brought down on him increasingly vicious personal attacks in the official media as well as unrelenting police harassment. On January 1, 1977, Havel joined Patočka and Jiří Hajek as a spokesman for the Charter 77 movement. The rest is a story of interrogations, investigations, detentions, provocations, searches, house arrests, buggings, prosecutor's charges, trials, jail sentences, labor camps, prison hospitals, and, amid all this turmoil, more writing.

As we all know, this particular story has a happy ending, the impeccable symmetry of which—the nation's most persecuted writer turns overnight into the nation's president—looks downright suspicious. Were Havel's life a novel, it might be the most naive piece of literary kitsch in the twentieth century. A clear-headed observer of the world's ways knows that there is no such neat example of virtue miraculously rewarded in real life. Is Havel's life a fairy tale, a dream? The honest and the brave, after all, are supposed to get beaten to death by unknown assailants, to disappear without trace, to be found in the trunk of an abandoned car with bullets in their heads. Havel's triumph is so unequivocally well deserved that it looks utterly outlandish.

And no wonder: this particular writer, again, is a walking paradox. This is true not merely of the course of his life, but also of his inner nature. Havel's role seems to have been delineated from the very beginning of his public and literary activity by his mind's preoccupation with two seemingly incompatible inclinations. His works and his actions reflect, on the one hand, a strong sense of moral order and of the need for justice, and on the other, a good-natured tolerance mixed with an absurd, zany sense of humor. An episode mentioned in *Disturbing the Peace* nicely illustrates the constant coexistence of these two inclinations. At one point early in Husák's rule, Havel took part in a general assembly of the governing boards of the unions of writers and artists, which feared—not without foundation, it soon turned out—that their forcible dissolution was imminent. Havel was included in a three-member committee charged with drafting a strong statement to protest, and to try to deflect, the blow:

Unfortunately, I was also expected to participate

in the opening of a show of paintings by a friend of mine in the Spálená Gallery, on Spálená Street, not far away. I wasn't going to give a serious speech—there were art historians for that— just take part in a little program of verses and songs. This was the dadaist wish of my friend, who loved the way I sang patriotic songs out of tune and gave impassioned recitations from our national literary classics at parties. And so, pretending that I had to go to the bathroom, I fled from the task of writing the historic manifesto and I ran to the gallery opening, where I sang and recited to a shocked audience, then rushed back to the film club to write the final paragraph.

Havel proceeds to note "something symbolic in this accidental juxtaposition." It illustrates, he suggests, certain fusions of a more general scope: the way the Czechs' sense— and more generally, the Central Europeans' sense—of misery about their existence is wed to a "sense of irony and self-deprecation." "Don't these two things somehow belong essentially together?" asks Havel. "Don't they condition each other?" The Central European writer's taste for the absurd, for dark humor, produces in him the saving art of "maintaining constant distance" from the world while never completely disengaging from it. Paradoxically, it is exactly the art of distance that allows you to see your subject from up close. As Havel puts it, "The outlines of genuine meaning can only be perceived from the bottom of absurdity."

In truth, the episode says more about Havel himself than about Central European culture. The distinguishing feature of his life and his art seems to be the nearly perfect balance between the seriousness of his moral imperatives and the boundlessness of his self-irony. That irony is not just his mind's innate inclination. It also stems from his recognition that his own vision of the truth—no matter how scrupulously precise he tries to make it, no matter how much he is himself sure of its accuracy—is still only one of many individual human truths.

It is by now quite obvious how much this balance of moral strength without fanaticism and pluralistic tolerance without relativism has affected Havel's progress along his political path. It is perhaps less clear how this same balance is reflected in his art. There, just as in Havel's politics, the equilibrium of opposites keeps the forces in check, so that the extreme manifestations of each can cancel the other out.

An artist of Havel's sort is truly himself when he submits to his moral impulses, when his work originates from his fundamental objection to the world's injustice. But if that were all it took, the art might easily lapse into dogmatic and self-righteous didacticism, the work would be noble yet tedious moral instruction. Another condition, clearly, must be met. In the arts, the moralist needs to have a sense of humor. (pp. 27-9)

Havel the playwright cannot really be squeezed into either of the two familiar drawers, "Theater of the Absurd" or "Protest Theater." He is too embedded in a stable bedrock of moral principles to fit into the first, and he is too irreverent and self-ironic to fit into the second. More precisely, his plays fall into two different categories, one stemming from the tradition of political theater, the other suggesting some superficial affinities with the Theater of the Absurd. The first category is represented by more or less realistic works such as the series of three one-act "Vaněk plays," inaugurated in 1975 by the famed *Audience. Largo Desolato,* one of Havel's relatively recent creations, also belongs here. In plays of this sort, realism takes a deep whiff of grotesque exaggeration, but there is no doubt, particularly in the Vaněk trilogy, that the action takes place in Husák's Czechoslovakia and that the characters' behavior is motivated by circumstances of that time and that place. (p. 29)

The other category, which includes *The Memorandum* and *Temptation,* is represented by plays, usually of greater length and based on more developed plots, that are parabolic rather than realistic. Sometimes they border on anti-utopian fantasy. Instead of a realistic setting, the typical drama revolves around a fictitious institution such as the Orwellian office in *The Memorandum,* complete with watchmen hidden in the hollow walls to keep an eye on employees through special cracks, and the scientific institute at war with society's "irrational tendencies" in *Temptation.* What goes beyond realism, actually, is not so much the setting as the plot's starting device: the introduction of Ptydepe, the artificial language for interoffice communication, in *The Memorandum* and the bureaucratic forms of idolatry of "rational science" that produce the Faustian rebellion of the protagonist in *Temptation.*

The difference between Havel's two types of plays, however, is one of degree. Both deal with essentially the same issues; the parabolic differs from the realistic perhaps only in that the grotesque and the absurd are turned up a notch. But the grotesque and the absurd are intrinsically present even in the most "realistic" of Havel's plays. In the strictly realistic *Audience,* a play that utilizes Havel's own first-hand experience of work at the Trutnov brewery, a socialist workplace that re-educates its employees by making them submit regular reports on themselves to the secret police cannot help but seem like a profoundly aberrant institution. And it is no less so than the imaginary office in *The Memorandum* that forces its employees to learn a special language, one that would help them produce more precise memos if its utter precision did not make it impossible to use. The only difference is that *Audience* could really have happened in Husák's Czechoslovakia, while something not so blatantly idiotic as *The Messenger,* but something similar in spirit, could perhaps have happened there.

Another striking similarity between Havel's "realistic" and "parabolic" plays lies in their protagonists. In fact, it would only be a slight oversimplification to say that whatever sort of play Havel writes, a single protagonist by the name of Ferdinand Vaněk always pops up at the center of its plot. The now legendary figure of Vaněk appeared first in *Audience* (to my mind, still the most perfectly executed accomplishment of Havel's wit), to reappear in his next two one-act plays, *Unveiling* and *Protest.* At the same time, the underground success of *Audience* gave rise to a one-of-a-kind literary phenomenon: a constellation of plays employing the same protagonist but written by different authors. ("The Vaněk plays" in that broader sense include pieces written by Pavel Kohout, Pavel Landovský, and Jiří Dienstbier, and they are all reprinted in [*The Vaněk Plays: Four Authors, One Character*]). But Leopold Nettles of *Largo Desolato* is also, to a large extent, another incarnation of Vaněk, and Vaněk-like characters spur the dramatic action in Havel's "parabolic" plays as well.

What these characters share is a position in society. All of them can be roughly defined as dissidents in a totalitarian state, or at least (as in the cases of Josef Gross in *The Memorandum* and Dr. Foustka in *Temptation*) jammed cogwheels in the otherwise smoothly functioning machine of a powerful institution. This position entails a number of consequences. The most crucial is that the Vaněk-like character represents, obviously, a political and moral minority. He is one of the last Mohicans of common sense, truthfulness, and human decency in a society that has laboriously adopted, in lieu of those simple principles, a Darwinian methodology of survival. Blind obedience to authority, thoughtless concentration on necessities of everyday life, and deep-seated distrust of any protester or reformer are the chief precepts of this methodology. Thus Vaněk is by no means a valiant knight in shining armor or a modern Robin Hood whom the wretched of the earth look up to. Despite all the words of cautious support and solidarity that some of his acquaintances occasionally dare whisper into his ear, Vaněk is hated and despised. Hated, because he is "disturbing the peace" of pacified minds; despised, because he is—cannot help being—a loser. The forces that he opposes are too powerful; he will certainly be crushed in the foreseeable future.

Hence the central paradox of Havel's literary universe: it is not Vaněk who, from the heights of his moral purity as a fighter for human rights, accuses the corrupt society of indifference; it is his society that accuses Vaněk of the same—yes, of indifference. In the eyes of a citizen whose main concerns are promotion at his workplace, getting his daughter into a university, and building himself a dacha in the country, Vaněk looks like a dangerous instigator and rabblerouser. What the Brewmaster in *Audience* says to his face would be echoed with equal sincerity by other characters in other plays, had their tongues been similarly loosened by the heavy intake of beer: "Principles! Principles! Damn right you gonna fight for your damn principles . . .—but what about me? I only get my ass busted for having principles!" Vaněk's original sin, all of them seem to think, is his indifference to other people, an attitude that he demonstrates merely by living among them and irritating them with his inflated conscience. He can afford to stick his neck out; we can't.

In specific plays, this reverberating "He can, we can't" is wrapped in different words, depending on the accuser's social status, intellectual acumen, and degree of cowardice. The Brewmaster's argument runs along the lines of social division: you can, but I can't, because I'm a simple worker whom nobody will care to defend and whose protest will go unheard anyway. In *Unveiling,* a married couple of friends who invited Vaněk for the "unveiling" of their newly decorated apartment resort to an argument that re-

flects their philosophy of life: you can, but we can't, because we need to live our lives to the full, while the pleasures of life apparently do not matter much to you. In *Protest,* a well-to-do screenwriter wriggles out of a moral obligation to sign a petition in defense of an imprisoned artist by involving sophisticated arguments related to political tactics (he ends up endorsing "the more beneficial effect which the protest would have *without* my signature"), which essentially come down to the following: you can, but I can't, because your career has gone to the dogs anyway, while mine is still something I have to take care of.

These are all voices of human normalcy. Havel the pluralist has no choice but to register them, and even partly to agree with them. But Havel the moralist counters with a more powerful argument of his own: that in a totalitarian society it is precisely the "abnormal" troublemakers who have preserved the last vestiges of normalcy. Theirs is the ordinary human striving for freedom and dignity, the kind that ultimately matters more than the misleading normalcy of a full stomach. And Havel the self-ironist acknowledges, and brings into dramatic relief, the intrinsic irony of the dissidents' position: they may well be the only normal human beings around, but since they constitute a ridiculously powerless minority, their cause, noble though it is, will always be doomed to defeat.

In Havel's plays, Vaněk serves as the central point around which these three lines of argument interlock, forming a triangular trap with no way out. He has no choice but to admit that people have basic rights to food on their tables and to a TV show after dinner. He realizes that his actions make people uneasy or put them at a risk. At the same time, he has no choice; he must stick to his own basic right to follow the voice of his conscience. That is not because of moral haughtiness, but for the simple reason that he is unable to force himself to do things or utter words that he considers wrong or false. . . . Finally Vaněk has no choice but to realize his own comical awkwardness. In a society like his, he will always be the odd man out, a laughable exception to the prevailing rule.

The combination of these three necessities makes Vaněk a highly complex dramatic character. This is clear even in the Vaněk trilogy, in which Havel's protagonist is, in terms of sheer stage presence, the least exposed among all the characters. He might seem like little more than a taciturn straight man opposite his rambling and dramatically more developed counterparts. Yet his psychological profile would fill volumes. He is, oddly yet convincingly, heroic and anti-heroic, a centerpiece of tragedy as well as farce. He is never so blindly self-righteous as to forget that, after all, he shares with people their trivial needs, that therefore he is one of them. If his moral backbone is a little more erect than most people's, it is also a backbone that aches.

Vaněk, in sum, is not comfortable with his nagging conscience, and he is not terribly proud of it, either. He realizes how little separates him from the less heroic human mass. In *Audience,* Vaněk, apparently blacklisted, barred from any white-collar job, and forced to take up physical labor in a provincial brewery, does not wish at all to be a martyr; and it is this reluctance that motivates the entire plot. He would gladly swallow the bait of the less exhausting clerical position that the Brewmaster dangles in front of him, even at the cost of the fellow worker whom he would replace. The only reason that he rejects the offer is that the torture of toiling in the brewery's cold cellar is ultimately more bearable than the torture of the nonsensical informing on himself, which the Brewmaster requires as part of the deal.

In *Largo Desolato,* Havel's tendency to endow his dissident hero with anti-heroic features reaches an even greater extreme. Leopold Nettles is a dissident *malgré lui,* one who is not only aware of his weaknesses, like Vaněk, but also doubtful about whether he is up to the task at all. He did not really become a dissident; he was made one. Some of his philosophical writings were denounced by the regime as ideologically harmful, and his quiet life of an introspective bookworm was irrevocably changed. We see him at the point of total exhaustion, on the verge of a nervous breakdown.

Ironically, his new status as a dissident has deprived him of his previous independence. Now everyone, his supporters and persecutors alike, expects something from him. His apartment is visited by an unending stream of friends who worry about his doing nothing, friends who worry about his not doing enough, friends who worry about his doing too much, friends who worry about his worrying. While expecting a secret police search and arrest any minute, he has to entertain his far-from-satisfied lover and at the same time handle a visit from a pair of suspiciously enthusiastic working-class supporters who bear the unmistakable signs of *agents provocateurs.*

When the police finally turn up, their only demand is that Nettles renounce the authorship of his paper. When he refuses, the final blow falls: the police declare that his case has been adjourned "indefinitely for the time being," since it has become clear that his denial of his own identity "would be superfluous." Nettles cries, "Are you trying to say that I am no longer me?" The words aptly sum up what has happened to him. His self has been transformed into (to use the word Havel has applied elsewhere to his own life) a role. A role, in this case, definitely "assigned to him by destiny" rather than "invented by himself," but a role that he has been unable to "play well."

To what extent does Nettles personify the playwright's own doubts? Just as Havel the president is not a man of marble, Havel the dissident was not a man of iron. He has had his crises, his failures, his moments of despair. *Largo Desolato* was written in four days in July 1984, precisely at the low point of a bout of acute "postprison despair." Yet in *Disturbing the Peace* Havel plays down the autobiographical import of his play: "It is not about me, or only about me as such. The play has ambitions to be a human parable, and in that sense it's about man in general."

For Havel, though, writing "about man in general" never means distilling some abstract concept of humanity out of concrete and individual experience. On the contrary, it means portraying man in his concrete surroundings, in the web of his innumerable entanglements, from the metaphysical to the trivial. (*Temptation,* with its Mephistopheles suffering from smelly feet, and its Faust immersed in

the vulgarity of power games and sycophancy of his colleagues, is a particularly apt illustration of that range of vision.) Central among those entanglements is the individual's relationship to society and its institutions. In Havel, who is a matchless literary expert on the ironies of totalitarianism, this relationship takes on, as a rule, the shape of the most ironic of oppressions: the constant oppression of the individual by the institutions that he helped create.

Seen from this point of view, Havel's entire dramatic output may not seem to have progressed much beyond, say, Ionesco's *The Rhinoceros* or *The Bald Singer.* The similarities extend even to characteristic techniques in construing dialogue and dramatic situations. Not unlike Ionesco, Havel's favorite device is mechanical repetition. His plays are organized masterfully, almost like musical pieces, around recurring, intercrossing, and clashing refrains, usually utterances from a small-talk phrase book; the more frequently repeated, the more meaningless they are. The Brewmaster's "Them's the paradoxes of life, right?" and similar verbal refrains find their counterparts in repetitive elements of stage action (for example, the way certain characters conspicuously hold hands in *Temptation*). The despotic oppression of language, custom, stereotype, institution, any automatism with which man replaces the irregularity, spontaneity, and uniqueness of his self is a theme that runs through the Theater of the Absurd. Havel did not invent it, he merely transplanted the theme and its corresponding dramatic techniques onto the ground of the specific experience of the inhabitant of a Central European police state.

What he did invent was his counterbalance to the oppressive weight of that experience. That counterbalance is the weak, confused, laughable, and oddly heroic Vaněk, in all his incarnations. Havel the moralist, Havel the pluralist, and Havel the ironist joined forces to produce a deeply human and exquisitely equivocal character. Precisely because Vaněk is safe from the excesses of relativistic immoralism, he is able to help us put things in perspective. Precisely because he is safe from the excesses of dogmatic didacticism and self-righteous seriousness, he remains someone who teaches us something, who has to be taken seriously.

If he is an anti-heroic and comical version of Camus's Rebel, he is nonetheless a Rebel with a cause—and a Rebel with no streak of single-minded obsessiveness. A Rebel essentially powerless, true; but Vaněk's obstinate defense of the core of his humanity expresses something more essential than the need for power: the need for values. In Central Europe in the mid-1970s, it was enough to realize the genuine presence of this need in the human world to begin to believe that "the power of the powerless," prophesied rather than described by Havel in his epoch-making essay of 1978, may one day manifest itself in real life. Last year it did. People very much like Havel's protagonist have woken up the rest of their society and won their seemingly lost cause. The symbolic credit for today's Czechoslovakia is owed not to Švejk, the bumbling soldier and relativistic philosopher of compromise. It is owed to Vaněk. (pp. 29-32)

Stanislaw Baranczak, "All the President's

Plays,"in The New Republic, *Vol. 203, No. 4, July 23, 1990, pp. 27-32.*

George Galt

Living in Truth, first published in English in 1987, is a collection of [Havel's] political texts accompanied by the reflections of some fellow writers. It includes Havel's brilliant 1978 essay **"The Power of the Powerless,"** which may now be read as a clairvoyant autopsy of the moral lies and mental stagnation that were the atrophying organs of what has become the corpse of Czechoslovakian Communism. For the sheer force of its honesty and intelligence this precise dissection of the paralysed totalitarian mind and the possible antidotes can have few equals in twentieth-century writing. Since it is a dense and demanding polemic that not many readers in the West are likely to pick up, Havel's new book is all the more welcome. *Disturbing the Peace* amounts to a narrative self-portrait with digressions into the author's political philosophy, though it is in fact a long, shifting interview conducted by the exiled Czech journalist Karel Hvíždala. Completed in 1986, the book in no way anticipates Havel's recent election to high office. His revised fate gives these reflections of a dogged dissident approaching his fiftieth birthday an even sharper edge.

Havel has not always considered himself a dissident—the term wasn't applied to the dignified, legally prepared protesters of the Soviet bloc much before 1975—but these reminiscences make it clear that he always considered himself an outsider. The son of wealthy parents, he was denied higher education because of the class bias of the Communists who took power in Prague in 1948. With a day job as a laboratory assistant, he quickly discovered a loophole in the new system when he was able to enroll in night classes and finish high school. (He remembers that "things were still disorganized" and that this "could not have happened two years later.") Barred from studying the humanities at any institute of higher learning, he nonetheless hung on to his dream of becoming a writer and caused a stir at one of the early Party-sponsored writers' congresses in 1956 when he challenged the assembly to give the unofficial, suppressed poets their due. After serving two years in the army, he took a job as a stagehand in one of the Prague theatres and in this milieu began to establish himself as a playwright. He took naturally to the role of thorn in the side of officialdom. From 1965, when he first joined the Writers' Union, until his third prison sentence in the first half of last year, he spoke out continually in defence of democratic practices at every level of society.

A cursory outline of Havel's career can lead to the quick conclusion that he's been a lifelong agitator with a hero complex, and maybe a professional malcontent. But this would be to misconstrue all his political efforts. Generally regarded as a quiet, reserved man, Havel never planned to occupy centre stage, nor to howl down the government. He merely refused to bend, whether to official literary dogma or to official pressure in the larger social arena that pitted free-thinkers of all kinds against the hide-bound Party apparatchiks who wanted to dictate the form and

content of all culture. He makes clear in his memoir that since the 1960s he has guarded against giving in on specific, concrete issues in the name of the large and vague future reforms the Communists were habitually promising. He argued early on that "the best way to liberalize conditions is to be uncompromising precisely in those 'minor' and 'unimportant' details, such as the publication of this or that book or this or that little magazine." Thus, his most ambitious human-rights initiative, the co-founding of Charter 77, grew not out of literary theorizing about how to improve the structure of society but out of his adoption of the cause of a relatively unknown musician, Ivan Jirous, whom the authorities decided to prosecute only because his music fell outside the prescribed norms of official culture.

Havel's memoir is a frank, human document; it tells the tale of an extraordinary life that has cut across all the great issues of our century. Another powerful volume, *Letters to Olga,* a collection of his prison letters to his wife, published here in 1988, also gave rare insights into this unique career, but the prison correspondence was written with the censors in mind and the author had to resort to literary contortions to get his ideas through the walls. A personal triumph because they were penned in such harsh conditions, the letters are nonetheless painfully cramped and their thoughts sometimes difficult to penetrate. *Disturbing the Peace* is by contrast a completely natural book that takes us behind the public image and explores the private world of one of the great men of our time. Not that he sees himself as the embodiment of greatness. It's unlikely that before last fall Havel ever thought for a moment he would be elevated to high political office. Yet ironically his appointment is foreshadowed in a passage of his memoir. Discussing the place of the writer in Czechoslovakia, he remarks that "more is expected of writers than merely writing readable books. The idea that a writer is the conscience of his nation has its own logic and its own tradition here. For years writers have stood in for politicians: they were renewers of the national community, maintainers of the national language, awakeners of the national conscience, interpreters of the national will." The man who wrote those words can't have been entirely surprised when crowds in the streets of Prague last fall began to chant his name. (pp. 62-3)

George Galt, "Gentle Revolutionary," in Saturday Night, *Vol. 105, No. 7, September, 1990, pp. 61-3.*

Peter Sherwood

[*Disturbing the Peace: A Conversation with Karel Hvíždala*] first appeared four years ago, when most Havel-watchers were interested mainly in the theatre and many knew Czech (though he was by no means a household name at home). Now that all the world is his stage, this translation—which comes with introduction, glossary and index—will be keenly scanned by a much wider audience for clues to that miraculously bloodless transition from communist dictatorship to pluralistic democracy so neatly symbolized by Havel's move from prison to president.

They will not be disappointed. This is the most detailed commentary Havel has so far given on his life and work, thanks in part to the often unfocused questions of the émigré journalist, Karel Hvížďala, which allow the famously polite but firm Havel to elaborate on topics of his choice. He ranges widely over personal and public matters with revealing autobiographical detail, an insider's account of cultural life in Czechoslovakia since the late 1960s and valuable insights into his own works and philosophy. It is particularly illuminating, as might be expected, on the link between Havel the playwright and Havel the "dissident"; at least as much light is shed on this by the style of presentation as by his explicit addressing of the issue. There is, of course, a great deal about the theatre, both in terms of material on his own plays and on the history of the small theatres in Prague from the late 1950s onwards, but also about what "theatre" means for him.

> a living spiritual and intellectual focus, a place for social self-awareness, a vanishing point where all the lines of force of the age meet, a seismograph of the times, a space, an area of freedom, an instrument of human liberation. . . . Inseparable from my kind of theatre is a touch of obscurity, of decay or degeneration, of frivolity, I don't know quite what to call it; I think theatre should always be somewhat suspect.

This, he suggests, should be seen against the background of his childhood. One grandfather was a property developer, another a financial journalist, while his father and uncle developed the exclusive Prague suburb of Barrandov. Havel grew up in a family with a cook, a maid, a gardener and a chauffeur, and had a governess. Ashamed of these advantages, he felt a distance between himself and those around him: his sense of exclusion, "outsiderhood", of the "instability of [his] place in the world" is, he avers, a key to his plays.

But if theatre means as much to him as it appears to, it is likely to be a key to the whole of his personality. The sense of being an outsider lurks in his avowal that "the intellectual doesn't belong anywhere". He repeatedly claims he is not a politician, demurring, for instance, when asked about his position on the political spectrum ("I don't know whether I'm right-wing or left-wing"). Yet there is evidence here of an acute political awareness and an interest in what can only be called political action from (at least) the mid-1960s, when he joined the editorial board of the journal *Tvář*. In the fight for the survival of this important precursor of the Prague Spring, here detailed for the first time, Havel learnt "a new model of behaviour": ignore the ideological froth and fight only for a concrete cause—and be prepared to fight for it to the end.

These concrete causes are often described in the same language as that he uses to write about theatre and childhood. This is most striking in the case of his support for the Czech punk band Plastic People of the Universe (whose trial was decisive in bringing about the solidarity needed to launch Charter 77):

> Somewhere in this group, their attitudes and their creations, I sensed a special purity, a shame and a vulnerability; in their music was an experience of metaphysical sorrow and a longing for salvation. . . . this . . . was an attempt to give hope to those who had been most excluded.

Similarly, his conviction that "a purely moral act . . . can gradually and indirectly . . . gain in political significance" echoes his description of theatrical performance as "a living and unrepeatable social event, transcending in far-reaching ways what seems at first sight to be its significance". His main criticism of Kundera, for example, is ultimately of his "refusal to see the indirect and long-term significance" of acts motivated by moral factors.

Despite an obviously hurried translation into a mixture of American and British English, and poor editing, ***Disturbing the Peace*** provides a fine double perspective on Havel, bringing out reassuring traits which will, if anything, increase a careful reader's admiration and support for a most unusual man. As Civic Forum begins to creak in Bohemia and Moravia, the Slovaks make secessionist noises, and the Hungarian minority stake their cultural claims, President Havel will need all the admiration and support he can get.

Paul Sherwood, "A Goal Lost Sight of," in The Times Literary Supplement, *No. 4573, November 23-29, 1990, p. 1262.*

Excerpts from Havel's address to the U. S. Congress

"We still don't know how to put morality ahead of politics, science and economics."

"We are still destroying the planet that was entrusted to us, and its environment. We still close our eyes to growing social, ethnic, and cultural conflicts in the world."

"The worst thing is that we are living in a decayed moral environment. We have become morally ill, because we have become accustomed to saying one thing and thinking another. We have learned not to believe in anything, not to have consideration for one another and only to look after ourselves. Notions such as love, friendship, compassion, humility, and forgiveness have lost their depth and dimension, and for many of us they represent merely some kind of psychological idiosyncrasy, or appear to be some kind of stray relic from times past, something rather comical in the era of computers and space rockets. . . ."

"Without a global revolution in the sphere of human consciousness nothing will change for the better in the sphere of our Being as humans, and the catastrophe toward which this world is headed, be it ecological, social, demographic or a general breakdown of civilization, will be unavoidable."

The 1990
Young Playwrights Festival

Sponsored by the Foundation of the Dramatists Guild, the Young Playwrights Festival is an annual event open to American youths aged nineteen and under. Writers meeting this qualification are invited to submit their original plays to the Foundation of the Dramatists Guild following specific guidelines. All entrants receive a detailed evaluation of their work. A committee chooses several plays each year for professional engagements in New York City, and the productions are reviewed by noted drama critics. The Young Playwrights Festival was established in 1981 through the efforts of noted dramatist and lyricist Stephen Sondheim, Ruth Goetz of the Dramatists Guild, and Gerald Chapman, who administered a similar festival in London during the mid-1970s. Mr. Sondheim stated: "The festival allows young people to use their creative imagination and to see their work done in collaboration with professionals. . . . But never are the playwrights treated as, quote, kids. Like all writers in the Dramatists Guild, they have total control over their material." Sondheim added: "These young playwrights are the theater's future."

650 plays were submitted for consideration in 1990 and four were chosen for full production in the ninth annual Young Playwrights Festival in autumn, 1990. The four plays included Gregory Clayman's *Mutterschaft,* which examines the untraditional relationship between a precocious daughter and her irresponsible mother. *Believing,* by Allison Birch, is a harrowing account of two Trinidadian women's struggles against abuse by their husbands. In Gilbert David Feke's farce *Psychoneurotic Phantasies,* the love affair and fantasies of two high school classmates are dramatized in comic exaggeration and include the appearance of Sigmund Freud. *Hey Little Walter,* by Carla D. Alleyne, is set in a New York City housing project and follows a boy's downfall when he succumbs to various pressures and becomes a drug dealer.

For further information about the Young Playwrights Festival, including guidelines and helpful advice, please write to the following address:

Young Playwrights Festival
The Foundation of the Dramatists Guild
321 West 44th Street, Suite 906
New York, NY 10036

(See also *Contemporary Literary Criticism,* Vol. 55: *Yearbook 1988* and *Contemporary Literary Criticism,* Vol. 59: *Yearbook 1989* for discussions of past Young Playwrights Festivals.)

Jan Stuart

At 9 years of age, the Young Playwrights Festival is experiencing growing pains.

Attending this worthiest of New York's short play fests is often like having ice poured down your back. The neophyte writers have never been afraid to stare into the truth. The dicey issues of adolescence—sexual uncertainty, peer pressures, religious conflicts, suicide, alienation—are treated with a candor and directness that make you shudder: How does anyone survive growing up?

Yet for all of their angst, these playwrights always seemed to have a safety net. The plays have reflected a disproportionately white, middle-class milieu in which, when the going got rough, one could always afford to see a shrink. In fact, the most facile of this year's one-acts is an analytic *Hellzapoppin.* That play, **Psychoneurotic Phantasies,** displays the qualities that were most appealing in the earliest festival plays, a deceptively naive, anything-goes regard for plotting and structure. If a character became muddled or uninteresting in one scene, not to worry, he or she might turn into a tarantula in the next.

This year, the festival is finally acknowledging the malaise of the disenfranchised, with two out of four plays that confront domestic violence and the urban crack plague. Their sincerity is unquestionable, but their passion does not always ignite into theatrical fire.

Allison Birch's **Believing** is an unblinking portrait of a West Indies peasant society in which poverty and patriarchal domination combine with tragic results. Birch methodically sets up an intractable landscape of female victims and male victimizers, epitomized by a bullying laborer Frank (Michael Rogers) and his cowering common-law wife, Thelma (Cynthia Martells). Frank's primitive notions of manhood reach their nadir when he rapes his stepdaughter and throws Thelma out of the house for suspected infidelity. Heady stuff, but the writer piles on a surfeit of violence, underscored by thunder and lightning. It's as enervating as it is noisy. Birch has the anger and insight of Ntozake Shange, but not yet her eloquence.

In **Hey Little Walter,** 16-year-old Carla D. Alleyne's study of the makings of a teenage crack dealer could illustrate a sociology text. Walter (Harold Perrineau) is a basically good kid who, lacking a paternal role model, buckles under group pressures to own $120 sneakers and impress his girlfriend (Lisa Carson in a fine, nervy performance). The predictability of Walter's downward spiral is offset by

Left to right: Young playwrights Carla D. Alleyne, Gregory Clayman, Gilbert David Feke, and Allison Birch.

great vitality in the dialogue. Alleyne also reveals a precocious awareness of the manifestations of urban paranoia.

A fatherless household of a very different sort is at the
heart of *Mutterschaft,* Gregory Clayman's little comedy
of a teenager who can't get her spirited mom to behave like
a mother. She is so starved for discipline that she goes after
mom's artist boyfriend Klaus (Victor Slezak) just to get
a rise out of her. *Mutterschaft* plays better than the slick
TV Guide listing it resembles, thanks to some droll acting.

In the midst of this agenda-heavy festival, the self-
conscious anarchy of Gilbert David Feke's *Psychoneurotic Phantasies,* comes as a tonic. *Phantasies* traces the
skewed romantic path followed by two high-school students (Christopher Shaw and Jane Adams) who share a
taste for awful kiddie programs. In Feke's fevered imagination, life is a never-ending Freudian game show filled
with Mad Hatter reversals of logic. This is a dippy fun
house of a play, reveling in language games ("It's an Eggo
with an ego" says a character tossing a waffle) and rude
conceits ("Stick puppets get hemorrhoids"). Feke was 15
when he wrote this thing, which is about 25 years younger
than George S. Kaufman when he wrote *The Cocoanuts.*
The mind boggles. (pp. 5, 11)

Jan Stuart, "Young Playwrights Work without

a Net," in Newsday, *September 19, 1990, pp.
5, 11.*

William A. Raidy

The combined ages of the four authors whose works are
currently being presented at the Young Playwrights Festival add up to less than the individual ages of several of our
distinguished older dramatists. . . .

And several of the pieces show both surprising sophistication and know-how in these fully staged productions presented by 26 actors. The plays and their creators are *Mutterschaft,* by Gregory Clayman; Allison Birch's *Believing*;
Psychoneurotic Phantasies by Gilbert David Feke, and
Hey Little Walter, by Carla D. Alleyne. . . .

This year's selection of short dramas ranges from the stark
realism of two of them—one involving a teenager and his
baby brother, caught up in the easy money of drug ped-
dling, the other a documentary on the abuse West Indian
men, smothering in poverty and frustration, pile on their
own—to a mad little romp in which Siggy Freud plays
master of ceremonies.

The most successful of the quartet is Gregory Clayman's
Mutterschaft, a cruel comedy about a high school girl and

her mother, a divorcee who seems to think she's a high school girl, too. Anyway, Mom can't understand why her attractive teenaged daughter doesn't have more fun with the boys. (She's busy living a sexually liberated life herself, after being strapped in by a domineering mother of her own, and sometimes even gives her daughter's dates a second glance).

[Daughter Opal] explains she's really not that interested in boys, adding that often "Guys are too much trouble." And when her pal, Evan, asks her: "Isn't sex fun?" she answers; "I guess so . . . but what about afterward? You have to talk to them." Then one night, Mom brings home a leather-suited avant garde artist type by the name of Klaus, who talks an amazing arty gibberish . . . and in a German accent too. . . .

Klaus, obviously more of a sexual athlete than an artist, immediately makes a play for Opal, who skips school the next day to have a sexual rendezvous with him while Mom's out to work. Later the two agree to have a date and when the doorbell rings that night is when Mom's sense of "Mutterschaft" really blossoms. It's a very funny little play. . . .

Believing, set in the West Indies, has obviously been written from first-hand observation. Allison Birch, who was 17 when she wrote it, had only left her native Trinidad two years earlier. Its power lies in the raw truth of the play, which depicts several men physically abusing the women who cook their food, wash their clothes and keep their meager shacks standing, while they drink rum and chase after other women. The cruelest of them is Frank, once a steel band musician and later a dock worker fired from his job, who takes his frustration out by beating on "his woman" and raping her daughter by another man. While the play is often turgid, Birch has a strong talent for characterization. A program note, incidentally, tells us that she plans to attend Grinnell College to become a physician.

Gilbert David Feke's comedy, *Psychoneurotic Phantasies* is more or less what it sounds like—an excursion to the wilder shores of fantasy psychiatry and the bearded prophet from Vienna, delightfully portrayed by Walter Bobbie, who sings a bit of "Swanee," plays host to a television game show, featuring the feuding Adler and Jung families, and sort of stage-manages a TV kiddie puppet show. Underneath it all is the quest for true love, which understandably seems to be in the minds of all the playwrights in the current festival. . . .

Carla D. Alleyne's *Hey Little Walter,* a fast-paced docuplay about two very young brothers who get caught up in crack dealing because the money seems so easy and is so good, doesn't exactly present a new theme. But one interesting note, repeated and repeated by Little Walter, comes home. It is his conviction that dope dealing, in a way, is a revenge against the white man and that this is one business the white man can't take over on the street level.

[Little Walter] is a young man who cares about his mother and his brother and his sister, living in abject poverty. To help pay a big bill when the electricity is about to be turned off, Little Walter decides to make a deal. It turns

sour (a murder adds to the trouble) but suddenly Walter finds himself "in business." And his little brother, Albert, soon to be known as Little Walter as well, eventually becomes a drug runner, too. Albert desperately needs a pair of $120 sneakers. Naturally, it all ends up in a funeral with the second Little Walter, no more than age 10 or 11, heading for the streets to make his drug fortune and repeating the same litany his dead brother did. What gives the play its strength is its truth!

William A. Raidy, "Young Playwrights Hit Home on Love, Lack of It," in The Star-Ledger, *September 20, 1990, p. 69.*

Mel Gussow

Of the four writers in the 1990 Young Playwrights Festival, two keep their ambition in check—and tongue in cheek—and demonstrate their promise with comedy. The two others, tackling more overtly dramatic material, are overcome by their ambition and veer into melodrama. . . .

The most engaging of the plays is the satiric curtain raiser, *Mutterschaft,* by Gregory Clayman. In this zestful variation on the mother-daughter relationship, it is the mother who is the mess, the teen-age daughter [Opal] who is both competent and supervisory. She keeps trying to encourage her mother to straighten out her life, and to straighten up her room. . . .

Conflict arises with the entrance of the mother's suitor, an empty-headed avant-garde artist who might easily be mistaken for a Nazi. Dressed in black and issuing curt orders, he quickly shifts his attentions from the mother to the daughter. On the sidelines is [Evan], one of [Opal's] schoolmates. The bearer of good sense, he notices that the daughter is getting back at her mother "by turning into her."

The author demonstrates an insightfulness into family attachments and rivalries, though occasionally he settles for an easy joke. Rough edges in the play are polished in the performance by the quartet of actors, nimbly led by Michael Mayer as director.

Gilbert David Feke's *Psychoneurotic Phantasies* is a breezy and at times sophomoric spoof of post-Freudian psychology, in which Freud himself plays a pivotal role. Two youngsters have wild fantasies, which are acted out by a vociferous team of cartoonlike players.

Freud frequently frolics, psychoanalyzing a patient on the kitchen table, and popping up in the classroom. At one point, he becomes the emcee of a television game show called *Family Freud,* which pits the Adlers against the Jungs. [Some] of this is amusing, in the *Saturday Night Live* mode. But the funniest bit has nothing to do with teen-age sexuality or Freud. The scene takes place at breakfast as Mr. Shaw is bedeviled by a frozen waffle that insists on talking back to him from the toaster.

Each of the over-reaching plays, Allison Birch's *Believing* and Carla D. Alleyne's *Hey Little Walter,* has enough plot to be full-length combined with a chaotic sense of theater. The setting for *Believing* is a West Indian community where women are subjugated to male domination and repression. The play plunges from wife abuse to rape to murder.

There are sparks of local flavor, but the play, as conceived, is too much for the playwright to handle, especially in 45 minutes. . . .

With *Hey Little Walter,* the family trauma moves to the city for a story of a young man's self-abandonment. Blockaded by poverty, the title character takes up drug selling as an easy road to remuneration, and he pays a heavy price. Though the subject is worn through familiarity, it always needs restating.

Unfortunately, Ms. Alleyne is unable to sustain our interest even for the play's brief duration. She does have an ear for urban language, just as the actors have a feeling for urban characters.

> *Mel Gussow, "Of Ambition, Melodrama and Youth," in* The New York Times, *September 21, 1990, p. C14.*

John Simon

For nine years now, the Young Playwrights Festival has turned up promising, indeed accomplished, young dramatists, and this year the results may be better than ever: All four plays are worthy, two of them remarkable. . . .

The best this time is Gregory Clayman's *Mutterschaft,* directed by Michael Mayer. It concerns Opal, a high-school student who finds that the only way she can gain the attention of her divorced mother, with whom she lives, is by seducing Mom's new boyfriend. This is a very mature, sophisticated piece, enhanced by the kind of subtlety not readily found in the work of successful adult playwrights. Nothing is overstated, much is merely (but powerfully) suggested, and we are always allowed—or compelled—to make our own inferences.

Clayman wisely avoids oversimplification and, though we know where his sympathies lie, states fairly the cases of both mother and daughter. Even Klaus, the amoral and fatuous artist (probably, but not necessarily, untalented), who would like nothing better than a two-generation threesome—separately, each woman bores him already—is allowed a modicum of amused tolerance. And that Clayman's protagonist is a young woman sympathetically imagined down to the most elusive detail fills me with admiration. . . .

Scarcely less effective in an antithetic way is Allison Birch's *Believing.* Like Clayman, Miss Birch was seventeen at the time of submission, and she, too, writes about what she knows: the grim lives of oppressed women in Trinidad, whence she came with her mother a few years ago. Unlike Clayman's, however, her play is graphic, confrontational, and shocking. Because it is so compressed in time and space (on a small stage), it skirts melodrama. Yet such is Miss Birch's command that even at the fringe—some would say core—of melodrama, she endows her women with redolent humanity and pathos. And the

men—however shiftless, selfish, violent—are entirely three-dimensional and fully understood. Furthermore, one gets a sense of the social conditions behind the injustices, and even a glimmer, faint but heartening, of hope. . . .

The author plans to go to medical school; let me hope it will no more impede her playwriting than it did Chekhov's.

Psychoneurotic Phantasies, an absurdist farce by Gilbert David Feke, takes up two romantically starved teenagers and their intertwining lives and imaginings, with Dr. Freud as therapist, chorus, and deus ex machina and a cast of eight as parents, teachers, fellow students, TV performers, famous psychiatrists, and what-not. There is a good deal of originality and wit here, but also cutesiness, prolixity, self-indulgence. Still, given Gloria Muzio's savvy staging and the lively acting (including cross-dressing) . . . , it's all far from unenjoyable and, from a fifteen-year-old, far from unimpressive. I am still chortling over the line "How can you misspell 'Id'?"

Hey Little Walter, by Carla D. Alleyne (sixteen), is the least noteworthy work. It is poster art—a sort of recruiting poster for black teenagers to enlist in the war on juvenile drug traffic. As such, it exhibits firsthand knowledge, total commitment, and true horror but little originality or artistry. (p. 54)

> *John Simon, "Babes Off Broadway," in* New York Magazine, *Vol. 23, No. 38, October 1, 1990, pp. 54-5.*

Kevin Grubb

The small miracle of the 9th Annual Young Playwrights Festival is that its quartet of authors refrains from patronizing their subjects—something adults writing about young people do with alarming frequency. From the curtain-raiser, *Mutterschaft,* to the finale, *Hey Little Walter,* the playwrights tackle issues some would consider beyond their years, among them incest and infanticide (*Believing*) and psychotherapy (*Psychoneurotic Phantasies*). In three of the plays, the nuclear family has dissolved into one-parent households where teenagers are catapulted into adulthood without the benefit of instruction. They are just as likely to be wearing "Banned in the U.S.A." anti-censorship T-shirts as Ninja Turtle baseball caps. Perhaps most startling, they have stepped into the ill-fitting roles of parents for parents who haven't the vaguest idea of how to raise their children.

Gregory Clayman's *Mutterschaft* explores the parent-child travails of a flower-childish mother and her pragmatic teenage daughter, Opal, who seems far more capable of managing the fatherless household. Mother gives her bright, pretty daughter the freedom to explore her options and make the hard choices she herself was denied as a teenager. Opal, however, finds her mother's yin-yang, matter-of-fact attitude too unstable and jolts her into taking a stronger parental role by pursuing Klaus, her mother's boyfriend, who is only too happy to deflower her.

This play's denouement—a parent forced to confront the

physical danger surrounding her child—is echoed in Allison Birch's stunning *Believing.* Set in the West Indies, Birch's play concerns the plight of poor black women who endure constant physical and emotional assault by their husbands. At the core of the story are Thelma and Lawna, one who sees her son killed in the hands of her male lover; one who learns her teenage sister has been raped by her husband. The crisp, spare dialogue—with convincing patois by the cast—is brutally frank and unflinching ("I am the one with the cock. I am the one to give; you are the one to take.")

Psychoneurotic Phantasies by Gilbert David Feke is a *Heathers*-type "revenge fantasy" involving high school students and their eccentric teachers, led by Sigmund Freud. A series of comedic blackouts, the play's best moment is a send-up of the game show *Family Feud* called *Family Freud,* which pits the family of Alfred Adler against that of Karl Jung with predictably scandalous results. Equally entertaining are the *Carrie*-worthy tortures of an arrogant athlete by "jock strangulation" with an athletic supporter and a cheerleader burned at the stake.

Based on the popular rap song of a few summers back, *Little Walter* by Carla D. Alleyne dramatizes the song's lyrics about an urban black teenager who puts his life and his family's in jeopardy by selling drugs. Although it's a familiar tale, Alleyne's dry-eyed portrayal of a single working mother struggling to support her three children manages to be sincere and convincing. . . . The play's coda—Walter's little brother is seen beginning his own 'career' as a drug runner—gives little hope to a family victimized by life in the projects.

With the exception of *Psychoneurotic Phantasies,* all of the plays in this festival could be expanded to full-evening works. Their verisimilitude leaves us anticipating future work by these talented teens. Amazingly, the oldest playwrights in the lot were 17 when their work was written. Maybe if adults will leave them alone, they won't end up writing the next episodes of *Roseanne.*

Kevin Grubb, "Young Enough to Know Better," in New York Native, *October 1, 1990, p. 40.*

Michael Feingold

The most exciting of the Young Playwrights Festival's finds this year, Carla Alleyne's *Hey Little Walter,* is set on the same mean streets as [Kurt] Weill's opera [*Street Scene*]. Apart from the up-to-date diction, the only changes are the absence of all idealistic hopes, the increase in destructive firepower, and the lowered life expectancy. Sixteen-year-old Alleyne's characters are teens and preteens in the crack trade, and her brief, incisive cautionary tale, which should be seen in every New York City school, spares only enough time on their feelings to confirm their humanity, and then lays out their inevitable fate with painful, blunt lucidity. . . .

Alleyne has promise as a journalist-dramatist, not an unworthy thing to be. Higher hopes may rest in Gregory Clayman, whose *Mutterschaft* deals, often comically, with an ex-hippie mom and teenage daughter sexually involved with the same man, a cold German art-faker. On trickier ground than Alleyne, Clayman is sometimes less sure-footed, but his compassionate perception of his characters . . . makes up for it. . . . Gilbert David Feke's *Psychoneurotic Phantasies* [is] a dribbling TV skit about two sexually nervous high-school psych students. Feke brings off a few good jokes (the Adler and Jung clans compete on a nightmare quiz show called *Family Freud,* but must there always be one of these sub-*SCTV* items to remind us that a committee chooses the YPF's plays?

Far more honorable, despite the sententious sloganeering of its last scene, is Allison Birch's *Believing,* which sets out some ugly truths about women's status in the West Indies by means of a melodramatically compressed but not implausible story. Birch is bursting with newfound dogmas that tempt her into schematism; the real measure of her ability is that this hasn't stopped her from giving . . . [her chief male villain] the evening's showiest acting opportunity, which he milks, in a dazzling turn, for every ounce of island-accented juice he can squeeze out of it.

Michael Feingold, "Same Streets, Other Scenes," in The Village Voice, *Vol. XXXV, No. 40, October 2, 1990, p. 111.*

□ Contemporary
Literary Criticism
Indexes

Literary Criticism Series
    Cumulative Author Index
Cumulative Topic Index
Cumulative Nationality Index
Title Index, Volume 65

This Index Includes References to Entries in These Gale Series

Contemporary Literary Criticism presents excerpts of criticism on the works of novelists, poets, dramatists, short story writers, scriptwriters, and other creative writers who are now living or who have died since 1960. Cumulative indexes to authors and nationalities are included, as well as an index to titles discussed in the individual volume.

Twentieth-Century Literary Criticism contains critical excerpts by the most significant commentators on poets, novelists, short story writers, dramatists, and philosophers who died between 1900 and 1960. Indexes to authors, nationalities, and titles discussed are included in each new volume.

Nineteenth-Century Literature Criticism offers significant passages from criticism on authors who died between 1800 and 1899. Indexes to authors, nationalities, and titles discussed are included in each new volume.

Literature Criticism from 1400 to 1800 compiles significant passages from the most noteworthy criticism on authors of the fifteenth through the eighteenth centuries. Cumulative indexes to authors, nationalities, and titles discussed are included in each new volume.

Classical and Medieval Literature Criticism offers excerpts of criticism on the works of world authors from classical antiquity through the fourteenth century. Cumulative indexes to authors, titles and critics are included in each volume.

Short Story Criticism combines excerpts of criticism on short fiction by writers of all eras and nationalities. Cumulative indexes to authors, nationalities, and titles discussed are included in each new volume.

Poetry Criticism presents excerpts of criticism on the works of poets from all eras, movements, and nationalities.

Children's Literature Review includes excerpts from reviews, criticism, and commentary on works of authors and illustrators who create books for children. Cumulative indexes to authors, nationalities, and titles discussed are included in each new volume.

Contemporary Authors Series encompasses five related series. *Contemporary Authors* provides biographical and bibliographical information on more than 92,000 writers of fiction, nonfiction, poetry, journalism, drama, film, and other related fields. Each new volume contains sketches on authors not previously covered in the series. *Contemporary Authors New Revision Series* provides completely updated information on active authors covered in previously published volumes of *CA*. Only entries requiring significant change are revised for *CA New Revision Series*. *Contemporary Authors Permanent Series* consists of updated listings for deceased and inactive authors removed from the original volumes 9-36 when those volumes were revised. *Contemporary Authors Autobiography Series* presents specially commissioned autobiographies by leading contemporary writers. *Contemporary Authors Bibliographical Series* contains primary and secondary bibliographies as well as analytical bibliographical essays by authorities on major modern authors.

Dictionary of Literary Biography encompasses three related series. *Dictionary of Literary Biography* furnishes illustrated overviews of authors' lives and works and places them in the larger perspective of literary history. *Dictionary of Literary Biography Documentary Series* illuminates the careers of major figures through a selection of literary documents, including letters, notebook and diary entries, interviews, book reviews, and photographs. *Dictionary of Literary Biography Yearbook* summarizes the past year's literary activity with articles on genres, major prizes, conferences, and other timely subjects and includes updated and new entries on individual authors. A cumulative index to authors and articles is included in each new volume. *Concise Dictionary of Literary Biography,* a six-volume series, collects revised and updated sketches on major American authors that were originally presented in *Dictionary of Literary Biography.*

Something about the Author Series encompasses three related series. *Something about the Author* contains heavily illustrated biographical sketches on authors and illustrators of juvenile and young adult literature from all eras. *Something about the Author Autobiography Series* presents specially commissioned autobiographies by prominent authors and illustrators of books for children and young adults. *Authors and Artists for Young Adults* provides high school and junior high school students with profiles of their favorite creative artists in the media of print, film, television, drama, song lyrics, and cartoons.

Yesterday's Authors of Books for Children contains heavily illustrated entries on children's writers who died before 1961. Complete in two volumes.

Literary Criticism Series
Cumulative Author Index

This index lists all author entries in the Gale Literary Criticism Series and includes cross-references to other Gale sources. References in the index are identified as follows:

Author Index

Author Index

Author Index

Author Index

Author Index

Author Index

Author Index

Author Index

Literary Criticism Series
Cumulative Topic Index

This index lists all topic entries in the Gale Literary Criticism Series *Contemporary Literary Criticism, Literature Criticism from 1400 to 1800, Nineteenth-Century Literature Criticism,* and *Twentieth-Century Literary Criticism.*

CLC Cumulative Nationality Index

Nationality Index

Nationality Index

Nationality Index

Nationality Index

Nationality Index

CLC-65 Title Index